Collins
gem

T0327777

English
School
Dictionary
& Thesaurus

Published by Collins
An imprint of HarperCollins
Publishers
Westerhill Road
Bishopbriggs
Glasgow
G64 2QT

HarperCollins Publishers
Macken House
39/40 Mayor Street Upper
Dublin 1, D01 C9W8, Ireland

Third edition 2019

10 9 8 7 6

ISBN 978-0-00-832116-1

Collins ® is a registered trademark of
HarperCollins Publishers Limited

www.collins.co.uk

Typeset by Davidson Publishing
Solutions

Printed in India

If you would like to comment on any
aspect of this book, please contact us
at the given address or online.
E-mail: dictionaries@harpercollins.co.uk

Acknowledgements
We would like to thank those authors
and publishers who kindly gave
permission for copyright material
to be used in the Collins Corpus.
We would also like to thank Times
Newspapers Ltd for providing
valuable data.

MIX
Paper | Supporting
responsible forestry
FSC™ C007454
www.fsc.org

Contents

Introduction

The ability to read, understand, and write good English is vital for both success in exams and, ultimately, success in the world beyond school. *Collins Gem School Dictionary & Thesaurus* is an essential tool in achieving that knowledge.

Collins Gem School Dictionary & Thesaurus has been researched with teachers and students to ensure that it includes the information on language that students need to allow them to improve their performance and achieve exam success, not just in English but in all other school subjects.

The up-to-date dictionary allows students to find out what a word means and how to spell it correctly. The thesaurus entries are a perfect complement, offering students thousands of synonyms to use in order to make their writing more vibrant.

In addition, a section called **Get It Right** recognises the importance of grammar, punctuation, and spelling. It explains the use and relevance of word classes, sentence types, and punctuation marks, and it lists words that students have been found to misspell, helping them to master the trickiest spelling problems.

Collins Gem School Dictionary & Thesaurus is accessible and student-friendly, and it provides two essential resources in a handy format.

How to Use the Dictionary & Thesaurus

In the Dictionary Entries

The headword is the word you are looking up.

The word class tells you if the headword is, for example, a noun, verb, adjective, adverb, or pronoun.

An example shows how the word is used.

Sometimes entries include a label, such as *formal*, *informal*, or *slang*, to give the appropriate context for a word.

Headwords with small numbers beside them have different origins.

Other words that come from the main headword show word connections.

along *preposition* **1** moving, happening or existing continuously from one end to the other of something, or at various points beside it: *houses along the river.* ▶ *adverb* **2** moving forward: *We marched along, singing as we went.* **3** with someone: *Why could she not take her along?* ▶ *phrase* **4 All along** means from the beginning of a period of time right up to now.

phoney phonier, phoniest; phoneys; also spelt **phony** (*informal*) *adjective* **1** false and intended to deceive. ▶ *noun* **2** Someone who is a phoney pretends to have qualities they do not possess.

desert¹ *noun* GEOGRAPHY a region of land with very little plant life, usually because of low rainfall.

desert² *verb* To desert a person means to leave or abandon them. ▷ **desertion** *noun*

The definition tells you what the word means.

There can be other forms of the word after the headword. These might be the plural of a noun, tenses of a verb, or comparative and superlative forms of adjectives.

Some words can have more than one spelling or form.

Core vocabulary from all curriculum subjects is labelled. See page viii for a full list of curriculum subject labels in the dictionary.

In the Thesaurus Entries

blank *adjective* **1** Something that is blank has nothing on it. **2** If you look blank, your face shows no feeling or interest. ▶ *noun* **3** If your mind is a blank, you cannot think of anything or remember anything.

> **blank** *adjective*
> **1** = bare, clean, clear, empty, plain, unmarked **2** = deadpan, dull, empty, impassive, vacant

bravery *noun* the quality of being courageous.

> **bravery** *noun*
> = boldness, courage, fortitude, heroism, pluck, valour

brag brags, bragging, bragged *verb* When someone brags, they boast about their achievements.

> **brag** *verb*
> = boast, crow (*informal*), skite (*Australian and New Zealand; informal*)

Numbers match the meanings in the dictionary entry, so you can find alternative words for the meaning you want.

Synonyms, which are indicated by =, are words with a similar meaning that that you can use instead.

A label, such *formal*, *informal*, or *slang*, tells you when it is appropriate to use the synonym.

The word class tells you if the headword is, for example, a noun, verb, adjective, adverb, or pronoun.

Some labels tell you where in the world a word is used.

Curriculum Subject Labels

Curriculum subject labels show when an entry word is core vocabulary for a curriculum subject.

An entry may also have a label if the word is particularly relevant to exams or using the library.

Here is a list of the subject labels used.

ART	Art
CITIZENSHIP	Citizenship
D&T	Design and technology
DRAMA	Drama
ENGLISH	English
EXAM TERM	Word used in exam questions
GEOGRAPHY	Geography
HISTORY	History
ICT	Information and communication technology
LIBRARY	Library skills
MATHS	Maths
MFL	Modern foreign languages
MUSIC	Music
PE	Physical education
PSHE	Personal, social, and health education
RE	Religious education
SCIENCE	Science

Dictionary &
Thesaurus
A–Z

Aa

a or **an** The indefinite article 'a', or 'an' if the next sound is a vowel, is used when you are talking about one of something: *an apple*; *There was a car parked behind the hedge.*

aback *adverb* If you are taken aback, you are very surprised.

abalone *noun* a shellfish which can be eaten.

abandon *verb* 1 If you abandon someone or something, you leave them or give them up for good. ▶ *noun* 2 If you do something with abandon, you do it in an uncontrolled way. > **abandoned** *adjective* > **abandonment** *noun*

> **abandon** *verb*
> 1 = desert, jilt, leave, leave behind
> ▶ *noun* 2 = recklessness, wildness

abate *verb* If something abates, it becomes less.

> **abate** *verb*
> = decrease, diminish, ebb, lessen, subside, wane

abattoir *noun* a place where animals are killed for meat.

abbey *noun* a church with buildings attached to it in which monks or nuns live.

abbot *noun* the monk or priest in charge of all the monks in a monastery.

abbreviate *verb* To abbreviate something is to make it shorter.

abbreviation *noun* a short form of a word or phrase. An example is 'W', which is short for 'West'.

abdicate *verb* If a king or queen abdicates, he or she gives up being a king or queen. > **abdication** *noun*

abdomen *noun* the front part of your body below your chest, containing your stomach and intestines. > **abdominal** *adjective*

abduct *verb* To abduct someone is to take them away by force. > **abduction** *noun*

aberration *noun* something that is not normal or usual.

abet abets, abetting, abetted *verb* If you abet someone, you help them to do something.

abhor abhors, abhorring, abhorred *verb* (formal) If you abhor something, you hate it. > **abhorrence** *noun* > **abhorrent** *adjective*

abide abides, abiding, abided *verb* 1 If you can't abide something, you dislike it very much. 2 If you abide by a decision or law, you act in agreement with it.

abiding *adjective* lasting for ever.

ability abilities *noun* the intelligence or skill needed to do something.

> **ability** *noun*
> = capability, competence, expertise, skill, talent

abject *adjective* very bad. > **abjectly** *adverb*

ablaze *adjective* on fire.

able abler, ablest *adjective* 1 If you are able to do something, you can do it. 2 (PSHE) Someone who is able is very clever or talented.

A

able *adjective*
2 = accomplished, capable,
efficient, expert, first-rate,
skilled, talented

-able *suffix* 1 forming adjectives
which have the meaning 'capable
of' an action: *enjoyable*; *breakable*.
2 forming adjectives with the
meaning 'able to' or 'causing':
comfortable; *miserable*.

ably *adverb* skilfully and successfully.

abnormal *adjective* not normal or
usual. > **abnormally** *adverb*

abnormality abnormalities *noun*
something that is not normal or
usual.

aboard *preposition, adverb* on a ship
or plane.

abode *noun* (old-fashioned) Your
abode is your home.

abolish *verb* To abolish something
is to do away with it. > **abolition**
noun

abolish *verb*
= annul, do away with,
overturn, put an end to

abominable *adjective* very
unpleasant or shocking.
> **abominably** *adverb*

Aboriginal *adjective* Aboriginal
people are descended from the
people who lived in Australia
before European settlers arrived.

abort *verb* If a plan or activity is
aborted, it is stopped before it is
finished.

abortion *noun* If a woman has an
abortion, the pregnancy is ended
deliberately before the foetus can
live independently.

abortive *adjective* unsuccessful.

abound *verb* If things abound,
there are very large numbers
of them.

about *preposition, adverb* 1 of or
concerning. 2 approximately and
not exactly. ▶ *adverb* 3 in different
directions: *There were some bottles
scattered about.* ▶ *adjective* 4 present
or in a place: *Is Jane about?* ▶ *phrase*
5 If you are about to do something,
you are just going to do it.

about *preposition, adverb*
1 = concerning, on, regarding,
relating to 2 = almost,
approximately, around, nearly,
roughly

above *preposition, adverb* 1 directly
over or higher than something.
2 greater than a level or amount.

above *preposition, adverb*
1 = higher than, over
2 = beyond, exceeding

abrasion *noun* 1 an area where
your skin has been broken.
2 (GEOGRAPHY) erosion caused by
the small stones, etc. carried by a
river or glacier scraping against a
surface.

abrasive *adjective* 1 An abrasive
substance is rough and can be
used to clean hard surfaces.
2 Someone who is abrasive is
unpleasant and rude.

abreast *adjective* 1 side by side. 2 If
you keep abreast of a subject, you
know all the most recent facts
about it.

abroad *adverb* in a foreign
country.

abrupt *adjective* 1 sudden and
quick. 2 not friendly or polite.
> **abruptly** *adverb* > **abruptness**
noun

abrupt *adjective*
1 = sudden, unexpected,
unforeseen 2 = curt, rude,
short, terse

abscess *noun* a painful swelling filled with pus.

abseiling *noun* Abseiling is the sport of going down a cliff or a tall building by sliding down ropes.

absent *adjective* Something that is absent is not present in a place or situation. > **absence** *noun*

> **absent** *adjective*
> = away, elsewhere, gone, missing

absentee *noun* someone who is not present when they should be.

absent-minded *adjective* forgetful and not paying attention.

> **absent-minded** *adjective*
> = distracted, forgetful, random (New Zealand)

absolute *adjective* total and complete. > **absolutely** *adverb*

> **absolute** *adjective*
> = complete, downright, pure, sheer, thorough, total, utter

absolve *verb* To absolve someone of something is to state they are not to blame for it.

absorb *verb* (SCIENCE) If something absorbs liquid or gas, it soaks it up or takes it in.

> **absorb** *verb*
> = digest, soak up, take in

absorbent *adjective* Absorbent materials soak up liquid easily.

absorption *noun* **1** the soaking up of a liquid or taking in of a gas. **2** great interest in something.

abstain *verb* **1** If you abstain from something, you do not do it or have it. **2** If you abstain in a vote, you do not vote. > **abstention** *noun*

abstain *verb*
1 = avoid, deny yourself, forgo, give up, refrain

abstinence *noun* Abstinence is deliberately not doing something you enjoy.

abstract *adjective* **1** An abstract idea is based on thoughts and ideas rather than physical objects or events, for example 'bravery'. **2** (ART) Abstract art is a style of art which uses shapes rather than images of people or objects. **3** Abstract nouns refer to qualities or ideas rather than to physical objects, for example 'happiness' or 'a question'. > **abstraction** *noun*

absurd *adjective* ridiculous and stupid. > **absurdly** *adverb* > **absurdity** *noun*

> **absurd** *adjective*
> = crazy (informal), illogical, ludicrous, nonsensical, ridiculous

abundance *noun* Something that exists in abundance exists in large numbers.

> **abundance** *noun*
> = bounty, plenty, wealth

abundant *adjective* present in large quantities. > **abundantly** *adverb*

> **abundant** *adjective*
> = ample, copious, plentiful

abuse *verb* **1** If you abuse someone, you speak insultingly to them. **2** (PSHE) To abuse someone also means to treat them cruelly. **3** If you abuse something, you use it wrongly or for a bad purpose. ▶ *noun* **4** (PSHE) prolonged cruel treatment of someone. **5** rude and unkind remarks directed towards

A

someone. **6** the wrong use of something. > **abuser** noun

abuse noun
4 = exploitation, harm, hurt, ill-treatment, oppression
5 = curses, derision, insults, invective

abusive adjective rude and unkind. > **abusively** adverb
> **abusiveness** noun

abusive adjective
= disparaging, insulting, offensive, rude, scathing

abysmal adjective very bad indeed.
> **abysmally** adverb

abyss noun a very deep hole.

abyss noun
= chasm, fissure, gorge, pit, void

acacia noun a type of thorny shrub with small yellow or white flowers.

academic adjective **1** Academic work is work done in a school, college or university. ▶ noun
2 someone who teaches or does research in a college or university.
> **academically** adverb

academy academies noun **1** a school or college, especially one that specialises in one particular subject. **2** in England, a school that is funded by the central government rather than by a local authority. **3** an organisation of scientists, artists, writers or musicians.

accelerate verb (SCIENCE) To accelerate is to go faster.

accelerate verb
= hurry, quicken, speed up

acceleration noun the rate at which the speed of something is increasing.

accelerator noun the pedal in a vehicle which you press to make it go faster.

accent noun **1** a way of pronouncing a language. **2** (MFL) a mark placed above or below a letter in some languages, which affects the way the letter is pronounced. **3** (ENGLISH) stress placed on a particular word, syllable or note. **4** an emphasis on something.

accentuate verb To accentuate a feature of something is to make it more noticeable.

accept verb **1** If you accept something, you say yes to it or take it from someone. **2** If you accept a situation, you realise that it cannot be changed. **3** If you accept a statement or story, you believe it is true. **4** If a group accepts you, they treat you as one of the group. > **acceptance** noun

accept verb
1 = acknowledge, agree to, concur with (formal), consent to, take

acceptable adjective good enough to be accepted. > **acceptably** adverb

acceptable adjective
= adequate, all right, fair, good enough, passable, satisfactory, tolerable

access noun **1** the right or opportunity to enter a place or to use something. ▶ verb **2** If you access information from a computer, you get it.

accessible adjective **1** easily reached or seen. **2** easily understood or used.
> **accessibility** noun

accession *noun* A ruler's accession is the time when he or she becomes the ruler of a country.

accessory accessories *noun* 1 an extra part. 2 someone who helps another person commit a crime.

accident *noun* 1 an unexpected event in which people are injured or killed. 2 Something that happens by accident happens by chance.

accidental *adjective* happening by chance. > **accidentally** *adverb*

> **accidental** *adjective*
> = casual, chance, inadvertent, random

accolade *noun* (*formal*) great praise or an award given to someone.

accommodate *verb* 1 If you accommodate someone, you provide them with a place to sleep, live or work. 2 If a place can accommodate a number of things or people, it has enough room for them.

> **accommodate** *verb*
> 1 = house, put up, shelter

accommodating *adjective* willing to help and to adjust to new situations.

> **accommodating** *adjective*
> = considerate, helpful, hospitable, kind, obliging

accommodation *noun* a place provided for someone to sleep, live or work in.

> **accommodation** *noun*
> = house, housing, lodgings, quarters

accompaniment *noun* 1 The accompaniment to a song is the music played to go with it. 2 An accompaniment to something is another thing that comes with it.

accompany accompanies, accompanying, accompanied *verb* 1 If you accompany someone, you go with them. 2 If one thing accompanies another, the two things exist at the same time. 3 If you accompany a singer or musician, you play an instrument while they sing or play the main tune.

> **accompany** *verb*
> 1 = conduct (*formal*), escort, go with, usher 2 = come with, go together with

accomplice *noun* a person who helps someone else to commit a crime.

accomplish *verb* If you accomplish something, you succeed in doing it.

> **accomplish** *verb*
> = achieve, bring about, complete, do, fulfil, manage

accomplished *adjective* very talented at something.

accomplishment *noun* Someone's accomplishments are the skills they have gained.

accord *verb* 1 If you accord someone or something a particular treatment, you treat them in that way. ▶ *noun* 2 agreement. ▶ *phrase* 3 If you do something **of your own accord**, you do it willingly and not because you have been forced to do it.

accordance *phrase* If you act in **accordance with** a rule or belief, you act in the way the rule or belief says you should.

accordingly *adverb* in a way that is appropriate for the circumstances.

according to *preposition* 1 If something is true according to a particular person, that person says that it is true. 2 If something is done according to a principle or plan, that principle or plan is used as the basis for it.

accordion *noun* a musical instrument like an expanding box. It is played by squeezing the two sides together while pressing the keys on it.

accost *verb* If someone accosts you, especially someone you do not know, they come up and speak to you.

account *noun* 1 a written or spoken report of something. 2 If you have a bank account, you can leave money in the bank and take it out when you need it. 3 (*in plural*) Accounts are records of money spent and received by a person or business. ▶ *phrase* 4 If you **take something into account**, you include it in your planning. 5 **On account of** means because of. ▶ *verb* 6 To account for something is to explain it. 7 If something accounts for a particular amount of something, it is that amount.

accountable *adjective* If you are accountable for something, you are responsible for it and have to explain your actions.
> **accountability** *noun*

accountancy *noun* the job of keeping or inspecting financial accounts.

accountant *noun* a person whose job is to keep or inspect financial accounts.

accounting *noun* the keeping and checking of financial accounts.

accumulate *verb* If you accumulate things or they accumulate, they collect over a period of time.

accurate *adjective* completely correct or precise. > **accurately** *adverb* > **accuracy** *noun*

> **accurate** *adjective*
> = correct, exact, faithful, precise, right, strict, true

accuse *verb* If you accuse someone of doing something wrong, you say they have done it.
> **accusation** *noun* > **accuser** *noun*

> **accuse** *verb*
> = blame, censure (*formal*), charge, cite, denounce

accustom *verb* If you accustom yourself to something new or different, you get used to it.

accustomed *adjective* used to something.

> **accustomed** *adjective*
> = adapted, familiar, used

ace *noun* 1 In a pack of cards, an ace is a card with a single symbol on it. ▶ *adjective* 2 (*informal*) good or skilful.

acerbic *adjective* (*formal*) Acerbic remarks are harsh and bitter.

ache *verb* 1 If you ache, you feel a continuous dull pain in a part of your body. 2 If you are aching for something, you want it very much. ▶ *noun* 3 a continuous dull pain.

achieve *verb* (PSHE) If you achieve something, you successfully do it or cause it to happen.

achieve verb
= accomplish, carry out, complete, do, fulfil, perform

achievement noun (PSHE)
something which you succeed in doing, especially after a lot of effort.

achievement noun
= accomplishment, deed, exploit, feat

acid noun 1 (SCIENCE) An acid is a substance with a pH value of less than 7. There are many different acids; some are used in chemical processes and others in household substances.
▶ adjective 2 Acid tastes are sharp or sour. 3 Acid comments are unkind and critical.
> **acidly** adverb > **acidic** adjective
> **acidity** noun

acid rain noun (GEOGRAPHY)
rain polluted by acid in the atmosphere which has come from factories.

acknowledge verb 1 If you acknowledge a fact or situation, you agree or admit it is true.
2 If you acknowledge someone, you show that you have seen and recognised them. 3 If you acknowledge a message, you tell the person who sent it that you have received it.
> **acknowledgment**; also spelt **acknowledgement** noun

acne noun lumpy spots that cover someone's face.

acoustic adjective 1 relating to sound or hearing. 2 An acoustic guitar is not made louder with an electric amplifier.

acoustics plural noun The acoustics of a room are its structural features which are responsible for how clearly you can hear sounds made in it.

acquaintance noun someone you know slightly but not well.

acquire verb If you acquire something, you obtain it.

acquire verb
= attain, gain, get, obtain, pick up, procure, secure

acquisition noun something you have obtained.

acquit acquits, acquitting, acquitted verb 1 If someone is acquitted of a crime, they have been tried in a court and found not guilty. 2 If you acquit yourself well on a particular occasion, you behave or perform well.
> **acquittal** noun

acre noun a unit for measuring areas of land. One acre is equal to 4840 square yards or about 4047 square metres.

acrid adjective sharp and bitter.

acrimony noun (formal) bitterness and anger. > **acrimonious** adjective

acrobat noun an entertainer who performs gymnastic tricks.
> **acrobatic** adjective

acronym noun a word made up of the initial letters of a phrase. An example of an acronym is 'BAFTA', which stands for 'British Academy of Film and Television Arts'.

across preposition, adverb 1 going from one side of something to the other. 2 on the other side of a road or river.

acrylic noun 1 Acrylic is a type of synthetic cloth. 2 (ART) Acrylics, or acrylic paints, are thick artists' paints which can be used like oil paints or thinned down with water.

act *verb* **1** If you act, you do something. **2** If you act in a particular way, you behave in that way. **3** If a person or thing acts as something else, they have the function or do the job of that thing. **4** If you act in a play or film, you play a part. ▶ *noun* **5** a single thing someone does. **6** An Act of Parliament is a law passed by the government. **7** In a play, ballet or opera, an act is one of the main parts into which it is divided into.

> **act** *verb*
> **1** = function, operate, perform, work **4** = act out, perform, play, play the part of, portray
> ▶ *noun* **5** = accomplishment, achievement, deed, feat, undertaking

acting *noun* the profession of performing in plays or films.

action *noun* **1** the process of doing something. **2** something that is done. **3** a physical movement. **4** In law, an action is a legal proceeding.

> **action** *noun*
> **1** = activity, operation, process **2** = accomplishment, achievement, deed, exploit, feat

activate *verb* To activate something is to make it start working.

active *adjective* **1** (PE) full of energy. **2** busy and hard-working. **3** (ENGLISH) In grammar, a verb in the active voice is one where the subject does the action, rather than having it done to them.
> **actively** *adverb*

> **active** *adjective*
> **1** = energetic, lively, restless, sprightly, vivacious **2** = busy,

engaged, enthusiastic, hardworking, industrious, involved, occupied

activist *noun* a person who tries to bring about political and social change.

activity activities *noun* **1** Activity is a situation in which a lot of things are happening at the same time. **2** (PE) something you do for pleasure.

> **activity** *noun*
> **1** = action, bustle, energy, liveliness **2** = hobby, interest, pastime, pursuit

actor *noun* a man or woman whose profession is acting.

actress *noun* a woman whose profession is acting.

actual *adjective* real, rather than imaginary or guessed at.
> **actually** *adverb*

> **actual** *adjective*
> = authentic, genuine, realistic, true, verified

acupuncture *noun* the treatment of illness or pain by sticking small needles into specific places on a person's body.

acute *adjective* **1** severe or intense. **2** very intelligent. **3** (MATHS) An acute angle is less than 90°. **4** (MFL) In French and some other languages, an acute accent is a line sloping upwards from left to right placed over a vowel to indicate a change in pronunciation, as in the word *café*.

> **acute** *adjective*
> **1** = critical, extreme, grave (*formal*), great, intense, serious, severe **2** = alert, astute, bright, keen, perceptive, quick, sharp, shrewd

ad *noun (informal)* an advertisement.

AD You use 'AD' in dates to indicate the number of years after the birth of Jesus Christ.

adage *noun* a saying that expresses some general truth about life.

adamant *adjective* If you are adamant, you are determined not to change your mind.

adapt *verb* 1 If you adapt to a new situation, you change so you can deal with it successfully. 2 If you adapt something, you change it so it is suitable for a new purpose or situation. > **adaptable** *adjective* > **adaptation** *noun*

> **adapt** *verb*
> 2 = adjust, alter, change, convert, modify

adaptor; also spelt **adapter** *noun* a type of electric plug which can be used to connect two or more plugs to one socket.

add *verb* 1 If you add something to a number of things, you put it with the things. 2 If you add numbers together or add them up, you work out the total.

> **add** *verb*
> 1 = attach, include, supplement
> 2 = add up, count up, total

addict *noun* (PSHE) someone who cannot stop doing something, especially something harmful. > **addicted** *adjective* > **addiction** *noun*

addictive *adjective* If something is addictive, people cannot stop once they have started to do it.

addition *noun* 1 something that has been added to something else. 2 (MATHS) the process of adding numbers together.

addition *noun*
1 = increase, supplement

additional *adjective* extra or more. > **additionally** *adverb*

additive *noun* something added to something else, usually in order to improve it.

address *noun* 1 the number of the house where you live, together with the name of the street and the town or village. 2 a group of words or letters that identifies a location on the internet. 3 a speech given to a group of people. ▶ *verb* 4 If a letter is addressed to you, it has your name and address written on it. 5 If you address a problem or task, you start to deal with it.

adept *adjective* very skilful at doing something.

adequate *adjective* enough in amount or good enough for a purpose. > **adequately** *adverb* > **adequacy** *noun*

> **adequate** *adjective*
> = acceptable, ample, enough, satisfactory, sufficient

adhere *verb* 1 If one thing adheres to another, it sticks firmly to it. 2 If you adhere to a rule or agreement, you do what it says. 3 If you adhere to an opinion or belief, you firmly hold that opinion or belief. > **adherence** *noun*

adherent *noun* An adherent of a belief is someone who holds that belief.

adhesive *noun* 1 any substance used to stick two things together, for example glue. ▶ *adjective* 2 Adhesive substances are sticky and able to stick to things.

A

adjacent *adjective* (formal) 1 If two things are adjacent, they are next to each other. 2 (MATHS) Adjacent angles share one side and have the same point opposite to their bases.

adjective *noun* (ENGLISH) (MFL) a word that adds to the description given by a noun. For example, in 'They live in a large white Georgian house', 'large', 'white' and 'Georgian' are all adjectives. > **adjectival** *adjective*

adjoining *adjective* If two rooms are next to each other and are connected, they are adjoining.

adjourn *verb* 1 If a meeting or trial is adjourned, it stops for a time. 2 If people adjourn to another place, they go there together after a meeting. > **adjournment** *noun*

adjust *verb* 1 If you adjust something, you change its position or alter it in some other way. 2 If you adjust to a new situation, you get used to it. > **adjustment** *noun* > **adjustable** *adjective*

administer *verb* 1 To administer an organisation is to be responsible for managing it. 2 To administer the law or administer justice is to put it into practice and apply it.

> **administer** *verb*
> 1 = be in charge of, command, control, direct, manage, run, supervise 2 = carry out, deal, dispense, execute, impose, inflict, perform

administration *noun* 1 Administration is the work of organising and supervising an organisation. 2 Administration is also the process of administering

something. 3 The administration is the group of people that manages an organisation or a country. > **administrative** *adjective* > **administrator** *noun*

admirable *adjective* very good and deserving to be admired. > **admirably** *adverb*

admiral *noun* the commander of a navy.

admiration *noun* a feeling of great liking and respect.

> **admiration** *noun*
> = appreciation, approval, esteem, regard, respect

admire *verb* If you admire someone or something, you respect and approve of them. > **admirer** *noun*

> **admire** *verb*
> = appreciate, look up to, respect, value

admission *noun* 1 If you are allowed admission to a place, you are allowed to go in. 2 If you make an admission of something, you agree, often reluctantly, it is true.

admit admits, admitting, admitted *verb* 1 If you admit something, you agree, often reluctantly, it is true. 2 To admit someone or something to a place or organisation is to allow them to enter it. 3 If you are admitted to hospital, you are taken there to stay until you are better.

> **admit** *verb*
> 1 = accept, acknowledge, grant 2 = accept, let in, receive, take in

admittedly *adverb* People use 'admittedly' to show that what they are saying contrasts with something they have already said or are about to say, and weakens their argument.

adolescent *noun* (SCIENCE) a young person who is no longer a child but who is not yet an adult. > **adolescence** *noun*

adopt *verb* **1** If you adopt a child that is not your own, you take him or her into your family as your son or daughter. **2** (*formal*) If you adopt a particular attitude, you start to have it. > **adoption** *noun*

adorable *adjective* sweet and attractive.

adore *verb* If you adore someone, you feel deep love and admiration for them. > **adoration** *noun*

adorn *verb* To adorn something is to decorate it. > **adornment** *noun*

adrenalin; also spelt **adrenaline** *noun* Adrenalin is a hormone which is produced by your body when you are angry, nervous or excited. Adrenalin makes your heart beat faster and gives you more energy.

adrift *adjective, adverb* If a boat is adrift or goes adrift, it floats on the water without being controlled.

adulation *noun* great admiration and praise for someone. > **adulatory** *adjective*

adult *noun* a mature and fully developed person or animal.

> **adult** *noun*
> = grown-up, man, woman

adulthood *noun* the time during someone's life when they are an adult.

advance *verb* **1** To advance is to move forward. **2** To advance a cause or interest is to help it to be successful. ▶ *noun* **3** Advance in something is progress in it. ▶ *adjective* **4** happening before

an event. ▶ *phrase* **5** If you do something **in advance**, you do it before something else happens.

> **advance** *verb*
> **1** = make inroads, press on, proceed (*formal*), progress
> ▶ *noun* **3** = breakthrough, development, gain, progress, step

advantage *noun* **1** a benefit or something that puts you in a better position. ▶ *phrase* **2** If you **take advantage** of someone, you treat them unfairly for your own benefit. **3** If you **take advantage** of something, you make use of it.

> **advantage** *noun*
> **1** = ascendancy (*formal*), benefit, dominance, superiority

advantageous *adjective* likely to benefit you in some way.

advent *noun* **1** The advent of something is its start or its coming into existence. **2** Advent is the season just before Christmas in the Christian calendar.

adventure *noun* a series of events that are unusual and exciting.

adventurer *noun* someone who enjoys doing dangerous and exciting things.

adventurous *adjective* willing to take risks and do new and exciting things. > **adventurously** *adverb*

adverb *noun* (ENGLISH) (MFL) a word that adds information about a verb or a following adjective or other adverb, for example, 'slowly', 'now' and 'here', which say how, when or where something is done. > **adverbial** *adjective*

adversary adversaries *noun* someone who is your enemy or who opposes what you are doing.

adverse *adjective* not helpful to you, or opposite to what you want or need. > **adversely** *adverb*

adversity adversities *noun* a time of danger or difficulty.

advert *noun* (*informal*) an advertisement.

advertise *verb* **1** If you advertise something, you tell people about it in a newspaper or poster, or on TV or the internet. **2** To advertise is to make an announcement in a newspaper or poster, or on TV or the internet. > **advertiser** *noun* > **advertising** *noun*

> **advertise** *verb*
> **1** = plug (*informal*), promote, publicise, push

advertisement *noun* an announcement about something in a newspaper or poster, or on TV or the internet.

> **advertisement** *noun*
> = ad (*informal*), advert (*informal*), banner ad, commercial, notice, plug (*informal*)

advice *noun* a suggestion from someone about what you should do.

> **advice** *noun*
> = counsel (*formal*), drum (*Australian; informal*), guidance, opinion, suggestion

advisable *adjective* sensible and likely to achieve the result you want.

advise *verb* **1** If you advise someone to do something, you tell them you think they should do it. **2** (*formal*) If you advise someone of something, you

inform them of it. > **advisory** *adjective*

> **advise** *verb*
> **1** = caution, counsel, recommend, suggest, urge
> **2** = inform, make known, notify

adviser *noun* a person whose job is to give advice.

> **adviser** *noun*
> = aide, consultant, guru, mentor, tutor

advocate *verb* **1** If you advocate a course of action or plan, you support it publicly. ▶ *noun* **2** An advocate of something is someone who supports it publicly. **3** (*formal*) a lawyer who represents clients in court. > **advocacy** *noun*

> **advocate** *verb*
> **1** = back, champion, endorse, favour, promote, recommend, support, uphold

aerial *adjective* **1** Aerial means happening in the air. ▶ *noun* **2** a piece of wire for receiving television or radio signals.

aerobic *adjective* (SCIENCE) Aerobic respiration is a type of breathing that uses oxygen.

aerodynamic *adjective* having a streamlined shape that moves easily through the air.

aeroplane *noun* a vehicle with wings and engines that enable it to fly.

aerosol *noun* (SCIENCE) a small metal container in which liquid is kept under pressure so that it can be forced out as a spray.

aerospace *adjective* involved in making and designing aeroplanes and spacecraft.

aesthetic; also spelt **esthetic** adjective ⒟ⒼⓉ (formal) relating to the appreciation of beauty or art. > **aesthetically** or **esthetically** adverb

afar noun (literary) From afar means from a long way away.

affable adjective pleasant and easy to talk to. > **affably** adverb

affair noun 1 an event or series of events. 2 (in plural) Your affairs are your private and personal life.

> **affair** noun
> 1 = business, event, issue, matter, question, situation, subject

affect verb 1 If something affects you, it influences you in some way. 2 (formal) If you affect a particular way of behaving, you behave in that way.

> **affect** verb
> 1 = act on, alter, change, impinge on

affectation noun An affectation is behaviour that is not genuine but is put on to impress people.

affection noun a feeling of love and fondness for someone.

> **affection** noun
> = attachment, fondness, liking, love, warmth

affectionate adjective full of fondness for someone. > **affectionately** adverb

> **affectionate** adjective
> = caring, fond, loving, tender

affiliate verb If a group affiliates itself to another, larger group, it forms a close association with it. > **affiliation** noun

affinity affinities noun a close similarity or understanding

between two things or people.

affirm verb If you affirm an idea or belief, you clearly indicate your support for it. > **affirmation** noun

affirmative adjective An affirmative word or gesture is one that means yes.

afflict verb If illness or pain afflicts someone, they suffer from it. > **affliction** noun

affluent adjective having a lot of money and possessions. > **affluence** noun

afford verb 1 If you can afford to do something, you have enough money or time to do it. 2 If you cannot afford something to happen, it would be harmful or embarrassing for you if it happened.

affordable adjective If something is affordable, most people have enough money to buy it.

affray noun (formal) a noisy and violent fight.

affront verb 1 If you are affronted by something, you are insulted and angered by it. ▶ noun 2 something that is an insult.

afield adverb Far afield means a long way away.

afloat adverb, adjective 1 floating on water. 2 successful and making enough money.

afoot adjective, adverb happening or being planned, especially secretly.

afraid adjective 1 If you are afraid, you think that something bad is going to happen. 2 If you are afraid something might happen, you are worried it might happen.

> **afraid** adjective
> 1 = apprehensive, fearful, frightened, nervous, scared

afresh *adverb* again and in a new way.

Africa *noun* Africa is the second largest continent. It is almost surrounded by sea, with the Atlantic on its west side, the Mediterranean to the north, and the Indian Ocean and the Red Sea to the east.

African *adjective* 1 belonging or relating to Africa. ▶ *noun* 2 someone, especially a Black person, who comes from Africa.

African American an American whose ancestors came from Africa.

Afrikaans *noun* a language spoken in South Africa, similar to Dutch.

Afrikaner *noun* a white South African with Dutch ancestors.

aft *adverb, adjective* towards the back of a ship or boat.

after *preposition, adverb* 1 later than a particular time, date or event. 2 behind and following someone or something.

> **after** *preposition, adverb*
> 1 = afterwards, following, later, subsequently

afterlife *noun* The afterlife is a life some people believe begins when you die.

aftermath *noun* The aftermath of a disaster is the situation that comes after it.

afternoon *noun* the part of the day between noon and about six o'clock.

aftershave *noun* a pleasant-smelling liquid men put on their faces after shaving.

afterthought *noun* something you do or say as an addition to something else you have already done or said.

afterwards *adverb* after an event or time.

again *adverb* 1 happening one more time. 2 returning to the same state or place as before.

> **again** *adverb*
> 1 = afresh, anew, once more

against *preposition* 1 touching and leaning on: *He leaned against the wall.* 2 in opposition to: *the Test match against England.* 3 in preparation for or in case of something: *precautions against fire.* 4 in comparison with: *The pound is now at its lowest rate against the dollar.*

> **against** *preposition*
> 2 = averse to, hostile to, in opposition to, versus 3 = in anticipation of, in expectation of, in preparation for

age ages, ageing or aging, aged *noun* 1 The age of someone or something is the number of years they have lived or existed. 2 Age is the quality of being old. 3 a particular period in history. 4 (*in plural, informal*) Ages means a very long time. ▶ *verb* 5 To age is to grow old or to appear older.

aged *adjective* 1 having a particular age. 2 very old.

agency agencies *noun* an organisation or business which provides certain services.

agenda *noun* a list of items to be discussed at a meeting.

agent *noun* 1 someone who arranges work or business for other people, especially actors or singers. 2 someone who works for their country's secret service.

aggravate verb 1 To aggravate a bad situation is to make it worse. 2 (informal) If someone or something aggravates you, they make you annoyed.
> **aggravating** adjective
> **aggravation** noun

aggregate noun a total that is made up of several smaller amounts.

aggression noun violent and hostile behaviour.

aggressive adjective full of hostility and violence.
> **aggressively** adverb
> **aggressiveness** noun

> **aggressive** adjective
> = assertive, hostile

aggressor noun a person or country that starts a fight or a war.

aggrieved adjective upset and angry about the way you have been treated.

aghast adjective shocked and horrified.

agile adjective (PE) able to move quickly and easily. > **agilely** adverb
> **agility** noun

> **agile** adjective
> = lithe, nimble, sprightly, supple

agitate verb 1 If you agitate for something, you campaign energetically to get it. 2 If something agitates you, it worries you. > **agitation** noun
> **agitator** noun

> **agitate** verb
> 1 = campaign, demonstrate, protest, push 2 = bother, distress, disturb, trouble, upset, worry

agnostic noun (RE) someone who believes we cannot know definitely whether God exists or not. > **agnosticism** noun

ago adverb in the past: He came to Britain six years ago.

agog adjective excited and eager to know more about an event or situation.

agonising; also spelt **agonizing** adjective extremely painful, either physically or mentally.

agony noun very great physical or mental pain.

agrarian adjective (formal) relating to farming and agriculture.

agree agrees, agreeing, agreed verb 1 If you agree with someone, you have the same opinion as them. 2 If you agree to do something, you say you will do it. 3 If two stories or totals agree, they are the same. 4 Food that doesn't agree with you makes you ill.

> **agree** verb
> 1 = assent (formal), be of the same opinion, concur (formal), see eye to eye 3 = accord (formal), conform, match, square, tally

agreeable adjective 1 pleasant or enjoyable. 2 If you are agreeable to something, you are willing to allow it or to do it. > **agreeably** adverb

> **agreeable** adjective
> 1 = delightful, enjoyable, lovely, nice, pleasant, pleasurable
> 2 = game, happy, prepared, ready, willing

agreement noun 1 a decision that has been reached by two or more people. 2 Two people who are in agreement have the same opinion about something.

agreement noun
1 = arrangement, contract, deal (informal), pact, settlement, treaty

agriculture noun Agriculture is farming. > **agricultural** adjective

aground adverb If a boat runs aground, it becomes stuck in the ground in a shallow stretch of water.

ahead adverb 1 in front: He looked ahead. 2 more advanced than someone or something else: We are five years ahead of the competition. 3 in the future: I haven't had time to think far ahead.

aid noun 1 Aid is money, equipment or services provided for people in need. 2 something that makes a task easier. ▸ verb 3 (formal) If you aid a person or an organisation, you help or support them.

aide noun an assistant to an important person, especially in the government or the army.

AIDS noun a disease which destroys the body's natural system of immunity to diseases. AIDS is an abbreviation for 'acquired immune deficiency syndrome'.

ailing adjective 1 sick or ill, and not getting better. 2 getting into difficulties, especially with money.

ailment noun a minor illness.

aim verb 1 If you aim an object or weapon at someone or something, you point it at them. 2 If you aim to do something, you are planning or hoping to do it. ▸ noun 3 Your aim is what you intend to achieve. 4 If you take aim, you point an object or weapon at someone or something.

aim verb
2 = aspire, attempt, intend, plan, propose, strive
▸ noun 3 = ambition, goal, intention, objective, plan, target

aimless adjective having no clear purpose or plan. > **aimlessly** adverb > **aimlessness** noun

air noun 1 Air is the mixture of oxygen and other gases which we breathe and which forms the earth's atmosphere. 2 'Air' is used to refer to travel in aircraft: I have to travel by air a great deal. 3 An air someone or something has is the impression they give: an air of defiance. ▸ verb 4 If you air your opinions, you talk about them to other people.

airborne adjective in the air and flying.

air-conditioning noun a system of providing cool, clean air in buildings. > **air-conditioned** adjective

aircraft noun any vehicle which can fly.

airfield noun an open area of ground with runways where small aircraft take off and land.

air force noun the part of a country's armed services that fights using aircraft.

airlift noun an operation to move people or goods by air, especially in an emergency.

airline noun a company which provides air travel.

airman airmen noun a man who serves in his country's air force.

airport noun a place where people go to catch planes.

air raid noun an attack by enemy aircraft in which bombs are dropped.

airship noun a large, light aircraft consisting of a rigid balloon filled with gas and powered by an engine, with a passenger compartment underneath.

airstrip noun a stretch of land that has been cleared for aircraft to take off and land.

airtight adjective not letting air in or out.

airy airier, airiest adjective full of fresh air and light. > **airily** adverb

aisle noun a long narrow gap that people can walk along between rows of seats or shelves.

ajar adjective A door or window that is ajar is slightly open.

akin adjective (formal) similar.

alacrity noun (formal) eager willingness.

alarm noun 1 a feeling of fear and worry. 2 an automatic device used to warn people of something. ▶ verb 3 If something alarms you, it makes you worried and anxious. > **alarming** adjective

> **alarm** noun
> 1 = anxiety, apprehension, fright, nervousness, panic, scare 2 = distress signal, siren, warning
> ▶ verb 3 = distress, frighten, panic, scare, startle, unnerve

alas adverb unfortunately or regrettably.

albatross noun a large white sea bird.

albeit conjunction (formal) although.

albino albinos noun a person or animal with very white skin, white hair, and pink eyes.

album noun 1 a recording with a number of songs on it. 2 a book in which you keep a collection of things such as photographs or stamps.

alchemy noun a medieval science that attempted to change ordinary metals into gold. > **alchemist** noun

alcohol noun Alcohol is any drink that can make people drunk; also the colourless flammable liquid found in these drinks, produced by fermenting sugar.

alcoholic adjective 1 An alcoholic drink contains alcohol. ▶ noun 2 someone who is addicted to alcohol. > **alcoholism** noun

alcove noun an area of a room which is set back slightly from the main part.

ale noun a type of beer.

alert adjective 1 paying full attention to what is happening. ▶ noun 2 a situation in which people prepare themselves for danger. ▶ verb 3 If you alert someone to a problem or danger, you warn them of it. > **alertness** noun

> **alert** adjective
> 1 = attentive, observant, on guard, vigilant, wary
> ▶ verb 3 = forewarn, inform, notify, warn

A level noun an advanced exam taken by students in many British schools and colleges.

algae plural noun plants that grow in water or on damp surfaces.

algebra noun (MATHS) a branch of mathematics in which symbols

A

and letters are used instead of numbers to express relationships between quantities. > **algebraic** *adjective*

Algerian *adjective* 1 belonging or relating to Algeria. ▶ *noun* 2 someone who comes from Algeria.

alias aliases *noun* a false name.

alibi alibis *noun* An alibi is evidence proving you were somewhere else when a crime was committed.

alien *adjective* 1 not familiar to you. ▶ *noun* 2 someone who is not a citizen of the country in which he or she lives. 3 In science fiction, an alien is a creature from outer space.

alienate *verb* If you alienate someone, you do something that makes them stop being sympathetic to you.

alight *adjective* 1 Something that is alight is burning. ▶ *verb* 2 If a bird or insect alights somewhere, it lands there.

align *verb* 1 If you align yourself with a particular group, you support them. 2 If you align things, you place them in a straight line. > **alignment** *noun*

alike *adjective* 1 Things that are alike are similar in some way. ▶ *adverb* 2 If people or things are treated alike, they are treated in a similar way.

> **alike** *adjective*
> 1 = analogous, close, identical, similar, the same
> ▶ *adverb* 2 = equally, in the same way, similarly, uniformly

alimony *noun* money someone has to pay regularly to their wife or husband after they are divorced.

alive *adjective* 1 living. 2 lively and active.

> **alive** *adjective*
> 1 = animate, breathing, living
> 2 = active, alert, animated, energetic, full of life, lively, vivacious

alkali *noun* (SCIENCE) a chemical substance that turns litmus paper blue. > **alkaline** *adjective*

all *adjective, pronoun, adverb* 1 used when referring to the whole of something: *She managed to finish it all.* ▶ *adverb* 2 'All' is also used when saying the two sides in a game or contest have the same score: *The final score was six points all.*

> **all** *adjective, pronoun, adverb*
> 1 = each, every one, everything, the whole amount, the (whole) lot

Allah *proper noun* (RE) the Arabic word for God.

allay *verb* To allay someone's fears or doubts is to stop them feeling afraid or doubtful.

allege *verb* If you allege that something is true, you say it is true but do not provide any proof. > **allegation** *noun*

allegiance *noun* loyal support for a person or organisation.

allegory allegories *noun* a piece of writing or art in which the characters and events are symbols for something else. Allegories usually make some moral, religious or political point. For example, George Orwell's novel *Animal Farm* is an allegory in that the animals who revolt in the farmyard are symbols of the political leaders in the Russian Revolution. > **allegorical** *adjective*

allergy allergies noun a sensitivity someone has to something, so that they become ill when they eat it or touch it. ▷ **allergic** adjective

alleviate verb To alleviate pain or a problem is to make it less severe. ▷ **alleviation** noun

alley noun a narrow passage between buildings.

alliance noun a group of people, organisations or countries working together for similar aims.

alligator noun a large animal, similar to a crocodile.

alliteration noun (ENGLISH) the use of several words together which all begin with the same sound, for example 'around the rugged rock the ragged rascal ran'.

allocate verb If you allocate something, you decide it should be given to a person or place, or used for a particular purpose. ▷ **allocation** noun

allot allots, allotting, allotted verb If something is allotted to you, it is given to you as your share.

allotment noun a piece of land which people can rent to grow vegetables on.

allow verb 1 If you allow something, you say it is all right or let it happen. 2 If you allow a period of time or an amount of something, you set it aside for a particular purpose. ▷ **allowable** adjective

allow verb
1 = approve, authorise, let, permit, stand for, tolerate
2 = allocate, allot, assign, grant, set aside

allowance noun 1 money given regularly to someone for a particular purpose. ▶ phrase 2 If you **make allowances** for something, you take it into account.

alloy noun (SCIENCE) a mixture of two or more metals.

all right; also spelt **alright** adjective 1 If something is all right, it is acceptable. 2 If someone is all right, they are safe and not harmed.

all right adjective
1 = acceptable, adequate, average, fair, okay or OK (informal)

allude verb If you allude to something, you refer to it in an indirect way.

allure noun The allure of something is an exciting quality that makes it attractive. ▷ **alluring** adjective

allusion noun (ENGLISH) an indirect reference to or comment about something.

ally allies, allying, allied noun 1 a person or country that helps and supports another. ▶ verb 2 If you ally yourself with someone, you agree to help and support each other.

almighty adjective 1 very great or serious. ▶ proper noun 2 The Almighty is another name for God.

almond noun a pale brown oval nut.

almost adverb very nearly.

almost adverb
= about, approximately, close to, nearly, not quite, practically

aloft adverb up in the air or in a high position.

A

alone *adjective, adverb* not with other people or things.

> **alone** *adjective, adverb*
> = detached, isolated, separate, single

along *preposition* **1** moving, happening or existing continuously from one end to the other of something, or at various points beside it: *houses along the river.* ▶ *adverb* **2** moving forward: *We marched along, singing as we went.* **3** with someone: *Why could she not take her along?* ▶ *phrase* **4 All along** means from the beginning of a period of time right up to now.

alongside *preposition, adverb* **1** next to something. ▶ *preposition* **2** If you work alongside other people, you are working in the same place and cooperating with them.

aloof *adjective* emotionally distant from someone or something.

aloud *adverb* When you read or speak aloud, you speak loudly enough for other people to hear you.

> **aloud** *adverb*
> = audibly, out loud

alphabet *noun* (LIBRARY) a set of letters in a fixed order that is used in writing a language.
> **alphabetical** *adjective*
> **alphabetically** *adverb*

alpine *adjective* existing in or relating to high mountains.

already *adverb* having happened before the present time or earlier than expected.

alright another spelling of **all right**.

also *adverb* in addition to something that has just been mentioned.

also *adverb*
= as well, besides, furthermore, into the bargain, moreover, too

altar *noun* a holy table in a church or temple.

alter *verb* If something alters or if you alter it, it changes.
> **alteration** *noun*

altercation *noun* (formal) a noisy disagreement.

alternate *verb* **1** If one thing alternates with another, the two things regularly occur one after the other. ▶ *adjective* **2** If something happens on alternate days, it happens on the first day but not the second, and happens again on the third day but not the fourth, and so on. **3** (MATHS) Alternate angles are two angles on opposite sides of a line that crosses two other lines.
> **alternately** *adverb*

alternative *noun* **1** something you can do or have instead of something else. ▶ *adjective* **2** Alternative plans or actions can happen or be done instead of what is already happening or being done. > **alternatively** *adverb*

although *conjunction* in spite of the fact that.

altitude *noun* (GEOGRAPHY) The altitude of something is its height above sea level.

altogether *adverb* **1** entirely. **2** in total; used of amounts.

aluminium *noun* (SCIENCE) Aluminium is a light silvery-white metallic element. It is used to make aircraft and other equipment, usually in the form of alloys.

always *adverb* all the time or for ever.

always *adverb*
= continually, every time, forever, invariably, perpetually

am the first person singular, present tense of **be**.

a.m. used to specify times between 12 midnight and 12 noon, eg *I get up at 6 a.m.* It is an abbreviation for the Latin phrase 'ante meridiem', which means 'before noon'.

amalgamate *verb* If two organisations amalgamate, they join together to form one new organisation. > **amalgamation** *noun*

amass *verb* If you amass something such as money or information, you collect large quantities of it.

amateur *noun* someone who does something as a hobby rather than as a job.

amateurish *adjective* not skilfully made or done.

amaze *verb* If something amazes you, it surprises you very much.

> **amaze** *verb*
> = astonish, astound, shock, stagger, stun, surprise

amazement *noun* complete surprise.

> **amazement** *noun*
> = astonishment, shock, surprise, wonder

amazing *adjective* very surprising or remarkable. > **amazingly** *adverb*

> **amazing** *adjective*
> = astonishing, astounding, staggering, startling, stunning, surprising

ambassador *noun* a person sent to a foreign country as the representative of his or her own government.

amber *noun* 1 a hard, yellowish-brown substance used for making jewellery. ▶ *noun, adjective* 2 orange-brown.

ambience *noun (formal)* The ambience of a place is its atmosphere.

ambiguous *adjective* A word or phrase that is ambiguous has more than one meaning.
> **ambiguously** *adverb*
> **ambiguity** *noun*

ambition *noun* 1 If you have an ambition to achieve something, you want very much to achieve it. 2 a great desire for success, power and wealth.

ambitious *adjective* 1 Someone who is ambitious has a strong desire for success, power and wealth. 2 An ambitious plan is a large one and requires a lot of work.

ambivalent *adjective* having or showing two conflicting attitudes or emotions.
> **ambivalence** *noun*

amble *verb* If you amble, you walk slowly and in a relaxed manner.

ambulance *noun* a vehicle for taking sick and injured people to hospital.

ambush *verb* 1 To ambush someone is to attack them after hiding and lying in wait for them. ▶ *noun* 2 an attack on someone after hiding and lying in wait for them.

amenable *adjective* willing to listen to suggestions, or to

A

cooperate with someone.
> **amenably** adverb

amend verb To amend something that has been written or said is to alter it slightly. > **amendment** noun

amenity amenities noun (GEOGRAPHY) Amenities are things that are available for the public to use, such as sports facilities or shopping centres.

America noun America refers to the United States or to the whole of North, South and Central America.

American adjective 1 belonging or relating to the United States or to the whole of North, South and Central America. ▶ noun 2 someone who comes from the United States.

amiable adjective pleasant and friendly. > **amiably** adverb

amicable adjective fairly friendly. > **amicably** adverb

amid or **amidst** preposition (formal) 1 If something happens amid events of some kind, it happens at the same time as those events. 2 surrounded by: The house is set amid trees and bushes.

amiss adjective If something is amiss, there is something wrong.

ammonia noun Ammonia is a colourless, strong-smelling gas or alkaline liquid. It is used in household cleaning materials, explosives and fertilisers. It has the chemical formula NH_3.

ammunition noun anything that can be fired from a gun or other weapon, for example bullets and shells.

amnesia noun loss of memory.

amnesty amnesties noun an official pardon for political or other prisoners.

amok phrase If a person or animal runs amok, they behave in a violent and uncontrolled way.

among or **amongst** preposition 1 surrounded by. 2 in the company of. 3 between more than two: The money will be divided among seven charities.

> **among** preposition
> 1 = amid, amidst, in the middle of, in the thick of, surrounded by 3 = between, to each of

amoral adjective Someone who is amoral has no moral standards by which to live.

amorous adjective passionately affectionate. > **amorously** adverb

amount noun 1 An amount of something is how much there is of it. ▶ verb 2 If something amounts to a particular total, all the parts of it add up to that total.

> **amount** noun
> 1 = expanse, quantity, volume

amp noun An amp is the same as an amplifier.

amphetamine noun a drug that increases people's energy and makes them excited. It can have dangerous and unpleasant side effects.

amphibian noun (SCIENCE) a creature that lives partly on land and partly in water, for example a frog.

amphibious adjective An amphibious animal, such as a frog, lives partly on land and partly in water.

amphitheatre noun (HISTORY) An amphitheatre is a large, circular open area with sloping sides covered with rows of seats. Amphitheatres were built originally by the Greeks and Romans as venues for sport and entertainment.

ample *adjective* If there is an ample amount of something, there is more than enough of it. > **amply** *adverb*

> **ample** *adjective*
> = abundant, enough, plenty of, sufficient

amplifier *noun* a piece of equipment which causes sounds or electrical signals to become louder.

amplify amplifies, amplifying, amplified *verb* If you amplify a sound, you make it louder. > **amplification** *noun*

amputate *verb* To amputate an arm or a leg is to cut it off as a surgical operation. > **amputation** *noun*

amuse *verb* **1** If something amuses you, you think it is funny. **2** If you amuse yourself, you find things to do which stop you from being bored. > **amusing** *adjective*

amusement *noun* **1** Amusement is the state of thinking something is funny. **2** Amusement is also the pleasure you get from being entertained or from doing something interesting.

an *adjective* 'An' is used instead of 'a' in front of words that begin with a vowel sound.

-an *suffix* '-an' comes at the end of nouns and adjectives which show where or what someone or something comes from or belongs to: *American*; *Victorian*.

anachronism *noun* something that belongs or seems to belong to another time. > **anachronistic** *adjective*

anaemia *noun* a medical condition resulting from too few red cells in a person's blood. People with anaemia look pale and feel very tired. > **anaemic** *adjective*

anaerobic *adjective* (SCIENCE) Anaerobic respiration is a type of breathing that does not use oxygen.

anaesthetic *noun* a substance that stops you feeling pain. A general anaesthetic stops you from feeling pain in the whole of your body by putting you to sleep, and a local anaesthetic makes just one part of your body go numb.

anaesthetist *noun* a doctor who is specially trained to give anaesthetics.

anagram *noun* a word or phrase formed by changing the order of the letters of another word or phrase. For example, 'triangle' is an anagram of 'integral'.

anal *adjective* relating to the anus.

analogy analogies *noun* a comparison showing that two things are similar in some ways. > **analogous** *adjective*

analyse *verb* (EXAM TERM) To analyse something is to break it down into parts or investigate it carefully, so that you can describe its main aspects or find out what it consists of.

analysis analyses *noun* the process of investigating something in order to understand it or find out what it consists of.

analyst *noun* a person whose job is to analyse things and to find out about them.

analytic or **analytical** *adjective* using logical reasoning.

anarchy *noun* a situation where nobody obeys laws or rules.

anatomy anatomies *noun* 1 the study of the structure of the human body or of the bodies of animals. 2 An animal's anatomy is the structure of its body.
> **anatomical** *adjective*
> **anatomically** *adverb*

ANC *noun* one of the main political parties in South Africa. ANC is an abbreviation for 'African National Congress'.

ancestor *noun* Your ancestors are the members of your family who lived many years ago and from whom you are descended.

> **ancestor** *noun*
> = forebear, forefather

ancestry ancestries *noun* Your ancestry consists of the people from whom you are descended.

anchor *noun* 1 a heavy, hooked object at the end of a chain, dropped from a boat into the water to keep the boat in one place. ▶ *verb* 2 To anchor a boat or another object is to stop it from moving by dropping an anchor or attaching it to something.

anchorage *noun* a place where a boat can safely be anchored.

anchovy anchovies *noun* a type of small edible fish with a very strong salty taste.

ancient *adjective* 1 existing or happening in the distant past. 2 very old or having a very long history.

ancillary *adjective* The ancillary workers in an institution are the people such as cooks and cleaners, whose work supports the main work of the institution.

and *conjunction* You use 'and' to link two or more words or phrases together.

androgynous *adjective* (formal) having both male and female characteristics.

android *noun* In science fiction, an android is a robot that looks like a human being.

anecdote *noun* a short, entertaining story about a person or event. > **anecdotal** *adjective*

anew *adverb* If you do something anew, you do it again.

angel *noun* Angels are spiritual beings some people believe live in heaven and act as messengers for God. > **angelic** *adjective*

anger *noun* 1 the strong feeling you get when you feel someone has behaved in an unfair or cruel way. ▶ *verb* 2 If something angers you, it makes you feel angry.

> **anger** *noun*
> 1 = fury, outrage, rage, wrath
> ▶ *verb* 2 = enrage, infuriate, outrage

angina *noun* a brief but very severe heart pain, caused by lack of blood supply to the heart.

angle *noun* 1 (MATHS) the difference in direction between two lines or surfaces. Angles are measured in degrees. 2 the direction from which you look at something. 3 An angle on something is a particular way of considering it.

angler *noun* someone who fishes with a fishing rod as a hobby.
> **angling** *noun*

Anglican noun, adjective (RE) (a member of one of the churches) belonging to the Anglican Communion, a group of Protestant churches which includes the Church of England.

Anglo-Saxon noun 1 (HISTORY) The Anglo-Saxons were a race of people who settled in England from the fifth century AD and were the dominant people until the Norman invasion in 1066. They were composed of three West Germanic tribes, the Angles, Saxons and Jutes. 2 Anglo-Saxon is another name for **Old English**.

Angolan adjective 1 belonging or relating to Angola. ▶ noun 2 someone who comes from Angola.

angry angrier, angriest adjective very cross or annoyed. > **angrily** adverb

> **angry** adjective
> = cross, enraged, furious, mad (informal)

anguish noun extreme suffering. > **anguished** adjective

angular adjective Angular things have straight lines and sharp points.

animal noun any living being except a plant, or any mammal except a human being.

> **animal** noun
> = beast, creature

animate verb To animate something is to make it lively and interesting.

animated adjective lively and interesting.

animation noun 1 a method of film-making in which a series of drawings are photographed.

When the film is projected, the characters in the drawings appear to move. 2 Someone who has animation shows liveliness in the way they speak and act. > **animator** noun

animosity animosities noun a feeling of strong dislike and anger towards someone.

> **animosity** noun
> = antagonism, antipathy (formal), dislike, hatred, hostility, ill will, malice, resentment

ankle noun the joint which connects your foot to your leg.

annex; also spelt **annexe** noun 1 an extra building which is joined to a larger main building. 2 an extra part added to a document. ▶ verb 3 If one country annexes another, it seizes the other country and takes control of it. > **annexation** noun

annihilate verb If something is annihilated, it is completely destroyed. > **annihilation** noun

anniversary anniversaries noun a date which is remembered because something special happened on that date in a previous year.

announce verb If you announce something, you tell people about it publicly or officially.

> **announce** verb
> = advertise, make known, proclaim, reveal, tell

announcement noun a statement giving information about something.

> **announcement** noun
> = advertisement, broadcast, bulletin, declaration, report, statement

A

announcer noun someone who introduces programmes on radio or television.

annoy verb If someone or something annoys you, they irritate you and make you fairly angry.

> **annoy** verb
> = bother, displease, get on someone's nerves (informal), hack off (British and New Zealand; slang), irritate, plague, vex

annoyance noun 1 a feeling of irritation. 2 something that causes irritation.

> **annoyance** noun
> 1 = displeasure, irritation
> 2 = bore, drag (informal), nuisance, pain (informal), pain in the neck (informal), pest

annual adjective 1 happening or done once a year. 2 happening or calculated over a period of one year. ▶ noun 3 a book or magazine published once a year. 4 a plant that grows, flowers and dies within one year. > **annually** adverb

annul annuls, annulling, annulled verb If a marriage or contract is annulled, it is declared invalid, so that legally it is considered never to have existed. > **annulment** noun

anoint verb To anoint someone is to put oil on them as part of a ceremony. > **anointment** noun

anomaly anomalies noun Something is an anomaly if it is unusual or different from normal. > **anomalous** adjective

anon. an abbreviation for **anonymous**.

anonymous adjective If something is anonymous, nobody knows who is responsible for it.
> **anonymously** adverb
> **anonymity** noun

anorak noun a warm waterproof jacket, usually with a hood.

anorexia noun a psychological condition in which a person may eat too little in order to keep their weight as low as possible.
> **anorexic** adjective

another adjective, pronoun Another thing or person is an additional thing or person.

answer verb 1 If you answer someone, you reply to them using words or actions or in writing. ▶ noun 2 the reply you give when you answer someone. 3 a solution to a problem.

> **answer** verb
> 1 = reply, respond, retort
> ▶ noun 2 = reply, response, retort

answerable adjective If you are answerable to someone for something, you are responsible for it.

ant noun Ants are small insects that live in large groups.

-ant suffix '-ant' is used to form adjectives: important.

antagonise; also spelt **antagonize** verb If someone is antagonised, they are made to feel anger and hostility.

antagonism noun hatred or hostility.

antagonist noun an enemy or opponent.

antagonistic adjective Someone who is antagonistic towards you shows hate or hostility.

Antarctic noun The Antarctic is the region south of the Antarctic Circle.

Antarctic Circle noun The Antarctic Circle is an imaginary circle around the southern part of the world.

ante- prefix 'Ante-' means 'before'. For example, antenatal means 'before birth'.

antelope noun an animal which looks like a deer.

antenatal adjective concerned with the care of pregnant women and their unborn children.

antenna antennae or antennas noun 1 The antennae of insects and certain other animals are the two long, thin parts attached to their heads which they use to feel with. 2 In Australian, New Zealand and American English, an antenna is a radio or television aerial.

anthem noun a hymn written for a special occasion.

anthology anthologies noun (LIBRARY) a collection of writings by various authors published in one book.

anthropology noun the study of human beings and their society and culture. > **anthropological** adjective > **anthropologist** noun

anti- prefix 'Anti-' means opposed to or opposite to something: antiwar marches.

antibiotic noun a drug or chemical used in medicine to kill bacteria and cure infections.

antibody antibodies noun a substance produced in the blood which can kill the harmful bacteria that cause disease.

anticipate verb If you anticipate an event, you are expecting it and are prepared for it. > **anticipation** noun

anticlimax noun something that disappoints you because it is not as exciting as expected, or because it occurs after something that was very exciting.

anticlockwise adjective, adverb moving in the opposite direction to the hands of a clock.

antics plural noun funny or silly ways of behaving.

antidote noun a chemical substance that acts against the effect of a poison.

antipathy noun a strong feeling of dislike or hostility towards something or someone.

antiquarian adjective relating to or involving old and rare objects.

antiquated adjective very old-fashioned.

antique noun 1 an object from the past that is collected because of its value or beauty. ▶ adjective 2 from or concerning the past.

antiquity antiquities noun 1 Antiquity is the distant past, especially the time of the ancient Egyptians, Greeks and Romans. 2 Antiquities are works of art and buildings from the distant past.

anti-Semitism noun hatred of Jewish people. > **anti-Semitic** adjective > **anti-Semite** noun

antiseptic adjective Something that is antiseptic kills germs.

antisocial adjective 1 An antisocial person is unwilling to meet and be friendly with other people. 2 Antisocial behaviour is annoying or upsetting to other people.

A

antithesis antitheses noun
(formal) The antithesis of
something is its exact opposite.

anus noun the hole between the
buttocks.

anvil noun a heavy iron block on
which hot metal is beaten into
shape.

anxiety anxieties noun
nervousness or worry.

> **anxiety** noun
> = apprehension, concern, fear,
> misgiving, nervousness,
> unease, worry

anxious adjective 1 If you are
anxious, you are nervous or
worried. 2 If you are anxious to do
something or anxious that
something should happen, you
very much want to do it or want it
to happen. > **anxiously** adverb

> **anxious** adjective
> 1 = apprehensive, bothered,
> concerned, fearful, nervous,
> troubled, uneasy, worried

any adjective, pronoun 1 one, some or
several: Do you have any paperclips I
could borrow? 2 even the smallest
amount or even one: He was unable
to tolerate any dairy products.
3 whatever or whichever, no
matter what or which: Any cooking
oil will do.

anybody pronoun any person.

anyhow adverb 1 in any case.
2 in a careless way.

anyone pronoun any person.

anything pronoun any object,
event, situation or action.

anyway adverb in any case.

anywhere adverb in, at or to any
place.

Anzac noun 1 (HISTORY) In World
War I, an Anzac was a soldier with
the Australia and New Zealand
Army Corps. 2 an Australian or
New Zealand soldier.

aorta noun (SCIENCE) the main
artery in the body, which carries
blood away from the heart.

apart adverb, adjective 1 When
something is apart from
something else, there is a space or
a distance between them. ▶ adverb
2 If you take something apart, you
separate it into pieces.

apartheid noun (HISTORY) In
South Africa, apartheid was the
government policy and laws
which kept people of different
races apart. It was abolished in
1994.

apartment noun a set of rooms
for living in, usually on one floor
of a building.

apathetic adjective not interested
in anything.

> **apathetic** adjective
> = cool, indifferent, passive,
> uninterested

apathy noun a state of mind in
which you do not care about
anything.

ape noun 1 Apes are animals with
a very short tail or no tail. They
are closely related to humans.
Apes include chimpanzees,
gorillas and gibbons. ▶ verb 2 If
you ape someone's speech or
behaviour, you imitate it.

aphid noun a small insect that feeds
by sucking the juices from plants.

apiece adverb If people have a
particular number of things
apiece, they have that number
each.

aplomb noun If you do something
with aplomb, you do it with
great confidence.

apocalypse *noun* The Apocalypse is the end of the world.
> **apocalyptic** *adjective*

apocryphal *adjective* A story that is apocryphal is generally believed not to have really happened.

apolitical *adjective* not interested in politics.

apologetic *adjective* showing or saying you are sorry.
> **apologetically** *adverb*

apologise; also spelt **apologize** *verb* When you apologise to someone, you say you are sorry for something you have said or done.

> **apologise** *verb*
> = ask forgiveness, beg someone's pardon, express regret, say sorry

apology apologies *noun* something you say or write to tell someone you are sorry.

apostle *noun* (RE) The apostles are the twelve followers who were chosen by Christ.

apostrophe *noun* (ENGLISH) the punctuation mark (') which is used to show that one or more letters have been missed out of a word. Apostrophes are also used with -s at the end of a noun to show that what follows belongs to or relates to the noun.

app *noun* (ICT) a computer program designed to do a particular task, especially one that you can download to a mobile electronic device.

appal appals, appalling, appalled *verb* If something appals you, it shocks you because it is very bad.

appalling *adjective* so bad as to be shocking.

apparatus *noun* The apparatus for a particular task is the equipment used for it.

apparent *adjective* 1 seeming real rather than actually being real. 2 obvious. > **apparently** *adverb*

apparition *noun* something you think you see but that is not really there.

appeal *verb* 1 If you appeal for something, you make an urgent request for it. 2 If you appeal to someone in authority against a decision, you formally ask them to change it. 3 If something appeals to you, you find it attractive or interesting. ▶ *noun* 4 a formal or serious request. 5 The appeal of something is the quality it has which people find attractive or interesting.
> **appealing** *adjective*

> **appeal** *verb*
> 1 = beg, call upon, plead, request
> 3 = attract, fascinate, interest, please
> ▶ *noun* 4 = petition, plea, request

appear *verb* 1 When something which you could not see appears, it moves (or you move) so that you can see it. 2 When something new appears, it begins to exist. 3 When an actor or actress appears in a film or show, they take part in it. 4 If something appears to be a certain way, it seems or looks that way.

> **appear** *verb*
> 1 = come into view, crop up (informal), emerge, show up (informal), surface, turn up
> 2 = become available, be invented, come into being, come into existence, come out

appearance *noun* **1** The appearance of someone in a place is their arrival there, especially when it is unexpected. **2** The appearance of something new is the time when it begins to exist. **3** Someone's or something's appearance is the way they look to other people.

> **appearance** *noun*
> **2** = advent, arrival, coming, debut, emergence, introduction **3** = bearing, image, look, looks

appease *verb* If you try to appease someone, you try to calm them down when they are angry, for example by giving them what they want. > **appeasement** *noun*

appendage *noun* a less important part attached to a main part.

appendicitis *noun* a painful illness in which a person's appendix becomes infected.

appendix appendices or **appendixes** *noun* **1** a small closed tube forming part of your digestive system. **2** An appendix to a book is extra information placed after the end of the main text.

appetising; also spelt **appetizing** *adjective* Food that is appetising looks and smells good, and makes you want to eat it.

appetite *noun* **1** Your appetite is your desire to eat. **2** If you have an appetite for something, you have a strong desire for it and enjoyment of it.

applaud *verb* **1** When a group of people applaud, they clap their hands in approval or praise.

2 When an action or attitude is applauded, people praise it.

applause *noun* Applause is clapping by a group of people.

apple *noun* a round fruit with smooth skin and firm white flesh.

appliance *noun* any machine in your home you use to do a job like cleaning or cooking.

applicable *adjective* Something that is applicable to a situation is relevant to it.

applicant *noun* someone who is applying for something.

application *noun* **1** a formal request for something, usually in writing. **2** The application of a rule, system or skill is the use of it in a particular situation.

apply applies, applying, applied *verb* **1** If you apply for something, you formally ask for it, usually by sending an email or writing a letter. **2** If you apply a rule or skill, you use it in a situation. **3** If something applies to a person or a situation, it is relevant to that person or situation. **4** If you apply something to a surface, you put it on it.

appoint *verb* **1** If you appoint someone to a job or position, you formally choose them for it. **2** If you appoint a time or place for something to happen, you decide when or where it will happen.

appointment *noun* **1** an arrangement you have with someone to meet them. **2** The appointment of a person to do a particular job is the choosing of that person to do it. **3** a job or a position of responsibility.

5 Your command of something is your knowledge of it and your ability to use this knowledge.

> **command** verb
> **1** = bid, demand, direct, order
> **3** = control, head, lead, manage, supervise
> ▶ noun **4** = bidding, decree, directive, injunction (formal), instruction, order **5** = grasp, knowledge, mastery

commandant noun an army officer in charge of a place or group of people.

commander noun an officer in charge of a military operation or organisation.

commandment noun (RE) The Ten Commandments are ten important rules of behaviour that, according to the Old Testament, people should obey.

commando commandos noun Commandos are soldiers who have been specially trained to carry out raids.

commemorate verb **1** An object that commemorates a person or an event is intended to remind people of that person or event. **2** If you commemorate an event, you do something special to show that you remember it.
> **commemorative** adjective
> **commemoration** noun

> **commemorate** verb
> **2** = celebrate, honour

commence verb (formal) To commence is to begin.

commend verb To commend someone or something is to praise them. > **commendation** noun > **commendable** adjective

comment verb **1** If you comment on something, you make a remark about it. ▶ noun **2** a remark about something.

> **comment** verb
> **1** = mention, note, observe, point out, remark, say
> ▶ noun **2** = observation, remark, statement

commentary commentaries noun a description of an event which is broadcast on radio or television while the event is happening.

commentator noun someone who gives a radio or television commentary.

commerce noun Commerce is the buying and selling of goods.

commercial adjective **1** relating to commerce. **2** Commercial activities involve producing goods on a large scale in order to make money. ▶ noun **3** an advertisement on television or radio. > **commercially** adverb

commission verb **1** If someone commissions a piece of work, they formally ask someone to do it. ▶ noun **2** a piece of work that has been commissioned. **3** Commission is money paid to a salesperson each time a sale is made. **4** an official body appointed to investigate or control something.

commit commits, committing, committed verb **1** To commit a crime or sin is to do it. **2** If you commit yourself, you state an opinion or state that you will do something. **3** If someone is committed to hospital or prison, they are officially sent there.

commit verb
1 = carry out, do, perform, perpetrate

commitment noun 1 Commitment is a strong belief in an idea or system. 2 something that regularly takes up some of your time.

committed adjective A committed person has strong beliefs.

committee noun a group of people who make decisions on behalf of a larger group.

commodity commodities noun (formal) Commodities are things that are sold.

common adjective 1 Something that is common exists in large numbers or happens often. 2 If something is common to two or more people, they all have it or use it. 3 'Common' is used to indicate that something is of the ordinary kind and not special. 4 If you describe someone as common, you mean they do not have good taste or good manners. ▶ noun 5 an area of grassy land where everyone can go. ▶ phrase 6 If two things or people have something in common, they both have it.

common adjective
1 = general, popular, prevailing, prevalent, universal, widespread 3 = average, commonplace, everyday, ordinary, plain, standard, usual 4 = coarse, rude, vulgar

commonplace adjective Something that is commonplace happens often.

common sense noun Your common sense is your natural ability to behave sensibly and make good judgments.

common sense noun
= good sense, judgment, level-headedness, prudence, wit

commotion noun A commotion is a lot of noise and excitement.

communal adjective shared by a group of people.

commune noun a group of people who live together and share everything.

communicate verb 1 If you communicate with someone, you keep in touch with them. 2 If you communicate information or a feeling to someone, you make them aware of it.

communicate verb
1 = be in contact, be in touch, correspond 2 = convey (formal), impart (formal), inform, pass on, spread, transmit, tweet

communication noun 1 (PSHE) Communication is the process by which people or animals exchange information. 2 (in plural) Communications are the systems by which people communicate or broadcast information, especially using electricity or radio waves. 3 (formal) a letter or telephone call.

communicative adjective Someone who is communicative is willing to talk to people.

communion noun 1 Communion is the sharing of thoughts and feelings. 2 (RE) In Christianity, Communion is a religious service in which people share bread and wine in remembrance of the death and resurrection of Jesus Christ.

communism noun Communism is the doctrine that the state should own the means of

production and that there should be no private property.
> **communist** adjective, noun

community communities noun (CITIZEN) all the people living in a particular area; also used to refer to particular groups within a society.

commute verb People who commute travel a long distance to work every day. > **commuter** noun

compact adjective taking up very little space.

compact disc noun a music or video recording in the form of a plastic disc which is played using a laser on a special machine, and gives good quality sound or pictures.

companion noun someone you travel or spend time with.
> **companionship** noun

> **companion** noun
> = comrade, crony (old-fashioned), friend, mate (informal), pal (informal), partner

company companies noun 1 a business that sells goods or provides a service. 2 a group of actors, opera singers or dancers. 3 If you have company, you have a friend or visitor with you.

> **company** noun
> 1 = business, corporation, establishment, firm, house
> 2 = assembly, band, circle, community, crowd, ensemble, group, party, troupe
> 3 = companionship, presence

comparable adjective If two things are comparable, they are similar in size or quality.

comparative adjective 1 You add comparative to indicate that

something is true only when compared with what is normal: *eight years of comparative calm.* ▶ noun 2 (ENGLISH) In grammar, the comparative is the form of an adjective which indicates that the person or thing described has more of a particular quality than someone or something else. For example, 'quicker', 'better' and 'easier' are all comparatives.

compare verb 1 (EXAM TERM) When you compare things, you look at them together and see in what ways they are different or similar. 2 If you compare one thing to another, you say it is like the other thing.

> **compare** verb
> 1 = contrast, juxtapose, weigh up

comparison noun (ENGLISH) When you make a comparison, you consider two things together and see in what ways they are different or similar.

compartment noun 1 a section of a railway carriage. 2 one of the separate parts of an object.

> **compartment** noun
> 2 = bay, chamber, division, section

compass noun 1 (SCIENCE) an instrument with a magnetic needle for finding directions. 2 (in plural) Compasses are a hinged instrument for drawing circles.

compassion noun pity and sympathy for someone who is suffering.

compassionate adjective feeling or showing sympathy and pity for others. > **compassionately** adverb

compassionate *adjective*
= caring, humane, kind,
kind-hearted, merciful,
sympathetic, tender

compatible *adjective* If people or
things are compatible, they can
live or work together successfully.
> **compatibility** *noun*

compatible *adjective*
= congenial, harmonious

compatriot *noun* Your
compatriots are people from your
own country.

compel compels, compelling,
compelled *verb* To compel
someone to do something is to
force them to do it.

compelling *adjective* 1 If a story
or event is compelling, it is
extremely interesting. 2 A
compelling argument or reason
makes you believe that something
is true or should be done.

compensate *verb* 1 To compensate
someone is to give them money
to replace something lost or
damaged. 2 If one thing
compensates for another, it
cancels out its bad effects.

compensate *verb*
1 = atone, refund, repay, reward
2 = balance, cancel out,
counteract, make up for, offset

compensation *noun* something
that makes up for loss or damage.

compensation *noun*
= amends, atonement,
damages, payment

compere *noun* 1 the person
who introduces the guests or
performers in a show. ▶ *verb* 2 To
compere a show is to introduce
the guests or performers.

compete *verb* 1 When people or
firms compete, each tries to prove
that they or their products are the
best. 2 If you compete in a contest
or game, you take part in it.

compete *verb*
1 = contend, contest, fight, vie

competent *adjective* Someone
who is competent at something
can do it satisfactorily.
> **competence** *noun*

competition *noun* 1 When there
is competition between people or
groups, they are all trying to get
something that not everyone can
have. 2 an event in which people
take part to find who is best at
something. 3 When there is
competition between firms, each
firm is trying to get people to buy
its own goods.

competition *noun*
1 = contention, contest,
opposition, rivalry, struggle
2 = championship, contest,
event, tournament

competitive *adjective* 1 A
competitive situation is one in
which people or firms are
competing with each other. 2 A
competitive person is eager to be
more successful than others.
3 Goods sold at competitive prices
are cheaper than other goods of
the same kind.

competitor *noun* a person or firm
that is competing to become the
most successful.

competitor *noun*
= adversary, challenger,
competition, contestant,
opponent, opposition, rival

compilation *noun* A compilation
is a book, recording or

programme consisting of several items that were originally produced separately.

compile *verb* When someone compiles a book or report, they make it by putting together several items.

complacent *adjective* If someone is complacent, they are unconcerned about a serious situation and do nothing about it.
> **complacently** *adverb*
> **complacency** *noun*

complain *verb* 1 If you complain, you say that you are not satisfied with something. 2 If you complain of pain or illness, you say that you have it.

> **complain** *verb*
> 1 = carp, find fault, grouse, grumble, kick up a fuss (*informal*), moan, whine, whinge (*informal*)

complaint *noun* If you make a complaint, you complain about something.

> **complaint** *noun*
> = criticism, grievance, grumble, objection, protest

complement *verb* 1 If one thing complements another, the two things go well together. ▶ *noun* 2 If one thing is a complement to another, it goes well with it. 3 In grammar, a complement is a word or phrase that gives information about the subject or object of a sentence. For example, in the sentence 'Rover is a dog', 'a dog' is the complement.
> **complementary** *adjective*

complete *adjective* 1 to the greatest degree possible. 2 If something is complete, none of it is missing. 3 When a task is

complete, it is finished. ▶ *verb* 4 If you complete something, you finish it. 5 If you complete a form, you fill it in. > **completion** *noun*

> **complete** *adjective*
> 1 = absolute, consummate, outright, perfect, thorough, total, utter 2 = entire, full, intact, undivided, whole
> ▶ *verb* 4 = conclude, end, finish

complex *adjective* 1 Something that is complex has many different parts. 2 In grammar, a complex sentence consists of a main clause with one or more subordinate clauses joined to it. ▶ *noun* 3 A complex is a group of buildings, roads or other things connected with each other in some way. 4 If someone has a complex, they have an emotional problem because of a past experience. > **complexity** *noun*

> **complex** *adjective*
> 1 = complicated, difficult, intricate, involved, tangled
> ▶ *noun* 4 = fixation, obsession, phobia, preoccupation, problem, thing

complexion *noun* the quality of the skin on your face.

complicate *verb* To complicate something is to make it more difficult to understand or deal with.

complicated *adjective* Something that is complicated has so many parts or aspects that it is difficult to understand or deal with.

> **complicated** *adjective*
> = complex, convoluted, elaborate, intricate, involved

complication *noun* something that makes a situation more difficult to deal with.

compliment noun **1** If you pay someone a compliment, you tell them you admire something about them. **2** (in plural, formal) When someone sends their compliments, they formally express their good wishes. ▶ verb **3** If you compliment someone, you pay them a compliment.

complimentary adjective **1** If you are complimentary about something, you express admiration for it. **2** A complimentary seat, ticket or magazine is given to you free.

comply complies, complying, complied verb If you comply with an order or rule, you obey it. > **compliance** noun

component noun (DGT)(SCIENCE) The components of something are the parts it is made of.

compose verb **1** If something is composed of particular things or people, it is made up of them. **2** To compose a piece of music, letter or speech means to write it. **3** If you compose yourself, you become calm after being excited or upset.

> **compose** verb
> **2** = create, devise, invent, produce, write

composed adjective calm and in control of your feelings.

composer noun someone who writes music.

composition noun **1** The composition of something is the things it consists of. **2** (ENGLISH) (MUSIC) The composition of a poem or piece of music is the writing of it. **3** (ENGLISH) (MUSIC) a piece of music or writing.

compost noun Compost is a mixture of decaying plants and manure added to soil to help plants grow.

composure noun Someone's composure is their ability to stay calm.

compound noun **1** an enclosed area of land with buildings used for a particular purpose. **2** (SCIENCE) In chemistry, a compound is a substance consisting of two or more different substances or chemical elements. ▶ verb **3** To compound something is to put together different parts to make a whole. **4** To compound a problem is to make it worse by adding to it. ▶ adjective **5** consisting of two or more parts. **6** In grammar, a compound sentence consists of two or more main clauses joined by a conjunction.

comprehend verb (formal) To comprehend something is to understand or appreciate it. > **comprehension** noun

> **comprehend** verb
> = appreciate, fathom, grasp, see, take in, understand, work out

comprehensible adjective able to be understood.

comprehensive adjective **1** Something that is comprehensive includes everything necessary or relevant. ▶ noun **2** a school where children of all abilities are taught together.

compress verb To compress something is to squeeze it or shorten it so that it takes up less space. > **compression** noun

comprise verb (formal) What something comprises is what it consists of.

compromise noun 1 an agreement in which people accept less than they originally wanted. ▶ verb 2 When people compromise, they agree to accept less than they originally wanted.

compulsion noun a very strong desire to do something.

compulsive adjective 1 You use 'compulsive' to describe someone who cannot stop doing something: *a compulsive letter writer*. 2 If you find something such as a book or television programme compulsive, you cannot stop reading or watching it.

compulsory adjective If something is compulsory, you have to do it.

> **compulsory** adjective
> = mandatory, obligatory, required, requisite

computer noun an electronic machine that can quickly make calculations or store and find information.

computerise; also spelt **computerize** verb When a system or process is computerised, the work is done by computers.

computing noun Computing is the use of computers and the writing of programs for them.

comrade noun A soldier's comrades are his or her fellow soldiers, especially in battle. > **comradeship** noun

con cons, conning, conned (informal) verb 1 If someone cons you, they trick you into doing or believing something. ▶ noun 2 a trick in which someone deceives you into doing or believing something.

> **con** verb
> 1 = cheat, deceive, mislead, swindle, trick
> ▶ noun 2 = bluff, deception, fraud, swindle, trick

concave adjective (MATHS) A concave surface curves inwards, rather than being level or bulging outwards.

conceal verb To conceal something is to hide it.

concede verb 1 If you concede something, you admit that it is true. 2 When someone concedes defeat, they accept that they have lost something such as a contest or an election.

conceit noun Conceit is someone's excessive pride in their appearance or abilities.

> **conceit** noun
> = egotism, pride, self-importance, vanity

conceited adjective Someone who is conceited is too proud of their appearance or abilities.

> **conceited** adjective
> = bigheaded (informal), cocky, egotistical, self-important, vain

conceivable adjective If something is conceivable, you can believe that it could exist or be true. > **conceivably** adverb

conceive verb 1 If you conceive of something, you can imagine it or believe it. 2 If you conceive something such as a plan, you think of it and work out how it could be done. 3 When a woman conceives, she becomes pregnant.

concentrate verb 1 If you concentrate on something, you give it all your attention. 2 When something is concentrated in one place, it is all there rather than in several places. > **concentration** noun

> **concentrate** verb
> 1 = be engrossed in, focus your attention on, give your attention to, put your mind to
> 2 = accumulate, collect, gather

concentrated adjective A concentrated liquid has been made stronger by having water removed from it.

concentration camp noun (HISTORY) a prison camp, especially one set up by the Nazis during World War Two.

concept noun an abstract or general idea. > **conceptual** adjective > **conceptually** adverb

conception noun 1 Your conception of something is the idea you have of it. 2 Conception is the process by which a woman becomes pregnant.

concern noun 1 Concern is a feeling of worry about something or someone. 2 If something is your concern, it is your responsibility. 3 a business. ▶ verb 4 If something concerns you or if you are concerned about it, it worries you. 5 You say that something concerns you if it affects or involves you. ▶ phrase 6 If something is of concern to you, it is important to you.

> **concern** noun
> 1 = anxiety, apprehension, disquiet, worry 2 = affair, business, responsibility

▶ verb 4 = bother, distress, disturb, trouble, worry
5 = affect, apply to, be relevant to, involve

concerning preposition You use 'concerning' to show what something is about.

concert noun a public performance by musicians.

concerted adjective A concerted action is done by several people working together.

concerto concertos or concerti noun (MUSIC) a piece of music for a solo instrument and an orchestra.

concession noun If you make a concession, you agree to let someone have or do something.

concise adjective giving all the necessary information using as few words as necessary.

> **concise** adjective
> = brief, short, succinct, terse

conclude verb 1 If you conclude something, you decide that it is so because of the other things that you know. 2 When you conclude something, you finish it.
> **concluding** adjective

> **conclude** verb
> 1 = decide, deduce, infer, judge, reckon (informal), suppose, surmise (formal) 2 = close, end, finish, round off, wind up

conclusion noun 1 a decision made after thinking carefully about something. 2 the finish or ending of something.

> **conclusion** noun
> 1 = deduction, inference, judgment, verdict 2 = close, end, ending, finish, termination (formal)

conclusive *adjective* Facts that are conclusive show that something is certainly true.

concoct *verb* 1 If you concoct an excuse or explanation, you invent one. 2 If you concoct something, you make it by mixing several things together. > **concoction** *noun*

concourse *noun* a wide hall in a building where people walk about or gather together.

concrete *noun* 1 Concrete is a solid building material made by mixing cement, sand and water. ▶ *adjective* 2 definite, rather than general or vague. 3 real and physical, rather than abstract.

concur concurs, concurring, concurred *verb* (*formal*) To concur is to agree.

concurrent *adjective* If things are concurrent, they happen at the same time. > **concurrently** *adverb*

concussed *adjective* confused or unconscious because of a blow to the head. > **concussion** *noun*

condemn *verb* 1 If you condemn something, you say it is bad and unacceptable. 2 If someone is condemned to a punishment, they are given it. 3 If you are condemned to something unpleasant, you must suffer it. 4 When a building is condemned, it is going to be pulled down because it is unsafe. > **condemnation** *noun*

> **condemn** *verb*
> 1 = blame, censure (*formal*), criticise, damn, denounce
> 2 = damn, doom, sentence

condensation *noun* (SCIENCE) Condensation is a coating of tiny

drops formed on a surface by steam or vapour.

condense *verb* 1 If you condense a piece of writing or a speech, you shorten it. 2 (SCIENCE) When a gas or vapour condenses, it changes into a liquid.

condescending *adjective* If you are condescending, you behave in a way that shows you think you are superior to other people.

condition *noun* 1 the state someone or something is in. 2 (*in plural*) The conditions in which something is done are the location and other factors likely to affect it. 3 a requirement that must be met for something else to be possible: *He had to report to the police each week as a condition of bail.* 4 You can refer to an illness or other medical problem as a condition. ▶ *phrase* 5 If you are **out of condition**, you are unfit. ▶ *verb* 6 If someone is conditioned to behave or think in a certain way, they do it as a result of their upbringing or training.

> **condition** *noun*
> 1 = form, shape, state
> 3 = prerequisite, provision, proviso, qualification, requirement, requisite, stipulation, term

conditional *adjective* If one thing is conditional on another, it can only happen if the other thing happens.

condolence *noun* Condolence is sympathy expressed for a bereaved person.

condominium *noun* In Canadian, American, Australian and New Zealand English, a condominium is an apartment block in which each apartment is owned by the person who lives in it.

condone *verb* If you condone someone's bad behaviour, you accept it and do not try to stop it.

conducive *adjective* If something is conducive to something else, it makes it likely to happen.

conduct *verb* 1 To conduct an activity or task is to carry it out. 2 (*formal*) The way you conduct yourself is the way you behave. 3 (MUSIC) When someone conducts an orchestra or choir, they stand in front of it and direct it. 4 (SCIENCE) If something conducts heat or electricity, heat or electricity can pass through it. ▶ *noun* 5 If you take part in the conduct of an activity or task, you help to carry it out. 6 Your conduct is your behaviour.

> **conduct** *verb*
> 1 = carry out, direct, do, manage, organise, perform, run 2 = act, behave
> ▶ *noun* 6 = attitude, behaviour, manners, ways

conductor *noun* 1 (MUSIC) someone who conducts an orchestra or choir. 2 someone who moves round a train, bus or tram checking or selling tickets. 3 (SCIENCE) a substance that conducts heat or electricity.

cone *noun* 1 a regular three-dimensional shape with a circular base and a point at the top. 2 A fir cone or pine cone is the fruit of a fir or pine tree.

confectionery *noun* Confectionery is sweets.

confederation *noun* an organisation formed for business or political purposes.

confer confers, conferring, conferred *verb* When people confer, they discuss something in order to make a decision.

conference *noun* a meeting at which formal discussions take place.

> **conference** *noun*
> = congress, convention, discussion, forum, meeting

confess *verb* If you confess to something, you admit it.

> **confess** *verb*
> = acknowledge, admit, own up

confession *noun* 1 If you make a confession, you admit you have done something wrong. 2 Confession is the act of confessing something, especially a religious act in which people confess their sins to a priest.

> **confession** *noun*
> 2 = acknowledgment, admission

confessional *noun* (RE) a small room in some churches where people confess their sins to a priest.

confetti *noun* Confetti is small pieces of coloured paper thrown over the newly married couple after a wedding ceremony.

confidant *noun* (*formal*) a person you discuss your private problems with.

confide *verb* If you confide in or to someone, you tell them a secret.

confidence *noun* 1 If you have confidence in someone, you feel you can trust them. 2 Someone who has confidence is sure of their own abilities or qualities. 3 a secret you tell someone.

confidence noun
1 = belief, faith, reliance, trust
2 = aplomb, assurance,
self-assurance, self-possession

confident adjective 1 If you are
confident about something, you
are sure it will happen the way
you want it to. 2 People who are
confident are sure of their own
abilities or qualities.
> **confidently** adverb

confident adjective
1 = certain, convinced, positive,
satisfied, secure, sure
2 = assured, self-assured,
self-possessed

confidential adjective
Confidential information is
meant to be kept secret.
> **confidentially** adverb

confine verb 1 If something is
confined to one place, person or
thing, it exists only in that place
or affects only that person or
thing. 2 If you confine yourself to
doing or saying something, it is
the only thing you do or say. 3 If
you are confined to a place, you
cannot leave it. ▶ plural noun 4 The
confines of a place are its
boundaries. > **confinement** noun

confine verb
2 = limit, restrict 3 = hem in,
imprison, restrict, shut up

confined adjective A confined
space is small and enclosed by
walls.

confirm verb 1 To confirm
something is to say or show that
it is true. 2 If you confirm an
arrangement or appointment,
you say it is definite. 3 (RE)
When someone is confirmed,
they are formally accepted as a
member of a Christian Church.
> **confirmation** noun

confirm verb
1 = bear out, endorse, prove,
substantiate, validate, verify
2 = fix, settle

confirmed adjective You use
'confirmed' to describe someone
who has a belief or way of life that
is unlikely to change: a confirmed
bachelor.

confiscate verb To confiscate
something is to take it away from
someone as a punishment.

conflict noun 1 Conflict is
disagreement and argument.
2 (HISTORY) a war or battle.
3 When there is a conflict of ideas
or interests, people have different
ideas or interests which cannot
all be satisfied. ▶ verb 4 When
ideas or interests conflict, they
are different and cannot all be
satisfied.

conflict noun
1 = antagonism, disagreement,
discord, friction, hostility,
opposition, strife 2 = battle,
combat, fighting, strife, war
▶ verb 4 = be at variance, be
incompatible, clash, differ,
disagree

conform verb 1 If you conform,
you behave the way people expect
you to. 2 If something conforms
to a law or to someone's wishes, it
is what is required or wanted.
> **conformist** noun, adjective

confound verb If someone or
something confounds you, they
make you feel surprised or
confused.

confront verb 1 If you are
confronted with a problem or
task, you have to deal with it.

2 If you confront someone, you meet them face to face like an enemy. **3** If you confront someone with evidence or a fact, you present it to them in order to accuse them of something.

confrontation *noun* a serious dispute or fight.

confuse *verb* **1** If you confuse two things, you mix them up and think one of them is the other. **2** To confuse someone means to make them uncertain about what is happening or what to do. **3** To confuse a situation means to make it more complicated.

> **confuse** *verb*
> 1 = mistake, mix up, muddle up
> 2 = baffle, bewilder, mystify, puzzle

confused *adjective* **1** uncertain about what is happening or what to do. **2** in an untidy mess.

> **confused** *adjective*
> 1 = baffled, bewildered, muddled, perplexed, puzzled
> 2 = chaotic, disordered, disorganised, untidy

confusing *adjective* puzzling or bewildering.

> **confusing** *adjective*
> = baffling, bewildering, complicated, puzzling

confusion *noun* **1** a bewildering state. **2** an untidy mess.

> **confusion** *noun*
> 2 = chaos, disarray, disorder, disorganisation, mess

congenital *adjective* If someone has a congenital disease or disability, they have had it from birth but did not inherit it.

congested *adjective* **1** When a road is congested, it is so full of traffic that normal movement is impossible. **2** If your nose is congested, it is blocked and you cannot breathe properly.
> **congestion** *noun*

conglomerate *noun* a large business organisation consisting of several companies.

congratulate *verb* If you congratulate someone, you express pleasure at something good that has happened to them, or praise them for something they have achieved.
> **congratulation** *noun*

congregate *verb* When people congregate, they gather together somewhere.

congregation *noun* the congregation are the people attending a service in a church.

congress *noun* a large meeting held to discuss ideas or policies.

conical *adjective* shaped like a cone.

conifer *noun* any type of evergreen tree that produces cones.
> **coniferous** *adjective*

conjecture *noun* Conjecture is guesswork about something.

conjunction *noun* **1** (ENGLISH) (MFL) In grammar, a conjunction is a word that links two other words or two clauses, for example 'and', 'but', 'while' and 'that'.
▶ *phrase* **2** If two or more things are done **in conjunction**, they are done together.

connect *verb* **1** To connect two things is to join them together. **2** If you connect something with something else, you think of them as being linked.

connect verb
1 = affix, attach, couple, fasten, join, link 2 = ally, associate, link, relate

connection; also spelt **connexion** noun 1 a link or relationship between things. 2 the point where two wires or pipes are joined together. 3 (in plural) Someone's connections are the people they know.

connection noun
1 = affiliation, association, bond, correlation, correspondence, link, relation, relationship 2 = coupling, fastening, junction, link

connective noun (ENGLISH) (MFL) a word or short phrase that connects clauses, phrases or words.

connoisseur noun someone who knows a lot about the arts, or about food or drink.

connotation noun (ENGLISH) The connotations of a word or name are what it makes you think of: *The word 'grey' has connotations of dullness.*

conquer verb 1 To conquer people is to take control of their country by force. 2 If you conquer something difficult or dangerous, you succeed in controlling it.
> **conqueror** noun

conquest noun 1 Conquest is the conquering of a country or group of people. 2 Conquests are lands captured by conquest.

conscience noun the part of your mind that tells you what is right and wrong.

conscience noun
= principles, scruples, sense of right and wrong

conscientious adjective Someone who is conscientious is very careful to do their work properly.

conscious adjective 1 If you are conscious of something, you are aware of it. 2 A conscious action or effort is done deliberately. 3 Someone who is conscious is awake, rather than asleep or unconscious.

consecrated adjective A consecrated building or place is one that has been officially declared to be holy.

consecutive adjective Consecutive events or periods of time happen one after the other.

consensus noun Consensus is general agreement among a group of people.

consent noun 1 (PSHE) Consent is permission to do something. 2 Consent is also agreement between two or more people.
▶ verb 3 (PSHE) If you consent to something, you agree to it or allow it.

consequence noun 1 The consequences of something are its results or effects. 2 (formal) If something is of consequence, it is important.

consequent adjective Consequent describes something as being the result of something else.
> **consequently** adverb

conservation noun Conservation is the preservation of the environment. > **conservationist** noun, adjective

conservative noun 1 In Britain, a Conservative is a member or supporter of the Conservative Party, a political party that believes that the government should interfere as little as possible in the running of the economy. ▶ *adjective* 2 In Britain, Conservative views and policies are those of the Conservative Party. 3 Someone who is conservative is opposed to radical change and values tradition and stability. 4 A conservative estimate or guess is a cautious or moderate one. > **conservatism** *noun*

conservative *adjective*
3 = conventional, traditional

conservatory conservatories *noun* a room with glass walls and a glass roof attached to a house.

conserve *verb* If you conserve a supply of something, you make it last.

consider *verb* 1 If you consider something to be the case, you think or judge it to be so. 2 (EXAM TERM) To consider something is to think about it carefully. 3 If you consider someone's needs or feelings, you take account of them.

consider *verb*
1 = believe, judge, rate, regard as, think 2 = contemplate, deliberate, meditate, muse, ponder, reflect, think about 3 = bear in mind, make allowances for, respect, take into account, think about

considerable *adjective* A considerable amount of something is a lot of it.
> **considerably** *adverb*

considerate *adjective* Someone who is considerate pays attention to other people's needs and feelings.

consideration *noun*
1 Consideration is careful thought

about something. 2 If you show consideration for someone, you take account of their needs and feelings. 3 something that has to be taken into account.

consideration *noun*
1 = attention, contemplation, deliberation, study, thought 2 = concern, kindness, respect, tact 3 = factor, issue, point

considered *adjective* A considered opinion or judgment is arrived at by careful thought.

considering *conjunction, preposition* You say 'considering' to indicate that you are taking something into account: *It's a great game considering that it's free.*

consign *verb* (formal) To consign something to a particular place is to send or put it there.

consignment *noun* A consignment of goods is a load of them being delivered somewhere.

consist *verb* What something consists of is its different parts or members.

consist *verb*
consist of = be composed of, be made up of, comprise

consistency consistencies *noun* 1 Consistency is the quality of being consistent. 2 The consistency of a substance is how thick or smooth it is.

consistent *adjective* 1 If you are consistent, you keep doing something the same way. 2 If something such as a statement or argument is consistent, there are no contradictions in it.
> **consistently** *adverb*

console *verb* 1 To console someone who is unhappy is to make them

more cheerful. ▶ *noun* **2** A panel with switches or knobs for operating a machine.
> **consolation** *noun*

consolidate *verb* To consolidate something you have gained or achieved is to make it more secure.

consonant *noun* (ENGLISH) a sound such as 'p' or 'm' which you make by stopping the air flowing freely through your mouth.

consort *verb* **1** (*formal*) If you consort with someone, you spend a lot of time with them. ▶ *noun* **2** the wife or husband of the king or queen.

consortium consortia or consortiums *noun* a group of businesses working together.

conspicuous *adjective* If something is conspicuous, people can see or notice it very easily.

> **conspicuous** *adjective*
> = apparent, blatant, evident, noticeable, obvious, perceptible

conspiracy conspiracies *noun* When there is a conspiracy, a group of people plan something illegal, often for a political purpose.

conspirator *noun* someone involved in a conspiracy.

conspire *verb* **1** When people conspire, they plan together to do something illegal, often for a political purpose. **2** (*literary*) When events conspire towards a particular result, they seem to work together to cause it.

constable *noun* a police officer of the lowest rank.

constabulary constabularies *noun* a police force.

constant *adjective* **1** Something

that is constant happens all the time or is always there. **2** If an amount or level is constant, it stays the same. **3** People who are constant stay loyal to a person or idea. > **constantly** *adverb*

> **constant** *adjective*
> **1** = continual, continuous, eternal, nonstop, perpetual, relentless **2** = even, fixed, regular, stable, steady, uniform

constellation *noun* a group of stars.

constituency constituencies *noun* a town or area represented by an MP.

constituent *noun* **1** An MP's constituents are the voters who live in his or her constituency. **2** The constituents of something are its parts.

constitute *verb* If a group of things constitute something, they are what it consists of.

constitution *noun* **1** (HISTORY) The constitution of a country is a system of laws and principles by which the country should be governed. **2** Your constitution is your health. > **constitutional** *adjective* > **constitutionally** *adverb*

constrained *adjective* If a person feels constrained to do something, they feel that they should do that.

constraint *noun* something that limits someone's freedom of action.

constrict *verb* To constrict something is to squeeze it tightly.

construct *verb* To construct something is to build or make it.

> **construct** *verb*
> = assemble, build, create, erect, make, put together, put up

construction noun 1 The construction of something is the building or making of it. 2 something built or made.

constructive adjective Constructive criticisms and comments are helpful.
> **constructively** adverb

consul noun an official who lives in a foreign city and who looks after people there who are citizens of his or her own country.

consulate noun the place where a consul works.

consult verb 1 If you consult someone, you ask for their opinion or advice. 2 When people consult each other, they exchange ideas and opinions. 3 If you consult a book or map, you look at it for information.

> **consult** verb
> 1 = ask for advice, confer with, refer to

consultancy consultancies noun an organisation whose members give expert advice on a subject.

consultant noun 1 an experienced doctor who specialises in one type of medicine. 2 someone who gives expert advice.

consultation noun 1 a meeting held to discuss something. 2 Consultation is discussion or the seeking of advice.
> **consultative** adjective

consume verb 1 (formal) If you consume something, you eat or drink it. 2 To consume fuel or energy is to use it up.

consumer noun someone who buys things or uses services.

consumerism noun Consumerism is the belief that a country will

have a strong economy if its people buy a lot of goods and spend a lot of money.

consuming adjective A consuming passion or interest is more important to you than anything else.

consummate verb 1 To consummate something is to make it complete. ▶ adjective 2 You use 'consummate' to describe someone who is very good at something.

consumption noun The consumption of fuel or food is the using of it, or the amount used.

contact noun 1 If you are in contact with someone, you regularly talk to them or write to them. 2 When things are in contact, they are touching each other. 3 someone you know in a place or organisation from whom you can get help or information. ▶ verb 4 If you contact someone, you telephone them or write to them.

> **contact** noun
> 1 = communication, touch
> 3 = acquaintance, connection
> ▶ verb 4 = approach, communicate with, get hold of, get in touch with, reach

contagious adjective A contagious disease can be caught by touching people or things infected with it.

contain verb 1 If a substance contains something, that thing is a part of it. 2 The things a box or room contains are the things inside it. 3 (formal) To contain something also means to stop it increasing or spreading.
> **containment** noun

contain *verb*
1 = comprise, include
3 = control, curb, repress, restrain, stifle

container *noun* 1 something such as a box or a bottle that you keep things in. 2 a large sealed metal box for transporting things.

container *noun*
1 = holder, vessel

contaminate *verb* If something is contaminated by dirt, chemicals or radiation, it is made impure and harmful. > **contamination** *noun*

contemplate *verb* 1 To contemplate is to think carefully about something for a long time. 2 If you contemplate doing something, you consider doing it. 3 If you contemplate something, you look at it for a long time. > **contemplation** *noun*

contemplate *verb*
1 = consider, examine, muse on, ponder, reflect on, think about
2 = consider, envisage, plan, think of

contemporary contemporaries *adjective* 1 produced or happening now: *contemporary literature*. 2 produced or happening at the time you are talking about: *contemporary descriptions of Lizzie Borden*. ▶ *noun* 3 Someone's contemporaries are other people living or active at the same time as them.

contempt *noun* If you treat someone or something with contempt, you show no respect for them at all.

contempt *noun*
= derision, disdain, disregard, disrespect, scorn

contemptible *adjective* not worthy of any respect.

contemptuous *adjective* showing contempt.

contend *verb* 1 To contend with a difficulty is to deal with it. 2 (*formal*) If you contend that something is true, you say firmly that it is true. 3 When people contend for something, they compete for it. > **contender** *noun*

content *noun* 1 (*in plural*) The contents of something are the things inside it. 2 Content is also the information or material presented on a website. ▶ *adjective* 3 happy and satisfied with your life. 4 willing to do or have something. ▶ *verb* 5 If you content yourself with doing something, you do it and do not try to do anything else.

contented *adjective* happy and satisfied with your life. > **contentment** *noun*

contention *noun* (*formal*) 1 Someone's contention is the idea or opinion they are expressing. 2 Contention is disagreement and argument about something.

contest *noun* 1 a competition or game. 2 a struggle for power. ▶ *verb* 3 If you contest a statement or decision, you object to it formally.

contest *noun*
1 = competition, game, match, tournament 2 = battle, fight, struggle
▶ *verb* 3 = challenge, dispute, oppose, question

contestant *noun* someone taking part in a competition.

context *noun* 1 The context of something consists of matters related to it which help to explain it. 2 (ENGLISH) The context of a word or sentence consists of the words or sentences before and after it.

continent *noun* 1 a very large area of land, such as Africa or Asia. 2 The Continent is the mainland of Europe. > **continental** *adjective*

contingency contingencies *noun* something that might happen in the future.

contingent *noun* 1 a group of people representing a country or organisation. 2 a group of police or soldiers.

continual *adjective* 1 happening all the time without stopping. 2 happening again and again. > **continually** *adverb*

> **continual** *adjective*
> 1 = constant, endless, eternal, nagging, perpetual, uninterrupted 2 = frequent, recurrent, regular, repeated

continuation *noun* 1 The continuation of something is the continuing of it. 2 Something that is a continuation of an event follows it and seems like a part of it.

continue continues, continuing, continued *verb* 1 If you continue to do something, you keep doing it. 2 If something continues, it does not stop. 3 You also say something continues when it starts again after stopping.

> **continue** *verb*
> 1 = carry on, go on, keep on, persist 2 = carry on, endure, last, persist, remain, survive 3 = carry on, recommence, resume

continuous *adjective* 1 Continuous means happening or existing without stopping. 2 (MATHS) A continuous line or surface has no gaps or holes in it. 3 (MATHS) A continuous set of data has an unlimited amount of numbers or items in it. > **continuously** *adverb* > **continuity** *noun*

> **continuous** *adjective*
> 1 = constant, continued, extended, prolonged, uninterrupted

contorted *adjective* twisted into an unnatural, unattractive shape.

contour *noun* 1 The contours of something are its general shape. 2 (GEOGRAPHY) On a map, a contour is a line joining points of equal height.

contraception *noun* Contraception is methods of preventing pregnancy.

contraceptive *noun* a device or pill for preventing pregnancy.

contract *noun* 1 a written legal agreement about the sale of something or work done for money. ▶ *verb* 2 When something contracts, it gets smaller or shorter. 3 (*formal*) If you contract an illness, you get it. > **contractual** *adjective*

contractor *noun* a person who or company that does work for other people or companies.

contradict *verb* If you contradict someone, you say that what they have just said is not true, and that something else is. > **contradiction** *noun* > **contradictory** *adjective*

contraption *noun* a strange-looking machine or piece of equipment.

contrary *adjective* 1 Contrary ideas or opinions are opposed to each other and cannot be held by the same person. ▶ *phrase* 2 You say **on the contrary** when you are contradicting what someone has just said.

contrast *noun* 1 a great difference between things. 2 If one thing is a contrast to another, it is very different from it. ▶ *verb* 3 (EXAM TERM) If you contrast things, you describe or emphasise the differences between them. 4 If one thing contrasts with another, it is very different from it.

contravene *verb* (*formal*) If you contravene a law or rule, you do something that it forbids.

contribute *verb* 1 If you contribute to something, you do things to help it succeed. 2 If you contribute money, you give it to help to pay for something. 3 If something contributes to an event or situation, it is one of its causes. > **contribution** *noun* > **contributor** *noun* > **contributory** *adjective*

contrive *verb* (*formal*) If you contrive to do something difficult, you succeed in doing it.

contrived *adjective* Something that is contrived is unnatural.

control controls, controlling, controlled *noun* 1 Control of a country or organisation is the power to make the important decisions about how it is run. 2 Your control over something is your ability to make it work the way you want it to. 3 The controls on a machine are knobs or other devices used to work it. ▶ *verb* 4 To control a country or organisation

means to have the power to make decisions about how it is run. 5 To control something such as a machine or system means to make it work the way you want it to. 6 If you control yourself, you make yourself behave calmly when you are angry or upset. ▶ *phrase* 7 If something is **out of control**, nobody has any power over it. > **controller** *noun*

> **control** *noun*
> 1 = authority, command, direction, government, management, power, rule, supremacy
> ▶ *verb* 4 = administer, be in charge of, command, direct, govern, have power over, manage, rule

controversial *adjective* Something that is controversial causes a lot of discussion and argument, because many people disapprove of it.

controversy controversies *noun* discussion and argument because many people disapprove of something.

conundrum *noun* (*formal*) a puzzling problem.

convection *noun* (SCIENCE) Convection is the process by which heat travels through gases and liquids.

convene *verb* 1 (*formal*) To convene a meeting is to arrange for it to take place. 2 When people convene, they come together for a meeting.

convenience *noun* 1 The convenience of something is the fact that it is easy to use or that it makes something easy to do. 2 something useful.

convenient adjective If something is convenient, it is easy to use or it makes something easy to do.
> **conveniently** adverb

> **convenient** adjective
> = handy, helpful, useful, user-friendly

convent noun a building where nuns live, or a school run by nuns.

convention noun 1 an accepted way of behaving or doing something. 2 a large meeting of an organisation or political group.

> **convention** noun
> 1 = code, custom, etiquette, practice, tradition
> 2 = assembly, conference, congress, meeting

conventional adjective 1 You say that people are conventional when there is nothing unusual about their way of life. 2 Conventional methods are the ones that are usually used.

> **conventional** adjective
> 1 = conformist, conservative, unadventurous 2 = customary, ordinary, orthodox, regular, standard, traditional

converge verb To converge is to meet or join at a particular place.

conversation noun If you have a conversation with someone, you spend time talking to them.

converse verb 1 (formal) When people converse, they talk to each other. ▶ noun 2 The converse of something is its opposite.
> **conversely** adverb

convert verb 1 To convert one thing into another is to change it

so that it becomes the other thing. 2 (MATHS) If you convert a unit or measurement, you express it in terms of another unit or scale of measurement. For example, you can convert inches to centimetres by multiplying by 2.54. 3 If someone converts you, they persuade you to change your religious or political beliefs. ▶ noun 4 someone who has changed their religious or political beliefs. > **conversion** noun

convey verb 1 To convey information or ideas is to cause them to be known or understood. 2 (formal) To convey someone or something to a place is to transport them there.

> **convey** verb
> 1 = communicate, express, get across, impart (formal)

conveyor belt noun a moving strip used in factories for moving objects along.

convict verb 1 To convict someone of a crime is to find them guilty. ▶ noun 2 someone serving a prison sentence.

conviction noun 1 a strong belief or opinion. 2 The conviction of someone is what happens when they are found guilty in a court of law.

convince verb To convince someone of something is to persuade them that it is true.

> **convince** verb
> = assure, persuade, satisfy

convincing adjective 'Convincing' is used to describe things or people that can make you believe something is true.
> **convincingly** adverb

convincing *adjective*
= conclusive, effective,
persuasive, plausible,
powerful, telling

convoluted *adjective* Something
that is convoluted has many
twists and bends.

convoy *noun* a group of vehicles
or ships travelling together.

convulsion *noun* If someone has
convulsions, their muscles move
violently and uncontrollably.

coo *verb* When pigeons coo, they
make a soft flutelike sound.

cook *verb* 1 To cook food is to
prepare it for eating by heating it.
▶ *noun* 2 someone who prepares
and cooks food, often as their job.

cook *verb*
1 = bake, barbecue, boil, fry,
grill, microwave, poach, roast,
steam, stew, toast

cooker *noun* a device for cooking
food.

cookery *noun* Cookery is the
activity of preparing and cooking
food.

cookie *noun* 1 a sweet biscuit.
2 a small file placed on a user's
computer by a website,
containing information about
the user's preferences that will be
used on any future visits he or she
may make to the site.

cool *adjective* 1 Something cool has
a low temperature but is not cold.
2 If you are cool in a difficult
situation, you stay calm and
unemotional. ▶ *verb* 3 When
something cools or when you
cool it, it becomes less warm.
> **coolly** *adverb*

cool *adjective*
1 = chilled, chilly, cold,

refreshing 2 = calm, collected,
composed, level-headed,
relaxed, serene
▶ *verb* 3 = chill, cool off, freeze,
refrigerate

coop *noun* a cage for chickens or
rabbits.

cooperate *verb* 1 When people
cooperate, they work or act
together. 2 To cooperate also
means to do what someone asks.
> **cooperation** *noun*

cooperate *verb*
1 = collaborate, join forces, pull
together, work together

cooperative *noun* 1 a business or
organisation run by the people
who work for it and who share its
benefits or profits. ▶ *adjective* 2 A
cooperative activity is done by
people working together.
3 Someone who is cooperative
does what you ask them to.

coordinate coordinates,
coordinating, coordinated *verb*
1 To coordinate an activity is to
organise the people or things
involved in it. ▶ *noun* 2 (MATHS)
(*in plural*) Coordinates are a pair of
numbers or letters which tell you
how far along and up or down a
point is on a grid. > **coordination**
noun > **coordinator** *noun*

cop *noun* (*slang*) a police officer.

cope *verb* If you cope with a
problem or task, you deal with it
successfully.

copious *adjective* (*formal*) existing
or produced in large quantities.

copper *noun* (SCIENCE) Copper
is a reddish-brown metallic
element. Its atomic number
is 29 and its symbol is Cu.
2 Coppers are brown metal
coins of low value.

copy copies, copying, copied *noun*
1 something made to look like
something else. 2 A copy of
something such as a book,
magazine or DVD is one of many
identical ones produced at the
same time. ▶ *verb* 3 If you copy
what someone does, you do the
same thing. 4 If you copy
something, you make a copy of it.
▷ **copier** *noun*

> **copy** *noun*
> 1 = counterfeit, duplicate, fake,
> forgery, imitation, replica,
> reproduction
> ▶ *verb* 3 = ape, emulate, follow,
> imitate, mimic 4 = counterfeit,
> duplicate, reproduce

copyright *noun* (LIBRARY) If
someone has the copyright on a
piece of writing or music, it
cannot be copied or performed
without their permission.

coral *noun* Coral is a hard
substance that forms in the sea
from the skeletons of tiny
animals called corals.

cord *noun* 1 Cord is strong, thick
string. 2 Electrical wire covered
in rubber or plastic is also called
cord.

cordial *adjective* 1 warm and
friendly. ▶ *noun* 2 a sweet drink
made from fruit juice.

cordon *noun* 1 a line or ring of
police or soldiers preventing
people entering or leaving a
place. ▶ *verb* 2 If police or soldiers
cordon off an area, they stop
people entering or leaving by
forming themselves into a line
or ring.

corduroy *noun* Corduroy is a thick
cloth with parallel raised lines on
the outside.

core *noun* 1 the hard central part
of a fruit such as an apple.
2 the most important part of
something. 3 (GEOGRAPHY) the
central part of the earth that lies
beneath the mantle.

cork *noun* 1 Cork is the very l
ight, spongelike bark of a
Mediterranean tree. 2 a piece of
cork pushed into the end of a
bottle to close it.

corn *noun* 1 Corn refers to crops
such as wheat and barley and to
their seeds. 2 a small painful area
of hard skin on your foot.

cornea *noun* the transparent skin
that covers the outside of your
eyeball.

corner *noun* 1 a place where two
sides or edges of something meet.
▶ *verb* 2 To corner a person or
animal is to get them into a place
they cannot escape from.

corny cornier, corniest *adjective*
very obvious or sentimental and
not at all original.

> **corny** *adjective*
> = banal, hackneyed, sentimental,
> stale, stereotyped, trite

coronary coronaries *noun* If
someone has a coronary, blood
cannot reach their heart because
of a blood clot.

coronation *noun* the ceremony
at which a king or queen is
crowned.

coronavirus *noun* a type of virus
that causes colds and diseases
such as COVID-19.

coroner *noun* an official who
investigates the deaths of people
who have died in a violent or
unusual way.

corporal *noun* an officer of low
rank in the army or air force.

corporal punishment *noun*
Corporal punishment is the punishing of people by beating them.

corporate *adjective* (*formal*) belonging to or done by all members of a group together.

corporation *noun* **1** a large business. **2** a group of people responsible for running a city.

corps *noun* **1** a part of an army with special duties. **2** a small group of people who do a special job.

corpse *noun* a dead body.

correct *adjective* **1** If something is correct, there are no mistakes in it. **2** The correct thing in a particular situation is the right one. **3** Correct behaviour is considered to be socially acceptable. ▶ *verb* **4** If you correct something which is wrong, you make it right. > **correctly** *adverb*

> **correct** *adjective*
> **1** = accurate, exact, faultless, flawless, precise, right, true
> **3** = acceptable, appropriate, fitting, okay *or* OK (*informal*), proper, seemly (*old-fashioned*)
> ▶ *verb* **4** = amend, cure, improve, rectify, reform, remedy, right

correction *noun* the act of making something right.

> **correction** *noun*
> = adjustment, amendment, righting

correlate *verb* If two things correlate or are correlated, they are closely connected or strongly influence each other.

correspond *verb* **1** If one thing corresponds to another, it has a similar purpose, function or status. **2** (MATHS) If numbers or amounts correspond, they are the same. **3** When people correspond, they write to each other.

> **correspond** *verb*
> **1** = agree, be related, coincide, correlate, fit, match, tally

correspondence *noun*
1 Correspondence is the writing of letters; also the letters written. **2** If there is a correspondence between two things, they are closely related or very similar.

correspondent *noun* a newspaper, television or radio reporter.

corresponding *adjective* **1** You use 'corresponding' to describe a change that results from a change in something else: *the rise in inflation and corresponding rise in prices.* **2** You also use 'corresponding' to describe something which has a similar purpose or status to something else: *Sales were up 8 per cent on the corresponding period last year.*

corridor *noun* a passage that connects different parts of a building.

corrode *verb* (SCIENCE) When metal corrodes, it is gradually destroyed by a chemical or rust. > **corrosion** *noun*

corrugated *adjective* Corrugated metal or cardboard is made in parallel folds to make it stronger.

corrupt *adjective* **1** Corrupt people act dishonestly or illegally in return for money or power. ▶ *verb* **2** To corrupt someone means to make them dishonest. **3** To corrupt someone also means to make them immoral.

corrupt adjective
1 = crooked, dishonest, fraudulent, shady (informal), unscrupulous
▶ verb 2 = bribe, buy off, fix (informal)

corruption noun Corruption is dishonesty and illegal behaviour by people in positions of power.

corruption noun
= bribery, dishonesty, fraud

corset noun Corsets are stiff underwear worn round the hips and waist to make them look slimmer.

cosmetic noun 1 Cosmetics are substances such as lipstick and face powder which are intended to make someone more attractive. ▶ adjective 2 Cosmetic changes improve the appearance of something without changing its basic nature.

cosmic adjective belonging or relating to the universe.

cosmopolitan adjective A cosmopolitan place is full of people from many countries.

cosmos noun The cosmos is the universe.

cost costs, costing, cost noun 1 The cost of something is the amount of money needed to buy it, do it, or make it. 2 The cost of achieving something is the loss or injury in achieving it. ▶ verb 3 You use 'cost' to talk about the amount of money you have to pay for things. 4 If a mistake costs you something, you lose that thing because of the mistake.

cost noun
1 = charge, expense, outlay, payment, price, rate

2 = detriment, expense, penalty
▶ verb 3 = come to, sell at, set someone back (informal)

costly costlier, costliest adjective expensive.

costume noun 1 (DRAMA) a set of clothes worn by an actor. 2 Costume is the clothing worn in a particular place or during a particular period.

cosy cosier, cosiest adjective 1 warm and comfortable. 2 Cosy activities are pleasant and friendly. > **cosily** adverb > **cosiness** noun

cosy adjective
1 = comfortable, snug, warm
2 = friendly, informal, intimate, relaxed

cot noun a small bed for a baby, with bars or panels round it to stop the baby falling out.

cottage noun a small house in the country.

cottage cheese noun Cottage cheese is a type of soft white lumpy cheese.

cotton noun 1 Cotton is cloth made from the soft fibres of the cotton plant. 2 Cotton is also thread used for sewing.

cotton wool noun Cotton wool is soft fluffy cotton, often used for dressing wounds.

couch noun 1 a long, soft piece of furniture which more than one person can sit on. ▶ verb 2 If a statement is couched in a particular type of language, it is expressed in that language.

cough verb 1 When you cough, you force air out of your throat with a sudden harsh noise. ▶ noun 2 an illness that makes you cough a lot; also the noise you make when you cough.

could *verb* 1 You use 'could' to say that you were able or allowed to do something: *He could hear voices*; *She could come and go as she wanted.* 2 You also use 'could' to say that something might happen or might be the case: *It could rain.* 3 You use 'could' when you are asking for something politely: *Could you tell me the name of that film?*

council *noun* (CITIZENSHIP) a group of people elected to look after the affairs of a town, district or county.

> **council** *noun*
> = assembly, board, committee, panel

councillor *noun* (CITIZENSHIP) an elected member of a local council.

counsel counsels, counselling, counselled *noun* 1 (*formal*) To give someone counsel is to give them advice. ▶ *verb* 2 To counsel people is to give them advice about their problems. > **counsellor** *noun*

count *verb* 1 To count is to say all the numbers in order up to a particular number. 2 If you count all the things in a group, you add them up to see how many there are. 3 What counts in a situation is whatever is most important. 4 To count as something means to be regarded as that thing. 5 If you can count on someone or something, you can rely on them. ▶ *noun* 6 a number reached by counting. 7 (*formal*) If something is wrong on a particular count, it is wrong in that respect. 8 a European nobleman.

> **count** *verb*
> 2 = add up, calculate, tally
> 3 = carry weight, matter, rate, signify, weigh
> ▶ *noun* 6 = calculation, reckoning, sum, tally

countdown *noun* the counting aloud of numbers in reverse order before something happens, especially before a spacecraft is launched.

countenance (*formal*) *noun* 1 Someone's countenance is their face. ▶ *verb* 2 To countenance something means to allow or accept it.

counter *noun* 1 a long, flat surface over which goods are sold in a shop. 2 a small, flat, round object used in board games. ▶ *verb* 3 If you counter something that is being done, you take action to make it less effective.

counteract *verb* To counteract something is to reduce its effect by producing an opposite effect.

> **counteract** *verb*
> = act against, offset

counterfeit *adjective* 1 Something counterfeit is not genuine but has been made to look genuine to deceive people. ▶ *verb* 2 To counterfeit something is to make a counterfeit version of it.

counterpart *noun* The counterpart of a person or thing is another person or thing with a similar function in a different place.

countess *noun* the wife of a count or earl, or a woman with the same rank as a count or earl.

counting *preposition* You say 'counting' when including something in a calculation.

countless *adjective* too many to count.

> **countless** *adjective*
> = infinite, innumerable, myriad, untold

country countries *noun*
1 (GEOGRAPHY) one of the political areas the world is divided into. **2** The country is land away from towns and cities.

> **country** *noun*
> **1** = kingdom, land, state
> **2** = bush (*Australian, New Zealand and South African*), countryside, outback (*Australian and New Zealand*), outdoors

countryman countrymen *noun* Your countrymen are people from your own country.

countryside *noun* The countryside is land away from towns and cities.

county counties *noun* (GEOGRAPHY) a region with its own local government.

coup or **coup d'état** *noun* (HISTORY) When there is a coup, a group of people seize power in a country.

couple *noun* **1** two people who are married or are involved in a romantic relationship. **2** A couple of things or people means two of them. ▶ *verb* **3** If one thing is coupled with another, the two things are done or dealt with together.

coupon *noun* **1** a piece of printed paper which, when you hand it in, entitles you to pay less than usual for something. **2** a form you fill in to ask for information or to enter a competition.

courage *noun* Courage is the quality shown by people who do things knowing they are dangerous or difficult.
> **courageous** *adjective*
> **courageously** *adverb*

> **courage** *noun*
> = bravery, daring, guts (*informal*), heroism, nerve, pluck, valour

courgette *noun* a type of small marrow with dark green skin. Courgettes are also called zucchini.

courier *noun* someone employed to collect and deliver letters and packages.

course *noun* **1** a series of lessons or lectures. **2** a series of medical treatments. **3** one of the parts of a meal. **4** A course or a course of action is one of the things you can do in a situation. **5** a piece of land where a sport such as golf is played. **6** the route a ship or aircraft takes. **7** If something happens in the course of a period of time, it happens during that period. ▶ *phrase* **8** If you say of course, you are showing that something is totally expected or that you are sure about something.

> **course** *noun*
> **1** = classes, curriculum **4** = plan, policy, procedure **6** = direction, line, path, route, trajectory, way

court *noun* **1** (CITIZENSHIP) a place where legal matters are decided by a judge and jury or a magistrate. The judge and jury or magistrate can also be referred to as the court. **2** a place where a game such as tennis or badminton is played. **3** the place where a king or queen lives and carries out ceremonial duties.

court noun
1 = bench, law court, tribunal

courteous adjective Courteous behaviour is polite and considerate.

courtesy noun Courtesy is polite, considerate behaviour.

courtesy noun
= civility, courteousness, gallantry, good manners, grace, graciousness, politeness

courtier noun Courtiers were noblemen and noblewomen at the court of a king or queen.

courtyard noun a flat area of ground surrounded by buildings or walls.

cousin noun Your cousin is the child of your uncle or aunt.

cove noun a small bay.

covenant noun a formal written agreement or promise.

cover verb 1 If you cover something, you put something else over it to protect it or hide it. 2 If something covers something else, it forms a layer over it. 3 If you cover a particular distance, you travel that distance. ▶ noun 4 something put over an object to protect it or keep it warm. 5 The cover of a book or magazine is its outside. 6 Insurance cover is a guarantee that money will be paid if something is lost or harmed. 7 In the open, cover consists of trees, rocks or other places where you can shelter or hide. ▶ **cover up** verb If you cover up something you do not want people to know about, you hide it from them.

cover verb
1 = cloak, conceal, cover up, hide, mask, obscure, screen, shade 2 = coat, overlay
▶ noun 4 = case, coating, covering, jacket, mask, screen, wrapper

coverage noun The coverage of something in the news is the reporting of it.

covering noun a layer of something which protects or conceals something else.

covert adjective (formal) Covert activities are secret, rather than open. > **covertly** adverb

COVID-19; also spelt **Covid-19** noun a serious infectious disease that affects the lungs.

cow noun a large animal kept on farms for its milk.

cow noun
= bovine (formal), cattle

coward noun someone who is easily frightened and who avoids dangerous or difficult situations. > **cowardice** noun

coward noun
= chicken (slang), wimp (informal)

cowardly adjective easily scared.

cowardly adjective
= chicken (slang), faint-hearted, gutless (informal), sookie (New Zealand)

cowboy noun a man employed to look after cattle in America.

cower verb When someone cowers, they crouch or move backwards because they are afraid.

cower verb
= cringe, quail, shrink

coy *adjective* If someone is coy, they pretend to be shy and modest.

coyote *noun* A North American animal like a small wolf.

crab *noun* a sea creature with four pairs of legs, two pincers, and a flat, round body covered by a shell.

crack *verb* **1** If something cracks, it becomes damaged, with lines appearing on its surface. **2** If you crack a joke, you tell it. **3** If you crack a problem or code, you solve it. ▶ *noun* **4** one of the lines appearing on something when it cracks. **5** a narrow gap. ▶ *adjective* **6** A crack soldier or sportsperson is highly trained and skilful.

> **crack** *verb*
> **1** = break, fracture, snap
> **3** = decipher, solve, work out
> ▶ *noun* **4** = break, cleft, crevice, fracture

cracker *noun* **1** a thin, crisp biscuit that is often eaten with cheese. **2** a paper-covered tube that pulls apart with a bang and usually has a toy and paper hat inside.

crackle *verb* **1** If something crackles, it makes a rapid series of short, harsh noises. ▶ *noun* **2** a short, harsh noise.

cradle *noun* **1** a box-shaped bed for a baby. ▶ *verb* **2** If you cradle something in your arms or hands, you hold it there carefully.

craft *noun* **1** an activity such as weaving, carving or pottery. **2** a skilful occupation. **3** a boat, plane or spacecraft.

craftsman craftsmen *noun* a man who makes things skilfully with his hands. > **craftsmanship** *noun*

craftswoman craftswomen *noun* a woman who makes things skilfully with her hands.

crafty craftier, craftiest *adjective* Someone who is crafty gets what they want by tricking people in a clever way.

> **crafty** *adjective*
> = artful, cunning, devious, scheming, slippery, sly, wily

craggy craggier, craggiest *adjective* A craggy mountain or cliff is steep and rocky.

cram crams, cramming, crammed *verb* If you cram people or things into a place, you put more in than there is room for.

> **cram** *verb*
> = jam, pack, squeeze, stuff

cramp *noun* Cramp or cramps is a pain caused by a muscle contracting.

cramped *adjective* If a room or building is cramped, it is not big enough for the people or things in it.

cranberry cranberries *noun* Cranberries are sour-tasting red berries, often made into a sauce.

crane *noun* **1** a machine that moves heavy things by lifting them in the air. **2** a large bird with a long neck and long legs. ▶ *verb* **3** If you crane your neck, you extend your head in a particular direction to see or hear something better.

crank *noun* **1** (*informal*) someone with strange ideas who behaves in an odd way. **2** a device you turn to make something move. ▶ *verb* **3** If you crank something, you make it move by turning a handle.

cranny crannies *noun* a very narrow opening in a wall or rock.

crash *noun* **1** an accident in which

a moving vehicle hits something violently. **2** a sudden loud noise. **3** the sudden failure of a business or financial institution. ▶ verb **4** When a vehicle crashes, it hits something and is badly damaged. **5** If a computer or a computer program crashes, it fails suddenly.

crash noun
1 = accident, bump (informal), collision, pile-up (informal), smash (informal) **2** = bang, clash, din, smash **3** = bankruptcy, collapse, depression, failure, ruin
▶ verb **4** = bump (informal), collide, drive into, have an accident, plough into (informal), wreck

crate noun a large box used for transporting or storing things.

crater noun (GEOGRAPHY) a wide hole in the ground caused by something hitting it or by an explosion.

crave verb If you crave something, you want it very much. > **craving** noun

crawl verb **1** When you crawl, you move forward on your hands and knees. **2** When a vehicle crawls, it moves very slowly. **3** (informal) If a place is crawling with people or things, it is full of them.

crawl verb
3 = be alive with, be full of, be overrun, swarm, teem

crayfish crayfishes or crayfish noun a small shellfish like a lobster.

crayon noun a coloured pencil or a stick of coloured wax.

craze noun something that is very popular for a short time.

craze noun
= fad, fashion, trend, vogue

crazy crazier, craziest adjective (informal) **1** very strange or foolish. **2** If you are crazy about something, you are very keen on it. > **crazily** adverb > **craziness** noun

crazy adjective
1 = foolish, insane, mad, ridiculous, wild, zany **2** = fanatical, mad, obsessed, passionate, smitten, wild

creak verb **1** If something creaks, it makes a harsh sound when it moves or when you stand on it.
▶ noun **2** a harsh squeaking noise. > **creaky** adjective

cream noun **1** Cream is a thick, yellowish-white liquid taken from the top of milk. **2** Cream is also a substance people can rub on their skin. ▶ adjective **3** yellowish-white.

crease noun **1** an irregular line that appears on cloth or paper when it is crumpled. **2** a straight line on something that has been pressed or folded neatly. ▶ verb **3** To crease something is to make lines appear on it. > **creased** adjective

create verb **1** To create something is to cause it to happen or exist. **2** When someone creates a new product or process, they invent it. > **creator** noun > **creation** noun

create verb
1 = bring about, cause, lead to, occasion (formal) **2** = coin, compose, devise, formulate, invent, originate

creative adjective **1** Creative people are able to invent and develop original ideas. **2** Creative activities involve the inventing and developing of original ideas.

creative adjective
1 = fertile, imaginative, inspired, inventive

creature noun any living thing that moves about.

credence noun (formal) If something gives credence to a theory or story, it makes it easier to believe.

credentials plural noun Your credentials are your past achievements or other things in your background that make you qualified for something.

credible adjective If someone or something is credible, you can believe them. ▶ **credibility** noun

credit noun 1 If you are allowed credit, you can take something and pay for it later. 2 If you get the credit for something, people praise you for it. 3 If you say someone is a credit to their family or school, you mean that their family or school should be proud of them. 4 (in plural) The list of people who helped make a film, recording or television programme is called the credits. ▶ phrase 5 If someone or their bank account is **in credit**, their account has money in it. ▶ verb 6 If you are credited with an achievement, people believe that you were responsible for it.

credit noun
2 = commendation, glory, praise, recognition, thanks

creditable adjective satisfactory or fairly good.

credit card noun a plastic card that allows someone to buy goods on credit.

creditor noun Your creditors are the people you owe money to.

creed noun 1 a religion. 2 any set of beliefs.

creek noun a narrow inlet where the sea comes a long way into the land.

creep creeps, creeping, crept verb To creep is to move quietly and slowly.

creepy creepier, creepiest adjective (informal) strange and frightening.

creepy adjective
= disturbing, eerie, macabre, scary (informal), sinister, spooky, unnatural

cremate verb When someone is cremated, their dead body is burned during a funeral service. ▶ **cremation** noun

crematorium crematoriums or crematoria noun a building in which the bodies of dead people are burned.

crepe noun 1 Crepe is a thin ridged material made from cotton, silk or wool. 2 Crepe is also a type of rubber with a rough surface.

crept the past tense and past participle of **creep**.

crescendo crescendos noun (MUSIC) When there is a crescendo in a piece of music, the music gets louder.

crescent noun a curved shape that is wider in its middle than at the ends, which are pointed.

crest noun 1 The crest of a hill or wave is its highest part. 2 a tuft of feathers on top of a bird's head. 3 a small picture or design that is the emblem of a noble family, a town, or an organisation. ▶ **crested** adjective

crevice noun a narrow crack in rock.

crew noun 1 The crew of a ship, aeroplane or spacecraft are the people who operate it. 2 people with special technical skills who work together.

crib cribs, cribbing, cribbed verb 1 (informal) If you crib, you copy what someone else has written and pretend it is your own work. ▶ noun 2 (old-fashioned) a baby's cot.

cricket noun 1 Cricket is an outdoor game played by two teams who take turns at scoring runs by hitting a ball with a bat. 2 a small jumping insect that produces sounds by rubbing its wings together. > **cricketer** noun

crime noun an action for which you can be punished by law.

> **crime** noun
> = misdemeanour, offence, violation, wrong

criminal noun 1 someone who has committed a crime. ▶ adjective 2 involving or related to crime.

> **criminal** noun
> 1 = crook (informal), culprit, delinquent, offender, skelm (South African), villain
> ▶ adjective 2 = corrupt, crooked, illegal, illicit, unlawful

criminology noun the scientific study of crime and criminals. > **criminologist** noun

crimson noun, adjective dark purplish-red.

cringe verb If you cringe, you back away from someone or something because you are afraid or embarrassed.

cripple verb 1 To cripple someone is to injure them severely. 2 To cripple a company or country is to prevent it from working.

> **cripple** verb
> 2 = bring to a standstill, impair, put out of action

crisis crises noun a serious or dangerous situation.

crisp adjective 1 Something that is crisp is pleasantly fresh and firm. 2 If the air or the weather is crisp, it is pleasantly fresh, cold and dry. ▶ noun 3 Crisps are thin slices of potato fried until they are hard and crunchy.

crispy crispier, crispiest adjective Crispy food is pleasantly hard and crunchy.

criterion criteria noun a standard by which you judge or decide something.

critic noun 1 someone who writes reviews of books, films, plays or musical performances. 2 A critic of a person or system is someone who criticises them publicly.

critical adjective 1 A critical time is one which is very important in determining what happens in the future. 2 A critical situation is a very serious one. 3 If an ill or injured person is critical, they are in danger of dying. 4 If you are critical of something or someone, you express severe judgments or opinions about them. 5 If you are critical, you examine and judge something carefully. > **critically** adverb

> **critical** adjective
> 1 = crucial, deciding, decisive, momentous, pivotal, vital
> 2 = grave (formal), precarious, serious 4 = carping, derogatory, disapproving, disparaging, scathing

criticise; also spelt **criticize** verb
If you criticise someone or
something, you say what you
think is wrong with them.

> **criticise** verb
> = censure (formal), condemn,
> find fault with, knock (informal),
> pan (informal), put down
> (informal)

criticism noun 1 When there is
criticism of someone or
something, people express
disapproval of them. 2 If you
make a criticism, you point out a
fault you think someone or
something has.

> **criticism** noun
> 1 = censure (formal), disapproval,
> disparagement, fault-finding,
> flak (informal), panning
> (informal)

croak verb 1 When animals and
birds croak, they make harsh, low
sounds. ▶ noun 2 a harsh, low
sound.

Croatian adjective 1 belonging or
relating to Croatia. ▶ noun
2 someone who comes from
Croatia. 3 Croatian is the form of
Serbo-Croat spoken in Croatia.

crochet crochets, crocheting,
crocheted noun 1 Crochet is a way
of making clothes and other
things out of thread using a
needle with a small hook at the
end. ▶ verb 2 If someone crochets
clothes, they make them out of
thread using a needle with a
small hook at the end.

crockery noun Crockery is plates,
cups and saucers.

crocodile noun a large, scaly,
meat-eating reptile which lives
in tropical rivers.

croissant noun a light,
crescent-shaped roll.

crony cronies noun (old-fashioned)
Your cronies are the friends you
spend a lot of time with.

crook noun 1 (informal) a criminal.
2 The crook of your arm or leg is
the soft inside part where you
bend your elbow or knee.
▶ adjective 3 In Australian English,
crook means ill.

> **crook** noun
> 1 = cheat, rogue, scoundrel
> (old-fashioned), shark (informal),
> swindler, thief, villain
> ▶ adjective 3 = ill, nauseous,
> poorly (British; informal), queasy,
> sick, under the weather
> (informal), unwell

crooked adjective 1 bent or
twisted. 2 (informal) Someone who
is crooked is dishonest.

> **crooked** adjective
> 1 = bent, deformed, distorted,
> irregular, out of shape, twisted,
> warped 2 = corrupt, criminal,
> dishonest, fraudulent, illegal,
> shady (informal)

crop crops, cropping, cropped noun
1 Crops are plants such as wheat
and potatoes that are grown for
food. 2 the plants collected at
harvest time. ▶ verb 3 To crop
someone's hair is to cut it very
short. > **crop up** verb (informal) If
something crops up, it happens
unexpectedly.

croquet noun Croquet is a game
in which the players use
long-handled mallets to hit balls
through arches pushed into a
lawn.

cross verb 1 If you cross something
such as a room or a road, you go to
the other side of it. 2 Lines or

roads that cross meet and go across each other. **3** If a thought crosses your mind, you think of it. **4** If you cross your arms, legs or fingers, you put one on top of the other. ▸ *noun* **5** a vertical bar or line crossed by a shorter horizontal bar or line; also used to describe any object shaped like this. **6** (RE) The Cross is the cross-shaped structure on which Christians believe that Jesus Christ was crucified. A cross is also any symbol representing Christ's Cross. **7** a written mark shaped like an X. **8** Something that is a cross between two things is neither one thing nor the other, but a mixture of both. ▸ *adjective* **9** Someone who is cross is rather angry. > **cross out** *verb* If you cross out words on a page, you draw a line through them because they are wrong or because you do not want people to read them.

cross *verb*
1 = ford, go across, span, traverse **2** = crisscross, intersect
▸ *noun* **8** = blend, combination, mixture
▸ *adjective* **9** = angry, annoyed, fractious, fretful, grumpy, in a bad mood, irritable

crossbow *noun* (HISTORY) a weapon consisting of a small bow fixed at the end of a piece of wood.

cross-country *noun*
1 Cross-country is the sport of running across open countryside, rather than on roads or on a track.
▸ *adverb, adjective* **2** across open countryside.

crossfire *noun* Crossfire is gunfire crossing the same place from opposite directions.

crossing *noun* **1** a place where you can cross a road safely. **2** a journey by ship to a place on the other side of the sea.

cross-legged *adjective* If you are sitting cross-legged, you are sitting on the floor with your knees pointing outwards and your feet tucked under them.

cross section *noun* A cross section of a group of people is a representative sample of them.

crossword *noun* a puzzle in which you work out the answers to clues and write them in the white squares of a pattern of black and white squares.

crotch *noun* the part of your body between the tops of your legs.

crouch *verb* If you are crouching, you are leaning forward with your legs bent under you.

crouch *verb*
= bend down, squat

crow *noun* **1** a large black bird which makes a loud, harsh noise. ▸ *verb* **2** When a cock crows, it utters a loud squawking sound.

crowbar *noun* a heavy iron bar used as a lever or for forcing things open.

crowd *noun* **1** a large group of people gathered together. ▸ *verb* **2** When people crowd somewhere, they gather there close together or in large numbers.

crowd *noun*
1 = horde, host, mass, mob, multitude, swarm, throng
▸ *verb* **2** = congregate, gather, swarm, throng

crowded *adjective* A crowded place is full of people.

crowded *adjective*
= congested, full, overflowing,
packed

crown *noun* 1 a circular ornament
worn on a royal person's head.
2 The crown of something such as
your head is the top part of it.
▶ *verb* 3 When a king or queen is
crowned, a crown is put on their
head during their coronation
ceremony. 4 When something
crowns an event, it is the final
part of it.

crucial *adjective* If something is
crucial, it is very important in
determining how something else
will be in the future.

crucial *adjective*
= central, critical, decisive,
momentous, pivotal, vital

crucifix *noun* (RE) a cross with a
figure representing Jesus Christ
being crucified on it.

crucify crucifies, crucifying,
crucified *verb* (RE) To crucify
someone is to tie or nail them to a
large wooden cross and leave them
there to die. > **crucifixion** *noun*

crude *adjective* 1 rough and simple.
2 A crude person speaks or behaves
in a rude and offensive way.

crude *adjective*
1 = primitive, rough,
rudimentary, simple 2 = coarse,
tasteless, vulgar

cruel *adjective* Cruel people
deliberately cause pain or distress
to other people or to animals.
> **cruelly** *adverb*

cruel *adjective*
= barbarous, brutal, callous,
cold-blooded, heartless,
inhumane, sadistic, savage,
vicious

cruelty *noun* cruel behaviour.

cruelty *noun*
= barbarity, brutality,
callousness, inhumanity,
savagery, viciousness

cruise *noun* 1 a holiday in which
you travel on a ship and visit
places. ▶ *verb* 2 When a vehicle
cruises, it moves at a constant
moderate speed.

cruiser *noun* 1 a motor boat with a
cabin you can sleep in. 2 a large,
fast warship.

crumb *noun* Crumbs are very
small pieces of bread or cake.

crumble *verb* When something
crumbles, it breaks into small
pieces.

crumbly crumblier, crumbliest
adjective Something crumbly
easily breaks into small pieces.

crumple *verb* To crumple paper or
cloth is to squash it so that it is
full of creases and folds.

crumple *verb*
= crease, crush, screw up,
wrinkle

crunch *verb* If you crunch
something, you crush it noisily,
for example between your teeth
or under your feet.

crunchy crunchier, crunchiest
adjective Crunchy food is hard or
crisp and makes a noise when you
eat it.

crusade *noun* a long and
determined attempt to achieve
something.

crush *verb* 1 To crush something is
to destroy its shape by squeezing
it. 2 To crush a substance is to
turn it into liquid or powder by
squeezing or grinding it. 3 To
crush an army or political

organisation is to defeat it completely. ▶ *noun* **4** a dense crowd of people.

> **crush** *verb*
> **1** = crumble, crumple, mash, squash **3** = overcome, put down, quell, stamp out, vanquish (*literary*)

crust *noun* **1** the hard outside part of a loaf. **2** a hard layer on top of something. **3** (GEOGRAPHY) the outer layer of the earth.

crusty crustier, crustiest *adjective* **1** Something that is crusty has a hard outside layer. **2** Crusty people are impatient and irritable.

crutch *noun* a support like a long stick which you lean on to help you walk when you have an injured foot or leg.

crux cruxes *noun* the most important or difficult part of a problem or argument.

cry cries, crying, cried *verb* **1** When you cry, tears appear in your eyes. **2** To cry something is to shout it or say it loudly. ▶ *noun* **3** If you have a cry, you cry for a period of time. **4** a shout or other loud sound made with your voice. **5** a loud sound made by some birds.

> **cry** *verb*
> **1** = blubber, howl, sob, wail, weep **2** = call, exclaim, shout, yell
> ▶ *noun* **4** = call, exclamation, shout, yell

crypt *noun* an underground room beneath a church, usually used as a burial place.

cryptic *adjective* A cryptic remark or message has a hidden meaning.

crystal *noun* **1** a piece of a mineral that has formed naturally into a regular shape. **2** Crystal is a type of transparent rock, used in jewellery. **3** Crystal is also a kind of very high-quality glass.
> **crystalline** *adjective*

crystallise; also spelt **crystallize** *verb* If a substance crystallises, it turns into crystals.

cub *noun* **1** Some young wild animals are called cubs. **2** The Cubs is an organisation for young boys before they join the Scouts.

Cuban *adjective* **1** belonging or relating to Cuba. ▶ *noun* **2** someone who comes from Cuba.

cube (MATHS) *noun* **1** a three-dimensional shape with six equal-sized surfaces. **2** The cube of a number is the number multiplied by itself twice. For example, the cube of 4, written 4^3, is $4 \times 4 \times 4$. ▶ *verb* **3** To cube a number is to multiply it by itself twice.

cubic *adjective* (MATHS) used in measurements of volume: *cubic centimetres*.

cubicle *noun* a small enclosed area in a place such as a sports centre, where you can dress and undress.

cuckoo cuckoos *noun* a grey bird with a two-note call that lays its eggs in other birds' nests.

cucumber *noun* a long, thin, green-skinned fruit, used as a vegetable and eaten raw.

cuddle *verb* **1** If you cuddle someone, you hold them affectionately in your arms. ▶ *noun* **2** If you give someone a cuddle, you hold them affectionately in your arms.

cuddly cuddlier, cuddliest *adjective* Cuddly people, animals or toys are soft or pleasing in some way so that you want to cuddle them.

cue *noun* 1 something said or done by a performer that is a signal for another performer to begin. 2 a long stick used to hit the balls in snooker.

cuff *noun* the end part of a sleeve.

cuisine *noun* The cuisine of a region is the style of cooking that is typical of it.

cul-de-sac *noun* a road that does not lead to any other roads because one end is blocked off.

culinary *adjective (formal)* connected with the kitchen or cooking.

cull *verb* 1 If you cull things, you gather them from different places or sources. 2 If you cull animals, you kill them in order to reduce their numbers. ▶ *noun* 3 When there is a cull, weaker animals are killed to reduce the numbers in a group.

culminate *verb* To culminate in something is to finally develop into it.

culprit *noun* someone who has done something harmful or wrong.

cult *noun* 1 A cult is a religious group with special rituals, usually connected with the worship of a particular person. 2 'Cult' is used to refer to any situation in which someone or something is very popular with a large group of people.

cultivate *verb* 1 To cultivate land is to grow crops on it. 2 If you cultivate a feeling or attitude, you try to develop it in yourself or other people. ▶ **cultivation** *noun*

cultural *adjective* 1 of or relating to artistic activities. 2 of or relating to a culture or civilisation.

culture *noun* 1 Culture refers to the arts and to people's appreciation of them. 2 The culture of a particular society is its ideas, customs and art. 3 In science, a culture is a group of bacteria or cells grown in a laboratory. ▶ **cultured** *adjective*

cumulative *adjective* Something that is cumulative keeps being added to.

cunning *adjective* 1 Someone who is cunning uses clever and deceitful methods to get what they want. ▶ *noun* 2 Cunning is the ability to get what you want using clever and deceitful methods.

> **cunning** *adjective*
> 1 = artful, crafty, devious, sly, wily
> ▶ *noun* 2 = deviousness, guile

cup cups, cupping, cupped *noun* 1 a small, round container with a handle, which you drink out of. 2 a large metal container with two handles, given as a prize. ▶ *verb* 3 If you cup your hands, you put them together to make a shape like a cup.

cupboard *noun* a piece of furniture with doors and shelves.

curable *adjective* If a disease or illness is curable, it can be cured.

curate *noun* a member of the clergy who helps a vicar or a priest.

curator *noun* the person in a museum or art gallery in charge of its contents.

curb *verb* 1 To curb something is to keep it within limits. ▶ *noun*

2 If a curb is placed on something, it is kept within limits.

curb verb
1 = check, contain, control, limit, restrain, suppress
▶ noun **2** = brake, control, limit, limitation, restraint

cure verb **1** To cure an illness is to end it. **2** To cure a sick or injured person is to make them well. **3** If something cures you of a habit or attitude, it stops you having it. **4** To cure food, tobacco or animal skin is to treat it in order to preserve it. ▶ noun **5** A cure for an illness is something that cures it.

cure verb
2 = heal, remedy
▶ noun **5** = medicine, remedy, treatment

curfew noun If there is a curfew, people must stay indoors between particular times at night.

curiosity curiosities noun
1 Curiosity is the desire to know about something or about many things. **2** something unusual and interesting.

curiosity noun
1 = inquisitiveness, interest
2 = freak, marvel, novelty, oddity, rarity

curious adjective **1** Someone who is curious wants to know more about something. **2** Something that is curious is unusual and hard to explain. ▶ **curiously** adverb

curious adjective
1 = inquiring, inquisitive, interested, nosy (informal)
2 = bizarre, extraordinary, odd, peculiar, singular, strange, unusual

curl noun **1** Curls are lengths of hair shaped in tight curves and circles. **2** a curved or spiral shape. ▶ verb **3** If something curls, it moves in a curve or spiral. > **curly** adjective

curler noun Curlers are plastic or metal tubes that you roll your hair round to make it curly.

currency currencies noun **1** A country's currency is its coins and banknotes or its monetary system generally. **2** If something such as an idea has currency, it is used a lot at a particular time.

current noun **1** (GEOGRAPHY) a strong continuous movement of the water in or in the sea. **2** (GEOGRAPHY) An air current is a flowing movement in the air. **3** (SCIENCE) An electric current is a flow of electricity through a wire or circuit. ▶ adjective **4** Something that is current is happening, being done, or being used now. > **currently** adverb

current noun
1 = flow, tide, undertow
▶ adjective **4** = contemporary, fashionable, ongoing, present, present-day, today's, up-to-the-minute

current affairs plural noun Current affairs are political and social events discussed in newspapers and on television and radio.

curriculum curriculums or curricula noun the different courses taught at a school or university.

curriculum vitae curricula vitae noun Someone's curriculum vitae is a written account of their personal details, education and work experience which they send when they apply for a job.

curry curries, currying, curried
noun 1 Curry is an Indian dish made with hot spices. ▶ phrase
2 To curry favour with someone means to try to please them by flattering them or doing things to help them.

curse verb 1 To curse is to swear because you are angry. 2 If you curse someone or something, you say angry things about them using rude words. ▶ noun
3 what you say when you curse.
4 something supernatural that is supposed to cause unpleasant things to happen to someone.
5 a thing or person that causes a lot of trouble.

cursor noun (ICT) an arrow or box on a computer screen which indicates where the next letter or symbol will be inserted.

cursory adjective When you give something a cursory glance or examination, you look at it briefly without paying attention to detail.

curt adjective If someone is curt, they speak in a brief and rather rude way.

curtail verb (formal) To curtail something is to reduce or restrict it.

curtain noun 1 a hanging piece of material which can be pulled across a window for privacy or to keep out the light. 2 (DRAMA) a large piece of material which hangs in front of the stage in a theatre until a performance begins.

curve noun 1 a smooth, gradually bending line. ▶ verb 2 When

something curves, it moves in a curve or has the shape of a curve.

> **curve** noun
> 1 = arc, bend, trajectory, turn
> ▶ verb 2 = arc, arch, bend, swerve

cushion noun 1 a soft object put on a seat to make it more comfortable. ▶ verb 2 To cushion something is to reduce its effect.

custard noun Custard is a sweet yellow sauce made from milk and eggs or milk and a powder.

custodian noun the person in charge of a collection in an art gallery or a museum.

custody noun 1 To have custody of a child means to have the legal right to keep it and look after it.
▶ phrase 2 Someone who is in custody is being kept in prison until they can be tried in a court.
> **custodial** adjective

custom noun 1 a traditional activity. 2 something usually done at a particular time or in particular circumstances by a person or by the people in a society. 3 Customs is the place at a border, airport or harbour where you have to declare any goods you are bringing into a country.
4 (formal) If a shop or business has your custom, you buy things or go there regularly.

> **custom** noun
> 1 = convention, practice, ritual, tradition 2 = habit, practice, routine, wont (formal)

customary adjective usual.
> **customarily** adverb

custom-built or **custom-made** adjective Something that is custom-built or custom-made is made to someone's special requirements.

customer noun 1 A shop's or firm's customers are the people who buy its goods. 2 (informal) You can use 'customer' to refer to someone when describing what they are like to deal with: a tough customer.

customer noun
1 = buyer, client, consumer, patron, purchaser, shopper

cut cuts, cutting, cut verb 1 If you cut something, you use a knife, scissors or some other sharp tool to mark it or remove parts of it. 2 If you cut yourself, you injure yourself on a sharp object. 3 If you cut the amount of something, you reduce it. 4 When writing is cut, parts of it are not printed or broadcast. 5 To cut from one scene or shot to another in a film is to go instantly to the other scene or shot. ▶ noun 6 a mark or injury made with a knife or other sharp tool. 7 a reduction. 8 a part in something written that is not printed or broadcast. > **cut back** verb To cut back or cut back on spending means to reduce it. > **cutback** noun > **cut down** verb If you cut down on an activity, you do it less often. > **cut off** verb 1 To cut someone or something off means to separate them from things they are normally connected with. 2 If a supply of something is cut off, you no longer get it. 3 If your telephone or telephone call is cut off, it is disconnected. > **cut out** verb 1 If you cut out something you are doing, you stop doing it. 2 If an engine cuts out, it suddenly stops working.

cut verb
1 = chop, clip, nick, slice, trim

3 = cut back, decrease, lower, reduce, slash
▶ noun 6 = gash, incision, slash, slit 7 = cutback, decrease, lowering, reduction, saving

cute adjective pretty or attractive.

cute adjective
= appealing, attractive, charming, dear, good-looking, gorgeous, pretty

cutlery noun Cutlery is knives, forks and spoons.

cutlet noun a small piece of meat which you fry or grill.

cutting noun 1 something cut from a newspaper or magazine. 2 a part cut from a plant and used to grow a new plant. ▶ adjective 3 A cutting remark is unkind and likely to hurt someone.

CV an abbreviation for **curriculum vitae**.

cyanide noun Cyanide is an extremely poisonous chemical.

cyber- prefix Words that begin with 'cyber-' have something to do with computers in their meaning. For example cybercrime is crime that involves the use of computers.

cycle verb 1 When you cycle, you ride a bicycle. ▶ noun 2 a bicycle or a motorcycle. 3 a series of events which is repeated again and again in the same order.

cyclical or **cyclic** adjective happening over and over again in cycles.

cyclist noun someone who rides a bicycle.

cyclone noun a violent tropical storm.

cylinder noun 1 (MATHS) a three-dimensional shape with

two equal-sized flat circular ends joined by a curved surface. **2** the part in a motor engine in which the piston moves backwards and forwards. ▸ **cylindrical** *adjective*

cynic *noun* a cynical person.

cynical *adjective* believing that people always behave selfishly or dishonestly. ▸ **cynically** *adverb*

> **cynical** *adjective*
> = distrustful, sceptical

cypress *noun* a type of evergreen tree with small dark green leaves and round cones.

cyst *noun* a growth containing liquid that can form under your skin or inside your body.

czar another spelling of **tsar**.

Czech *adjective* **1** belonging or relating to the Czech Republic. ▸ *noun* **2** someone who comes from the Czech Republic. **3** Czech is the language spoken in the Czech Republic.

Dd

dab dabs, dabbing, dabbed *verb* **1** If you dab something, you touch it with quick, light strokes. ▸ *noun* **2** a small amount of something that is put on a surface.

dabble *verb* If you dabble in something, you work or play at it without being seriously involved in it.

dad or **daddy** daddies *noun* (*informal*) Your dad or your daddy is your father.

daffodil *noun* A daffodil is an early spring flowering plant, with a yellow trumpet-shaped flower grown from a bulb.

daft *adjective* (*informal*) stupid and not sensible.

> **daft** *adjective*
> = crazy (*informal*), foolish, ludicrous, preposterous, ridiculous, silly, stupid

dagger *noun* a weapon like a short knife.

daily *adjective* **1** happening or appearing every day. ▸ *adverb* **2** every day.

dainty daintier, daintiest *adjective* very delicate and pretty. ▸ **daintily** *adverb*

dairy dairies *noun* **1** a shop or company that supplies milk and milk products. **2** in New Zealand, a small shop selling groceries, often outside usual opening hours. ▶ *adjective* **3** Dairy products are foods made from milk, such as butter, cheese, cream and yogurt. **4** A dairy farm is one which keeps cattle to produce milk.

dais *noun* a raised platform, normally at one end of a hall and used by a speaker.

daisy daisies *noun* a small wild flower with a yellow centre and small white petals.

dale *noun* a valley.

dam *noun* a barrier built across a river to hold back water.

damage *verb* **1** To damage something means to harm or spoil it. ▶ *noun* **2** Damage to something is injury or harm done to it. **3** Damages is the money awarded by a court to compensate someone for loss or harm.
> **damaging** *adjective*

> **damage** *verb*
> **1** = harm, hurt, injure
> ▶ *noun* **2** = harm, injury

dame *noun* the title given to a woman who has been awarded the OBE or one of the other British orders of chivalry.

damn *verb* **1** To damn something or someone means to curse or condemn them. ▶ *interjection* **2** 'Damn' is a swearword.
> **damned** *adjective*

damnation *noun* According to some religions, damnation is eternal punishment in Hell after death.

damp *adjective* **1** slightly wet. ▶ *noun* **2** Damp is slight wetness, especially in the air or in the walls of a building.

> **damp** *adjective*
> **1** = clammy, dank, humid, moist, sodden, soggy, wet

▶ *noun* **2** = dampness, humidity, moisture

dampen *verb* **1** If you dampen something, you make it slightly wet. **2** To dampen something also means to reduce its liveliness or strength.

damper *phrase* (*informal*) To **put a damper on** something means to stop it being enjoyable.

dance *verb* **1** To dance means to move your feet and body rhythmically in time to music. ▶ *noun* **2** a series of rhythmic movements or steps in time to music. **3** a social event where people dance with each other.

dandelion *noun* a wild plant with yellow flowers which form a ball of fluffy seeds.

dandruff *noun* Dandruff is small, loose scales of dead skin in someone's hair.

Dane *noun* someone who comes from Denmark.

danger *noun* **1** Danger is the possibility that someone may be harmed or killed. **2** something or someone that can hurt or harm you.

> **danger** *noun*
> **1** = hazard, jeopardy, menace, peril, risk, threat

dangerous *adjective* able to or likely to cause hurt or harm.

> **dangerous** *adjective*
> = hazardous, perilous, risky, treacherous

dangle *verb* When something dangles or when you dangle it, it swings or hangs loosely.

Danish *adjective* **1** belonging or relating to Denmark. ▶ *noun* **2** Danish is the main language spoken in Denmark.

dank *adjective* A dank place is unpleasantly damp and chilly.

dapper *adjective* slim and neatly dressed.

dappled *adjective* marked with patches of a darker shade.

dare *verb* 1 To dare someone means to challenge them to do something in order to prove their courage. 2 To dare to do something means to have the courage to do it. ▶ *noun* 3 a challenge to do something dangerous.

> **dare** *verb*
> 1 = challenge, defy, throw down the gauntlet 2 = risk, venture

daredevil *noun* a person who enjoys doing dangerous things.

daring *adjective* 1 bold and willing to take risks. ▶ *noun* 2 the courage required to do things which are dangerous.

> **daring** *adjective*
> 1 = adventurous, audacious, bold, brave, fearless
> ▶ *noun* 2 = audacity, boldness, bravery, courage, guts (*informal*), nerve (*informal*)

dark *adjective* 1 If it is dark, there is not enough light to see properly. 2 Dark colours or surfaces reflect little light and so look deep-coloured or dull. 3 'Dark' is also used to describe thoughts or ideas which are sinister or unpleasant. ▶ *noun* 4 The dark is the lack of light in a place.

> **dark** *adjective*
> 1 = cloudy, dim, dingy, murky, overcast, shadowy 2 = black, swarthy
> ▶ *noun* 4 = darkness, dimness, dusk, gloom

darken *verb* If something darkens, or if you darken it, it becomes darker than it was.

darling *noun* 1 Someone who is lovable or a favourite may be called a darling. ▶ *adjective* 2 much admired or loved.

darn *verb* 1 To darn a hole in a garment means to mend it with crossing stitches. ▶ *noun* 2 a part of a garment that has been darned.

dart *noun* 1 a small pointed arrow. 2 Darts is a game in which the players throw darts at a round board divided into numbered sections. ▶ *verb* 3 To dart about means to move quickly and suddenly from one place to another.

dash *verb* 1 To dash somewhere means to rush there. 2 If something is dashed against something else, it strikes it or is thrown violently against it. 3 If hopes or ambitions are dashed, they are ruined or frustrated. ▶ *noun* 4 a sudden movement or rush. 5 a small quantity of something. 6 (ENGLISH) the punctuation mark (—) which shows a change of subject, or which may be used in pairs instead of brackets.

> **dash** *verb*
> 1 = bolt, fly, race, run, rush, sprint, tear 2 = break, crash, hurl, slam, smash 3 = crush, destroy, disappoint, foil, frustrate, shatter, thwart
> ▶ *noun* 4 = bolt, race, run, rush, sprint, stampede 5 = drop, pinch, splash, sprinkling

dashboard *noun* the instrument panel in a motor vehicle.

dashing *adjective* A dashing man is stylish and confident.

data *noun* 1 information, usually in the form of facts or statistics. 2 (ICT) any information put into a computer and which the computer works on or processes.

database *noun* (ICT) a collection of information stored in a computer.

date *noun* 1 a particular day or year that can be named. 2 If you have a date, you have an appointment to meet someone; also used to refer to the person you are meeting. 3 a small dark-brown sticky fruit with a stone inside, which grows on palm trees. ▶ *verb* 4 If you are dating someone, you have a romantic relationship with them. 5 If you date something, you find out the time when it began or was made. 6 If something dates from a particular time, that is when it happened or was made. ▶ *phrase* 7 If something is **out of date**, it is old-fashioned or no longer valid.

dated *adjective* no longer fashionable.

datum the singular form of **data**.

daub *verb* If you daub something such as mud or paint on a surface, you smear it there.

daughter *noun* Someone's daughter is their female child.

daughter-in-law daughters-in-law *noun* Someone's daughter-in-law is the wife of their grown-up child.

daunt *verb* If something daunts you, you feel worried about whether you can succeed in doing it. ▷ **daunting** *adjective*

dawn *noun* 1 the time in the morning when light first appears in the sky. 2 the beginning of something. ▶ *verb* 3 If day is dawning, morning light is beginning to appear. 4 If an idea or fact dawns on you, you realise it.

day *noun* 1 one of the seven 24-hour periods of time in a week, measured from one midnight to the next. 2 Day is the period of light between sunrise and sunset. 3 You can refer to a particular day or days meaning a particular period in history.

daybreak *noun* Daybreak is the time in the morning when light first appears in the sky.

daydream *noun* 1 a series of pleasant thoughts about things that you would like to happen. ▶ *verb* 2 When you daydream, you drift off into a daydream.

> **daydream** *noun*
> 1 = dream, fantasy
> ▶ *verb* 2 = dream, fantasise

daylight *noun* 1 Daylight is the period during the day when it is light. 2 Daylight is also the light from the sun.

day-to-day *adjective* happening every day as part of routine life.

day trip *noun* a journey for pleasure to a place and back again on the same day.

daze *phrase* If you are **in a daze**, you are confused and bewildered.

dazed *adjective* If you are dazed, you are stunned and unable to think clearly.

> **dazed** *adjective*
> = bewildered, confused, dizzy, light-headed, numbed, stunned

D

dazzle verb 1 If someone or something dazzles you, you are very impressed by their brilliance. 2 If a bright light dazzles you, it blinds you for a moment. > **dazzling** adjective

deacon noun 1 In the Church of England or Roman Catholic Church, a deacon is a member of the clergy below the rank of priest. 2 In some other churches, a deacon is a church official appointed to help the minister. > **deaconess** noun

dead adjective 1 no longer living or supporting life. 2 no longer used or no longer functioning. 3 If part of your body goes dead, it loses sensation and feels numb. ▶ phrase 4 **The dead of night** is the middle part of the night, when it is most quiet and dark.

> **dead** adjective
> 1 = deceased (formal), departed, extinct, late 2 = defunct, not working

dead end noun a street that is closed off at one end.

deadline noun a time or date before which something must be completed.

deadlock noun a situation in which neither side in a dispute is willing to give in.

deadly deadlier, deadliest adjective likely or able to cause death.

> **deadly** adjective
> = destructive, fatal, lethal, mortal

deadpan adjective, adverb showing no emotion or expression.

deaf adjective 1 partially or totally unable to hear. 2 refusing to listen or pay attention to something: *She was deaf to all pleas for financial help.*

deafening adjective If a noise is deafening, it is so loud that you cannot hear anything else.

deal deals, dealing, dealt noun 1 an agreement or arrangement, especially in business. ▶ verb 2 If you deal with something, you do what is necessary to sort it out. 3 If you deal in a particular type of goods, you buy and sell those goods.

> **deal** verb
> 2 = attend to, cope with, handle, manage, see to, take care of

dealer noun a person or firm whose business involves buying or selling things.

dealings plural noun Your dealings with people are the relations you have with them or the business you do with them.

dean noun 1 In a university or college, a dean is a person responsible for administration or for the welfare of students. 2 In the Church of England, a dean is a member of the clergy who is responsible for administration.

dear noun 1 'Dear' is used as a sign of affection. ▶ adjective 2 much loved. 3 Something that is dear is expensive. 4 You use 'dear' at the beginning of a letter before the name of the person you are writing to. > **dearly** adverb

> **dear** noun
> 1 = angel, beloved (old-fashioned), darling, treasure (informal)
> ▶ adjective 2 = beloved, cherished, darling, esteemed, precious, prized, treasured
> 3 = costly, expensive, pricey (informal)

dearth noun a shortage of something.

death noun Death is the end of the life of a person or animal.

debacle noun (formal) a sudden disastrous failure.

debatable adjective not absolutely certain.

debate noun 1 Debate is argument or discussion. 2 (CITIZENSHIP) a formal discussion in which opposing views are expressed. ▶ verb 3 When people debate something, they discuss it in a fairly formal manner. 4 If you are debating whether or not to do something, you are considering it.

debilitating adjective (formal) If something is debilitating, it makes you very weak.

debit verb 1 to take money from a person's bank account. ▶ noun 2 a record of the money that has been taken out of a person's bank account.

debrief verb When someone is debriefed, they are asked to give a report on a task they have just completed. > **debriefing** noun

debris noun Debris is fragments or rubble left after something has been destroyed.

debt noun 1 a sum of money that is owed to one person by another. 2 Debt is the state of owing money.

debtor noun a person who owes money.

debut noun a performer's first public appearance.

debutante noun (old-fashioned) a girl from the upper classes who has started going to social events.

decade noun a period of ten years.

decadence noun Decadence is a decline in standards of morality and behaviour. > **decadent** adjective

decapitate verb To decapitate someone means to cut off their head.

decathlon noun a sports contest in which athletes compete in ten different events.

decay verb 1 When things decay, they rot or go bad. ▶ noun 2 Decay is the process of decaying.

deceased (formal) adjective 1 A deceased person is someone who has recently died. ▶ noun 2 The deceased is someone who has recently died.

deceit noun Deceit is behaviour that is intended to make people believe something that is not true. > **deceitful** adjective

deceive verb If you deceive someone, you make them believe something that is not true.

> **deceive** verb
> = con (informal), double-cross, dupe, fool, mislead, take in, trick

December noun December is the twelfth and last month of the year. It has 31 days.

decency noun 1 Decency is behaviour that is respectable and follows accepted moral standards. 2 Decency is also behaviour which shows kindness and respect towards people.

decent adjective 1 of an acceptable standard or quality. 2 Decent people are honest and respectable.

D

decent *adjective*
1 = adequate, passable,
reasonable, respectable,
satisfactory, tolerable
2 = proper, respectable

deception *noun* 1 something that
is intended to trick or deceive
someone. 2 Deception is the act
of deceiving someone.

deceptive *adjective* likely to make
people believe something that is
not true. > **deceptively** *adverb*

deceptive *adjective*
= false, fraudulent, illusory,
misleading, unreliable

decibel *noun* (SCIENCE) a unit of
the intensity of sound.

decide *verb* If you decide to do
something, you choose to do it.

decide *verb*
= choose, come to a decision,
determine (*formal*), elect
(*formal*), make up your mind,
reach a decision, resolve (*formal*)

deciduous *adjective* Deciduous
trees lose their leaves in the
autumn every year.

decimal (MATHS) *adjective* 1 The
decimal system expresses
numbers using all the digits from
0 to 9. ▶ *noun* 2 a fraction in
which a dot called a decimal
point is followed by numbers
representing tenths, hundredths
and thousandths. For example,
0.5 represents $^5/_{10}$ (or $^1/_2$); 0.05
represents $^5/_{100}$ (or $^1/_{20}$).

decimate *verb* To decimate a
group of people or animals means
to kill or destroy a large number
of them.

decipher *verb* If you decipher a
piece of writing or a message, you
work out its meaning.

decision *noun* a choice or judgment
that is made about something.

decision *noun*
= conclusion, finding,
judgment, resolution, ruling,
verdict

decisive *adjective* 1 having great
influence on the result of
something. 2 A decisive person is
able to make decisions firmly and
quickly.

deck *noun* 1 a floor or platform
built into a ship, or one of the two
floors on a bus. 2 a pack of cards.

declaration *noun* a firm, forceful
statement, often an official
announcement.

declaration *noun*
= affirmation, protestation
(*formal*), statement, testimony

declare *verb* 1 If you declare
something, you state it forcefully
or officially. 2 If you declare goods
or earnings, you state what you
have bought or earned, in order to
pay tax or duty.

declare *verb*
1 = affirm, announce, assert,
certify, proclaim, profess
(*formal*), pronounce, state

decline *verb* 1 If something
declines, it becomes smaller or
weaker. 2 If you decline
something, you politely refuse to
accept it or do it. ▶ *noun* 3 a
gradual weakening or decrease.

decline *verb*
1 = decrease, diminish, drop,
fall, go down, plummet, reduce
2 = abstain (*formal*), excuse
yourself, refuse, turn down
▶ *noun* 3 = decrease, downturn,
drop, fall, recession, shrinkage,
slump

decode verb If you decode a coded message, you convert it into ordinary language. > **decoder** noun

decommission verb When something such as a nuclear reactor is decommissioned, it is taken to pieces or removed from service because it is no longer going to be used.

decompose verb (SCIENCE) If something decomposes, it decays through chemical or bacterial action. > **decomposition** noun

decor noun The decor of a room or house is the style in which it is decorated and furnished.

decorate verb 1 If you decorate something, you make it more attractive by adding some ornament or colour to it. 2 If you decorate a room or building, you paint or wallpaper it.

> **decorate** verb
> 1 = adorn, deck, ornament
> 2 = do up (informal), renovate

decoration noun 1 Decorations are features added to something to make it more attractive. 2 The decoration in a building or room is the style of the furniture and wallpaper.

decorative adjective intended to look attractive.

decorator noun a person whose job is painting and putting up wallpaper in rooms and buildings.

decorum noun (formal) Decorum is polite and correct behaviour.

decoy noun a person or object that is used to lead someone or something into danger.

decrease verb 1 If something decreases or if you decrease it, it becomes less in quantity or size. ▶ noun 2 a lessening in the amount of something; also the amount by which something becomes less.

> **decrease** verb
> 1 = cut down, decline, diminish, drop, dwindle, lessen, lower, reduce, shrink
> ▶ noun 2 = cutback, decline, drop, lessening, reduction

decree decrees, decreeing, decreed verb 1 If someone decrees something, they state formally that it will happen. ▶ noun 2 an official decision or order, usually by governments or rulers.

dedicate verb If you dedicate yourself to something, you devote your time and energy to it. > **dedication** noun

deduce verb If you deduce something, you work it out from other facts that you know are true.

deduct verb To deduct an amount from a total amount means to subtract it from the total.

deduction noun 1 an amount which is taken away from a total. 2 a conclusion that you have reached because of other things that you know are true.

deed noun 1 something that is done. 2 a legal document, especially concerning the ownership of land or buildings.

deem verb (formal) If you deem something to be the case, you judge or consider it to be the case.

deep adjective 1 situated or extending a long way down from the top surface of something, or a

long way inwards: *a deep hole.*
2 great or intense: *deep suspicion.*
3 low in pitch. **4** strong and fairly dark in colour.

> **deep** *adjective*
> **1** = bottomless, yawning
> **2** = extreme, grave (*formal*),
> great, intense, profound,
> serious **3** = bass, low

deepen *verb* If something deepens or is deepened, it becomes deeper or more intense.

deer deer *noun* a large, hoofed mammal that lives in the wild.

deface *verb* If you deface a wall or notice, you spoil it by writing or drawing on it.

default *verb* **1** If someone defaults on something they have legally agreed to do, they fail to do it.
▶ *phrase* **2** If something happens **by default**, it happens because something else which might have prevented it has failed to happen.

defeat *verb* **1** If you defeat someone or something, you win a victory over them or cause them to fail. ▶ *noun* **2** the state of being beaten or of failing, or an occasion on which someone is beaten or fails to achieve something.

> **defeat** *verb*
> **1** = beat, conquer, crush, rout,
> trounce, vanquish (*literary*)
> ▶ *noun* **2** = conquest, debacle
> (*formal*), rout, trouncing

defect *noun* **1** a fault or flaw in something. ▶ *verb* **2** If someone defects, they leave their own country or organisation and join an opposing one.
> **defection** *noun*

> **defect** *noun*
> **1** = deficiency, failing, fault,
> flaw, imperfection,
> shortcoming, weakness

defective *adjective* imperfect or faulty.

defence *noun* **1** Defence is action that is taken to protect someone or something from attack.
2 any arguments used in support of something that has been criticised or questioned. **3** the case presented, in a court of law, by a lawyer for the person on trial; also the person on trial and his or her lawyers. **4** (HISTORY) A country's defences are its military resources, such as its armed forces and weapons.

> **defence** *noun*
> **1** = cover, protection, resistance,
> safeguard, security
> **2** = argument, excuse,
> explanation, justification, plea

defend *verb* **1** To defend someone or something means to protect them from harm or danger. **2** If you defend a person or their ideas and beliefs, you argue in support of them. **3** To defend someone in court means to represent them and argue their case for them.
4 In a game such as football or hockey, to defend means to try to prevent goals being scored by your opponents.

> **defend** *verb*
> **1** = cover, guard, protect,
> safeguard, shelter, shield
> **2** = endorse, justify, stick up for
> (*informal*), support, uphold

defendant *noun* a person who has been accused of a crime in a court of law.

defender *noun* 1 a person who protects someone or something from harm or danger. 2 a person who argues in support of something. 3 a person who tries to stop goals being scored in certain sports.

> **defender** *noun*
> 2 = advocate, champion, supporter

defensible *adjective* able to be defended against criticism or attack.

defensive *adjective* 1 intended or designed for protection. 2 Someone who is defensive feels unsure and threatened by other people's opinions and attitudes. > **defensively** *adverb*

defer defers, deferring, deferred *verb* 1 If you defer something, you delay or postpone it until a future time. 2 If you defer to someone, you agree with them or do what they want because you respect them.

deference *noun* Deference is polite and respectful behaviour. > **deferential** *adjective*

defiance *noun* Defiance is behaviour which shows that you are not willing to obey or behave in the expected way. > **defiant** *adjective* > **defiantly** *adverb*

deficiency deficiencies *noun* a lack of something.

> **deficiency** *noun*
> = deficit, deprivation, inadequacy, lack, want (formal)

deficient *adjective* lacking in something.

> **deficient** *adjective*
> = inadequate, lacking, poor, short, wanting

deficit *noun* the amount by which money received by an organisation is less than money spent.

define *verb* (EXAM TERM) If you define something, you say clearly what it is or what it means.

definite *adjective* 1 firm and unlikely to be changed. 2 certain or true rather than guessed or imagined. > **definitely** *adverb*

> **definite** *adjective*
> 1 = assured, certain, decided, fixed, guaranteed, settled
> 2 = clear, positive

definition *noun* a statement explaining the meaning of a word or idea.

definitive *adjective* 1 final and unable to be questioned or altered. 2 most complete, or the best of its kind.

deflate *verb* 1 If you deflate something such as a tyre or balloon, you let out all the air or gas in it. 2 If you deflate someone, you make them seem less important.

deflect *verb* To deflect something means to turn it aside or make it change direction. > **deflection** *noun*

deforestation *noun* (GEOGRAPHY) Deforestation is the cutting down of all the trees in an area.

deformed *adjective* disfigured or not naturally shaped.

> **deformed** *adjective*
> = disfigured, distorted

defraud *verb* If someone defrauds you, they cheat you out of something that should be yours.

defrost *verb* 1 If you defrost a freezer or refrigerator, you remove the ice from it. **2** If you defrost frozen food, you let it thaw out.

deft *adjective* Someone who is deft is quick and skilful in their movements.

defunct *adjective* no longer existing or functioning.

defuse *verb* **1** To defuse a dangerous or tense situation means to make it less dangerous or tense. **2** To defuse a bomb means to remove its fuse or detonator so that it cannot explode.

defy defies, defying, defied *verb* **1** If you defy a person or a law, you openly refuse to obey. **2** (*formal*) If you defy someone to do something that you think is impossible, you challenge them to do it.

degenerate *verb* **1** If something degenerates, it becomes worse. ▶ *adjective* **2** having low standards of morality. ▶ *noun* **3** someone whose standards of morality are so low that people find their behaviour shocking or disgusting. > **degeneration** *noun*

degradation *noun* Degradation is a state of poverty and misery.

degrade *verb* If something degrades people, it humiliates them and makes them feel that they are not respected. > **degrading** *adjective*

degrade *verb*
= demean, humiliate

degree *noun* **1** an amount of a feeling or quality. **2** (SCIENCE) a unit of measurement of temperature; often written as ° after a number. **3** (MATHS) (GEOGRAPHY) a unit of measurement of angles in

mathematics, and of latitude and longitude in geography. **4** a course of study at a university or college; also the qualification awarded after passing the course.

dehydrate *verb* **1** If something is dehydrated, water is removed or lost from it. **2** If someone is dehydrated, they are weak or ill because they have lost too much water from their body. > **dehydration** *noun*

deity deities *noun* a god or goddess.

deja vu *noun* Deja vu is the feeling that you have already experienced in the past exactly the same sequence of events as is happening now.

dejected *adjective* miserable and unhappy. > **dejection** *noun*

delay *verb* **1** If you delay doing something, you put it off until a later time. **2** If something delays you, it hinders you or slows you down. ▶ *noun* **3** Delay is time during which something is delayed.

delay *verb*
1 = defer, postpone, put off, shelve, suspend **2** = check, hinder, impede, obstruct, set back
▶ *noun* **3** = interruption, obstruction, setback

delectable *adjective* very pleasing.

delegate *noun* **1** a person appointed to vote or to make decisions on behalf of a group of people. ▶ *verb* **2** If you delegate duties, you give them to someone who can then act on your behalf.

delegation *noun* **1** a group of people chosen to represent a larger group of people.

2 Delegation is the giving of duties, responsibilities or power to someone who can then act on your behalf.

delete verb (ICT) To delete something means to cross it out or remove it. > **deletion** noun

> **delete** verb
> = cross out, erase, rub out

deliberate adjective 1 done on purpose or planned in advance. 2 careful and not hurried in speech and action. ▶ verb 3 If you deliberate about something, you think about it seriously and carefully. > **deliberately** adverb

> **deliberate** adjective
> 1 = calculated, conscious, intentional, premeditated, studied 2 = careful, cautious, measured, methodical
> ▶ verb 3 = debate, meditate, mull over, ponder, reflect

deliberation noun Deliberation is careful consideration of a subject.

delicacy delicacies noun 1 Delicacy is grace and attractiveness. 2 Something said or done with delicacy is said or done tactfully so that nobody is offended. 3 Delicacies are rare or expensive foods that are considered especially nice to eat.

delicate adjective 1 fine, graceful or subtle in character. 2 fragile and needing to be handled carefully. > **delicately** adverb

delicatessen noun a shop selling unusual or imported foods.

delicious adjective very pleasing, especially to taste.

> **delicious** adjective
> = appetising, delectable, luscious, tasty

delight noun 1 Delight is great pleasure or joy. ▶ verb 2 If something delights you or if you are delighted by it, it gives you a lot of pleasure. > **delighted** adjective

> **delight** noun
> 1 = glee, happiness, joy, pleasure, rapture, satisfaction
> ▶ verb 2 = amuse, captivate, charm, enchant, please, thrill

delightful adjective very pleasant and attractive. > **delightfully** adverb

delinquent noun a young person who commits minor crimes.

delirious adjective 1 unable to speak or act in a rational way because of illness or fever. 2 wildly excited and happy. > **deliriously** adverb

deliver verb 1 If you deliver something to someone, you take it to them and give them it. 2 To deliver a lecture or speech means to give it.

delivery deliveries noun 1 Delivery or a delivery is the bringing of letters or goods to a person or firm. 2 Someone's delivery is the way in which they give a speech.

delta noun (GEOGRAPHY) a low, flat area at the mouth of a river where the river has split into several branches to enter the sea.

delude verb To delude people means to deceive them into believing something that is not true.

deluge noun 1 a sudden, heavy downpour of rain. ▶ verb 2 To be deluged with things means to be overwhelmed by a great number of them.

delusion noun a mistaken or misleading belief or idea.

delve verb If you delve into something, you seek out more information about it.

demand verb 1 If you demand something, you ask for it forcefully and urgently. 2 If a job or situation demands a particular quality, it needs it. ▶ noun 3 a forceful request for something. 4 If there is a demand for something, a lot of people want to buy it or have it.

> **demand** verb
> 2 = involve, need, require, take, want

demean verb If you demean yourself, you do something which makes people have less respect for you. > **demeaning** adjective

demeanour noun Your demeanour is the way you behave and the impression that this creates.

demented adjective Someone who is demented behaves in a wild or violent way.

dementia noun Dementia is a serious illness of the brain that affects people's ability to think clearly and remember things.

demise noun (formal) Someone's demise is their death.

demo demos noun (informal) a demonstration.

democracy democracies noun (CITIZENSHIP) Democracy is a system of government in which the people choose their leaders by voting for them in elections.

democrat noun a person who believes in democracy, personal freedom and equality.

democratic adjective having

representatives elected by the people. > **democratically** adverb

demolish verb To demolish a building means to pull it down or break it up. > **demolition** noun

demon noun an evil spirit or devil. > **demonic** adjective

demonstrate verb 1 (EXAM TERM) To demonstrate a fact or theory means to prove or show it to be true. 2 If you demonstrate something to somebody, you show and explain it by using or doing the thing itself. 3 If people demonstrate, they take part in a march or rally to show their opposition or support for something.

demonstration noun 1 a talk or explanation to show how to do or use something. 2 Demonstration is proof that something exists or is true. 3 a public march or rally in support of or opposition to something. > **demonstrator** noun

demote verb A person who is demoted is put in a lower rank or position, often as a punishment. > **demotion** noun

demure adjective Someone who is demure is quiet and shy and behaves very modestly. > **demurely** adverb

den noun 1 the home of some wild animals such as lions or foxes. 2 a secret place where people meet.

denial noun 1 A denial of something is a statement that it is untrue. 2 The denial of a request or something to which you have a right is the refusal of it.

denigrate verb (formal) To denigrate someone or something means to criticise them in order to damage their reputation.

denim noun 1 Denim is strong cotton cloth, used for making clothes. 2 (in plural) Denims are jeans made from denim.

denomination noun 1 a particular group which has slightly different religious beliefs from other groups within the same faith. 2 a unit in a system of weights, values or measures.

denominator noun (MATHS) In maths, the denominator is the bottom part of a fraction.

denote verb If one thing denotes another, it is a sign of it or it represents it.

denounce verb 1 If you denounce someone or something, you express very strong disapproval of them. 2 If you denounce someone, you give information against them.

dense adjective 1 thickly crowded or packed together. 2 difficult to see through.

density densities noun the degree to which something is filled or occupied.

dent verb 1 To dent something means to damage it by hitting it and making a hollow in its surface. ▶ noun 2 a hollow in the surface of something.

dental adjective relating to the teeth.

dentist noun a person who is qualified to treat people's teeth.

dentistry noun Dentistry is the branch of medicine concerned with disorders of the teeth.

dentures plural noun Dentures are false teeth.

denunciation noun A denunciation of someone or something is severe public criticism of them.

deny denies, denying, denied verb 1 If you deny something that has been said, you state that it is untrue. 2 If you deny that something is the case, you refuse to believe it. 3 If you deny someone something, you refuse to give it to them.

> **deny** verb
> 1 = contradict, refute 2 = reject, renounce 3 = refuse, withhold

deodorant noun a substance used to hide the smell of sweat.

depart verb When you depart, you leave. > **departure** noun

department noun one of the sections into which an organisation is divided.

> **department** noun
> = division, office, section, unit

depend verb 1 If you depend on someone or something, you trust them and rely on them. 2 If one thing depends on another, it is influenced by it.

> **depend** verb
> 1 = bank on, count on, rely on, trust 2 = be determined by, hinge on

dependable adjective reliable and trustworthy.

dependant noun (PSHE) someone who relies on another person for financial support.

dependence noun Dependence is a constant need that someone has for something or someone in order to survive or operate properly.

dependency dependencies noun 1 (PSHE) Dependency is relying on someone or something to give you what you need. 2 a country or area controlled by another country.

dependent *adjective* reliant on someone or something.

depict *verb* To depict someone or something means to represent them in painting or sculpture.

deplete *verb* To deplete something means to reduce greatly the amount of it available. > **depletion** *noun*

deplorable *adjective* shocking or regrettable.

deplore *verb* If you deplore something, you condemn it because you feel it is wrong.

deploy *verb* To deploy troops or resources means to organise them so that they can be used effectively. > **deployment** *noun*

deport *verb* If a government deports someone, it sends them out of the country because they have committed a crime or because they do not have the right to be there. > **deportation** *noun*

depose *verb* If someone is deposed, they are removed from a position of power.

deposit *verb* 1 If you deposit something, you put it down or leave it somewhere. 2 If you deposit money or valuables, you put them somewhere for safekeeping. 3 (GEOGRAPHY) If something is deposited on a surface, a layer of it is left there as a result of chemical or geological action. ▶ *noun* 4 a sum of money given in part payment for goods or services.

> **deposit** *verb*
> 1 = drop, lay, leave, place, put down

depot *noun* a place where large

supplies of materials or equipment may be stored.

depraved *adjective* morally bad.

depress *verb* 1 If something depresses you, it makes you feel sad and gloomy. 2 If wages or prices are depressed, their value falls. > **depressive** *adjective*

depressed *adjective* 1 unhappy and gloomy. 2 A place that is depressed has little economic activity and therefore low incomes and high unemployment.

depression *noun* 1 a state of mind in which someone feels unhappy and has no energy or enthusiasm. 2 a time of industrial and economic decline. 3 (GEOGRAPHY) In meteorology, a depression is a mass of air that has low pressure and brings cloud, wind and rain. 4 (GEOGRAPHY) A depression in the surface of something is a part which is lower than the rest.

deprive *verb* If you deprive someone of something, you take it away or prevent them from having it. > **deprivation** *noun*

depth *noun* 1 The depth of something is the measurement or distance between its top and bottom, or between its front and back. 2 The depth of something such as emotion is its intensity.

deputy deputies *noun* Someone's deputy is a person appointed to act in their place.

deranged *adjective* behaving in a wild and uncontrolled way.

derby derbies *noun* A local derby is a sporting event between two teams from the same area.

derelict *adjective* abandoned and falling into ruins.

derelict *adjective*
= abandoned, dilapidated, neglected, ruined

deride *verb* To deride someone or something means to mock or jeer at them with contempt.

derision *noun* Derision is an attitude of contempt or scorn towards something or someone.

derivative *noun* **1** something which has developed from an earlier source. ▶ *adjective* **2** not original, but based on or copied from something else.

derive *verb* **1** (*formal*) If you derive something from someone or something, you get it from them. **2** If something derives from something else, it develops from it.

derogatory *adjective* critical and scornful.

descend *verb* **1** To descend means to move downwards. **2** If you descend on people or on a place, you arrive unexpectedly.

descend *verb*
1 = dip, dive, fall, go down, plummet, sink

descendant *noun* A person's descendants are the people in later generations who are related to them.

descent *noun* **1** a movement or slope from a higher to a lower position or level. **2** Your descent is your family's origins.

describe *verb* To describe someone or something means to give an account or a picture of them in words.

describe *verb*
= define, depict, portray

description *noun* an account or picture of something in words.
> **descriptive** *adjective*

desert[1] *noun* (GEOGRAPHY) a region of land with very little plant life, usually because of low rainfall.

desert[2] *verb* To desert a person means to leave or abandon them.
> **desertion** *noun*

deserter *noun* someone who leaves the armed forces without permission.

deserve *verb* If you deserve something, you are entitled to it or earn it because of your qualities, achievements or actions.

deserve *verb*
= be entitled to, be worthy of, earn, justify, merit, warrant

deserving *adjective* worthy of being helped, rewarded or praised.

design (DGT) *verb* **1** To design something means to plan it, especially by preparing a detailed sketch or drawings from which it can be built or made. ▶ *noun* **2** a drawing or plan from which something can be built or made. **3** The design of something is its shape and style.
> **designer** *noun*

design *verb*
1 = draft, draw up, plan
▶ *noun* **2** = model, plan **3** = form, pattern, shape, style

designate *verb* **1** To designate someone or something means to formally label or name them. **2** If you designate someone to do something, you appoint them to do it.

d

designation noun a name or title.

designing adjective crafty and cunning.

desirable adjective worth having or doing.

desire verb 1 If you desire something, you want it very much. ▶ noun 2 a strong feeling of wanting something.

> **desire** verb
> 1 = crave, fancy, long for, want, wish, yearn
> ▶ noun 2 = appetite, craving, hankering, longing, wish, yearning, yen (informal)

desist verb (formal) To desist from doing something means to stop doing it.

desk noun 1 a piece of furniture designed for working at or writing on. 2 a counter or table in a public building behind which a receptionist sits.

desktop adjective of a convenient size to be used on a desk or table.

desolate adjective 1 deserted and bleak. 2 lonely, very sad, and without hope. > **desolation** noun

despair noun 1 Despair is a total loss of hope. ▶ verb 2 If you despair, you lose hope.

> **despair** noun
> 1 = dejection, despondency, gloom, hopelessness
> ▶ verb 2 = feel dejected, feel despondent, lose heart, lose hope

despatch another spelling of **dispatch**.

desperate adjective 1 If you are desperate, you are so worried or frightened that you will try anything to improve your situation. 2 A desperate person is violent and dangerous. 3 A desperate situation is extremely dangerous or serious.
> **desperately** adverb
> **desperation** noun

despicable adjective deserving contempt.

despise verb If you despise someone or something, you dislike them very much.

despite preposition in spite of.

> **despite** preposition
> = in spite of, notwithstanding (formal), regardless of

despondent adjective dejected and unhappy. > **despondency** noun

dessert noun a sweet food served after the main course of a meal.

destination noun a place to which someone or something is going or is being sent.

destined adjective meant or intended to happen.

destiny destinies noun 1 Your destiny is all the things that happen to you in your life, especially when they are considered to be outside human control. 2 Destiny is the force which some people believe controls everyone's life.

destitute adjective without money or possessions, and therefore in great need.
> **destitution** noun

destroy verb To destroy something means to damage it so much that it is completely ruined.

> **destroy** verb
> = annihilate, demolish, devastate, obliterate, raze, ruin, wreck

destruction noun Destruction is the act of destroying something or the state of being destroyed.

> **destruction** noun
> = annihilation, demolition, devastation, obliteration

destructive adjective causing or able to cause great harm, damage or injury. > **destructiveness** noun

detach verb To detach something means to remove it. > **detachable** adjective

detached adjective 1 separate or standing apart. 2 having no real interest or emotional involvement with something.

detachment noun 1 Detachment is the feeling of not being personally involved with something. 2 a small group of soldiers sent to do a special job.

detail noun 1 an individual fact or feature of something. 2 Detail is all the small features that make up the whole of something. > **detailed** adjective

> **detail** noun
> 1 = aspect, element, particular, point, respect

detain verb 1 To detain someone means to force them to stay. 2 If you detain someone, you delay them.

detect verb 1 If you detect something, you notice it. 2 To detect something means to find it.

detection noun 1 Detection is the act of noticing, discovering or sensing something. 2 Detection is also the work of investigating crime.

detective noun a person, usually a police officer, whose job is to investigate crimes.

detector noun an instrument which is used to detect the presence of something.

detention noun The detention of someone is their arrest or imprisonment.

deter deters, deterring, deterred verb To deter someone means to discourage or prevent them from doing something by creating a feeling of fear or doubt.

detergent noun a chemical substance used for washing or cleaning things.

deteriorate verb If something deteriorates, it gets worse. > **deterioration** noun

determination noun Determination is great firmness, after you have made up your mind to do something.

> **determination** noun
> = perseverance, persistence, resolution, resolve (formal), tenacity

determine verb 1 If something determines a situation or result, it causes it or controls it. 2 To determine something means to decide or settle it firmly. 3 To determine something means to find out or calculate the facts about it.

> **determine** verb
> 1 = control, decide, dictate, govern, shape 2 = arrange, choose, decide, fix, resolve, settle 3 = ascertain (formal), confirm, discover, establish, find out, verify

determined adjective firmly decided.

D

determined adjective
= bent on, dogged, intent on, persistent, purposeful, resolute (formal), single-minded, tenacious

deterrent noun something that prevents you from doing something by making you afraid of what will happen if you do it.

detest verb If you detest someone or something, you strongly dislike them.

detonate verb To detonate a bomb or mine means to cause it to explode. ▷ **detonator** noun

detour noun an alternative, less direct route.

detract verb To detract from something means to make it seem less good or valuable.

detriment noun Detriment is disadvantage or harm.
▷ **detrimental** adjective

deuce noun In tennis, deuce is the score of forty all.

devalue verb To devalue something means to lower its status, importance or worth.
▷ **devaluation** noun

devastate verb To devastate an area or place means to damage it severely or destroy it.
▷ **devastation** noun

devastated adjective very shocked or upset.

develop verb 1 When something develops or is developed, it grows or becomes more advanced. 2 To develop an area of land means to build on it. 3 To develop an illness or a fault means to become affected by it.

develop verb
1 = advance, evolve, grow, mature, progress, result, spring

3 = catch, contract (formal), fall ill with, get, go down with, pick up, succumb to (formal)

developer noun a person or company that builds on land.

development noun
1 Development is gradual growth or progress. 2 The development of land is the process of making it more useful or profitable by the expansion of industry or housing. 3 a new stage in a series of events.

deviant adjective 1 Deviant behaviour is unacceptable or different from what people consider as normal. ▶ noun 2 someone whose behaviour or beliefs are different from what people consider to be acceptable.
▷ **deviance** noun

deviate verb To deviate means to differ or depart from what is usual or acceptable. ▷ **deviation** noun

device noun 1 a machine or tool that is used for a particular purpose. 2 a plan or scheme.

devil noun 1 (RE) In Christianity and Judaism, the Devil is the spirit of evil and enemy of God. 2 an evil spirit.

devious adjective insincere and dishonest. ▷ **deviousness** noun

devious adjective
= calculating, scheming, underhand, wily

devise verb To devise something means to work it out.

devoid adjective lacking in a particular thing or quality.

devolution noun Devolution is the transfer of power from a central government or organisation to local government departments or smaller organisations.

devote *verb* If you devote yourself to something, you give all your time, energy or money to it.

devoted *adjective* very loving and loyal.

> **devoted** *adjective*
> = constant, dedicated, doting, faithful, loving, loyal, true

devotee *noun* a fanatical or enthusiastic follower of something.

devotion *noun* Devotion to someone or something is great love or affection for them.

devour *verb* If you devour something, you eat it hungrily or greedily.

devout *adjective* deeply and sincerely religious.

dew *noun* Dew is drops of moisture that form on the ground and other cool surfaces at night.

dexterity *noun* Dexterity is skill or agility in using your hands or mind. > **dexterous** *adjective*

diabetes *noun* Diabetes is a disease in which someone has too much sugar in their blood, because they do not produce enough insulin to absorb it. > **diabetic** *adjective*

diabolical *adjective* 1 (*informal*) dreadful and very annoying. 2 extremely wicked and cruel.

diagnose *verb* To diagnose an illness or problem means to identify exactly what is wrong.

diagnosis *noun* the identification of what is wrong with someone who is ill. > **diagnostic** *adjective*

diagonal *adjective* in a slanting direction. > **diagonally** *adverb*

diagram *noun* a drawing that shows or explains something.

dial dials, dialling, dialled *noun* 1 the face of a clock or meter, with divisions marked on it so that a time or measurement can be recorded and read. 2 a part of a device, such as a radio, used to control or tune it. ▶ *verb* 3 To dial a telephone number means to press the number keys to select the required number.

dialect *noun* a form of a language spoken in a particular area.

dialogue *noun* 1 (ENGLISH) In a novel, play or film, dialogue is conversation. 2 Dialogue is communication or discussion between people or groups of people.

dialysis *noun* Dialysis is a treatment used for some kidney diseases, in which blood is filtered by a special machine to remove waste products.

diameter *noun* (MATHS) The diameter of a circle is the length of a straight line drawn across it through its centre.

diamond *noun* 1 A diamond is a precious stone made of pure carbon. Diamonds are the hardest known substance in the world and are used for cutting substances and for making jewellery. 2 A diamond is also a shape with four straight sides of equal length forming two opposite angles less than 90° and two opposite angles greater than 90°. 3 Diamonds is one of the four suits in a pack of playing cards. It is marked by a red diamond-shaped symbol. ▶ *adjective* 4 A diamond anniversary is the 60th anniversary of an event.

diaphragm noun (SCIENCE)
In mammals, the diaphragm is the muscular wall that separates the lungs from the stomach.

diarrhoea noun Diarrhoea is a condition in which the faeces are more liquid and frequent than usual.

diary diaries noun a book which has a separate space or page for each day of the year on which to keep a record of appointments. > **diarist** noun

dice noun 1 a small cube which has each side marked with dots representing the numbers one to six. ▶ verb 2 To dice food means to cut it into small cubes. > **diced** adjective

dictate verb 1 If you dictate something, you say or read it aloud for someone else to write down. 2 To dictate something means to command or state what must happen. > **dictation** noun

dictator noun (HISTORY) A dictator is a ruler who has complete power in a country, especially one who has taken power by force. > **dictatorial** adjective

diction noun Someone's diction is the clarity with which they speak or sing.

dictionary dictionaries noun (LIBRARY) a book in which words are listed alphabetically and explained, or equivalent words are given in another language.

did the past tense of **do**.

didgeridoo noun an Australian musical wind instrument made in the shape of a long wooden tube.

die dies, dying, died verb
1 When people, animals or plants die, they stop living. 2 When something dies, dies away or dies down, it gradually fades away. ▶ noun 3 a dice. > **die out** verb When something dies out, it ceases to exist.

> **die** verb
> 1 = cark it (Australian and New Zealand; informal), expire (formal), pass away, pass on, perish (formal) 2 = fade away, fade out, peter out
> ▶ **die out** = disappear, fade, vanish

diesel noun 1 a fuel used in trains, buses, lorries and some cars. 2 a vehicle with a diesel engine.

diet noun 1 Someone's diet is the usual food that they eat. 2 (PSHE) a special restricted selection of foods that someone eats to improve their health or regulate their weight. > **dietary** adjective > **dieter** noun

dietician; also spelt **dietitian** noun a person trained to advise people about healthy eating.

differ verb 1 If two or more things differ, they are unlike each other. 2 If people differ, they have opposing views or disagree about something.

difference noun 1 The difference between things is the way in which they are unlike each other. 2 The difference between two numbers is the amount by which one is less than another. 3 A difference in someone or something is a significant change in them.

difference noun
1 = contrast, discrepancy, disparity, distinction, divergence, variation
2 = balance, remainder

different adjective 1 unlike something else. 2 unusual and out of the ordinary. 3 distinct and separate, although of the same kind.

different adjective
1 = contrasting, disparate (formal), dissimilar, divergent (formal), opposed, unlike
2 = special, unique 3 = another, discrete (formal), distinct, individual, separate

differentiate verb 1 To differentiate between things means to recognise or show how one is unlike the other. 2 Something that differentiates one thing from another makes it distinct and unlike the other.

difficult adjective 1 not easy to do, understand or solve. 2 hard to deal with, especially because of being unreasonable or unpredictable.

difficult adjective
1 = arduous, demanding, hard, intractable (formal), laborious, uphill 2 = demanding, troublesome, trying

difficulty difficulties noun 1 a problem. 2 Difficulty is the fact or quality of being difficult.

difficulty noun
1 = complication, hassle (informal), hurdle, obstacle, pitfall, problem, snag, trouble
2 = hardship, strain, tribulation (formal)

diffident adjective timid and lacking in self-confidence.
> **diffidently** adverb > **diffidence** noun

diffuse verb 1 If something diffuses, it spreads out or scatters in all directions. 2 (SCIENCE) If particles of a gas, liquid or solid diffuse, they mix together, especially by moving from an area where they are very concentrated to one where there are fewer of them. ▶ adjective 3 spread out over a wide area.
> **diffusion** noun

dig verb 1 If you dig, you break up soil or sand, especially with a spade or garden fork. 2 To dig something into an object means to push, thrust or poke it in. ▶ noun 3 a prod or jab, especially in the ribs. 4 (informal) A dig at someone is a spiteful or unpleasant remark intended to hurt or embarrass them.

dig verb
1 = burrow, excavate, gouge, hollow out, quarry, till, tunnel
2 = jab, poke, thrust
▶ noun 3 = jab, poke, prod, thrust

digest verb 1 To digest food means to break it down in the gut so that it can be easily absorbed and used by the body. 2 If you digest information or a fact, you understand it and take it in.
> **digestible** adjective

digestion noun (SCIENCE) Digestion is the process of digesting food. > **digestive** adjective

digger noun In Australian English, digger is a friendly name to call a man.

digit noun 1 (*formal*) Your digits are your fingers or toes. 2 (MATHS) a written symbol for any of the numbers from 0 to 9.

digital *adjective* 1 Digital technology involves recording or transmitting information in the form of thousands of very small electronic signals. 2 Digital displays show information, especially time, by numbers, rather than by a pointer moving round a dial. > **digitally** *adverb*

dignified *adjective* full of dignity.

dignitary dignitaries *noun* a person who holds a high official position.

dignity *noun* Dignity is behaviour which is serious, calm and controlled.

dilapidated *adjective* falling to pieces and generally in a bad condition.

dilemma *noun* (PSHE) a situation in which a choice has to be made between alternatives that are equally difficult or unpleasant.

diligent *adjective* hard-working, and showing care and perseverance. > **diligence** *noun*

dill *noun* Dill is a herb with yellow flowers and a strong sweet smell.

dilute *verb* To dilute a liquid means to add water or another liquid to it to make it less concentrated. > **dilution** *noun*

dim dimmer, dimmest; dims, dimming, dimmed *adjective* 1 badly lit and lacking in brightness. 2 very vague and unclear in your mind. ▶ *verb* 3 If lights dim or are dimmed, they become less bright. > **dimly** *adverb*

> **dim** *adjective*
> 1 = dark, dull, grey, murky, poorly lit, shadowy 2 = faint, hazy, indistinct, obscure, shadowy, vague

dimension *noun* 1 A dimension of a situation is an aspect or factor that influences the way you understand it. 2 (ART) The dimensions of something are also its measurements, for example its length, breadth, height or diameter.

diminish *verb* If something diminishes or if you diminish it, it becomes reduced in size or importance.

> **diminish** *verb*
> = contract, decrease, lessen, lower, reduce, shrink, weaken

diminutive *adjective* very small.

din *noun* a loud and unpleasant noise.

dinar *noun* a unit of currency in several countries in southern Europe, North Africa and the Middle East.

dine *verb* (*formal*) To dine means to eat dinner in the evening.

diner *noun* 1 a person who is having dinner in a restaurant. 2 a small restaurant.

dinghy dinghies *noun* a small boat which is rowed, sailed or powered by outboard motor.

dingo dingoes *noun* an Australian wild dog.

dingy dingier, dingiest *adjective* dusty, dark and rather depressing.

dinkum *adjective* (*informal*) In Australian and New Zealand English, dinkum means genuine or right.

> **dinkum** *adjective*
> = genuine, guileless, honest, sincere

dinner *noun* 1 the main meal of the day, eaten either in the evening or at lunchtime. 2 a formal social occasion in the evening, at which a meal is served.

dinosaur *noun* a large reptile which lived in prehistoric times.

diocese *noun* a district controlled by a bishop. > **diocesan** *adjective*

dip dips, dipping, dipped *verb* 1 If you dip something into a liquid, you lower it or plunge it quickly into the liquid. 2 If something dips, it slopes downwards or goes below a certain level. 3 To dip also means to make a quick, slight downward movement. ▶ *noun* 4 a rich creamy mixture which you scoop up with biscuits or raw vegetables and eat. 5 (*informal*) a swim.

diploma *noun* a certificate awarded to a student who has successfully completed a course of study.

diplomacy *noun* 1 Diplomacy is the managing of relationships between countries. 2 Diplomacy is also skill in dealing with people without offending or upsetting them. > **diplomatic** *adjective* > **diplomatically** *adverb*

diplomat *noun* an official who negotiates and deals with another country on behalf of his or her own country.

dire *adjective* disastrous, urgent or terrible.

direct *adjective* 1 moving or aimed in a straight line or by the shortest route. 2 straightforward, and without delay or evasion: *his direct manner.* 3 without anyone or anything intervening: *direct control.* 4 exact: *the direct opposite.*

▶ *verb* 5 To direct something means to guide and control it. 6 To direct people or things means to send them, tell them, or show them the way. 7 To direct a film, a play, or a television programme means to organise the way it is made and performed.

direct *adjective*
1 = straight, uninterrupted
2 = blunt, candid, forthright, frank, straight, straightforward 3 = first-hand, immediate, personal
▶ *verb* 5 = control, guide, lead, manage, oversee, run, supervise

direction *noun* 1 the general line that someone or something is moving or pointing in. 2 Direction is the controlling and guiding of something. 3 (*in plural*) Directions are instructions that tell you how to do something or how to get somewhere.

direction *noun*
1 = course, path, route, way
2 = charge, command, control, guidance, leadership, management

directive *noun* an instruction that must be obeyed.

directly *adverb* in a straight line or immediately.

director *noun* 1 a member of the board of a company or institution. 2 (DRAMA) the person responsible for the making and performance of a programme, play or film.

directorate *noun* a board of directors of a company or organisation.

directory directories *noun* 1 a book which gives lists of facts, such as names and addresses, and is usually arranged in alphabetical order. **2** (ICT) another name for **folder**.

dirt noun **1** Dirt is any unclean substance, such as dust, mud or stains. **2** Dirt is also earth or soil.

> **dirt** noun
> **1** = dust, filth, grime, muck, mud **2** = earth, soil

dirty dirtier, dirtiest adjective **1** marked or covered with dirt. **2** unfair, unscrupulous or dishonest.

> **dirty** adjective
> **1** = filthy, grimy, grubby, mucky, muddy, soiled, unclean **2** = corrupt, crooked

disability disabilities noun a physical or mental condition or illness that restricts someone's ability to move or use his or her senses.

disable verb **1** If something disables someone, it restricts his or her ability to move or use his or her senses. **2** If someone or something disables a system or mechanism, they stop it working, usually temporarily.

disabled adjective having a physical or mental condition that restricts your ability to move or use your senses.

disadvantage noun an unfavourable or harmful circumstance. > **disadvantaged** adjective

> **disadvantage** noun
> = drawback, handicap, minus, weakness

disaffected adjective If someone is disaffected with an idea or organisation, they no longer believe in it or support it.

disagree disagrees, disagreeing, disagreed verb **1** If you disagree with someone, you have a different view or opinion from theirs. **2** If you disagree with an action or proposal, you disapprove of it and believe it is wrong. **3** If food or drink disagrees with you, it makes you feel unwell.

> **disagree** verb
> **1** = differ, dispute, dissent **2** = object, oppose, take issue with

disagreeable adjective unpleasant or unhelpful and unfriendly.

> **disagreeable** adjective
> = horrible, horrid (old-fashioned), nasty, objectionable, obnoxious, unfriendly, unpleasant

disagreement noun **1** a dispute about something. **2** an objection to something.

> **disagreement** noun
> **1** = altercation (formal), argument, difference, dispute, quarrel, row, squabble, tiff **2** = dissent, objection, opposition

disappear verb **1** If something or someone disappears, they go out of sight or become lost. **2** To disappear also means to stop existing or happening. > **disappearance** noun

> **disappear** verb
> **1** = be lost to view, drop out of sight, fade, recede, vanish **2** = cease (formal), die out, go away, melt away, pass, vanish

disappoint verb If someone or something disappoints you, it fails to live up to what you expected of it.

disappointed adjective sad because something has not happened.

disappointed adjective
= dejected, despondent, disenchanted, disillusioned, downcast, saddened

disappointment noun 1 a feeling of being disappointed.
2 something that disappoints you.

disappointment noun
1 = dejection, despondency, regret 2 = blow, setback

disapproval noun the belief that something is wrong or inappropriate.

disapproval noun
= censure (formal), condemnation, criticism

disapprove verb To disapprove of something or someone means to believe they are wrong or bad.
> **disapproving** adjective

disapprove verb
= condemn, deplore (formal), dislike, find unacceptable, take a dim view of

disarm verb 1 To disarm means to get rid of weapons. 2 If someone disarms you, they overcome your anger or doubt by charming or soothing you. > **disarming** adjective

disarmament noun
Disarmament is the reducing or getting rid of military forces and weapons.

disarray noun Disarray is a state of disorder and confusion.

disaster noun 1 an event or accident that causes great distress or destruction.

2 a complete failure. > **disastrous** adjective

disaster noun
1 = calamity (formal), catastrophe, misfortune, tragedy

disband verb When a group of people disbands, it officially ceases to exist.

disc noun 1 a flat round object. 2 one of the thin circular pieces of cartilage that separate the bones in your spine. 3 (ICT) in computing, another spelling of **disk**.

discard verb To discard something means to get rid of it, because you no longer want it or find it useful.

discard verb
= cast aside, dispose of, dump (informal), jettison, shed, throw away, throw out

discern verb (formal) To discern something means to notice or understand it clearly.

discern verb
= detect, make out, notice, observe, perceive, see, spot

discernible adjective able to be seen or recognised.

discerning adjective having good taste and judgment.
> **discernment** noun

discharge verb 1 If something discharges or is discharged, it is given or sent out. 2 To discharge someone from hospital, prison or the armed forces means to allow them to leave. 3 If someone is discharged from a job, they are dismissed from it. ▶ noun 4 a substance that is released from the inside of something. 5 a dismissal or release from a job or an institution.

discharge *verb*
1 = emit, empty, expel, flush, give off, release 2 = free, let go, liberate, release, set free 3 = dismiss, eject, fire (*informal*), sack (*informal*)
▶ *noun* 5 = dismissal, ejection, expulsion, the sack (*informal*)

disciple *noun* (RE) a follower of someone or something, especially one of the twelve men who were followers of Christ.

discipline *noun* 1 Discipline is making people obey rules and punishing them when they break them. 2 Discipline is the ability to behave and work in a controlled way. ▶ *verb* 3 If you discipline yourself, you train yourself to behave and work in an ordered way. 4 To discipline someone means to punish them.
> **disciplinary** *adjective*
> **disciplined** *adjective*

disc jockey *noun* someone who introduces and plays music on the radio or at a night club.

disclose *verb* To disclose something means to make it known or allow it to be seen.
> **disclosure** *noun*

disco discos *noun* a party or a club where people dance to recorded music.

discomfort *noun* 1 Discomfort is distress or slight pain. 2 Discomfort is also a feeling of worry or embarrassment. 3 Discomforts are things that make you uncomfortable.

disconcert *verb* If something disconcerts you, it makes you feel uneasy or embarrassed.
> **disconcerting** *adjective*

disconnect *verb* 1 To disconnect something means to detach it from something else. 2 If someone disconnects your fuel supply or telephone, they cut it off.

discontent *noun* Discontent is a feeling of dissatisfaction with conditions or with life in general.
> **discontented** *adjective*

discontinue discontinues, discontinuing, discontinued *verb* To discontinue something means to stop doing it.

discord *noun* Discord is unpleasantness or quarrelling between people.

discount *noun* 1 a reduction in the price of something. ▶ *verb* 2 If you discount something, you reject it or ignore it.

discourage *verb* To discourage someone means to take away their enthusiasm to do something. > **discouraging** *adjective* > **discouragement** *noun*

discourage *verb*
= daunt, deter, dissuade, put off

discourse (*formal*) *noun* 1 a formal talk or piece of writing intended to teach or explain something. 2 Discourse is serious conversation between people on a particular subject.

discover *verb* When you discover something, you find it or find out about it. > **discovery** *noun*

discover *verb*
= come across, find, find out, learn, realise, stumble on *or* stumble across, unearth

discredit *verb* 1 To discredit someone means to damage their reputation. 2 To discredit an idea means to cause it to be doubted or not believed.

discreet *adjective* If you are discreet, you avoid causing embarrassment when dealing with secret or private matters. > **discreetly** *adverb*

discrepancy discrepancies *noun* a difference between two things which ought to be the same.

discrete *adjective* 1 (*formal*) separate and distinct. 2 (MATHS) A discrete line or set of data is made up of a limited number of separate points or items.

discretion *noun* 1 Discretion is the quality of behaving with care and tact so as to avoid embarrassment or distress to other people. 2 Discretion is also freedom and authority to make decisions and take action according to your own judgment. > **discretionary** *adjective*

discriminate *verb* 1 To discriminate between things means to recognise and understand the differences between them. 2 (PSHE) To discriminate against a person or group means to treat them unfairly, for example because of their gender, race or colour. 3 To discriminate in favour of a person or group means to treat them more favourably than others. > **discrimination** *noun*

discus discuses *noun* a disc-shaped object with a heavy middle, thrown by athletes.

discuss *verb* 1 When people discuss something, they talk about it in detail. 2 (EXAM TERM) To discuss a question is to look at the points or arguments of both sides and try to reach your own opinion.

discuss *verb*
1 = debate, exchange views on, go into, talk about

discussion *noun* (PSHE) a conversation or piece of writing in which a subject is considered in detail.

discussion *noun*
= consultation, conversation, debate, dialogue, discourse, talk

disdain *noun* Disdain is a feeling of superiority over or contempt for someone or something. > **disdainful** *adjective*

disease *noun* (SCIENCE) an unhealthy condition in people, animals or plants. > **diseased** *adjective*

disembark *verb* To disembark means to land or unload from a ship, aircraft or bus.

disembodied *adjective* 1 separate from or existing without a body. 2 seeming not to be attached to or to come from anyone.

disenchanted *adjective* disappointed with something, and no longer believing that it is good or worthwhile. > **disenchantment** *noun*

disfigure *verb* To disfigure something means to spoil its appearance.

disgrace *noun* 1 Disgrace is a state in which people disapprove of someone. 2 If something is a disgrace, it is unacceptable. 3 If someone is a disgrace to a group of people, their behaviour makes the group feel ashamed. ▶ *verb* 4 If you disgrace yourself or disgrace someone else, you cause yourself or them to be strongly disapproved of by other people.

disgrace noun
1 = scandal, shame
▶ verb 4 = discredit, shame

disgraceful adjective If something is disgraceful, people disapprove of it strongly and think that those who are responsible for it should be ashamed. > **disgracefully** adverb

disgraceful adjective
= scandalous, shameful, shocking

disgruntled adjective discontented or in a bad mood.

disguise verb 1 To disguise something means to change its appearance so that people do not recognise it. 2 To disguise a feeling means to hide it. ▶ noun 3 something you wear or something you do to alter your appearance so that you cannot be recognised by other people.

disgust noun 1 Disgust is a strong feeling of dislike or disapproval. ▶ verb 2 To disgust someone means to make them feel a strong sense of dislike or disapproval. > **disgusted** adjective

disgust noun
1 = loathing, repulsion, revulsion
▶ verb 2 = repel, revolt, sicken

disgusting adjective very unpleasant and offensive.

disgusting adjective
= foul, gross, obnoxious, repellent, revolting, sickening, vile

dish noun 1 a shallow container for cooking or serving food. 2 food of a particular kind or food cooked in a particular way.

dishearten verb If you dishearten someone, you take away their hope and confidence in something.

dishevelled adjective If someone looks dishevelled, their clothes or hair look untidy.

dishonest adjective not truthful or able to be trusted.

dishonest adjective
= corrupt, crooked, deceitful, fraudulent, lying

dishonesty noun Dishonesty is behaviour which is meant to deceive people, either by not telling the truth or by cheating.

dishonesty noun
= cheating, corruption, deceit, trickery

disillusion verb If something or someone disillusions you, you discover that you were mistaken about something you valued, and so you feel disappointed with it. > **disillusionment** noun

disillusioned adjective If you are disillusioned with something, you are disappointed because it is not as good as you had expected.

disinfectant noun a chemical substance that kills germs.

disintegrate verb 1 If something disintegrates, it becomes weakened and is not effective. 2 If an object disintegrates, it breaks into many pieces and so is destroyed. > **disintegration** noun

disintegrate verb
2 = break up, crumble, fall apart, fall to pieces, fragment

disinterest noun 1 Disinterest is a lack of interest. 2 Disinterest is also a lack of personal involvement in a situation.

disinterested *adjective* If someone is disinterested, they are not going to gain or lose from the situation they are involved in, and so can act in a way that is fair to both sides.

disjointed *adjective* If thought or speech is disjointed, it jumps from subject to subject and so is difficult to follow.

disk *noun* 1 (ICT) In a computer, the disk is the part where information is stored. 2 another spelling of **disc**.

dislike *verb* 1 If you dislike something or someone, you think they are unpleasant and do not like them. ▶ *noun* 2 Dislike is a feeling that you have when you do not like someone or something.

> **dislike** *verb*
> 1 = abhor (*formal*), be averse to, detest, hate, loathe, not be able to abide, not be able to bear, not be able to stand
> ▶ *noun* 2 = animosity, antipathy (*formal*), aversion, distaste, hatred, hostility, loathing

dislocate *verb* To dislocate your bone or joint means to put it out of place.

dislodge *verb* To dislodge something means to move it or force it out of place.

dismal *adjective* rather gloomy and depressing. > **dismally** *adverb*

dismantle *verb* To dismantle something means to take it apart.

dismay *noun* 1 Dismay is a feeling of fear and worry. ▶ *verb* 2 If someone or something dismays you, they fill you with alarm and worry.

dismember *verb* (*formal*) To dismember a person or animal means to cut or tear their body into pieces.

dismiss *verb* 1 If you dismiss something, you decide to ignore it because it is not important enough for you to think about. 2 To dismiss an employee means to ask that person to leave their job. 3 If someone in authority dismisses you, they tell you to leave. > **dismissal** *noun*

dismissive *adjective* If you are dismissive of something or someone, you show that you think they are of little importance or value.

disobey *verb* To disobey a person or an order means to deliberately refuse to do what you are told.

> **disobey** *verb*
> = break, defy, flout, infringe, violate

disorder *noun* 1 Disorder is a state of untidiness. 2 Disorder is also a lack of organisation. 3 a disease.

> **disorder** *noun*
> 1 = clutter, disarray, muddle
> 2 = chaos, confusion, disarray, turmoil 3 = affliction, complaint, condition, disease, illness

disorganised; also spelt **disorganized** *adjective* If something is disorganised, it is confused and badly prepared or arranged. > **disorganisation** *noun*

disown *verb* To disown someone or something means to refuse to admit any connection with them.

disparaging *adjective* critical and scornful.

disparate *adjective* (*formal*) Things that are disparate are utterly different from one another. > **disparity** *noun*

dispatch; also spelt **despatch**
verb 1 To dispatch someone or something to a particular place means to send them there for a special reason. ▶ _noun_ 2 an official written message, often sent to an army or government headquarters.

dispel dispels, dispelling, dispelled
verb To dispel fears or beliefs means to drive them away or to destroy them.

dispensary dispensaries _noun_ a place where medicines are prepared and given out.

dispense _verb_ 1 (_formal_) To dispense something means to give it out. 2 To dispense medicines means to prepare them and them out. 3 To dispense with something means to do without it or do away with it.

dispenser _noun_ a machine or container from which you can get things.

disperse _verb_ 1 When something disperses, it scatters over a wide area. 2 When people disperse or when someone disperses them, they move apart and go in different directions.

dispirited _adjective_ downhearted and having no enthusiasm for anything.

dispiriting _adjective_ Something dispiriting makes you downhearted.

displace _verb_ 1 If one thing displaces another, it forces the thing out of its usual place and occupies that place itself. 2 If people are displaced, they are forced to leave their home or country.

displacement _noun_ 1 Displacement is the removal of something from its usual or correct place or position. 2 (SCIENCE) In physics, displacement is the weight or volume of liquid displaced by an object submerged or floating in it.

display _verb_ 1 If you display something, you show it or make it visible to people. 2 If you display something such as an emotion, you behave in a way that shows you feel it. ▶ _noun_ 3 (ART) an arrangement of things designed to attract people's attention.

displease _verb_ If someone or something displeases you, they make you annoyed, dissatisfied or offended. ▷ **displeasure** _noun_

disposable _adjective_ designed to be thrown away after use.

disposal _noun_ Disposal is the act of getting rid of something that is no longer wanted or needed.

dispose _verb_ 1 To dispose of something means to get rid of it. 2 If you are not disposed to do something, you are not willing to do it.

> **dispose** _verb_
> 1 = discard, dispense with, dump, get rid of, jettison, throw away

disprove _verb_ If someone disproves an idea, belief or theory, they show that it is not true.

> **disprove** _verb_
> = discredit, give the lie to, invalidate, prove false, refute

dispute _noun_ 1 an argument. ▶ _verb_ 2 To dispute a fact or theory means to question the truth of it.

> **dispute** _noun_
> 1 = argument, clash, conflict, disagreement, feud, row, wrangle

▶ *verb* **2** = challenge, contest, contradict, deny, query, question

disqualify disqualifies, disqualifying, disqualified *verb* If someone is disqualified from a competition or activity, they are officially stopped from taking part in it. > **disqualification** *noun*

disquiet *noun* Disquiet is worry or anxiety. > **disquieting** *adjective*

disregard *verb* **1** To disregard something means to pay little or no attention to it. ▶ *noun* **2** Disregard is a lack of attention or respect for something.

disrepair *phrase* If something is in **disrepair** or in **a state of disrepair**, it is broken or in poor condition.

disrespect *noun* Disrespect is contempt or lack of respect. > **disrespectful** *adjective*

disrupt *verb* To disrupt something such as an event or system means to break it up or throw it into confusion. > **disruption** *noun* > **disruptive** *adjective*

dissatisfied *adjective* not pleased or not contented. > **dissatisfaction** *noun*

dissect *verb* To dissect a plant or a dead body means to cut it up so that it can be scientifically examined. > **dissection** *noun*

dissent *noun* **1** Dissent is strong difference of opinion. ▶ *verb* **2** When people dissent, they express a difference of opinion about something.

dissertation *noun* a long essay, especially for a university degree.

disservice *noun* To do someone a disservice means to do something that harms them.

dissident *noun* someone who

disagrees with and criticises the government of their country.

dissimilar *adjective* If things are dissimilar, they are unlike each other.

dissipate *verb* **1** (*formal*) When something dissipates or is dissipated, it completely disappears. **2** If someone dissipates time, money or effort, they waste it.

dissipated *adjective* Someone who is dissipated shows signs of indulging too much in things such as food and drink.

dissolve *verb* **1** (SCIENCE) If you dissolve something or if it dissolves in a liquid, it becomes mixed with and absorbed in the liquid. **2** To dissolve an organisation or institution means to officially end it.

dissuade *verb* To dissuade someone from doing something or from believing something means to persuade them not to do it or not to believe in it.

distance *noun* **1** The distance between two points is how far it is between them. **2** Distance is the fact of being far away in space or time. ▶ *verb* **3** If you distance yourself from someone or something or are distanced from them, you become less involved with them.

distant *adjective* **1** far away in space or time. **2** A distant relative is one who is not closely related to you. **3** Someone who is distant is cold and unfriendly. > **distantly** *adverb*

distant *adjective*
1 = far, outlying, out-of-the-way, remote **3** = aloof, detached, reserved, withdrawn

d

distaste noun Distaste is a dislike of something which you find offensive.

distasteful adjective If you find something distasteful, you think it is unpleasant or offensive.

distil distils, distilling, distilled verb (SCIENCE) When a liquid is distilled, it is heated until it evaporates and then cooled to enable purified liquid to be collected. > **distillation** noun

distillery distilleries noun a place where whisky or other strong alcoholic drink is made, using a process of distillation.

distinct adjective 1 If one thing is distinct from another, it is recognisably different from it. 2 If something is distinct, you can hear, smell or see it clearly and plainly. 3 If something such as a fact, idea or intention is distinct, it is clear and definite. > **distinctly** adverb

distinction noun 1 a difference between two things. 2 Distinction is a quality of excellence and superiority. 3 a special honour or claim. 4 A distinction is the highest level of achievement in an examination.

distinctive adjective Something that is distinctive has a special quality which makes it recognisable.

distinguish verb 1 To distinguish between things means to recognise the difference between them. 2 To distinguish something means to make it out by seeing, hearing or tasting it. 3 If you distinguish yourself, you do something that makes people think highly of you.

distinguish verb
1 = differentiate, discriminate, tell, tell apart, tell the difference 2 = discern, make out, pick out, recognise

distinguished adjective 1 dignified in appearance or behaviour. 2 having a very high reputation.

distort verb 1 If you distort a statement or an argument, you represent it in an untrue or misleading way. 2 If something is distorted, it is changed so that it seems strange or unclear. 3 If an object is distorted, it is twisted or pulled out of shape. > **distorted** adjective > **distortion** noun

distract verb If something distracts you, your attention is taken away from what you are doing.

distract verb
= divert, draw away

distraction noun 1 something that takes people's attention away from something. 2 an activity that is intended to amuse or relax someone.

distraught adjective so upset and worried that you cannot think clearly.

distress noun 1 Distress is great suffering caused by pain or sorrow. 2 Distress is also the state of needing help because of difficulties or danger. ▶ verb 3 To distress someone means to make them feel alarmed or unhappy.

distress noun
1 = heartache, pain, sorrow, suffering 2 = difficulty, need, straits, trouble
▶ verb 3 = bother, disturb, grieve, pain, sadden, trouble, upset, worry

distressing *adjective* very worrying or upsetting.

distribute *verb* 1 To distribute something such as leaflets means to hand them out or deliver them. 2 If things are distributed, they are spread throughout an area or space. 3 To distribute something means to divide it and share it out among a number of people.

> **distribute** *verb*
> 1 = circulate, hand out, pass around, pass round 2 = diffuse, disperse, scatter, spread
> 3 = allocate, allot, dispense (*formal*), divide, dole out, share out

distribution *noun* 1 Distribution is the delivering of something to various people or organisations. 2 Distribution is the sharing out of something to various people.

distributor *noun* a company that supplies goods to other businesses which then sell them to the public.

district *noun* an area of a town or country.

distrust *verb* 1 If you distrust someone, you are suspicious of them because you are not sure whether they are honest. ▶ *noun* 2 Distrust is suspicion.
> **distrustful** *adjective*

disturb *verb* 1 If you disturb someone, you break their peace or privacy. 2 If something disturbs you, it makes you feel upset or worried. 3 If something is disturbed, it is moved out of position or meddled with.
> **disturbing** *adjective*

> **disturb** *verb*
> 1 = bother, disrupt, intrude on
> 2 = agitate, distress, shake, trouble, unsettle, upset, worry

disturbance *noun* 1 Disturbance is the state of being disturbed. 2 a violent or unruly incident in public.

disuse *noun* Something that has fallen into disuse is neglected or no longer used. > **disused** *adjective*

ditch *noun* a channel at the side of a road or field, to drain away excess water.

dither *verb* To dither means to be unsure and hesitant.

ditto 'Ditto' means 'the same'. In written lists, 'ditto' is represented by a mark (″) to avoid repetition.

ditty ditties *noun* (*old-fashioned*) a short simple song or poem.

diva *noun* a great or leading female singer, especially in opera.

dive dives, diving, dived *verb* 1 To dive means to jump into water with your arms held straight above your head, usually head first. 2 If you go diving, you go down under the surface of the sea or a lake using special breathing equipment. 3 If an aircraft or bird dives, it flies in a steep downward path or drops sharply.

> **dive** *verb*
> 1 = jump, leap, submerge

diverge *verb* 1 If opinions or facts diverge, they differ. 2 If two things such as roads or paths which have been going in the same direction diverge, they separate and go off in different directions. > **divergence** *noun* > **divergent** *adjective*

diverse *adjective* 1 (CITIZENSHIP) If a group of people or things is diverse, it is made up of several different kinds. 2 People, ideas or objects that are diverse are very different from each other.
> **diversity** *noun*

diversify diversifies, diversifying, diversified *verb* To diversify means to increase the variety of something. ▶ **diversification** *noun*

diversion *noun* 1 a special route arranged for traffic when the usual route is closed. 2 something that takes your attention away from what you should be concentrating on. 3 a pleasant or amusing activity.

divert *verb* To divert something means to change the course or direction it is following.

divide *verb* 1 When something divides or is divided, it is split up and separated into two or more parts. 2 If something divides two areas, it forms a barrier between them. 3 If people divide over something or if something divides them, it causes strong disagreement between them. 4 (MATHS) When you divide one number by another, you calculate how many times the first number contains the other. ▶ *noun* 5 a separation.

> **divide** *verb*
> 1 = cut up, partition, segregate, separate, split, split up
> 2 = bisect, separate 3 = come between, set against one another, split

dividend *noun* 1 (MATHS) a number that is divided by another number. 2 a portion of a company's profits that is paid to shareholders.

divine *adjective* 1 having the qualities of a god or goddess. ▶ *verb* 2 To divine something means to discover it by guessing.
> **divinely** *adverb*

divinity divinities *noun* 1 Divinity is the study of religion. 2 Divinity is the state of being a god. 3 a god or goddess.

division *noun* 1 Division is the separation of something into two or more distinct parts. 2 (MATHS) Division is also the process of dividing one number by another. 3 a difference of opinion that causes separation between ideas or groups of people. 4 any one of the parts or groups into which something is split. ▶ **divisional** *adjective*

> **division** *noun*
> 1 = partition, separation
> 3 = breach, difference of opinion, rupture, split
> 4 = department, section, sector

divisive *adjective* causing hostility between people so that they split into different groups.

divorce *noun* 1 Divorce is the formal and legal ending of a marriage. ▶ *verb* 2 When a married couple divorce, their marriage is legally ended.
> **divorced** *adjective* > **divorcee** *noun*

divulge *verb* To divulge information means to reveal it.

DIY *noun* DIY is the activity of making or repairing things yourself. DIY is an abbreviation for 'do-it-yourself'.

dizzy dizzier, dizziest *adjective* having or causing a whirling sensation. > **dizziness** *noun*

> **dizzy** *adjective*
> = giddy, light-headed

DNA *noun* (SCIENCE) DNA is deoxyribonucleic acid, a substance found in the cells of all living things. It determines the structure of every cell and is responsible for characteristics being passed on from parents to their children.

do does, doing, did, done verb 1 'Do' is an auxiliary verb, which is used to form questions and negatives and to give emphasis to the main verb of a sentence. 2 If someone does a task or activity, they perform it and finish it. 3 If you ask what people do, you want to know what their job is. 4 If you do well at something, you are successful. If you do badly, you are unsuccessful. 5 If something will do, it is adequate but not the most suitable option. ▶ noun 6 (informal) a party or other social event. > **do away with** verb To do away with something means to get rid of it. > **do up** verb 1 To do something up means to fasten it. 2 To do up something old means to repair and decorate it.

> **do** verb
> 2 = carry out, execute (formal), perform, undertake 4 = fare, get on, manage 5 = be adequate, be sufficient, suffice (formal)

docile adjective quiet, calm and easily controlled.

dock noun 1 an enclosed area in a harbour where ships go to be loaded, unloaded or repaired. 2 In a court of law, the dock is the place where the accused person stands or sits. 3 a stand in which a portable electronic device can be placed to charge its battery or to connect it to other devices. ▶ verb 4 When a ship docks, it is brought into dock at the end of its voyage. 5 To dock someone's wages means to deduct an amount from the sum they would normally receive.

6 To dock an animal's tail means to cut part of it off. > **docker** noun

doctor noun 1 a person who is qualified in medicine and treats people who are ill. 2 A doctor of an academic subject is someone who has been awarded the highest academic degree. ▶ verb 3 To doctor something means to alter it in order to deceive people.

doctorate noun the highest university degree. > **doctoral** adjective

doctrine noun a set of beliefs or principles held by a group.

document noun 1 (HISTORY) a piece of paper which provides an official record of something. 2 (ICT) a piece of text or graphics stored in a computer as a file that can be amended or altered by document processing software. ▶ verb 3 (HISTORY) If you document something, you make a detailed record of it. > **documentation** noun

documentary documentaries noun 1 a radio or television programme or a film which gives information on real events. ▶ adjective 2 Documentary evidence is made up of written or official records.

dodge verb 1 If you dodge or dodge something, you move suddenly to avoid being seen, hit or caught. 2 If you dodge something such as an issue or accusation, you avoid dealing with it.

> **dodge** verb
> 1 = duck, swerve 2 = avoid, elude, evade, get out of 2 = shirk, sidestep

dodgy dodgier, dodgiest adjective (informal) dangerous, risky or unreliable.

D

dodo dodos *noun* A dodo was a large, flightless bird that lived in Mauritius and became extinct in the late 17th century.

doe *noun* a female deer, rabbit or hare.

does the third person singular of the present tense of **do**.

dog dogs, dogging, dogged *noun* 1 a four-legged, meat-eating animal, kept as a pet, or to guard property or go hunting. ▶ *verb* 2 If you dog someone, you follow them very closely and never leave them.

dog *noun*
1 = brak (*South African*), canine (*formal*), mongrel, mutt (*slang*), pooch (*slang*)

dogged *adjective* showing determination to continue with something, even if it is very difficult.

dogma *noun* a belief or system of beliefs held by a religious or political group.

dogmatic *adjective* Someone who is dogmatic about something is convinced that they are right about it. > **dogmatism** *noun*

doldrums *phrase* (*informal*) If you are in the doldrums, you are dispirited or bored.

dole *verb* If you dole something out, you give a certain amount of it to each individual in a group.

doll *noun* a child's toy which looks like a baby or person.

dollar *noun* the main unit of currency in Australia, New Zealand, the USA, Canada and some other countries. A dollar is worth 100 cents.

dollop *noun* an amount of food, served casually in a lump.

dolphin *noun* a mammal which lives in the sea and looks like a large fish with a long snout.

domain *noun* 1 a particular area of activity or interest. 2 an area over which someone has control or influence.

dome *noun* a round roof.

domestic *adjective* 1 happening or existing within one particular country. 2 involving or concerned with the home and family.

domesticated *adjective* If a wild animal or plant has been domesticated, it has been controlled or cultivated.

domesticity *noun* (*formal*) Domesticity is life at home with your family.

dominance *noun* 1 Dominance is power or control. 2 If something has dominance over other similar things, it is more powerful or important than they are.
> **dominant** *adjective*

dominate *verb* 1 If something or someone dominates a situation or event, they are the most powerful or important thing in it and have control over it. 2 If a person or country dominates other people or places, they have power or control over them. 3 If something dominates an area, it towers over it. > **domination** *noun*

domineering *adjective* Someone who is domineering tries to control other people.

dominion *noun* Dominion is control or authority that a person or a country has over other people.

domino dominoes *noun* Dominoes are small rectangular blocks marked with two groups of spots on one side, used for playing the game called dominoes.

don dons, donning, donned *verb* (*literary*) If you don clothing, you put it on.

donate *verb* To donate something to a charity or organisation means to give it as a gift.
> **donation** *noun*

done the past participle of **do**.

donkey *noun* an animal like a horse, but smaller and with longer ears.

donor *noun* **1** someone who gives some of their blood or an organ to be used to help someone who is ill. **2** someone who gives something such as money to a charity or other organisation.

doom *noun* Doom is a terrible fate or event in the future which you can do nothing to prevent.

doomed *adjective* If someone or something is doomed to an unpleasant or unhappy experience, they are certain to suffer it.

> **doomed** *adjective*
> = condemned, hopeless, ill-fated

doomsday *noun* Doomsday is the end of the world.

door *noun* a swinging or sliding panel for opening or closing the entrance to something; also the entrance itself.

doorway *noun* an opening in a wall for a door.

dope *noun* **1** (*informal*) Dope is an illegal drug. ▶ *verb* **2** If someone dopes you, they put a drug into your food or drink.

dormant *adjective* Something that is dormant is not active, growing or being used.

dormitory dormitories *noun* a large bedroom where several people sleep.

dosage *noun* the amount of a medicine or a drug that should be taken.

dose *noun* a measured amount of a medicine or drug.

dossier *noun* a collection of papers with information on a particular subject or person.

dot dots, dotting, dotted *noun* **1** a very small, round mark. ▶ *verb* **2** If things dot an area, they are scattered all over it. ▶ *phrase* **3** If you arrive somewhere **on the dot**, you arrive there at exactly the right time.

dotcom *noun* a company that does most of its business on the internet.

dote *verb* If you dote on someone, you love them very much.

double *adjective* **1** twice the usual size. **2** consisting of two parts. ▶ *verb* **3** If something doubles, it becomes twice as large. **4** To double as something means to have a second job or use as well as the main one. ▶ *noun* **5** Your double is someone who looks exactly like you. **6** Doubles is a game of tennis or badminton which two people play against two other people.
> **doubly** *adverb*

> **double** *adjective*
> **1** = twice, twofold **2** = dual, twin, twofold

double bass *noun* a musical instrument like a large violin, which you play standing up.

double-decker *adjective* **1** having two tiers or layers. ▶ *noun* **2** a bus with two floors.

double glazing noun Double glazing is a second layer of glass fitted to windows to keep the building quieter or warmer.

doubt noun 1 Doubt is a feeling of uncertainty about whether something is true or possible.
▶ verb 2 If you doubt something, you think that it is probably not true or possible.

> **doubt** noun
> 1 = misgiving, qualm, scepticism, uncertainty
> ▶ verb 2 = be dubious, be sceptical, query, question

doubtful adjective unlikely or uncertain.

> **doubtful** adjective
> = debatable, dubious, questionable, uncertain

dough noun Dough is a mixture of flour and water and sometimes other ingredients, used to make bread, pastry or biscuits.

doughnut noun a ring or ball of sweet dough cooked in hot fat.

dour adjective severe and unfriendly.

douse; also spelt **dowse** verb If you douse a fire, you stop it burning by throwing water over it.

dove noun a bird like a small pigeon.

dovetail verb If two things dovetail together, they fit together closely or neatly.

dowdy dowdier, dowdiest adjective wearing dull and unfashionable clothes.

down preposition, adverb 1 Down means towards the ground, towards a lower level, or in a lower place. 2 If you go down a road or river, you go along it.
▶ adverb 3 If you put something down, you place it on a surface.
4 If an amount of something goes down, it decreases. ▶ adjective 5 If you feel down, you feel unhappy.
▶ verb 6 If you down a drink, you drink it quickly. ▶ noun 7 Down is the small, soft feathers on young birds.

> **down** preposition, adverb
> 1 = downwards, downstairs
> ▶ adjective 5 = dejected, depressed, dispirited, fed up (informal), glum, melancholy (literary), miserable

downcast adjective 1 feeling sad and dejected. 2 If your eyes are downcast, they are looking towards the ground.

downfall noun 1 The downfall of a successful or powerful person or institution is their failure.
2 Something that is someone's downfall is the thing that causes their failure.

> **downfall** noun
> 1 = collapse, fall, ruin

downgrade verb If you downgrade something, you give it less importance or make it less valuable.

downhill adverb 1 moving down a slope. 2 becoming worse.

download (ICT) verb 1 If you download data, you transfer it from the memory of a large computer system to a smaller computer. ▶ noun 2 a piece of data transferred in this way.

downpour noun a heavy fall of rain.

downright adjective, adverb You use 'downright' to emphasise that something is extremely unpleasant or bad: *Staff are often discourteous and sometimes downright rude.*

downstairs *adverb* 1 If you go downstairs in a building, you go down to a lower floor. ▶ *adjective, adverb* 2 on a lower floor or on the ground floor. ▶ *noun* 3 The downstairs of a building is its lower floor or floors.

downstream *adverb* towards the mouth of a river.

down-to-earth *adjective* sensible and practical.

downtrodden *adjective* People who are downtrodden are treated badly by those with power and do not have the ability to fight back.

downturn *noun* a decline in the economy or in the success of a company or industry.

down under (*informal*) *noun* 1 Australia or New Zealand. ▶ *adverb* 2 in or to Australia or New Zealand.

downwards *adverb* 1 If you move or look downwards, you move or look towards the ground or towards a lower level. 2 If an amount or rate moves downwards, it decreases. > **downward** *adjective*

downwind *adverb* If something moves downwind, it moves in the same direction as the wind.

dowry *dowries* *noun* In some societies, a woman's dowry is money or property which her father gives to the man she marries.

doze *verb* 1 When you doze, you sleep lightly for a short period. ▶ *noun* 2 a short, light sleep.

dozen *noun* A dozen things are twelve of them.

Dr 1 'Dr' is short for 'Doctor' and is used before the name of someone with the highest form of academic degree or who practises medicine. 2 'Dr' is short for 'drive' in addresses.

drab *drabber*, *drabbest* *adjective* dull and unattractive. > **drabness** *noun*

> **drab** *adjective*
> = dingy, dismal, dreary, gloomy, grey, sombre

draft *noun* 1 an early rough version of a document or speech. ▶ *verb* 2 When you draft a document or speech, you write the first rough version of it. 3 To draft people somewhere means to move them there so that they can do a specific job. 4 In Australian and New Zealand English, to draft cattle or sheep is to select some from a herd or flock.

drag *drags*, *dragging*, *dragged* *verb* 1 If you drag a heavy object somewhere, you pull it slowly and with difficulty. 2 If you drag someone somewhere, you make them go although they may be unwilling. 3 If things trail along behind you, they trail along the ground as you move along. 4 If an event or a period of time drags, it is boring and seems to last a long time. ▶ *noun* 5 (SCIENCE) Drag is the resistance to the motion of a body passing through air or a fluid.

> **drag** *verb*
> 1 = draw, haul, lug, tow, trail

dragon *noun* In stories and legends, a dragon is a fierce animal like a large lizard with wings and claws that breathes fire.

drain verb 1 If you drain something, you cause liquid to flow out of it. 2 If you drain a glass, you drink all its contents. 3 If liquid drains somewhere, it flows there. 4 If something drains strength or resources, it gradually uses them up. ▶ noun 5 A pipe or channel that carries water or sewage away from a place. 6 A metal grid in a road, through which rainwater flows.

> **drain** verb
> 1 = draw off, pump
> 3 = discharge, empty, flow, seep
> 4 = consume, exhaust, sap, tax, use up

drainage noun 1 Drainage is the system of pipes, drains or ditches used to drain water or other liquid away from a place. 2 Drainage is also the process of draining water away, or the way in which a place drains.

drama noun 1 a serious play for the theatre, television or radio. 2 Drama is plays and the theatre in general. 3 You can refer to the exciting events or aspects of a situation as drama.

dramatic adjective A dramatic change or event happens suddenly and is very noticeable.
> **dramatically** adverb

dramatist noun (DRAMA) a person who writes plays.

drank the past tense of **drink**.

drape verb If you drape a piece of cloth, you arrange it so that it hangs down or covers something in loose folds.

drastic adjective A drastic course of action is very severe and is usually taken urgently.
> **drastically** adverb

> **drastic** adjective
> = extreme, harsh, radical, severe

draught noun 1 a current of cold air. 2 an amount of liquid that you swallow. 3 Draughts is a game for two people played on a chessboard with round pieces. ▶ adjective 4 Draught beer is served straight from barrels rather than in bottles.

draughtsman draughtsmen noun a person who prepares detailed drawings or plans.

draughty draughtier, draughtiest adjective A place that is draughty has currents of cold air blowing through it.

draw draws, drawing, drew, drawn verb 1 When you draw, you use a pencil, pen or crayon to make a picture or diagram. 2 To draw near means to move closer. To draw away or draw back means to move away. 3 If you draw something in a particular direction, you pull it there smoothly and gently. 4 If you draw a deep breath, you breathe in deeply. 5 If you draw the curtains, you pull them so that they cover or uncover the window. 6 If something such as water or energy is drawn from a source, it is taken from it. 7 If you draw a conclusion, you arrive at it from the facts you know. 8 If you draw a distinction or a comparison between two things, you point out that it exists. ▶ noun 9 the result of a game or competition in which nobody wins. > **draw up** verb To draw up a plan, document or list means to prepare it and write it out.

draw *verb*
1 = paint, sketch, trace
2 = move, pull 3 = drag, haul,
pull

drawback *noun* a problem that
makes something less acceptable
or desirable.

drawback *noun*
= difficulty, hitch, problem,
snag, trouble

drawer *noun* a sliding box-shaped
part of a piece of furniture used
for storing things.

drawing *noun* 1 a picture made
with a pencil, pen or crayon.
2 Drawing is the skill or work of
making drawings.

drawl *verb* If someone drawls,
they speak slowly with long
vowel sounds.

drawn Drawn is the past
participle of **draw**.

dread *verb* 1 If you dread
something, you feel very worried
and frightened about it. ▶ *noun*
2 Dread is a feeling of great fear
or anxiety.

dreadful *adjective* very bad or
unpleasant. ▶ **dreadfully** *adverb*

dreadful *adjective*
= appalling, atrocious, awful,
frightful (*old-fashioned*), ghastly,
horrendous, terrible

dream dreams, dreaming,
dreamed or dreamt *noun* 1 a series
of events that you experience in
your mind while asleep. 2 a
situation or event which you
often think about because you
would very much like it to
happen. ▶ *verb* 3 When you
dream, you see events in your
mind while you are asleep.
4 When you dream about

something happening, you
often think about it because
you would very much like it to
happen. 5 If someone dreams
up a plan or idea, they invent it.
6 If you say you would not dream
of doing something, you are
emphasising that you would
not do it. ▶ *adjective* 7 too good
to be true: *a dream holiday*.
▷ **dreamer** *noun*

dream *noun*
1 = hallucination, trance, vision
2 = ambition, aspiration,
daydream, fantasy

Dreamtime *noun* In Aboriginal
Australian culture, Dreamtime is
the time when the world was
being made and the first people
were created.

dreamy dreamier, dreamiest
adjective Someone with a dreamy
expression looks as if they are
thinking about something very
pleasant.

dreary drearier, dreariest *adjective*
dull or boring.

dreary *adjective*
= boring, drab, dull, humdrum,
monotonous, tedious,
uneventful

dregs *plural noun* The dregs of a
liquid are the last drops left at the
bottom of a container, and any
sediment left with it.

drenched *adjective* soaking wet.

dress *noun* 1 a piece of clothing
made up of a skirt and top
attached. 2 Dress is any clothing.
▶ *verb* 3 When you dress, you put
clothes on. 4 If you dress for a
special occasion, you put on
formal clothes. 5 To dress a
wound means to clean it up
and treat it.

dress noun
1 = frock, gown, robe 2 = attire (formal), clothes, clothing, costume, garb (formal)
▶ verb 3 = attire (formal), clothe, garb (formal)

dresser noun a piece of kitchen furniture with cupboards and drawers in the lower part and open shelves in the top part.

dressing gown noun an item of clothing shaped like a coat and put on over nightwear.

dressing room noun a room used for getting changed and putting on make-up, especially a backstage room at a theatre.

dress rehearsal noun the last rehearsal of a show or play, using costumes, scenery and lighting.

drew the past tense of **draw**.

dribble verb 1 When liquid dribbles down a surface, it trickles down it in drops or a thin stream. 2 If a person or animal dribbles, saliva trickles from their mouth. 3 In sport, to dribble a ball means to move it along by repeatedly tapping it with your foot or a stick. ▶ noun 4 a small quantity of liquid flowing in a thin stream or drops.

drift verb 1 When something drifts, it is carried along by the wind or by water. 2 When people drift somewhere, they wander or move there gradually. 3 When people drift in life, they move without any aims from place to place or from one activity to another. 4 If you drift off to sleep, you gradually fall asleep. ▶ noun 5 A snow drift is a pile of snow heaped up by the wind. 6 The drift of an argument or speech is its main point. > **drifter** noun

drill noun 1 (DGT) a tool for making holes. 2 Drill is a routine exercise or routine training. ▶ verb 3 (DGT) To drill into something means to make a hole in it using a drill. 4 If you drill people, you teach them to do something by repetition.

drink drinks, drinking, drank, drunk verb 1 When you drink, you take liquid into your mouth and swallow it. 2 To drink also means to drink alcohol. ▶ noun 3 an amount of liquid suitable for drinking. 4 an alcoholic drink.
> **drinker** noun

drink verb
1 = gulp, guzzle, sip, swig (informal)

drip drips, dripping, dripped verb 1 When liquid drips, it falls in small drops. 2 When an object drips, drops of liquid fall from it. ▶ noun 3 a drop of liquid falling from something. 4 a device for allowing liquid food or medicine to enter the bloodstream of a person who is ill.

drip verb
1 = dribble, splash, trickle
▶ noun 3 = bead, drop, droplet

drive drives, driving, drove, driven verb 1 To drive a vehicle means to operate it and control its movements. 2 If something or someone drives you to do something, they force you to do it. 3 If you drive a post or nail into something, you force it in by hitting it with a hammer. 4 If something drives a machine, it supplies the power that makes it work. ▶ noun 5 a journey in a vehicle. 6 a private road that leads from a public road to a person's house. 7 Drive is energy and determination. > **driver** noun

drive verb
1 = operate, pilot, power, propel, run, steer, work **2** = compel, force, lead, motivate, prompt, push, spur **3** = hammer, knock, ram, sink, thrust
▶ noun **5** = excursion, jaunt, journey, ride, run, spin (informal), trip **7** = ambition, determination, energy, enterprise, initiative, motivation, vigour

drive-in noun a restaurant, cinema or other commercial place that is specially designed for customers to use while staying in their cars.

drivel noun Drivel is nonsense.

drizzle noun Drizzle is light rain.

drone verb **1** If something drones, it makes a low, continuous humming noise. **2** If someone drones on, they keep talking or reading aloud in a boring way.
▶ noun **3** a low, continuous humming sound.

drool verb If someone drools, saliva dribbles from their mouth without them being able to stop it.

droop verb If something droops, it hangs or sags downwards with no strength or firmness.

drop drops, dropping, dropped verb **1** If you drop something, you let it fall. **2** If something drops, it falls straight down. **3** If a level or amount drops, it becomes less. **4** If your voice drops, or if you drop your voice, you speak more quietly. **5** If you drop something that you are doing or dealing with, you stop doing it or dealing with it. **6** If you drop a hint, you give someone a hint in a casual way. **7** If you drop something or

someone somewhere, you deposit or leave them there. ▶ noun **8** A drop of liquid is a very small quantity of it that forms or falls in a round shape. **9** a decrease. **10** the distance between the top and bottom of something tall, such as a cliff or building.

drop verb
2 = descend, fall, plummet, sink, tumble **3** = decline, decrease, diminish, fall, plummet, sink, slump, tumble
▶ noun **8** = bead, drip, droplet

droplet noun a small drop.

droppings plural noun Droppings are the faeces of birds and small animals.

drought noun (GEOGRAPHY) a long period during which there is no rain.

drove **1** Drove is the past tense of **drive**. ▶ verb **2** To drove cattle or sheep is to make them walk over a long distance.

drown verb **1** When someone drowns or is drowned, they die because they have gone under water and cannot breathe. **2** If a noise drowns a sound, it is louder than the sound and makes it impossible to hear it.

drowsy drowsier, drowsiest adjective sleepy.

drudgery noun Drudgery is hard boring work.

drug drugs, drugging, drugged noun **1** a chemical given to people to treat disease. **2** (PSHE) Drugs are chemical substances that some people smoke, swallow, inhale or inject because of their stimulating effects. ▶ verb **3** To drug a person or animal means to give them a drug to make them unconscious. **4** To drug food or drink means to add a drug to it in order to make someone unconscious. ▷ **drugged** adjective

> **drug** noun
> **1** = medication, medicine
> **2** = narcotic, stimulant

drum drums, drumming, drummed noun **1** a musical instrument consisting of a skin stretched tightly over a round frame. **2** an object or container shaped like a drum. **3** (informal) In Australian English, the drum is information or advice. ▶ verb **4** If something is drumming on a surface, it is hitting it regularly, making a continuous beating sound. **5** If you drum something into someone, you keep saying it to them until they understand it or remember it. ▷ **drummer** noun

drunk **1** Drunk is the past participle of **drink**. ▶ adjective **2** If someone is drunk, they have drunk so much alcohol that they cannot speak clearly or behave sensibly. ▶ noun **3** a person who is drunk, or who often gets drunk. ▷ **drunken** adjective

> **drunk** adjective
> **2** = babalas (South African), intoxicated (formal), tipsy

dry drier or dryer, driest or dryest; dries, drying, dried adjective **1** Something that is dry contains or uses no water or liquid. **2** Dry bread or toast is eaten without a topping. **3** Dry sherry or wine does not taste sweet. **4** Dry also means plain and sometimes boring. **5** Dry humour is subtle and sarcastic. ▶ verb **6** When you dry something, or when it dries, liquid is removed from it.

▷ **dryness** noun ▷ **drily** adverb
▷ **dry up** verb **1** If something dries up, it becomes completely dry. **2** (informal) If you dry up, you forget what you were going to say, or find that you have nothing left to say.

> **dry** adjective
> **1** = arid, dried-up, parched
> ▶ verb **6** = dehydrate, drain

dryer; also spelt **drier** noun a device for removing moisture from something by heating or by hot air.

dual adjective having two parts, functions or aspects.

dub dubs, dubbing, dubbed verb **1** If something is dubbed a particular name, it is given that name. **2** If a film is dubbed, the voices on the soundtrack are not those of the actors, but those of other actors speaking in a different language.

dubious adjective **1** not entirely honest, safe or reliable. **2** doubtful. ▷ **dubiously** adverb

> **dubious** adjective
> **1** = crooked, dishonest, questionable, suspect, suspicious, unreliable
> **2** = doubtful, nervous, sceptical, suspicious, unconvinced, undecided, unsure

duchess noun a woman who has the same rank as a duke, or who is a duke's wife or widow.

duck ducks, ducking, ducked noun **1** a bird that lives in water and has webbed feet and a large flat bill. ▶ verb **2** If you duck, you move your head quickly downwards in order to avoid being hit by something. **3** If you duck a duty or responsibility, you avoid it.

appointment *noun*
1 = date, interview, meeting, rendezvous 2 = election, naming, nomination, selection 3 = assignment, job, place, position, post

appraise *verb* If you appraise something, you think about it carefully and form an opinion about it. > **appraisal** *noun*

appreciable *adjective* large enough to be noticed.
> **appreciably** *adverb*

appreciate *verb* 1 If you appreciate something, you like it because you recognise its good qualities. 2 If you appreciate a situation or problem, you understand it and know what it involves. 3 If you appreciate something someone has done for you, you are grateful to them for it. 4 If something appreciates over a period of time, its value increases.

appreciate *verb*
1 = admire, prize, rate highly, respect, treasure, value 2 = be aware of, perceive, realise, recognise, understand

appreciation *noun* Appreciation is gratitude for something.

appreciative *adjective*
1 understanding and enthusiastic. 2 thankful and grateful.

apprehend *verb (formal)* 1 When the police apprehend someone, they arrest them and take them into custody. 2 If you apprehend something, you understand it fully.

apprehensive *adjective* afraid something bad may happen.
> **apprehensively** *adverb*
> **apprehension** *noun*

apprentice *noun* a person who works with someone for a period of time in order to learn their skill or trade. > **apprenticeship** *noun*

approach *verb* 1 To approach something is to come near or nearer to it. 2 When a future event approaches, it gradually gets nearer. 3 If you approach someone about something, you ask them about it. 4 If you approach a situation or problem in a particular way, you think about it or deal with it in that way. ▶ *noun* 5 The approach of something is the process of it coming closer. 6 An approach to a situation or problem is a way of thinking about it or dealing with it. 7 a road or path that leads to a place. > **approaching**

appropriate *adjective* 1 suitable or acceptable for a particular situation. ▶ *verb* 2 *(formal)* If you appropriate something which does not belong to you, you take it without permission.
> **appropriately** *adverb*
> **appropriation** *noun*

appropriate *adjective*
1 = apt, correct, fitting, proper, suitable

approval *noun* 1 Approval is agreement given to a plan or request. 2 (PSHE) Approval is also admiration.

approval *noun*
1 = agreement, authorisation, blessing, endorsement, permission, sanction 2 = admiration, esteem, favour, praise, respect

approve *verb* 1 (PSHE) If you approve of something or someone, you think that thing

A

or person is acceptable or good.
2 If someone in a position of
authority approves a plan or idea,
they formally agree to it.
> **approved** *adjective* > **approving**
adjective

> **approve** *verb*
> **1** = admire, favour, praise,
> respect, think highly of
> **2** = authorise, consent to,
> endorse, permit, sanction

approximate *adjective* (MATHS)
almost exact. > **approximately**
adverb

> **approximate** *adjective*
> = estimated, inexact, loose,
> rough

apricot *noun* a small, soft,
yellowish-orange fruit.

April *noun* the fourth month of the
year. April has 30 days.

apron *noun* a piece of clothing
worn over the front of normal
clothing to protect it.

apt *adjective* **1** suitable or relevant.
2 having a particular tendency:
*They are apt to jump to the wrong
conclusions.*

aptitude *noun* Someone's
aptitude for something is their
ability to learn it quickly and to
do it well.

aquarium aquaria or aquariums
noun a glass tank filled with water
in which fish are kept.

Aquarius *noun* Aquarius is the
eleventh sign of the zodiac,
represented by a person carrying
water. People born between
January 20th and February 18th
are born under this sign.

aquatic *adjective* **1** An aquatic
animal or plant lives or grows in
water. **2** involving water.

Arab *noun* a member of a group of
people who used to live in Arabia
but who now live throughout the
Middle East and North Africa.

Arabic *noun* a language spoken by
many people in the Middle East
and North Africa.

arable *adjective* Arable land is used
for growing crops.

arbiter *noun* the person who
decides about something.

arbitrary *adjective* An arbitrary
decision or action is one that is
not based on a plan or system.
> **arbitrarily** *adverb*

arc *noun* **1** a smoothly curving line.
2 (MATHS) in geometry, a section of
the circumference of a circle.

arcade *noun* a covered passage
with shops or market stalls along
one or both sides.

arcane *adjective* mysterious and
difficult to understand.

arch *noun* **1** a structure that has a
curved top supported on either
side by a pillar or wall. **2** The arch
of your foot is the curved section
at the bottom in the middle.
▶ *verb* **3** When something arches,
it forms a curved line or shape.
▶ *adjective* **4** most important.

archaeology; also spelt
archeology *noun* the study of
the past by digging up and
examining the remains of
buildings, tools and other things.
> **archaeological**; also spelt
archeological *adjective*
> **archaeologist**; also spelt
archeologist *noun*

archaic *adjective* very old or
old-fashioned.

archbishop *noun* (RE) a bishop
of the highest rank in a
Christian Church.

archeology another spelling of **archaeology**.

archer noun someone who shoots with a bow and arrow.

archery noun a sport in which people shoot at a target with a bow and arrow.

archipelago archipelagos noun a group of small islands.

architect noun (ART) a person who designs buildings.

architecture noun (ART) the art or practice of designing buildings.
> **architectural** adjective

archive noun Archives are collections of documents and records about the history of a family or some other group of people.

arctic noun 1 The Arctic is the region north of the Arctic Circle.
▶ adjective 2 Arctic means very cold indeed.

Arctic Circle noun The Arctic Circle is an imaginary circle around the northern part of the world.

ardent adjective full of enthusiasm and passion. > **ardently** adverb

> **ardent** adjective
> = avid, devoted, enthusiastic, fervent, intense, keen, passionate

ardour noun a strong and passionate feeling of love or enthusiasm.

arduous adjective tiring and needing a lot of effort.

are the plural form of the present tense of **be**.

area noun 1 a particular part of a place, country or the world. 2 The area of a piece of ground or a surface is the amount of space it covers, measured in square metres or square feet. 3 (MATHS) The area of a geometric object is the amount of space enclosed within its lines.

> **area** noun
> 1 = district, locality, neighbourhood, region, zone
> 2 = expanse, extent, range, size

arena noun 1 a place where sports and other public events take place. 2 A particular arena is the centre of attention or activity in a particular situation.

Argentinian adjective 1 belonging or relating to Argentina. ▶ noun 2 someone who comes from Argentina.

arguable adjective An arguable idea or point is not necessarily true or correct and should be questioned. > **arguably** adverb

argue argues, arguing, argued verb 1 If you argue with someone about something, you disagree with them about it, sometimes in an angry way. 2 If you argue that something is the case, you give reasons why you think it is so.

> **argue** verb
> 1 = bicker, disagree, fall out (informal), feud, fight, quarrel, row, squabble, wrangle
> 2 = assert, claim, debate, maintain, reason

argument noun 1 a disagreement between two people which causes a quarrel. 2 a point or a set of reasons you use to try to convince people about something.

> **argument** noun
> 1 = barney (British, Australian and

New Zealand; informal), blue (Australian; slang), clash, dispute, feud, fight, row, squabble
2 = case, grounds, logic, reasoning

argumentative adjective An argumentative person is always disagreeing with other people.

aria noun a song sung by one of the singers in an opera.

arid adjective Arid land is very dry because it has very little rain.

Aries noun Aries is the first sign of the zodiac, represented by a ram. People born between March 21st and April 19th are born under this sign.

arise arises, arising, arose, arisen verb **1** When something such as an opportunity or problem arises, it begins to exist. **2** (formal) To arise also means to stand up from a sitting, kneeling or lying position.

aristocracy aristocracies noun a class of people who have a high social rank and special titles.

aristocrat noun someone whose family has a high social rank, and who has a title. > **aristocratic** adjective

arithmetic noun the part of mathematics which is to do with the addition, subtraction, multiplication and division of numbers.

ark noun (RE) In the Bible, the ark was the boat built by Noah for his family and the animals during the Flood.

arm noun **1** Your arms are the part of your body between your shoulder and your wrist. **2** The arms of a chair are the parts on which you rest your arms.

3 An arm of an organisation is a section of it. **4** (in plural) Arms are weapons used in a war. ▶ verb **5** To arm someone is to provide them with weapons.

armada noun An armada is a large fleet of warships. In 1588, the Spanish Armada was sent against England by Philip II of Spain, but was defeated in the Channel by the English.

Armageddon noun In Christianity, Armageddon is the final battle between good and evil at the end of the world.

armament noun Armaments are the weapons and military equipment that belong to a country.

armchair noun a comfortable chair with a support on each side for your arms.

armed adjective A person who is armed is carrying a weapon or weapons.

armistice noun (HISTORY) an agreement in a war to stop fighting in order to discuss peace.

armour noun (HISTORY) In the past, armour was metal clothing worn for protection in battle.

armoured adjective covered with thick steel for protection from gunfire and other missiles.

armoury armouries noun a place where weapons are stored.

armpit noun the area under your arm where your arm joins your shoulder.

army armies noun a large group of soldiers organised into divisions for fighting on land.

aroma noun a strong, pleasant smell. > **aromatic** adjective

aromatherapy noun a type of

therapy that involves massaging the body with special fragrant oils.

arose the past tense of **arise**.

around *preposition* **1** placed at various points in a place or area: *There are many seats around the building.* **2** from place to place inside an area: *We walked around the showroom.* **3** at approximately the time or place mentioned: *The attacks began around noon.*
▸ *adverb* **4** here and there: *scattered around.*

arouse *verb* If something arouses a feeling in you, it causes you to begin to have this feeling.
> **arousal** *noun*

arrange *verb* **1** If you arrange to do something, you make plans for it. **2** If you arrange something for someone, you make it possible for them to have it or do it. **3** If you arrange objects, you set them out in a particular position.
> **arrangement** *noun*

arrange *verb*
1 = fix up, organise, plan, schedule **3** = classify, group, order, organise, sort

array *noun* An array of different things is a large number of them displayed together.

arrears *plural noun* **1** Arrears are amounts of money you owe.
▸ *phrase* **2** If you are paid in **arrears**, you are paid at the end of the period for which the payment is due.

arrest *verb* **1** If the police arrest someone, they take them into custody to decide whether to charge them with an offence.
▸ *noun* **2** An arrest is the act of taking a person into custody.
> **arresting** *adjective*

arrest *verb*
1 = apprehend, capture, nick (*British; slang*), seize, take prisoner
▸ *noun* **2** = apprehension, capture, seizure

arrival *noun* **1** the act or time of arriving. **2** something or someone that has arrived.

arrive *verb* **1** When you arrive at a place, you reach it at the end of your journey. **2** When a letter or a piece of news arrives, it is brought to you. **3** When you arrive at an idea or decision you reach it. **4** When a moment, event or new thing arrives, it begins to happen.

arrogant *adjective* Someone who is arrogant behaves as if they are better than other people.
> **arrogance** *noun*

arrow *noun* a long, thin weapon with a sharp point at one end, shot from a bow.

arsenal *noun* a place where weapons and ammunition are stored or produced.

arsenic *noun* (SCIENCE) Arsenic is a strongly poisonous element used in insecticides and weedkillers. Arsenic's atomic number is 33 and its symbol is As.

arson *noun* the crime of deliberately setting fire to something, especially a building.

art *noun* **1** Art is the creation of objects such as paintings and sculptures which are thought to be beautiful or which express a particular idea; also used to refer to the objects themselves. **2** An activity is called an art when it requires special skill or ability. **3** (*in plural*) The arts are literature, music, painting and sculpture, considered together.

artefact *noun* any object made by people.

artery arteries *noun* 1 Your arteries are the tubes that carry blood from your heart to the rest of your body. 2 a main road or major section of any system of communication or transport.

artful *adjective* clever and skilful, often in a cunning way. > **artfully** *adverb*

arthritis *noun* (SCIENCE) a condition in which the joints in someone's body become swollen and painful. > **arthritic** *adjective*

artichoke *noun* 1 the round, green, partly edible flower head of a thistle-like plant; the flower head is made up of clusters of leaves that have a soft fleshy part that is eaten as a vegetable. 2 A Jerusalem artichoke is a small yellowish-white vegetable that grows underground and looks like a potato.

article *noun* 1 (LIBRARY) a piece of writing in a newspaper or magazine. 2 a particular item. 3 In English grammar, 'a' and 'the' are sometimes called articles: 'a' (or 'an') is the indefinite article; 'the' is the definite article.

> **article** *noun*
> 1 = feature, item, piece, story
> 2 = item, object, thing

articulate *adjective* 1 If you are articulate, you are able to express yourself well in words. ▶ *verb* 2 When you articulate your ideas or feelings, you express in words what you think or feel. 3 When

you articulate a sound or word, you speak it clearly. > **articulation** *noun*

artificial *adjective* 1 created by people rather than occurring naturally. 2 pretending to have attitudes and feelings which other people realise are not real. > **artificially** *adverb*

artillery *noun* 1 Artillery consists of large, powerful guns such as cannons. 2 The artillery is the branch of an army which uses large, powerful guns.

artist *noun* 1 a person who draws or paints or produces other works of art. 2 a person who is very skilled at a particular activity.

artistic *adjective* 1 able to create good paintings, sculptures or other works of art. 2 concerning or involving art or artists. > **artistically** *adverb*

artistry *noun* Artistry is the creative skill of an artist, writer, actor or musician.

arty artier, artiest *adjective* (*informal*) interested in painting, sculpture and other works of art.

as *conjunction* 1 at the same time that: *She waved at fans as she arrived for the concert.* 2 in the way that: *They had talked as only the best of friends can.* 3 because: *The opening of a story is important, as it engages the reader.* 4 You use the structure **as ... as** when you are comparing things that are similar: *It was as big as four football pitches.* ▶ *preposition* 5 You use 'as' when you are saying what role someone or something has: *She worked as a waitress.* ▶ *phrase* 6 You use **as if** or **as though** when you are giving a possible explanation for something: *He shrugged as if he didn't know the answer.*

asbestos *noun* a grey heat-resistant material used in the past to make fireproof articles.

ascend *verb (formal)* To ascend is to move or lead upwards.

ascendancy *noun (formal)* If one group has ascendancy over another, it has more power or influence than the other.

ascendant *adjective* 1 rising or moving upwards. ▶ *phrase* 2 Someone or something **in the ascendant** is increasing in power or popularity.

ascent *noun* an upward journey, for example up a mountain.

ascertain *verb (formal)* If you ascertain that something is the case, you find out it is the case.

ascribe *verb* 1 If you ascribe an event or state of affairs to a particular cause, you think that it is the cause of it. 2 If you ascribe a quality to someone, you think they have it.

ash *noun* 1 the grey or black powdery remains of anything that has been burnt. 2 a tree with grey bark and hard tough wood used for timber.

ashamed *adjective* 1 feeling embarrassed or guilty. 2 If you are ashamed of someone, you feel embarrassed to be connected with them.

> **ashamed** *adjective*
> 1 = embarrassed, guilty, humiliated, sheepish, sorry

ashore *adverb* on land or onto the land.

ashtray *noun* a small dish for ash from cigarettes and cigars.

Asia *noun* Asia is the largest continent. It has Europe on its western side, with the Arctic to the north, the Pacific to the east, and the Indian Ocean to the south. Asia includes several island groups, including Japan, Indonesia and the Philippines.

Asian *adjective* 1 belonging or relating to Asia. ▶ *noun* 2 someone who comes from Asia.

aside *adverb* 1 If you move something aside, you move it to one side. ▶ *noun* 2 a comment made away from the main conversation or dialogue that all those talking are not meant to hear.

ask *verb* 1 If you ask someone a question, you put a question to them for them to answer. 2 If you ask someone to do something or give you something, you tell them you want them to do it or to give it to you. 3 If you ask someone's permission or forgiveness, you try to obtain it. 4 If you ask someone somewhere, you invite them there.

> **ask** *verb*
> 1 = inquire, interrogate, query, question, quiz 2 = appeal, beg, demand, implore, plead, seek 4 = bid (*literary*), invite

askew *adjective* not straight.

asleep *adjective* sleeping.

asparagus *noun* a vegetable that has long shoots which are cooked and eaten.

aspect *noun* 1 An aspect of something is one of its features. 2 The aspect of a building is the direction it faces.

> **aspect** *noun*
> 1 = consideration, element, factor, feature, part, point, side

asphalt noun a black substance used to make road surfaces and playgrounds.

aspiration noun Someone's aspirations are their desires and ambitions.

aspire verb If you aspire to something, you have an ambition to achieve it. > **aspiring** adjective

aspirin noun 1 a white drug used to relieve pain, fever and colds. 2 a tablet of this drug.

ass noun a donkey.

assailant noun someone who attacks another person.

assassin noun someone who has murdered a political or religious leader.

assassinate verb To assassinate a political or religious leader is to murder him or her. > **assassination** noun

assault noun 1 a violent attack on someone. ▶ verb 2 To assault someone is to attack them violently.

assemble verb 1 To assemble is to gather together. 2 If you assemble something, you fit the parts of it together.

> **assemble** verb
> 1 = collect, come together, congregate, convene, gather, mass 2 = build, construct, erect, make, put together

assembly assemblies noun 1 a group of people who have gathered together for a meeting. 2 The assembly of an object is the fitting together of its parts.

assent noun 1 If you give your assent to something, you agree to it. ▶ verb 2 If you assent to something, you agree to it.

assert verb 1 If you assert a fact or belief, you state it firmly and forcefully. 2 If you assert yourself, you speak and behave in a confident and direct way, so that people pay attention to you.

assertion noun a statement.

assertive adjective If you are assertive, you speak and behave in a confident and direct way, so that people pay attention to you.
> **assertively** adverb
> **assertiveness** noun

assess verb (EXAM TERM) If you assess something, you consider it carefully and make a judgment about it. > **assessment** noun

assessor noun someone whose job is to assess the value of something.

asset noun 1 a person or thing considered useful. 2 (in plural) The assets of a person or company are all the things they own that could be sold to raise money.

assign verb 1 To assign something to someone is to give it to them officially or to make them responsible for it. 2 If someone is assigned to do something, they are officially told to do it.

assignment noun a job someone is given to do.

assimilate verb 1 If you assimilate ideas or experiences, you learn and understand them. 2 When people are assimilated into a group, they become part of it. > **assimilation** noun

assist verb To assist someone is to help them do something. > **assistance** noun

assistant noun someone whose job is to help another person in their work.

assistant noun
= aide, ally, colleague, helper, right-hand man

associate verb 1 If you associate one thing with another, you connect the two things in your mind. 2 If you associate with a group of people, you spend a lot of time with them. ▶ noun 3 Your associates are the people you work with or spend a lot of time with.

associate verb
1 = connect, couple, identify, link 2 = hang out (informal), mingle, mix, run around (informal), socialise
▶ noun 3 = colleague, co-worker, workmate

association noun 1 an organisation for people who have similar interests, jobs or aims. 2 Your association with a person or group is the connection or involvement you have with them. 3 An association between two things is a link you make in your mind between them.

association noun
1 = body, club, company, confederation, group, institution, league, society, syndicate 2 = affiliation, attachment, bond, connection, relationship, tie

assorted adjective Assorted things are different in size and colour.

assortment noun a group of similar things that are different sizes and colours.

assume verb 1 If you assume that something is true, you accept it is true even though you have not thought about it. 2 To assume

responsibility for something is to put yourself in charge of it.

assume verb
1 = believe, guess (informal), imagine, suppose, think 2 = accept, shoulder, take on, undertake

assumption noun 1 a belief that something is true, without thinking about it. 2 Assumption of power or responsibility is the taking of it.

assurance noun 1 something said which is intended to make people less worried. 2 Assurance is a feeling of confidence. 3 Life assurance is a type of insurance that pays money to your dependants when you die.

assure verb If you assure someone that something is true, you tell them it is true.

asterisk noun the symbol (*) used in printing and writing.

astern adverb, adjective (Nautical) backwards or at the back.

asteroid noun one of the large number of very small planets that move around the sun between the orbits of Jupiter and Mars.

asthma noun (SCIENCE) a disease of the chest which causes wheezing and difficulty in breathing. > **asthmatic** adjective

astonish verb If something astonishes you, it surprises you very much. > **astonished** adjective
> **astonishing** adjective
> **astonishment** noun

astound verb If something astounds you, it shocks and amazes you. > **astounded** adjective
> **astounding** adjective

astray phrase 1 To lead someone astray is to influence them to do

A

something wrong. **2** If something **goes astray**, it gets lost.

astride *preposition* with one leg on either side of something.

astringent *noun* a liquid that makes skin less greasy and stops bleeding.

astrology *noun* the study of the planets, sun, moon and stars in the belief that they predict the future. > **astrological** *adjective* > **astrologer** *noun*

astronaut *noun* a person who operates a spacecraft.

astronomical *adjective* **1** involved with or relating to astronomy. **2** extremely large in amount. > **astronomically** *adverb*

astronomy *noun* the scientific study of stars and planets. > **astronomer** *noun*

astute *adjective* clever and quick at understanding situations and behaviour.

> **astute** *adjective*
> = alert, clever, keen, perceptive, quick, sharp, shrewd, smart

asunder *adverb* (*literary*) If something is torn asunder, it is violently torn apart.

asylum *noun* **1** (*old-fashioned*) a hospital for psychiatric patients. **2** Political asylum is protection given by a government to someone who has fled from their own country for political reasons.

asymmetrical or **asymmetric** *adjective* unbalanced or with one half not exactly the same as the other half.

at *preposition* **1** used to say where someone or something is: *Bert met us at the airport.* **2** used to mention the direction something is going in: *He threw his plate at the wall.*

3 used to say when something happens: *The game starts at 3 o'clock.* **4** used to mention the rate or price of something: *priced at fifty pence.*

ate the past tense of **eat**.

atheist *noun* (RE) someone who believes there is no God.

athlete *noun* (PE) someone who is good at sport and takes part in sporting events.

athletic *adjective* **1** (PE) strong, healthy and good at sports. **2** involving athletes or athletics.

athletics *plural noun* Sporting events such as running, jumping and throwing are called athletics.

Atlantic *noun* The Atlantic is the ocean separating North and South America from Europe and Africa.

atlas atlases *noun* (GEOGRAPHY) a book of maps.

atmosphere *noun* **1** (SCIENCE) (GEOGRAPHY) the air and other gases that surround a planet; also the air in a particular place. **2** The general mood of a place. **3** (ENGLISH) the mood created by the writer of a novel or play. > **atmospheric** *adjective*

atom *noun* (SCIENCE) the smallest part of an element that can take part in a chemical reaction.

atomic *adjective* relating to atoms or to the power released by splitting atoms.

atomic bomb *noun* an extremely powerful bomb which explodes because of the energy that comes from splitting atoms.

atone *verb* (*formal*) If you atone for something wrong you have done, you say you are sorry and try to make up for it. > **atonement** *noun*

atrocious *adjective* extremely bad.

atrocity atrocities noun an extremely cruel and shocking act.

attach verb If you attach something to something else, you join or fasten the two things together.

> **attach** verb
> = affix, connect, couple, fasten, join, link, tie

attached adjective If you are attached to someone, you are very fond of them.

attachment noun 1 Attachment to someone is a feeling of love and affection for them. 2 Attachment to a cause or ideal is a strong belief in it and support for it. 3 a piece of equipment attached to a tool or machine to do a particular job. 4 an extra document attached to or included with another document. 5 a file that is attached to an electronic message.

attack verb 1 To attack someone is to use violence against them so as to hurt or kill them. 2 If you attack someone or their ideas, you criticise them strongly. 3 If a disease or chemical attacks something, it damages or destroys it. 4 In a game such as football or hockey, to attack is to get the ball into a position from which a goal can be scored. ▶ noun 5 An attack is violent physical action against someone. 6 An attack on someone or on their ideas is strong criticism of them. 7 An attack of an illness is a short time in which you suffer badly with it. > **attacker** noun

> **attack** verb
> 1 = assault, charge, invade, raid, set upon, storm 2 = blast,

censure (formal), criticise, have a go at (British; informal), put down (informal), vilify (formal) ▶ noun 5 = assault, charge, invasion, offensive, onslaught, raid

attain verb (formal) If you attain something, you manage to achieve it. > **attainable** adjective > **attainment** noun

attempt verb 1 If you attempt to do something, you try to do it or achieve it, but may not succeed. ▶ noun 2 an act of trying to do something.

> **attempt** verb
> 1 = endeavour, seek, strive, try, try your hand at
> ▶ noun 2 = bid, crack (informal), go (informal), shot (informal), stab (informal), try

attend verb 1 If you attend an event, you are present at it. 2 To attend school, church or hospital is to go there regularly. 3 If you attend to something, you deal with it. > **attendance** noun

attendant noun someone whose job is to look after people in a place such as a cloakroom or swimming pool.

attention noun Attention is the thought or care you give to something.

attentive adjective paying close attention to something. > **attentively** adverb > **attentiveness** noun

attest verb (formal) To attest something is to show or declare it is true. > **attestation** noun

attic noun a room at the top of a house just below the roof.

attire noun (formal) Attire is clothing.

attitude noun Your attitude to someone or something is the way you think about them and behave towards them.

> **attitude** noun
> = outlook, perspective, point of view, position, stance

attorney noun In America, an attorney is the same as a lawyer.

attract verb 1 If something attracts people, it interests them and makes them want to go to it. 2 If someone attracts you, you like and admire them. 3 If something attracts support or publicity, it gets it. 4 (SCIENCE) If something attracts objects to it, it has a force that pulls them towards it.

> **attract** verb
> 1 = appeal to, draw, entice, lure, pull (informal), tempt

attraction noun 1 Attraction is a feeling of liking someone or something very much. 2 something people visit for interest or pleasure. 3 a quality that attracts.

attractive adjective 1 interesting and possibly advantageous. 2 pleasant to look at or be with.
> **attractively** adverb
> **attractiveness** noun

> **attractive** adjective
> 2 = appealing, charming, fetching, handsome, lovely, pretty

attribute verb 1 If you attribute something to a person or thing, you believe it was caused or created by that person or thing. ▶ noun 2 a quality or feature someone or something has.
> **attribution** noun
> **attributable** adjective

> **attribute** noun
> 2 = characteristic, feature, property, quality, trait

attrition noun 1 Attrition is the constant wearing down of an enemy. 2 (GEOGRAPHY) the process by which rocks gradually become smaller and smoother as they rub against one another in moving water.

attuned adjective accustomed or well adjusted to something.

aubergine noun a dark purple, pear-shaped fruit that is eaten as a vegetable. It is also called an eggplant.

auburn adjective Auburn hair is reddish brown.

auction noun 1 a public sale in which goods are sold to the person who offers the highest price. ▶ verb 2 To auction something is to sell it in an auction.

auctioneer noun the person in charge of an auction.

audacious adjective very daring.
> **audacity** noun

audible adjective loud enough to be heard. ▶ **audibly** adverb
> **audibility** noun

audience noun 1 the group of people who are watching or listening to a performance. 2 the group of people who are reached by a piece of writing, film or television programme. 3 a private or formal meeting with an important person.

audio adjective used in recording and reproducing sound.

audit verb 1 To audit a set of financial accounts is to examine them officially to check they are correct. ▶ noun 2 an official examination of an organisation's accounts. > **auditor** noun

audition noun a short performance given by an actor or musician, so that a director can decide whether they are suitable for a part in a play or film or for a place in an orchestra.

auditorium auditoriums or auditoria noun the part of a theatre where the audience sits.

augment verb (formal) To augment something is to add something to it.

> **augment** verb
> = add to, boost, complement, increase, reinforce, supplement, top up

August noun the eighth month of the year. August has 31 days.

aunt noun Your aunt is the sister of your mother or father, or the wife of one of your parents' siblings.

au pair noun a young foreign person who lives with a family to help with the children and housework and sometimes to learn the language.

aura noun an atmosphere that surrounds a person or thing.

aural adjective relating to or done through the sense of hearing.

auspicious adjective (formal) favourable and seeming to promise success.

austere adjective plain and simple, and without luxury.
> **austerity** noun

Australasia noun Australasia consists of Australia, New Zealand and neighbouring islands in the Pacific.
> **Australasian** adjective

Australia noun Australia is the smallest continent and the largest island in the world, situated between the Indian Ocean and the Pacific.

Austrian adjective 1 belonging or relating to Austria. ▶ noun 2 someone who comes from Austria.

authentic adjective real and genuine. > **authentically** adverb > **authenticity** noun

> **authentic** adjective
> = bona fide, dinkum (Australian and New Zealand; informal), genuine, real, true

author noun (ENGLISH) The author of a book is the person who wrote it.

authorise; also spelt **authorize** verb To authorise something is to give official permission for it to happen. > **authorisation** noun

authoritarian adjective believing in strict obedience.
> **authoritarianism** noun

authoritative adjective 1 having authority. 2 accepted as being reliable and accurate.
> **authoritatively** adverb

authority authorities noun 1 Authority is the power to control people. 2 In Britain, an authority is a local government department. 3 Someone who is an authority on something knows a lot about it. 4 (in plural) The authorities are the people who have the power to make decisions.

autobiography autobiographies noun Someone's autobiography is an account of their life which they have written themselves.
> **autobiographical** adjective

autograph noun the signature of a famous person.

automatic adjective 1 An automatic machine is programmed to perform tasks without needing a person to operate it. 2 Automatic actions or reactions take place without involving conscious thought. 3 A process or punishment that is automatic always happens as a direct result of something. > **automatically** adverb

automatic adjective
1 = automated, mechanical, robot, self-propelled
2 = instinctive, involuntary, natural, reflex

automobile noun In American English, an automobile is a car.

automobile noun
= car, motor (old-fashioned), vehicle

autonomous adjective An autonomous country governs itself rather than being controlled by anyone else. > **autonomy** noun

autopsy autopsies noun a medical examination of a dead body to discover the cause of death.

autumn noun the season between summer and winter. > **autumnal** adjective

auxiliary auxiliaries noun 1 a person employed to help other members of staff. ▶ adjective 2 Auxiliary equipment is used when necessary in addition to the main equipment.

avail phrase If something you do is **of no avail** or **to no avail**, it is not successful or helpful.

available adjective 1 Something that is available can be obtained. 2 Someone who is available is ready for work or free for people to talk to. > **availability** noun

available adjective
1 = accessible, at hand, at someone's disposal, free, handy, to hand

avalanche noun a huge mass of snow and ice that falls down a mountain side.

avant-garde adjective extremely modern or experimental, especially in art, literature or music.

avarice noun (formal) greed for money and possessions. > **avaricious** adjective

avenge verb If you avenge something harmful someone has done to you or your family, you punish or harm the other person in return. > **avenger** noun

avenue noun a street, especially one with trees along it.

average noun 1 (MATHS) a measure which represents the typical central or normal value in a set of data. ▶ adjective 2 Average means standard or typical. ▶ verb 3 To average a number is to produce that number as an average over a period of time. ▶ phrase 4 You say **on average** when mentioning what usually happens in a situation.

average adjective
2 = normal, regular, standard, typical, usual
▶ phrase 4 **on average** = as a rule, generally, normally, typically, usually

averse adjective unwilling to do something.

aversion noun If you have an aversion to someone or something, you dislike them very much.

avert verb 1 If you avert an unpleasant event, you prevent it from happening. 2 If you avert your eyes from something, you turn your eyes away from it.

aviary aviaries noun a large cage or group of cages in which birds are kept.

aviation noun the science of flying aircraft.

aviator noun (old-fashioned) a pilot of an aircraft.

avid adjective eager and enthusiastic for something.
> **avidly** adverb

avocado avocados noun a pear-shaped fruit, with dark green skin, soft greenish yellow flesh, and a large stone.

avoid verb 1 If you avoid doing something, you make a deliberate effort not to do it. 2 If you avoid someone, you keep away from them. > **avoidable** adjective
> **avoidance** noun

> **avoid** verb
> 1 = dodge, duck out of (informal), fight shy of, refrain from, shirk
> 2 = dodge, elude, eschew (formal), evade, shun, sidestep, steer clear of

avowed adjective (formal) 1 If you are an avowed supporter or opponent of something, you have declared that you support it or oppose it. 2 An avowed belief or aim is one you hold very strongly.

avuncular adjective friendly and helpful in manner towards younger people, rather like an uncle.

await verb 1 If you await something, you expect it. 2 If something awaits you, it will happen to you in the future.

awake awakes, awaking, awoke, awoken adjective 1 Someone who is awake is not sleeping. ▶ verb 2 When you awake, you wake up. 3 If you are awoken by something, it wakes you up.

awaken verb If something awakens an emotion or interest in you, you start to feel this emotion or interest.

award noun 1 a prize or certificate for doing something well. 2 a sum of money an organisation gives to students for training or study. ▶ verb 3 If you award someone something, you give it to them formally or officially.

aware adjective 1 If you are aware of something, you realise it is there. 2 If you are aware of something, you know about it.
> **awareness** noun

> **aware** adjective
> 1 aware of = acquainted with, conscious of, familiar with, mindful of 2 = informed, in the picture, knowledgeable

awash adjective, adverb covered with water.

away adverb 1 moving from a place. 2 at a distance from a place. 3 in its proper place. 4 not at home, school or work.

awe noun (formal) a feeling of great respect mixed with amazement and sometimes slight fear.

awesome adjective 1 Something that is awesome is very impressive and frightening. 2 (informal) Awesome also means excellent or outstanding.

B

awful adjective **1** very unpleasant or very bad. **2** (informal) very great. > **awfully** adverb

> **awful** adjective
> **1** = appalling, dreadful, frightful (old-fashioned), ghastly, horrendous, terrible

awkward adjective **1** clumsy and uncomfortable. **2** embarrassed or nervous. **3** difficult to deal with.

awning noun a large roof of canvas or plastic attached to a building or vehicle.

awoke the past tense of **awake**.

awoken the past participle of **awake**.

awry adjective wrong or not as planned.

axe axes, axing, axed noun **1** a tool with a handle and a sharp blade, used for chopping wood. ▶ verb **2** To axe something is to end it.

axis axes noun **1** (MATHS) an imaginary line through the centre of something, around which it moves. **2** (MATHS) one of the two sides of a graph.

axle noun the long bar that connects a pair of wheels on a vehicle.

azure adjective (literary) bright blue.

Bb

babble verb When someone babbles, they talk in a confused or excited way.

> **babble** verb
> = burble, chatter, gabble, prattle

baboon noun an African monkey with a pointed face, large teeth, and a long tail.

baby babies noun a child in the first year or two of life. > **babyhood** noun > **babyish** adjective

> **baby** noun
> = ankle-biter (Australian and New Zealand; slang), bairn (Scottish), child, infant

baby-sit baby-sits, baby-sitting, baby-sat verb To baby-sit for someone means to look after their children while that person is out.

bach noun **1** In New Zealand, a bach is a small holiday cottage. ▶ verb **2** (informal) In Australian and New Zealand English, to bach is to keep a house on your own, especially when you are not used to it.

bachelor noun a man who has never been married.

back adverb **1** When people or things move back, they move in the opposite direction from the one they are facing. **2** When people or things go back to a place or situation, they return to it: *She went back to sleep.* **3** If you get something back, it is returned to you. **4** If you do something back to someone, you do to them what they have done to you: *I smiled back at them.* **5** Back also means in the past: *It happened back in the early eighties.* ▶ *noun* **6** The rear part of your body. **7** The part of something that is behind the front: *the back of a postcard.* ▶ *adjective* **8** The back parts of something are the ones near the rear: *an animal's back legs.* ▶ *verb* **9** If a building backs onto something, its back faces in that direction. **10** When a car backs, it moves backwards. **11** To back a person or organisation means to support or finance that person or organisation. > **back down** *verb* If you back down on a demand or claim, you withdraw and give up. > **back out** *verb* If you back out of a promise or commitment, you decide not to do what you had promised to do. > **back up** *verb* **1** If you back up a claim or story, you produce evidence to show that it is true. **2** If you back someone up, you help and support them.

back *noun*
7 = end, rear, reverse, stern
▶ *verb* **11** = advocate, encourage, endorse, favour, promote, support

backbone *noun* **1** the column of linked bones along the middle of a person's or animal's back. **2** strength of character.

backdate *verb* If an arrangement is backdated, it is valid from a date earlier than the one on which it is completed or signed.

backdrop *noun* the background to a situation or event.

backer *noun* The backers of a project are the people who give it financial help.

backfire *verb* **1** If a plan backfires, it fails. **2** When a car backfires, there is a small but noisy explosion in its exhaust pipe.

background *noun* **1** the circumstances which help to explain an event or caused it to happen. **2** the kind of home you come from and your education and experience. **3** If sounds are in the background, they are there but no one really pays any attention to them.

background *noun*
2 = culture, environment, history, upbringing

backing *noun* support or help.

backlash *noun* a hostile reaction to a new development or a new policy.

backlog *noun* a number of things which have not yet been done, but which need to be done.

backpack *noun* a large bag that hikers or campers carry on their backs.

backside *noun* (*informal*) the part of your body that you sit on.

backward *adjective* **1** Backward means directed behind you: *a backward glance.* **2** A backward country or society is one that does not have modern industries or technology. > **backwardness** *noun*

backwards *adverb* **1** Backwards means behind you: *Lucille looked backwards.* **2** If you do something backwards, you do it the opposite of the usual way: *He instructed them to count backwards.*

bacon noun meat from the back or sides of a pig, which has been salted or smoked.

bacteria plural noun (SCIENCE) Bacteria are very tiny organisms which live in air, water, soil, plants and the bodies of animals. Some bacteria provide food for plants, others cause diseases such as typhoid. > **bacterial** adjective

bad worse, worst adjective
1 Anything harmful or upsetting can be described as bad.
2 insufficient or of poor quality.
3 evil or immoral in character or behaviour. 4 lacking skill in something: I was bad at sports.
5 Bad language consists of swearwords. 6 If you have a bad temper, you become angry easily.

> **bad** adjective
> 1 = damaging, disturbing, harmful, serious, severe, terrible, unpleasant 2 = faulty, imperfect, inferior, poor, unsatisfactory 3 = corrupt, depraved, evil, immoral, wicked

bade a form of the past tense of bid.

badge noun a piece of plastic or metal with a design or message on it that you can pin to your clothes.

badger noun 1 a wild animal that has a white head with two black stripes on it. ▶ verb 2 If you badger someone, you keep asking them questions or pestering them to do something.

badly adverb in an inferior or unimpressive way.

> **badly** adverb
> = inadequately, ineptly, poorly, shoddily, unsatisfactorily

badminton noun (PE) Badminton is a game in which two or four players use rackets to hit a shuttlecock over a high net. It was first played at Badminton House in Gloucestershire.

baffle verb If something baffles you, you cannot understand or explain it.

bag noun 1 a container for carrying things in. 2 (in plural, informal) Bags of something is a lot of it.

baggage noun the suitcases and bags that you take on a journey.

baggy baggier, baggiest adjective Baggy clothing hangs loosely.

bagpipes plural noun (MUSIC) a musical instrument played by squeezing air out of a bag through pipes, on which a tune is played.

bail noun 1 Bail is a sum of money paid to a court to allow an accused person to go free until the time of the trial. ▶ verb 2 If you bail water from a boat, you scoop it out.
> **bail out**; also spelt **bale out** verb 1 To bail out of an aircraft means to jump out of it with a parachute. 2 If you bail someone out, you help them out of a difficult situation.

bailiff noun 1 a law officer who makes sure that the decisions of a court are obeyed. 2 a person employed to look after land or property for the owner.

bait noun 1 a small amount of food placed on a hook or in a trap, to attract a fish or wild animal so that it gets caught. 2 something used to tempt a person to do something. ▶ verb 3 If you bait a hook or trap, you put some food on it to catch a fish or wild animal.

bait *noun*
2 = bribe, decoy, inducement, lure, temptation

bake *verb* 1 To bake food means to cook it in an oven without using liquid or fat. 2 To bake earth or clay means to heat it until it becomes hard.

baker *noun* a person who makes and sells bread and cakes.

bakery bakeries *noun* a building where bread and cakes are baked and sold.

bakkie *noun* In South African English, a bakkie is a small truck.

balance *verb* 1 When someone or something balances, they remain steady and do not fall over. ▸ *noun* 2 Balance is the state of being upright and steady. 3 Balance is also a situation in which all the parts involved have a stable relationship with each other. 4 The balance in someone's bank account is the amount of money in it.

balance *verb*
1 = level, stabilise, steady
▸ *noun* 3 = equilibrium, equity, parity

balanced *adjective* A balanced account or report presents information in a fair and objective way.

balcony balconies *noun* 1 a platform on the outside of a building with a wall or railing round it. 2 an area of upstairs seats in a theatre or cinema.

bald *adjective* 1 A bald person has little or no hair on their head. 2 A bald statement or question is made in the simplest way without any attempt to be polite.

bale *noun* 1 a large bundle of something, such as paper or hay, tied tightly. ▸ *verb* 2 If you bale water from a boat, you remove it using a container; also spelt **bail**. > **bale out**; also spelt **bail out** *verb* To bale out of an aircraft means to jump out of it with a parachute.

balk; also spelt **baulk** *verb* If you balk at something, you object to it and may refuse to do it.

ball *noun* 1 a round object, especially one used in games such as cricket and soccer. 2 The ball of your foot or thumb is the rounded part where your toes join your foot or your thumb joins your hand. 3 a large formal social event at which people dance.

ball *noun*
1 = drop, globe, pellet, sphere

ballad *noun* 1 (ENGLISH) a long song or poem which tells a story. 2 a slow, romantic pop song.

ballast *noun* any heavy material placed in a ship to make it more stable.

ballerina *noun* a female ballet dancer.

ballet *noun* Ballet is a type of artistic dancing based on precise steps.

balloon *noun* 1 a small bag made of thin rubber that you blow into until it becomes larger and rounder. 2 a large, strong bag filled with gas or hot air, which travels through the air carrying passengers in a compartment underneath.

ballot *noun* 1 a secret vote in which people select a candidate in an election, or express their opinion about something. ▸ *verb* 2 When a group of people are balloted, they are asked questions to find out what they think about a particular problem or question.

ballpoint noun a pen with a small metal ball at the end which transfers the ink onto the paper.

ballroom noun a very large room used for dancing or formal balls.

balmy balmier, balmiest adjective mild and pleasant.

balustrade noun a railing or wall on a balcony or staircase.

bamboo noun Bamboo is a tall tropical plant with hard, hollow stems used for making furniture. It is a species of giant grass. The young shoots can be eaten.

ban bans, banning, banned verb 1 If something is banned, or if you are banned from doing it or using it, you are not allowed to do it or use it. ▶ noun 2 If there is a ban on something, it is not allowed.

> **ban** verb
> 1 = bar, disqualify, exclude, forbid, outlaw, prohibit
> ▶ noun 2 = disqualification, embargo, prohibition, suppression

banal adjective very ordinary and not at all interesting.

banana noun a long curved fruit with a yellow skin.

band noun 1 a group of musicians who play jazz or pop music together, or a group who play brass instruments together. 2 a group of people who share a common purpose. 3 a narrow strip of something used to hold things together or worn as a decoration. > **band together** verb When people band together, they join together for a particular purpose.

> **band** noun
> 1 = group, orchestra 2 = bunch, company, crowd, gang, party, troupe

bandage noun 1 a strip of cloth wrapped round a wound to protect it. ▶ verb 2 If you bandage a wound, you tie a bandage round it.

bandit noun (old-fashioned) a member of an armed gang who rob travellers.

bandwagon phrase To jump on the bandwagon means to become involved in something because it is fashionable or likely to be successful.

bandwidth noun The bandwidth of a telecommunications signal is the range of frequencies used to transmit it.

bandy bandies, bandying, bandied verb If a name is bandied about, many people mention it.

bang verb 1 If you bang something, you hit or put it somewhere violently, so that it makes a loud noise. 2 If you bang a part of your body against something, you accidentally bump it. ▶ noun 3 a sudden, short, loud noise. 4 a hard or painful bump against something.

> **bang** verb
> 1 = beat, hammer, hit, knock, pound, slam, thump
> ▶ noun 3 = blast, boom, crack, detonation, explosion, thump
> 4 = blow, clout (informal), knock, thump, whack (informal)

Bangladeshi adjective 1 belonging or relating to Bangladesh. ▶ noun 2 someone who comes from Bangladesh.

bangle noun an ornamental band worn round someone's wrist or ankle.

banish verb To banish someone means to send them into exile.

> **banish** verb
> = deport, eject, evict, exile, expel, transport

banjo banjos or banjoes noun a musical instrument, like a small guitar with a round body.

bank noun 1 a business that looks after people's money. 2 A bank of something is a store of it kept ready for use. 3 the raised ground along the edge of a river or lake. 4 the sloping side of an area of raised ground. ▶ verb 5 When you bank money, you pay it into a bank. 6 If you bank on something happening, you expect it and rely on it.

> **bank** noun
> 2 = fund, hoard, reserve, stock, store 3 = brink, edge, shore, side

banker noun a senior worker in a bank.

bank holiday noun a public holiday, when banks are officially closed.

banking noun the business of looking after people's money.

banknote noun a piece of paper money.

bankrupt adjective 1 People or organisations that go bankrupt do not have enough money to pay their debts. ▶ noun 2 someone who has been declared bankrupt. ▶ verb 3 To bankrupt someone means to make them bankrupt.
> **bankruptcy** noun

banner noun a long strip of cloth with a message or slogan on it.

banquet noun a grand formal dinner, often followed by speeches.

banter noun Banter is friendly joking and teasing.

baptise; also spelt **baptize** verb When someone is baptised, water is sprinkled on them, or they are immersed in water, as a sign that they have become a Christian.

baptism (RE) a ceremony in which someone is baptised.

Baptist noun (RE) a member of a Protestant church that believes that people should be baptised when they are adults rather than when they are babies.

bar bars, barring, barred noun 1 a long, straight piece of metal. 2 a piece of something made in a rectangular shape: *a bar of soap.* 3 a counter or room where alcoholic drinks are served. 4 The bars in a piece of music are the many short parts of equal length that the piece is divided into. 5 (GEOGRAPHY) In meteorology, a bar is a unit of pressure equivalent to 100,000 newtons per square metre. ▶ verb 6 If you bar a door, you place something across it to stop it being opened. 7 If you bar someone's way, you stop them going somewhere by standing in front of them.

> **bar** noun
> 1 = pole, rail, rod, shaft
> ▶ verb 7 = obstruct, prevent

barb noun a sharp curved point on the end of an arrow or fish-hook.

barbarian noun a member of a wild or uncivilised people.

barbaric adjective cruel or brutal.
> **barbarity** noun

barbecue barbecues, barbecuing, barbecued *noun* **1** a grill with a charcoal fire on which you cook food, usually outdoors; also an outdoor party where you eat food cooked on a barbecue. ▶ *verb* **2** When food is barbecued, it is cooked over a charcoal grill.

barbed *adjective* A barbed remark is one that seems straightforward but is really unkind or spiteful.

barbed wire *noun* Barbed wire is strong wire with sharp points sticking out of it, used to make fences.

barber *noun* a person who cuts men's hair.

bar code *noun* a small pattern of numbers and lines on something you buy in a shop, which can be electronically scanned at a checkout to give the price.

bard *noun* (*literary*) A bard is a poet. Some people call Shakespeare the Bard.

bare barer, barest *adjective* **1** If a part of your body is bare, it is not covered by any clothing. **2** If something is bare, it has nothing on top of it or inside it. **3** When trees are bare, they have no leaves on them. **4** The bare minimum or bare essentials means the very least that is needed. ▶ *verb* **5** If you bare something, you uncover or show it.

> **bare** *adjective*
> **1** = exposed, uncovered
> **2** = empty, open, spartan

barefoot *adjective, adverb* not wearing anything on your feet.

barely *adverb* only just.

> **barely** *adverb*
> = almost, hardly, just, scarcely

bargain *noun* **1** an agreement in which two people or groups discuss and agree what each will do, pay or receive in a matter which involves them both. **2** something which is sold at a low price and which is good value. ▶ *verb* **3** When people bargain with each other, they discuss and agree terms about what each will do, pay or receive in a matter which involves both.
> **bargain for** *verb* If you had not bargained for or on something, you were not prepared for it.

barge *noun* **1** a boat with a flat bottom used for carrying heavy loads, especially on canals. ▶ *verb* **2** (*informal*) If you barge into a place, you push into it in a rough way.

bark *verb* **1** When a dog barks, it makes a short, loud noise, once or several times. ▶ *noun* **2** the short, loud noise that a dog makes. **3** the tough material that covers the outside of a tree.

barley *noun* a cereal that is grown for food and is also used for making beer and whisky.

barmy barmier, barmiest *adjective* (*slang*) eccentric or very foolish.

barn *noun* a large farm building used for storing crops or animal food.

barometer *noun* (GEOGRAPHY) an instrument that measures air pressure and shows when the weather is changing.

baron *noun* a member of the lowest rank of the nobility.

baroness *noun* a woman who has the rank of baron, or who is the wife of a baron.

barracks *plural noun* a building where soldiers live.

barrage noun 1 A barrage of questions or complaints is a lot of them all coming at the same time. 2 A barrage is continuous artillery fire over a wide area, to prevent the enemy from moving.

barrel noun 1 a wooden container with rounded sides and flat ends. 2 The barrel of a gun is the long tube through which the bullet is fired.

barren adjective 1 Barren land has soil of such poor quality that plants cannot grow on it. 2 A barren female animal is not able to have young. ▷ **barrenness** noun

> **barren** adjective
> 1 = arid, desert, desolate, dry, empty, waste

barricade noun 1 a temporary barrier put up to stop people getting past. ▶ verb 2 If you barricade yourself inside a room or building, you put something heavy against the door to stop people getting in.

barrier noun 1 a fence or wall that prevents people or animals getting from one area to another. 2 If something is a barrier, it prevents two people or groups from agreeing or communicating, or prevents something from being achieved.

> **barrier** noun
> 1 = barricade, fence, obstruction, wall 2 = handicap, hindrance, hurdle, impediment, obstacle

barrister noun a lawyer who is qualified to represent people in the higher courts.

barrow noun 1 the same as a **wheelbarrow**. 2 a large cart from which fruit or other goods are sold in the street.

barter verb 1 If you barter goods, you exchange them for other goods, rather than selling them for money. ▶ noun 2 Barter is the activity of exchanging goods.

base noun 1 the lowest part of something, which often supports the rest. 2 a place which part of an army, navy or air force works from. 3 (SCIENCE) In chemistry, a base is any compound that reacts with an acid to form a salt. 4 (MATHS) In mathematics, a base is a system of counting and expressing numbers. The decimal system uses base 10, and the binary system uses base 2. 5 (MATHS) The base of a shape is the side or face that is at the bottom. ▶ verb 6 To base something on something else means to use the second thing as a foundation or starting point of the first: The film is based on a traditional folk tale. 7 If you are based somewhere, you live there or work from there.

> **base** noun
> 1 = bed, bottom, foot, foundation, pedestal, stand 2 = camp, centre, headquarters, post, station
> ▶ verb 6 = build, derive, found, ground, hinge

baseball noun Baseball is a team game played with a bat and a ball, similar to rounders.

basement noun a floor of a building built completely or partly below the ground.

bases plural noun 1 the plural of **basis**. 2 the plural of **base**.

B

bash (*informal*) *verb* 1 If you bash someone or bash into them, you hit them hard. ▶ *noun* 2 A bash is a hard blow. ▶ *phrase* 3 If you **have a bash** at something, you try to do it.

bashful *adjective* shy and easily embarrassed.

basic *adjective* 1 The basic aspects of something are the most necessary ones. 2 Something that is basic has only the necessary features without any extras or luxuries. > **basically** *adverb*

> **basic** *adjective*
> 1 = elementary, essential, fundamental, key, necessary, vital

basics *plural noun* The basics of something are the things you need to know or understand.

basin *noun* 1 a round wide container which is open at the top. 2 The basin of a river is an area of land from which water runs into the river.

basis bases *noun* 1 The basis of something is the essential main principle from which it can be developed. 2 The basis for a belief is the facts that support it.

> **basis** *noun*
> 1 = core, fundamental, heart, premise, principle

bask *verb* If you bask in the sun, you sit or lie in it, enjoying its warmth.

basket *noun* a container made of thin strips of cane woven together.

basketball *noun* Basketball is a game in which two teams try to score goals by throwing a large ball through one of two circular nets suspended high up at each end of the court.

bass¹ *noun* 1 (MUSIC) a man with a very deep singing voice. 2 (MUSIC) A bass is also a musical instrument that provides the rhythm and lowest part in the harmonies. A bass may be either a large guitar or a very large member of the violin family.

bass² *noun* a type of edible sea fish.

bat bats, batting, batted *noun* 1 a specially shaped piece of wood with a handle, used for hitting the ball in a game such as cricket or table tennis. 2 a small flying animal, active at night, that looks like a mouse with wings. ▶ *verb* 3 In certain sports, when someone is batting, it is their turn to try to hit the ball and score runs.

batch *noun* a group of things of the same kind produced or dealt with together.

bated *phrase* With bated breath means very anxiously.

bath *noun* a long container which you fill with water and sit in to wash yourself.

bathe *verb* 1 When you bathe, you swim or play in open water. 2 When you bathe a wound, you wash it gently. 3 (*literary*) If a place is bathed in light, a lot of light reaches it.

bathroom *noun* a room with a bath or shower, a washbasin, and often a toilet in it.

baton *noun* 1 a light, thin stick that a conductor uses to direct an orchestra or choir. 2 In athletics, the baton is the short stick passed from one runner to another in a relay race. 3 A baton is also a stick used as a weapon by police officers in some countries.

battalion noun an army unit consisting of three or more companies.

batten noun a strip of wood that is fixed to something to strengthen it or hold it firm.

batter verb 1 To batter someone or something means to hit them many times. ▶ noun 2 Batter is a mixture of flour, eggs and milk, used to make pancakes, or to coat food before frying it. 3 In cricket, the batter is the person who is batting. > **battering** noun

battery batteries noun 1 a device, containing two or more cells, for storing and producing electricity, for example in a torch or a car. 2 a large group of things or people. ▶ adjective 3 A battery hen is one of a large number of hens kept in small cages for the mass production of eggs.

battle noun 1 (HISTORY) a fight between armed forces or a struggle between two people or groups with conflicting aims. 2 A battle for something difficult is a determined attempt to obtain or achieve it.

battlefield noun a place where a battle is or has been fought.

battleship noun a large, heavily armoured warship.

batty battier, battiest adjective (informal) foolish or eccentric.

bauble noun a pretty but cheap ornament or piece of jewellery.

baulk another spelling of **balk**.

bawl verb 1 (informal) To bawl at someone means to shout at them loudly and harshly. 2 When a child is bawling, it is crying very loudly.

bay noun 1 (GEOGRAPHY) a part of a coastline where the land curves inwards. 2 a space or area used for a particular purpose: a loading bay. 3 Bay is a kind of tree similar to the laurel, with leaves used for flavouring in cooking. ▶ phrase 4 If you **keep something at bay**, you prevent it from reaching you. ▶ verb 5 When a hound or wolf bays, it makes a deep howling noise.

> **bay** noun
> 1 = cove, gulf, inlet, sound
> ▶ verb 5 = bark, cry, howl, yelp

bayonet noun a sharp blade that can be fixed to the end of a rifle and used for stabbing.

bazaar noun 1 an area with many small shops and stalls, especially in Asia or North Africa. 2 a sale to raise money for charity.

BC BC means 'before Christ'. You use 'BC' in dates to indicate the number of years before the traditional date of the birth of Jesus Christ.

be am, is, are; being; was, were; been auxiliary verb 1 'Be' is used with a present participle to form the continuous tense: Crimes of violence are increasing. 2 'Be' is also used to say that something will happen: We are going to America next month. 3 'Be' is used to form the passive voice: The walls were being repaired. ▶ verb 4 'Be' is used to give more information about the subject of a sentence: Her name is Melanie.

beach noun an area of sand or pebbles beside the sea.

> **beach** noun
> = coast, sands, seashore, seaside, shore, strand

beacon noun In the past, a beacon was a light or fire on a hill, which acted as a signal or warning.

bead noun 1 Beads are small pieces of coloured glass or wood with a hole through the middle, strung together to make necklaces. 2 Beads of liquid are drops of it.

beady beadier, beadiest adjective Beady eyes are small and bright like beads.

beagle noun a short-haired dog with long ears and short legs.

beak noun A bird's beak is the hard part of its mouth that sticks out.

beam noun 1 A broad smile. 2 A beam of light is a band of light that shines from something such as a torch. 3 a long, thick bar of wood or metal, especially one that supports a roof. ▶ verb 4 If you beam, you smile because you are happy.

bean noun Beans are the seeds or pods of a climbing plant, which are eaten as a vegetable; also used of some other seeds, for example the seeds from which coffee is made.

bear bears, bearing, bore, borne noun 1 a large, strong wild animal with thick fur and sharp claws. ▶ verb 2 (formal) To bear something means to carry it or support its weight. 3 If something bears a mark or typical feature, it has it. 4 If you bear something difficult, you accept it and are able to deal with it. 5 If you can't bear someone or something, you dislike them very much. 6 (formal) When a plant or tree bears flowers, fruit or leaves, it produces them. > **bearable** adjective > **bear out** verb To bear someone out or to bear out their story or report means to support what they are saying: *These claims are not borne out by the evidence.*

> **bear** verb
> 2 = carry, convey (formal), hold, support, take 3 = exhibit, harbour, have 4 = abide, endure, stand, stomach, suffer, tolerate

beard noun the hair that grows on the lower part of a man's face.

bearer noun The bearer of something is the person who carries or presents it.

bearing noun 1 If something has a bearing on a situation, it is relevant to it. 2 the way in which a person moves or stands.

beast noun 1 (old-fashioned) a large wild animal. 2 (informal) If you call someone a beast, you mean that they are cruel or spiteful.

beastly beastlier, beastliest adjective (old-fashioned, informal) cruel or spiteful.

beat beats, beating, beat, beaten verb 1 To beat someone or something means to hit them hard and repeatedly. 2 If you beat someone in a race or game, you defeat them or do better than them. 3 When a bird or insect beats its wings, it moves them up and down. 4 When your heart is beating, it is pumping blood with a regular rhythm. 5 If you beat eggs or butter, you mix them vigorously using a fork or a whisk. ▶ noun 6 The beat of your heart is its regular pumping action. 7 (MUSIC) The beat of a piece of music is its main rhythm. 8 A police officer's beat is the area which he or she patrols. > **beater** noun > **beating** noun > **beat up** verb

To beat someone up means to hit or kick them repeatedly.

beat *verb*
1 = batter, buffet, hit, pound, strike, thrash 2 = defeat, outdo, outstrip, overcome, overwhelm, vanquish (*literary*)
▸ *noun* 7 = cadence, metre, rhythm, stress, time

beaut (*informal*) *noun* 1 In Australian and New Zealand English, a beaut is an outstanding person or thing.
▸ *adjective* 2 In Australian and New Zealand English, beaut means good or excellent.

beautiful *adjective* very attractive or pleasing. ▸ **beautifully** *adverb*

beautiful *adjective*
= attractive, delightful, fine, gorgeous, lovely, pleasing

beauty beauties *noun* 1 Beauty is the quality of being beautiful. 2 (*old-fashioned*) a very attractive woman. 3 The beauty of an idea or plan is what makes it attractive or worthwhile.

beauty *noun*
1 = attractiveness, charm, elegance, loveliness
3 = advantage, asset, attraction, benefit

beaver *noun* an animal with a big, flat tail and webbed hind feet. Beavers build dams.

became the past tense of **become**.

because *conjunction* 1 'Because' is used with a clause that gives the reason for something: *I went home because I was tired.* ▸ *phrase* 2 **Because of** is used with a noun that gives the reason for something: *He quit playing because of a knee injury.*

because *conjunction*
1 = as, since

beck *phrase* If you are at someone's **beck and call**, you are always available to do what they ask.

become becomes, becoming, became, become *verb* To become something means to start feeling or being that thing: *I became very angry.*

bed *noun* 1 a piece of furniture that you lie on when you sleep. 2 A bed in a garden is an area of ground in which plants are grown. 3 The bed of a sea or river is the ground at the bottom of it.

bedding *noun* Bedding is sheets, blankets and other covers that are used on beds.

bedlam *noun* You can refer to a noisy and disorderly place or situation as bedlam.

bedraggled *adjective* A bedraggled person or animal is in a messy or untidy state.

bedridden *adjective* Someone who is bedridden is too ill to get out of bed.

bedroom *noun* a room used for sleeping in.

bedspread *noun* a cover put over a bed, on top of the blankets.

bee *noun* a winged insect that makes honey and lives in large groups.

beech *noun* a tree with a smooth grey trunk and shiny leaves.

beef *noun* Beef is the meat of a cow, bull or ox.

beefy beefier, beefiest *adjective* (*informal*) A beefy person is strong and muscular.

beehive *noun* a container in which bees live and make their honey.

B

beeline *phrase* (*informal*) If you **make a beeline** for a place, you go there as quickly and directly as possible.

been the past participle of **be**.

beer *noun* an alcoholic drink made from malt and flavoured with hops.

beetle *noun* a flying insect with hard wings which cover its body when it is not flying.

beetroot *noun* A beetroot is the round, dark red root of a type of beet. It is cooked and eaten, especially cold as a salad vegetable or preserved in vinegar.

befall befalls, befalling, befell, befallen *verb* (*old-fashioned*) If something befalls you, it happens to you.

before *adverb, preposition, conjunction* **1** 'Before' is used to refer to a previous time: *Apply the ointment before going to bed.* ▶ *adverb* **2** If you have done something before, you have done it on a previous occasion. ▶ *preposition* **3** (*formal*) Before also means in front of: *They stopped before a large white villa.*

> **before** *adverb, preposition, conjunction*
> **1** = earlier, formerly, in advance, previously, sooner

beforehand *adverb* before.

befriend *verb* If you befriend someone, you act in a kind and helpful way and so become friends with them.

beg begs, begging, begged *verb* **1** When people beg, they ask for food or money, because they are very poor. **2** If you beg someone to do something, you ask them very anxiously to do it.

beg *verb*
2 = beseech (*literary*), implore, petition, plead

began the past tense of **begin**.

beggar *noun* someone who lives by asking people for money or food.

begin begins, beginning, began, begun *verb* If you begin to do something, you start doing it. When something begins, it starts.

> **begin** *verb*
> = commence (*formal*), inaugurate (*formal*), initiate, originate, set about, start

beginner *noun* someone who has just started learning to do something and cannot do it very well yet.

> **beginner** *noun*
> = apprentice, learner, novice, starter, trainee

beginning *noun* The beginning of something is the first part of it or the time when it starts.

> **beginning** *noun*
> = birth, commencement (*formal*), opening, origin, outset, start

begrudge *verb* If you begrudge someone something, you are angry or envious because they have it.

begun the past participle of **begin**.

behalf *phrase* To do something on behalf of someone or something means to do it for their benefit or as their representative.

behave *verb* **1** If you behave in a particular way, you act in that way. **2** To behave yourself means to act correctly or properly.

behave verb
1 = act, function, operate, work

behaviour noun Your behaviour is the way in which you behave.

behead verb To behead someone means to cut their head off.

behind preposition 1 at the back of: He was seated behind the desk. 2 responsible for or causing: He was the driving force behind the move. 3 supporting someone: The whole country was behind him. ▶ adverb 4 If you stay behind, you remain after other people have gone. 5 If you leave something behind, you do not take it with you.

behold beholds, beholding, beheld (literary) verb 1 To behold something means to notice it or look at it. ▶ interjection 2 You say 'behold' when you want someone to look at something. > **beholder** noun

beige noun, adjective pale creamy-brown.

being 1 Being is the present participle of **be**. ▶ noun 2 Being is the state or fact of existing: The party came into being in 1923. 3 a living creature, either real or imaginary.

belated adjective (formal) A belated action happens later than it should have done.

belch verb 1 If you belch, you make a sudden noise in your throat because air has risen up from your stomach. 2 If something belches smoke or fire, it sends it out in large amounts. ▶ noun 3 the noise you make when you belch.

beleaguered adjective struggling against difficulties or criticism.

Belgian adjective 1 belonging or relating to Belgium. ▶ noun

2 someone who comes from Belgium.

belief noun 1 a feeling of certainty that something exists or is true. 2 one of the principles of a religion or moral system.

> **belief** noun
> 1 = confidence, conviction, judgment, opinion, trust, view
> 2 = creed, doctrine, dogma, faith, ideology, principle, tenet (formal)

believable adjective possible or likely to be the case.

> **believable** adjective
> = credible, imaginable, likely, plausible, possible, probable

believe verb 1 If you believe that something is true, you accept that it is true. 2 If you believe someone, you accept that they are telling the truth. 3 If you believe in things such as God and miracles, you accept that they exist or happen. 4 If you believe in something such as a plan or system, you are in favour of it. > **believer** noun

> **believe** verb
> 1 = accept, assume, presume, swallow (informal), trust

belittle verb If you belittle someone or something, you make them seem unimportant.

> **belittle** verb
> = deride (formal), detract from, downgrade, scorn, undervalue

bell noun 1 a cup-shaped metal object with a piece inside that swings and hits the sides, producing a ringing sound. 2 an electrical device that rings or buzzes in order to attract attention.

belligerent *adjective* aggressive and keen to start a fight or an argument. ▸ **belligerence** *noun*

bellow *verb* **1** When an animal such as a bull bellows, it makes a loud, deep roaring noise. **2** If someone bellows, they shout in a loud, deep voice.

belly bellies *noun* **1** Your belly is your stomach or the front of your body below your chest. **2** An animal's belly is the underneath part of its body.

belong *verb* **1** If something belongs to you, it is yours and you own it. **2** To belong to a group means to be a member of it. **3** If something belongs in a particular place, that is where it should be.

belongings *plural noun* Your belongings are the things that you own.

beloved *adjective* A beloved person or thing is one that you feel great affection for.

> **beloved** *adjective*
> = adored, cherished, darling, dearest, precious, treasured

below *preposition, adverb* **1** If something is below a line or on the surface of something else, it is lower down: *six inches below soil level*. **2** Below also means at or to a lower point, level or rate: *The temperature fell below zero degrees*.

> **below** *preposition, adverb*
> **1** = beneath, down, lower, under, underneath

belt *noun* **1** a strip of leather or cloth that you fasten round your waist to hold your trousers or skirt up. **2** In a machine, a belt is a

circular strip of rubber that drives moving parts or carries objects along. **3** a specific area of a country: *Poland's industrial belt*.
▸ *verb* **4** (*informal*) To belt someone means to hit them very hard.

bemused *adjective* If you are bemused, you are puzzled or confused.

bench *noun* **1** a long seat that two or more people can sit on. **2** a long, narrow table for working at, for example in a laboratory.

bend bends, bending, bent *verb* **1** When you bend something, you use force to make it curved or angular. **2** When you bend, you move your head and shoulders forwards and downwards. ▸ *noun* **3** a curved part of something.

> **bend** *verb*
> **1** = buckle, curve, turn, twist, warp **2** = arch, bow, crouch, incline, lean, stoop
> ▸ *noun* **3** = arc, corner, curve, loop, turn

beneath *preposition, adjective, adverb* **1** an old-fashioned word for **underneath**. ▸ *preposition* **2** If someone thinks something is beneath them, they think that it is too unimportant for them to bother with.

benefactor *noun* a person who helps to support a person or institution by giving money.

beneficial *adjective* Something that is beneficial is good for people. ▸ **beneficially** *adverb*

> **beneficial** *adjective*
> = advantageous, good for you, healthy, helpful, useful, wholesome

beneficiary beneficiaries *noun* A beneficiary of something is someone who receives money or other benefits from it.

benefit noun 1 The benefits of something are the advantages that it brings to people.
2 Benefit is money given by the government to people who are unemployed or ill. ▶ verb 3 If you benefit from something or something benefits you, it helps you.

> **benefit** noun
> 1 = advantage, asset, boon, gain, good, help, profit, use
> ▶ verb 3 = aid, assist, enhance, further, help, profit

benevolent adjective kind and helpful. > **benevolence** noun

> **benevolent** adjective
> = benign, charitable, compassionate, humane, kind

benign adjective 1 Someone who is benign is kind and gentle. 2 A benign tumour is one that will not cause death or serious illness. > **benignly** adverb

bent 1 Bent is the past tense and past participle of **bend**. ▶ phrase 2 If you are bent on doing something, you are determined to do it.

berate verb (formal) If you berate someone, you scold them angrily.

bereaved adjective (formal) You say that someone is bereaved when a close relative or friend of theirs has recently died. > **bereavement** noun

bereft adjective (literary) If you are bereft of something, you no longer have it.

beret noun a circular flat hat with no brim.

berry berries noun Berries are small, round fruits that grow on bushes or trees.

berserk phrase If someone **goes berserk**, they lose control of themselves and become very violent.

berth noun 1 a space in a harbour where a ship stays when it is being loaded or unloaded.
2 In a boat or caravan, a berth is a bed.

beset adjective (formal) If you are beset by difficulties or doubts, you have a lot of them.

beside preposition If one thing is beside something else, they are next to each other.

> **beside** preposition
> = adjacent to, alongside, close to, near, next to

besiege verb 1 When soldiers besiege a place, they surround it and wait for the people inside to surrender. 2 If you are besieged by people, many people want something from you and continually bother you.

best adjective, adverb 1 the superlative of **good** and **well**.
▶ adverb 2 The thing that you like best is the thing that you prefer to everything else. ▶ noun 3 the thing most preferred.

> **best** adjective, adverb
> 1 = finest, first-rate, foremost, greatest, leading, outstanding, pre-eminent, principal, superlative, supreme, top
> ▶ noun 3 = cream, elite, finest, pick

best man noun The best man at a wedding is the man who acts as the bridegroom's attendant.

bestow verb (formal) If you bestow something on someone, you give it to them.

bet bets, betting, bet verb 1 If you bet on the result of an event, you will win money if something happens and lose money if it does not. ▶ noun 2 the act of betting on something, or the amount of money that you agree to risk. ▶ phrase 3 (informal) You say I bet to indicate that you are sure that something is or will be so: I bet the answer is no. > **betting** noun

betray verb 1 If you betray someone who trusts you, you do something which harms them, such as helping their enemies. 2 If you betray your feelings or thoughts, you show them without intending to. > **betrayal** noun > **betrayer** noun

> **betray** verb
> 1 = break your promise, double-cross (informal), inform on 2 = expose, manifest (formal), reveal, show

better adjective, adverb 1 the comparative of **good** and **well**. ▶ adverb 2 If you like one thing better than another, you like it more than the other thing. ▶ adjective 3 If you are better after an illness, you are no longer ill.

> **better** adjective, adverb
> 1 = finer, grander, greater, higher-quality, nicer, preferable, superior, surpassing, worthier
> ▶ adjective 3 = cured, fitter, fully recovered, healthier, improving, on the mend (informal), recovering, stronger, well

between preposition, adverb 1 If something is between two other things, it is situated or happens in the space or time that separates them. 2 A relationship or difference between two people or things involves only those two.

beverage noun (formal) a drink.

bevy bevies noun a group of people.

beware verb If you tell someone to beware of something, you are warning them that it might be dangerous or harmful.

> **beware** verb
> = be careful, be cautious, be wary, guard against, look out, watch out

bewilder verb If something bewilders you, it is too confusing or difficult for you to understand.

bewitch verb 1 To bewitch someone means to cast a spell on them. 2 If something bewitches you, you are so attracted to it that you cannot pay attention to anything else.

beyond preposition 1 If something is beyond a certain place, it is on the other side of it. 2 If something continues beyond a particular point, it continues further than that point. 3 If someone or something is beyond understanding or help, they cannot be understood or helped.

bias noun Someone who shows bias favours one person or thing unfairly.

> **bias** noun
> = bigotry, favouritism, prejudice

biased; also spelt **biassed** adjective favouring one person or thing unfairly.

biased *adjective*
= one-eyed (*Australian and New Zealand*), one-sided, partial, prejudiced, slanted, weighted

bib *noun* a piece of cloth or plastic which is worn under the chin of very young children when they are eating, to keep their clothes clean.

Bible *noun* (RE) The Bible is the sacred book of the Christian and Jewish religions. > **biblical** *adjective*

bicentenary bicentenaries *noun* The bicentenary of an event is its two-hundredth anniversary.

biceps *noun* (PE) the large muscle on your upper arms.

bicker *verb* When people bicker, they argue or quarrel about unimportant things.

bicycle *noun* a two-wheeled vehicle which you ride by pushing two pedals with your feet.

bid bids, bidding, bade or bid, bidden or bid *noun* 1 an attempt to obtain or do something. 2 an offer to buy something for a certain sum of money. ▶ *verb* 3 If you bid for something, you agree to pay a certain sum of money for it. 4 (*old-fashioned*) If you bid someone a greeting or a farewell, you say it to them.

bide bides, biding, bided *phrase* If you **bide your time**, you wait for a good opportunity before doing something.

big bigger, biggest *adjective* 1 of a large size. 2 of great importance. > **biggish** *adjective* > **bigness** *noun*

big *adjective*
1 = enormous, huge, immense, massive, vast 2 = important, major, powerful, prominent, significant

bigot *noun* someone who has strong and unreasonable opinions which they refuse to change. > **bigoted** *adjective* > **bigotry** *noun*

bike *noun* (*informal*) a bicycle or motorcycle.

bikini bikinis *noun* a small two-piece swimming costume worn by women.

bilateral *adjective* A bilateral agreement is one made between two groups or countries.

bile *noun* Bile is a bitter yellow liquid produced by the liver which helps the digestion of fat. In the Middle Ages, it was believed to cause anger.

bilge *noun* the lowest part of a ship, where dirty water collects.

bilingual *adjective* involving or using two languages.

bill *noun* 1 a written statement of how much is owed for goods or services. 2 a formal statement of a proposed new law that is discussed and then voted on in Parliament. 3 a notice or a poster. 4 A bird's bill is its beak. ▶ *verb* 5 If you bill someone, you give or send them a bill for goods or services you have supplied.

bill *noun*
1 = account, charges, invoice, statement

billboard *noun* a large board on which advertisements are displayed.

billiards *noun* Billiards is a game played on a large table, in which a long stick called a cue is used to strike one of three balls. The aim is to hit a second ball with the first so that either the third ball is also hit or one of the balls goes

B

into one of the six pockets at the edges of the table.

billion *noun* a thousand million. Formerly, a billion was a million million. > **billionth** *adjective*

billow *verb* 1 When things made of cloth billow, they swell out and flap slowly in the wind. 2 When smoke or cloud billows, it spreads upwards and outwards.

bin *noun* a container, especially one that you put rubbish in.

binary *adjective* (ICT) The binary system expresses numbers using only two digits, 0 and 1.

bind binds, binding, bound *verb* 1 If you bind something, you tie rope or string round it so that it is held firmly. 2 If something binds you to a course of action, it makes you act in that way.

binding *adjective* 1 If a promise or agreement is binding, it must be obeyed. ▶ *noun* 2 The binding of a book is its cover.

binge *noun* (*informal*) a wild bout of drinking or eating too much.

bingo *noun* Bingo is a game in which players aim to match the numbers that someone calls out with the numbers on the card that they have been given.

binoculars *plural noun* Binoculars are an instrument with lenses for both eyes, which you look through in order to see objects far away.

biochemistry *noun* Biochemistry is the study of the chemistry of living things. > **biochemical** *adjective* > **biochemist** *noun*

biodegradable *adjective* If something is biodegradable, it can be broken down into its natural elements by the action of bacteria.

biodiversity *noun* (SCIENCE) the existence of a wide variety of species in a particular area.

biography biographies *noun* A biography is an account of someone's life, written by someone else. Compare **autobiography**. > **biographer** *noun* > **biographical** *adjective*

biology *noun* Biology is the study of living things. > **biological** *adjective* > **biologically** *adverb* > **biologist** *noun*

bionic *adjective* having a part of the body that works electronically.

biopsy biopsies *noun* an examination under a microscope of tissue from a living body to find out the cause of a disease.

birch *noun* a tall deciduous tree with thin branches and thin bark.

bird *noun* an animal with two legs, two wings, and feathers.

birth *noun* 1 The birth of a baby is when it comes out of its mother's womb at the beginning of its life. 2 The birth of something is its beginning.

birthday *noun* Your birthday is the anniversary of the date on which you were born.

biscuit *noun* a small flat cake made of baked dough.

bisexual *adjective* attracted to people of different genders.

bishop *noun* 1 (RE) a high-ranking member of the clergy in some Christian Churches. 2 In chess, a bishop is a piece that is moved diagonally across the board.

bison *noun* A bison is a large hairy animal, related to cattle, with a large head and shoulders. Bison used to be very common on the prairies in North America, but they are now almost extinct.

bistro bistros *noun* a small informal restaurant.

bit 1 Bit is the past tense of **bite**. ▶ *noun* 2 A bit of something is a small amount of it. ▶ *phrase* 3 A bit means slightly or to a small extent.

> **bit** *noun*
> 2 = crumb, fragment, grain, part, piece, scrap

bitch *noun* a female dog.

bite bites, biting, bit, bitten *verb* 1 To bite something or someone is to cut it or cut through it with the teeth. ▶ *noun* 2 A small amount that you bite off something with your teeth. 3 The injury you get when an animal or insect bites you.

> **bite** *verb*
> 1 = chew, gnaw, nibble, nip

bitter *adjective* 1 If someone is bitter, they feel angry and resentful. 2 A bitter disappointment or experience makes people feel angry or unhappy for a long time afterwards. 3 In a bitter argument or war, people argue or fight fiercely and angrily. 4 A bitter wind is an extremely cold wind. 5 Something that tastes bitter has a sharp, unpleasant taste.

> **bitter** *adjective*
> 1 = acrimonious (*formal*), begrudging, embittered, rancorous (*formal*), resentful, sour 5 = acid, acrid, astringent, sharp, sour, tart

bizarre *adjective* very strange or eccentric.

bizarre *adjective* = curious, eccentric, extraordinary, odd, outlandish, peculiar, queer (*old-fashioned*), strange, weird

black *noun*, *adjective* 1 Black is the darkest possible colour, like tar or soot. 2 Someone who is Black is a member of a dark-skinned race. 3 Black coffee or tea has no milk or cream added to it. 4 Black humour involves jokes about death and suffering. > **black out** *verb* If you black out, you lose consciousness.

blackberry blackberries *noun* Blackberries are small black fruits that grow on prickly bushes called brambles.

blackboard *noun* a dark-coloured board on which people can write or draw using chalk.

black box *noun* A black box is an electronic device in an aircraft which collects and stores information during flights. This information can be used to provide evidence if an accident occurs.

blackcurrant *noun* Blackcurrants are very small dark purple fruits that grow in bunches on bushes.

blacken *verb* To blacken something means to make it black.

blacklist *noun* 1 a list of people or organisations who are thought to be untrustworthy or disloyal. ▶ *verb* 2 When someone is blacklisted, they are put on a blacklist.

blackmail *verb* 1 If someone blackmails another person, they threaten to reveal an unpleasant secret about them unless that

B

person gives them money or does something for them. ▶ noun
2 Blackmail is the action of blackmailing people.

black market noun If something is bought or sold on the black market, it is bought or sold illegally.

blackout noun If you have a blackout, you lose consciousness for a short time.

blacksmith noun a person whose job is making things out of iron, such as horseshoes.

bladder noun the part of your body where urine is held until it leaves your body.

blade noun 1 The blade of a weapon or cutting tool is the sharp part of it. 2 The blades of a propeller are the thin, flat parts that turn round. 3 A blade of grass is a single piece of it.

blame verb 1 If someone blames you for something bad that has happened, they believe you caused it. ▶ noun 2 The blame for something bad that happens is the responsibility for letting it happen.

> **blame** verb
> 1 = accuse, charge, hold responsible
> ▶ noun 2 = accountability, fault, guilt, liability, rap (slang), responsibility

blameless adjective Someone who is blameless has not done anything wrong.

blanch verb If you blanch, you suddenly become very pale.

bland adjective tasteless, dull or boring.

blank adjective 1 Something that is blank has nothing on it. 2 If you

look blank, your face shows no feeling or interest. ▶ noun 3 If your mind is a blank, you cannot think of anything or remember anything.

> **blank** adjective
> 1 = bare, clean, clear, empty, plain, unmarked 2 = deadpan, dull, empty, impassive, vacant

blanket noun 1 a large rectangle of thick cloth that is put on a bed to keep people warm. 2 A blanket of something such as snow is a thick covering of it.

blare verb To blare means to make a loud, unpleasant noise.

blasphemy noun Blasphemy is speech or behaviour that shows disrespect for God or religion.
> **blasphemous** adjective

blast verb 1 When people blast a hole in something, they make a hole with an explosion. ▶ noun 2 a big explosion, especially one caused by a bomb. 3 a sudden strong rush of wind or air.

blatant adjective If you describe something you think is bad as blatant, you mean that rather than hide it, those responsible actually seem to be making it obvious.

blaze noun 1 a large, hot fire. 2 A blaze of light or colour is a great or strong amount of it. 3 A blaze of publicity or attention is a lot of it. ▶ verb 4 If something blazes, it burns or shines brightly.

blazer noun a kind of jacket, often in the colours of a school or sports team.

bleach verb 1 To bleach material or hair means to make it white or lighter in colour, usually by using a chemical. ▶ noun 2 Bleach is a chemical that is used to make material white or to clean thoroughly and kill germs.

bleak *adjective* 1 If a situation is bleak, it is bad and seems unlikely to improve. 2 If a place is bleak, it is cold, bare and exposed to the wind.

bleat *verb* 1 When sheep or goats bleat, they make a high-pitched cry. ▶ *noun* 2 the high-pitched cry that a sheep or goat makes.

bleed bleeds, bleeding, bled *verb* When you bleed, you lose blood as a result of an injury.

bleep *noun* a short high-pitched sound made by an electrical device such as an alarm.

blemish *noun* a mark that spoils the appearance of something.

blend *verb* 1 When you blend substances, you mix them together to form a single substance. 2 When colours or sounds blend, they combine in a pleasing way. ▶ *noun* 3 A blend of things is a mixture of them, especially one that is pleasing. 4 a word formed by joining together the beginning and the end of two other words; for example, 'brunch' is a blend of 'breakfast' and 'lunch'.

blend *verb*
1 = combine, merge, mingle, mix 2 = go well, harmonise
▶ *noun* 3 = alloy, amalgamation, combination, compound, fusion, mix, mixture

blender *noun* a machine used for mixing liquids and foods at high speed.

bless blesses, blessing, blessed or blest *verb* When a priest blesses

people or things, he or she asks for God's protection for them.

bless *verb*
= anoint, consecrate, dedicate, hallow

blessed *adjective* If someone is blessed with a particular quality or skill, they have it.

blessing *noun* 1 something good that you are thankful for. 2 If something is done with someone's blessing, they approve of it and support it.

blessing *noun*
1 = benefit, boon, gift, godsend, help 2 = approval, backing, consent, leave, permission, support

blew the past tense of **blow**.

blight *noun* 1 something that damages or spoils other things.
▶ *verb* 2 When something is blighted, it is seriously harmed.

blind *adjective* 1 Someone who is blind cannot see. 2 If someone is blind to a particular fact, they are not aware of it. ▶ *verb* 3 If something blinds you, you become unable to see, either for a short time or permanently. ▶ *noun* 4 a roll of cloth or paper that you pull down over a window to keep out the light.

blindfold *noun* 1 a strip of cloth tied over someone's eyes so that they cannot see. ▶ *verb* 2 To blindfold someone means to cover their eyes with a strip of cloth.

blinding *adjective* A blinding light is so bright that it hurts your eyes.

blindingly *adverb* (*informal*) If something is blindingly obvious, it is very obvious indeed.

bling (*informal*) *noun* **1** jewellery that looks expensive in a vulgar way. ▶ *adjective* **2** flashy; expensive-looking in a vulgar way.

blink *verb* When you blink, you close your eyes rapidly for a moment. Blinking is an involuntary action that keeps the eyes moist.

blinkers *plural noun* Blinkers are two pieces of leather placed at the side of a horse's eyes so that it can only see straight ahead.

bliss *noun* Bliss is a state of complete happiness. > **blissful** *adjective* > **blissfully** *adverb*

blister *noun* **1** a small bubble on your skin containing watery liquid, caused by a burn or rubbing. ▶ *verb* **2** If someone's skin blisters, blisters appear on it as result of burning or rubbing.

blistering *adjective* **1** Blistering heat is very hot. **2** A blistering remark expresses great anger or criticism.

blitz *noun* **1** (HISTORY) a bombing attack by enemy aircraft on a city. **2** a sudden intensive attack or concerted effort.

blizzard *noun* a heavy snowstorm with strong winds.

bloated *adjective* Something that is bloated is much larger than normal, often because there is a lot of liquid or gas inside it.

blob *noun* a small amount of a thick or sticky substance.

> **blob** *noun*
> = bead, dab, drop, droplet

bloc *noun* A group of countries or political parties with similar aims acting together is often called a bloc.

block *noun* **1** A block of flats or offices is a large building containing flats or offices. **2** In a town, a block is an area of land with streets on all its sides. **3** A block of something is a large rectangular piece of it. ▶ *verb* **4** To block a road or channel means to put something across it so that nothing can get through. **5** If something blocks your view, it is in the way and prevents you from seeing what you want to see. **6** If someone blocks something, they prevent it from happening.

> **block** *noun*
> **3** = bar, brick, chunk, ingot, lump, piece
> ▶ *verb* **4** = choke, clog, obstruct, plug **6** = bar, check, halt, obstruct, stop, thwart

blockade *noun* **1** an action that prevents goods from reaching a place. ▶ *verb* **2** When a place is blockaded, supplies are prevented from reaching it.

blockage *noun* When there is a blockage in a pipe or tunnel, something is clogging it.

> **blockage** *noun*
> = block, obstruction, stoppage

blog blogs, blogging, blogged *noun* **1** a person's online diary that he or she puts on the internet so that other people can read it. ▶ *verb* **2** If you blog, you write a blog. > **blogging** *verb*

blogger *noun* a person who keeps a blog.

bloke *noun* (*informal*) a man.

blonde; also spelt **blond** *adjective* **1** Blonde hair is pale yellow in colour. The spelling 'blond' is used when referring to men. ▶ *noun* **2** A blonde, or blond, is a person with light-coloured hair.

blood *noun* 1 Blood is the red liquid that is pumped by the heart round the bodies of human beings and other mammals.
▶ *phrase* 2 If something cruel is done **in cold blood**, it is done deliberately and without showing any emotion.

bloodless *adjective* 1 If someone's face or skin is bloodless, it is very pale. 2 In a bloodless coup or revolution, nobody is killed.

blood pressure *noun* Your blood pressure is a measure of the force with which your blood is being pumped round your body.

bloodshed *noun* When there is bloodshed, people are killed or wounded.

bloodshot *adjective* If a person's eyes are bloodshot, the white parts have become red.

bloodstream *noun* the flow of blood through your body.

bloodthirsty *adjective* Someone who is bloodthirsty enjoys using or watching violence.

blood transfusion *noun* a process in which blood is injected into the body of someone who has lost a lot of blood.

blood vessel *noun* Blood vessels are the narrow tubes in your body through which your blood flows.

bloody **bloodier**, **bloodiest** *adjective, adverb* 1 'Bloody' is a common swearword, used to express anger or annoyance.
▶ *adjective* 2 A bloody event is one in which a lot of people are killed. 3 Bloody also means covered with blood.

bloom *noun* 1 a flower on a plant. ▶ *verb* 2 When a plant blooms, it

produces flowers. 3 When something like a feeling blooms, it grows.

blossom *noun* 1 Blossom is the growth of flowers that appears on a tree before the fruit. ▶ *verb* 2 When a tree blossoms, it produces blossom.

blot **blots**, **blotting**, **blotted** *noun* 1 a drop of ink that has been spilled on a surface. 2 A blot on someone's reputation is a mistake or piece of bad behaviour that spoils their reputation.
> **blot out** *verb* To blot something out means to be in front of it and prevent it from being seen.

blotch *noun* a stain or a patch of a different colour. > **blotchy** *adjective*

blouse *noun* a light shirt, worn by a girl or a woman.

blow **blows**, **blowing**, **blew**, **blown** *verb* 1 When the wind blows, the air moves. 2 If something blows or is blown somewhere, the wind moves it there. 3 If you blow a whistle or horn, you make a sound by blowing into it. ▶ *noun* 4 If you receive a blow, someone or something hits you. 5 something that makes you very disappointed or unhappy. > **blow up** *verb* 1 To blow something up means to destroy it with an explosion. 2 To blow up a balloon or a tyre means to fill it with air.

---

blow *verb*

2 = buffet, drive, flutter, sweep, waft, whirl
▶ *noun* 4 = bang, clout (*informal*), knock, smack, thump, whack (*informal*) 5 = bombshell, disappointment, misfortune, setback, shock, upset

blubber *noun* The blubber of animals such as whales and seals is the layer of fat that protects them from the cold.

bludgeon *verb* To bludgeon someone means to hit them several times with a heavy object.

blue bluer, bluest *adjective, noun* 1 Blue is the colour of the sky on a clear, sunny day. ▶ *phrase* 2 If something happens **out of the blue**, it happens suddenly and unexpectedly.

blue-collar *adjective* Blue-collar workers do physical work as opposed to office work.

blueprint *noun* a plan of how something is expected to work.

blues *noun* The blues is a type of music which is similar to jazz, but is always slow and sad.

bluff *noun* 1 an attempt to make someone wrongly believe that you are in a strong position. ▶ *verb* 2 If you are bluffing, you are trying to make someone believe that you are in a position of strength.

blunder *verb* 1 If you blunder, you make a silly mistake. ▶ *noun* 2 a silly mistake.

blunt *adjective* 1 A blunt object has a rounded point or edge, rather than a sharp one. 2 If you are blunt, you say exactly what you think, without trying to be polite.

> **blunt** *adjective*
> 1 = dull, rounded, unsharpened
> 2 = bluff, brusque, forthright, frank, outspoken, straightforward

blur blurs, blurring, blurred *noun* 1 a shape or area which you cannot see clearly because it has no distinct outline or because it is moving very fast. ▶ *verb* 2 To blur the differences between things means to make them no longer clear.

blush *verb* 1 If you blush, your face becomes red, because you are embarrassed or ashamed. ▶ *noun* 2 the red colour on someone's face when they are embarrassed or ashamed.

> **blush** *verb*
> 1 = colour, flush, go red, turn crimson, turn red, turn scarlet
> ▶ *noun* 2 = colour, flush, glow

bluster *verb* 1 When someone blusters, they behave aggressively because they are angry or frightened. ▶ *noun* 2 Bluster is aggressive behaviour by someone who is angry or frightened.

blustery *adjective* Blustery weather is rough and windy.

boa *noun* 1 A boa, or a boa constrictor, is a large snake that kills its prey by coiling round it and crushing it. 2 a long thin scarf of feathers or fur.

boar *noun* a male wild pig, or a male domestic pig used for breeding.

board *noun* 1 a long, flat piece of wood. 2 the group of people who control a company or organisation. 3 Board is the meals provided when you stay somewhere. ▶ *verb* 4 If you board a ship or aircraft, you get on it or in it. ▶ *phrase* 5 If you are **on board** a ship or aircraft, you are on it or in it.

boarder *noun* a pupil who lives at school during the term.

boarding school *noun* a school where the pupils live during the term.

boardroom *noun* a room where the board of a company meets.

boast *verb* 1 If you boast about your possessions or achievements, you talk about them proudly. ▶ *noun* 2 something that you say which shows that you are proud of what you own or have done.

> **boast** *verb*
> 1 = brag, crow (*informal*), skite (*Australian and New Zealand*; *informal*)

boastful *adjective* tending to brag about things.

> **boastful** *adjective*
> = bragging, cocky, conceited, crowing, egotistical, swaggering

boat *noun* a small vehicle for travelling across water.

bob bobs, bobbing, bobbed *verb* 1 When something bobs, it moves up and down. ▶ *noun* 2 a woman's hair style in which her hair is cut level with her chin.

bode *phrase* (*literary*) If something bodes well, or bodes ill, it makes you think that something bad, or good, will happen.

bodice *noun* the upper part of a dress.

bodily *adjective* 1 relating to the body. ▶ *adverb* 2 involving the whole of someone's body.

body bodies *noun* 1 Your body is either all your physical parts, or just the main part not including your head, arms and legs. 2 a person's dead body. 3 the main part of a car or aircraft, not including the engine. 4 A body of people is an organised group.

> **body** *noun*
> 1 = build, figure, form, frame, physique, shape 2 = carcass, corpse, dead body, remains 4 = association, band, company, confederation, organisation, society

bodyguard *noun* a person employed to protect someone.

bodywork *noun* the outer part of a motor vehicle.

bog *noun* an area of land which is always wet and spongy.

boggle *verb* If your mind boggles at something, you find it difficult to imagine or understand.

bogus *adjective* not genuine: *a bogus doctor.*

bohemian *adjective* Someone who is bohemian does not behave in the same way as most other people in society, and is usually involved in the arts.

boil *verb* 1 When a hot liquid boils, bubbles appear in it and it starts to give off steam. 2 When you boil a kettle, you heat it until the water in it boils. 3 When you boil food, you cook it in boiling water. ▶ *noun* 4 a red swelling on your skin.

> **boil** *verb*
> 1 = bubble, fizz, foam, froth
> ▶ *noun* 4 = blister, swelling, tumour

boiler *noun* a piece of equipment which burns fuel to provide hot water.

boiling *adjective* (*informal*) very hot.

boisterous *adjective* Someone who is boisterous is noisy and lively.

bold *adjective* 1 confident and not shy or embarrassed. 2 not afraid of risk or danger. **3** clear and noticeable: *bold colours.*

bold *adjective*
1 = brash, brazen, cheeky, confident, forward, impudent **2** = adventurous, brave, courageous, daring, fearless, intrepid **3** = bright, flashy, loud, striking, strong, vivid

bolster *verb* To bolster something means to support it or make it stronger.

bolt *noun* **1** a metal bar that you slide across a door or window in order to fasten it. **2** a metal object which screws into a nut and is used to fasten things together. ▶ *verb* **3** If you bolt a door or window, you fasten it using a bolt. If you bolt things together, you fasten them together using a bolt. **4** To bolt means to escape or run away. **5** To bolt food means to eat it quickly.

bolt *verb*
4 = dash, escape, flee, fly, run away, run off, rush

bomb *noun* **1** a container filled with material that explodes when it hits something or is set off by a timer. ▶ *verb* **2** When a place is bombed, it is attacked with bombs.

bomb *noun*
1 = device, explosive, missile, rocket, shell, torpedo
▶ *verb* **2** = attack, blow up, bombard, destroy, shell, torpedo

bombard *verb* **1** To bombard a place means to attack it with heavy gunfire or bombs. **2** If you are bombarded with something, you are made to face a great deal of it.

bomber *noun* **1** an aircraft that drops bombs. **2** a person who plants or detonates bombs.

bombshell *noun* a sudden piece of shocking or upsetting news.

bond *noun* **1** a close relationship between people. **2** (*literary*) Bonds are chains or ropes used to tie a prisoner up. **3** a certificate which records that you have lent money to a business and that it will repay you the loan with interest. **4** (SCIENCE) In chemistry, a bond is the means by which atoms or groups of atoms are combined in molecules. **5** Bonds are also feelings or obligations that force you to behave in a particular way: *the social bonds of community.* ▶ *verb* **6** When two things bond or are bonded, they become closely linked or attached.

bond *noun*
1 = attachment, connection, link, relation, tie, union **5** = agreement, contract, obligation, pledge, promise, word
▶ *verb* **6** = bind, fasten, fuse, glue, paste

bondage *noun* Bondage is the condition of being someone's slave.

bone *noun* Bones are the hard parts that form the framework of a person's or animal's body.

bonfire *noun* a large fire made outdoors, often to burn rubbish.

bonnet *noun* **1** the metal cover over a car's engine. **2** a baby's or woman's hat tied under the chin.

bonus *noun* **1** an amount of money added to your usual pay. **2** Something that is a bonus is a good thing that you get in addition to something else.

bony *noun* **bonier, boniest** *adjective* Bony people or animals are thin, with very little flesh covering their bones.

boo *noun* 1 a shout of disapproval.
▶ *verb* 2 When people boo, they shout 'boo' to show their disapproval.

book *noun* 1 a number of pages held together inside a cover.
▶ *verb* 2 When you book something such as a room, you arrange to have it or use it at a particular time.

> **book** *noun*
> 1 = publication, textbook, volume, work
> ▶ *verb* 2 = charter, engage, organise, reserve, schedule

bookcase *noun* a piece of furniture with shelves for books.

booking *noun* an arrangement to book something such as a hotel room.

booklet *noun* a small book with a paper cover.

bookmaker *noun* a person who makes a living by taking people's bets and paying them when they win.

bookmark *noun* 1 a piece of card which you put between the pages of a book to mark your place. 2 In computing, a bookmark is the address of a website that you put into a list on your computer so that you can return to it easily.
▶ *verb* 3 If you bookmark a website, you put its address into a list on your computer so that you can return to it easily.

boom *noun* 1 a rapid increase in something. 2 a loud deep echoing sound. ▶ *verb* 3 When something booms, it increases rapidly. 4 To

boom means to make a loud, deep, echoing sound.

boomerang *noun* a curved wooden missile that can be thrown so that it returns to the thrower, originally used as a weapon by Aboriginal Australians.

boon *noun* Something that is a boon makes life better or easier.

boost *verb* 1 To boost something means to cause it to improve or increase. ▶ *noun* 2 an improvement or increase.
> **booster** *noun*

boot *noun* 1 Boots are strong shoes that come up over your ankle and sometimes your calf. 2 the covered space in a car, usually at the back, for carrying things in.
▶ *verb* 3 (*informal*) If you boot something, you kick it.

booth *noun* 1 a small partly enclosed area: *a photo booth*. 2 a stall where you can buy goods.

booty *noun* Booty is valuable things taken from a place, especially by soldiers after a battle.

booze (*informal*) *noun* 1 Booze is alcoholic drink. ▶ *verb* 2 When people booze, they drink alcohol.
> **boozer** *noun* > **boozy** *adjective*

border *noun* 1 the dividing line between two places or things. 2 a strip or band round the edge of something. 3 a long flower bed in a garden. ▶ *verb* 4 To border something means to form a boundary along the side of it.

> **border** *noun*
> 1 = borderline, boundary, frontier, line 2 = bounds, edge, limits, margin, rim
> ▶ *verb* 4 = edge, fringe, hem, rim, trim

borderline *adjective* only just acceptable as a member of a class or group.

bore *verb* 1 If something bores you, you find it dull and not at all interesting. 2 If you bore a hole in something, you make it using a tool such as a drill. 3 Bore is also the past tense of **bear**. ▶ *noun* 4 someone or something that bores you.

bored *adjective* If you are bored, you are impatient because you do not find something interesting or because you have nothing to do.

> **bored** *adjective*
> = fed up, tired, uninterested,
> wearied

boredom *noun* a lack of interest.

> **boredom** *noun*
> = apathy, dullness, flatness,
> monotony, tedium, weariness

boring *adjective* lacking interest.

> **boring** *adjective*
> = dull, flat, humdrum,
> monotonous, tedious, tiresome

born *verb* 1 When a baby is born, it comes out of its mother's womb at the beginning of its life. ▶ *adjective* 2 You use 'born' to mean that someone has a particular quality from birth: *a born pessimist*.

borne the past participle of **bear**.

borough *noun* a town, or a district within a large town, that has its own council.

borrow *verb* If you borrow something that belongs to someone else, they let you have it for a period of time. > **borrower** *noun*

Bosnian *adjective* 1 belonging or relating to Bosnia. ▶ *noun*

2 someone who comes from Bosnia.

bosom *noun* 1 A woman's bosom is her chest. ▶ *adjective* 2 A bosom friend is a very close friend.

boss bosses, bossing, bossed *noun* 1 Someone's boss is the person in charge of the place where they work. ▶ *verb* 2 If someone bosses you around, they keep telling you what to do.

> **boss** *noun*
> 1 = chief, director, employer,
> head, leader, manager

bossy bossier, bossiest *adjective* A bossy person enjoys telling other people what to do. > **bossiness** *noun*

> **bossy** *adjective*
> = authoritarian, dictatorial,
> domineering, imperious,
> overbearing

botany *noun* Botany is the scientific study of plants.
> **botanic** or **botanical** *adjective*
> **botanist** *noun*

botch *verb* (*informal*) If you botch something, you do it badly or clumsily.

> **botch** *verb*
> = bungle (*informal*), mar, mess
> up

both *adjective*, *pronoun* 'Both' is used when saying something about two things or people.

bother *verb* 1 If you do not bother to do something, you do not do it because it takes too much effort or it seems unnecessary. 2 If something bothers you, you are worried or concerned about it. If you do not bother about it, you are not concerned about it. 3 If you bother someone, you interrupt

them when they are busy. ▶ *noun*
4 Bother is trouble, fuss or
difficulty. > **bothersome** *adjective*

bother *verb*
2 = annoy, concern, disturb, get
on someone's nerves (*informal*),
trouble, worry
▶ *noun* **4** = annoyance,
difficulty, inconvenience,
irritation, trouble, worry

bottle *noun* **1** a glass or plastic
container for keeping liquids in.
▶ *verb* **2** To bottle something
means to store it in bottles.
> **bottle up** *verb* If you bottle up
strong feelings, you do not let
yourself think about them.

bottleneck *noun* a narrow section
of road where traffic has to slow
down or stop.

bottom *noun* **1** The bottom of
something is its lowest part.
2 Your bottom is your buttocks.
▶ *adjective* **3** The bottom thing in a
series of things is the lowest one.

bottom *noun*
1 = base, bed, depths, floor, foot
▶ *adjective* **3** = base, basement,
ground, lowest

bought the past tense and past
participle of **buy**.

boulder *noun* a large rounded
rock.

boulevard *noun* a wide street in a
city, usually with trees along each
side.

bounce *verb* When an object
bounces, it springs back from
something after hitting it.

bounce *verb*
= rebound, ricochet

bouncy bouncier, bounciest
adjective **1** Someone who is bouncy
is lively and enthusiastic.

2 Something that is bouncy is
capable of bouncing or being
bounced on.

bound *adjective* **1** If you say that
something is bound to happen,
you mean that it is certain to
happen. **2** If a person or a vehicle
is bound for a place, they are
going there. **3** If someone is
bound by an agreement or
regulation, they must obey it.
▶ *noun* **4** a large leap. **5** (*in plural*)
Bounds are limits which restrict
or control something. ▶ *phrase*
6 If a place is **out of bounds**, you
are forbidden to go there. ▶ *verb*
7 When animals or people bound,
they move quickly with large
leaps. **8** Bound is also the past
tense and past participle of **bind**.

boundary boundaries *noun*
something that indicates the
farthest limit of anything.

boundless *adjective* without end
or limit.

bountiful *adjective* (*literary*) freely
available in large amounts.

bounty *noun* **1** (*literary*) Bounty is a
generous supply. **2** Someone's
bounty is their generosity in
giving a lot of something.

bouquet *noun* an attractively
arranged bunch of flowers.

bout *noun* **1** If you have a bout of
something such as an illness, you
have it for a short time. **2** If you
have a bout of doing something,
you do it enthusiastically for a
short time. **3** a boxing or
wrestling match.

boutique *noun* a small shop that
sells fashionable clothes.

bovine *adjective* (*technical*) relating
to cattle.

bow¹ *verb* **1** When you bow, you
bend your body or lower your

head as a sign of respect or greeting. **2** If you bow to something, you give in to it. ▶ *noun* **3** the movement you make when you bow. **4** the front part of a ship.

bow² *noun* **1** a knot with two loops and two loose ends. **2** a long thin piece of wood with horsehair stretched along it, which you use to play a violin. **3** a long flexible piece of wood used for shooting arrows.

bowel *noun* Your bowels are the tubes leading from your stomach, through which waste passes before it leaves your body.

bowl *noun* **1** A bowl is a round container with a wide uncovered top, used for holding liquid or for serving food. **2** A bowl is also the hollow, rounded part of something. **3** (PE) A bowl is a large heavy ball used in the game of bowls or in bowling. ▶ *verb* **4** (PE) In cricket, to bowl means to throw the ball towards the batter; if a batter is bowled, or bowled out, their wicket is knocked over by the ball and they are out. > **bowler** *noun*

bowling *noun* Bowling is a game in which you roll a heavy ball down a narrow track towards a group of wooden objects called pins and try to knock them down.

bowls *noun* Bowls is a game in which the players try to roll large wooden balls as near as possible to a small ball.

box *noun* **1** a container with a firm base and sides and usually a lid. **2** On a form, a box is a rectangular space which you have to fill in. **3** In a theatre, a box is a small separate area where a few people can watch the performance together. ▶ *verb* **4** To box means to fight someone according to the rules of boxing.

> **box** *noun*
> **1** = carton, case, chest, container, trunk

boxer *noun* **1** a person who boxes. **2** a type of medium-sized, smooth-haired dog with a flat face.

boxing *noun* Boxing is a sport in which two people fight using their fists, wearing padded gloves.

box office *noun* the place where tickets are sold in a theatre or cinema.

boy *noun* a male child. > **boyhood** *noun* > **boyish** *adjective*

> **boy** *noun*
> = kid (*informal*), lad (*informal*), schoolboy, youngster, youth

boycott *verb* **1** If you boycott an organisation or event, you refuse to have anything to do with it. ▶ *noun* **2** the boycotting of an organisation or event.

> **boycott** *verb*
> **1** = blacklist, embargo, exclude

boyfriend *noun* Someone's boyfriend is the man or boy with whom they are having a romantic relationship.

bra *noun* a piece of underwear worn by a woman to support her breasts.

braaivleis or **braai** *braais noun* In South African English, a braaivleis is a picnic where meat is cooked on an open fire.

brace *verb* **1** When you brace yourself, you stiffen your body to steady yourself. **2** If you brace yourself for something unpleasant, you prepare yourself to deal with it. ▶ *noun* **3** an object fastened to something to straighten or support it. **4** (*in plural*) Braces are a pair of straps worn over the shoulders and fastened to the trousers to hold them up.

bracelet *noun* a chain or band worn around someone's wrist as an ornament.

bracing *adjective* Something that is bracing makes you feel fit and full of energy.

bracken *noun* Bracken is a plant like a large fern that grows on hills and in woods.

bracket *noun* **1** (ENGLISH) Brackets are a pair of written marks, ( ) or [ ], placed round a word or sentence that is not part of the main text, or to show that the items inside the brackets belong together. **2** a range between two limits, for example of ages or prices: *the four-figure price bracket.* **3** a piece of metal or wood fastened to a wall to support something such as a shelf.

brag brags, bragging, bragged *verb* When someone brags, they boast about their achievements.

> **brag** *verb*
> = boast, crow (*informal*), skite (*Australian and New Zealand*; *informal*)

braid *noun* **1** Braid is a strip of decorated cloth used to decorate clothes or curtains. **2** a length of hair which has been plaited and tied. ▶ *verb* **3** To braid hair or thread means to plait it.

Braille *noun* Braille is a system of printing for blind people in which letters are represented by raised dots that can be felt with the fingers. It was created by the French inventor Louis Braille.

brain *noun* **1** Your brain is the mass of nerve tissue inside your head that controls your body and enables you to think and feel; also used to refer to your mind and the way that you think: *I admired his legal brain.* **2** (*in plural*) If you say that someone has brains, you mean that they are very intelligent.

brainchild *noun* (*informal*) Someone's brainchild is something that they have invented or created.

brainwash *verb* If people are brainwashed into believing something, they accept it without question because they are told it repeatedly.
> **brainwashing** *noun*

brainwave *noun* (*informal*) a clever idea you think of suddenly.

brainy brainier, brainiest *adjective* (*informal*) clever.

braise *verb* To braise food means to fry it for a short time, then cook it slowly in a little liquid.

brake *noun* **1** a device for making a vehicle stop or slow down. ▶ *verb* **2** When a driver brakes, he or she makes a vehicle stop or slow down by using its brakes.

bran *noun* Bran is the ground husks that are left over after flour has been made from wheat grains.

branch *noun* **1** The branches of a tree are the parts that grow out from its trunk. **2** A branch of an organisation is one of a number of its offices or shops. **3** A branch of a subject is one of its areas of study or activity. ▶ verb **4** A road that branches off from another road splits off from it to lead in a different direction. > **branch out** verb To branch out means to take up an additional pursuit.

brand noun **1** A brand of something is a particular kind or make of it. ▶ verb **2** When an animal is branded, a mark is burned on its skin to show who owns it.

brandish verb (literary) If you brandish something, you wave it vigorously.

brand-new adjective completely new.

brandy brandies noun a strong alcoholic drink, usually made from wine.

brash adjective If someone is brash, they are overconfident or rather rude.

brass noun **1** Brass is a yellow-coloured metal made from copper and zinc. **2** In an orchestra, the brass or brass section consists of instruments made of brass such as trumpets and trombones.

brat noun (informal) A badly behaved child may be referred to as a brat.

bravado noun Bravado is a display of courage intended to impress other people.

brave adjective **1** A brave person is willing to do dangerous things and does not show any fear. ▶ verb **2** If you brave an unpleasant or dangerous situation, you face up to it in order to do something.

> **brave** adjective
> **1** = bold, courageous, fearless, heroic, plucky, valiant
> ▶ verb **2** = face, stand up to

bravery noun the quality of being courageous.

> **bravery** noun
> = boldness, courage, fortitude, heroism, pluck, valour

brawl noun **1** a rough fight. ▶ verb **2** When people brawl, they take part in a rough fight.

brawn noun Brawn is physical strength. > **brawny** adjective

brazen adjective When someone's behaviour is brazen, they do not care if other people think they are behaving wrongly.

Brazilian adjective **1** belonging or relating to Brazil. ▶ noun **2** someone who comes from Brazil.

breach verb **1** (formal) If you breach an agreement or law, you break it. **2** To breach a barrier means to make a gap in it. ▶ noun **3** A breach of an agreement or law is an action that breaks it. **4** a gap or break.

> **breach** noun
> **3** = infringement, offence, trespass, violation **4** = crack, gap, hole, opening, rift, split

bread noun a food made from flour and water, usually raised with yeast, and baked.

breadth noun The breadth of something is the distance between its two sides.

breadwinner noun the person who earns the money in a family.

break breaks, breaking, broke, broken ▶ verb **1** When an object breaks, it is damaged and separates into pieces. **2** If you break a rule or promise, you fail to keep it. **3** To break something means to end or interrupt it: *Radio contact was broken.* **4** When a boy's voice breaks, it becomes permanently deeper. **5** When a wave breaks, it falls and becomes foam. ▶ *noun* **6** A short period during which you rest or do something different. > **breakable** *adjective* > **break down** *verb* **1** When a machine or a vehicle breaks down, it stops working. **2** When a discussion or relationship breaks down, it ends because of problems or disagreements. > **break up** *verb* If something breaks up, it ends.

> **break** *verb*
> **1** = crack, shatter, smash, snap, split, wreck **2** = breach, contravene, infringe, violate
> ▶ *noun* **6** = interlude, interval, pause, recess, respite, rest

breakaway *adjective* A breakaway group is one that has separated from a larger group.

breakdown *noun* **1** The breakdown of something such as a system is its failure. **2** the same as a nervous breakdown. **3** If a driver has a breakdown, their car stops working. **4** A breakdown of something complex is a summary of its important points.

breaker *noun* Breakers are big sea waves.

breakfast *noun* the first meal of the day.

break-in *noun* the illegal entering of a building, especially by a burglar.

breakneck *adjective* (*informal*) Someone or something that is

travelling at breakneck speed is travelling dangerously fast.

breakthrough *noun* a sudden important development.

breakwater *noun* a wall extending into the sea that protects a coast from the force of the waves.

bream *noun* an edible fish.

breast *noun* **1** A woman's breasts are the two soft, fleshy parts on her chest, which secrete milk after she has had a baby. **2** (*literary or old-fashioned*) The human breast is the upper front part of the body, sometimes regarded as the place where emotions are felt.

breath *noun* **1** Your breath is the air you take into your lungs and let out again when you breathe. ▶ *phrase* **2** If you are **out of breath**, you are breathing with difficulty after doing something energetic. **3** If you say something **under your breath**, you say it in a very quiet voice.

breathe *verb* When you breathe, you take air into your lungs and let it out again.

breathless *adjective* If you are breathless, you are breathing fast or with difficulty.

breathtaking *adjective* If you say that something is breathtaking, you mean that it is very beautiful or exciting.

bred the past tense and past participle of **breed**.

breeches *plural noun* Breeches are trousers reaching to just below the knee, worn especially for riding.

breed breeds, breeding, bred *noun* **1** A breed of a species of domestic animal is a particular type of it.

B

▶ *verb* **2** Someone who breeds animals or plants keeps them in order to produce more animals or plants with particular qualities. **3** When animals breed, they mate and produce offspring.

> **breed** *noun*
> **1** = kind, species, stock, strain, type, variety
> ▶ *verb* **2** = cultivate, develop, keep, nurture, raise, rear
> **3** = multiply, produce, propagate, reproduce

breeze *noun* a gentle wind.

brevity *noun (formal)* Brevity means shortness.

brew *verb* **1** If you brew tea or coffee, you make it in a pot by pouring hot water over it. **2** To brew beer means to make it by boiling and fermenting malt. **3** If an unpleasant situation is brewing, it is about to happen. > **brewer** *noun*

brewery breweries *noun* a place where beer is made, or a company that makes it.

Brexit *noun* 'Brexit' is used to refer to the United Kingdom leaving the European Union.

bribe *noun* **1** a gift or money given to an official to persuade them to make a favourable decision. ▶ *verb* **2** To bribe someone means to give them a bribe. > **bribery** *noun*

bric-a-brac *noun* Bric-a-brac consists of small ornaments or pieces of furniture of no great value.

brick *noun* Bricks are rectangular blocks of baked clay used in building.

bricklayer *noun* a person whose job is to build with bricks.

bride *noun* a woman who is getting married or who has just got married. > **bridal** *adjective*

bridegroom *noun* a man who is getting married or who has just got married.

bridesmaid *noun* a woman who helps and accompanies a bride on her wedding day.

bridge *noun* **1** a structure built over a river, road or railway so that vehicles and people can cross. **2** the platform from which a ship is steered and controlled. **3** the hard ridge at the top of your nose. **4** Bridge is a card game for four players based on whist.

bridle *noun* a set of straps around a horse's head and mouth, which the rider uses to control the horse.

brief *adjective* **1** Something that is brief lasts only a short time. ▶ *verb* **2** (DGT) When you brief someone on a task, you give them all the instructions and information about it. > **briefly** *adverb*

> **brief** *adjective*
> **1** = fleeting, momentary, quick, short, swift
> ▶ *verb* **2** = advise, fill in (*informal*), inform, instruct, prepare, prime

briefcase *noun* a small flat case for carrying papers.

briefing *noun* a meeting at which information and instructions are given.

brigade *noun* an army unit consisting of three battalions.

brigadier *noun* an army officer of the rank immediately above colonel.

bright *adjective* **1** strong and startling. **2** clever. **3** cheerful.

bright adjective
1 = brilliant, dazzling, glowing, luminous, radiant, vivid 2 = brainy (informal), brilliant, clever, ingenious, intelligent, smart 3 = cheerful, happy, jolly, light-hearted, lively, merry

brighten verb 1 If something brightens, it becomes brighter. 2 If someone brightens, they suddenly look happier.
> **brighten up** verb To brighten something up means to make it more attractive and cheerful.

brilliant adjective 1 A brilliant light or colour is extremely bright. 2 A brilliant person is extremely clever. 3 A brilliant career is extremely successful.
> **brilliance** noun

brilliant adjective
1 = bright, dazzling, gleaming, glowing, luminous, radiant, sparkling, vivid 2 = acute, brainy (informal), bright, clever, intelligent, perceptive, sharp, smart 3 = first-class, great, magnificent, marvellous, outstanding, superb, tremendous, wonderful

brim noun 1 the wide part of a hat that sticks outwards at the bottom. ▶ phrase 2 If a container is filled **to the brim**, it is filled right to the top.

brine noun Brine is salt water.

bring brings, bringing, brought verb 1 If you bring something or someone with you when you go to a place, you take them with you. 2 To bring something to a particular state means to cause it to be like that. > **bring about** verb To bring something about means to cause it to happen. > **bring off**

verb If you bring off something difficult, you succeed in doing it.
> **bring out** verb 1 To bring out a new product means to produce it and offer it for sale. 2 If something brings out a particular kind of behaviour, it causes it to occur. > **bring up** verb 1 To bring up children means to look after them while they grow up. 2 If you bring up a subject, you introduce it into the conversation.

bring verb
1 = bear, carry, convey (formal), lead, take, transport 2 = cause, create, inflict, produce, result in, wreak
▶ **bring about** = cause, create, generate, make happen, produce, provoke

brink noun If you are on the brink of something, you are just about to do it or experience it.

brisk adjective 1 A brisk action is done quickly and energetically. 2 If someone's manner is brisk, it shows that they want to get things done quickly and efficiently.

bristle noun 1 Bristles are strong animal hairs used to make brushes. ▶ verb 2 If the hairs on an animal's body bristle, they rise up, because it is frightened.
> **bristly** adjective

British adjective belonging or relating to the United Kingdom of Great Britain and Northern Ireland.

Briton noun someone who comes from the United Kingdom of Great Britain and Northern Ireland.

brittle adjective An object that is brittle is hard but breaks easily.

broach verb When you broach a subject, you introduce it into a discussion.

broad adjective 1 wide. 2 having many different aspects or concerning many different people: *A broad range of issues was discussed.* 3 general rather than detailed: *the broad concerns of the movement.* 4 If someone has a broad accent, the way that they speak makes it very clear where they come from.

> **broad** adjective
> 1 = expansive, extensive, large, thick, vast, wide
> 2 = comprehensive, extensive, general, sweeping, universal, wide, wide-ranging
> 3 = approximate, general, non-specific, rough, sweeping, vague

broadband noun Broadband is a digital system used on the internet and in other forms of telecommunication which can process and transfer information input from various sources, such as from telephones, computers or televisions.

broadcast broadcasts, broadcasting, broadcast noun 1 a programme or announcement on radio or television. ▶ verb 2 To broadcast something means to send it out by radio waves, so that it can be seen on television or heard on radio. > **broadcaster** noun > **broadcasting** noun

broaden verb 1 When something broadens, it becomes wider. 2 To broaden something means to cause it to involve more things or concern more people.

broadly adverb true to a large extent or in most cases: *There are broadly two schools of thought on this.*

broadsheet noun (ENGLISH) a newspaper with large pages and detailed news stories.

brocade noun Brocade is a heavy, expensive material, often made of silk, with a raised pattern.

broccoli noun Broccoli is a green vegetable, similar to cauliflower.

brochure noun a booklet which gives information about a product or service.

broke 1 the past tense of **break**. ▶ adjective 2 (informal) If you are broke, you have no money.

broken 1 the past participle of **break**. ▶ adjective 2 in pieces. 3 A broken promise or rule is not kept.

broker noun a person whose job is to buy and sell shares for other people.

bronchitis noun Bronchitis is an illness in which the two tubes which connect your windpipe to your lungs become infected, making you cough.

bronze noun Bronze is a yellowish-brown metal which is a mixture of copper and tin; also the yellowish-brown colour of this metal.

brooch noun a piece of jewellery with a pin at the back for attaching to clothes.

brood noun 1 a family of baby birds. ▶ verb 2 If you brood about something, you keep thinking about it in a serious or unhappy way.

brook noun a stream.

broom noun a long-handled brush.

broth noun Broth is soup, usually with vegetables in it.

brother noun Your brother is a boy or man who has the same parents as you. ▶ **brotherly** adjective

brotherhood noun 1 Brotherhood is the affection and loyalty that brothers or close male friends feel for each other. 2 a group of men with common interests or beliefs.

brother-in-law brothers-in-law noun Someone's brother-in-law is the brother of their husband or wife, or their sibling's husband.

brought the past tense and past participle of **bring**.

brow noun 1 Your brow is your forehead. 2 Your brows are your eyebrows. 3 The brow of a hill is the top of it.

brown adjective, noun Brown is the colour of earth or wood.

browse verb 1 If you browse through a book or magazine, you look through it in a casual way. 2 If you browse in a shop, you look at the things in it for interest rather than because you want to buy something. 3 If you browse on a computer, you search for information on the World Wide Web.

browser noun a piece of computer software that lets you look at websites on the World Wide Web.

bruise noun 1 a purple mark that appears on your skin after something has hit it. ▶ verb 2 If something bruises you, it hits you so that a bruise appears on your skin.

brumby brumbies noun In Australia, a brumby is a wild horse.

brunette noun a girl or woman with dark brown hair.

brunt phrase If you **bear the brunt** of something unpleasant, you are the person who suffers most.

brush noun 1 an object with bristles which you use for cleaning things, painting, or tidying your hair. ▶ verb 2 If you brush something, you clean it or tidy it with a brush. 3 To brush against something means to touch it while passing it. ▶ **brush up** verb If you brush up on a subject, you improve your knowledge of it.

brusque adjective Someone who is brusque deals with people quickly and without considering their feelings.

Brussels sprout noun Brussels sprouts are vegetables that look like tiny cabbages.

brutal adjective Brutal behaviour is cruel and violent. ▶ **brutally** adverb ▶ **brutality** noun

brute noun 1 a rough and insensitive man. ▶ adjective 2 Brute force is strength alone, without any skill.

bubble noun 1 a ball of air in a liquid. 2 a hollow, delicate ball of soapy liquid. ▶ verb 3 When a liquid bubbles, bubbles form in it. 4 If you are bubbling with something like excitement, you are full of it. ▶ **bubbly** adjective

bucket noun a deep round container with an open top and a handle.

buckle noun 1 a fastening on the end of a belt or strap. ▶ verb 2 If you buckle a belt or strap, you fasten it. 3 If something buckles, it becomes bent because of severe heat or pressure.

bud buds, budding, budded noun 1 a small, tight swelling on a tree or plant, which develops into a

B

flower or a cluster of leaves. ▶ verb 2 When a tree or plant buds, new buds appear on it.

Buddhism noun (RE) An Eastern religion which teaches that the way to end suffering is by overcoming your desires. It was founded in the 6th century BC by the Buddha (a title meaning 'the enlightened one'), Gautama Siddhartha, a nobleman and religious teacher of northern India. > **Buddhist** noun, adjective

budding adjective just beginning to develop.

buddy buddies noun (informal) a friend.

budge verb If something will not budge, you cannot move it.

budgerigar noun A budgerigar is a small brightly coloured pet bird. Budgerigars originated in Australia.

budget noun 1 (CITIZENSHIP) a plan showing how much money will be available and how it will be spent. ▶ verb 2 (CITIZENSHIP) If you budget for something, you plan your money carefully, so that you are able to afford it. > **budgetary** adjective

budgie noun (informal) a budgerigar.

buff adjective 1 a pale brown colour. ▶ noun 2 (informal) someone who knows a lot about a subject.

buffalo buffaloes noun a wild animal like a large cow with long curved horns.

buffer noun 1 Buffers on a train or at the end of a railway line are metal discs on springs that reduce shock when they are hit. 2 something that prevents something else from being harmed.

buffet¹ noun 1 a café at a station. 2 a meal at which people serve themselves.

buffet² verb If the wind or sea buffets a place or person, it strikes them violently and repeatedly.

bug bugs, bugging, bugged noun 1 an insect, especially one that causes damage. 2 a small error in a computer program which means that the program will not work properly. 3 (informal) a virus or minor infection. ▶ verb 4 If a place is bugged, tiny microphones are hidden there to pick up what people are saying.

buggy buggies noun a small lightweight vehicle or carriage.

bugle noun (MUSIC) a brass musical instrument that looks like a small trumpet. > **bugler** noun

build builds, building, built verb 1 To build something such as a house means to make it from its parts. 2 To build something such as an organisation means to develop it gradually. ▶ noun 3 Your build is the shape and size of your body.

> **build** verb
> 1 = assemble, construct, erect, fabricate, form, make
> 2 = develop, extend, increase, intensify, strengthen
> ▶ noun 3 = body, figure, form, frame, physique, shape

building noun a structure with walls and a roof.

> **building** noun
> = edifice

bulb noun 1 the glass part of an electric lamp. 2 an onion-shaped root that grows into a flower or plant.

Bulgarian *adjective* **1** belonging or relating to Bulgaria. ▶ *noun* **2** someone who comes from Bulgaria. **3** the main language spoken in Bulgaria.

bulge *verb* **1** If something bulges, it swells out from a surface. ▶ *noun* **2** a lump on a normally flat surface.

> **bulge** *verb*
> **1** = expand, protrude (*formal*), stick out, swell
> ▶ *noun* **2** = bump, hump, lump, protrusion, swelling

bulk *noun* **1** a large mass of something. **2** The bulk of something is most of it. ▶ *phrase* **3** To buy something in bulk means to buy it in large quantities.

bulky bulkier, bulkiest *adjective* large and heavy.

bull *noun* the male of some species of animals, including the cow family, elephants and whales.

bulldog *noun* a squat dog with a broad head and muscular body.

bulldozer *noun* a powerful tractor with a broad blade in front, which is used for moving earth and knocking things down.

bullet *noun* a small piece of metal fired from a gun.

bulletin *noun* **1** a short news report on radio or television. **2** a leaflet or small newspaper regularly produced by a group or organisation.

bullion *noun* Bullion is gold or silver in the form of bars.

bully bullies, bullying, bullied *noun* **1** someone who repeatedly tries to hurt or frighten other people. ▶ *verb* **2** If you bully someone, you frighten or hurt them deliberately. **3** If someone bullies you into doing something, they make you do it by using force or threats.

> **bully** *noun*
> **1** = oppressor, persecutor
> ▶ *verb* **2** = intimidate, oppress, persecute, pick on, tease, torment **3** = force, intimidate, pressurise

bump *verb* **1** If you bump or bump into something, you knock it with a jolt. ▶ *noun* **2** a soft or dull noise made by something knocking into something else. **3** a raised, uneven part of a surface. > **bumpy** *adjective*
> **bump off** *verb* (*informal*) To bump someone off means to kill them.

> **bump** *verb*
> **1** = bang, collide, hit, jolt, knock, strike
> ▶ *noun* **2** = bang, knock, thud, thump **3** = bulge, hump, knob, lump, swelling

bumper *noun* **1** Bumpers are bars on the front and back of a vehicle which protect it if there is a collision. ▶ *adjective* **2** A bumper crop or harvest is larger than usual.

bun *noun* a small, round cake.

bunch *noun* **1** a group of people. **2** a number of flowers held or tied together. **3** a group of things. **4** a group of bananas or grapes growing on the same stem. ▶ *verb* **5** When people bunch together or bunch up, they stay very close to each other.

> **bunch** *noun*
> **1** = band, crowd, gaggle, gang, group, lot, multitude
> **2** = bouquet, posy, spray
> **3** = batch, bundle, cluster, heap, load, pile, set

b

B

bundle noun 1 a number of things tied together or wrapped up in a cloth. ▶ verb 2 If you bundle someone or something somewhere, you push them there quickly and roughly.

bung noun 1 a stopper used to close a hole in something such as a barrel. ▶ verb 2 (informal) If you bung something somewhere, you put it there quickly and carelessly.

bungalow noun a one-storey house.

bungle verb To bungle something means to fail to do it properly.

bunk noun a bed fixed to a wall in a ship or caravan.

bunker noun 1 On a golf course, a bunker is a large hole filled with sand. 2 an underground shelter with strong walls to protect it from bombing.

bunting noun Bunting is strips of small coloured flags displayed on streets on special occasions.

buoy noun a floating object anchored to the bottom of the sea, marking a channel or warning of danger.

buoyant adjective 1 able to float. 2 lively and cheerful. > **buoyancy** noun

burden noun 1 a heavy load. 2 If something is a burden to you, it causes you a lot of worry or hard work. > **burdensome** adjective

> **burden** noun
> 1 = load, weight 2 = anxiety, care, strain, stress, trouble, worry

bureau bureaux noun an office that provides a service.

bureaucracy noun Bureaucracy is the complex system of rules and procedures which operates in government departments.
> **bureaucratic** adjective

> **bureaucracy** noun
> = administration, officialdom, red tape (informal), regulations

bureaucrat noun a person who works in a government department, especially one who follows rules and procedures strictly.

burger noun a flat round mass of minced meat or vegetables which is fried and often eaten in a bread roll.

burglar noun a thief who breaks into a building.

burglary burglaries noun Burglary is the act of breaking into a building in order to steal things.

burgle verb If your house is burgled, someone breaks into it and steals things.

burial noun a ceremony held when a dead person is buried.

burly burlier, burliest adjective If you are burly, you have a broad body and strong muscles.

burn burns, burning, burned or burnt verb 1 If something is burning, it is on fire. 2 To burn something means to destroy it with fire. 3 If you burn yourself or are burned, you are injured by fire or by something hot. ▶ noun 4 an injury caused by fire or by something hot.

> **burn** verb
> 1 = be ablaze, be on fire, blaze, flame, flare, flicker 2 = char, incinerate, scorch, shrivel, singe

burrow noun 1 a tunnel or hole in the ground dug by a small animal. ▸ *verb* 2 When an animal burrows, it digs a burrow.

bursary bursaries *noun* a sum of money given to someone to help fund their education.

burst bursts, bursting, burst *verb* 1 When something bursts, it splits open because of pressure from inside it. 2 If you burst into a room, you enter it suddenly. 3 To burst means to happen or come suddenly and with force: *The aircraft burst into flames.* 4 (*informal*) If you are bursting with something, you find it difficult to keep it to yourself. ▸ *noun* 5 A burst of something is a short period of it.

> **burst** *verb*
> 1 = break, crack, explode, puncture, rupture, split
> 2 = barge, rush 3 = break, erupt
> ▸ *noun* 5 = fit, outbreak, rush, spate, surge, torrent

bury buries, burying, buried *verb* 1 When a dead person is buried, their body is put into a grave and covered with earth. 2 To bury something means to put it in a hole in the ground and cover it up. 3 If something is buried under something, it is covered by it.

bus *noun* a large motor vehicle that carries passengers.

bush *noun* 1 a thick plant with many stems branching out from ground level. 2 In Australia and South Africa, the bush is an area of land in its natural state outside of city areas. 3 In New Zealand, the bush is land covered with rainforest.

bushman bushmen *noun* 1 In Australia and New Zealand, a bushman is someone who lives or travels in the bush. 2 In New Zealand, a bushman is also someone whose job it is to clear the bush for farming.

Bushman Bushmen *noun* A Bushman is a member of a group of people in southern Africa who live by hunting and gathering food.

bushranger *noun* In Australia and New Zealand in the past, a bushranger was an outlaw living in the bush.

bushy bushier, bushiest *adjective* Bushy hair or fur grows very thickly.

business *noun* 1 Business is work relating to the buying and selling of goods and services. 2 an organisation which produces or sells goods or provides a service. 3 You can refer to any event, situation or activity as a business: *This whole business has upset me.*
> **businessman** *noun*
> **businesswoman** *noun*

> **business** *noun*
> 1 = commerce, dealings, industry, trade, trading, transaction 2 = company, corporation, enterprise, establishment, firm, organisation 3 = affair, issue, matter, problem, question, subject

businesslike *adjective* dealing with things in an efficient way.

busker *noun* someone who plays music or sings for money in public places.

bust busts, busting, bust or busted *noun* 1 a statue of someone's head and shoulders. 2 A woman's bust is her chest and her breasts.
▸ *adjective* 3 (*informal*) If a business

goes bust, it becomes bankrupt and closes down.

bustle verb 1 When people bustle, they move in a busy, hurried way. ▶ noun 2 Bustle is busy, noisy activity.

> **bustle** verb
> 1 = dash, fuss, hurry, rush, scurry, scuttle
> ▶ noun 2 = activity, commotion, excitement, flurry, fuss, hurry

busy busier, busiest; busies, busying, busied adjective 1 If you are busy, you are in the middle of doing something. 2 A busy place is full of people doing things or moving about. ▶ verb 3 If you busy yourself with something, you occupy yourself by doing it.
> **busily** adverb

> **busy** adjective
> 1 = active, employed, engaged, engrossed, occupied, working
> 2 = active, full, hectic, lively, restless
> ▶ verb 3 = absorb, employ, engage, immerse, occupy

but conjunction 1 used to introduce an idea that is opposite to what has gone before: I don't like apples, but I do like oranges. 2 used when apologising: I'm sorry, but I can't come tonight. 3 except: We can't do anything but wait.

> **but** conjunction
> 1 = although, though, while, yet
> 3 = except, except for, other than, save

butcher noun a shopkeeper who sells meat.

butler noun the chief male servant in a rich household.

butt noun 1 The butt of a weapon is the thick end of its handle. 2 If

you are the butt of teasing, you are the target of it. ▶ verb 3 If you butt something, you ram it with your head. > **butt in** verb If you butt in, you join in a private conversation or activity without being asked to.

butter noun 1 Butter is a soft fatty food made from cream, which is spread on bread and used in cooking. ▶ verb 2 To butter bread means to spread butter on it.

butterfly butterflies noun a type of insect with large colourful wings.

buttocks plural noun Your buttocks are the part of your body that you sit on.

button noun 1 Buttons are small, hard objects sewn on to clothing, and used to fasten two surfaces together. 2 a small object on a piece of equipment that you press to make it work. ▶ verb 3 If you button a piece of clothing, you fasten it using its buttons.

buxom adjective A buxom woman is large, healthy and attractive.

buy buys, buying, bought verb If you buy something, you obtain it by paying money for it. > **buyer** noun

> **buy** verb
> = acquire, get, invest in, pay for, procure, purchase

buzz verb 1 If something buzzes, it makes a humming sound, like a bee. ▶ noun 2 the sound something makes when it buzzes.

buzzer noun a device that makes a buzzing sound, to attract attention.

by preposition 1 used to indicate who or what has done something: The class was taken by a new teacher.

2 used to indicate how something is done: *He frightened her by hiding behind the door.* **3** located next to: *I sat by her bed.* **4** before a particular time: *It should be ready by next spring.*
▶ *preposition, adverb* **5** going past.

by-election *noun* an election held to choose a new member of parliament after the previous member has resigned or died.

bygone *adjective* (literary) happening or existing a long time ago.

bypass *noun* a main road which takes traffic round a town rather than through it.

bystander *noun* someone who is not included or involved in something but is there to see it happen.

byte *noun* (ICT) a unit of computer memory size.

Cc

cab *noun* **1** a taxi. **2** In a lorry, bus or train, the cab is where the driver sits.

cabaret *noun* a show consisting of dancing, singing or comedy acts.

cabbage *noun* a large green or reddish-purple leafy vegetable.

cabin *noun* **1** a room in a ship where a passenger sleeps. **2** a small house, usually in the country and often made of wood. **3** the area where the passengers or the crew sit in a plane.

cabinet *noun* **1** a small cupboard. **2** The cabinet in a government is a group of ministers who advise the leader and decide policies.

cable *noun* **1** a strong, thick rope or chain. **2** a bundle of wires with a rubber covering, which carries electricity. **3** a message sent abroad by using electrical signals sent along a wire.

cable car *noun* a vehicle pulled by a moving cable, for taking people up and down mountains.

cable television *noun* a television service people can receive from underground wires which carry the signals.

cache *noun* a store of things hidden away.

cachet *noun* (formal) Cachet is the status and respect something has.

C

cackle verb 1 If you cackle, you laugh harshly. ▶ noun 2 A harsh laugh.

cacophony noun (formal) A loud, unpleasant noise.

cactus cacti or cactuses noun a thick, fleshy plant that grows in deserts and is usually covered in spikes.

caddie; also spelt **caddy** noun 1 a person who carries golf clubs for a golf player. 2 A tea caddy is a container for keeping tea in.

cadence noun The cadence of someone's voice is the way it goes up and down as they speak.

cadet noun a young person being trained in the armed forces or police.

caesarean; also spelt **caesarian** or **cesarean** noun A caesarean or caesarean section is an operation in which a baby is lifted out of a woman's womb through a cut in her abdomen.

café noun 1 a place where you can buy light meals and drinks. 2 In South African English, a café is a corner shop or grocer's shop.

cafeteria noun a restaurant where you serve yourself.

caffeine noun Caffeine is a chemical in coffee and tea which makes you more active.

cage noun a box made of wire or bars in which birds or animals are kept.

cagey cagier, cagiest adjective (informal) cautious and not open.

cahoots phrase (informal) If you are **in cahoots** with someone, you are working closely with them on a secret plan.

cajole verb If you cajole someone into doing something, you persuade them to do it by saying nice things to them.

cake noun 1 a sweet food made by baking flour, eggs, fat and sugar. 2 a block of a hard substance such as soap. ▶ verb 3 If something cakes or is caked, it forms or becomes covered with a solid layer.

calamity calamities noun an event that causes disaster or distress. > **calamitous** adjective

calcium noun (SCIENCE) Calcium is a soft white element found in bones and teeth. Its atomic number is 20 and its symbol is Ca.

calculate verb (MATHS) If you calculate something, you work it out, by doing some arithmetic. > **calculation** noun

> **calculate** verb
> = count, determine, reckon, work out

calculating adjective carefully planning situations to get what you want.

calculator noun a small electronic machine used for doing mathematical calculations.

calculus noun Calculus is a branch of mathematics concerned with amounts that can change and rates of change.

calendar noun 1 a chart showing the date of each day in a particular year. 2 a system of dividing time into fixed periods of days, months and years.

calf calves noun 1 a young cow, bull, elephant, whale or seal. 2 the thick part at the back of your leg below your knee.

calibre noun 1 the ability or intelligence someone has. 2 The calibre of a gun is the width of the inside of the barrel of the gun.

call *verb* 1 If someone or something is called a particular name, that is their name. 2 If you call people or situations something, you use words to describe your opinion of them: *They called me unfriendly.* 3 If you call someone, you telephone them. 4 If you call or call out something, you say it loudly. 5 If you call on someone, you pay them a short visit. ▶ *noun* 6 If you get a call from someone, they telephone you or pay you a visit. 7 a cry or shout. 8 a demand for something. > **call off** *verb* If you call something off, you cancel it. > **call up** *verb* If someone is called up, they are ordered to join the army, navy or air force.

> **call** *verb*
> 1 = christen, designate, dub, name 3 = contact, phone, ring, telephone 4 = announce, cry, cry out, shout, yell
> ▶ *noun* 7 = cry, shout, yell

call centre *noun* an office in which most staff are employed to answer telephone calls on behalf of a particular company or organisation.

calling *noun* 1 a profession or career. 2 If you have a calling to a particular job, you have a strong feeling that you should do it.

callous *adjective* cruel and not concerned with other people's feelings.

> **callous** *adjective*
> = cold, heartless, indifferent, insensitive

calm *calmest adjective* 1 Someone who is calm is quiet and does not show any worry or excitement. 2 If the weather or the sea is calm,

it is still because there is no strong wind. ▶ *noun* 3 Calm is a state of quietness and peacefulness. ▶ *verb* 4 To calm someone means to make them less upset or excited.

> **calm** *adjective*
> 1 = collected, composed, cool, impassive, relaxed 2 = balmy, mild, still, tranquil
> ▶ *noun* 3 = calmness, peace, peacefulness, quiet, serenity, stillness
> ▶ *verb* 4 = quieten, relax, soothe

calorie *noun* a unit of measurement for the energy food and drink gives you.

calves the plural of **calf**.

calypso *calypsos noun* a type of song originally from Trinidad, accompanied by a rhythmic beat, about something happening at the time.

camaraderie *noun* Camaraderie is a feeling of trust and friendship between a group of people.

came the past tense of **come**.

camel *noun* a large mammal with either one or two humps on its back. Camels live in hot desert areas and are used for carrying things.

cameo *cameos noun* 1 a small but important part in a play or film played by a well-known actor or actress. 2 a brooch with a raised stone design on a flat stone of another colour.

camera *noun* a piece of equipment used for taking photographs or for filming.

camouflage *noun* 1 Camouflage is a way of avoiding being seen by having the same colour or appearance as the surroundings.

▶ *verb* **2** To camouflage something is to hide it by giving it the same colour or appearance as its surroundings.

camp *noun* **1** a place where people live in tents or stay in tents on holiday. **2** a collection of buildings for a particular group of people such as soldiers or prisoners. **3** a group of people who support a particular idea or belief: *the pro-government camp.*
▶ *verb* **4** If you camp, you stay in a tent.

campaign *noun* **1** a set of actions aiming to achieve a particular result. ▶ *verb* **2** To campaign means to carry out a campaign.

> **campaign** *noun*
> **1** = crusade, movement, operation, push

campus campuses *noun* the area of land and the buildings that make up a university or college.

can[1] **could** *verb* **1** If you can do something, it is possible for you to do it or you are allowed to do it. **2** If you can do something, you have the ability to do it.

can[2] **cans, canning, canned** *noun* **1** a metal container, often a sealed one with food or drink inside.
▶ *verb* **2** To can food or drink is to seal it in cans.

Canadian *adjective* **1** belonging or relating to Canada. ▶ *noun* **2** someone who comes from Canada.

canal *noun* a long, narrow man-made stretch of water.

canary canaries *noun* a small yellow bird.

cancel cancels, cancelling, cancelled *verb* **1** If you cancel something that has been arranged, you stop it from happening. **2** If you cancel a cheque or an agreement, you make sure that it is no longer valid. > **cancellation** *noun*

> **cancel** *verb*
> **1** = abandon, call off **2** = annul, quash, repeal, revoke

cancer *noun* **1** a serious disease in which abnormal cells in a part of the body increase rapidly, causing growths. **2** Cancer is also the fourth sign of the zodiac, represented by a crab. People born between June 21st and July 22nd are born under this sign.
> **cancerous** *adjective*

candelabra or **candelabrum** *noun* an ornamental holder for a number of candles.

candid *adjective* honest and frank.
> **candidly** *adverb* > **candour** *noun*

> **candid** *adjective*
> = blunt, frank, honest, open, straightforward, truthful

candidate *noun* **1** a person who is being considered for a job. **2** a person taking an examination.
> **candidacy** *noun*

> **candidate** *noun*
> **1** = applicant, competitor, contender

candied *adjective* covered in sugar.

candle *noun* a stick of hard wax with a wick through the middle. The lighted wick gives a flame that provides light.

candy candies *noun* In America, candy is sweets.

cane *noun* **1** Cane is the long, hollow stems of a plant such as bamboo. **2** Cane is also strips of cane used for weaving things such as baskets. **3** a long narrow stick, often used to beat people as a punishment. ▶ verb **4** To cane someone means to beat them with a cane as a punishment.

canine adjective relating to dogs.

canister noun A container with a lid, used for storing foods such as sugar.

cannabis noun Cannabis is an illegal drug made from the hemp plant, which some people smoke.

canned adjective **1** Canned food is kept in cans. **2** Canned music or laughter on a television or radio show is recorded beforehand.

cannibal noun a person who eats other human beings; also used of animals that eat animals of their own type. > **cannibalism** noun

cannon noun A cannon is a large gun, usually on wheels, used in battles to fire heavy metal balls.

cannot verb Cannot is the same as can not.

canny cannier, canniest adjective clever and cautious. > **cannily** adverb

canoe noun a small, narrow boat that you move through the water using a paddle.

canon noun **1** a member of the clergy in a cathedral. **2** a basic rule or principle. **3** In literature, a canon is all the writings by a particular author which are known to be genuine.

canopy canopies noun a cover for something, used for shelter or decoration.

cantankerous adjective Cantankerous people are quarrelsome and bad-tempered.

canteen noun **1** In a place such as a school or office, the canteen is a place where people can go to eat. **2** A canteen of cutlery is a set of cutlery in a box.

canter verb When a horse canters, it moves at a speed between a gallop and a trot.

canvas noun **1** Canvas is strong, heavy cloth used for making things such as sails. **2** a piece of canvas on which an artist does a painting.

canvass verb **1** If you canvass people or a place, you go round trying to persuade people to vote for a particular candidate or party in an election. **2** If you canvass opinion, you find out what people think about a particular subject.

canyon noun (GEOGRAPHY) a narrow river valley with steep sides.

cap caps, capping, capped noun **1** a soft, flat hat, often with a peak at the front. **2** the top of a bottle. **3** Caps are small explosives used in toy guns. ▶ verb **4** To cap something is to cover it with something. **5** If you cap a story or a joke that someone has just told, you tell a better one.

capable adjective **1** able to do something. **2** skilful or talented. > **capably** adverb > **capability** noun

> **capable** adjective
> **2** = able, accomplished, adept, competent, efficient, proficient, skilful

capacity capacities noun **1** the maximum amount that something can hold or produce. **2** a person's power or ability to do something. **3** someone's position or role.

capacity noun
1 = dimensions, room, size, space, volume 2 = ability, capability, facility, gift, potential, power

cape noun 1 a short cloak with no sleeves. 2 a large piece of land sticking out into the sea.

caper noun 1 Capers are the flower buds of a spiky Mediterranean shrub, which are pickled and used to flavour food. 2 a light-hearted practical joke.

capital noun 1 The capital of a country is the city where the government meets. 2 Capital is the amount of money or property owned or used by a business. 3 Capital is also a sum of money that you save or invest in order to gain interest. 4 A capital or capital letter is a larger letter used at the beginning of a sentence or a name.

capitalise; also spelt **capitalize** verb If you capitalise on a situation, you use it to get an advantage.

capitalism noun Capitalism is an economic and political system where businesses and industries are not owned and run by the government, but by individuals who can make a profit from them. > **capitalist** adjective, noun

capital punishment noun Capital punishment is legally killing someone as a punishment for a crime they have committed.

capitulate verb To capitulate is to give in and stop fighting or resisting. > **capitulation** noun

cappuccino cappuccinos noun coffee made with frothy milk.

capricious adjective often changing unexpectedly.

Capricorn noun Capricorn is the tenth sign of the zodiac, represented by a goat. People born between December 22nd and January 19th are born under this sign.

capsize verb If a boat capsizes, it turns upside down.

capsule noun 1 a small container with medicine inside which you swallow. 2 the part of a spacecraft in which astronauts travel.

captain noun 1 the officer in charge of a ship or aeroplane. 2 an army officer of the rank immediately above lieutenant. 3 a navy officer of the rank immediately above commander. 4 the leader of a sports team. ▶ verb 5 If you captain a group of people, you are their leader.

caption noun a title printed underneath a picture or photograph.

captivate verb To captivate someone is to fascinate or attract them so that they cannot take their attention away. > **captivating** adjective

captive noun 1 a person who has been captured and kept prisoner. ▶ adjective 2 imprisoned or enclosed. > **captivity** noun

captor noun someone who has captured a person or animal.

capture verb 1 To capture someone is to take them prisoner. 2 To capture a quality or mood means to succeed in representing or describing it. ▶ noun 3 The capture of someone or something is the action of taking them prisoner.

capture verb
1 = apprehend, arrest, catch, seize, take
▶ noun 3 = arrest, seizure, taking, trapping

car noun 1 a four-wheeled road vehicle with room for a small number of people. 2 a railway carriage used for a particular purpose.

car noun
1 = automobile (American), motor (old-fashioned), vehicle

caramel noun 1 a chewy sweet made from sugar, butter and milk. 2 Caramel is burnt sugar used for colouring or flavouring food.

carat noun 1 A carat is a unit for measuring the weight of diamonds and other precious stones, equal to 0.2 grams. 2 A carat is also a unit for measuring the purity of gold. The purest gold is 24 carats.

caravan noun 1 a vehicle pulled by a car in which people live or spend their holidays. 2 a group of people and animals travelling together, usually across a desert.

carbohydrate noun (DGT) (SCIENCE) Carbohydrate is a substance that gives you energy. It is found in foods like sugar and bread.

carbon noun (SCIENCE) Carbon is a chemical element that is pure in diamonds and also found in coal. All living things contain carbon. Its atomic number is 6 and its symbol is C.

carbonated adjective Carbonated drinks contain bubbles of carbon dioxide that make them fizzy.

carbon dioxide noun (SCIENCE) Carbon dioxide is a colourless, odourless gas that humans and animals breathe out. It is used in industry, for example in making fizzy drinks and in fire extinguishers.

carcass; also spelt **carcase** noun the body of a dead animal.

card noun 1 a piece of stiff paper or plastic with information or a message on it. 2 Cards can mean playing cards. 3 When you play cards, you play any game using playing cards. 4 Card is thick, stiff paper.

cardboard noun Cardboard is thick, stiff paper.

cardiac adjective relating to the heart.

cardigan noun a knitted jacket that fastens up the front.

cardinal noun 1 a high-ranking member of the Roman Catholic clergy who chooses and advises the Pope. ▶ adjective 2 extremely important.

care verb 1 If you care about something, you are concerned about it and interested in it. 2 If you care about someone, you feel affection towards them. 3 If you care for someone, you look after them. ▶ noun 4 Care is concern or worry. 5 Care of someone or something is treatment for them or looking after them. 6 If you do something with care, you do it with close attention.

care verb
1 = be bothered, be concerned, be interested, mind
▶ noun 4 = anxiety, concern, stress, trouble, woe, worry
6 = attention, caution, pains

career noun **1** (PSHE) the series of jobs that someone has in life, usually in the same occupation.
▶ verb **2** To career somewhere is to move very quickly, often out of control.

carefree adjective having no worries or responsibilities.

careful adjective **1** acting sensibly and with care. **2** complete and well done: *careful planning*.
> **carefully** adverb

> **careful** adjective
> **1** = cautious, prudent
> **2** = meticulous, painstaking, precise, thorough

careless adjective **1** done badly without enough attention. **2** relaxed and unconcerned: *careless laughter*.

> **careless** adjective
> **1** = irresponsible, neglectful, sloppy (*informal*) **2** = casual, nonchalant, offhand

carer noun a person who looks after someone who is ill or elderly, often a relative.

caress verb **1** If you caress someone, you stroke them gently and affectionately.
▶ noun **2** a gentle, affectionate stroke.

caretaker noun a person who looks after a large building such as a school.

cargo cargoes noun the goods carried on a ship or plane.

caricature noun **1** a drawing or description of someone that exaggerates striking parts of their appearance or personality.
▶ verb **2** To caricature someone is to give a caricature of them.

carnage noun Carnage is the violent killing of large numbers of people.

carnival noun a public festival with music, processions and dancing.

carnivore noun an animal that eats meat. > **carnivorous** adjective

carol noun a religious song sung at Christmas time.

carousel noun a merry-go-round.

carp noun **1** a large edible freshwater fish. ▶ verb **2** To carp means to complain about unimportant things.

carpenter noun a person who makes and repairs wooden structures. > **carpentry** noun

carpet noun **1** a thick covering for a floor, usually made of a material like wool. ▶ verb **2** To carpet a floor means to cover it with a carpet.

carriage noun **1** one of the separate sections of a passenger train. **2** an old-fashioned vehicle for carrying passengers, usually pulled by horses.

carriageway noun one of the sides of a road which traffic travels along in one direction only.

carrier noun **1** a vehicle that is used for carrying things. **2** A carrier of a germ or disease is a person or animal that can pass it on to others.

carrier bag noun a bag made of plastic or paper, which is used for carrying shopping.

carrot noun a long, thin orange root vegetable.

carry carries, carrying, carried **1** To carry something is to hold it and take it somewhere. **2** When a vehicle carries people, they travel in it. **3** If a person or animal carries a germ, they can pass it on to other people or animals. **4** If a sound carries, it can be heard far away. **5** In a meeting, if a proposal is carried, it is accepted by a majority of the people there. > **carry away** *verb* If you are carried away, you are so excited by something that you do not behave sensibly. > **carry on** *verb* To carry on doing something means to continue doing it. > **carry out** *verb* To carry something out means to do it and complete it.

> **carry** *verb*
> 1 = bear, convey (*formal*), lug, take, transport
> ▶ **carry out** = accomplish, achieve, fulfil, perform

cart *noun* a vehicle with wheels, used to carry goods and often pulled by horses or cattle.

cartilage *noun* (SCIENCE) Cartilage is a strong, flexible substance found around the joints and in the nose and ears.

carton *noun* a cardboard or plastic container.

cartoon *noun* **1** a drawing or a series of drawings which are funny or make a point. **2** a film in which the characters and scenes are drawn. > **cartoonist** *noun*

cartridge *noun* **1** a tube containing a bullet and an explosive substance, used in guns. **2** a plastic container full of ink that you put in a printer or pen.

carve *verb* **1** To carve an object means to cut it out of a substance such as stone or wood. **2** To carve meat means to cut slices from it.

> **carve** *verb*
> 1 = chisel, cut, engrave, inscribe, sculpt

carving *noun* a carved object.

cascade *noun* **1** a waterfall or group of waterfalls. ▶ *verb* **2** To cascade means to flow downwards quickly.

case *noun* **1** a particular situation, event or example: *a clear case of mistaken identity*. **2** a container for something, or a suitcase. **3** Doctors sometimes refer to a patient as a case. **4** Police detectives refer to a crime they are investigating as a case. **5** In an argument, the case for an idea is the reasons used to support it. **6** In law, a case is a trial or other inquiry. **7** In grammar, the case of a noun or pronoun is the form of it which shows its relationship with other words in a sentence: *the accusative case*. ▶ *phrase* **8** You say **in case** to explain something that you do because a particular thing might happen: *I didn't want to shout in case I startled you*. **9** You say **in that case** to show that you are assuming something said before is true: *In that case we won't do it*.

> **case** *noun*
> 1 = example, illustration, instance, occasion, occurrence
> 2 = box, container 6 = action, lawsuit, proceedings, trial

cash *noun* Cash is money in notes and coins.

cashew *noun* a curved, edible nut.

cash flow *noun* Cash flow is the money that a business makes and spends.

cashier *noun* the person that customers pay in a shop or get money from in a bank.

cashmere *noun* Cashmere is very soft, fine wool from goats.

cash register *noun* a machine in a shop which records sales, and where the money is kept.

casing *noun* a protective covering for something.

casino casinos *noun* a place where people go to play gambling games.

cask *noun* a wooden barrel.

casket *noun* a small box for jewellery or other valuables.

casserole *noun* a dish made by cooking a mixture of meat and vegetables slowly in an oven; also used to refer to the pot a casserole is cooked in.

cassowary cassowaries *noun* a large bird found in Australia with black feathers and a brightly coloured neck. Cassowaries cannot fly.

cast casts, casting, cast *noun* 1 all the people who act in a play or film. 2 an object made by pouring liquid into a mould and leaving it to harden. 3 a stiff plaster covering put on broken bones to keep them still so that they heal properly. ▶ *verb* 4 To cast actors is to choose them for roles in a play or film. 5 When people cast their votes in an election, they vote. 6 To cast something is to throw it. 7 If you cast your eyes somewhere, you look there. 8 To cast an object is to make it by pouring liquid into a mould and leaving it to harden. > **cast off** *verb* If you cast off, you untie the rope fastening a boat to a harbour or shore.

caste *noun* 1 (RE) one of the four classes into which Hindu society is divided. 2 Caste is a system of social classes decided according to family, wealth and position.

castigate *verb* (formal) To castigate someone is to criticise them severely.

castle *noun* 1 (HISTORY) a large building with walls or ditches round it to protect it from attack. 2 In chess, a castle is the same as a rook.

castor; also spelt **caster** *noun* a small wheel fitted to furniture so that it can be moved easily.

casual *adjective* 1 happening by chance without planning. 2 careless or without interest. 3 Casual clothes are suitable for informal occasions. 4 Casual work is not regular or permanent. > **casually** *adverb*

> **casual** *adjective*
> 1 = accidental, chance, incidental 2 = careless, cursory, nonchalant, offhand, relaxed

casualty casualties *noun* a person killed or injured in an accident or war.

cat *noun* 1 a small furry animal with whiskers, a tail, and sharp claws, often kept as a pet. 2 any of the family of mammals that includes lions and tigers.

> **cat** *noun*
> 1 = feline (formal), kitty (informal), moggy or moggie (British and New Zealand; slang), pussy or puss or pussycat (informal)

catalogue catalogues, cataloguing, catalogued *noun* 1 a book containing pictures and descriptions of goods that you can buy in a shop or through the post. 2 (LIBRARY) a list of things such as the objects in a museum or the books in a library. ▶ *verb* 3 To catalogue a collection of things means to list them in a catalogue.

catalyst noun 1 something that causes a change to happen. 2 (SCIENCE) a substance that speeds up a chemical reaction without changing itself.

catamaran noun a sailing boat with two hulls connected to each other.

catapult noun 1 a Y-shaped object with a piece of elastic tied between the two top ends, used for shooting small stones. ▶ verb 2 To catapult something is to throw it violently through the air. 3 If someone is catapulted into a situation, they find themselves unexpectedly in that situation.

cataract noun an area of the lens of someone's eye that has become white instead of clear, so that they cannot see properly.

catastrophe noun a terrible disaster. ▷ **catastrophic** adjective

catch catches, catching, caught verb 1 If you catch a ball moving in the air, you grasp hold of it when it comes near you. 2 To catch an animal means to trap it. 3 When the police catch criminals, they find them and arrest them. 4 If you catch someone doing something they should not be doing, you discover them doing it. 5 If you catch a bus or train, you get on it and travel somewhere. 6 If you catch a cold or a disease, you become infected with it. 7 If something catches on an object, it sticks to it or gets trapped. ▶ noun 8 a device that fastens something. 9 a problem or hidden complication in something. ▷ **catch on** verb 1 If you catch on to something, you understand it. 2 If something catches on, it becomes popular.

▷ **catch out** verb To catch someone out is to trick them or trap them.

▷ **catch up** verb 1 To catch up with someone in front of you is to reach the place where they are by moving slightly faster than them. 2 To catch up with someone is also to reach the same level or standard as them.

> **catch** verb
> 2 = capture, snare, trap
> 3 = apprehend, arrest
> ▶ noun 8 = bolt, clasp, clip, latch
> 9 = disadvantage, drawback, snag

catching adjective tending to spread very quickly.

catchy catchier, catchiest adjective attractive and easily remembered.

categorise; also spelt **categorize** verb To categorise things is to arrange them in different categories.

category categories noun a set of things with a particular characteristic in common.

> **category** noun
> = class, classification, group, set, sort, type

cater verb To cater for people is to provide them with what they need, especially food.

caterer noun a person or business that provides food for parties and groups.

caterpillar noun the larva of a butterfly or moth. It looks like a small coloured worm and feeds on plants.

catharsis catharses noun (formal) Catharsis is the release of strong emotions and feelings by expressing them through drama or literature.

cathedral noun (HISTORY) an important church with a bishop in charge of it.

Catholic noun, adjective (a) Roman Catholic. > **Catholicism**

cattle plural noun Cattle are cows and bulls kept by farmers.

catty cattier, cattiest adjective unpleasant and spiteful. > **cattiness** noun

catwalk noun a narrow pathway that people walk along, for example over a stage.

Caucasian noun a person belonging to a race of people with fair or light-brown skin.

caught the past tense and past participle of **catch**.

cauldron noun a large, round, metal cooking pot, especially one that sits over a fire.

cauliflower noun a large, round, white vegetable surrounded by green leaves.

cause noun 1 The cause of something is the thing that makes it happen. 2 an aim or principle which a group of people are working for. 3 If you have cause for something, you have a reason for it. ▶ verb 4 To cause something is to make it happen. > **causal** adjective

> **cause** noun
> 1 = origin, root, source 2 = aim, ideal, movement 3 = basis, grounds, justification, motivation, motive, reason
> ▶ verb 4 = bring about, create, generate, produce, provoke

causeway noun a raised path or road across water or marshland.

caustic adjective 1 A caustic chemical can destroy substances. 2 bitter or sarcastic.

caution noun 1 Caution is great care which you take to avoid danger. 2 a warning. ▶ verb 3 If someone cautions you, they warn you, usually not to do something again.

> **caution** noun
> 1 = care, prudence
> ▶ verb 3 = reprimand, tick off (informal), warn

cautious adjective acting very carefully to avoid danger. > **cautiously** adverb

> **cautious** adjective
> = careful, guarded, tentative, wary

cavalcade noun a procession of people on horses or in cars or carriages.

cavalry noun The cavalry is the part of an army that uses armoured vehicles or horses.

cave noun 1 a large hole in rock, that is underground or in the side of a cliff. ▶ verb 2 If a roof caves in, it collapses inwards.

caveman cavemen noun Cavemen were people who lived in caves in prehistoric times.

cavern noun a large cave.

cavernous adjective large, deep and hollow.

caviar noun Caviar is the tiny salted eggs of a fish called the sturgeon.

cavity cavities noun a small hole in something solid.

cavort verb When people cavort, they jump around excitedly.

cc an abbreviation for 'cubic centimetres'.

CD an abbreviation for 'compact disc'.

cease verb 1 If something ceases, it stops happening. 2 If you cease to do something, or cease doing it, you stop doing it.

cease verb
1 = be over, come to an end, die away, end, finish, stop
2 = desist from, discontinue, finish, give up, stop, suspend

ceaseless adjective going on without stopping.

cedar noun a large evergreen tree with wide branches and needle-shaped leaves.

cede verb To cede something is to give it up to someone else.

ceiling noun the top inside surface of a room.

celebrate verb 1 If you celebrate or celebrate something, you do something special and enjoyable because of it. 2 When a priest celebrates Mass, he performs the ceremonies of the Mass.

celebrate verb
1 = commemorate, party, rejoice

celebrated adjective famous.

celebration noun an event in honour of a special occasion.
> **celebratory** adjective

celebration noun
= festival, festivity, gala, party

celebrity celebrities noun a famous person.

celebrity noun
= big name, name, personality, star, superstar, VIP

celery noun Celery is a vegetable with long, pale green stalks.

celestial adjective (formal) concerning the sky or heaven.

celibate adjective Someone who is celibate does not marry.
> **celibacy** noun

cell noun 1 (SCIENCE) In biology, a cell is the smallest part of an animal or plant that can exist by itself. Each cell contains a nucleus. 2 a small room where a prisoner is kept in a prison or police station. 3 a small group of people set up to work together as part of a larger organisation. 4 (DGT) a device that converts chemical energy to electricity.

cellar noun a room underneath a building, often used to store wine.

cello cellos noun (MUSIC) a large musical stringed instrument which you play sitting down, holding the instrument upright with your knees. > **cellist** noun

cellular adjective Cellular means relating to the cells of animals or plants.

Celsius noun (SCIENCE) Celsius is a scale for measuring temperature in which water freezes at 0 degrees (0°C) and boils at 100 degrees (100°C). It is named after Anders Celsius (1701–1744), who invented it. Celsius is the same as 'Centigrade'.

Celtic adjective A Celtic language is one of a group of languages that includes Gaelic and Welsh.

cement noun 1 Cement is a fine powder made from limestone and clay, which is mixed with sand and water to make concrete.
▶ verb 2 To cement things is to stick them together with cement or cover them with cement. 3 Something that cements a relationship makes it stronger.

cemetery cemeteries noun an area of land where dead people are buried.

cenotaph *noun* a monument built in memory of dead people, especially soldiers buried elsewhere.

censor *noun* 1 a person officially appointed to examine books or films and to ban parts that are considered unsuitable. ▶ *verb* 2 If someone censors a book or film, they cut or ban parts of it that are considered unsuitable for the public. > **censorship** *noun*

censure *noun* 1 Censure is strong disapproval of something. ▶ *verb* 2 To censure someone is to criticise them severely.

> **censure** *noun*
> 1 = blame, condemnation, criticism, disapproval, reproach
> ▶ *verb* 2 = condemn, criticise, denounce, reproach

census censuses *noun* an official survey of the population of a country.

cent *noun* a unit of currency. In the USA and the Caribbean, a cent is worth one hundredth of a dollar; in Europe, it is worth one hundredth of a euro.

centenary centenaries *noun* the hundredth anniversary of something.

centimetre *noun* a unit of length equal to ten millimetres or one hundredth of a metre.

central *adjective* 1 in or near the centre of an object or area. 2 main or most important. > **centrally** *adverb*

Central America *noun* Central America is the area of land joining North America to South America.

central heating *noun* Central heating is a system of heating a building in which water or air is heated in a tank and travels through pipes and radiators round the building.

centralise; also spelt **centralize** *verb* To centralise a system is to bring the organisation of it under the control of one central group. > **centralisation** *noun*

centre *noun* 1 the middle of an object or area. 2 a building where people go for activities, meetings or help. 3 Someone or something that is the centre of attention attracts a lot of attention. ▶ *verb* 4 To centre something is to move it so that it is balanced or at the centre of something else. 5 If something centres on or around a particular thing, that thing is the main subject of attention.

> **centre** *noun*
> 1 = core, focus, heart, hub, middle
> ▶ *verb* 5 = concentrate, focus, revolve

centurion *noun* (HISTORY) an ancient Roman officer in charge of a hundred soldiers.

century centuries *noun* 1 a period of one hundred years. 2 In cricket, a century is one hundred runs scored by a batter.

ceramic *noun* 1 (SCIENCE) Ceramic is a hard material made by baking clay to a very high temperature. 2 Ceramics is the art of making objects out of clay.

cereal *noun* 1 a food made from grain, often eaten with milk for breakfast. 2 a plant that produces edible grain, such as wheat or oats.

cerebral *adjective* (formal) relating to the brain.

cerebral palsy noun Cerebral palsy is an illness caused by damage to a baby's brain, which makes its muscles and limbs very weak.

ceremonial adjective relating to a ceremony.

ceremony ceremonies noun 1 a set of formal actions performed at a special occasion or important public event. 2 Ceremony is very formal and polite behaviour.

> **ceremony** noun
> 1 = observance, pomp, rite, ritual, service 2 = decorum, etiquette, formality, niceties, protocol

certain adjective 1 definite or reliable. 2 having no doubt in your mind. 3 You use 'certain' to refer to a specific person or thing. 4 You use 'certain' to suggest that a quality is noticeable but not obvious.

> **certain** adjective
> 1 = definite, established, guaranteed, inevitable, known, sure, undeniable 2 = clear, confident, convinced, definite, positive, satisfied, sure

certainly adverb without doubt.

> **certainly** adverb
> = definitely, undeniably, undoubtedly, unquestionably, without doubt

certainty certainties noun 1 Certainty is the state of being certain. 2 something that is known without doubt.

certificate noun a document stating particular facts, for example of someone's birth or death.

certify certifies, certifying, certified verb 1 To certify something means to declare formally that it is true. 2 To certify someone means to declare officially that they are insane.

cervical adjective (technical) relating to the cervix.

cervix cervixes or cervices noun (technical) The cervix is the entrance to the womb.

cessation noun (formal) The cessation of something is the stopping of it.

cf. cf. means 'compare'. It is written after something in a text to mention something else which the reader should compare with what has just been written.

chaff noun Chaff is the outer parts of grain separated from the seeds by beating.

chagrin noun (formal) Chagrin is a feeling of annoyance or disappointment.

chain noun 1 a number of metal rings connected together in a line. 2 a number of things in a series or connected to each other. ▶ verb 3 If you chain one thing to another, you fasten them together with a chain.

chair noun 1 a seat with a back and four legs for one person. 2 the person in charge of a meeting who decides when each person may speak. ▶ verb 3 A person who chairs a meeting is in charge of it.

chairperson chairpersons noun 1 the person in charge of a meeting who decides when each person may speak. 2 the head of a company or committee. ▷ **chairman** noun ▷ **chairwoman** noun

chalet *noun* a wooden house with a sloping roof, especially in a mountain area or a holiday camp.

chalice *noun* (RE) a gold or silver cup used in churches to hold the Communion wine.

chalk *noun* 1 (ART) Chalk is a soft white rock. Small sticks of chalk are used for writing or drawing on a blackboard. ▶ *verb* 2 To chalk up a result is to achieve it.
> **chalky** *adjective*

challenge *noun* 1 something that is new and exciting but requires a lot of effort. 2 a suggestion from someone to compete with them. 3 A challenge to something is a questioning of whether it is correct or true. ▶ *verb* 4 If someone challenges you, they suggest that you compete with them in some way. 5 If you challenge something, you question whether it is correct or true.
> **challenger** *noun* > **challenging** *adjective*

> **challenge** *noun*
> 2 = dare
> ▶ *verb* 4 = dare, defy 5 = dispute, question

chamber *noun* 1 a large room, especially one used for formal meetings. 2 a group of people chosen to decide laws or administrative matters. 3 a hollow place or compartment inside something, especially inside an animal's body or inside a gun. 4 (*in plural*) Chambers are a room where judges hear cases that are not being heard in an open court.

chameleon *noun* a lizard which is able to change the colour of its skin to match the colour of its surroundings.

champagne *noun* Champagne is a sparkling white wine made in France.

champion *noun* 1 a person who wins a competition. 2 someone who supports or defends a cause or principle. ▶ *verb* 3 Someone who champions a cause or principle supports or defends it.

> **champion** *noun*
> 1 = hero, title holder, victor, winner 2 = advocate, defender, guardian, protector
> ▶ *verb* 3 = defend, fight for, promote, stick up for (*informal*), support, uphold

championship *noun* a competition to find the champion of a sport.

chance *noun* 1 The chance of something happening is how possible or likely it is. 2 an opportunity to do something. 3 a possibility that something dangerous or unpleasant may happen: *Don't take chances: he's armed.* 4 Chance is also the way things happen unexpectedly without being planned. ▶ *verb* 5 If you chance something, you try it although you are taking a risk.

> **chance** *noun*
> 1 = likelihood, odds, possibility, probability, prospect
> 2 = occasion, opening, opportunity, time 4 = accident, coincidence, fortune, luck

chancellor *noun* 1 the head of government in some European countries. 2 In Britain, the Chancellor is the Chancellor of the Exchequer. 3 the honorary head of a university.

Chancellor of the Exchequer *noun* In Britain, the Chancellor of the Exchequer is the minister responsible for finance and taxes.

chandelier noun an ornamental light fitting which hangs from the ceiling.

change noun 1 a difference or alteration in something. 2 a replacement of something by something else. 3 Change is money you get back when you have paid more than the actual price of something. ▶ verb 4 When something changes or when you change it, it becomes different. 5 If you change something, you exchange it for something else. 6 When you change, you put on different clothes. 7 To change money means to exchange it for smaller coins of the same total value, or to exchange it for foreign currency.

> **change** noun
> 1 = alteration, difference, modification, transformation
> ▶ verb 4 = alter, convert, moderate, modify, reform, transform 5 = barter, exchange, interchange, replace, substitute, swap, trade

changeable adjective likely to change all the time.

> **changeable** adjective
> = erratic, fickle, irregular, unpredictable, unstable, variable, volatile

changeover noun a change from one system or activity to another.

channel channels, channelling, channelled noun 1 a wavelength used to receive programmes broadcast by a television or radio station; also the station itself. 2 a passage along which water flows or along which something is carried. 3 The Channel or the English Channel is the stretch of sea between England and France. 4 a method of achieving something. ▶ verb 5 To channel something such as money or energy means to direct it in a particular way.

chant noun 1 a group of words repeated over and over again. 2 a religious song sung on only a few notes. ▶ verb 3 If people chant a group of words, they repeat them over and over again.

chaos noun Chaos is a state of complete disorder and confusion. > **chaotic** adjective

chap chaps, chapping, chapped noun 1 (informal) a man. ▶ verb 2 If your skin chaps, it becomes dry and cracked, usually as a result of cold or wind.

chapel noun 1 a section of a church or cathedral with its own altar. 2 a type of small church.

chaperone; also spelt **chaperon** noun an older woman who accompanies a young unmarried woman on social occasions, or any person who accompanies a group of younger people.

chaplain noun a member of the Christian clergy who regularly works in a hospital, school or prison.

chapter noun 1 one of the parts into which a book is divided. 2 a particular period in someone's life or in history.

char chars, charring, charred verb If something chars, it gets partly burned and goes black.

character noun 1 all the qualities which combine to form the personality of a person or the atmosphere of a place. 2 A person or place that has character has an interesting, attractive or admirable quality. 3 (ENGLISH) The characters in a film, play or book are the people in it. 4 a person. 5 a letter, number or other written symbol.

> **character** noun
> 1 = make-up, nature, personality, temperament
> 2 = honour, integrity, strength

characterise; also spelt **characterize** verb A quality that characterises something is typical of it.

characteristic noun 1 a quality that is typical of a particular person or thing. 2 (SCIENCE) a feature that is typical of a particular living thing. ▶ adjective 3 Characteristic means typical of a particular person or thing. > **characteristically** adverb

> **characteristic** noun
> 1 = attribute, feature, property, quality, trait
> ▶ adjective 3 = distinctive, distinguishing, typical

charade noun a ridiculous and unnecessary activity or pretence.

charcoal noun Charcoal is a black form of carbon made by burning wood without air, used as a fuel and also for drawing.

charge verb 1 If someone charges you money, they ask you to pay it for something you have bought or received. 2 To charge someone means to accuse them formally of having committed a crime. 3 To charge the battery of an electrical device means to pass an electrical current through it to make it store electricity. 4 To charge somewhere means to rush

forward, often to attack someone. ▶ noun 5 the price that you have to pay for something. 6 a formal accusation that a person is guilty of a crime and has to go to court. 7 To have charge or be in charge of someone or something means to be responsible for them and be in control of them. 8 an explosive put in a gun or other weapon. 9 (SCIENCE) An electrical charge is the amount of electricity that something carries.

> **charge** verb
> 1 = ask (for), bill, levy 4 = dash, rush, stampede, storm
> ▶ noun 5 = cost, fee, payment, price

charger noun a device for charging or recharging batteries.

chariot noun a two-wheeled open vehicle pulled by horses.

charisma noun Charisma is a special ability to attract or influence people by your personality. > **charismatic** adjective

charity charities noun 1 an organisation that raises money to help people or animals in need. 2 Charity is money or other help given to people or animals in need. 3 Charity is also a kind, sympathetic attitude towards people. > **charitable** adjective

charlatan noun someone who pretends to have skill or knowledge that they do not really have.

charm noun 1 Charm is an attractive and pleasing quality that some people and things have. 2 a small ornament worn on a bracelet. 3 a magical spell or an object that is supposed to bring good luck. ▶ verb 4 If you charm someone, you use your charm to please them.

> **charm** noun
> 1 = allure, appeal, attraction, fascination, magnetism
> ▶ verb 4 = bewitch, captivate, delight, entrance

charmer noun someone who uses their charm to influence people.

charming adjective very pleasant and attractive.

chart noun 1 a diagram or table showing information. 2 a map of the sea or stars. ▶ verb 3 If you chart something, you observe and record it carefully.

charter noun 1 a document stating the rights or aims of a group or organisation, often written by the government. ▶ verb 2 To charter transport such as a plane or boat is to hire it for private use.

chase verb 1 If you chase someone or something, you run after them in order to catch them. 2 If you chase someone, you force them to go somewhere else. ▶ noun 3 the activity of chasing or hunting someone or something.

> **chase** verb
> 1 = hunt, pursue 2 = drive, hound

chasm noun 1 a deep crack in the earth's surface. 2 a very large difference between two ideas or groups of people.

chassis noun the frame on which a vehicle is built.

chaste adjective (old-fashioned) pure and well-behaved. > **chastity** noun

chastise verb (formal) If someone chastises you, they criticise you or punish you for something that you have done.

chat chats, chatting, chatted noun 1 a friendly talk with someone, usually about things that are not very important. 2 an exchange of messages on a computer network. ▶ verb 3 When people chat, they talk to each other in a friendly way. > **chat up** verb (informal) If you chat up someone, you talk to them in a friendly way, because you are attracted to them.

> **chat** noun
> 1 = conversation, gossip, natter (informal), talk
> ▶ verb 3 = gossip, natter (informal), talk

chateau chateaux noun a large country house or castle in France.

chatroom noun an internet site where people read and post messages.

chatter verb 1 When people chatter, they talk very fast. 2 If your teeth are chattering, they are knocking together and making a clicking noise because you are cold. ▶ noun 3 Chatter is a lot of fast unimportant talk.

chatty chattier, chattiest adjective talkative and friendly.

chauffeur noun a person whose job is to drive another person's car.

chauvinist noun 1 a person who thinks their country is always right. 2 A male chauvinist is a man who believes that men are superior to women.
> **chauvinistic** adjective
> **chauvinism** noun

cheap adjective 1 costing very little money. 2 inexpensive but of poor quality. 3 A cheap joke or cheap remark is unfair and unkind.

cheap *adjective*
1 = bargain, economical, inexpensive, reasonable
2 = inferior, second-rate, tawdry

cheat *verb* 1 If someone cheats, they do wrong or unfair things to win or get something that they want. 2 If you are cheated of or out of something, you do not get what you are entitled to. ▶ *noun* 3 a person who cheats.

cheat *verb*
1 = con (*informal*), deceive, defraud, dupe, fleece, rip off (*slang*), swindle

check *verb* 1 To check something is to examine it in order to make sure that everything is all right. 2 To check the growth or spread of something is to make it stop. ▶ *noun* 3 an inspection to make sure that everything is all right. 4 (*in plural*) Checks are different coloured squares which form a pattern. ▶ *phrase* 5 If you keep something **in check**, you keep it under control. ▶ *adjective* 6 Check or checked means marked with a pattern of squares. > **check in** *verb* When you check in at a hotel or airport, you arrive and sign your name or show your ticket. > **check out** *verb* 1 If you check something out, you inspect it and find out whether everything about it is right. 2 When you check out of a hotel, you pay the bill and leave.

check *verb*
1 = check out, examine, inspect, test 2 = control, curb, halt, inhibit, restrain, stop
▶ *noun* 3 = examination, inspection, test

checkout *noun* a counter in a supermarket where the customers pay for their goods.

checkpoint *noun* a place where traffic has to stop in order to be checked.

checkup *noun* an examination by a doctor or dentist to see if you are healthy.

cheek *noun* 1 Your cheeks are the sides of your face below your eyes. 2 Cheek is speech or behaviour that is rude or disrespectful.

cheek *noun*
2 = audacity, gall, impudence, insolence, nerve, rudeness

cheeky cheekier, cheekiest *adjective* rather rude and disrespectful.

cheeky *adjective*
= impertinent, impudent, insolent, rude

cheer *verb* 1 When people cheer, they shout with approval or in order to show support for a person or team. ▶ *noun* 2 a shout of approval or support. > **cheer up** *verb* When you cheer up, you feel more cheerful.

cheerful *adjective* 1 happy and in good spirits. 2 bright and pleasant-looking. > **cheerfully** *adverb*

cheerful *adjective*
1 = bright, buoyant, cheery, happy, jaunty, jolly, light-hearted, merry

cheery cheerier, cheeriest *adjective* happy and cheerful.

cheery *adjective*
= cheerful, chirpy, good-humoured, happy, jolly, sunny, upbeat

cheese noun a hard or creamy food made from milk.

cheesecake noun a dessert made of biscuit covered with smooth soft cheese.

cheetah noun a wild animal like a large cat with black spots.

chef noun a head cook in a restaurant or hotel.

chemical noun (SCIENCE)
1 Chemicals are substances manufactured by chemistry.
▶ adjective 2 involved in chemistry or using chemicals. > **chemically** adverb

chemist noun 1 a person who is qualified to make up drugs and medicines prescribed by a doctor. 2 a shop where medicines and cosmetics are sold. 3 a scientist who does research in chemistry.

chemistry noun Chemistry is the scientific study of substances and the ways in which they change when they are combined with other substances.

chemotherapy noun Chemotherapy is a way of treating diseases such as cancer by using chemicals.

cheque noun a printed form on which you write an amount of money that you have to pay. You sign the cheque and your bank pays the money from your account.

chequered adjective 1 covered with a pattern of squares. 2 A chequered career is a varied career that has both good and bad parts.

cherish verb 1 If you cherish something, you care deeply about it and want to keep it or look after it lovingly. 2 If you cherish a

memory or hope, you have it in your mind and care deeply about it.

cherry cherries noun 1 a small, juicy fruit with a red or black skin and a hard stone in the centre. 2 a tree that produces cherries.

chess noun Chess is a board game for two people in which each player has 16 pieces and tries to move his or her pieces so that the other player's king cannot escape.

chest noun 1 the front part of your body between your shoulders and your waist. 2 a large wooden box with a hinged lid.

chestnut noun 1 Chestnuts are reddish-brown nuts that grow inside a prickly green outer covering. 2 a tree that produces these nuts. ▶ adjective 3 Something that is chestnut is reddish-brown.

chest of drawers noun a piece of furniture with drawers in it, used for storing clothes.

chew verb When you chew something, you use your teeth to break it up in your mouth before swallowing it. > **chewy** adjective

> **chew** verb
> = crunch, gnaw, munch

chewing gum noun Chewing gum is a kind of sweet that you chew for a long time, but which you do not swallow.

chic adjective elegant and fashionable.

chick noun a young bird.

chicken noun a bird kept on a farm for its eggs and meat; also the meat of this bird. > **chicken out** verb (informal) If you chicken out of something, you do not do it because you are afraid.

chickenpox *noun* Chickenpox is an illness which produces a fever and blister-like spots on the skin.

chicory *noun* Chicory is a plant with bitter leaves that are used in salads.

chide chides, chiding, chided *verb* (*old-fashioned*) To chide someone is to tell them off.

chief *noun* 1 the leader of a group or organisation. ▸ *adjective* 2 most important. > **chiefly** *adverb*

> **chief** *noun*
> 1 = boss, chieftain, director, governor, head, leader, manager
> ▸ *adjective* 2 = foremost, key, main, prevailing, primary, prime, principal

chieftain *noun* the leader of a tribe or clan.

chiffon *noun* Chiffon is a very thin lightweight cloth made of silk or nylon.

chihuahua *noun* a breed of very small dog with short hair and pointed ears.

child children *noun* 1 a young person who is not yet an adult. 2 Someone's child is their son or daughter.

> **child** *noun*
> 1 = ankle-biter (*Australian and New Zealand; slang*), baby, bairn (*Scottish*), infant, juvenile (*formal*), kid (*informal*), minor (*formal*), offspring, toddler, tot (*informal*), youngster

childbirth *noun* Childbirth is the act of giving birth to a child.

childhood *noun* Someone's childhood is the time when they are a child.

childish *adjective* immature and foolish.

> **childish** *adjective*
> = immature, infantile, juvenile, puerile

childless *adjective* having no children.

childlike *adjective* like a child in appearance or behaviour.

Chilean *adjective* 1 belonging or relating to Chile. ▸ *noun* 2 someone who comes from Chile.

chill *verb* 1 To chill something is to make it cold. 2 If something chills you, it makes you feel worried or frightened. ▸ *noun* 3 a feverish cold. 4 a feeling of cold.

chilli chillies *noun* the red or green seed pod of a type of pepper which has a very hot, spicy taste.

chilly chillier, chilliest *adjective* 1 rather cold. 2 unfriendly and without enthusiasm.

chime *verb* When a bell chimes, it makes a clear ringing sound.

chimney *noun* a vertical pipe or other hollow structure above a fireplace or furnace through which smoke from a fire escapes.

chimpanzee *noun* a small ape with dark fur that lives in forests in Africa.

chin *noun* the part of your face below your mouth.

china *noun* 1 China is items like cups, saucers and plates made from very thin clay. 2 (*informal*) In British and South African English, a china is a friend.

> **china** *noun*
> 2 = buddy (*informal*), chum (*informal*), crony (*old-fashioned*), friend, mate (*informal*), pal (*informal*)

Chinese *adjective* 1 belonging or relating to China. ▶ *noun* 2 someone who comes from China. 3 Chinese refers to any of a group of related languages and dialects spoken by Chinese people.

chink *noun* 1 a small, narrow opening. 2 a short, light, ringing sound, like one made by glasses touching each other.

chip chips, chipping, chipped *noun* 1 Chips are thin strips of fried potato. 2 In electronics, a chip is a tiny piece of silicon inside a computer which is used to form electronic circuits. 3 a small piece broken off an object, or the mark made when a piece breaks off. ▶ *verb* 4 If you chip an object, you break a small piece off it.

chirp *verb* When a bird chirps, it makes a short, high-pitched sound.

chisel chisels, chiselling, chiselled *noun* 1 a tool with a long metal blade and a sharp edge at the end which is used for cutting and shaping wood, stone or metal. ▶ *verb* 2 To chisel wood, stone or metal is to cut or shape it using a chisel.

chivalry *noun* Chivalry is polite and helpful behaviour, especially by men towards women. > **chivalrous** *adjective*

chive *noun* Chives are grasslike hollow leaves that have a mild onion flavour.

chlorine *noun* (SCIENCE) Chlorine is a chemical element which is a poisonous greenish-yellow gas with a strong, unpleasant smell. It is used to disinfect water and to make bleach. Its atomic number is 17 and its symbol is Cl.

chlorophyll *noun* (SCIENCE) Chlorophyll is a green substance in plants which enables them to use the energy from sunlight in order to grow.

chocolate *noun* 1 Chocolate is a sweet food made from cacao seeds. 2 a sweet made of chocolate. ▶ *adjective* 3 dark brown.

choice *noun* 1 a range of different things that are available to choose from. 2 something that you choose. 3 Choice is the power or right to choose.

> **choice** *noun*
> 1 = range, selection, variety
> 3 = alternative, option, say

choir *noun* (MUSIC) a group of singers, for example in a church.

choke *verb* 1 If you choke, you stop being able to breathe properly, usually because something is blocking your windpipe. 2 If things choke a place, they fill it so much that it is blocked or clogged up.

cholera *noun* Cholera is a serious disease causing severe diarrhoea and vomiting. It is caused by infected food or water.

cholesterol *noun* Cholesterol is a substance found in all animal fats, tissues and blood.

chook *noun* (informal) In Australian and New Zealand English, a chook is a chicken.

choose chooses, choosing, chose, chosen *verb* To choose something is to decide to have it or do it.

> **choose** *verb*
> = opt for, pick, select, take

choosy choosier, choosiest *adjective* fussy and difficult to satisfy.

chop chops, chopping, chopped
verb 1 To chop something is to cut it with quick, heavy strokes using an axe or a knife. ▶ *noun* 2 a small piece of lamb or pork containing a bone, usually cut from the ribs.

> **chop** *verb*
> 1 = cut, fell, hack, lop

chopper *noun* (*informal*) a helicopter.

choppy choppier, choppiest
adjective Choppy water has a lot of waves because it is windy.

choral *adjective* relating to singing by a choir.

chord *noun* (MUSIC) a group of three or more musical notes played together.

chore *noun* an uninteresting job that has to be done.

choreography *noun*
Choreography is the art of composing dance steps and movements. > **choreographer** *noun*

chorus choruses, chorusing, chorused (MUSIC) *noun* 1 a large group of singers; also a piece of music for a large group of singers. 2 a part of a song which is repeated after each verse. ▶ *verb* 3 If people chorus something, they all say or sing it at the same time.

chose the past tense of **choose**.

chosen the past participle of **choose**.

Christ *proper noun* (RE) Christ is the name for Jesus. Christians believe that Jesus is the son of God.

christen *verb* (RE) When a baby is christened, it is named by a member of the clergy in a religious ceremony.

Christian *noun* (RE) 1 a person who believes in Jesus Christ and his teachings. ▶ *adjective* 2 relating to Christ and his teachings. 3 good, kind and considerate.
> **Christianity** *noun*

Christmas *noun* (RE) the Christian festival celebrating the birth of Christ, falling on December 25th.

chrome *noun* Chrome is metal plated with chromium, a hard grey metal.

chromosome *noun* (SCIENCE) In biology, a chromosome is one of a number of rod-shaped parts in the nucleus of a cell which contains genes that determine the characteristics of an animal or plant.

chronic *adjective* lasting a very long time or never stopping.
> **chronically** *adverb*

chronicle *noun* 1 a record of a series of events described in the order in which they happened. ▶ *verb* 2 To chronicle a series of events is to record or describe them in the order in which they happened.

chronological *adjective* (HISTORY) arranged in the order in which things happened.
> **chronologically** *adverb*

chronology *noun* (HISTORY) The chronology of events is the order in which they happened.

chubby chubbier, chubbiest
adjective plump and round.

chuck *verb* (*informal*) To chuck something is to throw it casually.

chuckle *verb* When you chuckle, you laugh quietly.

chug chugs, chugging, chugged
verb When a machine or engine

chugs, it makes a continuous dull thudding sound.

chum *noun* (*informal*) a friend.

chunk *noun* a thick piece of something.

chunky chunkier, chunkiest *adjective* Someone who is chunky is broad and heavy but usually short.

church *noun* **1** a building where Christians go for religious services and worship. **2** In the Christian religion, a church is one of the groups with their own particular beliefs, customs and clergy.

Church of England *noun* (RE) The Church of England is the Anglican church in England, where it is the state church, with the King or Queen as its head.

churchyard *noun* an area of land around a church, often used as a graveyard.

churn *noun* a container used for making milk or cream into butter.

chute *noun* a steep slope or channel used to slide things down.

chutney *noun* Chutney is a strong-tasting thick sauce made from fruit, vinegar and spices.

cider *noun* Cider is an alcoholic drink made from apples.

cigar *noun* a roll of dried tobacco leaves which people smoke.

cigarette *noun* a thin roll of tobacco covered in thin paper which people smoke.

cinema *noun* **1** a place where people go to watch films. **2** Cinema is the business of making films.

cinnamon *noun* Cinnamon is a sweet spice which comes from the bark of an Asian tree.

circa *preposition* (*formal*) about or approximately; used especially before dates.

circle *noun* **1** (MATHS) a completely regular round shape. Every point on its edge is the same distance from the centre. **2** a group of people with the same interest or profession. **3** an area of seats on an upper floor of a theatre. ▶ *verb* **4** To circle is to move round and round as though going round the edge of a circle.

circuit *noun* **1** any closed line or path, often circular, for example a racing track; also the distance round this path. **2** (SCIENCE) An electrical circuit is a complete route around which an electric current can flow. A **closed circuit** is a complete electrical circuit around which current can flow; a **parallel circuit** is a closed circuit in which the current divides into two or more paths before coming back together to complete the circuit; a **series circuit** is an electrical circuit in which the elements are connected one after the other so that the same current flows through them all.

circular *adjective* **1** in the shape of a circle. **2** A circular argument or theory is not valid because it uses a statement to prove a conclusion and the conclusion to prove the statement. ▶ *noun* **3** a letter or advertisement sent to a lot of people at the same time. > **circularity** *noun*

circulate *verb* **1** When something circulates or when you circulate it, it moves easily around an area. **2** When you circulate something among people, you pass it round or tell it to all the people.

circulate *verb*
2 = distribute, propagate, spread

circulation *noun* 1 The circulation of something is the act of circulating it or the action of it circulating. 2 The circulation of a newspaper or magazine is the number of copies that are sold of each issue. 3 (SCIENCE) Your circulation is the movement of blood through your body.

circumference *noun* (MATHS) The circumference of a circle is its outer line or edge; also the length of this line.

circumstance *noun* 1 The circumstances of a situation or event are the conditions that affect what happens.
2 Someone's circumstances are their position and conditions in life.

circus *noun* circuses a show given by a travelling group of entertainers such as clowns, acrobats and specially trained animals.

cistern *noun* a tank in which water is stored, for example one in the roof of a house or above a toilet.

citadel *noun* a fortress in or near a city.

cite *verb* 1 (*formal*) If you cite something, you quote it or refer to it. 2 If someone is cited in a legal action, they are officially called to appear in court.

citizen *noun* (CITIZENSHIP) The citizens of a country or city are the people who live in it or belong to it.

citizenship *noun* (CITIZENSHIP) the status of being a citizen, with all the rights and duties that go with it.

citrus fruit *noun* Citrus fruits are juicy, sharp-tasting fruits such as oranges, lemons and grapefruit.

city cities *noun* a large town where many people live and work.

city *noun*
= metropolis, town

civic *adjective* relating to a city or citizens.

civil *adjective* 1 relating to the citizens of a country. 2 relating to people or things that are not connected with the armed forces. 3 polite. › **civility** *noun*

civil engineering *noun* Civil engineering is the design and construction of roads, bridges and public buildings.

civilian *noun* a person who is not in the armed forces.

civilisation; also spelt **civilization** *noun* 1 (HISTORY) a society which has a highly developed organisation and culture. 2 Civilisation is an advanced state of social organisation and culture.

civilised; also spelt **civilized** *adjective* 1 A civilised society is one with a developed social organisation and way of life.
2 A civilised person is polite and reasonable.

civilised *adjective*
1 = cultured, enlightened

civil servant *noun* a person who works in the civil service.

civil service *noun* The civil service is the government departments responsible for the administration of a country.

civil war *noun* a war between groups of people who live in the same country.

clad *adjective* (literary) Someone who is clad in particular clothes is wearing them.

claim *verb* **1** If you claim that something is the case, you say that it is the case. **2** If you claim something, you ask for it because it belongs to you or you have a right to it. ▶ *noun* **3** a statement that something is the case, or that you have a right to something.

> **claim** *verb*
> **1** = allege, assert, hold, insist, maintain, profess
> ▶ *noun* **3** = allegation, assertion

claimant *noun* someone who is making a claim, especially for money.

clairvoyant *adjective* **1** able to know about things that will happen in the future. ▶ *noun* **2** a person who is, or claims to be, clairvoyant.

clam *noun* a kind of shellfish.

clamber *verb* If you clamber somewhere, you climb there with difficulty.

clammy clammier, clammiest *adjective* unpleasantly damp and sticky.

clamour *verb* **1** If people clamour for something, they demand it noisily or angrily. ▶ *noun* **2** Clamour is noisy or angry shouts or demands by a lot of people.

clamp *noun* **1** an object with movable parts that are used to hold two things firmly together.

▶ *verb* **2** To clamp things together is to fasten them or hold them firmly with a clamp.

> **clamp down on** *verb* To clamp down on something is to become stricter in controlling it.

clan *noun* a group of families related to each other by being descended from the same ancestor.

clandestine *adjective* secret and hidden.

clap claps, clapping, clapped *verb* **1** When you clap, you hit your hands together loudly to show your appreciation. **2** If you clap someone on the back or shoulder, you hit them in a friendly way. **3** If you clap something somewhere, you put it there quickly and firmly. ▶ *noun* **4** a sound made by clapping your hands. **5** A clap of thunder is a sudden loud noise of thunder.

claret *noun* a type of red wine, especially one from the Bordeaux region of France.

clarify clarifies, clarifying, clarified *verb* (EXAM TERM) To clarify something is to make it clear and easier to understand.
> **clarification** *noun*

clarinet *noun* (MUSIC) a woodwind instrument with a straight tube and a single reed in its mouthpiece.

clarity *noun* The clarity of something is its clearness.

clash *verb* **1** If people clash with each other, they fight or argue. **2** Ideas or styles that clash are so different that they do not go together. **3** If two events clash, they happen at the same time so you cannot go to both. **4** When metal objects clash, they hit each

other with a loud noise. ▶ noun
5 a fight or argument. 6 A clash
of ideas, styles or events is a
situation in which they do not go
together.

> **clash** verb
> 1 = battle, fight, quarrel,
> wrangle 2 = conflict, contradict,
> differ, disagree, go against, jar
> ▶ noun 5 = battle, conflict,
> confrontation, fight, skirmish,
> squabble, struggle

clasp verb 1 To clasp something
means to hold it tightly or fasten
it. ▶ noun 2 a fastening such as a
hook or catch.

> **clasp** verb
> 1 = clutch, embrace, grip, hold,
> hug, press, squeeze
> ▶ noun 2 = buckle, catch, clip,
> fastener, fastening

class noun 1 A class of people
or things is a group of them
of a particular type or quality.
2 a group of pupils or students
taught together, or a lesson that
they have together. 3 Someone
who has class is elegant in
appearance or behaviour. ▶ verb
4 To class something means to
arrange it in a particular group or
to consider it as belonging to a
particular group.

> **class** noun
> 1 = category, genre, grade,
> group, kind, set, sort, type
> ▶ verb 4 = categorise, classify,
> designate, grade, rank, rate

classic adjective 1 typical and
therefore a good model or
example of something. 2 of very
high quality. 3 simple in style and
form. ▶ noun 4 something of the
highest quality. 5 Classics is the
study of Latin and Greek, and the

literature of ancient Greece and
Rome.

classical adjective 1 traditional in
style, form and content.
2 Classical music is serious music
considered to be of lasting value.
3 characteristic of the style of
ancient Greece and Rome.
> **classically** adverb

classified adjective officially
declared secret by the
government.

classify classifies, classifying,
classified verb (LIBRARY) To classify
things is to arrange them into
groups with similar
characteristics. > **classification**
noun

> **classify** verb
> = arrange, categorise, grade,
> rank, sort

classroom noun a room in a
school where pupils have lessons.

classy classier, classiest adjective
(informal) stylish and elegant.

clatter verb 1 When things clatter,
they hit each other with a loud
rattling noise. ▶ noun 2 a loud
rattling noise made by hard
things hitting each other.

clause noun 1 a section of a legal
document. 2 (ENGLISH) In
grammar, a clause is a group of
words with a subject and a verb,
which may be a complete
sentence or one of the parts of a
sentence.

claustrophobia noun
Claustrophobia is a fear of being
in enclosed spaces.
> **claustrophobic** adjective

claw noun 1 An animal's claws are
hard, curved nails at the end of its
feet. 2 The claws of a crab or
lobster are the two jointed parts,

used for grasping things. ▶ *verb*
3 If an animal claws something,
it digs its claws into it.

clay *noun* Clay is a type of earth
that is soft and sticky when wet
and hard when baked dry. It is
used to make pottery and bricks.

clean *adjective* **1** free from dirt or
marks. **2** free from germs or
infection. **3** If humour is clean, it
is not rude and does not involve
bad language. **4** A clean
movement is skilful and accurate.
5 Clean also means free from
fault or error. ▶ *verb* **6** To clean
something is to remove dirt
from it. > **cleanly** *adverb*
> **cleaner** *noun*

> **clean** *adjective*
> **1** = immaculate, impeccable,
> laundered, spotless, washed
> **2** = antiseptic, hygienic,
> purified, sterilised,
> uncontaminated, unpolluted
> ▶ *verb* **6** = cleanse, dust, scour,
> scrub, sponge, swab, wash,
> wipe

cleanliness *noun* Cleanliness is
the practice of keeping yourself
and your surroundings clean.

cleanse *verb* To cleanse
something is to make it
completely free from dirt.

clear *adjective* **1** easy to understand,
see or hear. **2** easy to see through.
3 free from obstructions or
unwanted things. ▶ *verb* **4** To
clear an area is to remove
unwanted things from it. **5** If you
clear a fence or other obstacle, you
jump over it without touching it.
6 When fog or mist clears, it
disappears. **7** If someone is
cleared of a crime, they are proved
to be not guilty. > **clearly** *adverb*
> **clear out** *verb* **1** If you clear out a

room or cupboard, you tidy it and
throw away unwanted things.
2 (*informal*) To clear out means to
leave. > **clear up** *verb* **1** If you clear
up, you tidy a place and put
things away. **2** When a problem
or misunderstanding is cleared
up, it is solved or settled.

> **clear** *adjective*
> **1** = apparent, blatant,
> conspicuous, definite, evident,
> explicit, obvious, plain
> **2** = crystalline, glassy,
> translucent, transparent
> ▶ *verb* **7** = absolve, acquit

clearance *noun* **1** Clearance is the
removal of old buildings in an
area. **2** If someone is given
clearance to do something, they
get official permission to do it.

clearing *noun* an area of bare
ground in a forest.

cleaver *noun* a knife with a large
square blade, used especially by
butchers.

cleft *noun* a narrow opening in a
rock.

clench *verb* **1** When you clench
your fist, you curl your fingers up
tightly. **2** When you clench your
teeth, you squeeze them together
tightly.

clergy *plural noun* (RE) The clergy
are the ministers of the Christian
Church.

clergyman **clergymen** *noun* a
male member of the clergy.

clerical *adjective* **1** relating to work
done in an office. **2** relating to the
clergy.

clerk *noun* a person who keeps
records or accounts in an office,
bank or law court.

clever *adjective* **1** intelligent and
quick to understand things.

2 very effective or skilful: *a clever plan*.

> **clever** *adjective*
> **1** = brainy (*informal*), bright, intelligent, shrewd, smart

cliché *noun* (ENGLISH) an idea or phrase which is no longer effective because it has been used so much.

click *verb* **1** When something clicks or when you click it, it makes a short snapping sound. **2** When you click on an area of a computer screen, you point the cursor at it and press one of the buttons on the mouse in order to make something happen. ▶ *noun* **3** a sound of something clicking.

client *noun* someone who pays a professional person or company for a service.

clientele *plural noun* The clientele of a place are its customers.

cliff *noun* a steep, high rock face by the sea.

climate *noun* **1** (GEOGRAPHY) The climate of a place is the average weather conditions there. **2** the general attitude and opinion of people at a particular time.
> **climatic** *adjective*

climax *noun* (ENGLISH) The climax of a process, story or piece of music is the most exciting moment in it, usually near the end.

climb *verb* **1** To climb is to move upwards. **2** If you climb somewhere, you move there with difficulty: *She climbed out of the driving seat*. ▶ *noun* **3** a movement upwards. > **climber** *noun*

> **climb** *verb*
> **1** = ascend, clamber, mount, scale

clinch *verb* If you clinch an agreement or an argument, you settle it in a way.

cling clings, clinging, clung *verb* To cling to something is to hold onto it or stay closely attached to it.

clinic *noun* a building where people go for medical treatment.

clinical *adjective* **1** relating to the medical treatment of patients. **2** Clinical behaviour or thought is logical and unemotional.
> **clinically** *adverb*

clip clips, clipping, clipped *noun* **1** a small metal or plastic object used for holding things together. **2** a short piece of a film shown by itself. ▶ *verb* **3** If you clip things together, you fasten them with clips. **4** If you clip something, you cut bits from it to shape it.

clipping *noun* an article cut from a newspaper or magazine.

clique *noun* a small group of people who stick together and do not mix with other people.

cloak *noun* **1** a wide, loose coat without sleeves. ▶ *verb* **2** To cloak something is to cover or hide it.

cloakroom *noun* a room for coats or a room with toilets and washbasins in a public building.

clock *noun* **1** a device that measures and shows the time. ▶ *phrase* **2** If you work round the clock, you work all day and night.

clockwise *adjective, adverb* in the same direction as the hands on a clock rotate.

clockwork *noun* **1** Toys that work by clockwork move when they are wound up with a key. ▶ *phrase* **2** If something happens like clockwork, it happens with no problems or delays.

clog clogs, clogging, clogged *verb*
1 To clog something is to block it.
▶ *noun* 2 Clogs are heavy wooden shoes.

clone (SCIENCE) *noun* 1 In biology, a clone is an animal or plant that has been produced artificially from the cells of another animal or plant and is therefore identical to it. ▶ *verb* 2 To clone an animal or plant is to produce it as a clone.

close *verb* 1 To close something is to shut it. 2 To close a road or entrance is to block it so that no-one can go in or out. 3 If a shop closes at a certain time, then it does not do business after that time. ▶ *adjective, adverb* 4 near to something. ▶ *adjective* 5 People who are close to each other are very friendly and know each other well. 6 You say the weather is close when it is uncomfortably warm and there is not enough air.
> **close down** *verb* If a business closes down, all work stops there permanently.

close *verb*
1 = secure, shut 2 = bar, block, obstruct, seal
▶ *adjective, adverb* 4 = adjacent, adjoining, at hand, handy, near, nearby, neighbouring
▶ *adjective* 5 = attached, dear, devoted, friendly, intimate, loving

closet *noun* 1 a cupboard.
▶ *verb* 2 If you are closeted somewhere, you shut yourself away alone or in private with another person. ▶ *adjective* 3 Closet beliefs, feelings or habits are kept private and secret.

close-up *noun* a detailed close view of something, especially a photograph taken close to the subject.

closure *noun* 1 The closure of a business is the permanent shutting of it. 2 The closure of a road is the blocking of it so it cannot be used.

clot clots, clotting, clotted *noun*
1 a lump, especially one that forms when blood thickens. ▶ *verb* 2 When a substance such as blood clots, it thickens and forms a lump.

cloth *noun* 1 Cloth is fabric made by a process such as weaving. 2 a piece of material used for wiping or protecting things.

cloth *noun*
1 = fabric, material, textile

clothe clothes, clothing, clothed *verb* To clothe someone is to give them clothes to wear.

clothes *plural noun* the things people wear on their bodies.

clothes *plural noun*
= attire (*formal*), clothing, costume, dress, garments, gear (*informal*), outfit, wardrobe, wear

clothing *noun* the clothes people wear.

cloud *noun* 1 a mass of water vapour, smoke or dust that forms in the air and is seen floating in the sky. 2 (ICT) The cloud is a name for a network of servers on the internet used to store data and services. ▶ *verb* 3 If something clouds or is clouded, it becomes cloudy or difficult to see through. 4 Something that clouds an issue makes it more confusing.

cloud noun
1 = billow, fog, haze, mist, vapour
▶ verb 4 = confuse, distort, muddle

cloud computing noun (ICT)
Cloud computing is a system where a person's files and programs are stored on the internet so that the person can use them at any time from any place.

cloudy cloudier, cloudiest adjective
1 full of clouds. 2 difficult to see through.

cloudy adjective
1 = dull, gloomy, leaden, overcast 2 = muddy, murky, opaque

clout (informal) noun 1 Someone who has clout has influence.
2 A clout is a hit. ▶ verb 3 If you clout someone, you hit them.

clove noun 1 Cloves are small, strong-smelling dried flower buds from a tropical tree, used as a spice in cooking. 2 A clove of garlic is one of the separate sections of the bulb.

clover noun Clover is a small plant with leaves made up of three similar parts.

clown noun 1 a circus performer who wears funny clothes and make-up and does silly things to make people laugh. ▶ verb 2 If you clown around, you do silly things to make people laugh.

cloying adjective unpleasantly sickly, sweet or sentimental.

club clubs, clubbing, clubbed noun
1 an organisation of people with a particular interest who meet regularly; also the place where they meet. 2 a thick, heavy stick

used as a weapon. 3 a stick with a shaped head that a golf player uses to hit the ball. 4 Clubs is one of the four suits in a pack of playing cards. It is marked by a black symbol in the shape of a clover leaf. ▶ verb 5 To club someone is to hit them hard with a heavy object. > **club together** verb If people club together, they all join together to give money to buy something.

club noun
1 = association, circle, group, guild, society, union 2 = bat, stick, truncheon

clue noun something that helps to solve a problem or mystery.

clump noun 1 a small group of things close together. ▶ verb 2 If you clump about, you walk with heavy footsteps.

clumsiness noun awkwardness in the way someone or something moves.

clumsiness noun
= awkwardness, ungainliness

clumsy clumsier, clumsiest adjective 1 moving awkwardly and carelessly. 2 said or done without thought or tact. > **clumsily** adverb

clumsy adjective
1 = awkward, gauche, lumbering, uncoordinated, ungainly

clung the past tense and past participle of **cling**.

cluster noun 1 A cluster of things is a group of them together. ▶ verb 2 If people cluster together, they stay together in a close group.

clutch verb If you clutch something, you hold it tightly or seize it.

clutter noun 1 Clutter is an untidy mess. ▶ verb 2 Things that clutter a place fill it and make it untidy.

cm an abbreviation for 'centimetres'.

co- prefix 'Co-' means 'together': Paula is now co-writing a book with Pierre.

coach noun 1 a long motor vehicle used for taking passengers on long journeys. 2 a section of a train that carries passengers. 3 a four-wheeled vehicle with a roof pulled by horses, which people used to travel in. 4 a person who coaches a sport or a subject. ▶ verb 5 If someone coaches you, they teach you and help you to get better at a sport or a subject.

coal noun 1 Coal is a hard black rock obtained from under the earth and burned as a fuel. 2 Coals are burning pieces of coal.

coalition noun a temporary alliance, especially between different political parties forming a government.

coarse adjective 1 Something that is coarse is rough in texture, often consisting of large particles. 2 Someone who is coarse talks or behaves in a rude or rather offensive way.

coast noun 1 the edge of the land where it meets the sea. ▶ verb 2 A vehicle that is coasting is moving without engine power. > **coastal** adjective

> **coast** noun
> 1 = beach, border, coastline, seaside, shore, strand

coastguard noun an official who watches the sea near a coast to get help for sailors when they need it, and to prevent smuggling.

coastline noun the outline of a coast, especially its appearance as seen from the sea or air.

coat noun 1 a piece of clothing with sleeves which you wear over your other clothes. 2 An animal's coat is the fur or hair on its body. 3 A coat of paint or varnish is a layer of it. ▶ verb 4 To coat something means to cover it with a thin layer of something.

> **coat** noun
> 2 = fleece, fur, hair, hide, pelt, skin, wool

coating noun a layer of something.

> **coating** noun
> = coat, covering, layer

coax verb If you coax someone to do something, you gently persuade them to do it.

> **coax** verb
> = cajole, persuade, talk into

cobalt noun (SCIENCE) Cobalt is a hard silvery-white metallic element which is used in alloys and for producing a blue dye. Its atomic number is 27 and its symbol is Co.

cobble noun Cobbles or cobblestones are stones with a rounded surface that were used in the past for making roads.

cobbler noun a person who makes or mends shoes.

cobra noun a type of large poisonous snake from Africa and Asia.

cobweb noun the very thin net that a spider spins for catching insects.

cocaine noun Cocaine is an illegal addictive drug.

cock noun an adult male chicken; also used of any male bird.

cockatoo cockatoos noun a type of parrot with a crest, found in Australia and New Guinea.

Cockney noun a person born in the East End of London.

cockpit noun The place in a small plane where the pilot sits.

cockroach noun a large dark-coloured insect often found in dirty rooms.

cocktail noun an alcoholic drink made from several ingredients.

cocky cockier, cockiest; cockies (informal) adjective 1 cheeky or too self-confident. ▶ noun 2 in Australian English, a cockatoo. 3 in Australian and New Zealand English, a farmer, especially one whose farm is small. > **cockiness** noun

> **cocky** adjective
> 1 = arrogant, brash, conceited, overconfident
> ▶ noun 3 = crofter (Scottish), farmer

cocoa noun Cocoa is a brown powder made from the seeds of a tropical tree and used for making chocolate; also a hot drink made from this powder.

coconut noun a very large nut with white flesh, milky juice, and a hard hairy shell.

cocoon noun a silky covering over the larvae of moths and some other insects.

cod noun a large edible fish.

code noun 1 a system of replacing the letters or words in a message with other letters or words, so that nobody can understand the message unless they know the

system. 2 a group of numbers and letters which is used to identify something. 3 (ICT) Code is the instructions used to create a computer program. ▶ verb 4 If you code a message, you put it into code. 5 To code is also to write computer programs. > **coded** adjective

coffee noun Coffee is a substance made by roasting and grinding the beans of a tropical shrub; also a hot drink made from this substance.

coffin noun a box in which a dead body is buried or cremated.

cog noun a wheel with teeth which turns another wheel or part of a machine.

coherent adjective 1 If something such as a theory is coherent, its parts fit together well and do not contradict each other. 2 If someone is coherent, what they are saying makes sense and is not jumbled or confused. > **coherence** noun

cohesive adjective If something is cohesive, its parts fit together well. > **cohesion** noun

coil noun 1 a length of rope or wire wound into a series of loops; also one of the loops. ▶ verb 2 If something coils, it turns into a series of loops.

> **coil** verb
> 2 = curl, loop, spiral, twine, twist, wind

coin noun 1 a small metal disc which is used as money. ▶ verb 2 If you coin a word or a phrase, you invent it.

coinage noun The coinage of a country is the coins that are used there.

coincide verb 1 If two events coincide, they happen at about the same time. 2 When two people's ideas or opinions coincide, they agree.

coincidence noun 1 what happens when two similar things occur at the same time by chance. 2 the fact that two things are surprisingly the same.
> **coincidental** adjective
> **coincidentally** adverb

coke noun Coke is a grey solid fuel produced from coal.

colander noun a bowl-shaped container with holes in it, used for washing or draining food.

cold adjective 1 having a low temperature. 2 Someone who is cold does not show much affection. ▶ noun 3 You can refer to cold weather as the cold. 4 a minor illness in which you sneeze and may have a sore throat.

> **cold** adjective
> 1 = arctic, biting, bitter, bleak, chilly, freezing, icy, raw, wintry
> 2 = aloof, distant, frigid, lukewarm, reserved, stony

cold-blooded adjective 1 Someone who is cold-blooded does not show any pity. 2 A cold-blooded animal has a body temperature that changes according to the surrounding temperature.

cold war noun Cold war is a state of extreme unfriendliness between countries not actually at war.

coleslaw noun Coleslaw is a salad of chopped cabbage and other vegetables in mayonnaise.

colic noun Colic is pain in a baby's stomach.

collaborate verb When people collaborate, they work together to produce something.
> **collaboration** noun
> **collaborator** noun

collage noun (ART) a picture made by sticking pieces of paper or cloth onto a surface.

collapse verb 1 If something such as a building collapses, it falls down suddenly. If a person collapses, they fall down suddenly because they are ill. 2 If something such as a system or a business collapses, it suddenly stops working. ▶ noun 3 The collapse of something is what happens when it stops working.

> **collapse** verb
> 1 = fall down, give way 2 = fail, fold, founder
> ▶ noun 3 = downfall, failure

collapsible adjective A collapsible object can be folded flat when it is not in use.

collar noun 1 The collar of a shirt or coat is the part round the neck which is usually folded over. 2 a leather band round the neck of a dog or cat.

collateral noun Collateral is money or property which is used as a guarantee that someone will repay a loan, and which the lender can take if the loan is not repaid.

colleague noun A person's colleagues are the people he or she works with.

> **colleague** noun
> = associate, co-worker, partner, workmate

collect verb 1 To collect things is to gather them together for a special

purpose or as a hobby. **2** If you collect someone or something from a place, you call there and take them away. **3** When things collect in a place, they gather there over a period of time.
> **collector** *noun*

> **collect** *verb*
> 1 = accumulate, assemble, gather, raise

collected *adjective* calm and self-controlled.

collection *noun* **1** (ART) a group of things collected over a period of time. **2** Collection is the collecting of something. **3** the organised collecting of money, for example for charity, or the sum of money collected.

> **collection** *noun*
> 1 = assortment, group, store

collective *adjective* **1** involving every member of a group of people. ▸ *noun* **2** a group of people who share the responsibility both for running something and for doing the work. > **collectively** *adverb*

college *noun* **1** a place where students study after they have left school. **2** a name given to some secondary schools. **3** one of the institutions into which some universities are divided. **4** In New Zealand English, a college can also refer to a teacher training college.

collide *verb* If a moving object collides with something, it hits it.

collie *noun* a dog that is used for rounding up sheep.

colliery collieries *noun* a coal mine.

collision *noun* A collision occurs when a moving object hits something.

colloquial *adjective* (ENGLISH) Colloquial words and phrases are informal and used especially in conversation.

> **colloquial** *adjective*
> = conversational, everyday, informal

cologne *noun* Cologne is a kind of weak perfume.

colon *noun* **1** (ENGLISH) the punctuation mark (:) which is used to introduce a list or an explanation of a statement. **2** part of your intestine.

colonel *noun* an army officer with a fairly high rank.

colonial *adjective* **1** relating to a colony. **2** In Australia, 'colonial' is used to relate to the period of Australian history before the Federation in 1901.

colonise; also spelt **colonize** *verb* **1** (HISTORY) When people colonise a place, they go to live there and take control of it. **2** When a lot of animals colonise a place, they go there and make it their home.
> **colonisation** *noun* > **colonist** *noun*

colony colonies *noun* **1** (HISTORY) a country controlled by a more powerful country. **2** a group of people who settle in a country controlled by their homeland.

> **colony** *noun*
> 1 = dependency, dominion, territory **2** = community, outpost, settlement

colossal *adjective* very large indeed.

colossal *adjective*
= enormous, gigantic, huge, immense, mammoth, massive, vast

colour *noun* 1 (ART) the appearance something has as a result of reflecting light. 2 a substance used to give colour. 3 Someone's colour is the normal colour of their skin. 4 Colour is also a quality that makes something interesting or exciting. ▶ *verb* 5 If you colour something, you give it a colour. 6 If something colours your opinion, it affects the way you think about something.
> **colouring** *noun*

colour *noun*
1 = hue, pigmentation, shade, tint 2 = dye, paint, pigment ▶ 5 = dye, paint, stain, tint 6 = bias, distort, prejudice, slant

colourful *adjective* 1 full of colour. 2 interesting or exciting.

colourful *adjective*
1 = bright, brilliant, intense, jazzy (*informal*), rich, vibrant, vivid 2 = graphic, interesting, lively, rich, vivid

colt *noun* a young male horse.

column *noun* 1 a tall solid upright cylinder, especially one supporting a part of a building. 2 a group of people moving in a long line. 3 a vertical section of writing. 4 a regular article in a newspaper or magazine.

columnist *noun* a journalist who writes a regular article in a newspaper or magazine.

coma *noun* Someone who is in a coma is in a state of deep unconsciousness.

comb *noun* 1 a flat object with pointed teeth used for tidying your hair. ▶ *verb* 2 When you comb your hair, you tidy it with a comb. 3 If you comb a place, you search it thoroughly to try to find someone or something.

combat *noun* 1 Combat is fighting. ▶ *verb* 2 To combat something means to try to stop it happening or developing.

combination *noun* 1 a mixture of things. 2 a series of letters or numbers used to open a special lock.

combination *noun*
1 = amalgamation, blend, mix, mixture

combine *verb* 1 To combine things is to cause them to exist together. 2 To combine things also means to join them together to make a single thing. 3 If something combines two qualities or features, it has them both.

combine *verb*
2 = amalgamate, blend, fuse, integrate, merge, mix, unite

combustion *noun* (SCIENCE) Combustion is the act of burning something or the process of burning.

come comes, coming, came, come *verb* 1 To come to a place is to move there or arrive there. 2 To come to a place also means to reach as far as that place: *The sea water came up to his waist.* 3 'Come' is used to say that someone or something reaches a particular state: *They came to power in 2016.* 4 When a particular time or event comes, it happens. 5 If you come from a place, you were born there or it is your home. ▶ *phrase* 6 A time or event **to come** is a future time or event. ▸ **come about** verb The way something comes about is the way it happens: *The discussion came about because of the proposed changes.* ▸ **come across** verb If you come across something, you find it by chance. ▸ **come off** verb If something comes off, it succeeds. ▸ **come on** verb If something is coming on, it is making progress. ▸ **come round** verb 1 To come round means to recover consciousness. 2 To come round to an idea or situation means to eventually accept it. 3 When a regular event comes round, it happens. ▸ **come to** verb To come to means to recover consciousness. ▸ **come up** verb If something comes up in a conversation or meeting, it is mentioned or discussed. ▸ **come up with** verb If you come up with a plan or idea, you suggest it.

> **come** verb
> 1 = appear, arrive, enter, materialise, show up (*informal*), turn up (*informal*) 4 = happen, occur, take place

comeback noun To make a comeback means to be popular or successful again.

comedian noun an entertainer whose job is to make people laugh.

comedienne noun a female comedian.

comedy comedies noun a light-hearted play or film with a happy ending.

comet noun an object that travels around the sun leaving a bright trail behind it.

comfort noun 1 Comfort is the state of being physically relaxed. 2 Comfort is also a feeling of relief from worries or unhappiness. 3 (*in plural*) Comforts are things which make your life easier and more pleasant. ▸ verb 4 To comfort someone is to make them less worried or unhappy.

> **comfort** noun
> 1 = ease, luxury, wellbeing
> 2 = consolation, help, relief, satisfaction, support
> ▸ verb 4 = cheer, console, reassure, soothe

comfortable adjective 1 If you are comfortable, you are physically relaxed. 2 Something that is comfortable makes you feel relaxed. 3 If you feel comfortable in a particular situation, you are not afraid or embarrassed. ▸ **comfortably** adverb

> **comfortable** adjective
> 2 = cosy, homely, relaxing, restful 3 = at ease, at home, contented, happy, relaxed

comic adjective 1 funny. ▸ noun 2 someone who tells jokes. 3 a magazine that contains stories told in pictures.

comical adjective funny.

comma noun (ENGLISH) the punctuation mark (,) which is used to separate different parts of a sentence or items in a list.

command verb 1 To command someone to do something is to order them to do it. 2 If you command something such as respect, you receive it because of your personal qualities. 3 An officer who commands part of an army or navy is in charge of it. ▸ noun 4 an order to do something.

4 To duck someone means to push them briefly under water.

duckling *noun* a young duck.

duct *noun* **1** a pipe or channel through which liquid or gas is sent. **2** a bodily passage through which liquid such as tears can pass.

dud *noun* something which does not function properly.

due *adjective* **1** expected to happen or arrive. **2** If you give something due consideration, you give it the consideration it needs. ▶ *phrase* **3** Due to means caused by. ▶ *adverb* **4** Due means exactly in a particular direction: *About a mile due west lay the ocean.* ▶ *noun* **5** (in plural) Dues are sums of money that you pay regularly to an organisation you belong to.

duel *noun* **1** a fight arranged between two people using deadly weapons, to settle a quarrel. **2** Any contest or conflict between two people can be referred to as a duel.

duet *noun* (MUSIC) a piece of music sung or played by two people.

dug Dug is the past tense and past participle of **dig**.

dugout *noun* **1** a canoe made by hollowing out a log. **2** (*Military*) a shelter dug in the ground for protection.

duke *noun* a nobleman with a rank just below that of a prince.

dull *adjective* **1** not at all interesting in any way. **2** not bright, sharp or clear. **3** A dull day or dull sky is very cloudy. **4** Dull feelings are weak and not intense. ▶ *verb* **5** If something dulls or is dulled, it becomes less bright, sharp or clear. ▷ **dully** *adverb*

dull *adjective*
1 = boring, drab, humdrum, monotonous, tedious, uninteresting **2** = drab, gloomy, muted, sombre, subdued **3** = cloudy, leaden, murky, overcast

duly *adverb* **1** (*formal*) If something is duly done, it is done in the correct way. **2** If something duly happens, it is something that you expected to happen.

dumb *adjective* **1** unable to speak. **2** (*informal*) slow to understand or stupid.

dumb *adjective*
1 = mute, silent, speechless **2** = dim, obtuse (*formal*), stupid, thick (*informal*)

dumbfounded *adjective* speechless with amazement.

dummy *dummies* *noun* **1** a rubber teat which a baby sucks or bites on. **2** an imitation or model of something which is used for display. ▶ *adjective* **3** imitation or substitute.

dump *verb* **1** When unwanted waste is dumped, it is left somewhere. **2** If you dump something, you throw it down or put it down somewhere in a careless way. ▶ *noun* **3** a place where rubbish is left. **4** a storage place, especially used by the military for storing supplies. **5** (*informal*) You refer to a place as a dump when it is unattractive and unpleasant to live in.

dump *verb*
1 = discharge, dispose of, get rid of, jettison, throw away, throw out **2** = deposit, drop

dumpling *noun* a small lump of dough that is cooked and eaten with meat and vegetables.

dunce *noun* a person who cannot learn what someone is trying to teach them.

dune *noun* A dune or sand dune is a hill of sand near the sea or in the desert.

dung *noun* Dung is the faeces from large animals.

dungeon *noun* an underground prison.

dunk *verb* To dunk something means to dip it briefly into a liquid.

duo *duos noun* 1 a pair of musical performers; also a piece of music written for two players. 2 Any two people doing something together can be referred to as a duo.

dupe *verb* If someone dupes you, they trick you.

> **dupe** *verb*
> = cheat, con (*informal*), deceive, delude, fool, play a trick on, trick

duplicate *verb* 1 To duplicate something means to make an exact copy of it. ▶ *noun* 2 something that is identical to something else. ▶ *adjective* 3 identical to or an exact copy of. > **duplication** *noun*

durable *adjective* strong and lasting for a long time. > **durability** *noun*

duration *noun* The duration of something is the length of time during which it happens or exists.

duress *noun* If you do something under duress, you are forced to do it, and you do it very unwillingly.

during *preposition* happening throughout a particular time or at a particular point in time.

dusk *noun* Dusk is the time just before nightfall when it is not completely dark.

dust *noun* 1 Dust is dry fine powdery material such as particles of earth, dirt or pollen. ▶ *verb* 2 When you dust furniture or other objects, you remove dust from them using a duster. 3 If you dust a surface with powder, you cover it lightly with the powder.

dustbin *noun* a large container for rubbish.

duster *noun* a cloth used for removing dust from furniture and other objects.

dusty *dustier, dustiest adjective* covered with dust.

Dutch *adjective* 1 belonging or relating to Holland. ▶ *noun* 2 Dutch is the main language spoken in Holland.

dutiful *adjective* doing everything you are expected to do. > **dutifully** *adverb*

duty *duties noun* 1 something you ought to do or feel you should do, because it is your responsibility. 2 a task which you do as part of your job. 3 Duty is tax paid to the government on some goods, especially imports.

> **duty** *noun*
> 1 = obligation, responsibility
> 2 = assignment, job, responsibility, role 3 = excise, levy (*formal*), tariff, tax

duty-free *adjective* Duty-free goods are sold at airports or on planes or ships at a cheaper price than usual because they are not taxed.

duvet noun a cotton quilt filled with feathers or other material, which you put over yourself in bed.

DVD noun A DVD is a disc that can store video and sound information. DVD is an abbreviation for 'digital video disc' or 'digital versatile disc'.

dwarf verb 1 If one thing dwarfs another, it is so much bigger that it makes it look very small.
▶ adjective 2 smaller than average.
▶ noun 3 a person who is much smaller than average size.

dwell dwells, dwelling, dwelled or dwelt verb 1 (literary) To dwell somewhere means to live there. 2 If you dwell on something or dwell upon it, you think or write about it a lot.

dwelling noun (formal) Someone's dwelling is the house or other place where they live.

dwindle verb If something dwindles, it becomes smaller or weaker.

dye dyes, dyeing, dyed verb 1 To dye something means to change its colour by applying coloured liquid to it. ▶ noun 2 a colouring substance which is used to change the colour of something such as cloth or hair.

dying adjective 1 likely to die soon. 2 (informal) If you are **dying for something**, you want it very much.

> **dying** adjective
> 2 **be dying for** = ache for, be hungry for, long for, pine for, yearn for

dyke; also spelt **dike** noun a thick wall that prevents water flooding onto land from a river or the sea.

dynamic adjective 1 A dynamic person is full of energy, ambition and new ideas. 2 relating to energy or forces which produce motion.

dynamics plural noun 1 The dynamics of a society or a situation are the forces that cause it to change. 2 (MUSIC) Dynamics is the various degrees of loudness needed in the performance of a piece of music, or the symbols used to indicate this in written music.

dynamite noun Dynamite is an explosive made of nitroglycerine.

dynamo dynamos noun (SCIENCE) a device that converts mechanical energy into electricity.

dynasty dynasties noun (HISTORY) a series of rulers of a country all belonging to the same family.

dysentery noun an infection of the bowel which causes fever, stomach pain and severe diarrhoea.

dyslexia noun Dyslexia is a learning difficulty that causes problems with reading and spelling.
> **dyslexic** adjective

Ee

each adjective, pronoun **1** every one taken separately: *Each time she went out, she would buy a plant.* ▶ phrase **2** If people do something to **each other**, each person does it to the other or others.

eager adjective wanting very much to do or have something.

> **eager** adjective
> = anxious, ardent, avid, enthusiastic, keen, raring to go (informal)

eagle noun a large bird of prey.

ear noun **1** the parts of your body on either side of your head with which you hear sounds. **2** An ear of corn or wheat is the top part of the stalk which contains seeds.

earl noun a British nobleman.

early earlier, earliest adjective **1** before the arranged or expected time. **2** near the beginning of a day, evening or other period of time. ▶ adverb **3** before the arranged or expected time.

> **early** adjective
> **1** = advance, premature, untimely
> ▶ adverb **3** = ahead of time, beforehand, in advance, in good time, prematurely

earmark verb If you earmark something for a special purpose, you keep it for that purpose.

earn verb **1** If you earn money, you get it in return for work that you do. **2** If you earn something such as praise, you receive it because you deserve it. > **earner** noun

> **earn** verb
> **1** = bring in, draw, get, make, obtain **2** = acquire, attain (formal), win

earnest adjective **1** sincere in what you say or do. ▶ phrase **2** If something begins **in earnest**, it happens to a greater or more serious extent than before.

earnings plural noun Your earnings are money that you earn.

earphones plural noun small speakers which you wear on your ears to listen to sounds from an electronic device.

earring noun Earrings are pieces of jewellery that you wear on your ear lobes.

earshot phrase If you are **within earshot** of something, you can hear it.

earth noun **1** The earth is the planet on which we live. **2** Earth is the dry land on the surface of the earth, especially the soil in which things grow. **3** a hole in the ground where a fox lives. **4** The earth in a piece of electrical equipment is the wire through which electricity can pass into the ground and so make the equipment safe for use.

> **earth** noun
> **1** = globe, planet, world **2** = clay, dirt, ground, soil

earthenware noun pottery made of baked clay.

earthly earlier, earliest *adjective* concerned with life on earth rather than heaven or life after death.

earthquake *noun* (SCIENCE) (GEOGRAPHY) a shaking of the ground caused by movement of the earth.

earthy earlier, earliest *adjective* 1 looking or smelling like earth. 2 Someone who is earthy is open and direct, often in a crude way.

ease *noun* 1 lack of difficulty, worry or hardship. ▶ *verb* 2 When something eases, or when you ease it, it becomes less severe or less intense. 3 If you ease something somewhere, you move it there slowly and carefully.

> **ease** *noun*
> 1 = leisure, relaxation, simplicity
> ▶ *verb* 2 = abate, calm, relax, relieve, slacken 3 = creep, edge, guide, inch, lower, manoeuvre, squeeze

easel *noun* (ART) an upright frame which supports a picture that someone is painting.

easily *adverb* 1 without difficulty. 2 without a doubt: *The song is easily one of their best.*

east *noun* 1 East is the direction in which you look to see the sun rise. 2 The east of a place is the part which is towards the east when you are in the centre. 3 The East is the countries in the south and east of Asia. ▶ *adjective, adverb* 4 East means in or towards the east. ▶ *adjective* 5 An east wind blows from the east.

Easter *noun* (RE) a religious festival when Christians celebrate Christ's coming back

to life after he had been killed.

easterly *adjective* 1 Easterly means to or towards the east. 2 An easterly wind blows from the east.

eastern *adjective* in or from the east.

eastward or **eastwards** *adverb* 1 Eastward or eastwards means towards the east. ▶ *adjective* 2 The eastward part of something is the east part.

easy easier, easiest *adjective* 1 able to be done without difficulty. 2 comfortable and without any worries: *an easy life.*

> **easy** *adjective*
> 1 = light, painless, simple, smooth, straightforward
> 2 = carefree, comfortable, leisurely, quiet, relaxed

eat eats, eating, ate, eaten *verb* 1 To eat means to chew and swallow food. 2 When you eat, you have a meal. > **eat away** *verb* If something is eaten away, it is slowly destroyed.

> **eat** *verb*
> 1 = chew, consume, devour, feed on, scoff, swallow 2 = breakfast (formal), dine (formal), feed, have a meal, lunch (formal), picnic
> ▶ **eat away** = corrode, destroy, dissolve, erode, rot, wear away

eaves *plural noun* The eaves of a roof are the lower edges which jut out over the walls.

eavesdrop eavesdrops, eavesdropping, eavesdropped *verb* If you eavesdrop, you listen secretly to what other people are saying.

ebb *verb* 1 When the sea or the tide ebbs, it flows back. 2 If a person's feeling or strength ebbs, it gets weaker.

ebony noun 1 a hard, dark-coloured wood, used for making furniture. ▶ noun, adjective 2 very deep black.

ebullient adjective (formal) lively and full of enthusiasm.

eccentric adjective 1 having habits or opinions which other people think are odd or peculiar. ▶ noun 2 someone who is eccentric.
> **eccentricity** noun
> **eccentrically** adverb

> **eccentric** adjective
> 1 = bizarre, outlandish, quirky, strange, weird, whimsical
> ▶ noun 2 = character (informal), crank

ecclesiastical adjective of or relating to the Christian Church.

echelon noun 1 An echelon is a level of power or responsibility in an organisation; also used of the group of people at that level. 2 An echelon is also a military formation in the shape of an arrowhead.

echidna echidnas or echidnae noun a small, spiny mammal that lays eggs and has a long snout and claws, found in Australia.

echo echoes, echoing, echoed noun 1 (SCIENCE) a sound which is caused by sound waves reflecting off a surface. 2 a repetition, imitation or reminder of something. ▶ verb 3 If a sound echoes, it is reflected off a surface so that you can hear it again after the original sound has stopped.

eclipse noun An eclipse occurs when one planet passes in front of another and hides it from view for a short time.

eco-friendly eco-friendlier, eco-friendliest adjective If a product is eco-friendly, it does not cause any damage to the environment.

ecology noun (SCIENCE) the relationship between living things and their environment; also used of the study of this relationship. > **ecological** adjective > **ecologically** adverb > **ecologist** noun

economic adjective 1 concerning the management of the money, industry and trade of a country. 2 concerning making a profit.

> **economic** adjective
> 1 = budgetary, commercial, financial 2 = productive, profitable, viable

economical adjective 1 another word for **economic**. 2 Something that is economical is cheap to use or operate. 3 Someone who is economical spends money carefully and sensibly.
> **economically** adverb

> **economical** adjective
> 2 = cheap, cost-effective, economic, inexpensive
> 3 = careful, frugal, prudent, thrifty

economics noun Economics is the study of the production and distribution of goods, services and wealth in a society and the organisation of its money, industry and trade.

economist noun a person who studies or writes about economics.

economy economies noun 1 (HISTORY) The economy of a country is the system it uses to organise and manage its money, industry and trade; also used of the wealth that a country gets from business and industry. **2** Economy is the careful use of things to save money, time or energy.

> **economy** *noun*
> **2** = frugality *(formal)*, prudence, restraint, thrift

ecosystem *noun* (SCIENCE) the relationship between plants and animals and their environment.

ecstasy ecstasies *noun* Ecstasy is a feeling of extreme happiness. ▸ **ecstatic** *adjective* ▸ **ecstatically** *adverb*

> **ecstasy** *noun*
> = bliss, delight, elation, euphoria, exaltation, joy, rapture

eczema *noun* a skin disease that causes the surface of the skin to become rough and itchy.

edge *noun* **1** The edge of something is a border or line where it ends or meets something else. **2** The edge of a blade is its thin, sharp side. **3** If you have the edge over someone, you have an advantage over them. ▸ *verb* **4** If you edge something, you make a border for it. **5** If you edge somewhere, you move there very gradually.

> **edge** *noun*
> **1** = border, boundary, brim, fringe, lip, margin, rim
> ▸ *verb* **5** = creep, inch, sidle

edgy edgier, edgiest *adjective* anxious and irritable.

edible *adjective* safe and pleasant to eat.

edifice *noun (formal)* a large and impressive building.

edit *verb* **1** If you edit a piece of writing, you correct it so that it is fit for publishing. **2** To edit a film or television programme means to select different parts of it and arrange them in a particular order. **3** Someone who edits a newspaper or magazine is in charge of it.

edition *noun* **1** (ENGLISH) An edition of a book, magazine or newspaper is a particular version of it printed at one time; also the total number of copies printed at one time. **2** An edition of a television or radio programme is a single programme that is one of a series.

editor *noun* **1** a person who is responsible for the content of a newspaper or magazine. **2** (LIBRARY) a person who checks books and makes corrections to them before they are published. **3** a person who selects different parts of a television programme or a film and arranges them in a particular order.

editorial *adjective* **1** involved in preparing a newspaper, book or magazine for publication. **2** involving the contents and the opinions of a newspaper or magazine. ▸ *noun* **3** an article in a newspaper or magazine which gives the opinions of the editor or publisher on a particular topic. ▸ **editorially** *adverb*

educate *verb* To educate someone means to teach them so that they gain knowledge about something.

educated *adjective* having a high standard of learning and culture.

> **educated** *adjective*
> = cultivated, cultured, intellectual, learned

education noun the process of gaining knowledge and understanding through learning or the system of teaching people.
> **educational** adjective
> **educationally** adverb

> **education** noun
> = coaching, e-learning, instruction, schooling, training, tuition

eel noun a long, thin, snakelike fish.

eerie eerier, eeriest adjective strange and frightening.
> **eerily** adverb

effect noun 1 a direct result of someone or something on another person or thing. 2 An effect that someone or something has is the overall impression or result that they have. ▶ phrase 3 If something **takes effect** at a particular time, it starts to happen or starts to produce results at that time.

> **effect** noun
> 1 = consequence, end result, fruit, result, upshot

effective adjective 1 working well and producing the intended results. 2 coming into operation or beginning officially.

effeminate adjective A man who is effeminate behaves, looks or sounds like a woman.

efficient adjective capable of doing something well without wasting time or energy. > **efficiency** noun

> **efficient** adjective
> = businesslike, competent, economic, effective, organised, productive

effigy effigies noun a statue or model of a person.

effluent noun Effluent is liquid waste that comes out of factories or sewage works.

effort noun 1 (PSHE) Effort is the physical or mental energy needed to do something. 2 an attempt or struggle to do something.

> **effort** noun
> 1 = application, energy, exertion, trouble, work
> 2 = attempt, bid, stab (informal), struggle

effortless adjective done easily.

eg or **e.g.** Eg means 'for example', and is abbreviated from the Latin expression 'exempli gratia'.

egalitarian adjective favouring equality for all people.

egg noun 1 an oval or rounded object laid by female birds, reptiles, fishes and insects. A baby creature develops inside the egg until it is ready to be born. 2 a hen's egg used as food. 3 In a female animal, an egg is a cell produced in its body which can develop into a baby if it is fertilised. > **egg on** verb If you egg someone on, you encourage them to do something foolish or daring.

eggplant noun a dark purple pear-shaped fruit eaten as a vegetable. It is also called aubergine.

ego egos noun Your ego is your opinion of what you are worth.

egocentric adjective only thinking of yourself.

egoism or **egotism** noun Egoism is behaviour and attitudes which show that you believe that you are more important than other people. > **egoist** or **egotist** noun
> **egoistic** or **egotistic** or **egotistical** adjective

Egyptian *adjective* 1 belonging or relating to Egypt. ▶ *noun* 2 An Egyptian is someone who comes from Egypt.

Eid ul-Fitr *noun* (RE) an annual Muslim festival marking the end of Ramadan.

eight 1 the number 8. ▶ *noun* 2 In rowing, an eight is the crew of a narrow racing boat, consisting of eight rowers.
> **eighth** *adjective*

eighteen the number 18.
> **eighteenth** *adjective*

eighty *eighties* the number 80.
> **eightieth** *adjective*

either *adjective, pronoun, conjunction* 1 one or the other of two possible alternatives: *You can spell it either way.* ▶ *adjective* 2 both one and the other: *on either side of the head.*

eject *verb* If you eject something or someone, you forcefully push or send them out. > **ejection** *noun*

elaborate *adjective* 1 having many different parts. 2 carefully planned, detailed and exact. 3 highly decorated and complicated. ▶ *verb* 4 If you elaborate on something, you add more information or detail about it.

> **elaborate** *adjective*
> 1 = complex, complicated, detailed, intricate, involved
> 3 = fancy, fussy, ornate
> ▶ *verb* 4 = develop, enlarge, expand

elapse *verb* When time elapses, it passes by.

elastic *adjective* 1 able to stretch easily. ▶ *noun* 2 Elastic is rubber material which stretches and returns to its original shape.
> **elasticity** *noun*

elation *noun* Elation is a feeling of great happiness. > **elated** *adjective*

elbow *noun* 1 Your elbow is the joint between the upper part of your arm and your forearm. ▶ *verb* 2 If you elbow someone aside, you push them away with your elbow.

elder *adjective* 1 Your elder brother or sister is older than you. ▶ *noun* 2 a senior member of a group who has influence or authority. 3 a bush or small tree with dark purple berries.

elderly *adjective* Elderly is a polite way to describe an old person.

elect *verb* 1 (CITIZENSHIP) If you elect someone, you choose them to fill a position by voting for them. 2 (*formal*) If you elect to do something, you choose to do it. ▶ *adjective* 3 (*formal*) voted into a position, but not yet carrying out the duties of the position.

election *noun* (CITIZENSHIP) the selection of one or more people for an official position by voting.
> **electoral** *adjective*

electorate *noun* all the people who have the right to vote in an election.

electric *adjective* 1 powered or produced by electricity. 2 very tense or exciting.

electrical *adjective* using or producing electricity.
> **electrically** *adverb*

electrician *noun* a person whose job is to install and repair electrical equipment.

electricity *noun* Electricity is a form of energy used for heating and lighting, and to provide power for machines.

electrified *adjective* connected to a supply of electricity.

E

electrifying adjective Something that is electrifying makes you feel very excited.

electrocute verb If someone is electrocuted, they are killed by touching something that is connected to electricity. > **electrocution** noun

electrode noun a small piece of metal which allows an electric current to pass between a source of power and a piece of equipment.

electron noun (SCIENCE) 1 In physics, an electron is a tiny particle of matter, smaller than an atom. 2 An **electron shell** is the orbit of an electron around the nucleus of an atom.

electronic adjective (ICT) having transistors or silicon chips which control an electric current. > **electronically** adverb

electronics noun Electronics is the technology of electronic devices such as televisions and computers; also the study of how these devices work.

elegant adjective attractive and graceful or stylish. > **elegantly** adverb > **elegance** noun

element noun 1 a part of something which combines with others to make a whole. 2 (SCIENCE) In chemistry, an element is a substance that is made up of only one type of atom. 3 A particular element within a large group of people is a section of it which is similar. 4 An element of a quality is a certain amount of it. 5 The elements of a subject are the basic and most important points. 6 The elements are the weather conditions.

elementary adjective simple, basic and straightforward.

elephant noun a very large four-legged mammal with a long trunk, large ears, and ivory tusks.

elevate verb 1 To elevate someone to a higher status or position means to give them greater status or importance. 2 To elevate something means to raise it up.

elevation noun 1 The elevation of someone or something is the raising of them to a higher level or position. 2 The elevation of a place is its height above sea level or above the ground.

eleven 1 the number 11. ▸ noun 2 a team of cricket or soccer players. > **eleventh** adjective

elf elves noun In folklore, an elf is a small mischievous fairy.

elicit verb 1 (formal) If you elicit information, you find it out by asking careful questions. 2 If you elicit a response or reaction, you make it happen.

eligible adjective suitable or having the right qualifications for something. > **eligibility** noun

eliminate verb 1 If you eliminate something or someone, you get rid of them. 2 If a team or a person is eliminated from a competition, they can no longer take part. > **elimination** noun

> **eliminate** verb
> 1 = cut out, do away with, eradicate, get rid of, remove, stamp out 2 = knock out, put out

elite noun a group of the most powerful, rich or talented people in a society.

Elizabethan (HISTORY) adjective Someone or something that is

Elizabethan lived or was made during the reign of Elizabeth I.

elk *noun* a kind of large deer.

elm *noun* a tall tree with broad leaves.

elongated *adjective* long and thin.

eloquent *adjective* able to speak or write skilfully and with ease.
> **eloquence** *noun*

else *adverb* 1 other than this or more than this: *Can you think of anything else?* ▶ *phrase* 2 You say **or else** to introduce a possibility or an alternative.

elsewhere *adverb* in or to another place.

elude *verb* 1 If a fact or idea eludes you, you cannot understand it or remember it. 2 If you elude someone or something, you avoid them or escape from them.

elusive *adjective* difficult to find, achieve, describe or remember.

elves the plural of **elf**.

emaciated *adjective* extremely thin and weak, because of illness or lack of food.

email; also spelt **e-mail** *noun* 1 the sending of messages from one computer to another. 2 a message sent in this way. ▶ *verb* 3 If you email someone, you send an email to them. 4 If you email something to someone, you send it to them by email.

emancipation *noun* The emancipation of a person means the act of freeing them from harmful or unpleasant restrictions.

embargo embargoes *noun* an order made by a government to stop trade with another country.

embark *verb* 1 If you embark, you go onto a ship at the start of a journey. 2 If you embark on something, you start it.

embarrass *verb* If you embarrass someone, you make them feel ashamed or awkward.
> **embarrassing** *adjective*

> **embarrass** *verb*
> = disconcert, fluster, humiliate, shame

embarrassed *adjective* ashamed or awkward.

> **embarrassed** *adjective*
> = ashamed, awkward, humiliated, red-faced, self-conscious, sheepish

embarrassment *noun* shame and awkwardness.

> **embarrassment** *noun*
> = awkwardness, bashfulness, humiliation, self-consciousness, shame

embassy embassies *noun* the building in which an ambassador and his or her staff work; also used of the ambassador and his or her staff.

embedded *adjective* Something that is embedded is fixed firmly and deeply.

ember *noun* Embers are glowing pieces of coal or wood from a dying fire.

embittered *adjective* If you are embittered, you are angry and resentful about things that have happened to you.

emblazoned *adjective* If something is emblazoned with designs, it is decorated with them.

emblem *noun* an object or a design representing an organisation or an idea.

e

embody embodies, embodying, embodied verb 1 To embody a quality or idea means to contain it or express it. 2 If a number of things are embodied in one thing, they are contained in it. > **embodiment** noun

embossed adjective decorated with designs that stand up slightly from the surface.

embrace verb 1 If you embrace someone, you hug them to show affection or as a greeting. 2 If you embrace a belief or cause, you accept it and believe in it. ▶ noun 3 a hug.

embroider verb If you embroider fabric, you sew a decorative design onto it.

embroidery noun Embroidery is decorative designs sewn onto fabric; also the art or skill of embroidering.

embroiled adjective If someone is embroiled in an argument or conflict, they are deeply involved in it and cannot get out of it.

embryo embryos noun (SCIENCE) an animal or human being in the very early stages of development in the womb. > **embryonic** adjective

emerald noun 1 a bright green precious stone. ▶ noun, adjective 2 bright green.

emerge verb 1 If someone emerges from a place, they come out of it so that they can be seen. 2 If something emerges, it becomes known or begins to be recognised as existing. > **emergence** noun

emergency emergencies noun an unexpected and serious event which needs immediate action to deal with it.

emergency noun
= crisis, pinch

emigrant noun (HISTORY) someone who leaves their native country and goes to live permanently in another one. > **emigrate** verb > **emigration** noun

eminence noun 1 Eminence is the quality of being well-known and respected for what you do. 2 'Your Eminence' is a title of respect used to address a Roman Catholic cardinal.

eminent adjective well-known and respected for what you do.

eminently adverb (formal) very.

emir noun a Muslim ruler or nobleman.

emission noun (formal) The emission of something such as gas or radiation is the release of it into the atmosphere.

emit emits, emitting, emitted verb To emit something means to give it out or release it.

emit verb
= exude, give off, give out, release, send out, utter

emoji emojis noun an image used in electronic communication to represent an emotion.

emotion noun (PSHE) a strong feeling, such as love or fear.

emotional adjective 1 causing strong feelings. 2 (PSHE) to do with feelings rather than your physical condition: emotional support. 3 showing your feelings openly. > **emotionally** adverb

emotive adjective concerning emotions, or stirring up strong emotions.

empathise; also spelt **empathize**

verb (PSHE) If you empathise with someone, you understand how they are feeling. > **empathy** noun

emperor noun a male ruler of an empire.

emphasis emphases noun Emphasis is special importance or extra stress given to something.

> **emphasis** noun
> = accent, importance, prominence, weight

emphasise; also spelt **emphasize** verb If you emphasise something, you make it known that it is very important.

> **emphasise** verb
> = accent, accentuate, highlight, play up, stress, underline

emphatic adjective expressed strongly and with force to show how important something is. > **emphatically** adverb

empire noun 1 a group of countries controlled by one country. 2 a powerful group of companies controlled by one person.

employ verb 1 If you employ someone, you pay them to work for you. 2 If you employ something for a particular purpose, you make use of it.

> **employ** verb
> 1 = appoint, commission, engage (formal), hire, take on
> 2 = bring to bear, make use of, use, utilise

employee noun a person who is paid to work for another person or for an organisation.

> **employee** noun
> = hand, worker, workman

employer noun Someone's employer is the person or organisation that they work for.

> **employer** noun
> = boss, gaffer (informal)

employment noun (GEOGRAPHY) Employment is the state of having a paid job, or the activity of recruiting people for a job.

> **employment** noun
> = engagement, enlistment, hiring, recruitment, taking on

empower verb If you are empowered to do something, you have the authority or power to do it.

empress noun a woman who rules an empire, or the wife of an emperor.

empty emptier, emptiest; empties, emptying, emptied adjective 1 having nothing or nobody inside. 2 without purpose, value or meaning. ▶ verb 3 If you empty something, or empty its contents, you remove the contents. > **emptiness** noun

> **empty** adjective
> 1 = bare, blank, clear, deserted, unfurnished, uninhabited, vacant 2 = inane, meaningless, worthless
> ▶ verb 3 = clear, drain, evacuate, unload

emu noun a large Australian bird which can run fast but cannot fly.

emulate verb If you emulate someone or something, you imitate them because you admire them.

emulsion noun a water-based paint.

enable verb To enable something to happen means to make it possible.

enact verb 1 If a government enacts a law or bill, it officially passes it so that it becomes law. 2 If you enact a story or play, you act it out.

enamel enamels, enamelling, enamelled noun 1 a substance like glass, used to decorate or protect metal or china. 2 The enamel on your teeth is the hard, white substance that forms the outer part. ▶ verb 3 If you enamel something, you decorate or cover it with enamel.
> **enamelled** adjective

enamoured adjective If you are enamoured of someone or something, you like them very much.

encapsulate verb If something encapsulates facts or ideas, it contains or represents them in a small space.

encased adjective Something that is encased is surrounded or covered with a substance.

enchanted adjective If you are enchanted by something or someone, you are fascinated or charmed by them.

enchanting adjective attractive, delightful or charming.

encircle verb To encircle something or someone means to completely surround them.

enclave noun a place that is surrounded by areas that are different from it in some important way, for example because the people there are from a different culture.

enclose verb To enclose an object or area means to surround it with something solid.

enclose verb
= encircle, fence off, hem in, surround, wrap

enclosure noun an area of land surrounded by a wall or fence and used for a particular purpose.

encompass verb To encompass a number of things means to include all of those things.

encore noun a short extra performance given by an entertainer because the audience asks for it.

encounter verb 1 If you encounter someone or something, you meet them or are faced with them. ▶ noun 2 a meeting, especially when it is difficult or unexpected.

encourage verb 1 (PSHE) If you encourage someone, you give them courage and confidence to do something. 2 If someone or something encourages a particular activity, they support it. > **encouraging** adjective > **encouragement** noun

encourage verb
1 = cheer, hearten, reassure
2 = aid, boost, favour, help, incite, support

encroach verb If something encroaches on a place or on your time or rights, it gradually takes up or takes away more and more of it. > **encroachment** noun

encrusted adjective covered with a crust or layer of something.

encyclopedia; also spelt **encyclopaedia** noun (LIBRARY) a book or set of books giving information about many different subjects.

encyclopedic; also spelt **encyclopaedic** adjective knowing or giving information about many different things.

end noun 1 The end of a period of time or an event is the last part. 2 The end of something is the farthest point of it. 3 the purpose for which something is done.
▶ verb 4 If something ends or if you end it, it comes to a finish.

end noun
1 = climax, close, conclusion, culmination, ending, expiry, finale, finish 2 = boundary, bounds, edge, extremity, limit, margin 3 = aim, goal, intention, object, objective, purpose, reason
▶ verb 4 = bring to an end, cease, conclude, finish, stop, terminate (formal)

endanger verb To endanger something means to cause it to be in a dangerous and harmful situation.

endanger verb
= compromise, jeopardise, put at risk, risk, threaten

endear verb If someone's behaviour endears them to you, it makes you fond of them.
> **endearing** adjective

endeavour verb 1 (formal) If you endeavour to do something, you try very hard to do it. ▶ noun 2 an effort to do or achieve something.

endless adjective having or seeming to have no end.
> **endlessly** adverb

endorse verb 1 If you endorse someone or something, you give approval and support to them. 2 If you endorse a document, you write your signature on it or a comment on it, to show that you approve of it.
> **endorsement** noun

endowed adjective If someone is endowed with a quality or ability, they have it or are given it.

endurance noun Endurance is the ability to put up with a difficult situation for a period of time.

endure verb 1 If you endure a difficult situation, you put up with it calmly and patiently. 2 If something endures, it lasts or continues to exist.

endure verb
1 = cope with, experience, go through, stand, suffer 2 = last, live on, remain, survive

enemy enemies noun a person or group that is hostile or opposed to another person or group.

enemy noun
= adversary, antagonist, foe, opponent

energetic adjective having or showing energy or enthusiasm.
> **energetically** adverb

energetic adjective
= animated, dynamic, indefatigable, spirited, tireless, vigorous

energy energies noun 1 the physical strength to do active things. 2 the power which drives machinery. 3 (SCIENCE) In physics, energy is the capacity of a body or system to do work. It is measured in joules.

energy noun
1 = drive, life, spirit, strength, vigour, vitality

enforce verb If you enforce a law or a rule, you make sure that it is obeyed. > **enforcement** noun

engage verb 1 If you engage in an activity, you take part in it.

2 To engage someone or their attention means to make or keep someone interested in something.

engaged *adjective* **1** When two people are engaged, they have agreed to marry each other. **2** If someone or something is engaged, they are occupied or busy.

engagement *noun* **1** an appointment that you have with someone. **2** an agreement that two people have made with each other to get married.

engine *noun* **1** a machine designed to convert heat or other kinds of energy into mechanical movement. **2** a railway locomotive.

engineer *noun* **1** a person trained in designing and building machinery and electrical devices, or roads and bridges. **2** a person who repairs mechanical or electrical devices. ▶ *verb* **3** If you engineer an event or situation, you arrange it cleverly, usually for your own advantage.

engineering *noun* Engineering is the profession of designing and constructing machinery and electrical devices, or roads and bridges.

English *adjective* **1** belonging or relating to England. ▶ *noun* **2** English is the main language spoken in the United Kingdom, the USA, Canada, Australia, New Zealand and many other countries.

Englishman Englishmen *noun* a man who comes from England.

Englishwoman Englishwomen *noun* a woman who comes from England.

engrave *verb* To engrave means to cut letters or designs into a hard surface with a tool.

engraving *noun* a picture or design that has been cut into a hard surface. ▶ **engraver** *noun*

engrossed *adjective* If you are engrossed in something, it holds all your attention.

engulf *verb* To engulf something means to completely cover or surround it.

enhance *verb* To enhance something means to make it more valuable or attractive. ▶ **enhancement** *noun*

enigma *noun* anything which is puzzling or difficult to understand.

enigmatic *adjective* mysterious, puzzling or difficult to understand. ▶ **enigmatically** *adverb*

enjoy *verb* If you enjoy something, you find pleasure and satisfaction in it.

> **enjoy** *verb*
> = appreciate, delight in, like, love, relish, revel in, take pleasure from, take pleasure in

enjoyable *adjective* giving pleasure or satisfaction.

enjoyment *noun* Enjoyment is the feeling of pleasure or satisfaction you get from something nice.

enlarge *verb* **1** When you enlarge something, it gets bigger. **2** If you enlarge on a subject, you give more details about it.

> **enlarge** *verb*
> **1** = add to, expand, extend, increase, magnify **2** = develop, elaborate on, expand on

enlargement noun 1 The enlargement of something is the action of making it bigger. 2 something, especially a photograph, which has been made bigger.

enlighten verb To enlighten someone means to give them more knowledge or understanding of something.
> **enlightening** adjective
> **enlightenment** noun

enlightened adjective well-informed and willing to consider different opinions.

enlist verb 1 If someone enlists, they join the army, navy or air force. 2 If you enlist someone's help, you persuade them to help you in something you are doing.

enliven verb To enliven something means to make it more lively or more cheerful.

en masse adverb If a group of people do something en masse, they do it together and at the same time.

enormity enormities noun 1 The enormity of a problem or difficulty is its great size and seriousness. 2 something that is thought to be a terrible crime or offence.

enormous adjective very large in size or amount. > **enormously** adverb

> **enormous** adjective
> = colossal, gigantic, huge,
> immense, massive,
> tremendous, vast

enough adjective, adverb 1 as much or as many as required. ▶ noun 2 Enough is the quantity necessary for something. ▶ adverb 3 very or fairly: She could manage well enough without me.

enquire; also spelt **inquire** verb If you enquire about something or someone, you ask about them.

enquiry; also spelt **inquiry** noun 1 a question that you ask in order to find something out. 2 an investigation into something that has happened and that needs explaining.

enrage verb If something enrages you, it makes you very angry.

enrich verb To enrich something means to improve the quality or value of it. > **enriched** adjective
> **enrichment** noun

enrol enrols, enrolling, enrolled verb If you enrol for something such as a course or a college, you register to join or become a member of it. > **enrolment** noun

en route adverb If something happens en route to a place, it happens on the way there.

ensconced adjective If you are ensconced in a particular place, you are settled there firmly and comfortably.

ensemble noun 1 a group of things or people considered as a whole rather than separately. 2 a small group of musicians who play or sing together.

enshrine verb If something such as an idea or a right is enshrined in a society, constitution or a law, it is protected by it.

ensue ensues, ensuing, ensued verb If something ensues, it happens after another event, usually as a result of it.
> **ensuing** adjective

ensure verb To ensure that something happens means to make certain that it happens.

ensure verb
= guarantee, make certain, make sure

entangled adjective If you are entangled in problems or difficulties, they are involved in them.

enter verb 1 To enter a place means to go into it. 2 If you enter an organisation or institution, you join and become a member of it. 3 If you enter a competition or examination, you take part in it. 4 If you enter data into a form or database, you record it by writing or typing it in an empty space.

enterprise noun 1 a business or company. 2 a project or task, especially one that involves risk or difficulty.

enterprise noun
1 = business, company, concern, establishment, firm, operation
2 = effort, endeavour, operation, project, undertaking, venture

enterprising adjective ready to start new projects and tasks and full of boldness and initiative.

entertain verb 1 If you entertain people, you keep them amused or interested. 2 If you entertain guests, you receive them into your house and give them food and hospitality.

entertain verb
1 = amuse, charm, delight, enthral, please

entertainer noun someone whose job is to amuse and please audiences, for example a comedian or singer.

entertaining adjective 1 amusing and full of interest. ▶ noun

2 Entertaining is the hospitality that you give to guests.

entertainment noun anything people watch or do for pleasure.

entertainment noun
= amusement, enjoyment, fun, pleasure, recreation

enthral enthrals, enthralling, enthralled verb If you enthral someone, you hold their attention and interest completely. > **enthralling** adjective

enthuse verb If you enthuse about something, you talk about it with enthusiasm and excitement.

enthusiasm noun Enthusiasm is interest, eagerness or delight in something.

enthusiasm noun
= eagerness, excitement, interest, keenness, warmth

enthusiastic adjective showing great excitement, eagerness or approval for something.
> **enthusiastically** adverb

enthusiastic adjective
= ardent, avid, devoted, eager, excited, keen, passionate

entice verb If you entice someone to do something, you tempt them to do it.

enticing adjective extremely attractive and tempting.

entire adjective including all of something.

entirely adverb wholly and completely.

entirety phrase If something happens to something in its entirety, it happens to all of it.

entitle verb If something entitles you to have or do something, it gives you the right to have or do it. > **entitlement** noun

entity entities noun any complete thing that is not divided and not part of anything else.

entourage noun a group of people who follow or travel with a famous or important person.

entrails plural noun Entrails are the inner parts, especially the intestines, of people or animals.

entrance[1] noun 1 The entrance of a building or area is its doorway or gate. 2 A person's entrance is their arrival in a place, or the way in which they arrive. 3 (DRAMA) In the theatre, an actor makes his or her entrance when he or she comes onto the stage. 4 Entrance is the right to enter a place.

> **entrance** noun
> 1 = door, doorway, entry, gate, way in 2 = appearance, arrival, entry 4 = access, admission, entry

entrance[2] verb If something entrances you, it gives you a feeling of wonder and delight.
> **entrancing** adjective

> **entrance** verb
> = bewitch, captivate, charm, delight, enthral, fascinate

entrant noun a person who officially enters a competition or an organisation.

entrenched adjective If a belief, custom or power is entrenched, it is firmly established.

entrepreneur noun a person who sets up business deals, especially ones in which risks are involved, in order to make a profit.
> **entrepreneurial** adjective

entrust verb If you entrust something to someone, you give them the care and protection of it.

entry entries noun 1 Entry is the act of entering a place. 2 a place through which you enter somewhere. 3 anything which is entered or recorded.

> **entry** noun
> 1 = appearance, arrival, entrance 2 = door, doorway, entrance, gate, way in 3 = item, note, record

envelop verb To envelop something means to cover or surround it completely.

envelope noun a flat covering of paper with a flap that can be folded over to seal it, which is used to hold a letter.

enviable adjective If you describe something as enviable, you mean that you wish you had it yourself.

envious adjective full of envy.

environment noun 1 Your environment is the circumstances and conditions in which you live or work. 2 (SCIENCE) The environment is the natural world around us. > **environmental** adjective > **environmentally** adverb

environmentalist noun a person who is concerned with the problems of the natural environment, such as pollution.

envisage verb If you envisage a situation or state of affairs, you can picture it in your mind as being true or likely to happen.

envoy noun a messenger sent especially from one government to another.

envy envies, envying, envied noun 1 Envy is a feeling of resentment you have when you wish you could have what someone else has. ▶ verb 2 If you envy someone, you wish that you had what they have.

e

envy noun
1 = jealousy, resentment
▶ verb 2 = be envious, begrudge, be jealous, covet, resent

enzyme noun (SCIENCE) a chemical substance, usually a protein, produced by cells in the body.

ephemeral adjective lasting only a short time.

epic noun 1 a long story of heroic events and actions. ▶ adjective 2 very impressive or ambitious.

epidemic noun 1 an occurrence of a disease in one area, spreading quickly and affecting many people. 2 a rapid development or spread of something.

epilepsy noun Epilepsy is a condition of the brain which causes fits and periods of unconsciousness. > **epileptic** adjective

episode noun 1 an event or period. 2 (ENGLISH) one of several parts of a novel or drama appearing for example on television.

epitaph noun some words on a tomb about the person who has died.

epithet noun a word or short phrase used to describe some characteristic of a person.

epitome noun (formal) The epitome of something is the most typical example of its sort.

epoch noun a long period of time.

eponymous adjective (formal) The eponymous hero or heroine of a play or book is the person whose name forms its title.

equal equals, equalling, equalled adjective 1 having the same size, amount, value or standard. 2 If you are equal to a task, you have the necessary ability to deal with

it. ▶ noun 3 Your equals are people who have the same ability, status or rights as you. ▶ verb 4 If one thing equals another, it is as good or remarkable as the other.
> **equally** adverb > **equality** noun

equal adjective
1 = equivalent, identical, the same 2 **equal to** = capable of, up to
▶ verb 4 = be equal to, match

equate verb If you equate a particular thing with something else, you believe that it is similar or equal.

equation noun (MATHS) a mathematical statement showing that two expressions are equal.

equator noun (GEOGRAPHY) an imaginary line drawn round the middle of the earth, lying halfway between the North and South Poles. > **equatorial** adjective

equestrian adjective relating to or involving horses.

equilibrium noun a state of balance or stability in a situation.

equine adjective relating to horses.

equip equips, equipping, equipped verb If a person or thing is equipped with something, they have it or are provided with it.

equip verb
= arm, endow, fit out, provide, supply

equipment noun Equipment is all the things that are needed or used for a particular job or activity.

equipment noun
= apparatus, gear (informal), paraphernalia, stuff, tackle

equitable adjective fair and reasonable.

equivalent *adjective* 1 equal in use, size, value or effect. ▶ *noun* 2 something that has the same use, value or effect as something else. > **equivalence** *noun*

era *noun* a period of time distinguished by a particular feature: *a new era of prosperity.*

eradicate *verb* To eradicate something means to get rid of it or destroy it completely. > **eradication** *noun*

erase *verb* To erase something means to remove it.

erect *verb* 1 To erect something means to put it up or construct it. ▶ *adjective* 2 in a straight and upright position.

erection erections *noun* 1 the process of erecting something. 2 anything which has been erected.

erode *verb* If something erodes or is eroded, it is gradually worn or eaten away and destroyed.

> **erode** *verb*
> = corrode, destroy, deteriorate, disintegrate

erosion *noun* (GEOGRAPHY) the gradual wearing away and destruction of something.

err *verb* If you err, you make a mistake.

> **err** *verb*
> = blunder, go wrong, make a mistake, miscalculate

errand *noun* a short trip you make in order to do a job for someone.

erratic *adjective* not following a regular pattern or a fixed course. > **erratically** *adverb*

erroneous *adjective* Ideas or methods that are erroneous are incorrect or only partly correct.

error *noun* a mistake or something which you have done wrong.

> **error** *noun*
> = blunder, fault, lapse, mistake, slip

erudite *adjective* having great academic knowledge.

erupt *verb* 1 When a volcano erupts, it violently throws out a lot of hot lava and ash. 2 When a situation erupts, it starts up suddenly and violently. > **eruption** *noun*

escalate *verb* If a situation escalates, it becomes greater in size, seriousness or intensity.

escalator *noun* a mechanical moving staircase.

escapade *noun* an adventurous or daring incident that causes trouble.

escape *verb* 1 To escape means to get free from someone or something. 2 If you escape something unpleasant or difficult, you manage to avoid it. 3 If something escapes you, you cannot remember it. ▶ *noun* 4 an act of escaping from a particular place or situation. 5 a situation or activity which distracts you from something unpleasant.

> **escape** *verb*
> 1 = break free, break out, get away, make your escape, run away, run off 2 = avoid, dodge, duck, elude, evade
> ▶ *noun* 5 = distraction, diversion, relief

escapee *noun* someone who has escaped, especially an escaped prisoner.

escapism *noun* avoiding the real and unpleasant things in life by thinking about pleasant or exciting things. > **escapist** *adjective*

eschew *verb* (*formal*) If you eschew something, you deliberately avoid it or keep away from it.

escort *noun* 1 a person or vehicle that travels with another in order to protect or guide them. 2 a person who accompanies another person to a social event. ▶ *verb* 3 If you escort someone, you go with them somewhere, especially in order to protect or guide them.

Eskimo Eskimos *noun* (*offensive*) a name that was formerly used for the Inuit and their language.

especially *adverb* You say especially to show that something applies more to one thing, person or situation than to any other.

espionage *noun* Espionage is the act of spying to get secret information, especially to find out military or political secrets.

espresso *noun* Espresso is strong coffee made by forcing steam through ground coffee.

essay *noun* a short piece of writing on a particular subject, for example one done as an exercise by a student.

essence *noun* 1 The essence of something is its most basic and most important part, which gives it its identity. 2 a concentrated liquid used for flavouring food.

> **essence** *noun*
> 1 = core, heart, nature, soul, spirit 2 = concentrate, extract

essential *adjective* 1 vitally important and absolutely necessary. 2 very basic, important and typical. > **essentially** *adverb*

> **essential** *adjective*
> 1 = crucial, indispensable, vital
> 2 = basic, cardinal, fundamental, key, main, principal

establish *verb* 1 To establish something means to set it up in a permanent way. 2 If you establish yourself or become established as something, you achieve a strong reputation for a particular activity. 3 If you establish a fact or establish the truth of something, you discover it and can prove it.

establishment *noun* 1 The establishment of an organisation or system is the act of setting it up. 2 a shop, business or some other sort of organisation or institution. 3 The Establishment is the group of people in a country who have power and influence.

estate *noun* 1 a large area of privately owned land in the country, together with all the property on it. 2 an area of land, usually in or near a city, which has been developed for housing or industry. 3 (*Law*) A person's estate consists of all the possessions they leave behind when they die.

estate agent *noun* a person who works for a company that sells houses and land.

esteem *noun* admiration and respect that you feel for another person. > **esteemed** *adjective*

> **esteem** *noun*
> = admiration, estimation, regard, respect, reverence

estimate *verb* 1 (MATHS) If you estimate an amount or quantity, you calculate it approximately. 2 If you estimate something, you make a guess about it based on the evidence you have available. ▶ *noun* **3** a guess at an amount, quantity or outcome, based on the evidence you have available. **4** a formal statement from a company which may do some work for you, telling you how much it is likely to cost.

> **estimate** *noun*
> **3** = appraisal, assessment, estimation, guess, quote, reckoning, valuation

estimation *noun* **1** an approximate calculation of something that can be measured. **2** the opinion or impression you form about a person or situation.

estranged *adjective* **1** If someone is estranged from their husband or wife, they no longer live with them. **2** If someone is estranged from their family or friends, they have quarrelled with them and no longer keep in touch with them.

estrogen *noun* (SCIENCE) a female hormone which regulates the reproductive cycle.

estuary estuaries *noun* (GEOGRAPHY) the wide part of a river near where it joins the sea and where fresh water mixes with salt water.

etc. a written abbreviation for **et cetera**.

et cetera 'Et cetera' is used at the end of a list to indicate that other items of the same type you have mentioned could have been mentioned if there had been time or space.

etch *verb* **1** If you etch a design or pattern on a surface, you cut it into the surface by using acid or a sharp tool. **2** If something is etched on your mind or memory,

it has made such a strong impression on you that you feel you will never forget it.

etching *noun* a picture printed from a metal plate that has had a design cut into it.

eternal *adjective* lasting forever, or seeming to last forever. > **eternally** *adverb*

> **eternal** *adjective*
> = everlasting, immortal, unchanging

eternity eternities *noun* **1** Eternity is time without end, or a state of existing outside time, especially the state some people believe they will pass into when they die. **2** a period of time which seems to go on forever.

ether *noun* a colourless liquid that burns easily, used in industry as a solvent and in medicine as an anaesthetic.

ethereal *adjective* light and delicate. > **ethereally** *adverb*

ethical *adjective* in agreement with accepted principles of behaviour that are thought to be right. > **ethically** *adverb*

ethics *plural noun* Ethics are moral beliefs about right and wrong.

Ethiopian *adjective* **1** belonging or relating to Ethiopia. ▶ *noun* **2** someone who comes from Ethiopia.

ethnic *adjective* **1** involving different racial groups of people. **2** relating to a particular racial or cultural group, especially when very different from modern western culture. > **ethnically** *adverb* > **ethnicity** *noun*

ethos *noun* a set of ideas and attitudes that is associated with a particular group of people.

etiquette *noun* a set of rules for behaviour in a particular social situation.

EU an abbreviation for **European Union**.

eucalyptus eucalyptuses or **eucalypt** *noun* an evergreen tree, grown mostly in Australia; also the wood and oil from this tree.

Eucharist *noun* (RE) a religious ceremony in which Christians celebrate Christ's last meal with his disciples.

euphemism *noun* a polite word or expression that you can use instead of one that might offend or upset people. > **euphemistic** *adjective* > **euphemistically** *adverb*

euphoria *noun* a feeling of great happiness. > **euphoric** *adjective*

euro euros *noun* the official unit of currency in some countries of the European Union.

Europe *noun* Europe is the second smallest continent. It has Asia on its eastern side, with the Arctic to the north, the Atlantic to the west, and the Mediterranean Sea and Africa to the south.

European *adjective* 1 belonging or relating to Europe. ▶ *noun* 2 someone who comes from Europe.

European Union *noun* The group of countries which have joined together for economic and trade purposes are officially known as the European Union.

euthanasia *noun* Euthanasia is the act of painlessly killing a dying person in order to stop their suffering.

evacuate *verb* If someone is evacuated, they are removed from a place of danger to a place of safety. > **evacuation** *noun* > **evacuee** *noun*

evade *verb* 1 If you evade something or someone, you keep moving in order to keep out of their way. 2 If you evade a problem or question, you avoid dealing with it.

evaluate *verb* (EXAM TERM) If you evaluate something, you assess its strengths and weaknesses.

evaluation evaluations *noun* 1 Evaluation is assessing the strengths and weaknesses of something. 2 (DGT) To carry out an evaluation of a design, product or system is to do an assessment to find out how well it works or will work.

evangelical *adjective* Evangelical beliefs are Christian beliefs that stress the importance of the Gospels and a personal belief in Christ.

evangelist *noun* (RE) a person who travels from place to place preaching Christianity.

evaporate *verb* 1 (SCIENCE) When a liquid evaporates, it gradually changes into a gas. 2 (SCIENCE) If a substance has been evaporated, all the liquid has been taken out so that it is dry or concentrated. > **evaporation** *noun*

evasion *noun* deliberately avoiding doing something.

evasive *adjective* deliberately trying to avoid talking about or doing something.

eve *noun* the evening or day before an event or occasion.

even *adjective* 1 flat and level. 2 regular and without variation. 3 In maths, numbers that are even can be divided exactly by two. 4 Scores that are even are exactly the same. ▶ adverb 5 'Even' is used to suggest that something is unexpected or surprising: I haven't even got a bank account. 6 'Even' is also used to say that something is greater in degree than something else: This was an opportunity to obtain even more money. ▶ phrase 7 Even if or even though is used to introduce something that is surprising in relation to the main part of the sentence: She was too kind to say anything, even though he was jealous. > **evenly** adverb

> **even** adjective
> 1 = flat, horizontal, level, smooth 2 = constant, regular, smooth, steady, uniform
> 4 = equal, identical, level, neck and neck

evening noun the part of the day between late afternoon and night.

event noun 1 something that happens, especially when it is unusual or important. 2 one of the competitions that are part of an organised occasion, especially in sports. ▶ phrase 3 If you say in any event, you mean whatever happens.

> **event** noun
> 1 = affair, business, circumstance, episode, experience, incident, matter
> 2 = bout, competition, contest

eventful adjective full of interesting and important events.

eventual adjective happening or being achieved in the end.

eventuality eventualities noun a possible future event or result.

eventually adverb in the end.

ever adverb 1 at any time: Have you

ever seen anything like it? 2 more all the time: They grew ever further apart. 3 'Ever' is used to give emphasis to what you are saying: I'm as happy here as ever I was in England. ▶ phrase 4 (informal) Ever so means very.

evergreen noun a tree or bush which has green leaves all the year round.

everlasting adjective never coming to an end.

every adjective 1 'Every' is used to refer to all the members of a particular group, separately and one by one: We eat out every night. 2 'Every' is used to mean the greatest or the best possible degree of something: He has every reason to avoid the subject. 3 'Every' is also used to indicate that something happens at regular intervals: renewable every five years. ▶ phrase 4 Every other means each alternate.

everybody pronoun 1 all the people in a group. 2 all the people in the world.

everyday adjective usual or ordinary.

> **everyday** adjective
> = common, daily, day-to-day, mundane, ordinary, routine

everyone pronoun 1 all the people in a group. 2 all the people in the world.

everything pronoun all or the whole of something.

everywhere adverb in or to all places.

evict verb To evict someone means to officially force them to leave a place they are occupying. > **eviction** noun

evidence noun 1 Evidence is anything you see, read or are told which gives you reason to believe something. **2** Evidence is the information used in court to attempt to prove or disprove something.

evident *adjective* easily noticed or understood.

> **evident** *adjective*
> = apparent, clear, noticeable, obvious, palpable, plain, visible

evil *noun* **1** Evil is a force or power that is believed to cause wicked or bad things to happen. **2** a very unpleasant or harmful situation or activity. ▸ *adjective* **3** Someone or something that is evil is morally wrong or bad.

> **evil** *noun*
> **1** = badness, immorality, sin, vice, wickedness **2** = affliction, ill, misery, sorrow
> ▸ *adjective* **3** = bad, depraved, malevolent, sinful, vile, wicked

evoke *verb* To evoke an emotion, memory or reaction means to cause it.

evolution *noun* **1** (SCIENCE) Evolution is a process of gradual change taking place over many generations during which living things slowly change as they adapt to different environments. **2** Evolution is also any process of gradual change and development over a period of time.

evolve *verb* **1** If something evolves or if you evolve it, it develops gradually over a period of time. **2** When living things evolve, they gradually change and develop into different forms over a period of time.

ewe *noun* a female sheep.

ex- *prefix* 'Ex-' means 'former': *her ex-husband.*

exacerbate *verb* To exacerbate something means to make it worse.

exact *adjective* **1** correct and complete in every detail. **2** accurate and precise, as opposed to approximate: *Can you give an exact figure for the cost?* ▸ *verb* **3** (formal) If somebody or something exacts something from you, they demand or obtain it from you, especially through force.

> **exact** *adjective*
> **1** = accurate, authentic, faithful, faultless, precise, true
> ▸ *verb* **3** = command, extract, impose, insist on, insist upon, wring

exactly *adverb* **1** with complete accuracy and precision. **2** You can use 'exactly' to emphasise the truth of a statement, or a similarity or close relationship between one thing and another: *It's exactly the same colour.*
▸ *interjection* **3** an expression implying total agreement.

> **exactly** *adverb*
> **1** = accurately, faithfully, just, on the dot, precisely, quite
> ▸ *interjection* **3** = absolutely, indeed, precisely, quite

exaggerate *verb* **1** If you exaggerate, you make the thing you are describing seem better, worse, bigger or more important than it really is. **2** To exaggerate something means to make it more noticeable than usual.
> **exaggeration** *noun*

> **exaggerate** *verb*
> **1** = overdo, overestimate, overstate

exalted adjective (formal) Someone who is exalted is very important.

exam noun an official test set to find out your knowledge or skill in a subject.

> **exam** noun
> = examination, oral, test

examination noun 1 an exam. 2 If you make an examination of something, you inspect it very carefully. 3 A medical examination is a check by a doctor to find out the state of your health.

> **examination** noun
> 2 = analysis, inspection, study
> 3 = check, checkup, medical

examine verb 1 If you examine something, you inspect it very carefully. 2 (EXAM TERM) To examine a subject is to look closely at the issues involved and form your own opinion. 3 To examine someone means to find out their knowledge or skill in a particular subject by testing them. 4 If a doctor examines you, he or she checks your body to find out the state of your health.

> **examine** verb
> 1 = analyse, go over, go through, inspect, look over, study
> 4 = check, inspect, look at, test

examiner noun a person who sets or marks an exam.

example noun 1 something which represents or is typical of a group or set. 2 If you say someone or something is an example to people, you mean that people can imitate and learn from them.
▶ phrase 3 You use **for example** to give an example of something you are talking about.

example noun
1 = illustration, sample, specimen 2 = ideal, model, paragon, prototype

exasperate verb If someone or something exasperates you, they irritate you and make you angry. > **exasperation** noun

excavate verb To excavate means to remove earth from the ground by digging. > **excavation** noun

exceed verb To exceed something such as a limit means to go beyond it or to become greater than it.

exceedingly adverb extremely or very much.

excel excels, excelling, excelled verb If someone excels in something, they are very good at doing it.

Excellency Excellencies noun a title used to address an official of very high rank, such as an ambassador or a governor.

excellent adjective very good indeed. > **excellence** noun

> **excellent** adjective
> = beaut (Australian and New Zealand; informal), brilliant, cracking (British, Australian and New Zealand; informal), fine, first-class, great, outstanding, superb

except preposition Except or except for means other than or apart from.

> **except** preposition
> = apart from, but, other than, save (formal), with the exception of

exception noun somebody or something that is not included in a general statement or rule.

exceptional adjective 1 unusually talented or clever. 2 unusual and likely to happen very rarely. > **exceptionally** adverb

> **exceptional** adjective
> 1 = excellent, extraordinary, outstanding, phenomenal, remarkable, talented 2 = isolated, out of the ordinary, rare, special, unheard-of, unusual

excerpt noun a short piece of writing or music which is taken from a larger piece.

excess noun 1 Excess is behaviour which goes beyond normally acceptable limits. 2 a larger amount of something than is needed, usual or healthy. ▶ adjective 3 more than is needed, allowed or healthy. ▶ phrase 4 In excess of a particular amount means more than that amount. 5 If you do something to excess, you do it too much.

> **excess** noun
> 1 = extravagance, indulgence 2 = glut, overdose, surfeit, surplus
> ▶ adjective 3 = extra, superfluous, surplus

excessive adjective too great in amount or degree. > **excessively** adverb

> **excessive** adjective
> = exaggerated, undue, unreasonable

exchange verb 1 To exchange things means to give or receive one thing in return for another. ▶ noun 2 the act of giving or receiving something in return for something else.

> **exchange** verb
> 1 = barter, change, swap, switch, trade
> ▶ noun 2 = interchange, swap, switch, trade

exchequer noun The exchequer is the department in the government in Britain and other countries which is responsible for money belonging to the state.

excise noun Excise is a tax put on goods produced for sale in the country that produces them.

excitable adjective easily excited.

excite verb 1 If somebody or something excites you, they make you feel very happy and nervous or very interested and enthusiastic. 2 If something excites a particular feeling, it causes somebody to have that feeling.

> **excite** verb
> 1 = agitate, animate, thrill, titillate 2 = arouse, elicit, evoke, incite, inspire, provoke, stir up

excited adjective happy and unable to relax. > **excitedly** adverb

> **excited** adjective
> = agitated, enthusiastic, feverish, high (informal), thrilled

excitement noun happiness and enthusiasm.

> **excitement** noun
> = activity, adventure, agitation, commotion, enthusiasm, thrill

exciting adjective making you feel happy and enthusiastic.

> **exciting** adjective
> = dramatic, electrifying, exhilarating, rousing, stimulating, thrilling

exclaim *verb* When you exclaim, you cry out suddenly or loudly because you are excited or shocked.

exclamation *noun* (ENGLISH) a word or phrase spoken suddenly to express a strong feeling.

exclude *verb* 1 If you exclude something, you deliberately do not include it. 2 If you exclude somebody from a place or an activity, you prevent them from entering the place or taking part in the activity. > **exclusion** *noun*

> **exclude** *verb*
> 1 = eliminate, ignore, leave out, omit, rule out 2 = ban, bar, forbid, keep out

exclusive *adjective* 1 available to or for the use of a small group of rich or privileged people. 2 belonging to a particular person or group only. ▸ *noun* 3 a story or interview which appears in only one newspaper or on only one television programme.
> **exclusively** *adverb*

> **exclusive** *adjective*
> 1 = chic, classy, posh (*informal*), select, up-market

excrement *noun* Excrement is the solid waste matter that is passed out of a person's or animal's body through their bowels.

excrete *verb* (SCIENCE) When you excrete waste matter from your body, you get rid of it, for example by going to the lavatory or by sweating.

excruciating *adjective* unbearably painful.

excursion *noun* a short outing.

excuse *noun* 1 a reason which you give to explain why something has been done, has not been done, or will not be done. ▸ *verb* 2 If you excuse yourself or something that you have done, you give reasons defending your actions. 3 If you excuse somebody for something wrong they have done, you forgive them for it. 4 If you excuse somebody from a duty or responsibility, you free them from it. ▸ *phrase* 5 You say **excuse me** to try to catch somebody's attention or to apologise for an interruption or for rude behaviour.

> **excuse** *noun*
> 1 = explanation, justification, pretext, reason
> ▸ *verb* 3 = forgive, overlook, pardon, turn a blind eye to

execute *verb* 1 To execute somebody means to kill them as a punishment for a crime. 2 If you execute something such as a plan or an action, you carry it out or perform it. > **execution** *noun*

executioner *noun* a person whose job is to execute criminals.

executive *noun* 1 a person who is employed by a company at a senior level. 2 The executive of an organisation is a committee which has the authority to make decisions and ensure that they are carried out. ▸ *adjective* 3 concerned with making important decisions and ensuring that they are carried out.

executor *noun* a person you appoint to carry out the instructions in your will.

exemplary *adjective* 1 being a good example and worthy of imitation. 2 serving as a warning.

exemplify exemplifies,
exemplifying, exemplified *verb*
1 To exemplify something means
to be a typical example of it. 2 If
you exemplify something, you
give an example of it.

exempt *adjective* 1 excused from a
rule or duty. ▶ *verb* 2 To exempt
someone from a rule, duty or
obligation means to excuse them
from it. > **exemption** *noun*

> **exempt** *adjective*
> 1 = excused, immune, not liable

exercise *noun* 1 (PE) Exercise is
any activity which you do to get
fit or remain healthy. 2 Exercises
are also activities which you do to
practise and train for a particular
skill. ▶ *verb* 3 When you exercise,
you do activities which help you
to get fit and remain healthy. 4 If
you exercise your rights or
responsibilities, you use them.

> **exercise** *noun*
> 1 = activity, exertion, training,
> work

exert *verb* 1 To exert pressure
means to apply it. 2 If you exert
yourself, you make a physical or
mental effort to do something.

exertion *noun* Exertion is
vigorous physical effort or
exercise.

exhale *verb* (SCIENCE) When you
exhale, you breathe out.
> **exhalation** *noun*

exhaust *verb* 1 To exhaust
somebody means to make them
very tired. 2 If you exhaust
a supply of something such as
money or food, you use it up
completely. 3 If you exhaust a
subject, you talk about it so much
that there is nothing else to say
about it. ▶ *noun* 4 A pipe which

carries the gas or steam out of the
engine of a vehicle. 5 Exhaust is
the gas or steam produced by the
engine of a vehicle. > **exhaustion**
noun

> **exhaust** *verb*
> 1 = drain, fatigue, tire out, wear
> out 2 = consume, deplete, run
> through, use up

exhaustive *adjective* thorough
and complete.

exhibit *verb* 1 To exhibit things
means to show them in a public
place for people to see. 2 If you
exhibit your feelings or abilities,
you display them so that other
people can see them. ▶ *noun*
3 anything which is put on show
for the public to see.

exhibition *noun* (ART) a public
display of works of art, products
or skills.

exhibitor *noun* a person whose
work is being shown in an
exhibition.

exhilarating *adjective* Something
that is exhilarating makes you
feel very happy and excited.

exile *noun* 1 If somebody lives in
exile, they live in a foreign
country because they cannot live
in their own country, usually for
political reasons. 2 a person who
lives in exile. ▶ *verb* 3 If somebody
is exiled, they are sent away from
their own country and not
allowed to return.

exist *verb* If something exists, it is
present in the world as a real or
living thing.

existence *noun* 1 Existence is the
state of being or existing. 2 a way
of living or being: *an idyllic existence*.

exit *noun* 1 a way out of a place.
2 If you make an exit, you leave a

place. ▶ *verb* 3 To exit means to go out. 4 (DRAMA) An actor exits when he or she leaves the stage.

exodus *noun* An exodus is the departure of a large number of people from a place.

exotic *adjective* 1 attractive or interesting through being unusual. 2 coming from a foreign country.

expand *verb* 1 If something expands or you expand it, it becomes larger in number or size. 2 If you expand on something, you give more details about it. > **expansion** *noun*

> **expand** *verb*
> 1 = develop, enlarge, extend, fill out, grow, increase, swell
> 2 = develop, elaborate on, enlarge on

expanse *noun* a very large or widespread area.

expansive *adjective* 1 Something that is expansive is very wide or extends over a very large area. 2 Someone who is expansive is friendly, open or talkative.

expatriate *noun* someone who is living in a country which is not their own.

expect *verb* 1 If you expect something to happen, you believe that it will happen. 2 If you are expecting somebody or something, you believe that they are going to arrive or to happen. 3 If you expect something, you believe that it is your right to get it or have it.

> **expect** *verb*
> 1 = anticipate, assume, believe, imagine, presume, reckon (*informal*), think 3 = demand, rely on, require

expectancy *noun* Expectancy is the feeling that something is about to happen, especially something exciting.

expectant *adjective* 1 If you are expectant, you believe that something is about to happen, especially something exciting. 2 An expectant mother or father is someone whose baby is going to be born soon. > **expectantly** *adverb*

expectation *noun* Expectation or an expectation is a strong belief or hope that something will happen.

expedition *noun* 1 an organised journey made for a special purpose, such as to explore; also the party of people who make such a journey or outing. 2 a short journey or outing.

expel expels, expelling, expelled *verb* 1 If someone is expelled from a school or club, they are officially told to leave because they have behaved badly. 2 If a gas or liquid is expelled from a place, it is forced out of it.

expend *verb* To expend energy, time or money means to use it up or spend it.

expendable *adjective* no longer useful or necessary, and therefore able to be got rid of.

expenditure *noun* Expenditure is the total amount of money spent on something.

expense *noun* Expense is the money that something costs.

expensive *adjective* costing a lot of money. > **expensively** *adverb*

> **expensive** *adjective*
> = costly, dear, pricey (*informal*)

experience *noun* 1 Experience consists of all the things that you have done or that have happened to you. **2** the knowledge or skill you have in a particular activity. **3** something that you do or something that happens to you, especially something new or unusual. ▶ *verb* **4** If you experience a situation or feeling, it happens to you or you are affected by it.

> **experience** *noun*
> **2** = expertise, know-how, knowledge, training, understanding **3** = adventure, affair, encounter, episode, incident, ordeal
> ▶ *verb* **4** = encounter, have, meet, undergo

experienced *adjective* skilled or knowledgeable through doing something for a long time.

> **experienced** *adjective*
> = expert, knowledgeable, practised, seasoned, well-versed

experiment *noun* **1** the testing of something, either to find out its effect or to prove something. ▶ *verb* **2** If you experiment with something, you do a scientific test on it to prove or discover something. > **experimental** *adjective*

expert *noun* **1** a person who is very skilled at doing something or very knowledgeable about a particular subject. ▶ *adjective* **2** having or requiring special skill or knowledge. > **expertly** *adverb*

> **expert** *noun*
> **1** = ace (*informal*), authority, buff (*informal*), geek (*informal*), guru, master, professional, specialist, wizard
> ▶ *adjective* **2** = able, adept, experienced, knowledgeable, proficient, skilful, skilled

expertise *noun* Expertise is special skill or knowledge.

expire *verb* When something expires, it reaches the end of the period of time for which it is valid. > **expiry** *noun*

explain *verb* If you explain something, you give details about it or reasons for it so that it can be understood.

> **explain** *verb*
> = define, describe, illustrate

explanation *noun* a helpful or clear description. > **explanatory** *adjective*

> **explanation** *noun*
> = clarification, definition, description, exposition

explicit *adjective* shown or expressed clearly and openly. > **explicitly** *adverb*

explode *verb* **1** If something such as a bomb explodes, it bursts loudly and with great force, often causing damage. **2** If somebody explodes, they express strong feelings suddenly or violently. **3** When something increases suddenly and rapidly, it can be said to explode.

> **explode** *verb*
> **1** = blow up, burst, detonate, go off, set off **2** = blow up, go berserk, go mad **3** = rocket, shoot up, soar

exploit *verb* **1** If somebody exploits a person or a situation, they take advantage of them for their own ends. **2** If you exploit something, you make the best use of it, often for profit. ▶ *noun* **3** something daring or interesting that somebody has done. > **exploitation** *noun*

explore _verb_ 1 If you explore a place, you travel in it to find out what it is like. 2 If you explore an idea, you think about it carefully. > **exploration** _noun_ > **exploratory** _adjective_ > **explorer** _noun_

explosion _noun_ a sudden violent burst of energy, for example one caused by a bomb.

> **explosion** _noun_
> = bang, blast

explosive _adjective_ 1 capable of exploding or likely to explode. 2 happening suddenly and making a loud noise. 3 An explosive situation is one which is likely to have serious or dangerous effects. ▶ _noun_ 4 a substance or device that can explode.

exponent _noun_ 1 An exponent of an idea or plan is someone who puts it forward. 2 (_formal_) An exponent of a skill or activity is someone who is good at it.

export _verb_ 1 If you export goods, you send them to another country and sell them there. 2 (ICT) If you export data, you save it in a format that can be used by another software program. ▶ _noun_ 3 Exports are goods which are sent to another country and sold there. > **exporter** _noun_

expose _verb_ 1 To expose something means to uncover it and make it visible. 2 To expose a person to something dangerous means to put them in a situation in which it might harm them. 3 To expose a person or situation means to reveal the truth about them.

> **expose** _verb_
> 1 = reveal, show, uncover
> 3 = bring to light, reveal, show up, uncover, unearth

exposition _noun_ (ENGLISH) a detailed explanation.

exposure _noun_ 1 Exposure is the exposing of something. 2 Exposure is the harmful effect on the body caused by very cold weather.

express _verb_ 1 When you express an idea or feeling, you show what you think or feel by saying or doing something. 2 If you express a quantity in a particular form, you write it down in that form. ▶ _adjective_ 3 very fast. ▶ _noun_ 4 a fast train or coach which stops at only a few places.

> **express** _verb_
> 1 = communicate, couch, phrase, put, put across, voice
> ▶ _adjective_ 3 = direct, fast, high-speed, nonstop

expression _noun_ 1 Your expression is the look on your face which shows what you are thinking or feeling. 2 (ENGLISH) The expression of ideas or feelings is the showing of them through words, actions or art. 3 a word or phrase used in communicating. 4 (MATHS) A symbol or equation that represents a quantity or problem.

> **expression** _noun_
> 1 = countenance (_formal_), face
> 3 = idiom, phrase, remark, term

expressive _adjective_ 1 showing feelings clearly. 2 full of expression.

expressway _noun_ a road designed for fast-moving traffic.

expulsion _noun_ The expulsion of someone from a place or institution is the act of officially banning them from that place or institution.

exquisite *adjective* extremely beautiful and pleasing.

extend *verb* 1 If something extends for a distance, it continues and stretches into the distance. 2 If something extends from a surface or an object, it sticks out from it. 3 If you extend something, you make it larger or longer.

> **extend** *verb*
> 1 = continue, hang, reach, stretch 2 = jut out, project, protrude (*formal*), stick out
> 3 = add to, develop, enlarge, expand, widen

extension *noun* 1 a room or building which is added to an existing building. 2 an extra period of time for which something continues to exist or be valid. 3 an additional telephone connected to the same line as another telephone.

extensive *adjective* 1 covering a large area. 2 very great in effect.

> **extensive** *adjective*
> 1 = broad, expansive, large, spacious, sweeping, vast, wide
> 2 = comprehensive, considerable, far-reaching, great, pervasive, untold, widespread

extent *noun* The extent of something is its length, area or size.

> **extent** *noun*
> = degree, level, measure, scale, size

exterior *noun* 1 The exterior of something is its outside. 2 Your exterior is your outward appearance.

exterminate *verb* When animals or people are exterminated, they are deliberately killed.

external *adjective* existing or happening on the outside or outer part of something.
> **externally** *adverb*

extinct *adjective* 1 (SCIENCE) An extinct species of animal or plant is no longer in existence.
2 (SCIENCE) An extinct volcano is no longer likely to erupt.
> **extinction** *noun*

extinguish *verb* To extinguish a light or fire means to put it out.

extortionate *adjective* more expensive than you consider to be fair.

extra *adjective* 1 more than is usual, necessary or expected.
▶ *noun* 2 anything which is additional. 3 a person who is hired to play an unimportant part in a film.

> **extra** *adjective*
> 1 = added, additional, excess, further, more, new, spare
> ▶ *noun* 2 = accessory, addition, bonus

extract *verb* 1 To extract something from a place means to take it out or get it out, often by force. 2 If you extract information from someone, you get it from them with difficulty. ▶ *noun* (LIBRARY) 3 a small section taken from a book or piece of music.

> **extract** *verb*
> 1 = draw, mine, obtain, pull out, remove, take out 2 = draw, elicit (*formal*), get, glean, obtain
> ▶ *noun* 3 = excerpt, passage, reading, section, snatch, snippet

extraction *noun* 1 Your extraction is the country or people that your family originally comes from. 2 Extraction is the process of taking or getting something out of a place.

extraordinary *adjective* unusual or surprising. > **extraordinarily** *adverb*

> **extraordinary** *adjective*
> = amazing, bizarre, odd, singular, strange, surprising, unusual

extravagant *adjective* 1 spending or costing more money than is reasonable or affordable. 2 going beyond reasonable limits. > **extravagance** *noun*

extravaganza *noun* a spectacular and expensive public show.

extreme *adjective* 1 very great in degree or intensity. 2 going beyond what is usual or reasonable. 3 at the furthest point or edge of something. ▶ *noun* 4 the highest or furthest degree of something. > **extremely** *adverb*

> **extreme** *adjective*
> 1 = acute, deep, dire, great, intense, profound, severe
> 2 = drastic, exceptional, excessive, extravagant, radical, unreasonable
> ▶ *noun* 4 = boundary, depth, end, height, limit, ultimate

extremist *noun* a person who uses unreasonable or violent methods to bring about political change. > **extremism** *noun*

extremity extremities *noun* The extremities of something are its furthest ends or edges.

extricate *verb* To extricate someone from a place or a situation means to free them from it.

extrovert *noun* a person who is more interested in other people and the world around them than their own thoughts and feelings.

exuberant *adjective* full of energy and cheerfulness.

exude *verb* If someone exudes a quality or feeling, they seem to have it to a great degree.

eye eyes, eyeing or eying, eyed *noun* 1 the organ of sight. 2 the small hole at the end of a needle through which you pass the thread. ▶ *verb* 3 To eye something means to look at it carefully or suspiciously.

eyeball *noun* the whole of the ball-shaped part of the eye.

eyebrow *noun* Your eyebrows are the lines of hair which grow on the ridges of bone above your eyes.

eyelash *noun* Your eyelashes are hairs that grow on the edges of your eyelids.

eyelid *noun* Your eyelids are the folds of skin which cover your eyes when they are closed.

eyesight *noun* Your eyesight is your ability to see.

eyesore *noun* Something that is an eyesore is extremely ugly.

eyewitness *noun* a person who has seen an event and can describe what happened.

e

Ff

fable *noun* a story intended to teach a moral lesson.

fabric *noun* 1 (DGT) cloth. 2 The fabric of a building is its walls, roof and other parts. 3 The fabric of a society or system is its structure, laws and customs.

fabricate *verb* 1 If you fabricate a story or an explanation, you invent it in order to deceive people. 2 To fabricate something is to make it or manufacture it.
> **fabrication** *noun*

fabulous *adjective* 1 wonderful or very impressive. 2 not real, but happening in stories and legends.

facade *noun* 1 the front outside wall of a building. 2 a false outward appearance.

face *noun* 1 the front part of your head from your chin to your forehead. 2 the expression someone has or is making: *a grim face.* 3 a surface or side of something, especially the most important side. 4 the main aspect or general appearance of something: *We have changed the face of language study.* ▶ *verb* 5 To face something or someone is to be opposite them or to look at them or towards them. 6 If you face something difficult or unpleasant, you have to deal with it.

face *noun*
1 = countenance (*formal*), features, mug (*slang*) 3 = aspect, exterior, front, side, surface
▶ *verb* 5 = be opposite, look at, overlook

facet *noun* 1 a single part or aspect of something. 2 one of the flat, cut surfaces of a precious stone.

facial *adjective* appearing on or being part of the face.

facilitate *verb* To facilitate something is to make it easier for it to happen.

facility facilities *noun* 1 a service or piece of equipment which makes it possible to do something. 2 A facility for something is an ability to do it easily or well.

fact *noun* 1 a piece of knowledge or information that is true or something that has actually happened. ▶ *phrase* 2 In fact, as a matter of fact and in point of fact mean 'actually' or 'really' and are used for emphasis or when making an additional comment.
> **factual** *adjective* > **factually** *adverb*

fact *noun*
1 = certainty, reality, truth

faction *noun* a small group of people belonging to a larger group, but differing from the larger group in some aims or ideas.

fact of life *noun* 1 The facts of life are details about how babies are conceived and born. 2 If you say that something is a fact of life, you mean that it is something that people expect to happen, even though they might find it shocking or unpleasant.

factor noun 1 something that helps to cause a result. 2 The factors of a number are the whole numbers that will divide exactly into it. For example, 2 and 5 are factors of 10. 3 If something increases by a particular factor, it is multiplied that number of times.

> **factor** noun
> 1 = aspect, cause, consideration, element, influence, part

factory factories noun a building or group of buildings where goods are made in large quantities.

> **factory** noun
> = mill, plant, works

faculty faculties noun 1 Your faculties are your physical and mental abilities. 2 In some universities, a Faculty is a group of related departments.

fad noun a temporary fashion or craze.

fade verb If something fades, the intensity of its colour, brightness or sound is gradually reduced.

> **fade** verb
> = die away, dim, discolour, dull, wash out

faeces; also spelt **feces** plural noun the solid waste substances discharged from a person's or animal's body.

fag noun (informal) a cigarette.

Fahrenheit noun a scale of temperature in which the freezing point of water is 32° and the boiling point is 212°.

fail verb 1 If someone fails to achieve something, they are not successful. 2 If you fail an exam, your marks are too low and you do not pass. 3 If you fail to do

something that you should have done, you do not do it. 4 If something fails, it becomes less effective or stops working properly. ▶ noun 5 In an exam, a fail is a piece of work that is not good enough to pass. ▶ phrase 6 Without fail means definitely or regularly.

> **fail** verb
> 1 = be defeated, be in vain, be unsuccessful, come to grief, fall through, flunk (informal)
> 3 = neglect, omit 4 = crash, give out, stop working

failing noun 1 a fault in something or someone. ▶ preposition 2 used to introduce an alternative: Failing that, get a market stall.

failure noun 1 lack of success. 2 an unsuccessful person, thing or action. 3 Your failure to do something is not doing something that you were expected to do.

> **failure** noun
> 1 = breakdown, collapse, defeat, downfall 2 = disappointment, fiasco, flop (informal), loser (informal), no-hoper (informal)

faint adjective 1 A sound, colour or feeling that is faint is not very strong or intense. 2 If you feel faint, you feel weak, dizzy and unsteady. ▶ verb 3 If you faint, you lose consciousness for a short time. ▶ **faintly** adverb

> **faint** adjective
> 1 = dim, faded, indistinct, low, muted, vague 2 = dizzy, giddy, light-headed
> ▶ verb 3 = black out, collapse, pass out, swoon (literary)

fair adjective 1 reasonable and just.

2 quite large. **3** moderately good or likely to be correct. **4** having light-coloured hair or pale skin. **5** with pleasant and dry weather. ▶ *noun* **6** a form of entertainment that takes place outside, with stalls, sideshows and machines to ride on. **7** an exhibition of goods produced by a particular industry. > **fairly** *adverb*

> **fair** *adjective*
> **1** = equal, equitable, impartial, legitimate, proper, upright **4** = blonde *or* blond, light ▶ *noun* **6** = bazaar, carnival, exhibition, festival, fete, show

fairground *noun* an outdoor area where a fair is set up.

fairway *noun* the area of trimmed grass between a tee and a green on a golf course.

fairy *fairies noun* In stories, fairies are small, supernatural creatures with magical powers.

fairy tale *noun* a story of magical events.

faith *noun* **1** Faith is a feeling of confidence, trust or optimism about something. **2** (RE) Someone's faith is their religion.

> **faith** *noun*
> **1** = confidence, trust **2** = belief, creed, persuasion, religion

faithful *adjective* **1** loyal to someone or something and remaining firm in support of them. **2** accurate and truthful. > **faithfully** *adverb*

> **faithful** *adjective*
> **1** = devoted, loyal, staunch, true **2** = accurate, exact, strict, true

fake *noun* **1** an imitation of something made to trick people into thinking that it is genuine.

▶ *adjective* **2** imitation and not genuine. ▶ *verb* **3** If you fake a feeling, you pretend that you are experiencing it.

> **fake** *noun*
> **1** = copy, forgery, fraud, imitation, reproduction, sham ▶ *adjective* **2** = artificial, counterfeit, false, imitation, phoney *or* phony (*informal*) ▶ *verb* **3** = feign, pretend, simulate

falcon *noun* a bird of prey that can be trained to hunt.

fall *falls, falling, fell, fallen verb* **1** If someone or something falls or falls over, they drop towards the ground. **2** If something falls somewhere, it lands there. **3** If something falls in amount or strength, it becomes less. **4** If a person or group in a position of power falls, they lose their position and someone else takes control. **5** Someone who falls in battle is killed. **6** If, for example, you fall asleep, fall ill, or fall in love, you change quite quickly to that new state. **7** If you fall for someone, you become strongly attracted to them and fall in love. **8** If you fall for a trick or lie, you are deceived by it. **9** Something that falls on a particular date occurs on that date. ▶ *noun* **10** If you have a fall, you accidentally fall over. **11** A fall of snow, soot or other substance is a quantity of it that has fallen to the ground. **12** A fall in something is a reduction in its amount or strength. **13** In America, autumn is called fall. ▶ **fall down** *verb* An argument or idea that falls down on a particular point is weak on that point and as a result will be unsuccessful. > **fall out** *verb* If people fall out, they disagree and quarrel. > **fall through** *verb* If an arrangement or plan falls through, it fails or is abandoned.

fall *verb*
1 = collapse, drop, plunge, topple, trip 3 = decline, decrease, diminish, dwindle, plummet, subside
▶ *noun* 12 = decline, decrease, drop, reduction, slump

fallacy fallacies *noun* something false that is generally believed to be true.

fallout *noun* radioactive particles that fall to the earth after a nuclear explosion.

fallow *adjective* Land that is fallow is not being used for crop growing so that it has the chance to rest and improve.

false *adjective* 1 untrue or incorrect. 2 not real or genuine but intended to seem real. 3 unfaithful or deceitful. > **falsely** *adverb*

false *adjective*
1 = erroneous (*formal*), fictitious, incorrect, mistaken, untrue
2 = artificial, bogus, fake, forged, simulated 3 = deceitful, disloyal, insincere, unfaithful

falsehood *noun* 1 the quality or fact of being untrue. 2 a lie.

falsify falsifies, falsifying, falsified *verb* If you falsify something, you change it in order to deceive people. > **falsification** *noun*

falter *verb* If someone or something falters, they hesitate or become unsure or unsteady.

fame *noun* the state of being very well-known.

fame *noun*
= eminence, glory, prominence, renown, reputation

famed *adjective* very well-known.

familiar *adjective* 1 well-known or easy to recognise. 2 knowing or understanding something well. > **familiarity** *noun* > **familiarise** *verb*

familiar *adjective*
2 = acquainted with, aware of, knowledgeable about, versed in

family families *noun* 1 a group usually consisting of parents and their children; also all the people who are related to each other, including aunts and uncles, cousins and grandparents. 2 a group of related species of animals or plants. It is smaller than an order and larger than a genus. > **familial** *adjective*

family *noun*
1 = descendants, relations, relatives 2 = class, kind, classification

famine *noun* a serious shortage of food which may cause many deaths.

famous *adjective* very well-known.

famous *adjective*
= celebrated, distinguished, illustrious, legendary, noted, renowned

famously *adverb* (*old-fashioned*) If people get on famously, they enjoy each other's company very much.

fan fans, fanning, fanned *noun* 1 If you are a fan of someone or something, you like them very much and are very enthusiastic about them. 2 a hand-held or mechanical object which creates a draught of cool air when it moves. ▶ verb 3 To fan someone or something is to create a draught in their direction. ▶ **fan out** If things or people fan out, they move outwards in different directions.

fan noun
1 = adherent (formal), admirer, devotee, geek (informal), lover, supporter, zealot

fanatic noun a person who is very extreme in their support for a cause or in their enthusiasm for a particular activity. > **fanaticism** noun

fanatic noun
= activist, devotee, extremist, militant, zealot

fanatical adjective If you are fanatical about something, you are very extreme in your enthusiasm or support for it. > **fanatically** adverb

fanatical adjective
= fervent, obsessive, passionate, rabid, wild

fancy fancies, fancying, fancied; fancier, fanciest verb 1 If you fancy something, you want to have it or do it. ▶ adjective 2 special and elaborate.

fancy verb
1 = be attracted to, hanker after, have a yen for, would like
▶ adjective 2 = decorated, elaborate, extravagant, intricate, ornate

fancy dress noun clothing worn for a party at which people dress up to look like a particular character or animal.

fanfare noun a short, loud musical introduction to a special event, usually played on trumpets.

fantasise; also spelt **fantasize** verb If you fantasise, you imagine pleasant but unlikely events or situations.

fantastic adjective 1 wonderful and very pleasing. 2 extremely large in degree or amount. 3 strange and difficult to believe. > **fantastically** adverb

fantasy fantasies noun 1 an imagined story or situation. 2 Fantasy is the activity of imagining things or the things that you imagine. 3 In books and films, fantasy is the people or situations which are created in the writer's imagination and do not reflect reality.

far farther, farthest; further, furthest adverb 1 If something is far away from other things, it is a long distance away. 2 Far also means very much or to a great extent or degree: far more important. ▶ adjective 3 Far means very distant. 4 Far also describes the more distant of two things rather than the nearer one: the far corner of the goal. ▶ phrase 5 By far and far and away are used to say that something is so to a great degree. 6 So far means up to the present moment. 7 As far as, so far as and in so far as mean to the degree or extent that something is true.

far adverb
1 = afar, a great distance, a long way, deep, miles
2 = considerably, incomparably, much, very much
▶ adjective 3 = distant, long, outlying, remote

farce noun 1 a humorous play in

which ridiculous and unlikely situations occur. **2** a disorganised and ridiculous situation.
> **farcical** adjective

fare noun **1** the amount charged for a journey on a bus, train or plane. ▶ verb **2** How someone fares in a particular situation is how they get on.

Far East noun The Far East consists of the countries of East Asia, including China, Japan and Malaysia. > **Far Eastern** adjective

farewell interjection **1** Farewell means goodbye. ▶ adjective **2** A farewell act is performed by or for someone who is leaving a particular job or career.

far-fetched adjective unlikely to be true.

farm noun **1** an area of land together with buildings, used for growing crops and raising animals. ▶ verb **2** Someone who farms uses land to grow crops and raise animals. > **farmer** noun
> **farming** noun

farmhouse noun the main house on a farm.

farmyard noun an area surrounded by farm buildings.

fascinate verb If something fascinates you, it interests you very much. > **fascinating** adjective

fascinate verb
= absorb, bewitch, captivate, enthral, intrigue

fascism noun (HISTORY) an extreme political ideology or system of government with a powerful dictator and state control of most activities. Nationalism is encouraged and political opposition is not allowed. > **fascist** noun, adjective

fashion noun **1** a style of dress or way of behaving that is popular at a particular time. **2** The fashion in which someone does something is the way in which they do it. ▶ verb **3** If you fashion something, you make or shape it.

fashion noun
1 = craze, fad, style, trend, vogue
2 = manner, method, mode, way
▶ verb **3** = construct, create, make, mould, shape, work

fashionable adjective Something that is fashionable is very popular with a lot of people at the same time. > **fashionably** adverb

fashionable adjective
= current, in (informal), latest, popular, prevailing

fast adjective **1** moving or done at great speed. **2** If a clock is fast, it shows a time that is later than the real time. ▶ adverb **3** quickly and without delay. **4** Something that is held fast is firmly fixed. ▶ phrase **5** If you are **fast asleep**, you are in a deep sleep. ▶ verb **6** If you fast, you eat no food at all for a period of time, usually for religious reasons. ▶ noun **7** a period of time during which someone does not eat food.

fast adjective
1 = accelerated, hurried, quick, rapid, speedy, swift
▶ adverb **3** = hastily, hurriedly, quickly, rapidly, swiftly
4 = firmly, securely, tightly

fasten verb **1** To fasten something is to close it or attach it firmly to something else. **2** If you fasten your hands or teeth around or onto something, you hold it tightly with them. > **fastener** noun

> **fasten** verb
> 1 = attach, fix, join, lock, secure, tie

fast food noun hot food that is prepared and served quickly after you have ordered it.

fastidious adjective extremely choosy and concerned about neatness and cleanliness.

fast-track verb To fast-track something is to make it happen or put it into effect as quickly as possible, usually giving it priority over other things.

fat fatter, fattest; fats adjective
1 Someone who is fat has too much weight on their body.
2 large or great: a fat pile of letters.
▶ noun 3 Fat is the greasy, cream-coloured substance that animals and humans have under their skin, which is used to store energy and to help keep them warm. 4 Fat is also the greasy solid or liquid substance obtained from animals and plants and used in cooking. > **fatty** adjective

fatal adjective 1 causing death.
2 very important or significant and likely to have an undesirable effect. > **fatally** adverb

> **fatal** adjective
> 1 = deadly, incurable, lethal, mortal, terminal
> 2 = calamitous, catastrophic, disastrous, lethal

fatality fatalities noun a death caused by accident or violence.

fate noun 1 Fate is a power that is believed to control events.
2 Someone's fate is what happens to them.

fate noun
1 = chance, destiny, fortune, providence

fateful adjective having an important, often disastrous, effect.

father noun 1 A person's father is their male parent. 2 The father of something is the man who invented or started it. 3 'Father' is used to address a priest in some Christian churches. 4 Father is another name for God. > **fatherly** adjective > **fatherhood** noun

father-in-law fathers-in-law noun A person's father-in-law is the father of their husband or wife.

fathom noun 1 a unit for measuring the depth of water. It is equal to 6 feet or about 1.83 metres. ▶ verb 2 If you fathom something, you understand it after careful thought.

fatigue fatigues, fatiguing, fatigued noun 1 Fatigue is extreme tiredness. ▶ verb 2 If you are fatigued by something, it makes you extremely tired.

fault noun 1 If something bad is your fault, you are to blame for it.
2 a weakness or imperfection in someone or something.
3 (GEOGRAPHY) a large crack in rock caused by movement of the earth's crust. ▶ phrase 4 If you are at fault, you are mistaken or are to blame for something. ▶ verb 5 If you fault someone, you criticise them for what they are doing because they are not doing it well.

> **fault** noun
> 1 = blame, liability, responsibility 2 = blemish, defect, deficiency, drawback,

failing, flaw, imperfection, weakness
▶ verb 5 = blame, censure (formal), criticise

faulty faultier, faultiest adjective containing flaws or errors.

faulty adjective
= defective, flawed, imperfect, invalid, unsound

favour noun 1 If you regard someone or something with favour, you like or support them. 2 If you do someone a favour, you do something helpful for them. ▶ phrase 3 Something that is in someone's favour is a help or advantage to them. 4 If you are in favour of something, you agree with it and think it should happen. ▶ verb 5 If you favour something or someone, you prefer that person or thing.

favour noun
1 = approval, esteem, grace, support 2 = courtesy, good turn, kindness, service
▶ verb 5 = prefer, single out

favourable adjective 1 of advantage or benefit to someone. 2 positive and expressing approval. > **favourably** adverb

favourable adjective
1 = advantageous, beneficial, good, opportune, suitable
2 = affirmative, amicable, approving, friendly, positive, sympathetic, welcoming

favourite adjective 1 Your favourite person or thing is the one you like best. ▶ noun
2 Someone's favourite is the person or thing they like best. 3 the animal or person expected to win in a race or contest.

favourite adjective
1 = best-loved, dearest, favoured, preferred
▶ noun 2 = darling, idol, pet, pick

favouritism noun Favouritism is behaviour in which you are unfairly more helpful or more generous to one person than to other people.

favouritism noun
= bias, one-sidedness

fawn noun, adjective 1 pale yellowish-brown. ▶ noun 2 a very young deer. ▶ verb 3 To fawn on someone is to seek their approval by flattering them.

fear noun 1 Fear is an unpleasant feeling of danger. 2 a thought that something undesirable or unpleasant might happen. ▶ verb 3 If you fear someone or something, you are frightened of them. 4 If you fear something unpleasant, you are worried that it is likely to happen. > **fearless** adjective

fear noun
1 = alarm, awe, dread, fright, panic, terror
▶ verb 3 = be afraid, be frightened, be scared, dread, take fright

fearful adjective 1 afraid and full of fear. 2 extremely unpleasant or worrying. > **fearfully** adverb

fearsome adjective terrible or frightening.

feasible adjective possible and likely to happen. > **feasibility** noun

feast noun a large and special meal for many people.

feat noun an impressive and difficult achievement.

feather *noun* one of the light fluffy things covering a bird's body. ▸ **feathery** *adjective*

feature *noun* 1 an interesting or important part or characteristic of something. 2 Someone's features are the various parts of their face. 3 a special article or programme dealing with a particular subject. 4 the main film in a cinema programme. ▸ *verb* 5 To feature something is to include it or emphasise it as an important part or subject. ▸ **featureless** *adjective*

---
feature *noun*
1 = aspect, attribute, characteristic, mark, property, quality 3 = article, column, item, piece, report, story
▸ *verb* 5 = emphasise, give prominence to, spotlight, star

February *noun* February is the second month of the year. It has 28 days, except in a leap year, when it has 29 days.

fed the past tense and past participle of **feed**.

federal *adjective* relating to a system of government in which a group of states is controlled by a central government, but each state has its own local powers.

federation *noun* a group of organisations or states that have joined together for a common purpose.

fed up *adjective* (*informal*) unhappy or bored.

fee *noun* a charge or payment for a job, service or activity.

feeble *adjective* weak or lacking in power or influence.

feed feeds, feeding, fed *verb* 1 To feed a person or animal is to give

them food. 2 When an animal or baby feeds, it eats. 3 To feed something is to supply what is needed for it to operate or exist. ▸ *noun* 4 Feed is food for animals.

feedback *noun* 1 Feedback is comments and information about the quality or success of something. 2 Feedback is also a condition in which some of the power, sound or information produced by electronic equipment goes back into it.

feel feels, feeling, felt *verb* 1 If you feel an emotion or sensation, you experience it. 2 If you feel that something is the case, you believe it to be so. 3 If you feel something, you touch it. 4 If something feels warm or cold, for example, you experience its warmth or coldness through the sense of touch. 5 To feel the effect of something is to be affected by it. ▸ *noun* 6 The feel of something is how it feels to you when you touch it. ▸ *phrase* 7 If you **feel like** doing something, you want to do it.

---
feel *verb*
1 = experience, suffer, undergo 2 = believe, consider, deem, judge, think 3 = finger, fondle, stroke, touch
---

feeling *noun* 1 an emotion or reaction. 2 a physical sensation. 3 Feeling is the ability to experience the sense of touch in your body. 4 (*in plural*) Your feelings about something are your general attitudes or thoughts about it.

---
feeling *noun*
1 = emotion, fervour, heat, passion 2 = sensation, sense 4 = inclination, opinion, point of view, sentiment, view
---

feet the plural of **foot**.

feign *verb* If you feign an emotion or state, you pretend to experience it.

feisty feistier, feistiest *adjective* tough, independent and spirited.

feline *adjective* belonging or relating to the cat family.

fell 1 the past tense of **fall**. ▶ *verb* 2 To fell a tree is to cut it down.

fellow *noun* 1 (*old-fashioned, informal*) a man. 2 a senior member of a learned society or a university college. 3 Your fellows are the people who share work or an activity with you. ▶ *adjective* 4 You use 'fellow' to describe people who have something in common with you.

fellowship *noun* 1 a feeling of friendliness that a group of people have when they are doing things together. 2 a group of people that join together because they have interests in common. 3 an academic post at a university which involves research work.

> **fellowship** *noun*
> 1 = brotherhood, camaraderie, companionship 2 = association, brotherhood, club, league, society

felt 1 the past tense and past participle of **feel**. ▶ *noun* 2 Ⓓⓖⓣ Felt is a thick cloth made by pressing short threads together.

female *noun* 1 a person or animal that belongs to the sex that can have babies or lay eggs. ▶ *adjective* 2 concerning or relating to females.

> **female** *adjective*
> 2 = feminine, womanly

feminine *adjective* 1 relating to women or considered to be typical of women. 2 belonging to a particular class of nouns in some languages, such as French, German and Latin. > **femininity** *noun*

feminism *noun* Feminism is the belief that women should have the same rights and opportunities as men. > **feminist** *noun, adjective*

fence *noun* 1 a wooden or wire barrier between two areas of land. 2 a barrier or hedge for the horses to jump over in horse racing or show jumping. ▶ *verb* 3 To fence an area of land is to surround it with a fence. 4 When two people fence, they use special swords to fight each other as a sport.

fend *phrase* If you have to fend for **yourself**, you have to look after yourself. ▶ **fend off** *verb* If you fend off an attack or unwelcome questions or attention, you defend and protect yourself.

ferment *verb* When food or drink ferments, a chemical change takes place in it, often producing alcohol. > **fermentation** *noun*

fern *noun* a plant with long feathery leaves and no flowers.

ferocious *adjective* violent and fierce. > **ferocity** *noun*

ferret *noun* a small, fierce animal related to the weasel and kept for hunting rats and rabbits.

ferry ferries, ferrying, ferried *noun* 1 a boat that carries people and vehicles across short stretches of water. ▶ *verb* 2 To ferry people or goods somewhere is to transport them there, usually on a short, regular journey.

fertile *adjective* 1 capable of producing offspring or plants. 2 creative. > **fertility** *noun*

fertile *adjective*
1 = fruitful, productive, prolific, rich

fertilise; also spelt **fertilize** *verb*
1 (SCIENCE) When an egg, plant or female is fertilised, the process of reproduction begins with sperm joining with the egg, or by pollen coming into contact with the reproductive part of a plant. 2 To fertilise land is to put manure or chemicals onto it to feed the plants.

fertiliser; also spelt **fertilizer** *noun* (GEOGRAPHY) a substance put onto soil to improve plant growth.

fervent *adjective* showing strong, sincere and feeling.

fervent *adjective*
= ardent, committed, devout, enthusiastic, impassioned, passionate, zealous

fervour *noun* a very strong feeling for or belief in something.

fester *verb* If a wound festers, it becomes infected and produces pus.

festival *noun* 1 an organised series of events and performances. 2 (RE) a day or period of religious celebration.

festival *noun*
1 = carnival, entertainment, fair, fete, gala 2 = anniversary, holiday

festive *adjective* full of happiness and celebration.

festivity festivities *noun* celebration and happiness.

festooned *adjective* If something is festooned with objects, the objects are hanging across it in large numbers.

fetch *verb* 1 If you fetch something, you go to where it is and bring it back. 2 If something fetches a particular sum of money, it is sold for that amount.

fetching *adjective* attractive in appearance.

fete *noun* 1 an outdoor event with competitions, displays and goods for sale. ▶ *verb* 2 Someone who is feted receives a public welcome or entertainment as an honour.

feud *noun* 1 a long-term and very bitter quarrel, especially between families. ▶ *verb* 2 When people feud, they take part in a feud.

fever *noun* 1 Fever is a condition occurring during illness, in which the patient has a very high body temperature. 2 A fever is extreme excitement or agitation.

feverish *adjective* 1 in a state of extreme excitement or agitation. 2 suffering from a high body temperature. ▶ **feverishly** *adverb*

few *adjective, noun* 1 used to refer to a small number of things. ▶ *phrase* 2 Quite a few or a good few means quite a large number of things.

few *adjective, noun*
1 = infrequent, meagre, not many, scanty, scarce, sparse

fiancé *noun* A person's fiancé is the man to whom they are engaged.

fiancée *noun* A person's fiancée is the woman to whom they are engaged.

fiasco fiascos *noun* an event or attempt that fails completely, especially in a ridiculous or disorganised way.

fib fibs, fibbing, fibbed *noun* 1 a small, unimportant lie. ▶ *verb* 2 If you fib, you tell a small lie.

fibre noun 1 (DGT) a thin thread of a substance used to make cloth. 2 (SCIENCE) Fibre is also a part of plants that can be eaten but not digested; it helps food pass quickly through the body.
> **fibrous** adjective

fickle adjective A fickle person keeps changing their mind about who or what they like or want.

fiction noun 1 Fiction is stories about people and events that have been invented by the author. 2 something that is not true.
> **fictional** adjective > **fictitious** adjective

fiddle verb 1 If you fiddle with something, you keep moving it or touching it restlessly. 2 (informal) If someone fiddles something such as an account, they alter it dishonestly to get money for themselves. ▶ noun (informal) 3 a dishonest action or scheme to get money. 4 a violin.
> **fiddler** noun

fiddly fiddlier, fiddliest adjective small and difficult to do or use.

fidelity noun Fidelity is remaining firm in your beliefs, friendships or loyalty to another person.

fidget verb 1 If you fidget, you keep changing your position because of nervousness or boredom.
▶ noun 2 someone who fidgets.

> **fidget** verb
> 1 = fiddle (informal), jiggle, squirm, twitch

field noun 1 an area of land where crops are grown or animals are kept. 2 (PE) an area of land where sports are played. 3 A coal field, oil field or gold field is an area where coal, oil or gold is found. 4 a particular subject or area of interest. ▶ adjective 5 A field trip or a field study involves research or activity in the natural environment rather than theoretical or laboratory work. 6 In an athletics competition, the field events are the events such as the high jump and the javelin which do not take place on a running track. ▶ verb 7 In cricket, when you field the ball, you stop it after the batter has hit it. 8 To field questions is to answer or deal with them skilfully.

> **field** noun
> 1 = green, meadow, pasture
> 4 = area, department, domain, province, speciality, territory

fielder noun In cricket, the fielders are the team members who stand at various parts of the pitch and try to get the batters out or to prevent runs from being scored.

fieldwork noun Fieldwork is the study of something in the environment where it naturally lives or occurs, rather than in a class.

fiend noun 1 a devil or evil spirit. 2 a very wicked or cruel person. 3 (informal) someone who is very keen on a particular thing: a fitness fiend.

fierce adjective 1 very aggressive or angry. 2 extremely strong or intense.

> **fierce** adjective
> 1 = aggressive, dangerous, ferocious, murderous
> 2 = intense, keen, relentless, strong

fiery fierier, fieriest adjective 1 involving fire or seeming like fire. 2 showing great anger, energy or passion.

fifteen the number 15. ▸ **fifteenth** adjective

fifth adjective 1 The fifth item in a series is the one counted as number five. ▸ noun 2 one of five equal parts.

fifty fifties the number 50. ▸ **fiftieth** adjective

fig noun a soft, sweet fruit full of tiny seeds.

fight fights, fighting, fought verb 1 When people fight, they take part in a battle, a war, a boxing match, or in some other attempt to hurt or kill someone. 2 To fight for something is to try in a very determined way to achieve it. ▸ noun 3 a situation in which people hit or try to hurt each other. 4 a determined attempt to prevent or achieve something. 5 an angry disagreement.

> **fight** verb
> 1 = battle, brawl, grapple, struggle
> ▸ noun 3 = action, battle, bout, combat, duel, skirmish
> 5 = argument, blue (Australian; slang), dispute, row, squabble

fighter noun someone who physically fights another person.

> **fighter** noun
> = soldier, warrior

figurative adjective (ENGLISH) If you use a word or expression in a figurative sense, you use it with a more abstract or imaginative meaning than its ordinary one.

figure noun 1 a written number or the amount a number stands for. 2 a geometrical shape. 3 a diagram or table in a written text. 4 the shape of a human body, sometimes one that you cannot see properly. 5 a person. ▸ verb 6 To figure in something is to appear or be included in it. 7 (informal) If you figure that something is the case, you guess or conclude this.

> **figure** noun
> 1 = amount, digit, number, numeral, statistic, total
> 4 = body, build, form, physique, shape, silhouette 5 = character, dignitary, person, personality, player
> ▸ verb 7 = expect, guess, reckon (informal), suppose

figurehead noun the leader of a movement or organisation who has no real power.

file noun 1 a box or folder in which a group of papers or records is kept; also used of the information kept in the file. 2 In computing, a file is a stored set of related data with its own name. 3 a line of people one behind the other. 4 (DGT) a long steel tool with a rough surface, used for smoothing and shaping hard materials. ▸ verb 5 When someone files a document, they put it in its correct place with similar documents. 6 When a group of people file somewhere, they walk one behind the other in a line. 7 If you file something, you smooth or shape it with a file.

fill verb 1 If you fill something or if it fills up, it becomes full. 2 If something fills a need, it satisfies the need. 3 To fill a job vacancy is to appoint someone to do that job. ▸ noun 4 If you have had your fill of something, you do not want any more. > **fill in** verb 1 If you fill in a form, you write information in the appropriate spaces. 2 If you fill someone in, you give them information to bring them up to date.

fill *verb*
1 = cram, gorge, pack, stock, stuff

fillet *noun* 1 a strip of tender, boneless beef, veal or pork. 2 a piece of fish with the bones removed. ▶ *verb* 3 To fillet meat or fish is to prepare it by cutting out the bones.

filling *noun* 1 the soft food mixture inside a sandwich, cake or pie. 2 a small amount of metal or plastic put into a hole in a tooth by a dentist.

filly fillies *noun* a female horse or pony under the age of four.

film *noun* 1 a series of moving pictures projected onto a screen and shown at the cinema or on television. 2 a thin flexible strip of plastic used in some cameras to record images when exposed to light. 3 a very thin layer of powder or liquid on a surface. 4 Plastic film is a very thin sheet of plastic used for wrapping things. ▶ *verb* 5 If you film someone, you use a video camera to record their movements.

filter *noun* 1 a device that allows some things to pass through it, but not others. ▶ *verb* 2 To filter something is to pass it through a filter. 3 If something filters somewhere, it gets there slowly or faintly. > **filtration** *noun*

filth *noun* 1 Filth is disgusting dirt and muck. 2 People often use the word filth to refer to very bad language or to things that are thought to be crude and offensive. > **filthy** *adjective* > **filthiness** *noun*

fin *noun* a thin, flat structure on the body of a fish, used to help guide it through the water.

final *adjective* 1 last in a series or happening at the end of something. 2 A decision that is final cannot be changed or questioned. ▶ *noun* 3 the last game or contest in a series which decides the overall winner. 4 (in plural) Finals are the last and most important examinations of a university or college course.

final *adjective*
1 = closing, concluding, eventual, last, ultimate
2 = absolute, conclusive, definite, definitive

finale *noun* the last section of a piece of music or show.

finalise; also spelt **finalize** *verb* If you finalise something, you complete all the arrangements for it.

finalist *noun* a person taking part in the final of a competition.

finally *adverb* 1 If something finally happens, it happens after a long delay. 2 You use 'finally' to introduce a final point, question or topic that you are talking or writing about.

finally *adverb*
1 = at last, at the last moment, eventually, in the end, in the long run 2 = in conclusion, in summary, lastly

finance *verb* 1 To finance a project or a large purchase is to provide the money for it. ▶ *noun* 2 Finance for something is the money or loans used to pay for it. 3 Finance is also the management of money, loans and investments.

finance verb
1 = back, fund, pay for, support
▶ noun 3 = banking, budgeting, commerce, economics, investment

financial adjective relating to money. > **financially** adverb

financial adjective
= economic, fiscal, money

financier noun a person who deals with the finance for large businesses.

find finds, finding, found verb 1 If you find someone or something, you discover them, either as a result of searching or by coming across them unexpectedly. 2 If you find that something is the case, you become aware of it or realise it. 3 Something that is found in a particular place typically lives or exists there. 4 When a court or jury finds a person guilty or not guilty, they decide that the person is guilty or innocent. ▶ noun 5 If you describe something or someone as a find, you mean that you have recently discovered them and they are valuable or useful. > **finder** noun
> **find out** verb 1 If you find out something, you learn or discover something that you did not know. 2 If you find someone out, you discover that they have been doing something they should not have been doing.

find verb
1 = come across, discover, locate, track down, turn up, unearth
2 = become aware, detect, discover, learn, realise

findings plural noun Someone's findings are the conclusions they reach as a result of investigation.

fine adjective 1 very good or very beautiful. 2 satisfactory or suitable. 3 very narrow or thin. 4 A fine detail, adjustment or distinction is very delicate, exact or subtle. 5 When the weather is fine, it is not raining and is bright or sunny. ▶ noun 6 a sum of money paid as a punishment. ▶ verb 7 Someone who is fined has to pay a sum of money as a punishment.

fine adjective
1 = admirable, beautiful, excellent, magnificent, outstanding, splendid
3 = delicate, lightweight, powdery, sheer, small
4 = fastidious, keen, precise, refined, sensitive, subtle

finery noun Finery is very beautiful clothing and jewellery.

finesse noun If you do something with finesse, you do it with skill and subtlety.

finger noun 1 Your fingers are the four long jointed parts of your hands, sometimes including the thumbs. ▶ verb 2 If you finger something, you feel it with your fingers.

fingernail noun Your fingernails are the hard coverings at the ends of your fingers.

fingerprint noun a mark made showing the pattern on the skin at the tip of a person's finger.

finish verb 1 When you finish something, you reach the end of it and complete it. 2 When something finishes, it ends or stops. ▶ noun 3 The finish of something is the end or last part of it. 4 (DGT) The finish that something has is the texture or appearance of its surface.

finish *verb*
1 = close, complete, conclude, end, finalise
▶ *noun* 3 = close, completion, conclusion, end, ending, finale
4 = grain, lustre, polish, shine, surface, texture

finite *adjective* having a particular size or limit which cannot be increased.

Finn *noun* someone who comes from Finland.

Finnish *adjective* 1 belonging or relating to Finland. ▶ *noun*
2 Finnish is the main language spoken in Finland.

fir *noun* a tall, pointed evergreen tree that has thin, needle-like leaves and produces cones.

fire *noun* 1 Fire is the flames produced when something burns.
2 a pile or mass of burning material. 3 a piece of equipment that is used as a heater. ▶ *verb* 4 If you fire a weapon or a bullet, you operate the weapon so that the bullet or missile is released. 5 If you fire questions at someone, you ask them a lot of questions very quickly. 6 (*informal*) If an employer fires someone, he or she dismisses that person from their job. ▶ *phrase* 7 If someone **opens fire**, they start shooting.

> **fire** *noun*
> 1 = blaze, combustion, flames, inferno
> ▶ *verb* 4 = detonate, explode, launch, set off, shoot
> 6 = discharge, dismiss, make redundant, sack (*informal*)

firearm *noun* a gun.

fire brigade *noun* the organisation which has the job of putting out fires.

fire engine *noun* a large vehicle that carries equipment for putting out fires.

fire extinguisher *noun* a metal cylinder containing water or foam for spraying onto a fire.

firefighter *noun* a person whose job is to put out fires and rescue trapped people.

fireplace *noun* the opening beneath a chimney where a fire can be lit.

fire station *noun* a building where fire engines are kept and where firefighters wait to be called out.

firewall *noun* a computer system or program that automatically prevents an unauthorised person from gaining access to a computer when it is connected to the internet.

firework *noun* a small container of gunpowder and other chemicals which explodes and produces coloured sparks or smoke when lit.

firm *adjective* 1 Something that is firm does not move easily when pressed or pushed, or when weight is put on it. 2 A firm grasp or push is one with controlled force or pressure. 3 A firm decision is definite. 4 Someone who is firm behaves with authority that shows they will not change their mind. ▶ *noun*
5 a business selling or producing something.

> **firm** *adjective*
> 1 = compressed, congealed, hard, rigid, set, solid, stiff
> 4 = adamant, determined, inflexible, resolute, staunch, unshakable
> ▶ *noun* 5 = business, company, corporation, enterprise, organisation

first *adjective* **1** done or in existence before anything else. **2** more important than anything else.
▸ *adverb* **3** before anything else.
▸ *noun* **4** something that has never happened or been done before. > **firstly** *adverb*

> **first** *adjective*
> **1** = earliest, initial, opening, original, primeval **2** = chief, foremost, leading, main, prime, principal
> ▸ *adverb* **3** = beforehand, earlier, firstly, initially, to begin with

first aid *noun* First aid is medical treatment given to an injured person.

first-class *adjective* **1** Something that is first-class is of the highest quality. **2** First-class services are more expensive and therefore faster or more comfortable than second-class ones.

first-hand *adjective* First-hand knowledge or experience is gained directly rather than from books or other people.

First Lady *noun* The First Lady of a country is the wife of its president.

first-rate *adjective* excellent.

> **first-rate** *adjective*
> = excellent, exceptional, first-class, marvellous, outstanding, splendid, superb

fiscal *adjective* involving government or public money, especially taxes.

fish fish or fishes *noun* **1** a cold-blooded creature living in water that has a spine, gills, fins and a scaly skin. **2** Fish is the flesh of fish eaten as food. ▸ *verb* **3** To fish is to try to catch fish for food or sport. **4** If you fish for information, you try to get it in an indirect way. > **fishing** *noun* > **fisherman** *noun*

fishery fisheries *noun* an area of the sea where fish are caught commercially.

fishmonger *noun* a shopkeeper who sells fish; also the shop itself.

fishy fishier, fishiest *adjective* **1** smelling of fish. **2** (*informal*) suspicious or doubtful.

fist *noun* a hand with the fingers curled tightly towards the palm.

fit fits, fitting, fitted; fitter, fittest *verb* **1** Something that fits is the right shape or size for a particular person or position. **2** If you fit something somewhere, you put it there carefully or securely. **3** If something fits a particular situation, person or thing, it is suitable or appropriate. ▸ *noun* **4** The fit of something is how it fits. **5** If someone has a fit, their muscles suddenly start contracting violently and they may lose consciousness. **6** A fit of laughter, coughing, anger or panic is a sudden uncontrolled outburst. ▸ *adjective* **7** good enough or suitable. **8** Someone who is fit is healthy and has strong muscles as a result of regular exercise. > **fitness** *noun* > **fit out** *verb* To fit out someone or something out means to provide them with the necessary equipment.

> **fit** *verb*
> **1** = belong, correspond, dovetail, go, match **2** = adapt, arrange, place, position
> ▸ *adjective* **8** = healthy, in good condition, robust, trim, well

fitful *adjective* happening at irregular intervals and not continuous.

fitter *noun* a person who assembles or installs machinery.

fitting *adjective* **1** right or suitable. ▶ *noun* **2** a small part that is fixed to a piece of equipment or furniture. **3** If you have a fitting, you try on a garment that is being made to see if it fits properly.

> **fitting** *adjective*
> **1** = appropriate, correct, proper, right, suitable
> ▶ *noun* **2** = accessory, attachment, component, part, unit

five **1** the number 5. ▶ *noun* **2** Fives is a ball game similar to squash, in which you hit the ball with your hand.

fix *verb* **1** If you fix something somewhere, you attach it or put it there securely. **2** If you fix something broken, you mend it. **3** If you fix your attention on something, you concentrate on it. **4** If you fix something, you make arrangements for it. **5** (*informal*) To fix something is to arrange the outcome unfairly or dishonestly. ▶ *noun* **6** (*informal*) something that has been unfairly or dishonestly arranged. **7** (*informal*) If you are in a fix, you are in a difficult situation. > **fixed** *adjective* > **fixedly** *adverb*

> **fix** *verb*
> **1** = attach, bind, fasten, secure, stick **2** = correct, mend, patch up, repair
> ▶ *noun* **7** = difficulty, mess, predicament, quandary

fixation *noun* an extreme and obsessive interest in something.

fixture *noun* **1** a piece of furniture or equipment that is fixed into position in a house. **2** a sports event due to take place on a particular date.

fizz *verb* Something that fizzes makes a hissing sound.

fizzle *verb* Something that fizzles makes a weak hissing or spitting sound.

fizzy fizzier, fizziest *adjective* Fizzy drinks have carbon dioxide in them to make them bubbly.

fjord; also spelt **fiord** *noun* a long, narrow inlet of the sea between very high cliffs, especially in Norway.

flab *noun* Flab is large amounts of surplus fat on someone's body.

flabbergasted *adjective* extremely surprised.

flabby flabbier, flabbiest *adjective* Someone who is flabby is rather fat, with loose flesh on their body.

> **flabby** *adjective*
> = sagging, slack

flag flags, flagging, flagged *noun* **1** a rectangular or square cloth which has a particular colour and design, and is used as the symbol of a nation or as a signal. ▶ *verb* **2** If you or your spirits flag, you start to lose energy or enthusiasm. > **flag down** *verb* If you flag down a vehicle, you signal to the driver to stop.

flagrant *adjective* very shocking and bad in an obvious way.

flagship *noun* **1** a ship carrying the commander of the fleet. **2** the most modern or impressive product or asset of an organisation.

flail *verb* If someone's arms or legs flail about, they move in a wild, uncontrolled way.

flair *noun* Flair is a natural ability to do something well or stylishly.

flak *noun* 1 Flak is anti-aircraft fire. 2 If you get flak for doing something, you get a lot of severe criticism.

flake *noun* 1 a small, thin piece of something. ▶ *verb* 2 When something such as paint flakes, small thin pieces of it come off. > **flake out** *verb* (*informal*) If you flake out, you collapse, go to sleep, or lose consciousness.

flamboyant *adjective* behaving in a very showy and confident way.

flame *noun* 1 a hot, bright stream of burning gas. 2 A flame of passion, desire or anger is a sudden strong feeling.

flamenco *noun* Flamenco is a type of very lively, fast Spanish dancing, accompanied by guitar music.

flammable *adjective* likely to catch fire and burn easily.

flan *noun* an open sweet or savoury tart with a pastry or cake base.

flank *noun* 1 the side of an animal between the ribs and the hip. ▶ *verb* 2 Someone or something that is flanked by a particular thing or person has them at their side.

flannel *noun* 1 Flannel is a lightweight woollen fabric. 2 a small square of towelling, used for washing yourself. In Australian English it is called a **washer**.

flap flaps, flapping, flapped *verb* 1 Something that flaps moves up and down or from side to side with a snapping sound. ▶ *noun* 2 a loose piece of something such as paper or skin that is attached at one edge.

flare *noun* 1 a device that produces a brightly coloured flame, used especially as an emergency signal. ▶ *verb* 2 If a fire flares, it suddenly burns much more vigorously. 3 If violence or a conflict flares or flares up, it suddenly starts or becomes more serious.

flash *noun* 1 a sudden, short burst of light. ▶ *verb* 2 If a light flashes, it shines for a very short period, often repeatedly. 3 Something that flashes past moves or happens so fast that you almost miss it. 4 If you flash something, you show it briefly. ▶ *phrase* 5 Something that happens **in a flash** happens suddenly and lasts a very short time.

> **flash** *noun*
> 1 = burst, flare, sparkle
> ▶ *verb* 2 = flare, glint, glitter, sparkle, twinkle

flashback *noun* a scene in a film, play or book that returns to events in the past.

flashlight *noun* a large, powerful torch.

flashy flashier, flashiest *adjective* expensive and fashionable in appearance, in a vulgar way.

> **flashy** *adjective*
> = flamboyant, garish, showy, tacky (*informal*), tasteless

flask *noun* a bottle used for carrying hot drinks around with you.

flat *noun* 1 a self-contained set of rooms, usually on one level, for living in. 2 In music, a flat is a note or key a semitone lower than that described by the same letter. It is represented by the symbol (♭). ▶ *verb* 3 In Australian and New

Zealand English, to flat is to live in a flat. ▶ *adjective* **4** Something that is flat is level and smooth. **5** A flat object is not very tall or deep. **6** A flat tyre or ball has not got enough air in it. **7** A flat battery has lost its electrical charge. **8** A flat refusal or denial is complete and firm. **9** Something that is flat is without emotion or interest. **10** A flat rate or price is fixed and the same for everyone. **11** A musical instrument or note that is flat is slightly too low in pitch. ▶ *adverb* **12** Something that is done in a particular time flat, takes exactly that time. > **flatly** *adverb*

flat *noun*
1 = apartment, rooms
▶ *adjective* **4** = horizontal, level, levelled, smooth, unbroken
9 = boring, dull, insipid, monotonous, weak

flathead *noun* a common Australian edible fish.

flatten *verb* If you flatten something or if it flattens, it becomes flat or flatter.

flatter *verb* **1** If you flatter someone, you praise them in an exaggerated way, either to please them or to persuade them to do something. **2** If you are flattered by something, it makes you feel pleased and important. **3** If you flatter yourself that something is the case, you believe, perhaps mistakenly, something good about yourself or your abilities. **4** Something that flatters you makes you appear more attractive. > **flattering** *adjective*

flatter *verb*
1 = compliment, fawn
4 = enhance, set off, suit

flattery *noun* Flattery is flattering words or behaviour.

flattery *noun*
= adulation, fawning

flatulence *noun* Flatulence is the uncomfortable state of having too much gas in your intestine.

flaunt *verb* If you flaunt your possessions or talents, you display them too obviously or proudly.

flautist *noun* someone who plays the flute.

flavour *noun* **1** (DGT) The flavour of food is its taste. **2** The flavour of something is its distinctive characteristic or quality. ▶ *verb* **3** (DGT) If you flavour food with a spice or herb, you add it to the food to give it a particular taste.

flaw *noun* **1** a fault or mark in a piece of fabric or glass, or in a decorative pattern. **2** a weak point or undesirable quality in a theory, plan or person's character.

flaw *noun*
1 = blemish, defect, fault, imperfection

flax *noun* Flax is a plant used for making rope and cloth.

flea *noun* a small wingless jumping insect which feeds on blood.

fled the past tense and past participle of **flee**.

fledgling *noun* **1** a young bird that is learning to fly. ▶ *adjective* **2** Fledgling means new, or young and inexperienced.

flee flees, fleeing, fled *verb* To flee from someone or something is to run away from them.

flee *verb*
= bolt, escape, fly, leave, run away, take flight

fleece noun 1 A sheep's fleece is its coat of wool. ▶ verb 2 (informal) To fleece someone is to swindle them or charge them too much money.

fleet noun a group of ships or vehicles owned by the same organisation or travelling together.

fleeting adjective lasting for a very short time.

Flemish noun Flemish is a language spoken in many parts of Belgium.

flesh noun 1 Flesh is the soft part of the body. 2 The flesh of a fruit or vegetable is the soft inner part that you eat. ▶ **fleshy** adjective

flew the past tense of **fly**.

flex noun 1 a length of wire covered in plastic, which carries electricity to an appliance. ▶ verb 2 If you flex your muscles, you bend and stretch them.

flexible adjective 1 able to be bent easily without breaking. 2 able to adapt to changing circumstances. > **flexibility** noun

> **flexible** adjective
> 1 = elastic, lithe, pliable, supple
> 2 = adaptable, discretionary, open

flick verb 1 If you flick something, you move it sharply with your finger. 2 If something flicks somewhere, it moves with a short sudden movement. ▶ noun 3 a short sudden movement or sharp touch with the finger.

flicker verb 1 If a light or a flame flickers, it shines and moves unsteadily. ▶ noun 2 a short unsteady light or movement of light. 3 A flicker of a feeling is a very brief experience of it.

flight noun 1 a journey made by aeroplane. 2 Flight is the action of flying or the ability to fly. 3 Flight is also the act of running away. 4 A flight of stairs or steps is a set running in a single direction.

flight attendant noun a person who looks after passengers on an aircraft.

flimsy flimsier, flimsiest adjective 1 made of something very thin or weak and not providing much protection. 2 not very convincing.

flinch verb If you flinch, you make a sudden small movement in fear or pain.

> **flinch** verb
> = cringe, shrink, start, wince

fling flings, flinging, flung verb 1 If you fling something, you throw it with a lot of force. ▶ noun 2 a short period devoted to pleasure and free from any restrictions or rules.

flint noun Flint is a hard greyish-black form of quartz. It produces a spark when struck with steel.

flip flips, flipping, flipped verb If you flip something, you turn or move it quickly and sharply.

flippant adjective showing an inappropriate lack of seriousness.

flipper noun 1 one of the broad, flat limbs of sea animals, for example seals or penguins, used for swimming. 2 Flippers are broad, flat pieces of rubber that you can attach to your feet to help you swim.

flirt verb 1 If you flirt with someone, you behave as if you are attracted to them but without serious intentions. 2 If you flirt with an idea, you consider it without seriously intending to do anything about it. ▶ *noun* **3** someone who often flirts with people. > **flirtation** *noun* > **flirtatious** *adjective*

flit flits, flitting, flitted *verb* To fly or move there with quick, light movements.

float *verb* **1** Something that floats is supported by water. **2** Something that floats through the air moves along gently, supported by the air. **3** If a company is floated, shares are sold to the public for the first time and the company gains a listing on the stock exchange. ▶ *noun* **4** a light object that floats and either supports something or someone or regulates the level of liquid in a tank or cistern. **5** In Australian English, a float is also a vehicle for transporting horses.

float *verb*
1 = be on the surface, bob, drift, lie on the surface, stay afloat **2** = drift, glide, hang, hover

flock *noun* **1** a group of birds, sheep or goats. ▶ *verb* **2** If people flock somewhere, they go there in large numbers.

flog flogs, flogging, flogged *verb* **1** (*informal*) If you flog something, you sell it. **2** To flog someone is to beat them with a whip or stick. > **flogging** *noun*

flood *noun* **1** a large amount of water covering an area that is usually dry. **2** A flood of something is a large amount of it suddenly occurring. ▶ *verb* **3** If liquid floods an area, or if a river floods, the water or liquid overflows, covering the surrounding area. **4** If people or

things flood into a place, they come there in large numbers.

flood *noun*
1 = deluge, downpour, spate, torrent **2** = rush, stream, torrent
▶ *verb* **3** = deluge, drown, overflow, submerge, swamp

floodgates *phrase* To **open the floodgates** is suddenly to give a lot of people the opportunity to do something they could not do before.

floodlight *noun* a very powerful outdoor lamp used to light up public buildings and sports grounds. > **floodlit** *adjective*

floor *noun* **1** the part of a room you walk on. **2** one of the levels in a building. **3** the ground at the bottom of a valley, forest or the sea. ▶ *verb* **4** If a remark or question floors you, you are completely unable to deal with it or answer it.

floorboard *noun* one of the long planks of wood from which a floor is made.

flop flops, flopping, flopped *verb* **1** If someone or something flops, they fall loosely and rather heavily. **2** (*informal*) Something that flops fails. ▶ *noun* **3** (*informal*) something that is completely unsuccessful.

floppy floppier, floppiest *adjective* tending to hang downwards in a rather loose way.

floral *adjective* patterned with flowers or made from flowers.

florid *adjective* **1** highly elaborate and extravagant. **2** having a red face.

florist *noun* a person or shop selling flowers.

floss *noun* Dental floss is soft silky threads or fibre which you use to clean between your teeth.

flotation *noun* 1 The flotation of a business is the issuing of shares in order to launch it or to raise money. 2 Flotation is the act of floating.

flotilla *noun* a small fleet or group of small ships.

flotsam *noun* Flotsam is rubbish or wreckage floating at sea or washed up on the shore.

flounder *verb* 1 To flounder is to struggle to move or stay upright, for example in water or mud. 2 If you flounder in a conversation or situation, you find it difficult to decide what to say or do. ▶ *noun* 3 a type of edible flatfish.

flour *noun* (DGT) Flour is a powder made from finely ground grain, usually wheat, and used for baking and cooking. ▷ **floury** *adjective*

flourish *verb* 1 Something that flourishes develops or functions successfully or healthily. 2 If you flourish something, you wave or display it so that people notice it. ▶ *noun* 3 a bold sweeping or waving movement.

> **flourish** *verb*
> 1 = bloom, boom, come on, do well, prosper, succeed, thrive
> 2 = brandish (*literary*), display, hold aloft, wave
> ▶ *noun* 3 = flick, sweep, wave

flout *verb* If you flout a convention or law, you deliberately disobey it.

flow *verb* 1 If something flows, it moves or happens in a steady continuous stream. ▶ *noun* 2 A flow of something is a steady continuous movement of it;

also the rate at which it flows.

> **flow** *verb*
> 1 = circulate, glide, roll, run, slide
> ▶ *noun* 2 = current, drift, flood, stream, tide

flower *noun* 1 (SCIENCE) the part of a plant containing the reproductive organs from which the fruit or seeds develop. A **complete flower** is a flower that has all the flower parts, particularly the stamens and pistils; an **incomplete flower** is a flower without one or more of the main flower parts; a **perfect flower** is a flower that has both stamens and pistils. ▶ *verb* 2 When a plant flowers, it produces flowers.

flowery *adjective* Flowery language is full of elaborate expressions.

flown the past participle of **fly**.

flu *noun* Flu is an illness similar to a very bad cold, which causes headaches, sore throat, weakness and aching muscles. Flu is short for 'influenza'.

fluctuate *verb* Something that fluctuates is irregular and changeable.

flue *noun* a pipe which takes fumes and smoke away from a stove or boiler.

fluent *adjective* 1 able to speak a foreign language correctly and without hesitation. 2 able to express yourself clearly and without hesitation. ▷ **fluently** *adverb*

> **fluent** *adjective*
> 2 = articulate, easy, effortless, flowing, ready

fluff noun 1 Fluff is soft, light, woolly threads or fibres bunched together. ▶ verb 2 If you fluff something up or out, you brush or shake it to make it seem larger and lighter. > **fluffy** adjective

fluid noun 1 a liquid. ▶ adjective 2 Fluid movement is smooth and flowing. 3 A fluid arrangement or plan is flexible and without a fixed structure. > **fluidity** noun

fluke noun an accidental success or piece of good luck.

flung the past tense and past participle of **fling**.

fluorescent adjective 1 having a very bright appearance when light is shone on it, as if it is shining itself. 2 A fluorescent light is in the form of a tube and shines with a hard bright light.

fluoride noun Fluoride is a mixture of chemicals that is used to prevent tooth decay.

flurry flurries noun a short rush of activity or movement.

flush noun 1 A flush is a rosy red colour. 2 In cards, a flush is a hand all of one suit. ▶ verb 3 If you flush, your face goes red. 4 If you flush a toilet or something such as a pipe, you force water through it to clean it. ▶ adjective 5 (informal) Someone who is flush has plenty of money. 6 Something that is flush with a surface is level with it or flat against it.

flustered adjective If you are flustered, you feel confused, nervous and rushed.

flute noun a musical wind instrument consisting of a long metal tube with holes and keys. It is held sideways to the mouth and played by blowing across a hole in its side.

flutter verb 1 If something flutters, it flaps or waves with small, quick movements. ▶ noun 2 If you are in a flutter, you are excited and nervous. 3 (informal) If you have a flutter, you have a small bet.

flux noun Flux is a state of constant change.

fly flies, flying, flew, flown noun 1 an insect with two pairs of wings. 2 The front opening on a pair of trousers is the fly or the flies. 3 The fly or fly sheet of a tent is either a flap at the entrance or an outer layer providing protection from rain. ▶ verb 4 When a bird, insect or aircraft flies, it moves through the air. 5 If someone or something flies, they move or go very quickly. 6 If you fly at someone or let fly at them, you attack or criticise them suddenly and aggressively. > **flyer** noun

fly verb
4 = flit, flutter, sail, soar
5 = dart, dash, hurry, race, rush, speed, tear

fly-fishing noun Fly-fishing is a method of fishing using imitation flies as bait.

flying fox noun 1 a large bat that eats fruit, found in Australia and Africa. 2 In Australia and New Zealand, a flying fox is a cable car used to carry people over rivers and gorges.

flyover noun a structure carrying one road over another at a junction or intersection.

foal noun 1 a young horse. ▶ verb 2 When a female horse foals, she gives birth.

foam noun 1 Foam is a mass of tiny bubbles. 2 (DGT) Foam is light spongy material used, for example, in furniture or packaging. ▶ *verb* **3** When something foams, it forms a mass of small bubbles.

>**foam** *noun*
>**1** = bubbles, froth, lather
>▶ *verb* **3** = bubble, fizz, froth

focus focuses or focusses, focusing or focussing, focused or focussed; focuses or foci *verb* **1** If you focus your eyes or an instrument on an object, you adjust them so that the image is clear. ▶ *noun* **2** The focus of something is its centre of attention. > **focal** *adjective*

>**focus** *verb*
>**1** = aim, concentrate, direct, fix
>▶ *noun* **2** = centre, focal point, hub, target

fodder *noun* Fodder is food for farm animals or horses.

foe *noun* an enemy.

foetus; also spelt **fetus** *noun* (SCIENCE) an unborn child or animal in the womb. > **foetal** *adjective*

fog fogs, fogging, fogged *noun* **1** Fog is a thick mist of water droplets suspended in the air. ▶ *verb* **2** If glass fogs up, it becomes clouded with steam or condensation. > **foggy** *adjective*

foil *verb* **1** If you foil someone's attempt at something, you prevent them from succeeding. ▶ *noun* **2** Foil is thin, paper-like sheets of metal used to wrap food. **3** Something that is a good foil for something else contrasts with it and makes its good qualities more noticeable. **4** a thin, light sword with a button on the tip, used in fencing.

foil *verb*
1 = check, counter, defeat, frustrate, thwart
▶ *noun* **3** = antithesis, background, complement, contrast

foist *verb* If you foist something on someone, you force it on them.

fold *verb* **1** If you fold something, you bend it so that one part lies over another. **2** (*informal*) If a business folds, it fails and closes down. **3** In cooking, if you fold one ingredient into another, you mix it in gently. ▶ *noun* **4** a crease or bend in paper or cloth. **5** a small enclosed area for sheep.

>**fold** *verb*
>**1** = bend, crease, crumple, tuck, turn under
>▶ *noun* **4** = bend, crease, pleat, wrinkle

folder *noun* **1** a thin piece of folded cardboard for keeping loose papers together. **2** In computing, a folder is a named area of a computer disk where you can group together files and subdirectories.

foliage *noun* Foliage is leaves and plants.

folk *plural noun* **1** Folk or folks are people. ▶ *adjective* **2** Folk music, dance or art is traditional or representative of the ordinary people of an area.

folklore *noun* Folklore is the traditional stories and beliefs of a community.

follicle *noun* a small sac or cavity in the body.

follow *verb* **1** If you follow someone, you move along behind them. If you follow a path or a sign, you move along in that direction. **2** Something that follows a particular thing happens after it. **3** Something that follows is true or logical as a result of something else being the case: *Just because she is pretty, it doesn't follow that she can sing.* **4** If you follow instructions or advice, you do what you are told. **5** If you follow an explanation or the plot of a story, you understand each stage of it. **6** If you follow a person on a social networking site, you regularly read the messages he or she writes. > **follow up** *verb* If you follow up a suggestion or discovery, you find out more about it or act upon it.

> **follow** *verb*
> **1** = hound, pursue, stalk, track
> **2** = come after, succeed, supersede **4** = comply, conform, obey, observe

follower *noun* **1** The followers of a person or belief are the people who support them. **2** On a social networking site, the followers of a person are the people who regularly read their messages.

> **follower** *noun*
> **1** = believer, disciple, fan, henchman, supporter

folly follies *noun* Folly is a foolish act or foolish behaviour.

fond *adjective* **1** If you are fond of someone or something, you like them. **2** A fond hope or belief is thought of with happiness but is unlikely to happen.

> **fond** *adjective*
> **1** = adoring, affectionate, devoted, doting, having a liking for, loving **2** = deluded, empty, foolish, naive, vain

fondle *verb* To fondle something is to stroke it affectionately.

font *noun* **1** In printing, a font is a set of characters of the same style and size. **2** a large stone bowl in a church that holds the water for baptisms.

food *noun* Food is any substance consumed by an animal or plant to provide energy.

> **food** *noun*
> = diet, fare, foodstuffs, grub (*informal*), kai (*New Zealand; informal*), nourishment, provisions, refreshment, tucker (*Australian and New Zealand; informal*)

food chain *noun* (SCIENCE) a series of living things which are linked because each one feeds on the next one in the series. For example, a plant may be eaten by a rabbit which may be eaten by a fox.

foodstuff *noun* anything used for food.

fool *noun* **1** someone who behaves in a silly or stupid way. **2** a dessert made from fruit, cream and sugar whipped together. ▶ *verb* **3** If you fool someone, you trick them.

> **fool** *noun*
> **1** = dope (*informal*), dunce, idiot, ignoramus
> ▶ *verb* **3** = con (*informal*), deceive, dupe, mislead, trick

foolhardy *adjective* foolish and involving too great a risk.

foolish *adjective* very silly or unwise.

> **foolish** *adjective*
> = inane, nonsensical, senseless, silly, unintelligent, unwise

foolproof adjective Something that is foolproof is so well designed or simple to use that it cannot fail.

foot noun 1 the part of your body at the end of your leg. 2 the bottom, base or lower end of something. 3 a unit of length equal to 12 inches or about 30.5 centimetres. 4 (ENGLISH) In poetry, a foot is the basic unit of rhythm containing two or three syllables. ▶ adjective 5 A foot brake, pedal or pump is operated by your foot.

footage noun Footage is a length of film.

football noun 1 Football is any game in which the ball can be kicked, such as soccer, Australian Rules, rugby union and American football. 2 a ball used in any of these games. > **footballer** noun

foothills plural noun (GEOGRAPHY) Foothills are hills at the base of mountains.

foothold noun 1 a place where you can put your foot when climbing. 2 a position from which further progress can be made.

footing noun 1 Footing is a secure grip by or for your feet. 2 a footing is the basis or nature of a relationship or situation.

footman footmen noun a male servant in a large house who wears a uniform.

footnote noun a note at the bottom of a page or an additional comment giving extra information.

footpath noun a path to walk on.

footprint noun a mark left by a foot or shoe.

footstep noun the sound or mark made by someone walking.

for preposition 1 meant to be given to or used by a particular person, or done in order to help or benefit them: *private beaches for their exclusive use.* 2 'For' is used when explaining the reason, cause or purpose of something: *This is my excuse for going to Italy.* 3 You use 'for' to express a quantity, time or distance: *I'll play for ages.* 4 If you are for something, you support it or approve of it.

forage verb When a person or animal forages, they search for food.

foray noun 1 a brief attempt to do or get something. 2 an attack or raid by soldiers.

forbid forbids, forbidding, forbade, forbidden verb If you forbid someone to do something, you order them not to do it. > **forbidden** adjective

> **forbid** verb
> = ban, exclude, outlaw, prohibit, veto

force verb 1 To force someone to do something is to make them do it. 2 To force something is to use violence or great strength to move or open it. ▶ noun 3 a pressure to do something, sometimes with the use of violence or great strength. 4 The force of something is its strength or power. 5 a person or thing that has a lot of influence or effect. 6 an organised group of soldiers or police. 7 (SCIENCE) In physics, force is a pushing or pulling influence that changes a body from a state of rest to one of motion, or changes its rate of motion. ▶ phrase 8 A law or rule that is **in force** is currently valid and must be obeyed.

force *verb*
1 = compel, drive, make, oblige, pressurise
▶ *noun* 3 = compulsion, duress, pressure 4 = impact, might, power, pressure, strength

forceful *adjective* powerful and convincing. > **forcefully** *adverb*

forceps *plural noun* Forceps are a pair of long tongs or pincers used by a doctor or surgeon.

forcible *adjective* 1 involving physical force or violence. 2 convincing and making a strong impression. > **forcibly** *adverb*

ford *noun* 1 a shallow place in a river where it is possible to cross on foot or in a vehicle. ▶ *verb* 2 To ford a river is to cross it on foot or in a vehicle.

fore *phrase* Someone or something that comes **to the fore** becomes important or popular.

forearm *noun* the part of your arm between your elbow and your wrist.

forebear *noun* Your forebears are your ancestors.

foreboding *noun* a strong feeling of approaching disaster.

forecast forecasts, forecasting, forecast or forecasted *noun* 1 a prediction of what will happen, especially a statement about what the weather will be like. ▶ *verb* 2 To forecast an event is to predict what will happen.

forecourt *noun* an open area at the front of a petrol station or large building.

forefinger *noun* the finger next to your thumb.

forefront *noun* The forefront of something is the most important and progressive part of it.

forego foregoes, foregoing, forewent, foregone; also spelt **forgo** *verb* If you forego something pleasant, you give it up or do not insist on having it.

foregone conclusion *noun* A foregone conclusion is a result or conclusion that is bound to happen.

foreground *noun* (ART) In a picture, the foreground is the part that seems nearest to you.

forehand *noun, adjective* (PE) (a stroke in tennis, squash or badminton) made with the palm of your hand facing in the direction that you hit the ball.

forehead *noun* the area at the front of your head, above your eyebrows and below your hairline.

foreign *adjective* 1 belonging to or involving countries other than your own. 2 unfamiliar or uncharacteristic. 3 A foreign object has got into something, usually by accident, and should not be there. > **foreigner** *noun*

foreign *adjective*
1 = distant, exotic, overseas

foreman foremen *noun* 1 a person in charge of a group of workers, for example on a building site. 2 The foreman of a jury is its spokesperson.

foremost *adjective* The foremost of a group of things is the most important or the best.

foremost *adjective*
= best, chief, first, greatest, leading, most important, prime, principal, top

forensic *adjective* 1 relating to or involving the scientific examination of objects involved in a crime. 2 relating to the legal profession.

forerunner *noun* The forerunner of something is the person who first introduced or achieved it, or the first example of it.

foresee foresees, foreseeing, foresaw, foreseen *verb* If you foresee something, you predict or expect that it will happen.

foresight *noun* Foresight is the ability to know what is going to happen in the future.

forest *noun* a large area of trees growing close together.

forestry *noun* Forestry is the study and work of growing and maintaining forests.

foretaste *noun* a slight taste or experience of something in advance.

forever *adverb* permanently or continually.

forewent the past tense of **forego**.

foreword *noun* an introduction in a book.

forfeit *verb* 1 If you forfeit something, you have to give it up as a penalty. ▶ *noun* 2 something that you have to give up or do as a penalty.

forgave the past tense of **forgive**.

forge *noun* 1 a place where a blacksmith works making metal goods by hand. ▶ *verb* 2 To forge metal is to hammer and bend it into shape while it is hot. 3 To forge a relationship is to create a strong and lasting relationship. 4 To forge money, documents or paintings is to make illegal copies of them. 5 To forge ahead is to progress quickly.

forgery forgeries *noun* Forgery is the crime of forging money, documents or paintings; also something that has been forged.

forget forgets, forgetting, forgot, forgotten *verb* 1 If you forget something, you fail to remember or think about it. 2 If you forget yourself, you behave in an unacceptable, uncontrolled way. > **forgetful** *adjective*

> **forget** *verb*
> 1 = fail to remember, omit, overlook

forgive forgives, forgiving, forgave, forgiven *verb* If you forgive someone for doing something bad, you stop feeling angry and resentful towards them. > **forgiving** *adjective*

> **forgive** *verb*
> = absolve, condone, excuse, pardon

forgiveness *noun* the act of forgiving.

> **forgiveness** *noun*
> = mercy, pardon

forgo another spelling of **forego**.

forgot the past tense of **forget**.

forgotten the past participle of **forget**.

fork *noun* 1 a pronged instrument used for eating food. 2 a large garden tool with three or four prongs. 3 a Y-shaped junction or division in a road, river or branch. ▶ *verb* 4 To fork something is to move or turn it with a fork. > **fork out** *verb* (*informal*) If you fork out for something, you pay for it, often unwillingly.

forlorn *adjective* 1 lonely, unhappy and pitiful. 2 desperate and without any expectation of success.

form *noun* 1 A particular form of something is a type or kind of it. 2 The form of something is the shape or pattern of something. 3 a sheet of paper with questions and spaces for you to fill in the answers. 4 a class in a school.
▶ *verb* 5 The things that form something are the things it consists of. 6 When someone forms something or when it forms, it is created, organised or started.

> **form** *noun*
> 1 = class, kind, sort, type, variant, variety 2 = contours, layout, outline, shape, structure
> ▶ *verb* 5 = compose, constitute, make up, serve as 6 = assemble, create, develop, draw up, establish, fashion, make

formal *adjective* 1 correct, serious and conforming to accepted conventions. 2 official and publicly recognised. > **formally** *adverb*

> **formal** *adjective*
> 1 = conventional, correct, precise, stiff 2 = approved, legal, official, prescribed, regular

formaldehyde *noun* Formaldehyde is a poisonous, strong-smelling gas, used for preserving biological specimens. Its formula is HCHO.

formality formalities *noun* an action or process that is carried out as part of an official procedure.

format *noun* 1 the way in which something is arranged or presented. 2 (ICT) The format of a computer file is the way in which the data is stored in it.

formation *noun* 1 The formation of something is the process of developing and creating it. 2 the pattern or shape of something.

formative *adjective* having an important and lasting influence on character and development.

former *adjective* 1 happening or existing before now or in the past.
▶ *noun* 2 You use 'the former' to refer to the first of two things just mentioned: *If I had to choose between happiness and money, I would have the former.* > **formerly** *adverb*

> **former** *adjective*
> 1 = ancient, bygone, old, past

formidable *adjective* very difficult to deal with or overcome, and therefore rather frightening or impressive.

> **formidable** *adjective*
> = challenging, daunting, difficult, intimidating, mammoth, onerous

formula formulae or formulas *noun* 1 (MATHS) a group of letters, numbers and symbols which stand for a mathematical or scientific rule. 2 (SCIENCE) a list of quantities of substances that when mixed make another substance, for example in chemistry. 3 a plan or set of rules for dealing with a particular problem.

formulate *verb* If you formulate a plan or thought, you create it and express it in a clear and precise way.

f

forsake forsakes, forsaking, forsook, forsaken *verb* To forsake someone or something is to give them up or abandon them.

fort *noun* 1 a strong building built for defence. ▶ *phrase* 2 If you **hold the fort** for someone, you manage their affairs while they are away.

> **fort** *noun*
> 1 = castle, citadel, fortification, fortress

forte *adverb* 1 (MUSIC) In music, forte is an instruction to play or sing something loudly. ▶ *noun* 2 If something is your forte, you are particularly good at doing it.

forth *adverb* 1 out and forward from a starting place. 2 into view.

forthcoming *adjective* 1 planned to happen soon. 2 given or made available. 3 willing to give information.

forthright *adjective* Someone who is forthright is direct and honest about their opinions and feelings.

fortification *noun* Fortifications are buildings, walls and ditches used to protect a place.

fortitude *noun* Fortitude is calm and patient courage.

fortnight *noun* a period of two weeks. > **fortnightly** *adverb, adjective*

fortress *noun* a castle or well-protected town built for defence.

fortuitous *adjective* happening by good luck.

fortunate *adjective* 1 Someone who is fortunate is lucky. 2 Something that is fortunate brings success or advantage. > **fortunately** *adverb*

fortune *noun* 1 Fortune or good fortune is good luck. 2 A fortune is a large amount of money. ▶ *phrase* 3 If someone **tells your fortune**, they predict your future.

forty forties the number 40. > **fortieth** *adjective*

forum *noun* 1 a place or meeting in which people can exchange ideas and discuss public issues. 2 a website where people discuss a particular topic. 3 a square in Roman towns where people met to discuss business and politics.

forward *adverb, adjective* 1 Forward or forwards means in the front or towards the front. 2 Forward means in or towards a future time. 3 Forward or forwards also means developing or progressing: *The new committee would push forward government plans.* ▶ *adverb* 4 If someone or something is put forward, they are suggested as being suitable for something. ▶ *verb* 5 If you forward a message or document that you have received, you send it on to another person. ▶ *noun* 6 In a game such as football or hockey, a forward is a player in an attacking position.

fossil *noun* (SCIENCE) the remains or impression of an animal or plant from a previous age, preserved in rock. > **fossilise** *verb*

fossil fuel *noun* (GEOGRAPHY) (SCIENCE) Fossil fuels are fuels such as coal, oil and natural gas, which have been formed by rotting animals and plants from millions of years ago.

foster *verb* 1 If someone fosters a child, they are paid to look after the child for a period, but do not become its legal parent. 2 If you foster something such as an activity or an idea, you help its development and growth by encouraging people to do or think it. > **foster child** noun > **foster parent** noun

fought the past tense and past participle of **fight**.

foul adjective **1** Something that is foul is very unpleasant, especially because it is dirty, wicked or obscene. ▶ verb **2** To foul something is to make it dirty, especially with faeces. ▶ noun **3** In sport, a foul is an act of breaking the rules.

found 1 Found is the past tense and past participle of **find**. ▶ verb **2** If someone founds an organisation or institution, they start it and set it up.

foundation noun **1** The foundation of a belief or way of life is the basic ideas or attitudes on which it is built. **2** a solid layer of concrete or bricks in the ground, on which a building is built to give it a firm base. **3** an organisation set up by money donated to or left in someone's will for research or charity.

founder noun **1** The founder of an institution or organisation is the person who sets it up. ▶ verb **2** If something founders, it fails.

foundry foundries noun a factory where metal is melted and cast.

fountain noun an ornamental structure consisting of a jet of water forced into the air by a pump.

fountain pen noun a pen which is supplied with ink from a container inside the pen.

four 1 the number 4. ▶ phrase **2** If you are on **all fours**, you are on your hands and knees.

fourteen the number 14. > **fourteenth** adjective

fourth adjective The fourth item in a series is the one counted as number four.

fowl noun a bird such as chicken or duck that is kept or hunted for its meat or eggs.

fox noun **1** a dog-like wild animal with reddish-brown fur, a pointed face and ears, and a thick tail. ▶ verb **2** If something foxes you, it is too confusing or puzzling for you to understand.

foyer noun a large area just inside the main doors of a cinema, hotel or public building.

fracas noun a rough, noisy quarrel or fight.

fracking noun Fracking is the extraction of oil or gas by forcing liquid into rock at high pressure.

fraction noun **1** (MATHS) In arithmetic, a fraction is a part of a whole number. A **proper fraction** is a fraction in which the number above the line is lower than the number below it; an **improper fraction** has the greater number above the line. **2** a tiny proportion or amount of something.

fractious adjective When small children are fractious, they become upset or angry very easily, often because they are tired.

fracture noun **1** a crack or break in something, especially a bone. ▶ verb **2** If something fractures, it breaks.

fragile adjective easily broken or damaged. > **fragility** noun

> **fragile** adjective
> = breakable, dainty, delicate, flimsy, frail

fragment noun 1 a small piece or part of something. ▶ verb 2 If something fragments, it breaks into small pieces or different parts.

fragmentary adjective made up of small pieces, or parts that are not connected.

fragrance noun a sweet or pleasant smell.

> **fragrance** noun
> = aroma, perfume, scent, smell

fragrant adjective Something that is fragrant smells sweet or pleasant.

> **fragrant** adjective
> = aromatic, perfumed, sweet-smelling

frail adjective 1 Someone who is frail is not strong or healthy. 2 Something that is frail is easily broken or damaged. > **frailty** noun

frame noun 1 the structure surrounding a door, window or picture. 2 an arrangement of connected bars over which something is built. 3 The frames of a pair of glasses are the wire or plastic parts that hold the lenses. 4 Your frame is your body. 5 one of the many separate photographs of which a cinema film is made up. ▶ verb 6 To frame a picture is to put it into a frame. 7 The language something is framed in is the language used to express it.

framework noun 1 (D&T) a structure acting as a support or frame. 2 a set of rules, beliefs or ideas which you use to decide what to do.

franc noun the main unit of currency in Switzerland, and formerly in France and Belgium. A franc is worth 100 centimes.

franchise noun 1 The franchise is the right to vote in an election. 2 the right given by a company to someone to allow them to sell its goods or services.

frank adjective If you are frank, you say things in an open and honest way. > **frankly** adverb

> **frank** adjective
> = blunt, candid, honest, open, plain, straightforward

frantic adjective If you are frantic, you behave in a wild, desperate way because you are anxious or frightened. > **frantically** adverb

fraternal adjective 'Fraternal' is used to describe friendly actions and feelings between groups of people.

fraternity fraternities noun 1 Fraternity is friendship between groups of people. 2 a group of people with something in common.

fraud noun 1 Fraud is the crime of getting money by deceit or trickery. 2 something that deceives people in an illegal or immoral way. 3 someone who is not what they pretend to be.

> **fraud** noun
> 1 = deceit, deception, guile, trickery 2 = fake, forgery, hoax 3 = charlatan, cheat, imposter, quack

fraudulent adjective dishonest or deceitful.

fraught adjective If something is fraught with problems or difficulties, it is full of them.

fray verb 1 If cloth or rope frays, its threads or strands become worn and it is likely to tear or break. ▶ noun 2 a fight or argument.

freak noun 1 someone whose appearance or behaviour is very unusual. ▶ adjective 2 A freak event is very unusual and unlikely to happen.

freckle noun Freckles are small, light brown spots on someone's skin, especially their face.
> **freckled** adjective

free freer, freest; frees, freeing, freed adjective 1 not controlled or limited. 2 Someone who is free is no longer a prisoner. 3 To be free of something unpleasant is not to have it. 4 If someone is free, they are not busy or occupied. If a place, seat or machine is free, it is not occupied or not being used. 5 If something is free, you can have it without paying for it. ▶ verb 6 If you free someone or something that is imprisoned, fastened or trapped, you release them.

> **free** adjective
> 2 = at large, at liberty, liberated, loose 5 = complimentary, gratis, unpaid, without charge
> ▶ verb 6 = discharge, liberate, release, set at liberty, set loose

freedom noun 1 If you have the freedom to do something, you have the scope or are allowed to do it. 2 When prisoners gain their freedom, they escape or are released. 3 When there is freedom from something unpleasant, people are not affected by it.

> **freedom** noun
> 1 = discretion, latitude, leeway, licence, scope
> 2 = emancipation, liberty, release 3 = exemption, immunity

freehold noun the right to own a house or piece of land for life without conditions.

freelance adjective, adverb A freelance worker is not employed by one organisation, but is paid for each job he or she does.

freely adverb Freely means without restriction.

free-range adjective Free-range eggs are laid by hens that can move and feed freely on an area of open ground.

freestyle noun Freestyle refers to sports competitions, especially swimming, in which competitors can use any style or method.

freeway noun In Australia, South Africa and the United States, a freeway is a road designed for fast-moving traffic.

free will phrase If you do something of your own free will, you do it by choice and not because you are forced to.

freeze freezes, freezing, froze, frozen verb 1 (SCIENCE) When a liquid freezes, it becomes solid because it is very cold. 2 If you freeze, you suddenly become very still and quiet. 3 (DRAMA) To freeze the action in a film is to stop the film at a particular frame. 4 If you freeze food, you put it in a freezer to preserve it. 5 When wages or prices are frozen, they are officially prevented from rising. ▶ noun 6 an official action taken to prevent wages or prices from rising. 7 a period of freezing weather.

freezer noun a large refrigerator which freezes and stores food for a long time.

freezing *adjective* extremely cold.

freight *noun* Freight is goods moved by lorries, ships or other transport; also the moving of these goods.

French *adjective* 1 belonging or relating to France. 2 French is the main language spoken in France, and is also spoken by many people in Belgium, Switzerland and Canada.

Frenchman Frenchmen *noun* a man who comes from France.

Frenchwoman Frenchwomen *noun* a woman who comes from France.

frenetic *adjective* Frenetic behaviour is wild and excited.
> **frenetically** *adverb*

frenzy frenzies *noun* If someone is in a frenzy, their behaviour is wild and uncontrolled.
> **frenzied** *adjective*

> **frenzy** *noun*
> = agitation, fury, hysteria, madness, rage

frequency frequencies *noun* 1 The frequency of an event is how often it happens. 2 (SCIENCE) The frequency of a sound or radio wave is the rate at which it vibrates. 3 (MATHS) In statistics, the frequency of a particular class is the number of individuals in it.

frequent *adjective* 1 often happening. ► *verb* 2 If you frequent a place, you go there often. > **frequently** *adverb*

> **frequent** *adjective*
> 1 = common, continual, everyday, habitual, recurrent, repeated
> ► *verb* 2 = attend, haunt, patronise, visit

fresco frescoes *noun* a picture painted on a plastered wall while the plaster is still wet.

fresh *adjective* 1 A fresh thing replaces a previous one, or is added to it. 2 Fresh food is newly made or obtained, and not tinned or frozen. 3 Fresh water is not salty, for example the water in a stream. 4 If the weather is fresh, it is fairly cold and windy. 5 If you are fresh from something, you have experienced it recently.

freshwater *adjective* 1 A freshwater lake or pool contains water that is not salty. 2 A freshwater creature lives in a river, lake or pool that is not salty.

fret frets, fretting, fretted *verb* 1 If you fret about something, you worry about it. ► *noun* 2 The frets on a stringed instrument, such as a guitar, are the metal ridges across its neck. > **fretful** *adjective*

friction *noun* 1 (SCIENCE) the force that stops things from moving freely when they rub against each other. 2 Friction between people is disagreement and quarrels.

Friday *noun* the day between Thursday and Saturday.

fridge *noun* the same as a **refrigerator**.

friend *noun* 1 Your friends are people you know well and like to spend time with. 2 someone with whom you can exchange posts and messages on a social networking site.

> **friend** *noun*
> 1 = buddy (*informal*), china (*British and South African; informal*), chum (*informal*), companion, confidant or confidante, crony (*old-fashioned*), mate (*British; informal*), pal (*informal*)

friendly friendlier, friendliest
adjective **1** If you are friendly to
someone, you behave in a kind
and pleasant way to them.
2 People who are friendly with
each other like each other and
enjoy spending time together.
> **friendliness** *noun*

> **friendly** *adjective*
> **1** = affectionate, amiable, close,
> cordial, genial, welcoming

friendship *noun* **1** Your
friendships are the special
relationships that you have with
your friends. **2** Friendship is the
state of being friends with
someone.

> **friendship** *noun*
> **2** = affection, attachment,
> closeness, goodwill

frieze *noun* **1** a strip of decoration
or carving along the top of a wall
or column. **2** (ART) a picture on a
long strip of paper which is hung
along a wall.

frigate *noun* a small, fast warship.

fright *noun* Fright is a sudden
feeling of fear.

frighten *verb* If something
frightens you, it makes you
afraid.

> **frighten** *verb*
> = alarm, intimidate, scare,
> startle, terrify, terrorise,
> unnerve

frightened *adjective* having
feelings of fear about
something.

> **frightened** *adjective*
> = afraid, alarmed, petrified,
> scared, startled, terrified

frightening *adjective* causing
someone to feel fear.

> **frightening** *adjective*
> = alarming, hair-raising,
> intimidating, menacing,
> terrifying

frightful *adjective* very bad or
unpleasant.

frigid *adjective* Frigid behaviour is
cold and unfriendly.

frill *noun* a strip of cloth with
many folds, attached to
something as a decoration.
> **frilly** *adjective*

fringe *noun* **1** the hair that hangs
over a person's forehead. **2** a
decoration on clothes and other
objects, consisting of a row of
hanging strips or threads. **3** The
fringes of a place are the parts
farthest from its centre.

frisky friskier, friskiest *adjective*
A frisky animal or child is
energetic and wants to have
fun.

fritter *noun* **1** Fritters consist of
food dipped in batter and fried.
▶ *verb* **2** If you fritter away your
time or money, you waste it on
unimportant things.

frivolous *adjective* Someone who
is frivolous behaves in a silly way
especially when they should be
sensible. > **frivolity** *noun*

> **frivolous** *adjective*
> = flippant, foolish, juvenile,
> puerile, silly

frock *noun* (old-fashioned) a dress.

frog *noun* a small amphibious
creature with smooth skin,
prominent eyes, and long back
legs which it uses for jumping.

frolic frolics, frolicking, frolicked
verb When animals or children
frolic, they run and play in a
lively way.

from preposition 1 You use 'from' to say what the source, origin or starting point of something is: *a call from a mobile phone*. 2 If you take something from an amount, you reduce the amount by that much. 3 You also use 'from' when stating the range of something: *a score from one to five*.

front noun 1 The front of something is the part that faces forward. 2 In a war, the front is the place where two armies are fighting. 3 In meteorology, a front is the line where a mass of cold air meets a mass of warm air. 4 A front is an outward appearance, often one that is false. ▶ *phrase* 5 In front means ahead or further forward. 6 If you do something in front of someone, you do it when they are present. > **frontal** adjective

> **front** noun
> 1 = facade, face, frontage
> 4 = appearance, exterior, facade, face, show
> ▶ *phrase* 5 in front of = ahead of, before

frontage noun The frontage of a building is the wall that faces a street.

frontier noun a border between two countries.

frost noun When there is a frost, the temperature outside falls below freezing.

frostbite noun Frostbite is damage to your fingers, toes or ears caused by extreme cold.

frosty frostier, frostiest adjective 1 If it is frosty, the temperature outside is below freezing point. 2 If someone is frosty, they are unfriendly or disapproving. > **frostily** adverb

froth noun 1 Froth is a mass of small bubbles on the surface of a liquid. ▶ *verb* 2 If a liquid froths, small bubbles appear on its surface.

frown verb 1 If you frown, you move your eyebrows closer together, because you are annoyed, worried or concentrating. ▶ *noun* 2 a cross expression on someone's face.

> **frown** verb
> 1 = glare, glower, knit your brows, scowl

froze the past tense of **freeze**.

frozen 1 Frozen is the past participle of **freeze**. ▶ *adjective* 2 extremely cold.

> **frozen** adjective
> 2 = arctic, chilled, frigid, icy, numb

frugal adjective 1 Someone who is frugal spends very little money. 2 A frugal meal is small and cheap.

fruit noun 1 the part of a plant that develops after the flower and contains the seeds. Many fruits are edible. 2 (*in plural*) The fruits of something are its good results.

fruitful adjective Something that is fruitful has good and useful results.

fruitless adjective Something that is fruitless does not achieve anything.

fruit salad noun a mixture of pieces of different fruits served in a juice.

fruity fruitier, fruitiest adjective Something that is fruity smells or tastes of fruit.

frustrate verb 1 If something frustrates you, it prevents you doing what you want and makes you upset and angry. **2** To frustrate something such as a plan is to prevent it. **> frustration** noun

> **frustrate** verb
> **2** = block, check, foil, thwart

fry fries, frying, fried verb When you fry food, you cook it in a pan containing hot fat or oil.

fuchsia noun a plant or small bush with pink, purple or white flowers that hang downwards.

fudge noun **1** Fudge is a soft brown sweet made from butter, milk and sugar. ▶ verb **2** If you fudge something, you avoid making clear or definite decisions or statements about it.

fuel fuels, fuelling, fuelled noun **1** Fuel is a substance such as coal or petrol that is burned to provide heat or power. ▶ verb **2** A machine or vehicle that is fuelled by a substance works by burning the substance as a fuel.

fugitive noun someone who is running away or hiding, especially from the police.

-ful suffix **1** '-ful' is used to form adjectives with the meaning 'full of': careful. **2** '-ful' is used to form nouns which mean 'the amount needed to fill': spoonful.

fulcrum fulcrums or fulcra noun (DGT) the point at which something is balancing or pivoting.

fulfil fulfils, fulfilling, fulfilled verb **1** If you fulfil a promise, hope or duty, you carry it out or achieve it. **2** If something fulfils you, it gives you satisfaction. **> fulfilling** adjective

> **fulfil** verb
> **1** = accomplish, achieve, carry out, perform, realise, satisfy

full adjective **1** containing or having as much as it is possible to hold. **2** complete or whole: a full meal. **3** loose and made from a lot of fabric: full sleeves. ▶ adverb **4** completely and directly: Turn the taps full on. ▶ phrase **5** Something that has been done or described in full has been dealt with completely. **> fullness** noun **> fully** adverb

> **full** adjective
> **1** = filled, loaded, packed, saturated **2** = comprehensive, detailed, exhaustive, extensive, maximum, thorough **3** = baggy, loose, voluminous

full-blown adjective complete and fully developed.

full moon noun the moon when it appears as a complete circle.

full stop noun (ENGLISH) the punctuation mark (.) used at the end of a sentence or after an abbreviation or initial.

full-time adjective **1** involving work for the whole of each normal working week. ▶ noun **2** In games such as football, full time is the end of the match.

fully fledged adjective completely developed.

fulsome adjective exaggerated and elaborate, and often sounding insincere.

fumble verb If you fumble, you feel for or handle something clumsily.

fume noun **1** Fumes are unpleasant-smelling gases and smoke, often toxic, that are produced by burning and by some chemicals. ▶ *verb* **2** If you are fuming, you are very angry.

fun *noun* **1** Fun is pleasant, enjoyable and light-hearted activity. ▶ *phrase* **2** If you **make fun** of someone, you tease them or joke about them.

> **fun** *noun*
> **1** = amusement, enjoyment, entertainment, pleasure, recreation
> ▶ *phrase* **2** make fun of = deride (*formal*), laugh at, mock, ridicule, taunt, tease

function *noun* **1** The function of something or someone is their purpose or the job they have to do. **2** a large formal dinner, reception or party. **3** (MATHS) A function is a variable whose value depends on the value of other independent variables. 'y is a function of x' is written $y = f(x)$. ▶ *verb* **4** When something functions, it operates or works.

> **function** *noun*
> **1** = duty, job, purpose, remit, responsibility, role **2** = dinner, gathering, party, reception
> ▶ *verb* **4** = go, operate, perform, run, work

functional *adjective* **1** relating to the way something works. **2** designed for practical use rather than for decoration or attractiveness. **3** working properly.

fund *noun* **1** an amount of available money, usually for a particular purpose. A fund of something is a lot of it. ▶ *verb* **3** Someone who funds something provides money for it.

fund *noun* **1** = capital, foundation, pool, reserve, supply **2** = hoard, mine, reserve, reservoir, store ▶ *verb* **2** = finance, pay for, subsidise, support

fundamental *adjective* **1** basic and central. ▶ *noun* **2** The fundamentals of something are its most basic and important parts.

funeral *noun* a ceremony or religious service for the burial or cremation of a dead person.

funereal *adjective* depressing and gloomy.

funfair *noun* a place of entertainment with things like amusement arcades and rides.

fungicide *noun* a chemical used to kill or prevent fungus.

fungus fungi or funguses *noun* (SCIENCE) a plant such as a mushroom or mould that does not have leaves and grows on other living things. > **fungal** *adjective*

funnel funnels, funnelling, funnelled *noun* **1** an open cone narrowing to a tube, used to pour substances into containers. **2** a metal chimney on a ship or steam engine. ▶ *verb* **3** If something is funnelled somewhere, it is directed through a narrow space into that place.

funny funnier, funniest *adjective* **1** strange or puzzling. **2** causing amusement or laughter. > **funnily** *adverb*

> **funny** *adjective*
> **1** = mysterious, odd, peculiar, puzzling, strange, unusual, weird **2** = amusing, comic, comical, hilarious, humorous, witty

fur noun 1 Fur is the soft thick body hair of many animals. 2 a coat made from an animal's fur.
> **furry** adjective

furious adjective 1 extremely angry. 2 involving great energy, effort or speed.

> **furious** adjective
> 1 = enraged, fuming, infuriated, livid, mad, raging
> 2 = breakneck, fierce, frantic, frenzied, intense, manic

furlong noun a unit of length equal to 220 yards or about 201.2 metres.

furnace noun a container for a very large, hot fire used, for example, in the steel industry for melting ore.

furnish verb 1 If you furnish a room, you put furniture into it. 2 (formal) If you furnish someone with something, you provide it for them.

furnishings plural noun The furnishings of a room or house are the furniture and fittings in it.

furniture noun Furniture is movable objects such as tables, chairs and wardrobes.

furore noun an angry and excited reaction or protest.

furrow noun 1 a long, shallow trench made by a plough. ▶ verb 2 When someone furrows their brow, they frown.

further 1 a comparative form of **far**. ▶ adjective 2 additional or more. ▶ verb 3 If you further something, you help it to progress.

further education noun Further education is education at a college after leaving school, but not at a university.

furthermore adverb (formal) used to introduce additional information: There is no record of such a letter. Furthermore, it is company policy never to send such letters.

furthest a superlative form of **far**.

furtive adjective secretive, sly and cautious.

fury noun Fury is violent or extreme anger.

fuse noun 1 a safety device in a plug or electrical appliance consisting of a piece of wire which melts to stop the electrical current if a fault occurs. 2 a long cord attached to some types of simple bomb which is lit to detonate it. ▶ verb 3 When an electrical appliance fuses, it stops working because the fuse has melted to protect it. 4 If two things fuse, they join or become combined.

fuselage noun the main part of an aeroplane or rocket.

fusion noun 1 Fusion is what happens when two substances join by melting together. 2 Fusion is also nuclear fusion. ▶ adjective 3 Fusion is used to refer to food or a style of cooking that brings together ingredients or cooking techniques from several different countries.

fuss noun 1 Fuss is unnecessarily anxious or excited behaviour. ▶ verb 2 If someone fusses, they behave with unnecessary anxiety and concern for unimportant things.

> **fuss** noun
> 1 = agitation, bother, commotion, confusion, stir, to-do (informal)
> ▶ verb 2 = bustle, fidget, fret

fussy fussier, fussiest adjective
1 likely to fuss a lot. 2 with too much elaborate detail or decoration.

> **fussy** adjective
> 1 = choosy (informal),
> discriminating, exacting,
> fastidious, particular

futile adjective having no chance of success. ▷ **futility** noun

> **futile** adjective
> = abortive, forlorn,
> unsuccessful, useless, vain

future noun 1 The future is the period of time after the present. 2 Something that has a future is likely to succeed. ▷ adjective 3 relating to or occurring at a time after the present. 4 (ENGLISH) (MFL) The future tense of a verb is the form used to express something that will happen in the future.

> **future** adjective
> 3 = approaching, coming,
> forthcoming, impending, later,
> prospective

futuristic adjective very modern and strange, as if belonging to a time in the future.

fuzz noun short fluffy hair.

Gg

g an abbreviation for 'gram' or 'grams'.

gable noun Gables are the triangular parts at the top of the outside walls at each end of a house.

gadget noun a small machine or tool. ▷ **gadgetry** noun

> **gadget** noun
> = appliance, device, machine,
> tool

Gaelic noun a language spoken in some parts of Scotland and Ireland.

gaffe noun a social blunder or mistake.

gaffer noun (informal) a boss.

gag gags, gagging, gagged noun 1 a strip of cloth that is tied round someone's mouth to stop them speaking. 2 (informal) a joke told by a comedian. ▷ verb 3 To gag someone means to put a gag round their mouth. 4 If you gag, you choke and nearly vomit.

gaggle noun 1 a group of geese. 2 (informal) a noisy group.

gaiety noun liveliness and fun.

gaily adverb in a happy and cheerful way.

gain verb 1 If you gain something, you get it gradually. 2 If you gain from a situation, you get some advantage from it. 3 If you gain on someone, you gradually catch them up. ▶ noun **4** an increase. **5** an advantage that you get for yourself.

gain verb
1 = achieve, acquire, earn, obtain, secure (formal), win
2 = benefit, profit
▶ noun **4** = advance, growth, improvement, increase, rise

gait noun Someone's gait is their way of walking.

gala noun a special public celebration or performance.

galaxy galaxies noun (SCIENCE) A galaxy is an enormous group of stars that extends over many millions of miles. The galaxy to which the earth's solar system belongs is called the Milky Way.
> **galactic** adjective

gale noun an extremely strong wind.

gall noun **1** If someone has the gall to do something, they have enough courage or impudence to do it. ▶ verb **2** If something galls you, it makes you extremely annoyed.

gallant adjective **1** brave and honourable. **2** polite and considerate towards women.

gall bladder noun an organ in your body which stores bile and which is next to your liver.

gallery galleries noun **1** (ART) a building or room where works of art are shown. **2** In a theatre or large hall, the gallery is a raised area at the back or sides.

galley noun **1** a kitchen in a ship or aircraft. **2** a ship, driven by oars, used in ancient and medieval times.

Gallic adjective (formal or literary) French.

gallon noun a unit of liquid volume equal to eight pints or about 4.55 litres.

gallop verb **1** When a horse gallops, it runs very fast, so that during each stride all four feet are off the ground at the same time. ▶ noun **2** a very fast run.

gallows noun A gallows is a framework on which criminals used to be hanged.

galore adjective in very large numbers.

galvanised; also spelt **galvanized** adjective Galvanised metal has been coated with zinc by an electrical process to protect it from rust.

gambit noun something which someone does to gain an advantage in a situation.

gamble verb **1** When people gamble, they bet money on the result of a game or race. **2** If you gamble something, you risk losing it in the hope of gaining an advantage. ▶ noun **3** If you take a gamble, you take a risk in the hope of gaining an advantage.

gamble verb
1 = back, bet **2** = chance, risk, stake
▶ noun **3** = chance, lottery, risk

game noun **1** an enjoyable activity with a set of rules which is played by individuals or teams against each other. **2** an enjoyable imaginative activity played by small children. **3** You might describe something as a game when it is designed to gain advantage: playing the political game. **4** Game is wild animals or birds that are hunted for sport or for food. **5** (in plural) Games are sports

played at school or in a
competition. ▶ adjective 6 (informal)
Someone who is game is willing
to try something unusual or
difficult.

> **game** noun
> 1 = clash, contest, match

gamekeeper noun a person
employed to look after game
animals and birds on a country
estate.

gang noun a group of people who
join together for some purpose,
for example to commit a crime.
> **gang up** verb (informal) If people
gang up on you, they join
together to oppose you.

gangrene noun Gangrene is decay
in the tissues of part of the body,
caused by inadequate blood supply.

gangster noun a violent criminal
who is a member of a gang.

gap noun 1 a space between two
things or a hole in something
solid. 2 a period of time. 3 A gap
between things, people or ideas is
a great difference between them.

> **gap** noun
> 1 = break, chink, crack, hole,
> opening, space 2 = hiatus
> (formal), interlude, interval, lull,
> pause 3 = difference, disparity
> (formal), inconsistency

gape verb 1 If you gape at someone
or something, you stare at them
with your mouth open in
surprise. 2 Something that gapes
is wide open.

garage noun 1 a building where a
car can be kept. 2 a place where
cars are repaired and where petrol
is sold.

garb noun (formal) Someone's garb
is their clothes.

garbage noun 1 Garbage is
rubbish, especially household
rubbish. 2 (informal) If you say
something is garbage, you mean
it is nonsense.

> **garbage** noun
> 1 = debris, junk (informal), litter,
> refuse (formal), rubbish, trash,
> waste 2 = drivel, gibberish,
> nonsense, rubbish

garbled adjective Garbled
messages are jumbled and the
details may be wrong.

> **garbled** adjective
> = confused, distorted,
> incomprehensible, jumbled,
> unintelligible

garden noun 1 an area of land next
to a house, where flowers, fruit or
vegetables are grown. 2 (in plural)
Gardens are a type of park in a
town or around a large house.
▶ verb 3 If you garden, you do work
in your garden such as weeding or
planting.

gardener noun a person who
looks after a garden as a job or as a
hobby.

garish adjective bright and harsh
to look at.

garland noun a circle of flowers
and leaves which is worn around
the neck or head.

garlic noun Garlic is the small
white bulb of an onion-like plant
which has a strong taste and
smell.

garment noun a piece of clothing.

garnish noun 1 something, such
as a sprig of parsley, that is used
in cooking for decoration. ▶ verb
2 To garnish food means to
decorate it with a garnish.

garrison noun a group of soldiers

stationed in a town in order to guard it; also used of the buildings in which these soldiers live.

gas *gases; gasses, gassing, gassed noun* 1 (SCIENCE) any airlike substance that is not liquid or solid, such as oxygen or the gas used as a fuel in heating. 2 In American English, gas is petrol. ▶ *verb* 3 To gas people or animals means to kill them with poisonous gas.

gash *noun* 1 a long, deep cut. ▶ *verb* 2 If you gash something, you make a long, deep cut in it.

gasoline *noun* In American English, gasoline is petrol.

gasp *verb* 1 If you gasp, you quickly draw in your breath through your mouth because you are surprised or in pain. ▶ *noun* 2 a sharp intake of breath through the mouth.

gasp *verb*
1 = choke, gulp, pant, puff
▶ *noun* 2 = gulp, pant, puff

gastric *adjective* occurring in the stomach or involving the stomach.

gate *noun* 1 a barrier which can open and shut and is used to close the entrance to a garden or field. 2 The gate at a sports event is the number of people who have attended it.

gatecrash *verb* If you gatecrash a party, you go to it when you have not been invited.

gateway *noun* 1 an entrance through a wall or fence where there is a gate. 2 Something that is considered to be the entrance to a larger or more important thing can be described as the gateway to the larger thing.

gather *verb* 1 When people gather, they come together in a group. 2 If you gather a number of things, you bring them together in one place. 3 If something gathers speed or strength, it gets faster or stronger. 4 If you gather something, you learn it, often from what someone says.

gather *verb*
1 = assemble, congregate, flock, mass, round up 2 = accumulate, amass, collect, hoard, stockpile 4 = assume, conclude, hear, learn, understand

gathering *noun* a meeting of people who have come together for a particular purpose.

gathering *noun*
= assembly, congregation, get-together (*informal*), meeting, rally

gauche *adjective* (*formal*) socially awkward.

gaudy *gaudier, gaudiest adjective* very colourful in a vulgar way.

gaudy *adjective*
= bright, flashy, garish, loud, showy, tacky (*informal*), vulgar

gauge *verb* 1 If you gauge something, you estimate it or calculate it. ▶ *noun* 2 a piece of equipment that measures the amount of something. 3 something that is used as a standard by which you judge a situation. 4 On railways, the gauge is the distance between the two rails on a railway line.

gaunt *adjective* A person who looks gaunt is thin and bony.

gauntlet *noun* 1 Gauntlets are long thick gloves worn for protection, for example by motorcyclists. ▸ *phrase* **2** If you **throw down the gauntlet**, you challenge someone. **3** If you **run the gauntlet**, you have an unpleasant experience in which you are attacked or criticised by people.

gave the past tense of **give**.

gay *adjective* **1** Someone who is gay is homosexual. **2** (*old-fashioned*) Gay people or places are lively and full of fun.

gaze *verb* If you gaze at something, you look steadily at it for a long time.

gazette *noun* a newspaper or journal.

GB an abbreviation for **Great Britain**.

GCSE *noun* In Britain, the GCSE is an examination taken by school students aged 15 and 16. GCSE is an abbreviation for 'General Certificate of Secondary Education'.

gear *noun* **1** (DGT) a piece of machinery which controls the rate at which energy is converted into movement. Gears in vehicles control the speed and power of the vehicle. **2** (PE) The gear for an activity is the clothes and equipment that you need for it. ▸ *verb* **3** If someone or something is geared to a particular event or purpose, they are prepared for it.

geek *noun* (*informal*) a person who is obsessive about an interest.

geese the plural of **goose**.

gel gels, gelling, gelled *noun* **1** a smooth, soft, jelly-like substance. ▸ *verb* **2** If a liquid gels, it turns into a gel. **3** If a vague thought or plan gels, it becomes more definite.

gelatine or **gelatin** *noun* a clear tasteless substance, obtained from meat and bones, used to make liquids firm and jelly-like.

gem *noun* **1** a jewel or precious stone. **2** You can describe something or someone that is extremely good or beautiful as a gem.

Gemini *noun* Gemini is the third sign of the zodiac, represented by a pair of twins. People born between May 21st and June 20th are born under this sign.

gen *noun* (*informal*) The gen on something is information about it.

gender *noun* **1** (PSHE) the state of being a boy or a girl, including the way society expects you to behave because of that. **2** (MFL) the classification of nouns as masculine, feminine or neuter in certain languages.

gene *noun* (SCIENCE) one of the parts of a living cell which controls the physical characteristics of an organism, and which characteristics are passed on from one generation to the next.

genera the plural of **genus**.

general *adjective* **1** relating to the whole of something or to most things in a group: *your general health.* **2** true, suitable or relevant in most situations: *the general truth of science.* **3** including or involving a wide range of different things: *a general hospital.* **4** having complete responsibility over a wide area of work or a large number of people: *the general secretary.* ▸ *noun* **5** an army officer of very high rank. ▸ *phrase* **6** In general means usually. > **generally** *adverb*

general *adjective*
1 = broad, comprehensive, overall 2 = accepted, broad, common, universal, widespread

general election *noun* an election for a new government, which all the people of a country may vote in.

generalise; also spelt **generalize** *verb* To generalise means to say that something is true in most cases, ignoring minor details. > **generalisation** *noun*

general practitioner *noun* a doctor who works in the community rather than in a hospital.

generate *verb* To generate something means to create or produce it.

generation *noun* all the people of about the same age; also the period of time between one generation and the next, usually considered to be about 25–30 years.

generator *noun* a machine which produces electricity from another form of energy such as wind power.

generic *adjective* A generic term is a name that applies to all the members of a group of similar things.

generosity *noun* (PSHE) the willingness to give money, time or help.

generosity *noun*
= benevolence, charity, kindness

generous *adjective* 1 (PSHE) A generous person is very willing to give money or time. 2 Something that is generous is very large.

generous *adjective*
1 = charitable, hospitable, kind, lavish, liberal 2 = abundant, ample, plentiful

genesis *noun* (formal) The genesis of something is its beginning.

genetics *noun* (SCIENCE) Genetics is the science of the way that characteristics are passed on from generation to generation by means of genes. > **genetic** *adjective* > **genetically** *adverb*

genial *adjective* cheerful, friendly and kind. > **genially** *adverb*

genie *noun* a magical being that obeys the wishes of the person who controls it.

genitals *plural noun* The genitals are the reproductive organs. The technical name is **genitalia**. > **genital** *adjective*

genius *noun* 1 a highly intelligent, creative or talented person. 2 Genius is great intelligence, creativity or talent.

genius *noun*
1 = brain, master, mastermind, virtuoso 2 = brains, brilliance, intellect

genocide *noun* (formal) Genocide is the systematic murder of all members of a particular ethnic group.

genome *noun* (SCIENCE) all of the genes contained in a single cell of an organism.

genre *noun* (ENGLISH) (formal) a particular style in literature or art.

genteel *adjective* very polite and refined.

Gentile *noun* (RE) a person who is not Jewish.

gentle *adjective* mild and calm; not violent or rough. > **gently** *adverb*

> **gentle** *adjective*
> = benign, kind, kindly, meek, mild, placid, soft, tender

gentleman gentlemen *noun* a man who is polite and well-educated; also a polite way of referring to any man. > **gentlemanly** *adjective*

gentry *plural noun* The gentry are wealthy landowners who are not members of the nobility.

genuine *adjective* **1** real and not false or pretend. **2** A genuine person is sincere and honest.

> **genuine** *adjective*
> **1** = authentic, bona fide, dinkum (*Australian and New Zealand; informal*), real

genus genera *noun* (SCIENCE) In biology, a genus is a class of animals or closely related plants. It is smaller than a family and larger than a species.

geography *noun* the study of the physical features of the earth, together with the climate, natural resources and population in different parts of the world. > **geographic** or **geographical** *adjective* > **geographically** *adverb*

geology *noun* the study of the earth's structure, especially the layers of rock that make up the surface of the earth. > **geological** *adjective* > **geologist** *noun*

geometric or **geometrical** *adjective* **1** consisting of regular lines and shapes, such as squares, triangles and circles. **2** involving geometry.

geometry *noun* Geometry is the branch of mathematics that deals with lines, angles, curves and spaces.

Georgian *adjective* (HISTORY) belonging to or typical of the time from 1714 to 1830, when George I to George IV reigned in Britain.

geranium *noun* a garden plant with red, pink or white flowers.

geriatrics *noun* Geriatrics is the medical care of elderly people. > **geriatric** *adjective*

germ *noun* **1** a very small organism that causes disease. **2** (*formal*) The germ of an idea or plan is the beginning of it.

German *adjective* **1** belonging or relating to Germany. ▸ *noun* **2** someone who comes from Germany. **3** German is the main language spoken in Germany and Austria and is also spoken by many people in Switzerland.

Germanic *adjective* **1** typical of Germany or the German people. **2** The Germanic group of languages includes English, Dutch, German, Danish, Swedish and Norwegian.

germinate *verb* **1** (SCIENCE) When a seed germinates, it starts to grow. **2** When an idea germinates, it starts to develop. > **germination** *noun*

gestation *noun* (SCIENCE) Gestation is the time during which a foetus is growing inside its mother's womb.

gesture *noun* **1** a movement of your hands or head that conveys a message or feeling. **2** an action symbolising something: *a gesture of support.* ▸ *verb* **3** If you gesture, you move your hands or head in order to communicate a message or feeling.

get gets, getting, got verb 1 Get often means the same as become. 2 If you get into a particular situation, you put yourself in that situation. 3 If you get something done, you do it or someone does it for you. 4 If you get somewhere, you go there. 5 If you get something, you fetch it or are given it: *I'll get us all a cup of coffee.* 6 If you get a joke or get the point of something, you understand it. 7 If you get a train, bus or plane, you travel on it. > **get across** verb If you get an idea across, you make people understand it.
> **get at** verb 1 If someone is getting at you, they are criticising you in an unkind way. 2 If you ask someone what they are getting at, you are asking them to explain what they mean. > **get away with** verb If you get away with something dishonest, you are not found out or punished for doing it. > **get by** If you get by, you have just enough money to live on. > **get on** verb 1 If two people get on well together, they like each other's company. 2 If you get on with a task, you do it.
> **get over with** verb If you want to get something unpleasant over with, you want it to be finished quickly. > **get through** verb 1 If you get through to someone, you make them understand what you are saying. 2 If you get through to someone on the telephone, you succeed in talking to them.

> **get** verb
> 1 = become, grow, turn
> 5 = acquire, fetch, obtain, procure (formal), receive, secure (formal)
> ▶ **get on** 1 = be compatible, hit it off (informal)

getaway noun an escape made by criminals.

get-together noun (informal) an informal meeting or party.

Ghanaian adjective 1 belonging or relating to Ghana. ▶ noun 2 someone who comes from Ghana.

ghastly ghastlier, ghastliest adjective extremely horrible and unpleasant.

ghetto ghettoes or ghettos noun a part of a city where many poor people of a particular ethnic group live.

ghost noun the spirit of a dead person, believed to haunt people or places.

> **ghost** noun
> = apparition, phantom, spectre, spirit

ghoulish adjective very interested in unpleasant things such as death and murder.

giant noun 1 a huge person in a myth or legend. ▶ adjective 2 much larger than other similar things.

gibberish noun Gibberish is speech that makes no sense at all.

gibe; also spelt **jibe** noun an insulting remark.

giddy giddier, giddiest adjective If you feel giddy, you feel unsteady on your feet usually because you are ill.

gift noun 1 a present. 2 a natural skill or ability.

> **gift** noun
> 1 = bequest (formal), bonsela (South African), contribution, donation, legacy, present
> 2 = ability, aptitude, flair, talent

gifted adjective having a special ability.

g

gig noun a rock or jazz concert.

gigabyte noun (ICT) a unit of computer memory size, equal to 1024 megabytes.

gigantic adjective extremely large.

giggle verb 1 To giggle means to laugh in a silly or nervous way.
▶ noun 2 a silly or nervous laugh.

gilded adjective Something which is gilded is covered with a thin layer of gold.

gill noun The gills of a fish are the organs on its sides which it uses for breathing.

gilt noun 1 a thin layer of gold.
▶ adjective 2 covered with a thin layer of gold.

gimmick noun a device that is not really necessary but is used to attract interest. ▶ **gimmicky** adjective

gin noun Gin is a strong, colourless alcoholic drink made from grain and juniper berries.

ginger noun 1 Ginger is a plant root with a hot, spicy flavour, used in cooking. ▶ adjective 2 bright orange or red.

gingerbread noun Gingerbread is a sweet, ginger-flavoured cake.

gingerly adverb If you move gingerly, you move cautiously.

giraffe noun a tall, four-legged African mammal with a very long neck.

girl noun a female child. ▶ **girlhood** noun ▶ **girlish** adjective

girlfriend noun Someone's girlfriend is the woman or girl with whom they are having a romantic relationship.

girth noun The girth of something is the measurement round it.

gist noun the general meaning or most important points in a piece of writing or speech.

give gives, giving, gave, given verb 1 If you give someone something, you hand it to them or provide it for them. 2 'Give' is also used to express physical actions and speech: He gave a fierce smile. 3 If you give a party or a meal, you are the host at it. 4 If something gives, it collapses under pressure. ▶ noun 5 If material has give, it will bend or stretch when pulled or put under pressure. ▶ phrase 6 You use **give or take** to indicate that an amount you are mentioning is not exact. 7 If something **gives way** to something else, it is replaced by it. 8 If something **gives way**, it collapses. > **give in** verb If you give in, you admit that you are defeated. > **give out** verb If something gives out, it stops working. > **give up** verb 1 If you give something up, you stop doing it. 2 If you give up, you admit that you cannot do something. 3 If you give someone up, you let the police know where they are hiding.

> **give** verb
> 1 = award, deliver, donate, grant, hand, present, provide, supply 4 = buckle, cave in, collapse, give way, yield
> ▶ **give in** = capitulate, concede, submit, succumb (formal), surrender, yield (formal)

given 1 the past participle of **give**.
▶ adjective 2 fixed or specified.

glacier noun (GEOGRAPHY) a huge frozen river of slow-moving ice.

glad gladder, gladdest adjective happy and pleased.

glad *adjective*
= delighted, happy, joyful,
overjoyed, pleased

gladiator *noun* (HISTORY) In
ancient Rome, gladiators were
slaves trained to fight in arenas to
provide entertainment.

glamour *noun* The glamour of a
fashionable or attractive person
or place is the charm and
excitement that they have.
> **glamorous** *adjective*

glance *verb* 1 If you glance at
something, you look at it quickly.
2 If one object glances off another,
it hits it at an angle and bounces
away in another direction. ▶ *noun*
3 A quick look.

glance *verb*
1 = glimpse, look, peek, peep,
scan 2 = bounce, brush, skim
▶ *noun* 3 = glimpse, look, peek,
peep

gland *noun* an organ in your body,
such as the thyroid gland and the
sweat glands, which either
produce chemical substances for
your body to use or help to get rid
of waste products from your body.
> **glandular** *adjective*

glare *verb* 1 If you glare at someone,
you look at them angrily. ▶ *noun*
2 a hard, angry look. 3 Glare is
extremely bright light.

glare *verb*
1 = frown, glower, scowl
▶ *noun* 2 = frown, scowl
3 = blaze, glow

glass *noun* 1 Glass is a hard,
transparent substance that is
easily broken, used to make
windows and bottles. 2 a
container for drinking out of,
made from glass.

glasses *plural noun* Glasses are two
lenses in a frame, which some
people wear over their eyes to
improve their eyesight.

glassy **glassier**, **glassiest** *adjective*
1 smooth and shiny like glass.
2 A glassy look shows no feeling
or expression.

glaze *noun* 1 A glaze on pottery or
on food is a smooth shiny surface.
▶ *verb* 2 To glaze pottery or food
means to cover it with a glaze.
3 To glaze a window means to fit a
sheet of glass into a window
frame. > **glaze over** *verb* If your
eyes glaze over, they lose all
expression, usually because you
are bored.

glazed *adjective* Someone who has
a glazed expression looks bored.

gleam *verb* 1 If something gleams,
it shines and reflects light. ▶ *noun*
2 a pale shining light.

glean *verb* To glean information
means to collect it from various
sources.

glee *noun* Glee is joy and delight.

glen *noun* a deep, narrow valley,
especially in Scotland or Ireland.

glide *verb* 1 To glide means to
move smoothly. 2 When birds or
aeroplanes glide, they float on air
currents.

glider *noun* an aeroplane without
an engine, which flies by floating
on air currents.

glimmer *noun* 1 a faint, unsteady
light. 2 A glimmer of a feeling or
quality is a faint sign of it.

glimpse *noun* 1 a brief sight of
something. ▶ *verb* 2 If you
glimpse something, you see it
very briefly.

glint *verb* 1 If something glints,
it reflects quick flashes of light.

▶ *noun* **2** a quick flash of light. **3** A glint in someone's eye is a brightness expressing some emotion.

glisten *verb* If something glistens, it shines or sparkles.

glitter *verb* **1** If something glitters, it shines in a sparkling way. ▶ *noun* **2** Glitter is sparkling light.

gloat *verb* If you gloat, you cruelly show your pleasure about your own success or someone else's failure.

global *adjective* concerning the whole world.

globalisation; also spelt **globalization** *noun* **1** the process by which a company expands so that it can do business internationally. **2** the process by which cultures throughout the world become more and more similar for a variety of reasons, including increased global business and better international communications.

global warming *noun* (GEOGRAPHY) (SCIENCE) an increase in the world's overall temperature believed to be caused by the greenhouse effect.

globe *noun* **1** a ball-shaped object, especially one with a map of the earth on it. **2** (GEOGRAPHY) You can refer to the world as the globe. **3** In South African, Australian and New Zealand English, a globe is an electric light bulb.

gloom *noun* **1** Gloom is darkness or dimness. **2** Gloom is also a feeling of unhappiness or despair.

gloomy gloomier, gloomiest *adjective* **1** dark and depressing. **2** feeling very sad. ▶ **gloomily** *adverb*

gloomy *adjective*
1 = dark, dismal, dreary, dull
2 = dejected, down, glum, miserable, sad

glorify glorifies, glorifying, glorified *verb* If you glorify someone or something, you make them seem better than they really are. ▶ **glorification** *noun*

glorious *adjective* **1** beautiful and impressive to look at. **2** very pleasant and giving a feeling of happiness. **3** involving great fame and success.

glory glories, glorying, gloried *noun* **1** Glory is fame and admiration for an achievement. **2** magnificence or beauty. **3** something considered splendid or admirable. ▶ *verb* **4** If you glory in something, you take great delight in it.

glory *noun*
1 = fame, honour, immortality, praise, prestige **2** = grandeur, magnificence, majesty, splendour
▶ *verb* **4** = gloat, relish, revel

gloss *noun* **1** Gloss is a bright shine on a surface. **2** Gloss is also an attractive appearance which may hide less attractive qualities.

gloss *noun*
1 = brilliance, gleam, polish, sheen, shine

glossary glossaries *noun* (LIBRARY) a list of explanations of specialist words.

glossy glossier, glossiest *adjective* smooth and shiny.

glossy *adjective*
= bright, brilliant, polished, shiny, sleek

glove noun Gloves are coverings which you wear over your hands for warmth or protection.

glow noun **1** a dull, steady light. **2** a strong feeling of pleasure or happiness. ▶ verb **3** If something glows, it shines with a dull, steady light. **4** If you are glowing, you look very happy or healthy.

> **glow** noun
> **1** = gleam, glimmer, light
> ▶ verb **3** = gleam, glimmer, shine, smoulder

glowing adjective A glowing description praises or something very highly.

glucose noun (SCIENCE) Glucose is a type of sugar found in plants and that animals and people make in their bodies from food to provide energy.

glue glues, gluing or glueing, glued noun **1** a substance used for sticking things together. ▶ verb **2** If you glue one object to another, you stick them together using glue.

> **glue** verb
> **2** = fix, paste, seal, stick

glum glummer, glummest adjective miserable and downhearted.

glut noun a greater quantity of things than is needed.

gluten noun a sticky protein found in cereal grains, such as wheat.

gnarled adjective old, twisted and rough.

gnome noun a tiny old man in fairy stories.

go goes, going, went, gone verb **1** If you go somewhere, you move or travel there. **2** You can use 'go' to mean become: *She felt she was going insane.* **3** You can use 'go' to describe the state that someone or something is in: *Our arrival went unnoticed.* **4** If something goes well, it is successful. If it goes badly, it is unsuccessful. **5** If you are going to do something, you will do it. **6** If a machine or clock goes, it works and is not broken. **7** You use 'go' before giving the sound something makes or before quoting a song or saying: *The bell goes ding-dong.* **8** If something goes on something or to someone, it is allotted to them. **9** If one thing goes with another, they are appropriate together. **10** If one number goes into another, it can be divided into it. ▶ noun **11** an attempt at doing something. ▶ phrase **12** If someone is always **on the go**, they are always busy and active. **13** To go means remaining. > **go back on** verb If you go back on a promise or agreement, you do not do what you promised or agreed. > **go down** verb **1** If something goes down well, people like it. If it goes down badly, they do not like it. **2** If you go down with an illness, you catch it. > **go for** verb If someone goes for you, they attack you. > **go in for** verb If you go in for something, you decide to do it as your job. > **go off** verb **1** If you go off someone or something, you stop liking them. **2** If a bomb goes off, it explodes. > **go on** verb **1** If you go on doing something, you continue to do it. **2** If you go on about something, you keep talking about it in a rather boring way. **3** Something that is going on is happening. > **go out** verb If you go out with someone, you have a romantic relationship with them. > **go over** verb If you go over something, you think about it or discuss it carefully. > **go through** verb 1 If you go through an unpleasant event, you experience it. 2 If a law or agreement goes through, it is approved and becomes official. 3 If you go through with something, you do it even though it is unpleasant.

go verb
1 = advance, drive, fly, journey (formal), leave, set off, travel 6 = function, work
▶ noun 11 = attempt, shot (informal), stab (informal), try
▶ **go through** 1 = endure, experience, undergo

goad verb If you goad someone, you encourage them to do something by making them angry or excited.

go-ahead noun If someone gives you the go-ahead for something, they give you permission to do it.

goal noun 1 the space, in games like football or hockey, into which the players try to get the ball in order to score a point. 2 an instance of this. 3 Your goal is something that you hope to achieve.

goal noun
3 = aim, end, intention, object, objective, purpose, target

goalkeeper noun the player, in games like soccer or hockey, who stands in the goal and tries to stop the other team from scoring.

goat noun an animal like a sheep, with coarse hair, a beard and horns.

gob noun (informal) Your gob is your mouth.

gobble verb 1 If you gobble food, you eat it very quickly. 2 When a

turkey gobbles, it makes a loud gurgling sound.

gobble verb
1 = bolt, devour, wolf

god proper noun 1 (RE) The name God is given to the being who is worshipped by Christians, Jews and Muslims as the creator and ruler of the world. ▶ noun 2 any of the beings that are believed in many religions to have power over an aspect of life or a part of the world. 3 If someone is your god, you admire them very much. 4 (in plural) In a theatre, the gods are the highest seats farthest from the stage.

goddess noun a female god.

godsend noun something that comes unexpectedly and helps you very much.

goggles plural noun Goggles are special glasses that fit closely round your eyes to protect them.

gold noun 1 (SCIENCE) Gold is a valuable, yellow-coloured metallic element. It is used for making jewellery and as an international currency. Its atomic number is 79 and its symbol is Au. 2 'Gold' is also used to mean things that are made of gold. ▶ adjective 3 bright yellow.

golden adjective 1 gold in colour. 2 made of gold.

golden rule noun a very important rule to remember in order to be able to do something successfully.

goldfish noun a small orange-coloured fish, often kept in ponds or bowls.

golf noun Golf is a game in which players use special clubs to hit a small ball into holes that are spread out over a large area of grassy land. > **golfer** *noun*

golf course *noun* an area of grassy land where people play golf.

gondola *noun* a long narrow boat used in Venice, which is propelled with a long pole.

gone the past participle of **go**.

gong *noun* a flat, circular piece of metal that is hit with a hammer to make a loud sound, often as a signal for something.

good better, best *adjective*
1 pleasant, acceptable or satisfactory. **2** skilful or successful. **3** kind, thoughtful and loving. **4** well-behaved. **5** used to emphasise something: *a good few million pounds*. ▶ *noun* **6** Good is moral and spiritual justice and virtue. **7** Good also refers to anything that is desirable or beneficial as opposed to harmful. **8** (*in plural*) Goods are objects that people own or that are sold in shops. ▶ *phrase* **9** For good means for ever. **10** As good as means almost.

> **good** *adjective*
> **1** = excellent, fine, first-class, first-rate, splendid, superb
> **2** = able, capable, competent, skilful, talented **3** = decent, generous, kind, kind-hearted, thoughtful

goodbye *interjection* You say goodbye when you are leaving someone or ending a telephone conversation.

Good Friday *noun* (RE) Good Friday is the Friday before Easter, when Christians commemorate the crucifixion of Christ.

good-natured *adjective* friendly, pleasant and even-tempered.

goodness *noun* **1** Goodness is the quality of being kind. ▶ *interjection* **2** People say 'Goodness!' or 'My goodness!' when they are surprised.

goodwill *noun* Goodwill is kindness and helpfulness.

> **goodwill** *noun*
> = benevolence, favour, friendliness, friendship

goody goodies *noun* (*informal*) **1** Goodies are enjoyable things, often food. **2** You can call a hero in a film or book a goody.

goose geese *noun* a fairly large bird with webbed feet and a long neck.

gooseberry gooseberries *noun* a round, green berry that grows on a bush and has a sharp taste.

gore *verb* **1** If an animal gores someone, it wounds them badly with its horns or tusks. ▶ *noun* **2** Gore is clotted blood from a wound.

gorge *noun* **1** (GEOGRAPHY) a deep, narrow valley. ▶ *verb* **2** If you gorge yourself, you eat a lot of food greedily.

gorgeous *adjective* extremely pleasant or attractive.

gorilla *noun* a very large, strong ape with very dark fur.

gorse *noun* Gorse is a dark green wild shrub that has sharp prickles and small yellow flowers.

gory gorier, goriest *adjective* Gory situations involve people being injured in horrible ways.

gospel *noun* **1** (RE) The Gospels are the four books in the New Testament which describe the life and teachings of Jesus Christ. **2** a set of ideas that someone strongly believes in. ▶ *adjective* **3** Gospel music is a style of religious music popular among Black Christians in the United States.

gossip gossips, gossiping, gossiped *noun* 1 Gossip is informal conversation, often concerning people's private affairs.
2 Someone who is a gossip enjoys talking about other people's private affairs. ▶ *verb* 3 If you gossip, you talk informally with someone, especially about other people.

> **gossip** *noun*
> 1 = dirt (*informal*), hearsay

got 1 Got is the past tense and past participle of **get**. 2 You can use 'have got' instead of the more formal 'have' when talking about possessing things: *The director has got a map.* 3 You can use 'have got to' instead of the more formal 'have to' when talking about something that must be done: *He has got to win.*

gouge *verb* 1 If you gouge a hole in something, you make a hole in it with a pointed object. 2 If you gouge something out, you force it out of position with your fingers or a sharp tool.

gourmet *noun* a person who enjoys good food and drink and knows a lot about it.

govern *verb* 1 To govern a country means to control it. 2 Something that governs a situation influences it.

governess *noun* a woman who is employed to teach the children in a family and who lives with the family.

government *noun* 1 (CITIZENSHIP) The government is the group of people who govern a country.

2 (CITIZENSHIP) Government is the control and organisation of a country. > **governmental** *adjective*

governor *noun* 1 a person who controls and organises a state or an institution. 2 In Australia, the Governor is the representative of the King or Queen in a State.

gown *noun* 1 a long, formal dress. 2 a long, dark cloak worn by people such as judges and lawyers.

GP an abbreviation for **general practitioner**.

grab grabs, grabbing, grabbed *verb* 1 If you grab something, you take it or pick it up roughly. 2 If you grab an opportunity, you take advantage of it eagerly. 3 (*informal*) If an idea grabs you, it excites you. ▶ *noun* 4 A grab at an object is an attempt to grab it.

> **grab** *verb*
> 1 = clutch, grasp, seize, snatch

grace *noun* 1 Grace is an elegant way of moving. 2 Grace is also a pleasant, kind way of behaving. 3 Grace is also a short prayer of thanks said before a meal. 4 Dukes and archbishops are addressed as 'Your Grace' and referred to as 'His Grace'. ▶ *verb* 5 Something that graces a place makes it more attractive. 6 If someone important graces an event, they kindly agree to be present at it. > **graceful** *adjective*

> **grace** *noun*
> 1 = elegance, poise

gracious *adjective* kind, polite and pleasant. > **graciously** *adverb*

grade *verb* 1 To grade things means to arrange them according to quality. ▶ *noun* 2 The grade of something is its quality. 3 the mark that you get for an exam or piece of written work. **4** Your grade in a company or organisation is your level of importance or your rank.

> **grade** verb
> **1** = class, classify, group, rate, sort

gradient noun a slope or the steepness of a slope.

gradual adjective happening or changing slowly over a long period of time. > **gradually** adverb

> **gradual** adjective
> = continuous, progressive, slow, steady

graduate noun **1** a person who has completed a first degree at a university or college. ▶ verb **2** When students graduate, they complete a first degree at a university or college. **3** To graduate from one thing to another means to progress gradually towards the second thing. > **graduation** noun

graffiti noun Graffiti is slogans or drawings scribbled on walls.

graft noun **1** a piece of living tissue which is used to replace by surgery a damaged or unhealthy part of a person's body. **2** (informal) Graft is hard work. ▶ verb **3** To graft one thing on to another means to attach it.

grain noun **1** a cereal plant, such as wheat, that is grown as a crop and used for food. **2** Grains are seeds of a cereal plant. **3** A grain of sand or salt is a tiny particle of it. **4** The grain of a piece of wood is the pattern of lines made by the fibres in it. ▶ phrase **5** If something **goes against the grain**, you find it difficult to

accept because it is against your principles.

gram; also spelt **gramme** noun a unit of weight equal to one thousandth of a kilogram.

grammar noun (ENGLISH) (MFL) Grammar is the rules of a language relating to the ways you can combine words to form sentences.

grammar school noun
1 a secondary school for pupils of high academic ability.
2 In Australia, a grammar school is a private school, usually one controlled by a church.

grammatical adjective **1** relating to grammar. **2** following the rules of grammar correctly. > **grammatically** adverb

gran noun (informal) Your gran is your grandmother.

grand adjective **1** magnificent in appearance and size. **2** very important. **3** (informal) very pleasant or enjoyable. **4** A grand total is the final complete amount. ▶ noun **5** (informal) a thousand pounds or dollars. > **grandly** adverb

> **grand** adjective
> **1** = imposing, impressive, magnificent, majestic, monumental, splendid
> **3** = brilliant, fantastic (informal), great (informal), marvellous, terrific, tremendous, wonderful

grandad noun (informal) Your grandad is your grandfather.

grandchild grandchildren noun Someone's grandchildren are the children of their son or daughter.

granddaughter noun Someone's granddaughter is the daughter of their son or daughter.

grandeur noun Grandeur is great beauty and magnificence.

grandfather noun Your grandfather is your father's father or your mother's father.

grandiose adjective intended to be very impressive, but seeming ridiculous.

grandma noun (informal) Your grandma is your grandmother.

grandmother noun Your grandmother is your father's mother or your mother's mother.

grandparent noun Your grandparents are your parents' parents.

grand piano noun a large flat piano with horizontal strings.

grandson noun Someone's grandson is the son of their son or daughter.

grandstand noun a structure with a roof and seats for spectators at a sports ground.

granite noun Granite is a very hard rock used in building.

granny grannies noun (informal) Your granny is your grandmother.

grant noun 1 an amount of money that an official body gives to someone for a particular purpose. ▶ verb 2 If you grant something to someone, you allow them to have it. 3 If you grant that something is true, you admit that it is true. ▶ phrase 4 If you **take something for granted**, you believe it without thinking about it. If you **take someone for granted**, you benefit from them without showing that you are grateful.

grant noun
1 = allocation, allowance, award, handout, subsidy
▶ verb 2 = allocate, allow, award, give, permit 3 = accept, acknowledge, admit, allow, concede

grape noun a small green or purple fruit, eaten raw or used to make wine.

grapefruit noun a large, round, yellow citrus fruit.

grapevine noun 1 a climbing plant which grapes grow on. ▶ phrase 2 If you hear some news **on the grapevine**, it has been passed on from person to person, usually unofficially or secretly.

graph noun (MATHS) a diagram which shows how sets of numbers or measurements are related.

-graph suffix '-graph' means a writer or recorder of some sort or something made by writing, drawing or recording: autograph.

graphic adjective 1 A graphic description is very detailed and lifelike. 2 relating to drawing or painting. > **graphically** adverb

graphics plural noun (ICT) Graphics are drawings and pictures composed of simple lines and strong colours.

graphite noun a black form of carbon that is used in pencil leads.

grapple verb 1 If you grapple with someone, you struggle with them while fighting. 2 If you grapple with a problem, you try hard to solve it.

grasp verb 1 If you grasp something, you hold it firmly. 2 If you grasp an idea, you understand it. ▶ noun **3** a firm hold. **4** Your grasp of something is your understanding of it.

> **grasp** verb
> **1** = clutch, grab, grip, hold, seize, snatch **2** = absorb, appreciate, assimilate, realise, take in, understand
> ▶ noun **3** = clasp, embrace, grip, hold **4** = awareness, comprehension (formal), grip, knowledge, understanding

grass noun Grass is the common green plant that grows on lawns and in parks. > **grassy** adjective

grasshopper noun an insect with long back legs which it uses for jumping and making a high-pitched sound.

grate noun **1** a framework of metal bars in a fireplace. ▶ verb **2** To grate food means to shred it into small pieces by rubbing it against a metal tool. **3** When something grates on something else, it rubs against it making a harsh sound. **4** If something grates on you, it irritates you.

grateful adjective If you are grateful for something, you are glad you have it and want to thank the person who gave it to you. > **gratefully** adverb

> **grateful** adjective
> = appreciative, indebted, thankful

gratify gratifies, gratifying, gratified verb If you are gratified by something, you are pleased by it.

grating noun **1** a metal frame with bars across it fastened over a hole in a wall or in the ground.
▶ adjective **2** A grating sound is harsh and unpleasant.

gratitude noun Gratitude is the feeling of being grateful.

> **gratitude** noun
> = appreciation, recognition, thanks

gratuitous adjective unnecessary.

grave¹ noun **1** a place where a corpse is buried. ▶ adjective **2** (formal) very serious.

> **grave** noun
> **1** = mausoleum, pit, sepulchre (literary), tomb
> ▶ adjective **2** = acute, critical, heavy (informal), serious

grave² adjective (MFL) In French and some other languages, a grave accent is a line sloping downwards from left to right placed over a vowel to indicate a change in pronunciation, as in the word lièvre (a hare).

gravel noun Gravel is small stones used for making roads and paths.

gravestone noun a large stone placed over someone's grave, with their name on it.

graveyard noun an area of land where corpses are buried.

gravitate verb When people gravitate towards something, they go towards it because they are attracted to it.

gravity noun **1** (SCIENCE) Gravity is the force that makes things fall when you drop them. **2** The gravity of a situation is its seriousness.

gravy noun Gravy is a brown sauce made from meat juices.

graze verb **1** When animals graze, they eat grass. **2** If something grazes a part of your body, it scrapes against it, injuring you slightly. ▶ noun **3** a slight injury caused by something scraping against your skin.

graze *verb*
2 = scrape, scratch, skin
▶ *noun* 3 = abrasion (*formal*), scratch

grease *noun* 1 Grease is an oily substance used for lubricating machines. 2 Grease is also melted animal fat, used in cooking. 3 Grease is also an oily substance produced by your skin and found in your hair. ▶ *verb* 4 If you grease something, you lubricate it with grease. > **greasy** *adjective*

great *adjective* 1 very large. 2 very important. 3 (*informal*) very good.

great *adjective*
1 = big, colossal, huge, large, enormous, extensive, gigantic, immense, massive, stupendous, tremendous, vast
2 = celebrated, chief, distinguished, eminent, famed, famous, illustrious, important, main, major, momentous, notable, principal, prominent, renowned, serious, significant
3 = beaut (*Australian and New Zealand*; *informal*), excellent, fantastic (*informal*), fine, first-rate, marvellous, outstanding, superb, terrific, tremendous, wonderful

Great Britain *noun* Great Britain is the largest of the British Isles, consisting of England, Scotland and Wales.

great-grandfather *noun* Your great-grandfather is your father's or mother's grandfather.

great-grandmother *noun* Your great-grandmother is your father's or mother's grandmother.

greed *noun* Greed is a desire for more of something than you really need.

greedy greedier, greediest *adjective* wanting more of something than you really need. > **greedily** *adverb*

greedy *adjective*
= materialistic, snoep (*South African*; *informal*)

Greek *adjective* 1 belonging or relating to Greece. ▶ *noun* 2 someone who comes from Greece. 3 Greek is the main language spoken in Greece.

green *adjective, noun* 1 Green is a colour between yellow and blue on the spectrum. ▶ *noun* 2 an area of grass in the middle of a village. 3 A putting green or bowling green is a grassy area on which people putt or play bowls. 4 an area of smooth short grass around each hole on a golf course. 5 (*in plural*) Greens are green vegetables. ▶ *adjective* 6 'Green' is used to describe political movements which are concerned with environmental issues. 7 (*informal*) Someone who is green is young and inexperienced.

green *adjective*
6 = conservationist, ecological

greenery *noun* Greenery is a lot of trees, bushes or other green plants together in one place.

greengrocer *noun* a shopkeeper who sells vegetables and fruit.

greenhouse *noun* a glass building in which people grow plants that need to be kept warm.

greenhouse effect *noun* (GEOGRAPHY) (SCIENCE) the gradual rise in temperature in the earth's atmosphere due to heat being absorbed from the sun and being trapped by gases such as carbon dioxide in the air around the earth.

green paper noun In Britain, Australia and New Zealand, a green paper is a report published by the government containing proposals to be discussed before decisions are made about them.

greet verb 1 If you greet someone, you say something friendly like 'hello' to them when you meet them. 2 If you greet something in a particular way, you react to it in that way.

> **greet** verb
> 1 = meet, receive (formal), welcome

greeting noun something friendly that you say to someone when you meet them.

gregarious adjective (formal) Someone who is gregarious enjoys being with other people.

grenade noun a small bomb, containing explosive or tear gas, which can be thrown.

grew the past tense of **grow**.

grey adjective, noun 1 Grey is a colour between black and white. ▶ adjective 2 dull and boring. ▶ verb 3 If someone is greying, their hair is going grey.

greyhound noun a thin dog with long legs that can run very fast.

grid noun 1 a pattern of lines crossing each other to form squares. 2 The grid is the network of wires and cables by which electricity is distributed throughout a country.

grief noun 1 Grief is extreme sadness. ▶ phrase 2 If someone or

something **comes to grief**, they fail or are injured.

> **grief** noun
> 1 = distress, heartache, misery, sadness, sorrow, unhappiness

grievance noun a reason for complaining.

grieve verb 1 If you grieve, you are extremely sad, especially because someone has died. 2 If something grieves you, it makes you feel sad.

> **grieve** verb
> 1 = lament, mourn 2 = distress, pain, sadden, upset

grievous adjective (formal) extremely serious.

grill noun 1 a part on a cooker where food is cooked by strong heat from above. 2 a metal frame on which you cook food over a fire. ▶ verb 3 If you grill food, you cook it on or under a grill. 4 (informal) If you grill someone, you ask them a lot of questions in a very intense way.

grille; also spelt **grill** noun a metal framework over a window or piece of machinery, used for protection.

grim grimmer, grimmest adjective 1 If a situation or news is grim, it is very unpleasant and worrying. 2 Grim places are unattractive and depressing. 3 If someone is grim, they are very serious or stern.

> **grim** adjective
> 3 = grave (formal), severe, solemn, stern

grimace noun 1 a twisted facial expression indicating disgust or pain. ▶ verb 2 When someone grimaces, they make a grimace.

g

grime noun Grime is thick dirt which gathers on the surface of something. > **grimy** adjective

grin grins, grinning, grinned verb 1 If you grin, you smile broadly. ▶ noun 2 a broad smile. ▶ phrase 3 If you **grin and bear it**, you accept a difficult situation without complaining.

grind grinds, grinding, ground verb 1 If you grind something such as pepper, you crush it into a fine powder. 2 If you grind your teeth, you rub your upper and lower teeth together. ▶ phrase 3 If something **grinds to a halt**, it stops.

grip grips, gripping, gripped noun 1 a firm hold. 2 a handle on a bat or a racket. 3 Your grip on a situation is your control over it. ▶ verb 4 If you grip something, you hold it firmly. ▶ phrase 5 If you **get to grips with** a situation or problem, you start to deal with it effectively.

> **grip** noun
> 1 = clasp, grasp, hold
> 3 = clutches, control, influence, power
> ▶ verb 4 = clutch, grasp, hold

grisly grislier, grisliest adjective very nasty and horrible.

grit grits, gritting, gritted noun 1 Grit consists of very small stones. It is put on icy roads to make them less slippery. ▶ verb 2 When workers grit an icy road, they put grit on it. ▶ phrase 3 To **grit your teeth** means to decide to carry on in a difficult situation. > **gritty** adjective

grizzled adjective Grizzled hair is grey. A grizzled person has grey hair.

groan verb 1 If you groan, you make a long, low sound of pain, unhappiness or disapproval. ▶ noun 2 the sound you make when you groan.

grocer noun a shopkeeper who sells many kinds of food and other household goods.

grocery groceries noun 1 a grocer's shop. 2 (in plural) Groceries are the goods you buy in a grocer's shop.

grog noun (informal) In Australian and New Zealand English, grog is any alcoholic drink.

groin noun the area where your legs join the main part of your body at the front.

groom noun 1 someone who looks after horses in a stable. 2 a man who is getting married or who has just got married. ▶ verb 3 To groom an animal means to clean its fur. 4 If you groom someone for a job, you prepare them for it by teaching them the skills they will need.

groove noun a deep line cut into a surface. > **grooved** adjective

grope verb 1 If you grope for something you cannot see, you search for it with your hands. 2 If you grope for something such as the solution to a problem, you try to think of it.

gross adjective 1 extremely bad. 2 Gross speech or behaviour is very rude. 3 Gross things are ugly. 4 Someone's gross income is their total income before any deductions are made. 5 The gross weight of something is its total weight, including the weight of its container. ▶ verb 6 If you gross an amount of money, you earn that amount in total. > **grossly** adverb

grotesque *adjective* **1** exaggerated and absurd. **2** very strange and ugly.

grotto grottoes or grottos *noun* a small cave that people visit because it is attractive.

ground *noun* **1** The ground is the surface of the earth. **2** a piece of land that is used for a particular purpose. **3** The ground covered by a book or course is the range of subjects it deals with. **4** (*in plural*) The grounds of a large building are the land belonging to it and surrounding it. **5** (*in plural, formal*) The grounds for something are the reasons for it. ▶ *verb* **6** (*formal*) If something is grounded in something else, it is based on it. **7** If an aircraft is grounded, it has to remain on the ground. **8** Ground is the past tense and past participle of **grind**.

> **ground** *noun*
> **1** = dirt, earth, land, soil, terrain
> **4** = estate, gardens, land
> **5** = basis, cause, excuse, justification, reason

ground floor *noun* The ground floor of a building is the floor that is level with the ground.

grounding *noun* If you have a grounding in a skill or subject, you have had basic instruction in it.

groundless *adjective* not based on reason or evidence.

group *noun* **1** A group of things or people is a number of them that are linked together in some way. **2** a number of musicians who perform pop music together. ▶ *verb* **3** When things or people are grouped together, they are linked together in some way.

> **group** *noun*
> **1** = band, bunch, collection, crowd, gang, pack, party, set
> ▶ *verb* **3** = arrange, class, classify, organise, sort

grouping *noun* a number of things or people that are linked together in some way.

grouse grouse *noun* a fat brown or grey bird, often shot for sport.

grove *noun* (*literary*) a group of trees growing close together.

grovel grovels, grovelling, grovelled *verb* If you grovel, you behave in an unpleasantly humble way towards someone you regard as important.

grow grows, growing, grew, grown *verb* **1** To grow means to increase in size or amount. **2** If a tree or plant grows somewhere, it is alive there. **3** When people grow plants, they plant them and look after them. **4** If a man grows a beard or moustache, he lets it develop by not shaving. **5** To grow also means to pass gradually into a particular state. **6** If one thing grows from another, it develops from it. **7** (*informal*) If something grows on you, you gradually get to like it. ▶ **grow up** *verb* When a child grows up, he or she becomes an adult.

> **grow** *verb*
> **1** = develop, expand, increase, multiply **2** = flourish, germinate, sprout **5** = become, get, turn

growl *verb* **1** When an animal growls, it makes a low rumbling sound, usually because it is angry. **2** If you growl something, you say it in a low, rough, rather angry

voice. ▶ noun **3** the sound an animal makes when it growls.
grown-up noun **1** (*informal*) an adult. ▶ adjective **2** Someone who is grown-up is adult or behaves like an adult.
growth noun **1** When there is a growth in something, it gets bigger. **2** Growth is the process by which something develops to its full size. **3** an abnormal lump that grows inside or on a person, animal or plant.

> **growth** noun
> **1** = development, enlargement, expansion, increase

grub noun **1** a wormlike insect that has just hatched from its egg. **2** (*informal*) Grub is food.
grubby grubbier, grubbiest adjective rather dirty.
grudge noun **1** If you have a grudge against someone, you resent them because they have harmed you in the past. ▶ verb **2** If you grudge someone something, you give it to them unwillingly, or are displeased that they have it.
grudging adjective done or felt unwillingly.
gruelling adjective difficult and tiring.
gruesome adjective shocking and horrible.
gruff adjective If someone's voice is gruff, it sounds rough and unfriendly.
grumble verb **1** If you grumble, you complain in a bad-tempered way. ▶ noun **2** a bad-tempered complaint.

> **grumble** verb
> **1** = carp, complain, groan, moan, mutter, whine, whinge

▶ noun **2** = complaint, moan, murmur, objection, protest, whinge

grumpy grumpier, grumpiest adjective bad-tempered and fed-up.

> **grumpy** adjective
> = irritable, sulky, sullen, surly

grunt verb **1** If a person or a pig grunts, they make a short, low, gruff sound. ▶ noun **2** the sound a person or a pig makes when they grunt.
guarantee guarantees, guaranteeing, guaranteed noun **1** If something is a guarantee of something else, it makes it certain that it will happen. **2** a written promise that if a product develops a fault, it will be replaced or repaired free. ▶ verb **3** If something or someone guarantees something, they make certain that it will happen. > **guarantor** noun

> **guarantee** noun
> **1** = assurance, pledge, promise, undertaking, word
> ▶ verb **3** = ensure, pledge, promise

guard verb **1** If you guard a person or object, you stay near to them to protect them. **2** If you guard a person, you stop them making trouble or escaping. **3** If you guard against something, you are careful to avoid it happening. ▶ noun **4** a person or group of people who guard a person, object or place. **5** a railway official in charge of a train. **6** Any object which covers something to prevent it causing harm can be called a guard.

guard verb
1 = defend, protect, safeguard, shelter, shield, watch over
2 = patrol, police, supervise
▶ noun 4 = sentry, warden

guardian noun 1 someone who has been legally appointed to look after a child. 2 A guardian of something is someone who protects it. > **guardianship** noun

guernsey noun 1 In Australian and New Zealand English, a jersey. 2 a sleeveless top worn by an Australian Rules football player.

guerrilla; also spelt **guerilla** noun a member of a small unofficial army fighting an official army.

guess verb 1 If you guess something, you form or express an opinion that it is the case, without having much information. ▶ noun 2 an attempt to give the correct answer to something without having much information, or without working it out properly.

guess verb
1 = estimate, imagine, reckon (informal), speculate, suppose, suspect, think
▶ noun 2 = feeling, reckoning, speculation

guest noun 1 someone who stays at your home or who attends an occasion because they have been invited. 2 The guests in a hotel are the people staying there.

guidance noun Guidance is help and advice.

guide noun 1 someone who shows you round places, or leads the way through difficult country.
2 a book which gives you information or instructions.

3 A Guide is a girl who is a member of an organisation that encourages discipline and practical skills. ▶ verb 4 If you guide someone in a particular direction, you lead them in that direction. 5 If you are guided by something, it influences your actions or decisions.

guide verb
4 = accompany, direct, escort, lead 5 = counsel (formal), govern, influence

guidebook noun a book which gives information about a place.

guide dog noun a dog that has been trained to lead a blind person.

guideline noun a piece of advice about how something should be done.

guild noun a society of people.

guile noun Guile is cunning and deceit.

guillotine noun 1 (HISTORY) In the past, the guillotine was a machine used for beheading people, especially in France. It was named after Joseph-Ignace Guillotin, who first recommended its use. 2 A guillotine is also a piece of equipment with a long sharp blade, used for cutting paper.

guilt noun 1 Guilt is an unhappy feeling of having done something wrong. 2 Someone's guilt is the fact that they have done something wrong.

guilty guiltier, guiltiest adjective 1 If you are guilty of doing something wrong, you did it. 2 If you feel guilty, you are unhappy because you have done something wrong. > **guiltily** adverb

g

guilty *adjective*
1 = convicted, criminal
2 = ashamed, regretful, remorseful (*formal*), sorry

guinea pig *noun* 1 a small furry animal without a tail, often kept as a pet. 2 a person used to try something out on.

guise *noun* a misleading appearance.

guitar *noun* a musical instrument with six strings which are strummed or plucked.
> **guitarist** *noun*

gulf *noun* 1 (GEOGRAPHY) a very large bay. 2 a wide gap or difference between two things or people.

gull *noun* a sea bird with long wings, white and grey or black feathers, and webbed feet.

gullible *adjective* easily tricked.

gullible *adjective*
= naive, trusting

gully gullies *noun* a long, narrow valley.

gulp *verb* 1 If you gulp food or drink, you swallow large quantities of it. 2 If you gulp, you swallow air, because you are nervous. ▶ *noun* 3 A gulp of food or drink is a large quantity of it swallowed at one time.

gum *noun* 1 Gum is a soft flavoured substance that people chew but do not swallow. 2 Gum is also glue for sticking paper. 3 Your gums are the firm flesh in which your teeth are set.

gun *noun* a weapon which fires bullets or shells.

gunfire *noun* Gunfire is the repeated firing of guns.

gunpowder *noun* Gunpowder is an explosive powder made from a mixture of potassium nitrate and other substances.

gunshot *noun* the sound of a gun being fired.

gurgle *verb* 1 To gurgle means to make a bubbling sound. ▶ *noun* 2 a bubbling sound.

guru *noun* (RE) a spiritual teacher, especially in India.

gush *verb* 1 When liquid gushes from something, it flows out of it in large quantities. 2 When people gush, they express admiration in an exaggerated way.

gush *verb*
1 = flow, pour, spurt, stream

gust *noun* a sudden rush of wind.
> **gusty** *adjective*

gusto *noun* Gusto is energy and enthusiasm.

gut guts, gutting, gutted *noun* (in plural) 1 Your guts are your internal organs, especially your intestines. 2 (*informal*) Guts is courage. ▶ *verb* 3 To gut a dead fish means to remove its internal organs. 4 If a building is gutted, the inside of it is destroyed, especially by fire.

gutter *noun* 1 the edge of a road next to the pavement, where rain collects and flows away. 2 a channel fixed to the edge of a roof, where rain collects and flows away.

guy *noun* 1 (*informal*) a man or boy. 2 a crude model of Guy Fawkes that is burnt on top of a bonfire on Guy Fawkes Day (November 5).

guzzle *verb* To guzzle something means to drink or eat it quickly and greedily.

gym *noun* 1 a gymnasium. 2 (PE) Gym is gymnastics.

gymnasium *noun* a room with special equipment for physical exercises.

gymnast *noun* someone who is trained in gymnastics.
> **gymnastic** *adjective*

gymnastics *noun* (PE) Gymnastics is physical exercises, especially ones using equipment such as bars and ropes.

gynaecology; also spelt **gynecology** *noun* Gynaecology is the branch of medical science concerned with the female reproductive system.
> **gynaecologist** *noun*
> **gynaecological** *adjective*

habit *noun* 1 something that you do often. 2 something that you keep doing and find it difficult to stop doing. 3 A monk's or nun's habit is a garment like a loose dress. > **habitual** *adjective*

> **habit** *noun*
> 1 = convention, custom, practice, routine, tradition

habitat *noun* (GEOGRAPHY) the natural home of a plant or animal.

> **habitat** *noun*
> = environment, territory

hack *verb* 1 If you hack at something, you cut it using rough strokes. 2 If you hack into a computer system, you gain access to it without permission. ▶ *noun* 3 a writer or journalist who produces work fast without worrying about quality.

hacker *noun* someone who uses a computer to break into the computer system of a company or government.

hackles *plural noun* 1 A dog's hackles are the hairs on the back of its neck which rise when it is angry. ▶ *phrase* 2 Something that **makes your hackles rise** makes you angry.

hackneyed *adjective* A hackneyed phrase is meaningless because it has been used too often.

hackneyed *adjective*
= banal, clichéd, stale, tired, trite

had the past tense and past participle of **have**.

haddock *noun* an edible sea fish.

haemoglobin *noun* (SCIENCE) Haemoglobin is a substance in red blood cells which carries oxygen round the body.

haemorrhage *noun* A haemorrhage is serious bleeding, especially inside a person's body.

haggard *adjective* A person who is haggard looks very tired and ill.

haggis *noun* Haggis is a Scottish dish made of the internal organs of a sheep, boiled together with oatmeal and spices in a skin.

haggle *verb* If you haggle with someone, you argue with them, usually about the cost of something.

hail *noun* 1 Hail is frozen rain. 2 A hail of things is a lot of them falling together. ▶ *verb* 3 When it is hailing, frozen rain is falling. 4 If someone hails you, they call you to attract your attention or greet you.

hail *noun*
2 = barrage, bombardment, shower, storm, volley
▶ *verb* 4 = call, signal to, wave down

hair *noun* Hair consists of the long, threadlike strands that grow from the skin of animals and humans.

haircut *noun* the cutting of someone's hair; also the style in which it is cut.

hairdo *hairdos* *noun* a hairstyle.

hairdresser *noun* someone who is trained to cut and style people's hair; also a shop where this is done.

hairline *noun* 1 the edge of the area on your forehead where your hair grows. ▶ *adjective* 2 A hairline crack is so fine that you can hardly see it.

hairpin *noun* 1 a U-shaped wire used to hold hair in position. ▶ *adjective* 2 A hairpin bend is a U-shaped bend in the road.

hair-raising *adjective* very frightening or exciting.

hairstyle *noun* Someone's hairstyle is the way in which their hair is arranged or cut.

hairy *hairier, hairiest* *adjective* 1 covered in a lot of hair. 2 (*informal*) difficult, exciting and rather frightening.

hajj *noun* (RE) The hajj is the pilgrimage to Mecca that every Muslim must make at least once in their life if they are healthy and wealthy enough to do so.

haka *noun* 1 In New Zealand, a haka is a ceremonial Māori dance made up of various postures and accompanied by a chant. 2 an imitation of this dance performed by New Zealand sports teams before matches as a challenge.

halcyon *phrase* Halcyon days are a happy and carefree time in the past.

half *noun, adjective, adverb* 1 Half refers to one of two equal parts that make up a whole. ▶ *adverb* 2 You can use 'half' to say that something is only partly true: *I half expected him to explode in anger.*

half-baked *adjective* (*informal*) Half-baked ideas or plans have not been properly thought out.

half-brother noun Your half-brother is the son of either your mother or your father but not of your other parent.

half-hearted adjective showing no real effort or enthusiasm.

half-sister noun Your half-sister is the daughter of either your mother or your father but not of your other parent.

half-time noun Half-time is a short break between two parts of a game when the players have a rest.

halfway adverb at the middle of the distance between two points in place or time.

halibut noun a large edible flat fish.

hall noun 1 the room just inside the front entrance of a house which leads into other rooms. 2 a large room or building used for public events.

hallmark noun 1 The hallmark of a person or group is their most typical quality. 2 an official mark on gold or silver indicating the quality of the metal.

hallowed adjective respected as being holy.

Halloween noun Halloween is October 31st, and is celebrated by children dressing up, often as ghosts and witches.

hallucinate verb If you hallucinate, you see strange things in your mind because of illness or drugs. ▸ **hallucination** noun ▸ **hallucinatory** adjective

halo haloes or halos noun a circle of light around the head of a holy figure in art.

halt verb 1 To halt when moving means to stop. 2 To halt

development or action means to stop it. ▸ noun 3 a short standstill.

> **halt** verb
> 1 = draw up, pull up, stop
> 2 = cease, check, curb, cut short, end, terminate (formal)
> ▸ noun 3 = close, end, pause, standstill, stop, stoppage

halter noun a strap fastened round a horse's head so that it can be led easily.

halve verb 1 If you halve something, you divide it into two equal parts. 2 To halve something also means to reduce its size or amount by half.

ham noun 1 Ham is meat from the hind leg of a pig, salted and cured. 2 (informal) a bad actor who exaggerates emotions and gestures.

hamburger noun a flat disc of minced meat, seasoned and fried; often eaten in a bread roll.

hammer noun 1 a tool consisting of a heavy piece of metal at the end of a handle, used for hitting nails into things. ▸ verb 2 If you hammer something, you hit it repeatedly, with a hammer or with your fist. 3 If you hammer an idea into someone, you keep repeating it and telling them about it. 4 (informal) If you hammer someone, you criticise or attack them severely.

hammock noun a piece of net or canvas hung between two supports and used as a bed.

hamper noun 1 a rectangular wicker basket with a lid, used for carrying food. ▸ verb 2 If you hamper someone, you make it difficult for them to move or progress.

hamper *verb*
2 = frustrate, hinder, impede, obstruct, restrict

hamster *noun* a small furry rodent which is often kept as a pet.

hamstring *noun* (PE) Your hamstring is a tendon behind your knee joining your thigh muscles to the bones of your lower leg.

hand *noun* 1 Your hand is the part of your body beyond the wrist, with four fingers and a thumb. 2 Your hand is also your writing style. 3 If you have a hand in a situation, you influence it or play a part in it. 4 If you give someone a hand, you help them to do something. 5 When an audience gives someone a big hand, they applaud. 6 The hands of a clock or watch are the pointers that point to the numbers. 7 In cards, your hand is the cards you are holding. ▶ *verb* 8 If you hand something to someone, you give it to them. ▶ *phrase* 9 Something that is at hand, to hand or on hand is available, close by, and ready for use. 10 You use on the one hand to introduce the first part of an argument or discussion with two different points of view. 11 You use on the other hand to introduce the second part of an argument or discussion with two different points of view. 12 If you do something by hand, you do it using your hands rather than a machine. > **hand down** *verb* Something that is handed down is passed from one generation to another.

▶ **hand down** = bequeath, give, pass down, pass on

handbag *noun* a small bag used mainly by women to carry money and personal items.

handbook *noun* a book giving information and instructions about something.

handcuff *noun* Handcuffs are two metal rings linked by a chain which are locked around a prisoner's wrists.

handful *noun* 1 A handful of something is the amount of it you can hold in your hand. 2 a small quantity. 3 Someone who is a handful is difficult to control.

handicap handicaps, handicapping, handicapped *noun* 1 (old-fashioned, offensive) a physical or mental disability. 2 something that makes it difficult for you to achieve something. 3 In sport, a handicap is a disadvantage or advantage given to competitors according to their skill, in order to give them an equal chance of winning. ▶ *verb* 4 If something handicaps someone, it makes it difficult for them to achieve something.

handicap *noun*
2 = barrier, disadvantage, drawback, hindrance, impediment, obstacle
▶ *verb* 4 = burden, hamper, hinder, impede, restrict

handiwork *noun* Your handiwork is something that you have done or made yourself.

handkerchief *noun* a small square of fabric used for blowing your nose.

handle *noun* 1 The handle of an object is the part by which it is held or controlled. 2 a small lever used to open and close a door or window. ▶ *verb* **3** If you handle an object, you hold it in your hands to examine it. **4** If you handle something, you deal with it or control it.

handle *noun*
1 = grip, hilt
▶ *verb* **3** = feel, finger, grasp, hold, touch **4** = administer, conduct, deal with, manage, supervise, take care of

handlebar *noun* Handlebars are the bar and handles at the front of a bicycle, used for steering.

handout *noun* **1** a gift of food, clothing or money given to a person in need. **2** a piece of paper giving information about something.

hand-picked *adjective* carefully chosen.

handset *noun* The handset of a telephone is the part that you speak into and listen with.

handshake *noun* the grasping and shaking of a person's hand by another person.

handsome *adjective* **1** very attractive in appearance. **2** large and generous.

handsome *adjective*
1 = attractive, good-looking
2 = ample, considerable, generous, liberal, plentiful, sizable *or* sizeable

handwriting *noun* Someone's handwriting is their style of writing as it looks on the page.

handy handier, handiest *adjective*
1 conveniently near. **2** easy to handle or use. **3** skilful.

handy *adjective*
1 = at hand, at your fingertips, close, convenient, nearby, on

hand **2** = convenient, easy to use, helpful, neat, practical, useful, user-friendly

hang hangs, hanging, hung *verb*
1 If you hang something somewhere, you attach it to a high point. **2** If something is hanging on something, it is attached by its top to it. **3** If a future event or possibility is hanging over you, it worries or frightens you. **4** When you hang wallpaper, you stick it onto a wall. **5** To hang someone means to kill them by suspending them from a rope around the neck. ▶ *phrase* **6** When you **get the hang of something**, you understand it and are able to do it. > **hang about** or **hang around** *verb* **1** (*informal*) To hang about or hang around means to wait somewhere. **2** To hang about or hang around with someone means to spend a lot of time with them. > **hang back** *verb* To hang back means to wait or hesitate. > **hang on** *verb* **1** If you hang on to something, you hold it tightly or keep it. **2** (*informal*) To hang on means to wait. > **hang out** *verb* (*informal*) If you hang out somewhere or with someone, you spend a lot of time there or with them. > **hang up** *verb* When you hang up, you end a telephone call.

hang *verb*
1 = attach, drape, fasten, fix, suspend **2** = dangle, droop

hangar *noun* a large building where aircraft are kept.

hangover *noun* a feeling of sickness and headache after drinking too much alcohol.

h

hanker verb If you hanker after something, you continually want it.

hanky hankies noun a handkerchief.

Hanukkah; also spelt **Chanukah** noun (RE) Hanukkah is an eight-day Jewish festival of lights.

haphazard adjective not organised or planned.
> **haphazardly** adverb

hapless adjective (literary) unlucky.

happen verb 1 When something happens, it occurs or takes place. 2 If you happen to do something, you do it by chance. > **happening** noun

> **happen** verb
> 1 = come about, follow, occur, result, take place

happiness noun a feeling of great contentment or pleasure.

> **happiness** noun
> = delight, ecstasy, elation, joy, pleasure, satisfaction

happy happier, happiest adjective 1 feeling, showing or producing contentment or pleasure. 2 satisfied that something is right. 3 willing. 4 fortunate or lucky. > **happily** adverb

> **happy** adjective
> 1 = cheerful, delighted, jolly, joyful, jubilant, merry
> 4 = auspicious, convenient, favourable, fortunate, lucky, opportune, timely

happy-go-lucky adjective carefree and unconcerned.

harass verb If someone harasses you, they trouble or annoy you continually. > **harassed** adjective > **harassment** noun

harbinger noun a person or thing that announces or indicates the approach of a future event.

harbour noun 1 a protected area of deep water where boats can be moored. ▶ verb 2 To harbour someone means to hide them secretly in your house. 3 If you harbour a feeling, you have it for a long time.

hard adjective 1 Something that is hard is firm, solid or stiff. 2 requiring a lot of effort: hard work. 3 difficult. 4 Someone who is hard has no kindness or pity. 5 A hard colour or voice is harsh and unpleasant. 6 Hard evidence or facts can be proved to be true. 7 Hard water contains a lot of lime and does not easily produce a lather. ▶ adverb 8 earnestly or intently: They tried hard to attract tourists. 9 An event that follows hard upon something takes place immediately afterwards. > **hardness** noun

> **hard** adjective
> 1 = firm, rigid, solid, stiff, strong, tough 2 = arduous, exhausting, laborious, rigorous, strenuous, tough 3 = baffling, complex, complicated, difficult, puzzling

hard and fast adjective fixed and not able to be changed.

hardback noun a book with a stiff cover.

hard core noun The hard core in an organisation is the group of people who most resist change.

harden verb To harden means to become hard or get harder.

> **harden** verb
> = bake, cake, freeze, set, stiffen

hard labour noun physical work which is difficult and tiring, used in some countries as a punishment for a crime.

hardly adverb 1 almost not or not quite: *I could hardly believe it.* 2 certainly not: *It's hardly a secret.*

> **hardly** adverb
> 1 = barely, just, only just, scarcely

hardship noun Hardship is a time or situation of suffering and difficulty.

> **hardship** noun
> = adversity, destitution, difficulty, misfortune, want

hard shoulder noun the area at the edge of a motorway where a driver can stop in the event of a breakdown.

hard up adjective (informal) having hardly any money.

hardware noun 1 Hardware is tools and equipment for use in the home and garden. 2 (ICT) Hardware is also computer machinery rather than computer programs.

hard-wearing adjective strong, well-made and long-lasting.

hardwood noun strong, hard wood from a tree such as an oak; also the tree itself.

hardy hardier, hardiest adjective tough and able to endure very difficult or cold conditions.

hare noun 1 an animal like a large rabbit, but with longer ears and legs. ▶ verb 2 To hare means to run very fast.

harem noun in the past, the place in a Muslim house or palace where the women lived.

hark verb 1 (old-fashioned) To hark means to listen. 2 To hark back to

something in the past means to refer back to it or recall it.

harlequin adjective having many different colours.

harm verb 1 To harm someone or something means to injure or damage them. ▶ noun 2 Harm is injury or damage.

> **harm** verb
> 1 = abuse, damage, hurt, ill-treat, ruin, wound
> ▶ noun 2 = abuse, damage, hurt, injury

harmful adjective having a bad effect on something.

> **harmful** adjective
> = damaging, destructive, detrimental, hurtful, pernicious

harmless adjective 1 safe to use or be near. 2 unlikely to cause problems or annoyance.
> **harmlessly** adverb

> **harmless** adjective
> 1 = innocuous, nontoxic, not dangerous, safe

harmonic adjective using musical harmony.

harmonica noun a small musical instrument which you play by blowing and sucking while moving it across your lips.

harmonious adjective 1 showing agreement, peacefulness and friendship. 2 consisting of parts which blend well together making an attractive whole.
> **harmoniously** adverb

harmony harmonies noun 1 Harmony is a state of peaceful agreement and cooperation. 2 (MUSIC) Harmony is the structure and relationship of chords in a piece of music.

3 Harmony is the pleasant combination of two or more notes played at the same time.

harness noun **1** a set of straps and fittings fastened round a horse so that it can pull a vehicle, or fastened round someone's body to attach something. ▸ verb **2** If you harness something, you bring it under control to use it.

harp noun **1** a musical instrument consisting of a triangular frame with vertical strings which you pluck with your fingers. ▸ verb **2** (informal) If someone harps on about something, they keep talking about it, especially in a boring way. > **harpist** noun

harpoon noun a barbed spear attached to a rope, thrown or fired from a gun, and used for catching whales or large fish.

harpsichord noun a musical instrument like a small piano, with strings which are plucked when the keys are pressed.

harrowing adjective very upsetting or disturbing.

harsh adjective severe, difficult and unpleasant. > **harshly** adverb

> **harsh** adjective
> = austere, cruel, hard, ruthless, severe, stern

harvest noun **1** the cutting and gathering of a crop; also the ripe crop when it is gathered at the time of gathering. ▸ verb **2** To harvest food means to gather it when it is ripe. > **harvester** noun

has-been noun (informal) a person who is no longer important or successful.

hash phrase **1** If you **make a hash of** a job, you do it badly. ▸ noun **2** the name for the symbol #. **3** Hash is

a dish made of small pieces of meat and vegetables cooked together.

hashtag noun (ICT) a word or phrase that is used to indicate the topic of a post on a social networking website.

hassle (informal) noun **1** Something that is a hassle is difficult or causes trouble. ▸ verb **2** If you hassle someone, you annoy them by repeatedly asking them to do something.

> **hassle** noun
> **1** = bother, effort, inconvenience, trouble, upheaval
> ▸ verb **2** = badger, bother, go on at, harass, nag, pester

haste noun Haste is doing something quickly, especially too quickly.

hasten verb To hasten means to move quickly or do something quickly.

hasty hastier, hastiest adjective done or happening suddenly and quickly, often without enough care or thought. > **hastily** adverb

> **hasty** adjective
> = brisk, hurried, prompt, rapid, swift

hat noun a covering for the head.

hatch verb **1** When an egg hatches, or when a bird or reptile hatches, the egg breaks open and the young bird or reptile emerges. **2** To hatch a plot means to plan it. ▸ noun **3** a covered opening in a floor or wall.

hatchback noun a car with a door at the back which opens upwards.

hatchet noun **1** a small axe. ▸ phrase **2** To **bury the hatchet**

means to resolve a disagreement and become friends again.

hate verb 1 If you hate someone or something, you have a strong dislike for them. ▶ noun 2 Hate is a strong dislike.

> **hate** verb
> 1 = abhor (formal), be sick of, despise, detest, dislike, loathe
> ▶ noun 2 = animosity, aversion, dislike, hatred, hostility, loathing

hateful adjective extremely unpleasant.

> **hateful** adjective
> = abhorrent (formal), despicable, horrible, loathsome, obnoxious, offensive

hatred noun Hatred is an extremely strong feeling of dislike.

> **hatred** noun
> = animosity, antipathy (formal), aversion, dislike, hate, revulsion

hat trick noun In sport, a hat trick is three achievements, for example when a footballer scores three goals in a match.

haughty haughtier, haughtiest adjective showing excessive pride. > **haughtily** adverb

> **haughty** adjective
> = arrogant, conceited, disdainful, proud, snobbish, stuck-up (informal)

haul verb 1 To haul something somewhere means to pull it with great effort. ▶ noun 2 a quantity of something obtained. ▶ phrase 3 Something that you describe as **a long haul** takes a lot of time and effort to achieve.

haulage noun Haulage is the business or cost of transporting goods by road.

haunches plural noun Your haunches are your buttocks and the tops of your legs.

haunt verb 1 If a ghost is said to haunt a place, it is supposed to be seen or heard there regularly. 2 If a memory or a fear haunts you, it continually worries you. ▶ noun 3 A person's favourite haunt is a place they like to visit often.

haunted adjective 1 said to be regularly visited by a ghost. 2 very worried or troubled.

haunting adjective extremely beautiful or sad so that it makes a lasting impression on you.

have has, having, had verb 1 Have is an auxiliary verb, used to form the past tense or to express completed actions: They have never met. 2 If you have something, you own or possess it. 3 If you have something, you experience it, it happens to you, or you are affected by it: He had a marvellous time. 4 To have a child or baby animal means to give birth to it. ▶ phrase 5 If you **have to** do something, you must do it. If you **had better** do something, you ought to do it.

> **have** verb
> 2 = hold, keep, own, possess
> 3 = endure, enjoy, experience, feel, sustain, undergo

haven noun a safe place.

havoc noun 1 Havoc is disorder and confusion. ▶ phrase 2 To **play havoc** with something means to cause great disorder and confusion in it.

h

hawk noun 1 a bird of prey with short rounded wings and a long tail. ▶ verb 2 To hawk goods means to sell them by taking them around from place to place.

hawthorn noun a small, thorny tree producing white blossom and red berries.

hay noun Hay is grass which has been cut and dried and is used as animal feed.

hay fever noun Hay fever is an allergy to pollen, causing sneezing and watering eyes.

haystack noun a large, firmly built pile of hay, usually covered and left out in the open.

hazard noun 1 (SCIENCE) a substance, object or action which could be dangerous to you. ▶ verb 2 If you hazard something, you put it at risk. ▶ phrase 3 If you hazard a guess, you make a guess. > **hazardous** adjective

haze noun If there is a haze, you cannot see clearly because there is moisture or smoke in the air.

hazel noun 1 a small tree producing edible nuts. ▶ adjective 2 greenish brown in colour.

hazy hazier, haziest adjective dim or vague.

he pronoun 'He' is used to refer to a man, boy or male animal.

head noun 1 Your head is the part of your body which has your eyes, brain and mouth in it. 2 Your head is also your mind and mental abilities. 3 The head of something is the top, start or most important one. 4 The head of a group or organisation is the person in charge. 5 The head on beer is the layer of froth on the top. 6 The head on a computer or tape recorder is the part that can read or write information. 7 When you toss a coin, the side called heads is the one with the head on it. ▶ verb 8 To head a group or organisation means to be in charge. 9 To head in a particular direction means to move in that direction. 10 To head a ball means to hit it with your head. ▶ phrase 11 If you **lose your head**, you panic. 12 If you say that someone is **off their head**, you mean that they are behaving in a very strange or foolish way. 13 If something is **over someone's head**, it is too difficult for them to understand. 14 If you **can't make head nor tail of something**, you cannot understand it. > **head off** verb If you head off someone or something, you make them change direction or prevent something from happening.

head noun
2 = aptitude, brain, common sense, intelligence, mind, wits
3 = beginning, front, source, start, top 4 = boss, chief, director, leader, manager, president, principal
▶ verb 8 = be in charge of, control, direct, lead, manage, run

headache noun 1 a pain in your head. 2 Something that is a headache is causing a lot of difficulty or worry.

header noun A header in soccer is hitting the ball with your head.

heading noun a piece of writing that is written or printed at the top of a page or section.

headland noun (GEOGRAPHY) a narrow piece of land jutting out into the sea.

headlight *noun* The headlights on a motor vehicle are the large powerful lights at the front.

headline *noun* 1 A newspaper headline is the title of a newspaper article printed in large, bold type. 2 The headlines are the main points of the radio or television news.

headmaster *noun* a man who is the head teacher of a school.

headmistress *noun* a woman who is the head teacher of a school.

headphones *plural noun* Headphones are a pair of small speakers which you wear in or over your ears to listen to music without other people hearing.

headquarters *noun* The headquarters of an organisation is the main place or the place from which it is run.

headroom *noun* Headroom is the amount of space below a roof or surface under which an object must pass or fit.

headstone *noun* a large stone standing at one end of a grave and showing the name of the person buried there.

headstrong *adjective* determined to do something in your own way and ignoring other people's advice.

head teacher *noun* the teacher who is in charge of a school.

headway *phrase* If you are making headway, you are making progress.

headwind *noun* a wind blowing in the opposite direction to the way you are travelling.

heady headier, headiest *adjective* extremely exciting.

heal *verb* If something heals or if you heal it, it becomes healthy or normal again.

healer *noun* a person who heals people.

health *noun* 1 (PSHE) Your health is the condition of your body. 2 Health is also the state of being free from disease and feeling well.

> **health** *noun*
> 1 = condition, constitution, shape 2 = fitness, good condition, wellbeing

healthy healthier, healthiest *adjective* 1 (PSHE) Someone who is healthy is fit and strong and does not have any diseases. 2 Something that is healthy is good for you. 3 An organisation or system that is healthy is successful. > **healthily** *adverb*

> **healthy** *adjective*
> 1 = fit, in good shape (*informal*), robust, strong, well
> 2 = beneficial, bracing, good for you, nourishing, nutritious, wholesome

heap *noun* 1 a pile of things. 2 (*in plural, informal*) Heaps of something means plenty of it. ▶ *verb* 3 If you heap things, you pile them up. 4 To heap something such as praise on someone means to give them a lot of it.

> **heap** *noun*
> 1 = hoard, mass, mound, pile, stack 2 = loads (*informal*), lots (*informal*), plenty, stacks (*informal*), tons (*informal*)
> ▶ *verb* 3 = pile, stack

hear hears, hearing, heard *verb* 1 When you hear sounds, you are aware of them because they reach your ears. **2** When you hear from someone, they write to you or phone you. **3** When you hear about something, you are informed about it. **4** When a judge hears a case, he or she listens to it in court in order to make a decision on it. ▶ *phrase* **5** If you say that you **won't hear of** something, you mean you refuse to allow it. ▷ **hear out** *verb* If you hear someone out, you listen to all they have to say without interrupting.

> **hear** *verb*
> 1 = catch, eavesdrop, heed, listen in, listen to, overhear
> 3 = ascertain, discover, find out, gather, learn, understand

hearing *noun* **1** Hearing is the sense which makes it possible for you to be aware of sounds. **2** a court trial or official meeting to hear facts about an incident. **3** If someone gives you a hearing, they let you give your point of view and listen to you.

hearsay *noun* Hearsay is information that you have heard from other people rather than something that you know personally to be true.

hearse *noun* a large car that carries the coffin at a funeral.

heart *noun* **1** the organ in your chest that pumps the blood around your body. **2** Your heart is also thought of as the centre of your emotions. **3** Heart is courage, determination or enthusiasm. **4** The heart of something is the most central and important part of it. **5** a shape similar to a heart, used especially as a symbol of love.

6 Hearts is one of the four suits in a pack of playing cards. It is marked by a red heart-shaped symbol.

heartache *noun* Heartache is very great sadness and emotional suffering.

heart attack *noun* a serious medical condition in which the heart suddenly beats irregularly or stops completely.

heartbreak *noun* Heartbreak is great sadness and emotional suffering. ▷ **heartbreaking** *adjective*

heartbroken *adjective* very sad and emotionally upset.

heartburn *noun* Heartburn is a painful burning sensation in your chest, caused by indigestion.

heartening *adjective* encouraging or uplifting.

heart failure *noun* Heart failure is a serious condition in which someone's heart does not work as well as it should, sometimes stopping completely.

heartfelt *adjective* sincerely and deeply felt.

hearth *noun* the floor of a fireplace.

heartless *adjective* cruel and unkind.

heart-rending *adjective* causing great sadness and pity.

heart-throb *noun* someone who is attractive to a lot of people.

heart-to-heart *noun* a discussion in which two people talk about their deepest feelings.

hearty heartier, heartiest *adjective* **1** cheerful and enthusiastic. **2** strongly felt: *a hearty dislike for her teacher*. **3** A hearty meal is large and satisfying. ▷ **heartily** *adverb*

heat noun 1 Heat is warmth or the quality of something being hot; also the temperature of something that is warm or hot. 2 Heat is strength of feeling, especially of anger or excitement. 3 a contest or race in a competition held to decide who will play in the final. ▶ verb 4 To heat something means to raise its temperature. ▶ phrase 5 When a female animal is **on heat**, she is ready for mating.

> **heat** noun
> 1 = high temperature, warmth
> 2 = excitement, fervour, intensity, passion, vehemence
> ▶ verb 4 = reheat, warm up

heater noun a piece of equipment or a machine which is used to raise the temperature of something.

heath noun an area of open land covered with rough grass or heather.

heather noun a plant with small purple or white flowers that grows wild on hills and moorland.

heating noun Heating is the equipment used to heat a building; also the process and cost of running the equipment to provide heat.

heatwave noun a period of time during which the weather is much hotter than usual.

heave verb 1 To heave something means to move or throw it with a lot of effort. 2 If your stomach heaves, you vomit or suddenly feel sick. 3 If you heave a sigh, you sigh loudly. ▶ noun 4 If you give something a heave, you move or throw it with a lot of effort.

heaven noun 1 (RE) a place of happiness where God is believed to live and where good people are believed to go when they die. 2 (informal) If you describe something as heaven, you mean that it is wonderful.

> **heaven** noun
> 1 = next world, paradise
> 2 = bliss, ecstasy, paradise, rapture

heavenly adjective 1 relating to heaven. 2 (informal) wonderful.

heavy heavier, heaviest adjective 1 great in weight or force. 2 great in degree or amount: heavy casualties. 3 solid and thick in appearance: heavy shoes. 4 using a lot of something quickly: The van is heavy on petrol. 5 serious and difficult to deal with or understand: a heavy speech. 6 Food that is heavy is solid and difficult to digest. 7 When it is heavy, the weather is hot, humid and still. 8 Someone with a heavy heart is very sad. > **heavily** adverb

> **heavy** adjective
> 1 = bulky, massive 5 = deep, grave (formal), profound, serious, solemn, weighty

heavy-duty adjective Heavy-duty equipment is strong and hard-wearing.

heavyweight noun 1 a boxer in the heaviest weight group. 2 an important person with a lot of influence.

Hebrew noun 1 Hebrew is an ancient language now spoken in Israel, where it is the official language. 2 In the past, the Hebrews were Hebrew-speaking Jews who lived in Israel. ▶ adjective 3 relating to the Hebrews and their customs.

heckle *verb* If members of an audience heckle a speaker, they interrupt and shout rude remarks.

hectare *noun* a unit for measuring areas of land, equal to 10,000 square metres or about 2.471 acres.

hectic *adjective* involving a lot of rushed activity.

hedge *noun* 1 a row of bushes forming a barrier or boundary. ▶ *verb* 2 If you hedge against something unpleasant happening, you protect yourself. 3 If you hedge, you avoid answering a question or dealing with a problem. ▶ *phrase* 4 If you **hedge your bets**, you support two or more people or courses of action to avoid the risk of losing a lot.

hedgehog *noun* a small, brown animal with sharp spikes covering its back.

hedonism *noun* Hedonism is the belief that gaining pleasure is the most important thing in life. > **hedonistic** *adjective*

heed *verb* 1 If you heed someone's advice, you pay attention to it. ▶ *noun* 2 If you take or pay heed to something, you give it careful attention.

> **heed** *verb*
> 1 = follow, listen to, pay attention to, take notice of
> ▶ *noun* 2 = attention, notice

heel *noun* 1 the back part of your foot. 2 The heel of a shoe or sock is the part that fits over your heel. ▶ *verb* 3 To heel a pair of shoes means to put a new piece on the heel. ▶ *phrase* 4 A person or place that looks **down at heel** looks untidy and in poor condition.

hefty heftier, heftiest *adjective* of great size, force or weight.

height *noun* 1 The height of an object is its measurement from the bottom to the top. 2 a high position or place. 3 The height of something is its peak, or the time when it is most successful or intense. 4 (MATHS) In maths, the height of a triangle is the point where two sides meet at a peak opposite the base.

heighten *verb* If something heightens a feeling or experience, it increases its intensity.

heinous *adjective* evil and terrible.

heir *noun* A person's heir is the person who is entitled to inherit their property or title.

heiress *noun* a woman or girl with the right to inherit property or a title.

heirloom *noun* something belonging to a family that has been passed from one generation to another.

held the past tense and past participle of **hold**.

helicopter *noun* an aircraft with rotating blades above it which enable it to take off vertically, hover and fly.

helium *noun* (SCIENCE) Helium is an element which is a colourless inert gas. It occurs in some natural gases, and is used in balloons. Its atomic number is 2 and its symbol is He.

hell *noun* 1 (RE) Hell is the place where souls of evil people are believed to go to be punished after death. 2 (*informal*) If you say that something is hell, you mean it is very unpleasant.

hell *noun*
1 = abyss, inferno 2 = agony, anguish, misery, nightmare, ordeal

hell-bent *adjective* determined to do something whatever the consequences.

hellish *adjective* (*informal*) very unpleasant.

hello *interjection* You say 'Hello' as a greeting or when you answer the phone.

hello *interjection*
= gidday (*Australian and New Zealand*), good afternoon (*formal*), good evening (*formal*), good morning (*formal*), hi (*informal*), how do you do? (*formal*)

helm *noun* 1 The helm on a boat is the position from which it is steered and the wheel or tiller.
▶ *phrase* 2 **At the helm** means in a position of leadership or control.

helmet *noun* A hard hat worn to protect the head.

help *verb* 1 To help someone means to make something easier or better for them. ▶ *noun* 2 If you need or give help, you need or give assistance. 3 someone or something that helps you.
▶ *phrase* 4 If you **help yourself** to something, you take it. 5 If you **can't help** something, you cannot control it or change it.

help *verb*
1 = aid, assist, lend a hand, support
▶ *noun* 2 = advice, aid, assistance, guidance, helping hand, support

helper *noun* a person who gives assistance.

helper *noun*
= aide, assistant, deputy, henchman, right-hand man, supporter

helpful *adjective* 1 If someone is helpful, they help you by doing something for you. 2 Something that is helpful makes a situation more pleasant or easier to tolerate. > **helpfully** *adverb*

helpful *adjective*
1 = accommodating, cooperative, kind, supportive
2 = advantageous, beneficial, constructive, profitable, useful

helping *noun* an amount of food that you get in a single serving.

helpless *adjective* defenceless or unable to cope on your own.

helpless *adjective*
= defenceless, powerless, unprotected, vulnerable, weak

hem hems, hemming, hemmed
noun 1 The hem of a garment is an edge which has been turned over and sewn in place. ▶ *verb* 2 To hem something means to make a hem on it. > **hem in** *verb* If someone is hemmed in, they are surrounded and prevented from moving.

hemisphere *noun* one half of the earth, the brain or a sphere.
> **hemispherical** *adjective*

hemp *noun* Hemp is a tall plant, some varieties of which are used to make rope, and others to produce the drug cannabis.

hen *noun* a female chicken; also any female bird.

hence *adverb* 1 (*formal*) for this reason. 2 from now or from the time mentioned.

henchman henchmen *noun* The henchmen of a powerful person are the people employed to do violent or dishonest work for that person.

hepatitis noun Hepatitis is a serious infectious disease causing inflammation of the liver.

heptagon noun (MATHS) a shape with seven straight sides.
> **heptagonal** adjective

her pronoun, adjective 'Her' is used to refer to a woman, girl or female animal that has already been mentioned, or to show that something belongs to a particular female.

herald noun 1 In the past, a herald was a messenger. ▶ verb 2 Something that heralds a future event is a sign of that event.

herb noun a plant whose leaves are used in medicine or to flavour food. > **herbal** adjective > **herbalist** noun

herd noun 1 a large group of animals. ▶ verb 2 To herd animals or people means to make them move together as a group.

here adverb 1 at, to or in the place where you are, or the place mentioned or indicated. ▶ phrase 2 Here and there means in various unspecified places.

hereafter adverb (formal) after this time or point.

hereby adverb (formal) used in documents and statements to indicate that a declaration is official: All leave is hereby cancelled.

hereditary adjective passed on to a child from a parent.

herein adverb (formal) in this place or document.

heresy heresies noun Heresy is belief or behaviour considered to be wrong because it disagrees

with what is generally accepted, especially with regard to religion.
> **heretic** noun > **heretical** adjective

heritage noun the possessions or traditions that have been passed from one generation to another.

hermit noun a person who lives alone with a simple way of life, especially for religious reasons.

hernia noun a medical condition in which part of the intestine sticks through a weak point in the surrounding tissue.

hero heroes noun 1 the main male character in a book, film or play. 2 a person who has done something brave or good.

heroic adjective brave, courageous and determined. > **heroically** adverb

heroin noun Heroin is a powerful drug formerly used as an anaesthetic and now taken illegally by some people for pleasure.

heroine noun 1 the main female character in a book, film or play. 2 a woman who has done something brave or good.

heroism noun Heroism is great courage and bravery.

heron noun a wading bird with very long legs and a long beak and neck.

herring noun a silvery fish that lives in large shoals in northern seas.

hers pronoun 'Hers' refers to something that belongs or relates to a woman, girl or female animal.

herself pronoun 1 'Herself' is used when the same woman, girl or female animal does an action and is affected by it: She pulled herself out of the water. **2** 'Herself' is used to emphasise 'she': *She herself was not a keen gardener.*

hesitant *adjective* If you are hesitant, you do not do something immediately because you are uncertain or worried.

> **hesitant** *adjective*
> = diffident, doubtful, reluctant, unsure, wavering

hesitate *verb* To hesitate means to pause or show uncertainty.
> **hesitation** *noun*

> **hesitate** *verb*
> = dither, pause, waver

heterosexual *noun* **1** a person who is attracted to people of the opposite sex. ▶ *adjective* **2** attracted to people of the opposite sex.

hewn *adjective* carved from a substance.

hexagon *noun* (MATHS) a shape with six straight sides; a **regular hexagon** has six straight sides of the same length. ▶ **hexagonal** *adjective*

heyday *noun* The heyday of a person or thing is the period when they are most successful or popular.

hi *interjection* 'Hi!' is an informal greeting.

hiatus hiatuses *noun* (*formal*) a pause or gap.

hibernate *verb* Animals that hibernate spend the winter in a state like deep sleep.
> **hibernation** *noun*

hibiscus hibiscuses *noun* a type of tropical shrub with brightly coloured flowers.

hiccup hiccups, hiccupping, hiccupped *noun* **1** Hiccups are short, uncontrolled choking sounds in your throat that you sometimes get if you have been eating or drinking too quickly. **2** (*informal*) a minor problem. ▶ *verb* **3** When you hiccup, you make little choking sounds.

hide hides, hiding, hid, hidden *verb* **1** To hide something means to put it where it cannot be seen, or to prevent it from being discovered. ▶ *noun* **2** the skin of a large animal.

> **hide** *verb*
> 1 = cache, conceal, secrete, stash (*informal*)
> ▶ *noun* 2 = pelt, skin

hideous *adjective* extremely ugly or unpleasant.

hideout *noun* a hiding place.

hiding *noun* (*informal*) To give someone a hiding means to beat them severely.

hierarchy hierarchies *noun* a system in which people or things are ranked according to how important they are.
> **hierarchical** *adjective*

high *adjective* **1** tall or a long way above the ground. **2** great in degree, quantity or intensity: *high interest rates.* **3** towards the top of a scale of importance or quality: *high fashion.* **4** close to the top of a range of sound or notes. ▶ *adverb* **5** at or to a height. ▶ *noun* **6** a high point or level. ▶ *phrase* **7** (*informal*) Someone who is **on a high** is in a very excited and optimistic mood.

> **high** *adjective*
> 1 = elevated, lofty, soaring, steep, tall, towering 2 = acute, excessive, extraordinary, extreme, great, severe

h

highbrow *adjective* concerned with serious, intellectual subjects.

higher education *noun* Higher education is education at universities and colleges.

high jump *noun* The high jump is an athletics event involving jumping over a high bar.

highlands *plural noun* Highlands are mountainous or hilly areas of land.

highlight *verb* 1 If you highlight a point or problem, you emphasise and draw attention to it. ▶ *noun* 2 The highlight of something is the most interesting part of it. 3 (ART) a lighter area of a painting, showing where light shines on things. 4 Highlights are also light-coloured streaks in someone's hair.

highly *adverb* 1 extremely. 2 towards the top of a scale of importance, admiration or respect: *She thought highly of him.*

high-minded *adjective* Someone who is high-minded has strong moral principles.

Highness *noun* 'Highness' is used in titles and forms of address for members of a royal family other than a king or queen.

high-pitched *adjective* A high-pitched sound is high and often rather shrill.

high-rise *adjective* High-rise buildings are very tall.

high school *noun* a secondary school.

high tide *noun* On a coast, high tide is the time, usually twice a day, when the sea is at its highest level.

highway *noun* a road along which vehicles have the right to travel.

hijab *noun* a head-covering worn by some Muslim women.

hijack *verb* If someone hijacks a plane or vehicle, they illegally take control of it during a journey.

hike *noun* 1 a long country walk. ▶ *verb* 2 To hike means to walk long distances in the country.

hilarious *adjective* very funny.

hilarity *noun* Hilarity is great amusement and laughter.

hill *noun* a rounded area of land higher than the land surrounding it.

hilt *noun* The hilt of a sword or knife is its handle.

him *pronoun* You use 'him' to refer to a man, boy or male animal that has already been mentioned.

himself *pronoun* 1 'Himself' is used when the same man, boy or male animal does an action and is affected by it: *He discharged himself from hospital.* 2 'Himself' is used to emphasise 'he': *He himself was not keen to join the others.*

hind *adjective* 1 used to refer to the back part of an animal. ▶ *noun* 2 a female deer.

hinder *verb* If you hinder someone or something, you get in their way and make something difficult for them.

Hindi *noun* Hindi is a language spoken in northern India.

hindrance *noun* 1 Someone or something that is a hindrance causes difficulties or is an obstruction. 2 Hindrance is the act of hindering someone or something.

hindsight *noun* Hindsight is the ability to understand an event after it has actually taken place.

Hindu noun (RE) a person who believes in Hinduism, an Indian religion which has many gods and believes that people have another life on earth after death.
> **Hinduism** noun

hinge noun **1** the movable joint which attaches a door or window to its frame. ▶ verb **2** Something that hinges on a situation or event depends entirely on that situation or event.

hint noun **1** an indirect suggestion. **2** a helpful piece of advice. ▶ verb **3** If you hint at something, you suggest it indirectly.

> **hint** noun
> **1** = clue, indication, intimation, suggestion **2** = advice, pointer, suggestion, tip
> ▶ verb **3** = imply, indicate, insinuate, intimate, suggest

hinterland noun The hinterland of a coastline or a port is the area of land behind it or around it.

hip noun Your hips are the two parts at the sides of your body between your waist and your upper legs.

hippo hippos noun (informal) a hippopotamus.

hippopotamus hippopotamuses or **hippopotami** noun a large African animal with thick wrinkled skin and short legs that lives near rivers.

hippy hippies; also spelt **hippie** noun In the 1960s and 1970s hippies were people who rejected conventional society and tried to live a life based on peace and love.

hire verb **1** If you hire something, you pay money to be able to use it for a period of time. **2** If you hire

someone, you pay them to do a job for you. ▶ phrase **3** Something that is **for hire** is available for people to hire.

> **hire** verb
> **1** = charter, lease, rent
> **2** = appoint, commission, employ, engage, sign up

hirsute adjective (formal) hairy.

his adjective, pronoun 'His' refers to something that belongs or relates to a man, boy or male animal that has already been mentioned, and sometimes also to any person whose gender is not known.

hiss verb **1** To hiss means to make a long 's' sound, especially to show disapproval or aggression. ▶ noun **2** a long 's' sound.

historian noun a person who studies and writes about history.

historic adjective important in the past or likely to be seen as important in the future.

historical adjective **1** occurring in the past, or relating to the study of the past. **2** describing or representing the past.
> **historically** adverb

history histories noun History is the study of the past. A history is a record of the past.

histrionics plural noun Histrionics are dramatic behaviour full of exaggerated emotion.

hit hits, hitting, hit verb **1** If you hit someone, you strike them forcefully, usually causing hurt or damage. **2** If you hit an object, you collide with it. **3** To hit a ball or other object means to make it move by hitting it with something. **4** If something hits you, it affects you badly and suddenly. **5** If you hit on an idea or solution, you suddenly think of it. ▶ *noun* **6** a person or thing that is popular and successful. **7** the action of hitting something.

hit *verb*
1 = beat, knock, slap, smack, strike, thump, wallop **2** = bang into, bump, collide with, meet head-on, run into, smash into
▶ *noun* **7** = blow, knock, rap, slap, smack, stroke

hit and miss *adjective* happening in an unpredictable way or without being properly organised.

hit-and-run *adjective* A hit-and-run car accident is one in which the person who has caused the damage drives away without stopping.

hitch *noun* **1** A hitch is a slight problem or difficulty. ▶ *verb* **2** (*informal*) If you hitch, you hitchhike. **3** To hitch something somewhere means to hook it or fasten it there.

hitchhiking *noun* Hitchhiking is travelling by getting free lifts from passing vehicles.

hither (*old-fashioned*) *adverb* **1** used to refer to movement towards the place where you are. ▶ *phrase* **2** Something that moves **hither and thither** moves in all directions.

hitherto *adverb* (*formal*) until now.

HIV *noun* HIV is a virus that reduces people's resistance to illness and can cause AIDS. HIV is an abbreviation for 'human immunodeficiency virus'.

hive *noun* **1** a beehive. **2** A place that is a hive of activity is very busy with a lot of people working hard.

hoard *verb* **1** To hoard things means to save them even though they may no longer be useful.
▶ *noun* **2** a store of things that has been saved or hidden.

hoard *verb*
1 = save, stockpile, store
▶ *noun* **2** = cache, fund, reserve, stockpile, store, supply

hoarding *noun* a large advertising board by the side of the road.

hoarse *adjective* A hoarse voice sounds rough and unclear.

hoarse *adjective*
= croaky, gruff, husky, rasping

hoax *noun* **1** a trick or an attempt to deceive someone. ▶ *verb* **2** To hoax someone means to trick or deceive them. > **hoaxer** *noun*

hob *noun* a surface on top of a cooker which can be heated in order to cook things.

hobble *verb* **1** If you hobble, you walk awkwardly because of pain or injury. **2** If you hobble an animal, you tie its legs together to restrict its movement.

hobby hobbies *noun* something that you do for enjoyment in your spare time.

hobby *noun*
= diversion, leisure activity, leisure pursuit, pastime

hock *noun* The hock of a horse or other animal is the angled joint in its back leg.

hockey *noun* Hockey is a game in which two teams use long sticks with curved ends to try to hit a small ball into the other team's goal.

hoe hoes, hoeing, hoed *noun* **1** a long-handled gardening tool with a small square blade, used to remove weeds and break up the soil. ▶ verb 2 To hoe the ground means to use a hoe on it.

hog hogs, hogging, hogged noun 1 a male pig that has had its testicles removed. ▶ verb 2 (informal) If you hog something, you take more than your share of it, or keep it for too long. ▶ phrase 3 (informal) If you **go the whole hog**, you do something thoroughly in a bold or extravagant way.

hoist verb 1 To hoist something means to lift it, especially using a crane or other machinery. ▶ noun 2 a machine for lifting heavy things.

hold holds, holding, held verb 1 To hold something means to carry or keep it in place, usually with your hand or arms. 2 Someone who holds power, office or an opinion has it or possesses it. 3 If you hold something such as a meeting or an election, you arrange it and cause it to happen. 4 If something holds, it is still available or valid. 5 If you hold someone responsible for something, you consider them responsible for it. 6 If something holds a certain number or amount, it can contain that number or amount. 7 If you hold something such as theatre tickets, a telephone call, or the price of something, you keep or reserve it for a period of time. 8 To hold something down means to keep it or to keep it under control. 9 If you hold on to something, you continue it or keep it even though it might be difficult. 10 To hold something back means to prevent it, keep it under control, or not

reveal it. ▶ noun 11 If someone or something has a hold over you, they have power, control or influence over you. 12 a way of holding something or the act of holding it. 13 the place where cargo or luggage is stored in a ship or a plane. > **hold out** verb If you hold out, you stand firm and manage to resist opposition in difficult circumstances. > **hold up** verb If something holds you up, it delays you.

> **hold** verb
> 1 = carry, clasp, clutch, embrace, grasp, grip
> ▶ noun 11 = control, dominance, sway 12 = grasp, grip

holdall noun a large, soft bag for carrying clothing.

hole noun 1 an opening or hollow in something. 2 (informal) If you are in a hole, you are in a difficult situation. 3 (informal) A hole in a theory or argument is a weakness or error in it. 4 In golf, a hole is one of the small holes into which you have to hit the ball. ▶ verb 5 When you hole the ball in golf, you hit the ball into one of the holes.

> **hole** noun
> 1 = gap, hollow, opening, pit, split, tear 2 = fix (informal), hot water (informal), mess, predicament, tight spot (informal) 3 = defect, error, fault, flaw, loophole

holiday noun 1 a period of time spent away from home for enjoyment. 2 a time when you are not working or not at school. ▶ verb 3 When you holiday somewhere, you take a holiday there.

holiday noun
1 = break, leave, recess, staycation (informal), time off, vacation

holidaymaker noun a person who is away from home on holiday.

holiness noun 1 Holiness is the state or quality of being holy. 2 'Your Holiness' and 'His Holiness' are titles used to address or refer to the Pope or to leaders of some other religions.

hollow adjective 1 Something that is hollow has space inside it rather than being solid. 2 An opinion or situation that is hollow has no real value or worth. 3 A hollow sound is dull and has a slight echo. ▸ noun 4 a hole in something or a part of a surface that is lower than the rest. ▸ verb 5 To hollow means to make a hollow.

holly noun 1 a Holly is an evergreen tree or shrub with spiky leaves. It often has red berries in winter.

holocaust noun 1 a large-scale destruction or loss of life, especially as a result of war or fire. 2 (HISTORY) The Holocaust was the mass murder of Jews in Europe by the Nazis during World War II.

holster noun a holder for a gun, worn at the side of the body or under the arm.

holy holier, holiest adjective 1 (RE) relating to God or to a particular religion. 2 Someone who is holy is religious and leads a pure and good life.

holy adjective
1 = blessed, consecrated, hallowed, sacred, sacrosanct, venerated (formal) 2 = devout, pious, religious, saintly, virtuous

homage noun Homage is an act of respect and admiration.

home noun 1 Your home is the building or place in which you live or feel you belong. 2 a building in which elderly or ill people live and are looked after. ▸ adjective 3 connected with or involving your home or country. > **home in** verb If something homes in on a target, it moves directly and quickly towards it.

home noun
1 = abode (old-fashioned), dwelling (formal), house, residence (formal)
▸ adjective 3 = domestic, internal, national, native

homeland noun Your homeland is your native country.

homeless adjective 1 having no home. ▸ plural noun 2 The homeless are people who have no home.

homely homelier, homeliest adjective simple, ordinary and comfortable.

homely adjective
= comfortable, cosy, modest, simple, welcoming

homeopathy noun Homeopathy is a way of treating illness by giving the patient tiny amounts of a substance that would normally cause illness in a healthy person. > **homeopathic** adjective > **homeopath** noun

homeowner noun a person who owns the home in which he or she lives.

homesick adjective unhappy because of being away from home

and missing family and friends.
> **homesickness** noun

homespun adjective not sophisticated or complicated.

homestead noun a house and its land and other buildings, especially a farm.

homeward or **homewards** adjective, adverb towards home.

homework noun 1 Homework is school work given to pupils to be done in the evening at home. 2 Homework is also research and preparation.

homicide noun Homicide is the crime of murder. > **homicidal** adjective

homing adjective A homing device is able to guide itself to a target. An animal with a homing instinct is able to guide itself home.

homosexual noun 1 a person who is attracted to people of the same sex. ▶ adjective 2 attracted to people of the same sex. > **homosexuality** noun

hone verb 1 If you hone a tool, you sharpen it. 2 If you hone a quality or ability, you develop and improve it.

honest adjective truthful and trustworthy. > **honestly** adverb

> **honest** adjective
> = law-abiding, reputable, trustworthy, truthful, virtuous

honesty noun Honesty is the quality of being truthful and trustworthy.

honey noun 1 Honey is a sweet, edible, sticky substance produced by bees. 2 'Honey' means 'sweetheart' or 'darling'.

honeycomb noun a wax structure consisting of rows of six-sided cells made by bees for storage of honey and eggs.

honeymoon noun a holiday taken by a couple who have just got married.

honeysuckle noun Honeysuckle is a climbing plant with fragrant pink or cream flowers.

honk noun 1 a short, loud sound like that made by a car horn or a goose. ▶ verb 2 When something honks, it makes a short, loud sound.

honorary adjective An honorary title or job is given as a mark of respect, and does not involve the usual qualifications or work.

honour noun 1 Your honour is your good reputation and the respect that other people have for you. 2 an award or privilege given as a mark of respect. 3 Honours is a class of university degree which is higher than a pass or ordinary degree. ▶ phrase 4 If something is done in honour of someone, it is done out of respect for them. ▶ verb 5 If you honour someone, you give them special praise or attention, or an award. 6 If you honour an agreement or promise, you do what was agreed or promised.

> **honour** noun
> 1 = decency, goodness, honesty, integrity 2 = accolade, commendation, homage, praise, recognition, tribute
> ▶ verb 5 = commemorate, commend, decorate, glorify, praise

honourable adjective worthy of respect or admiration.

hood noun **1** a loose covering for the head, usually part of a coat or jacket. **2** a cover on a piece of equipment or vehicle, usually curved and movable. > **hooded** adjective

-hood suffix '-hood' is added at the end of words to form nouns that indicate a state or condition: childhood.

hoodie noun a type of casual jacket with a hood.

hoof hooves or hoofs noun the hard bony part of certain animals' feet.

hook noun **1** a curved piece of metal or plastic that is used for catching, holding or hanging things. **2** a curving movement, for example of the fist in boxing, or of a golf ball. ▶ verb **3** If you hook one thing onto another, you attach it there using a hook. ▶ phrase **4** If you are **let off the hook**, something happens so that you avoid punishment or a difficult situation.

hooked adjective addicted to something; also obsessed by something.

hooligan noun a destructive and violent young person. > **hooliganism** noun

> **hooligan** noun
> = delinquent, hoon (Australian and New Zealand; informal), lout, vandal, yob (British and Australian; slang)

hoop noun a large ring, often used as a toy.

hooray interjection another spelling of **hurray**.

hoot verb **1** To hoot means to make a long 'oo' sound like an owl. **2** If a car horn hoots, it makes a loud honking noise. ▶ noun **3** a sound like that made by an owl or a car horn.

hooves a plural of **hoof**.

hop hops, hopping, hopped verb **1** If you hop, you jump on one foot. **2** When animals or birds hop, they jump with two feet together. **3** (informal) If you hop into or out of something, you move there quickly and easily. ▶ noun **4** a jump on one leg. **5** Hops are flowers of the hop plant, which are dried and used for making beer.

hope verb **1** If you hope that something will happen or hope that it is true, you want it to happen or to be true. ▶ noun **2** Hope is a wish or feeling of desire and expectation.

> **hope** noun
> **2** = ambition, dream, expectation

hopeless adjective **1** having no hope. **2** certain to fail or be unsuccessful. **3** bad or inadequate.

> **hopeless** adjective
> **2** = forlorn, futile, impossible, pointless, useless, vain
> **3** = inadequate, pathetic, poor, useless (informal)

hopper noun a large, funnel-shaped container for storing things such as grain or sand.

horde noun a large group or number of people or animals.

horizon noun **1** the distant line where the sky seems to touch the land or sea. **2** Your horizons are the limits of what you want to do or are interested in. ▶ phrase **3** If something is **on the horizon**, it is almost certainly going to happen or be done in the future.

horizontal *adjective* (MATHS) flat and parallel with the horizon or with a line considered as a base.
> **horizontally** *adverb*

hormone *noun* a chemical made by one part of your body that stimulates or has a specific effect on another part of your body.
> **hormonal** *adjective*

horn *noun* **1** one of the hard, pointed growths on the heads of animals such as goats. **2** a musical instrument made of brass, consisting of a tube that is narrow at one end and wide at the other. **3** On vehicles, a horn is a warning device which makes a loud noise.

hornet *noun* a type of large wasp.

horoscope *noun* a prediction about what is going to happen to someone, based on the position of the stars when they were born.

horrendous *adjective* very unpleasant and shocking.

horrible *adjective* **1** disagreeable and unpleasant. **2** causing shock, fear or disgust.

horrible *adjective*
1 = awful, disagreeable, horrid (*old-fashioned*), mean, nasty, unpleasant 2 = appalling, dreadful, grim, gruesome, terrifying

horrid *adjective* (*old-fashioned*) very unpleasant indeed.

horrific *adjective* so bad or unpleasant that people are horrified.

horrify horrifies, horrifying, horrified *verb* If something horrifies you, it makes you feel dismay or disgust.
> **horrifying** *adjective*

horrify *verb*
= appal, disgust, dismay, outrage, shock, sicken

horror *noun* **1** a strong feeling of alarm, dismay and disgust. **2** If you have a horror of something, you fear it very much.

horror *noun*
1 = alarm, dread, fear, fright, panic, terror 2 = abhorrence (*formal*), aversion, disgust, hatred, loathing, revulsion

horse *noun* **1** a large animal with a mane and long tail, on which people can ride. **2** a piece of gymnastics equipment with four legs, used for jumping over.

horse *noun*
1 = brumby (*Australian and New Zealand*), equine (*formal*), moke (*Australian and New Zealand; slang*), nag (*informal*), pony

horseback *noun, adjective* You refer to someone who is riding a horse as someone 'on horseback', or a horseback rider.

horsepower *noun* Horsepower is a unit used for measuring how powerful an engine is, equal to about 746 watts.

horseradish *noun* Horseradish is the white root of a plant made into a hot-tasting sauce.

horseshoe *noun* a U-shaped piece of metal, nailed to the hard surface of a horse's hoof to protect it; also anything of this shape, often regarded as a good luck symbol.

horticulture *noun* Horticulture is the study and practice of growing flowers, fruit and vegetables.
> **horticultural** *adjective*

hose noun **1** a long flexible tube through which liquid or gas can be passed. ▶ verb **2** If you hose something, you wash or water it using a hose.

hosiery noun Hosiery consists of tights, socks and similar items, especially in shops.

hospice noun a hospital which provides care for people who are dying.

hospitable adjective friendly, generous and welcoming to guests or strangers. > **hospitality** noun

hospital noun a place where sick and injured people are treated and cared for.

host noun **1** The host of an event is the person that welcomes guests and provides food or accommodation for them. **2** The host of a radio or television show is the person who introduces it and talks to other people who take part in it. **3** a plant or animal with smaller plants or animals living on or in it. **4** A host of things is a large number of them. **5** In the Christian Church, the Host is the consecrated bread used in Mass or Holy Communion. ▶ verb **6** To host an event or programme means to act as its host.

hostage noun a person who is illegally held prisoner and threatened with injury or death unless certain demands are met by other people.

hostel noun a large building in which people can stay or live.

hostess noun a woman who welcomes guests or visitors and provides food or accommodation for them.

hostile adjective **1** unfriendly, aggressive and unpleasant. **2** relating to or involving the enemies of a country.

> **hostile** adjective
> **1** = antagonistic, belligerent, malevolent, unkind

hostility hostilities noun aggression or unfriendly behaviour towards a person or thing.

> **hostility** noun
> = animosity, antagonism, hatred, ill will, malice, resentment

hot hotter, hottest adjective **1** having a high temperature. **2** very spicy and causing a burning sensation in your mouth. **3** new, recent and exciting. **4** dangerous or difficult to deal with.

> **hot** adjective
> **1** = boiling, heated, scalding, scorching, warm **2** = peppery, spicy

hotbed noun A hotbed of some type of activity is a place that seems to encourage it.

hot dog noun a sausage served in a roll split lengthways.

hotel noun a building where people stay, paying for their room and sometimes also meals.

hothouse noun **1** a large heated greenhouse. **2** a place or situation of intense intellectual or emotional activity.

hot seat noun (informal) Someone who is in the hot seat has to make difficult decisions for which they will be held responsible.

hound noun **1** a dog, especially one used for hunting or racing. ▶ verb

2 If someone hounds you, they constantly pursue or trouble you.

hour noun **1** a unit of time equal to 60 minutes, of which there are 24 in a day. **2** The hour for something is the time when it happens. **3** The hour is also the time of day. ▷ **hourly** adjective, adverb

house noun **1** a building where a person or family lives. **2** a building used for a particular purpose: an auction house. **3** In a theatre or cinema, the house is the part where the audience sits; also the audience itself. ▷ verb **4** To house something means to keep it or contain it.

> **house** noun
> **1** = abode (old-fashioned), building, dwelling (formal), home, residence (formal)

houseboat noun a small boat which people live on that is tied up at a particular place on a river or canal.

household noun **1** all the people who live as a group in a house or flat. ▷ phrase **2** Someone who is **a household name** is very well-known. ▷ **householder** noun

housekeeper noun a person who is employed to do the cooking and cleaning in a house.

House of Commons noun The House of Commons is the more powerful of the two parts of the British Parliament. Its members are elected by the public.

House of Lords noun The House of Lords is the less powerful of the two parts of the British Parliament. Its members are unelected and come from noble families or are appointed as an honour for a life of public service.

House of Representatives noun **1** In Australia, the House of Representatives is the larger of the two parts of the Federal Parliament. **2** In New Zealand, the House of Representatives is the Parliament.

housewife housewives noun a married woman who does the chores in her home and does not have a paid job.

housing noun Housing is the buildings in which people live.

hover verb **1** When a bird, insect or aircraft hovers, it stays in the same position in the air. **2** If someone is hovering, they are hesitating because they cannot decide what to do.

hovercraft noun a vehicle which can travel over water or land supported by a cushion of air.

how adverb **1** 'How' is used to ask about, explain or refer to the way in which something is done, known or experienced: How did this happen? **2** 'How' is used to ask about or refer to a measurement or quantity: How much is it for the weekend? **3** 'How' is used to emphasise the following word or statement: How odd!

however adverb **1** You use 'however' when you are adding a comment that seems to contradict or contrast with what has just been said: For all his compassion, he is, however, surprisingly restrained. **2** You use 'however' to say that something makes no difference to a situation: However hard she tried, nothing seemed to work.

howl verb **1** To howl means to make a long, loud wailing noise such as that made by a dog when it is upset. ▷ noun **2** a long, loud wailing noise.

HQ an abbreviation for **headquarters**.

hub *noun* 1 the centre part of a wheel. 2 the most important or active part of a place or organisation.

hubbub *noun* Hubbub is great noise or confusion.

huddle *verb* 1 If you huddle up or are huddled, you are curled up with your arms and legs close to your body. 2 When people or animals huddle together, they sit or stand close to each other, often for warmth. ▶ *noun* 3 A huddle of people or things is a small group of them.

hue *noun* 1 (literary) a colour or a particular shade of a colour.
▶ *phrase* 2 If people raise a **hue and cry**, they are very angry about something and protest.

huff *phrase* (informal) If you are in a **huff**, you are sulking or offended about something. > **huffy** *adjective*

hug hugs, hugging, hugged *verb* 1 If you hug someone, you put your arms round them and hold them close to you. 2 To hug the ground or a stretch of water or land means to keep very close to it. ▶ *noun* 3 If you give someone a hug, you hold them close to you.

hug *verb*
1 = clasp, cuddle, embrace, squeeze
▶ *noun* 3 = cuddle, embrace

huge *adjective* extremely large in amount, size or degree.

huge *adjective*
= colossal, enormous, giant, immense, massive, vast

hulk *noun* 1 a large, heavy person or thing. 2 the body of a ship that

has been wrecked or abandoned.
> **hulking** *adjective*

hull *noun* The hull of a ship is the main part of its body that sits in the water.

hum hums, humming, hummed *verb* 1 To hum means to make a continuous low noise. 2 If you hum, you sing with your lips closed. ▶ *noun* 3 a continuous low noise.

human *adjective* 1 relating to, concerning or typical of people.
▶ *noun* 2 a person. > **humanly** *adverb*

human being *noun* a person.

humane *adjective* showing kindness and sympathy towards others.

humane *adjective*
= benevolent, caring, charitable, compassionate, kind, merciful, thoughtful

humanism *noun* (RE) Humanism is the belief in people's ability to achieve happiness and fulfilment without depending on religion or superstition.

humanitarian *noun* 1 a person who works for the welfare of humanity. ▶ *adjective* 2 concerned with the welfare of humanity.
> **humanitarianism** *noun*

humanity *noun* 1 Humanity is people in general. 2 Humanity is also the condition of being human. 3 Someone who has humanity is kind and sympathetic.

human rights *plural noun* (CITIZENSHIP) Human rights are the rights of individuals to freedom and justice.

humble *adjective* 1 A humble person is modest and thinks that he or she has very little value.

2 Something that is humble is small, or not very important or special. ▶ *verb* **3** To humble someone means to make them feel humiliated. ▶ **humbly** *adverb*

> **humble** *adjective*
> **1** = meek, modest, unassuming
> **2** = lowly, modest, ordinary, simple
> ▶ *verb* **3** = disgrace, humiliate

humbug *noun* **1** a hard black and white striped sweet that tastes of peppermint. **2** Humbug is speech or writing that is obviously dishonest or untrue.

humdrum *adjective* ordinary, dull and boring.

humid *adjective* If it is humid, the air feels damp, heavy and warm.

> **humid** *adjective*
> = clammy, muggy, steamy, sticky

humidity *noun* Humidity is the amount of moisture in the air, or the state of being humid.

humiliate *verb* To humiliate someone means to make them feel ashamed or appear stupid to other people. > **humiliation** *noun*

> **humiliate** *verb*
> = disgrace, embarrass, humble, put down, shame

humility *noun* Humility is the quality of being modest and humble.

humour *noun* **1** Humour is the quality of being funny. **2** Humour is also the ability to be amused by certain things. **3** Someone's humour is the mood they are in. ▶ *verb* **4** If you humour someone, you are especially kind to them and do whatever they want. > **humorous** *adjective*

humour *noun*
1 = comedy, wit **3** = frame of mind, mood, spirits, temper
▶ *verb* **4** = flatter, indulge, mollify, pander to

hump *noun* **1** a small, rounded lump or mound. ▶ *verb* **2** (*informal*) If you hump something heavy, you carry or move it with difficulty.

hunch *noun* **1** a feeling or suspicion about something, not based on facts or evidence. ▶ *verb* **2** If you hunch your shoulders, you raise your shoulders and lean forwards.

hundred the number 100. > **hundredth** *adjective*

hung a past tense and past participle of **hang**.

Hungarian *adjective* **1** belonging or relating to Hungary. ▶ *noun* **2** someone who comes from Hungary. **3** Hungarian is the main language spoken in Hungary.

hunger *noun* **1** Hunger is the need to eat or the desire to eat. **2** A hunger for something is a strong need or desire for it. ▶ *verb* **3** If you hunger for something, you want it very much.

hunger strike *noun* a refusal to eat anything at all, especially by prisoners, as a form of protest.

hungry hungrier, hungriest *adjective* needing or wanting to eat. > **hungrily** *adverb*

> **hungry** *adjective*
> = famished, ravenous, starving

hunk *noun* A hunk of something is a large piece of it.

hunt *verb* **1** To hunt means to chase wild animals to kill them for food or for sport. **2** If you hunt for something, you search for it. ▶ *noun* **3** the act of hunting. > **hunter** *noun* > **hunting** *adjective, noun*

hurdle *noun* **1** one of the frames or barriers that you jump over in an athletics race called hurdles. **2** a problem or difficulty: *hurdles exist for anyone seeking to do postgraduate study.*

hurl *verb* **1** To hurl something means to throw it with great force. **2** If you hurl insults at someone, you insult them aggressively and repeatedly.

hurray or **hurrah** or **hooray** *interjection* an exclamation of excitement or approval.

hurricane *noun* (GEOGRAPHY) A hurricane is a violent wind or storm, usually force 12 or above on the Beaufort scale.

hurry hurries, hurrying, hurried *verb* **1** To hurry means to move or do something as quickly as possible. **2** To hurry something means to make it happen more quickly. ▶ *noun* **3** Hurry is the speed with which you do something quickly. > **hurried** *adjective*

> **hurry** *verb*
> **1** = dash, fly, get a move on (*informal*), rush, scurry
> **2** = accelerate, hasten, quicken, speed up

hurt hurts, hurting, hurt *verb* **1** To hurt someone means to cause them physical pain. **2** If a part of your body hurts, you feel pain there. **3** If you hurt yourself, you injure yourself. **4** To hurt someone also means to make them unhappy by being unkind

or thoughtless towards them. ▶ *adjective* **5** If someone feels hurt, they feel unhappy because of someone's unkindness towards them. > **hurtful** *adjective*

> **hurt** *verb*
> **1** = harm, injure, wound
> **4** = distress, sadden, upset, wound
> ▶ *adjective* **5** = aggrieved, offended, upset, wounded

hurtle *verb* To hurtle means to move or travel very fast indeed, especially in an uncontrolled way.

husband *noun* A person's husband is the man they are married to.

husbandry *noun* **1** Husbandry is the art or skill of farming. **2** Husbandry is also the art or skill of managing something economically.

hush *verb* **1** If you tell someone to hush, you are telling them to be quiet. **2** To hush something up means to keep it secret, especially something dishonest involving important people. ▶ *noun* **3** If there is a hush, it is quiet and still. > **hushed** *adjective*

husk *noun* Husks are the dry outer coverings of grain or seed.

husky huskier, huskiest; huskies *adjective* **1** A husky voice is rough or hoarse. ▶ *noun* **2** a large, strong dog with a thick coat, often used to pull sledges across snow.

hustle *verb* To hustle someone means to make them move by pushing and jostling them.

hut *noun* a small, simple building with one or two rooms.

hybrid *noun* **1** a plant or animal that has been bred from two different types of plant or animal.

2 anything that is a mixture of two other things.

hydraulic *adjective* operated by water or other fluid which is under pressure.

hydraulics *noun* Hydraulics is the study and use of systems that work using hydraulic pressure.

hydrogen *noun* (SCIENCE) Hydrogen is the lightest gas and the simplest chemical element. It is colourless and odourless. Its atomic number is 1 and its symbol is H.

hyena; also spelt **hyaena** *noun* a wild doglike animal of Africa and Asia that hunts in packs.

hygiene *noun* (DGT) Hygiene is the practice of keeping yourself and your surroundings clean, especially to stop the spread of disease. > **hygienic** *adjective* > **hygienically** *adverb*

> **hygiene** *noun*
> = cleanliness, sanitation

hymn *noun* (RE) a Christian song in praise of God.

hype *noun* Hype is the use of a lot of publicity and advertising to make people interested in something.

hyperactive *adjective* A hyperactive person is unable to relax and is always in a state of restless activity.

hyperbole *noun* Hyperbole is a style of speech or writing which uses exaggeration.

hypertension *noun* Hypertension is a medical condition in which a person has high blood pressure.

hyphen *noun* (ENGLISH) the punctuation mark (-) which is used to join together words or

parts of words, as in the word 'left-handed'. > **hyphenate** *verb* > **hyphenation** *noun*

hypnosis *noun* Hypnosis is an artificially produced state of relaxation in which the mind is very receptive to suggestion.

hypocrisy hypocrisies *noun* Hypocrisy is pretending to have beliefs or qualities that you do not really have, so that you seem a better person than you are. > **hypocritical** *adjective* > **hypocrite** *noun*

hypothermia *noun* (SCIENCE) Hypothermia is a condition in which a person is very ill because their body temperature has unusually low for a long time.

hypothesis hypotheses *noun* (SCIENCE) an explanation or theory which has not yet been proved to be correct.

hypothetical *adjective* based on assumption rather than on fact or reality. > **hypothetically** *adverb*

hysterectomy hysterectomies *noun* an operation to remove a woman's womb.

hysteria *noun* Hysteria is a state of uncontrolled excitement or panic.

hysterical *adjective* **1** Someone who is hysterical is in a state of uncontrolled excitement or panic. **2** (*informal*) Something that is hysterical is extremely funny. > **hysterically** *adverb* > **hysterics** *noun*

> **hysterical** *adjective*
> **1** = frantic, frenzied, overwrought, raving
> **2** = comical, hilarious

Ii

I *pronoun* A speaker or writer uses 'I' to refer to himself or herself.

ibis ibises *noun* a large wading bird with a long, thin, curved bill that lives in warm countries.

-ible *suffix* another form of the suffix **-able**.

-ic or -ical *suffix* '-ic' and '-ical' form adjectives from nouns. For example, *ironic* or *ironical* can be formed from *irony*.

ice *noun* 1 water that has frozen solid. 2 an ice cream. ▶ *verb* 3 If you ice cakes, you cover them with icing. 4 If something ices over or ices up, it becomes covered with a layer of ice. ▶ *phrase* 5 If you do something to **break the ice**, you make people feel relaxed and comfortable.

Ice Age *noun* a period of time lasting thousands of years when a lot of the earth's surface was covered with ice.

iceberg *noun* a large mass of ice floating in the sea.

ice cream *noun* a very cold sweet food made from frozen cream.

ice hockey *noun* a type of hockey played on ice, with two teams of six players.

Icelandic *adjective* 1 belonging or relating to Iceland. ▶ *noun* 2 the main language spoken in Iceland.

icing *noun* a mixture of powdered sugar and water or egg whites, used to decorate cakes.

icon *noun* 1 (ICT) a picture on a computer screen representing a program that can be activated by moving the cursor over it. 2 in the Orthodox Churches, a holy picture of Christ, the Virgin Mary or a saint.

ICT an abbreviation for 'Information and Communication Technology'.

icy icier, iciest *adjective* 1 Something which is icy is very cold. 2 An icy road has ice on it. > **icily** *adverb*

ID *noun* (*informal*) ID is something which proves who you are, such as a passport. ID is an abbreviation for 'identification document'.

idea *noun* 1 a plan, suggestion or thought that you have after thinking about a problem. 2 an opinion or belief. 3 An idea of something is what you know about it.

> **idea** *noun*
> 1 = plan, recommendation, scheme, solution, suggestion
> 2 = belief, conviction, impression, notion, opinion, view 3 = clue, guess, hint, inkling, notion, suspicion

ideal *noun* 1 a principle or idea that you try to achieve because it seems perfect to you. 2 Your ideal of something is the person or thing that seems the best example of it. ▶ *adjective* 3 The ideal person or thing is the best possible person or thing for the situation.

ideal *noun*
1 = principle, standard, value
2 = epitome, example, model, paragon, prototype, standard
▶ *adjective* 3 = classic, complete, consummate, model, perfect, supreme

idealism *noun* behaviour that is based on a person's ideals. > **idealist** *noun* > **idealistic** *adjective*

ideally *adverb* 1 If you say that ideally something should happen, you mean that you would like it to happen but you know that it is not likely. 2 Ideally means perfectly.

identical *adjective* exactly the same. > **identically** *adverb*

identification *noun* 1 The identification of someone or something is the act of identifying them.
2 Identification is a document, such as a driving licence or passport, which proves who you are.

identify identifies, identifying, identified *verb* 1 To identify someone or something is to recognise them or name them. 2 If you identify with someone, you understand their feelings and ideas. > **identifiable** *adjective*

identify *verb*
1 = diagnose, label, name, pinpoint, place, recognise
2 identify with = associate with, empathise with, feel for, relate to, respond to

identity identities *noun* 1 the characteristics that make you who you are. 2 (MATHS) an equation that is valid for all values of its variables.

ideology ideologies *noun* a set of political beliefs. > **ideological** *adjective* > **ideologically** *adverb*

idiom *noun* (ENGLISH) a group of words whose meaning together is different from all the words taken individually. For example, 'It's raining cats and dogs' is an idiom.

idiot *noun* someone who is stupid or foolish.

idiot *noun*
= fool, galah (*Australian*; *informal*), imbecile, oaf, twit (*informal*)

idiotic *adjective* extremely foolish or silly. > **idiotically** *adverb*

idiotic *adjective*
= crazy (*informal*), daft (*British*; *informal*), dumb (*informal*), foolish, senseless, stupid

idle *adjective* If you are idle, you are doing nothing. > **idly** *adverb*

idle *adjective*
= jobless, redundant, unemployed

idol *noun* 1 a famous person who is loved and admired by fans. 2 (RE) a picture or statue which is worshipped as if it were a god.

idyll *noun* a situation which is peaceful and beautiful. > **idyllic** *adjective*

i.e. i.e. means 'that is', and is used before giving more information. It is an abbreviation for the Latin expression 'id est'.

if *conjunction* 1 on the condition that: *I shall stay if I can.* 2 whether: *I asked her if she wanted to go.*

igloo igloos *noun* a dome-shaped house built out of blocks of snow by Inuit.

ignite verb If you ignite something or if it ignites, it starts burning.

ignition noun In a car, the ignition is the part of the engine where the fuel is ignited.

ignominious adjective shameful or considered wrong.

ignorant adjective 1 If you are ignorant of something, you do not know about it. 2 Someone who is ignorant does not know about things in general.
> **ignorance** noun

> **ignorant** adjective
> 1 = inexperienced, innocent, oblivious, unaware, unconscious 2 = green (informal), naive, unaware

ignore verb If you ignore someone or something, you deliberately do not take any notice of them.

> **ignore** verb
> = blank (slang), discount, disregard, neglect, overlook

iguana noun a large, tropical lizard.

ill adjective 1 unhealthy or sick. 2 harmful or unpleasant: ill effects. ▶ plural noun 3 Ills are difficulties or problems. ▶ phrase 4 If you feel **ill at ease**, you feel unable to relax.

> **ill** adjective
> 1 = ailing, poorly (British; informal), queasy, sick, unhealthy, unwell

illegal adjective forbidden by the law. > **illegally** adverb > **illegality** noun

> **illegal** adjective
> = banned, criminal, illicit, outlawed, prohibited, unlawful

illegible adjective Writing which is illegible is unclear and very difficult to read.

ill-fated adjective doomed to end unhappily.

illicit adjective not allowed by law or not approved of by society.

illiterate adjective unable to read or write. > **illiteracy** noun

illness noun 1 Illness is the experience of being ill. 2 a particular disease.

> **illness** noun
> 2 = affliction, ailment, complaint, disease, disorder, lurgy (British, Australian and New Zealand; informal), sickness

illogical adjective An illogical feeling or action is not reasonable or sensible. > **illogically** adverb

illuminate verb To illuminate something is to shine light on it to make it easier to see.

illumination noun 1 Illumination is lighting. 2 Illuminations are the coloured lights put up to decorate a town, especially at Christmas.

illusion noun 1 a false belief which you think is true. 2 (ART) a false appearance of reality which deceives the eye.

> **illusion** noun
> 1 = delusion, fallacy, fancy, misconception
> 2 = hallucination, mirage, semblance

illusory adjective seeming to be true, but actually false.

illustrate verb 1 (EXAM TERM) If you illustrate a point, you explain it or make it clearer, often by using examples. 2 If you illustrate a book, you put pictures in it.

> **illustrator** *noun* > **illustrative** *adjective*

illustration *noun* 1 an example or a story which is used to make a point clear. 2 a picture in a book.

illustrious *adjective* An illustrious person is famous and respected.

ill will *noun* Ill will is a feeling of hostility.

image *noun* 1 a mental picture of someone or something. 2 the appearance which a person, group or organisation presents to the public.

imagery *noun* (ENGLISH) The imagery of a poem or book is the descriptive language used in it.

imaginary *adjective* Something that is imaginary exists only in your mind, not in real life.

> **imaginary** *adjective*
> = fictional, fictitious, hypothetical, ideal, illusory, invented, mythological

imagination *noun* the ability to form new and exciting ideas.

> **imagination** *noun*
> = creativity, ingenuity, inventiveness, originality, vision

imaginative *adjective* Someone who is imaginative can easily form new or exciting ideas in their mind.

imagine *verb* 1 If you imagine something, you form an idea of it in your mind, or you think you have seen or heard it but you have not really. 2 If you imagine that something is the case, you believe it is the case. > **imaginable** *adjective*

imagine *verb*
1 = conceive, envisage, fantasise, picture, visualise
2 = assume, believe, gather, guess (*informal*), suppose, suspect

imam *noun* (RE) a person who leads a group in prayer in a mosque.

imbalance *noun* If there is an imbalance between things, they are unequal.

imitate *verb* To imitate someone or something is to copy them.
> **imitator** *noun* > **imitative** *adjective*

> **imitate** *verb*
> = ape, copy, emulate, impersonate, mimic, simulate

imitation *noun* a copy of something else.

immaculate *adjective*
1 completely clean and tidy.
2 without any mistakes at all.

immaterial *adjective* Something that is immaterial is not important.

immature *adjective* 1 Something that is immature has not finished growing or developing. 2 A person who is immature does not behave in a sensible adult way.
> **immaturity** *noun*

immediate *adjective* 1 Something that is immediate happens or is done without delay. 2 Your immediate relatives and friends are the ones most closely connected or related to you.
> **immediacy** *noun*

> **immediate** *adjective*
> 1 = instant, instantaneous
> 2 = close, direct, near

immediately adverb 1 If something happens immediately, it happens right away.
2 Immediately means very near in time or position: *immediately behind the house.*

> **immediately** adverb
> 1 = at once, directly, instantly, now, promptly, right away, straight away 2 = closely, directly, right

immemorial adjective If something has been happening from time immemorial, it has been happening longer than anyone can remember.

immense adjective very large or huge. > **immensely** adverb

> **immense** adjective
> = colossal, enormous, giant, gigantic, huge, massive, vast

immerse verb 1 If you are immersed in an activity, you are completely involved in it. 2 If you immerse something in a liquid, you put it into the liquid so that it is completely covered.
> **immersion** noun

immigrant noun (HISTORY) someone who has come to live permanently in a new country.
> **immigrate** verb > **immigration** noun

imminent adjective If something is imminent, it is going to happen very soon. > **imminently** adverb

> **imminent** adjective
> = close, coming, forthcoming, impending, looming, near, upcoming

immobile adjective not moving.
> **immobility** noun

immoral adjective (RE) If you describe someone or their behaviour as immoral, you mean that they do not fit in with most people's idea of what is right and proper. > **immorality** noun

immortal adjective 1 Something that is immortal is famous and will be remembered for a long time. 2 In stories, someone who is immortal will never die.

immortality noun (RE) Immortality is never dying. In many religions, people believe that the soul of a person lives forever or continues to exist in some form.

immovable; also spelt **immoveable** adjective Something that is immovable is fixed and cannot be moved.

immune adjective 1 If you are immune to a particular disease, you cannot catch it. 2 If someone or something is immune to something, they are able to avoid it or are not affected by it.
> **immunity** noun

> **immune** adjective
> 2 = exempt, free, protected, resistant, safe, unaffected

immune system noun (SCIENCE) Your body's immune system consists of your white blood cells, which fight disease by producing antibodies or germs to kill germs which come into your body.

impact noun 1 The impact that someone or something has is the impression that they make or the effect that they have. 2 Impact is the action of one object hitting another, usually with a lot of force.

impair verb To impair something is to damage it so that it stops working properly.

impart verb (formal) To impart information to someone is to pass it on to them.

impartial adjective Someone who is impartial has a view of something which is fair or not biased. > **impartially** adverb > **impartiality** noun

impasse noun a difficult situation in which it is impossible to find a solution.

impassioned adjective full of emotion.

impassive adjective showing no emotion. > **impassively** adverb

impatient adjective 1 Someone who is impatient becomes annoyed easily or is quick to lose their temper when things go wrong. 2 If you are impatient to do something, you are eager and do not want to wait. > **impatiently** adverb > **impatience** noun

> **impatient** adjective
> 1 = brusque, curt, irritable
> 2 = eager, restless

impeccable adjective excellent, without any faults. > **impeccably** adverb

impede verb If you impede someone, you make their progress difficult.

> **impede** verb
> = block, delay, disrupt, get in the way, hamper, hinder, obstruct

impediment noun something that makes it difficult to move, develop or do something properly.

impending adjective (formal) You use 'impending' to describe something that is going to happen very soon.

impenetrable adjective impossible to get through.

imperative adjective 1 Something that is imperative is extremely urgent or important. ▶ noun 2 (ENGLISH) In grammar, an imperative is the form of a verb that is used for giving orders.

imperfect adjective 1 Something that is imperfect has faults or problems. ▶ noun 2 (ENGLISH) (MFL) In grammar, the imperfect is a tense used to describe continuous or repeated actions which happened in the past. > **imperfectly** adverb > **imperfection** noun

> **imperfect** adjective
> 1 = broken, damaged, defective, faulty, flawed

imperial adjective 1 (HISTORY) Imperial means relating to an empire or an emperor or empress. 2 The imperial system of measurement is the measuring system which uses inches, feet and yards, ounces and pounds, and pints and gallons.

imperialism noun HISTORY a system of rule in which a rich and powerful nation controls other nations. > **imperialist** adjective, noun

imperious adjective proud and domineering. > **imperiously** adverb

impersonal adjective Something that is impersonal makes you feel that individuals and their feelings do not matter.

> **impersonal** adjective
> = aloof, cold, detached, formal, neutral, remote

impersonate verb If you impersonate someone, you pretend to be that person.
> **impersonation** noun
> **impersonator** noun

impertinent adjective disrespectful and rude.
> **impertinently** adverb
> **impertinence** noun

impetuous adjective If you are impetuous, you act quickly without thinking. > **impetuously** adverb > **impetuosity** noun

impetus noun 1 An impetus is the stimulating effect that something has on a situation, which causes it to develop more quickly. 2 In physics, impetus is the force that starts an object moving and resists changes in speed or direction.

impinge verb If something impinges on your life, it has an effect on you and influences you.

implacable adjective Someone who is implacable is being harsh and refuses to change their mind.
> **implacably** adverb

implant verb 1 To implant something into a person's body is to put it there, usually by means of an operation. ▶ noun 2 something that has been implanted into someone's body.

implausible adjective very unlikely. > **implausibly** adverb

implement verb 1 If you implement something such as a plan, you carry it out. ▶ noun 2 An implement is a tool. > **implementation** noun

implicate verb If you are implicated in a crime, you are shown to be involved in it.

implication noun something that is suggested or implied but not stated directly.

implicit adjective 1 expressed in an indirect way. 2 If you have an implicit belief in something, you have no doubts about it.
> **implicitly** adverb

implore verb If you implore someone to do something, you beg them to do it.

> **implore** verb
> = beg, beseech (literary), plead with

imply implies, implying, implied verb If you imply that something is the case, you suggest it in an indirect way.

import verb 1 If you import something from another country, you bring it into your country or have it sent there. 2 ICT If you import data, you open it using a different software program. ▶ noun 3 Imports are goods that are made in another country and sent to your own country to be sold there. > **importer** noun

important adjective 1 Something that is important is very valuable, necessary or significant. 2 An important person has great influence or power.
> **importantly** adverb
> **importance** noun

> **important** adjective
> 1 = momentous, serious, significant, weighty
> 2 = eminent, foremost, influential, leading, notable, powerful

impose verb 1 If you impose something on people, you force it on them. 2 If someone imposes on you, they unreasonably expect

you to do something for them.
> **imposition** noun

> **impose** verb
> 1 = dictate, enforce, inflict, levy, ordain 2 **impose on** = abuse, take advantage of, use

imposing adjective having an impressive appearance or manner.

impossible adjective Something that is impossible cannot happen, be done, or be believed.
> **impossibly** adverb
> **impossibility** noun

> **impossible** adjective
> = absurd, hopeless, inconceivable, ludicrous, out of the question, unthinkable

imposter; also spelt **impostor** noun a person who pretends to be someone else in order to get things they want.

impotent adjective Someone who is impotent has no power to influence events or people.
> **impotently** adverb > **impotence** noun

impound verb If something you own is impounded, the police or other officials take it.

impoverished adjective Someone who is impoverished is very poor.

impractical adjective not practical, sensible or realistic.

impregnable adjective A building or other structure that is impregnable is so strong that it cannot be broken into or captured.

impress verb 1 If you impress someone, you make them admire or respect you. 2 If you impress something on someone, you make them understand the importance of it.

impression noun An impression of someone or something is the way they look or seem to you.

> **impression** noun
> = feeling, hunch, idea, notion, sense

impressionable adjective easy to influence.

> **impressionable** adjective
> = gullible, open, receptive, sensitive, susceptible, vulnerable

impressive adjective If something is impressive, it impresses you.

> **impressive** adjective
> = awesome, exciting, grand, powerful, stirring, striking

imprint noun 1 If something leaves an imprint on your mind, it has a strong and lasting effect. 2 the mark left by the pressure of one object on another. ▶ verb 3 If something is imprinted on your memory, it is firmly fixed there.

imprison verb If you are imprisoned, you are locked up, usually in a prison.
> **imprisonment** noun

> **imprison** verb
> = confine, detain, incarcerate, jail, lock up, send to prison

improbable adjective not probable or likely to happen.

> **improbable** adjective
> = doubtful, dubious, far-fetched, implausible, unbelievable, unlikely

impromptu adjective An impromptu action is one done without planning or organisation.

improper adjective 1 rude or shocking. 2 illegal or dishonest. 3 not suitable or correct.
> **improperly** adverb

impropriety noun (formal) Impropriety is improper behaviour.

improve verb If something improves or if you improve it, it gets better or becomes more valuable.

> **improve** verb
= advance, better, enhance, look up (informal), progress, upgrade

improvement noun 1 the fact or process of getting better. 2 An improvement in something is a change in something that makes it better.

> **improvement** noun
1 = advance, development, enhancement, progress, upturn

improvise verb 1 If you improvise something, you make or do something without planning in advance, and with whatever materials are available. 2 (DRAMA) (MUSIC) When musicians or actors improvise, they make up the music or words as they go along.

impudent adjective If someone is impudent, something they say or do is cheeky and lacking in respect. > **impudently** adverb

impulse noun a strong urge to do something.

impulsive adjective If you are impulsive, you do things suddenly, without thinking about them carefully.
> **impulsively** adverb

impure adjective Something which is impure contains small amounts of other things, such as dirt.

impurity impurities noun 1 Impurity is the quality of being impure. 2 If something contains impurities, it contains small amounts of dirt or other substances that should not be there.

in preposition, adverb 'In' is used to indicate position, direction, time and manner: boarding schools in England; in the past few years.

inability noun a lack of ability to do something.

> **inability** noun
= impotence, inadequacy, incompetence, ineptitude

inaccessible adjective impossible or very difficult to reach.

inaccurate adjective not accurate or correct.

inadequate adjective 1 If something is inadequate, there is not enough of it. 2 not good enough in quality for a particular purpose. 3 If someone feels inadequate, they feel they do not possess the skills necessary to do a particular job or to cope with life in general. > **inadequately** adverb > **inadequacy** noun

> **inadequate** adjective
1 = insufficient, lacking, poor, scarce, short 2 = deficient, incapable, incompetent, inept, pathetic, useless (informal)

inadvertent adjective not intentional. > **inadvertently** adverb

inane adjective silly or stupid.
> **inanely** adverb > **inanity** noun

inanimate *adjective* An inanimate object is not alive.

inappropriate *adjective* not suitable for a particular purpose or occasion.

> **inappropriate** *adjective*
> = improper, incongruous, unfit, unseemly, unsuitable, untimely

inarticulate *adjective* If you are inarticulate, you are unable to express yourself well or easily in speech.

inaudible *adjective* not loud enough to be heard. > **inaudibly** *adverb*

inaugurate *verb* 1 To inaugurate a new scheme is to start it. 2 To inaugurate a new leader is to officially establish them in their new position in a special ceremony. > **inauguration** *noun* > **inaugural** *adjective*

inbox *noun* a folder on a computer or phone where emails are received.

incandescent *adjective* Something which is incandescent gives out light when it is heated. > **incandescence** *noun*

incapable *adjective* 1 Someone who is incapable of doing something is not able to do it. 2 An incapable person is weak and helpless.

incarcerate *verb* To incarcerate someone is to lock them up. > **incarceration** *noun*

incendiary *adjective* An incendiary weapon is one which sets fire to things.

incense *noun* Incense is a spicy substance which is burned to create a sweet smell, especially during religious services.

incensed *adjective* If you are incensed by something, it makes you extremely angry.

incentive *noun* something that encourages you to do something.

> **incentive** *noun*
> = bait, encouragement, inducement, motivation, stimulus

inception *noun (formal)* The inception of a project is the start of it.

incessant *adjective* continuing without stopping. > **incessantly** *adverb*

inch *noun* 1 a unit of length equal to about 2.54 centimetres. ▶ *verb* 2 To inch forward is to move forward slowly.

incident *noun* an event.

> **incident** *noun*
> = circumstance, episode, event, happening, occasion, occurrence

incidental *adjective* occurring as a minor part of something. > **incidentally** *adverb*

incinerator *noun* a furnace for burning rubbish.

incision *noun* a sharp cut, usually made by a surgeon operating on a patient.

incisive *adjective* Incisive language is clear and forceful.

incite *verb* If you incite someone to do something, you encourage them to do it by making them angry or excited. > **incitement** *noun*

> **incite** *verb*
> = agitate for, goad, instigate, provoke, whip up

inclination noun If you have an inclination to do something, you want to do it.

incline verb 1 If you are inclined to behave in a certain way, you often behave that way or you want to behave that way. ▶ noun 2 a slope.

include verb If one thing includes another, it has the second thing as one of its parts. ▶ **including** preposition

> **include** verb
> = contain, cover, embrace, encompass, incorporate, involve

inclusion noun The inclusion of one thing in another is the act of making it part of the other thing.

inclusive adjective A price that is inclusive includes all the goods and services that are being offered, with no extra charge for any of them.

incognito adverb If you are travelling incognito, you are travelling in disguise.

incoherent adjective If someone is incoherent, they are talking in an unclear or rambling way.
> **incoherence** noun

income noun the money a person earns.

> **income** noun
> = earnings, pay, profits, salary, takings, wages

income tax noun Income tax is a part of someone's salary which they have to pay regularly to the state.

incoming adjective coming in.

incomparable adjective Something that is incomparable is so good that it cannot be compared with anything else.

> **incomparably** adverb

> **incomparable** adjective
> = inimitable, peerless (literary), superlative, supreme, unparalleled, unrivalled

incompatible adjective Two things or people are incompatible if they are unable to live or exist together because they are completely different.
> **incompatibility** noun

incompetent adjective Someone who is incompetent does not have the ability to do something properly. > **incompetently** adverb
> **incompetence** noun

> **incompetent** adjective
> = bungling, cowboy (British; informal), incapable, inept, unable, useless (informal)

incomplete adjective not complete or finished.
> **incompletely** adverb

> **incomplete** adjective
> = deficient, half-pie (New Zealand; informal), insufficient, partial

incomprehensible adjective not able to be understood.

inconceivable adjective impossible to believe.

inconclusive adjective not leading to a decision or to a definite result.

incongruous adjective Something that is incongruous seems strange because it does not fit in to a place or situation.
> **incongruously** adverb

inconsequential adjective Something that is inconsequential is not very important.

inconsistent *adjective* Someone or something that is inconsistent is unpredictable and behaves differently in similar situations.
> **inconsistently** *adverb*

inconspicuous *adjective* not easily seen or obvious.
> **inconspicuously** *adverb*

inconvenience *noun* 1 If something causes inconvenience, it causes difficulty or problems.
▶ *verb* 2 To inconvenience someone is to cause them trouble, difficulty or problems.
> **inconvenient** *adjective*
> **inconveniently** *adverb*

incorporate *verb* If something is incorporated into another thing, it becomes part of that thing.
> **incorporation** *noun*

incorrect *adjective* wrong or untrue. > **incorrectly** *adverb*

increase *verb* 1 If something increases, it becomes larger in amount. ▶ *noun* 2 a rise in the number, level or amount of something. > **increasingly** *adverb*

> **increase** *verb*
> 1 = enlarge, expand, extend, grow, multiply, swell
> ▶ *noun* 2 = gain, growth, increment, rise, upsurge

incredible *adjective* 1 totally amazing. 2 impossible to believe.
> **incredibly** *adverb*

> **incredible** *adjective*
> 1 = amazing, astonishing, astounding, extraordinary, marvellous, sensational (*informal*) 2 = absurd, far-fetched, improbable, unbelievable, unimaginable, unthinkable

incredulous *adjective* If you are incredulous, you are unable to believe something because it is very surprising or shocking.
> **incredulity** *noun*

increment *noun* the amount by which something increases, or a regular increase in someone's salary. > **incremental** *adjective*

incriminate *verb* If something incriminates you, it suggests that you are involved in a crime.

incubator *noun* a piece of hospital equipment in which sick or weak newborn babies are kept warm.

incumbent (*formal*) *adjective* 1 If it is incumbent on you to do something, it is your duty to do it.
▶ *noun* 2 the person in a particular official position.

incur incurs, incurring, incurred *verb* If you incur something unpleasant, you cause it to happen.

incurable *adjective* An incurable disease is one which cannot be cured.

indebted *adjective* If you are indebted to someone, you are grateful to them.

indecent *adjective* Something that is indecent is shocking or rude.
> **indecently** *adverb* > **indecency** *noun*

> **indecent** *adjective*
> = crude, improper, rude, vulgar

indeed *adverb* You use 'indeed' to strengthen a point that you are making: *very good indeed.*

indefatigable *adjective* People who never get tired of doing something are indefatigable.

indefinite *adjective* 1 If something is indefinite, no time to finish has been decided. 2 Indefinite

also means vague or not exact.
> **indefinitely** *adverb*

indelible *adjective* unable to be removed.

indemnity *noun* (formal) Indemnity is protection against damage or loss.

independence *noun*
1 Independence is not relying on anyone else. 2 (HISTORY) A nation or state gains its independence when it stops being ruled or governed by another country and has its own government and laws.

independent *adjective*
1 Something that is independent happens or exists separately from other people or things. 2 Someone who is independent does not need other people's help. 3 An independent nation is one that is not ruled or governed by another country. > **independently** *adverb*

> **independent** *adjective*
> 1 = autonomous, free, separate, unrelated 2 = individualistic, liberated, self-sufficient, unaided

indeterminate *adjective* not certain or definite.

index indexes or indices *noun*
1 (ENGLISH) An index is an alphabetical list at the back of a book, referring to items in the book. 2 (LIBRARY) An index is also an alphabetical list of all the books in a library, arranged by title, author or subject. 3 (MATHS) a number or symbol placed above and to the right of a number, indicating the number of times the number is to be multiplied by itself. ▶ *verb* 4 To index a book or collection of information

means to provide an index for it.

index finger *noun* your first finger, next to your thumb.

Indian *adjective* 1 belonging or relating to India. ▶ *noun* 2 someone who comes from India. 3 someone descended from the people who lived in North, South or Central America before Europeans arrived.

indicate *verb* 1 If something indicates something, it shows that it is true. 2 If you indicate something to someone, you point to it. 3 If you indicate a fact, you mention it. 4 If the driver of a vehicle indicates, they give a signal to show which way they are going to turn.

> **indicate** *verb*
> 1 = denote, reveal, show, signal, signify

indication *noun* a sign of what someone feels or what is likely to happen.

> **indication** *noun*
> = clue, hint, sign, signal, suggestion, warning

indicative *adjective* 1 If something is indicative of something else, it is a sign of that thing. ▶ *noun* 2 (ENGLISH) If a verb is used in the indicative, it is in the form used for making statements.

indicator *noun* 1 something which tells you what something is like or what is happening. 2 A car's indicators are the lights at the front and back which are used to show when it is turning left or right. 3 (SCIENCE) a substance used in chemistry that shows if another substance is an acid or alkali by changing colour when it comes into contact with it.

indict *verb* (*formal*) To indict someone is to charge them officially with a crime. > **indictment** *noun*

indifferent *adjective* 1 If you are indifferent to something, you have no interest in it. 2 If something is indifferent, it is of a poor quality or low standard. > **indifferently** *adverb* > **indifference** *noun*

indigenous *adjective* If something is indigenous to a country, it comes from that country.

indigestion *noun* Indigestion is a pain you get when you find it difficult to digest food.

indignant *adjective* If you are indignant, you feel angry about something that you think is unfair. > **indignantly** *adverb*

indignation *noun* Indignation is anger about something that you think is unfair.

indignity indignities *noun* something that makes you feel embarrassed or humiliated.

indigo indigos or indigoes *noun*, *adjective* dark violet-blue.

indirect *adjective* 1 not moving in a straight line or by the shortest route. 2 not done or caused directly by a particular person or thing, but by someone or something else. > **indirectly** *adverb*

> **indirect** *adjective*
> 1 = meandering, oblique, rambling, roundabout, tortuous, wandering

indiscriminate *adjective* not involving careful thought or choice. > **indiscriminately** *adverb*

indispensable *adjective* If something is indispensable, you cannot do without it.

indistinct *adjective* not clear.

individual *adjective* 1 relating to one particular person or thing. 2 Someone who is individual behaves quite differently from the way other people behave. ▶ *noun* 3 a person when considered as different from all other people. > **individually** *adverb*

> **individual** *adjective*
> 1 = discrete (*formal*), independent, separate, single
> 2 = characteristic, distinctive, idiosyncratic, original, personal, special, unique
> ▶ *noun* 3 = character, party, person, soul

individuality *noun* If something has individuality, it is different from all other things, and therefore is very interesting and noticeable.

Indonesian *adjective* 1 belonging or relating to Indonesia. ▶ *noun* 2 someone who comes from Indonesia. 3 Indonesian is the official language of Indonesia.

indoor *adjective* situated or happening inside a building.

indoors *adverb* If something happens indoors, it takes place inside a building.

induce *verb* 1 To induce a state is to cause it. 2 If you induce someone to do something, you persuade them to do it.

inducement *noun* something offered to encourage someone to do something.

indulge *verb* 1 If you indulge in something, you allow yourself to do something that you enjoy. 2 If you indulge someone, you let them have or do what they want, often in a way that is not good for them.

indulgence *noun* 1 something you allow yourself to have because it gives you pleasure. 2 Indulgence is the act of indulging yourself or another person.

indulgent *adjective* If you are indulgent, you treat someone with special kindness.

industrial *adjective* relating to industry.

industrial action *noun* Industrial action is action such as striking taken by workers in protest over pay or working conditions.

industrialist *noun* a person who owns or controls a lot of factories.

Industrial Revolution *noun* (HISTORY) The Industrial Revolution was a period when machines began to be used more in factories and more goods were produced as a result. It started in Britain in the late eighteenth and early nineteenth century.

industrious *adjective* An industrious person works very hard.

> **industrious** *adjective*
> = busy, conscientious, diligent, hard-working, tireless

industry industries *noun* 1 Industry is the work and processes involved in manufacturing things in factories. 2 all the people and processes involved in manufacturing a particular thing.

inedible *adjective* too nasty or poisonous to eat.

inefficient *adjective* badly organised, wasteful and slow.
> **inefficiently** *adverb*
> **inefficiency** *noun*

inefficient *adjective*
= disorganised, incapable, incompetent, inept, sloppy

inept *adjective* without skill.
> **ineptitude** *noun*

inequality inequalities *noun* a difference in size, status, wealth or position between different things, groups or people.

inert *adjective* 1 Something that is inert does not move and appears lifeless. 2 In chemistry, an inert gas does not react with other substances. The inert gases are also called **noble gases**.

inertia *noun* If you have a feeling of inertia, you feel very lazy and unwilling to do anything.

inevitable *adjective* certain to happen. > **inevitably** *adverb*
> **inevitability** *noun*

inexhaustible *adjective* Something that is inexhaustible will never be used up.

inexpensive *adjective* not costing much.

inexperienced *adjective* lacking experience of a situation or activity. > **inexperience** *noun*

inexperienced *adjective*
= green (*informal*), new, raw, unaccustomed

inexplicable *adjective* If something is inexplicable, you cannot explain it. > **inexplicably** *adverb*

inextricably *adverb* If two or more things are inextricably linked, they cannot be separated.

infallible *adjective* never wrong.

infamous *adjective* well-known because of something bad or evil.

infant *noun* 1 a baby or very young child. ▶ *adjective* 2 designed for young children. > **infancy** *noun*

> **infantile** adjective

infantry noun In an army, the infantry are soldiers who fight on foot rather than in tanks or on horses.

infatuated adjective If you are infatuated with someone, you have such strong feelings of love or passion that you cannot think sensibly about them.
> **infatuation** noun

infect verb To infect someone or something is to cause disease in them.

> **infect** verb
> = affect, blight, contaminate, taint

infection noun 1 a disease caused by germs. 2 Infection is the state of being infected.

infectious adjective spreading from one person to another.

> **infectious** adjective
> = catching, contagious, spreading

infer infers, inferring, inferred verb If you infer something, you work out that it is true on the basis of information that you already have. > **inference** noun

inferior adjective 1 having a lower position than something or someone else. 2 of low quality.
▶ noun 3 Your inferiors are people who may be regarded as less important than you, because they are in a lower position.
> **inferiority** noun

> **inferior** adjective
> 1 = lesser, lower, minor, secondary, second-class, subordinate 2 = mediocre, poor, second-class, second-rate, shoddy

▶ noun 3 = junior, menial, subordinate, underling

inferno infernos noun a very large dangerous fire.

infertile adjective 1 Infertile soil is of poor quality and plants cannot grow well in it. 2 Someone who is infertile cannot have children.
> **infertility** noun

infested adjective Something that is infested has a large number of animals or insects living on or in it and causing damage.
> **infestation** noun

infighting noun Infighting is quarrelling or rivalry between members of the same organisation.

infiltrate verb If people infiltrate an organisation, they gradually enter it in secret to spy on its activities. > **infiltrator** noun

infinite adjective without any limit or end. > **infinitely** adverb

> **infinite** adjective
> = boundless, endless, eternal, everlasting, inexhaustible, perpetual

infinity noun 1 Infinity is a number that is larger than any other number and can never be given an exact value. 2 Infinity is also a point that can never be reached, further away than any other point.

infirmary infirmaries noun a hospital.

inflamed adjective If part of your body is inflamed, it is red and swollen, usually because of infection.

inflammation noun Inflammation is painful redness or swelling of part of the body.

inflammatory *adjective*
Inflammatory actions are likely
to make people very angry.

inflate *verb* When you inflate
something, you fill it with air or
gas to make it swell. > **inflatable**
adjective

inflation *noun* Inflation is an
increase in the price of goods and
services in a country.

inflection; also spelt **inflexion**
noun (MFL) a change in the form
of a word that shows its
grammatical function, for
example a change that makes
a noun plural.

inflexible *adjective* fixed and
unable to be altered.

inflict *verb* If you inflict
something unpleasant on
someone, you make them
suffer it.

influence *noun* 1 Influence is
power that a person has over
other people. 2 An influence is
also the effect that someone or
something has. ▶ *verb* 3 To
influence someone or something
means to have an effect on them.

> **influence** *noun*
> 1 = authority, control,
> importance, power, sway
> 2 = effect, hold, magnetism,
> spell, weight
> ▶ *verb* 3 = affect, control, direct,
> guide, manipulate, sway

influential *adjective* Someone
who is influential has a lot of
influence over people.

influenza *noun* (*formal*) Influenza
is flu.

influx *noun* a steady arrival of
people or things.

inform *verb* 1 If you inform
someone of something, you tell

them about it. 2 If you inform on
a person, you tell the police about
a crime they have committed.
> **informant** *noun*

> **inform** *verb*
> 1 = advise (*formal*), enlighten,
> notify, tell 2 = betray, denounce,
> grass on (*British*; *slang*), tell on
> (*informal*)

informal *adjective* relaxed and
casual. > **informally** *adverb*
> **informality** *noun*

> **informal** *adjective*
> = casual, colloquial, easy,
> familiar, natural, relaxed

information *noun* If you have
information on or about
something, you know something
about it.

> **information** *noun*
> = data, drum (*Australian*;
> *informal*), facts, material, news,
> notice, word

informative *adjective* Something
that is informative gives you
useful information.

informer *noun* someone who tells
the police that another person
has committed a crime.

infrastructure *noun* (GEOGRAPHY)
The infrastructure of a country
consists of things like factories,
schools and roads, which show
how much money the country
has and how strong its
economy is.

infringe *verb* 1 If you infringe a
law, you break it. 2 To infringe
people's rights is to not allow
them the rights to which they are
entitled. > **infringement** *noun*

infuriate *verb* If someone
infuriates you, they make you
very angry. > **infuriating** *adjective*

infuse verb 1 If you infuse someone with a feeling such as enthusiasm or joy, you fill them with it. 2 If you infuse a substance such as a herb or medicine, you pour hot water onto it and leave it for the water to absorb the flavour. > **infusion** noun

ingenious adjective very clever and using new ideas. > **ingeniously** adverb

ingenuity noun Ingenuity is cleverness and skill at inventing things or working out plans.

ingrained adjective If habits and beliefs are ingrained, they are difficult to change or destroy.

ingredient noun (D&T) Ingredients are the things that something is made from, especially in cookery.

> **ingredient** noun
> = component, constituent, element

inhabit verb If you inhabit a place, you live there.

> **inhabit** verb
> = dwell (formal), live, lodge, occupy, populate, reside (formal)

inhabitant noun The inhabitants of a place are the people who live there.

> **inhabitant** noun
> = citizen, inmate, native, occupant, resident

inhale verb (SCIENCE) When you inhale, you breathe in. > **inhalation** noun

inherent adjective Inherent qualities or characteristics in something are a natural part of it. > **inherently** adverb

inherit verb 1 If you inherit money or property, you receive it from someone who has died. 2 (SCIENCE) If you inherit a quality or characteristic from a parent or ancestor, it is passed on to you at birth. > **inheritor** noun

inheritance noun something that is passed on from another person.

> **inheritance** noun
> = bequest, heritage, legacy

inhibit verb If you inhibit someone from doing something, you prevent them from doing it.

inhibited adjective People who are inhibited find it difficult to relax and to show their emotions.

inhibition noun Inhibitions are feelings of fear or embarrassment that make it difficult for someone to relax and to show their emotions.

inhospitable adjective 1 An inhospitable place is unpleasant or difficult to live in. 2 If someone is inhospitable, they do not make people who visit them feel welcome.

inhuman adjective not human or not behaving like a human.

inhumane adjective extremely cruel. > **inhumanity** noun

inimitable adjective If you have an inimitable characteristic, no one else can imitate it.

initial adjective 1 first, or at the beginning. ▶ noun 2 The first letter of a name. > **initially** adverb

initiate verb 1 If you initiate something, you make it start or happen. 2 If you initiate someone into a group or club, you allow them to become a member of it, usually by means of a special ceremony. > **initiation** noun

initiative *noun* 1 an attempt to get something done. 2 If you have initiative, you decide what to do and then do it, without needing the advice of other people.

inject *verb* 1 If a doctor or nurse injects you with a substance, they use a needle and syringe to put the substance into your body. 2 If you inject something new into a situation, you add it.
> **injection** *noun*

injunction *noun* an order issued by a court of law to stop someone doing something.

injure *verb* To injure someone is to damage part of their body.

> **injure** *verb*
> = harm, hurt, maim, wound

injury injuries *noun* (PE) hurt or damage, especially to part of a person's body or to their feelings.

> **injury** *noun*
> = damage, harm, wound

injustice *noun* 1 Injustice is lack of justice and fairness. 2 If you do someone an injustice, you judge them too harshly.

> **injustice** *noun*
> 1 = bias, discrimination, inequality, prejudice, unfairness, wrong

ink *noun* Ink is the coloured liquid used for writing or printing.

inkling *noun* a vague idea about something.

inlaid *adjective* decorated with small pieces of wood, metal or stone.

inland *adjective* 1 near the middle of a country, away from the sea.
▶ *adverb* 2 towards the middle of a country, away from the sea.

in-law *noun* Your in-laws are members of your husband's or wife's family.

inlet *noun* a narrow bay.

inmate *noun* someone who lives in a prison or psychiatric hospital.

inn *noun* a small old country pub or hotel.

innards *plural noun* The innards of something are its inside parts.

innate *adjective* An innate quality is one that you were born with.
> **innately** *adverb*

inner *adjective* contained inside a place or object.

innermost *adjective* deepest and most secret.

innings *noun* In cricket, an innings is a period when a particular team is batting.

innocence *noun* inexperience of evil or unpleasant things.

> **innocence** *noun*
> = gullibility, inexperience, naivety, simplicity

innocent *adjective* 1 not guilty of a crime. 2 without experience of evil or unpleasant things.
> **innocently** *adverb*

> **innocent** *adjective*
> 1 = blameless, clear, not guilty
> 2 = childlike, guileless, naive, pure, spotless

innocuous *adjective* not harmful.

innovation *noun* (DGT) a completely new idea, product or system of doing things.

innuendo innuendos or **innuendoes** *noun* an indirect reference to something rude or unpleasant.

innumerable *adjective* too many to be counted.

input *noun* 1 Input consists of all the money, information and other resources that are put into a job, project or company to make it work. 2 (ICT) In computing, input is information which is fed into a computer.

inquest *noun* an official inquiry to find out what caused a person's death.

inquire; also spelt **enquire** *verb* If you inquire about something, you ask for information about it.
> **inquiring** *adjective* > **inquiry** *noun*

inquisition *noun* an official investigation, especially one which is very thorough and uses harsh methods of questioning.

inquisitive *adjective* Someone who is inquisitive is keen to find out about things. > **inquisitively** *adverb*

inroads *plural noun* If something makes inroads on or into something, it starts affecting it.

insane *adjective* Someone who is insane has a serious mental illness that does not to work normally. > **insanely** *adverb* > **insanity** *noun*

> **insane** *adjective*
> = crazy (*informal*), foolhardy, foolish, mad

insatiable *adjective* A desire or urge that is insatiable is very great. > **insatiably** *adverb*

inscribe *verb* If you inscribe words on an object, you write or carve them on it.

inscription *noun* the words that are written or carved on something.

inscrutable *adjective* Someone who is inscrutable does not show what they are really thinking.

insect *noun* (SCIENCE) a small creature with six legs, and usually wings.

insecticide *noun* (SCIENCE) a poisonous chemical used to kill insects.

insecure *adjective* 1 If you are insecure, you feel unsure of yourself and doubt whether other people like you. 2 Something that is insecure is not safe or well protected. > **insecurity** *noun*

insensitive *adjective* If you are insensitive, you do not notice when you are upsetting people.
> **insensitivity** *noun*

insert *verb* If you insert an object into something, you put it inside.
> **insertion** *noun*

> **insert** *verb*
> = enter, implant, introduce, place, put, set

inshore *adjective* at sea but close to the shore.

inside *noun* 1 the part of something that is surrounded by the main part and often hidden. 2 (*in plural*) Your insides are the parts inside your body. ▶ *adjective* 3 surrounded by the main part and often hidden: *an inside pocket.* ▶ *preposition* 4 in or to the interior of. ▶ *phrase* 5 **Inside out** means with the inside part facing outwards.

> **inside** *noun*
> 2 = entrails, guts, innards, internal organs
> ▶ *adjective* 3 = inner, innermost, interior, internal

insider noun a person who is involved in a situation and so knows more about it than other people.

insidious adjective Something that is insidious is unpleasant and develops slowly without being noticed. > **insidiously** adverb

insight noun If you gain insight into a problem, you gradually get a deep and accurate understanding of it.

insignia noun the badge or sign of a particular organisation.

insignificant adjective small and unimportant. > **insignificance** noun

> **insignificant** adjective
> = irrelevant, little, minor, petty, trifling, trivial, unimportant

insincere adjective Someone who is insincere pretends to have feelings which they do not really have. > **insincerely** adverb > **insincerity** noun

> **insincere** adjective
> = deceitful, dishonest, false, two-faced

insinuate verb If you insinuate something unpleasant, you hint about it. > **insinuation** noun

insipid adjective 1 An insipid person or activity is dull and boring. 2 Food that is insipid has very little taste.

insist verb If you insist on something, you demand it forcefully. > **insistent** adjective > **insistence** noun

> **insist** verb
> = demand, press, urge

insolent adjective very rude and disrespectful. > **insolently** adverb > **insolence** noun

insoluble adjective 1 impossible to solve. 2 (SCIENCE) unable to dissolve.

insolvent adjective unable to pay your debts. > **insolvency** noun

insomnia noun Insomnia is difficulty in sleeping. > **insomniac** noun

inspect verb To inspect something is to examine it carefully to check that everything is all right. > **inspection** noun

> **inspect** verb
> = check, examine, eye, investigate, scan, survey

inspector noun 1 someone who inspects things. 2 a police officer just above a sergeant in rank.

inspire verb 1 If something inspires you, it gives you new ideas and enthusiasm to do something. 2 To inspire an emotion in someone is to make them feel this emotion. > **inspiration** noun

instability noun Instability is a lack of stability in a place.

install verb 1 If you install a piece of equipment in a place, you put it there so it is ready to be used. 2 If you install software on a computer, you transfer it there and make it ready to be used. 3 To install someone in an important job is to officially give them that position. > **installation** noun

instalment noun 1 If you pay for something in instalments, you pay small amounts of money regularly over a period of time. 2 one of the parts of a story or television series.

instance noun 1 a particular example or occurrence of an event, situation or person. ▶ phrase 2 You use **for instance** to give an example of something you are talking about.

instant noun 1 a moment or short period of time. ▶ adjective 2 immediate and without delay. > **instantly** adverb

> **instant** noun
> 1 = flash, minute, moment, second, split second, trice
> ▶ adjective 2 = immediate, instantaneous, prompt

instantaneous adjective happening immediately and without delay. > **instantaneously** adverb

instead adverb in place of something.

instigate verb Someone who instigates a situation makes it happen. > **instigation** noun > **instigator** noun

instil instils, instilling, instilled verb If you instil an idea or feeling into someone, you make them feel or think it.

instinct noun a natural tendency to do something. > **instinctive** adjective > **instinctively** adverb

> **instinct** noun
> = feeling, impulse, intuition, sixth sense, urge

institute noun 1 an organisation for teaching or research. ▶ verb 2 (formal) If you institute a rule or system, you introduce it.

institution noun 1 a custom or system regarded as an important tradition within a society. 2 a large, important organisation, for example a university or bank.

instruct verb 1 If you instruct someone to do something, you tell them to do it. 2 If someone instructs you in a subject or skill, they teach you about it. > **instructor** noun > **instruction** noun

> **instruct** verb
> 1 = command, direct, order, tell
> 2 = coach, educate, school, teach, train, tutor

instrument noun 1 a tool or device used for a particular job. 2 (MUSIC) A musical instrument is an object, such as a piano or flute, played to make music.

instrumental adjective 1 If you are instrumental in doing something, you help to make it happen. 2 (MUSIC) Instrumental music is performed using only musical instruments, and not voices.

insufficient adjective not enough for a particular purpose.

> **insufficient** adjective
> = deficient, inadequate, lacking, scant, short

insular adjective Someone who is insular is unwilling to meet new people or to consider new ideas. > **insularity** noun

insulate verb 1 If you insulate a person from harmful things, you protect them from those things. 2 If materials such as feathers, fur or foam insulate something, they keep it warm by covering it in a thick layer. 3 (SCIENCE) You insulate an electrical or metal object by covering it with rubber or plastic. This is to stop electricity passing through it and giving you an electric shock. > **insulation** noun > **insulator** noun

insulin *noun* Insulin is a substance which controls the level of sugar in the blood. People who have diabetes do not produce insulin naturally and have to take regular doses of it.

insult *verb* 1 If you insult someone, you offend them by being rude to them. ▶ *noun* 2 a rude remark which offends you. > **insulting** *adjective*

> **insult** *verb*
> 1 = abuse, affront, offend, put down, slag off (*British; informal*), slight, snub
> ▶ *noun* 2 = abuse, affront, offence, slight, snub

insure *verb* 1 If you insure something or yourself, you pay money regularly to a company so that if there is an accident or damage, the company will pay for medical treatment or repairs. 2 If you do something to insure against something unpleasant happening, you do it to prevent the unpleasant thing from happening or to protect yourself if it does happen. > **insurance** *noun*

insurrection *noun* a violent action taken against the rulers of a country.

intact *adjective* complete, and not changed or damaged in any way.

intake *noun* A person's intake of food, drink or air is the amount they take in.

integral *adjective* If something is an integral part of a whole thing, it is an essential part.

integrate *verb* 1 If a person integrates into a group, they become part of it. 2 To integrate things is to combine them so that

they become closely linked or form one thing. > **integration** *noun*

integrity *noun* 1 Integrity is the quality of being honest and following your principles. 2 The integrity of a group of people is their being united as one whole.

intellect *noun* Intellect is the ability to understand ideas and information.

intellectual *adjective* 1 involving thought, ideas and understanding. ▶ *noun* 2 someone who enjoys thinking about complicated ideas. > **intellectually** *adverb*

intelligence *noun* A person's intelligence is their ability to understand and learn things quickly and well.

> **intelligence** *noun*
> = cleverness, comprehension, intellect, perception, sense, understanding, wit

intelligent *adjective* able to understand and learn things quickly and well. > **intelligently** *adverb*

> **intelligent** *adjective*
> = acute, brainy (*informal*), bright, clever, quick, sharp, smart

intelligentsia *noun* The intelligentsia are intellectual people, considered as a group.

intelligible *adjective* able to be understood.

intend *verb* 1 If you intend to do something, you have decided or planned to do it. 2 If something is intended for a particular use, you have planned that it should have this use.

intend *verb*
1 = aim, be determined, mean, plan, propose, resolve 2 = aim, design, earmark, mean

intense *adjective* 1 very great in strength or amount. 2 If a person is intense, they take things very seriously and have very strong feelings. > **intensely** *adverb* > **intensity** *noun*

intense *adjective*
1 = acute, deep, extreme, fierce, great, powerful, profound, severe 2 = ardent, earnest, fervent, fierce, impassioned, passionate, vehement

intensify intensifies, intensifying, intensified *verb* To intensify something is to make it greater or stronger.

intensive *adjective* involving a lot of energy or effort over a very short time.

intent *noun* 1 (*formal*) A person's intent is their purpose or intention. ▸ *adjective* 2 If you are intent on doing something, you are determined to do it. > **intently** *adverb*

intention *noun* If you have an intention to do something, you have a plan of what you are going to do.

intention *noun*
= aim, goal, idea, object, objective, purpose

intentional *adjective* If something is intentional, it is done on purpose. > **intentionally** *adverb*

interact *verb* The way two people or things interact is the way they work together, communicate or react with each other. > **interaction** *noun*

interactive *adjective* (ICT) Interactive television, computers and games react to decisions taken by the viewer, user or player.

intercept *verb* If you intercept someone or something that is going from one place to another, you stop them.

interchange *noun* An interchange is the act or process of exchanging things or ideas. > **interchangeable** *adjective*

intercom *noun* a device consisting of a microphone and a loudspeaker, which you use to speak to people in another room.

interest *noun* 1 If you have an interest in something or if something is of interest, you want to learn or hear more about it. 2 Your interests are your hobbies. 3 If you have an interest in something being done, you want it to be done because it will benefit you. 4 Interest is an extra payment made to the lender by someone who has borrowed a sum of money, or by a bank or company to someone who has invested money in them. Interest is worked out as a percentage of the sum of money borrowed or invested. ▸ *verb* 5 Something that interests you attracts your attention so that you want to learn or hear more about it. > **interested** *adjective*

interest *noun*
1 = attention, concern, curiosity, fascination 2 = activity, hobby, pastime, pursuit
▸ *verb* 5 = appeal, captivate, fascinate, intrigue, stimulate

interesting *adjective* making you want to know, learn or hear more.

interesting adjective
= absorbing, compelling, entertaining, gripping, intriguing, stimulating

interface noun 1 The interface between two subjects or systems is the area in which they affect each other or are linked. 2 (ICT) The user interface of a computer program is how it is presented on the computer screen and how easy it is to operate.

interfere verb 1 If you interfere in a situation, you try to influence it, although it does not really concern you. 2 Something that interferes with a situation has a damaging effect on it. > **interference** noun > **interfering** adjective

interfere verb
1 = butt in, intervene, intrude, meddle, tamper 2 = conflict, disrupt

interim adjective intended for use only until something permanent is arranged.

interior noun 1 the inside part of something. ▸ adjective 2 Interior means inside.

interlude noun a short break from an activity.

intermediary intermediaries noun someone who tries to get two groups of people to come to an agreement.

intermediate adjective An intermediate level occurs in the middle, between two other stages.

interminable adjective If something is interminable, it goes on for a very long time. > **interminably** adverb

intermission noun an interval between two parts of a film or play.

intermittent adjective happening only occasionally. > **intermittently** adverb

internal adjective happening inside a person, place or object. > **internally** adverb

international adjective (GEOGRAPHY) 1 involving different countries. ▸ noun 2 a sports match between two countries. > **internationally** adverb

internet or **Internet** noun (ICT) The internet is a global communication system of interconnected computer networks which supports the World Wide Web, email and instant messaging.

interplay noun The interplay between two things is the way they react with one another.

interpret verb 1 If you interpret what someone writes, says or does, you decide what it means. 2 If you interpret a foreign language that someone is speaking, you translate it. > **interpretation** noun > **interpreter** noun

interrogate verb If you interrogate someone, you question them thoroughly to get information from them. > **interrogation** noun

interrogate verb
= examine, grill (informal), question, quiz

interrupt verb 1 If you interrupt someone, you start talking while they are talking. 2 If you interrupt a process or activity, you stop it continuing for a time. > **interruption** noun

interrupt verb
1 = butt in, heckle 2 = break, discontinue, suspend

intersect verb When two roads or lines intersect, they cross each other.

intersection noun 1 An intersection is where two roads meet. 2 (MATHS) In maths, an intersection is the point where two straight lines meet.

interspersed adjective If something is interspersed with things, these things occur at various points in it.

interval noun 1 the period of time between two moments or dates. 2 a short break during a play or concert. 3 (MUSIC) In music, an interval is the difference in pitch between two musical notes.

> **interval** noun
> 1 = break, gap, hiatus (formal), interlude, intermission, pause

intervene verb If you intervene in a situation, you step in to prevent conflict between people.
> **intervention** noun

> **intervene** verb
> = arbitrate, mediate

intervening adjective An intervening period of time is one which separates two events.

interview noun 1 a meeting at which someone asks you questions about yourself to see if you are suitable for a particular job. 2 a conversation in which a journalist asks a famous person questions. ▸ verb 3 If you interview someone, you ask them questions about themselves.
> **interviewer** noun > **interviewee** noun

intestine noun Your intestines are a long tube which carries food from your stomach through to

your bowels, and in which the food is digested. > **intestinal** adjective

intimate adjective 1 If two people are intimate, there is a close relationship between them. 2 An intimate matter is very private and personal. 3 An intimate knowledge of something is very deep and detailed. ▸ verb 4 If you intimate something, you hint at it. > **intimately** adverb > **intimacy** noun > **intimation** noun

intimidate verb If you intimidate someone, you frighten them in a threatening way. > **intimidated** adjective > **intimidating** adjective > **intimidation** noun

into preposition 1 If something goes into something else, it goes inside it. 2 If you bump or crash into something, you hit it. 3 (informal) If you are into something, you like it very much.

intolerable adjective If something is intolerable, it is so bad that it is difficult to put up with it.

intonation noun Your intonation is the way that your voice rises and falls as you speak.

intoxicated adjective If someone is intoxicated, they are drunk. > **intoxicating** adjective > **intoxication** noun

intractable adjective (formal) stubborn and difficult to deal with or control.

intravenous adjective Intravenous foods or drugs are given to sick people through their veins. > **intravenously** adverb

intrepid adjective not worried by danger.

intricate adjective Something that is intricate has many fine details. > **intricately** adverb > **intricacy** noun

intrigue noun 1 Intrigue is the making of secret plans, often with the intention of harming other people. ▶ verb 2 If something intrigues you, you are fascinated by it and curious about it. > **intriguing** adjective

intrinsic adjective (formal) The intrinsic qualities of something are its basic qualities. > **intrinsically** adverb

introduce verb 1 If you introduce one person to another, you tell them each other's name so that they can get to know each other. 2 When someone introduces a radio or television show, they say a few words at the beginning to tell you about it. 3 If you introduce someone to something, they learn about it for the first time. > **introductory** adjective

introduction noun 1 The introduction of someone or something is the act of presenting them for the first time. 2 (ENGLISH) a piece of writing at the beginning of a book, which usually tells you what the book is about.

> **introduction** noun
> 1 = establishment, inauguration (formal), initiation, institution, launch
> 2 = foreword, preface, prologue

introvert noun someone who spends more time thinking about their private feelings than about the world around them, and who often finds it difficult to talk to others. > **introverted** adjective

intrude verb To intrude on someone or something is to disturb them. > **intruder** noun > **intrusion** noun

intrude verb
= butt in, encroach, infringe, interrupt, trespass, violate

intuition noun Your intuition is a feeling you have about something that you cannot explain. > **intuitive** adjective

Inuit; also spelt **Innuit** noun one of a group of peoples who live in Northern Canada, Greenland, Alaska and Eastern Siberia.

inundated adjective If you are inundated by messages or requests, you receive so many that you cannot deal with them all.

invade verb 1 If an army invades a country, it enters it by force. 2 If someone invades your privacy, they disturb you when you want to be alone. > **invader** noun

invade verb
1 = attack, enter, occupy, violate

invalid[1] noun someone who is so ill that they need to be looked after by someone else.

invalid[2] adjective 1 If an argument or result is invalid, it is not acceptable because it is based on a mistake. 2 If a law, marriage or election is invalid, it is illegal because it has not been carried out properly. > **invalidate** verb

invaluable adjective extremely useful.

invariably adverb If something invariably happens, it almost always happens.

invasion noun 1 (HISTORY) The invasion of a country or territory is the act of entering it by force. 2 an unwanted disturbance or intrusion.

invective noun (formal) Invective is abusive language used by someone who is angry.

invent verb 1 If you invent a device or process, you are the first person to think of it or to use it. 2 If you invent a story or an excuse, you make it up. > **inventor** noun > **invention** noun > **inventive** adjective

> **invent** verb
> 1 = coin, come up with (informal), conceive, create, formulate, originate 2 = concoct, fabricate, make up, manufacture

inventory inventories noun a written list of all the objects in a place.

inverse adjective (formal) If there is an inverse relationship between two things, one decreases as the other increases.

invertebrate noun (SCIENCE) An invertebrate is a creature which does not have a spine. Some invertebrates, for example crabs, have an external skeleton.

inverted adjective upside down or back to front.

invest verb 1 If you invest money, you pay it into a bank or buy shares so that you will receive a profit. 2 If you invest in something useful, you buy it because it will help you do something better. 3 If you invest money, time or energy in something, you try to make it a success. > **investor** noun > **investment** noun

investigate verb To investigate something is to try to find out the facts about it. > **investigator** noun > **investigation** noun

investigate verb
= examine, explore, probe, research, sift, study

invincible adjective unable to be defeated. > **invincibility** noun

> **invincible** adjective
> = impregnable, indomitable, unbeatable

invisible adjective If something is invisible, you cannot see it, because it is hidden, very small or imaginary. > **invisibility** noun

> **invisible** adjective
> = concealed, disguised, hidden, inconspicuous, unseen

invite verb 1 If you invite someone to an event, you ask them to come to it. 2 If you invite someone to do something, you ask them to do it. > **inviting** adjective > **invitation** noun

invoice noun a bill for services or goods.

invoke verb 1 (formal) If you invoke a law, you use it to justify what you are doing. 2 If you invoke certain feelings, you cause someone to have these feelings.

involuntary adjective sudden and uncontrollable. > **involuntarily** adverb

involve verb (PSHE) If a situation involves someone or something, it includes them as a necessary part. > **involvement** noun

> **involve** verb
> = incorporate, require, take in

inward adjective, adverb 1 Inward means towards the inside or centre of something. ► adjective 2 Your inward thoughts and feelings are private. > **inwardly** adverb

inwards *adverb* towards the centre or inside.

iodine *noun* (SCIENCE) Iodine is a bluish-black element whose compounds are used in medicine and photography. Its atomic number is 53 and its symbol is I.

ion *noun* Ions are electrically charged atoms.

iota *noun* an extremely small amount.

IQ *noun* Your IQ is your level of intelligence shown by the results of a special test. IQ is an abbreviation for 'intelligence quotient'.

Iranian *adjective* **1** belonging or relating to Iran. ▶ *noun* **2** someone who comes from Iran. **3** Iranian is the main language spoken in Iran. It is also known as Farsi.

Iraqi *adjective* **1** belonging or relating to Iraq. ▶ *noun* **2** someone who comes from Iraq.

irate *adjective* very angry.

iris *noun* irises **1** the round, coloured part of your eye. **2** a tall plant with long leaves and large blue, yellow or white flowers.

Irish *adjective* **1** belonging or relating to the Irish Republic, or to the whole of Ireland. ▶ *noun* **2** Irish or Irish Gaelic is a language spoken in some parts of Ireland.

Irishman Irishmen *noun* a man who comes from Ireland.

Irishwoman Irishwomen *noun* a woman who comes from Ireland.

irk *verb* If something irks you, it annoys you. > **irksome** *adjective*

iron *noun* **1** (SCIENCE) Iron is a strong, hard metallic element found in rocks. It is used in making tools and machines, and is also an important component

of blood. Its atomic number is 26 and its symbol is Fe. **2** An iron is a device which heats up and which you rub over clothes to remove creases. ▶ *verb* **3** If you iron clothes, you use a hot iron to remove creases from them. > **ironing** *noun* > **iron out** *verb* If you iron out difficulties, you solve them.

Iron Age *noun* (HISTORY) The Iron Age was a time about 3000 years ago when people first started to make tools out of iron.

irony ironies *noun* **1** (ENGLISH) Irony is a form of humour in which you say the opposite of what you really mean. **2** There is irony in a situation when there is an unexpected or unusual connection between things or events. > **ironic** or **ironical** *adjective* > **ironically** *adverb*

irrational *adjective* **1** Irrational feelings are not based on logical reasons. **2** (MATHS) An irrational number is a number that cannot be expressed as the ratio of two whole numbers. > **irrationally** *adverb*

> **irrational** *adjective*
> **1** = absurd, crazy (*informal*), illogical, nonsensical, unsound

irregular *adjective* **1** not smooth or even. **2** not forming a regular pattern. **3** (MATHS) Irregular things are uneven or unequal, or are not symmetrical. > **irregularly** *adverb* > **irregularity** *noun*

> **irregular** *adjective*
> **1** = asymmetrical, bumpy, jagged, lopsided, ragged, uneven **2** = erratic, haphazard, occasional, patchy, random, variable

irrelevant *adjective* not directly connected with a subject.
> **irrelevance** *noun*

irrepressible *adjective* Someone who is irrepressible is lively and cheerful.

irresistible *adjective* 1 unable to be controlled. 2 extremely attractive.

irrespective *adjective* If you say something will be done irrespective of certain things, you mean it will be done without taking those things into account.

irresponsible *adjective* An irresponsible person does things without considering the consequences. > **irresponsibility** *noun*

> **irresponsible** *adjective*
> = careless, reckless, thoughtless, wild

irrigate *verb* To irrigate land is to supply it with water brought through pipes or ditches.
> **irrigation** *noun*

irritable *adjective* easily annoyed.

> **irritable** *adjective*
> = bad-tempered, cantankerous, petulant, ratty (*British and New Zealand; informal*)

irritate *verb* 1 If something irritates you, it annoys you. 2 If something irritates part of your body, it makes it tender, sore or itchy. > **irritant** *noun* > **irritation** *noun*

> **irritate** *verb*
> 1 = anger, annoy, bother, exasperate, needle (*informal*), ruffle

is the third person singular, present tense of **be**.

-ise or **-ize** *suffix* '-ise' and '-ize' form verbs. Most verbs can be spelt with either ending, though there are some that can only be spelt with '-ise', for example *advertise*, *improvise* and *revise*.

-ish *suffix* '-ish' forms adjectives that mean 'fairly' or 'rather': *smallish*.

Islam *noun* (RE) Islam is the Muslim religion, which teaches that there is only one God, Allah, and Mohammed is his prophet. The holy book of Islam is the Qur'an. > **Islamic** *adjective*

island *noun* a piece of land surrounded on all sides by water. > **islander** *noun*

isle *noun* (*literary*) an island.

-ism *suffix* 1 '-ism' forms nouns that refer to an action or condition: *criticism*. 2 '-ism' forms nouns that refer to a political or economic system or a system of beliefs: *Marxism*. 3 '-ism' forms nouns that refer to a type of prejudice: *racism*.

isolate *verb* 1 If something isolates you or if you isolate yourself, you are set apart from other people. 2 If you isolate something, you separate it from everything else. > **isolated** *adjective* > **isolation** *noun*

ISP an abbreviation for 'internet service provider'.

Israeli Israelis *adjective* 1 belonging or relating to Israel. ▸ *noun* 2 someone who comes from Israel.

issue issues, issuing, issued *noun* 1 an important subject that people are talking about. 2 a particular edition of a newspaper or magazine. ▸ *verb* 3 If you issue a statement or a warning, you say it formally and publicly.

4 If someone issues something, they officially give it.

issue noun
1 = concern, matter, problem, question, subject, topic
2 = copy, edition, instalment
▶ verb 3 = deliver, give, make, pronounce, read out, release
4 = equip, furnish (formal), give out, provide, supply

-ist suffix 1 '-ist' forms nouns and adjectives which refer to someone who is involved in a certain activity, or who believes in a certain system or religion: chemist. 2 '-ist' forms nouns and adjectives which refer to someone who has a certain prejudice: racist.

it pronoun 1 'It' is used to refer to something that has already been mentioned, or to a situation or fact: The course had become so wet that it was considered dangerous; It was a difficult decision. 2 'It' is used to refer to people or animals whose gender is not known: If a baby is thirsty, it feeds more often. 3 You use 'it' to make statements about the weather, time or date: It's noon.

IT noun IT is the use of computers to store and analyse information. IT is an abbreviation for 'information technology'.

Italian adjective 1 belonging or relating to Italy. ▶ noun 2 someone who comes from Italy. 3 Italian is the main language spoken in Italy.

italics plural noun Italics are letters printed in a special sloping way, and are often used to emphasise something. ▷ **italic** adjective

itch verb 1 When your skin itches, it has an unpleasant feeling and you want to scratch it. 2 If you are

itching to do something, you are impatient to do it. ▶ noun 3 an unpleasant feeling on your skin that you want to scratch. ▷ **itchy** adjective

item noun 1 one of a collection or list of objects. 2 a newspaper or magazine article.

item noun
1 = article, matter, point, thing
2 = article, feature, notice, piece, report

itinerary itineraries noun a plan of a journey, showing a route to follow and places to visit.

-itis suffix '-itis' is added to the name of a part of the body to refer to disease or inflammation in that part: tonsillitis.

its adjective, pronoun 'Its' refers to something belonging to or relating to things, children or animals that have already been mentioned: The lion lifted its head.

itself pronoun 1 'Itself' is used when the same thing, child or animal does an action and is affected by it: The cat was washing itself. 2 'Itself' is used to emphasise 'it'.

-ity suffix '-ity' forms nouns that refer to a state or condition: continuity.

-ive suffix '-ive' forms adjectives and some nouns: massive; detective.

ivory noun 1 the valuable creamy-white bone which forms the tusk of an elephant. It is used to make ornaments. ▶ noun, adjective 2 creamy-white.

ivy noun an evergreen plant which creeps along the ground and up walls.

iwi iwi or iwis noun In New Zealand, an iwi is a Māori tribe.

Jj

jab jabs, jabbing, jabbed *verb* 1 To jab something means to poke at it roughly. ▶ *noun* 2 a sharp or sudden poke. 3 (*informal*) an injection.

jack *noun* 1 a piece of equipment for lifting heavy objects, especially for lifting a car when changing a wheel. 2 In a pack of cards, a jack is a card with a picture of a young prince on it. ▶ *verb* 3 To jack up an object means to raise it, especially by using a jack. 4 (*informal*) In New Zealand English, to jack something up is to organise or prepare something.

jacket *noun* 1 a short coat reaching to the waist or hips. 2 an outer covering for something. 3 The jacket of a baked potato is its skin.

jackpot *noun* In a gambling game, the jackpot is the top prize.

jade *noun* Jade is a hard green stone used for making jewellery.

jagged *adjective* sharp and spiky.

> **jagged** *adjective*
> = barbed, craggy, rough, serrated

jaguar *noun* A jaguar is a large member of the cat family with spots on its back. Jaguars live in South and Central America.

jail; also spelt **gaol** *noun* 1 a building where people convicted

of a crime are locked up. ▶ *verb* 2 To jail someone means to lock them up in a jail.

> **jail** *noun*
> 1 = nick (*British, Australian and New Zealand*; *slang*), prison
> ▶ *verb* 2 = detain, imprison, incarcerate

jam jams, jamming, jammed *noun* 1 a food, made by boiling fruit and sugar together until it sets. 2 a situation in which it is impossible to move. 3 (*informal*) If someone is in a jam, they are in a difficult situation. ▶ *verb* 4 If people or things are jammed in a place, they are squeezed together so closely that they can hardly move. 5 To jam something somewhere means to push it there roughly. 6 If something is jammed, it is stuck or unable to work properly.

> **jam** *noun*
> 2 = crowd, crush, mass, mob, multitude, throng
> 3 = dilemma, fix (*informal*), hole (*slang*), plight, predicament, quandary, trouble
> ▶ *verb* 5 = cram, force, ram, stuff
> 6 = stall, stick

Jamaican *adjective* 1 belonging or relating to Jamaica. ▶ *noun* 2 someone who comes from Jamaica.

jamboree *noun* a large gathering of people enjoying themselves.

janitor *noun* the caretaker of a building.

January *noun* January is the first month of the year. It has 31 days.

Japanese *adjective* 1 belonging or relating to Japan. ▶ *noun* 2 someone who comes from Japan. 3 Japanese is the main language spoken in Japan.

jar jars, jarring, jarred noun 1 a glass container with a wide top used for storing food. ▶ verb 2 If something jars on you, you find it unpleasant or annoying.

jargon noun Jargon consists of words that are used in special or technical ways by particular groups of people.

jarrah noun An Australian eucalyptus tree that produces wood used for timber.

jasmine noun Jasmine is a climbing plant with small sweet-scented white flowers.

jaundice noun Jaundice is an illness affecting the liver, in which the skin and the whites of the eyes become yellow.

jaundiced adjective pessimistic and lacking enthusiasm.

jaunt noun a journey or trip you go on for pleasure.

jaunty jauntier, jauntiest adjective expressing cheerfulness and self-confidence. ▶ **jauntily** adverb

javelin noun a long spear that is thrown in sports competitions.

jaw noun 1 A person's or animal's jaw is the bone in which the teeth are set. 2 A person's or animal's jaws are their mouth and teeth.

jay noun a kind of noisy chattering bird.

jazz noun 1 Jazz is a style of popular music with a forceful rhythm. ▶ verb 2 (informal) To jazz something up means to make it more exciting.

jazzy jazzier, jazziest adjective (informal) bright and showy.

jealous adjective 1 If you are jealous, you feel bitterness towards someone who has something that you would like to have. 2 If you are jealous of something you have, you feel you must try to keep it from other people. ▶ **jealously** adverb

> **jealous** adjective
> 1 = envious, resentful

jeans plural noun Jeans are casual denim trousers.

Jeep noun (trademark) a small road vehicle with four-wheel drive.

jeer verb 1 If you jeer at someone, you insult them in a loud, unpleasant way. ▶ noun 2 Jeers are rude and insulting remarks.

Jehovah proper noun (RE) Jehovah is a name of God in the Old Testament.

jelly jellies noun 1 a clear, sweet food eaten as a dessert. 2 a type of clear, set jam.

jellyfish noun a sea animal with a clear soft body and tentacles which may sting.

jeopardise; also spelt
jeopardize verb To jeopardise something means to do something which puts it at risk.

jeopardy noun If someone or something is in jeopardy, they are at risk of failing or of being destroyed.

jerk verb 1 To jerk something means to give it a sudden, sharp pull. 2 If something jerks, it moves suddenly and sharply. ▶ noun 3 a sudden sharp movement. 4 (informal) If you call someone a jerk, you mean they are stupid. ▶ **jerky** adjective

jersey noun 1 a knitted garment for the upper half of the body. 2 Jersey is a type of knitted woollen or cotton fabric used to make clothing.

jest noun 1 a joke. ▶ verb 2 To jest means to speak jokingly.

jester noun In the past, a jester was a man who was kept to amuse the king or queen.

jet jets, jetting, jetted noun 1 a plane which is able to fly very fast. 2 a stream of liquid, gas or flame forced out under pressure. 3 Jet is a hard black stone, usually highly polished and used in jewellery and ornaments. ▶ verb 4 To jet somewhere means to fly there in a plane, especially a jet.

jet lag noun Jet lag is a feeling of tiredness or confusion that people have after a long flight across different time zones.

jettison verb If you jettison something, you throw it away because you no longer want it.

jetty jetties noun a wide stone wall or wooden platform at the edge of the sea or a river, where boats can be moored.

Jew noun (RE) a person who practises the religion of Judaism, or who is of Hebrew descent. > **Jewish** adjective

jewel noun a precious stone used to decorate valuable ornaments or jewellery. > **jewelled** adjective

jeweller noun a person who makes jewellery or who sells and repairs jewellery and watches.

jewellery noun Jewellery consists of ornaments that people wear, such as rings or necklaces, made of valuable metals and sometimes decorated with precious stones.

jib noun a small sail towards the front of a sailing boat.

jibe another spelling of **gibe**.

jig jigs, jigging, jigged noun 1 A jig is a type of lively folk dance; also the music that accompanies it. ▶ verb 2 If you jig, you dance or jump around in a lively bouncy manner.

jigsaw noun a puzzle consisting of a picture on cardboard that has been cut up into small pieces which have to be put together again.

jihad noun 1 (RE) a holy war waged to defend or further the ideals of Islam. 2 (RE) Jihad also means the personal struggle of a Muslim against sin.

jingle noun 1 a short, catchy phrase or rhyme set to music and used to advertise something on radio or television. 2 the sound of something jingling. ▶ verb 3 When something jingles, it makes a tinkling sound like small bells.

jinks plural noun High jinks is boisterous and mischievous behaviour.

jinx noun someone or something that is thought to bring bad luck.

jinxed adjective If something is jinxed it is considered to be unlucky.

jitters plural noun (informal) If you have got the jitters, you are feeling very nervous. > **jittery** adjective

job noun 1 the work that someone does to earn money. 2 a duty or responsibility. ▶ phrase 3 If something is **just the job**, it is exactly what you wanted.

> **job** noun
> 1 = employment, occupation, position, post, profession, trade
> 2 = concern, duty, function, responsibility, role, task

jobless *adjective* without any work.

jockey *noun* 1 someone who rides a horse in a race. ▶ *verb* 2 To jockey for position means to manoeuvre in order to gain an advantage over other people.

jocular *adjective* A jocular comment is intended to make people laugh.

jog jogs, jogging, jogged *verb* 1 To jog means to run slowly and rhythmically, often as a form of exercise. 2 If you jog something, you knock it slightly so that it shakes or moves. 3 If someone or something jogs your memory, they remind you of something. ▶ *noun* 4 a slow run. > **jogger** *noun* > **jogging** *noun*

join *verb* 1 When two things join, or when one thing joins another, they come together. 2 If you join a club or organisation, you become a member of it or start taking part in it. 3 To join two things means to fasten them. ▶ *noun* 4 a place where two things are fastened together. > **join up** *verb* If someone joins up, they become a member of the armed forces.

join *verb*
2 = enlist, enrol, sign up
3 = attach, connect, couple, fasten, link, tie

joiner *noun* a person who makes wooden window frames, doors and furniture.

joinery *noun* Joinery is the work done by a joiner.

joint *adjective* 1 shared by or belonging to two or more people. ▶ *noun* 2 (SCIENCE) a part of the body where two bones meet and are joined together so that they

can move, for example a knee or hip. 3 (DGT) a place where two things are fixed together. 4 a large piece of meat suitable for roasting. 5 (*informal*) any place of entertainment, such as a pub. ▶ *verb* 6 To joint meat means to cut it into large pieces according to where the bones are. > **jointly** *adverb*

joke *noun* 1 something that you say or do to make people laugh, such as a funny story. 2 anything that you think is ridiculous and not worthy of respect. ▶ *verb* 3 If you are joking, you are teasing someone. > **jokingly** *adverb*

joke *noun*
1 = gag (*informal*), jest, lark, prank, quip, wisecrack (*informal*), witticism

joker *noun* In a pack of cards, a joker is an extra card that does not belong to any of the four suits, but is used in some games.

jolly jollier, jolliest; jollies, jollying, jollied *adjective* 1 happy, cheerful and pleasant. ▶ *adverb* 2 (*informal*) Jolly also means very. ▶ *verb* 3 If you jolly someone along, you encourage them in a cheerful and friendly way. > **jolliness** *noun*

jolt *verb* 1 To jolt means to move or shake roughly and violently. 2 If you are jolted by something, it gives you an unpleasant surprise. ▶ *noun* 3 a sudden jerky movement. 4 an unpleasant shock or surprise.

jostle *verb* To jostle means to push roughly against people in a crowd.

jot jots, jotting, jotted *verb* 1 If you jot something down, you write it quickly in the form of a short informal note. ▶ noun 2 a very small amount. > jotting noun

journal noun 1 a magazine that deals with a particular subject, trade or profession. 2 a diary which someone keeps regularly.

journalism noun Journalism is the work of collecting, writing and publishing news in newspapers and magazines, and on television and radio. > journalist noun

journey noun 1 the act of travelling from one place to another. ▶ verb 2 (formal) To journey somewhere means to travel there.

> **journey** noun
> 1 = excursion, expedition, passage, tour, trek, trip, voyage
> ▶ verb 2 = go, proceed (formal), tour, travel, trek, voyage

joust (HISTORY) noun In medieval times, a joust was a competition between knights fighting on horseback, using lances.

jovial adjective cheerful and friendly.

joy noun 1 Joy is a feeling of great happiness. 2 (informal) Joy also means success or luck. 3 something that makes you happy or gives you pleasure.

> **joy** noun
> 1 = bliss, delight, ecstasy, elation, rapture

joyful adjective 1 causing pleasure and happiness. 2 Someone who is joyful is extremely happy. > joyfully adverb

> **joyful** adjective
> 2 = delighted, elated, jubilant, over the moon (informal)

joyous adjective (formal) joyful.

joyride noun a drive in a stolen car for pleasure. > joyrider noun

joystick noun 1 a lever in an aircraft which the pilot uses to control height and direction. 2 In some computer games, the joystick is the lever used to control the movement of objects on the screen.

jubilant adjective feeling or expressing great happiness or triumph. > jubilantly adverb

jubilation noun Jubilation is a feeling of great happiness and triumph.

jubilee noun a special anniversary of an event such as a coronation.

Judaism noun (RE) Judaism is the religion of the Jewish people. It is based on a belief in one God, and draws its laws and authority from the Old Testament. > Judaic adjective

judge noun 1 the person in a law court who decides how the law should be applied to people who appear in the court. 2 someone who decides the winner in a contest or competition. ▶ verb 3 If you judge someone or something, you form an opinion about them based on the evidence that you have. 4 To judge a contest or competition means to decide on the winner.

> **judge** noun
> 1 = justice, magistrate
> 2 = referee, umpire
> ▶ verb 3 = appraise, assess, consider, estimate, evaluate, rate 4 = referee, umpire

judgment; also spelt **judgement** noun an opinion or decision based on evidence.

> **judgment** noun
> = appraisal, assessment,
> conclusion, opinion, ruling,
> verdict, view

judicial *adjective* relating to judgment or to justice.

judiciary *noun* The judiciary is the branch of government concerned with justice and the legal system.

judicious *adjective* sensible and showing good judgment.

judo *noun* Judo is a sport in which two people try to force each other to the ground using special throwing techniques. It originated in Japan as a form of self-defence.

jug *noun* a container with a lip or spout used for holding or serving liquids.

juggernaut *noun* a large heavy lorry.

juggle *verb* 1 To juggle means to throw objects into the air, catching them in sequence, and tossing them up again so there are several in the air at one time. 2 If you juggle several different activities, you spend some time doing each of them rather than concentrating on just one.
> **juggler** *noun*

jugular *noun* The jugular or jugular vein is one of the veins in the neck which carry blood from the head back to the heart.

juice *noun* 1 Juice is the liquid that can be squeezed or extracted from fruit or other food. 2 Juices in the body are fluids.

juicy juicier, juiciest *adjective* 1 Juicy food has a lot of juice in it. 2 Something that is juicy is interesting, exciting or scandalous. > **juiciness** *noun*

jukebox *noun* a machine which automatically plays a selected piece of music when coins are inserted.

July *noun* July is the seventh month of the year. It has 31 days.

jumble *noun* 1 an untidy muddle of things. 2 Jumble consists of cheap articles that are given away to a charity so that they can be sold to raise money. ▶ *verb* 3 To jumble things means to mix them up untidily.

jumbo *noun* 1 A jumbo or jumbo jet is a large jet aeroplane that can carry several hundred passengers. ▶ *adjective* 2 very large.

jump *verb* 1 To jump means to spring off the ground using your leg muscles. 2 To jump something means to spring off the ground and move over or across it. 3 If you jump at something, such as an opportunity, you accept it eagerly. 4 If you jump on someone, you criticise them suddenly and forcefully. 5 If someone jumps, they make a sudden sharp movement of surprise. 6 If an amount or level jumps, it suddenly increases. ▶ *noun* 7 a spring into the air, sometimes over an object.

> **jump** *verb*
> 2 = bound, clear, hurdle, leap,
> spring, vault 6 = escalate,
> increase, rise, surge
> ▶ *noun* 7 = bound, leap, vault

jumper *noun* a knitted garment for the top half of the body.

jumpy jumpier, jumpiest *adjective* nervous and worried.

junction *noun* a place where roads or railway lines meet or cross.

June *noun* June is the sixth month of the year. It has 30 days.

jungle *noun* 1 a dense tropical forest. 2 a tangled mass of plants or other objects.

junior *adjective* 1 Someone who is junior to other people has a lower position in an organisation. 2 Junior also means younger. 3 relating to childhood. ▶ *noun* 4 someone who holds an unimportant position in an organisation.

> **junior** *adjective*
> 1 = inferior, lesser, lower, subordinate

juniper *noun* an evergreen shrub with purple berries used in cooking and medicine.

junk *noun* 1 Junk is old or second-hand articles which are sold cheaply or thrown away. 2 If you think something is junk, you think it is worthless rubbish. 3 a Chinese sailing boat with a flat bottom and square sails.

> **junk** *noun*
> 1 = clutter, odds and ends, refuse (*formal*), rubbish, scrap, trash

junk food *noun* Junk food is food low in nutritional value which is eaten as well as or instead of proper meals.

junkie *noun* (*slang*) a drug addict.

Jupiter *noun* Jupiter is the largest planet in the solar system and the fifth from the sun.

jurisdiction *noun* 1 (*formal*) Jurisdiction is the power or right of the courts to apply laws and make legal judgments.

2 Jurisdiction is power or authority.

juror *noun* a member of a jury.

jury *juries noun* a group of people in a court of law who have been selected to listen to the facts of a case on trial, and to decide whether the accused person is guilty or not.

just *adjective* 1 fair and impartial: *She arrived at a just decision.* 2 morally right or proper: *a just reward.* ▶ *adverb* 3 If something has just happened, it happened a very short time ago. 4 If you just do something, you do it by a very small amount: *They only just won.* 5 simply or only: *It was just an excuse not to work.* 6 exactly: *It's just what she wants.* ▶ *phrase* 7 In South African English, **just now** means in a little while.

justice *noun* 1 Justice is fairness and reasonableness. 2 (CITIZENSHIP) The system of justice in a country is the way in which laws are maintained by the courts. 3 a judge or magistrate.

> **justice** *noun*
> 1 = equity, fairness, impartiality
> 3 = judge, magistrate

justify *justifies, justifying, justified verb* 1 If you justify an action or idea, you prove or explain why it is reasonable or necessary. 2 (ICT) To justify text that you have typed or keyed into a computer is to adjust the spaces between the words so each full line in a paragraph fills the space between the left and right hand margins of the page.
> **justification** *noun*
> **justifiable** *adjective*

justify *verb*
1 = defend, excuse, explain, vindicate, warrant

jut juts, jutting, jutted *verb* If something juts out, it sticks out beyond a surface or edge.

juvenile *adjective* 1 suitable for young people. 2 childish and rather silly. ▶ *noun* 3 a young person not old enough to be considered an adult.

juxtapose *verb* If you juxtapose things or ideas, you put them close together, often to emphasise the difference between them.

Kk

kaleidoscope *noun* a toy consisting of a tube with a hole at one end. When you look through the hole and twist the other end of the tube, you can see a changing pattern of colours.

kamikaze *noun* (HISTORY) In the Second World War, a kamikaze was a Japanese pilot who flew an aircraft loaded with explosives directly into an enemy target knowing he would be killed doing so.

kangaroo kangaroos *noun* a large Australian animal with very strong back legs which it uses for jumping.

karate *noun* Karate is a sport in which people fight each other using only their hands, elbows, feet and legs.

karma *noun* (RE) In Buddhism, Hinduism and Sikhism, karma refers to the forces that influence people's fortune and rebirth.

Karoo Karoos; also spelt **Karroo** *noun* In South Africa, the Karoos are areas of very dry land.

kayak *noun* a covered canoe with a small opening for the person sitting in it, originally used by the Inuit.

kebab *noun* pieces of meat or vegetable stuck on a stick and grilled.

keel *noun* 1 the specially shaped bottom of a ship which supports the sides and sits in the water.
▶ *verb* 2 If someone or something keels over, they fall down sideways.

keen *adjective* 1 Someone who is keen shows great eagerness and enthusiasm. 2 If you are keen on someone or something, you are attracted to or fond of them. 3 quick to notice or understand things. 4 Keen senses let you see, hear, smell and taste things very clearly or strongly. > **keenly** *adverb*

> **keen** *adjective*
> 1 = ardent, avid, eager, enthusiastic, fond, into (*informal*) 3 = astute, brilliant, perceptive, quick, shrewd

keep keeps, keeping, kept *verb* 1 To keep someone or something in a particular condition means to make them stay in that condition. 2 If you keep something, you have it and look after it. 3 To keep something also means to store it in the usual place. 4 If you keep doing something, you do it repeatedly or continuously. 5 If you keep a promise, you do what you promised to do. 6 If you keep a secret, you do not tell anyone else. 7 If you keep a diary, you write something in it every day. 8 If you keep someone from going somewhere, you delay them so that they are late. 9 To keep someone means to provide them with money, food and clothing.
▶ *noun* 10 Your keep is the cost of the food you eat, your housing and your clothing. 11 (HISTORY) the main tower inside the walls of a castle. > **keep up** *verb* If you

keep up with other people, you move or work at the same speed as they do.

> **keep** *verb*
> 2 = care for, maintain, preserve
> 3 = deposit, hold, store 5 = carry out, fulfil, honour

keeper *noun* 1 a person whose job is to look after the animals in a zoo. 2 a goalkeeper in soccer or hockey.

keeping *noun* 1 If something is in your keeping, it has been given to you to look after for a while.
▶ *phrase* 2 If one thing is in keeping with another, the two things are suitable or appropriate together.

keepsake *noun* something that someone gives you to remind you of a particular person or event.

keg *noun* a small barrel.

kennel *noun* 1 a shelter for a dog. 2 A kennels is a place where dogs can be kept for a time, or where they are bred.

Kenyan *adjective* 1 belonging or relating to Kenya. ▶ *noun* 2 someone who comes from Kenya.

kept the past tense and past participle of **keep**.

kerb *noun* the raised edge at the point where a pavement joins onto a road.

kernel *noun* the part of a nut that is inside the shell.

kerosene *noun* Kerosene is the same as paraffin.

ketchup *noun* Ketchup is a cold sauce, usually made from tomatoes.

kettle *noun* a metal container with a spout, in which you boil water.

key noun 1 a shaped piece of metal that fits into a hole so that you can unlock a door, wind something that is clockwork, or start a car. 2 The keys on a computer keyboard, piano or cash register are the buttons that you press to use it. 3 an explanation of the symbols used in a map or diagram. 4 (MUSIC) In music, a key is a scale of notes. 5 The key to a situation or result is the way in which it can be achieved. ▶ verb 6 (ICT) If you key in information on a computer keyboard, you type it. ▶ adjective 7 The key person or thing in a group is the most important one.

keyboard noun (ICT) a row of buttons or levers on a computer, piano or cash register.

kg an abbreviation for 'kilogram' or 'kilograms'.

khaki noun 1 Khaki is a strong yellowish-brown material, used especially for military uniforms. ▶ noun, adjective 2 yellowish-brown.

kibbutz kibbutzim noun a place of work in Israel where the workers live together and share all the duties and income.

kick verb 1 If you kick something, you hit it with your foot. ▶ noun 2 If you give something a kick, you hit it with your foot. 3 (informal) If you get a kick out of doing something, you enjoy doing it. > **kick off** verb When players kick off, they start a soccer or rugby match. > **kick-off** noun

kid kids, kidding, kidded noun 1 (informal) a child. 2 a young goat. ▶ verb 3 If you kid people, you tease them by deceiving them in fun.

kidnap kidnaps, kidnapping, kidnapped verb To kidnap

someone is to take them away by force and demand a ransom in exchange for returning them. > **kidnapper** noun

> **kidnap** verb
> = abduct, capture, seize

kidney noun Your kidneys are two organs in your body that remove waste products from your blood.

kill verb 1 To kill a person, animal or plant is to make them die. 2 (informal) If something is killing you, it is causing you severe pain or discomfort. ▶ noun 3 The kill is the moment when a hunter kills an animal. > **killer** noun

> **kill** verb
> 1 = assassinate, butcher, destroy, execute, exterminate, massacre, murder, slaughter, slay (literary)

kiln noun (ART) an oven for baking china or pottery until it becomes hard and dry.

kilo kilos noun a kilogram.

kilobyte noun (ICT) a unit of computer memory size, equal to 1024 bytes.

kilogram noun a unit of weight equal to 1000 grams.

kilometre noun (MATHS) a unit of distance equal to 1000 metres.

kilowatt noun (SCIENCE) a unit of power equal to 1000 watts.

kilt noun a tartan skirt worn by men as part of Scottish Highland dress.

kimono kimonos noun a long, loose garment with wide sleeves and a sash, worn in Japan.

kin plural noun Your kin are your relatives.

kin *plural noun*
= family, kindred, people, relations, relatives

kind *noun* **1** A particular kind of thing is something of the same type or sort as other things.
▶ *adjective* **2** Someone who is kind is considerate and generous towards other people.

kind *noun*
1 = brand, breed, category, class, classification, genre, grade, sort, species, type, variety
▶ *adjective* **2** = benevolent, benign, charitable, compassionate, considerate, good, humane, kind-hearted, kindly, thoughtful, unselfish

kindergarten *noun* a school for children who are too young to go to primary school.

kindness *noun* the quality of being considerate towards other people.

kindness *noun*
= benevolence, charity, compassion, gentleness, humanity

kindred *adjective* If you say that someone is a kindred spirit, you mean that they have the same interests or opinions as you.

king *noun* **1** (HISTORY) The king of a country is a man who is the head of state in the country, and who inherited his position from his parents. **2** In chess, the king is a piece which can only move one square at a time. When a king cannot move away from a position where it can be taken, the game is lost. **3** In a pack of cards, a king is a card with a picture of a king on it.

kingdom *noun* **1** (HISTORY) a country that is governed by a king or queen. **2** The largest divisions of the living organisms in the natural world are called kingdoms.

king-size or **king-sized** *adjective* larger than the normal size.

kinship *noun* Kinship is a family relationship to other people.

kiosk *noun* a covered stall on a street where you can buy newspapers, sweets or cigarettes.

kip kips, kipping, kipped (*informal*) *noun* **1** a period of sleep. ▶ *verb* **2** When you kip, you sleep.

kiss *verb* **1** When you kiss someone, you touch them with your lips as a sign of love or affection. ▶ *noun* **2** When you give someone a kiss, you kiss them.

kiss of life *noun* The kiss of life is a method of reviving someone by blowing air into their lungs.

kit *noun* **1** a collection of things that you use for a sport or other activity. **2** a set of parts that you put together to make something.

kitchen *noun* a room used for cooking and preparing food.

kite *noun* **1** a frame covered with paper or cloth which is attached to a piece of string, and which you fly in the air. **2** a shape with four sides, with two pairs of the same length, and none of the sides parallel to each other. **3** a bird of prey with a long tail and long wings.

kitten *noun* a young cat.

kitty kitties *noun* a fund of money that has been given by a group of people who will use it to pay for or do things together.

kiwi kiwi or kiwis *noun* **1** a type of bird found in New Zealand.

k

Kiwis cannot fly. **2** (*informal*) someone who comes from New Zealand. The plural of this sense is 'kiwis'.

km an abbreviation for 'kilometres'.

▶ **knack** *noun* a skilful or clever way of doing something difficult.

knead *verb* If you knead dough, you press it and squeeze it with your hands before baking it.

knee *noun* the joint in your leg between your ankle and your hip.

kneecap *noun* Your kneecaps are the bones at the front of your knees.

kneel kneels, kneeling, knelt *verb* When you kneel, you bend your legs and lower your body until your knees are touching the ground.

knell *noun* (*literary*) the sound of a bell rung to announce a death or at a funeral.

knelt the past tense and past participle of **kneel**.

knew the past tense of **know**.

knickers *plural noun* Knickers are underpants worn by women and girls.

knife knives; knifes, knifing, knifed *noun* **1** (DGT) a sharp metal tool that you use to cut things. ▶ *verb* **2** To knife someone is to stab them with a knife.

knight *noun* **1** a man who has been given the title 'Sir' by the King or Queen. **2** (HISTORY) In medieval Europe, a knight was a man who served a monarch or lord as a mounted soldier. **3** a chess piece that is usually in the shape of a horse's head. ▶ *verb* **4** To knight a man is to give him the title 'Sir'.

knit knits, knitting, knitted *verb* **1** If you knit a piece of clothing, you make it by working lengths of wool together, either using needles held in the hand, or with a machine. **2** If you knit your brows, you frown. ▶ **knitting** *noun*

knob *noun* **1** a round handle. **2** a round switch on a machine.

knock *verb* **1** If you knock on something, you strike it with your hand or fist. **2** If you knock a part of your body against something, you bump into it quite forcefully. **3** (*informal*) To knock someone is to criticise them. ▶ *noun* **4** a firm blow on something solid. ▷ **knock out** *verb* To knock someone out is to hit them so hard that they become unconscious.

knockout *noun* **1** a punch in boxing which knocks a boxer unconscious. **2** a competition in which competitors are eliminated in each round until only the winner is left.

knot knots, knotting, knotted *noun* **1** a fastening made by looping a piece of string around itself and pulling the ends tight. **2** a small lump visible on the surface of a piece of wood. **3** A knot of people is a small group of them. **4** (*technical*) a unit of speed used for ships and aircraft. ▶ *verb* **5** If you knot a piece of string, you tie a knot in it.

know knows, knowing, knew, known *verb* **1** If you know a fact, you have it in your mind and you do not need to learn it. **2** People you know are not strangers because you have met them and spoken to them. ▶ *phrase* **3** (*informal*) If you are **in the know**, you are one of a small number of people who share a secret.

know *verb*
1 = apprehend, be aware of, comprehend, perceive, see, understand **2** = be acquainted with, be familiar with, recognise

know-how *noun* Know-how is the ability to do something that is quite difficult or technical.

knowing *adjective* A knowing look is one that shows that you know or understand something that other people do not. > **knowingly** *adverb*

knowledge *noun* Knowledge is all the information and facts that you know.

knowledge *noun*
= education, learning, scholarship, wisdom

knowledgeable *adjective* Someone who is knowledgeable knows a lot about a subject.

knuckle *noun* Your knuckles are the joints at the end of your fingers where they join your hand.

koala *noun* an Australian animal with grey fur and small tufted ears. Koalas live in trees and eat eucalyptus leaves.

Koran; also spelt **Qur'an** *noun* (RE) The Koran is the holy book of Islam.

Korean *adjective* **1** relating or belonging to Korea. ▶ *noun* **2** someone who comes from Korea. **3** Korean is the main language spoken in Korea.

kosher *adjective* (RE) Kosher food is acceptable for Jewish people to eat.

kung fu *noun* Kung fu is a Chinese style of fighting which involves using your hands and feet.

Kurd *noun* The Kurds are a group of people who live in eastern Turkey, northern Iraq and western Iran.

Kurdish *adjective* **1** belonging or relating to the Kurds. ▶ *noun* **2** Kurdish is the language spoken by the Kurds.

k

Ll

l an abbreviation for 'litres'.

lab noun (*informal*) a laboratory.

label labels, labelling, labelled noun **1** a piece of paper or plastic attached to something as an identification. ▶ verb **2** If you label something, you put a label on it.

> **label** noun
> **1** = sticker, tag, ticket
> ▶ verb **2** = flag, sticker, tag

laboratory laboratories noun a place where scientific experiments are carried out.

laborious adjective needing a lot of effort or time. > **laboriously** adverb

Labor Party noun In Australia, the Labor Party is one of the major political parties.

labour noun **1** Labour is hard work. **2** The workforce of a country or industry is sometimes called its labour. **3** In Britain, the Labour Party is a political party that believes that wealth and power should be shared more equally among the population. **4** In New Zealand, the Labour Party is one of the main political parties. **5** Labour is also the last stage of pregnancy, when a woman gives birth to a baby. ▶ verb **6** (*old-fashioned*) To labour means to work hard.

> **labour** noun
> **1** = effort, exertion, industry, toil, work **2** = employees, workers, workforce
> ▶ verb **6** = slave, toil, work

labrador noun a large dog with short black, golden or brown hair.

labyrinth noun a complicated series of paths or passages.

lace noun **1** Lace is a very fine decorated cloth made with a lot of holes in it. **2** Laces are cords with which you fasten your shoes. ▶ verb **3** When you lace up your shoes, you tie a bow in the laces. **4** To lace someone's food or drink means to put a small amount of alcohol, a drug, or poison in it. > **lacy** adjective

lack noun **1** If there is a lack of something, it is not present when or where it is needed. ▶ verb **2** If something is lacking, it is not present when or where it is needed. **3** If someone or something is lacking in something, they do not have it or do not have enough of it.

> **lack** noun
> **1** = absence, deficiency, scarcity, shortage, want

lacklustre adjective not interesting or exciting.

laconic adjective using very few words.

lacquer noun Lacquer is thin, clear paint that you put on wood to protect it and make it shiny.

lacrosse noun Lacrosse is an outdoor ball game in which two teams try to score goals using long sticks with nets on the end of them.

lad noun a boy or young man.

ladder *noun* 1 a wooden or metal frame used for climbing which consists of horizontal steps fixed to two vertical poles. 2 If your stockings or tights have a ladder in them, they have a vertical, ladder-like tear in them. ▶ *verb* 3 If you ladder your stockings or tights, you get a ladder in them.

laden *adjective* To be laden with something means to be carrying or holding a lot of it.

ladle *noun* 1 a long-handled spoon with a deep, round bowl, which you use to serve soup. 2 If you ladle out food, you serve it with a ladle.

lady ladies *noun* 1 a woman, especially one who is considered to be well-mannered. 2 Lady is a title used in front of the name of a woman from the nobility, such as a lord's wife.

lag lags, lagging, lagged *verb* 1 To lag behind is to make slower progress than other people. 2 To lag pipes is to wrap cloth round them to stop the water inside freezing in cold weather.

> **lag** *verb*
> 1 = fall behind, trail

lager *noun* Lager is light-coloured beer.

lagoon *noun* an area of water separated from the sea by reefs or sand.

laid the past tense and past participle of **lay**.

lain the past participle of some meanings of **lie**[1].

lair *noun* a place where a wild animal lives.

lake *noun* an area of fresh water surrounded by land.

lamb *noun* 1 a young sheep.

2 Lamb is the meat from a lamb.

lame *adjective* 1 unable to walk easily because of an injured leg. 2 A lame excuse is not very convincing.

> **lame** *adjective*
> 2 = feeble, flimsy, pathetic, poor, unconvincing, weak

lament *verb* 1 To lament something means to express sorrow or regret about it. ▶ *noun* 2 an expression of sorrow or regret. 3 a song or poem expressing grief at someone's death.

> **lament** *verb*
> 1 = grieve, mourn, wail, weep
> ▶ *noun* 2 = moan, wail

lamentable *adjective* disappointing and regrettable.

laminated *adjective* consisting of several thin sheets or layers stuck together.

lamp *noun* a device that produces light.

lamppost *noun* a tall column in a street, with a lamp at the top.

lance *noun* 1 To lance a boil or abscess means to stick a sharp instrument into it in order to release the fluid. ▶ *noun* 2 a long spear that used to be used by soldiers on horseback.

land *noun* 1 Land is an area of ground. 2 Land is also the part of the earth that is not covered by water. 3 a country. ▶ *verb* 4 When a plane lands, it arrives back on the ground after a flight. 5 If you land something you have been trying to get, you succeed in getting it. 6 To land a fish means to catch it while fishing. 7 If you land someone with something unpleasant, you cause them to have to deal with it.

land noun
1 = estate, grounds, property
3 = country, nation, province, region, territory
▶ verb 4 = alight, dock, touch down

landfill noun 1 Landfill is the disposing of rubbish by covering it with earth. 2 A landfill is an area where rubbish is disposed of in this way.

landing noun 1 a flat area in a building at the top of a flight of stairs. 2 The landing of an aeroplane is its arrival back on the ground after a flight.

landlady landladies noun a woman who owns a house or small hotel and who lets rooms to people.

landlord noun a man who owns a house or small hotel and who lets rooms to people.

landmark noun 1 a noticeable feature in a landscape, which you can use to check your position. 2 an important stage in the development of something.

landowner noun someone who owns land, especially a large area of the countryside.

landscape noun 1 (GEOGRAPHY) The landscape is the view over an area of open land. 2 (ART) a painting of the countryside.

landslide noun 1 a large amount of loose earth and rocks falling down a mountain side. 2 a victory in an election won by a large number of votes.

lane noun 1 a narrow road, especially in the country. 2 one of the strips on a road marked with lines to guide drivers.

language noun 1 the system of words that the people of a country use to communicate with each other. 2 Your language is the style in which you express yourself. 3 Language is the study of the words and grammar of a particular language.

language noun
1 = dialect, idiom, jargon, lingo (informal), tongue, vernacular, vocabulary 2 = phrasing, style, wording

languid adjective slow and lacking energy.

languish verb If you languish, you endure an unpleasant situation for a long time.

lanky lankier, lankiest adjective Someone who is lanky is tall and thin and moves rather awkwardly.

lantern noun a lamp in a metal frame with glass sides.

lap laps, lapping, lapped noun 1 Your lap is the flat area formed by your thighs when you are sitting down. 2 one circuit of a running track or racecourse.
▶ verb 3 When an animal laps up liquid, it drinks using its tongue to get the liquid into its mouth. 4 If you lap someone in a race, you overtake them when they are still on the previous lap. 5 When water laps against something, it gently moves against it in little waves.

lapel noun a flap which is joined on to the collar of a jacket or coat.

lapse noun 1 a moment of bad behaviour by someone who usually behaves well. 2 a slight mistake. 3 a period of time between two events. ▶ verb

4 If you lapse into a different way of behaving, you start behaving that way. **5** If a legal document or contract lapses, it is not renewed on the date when it expires.

laptop noun (ICT) a type of small portable computer.

lard noun Lard is fat from a pig, used in cooking.

larder noun a room in which you store food, often next to a kitchen.

large adjective **1** Someone or something that is large is much bigger than average. ▶ phrase **2** If a prisoner is **at large**, he or she has escaped from prison.

> **large** adjective
> **1** = big, colossal, enormous, giant, gigantic, great, huge, immense, massive, vast

largely adverb to a great extent.

lark noun **1** a small brown bird with a distinctive song. **2** If you do something for a lark, you do it in a high-spirited or mischievous way for fun.

larrikin noun (informal) In Australian and New Zealand English, a larrikin is a young person who behaves in a wild or irresponsible way.

larva larvae noun an insect, which looks like a short, fat worm, at the stage before it becomes an adult.

larynx larynxes or larynges noun the part of your throat containing the vocal cords, through which air passes between your nose and lungs.

lasagne noun Lasagne is an Italian dish made with wide flat sheets of pasta, meat and cheese sauce.

laser noun a machine that produces a powerful concentrated beam of light which is used to cut very hard materials and in some kinds of surgery.

lash noun **1** Your lashes are the hairs growing on the edge of your eyelids. **2** a strip of leather at the end of a whip. **3** Lashes are blows struck with a whip. ▶ **lash out** verb To lash out at someone means to criticise them severely.

lass noun a girl or young woman.

last adjective **1** The last thing or event is the most recent one: last year. **2** The last thing that remains is the only one left after all the others have gone. ▶ adverb **3** If you last did something on a particular occasion, you have not done it since then. **4** The thing that happens last in a sequence of events is the final one. ▶ verb **5** If something lasts, it continues to exist or happen. **6** To last also means to remain in good condition. ▶ phrase **7** At last means after a long time.
> **lastly** adverb

> **last** adjective
> **1** = latest, most recent, preceding, previous **2** = closing, concluding, final, ultimate
> ▶ verb **5** = carry on, continue, endure, persist, remain, survive

last-ditch adjective A last-ditch attempt to do something is a final attempt to succeed when everything else has failed.

latch noun **1** a simple door fastening consisting of a metal bar which falls into a hook. **2** a type of door lock which locks automatically when you close the door and which has to be opened with a key. ▶ verb **3** (informal) If you latch onto someone or something, you become attached to them.

late *adjective, adverb* **1** Something that happens late happens towards the end of a period of time: *the late evening.* **2** If you arrive late, or do something late, you arrive or do it after the time you were expected to. ▸ *adjective* **3** A late event happens after the time when it usually takes place: *a late breakfast.* **4** (*formal*) Late means dead: *my late grandmother.*

> **late** *adjective*
> **3** = behind, behind time, belated, delayed, last-minute, overdue **4** = dead, deceased (*formal*), departed

lately *adverb* Events that happened lately happened recently.

latent *adjective* A latent quality is hidden at the moment, but may emerge in the future.

lateral *adjective* relating to the sides of something, or moving in a sideways direction.

lathe *noun* a machine which holds and turns a piece of wood or metal against a tool to cut and shape it.

lather *noun* Lather is the foam that you get when you rub soap in water.

Latin *noun* **1** Latin is the language of ancient Rome. **2** Latins are people who speak languages closely related to Latin, such as French, Italian, Spanish and Portuguese.

Latin America *noun* Latin America consists of the countries in North, South and Central America where Spanish or Portuguese is the main language.

latitude *noun* (GEOGRAPHY) The latitude of a place is its distance north or south of the equator measured in degrees.

latter *adjective, noun* **1** You use 'latter' to refer to the second of two things that are mentioned: *They were eating sandwiches and cakes (the latter bought from Mrs Paul's bakery).* ▸ *adjective* **2** 'Latter' also describes the second or end part of something: *the latter part of his career.*

lattice *noun* a structure made of strips which cross over each other diagonally leaving holes in between.

laudable *adjective* (*formal*) deserving praise.

laugh *verb* **1** When you laugh, you make a noise which shows that you are amused or happy. ▸ *noun* **2** the noise you make when you laugh.

> **laugh** *verb*
> **1** = chortle, chuckle, giggle, guffaw, snigger, titter
> ▸ *noun* **2** = chortle, chuckle, giggle, guffaw, snigger, titter

laughable *adjective* quite absurd.

laughing stock *noun* someone who has been made to seem ridiculous.

laughter *noun* Laughter is a noise which shows that you are amused or happy.

launch *verb* **1** To launch a ship means to send it into the water for the first time. **2** To launch a rocket means to send it into space. **3** When a company launches a new product, they have an advertising campaign to promote it as they start to sell it. ▸ *noun* **4** a motorboat.

launch pad *noun* A launch pad, or a launching pad, is the place from which space rockets take off.

launder *verb (old-fashioned)* To launder clothes, sheets or towels means to wash and iron them.

laundry laundries *noun* 1 a business that washes and irons clothes and sheets. 2 Laundry is also the dirty clothes and sheets that are being washed, or are about to be washed.

laurel *noun* an evergreen tree with shiny leaves.

lava *noun* (GEOGRAPHY) Lava is the very hot liquid rock that comes shooting out of an erupting volcano and becomes solid as it cools.

lavatory lavatories *noun* a toilet.

lavender *noun* 1 Lavender is a small bush with bluish-pink flowers that have a strong, pleasant scent. ▶ *adjective* 2 bluish-pink.

lavish *adjective* 1 If you are lavish, you are very generous with your time, money or gifts. 2 A lavish amount is a large amount. ▶ *verb* 3 If you lavish money or affection on someone, you give them a lot of it.

law *noun* 1 (CITIZENSHIP) The law is the system of rules developed by the government of a country, which regulate what people may and may not do and deals with people who break these rules. 2 The law is also the profession of people such as lawyers, whose job involves the application of the laws of a country. 3 (CITIZENSHIP) one of the rules established by a government or a religion, which tells people what they may or may not do. 4 a scientific fact which

allows you to explain how things work in the physical world.
▶ *lawful adjective*

law *noun*
1 = charter, code, constitution
3 = act, code, decree, regulation, rule, statute

law-abiding *adjective* obeying the law and not causing any trouble.

lawless *adjective* having no regard for the law.

lawn *noun* an area of grass that is kept cut short.

lawnmower *noun* a machine for cutting grass.

lawsuit *noun* a civil court case between two people, as opposed to the police prosecuting someone for a criminal offence.

lawyer *noun* a person who is qualified in law, and whose job is to advise people about the law and represent them in court.

lawyer *noun*
= advocate, attorney, barrister, counsel, solicitor

lax *adjective* careless and not keeping to the usual standards.

lay lays, laying, laid *verb* 1 When you lay something somewhere, you put it down so that it lies there. 2 If you lay something, you arrange it or set it out. 3 If you lay the table, you put cutlery on the table ready for a meal. 4 When a bird lays an egg, it produces the egg out of its body. 5 If you lay a trap for someone, you create a situation in which you will be able to catch them out. 6 If you lay emphasis on something, you refer to it in a way that shows you think it is very important. 7 If you lay odds on something, you bet that it will happen. **8** Lay is the past tense of **lie¹**. ▸ *adjective* **9** You use 'lay' to describe people who are involved with a Christian church but are not members of the clergy. ▸ **lay off** *verb* **1** When workers are laid off, their employers tell them not to come to work for a while because there is a shortage of work. **2** (*informal*) If you tell someone to lay off, you want them to stop doing something annoying. ▸ **lay on** *verb* If you lay on a meal or entertainment, you provide it.

lay *verb*
1 = place, put, set, set down, settle, spread **2** = arrange, set out

lay-by *noun* **1** an area by the side of a main road where motorists can stop for a short while. **2** In Australia and New Zealand, lay-by is a system where you pay a deposit on an item in a shop so that it will be kept for you until you pay the rest of the price.

layer *noun* a single thickness of something.

layer *noun*
= blanket, coat, coating, covering, film, sheet, stratum

layman laymen *noun* **1** someone who has not specialised knowledge of a subject.
2 someone who belongs to the church but is not a member of the clergy.

layout *noun* The layout of something is the pattern in which it is arranged.

layout *noun*
= arrangement, design, format, plan

laze *verb* If you laze, you relax and do no work.

laze *verb*
= idle, loaf, lounge

lazy lazier, laziest *adjective* idle and unwilling to work. ▸ **lazily** *adverb* ▸ **laziness** *noun*

lazy *adjective*
= idle, slack

lb an abbreviation for 'pounds'.

lbw In cricket, lbw is a way of dismissing a batter when his or her legs prevent the ball from hitting the wicket. lbw is an abbreviation for 'leg before wicket'.

leach *verb* When minerals are leached from rocks, they are dissolved by water which filters through the rock.

lead¹ leads, leading, led *verb* **1** If you lead someone somewhere, you go in front of them in order to show them the way. **2** If one thing leads to another, it causes the second thing to happen. **3** a person who leads a group of people is in charge of them. ▸ *noun* **4** a length of leather or chain attached to a dog's collar, so that the dog can be kept under control. **5** If the police have a lead, they have a clue which might help them to solve a crime.

lead *verb*
1 = conduct (*formal*), escort, guide, steer, usher **2** = cause, contribute to, produce **3** = command, direct, govern, head, manage, supervise ▸ *noun* **5** = clue, indication, trace

lead² *noun* (SCIENCE) Lead is a soft metallic element. Its atomic number is 82 and its symbol is Pb.

leader noun 1 someone who is in charge of a country, an organisation, or a group of people. 2 the person who is winning in a competition or race. 3 a newspaper article that expresses the newspaper's opinions.

> **leader** noun
> 1 = boss, captain, chief, commander, director, head, principal, ringleader

leadership noun 1 the group of people in charge of an organisation. 2 Leadership is the ability to be a good leader.

leading adjective particularly important, respected or advanced.

> **leading** adjective
> = chief, eminent, key, main, major, principal, prominent, top

leaf leaves noun 1 the flat green growth on the end of a twig or branch of a tree or other plant. ▶ verb 2 If you leaf through a book, magazine or newspaper, you turn the pages over quickly.

leaflet noun a piece of paper with information or advertising printed on it.

> **leaflet** noun
> = booklet, brochure, circular, pamphlet

league noun 1 (PE) a group of countries, clubs or people who have joined together for a particular purpose or because they share a common interest. 2 a unit of distance used in former times, equal to about 3 miles.

leak verb 1 If a pipe or container leaks, it has a hole which lets gas or liquid escape. 2 If liquid or gas leaks, it escapes from a pipe or container. 3 If someone in an organisation leaks information, they give the information to someone who is not supposed to have it. ▶ noun 4 If a pipe or container has a leak, it has a hole which lets gas or liquid escape. 5 If there is a leak in an organisation, someone inside the organisation is giving information to people who are not supposed to have it.

> **leak** verb
> 2 = escape, ooze, seep, spill
> ▶ noun 4 = chink, crack, fissure, hole, puncture

leakage noun an escape of gas or liquid from a pipe or container.

lean leans, leaning, leant or leaned verb 1 When you lean in a particular direction, you bend your body in that direction. 2 When you lean on something, you rest your body against it for support. 3 If you lean on someone, you depend on them. 4 If you lean towards particular ideas, you approve of them and follow them. ▶ adjective 5 having little or no fat. 6 A lean period is a time when food or money is in short supply.

leap leaps, leaping, leapt or leaped verb 1 If you leap somewhere, you jump over a long distance or high in the air. ▶ noun 2 a jump over a long distance or high in the air.

> **leap** verb
> 1 = bounce, bound, jump, spring, vault
> ▶ noun 2 = bound, jump, spring

leap year noun a year, occurring every four years, in which there are 366 days.

learn learns, learning, learnt or learned *verb* 1 When you learn something, you gain knowledge or a skill through studying or training. 2 If you learn of something, you find out about it. ▶ **learner** *noun*

> **learn** *verb*
> 1 = grasp, master, pick up
> 2 = ascertain, determine, discover, find out, gather, hear, understand

learned *adjective* A learned person has a lot of knowledge gained from years of study.

> **learned** *adjective*
> = academic, erudite, intellectual, literate, scholarly

learning *noun* Learning is knowledge that has been acquired through serious study.

lease *noun* 1 an agreement which allows someone to use a house or flat in return for rent. ▶ *verb* 2 To lease property to someone means to allow them to use it in return for rent.

leash *noun* a length of leather or chain attached to a dog's collar so that the dog can be controlled.

least *noun* 1 The least is the smallest possible amount of something. ▶ *adjective* 2 as small or as few as possible. ▶ *adverb* 3 Least is a superlative form of **little**. ▶ *phrase* 4 You use at least to show that you are referring to the minimum amount of something, and that you think the true amount is greater.

> **least** *adjective*
> 2 = fewest, lowest, minimum, slightest, smallest

leather *noun* Leather is the tanned skin of some animals, used to make shoes and clothes. ▶ **leathery** *adjective*

leave leaves, leaving, left *verb* 1 When you leave a place, you go away from it. 2 If you leave someone somewhere, they stay behind after you go away. 3 If you leave a job or organisation, you stop being part of it. 4 If someone leaves money or possessions to someone, they arrange for them to be given to them after their death. 5 In subtraction, when you take one number from another, it leaves a third number. ▶ *noun* 6 a period of holiday or absence from a job.

> **leave** *verb*
> 1 = abandon, depart, desert, forsake, go, quit, withdraw
> ▶ *noun* 6 = holiday, time off, vacation

Lebanese *adjective* 1 belonging or relating to Lebanon. ▶ *noun* 2 someone who comes from Lebanon.

lectern *noun* a sloping desk which people use to rest books or notes on.

lecture *noun* 1 a formal talk intended to teach people about a particular subject. 2 a talk intended to tell someone off. ▶ *verb* 3 Someone who lectures teaches in a college or university.

> **lecture** *noun*
> 1 = address, discourse, presentation, sermon, speech, talk 2 = reprimand, scolding, telling-off (*informal*), warning
> ▶ *verb* 3 = give a talk, speak, talk, teach

lecturer *noun* a teacher in a college or university.

led the past tense and past participle of **lead**[1].

ledge noun a narrow shelf on the side of a cliff or rock face, or on the outside of a building, directly under a window.

ledger noun a book in which accounts are kept.

leech noun a small worm that lives in water and feeds by sucking the blood from other animals.

leek noun a long vegetable of the onion family which is white at one end and has green leaves at the other.

leeway noun If something gives you some leeway, it allows you more flexibility, for example by giving you time to finish an activity.

left noun 1 The left is one of two sides of something. For example, on a page, English writing begins on the left. 2 People and political groups who hold socialist or communist views are referred to as the Left. 3 Left is the past tense and past participle of **leave**.
▶ adjective, adverb 4 Left means on or towards the left side of something.

left-handed adjective, adverb Someone who is left-handed does things such as writing with their left hand.

leftist noun, adjective (a person) holding left-wing political views.

leftovers plural noun the bits of food which have not been eaten at the end of a meal.

left-wing adjective believing more strongly in socialism, or less strongly in capitalism or conservatism, than other members of the same party or group. > **left-winger** noun

> **left-wing** adjective
> = leftist, liberal, socialist

leg noun 1 Your legs are the two limbs which stretch from your hips to your feet. 2 The legs of a pair of trousers are the parts that cover your legs. 3 The legs of an object such as a table are the parts which rest on the floor and support the object's weight. 4 A leg of a journey is one part of it. 5 one of two matches played between two sports teams.

legacy legacies noun 1 property or money that someone gets in the will of a person who has died. 2 something that exists as a result of a previous event or time.

> **legacy** noun
> 1 = bequest, estate, heirloom, inheritance

legal adjective 1 relating to the law. 2 allowed by the law. > **legally** adverb

> **legal** adjective
> 1 = forensic, judicial, judiciary
> 2 = authorised, lawful, legitimate, permissible, rightful, valid

legal aid noun Legal aid is a system which provides the services of a lawyer cheaply to people who cannot afford the full fees.

legalise; also spelt **legalize** verb To legalise something that is illegal means to change the law so that it becomes legal. > **legalisation** noun

legality noun The legality of an action means whether or not it is allowed by the law.

legend noun **1** an old story which was once believed to be true, but which is probably untrue. **2** If you refer to someone or something as a legend, you mean they are very famous. > **legendary** adjective

leggings plural noun **1** Leggings are very close-fitting trousers made of stretch material. **2** Leggings are also a waterproof covering worn over ordinary trousers to protect them.

legible adjective Writing that is legible is clear enough to be read.

legion noun **1** (HISTORY) In ancient Rome, a legion was a military unit of between 3000 and 6000 soldiers. **2** a large military force. **3** Legions of people are large numbers of them.

legislate verb (formal) When a government legislates, it creates new laws.

legislation noun Legislation is a law or set of laws created by a government.

legislative adjective relating to the making of new laws.

legislator noun (formal) a person involved in making or passing laws.

legislature noun (formal) the parliament in a country, which is responsible for making new laws.

legitimate adjective Something that is legitimate is reasonable or acceptable according to existing laws or standards.

leisure noun **1** Leisure is time during which you do not have to work, and can do what you enjoy doing. ▶ phrase **2** If you do something **at leisure**, or **at your leisure**, you do it at a convenient time.

leisure noun
1 = free time, recreation, relaxation, time off

leisurely adjective, adverb A leisurely action is done in an unhurried way.

leisurely adjective, adverb
= comfortable, easy, gentle, relaxed, unhurried

lemon noun **1** a yellow citrus fruit with a sour taste. ▶ adjective **2** pale yellow.

lemonade noun a sweet, fizzy drink made from lemons, water and sugar.

lend lends, lending, lent verb **1** If you lend someone something, you give it to them for a period of time and then they give it back to you. **2** If a bank lends money, it gives the money to someone and the money has to be repaid in the future, usually with interest. ▶ phrase **3** If you **lend someone a hand**, you help them.

length noun **1** The length of something is the horizontal distance from one end to the other. **2** The length of an event or activity is the amount of time it lasts for. **3** The length of something is also the fact that it is long rather than short. **4** a long piece of something.

length noun
1 = distance, extent, span
2 = duration, period, space, span, term

lengthen verb To lengthen something means to make it longer.

lengthen verb
= extend, make longer, prolong, stretch

lengthways or **lengthwise**
adverb If you measure something lengthways, you measure the horizontal distance from one end to the other.

lengthy lengthier, lengthiest *adjective* Something that is lengthy lasts for a long time.

lenient *adjective* If someone in authority is lenient, they are less severe than expected. > **leniently** *adverb* > **leniency** *noun*

lens *noun* 1 a curved piece of glass designed to focus light in a certain way, for example in a camera, telescope or pair of glasses. 2 The lens in your eye is the part behind the iris that focuses light.

lent 1 the past tense and past participle of **lend**. ▶ *noun* 2 (RE) Lent is the period of forty days leading up to Easter, during which Christians give up something they enjoy.

lentil *noun* Lentils are small dried red, green or brown seeds which are cooked and eaten in soups and curries.

Leo *noun* Leo is the fifth sign of the zodiac, represented by a lion. People born between July 23rd and August 22nd are born under this sign.

leopard *noun* a wild Asian or African big cat with yellow fur and black or brown spots.

leotard *noun* A leotard is a tight-fitting costume covering the body, which is worn for dancing or exercise. It is named after a French acrobat called Jules Léotard.

leper *noun* (*offensive*) someone who has leprosy.

leprosy *noun* Leprosy is an infectious disease which attacks the skin and nerves, and which can lead to fingers or toes dropping off.

lesbian *noun* a homosexual woman.

lesion *noun* a wound or injury.

less *adjective, adverb* 1 Less means a smaller amount, or not as much in quality: *She had become less frightened of the dark now.* 2 Less is a comparative form of **little**.
▶ *preposition* 3 You use 'less' to show that you are subtracting one number from another: *Eight less two leaves six.*

-less *suffix* '-less' means without: *hopeless.*

lessen *verb* If something lessens, it is reduced in amount, size or quality.

> **lessen** *verb*
> = abate, decrease, diminish, dwindle, lower, minimise, reduce, shrink

lesser *adjective* smaller in importance or amount than something else.

lesson *noun* 1 a fixed period of time during which a class of pupils is taught by a teacher. 2 an experience that makes you understand something important which you had not realised before.

> **lesson** *noun*
> 1 = class, coaching, lecture, period, tutoring

let lets, letting, let *verb* 1 If you let someone do something, you allow them to do it. 2 If someone lets a house or flat that they own, they rent it out. 3 You can say 'let's' or 'let us' when you want to suggest doing something with someone else: *Let's go.* **4** If you let yourself in for something, you agree to do it although you do not really want to. > **let down** *verb* If you let someone down, you fail to do something you had agreed to do for them. > **let off** *verb* **1** If someone in authority lets you off, they do not punish you for something you have done wrong. **2** If you let off a firework or explosive, you light it or detonate it.

let *verb*
1 = allow, give permission, permit, sanction **2** = hire out, lease, rent

lethal *adjective* able to kill someone.

lethargic *adjective* If you feel lethargic, you have no energy or enthusiasm.

lethargy *noun* Lethargy is a lack of energy and enthusiasm.

letter *noun* **1** Letters are written symbols which go together to make words. **2** a piece of writing addressed to someone and usually sent through the post.

lettering *noun* Lettering is writing, especially when you are describing the type of letters used.

lettuce *noun* a vegetable with large green leaves eaten raw in salad.

leukaemia; also spelt **leukemia** *noun* Leukaemia is a serious illness which affects the blood.

level levels, levelling, levelled *adjective* **1** A surface that is level is smooth, flat and parallel to the ground. ▸ *verb* **2** To level a piece of

land means to make it flat. **3** If you level a criticism at someone, you say or write something critical about them. ▸ *adverb* **4** If you draw level with someone, you get closer to them so that you are moving next to them. ▸ *noun* **5** a point on a scale which measures the amount, importance or difficulty of something. **6** The level of a liquid is the height it comes up to in a container. > **level off** or **level out** *verb* If something levels off or levels out, it stops increasing or decreasing.

level *adjective*
1 = flat, horizontal
▸ *verb* **2** = flatten, plane, smooth
▸ *noun* **5** = grade, rank, stage, standard, status

level crossing *noun* a place where road traffic is allowed to drive across a railway track.

level-headed *adjective* Someone who is level-headed is sensible and calm in emergencies.

lever *noun* **1** a handle on a machine that you pull in order to make the machine work. **2** a long bar that you wedge underneath a heavy object and press down on to make the object move.

leverage *noun* Leverage is knowledge or influence that you can use to make someone do something.

levy levies, levying, levied *(formal)* *noun* **1** an amount of money that you pay in tax. ▸ *verb* **2** When a government levies a tax, it makes people pay the tax and organises the collection of the money.

liability liabilities *noun*
1 Someone's liability is their

responsibility for something they have done wrong. **2** In business, a company's liabilities are its debts. **3** (*informal*) If you describe someone as a liability, you mean that they cause a lot of problems or embarrassment.

liable *adjective* **1** If you say that something is liable to happen, you mean that you think it will probably happen. **2** If you are liable for something you have done, you are legally responsible for it.

liaise *verb* To liaise with someone or an organisation means to cooperate with them and keep them informed.

liaison *noun* Liaison is communication between two organisations or two sections of an organisation.

liar *noun* a person who tells lies.

libel libels, libelling, libelled *noun* **1** Libel is something written about someone which is not true, and for which the writer can be made to pay damages in court. ▶ *verb* **2** To libel someone means to write or say something untrue about them. > **libellous** *adjective*

liberal *noun* **1** someone who believes in political progress, social welfare and individual freedom. ▶ *adjective* **2** Someone who is liberal is tolerant of a wide range of behaviour, standards or opinions. **3** To be liberal with something means to be generous with it. **4** A liberal quantity of something is a large amount of it.

Liberal Democrat *noun* In Britain, the Liberal Democrats are a political party that believes that individuals should have more freedom.

liberate *verb* To liberate people means to free them from prison or from an unpleasant situation. > **liberation** *noun* > **liberator** *noun*

liberty *noun* (CITIZENSHIP) Liberty is the freedom to choose how you want to live, without government restrictions.

Libra *noun* Libra is the seventh sign of the zodiac, represented by a pair of scales. People born between September 23rd and October 22nd are born under this sign.

librarian *noun* (LIBRARY) a person who works in a library.

library libraries *noun* **1** a building in which books are kept for people to borrow. **2** a collection of things such as books or music.

Libyan *adjective* **1** belonging or relating to Libya. ▶ *noun* **2** someone who comes from Libya.

lice the plural of **louse**.

licence *noun* **1** an official document which entitles you to carry out a particular activity, for example to drive a car. **2** Licence is the freedom to do what you want, especially when other people consider that it is being used irresponsibly.

license *verb* To license an activity means to give official permission for it to be carried out.

lichen *noun* Lichen is a green, moss-like growth on rocks or tree trunks.

lick *verb* **1** If you lick something, you move your tongue over it. ▶ *noun* **2** the action of licking.

lid *noun* the top of a container, which you open in order to reach what is inside.

lie¹ lies, lying, lay, lain *verb* **1** To lie somewhere means to rest there horizontally. **2** If you say where something lies, you are describing where it is.

> **lie** *verb*
> 1 = loll, lounge, recline, sprawl

lie² lies, lying, lied *verb* **1** To lie means to say something that is not true. ► *noun* **2** something you say that is not true.

> **lie** *verb*
> 1 = fib (*informal*), perjure yourself, tell a lie
> ► *noun* 2 = deceit, fabrication, falsehood, fib (*informal*), fiction

lieu *phrase* If one thing happens in lieu of another, it happens instead of it.

lieutenant *noun* a junior officer in the army or navy.

life lives *noun* **1** Life is the quality of being able to grow and develop, which is present in people, plants and animals. **2** Your life is your existence from the time you are born until the time you die. **3** The life of a machine is the period of time for which it is likely to work. **4** If you refer to the life in a place, you are talking about the amount of activity there. **5** If criminals are sentenced to life, they are sent to prison for the rest of their lives, or until they are granted parole.

> **life** *noun*
> 2 = existence, life span, lifetime, time

life assurance *noun* Life assurance is an insurance which provides a sum of money in the event of the policy holder's death.

lifeblood *noun* The lifeblood of something is the most essential part of it.

lifeboat *noun* **1** a boat kept on shore, which is sent out to rescue people who are in danger at sea. **2** a small boat kept on a ship, which is used if the ship starts to sink.

life expectancy *noun* (GEOGRAPHY) Your life expectancy is the number of years you can expect to live.

lifeguard *noun* a person whose job is to rescue people who are in difficulty in the sea or in a swimming pool.

life jacket *noun* a sleeveless inflatable jacket that keeps you afloat in water.

lifeless *adjective* **1** Someone who is lifeless is dead. **2** If you describe a place or person as lifeless, you mean that they are dull.

lifelike *adjective* A picture or sculpture that is lifelike looks very real or alive.

lifeline *noun* **1** something which helps you to survive or helps an activity to continue. **2** a rope thrown to someone who is in danger of drowning.

lifelong *adjective* existing throughout someone's life.

lifesaver *noun* In Australia and New Zealand, a lifesaver is a person whose job is to rescue people who are in difficulty in the sea.

life span *noun* **1** Someone's life span is the length of time during which they are alive. **2** The life span of a product or organisation is the length of time it exists or is useful.

lifestyle noun (PSHE) the living conditions, behaviour and habits that a person chooses to have.

lifetime noun Your lifetime is the period of time during which you are alive.

lift verb 1 To lift something means to move it to a higher position. 2 When fog or mist lifts, it clears away. 3 To lift a ban on something means to remove it. 4 (informal) To lift things means to steal them. ▶ noun 5 a machine like a large box which carries passengers from one floor to another in a building. 6 If you give someone a lift, you drive them somewhere in a car.

lift verb
1 = elevate, hoist, pick up, raise
3 = cancel, end, relax, remove

ligament noun (SCIENCE) a piece of tough tissue in your body which connects your bones.

light lights, lighting, lighted or lit noun 1 Light is brightness from the sun, fire or lamps that enables you to see things. 2 a lamp or other device that gives out brightness. 3 If you give someone a light, you give them a match or lighter to light their cigarette. ▶ adjective 4 A place that is light is bright because of the sun or the use of lamps. 5 A light colour is pale. 6 A light object does not weigh much. 7 A light task is fairly easy. 8 Light books or music are entertaining and are not intended to be serious. ▶ verb 9 To light a place means to cause it to be filled with light. 10 To light a fire means to make it start burning. 11 To light upon something means to find it by accident. > **lightly** adverb

light noun
1 = brightness, brilliance, glare, glow, illumination, radiance
▶ adjective 5 = bleached, blonde or blond, fair, pale, pastel
6 = flimsy, lightweight, portable, slight
▶ verb 9 = brighten, illuminate, light up 10 = ignite, kindle

lighten verb 1 When something lightens, it becomes less dark. 2 To lighten a load means to make it less heavy.

lighter noun a device for lighting a cigarette or cigar.

light-hearted adjective Someone who is light-hearted is cheerful and has no worries.

lighthouse noun a tower by the sea which sends out a powerful light to guide ships.

lighting noun 1 The lighting in a room or building is the way that it is lit. 2 (DRAMA) Lighting in the theatre or for a film is the special lights that are directed on the performers or scene.

lightning noun Lightning is the bright flashes of light in the sky which are produced by natural electricity during a thunderstorm.

lightweight noun 1 a boxer in one of the lighter weight groups. ▶ adjective 2 Something that is lightweight does not weigh very much.

likable; also spelt **likeable** adjective Someone who is likable is very pleasant and friendly.

like preposition 1 If one thing is like another, it is similar to it. ▶ noun 2 'The like' means other similar things of the sort just mentioned. ▶ phrase 3 If you feel like something,

you want to do it or have it.
▶ *verb* 4 If you like something or someone, you find them pleasant.

like *preposition*
1 = akin, analogous, parallel, similar
▶ *verb* 4 = adore (*informal*), appreciate, be fond of, be keen on, be partial to, enjoy, go for, have a soft spot for, have a weakness for, love, relish, revel in

-like *suffix* '-like' means resembling or similar to: *a balloonlike object.*

likelihood *noun* If you say that there is a likelihood that something will happen, you mean that you think it will probably happen.

likely *adjective* Something that is likely will probably happen or is probably true.

likely *adjective*
= anticipated, expected, liable, possible, probable

liken *verb* If you liken one thing to another, you say that they are similar.

likeness *noun* If two things have a likeness to each other, they are similar in appearance.

likewise *adverb* Likewise means similarly.

liking *noun* If you have a liking for someone or something, you like them.

lilac *noun* 1 a shrub with large clusters of pink, white or mauve flowers. ▶ *adjective* 2 pale mauve.

lilt *noun* A lilt in someone's voice is a pleasant rising and falling sound in it. > **lilting** *adjective*

lily lilies *noun* a plant with trumpet-shaped flowers of various colours.

limb *noun* 1 Your limbs are your arms and legs. 2 The limbs of a tree are its branches. ▶ *phrase* 3 If you have gone **out on a limb**, you have said or done something risky.

limbo *noun* 1 If you are in limbo, you are in an uncertain situation over which you feel you have no control. 2 The limbo is a dance, originally from Trinidad, in which the dancer has to pass under a low bar while leaning backwards.

lime *noun* 1 a small, green citrus fruit, rather like a lemon. 2 A lime tree is a large tree with pale green leaves. 3 Lime is a chemical substance that is used in cement and as a fertiliser.

limelight *noun* If someone is in the limelight, they are getting a lot of attention.

limestone *noun* Limestone is a white rock which is used for building and making cement.

limit *noun* 1 a boundary or an extreme beyond which something cannot go. ▶ *verb* 2 To limit something means to prevent it from becoming bigger, spreading or making progress.

limit *noun*
1 = bounds, deadline, maximum, ultimate, utmost
▶ *verb* 2 = confine, curb, fix, ration, restrict

limitation *noun* 1 The limitation of something is the reducing or controlling of it. 2 If you talk about the limitations of a person or thing, you are talking about the limits of their abilities.

limited *adjective* Something that is limited is rather small in amount or extent.

limousine *noun* a large, luxurious car, usually driven by a chauffeur.

limp *verb* **1** If you limp, you walk unevenly because you have hurt your leg or foot. ▶ *noun* **2** an uneven way of walking. ▶ *adjective* **3** Something that is limp is soft and floppy, and not stiff or firm.

> **limp** *adjective*
> **3** = drooping, flabby, floppy, slack, soft

line *noun* **1** a long, thin mark. **2** a number of people or things positioned one behind the other. **3** a route along which someone or something moves: *a railway line.* **4** In a piece of writing, a line is a number of words together. **5** (MATHS) In maths, a line is the straight, one-dimensional space between two points. **6** Someone's line of work is the kind of work they do. **7** The line someone takes is the attitude they have towards something. **8** In a shop or business, a line is a type of product. ▶ *verb* **9** To line something means to cover its inside surface or edge with something. ▶ **line up** *verb* **1** When people line up, they stand in a line. **2** When you line something up, you arrange it for a special occasion.

> **line** *noun*
> **1** = rule, score, streak, stripe
> **2** = column, file, queue, rank, row **3** = course, path, route, track, trajectory

lineage *noun* Someone's lineage is all the people from whom they are directly descended.

linear *adjective* arranged in a line or in a strict sequence, or happening at a constant rate.

linen *noun* **1** (DGT) Linen is a type of cloth made from a plant called flax. **2** Linen is also household goods made of cloth, such as sheets and tablecloths.

liner *noun* a large passenger ship that makes long journeys.

linesman **linesmen** *noun* an official at a sports match who watches the lines of the field or court and indicates when the ball goes outside them.

-ling *suffix* '-ling' means 'small' or 'young': *duckling.*

linger *verb* To linger means to remain for a long time.

lingerie *noun* Lingerie is women's nightclothes and underclothes.

lingo **lingoes** *noun* (*informal*) a foreign language.

linguist *noun* (MFL) someone who studies foreign languages or the way in which language works.

lining *noun* any material used to line the inside of something.

link *noun* **1** a relationship or connection between two things. **2** a physical connection between two things or places. **3** one of the rings in a chain. **4** In computing, a link is a connection between different documents, or between different parts of the same document. ▶ *verb* **5** To link people, places or things means to join them together.

> **link** *noun*
> **1** = affiliation, association, attachment, bond, connection, relationship, tie
> ▶ *verb* **5** = attach, connect, couple, fasten, join, tie

lino *noun* Lino is the same as linoleum.

linoleum *noun* a floor covering with a shiny surface.

lint *noun* soft cloth made from linen, used to dress wounds.

lion *noun* a large member of the cat family which comes from Africa. Lions have light brown fur, and the male has a long mane. A female lion is called a lioness.

lip *noun* 1 Your lips are the edges of your mouth. 2 The lip of a jug is the slightly pointed part through which liquids are poured out.

lipstick *noun* a coloured substance which is worn on the lips.

liqueur *noun* a strong, sweet alcoholic drink, usually drunk after a meal.

liquid *noun* 1 (SCIENCE) any substance which is not a solid or a gas, and which can be poured.
▶ *adjective* 2 Something that is liquid is in the form of a liquid. 3 In commerce and finance, a person's or company's liquid assets are the things that can be sold quickly to raise cash.

> **liquid** *noun*
> 1 = fluid, liquor, solution
> ▶ *adjective* 2 = fluid, molten, runny

liquidate *verb* To liquidate a company means to close it down and use its assets to pay off its debts. > **liquidation** *noun*

liquor *noun* Liquor is any strong alcoholic drink.

liquorice *noun* Liquorice is a root used to flavour sweets; also the sweets themselves.

list *noun* 1 a set of words or items written one below the other.
▶ *verb* 2 If you list a number of things, you make a list of them.

> **list** *noun*
> 1 = catalogue, directory, index, inventory, listing, record, register
> ▶ *verb* 2 = catalogue, index, record, register

listen *verb* If you listen to something, you hear it and pay attention to it.

> **listen** *verb*
> = attend (*formal*), hark (*literary*), hear, pay attention

listless *adjective* lacking energy and enthusiasm. > **listlessly** *adverb*

lit a past tense and past participle of **light**.

litany litanies *noun* 1 a part of a church service in which the priest says or chants prayers and the people give responses. 2 something, especially a list of things, that is repeated often or in a boring or insincere way.

literacy *noun* Literacy is the ability to read and write. > **literate** *adjective*

literal *adjective* 1 (ENGLISH) The literal meaning of a word is its most basic meaning. 2 A literal translation from a foreign language is one that has been translated exactly word for word. > **literally** *adverb*

literary *adjective* (ENGLISH) connected with literature.

literature *noun* 1 (ENGLISH) Literature consists of novels, plays and poetry. 2 The literature on a subject is everything that has been written about it.

lithe *adjective* supple and graceful.

litmus noun (SCIENCE) In chemistry, litmus is a substance that turns red under acid and blue under alkali conditions.

litre noun (MATHS) A unit of liquid volume equal to about 1.76 pints.

litter noun 1 Litter is rubbish in the street and other public places. 2 Cat litter is a gravelly substance you put in a container where you want your cat to urinate and defecate. 3 a number of baby animals born at the same time to the same mother. ▶ verb 4 If things litter a place, they are scattered all over it.

little less, lesser, least adjective 1 small in size or amount. ▶ noun 2 A little is a small amount or degree. ▶ adverb 3 to a small amount or degree.

> **little** adjective
> 1 = dainty, dwarf, meagre, measly, mini, miniature, minute, paltry, pygmy, scant, small, tiny, wee (Scottish)
> ▶ noun 2 = hardly any, not much

live verb 1 If you live in a place, that is where your home is. 2 To live means to be alive. 3 If something lives up to your expectations, it is as good as you thought it would be. ▶ adjective, adverb 4 Live television or radio is broadcast while the event is taking place. ▶ adjective 5 Live animals or plants are alive, rather than dead or artificial. 6 Something is live if it is directly connected to an electricity supply. 7 Live bullets or ammunition have not yet been exploded. > **live down** verb If you cannot live down a mistake, you cannot make people forget it.

live verb 1 = dwell (formal), inhabit, reside (formal), stay (Scottish and South African) 2 = be alive, exist ▶ adjective 5 = alive, animate, living

livelihood noun Someone's livelihood is their job or the source of their income.

lively livelier, liveliest adjective full of life and enthusiasm. > **liveliness** noun

> **lively** adjective
> = active, animated, energetic, perky, sparkling, sprightly, vivacious

liver noun 1 Your liver is a large organ in your body which cleans your blood and helps digestion. 2 Liver is also the liver of some animals, which may be cooked and eaten.

livestock noun Livestock is farm animals.

livid adjective 1 extremely angry. 2 dark purple or bluish.

living adjective 1 If someone is living, they are alive. ▶ noun 2 The work you do for a living is the work you do in order to earn money to live.

living room noun the room where people relax and entertain in their homes.

lizard noun a long, thin, dry-skinned reptile found in hot, dry countries.

llama noun a South American animal related to the camel.

load noun 1 something being carried. 2 (informal) Loads means a lot. ▶ verb 3 To load a vehicle or animal means to put a large number of things into it or onto it.

load *noun*
1 = cargo, consignment, freight, shipment
▶ *verb* 3 = fill, pack, pile, stack

loaf loaves; loafs, loafing, loafed *noun* 1 a large piece of bread baked in a shape that can be cut into slices. ▶ *verb* 2 To loaf around means to be lazy and not do any work.

loan *noun* 1 a sum of money that you borrow. 2 the act of borrowing or lending something.
▶ *verb* 3 If you loan something to someone, you lend it to them.

loan *noun*
1 = advance, credit, mortgage
▶ *verb* 3 = advance, lend

loath *adjective* If you are loath to do something, you are very unwilling to do it.

loathe *verb* To loathe someone or something means to feel strong dislike for them. > **loathing** *noun*

lob lobs, lobbing, lobbed *verb* 1 If you lob something, you throw it high in the air. ▶ *noun* 2 In tennis, a lob is a stroke in which the player hits the ball high in the air.

lobby lobbies, lobbying, lobbied *noun* 1 The lobby in a building is the main entrance area with corridors and doors leading off it. 2 a group of people trying to persuade an organisation that something should be done. ▶ *verb* 3 To lobby an MP or an organisation means to try to persuade them to do something, for example by writing them letters.

lobe *noun* 1 The lobe of your ear is the rounded soft part at the bottom. 2 any rounded part of something.

lobster *noun* an edible shellfish with two front claws and eight legs.

local *adjective* 1 Local means in, near or belonging to the area in which you live. 2 A local anaesthetic numbs only one part of your body and does not send you to sleep. ▶ *noun* 3 The locals are the people who live in a particular area. 4 (*informal*) Someone's local is the pub nearest their home. > **locally** *adverb*

local *adjective*
1 = community, district, neighbourhood, parish, regional
▶ *noun* 3 = inhabitant, native, resident

localised; also spelt **localized** *adjective* existing or happening in only one place.

locality localities *noun* an area of a country or city.

locate *verb* 1 To locate someone or something means to find out where they are. 2 If something is located in a place, it is in that place.

locate *verb*
1 = find, pinpoint, track down
2 = placed, sited, situated

location *noun* 1 (GEOGRAPHY) a place, or the position of something. 2 In South Africa, a location was a small town where only Black people or Coloured people were allowed to live.
▶ *phrase* 3 If a film is made on location, it is made away from a studio.

location *noun*
1 = place, point, position, site, situation, spot, whereabouts

loch *noun* In Scottish English, a loch is a lake.

lock *verb* 1 If you lock something, you close it and fasten it with a key. 2 If something locks into place, it moves into place and becomes firmly fixed there. ▸ *noun* 3 A device on something which fastens it and prevents it from being opened except with a key. 4 A lock on a canal is a place where the water level can be raised or lowered to allow boats to go between two parts of the canal which have different water levels. 5 A lock is a small bunch of hair.

lockdown *noun* If there is a lockdown, or a place is in lockdown, people must stay indoors in order to keep themselves and other people safe.

locker *noun* a small cupboard for your personal belongings, for example in a changing room.

locomotive *noun* a railway engine.

locust *noun* an insect like a large grasshopper, which travels in huge swarms and eats crops.

lodge *noun* 1 a small house in the grounds of a large country house, or a small house used for holidays. ▸ *verb* 2 If you lodge in someone else's house, you live there and pay them rent. 3 If something lodges somewhere, it gets stuck there. 4 If you lodge a complaint, you formally make it.

lodger *noun* a person who lives in someone's house and pays rent.

loft *noun* the space immediately under the roof of a house, often used for storing things.

lofty *loftier, loftiest adjective* 1 very high. 2 very noble and important. 3 proud and superior.

log *logs, logging, logged noun* 1 a thick branch or piece of tree trunk which has fallen or been cut down. 2 the captain's official record of everything that happens on board a ship. ▸ *verb* 3 If you log something, you officially make a record of it, for example in a ship's log. 4 To log into a computer system means to gain access to it, usually by giving your name and password. To log out means to finish using the system.

logic *noun* Logic is a way of reasoning involving a series of statements, each of which must be true if the statement before it is true.

logical *adjective* 1 A logical argument uses logic. 2 A logical course of action or decision is sensible or reasonable in the circumstances. > **logically** *adverb*

> **logical** *adjective*
> 1 = consistent, rational, reasoned, sound, valid
> 2 = judicious (*formal*), obvious, plausible, reasonable, sensible, wise

logistics *noun* (*formal*) The logistics of a complicated undertaking is the skilful organisation of it.

logo *logos noun* The logo of an organisation is a special design that is put on all its products.

-logy *suffix* '-logy' is used to form words that refer to the study of something: *biology*.

loin *noun* 1 (*old-fashioned*) Your loins are the front parts of your body between your waist and your thighs. 2 Loin is a piece of meat from the back or sides of an animal.

loiter verb To loiter means to stand about idly with no real purpose.

lollipop noun a hard sweet on the end of a stick.

lolly lollies noun 1 a lollipop. 2 a piece of flavoured ice or ice cream on a stick. 3 In Australian and New Zealand English, a lolly is a sweet.

lone adjective A lone person or thing is the only one in a particular place.

lonely lonelier, loneliest adjective 1 If you are lonely, you are unhappy because you are alone. 2 A lonely place is an isolated one which very few people visit.
> **loneliness** noun

> **lonely** adjective
> 1 = alone, forlorn, forsaken, lonesome 2 = deserted, desolate, isolated, remote, secluded, uninhabited

loner noun a person who likes to be alone.

lonesome adjective lonely and sad.

long adjective 1 continuing for a great amount of time. 2 great in length or distance. ▶ adverb 3 for a certain period of time: How long will it last? 4 for an extensive period of time: long into the following year. ▶ phrase 5 If something no longer happens, it does not happen any more. 6 Before long means soon. 7 If one thing is true as long as another thing is true, it is true only if the other thing is true. ▶ verb 8 If you long for something, you want it very much.

> **long** adjective
> 1 = extended, interminable, lengthy, lingering,

long-drawn-out, prolonged, protracted, slow, sustained 2 = elongated, extensive, lengthy
> ▶ verb 8 = ache, covet, crave, hunger, lust, pine, yearn

longevity noun (formal) Longevity is long life.

longing noun a strong wish for something.

> **longing** noun
> = craving, desire, hankering, hunger, thirst, yearning

longitude noun (GEOGRAPHY) The longitude of a place is its distance east or west of a meridian line passing through Greenwich, measured in degrees.

long jump noun The long jump is an athletics event in which you jump as far as possible after taking a long run.

long-range adjective 1 able to be used over a great distance. 2 extending a long way into the future.

long-standing adjective having existed for a long time.

long-suffering adjective very patient.

long-term adjective continuing for a long time.

long-winded adjective long and boring.

loo noun (informal) a toilet.

look verb 1 If you look at something, you turn your eyes towards it so that you can see it. 2 If you look at a subject or situation, you study it or judge it. 3 If you look down on someone, you think that they are inferior to you. 4 If you are looking forward to something, you want it to happen because you think you will enjoy it. **5** If you look up to someone, you admire and respect them. **6** If you describe the way that something or someone looks, you are describing the appearance of it or them. ▶ *noun* **7** If you have a look at something, you look at it. **8** the way someone or something appears, especially the expression on a person's face. **9** If you talk about someone's looks, you are talking about how attractive they are. ▶ *interjection* **10** You say 'look out' to warn someone of danger. > **look after** *verb* If you look after someone or something, you take care of them. > **look for** *verb* If you look for someone or something, you try to find them. > **look up** *verb* **1** To look up information means to find it out in a book. **2** If you look someone up, you go to see them after not having seen them for a long time. **3** If a situation is looking up, it is improving.

look *verb*
1 = gaze, glance, glimpse, peek, peep, scan, stare, view
6 = appear, look like, seem, seem to be
▶ *noun* **7** = gaze, glance, glimpse, peek **8** = air, appearance, bearing, expression, face, semblance
▶ **look after** = care for, mind, nurse, take care of, tend, watch
▶ **look for** = forage, hunt, search, seek

lookalike *noun* a person who looks very like someone else.

lookalike *noun*
= dead ringer (*informal*), double, spitting image (*informal*)

lookout *noun* **1** someone who is watching for danger, or a place where they watch for danger. ▶ *phrase* **2** If you are on the lookout for something, you are watching for it or waiting expectantly for it.

loom *noun* **1** a machine for weaving cloth. ▶ *verb* **2** If something looms in front of you, it suddenly appears as a tall, unclear and sometimes frightening shape. **3** If a situation or event is looming, it is likely to happen soon and is rather worrying.

loop *noun* **1** a curved or circular shape in something long such as a piece of string. ▶ *verb* **2** If you loop rope or string around an object, you place it in a loop around the object.

loophole *noun* a small mistake or omission in the law which allows you to do something that the law intends that you should not do.

loose *adjective* **1** If something is loose, it is not firmly held, fixed or attached. **2** Loose clothes do not fit closely. ▶ *adverb* **3** To set animals loose means to set them free after they have been tied up or kept in a cage.

loose *adjective*
1 = free, unsecured, wobbly
2 = baggy, slack, sloppy

loosen *verb* To loosen something means to make it looser.

loosen *verb*
= slacken, undo, untie

loot *verb* **1** To loot shops and houses means to steal goods from them during a battle or riot. ▶ *noun* **2** Loot is stolen money or goods.

loot verb
1 = pillage, plunder, raid, ransack
▶ noun 2 = booty, haul, plunder, spoils, swag (slang)

lop lops, lopping, lopped verb If you lop something off, you cut it off with one quick stroke.

lopsided adjective Something that is lopsided is uneven because its two sides are different sizes or shapes.

lord noun 1 a nobleman. 2 Lord is a title used in front of the names of some noblemen, bishops, archbishops, judges and some high-ranking officials. 3 In Christianity, Lord is a name given to God and Jesus Christ.

Lordship noun You address a lord, judge or bishop as Your Lordship.

lore noun The lore of a place, people or subject is all the traditional knowledge and stories about it.

lorry lorries noun a large vehicle for transporting goods by road.

lose loses, losing, lost verb 1 If you lose something, you cannot find it, or you no longer have it because it has been taken away from you. 2 If you lose a relative or friend, they die. 3 If you lose a fight or an argument, you are beaten. 4 If a business loses money, it is spending more money than it is earning.

lose verb
1 = drop, mislay, misplace 3 = be beaten, be defeated

loser noun 1 a person who is defeated in a game, contest or struggle. 2 (informal) If you refer to someone as a loser, you have a low opinion of them because you

think they are always unsuccessful.

loss noun 1 The loss of something is the losing of it. ▶ phrase 2 If you are at a loss, you do not know what to do.

lost adjective 1 If you are lost, you do not know where you are. 2 If something is lost, you cannot find it. 3 Lost is the past tense and past participle of **lose**.

lost adjective
1 = adrift, astray, off course
2 = mislaid, misplaced, missing, vanished

lot phrase 1 A lot of something, or lots of something, is a large amount of it. 2 A lot means very much or very often. ▶ noun 3 an amount of something or a number of things. 4 In an auction, a lot is one of the things being sold.

lot phrase
1 a lot = abundance, a great deal, masses (informal), piles (informal), plenty, quantities, scores
▶ noun 3 = batch, bunch (informal), crowd, group, quantity, set

lotion noun a liquid that you put on your skin to protect or soften it.

lottery lotteries noun a method of raising money by selling tickets by which a winner is selected at random.

lotus noun a large water lily, found in Africa and Asia.

loud adjective 1 A loud noise has a high volume of sound. 2 If you describe clothing as loud, you mean that it is too bright.

loud *adjective, adverb*
1 = blaring, deafening, noisy, resounding, strident, thunderous **2** = flamboyant, flashy, garish, gaudy, lurid

loudspeaker *noun* a piece of equipment that makes your voice louder when you speak into a microphone connected to it.

lounge *noun* **1** a room in a house or hotel with comfortable chairs where people can relax. **2** The lounge or lounge bar in a pub or hotel is a comfortably furnished bar. ▶ *verb* **3** If you lounge around, you lean against something or sit or lie around in a lazy and comfortable way.

louse lice *noun* Lice are small insects that live on people's bodies.

lousy lousier, lousiest *adjective* (*informal*) **1** of bad quality or very unpleasant. **2** ill or unhappy.

lout *noun* a young man who behaves in an aggressive and rude way.

lovable; also spelt **loveable** *adjective* having very attractive qualities and therefore easy to love.

lovable *adjective*
= adorable, charming, enchanting, endearing, sweet

love *verb* **1** If you love someone, you have strong emotional feelings of affection for them. **2** If you love something, you like it very much. **3** If you would love to do something, you want very much to do it. ▶ *noun* **4** Love is a strong emotional feeling of affection for someone or something. **5** a strong liking for something. **6** In tennis, love is a score of zero. ▶ *phrase* **7** If you are in love with someone, you feel strongly attracted to them romantically.

love *verb*
1 = adore, cherish, worship **2** = appreciate, enjoy, like, relish ▶ *noun* **4** = adoration, affection, ardour, devotion, infatuation, passion **5** = devotion, fondness, liking, weakness

love affair *noun* a romantic relationship between two people.

love life *noun* a person's romantic relationships.

lovely lovelier, loveliest *adjective* very beautiful, attractive and pleasant. ▶ **loveliness** *noun*

lovely *adjective*
= attractive, beautiful, delightful, enjoyable, pleasant, pretty

lover *noun* Someone who is a lover of something, for example art or music, is very fond of it.

loving *adjective* feeling or showing love. ▶ **lovingly** *adverb*

loving *adjective*
= affectionate, devoted, doting, fond, tender, warm

low *adjective* **1** Something that is low is close to the ground, or measures a short distance from the ground to the top. **2** Low means small in value or amount. **3** 'Low' is used to describe people who are not considered respectable. ▶ *adverb* **4** in a low position, level or degree. ▶ *noun* **5** a level or amount that is less than before.

low *adjective*
1 = little, short, small, squat, stunted, sunken **2** = minimal,

modest, poor, reduced, scant,
small **3** = common,
contemptible, despicable,
disreputable, lowly, vulgar

lower *verb* **1** To lower something
means to move it downwards.
2 To lower something also means
to make it less in value or
amount.

> **lower** *verb*
> **1** = drop, let down, take down
> **2** = cut, decrease, diminish,
> lessen, minimise, reduce, slash

lowlands *plural noun* Lowlands are
an area of flat, low land.
> **lowland** *adjective*

lowly lowlier, lowliest *adjective* low
in importance, rank or status.

low tide *noun* On a coast, low tide
is the time, usually twice a day,
when the sea is at its lowest level.

loyal *adjective* firm in your
friendship or support for
someone or something.
> **loyalty** *noun*

> **loyal** *adjective*
> = constant, dependable,
> faithful, staunch, true, trusty

loyalist *noun* a person who
remains firm in their support for
a government or ruler.

Ltd an abbreviation for 'limited';
used after the names of some
companies.

lucid *adjective* **1** Lucid writing or
speech is clear and easy to
understand. **2** Someone who is
lucid after having been ill or
delirious is able to think clearly
again.

luck *noun* Luck is anything that
seems to happen by chance and
not through your own efforts.

luck *noun*
= accident, chance, destiny,
fate, fortune

luckless *adjective* unsuccessful or
unfortunate.

lucky luckier, luckiest *adjective*
1 Someone who is lucky has a lot
of good luck. **2** Something that is
lucky happens by chance and has
good effects or consequences.
> **luckily** *adverb*

> **lucky** *adjective*
> **1** = blessed, charmed, fortunate
> **2** = fortuitous, fortunate,
> opportune, timely

lucrative *adjective* Something
that is lucrative earns you a lot of
money.

ludicrous *adjective* completely
foolish, unsuitable or ridiculous.

lug lugs, lugging, lugged *verb* If you
lug a heavy object around, you
carry it with difficulty.

luggage *noun* Your luggage is the
bags and suitcases that you take
with you when you travel.

lukewarm *adjective* **1** slightly
warm. **2** not very enthusiastic or
interested.

lull *noun* **1** a pause in something,
or a short time when it is quiet
and nothing much happens.
▶ *verb* **2** If you are lulled into
feeling safe, someone or
something causes you to feel safe
at a time when you are not safe.

lullaby lullabies *noun* a song used
for sending a baby or child to
sleep.

lumber *noun* **1** Lumber is wood
that has been roughly cut up.
2 Lumber is also old unwanted
furniture and other items. ▶ *verb*
3 If you lumber around, you move

heavily and clumsily. **4** (*informal*) If you are lumbered with something, you are given it to deal with even though you do not want it.

luminary luminaries *noun* (*literary*) a person who is famous or an expert in a particular subject.

luminous *adjective* Something that is luminous glows in the dark, usually because it has been treated with a special substance. > **luminosity** *noun*

lump *noun* **1** A lump of something is a solid piece of it, of any shape or size. **2** a bump on the surface of something. ▶ *verb* **3** If you lump people or things together, you combine them into one group or consider them as being similar in some way. > **lumpy** *adjective*

> **lump** *noun*
> **1** = ball, cake, chunk, hunk, piece, wedge **2** = bulge, bump, hump, swelling

lump sum *noun* a large sum of money given or received all at once.

lunacy *noun* Lunacy is extremely foolish or eccentric behaviour.

lunar *adjective* relating to the moon.

lunatic *noun* **1** If you call someone a lunatic, you mean that they are very foolish. ▶ *adjective* **2** Lunatic behaviour is very stupid, foolish or dangerous.

lunch *noun* **1** a meal eaten in the middle of the day. ▶ *verb* **2** When you lunch, you eat lunch.

luncheon *noun* (*formal*) Luncheon is lunch.

lung *noun* Your lungs are the two organs inside your ribcage with which you breathe.

lunge *noun* **1** a sudden forward movement. ▶ *verb* **2** To lunge means to make a sudden movement in a particular direction.

lurch *verb* **1** To lurch means to make a sudden, jerky movement. ▶ *noun* **2** a sudden, jerky movement.

lure *verb* **1** To lure someone means to attract them into going somewhere or doing something. ▶ *noun* **2** something that you find very attractive.

> **lure** *verb*
> **1** = attract, beckon, draw, entice, tempt
> ▶ *noun* **2** = attraction, bait, magnet, pull, temptation

lurid *adjective* **1** involving a lot of sensational detail. **2** very brightly coloured or patterned.

lurk *verb* To lurk somewhere means to remain there hidden from the person you are waiting for.

> **lurk** *verb*
> = lie in wait, loiter, skulk

luscious *adjective* very tasty.

lush *adjective* In a lush field or garden, the grass or plants are healthy and growing thickly.

lust *noun* **1** A lust for something is a strong desire to have it. ▶ *verb* **2** If you lust for or after something, you have a very strong desire to possess it.

lustre *noun* Lustre is soft shining light reflected from the surface of something.

luxuriant *adjective* Luxuriant plants, trees and gardens are large, healthy and growing strongly.

luxurious *adjective* very expensive and full of luxury.

> **luxurious** *adjective*
> = de luxe, lavish, opulent, plush (*informal*), sumptuous

luxury luxuries *noun* 1 Luxury is great comfort in expensive and beautiful surroundings.
2 something that you enjoy very much but do not have very often, usually because it is expensive.

> **luxury** *noun*
> 1 = affluence, opulence, sumptuousness 2 = extra, extravagance, indulgence, treat

-ly *suffix* 1 '-ly' forms adjectives that describe a quality: *friendly*.
2 '-ly' forms adjectives or adverbs that refer to when something happens or is done: *yearly*. 3 '-ly' forms adverbs that refer to how or in what way something is done: *quickly*.

lying *noun* 1 Lying is telling lies.
▶ *adjective* 2 A lying person is telling lies. 3 Lying is also the present participle of **lie²**.

> **lying** *noun*
> 1 = deceit, dishonesty, fabrication, fibbing, perjury
> ▶ *adjective* 2 = deceitful, dishonest, false, untruthful

lynch *verb* If a crowd lynches someone, it kills them in a violent way without first holding a legal trial.

lynx lynxes *noun* a wildcat with a short tail and tufted ears.

lyric *noun* 1 (MUSIC) The lyrics of a song are the words. ▶ *adjective*
2 Lyric poetry is written in a simple and direct style, and is usually about love.

lyrical *adjective* poetic and romantic.

Mm

m an abbreviation for 'metres' or 'miles'.

macabre *adjective* A macabre event or story is strange and horrible.

macadamia *noun* an Australian tree, also grown in New Zealand, that produces edible nuts.

macaroni *noun* Macaroni is short hollow tubes of pasta.

mace *noun* an ornamental pole carried by an official during ceremonies as a symbol of authority.

machete *noun* a large, heavy knife with a big blade.

machine *noun* 1 (DGT) a piece of equipment which uses electricity or power from an engine to make it work. ▶ *verb* 2 If you machine something, you make it or work on it using a machine.

> **machine** *noun*
> 1 = apparatus, appliance, contraption, device, instrument, mechanism

machine-gun *noun* a gun that works automatically, firing bullets one after the other.

machinery *noun* Machinery is machines in general.

machismo *noun* Machismo is exaggerated aggressive male behaviour.

macho *adjective* A man who is described as macho behaves in an aggressively masculine way.

mackerel *noun* a sea fish with blue and silver stripes.

mad madder, maddest *adjective* 1 If you describe someone as mad, you mean that they are very eccentric or foolish. 2 (*informal*) Someone who is mad is angry. 3 (*informal*) If you are mad about someone or something, you like them very much.

> **mad** *adjective*
> 1 = barmy (*slang*), crazy (*informal*), daft (*British; informal*), foolhardy, foolish, stupid 2 = angry, enraged, fuming, furious, incensed, infuriated, irate, livid

madam *noun* 'Madam' is a very formal way of addressing a woman.

maddening *adjective* irritating or frustrating.

made the past tense and past participle of **make**.

madly *adverb* If you do something madly, you do it in a fast, excited way.

Mafia *noun* The Mafia is a large crime organisation operating in Italy and the USA.

magazine *noun* 1 (LIBRARY) a weekly or monthly publication with articles and photographs. 2 a compartment in a gun for cartridges.

magenta *noun, adjective* dark reddish-purple.

maggot *noun* a creature that looks like a small worm and lives on decaying things. Maggots turn into flies.

magic *noun* 1 In fairy stories, magic is a special power that can make impossible things happen. 2 Magic is the art of performing tricks to entertain people.

> **magic** *noun*
> 1 = sorcery, witchcraft

magical *adjective* wonderful and exciting. > **magically** *adverb*

> **magical** *adjective*
> = bewitching, enchanting

magician *noun* 1 a person who performs tricks as entertainment. 2 In fairy stories, a magician is a man with magical powers.

magistrate *noun* an official who acts as a judge in a law court that deals with less serious crimes.

magnanimous *adjective* generous and forgiving.

magnate *noun* someone who is very rich and powerful in business.

magnet *noun* (SCIENCE) a piece of iron which attracts iron or steel towards it, and which points towards north if allowed to swing freely. A **permanent magnet** is a magnet that is still magnetic when the magnetic field that produced it is taken away; a **temporary magnet** is a magnet that loses its magnetism when the magnetic field that produced it is taken away. > **magnetic** *adjective* > **magnetism** *noun*

magnificent *adjective* extremely beautiful or impressive.

magnify magnifies, magnifying, magnified *verb* (SCIENCE) When a microscope or lens magnifies something, it makes it appear bigger than it actually is.

magnifying glass *noun* a lens which makes things appear bigger than they really are.

m

magnitude *noun* The magnitude of something is its great size or importance.

magnolia *noun* a tree which has large white or pink flowers in spring.

magpie *noun* a large black and white bird with a long tail.

mahogany *noun* Mahogany is a hard, reddish-brown wood used for making furniture.

maid *noun* a female servant.

maiden *noun* **1** (literary) a young woman. ▶ *adjective* **2** first: *a maiden voyage.*

maiden name *noun* the surname a woman had before she married.

mail *noun* **1** Your mail is the letters and parcels delivered to you by the post office. ▶ *verb* **2** If you mail a letter, you send it by post.

mailbox *noun* On a computer, your mailbox is the file where your email is stored.

mail order *noun* Mail order is a system of buying goods by post.

maim *verb* To maim someone is to injure them very badly for life.

main *adjective* **1** most important. ▶ *noun* **2** The mains are large pipes or wires that carry gas, water or electricity.

> **main** *adjective*
> **1** = cardinal, chief, foremost, leading, major, predominant, primary, prime, principal

mainframe *noun* a large computer which can be used by many people at the same time.

mainland *noun* The mainland is the main part of a country in contrast to islands around its coast.

mainly *adverb* true in most cases.

> **mainly** *adverb*
> = chiefly, generally, largely, mostly, predominantly, primarily, principally

mainstay *noun* The mainstay of something is the most important part of it.

mainstream *noun* The mainstream is the most ordinary and conventional group of people or ideas in a society.

maintain *verb* **1** If you maintain something, you keep it going or keep it at a particular rate or level. **2** If you maintain someone, you provide them regularly with money for what they need. **3** To maintain a machine or a building is to keep it in good condition. **4** If you maintain that something is true, you believe it is true and say so.

maintenance *noun* **1** Maintenance is the process of keeping something in good condition. **2** Maintenance is also money that a person sends regularly to someone to provide for the things they need.

maize *noun* Maize is a tall plant which produces sweet corn.

majesty *noun* **1** Majesty is great dignity and impressiveness. **2** 'Majesty' is used in the title and form of address for kings and queens. ▷ **majestic** *adjective*

major *adjective* **1** more important or more significant than other things. **2** (MUSIC) A major key is one of the keys in which most European music is written. In a major key the third note is four semitones higher than the first. ▶ *noun* **3** an army officer of the rank immediately above captain.

major *adjective*
1 = critical, crucial, leading, outstanding, significant

majority majorities *noun* 1 The majority of people or things in a group is more than half of the group. 2 In an election, the majority is the difference between the number of votes gained by the winner and the number gained by the runner-up.

majority *noun*
1 = best part, better part, bulk, mass, most

make makes, making, made *verb*
1 To make something is to produce or construct it, or to cause it to happen. 2 To make something is to do it: *He was going to make a speech.* 3 To make something is to prepare it: *I'll make some salad dressing.* 4 If someone makes you do something, they force you to do it. ▶ *noun* 5 The make of a product is the name of the company that manufactured it.
> **make up** *verb* 1 If a number of things make up something, they form that thing. 2 If you make up a story, you invent it. 3 If you make yourself up, you put make-up on. 4 If two people make it up, they become friends again after a quarrel.

make *verb*
1 = assemble, build, construct, create, fabricate, fashion, form, manufacture, produce
4 = compel, drive, force, oblige
▶ *noun* 5 = brand, model
▶ **make up** 1 = compose, comprise, constitute, form
2 = concoct, fabricate, invent

make-up *noun* 1 Make-up is coloured creams and powders which people put on their faces to make themselves look more attractive. 2 Someone's make-up is their character or personality.

making *noun* 1 The making of something is the act or process of creating or producing it. ▶ *phrase* 2 When you describe someone as something **in the making**, you mean that they are gradually becoming that thing.

making *noun*
1 = assembly, building, construction, creation, fabrication, manufacture, production
▶ *phrase* 2 **in the making** = budding, emergent, potential, up-and-coming

malaise *noun* (*formal*) Malaise is a feeling of dissatisfaction or unhappiness.

malaria *noun* Malaria is a tropical disease caught from mosquitoes which causes fever and shivering.

Malaysian *adjective* 1 belonging or relating to Malaysia. ▶ *noun* 2 someone who comes from Malaysia.

male *noun* 1 a person or animal belonging to the sex that cannot give birth or lay eggs. ▶ *adjective* 2 concerning or relating to males.

male *adjective*
2 = manly, masculine

malevolent *adjective* (*formal*) wanting or intending to cause harm.

malfunction *verb* 1 If a machine or part of the body malfunctions, it fails to work properly. ▶ *noun* 2 the failure of a machine or part of the body to work properly.

malice noun Malice is a desire to cause harm to people.

malicious adjective Malicious talk or behaviour is intended to harm someone.

> **malicious** adjective
> = cruel, malevolent (formal), mean, spiteful, vicious

malign (formal) verb **1** To malign someone means to say unpleasant and untrue things about them. ▶ adjective **2** intended to harm someone.

malignant adjective **1** harmful and cruel. **2** A malignant disease or tumour could cause death if it is allowed to continue.

mall noun a very large enclosed shopping area.

mallet noun a wooden hammer with a square head.

malnutrition noun (SCIENCE) Malnutrition is not eating enough food, or enough healthy food.

malpractice noun If someone such as a doctor or lawyer breaks the rules of their profession, their behaviour is called malpractice.

malt noun Malt is roasted grain, usually barley, that is used in making beer and whisky.

malware noun Computer programs that are designed to damage or disrupt a system are known as malware.

mammal noun (SCIENCE) Animals that give birth to live babies and feed their young with milk from the mother's body are called mammals. Human beings, dogs and whales are all mammals.

mammoth adjective **1** very large indeed. ▶ noun **2** a huge animal that looked like a hairy elephant with long tusks. Mammoths became extinct a long time ago.

man men; mans, manning, manned; noun **1** an adult male human being. ▶ plural noun **2** 'Man' is sometimes used to refer to human beings in general, including men and women. Some people do not like this use and prefer to say humans or people. ▶ verb **3** To man something is to be in charge of it or operate it.

> **man** noun
> **1** = bloke (British, Australian and New Zealand; informal), chap (informal), gentleman, guy (informal), male
> ▶ plural noun **2** = humanity, human race, mankind

manage verb **1** If you manage to do something, you succeed in doing it. **2** If you manage an organisation or business, you are responsible for controlling it.

> **manage** verb
> **1** = cope with, succeed in **2** = be in charge of, command, control, direct, run

manageable adjective able to be dealt with.

management noun **1** The management of a business is the controlling and organising of it. **2** The people who control an organisation are called the management.

> **management** noun
> **1** = control, direction, running **2** = administration, board, bosses, directors, employers

manager noun a person responsible for running a business or organisation.

manager noun
= boss, director, executive

managing director noun a company director who is responsible for the way the company is managed.

mandarin noun a type of small orange which is easy to peel.

mandate noun (formal) A government's mandate is the authority it has to carry out particular policies as a result of winning an election.

mandatory adjective If something is mandatory, there is a law or rule stating that it must be done.

mandolin noun a musical instrument like a small guitar with a deep, rounded body.

mane noun the long hair growing from the neck of a lion or horse.

manger noun a feeding box in a barn or stable.

mangle verb 1 If something is mangled, it is crushed and twisted. ▶ noun 2 an old-fashioned piece of equipment consisting of two large rollers which squeeze water out of wet clothes.

mango mangoes or mangos noun a sweet yellowish fruit which grows in tropical countries.

manhole noun a covered hole in the ground leading to a drain or sewer.

manhood noun Manhood is the state of being a man rather than a boy.

mania noun 1 a strong liking for something. 2 a mental condition characterised by periods of great excitement.

maniac noun a person who is violent and dangerous.

manic adjective energetic and excited.

manicure verb 1 If you manicure your hands, you care for them by softening the skin and shaping and polishing the nails. ▶ noun 2 A manicure is a special treatment for the hands and nails.

manifest (formal) adjective
1 obvious or easily seen. ▶ verb 2 To manifest something is to make people aware of it.

> **manifest** adjective
> 1 = blatant, clear, conspicuous, glaring, obvious, patent, plain

manifestation noun (formal) A manifestation of something is a sign that it is happening or exists.

manifesto manifestoes or manifestos noun a published statement of the aims and policies of a political party.

manipulate verb 1 To manipulate people or events is to control or influence them to produce a particular result. 2 If you manipulate a piece of equipment, you control it in a skilful way.
> **manipulation** noun
> **manipulative** adjective

mankind noun 'Mankind' is used to refer to all human beings.

manly manlier, manliest adjective having qualities that are typically masculine.

manner noun 1 The manner in which you do something is the way you do it. 2 Your manner is the way in which you behave and talk. 3 (in plural) If you have good manners, you behave very politely.

> **manner** noun
> 1 = fashion, mode, style, way
> 2 = bearing, behaviour, conduct, demeanour

m

mannerism *noun* a gesture or a way of speaking which is characteristic of a person.

manoeuvre *verb* 1 If you manoeuvre something into a place, you skilfully move it there. ▶ *noun* 2 a clever move you make in order to change a situation to your advantage.

> **manoeuvre** *verb*
> 1 = guide, navigate, negotiate, steer
> ▶ *noun* 2 = dodge, ploy, ruse, tactic

manor *noun* a large country house with land.

manpower *noun* Workers can be referred to as manpower.

mansion *noun* a very large house.

manslaughter *noun* (*Law*) Manslaughter is the accidental killing of a person.

mantelpiece *noun* a shelf over a fireplace.

mantle *noun* 1 (*literary*) To take on the mantle of something is to accept the status or duties associated with it. 2 (GEOGRAPHY) the part of the earth between the crust and the core.

mantra *noun* (RE) a word or short piece of sacred text or prayer continually repeated to help concentration.

manual *adjective* 1 Manual work involves physical strength rather than mental skill. 2 operated by hand rather than by electricity or by motor. ▶ *noun* 3 an instruction book which tells you how to use a machine.

manufacture (DGT) *verb* 1 To manufacture goods is to make them in a factory. ▶ *noun* 2 The manufacture of goods is the making of them in a factory.
> **manufacturer** *noun*

> **manufacture** *verb*
> 1 = assemble, fabricate, make, mass-produce, process, produce
> ▶ *noun* 2 = assembly, fabrication, making, mass production, production

manure *noun* Manure is animal faeces used to fertilise the soil.

manuscript *noun* a handwritten or typed document, especially a version of a book before it is printed.

Manx *adjective* belonging or relating to the Isle of Man.

many *adjective* 1 If there are many people or things, there is a large number of them. 2 You also use 'many' to ask how great a quantity is or to give information about it: *How many tickets do you require?* ▶ *pronoun* 3 a large number of people or things.

> **many** *adjective*
> 1 = countless, innumerable, myriad, numerous, umpteen (*informal*)
> ▶ *pronoun* 3 = a lot, a mass, a multitude, large numbers, lots (*informal*), plenty, scores

Māori Māoris *noun* 1 someone descended from the people who lived in New Zealand before Europeans arrived. 2 Māori is a language spoken by Māoris. ▶ *adjective* 3 belonging or relating to Māoris.

map maps, mapping, mapped *noun* 1 a detailed drawing of an area as it would appear if you saw it from above. 2 (MATHS) the relationship between elements of a set and elements in the same or another set. > **map out** *verb* If you map out a plan, you work out in detail what you will do.

maple *noun* a tree that has large leaves with five points.

mar mars, marring, marred *verb* To mar something is to spoil it.

marathon *noun* 1 a race in which people run 26 miles along roads. ▶ *adjective* 2 A marathon task is a large one that takes a long time.

marble *noun* 1 Marble is a very hard, cold stone which is often polished to show the coloured patterns in it. 2 Marbles is a children's game played with small coloured glass balls. These balls are also called marbles.

march *noun* 1 March is the third month of the year. It has 31 days. 2 an organised protest in which a large group of people walk somewhere together. ▶ *verb* 3 When soldiers march, they walk with quick regular steps in time with each other. 4 To march somewhere is to walk quickly in a determined way.

mare *noun* an adult female horse.

margarine *noun* Margarine is a substance that is similar to butter but is made from vegetable oil and animal fats.

margin *noun* 1 If you win a contest by a large or small margin, you win it by a large or small amount. 2 the blank space at each side on a written or printed page.

marginal *adjective* small and not very important: *a marginal increase.* > **marginally** *adverb*

marijuana *noun* Marijuana is an illegal drug which people smoke.

marina *noun* a harbour for pleasure boats and yachts.

marinate *verb* To marinate food is to soak it in a mixture of oil, vinegar, spices and herbs before cooking.

marine *noun* 1 a soldier who serves with the navy. ▶ *adjective* 2 relating to or involving the sea.

marital *adjective* relating to or involving marriage.

maritime *adjective* relating to the sea and ships.

mark *noun* 1 a small stain or damaged area on a surface. 2 a written or printed symbol. 3 a letter or number showing how well you have done in homework or in an exam. ▶ *verb* 4 If something marks a surface, it damages it in some way. 5 If you mark something, you write a symbol on it or identify it in some other way. 6 When a teacher marks your work, he or she decides how good it is and gives it a mark. 7 To mark something is to be a sign of it. 8 In soccer or hockey, if you mark your opposing player, you stay close to them, trying to prevent them from getting the ball.

> **mark** *noun*
> 1 = blot, line, smudge, spot, stain, streak
> ▶ *verb* 4 = smudge, stain, streak

marked *adjective* very obvious.

market *noun* 1 a place where goods or animals are bought and sold. 2 The market for a product is the number of people who want to buy it. ▶ *verb* 3 To market a product is to organise its sale, by deciding its price, where it should be sold, and how it should be advertised.

> **market** *noun*
> 1 = bazaar, fair

marketing noun (DGT) Marketing is the part of a business concerned with the way a product is sold.

market research noun (DGT) Market research is research into what people want and buy.

marksman marksmen noun someone who can shoot very accurately.

marlin noun a large fish found in tropical seas which has a very long upper jaw.

marmalade noun Marmalade is a jam made from citrus fruit.

maroon noun, adjective dark reddish-purple.

marooned adjective If you are marooned in a place, you are stranded there and cannot leave it.

marquee noun a very large tent used at a fair or other outdoor entertainment.

marriage noun 1 the legal relationship between a couple. 2 Marriage is the act of marrying someone.

> **marriage** noun
> 1 = matrimony (formal), wedlock (formal)

marrow noun a long, thick, green-skinned fruit with cream-coloured flesh eaten as a vegetable.

marry marries, marrying, married verb 1 When two people marry, they become each other's partner during a special ceremony. 2 When a member of the clergy or a registrar marries a couple, he or she is in charge of their marriage ceremony.

Mars noun Mars is the planet in the solar system which is fourth from the sun.

marsh noun an area of land which is permanently wet.

marshal marshals, marshalling, marshalled verb 1 If you marshal things or people, you gather them together and organise them. ▶ noun 2 an official who helps to organise a public event.

marshmallow noun a soft, spongy, pink or white sweet made using gelatine.

marsupial noun an animal that carries its young in a pouch. Koalas and kangaroos are marsupials.

martial arts plural noun The martial arts are the techniques of self-defence that come from East Asia, for example karate or judo.

Martian noun an imaginary creature from the planet Mars.

martyr (RE) noun 1 someone who suffers or is killed rather than change their beliefs. ▶ verb 2 If someone is martyred, they are killed because of their beliefs. > **martyrdom** noun

marvel marvels, marvelling, marvelled verb 1 If you marvel at something, it fills you with surprise or admiration. ▶ noun 2 something that makes you feel great surprise or admiration.

marvellous adjective wonderful or excellent. > **marvellously** adverb

> **marvellous** adjective
> = brilliant, excellent, first-rate, magnificent, remarkable, splendid, superb, wonderful

Marxism noun Marxism is a political philosophy based on the writings of Karl Marx. It states that society will develop towards communism through the struggle between different social classes. > **Marxist** adjective, noun

marzipan noun Marzipan is a paste made of almonds, sugar and egg. It is put on top of cakes or used to make small sweets.

mascara noun Mascara is a substance that can be used to colour eyelashes and make them look longer.

mascot noun a person, animal or toy which is thought to bring good luck.

masculine adjective 1 relating to men or considered to be typical of men. 2 belonging to a particular class of nouns in some languages, such as French, German and Latin.

mash verb If you mash vegetables, you crush them after they have been cooked.

mask noun 1 something you wear over your face for protection or disguise. ▶ verb 2 If you mask something, you cover it so that it is protected or cannot be seen.

mason noun a person who is skilled at making things with stone.

masonry noun Masonry is pieces of stone which form part of a wall or building.

masquerade verb If you masquerade as something, you pretend to be it.

mass noun 1 a large amount of something. 2 The masses are the ordinary people in society considered as a group. 3 (SCIENCE) In physics, the mass of an object is the amount of physical matter that it has. 4 (RE) In the Roman Catholic Church, Mass is a religious service in which people share bread and wine in

remembrance of the death and resurrection of Jesus Christ.
▶ adjective 5 involving a large number of people. ▶ verb 6 When people mass, they gather together in a large group.

> **mass** noun
> 1 = crowd, heap, load, lump, mob, pile, throng
> ▶ adjective 5 = general, popular, universal, widespread
> ▶ verb 6 = assemble, congregate, gather, group

massacre noun 1 the killing of a very large number of people in a violent and cruel way. ▶ verb 2 To massacre people is to kill large numbers of them in a violent and cruel way.

massage verb 1 To massage someone is to rub their body in order to help them relax or to relieve pain. ▶ noun 2 A massage is treatment which involves rubbing the body.

massive adjective extremely large.

mast noun the tall upright pole that supports the sails of a boat.

master noun 1 a man who has authority over others, especially servants or slaves. 2 the owner of an animal. 3 If you are master of a situation, you have control over it. 4 a male teacher at some schools. ▶ verb 5 If you master a difficult situation, you succeed in controlling it. 6 If you master something, you learn how to do it properly.

> **master** noun
> 4 = instructor, teacher, tutor
> ▶ verb 6 = become proficient in, get the hang of (informal), grasp, learn

masterful *adjective* showing control and authority.

masterly *adjective* extremely clever or well done.

mastermind *verb* 1 If you mastermind a complicated activity, you plan and organise it.
▶ *noun* 2 The mastermind behind something is the person responsible for planning it.

masterpiece *noun* an extremely good painting or other work of art.

mat *noun* 1 a small round or square piece of cloth, card or plastic that is placed on a table to protect it from plates or glasses. 2 a small piece of carpet or other thick material that is placed on the floor.

matador *noun* a man who fights and tries to kill bulls as part of a public entertainment, especially in Spain.

match *noun* 1 an organised game of football, cricket or some other sport. 2 a small, thin stick of wood that produces a flame when you strike it against a rough surface. ▶ *verb* 3 If one thing matches another, the two things look the same or have similar qualities.

> **match** *noun*
> 1 = competition, contest, game
> ▶ *verb* 3 = agree, correspond, fit, go with, suit, tally

mate *noun* 1 (*informal*) Your mates are your friends. 2 The first mate on a ship is the officer who is next in importance to the captain. 3 An animal's mate is its partner for reproduction. ▶ *verb* 4 When a male and female animal mate, they come together in order to breed.

material *noun* 1 (DGT) Material is cloth. 2 (DGT) a substance from which something is made. 3 (DGT) The equipment for a particular activity can be referred to as materials. 4 Material for a book, play or film is the information or ideas on which it is based.
▶ *adjective* 5 involving possessions and money. > **materially** *adverb*

> **material** *noun*
> 1 = cloth, fabric 2 = matter, stuff, substance

materialise; also spelt **materialize** *verb* If something materialises, it actually happens or appears.

materialism *noun* Materialism is thinking that money and possessions are the most important things in life.
> **materialistic** *adjective*

maternal *adjective* relating to or involving a mother.

maternity *adjective* relating to or involving pregnant women and birth.

mathematics *noun* Mathematics is the study of numbers, quantities and shapes.
> **mathematical** *adjective*
> **mathematician** *noun*

maths *noun* Maths is mathematics.

Matilda *noun* (*old-fashioned, informal*) In Australia, Matilda is the pack of belongings carried by a swagman in the bush. The word is now used only in the phrase 'waltzing Matilda', meaning travelling in the bush with few possessions.

matrimony *noun* (*formal*) Matrimony is marriage.
> **matrimonial** *adjective*

M

matrix matrices *noun* 1 (*formal*) the framework in which something grows and develops. 2 (MATHS) a set of numbers or elements set out in rows and columns.

matron *noun* In a hospital, a senior nurse in charge of all the nursing staff used to be known as matron.

matt *adjective* A matt surface is dull rather than shiny.

matted *adjective* Hair that is matted is tangled with the strands sticking together.

matter *noun* 1 something that you have to deal with. 2 Matter is any substance. 3 Books and magazines are reading matter. ▶ *verb* 4 If something matters to you, it is important. ▶ *phrase* 5 If you ask **What's the matter?**, you are asking what is wrong.

> **matter** *noun*
> 1 = affair, business, issue, question, situation, subject
> 2 = material, stuff, substance
> ▶ *verb* 4 = be of consequence, count, make a difference

matter-of-fact *adjective* showing no emotion.

matting *noun* Matting is thick woven material such as rope or straw, used as a floor covering.

mattress *noun* a large thick pad filled with springs, foam or other material that is put on a bed to make it comfortable.

mature *verb* 1 When a child or young animal matures, it becomes an adult. 2 When something matures, it reaches complete development. ▶ *adjective* 3 Mature means fully developed and emotionally balanced.
> **maturity** *noun*

mature *verb*
1 = come of age, grow up, reach adulthood
▶ *adjective* 3 = adult, full-grown, fully-fledged, grown, grown-up

maudlin *adjective* Someone who is maudlin is sad and sentimental, especially when they are drunk.

maul *verb* If someone is mauled by an animal, they are savagely attacked and badly injured by it.

mausoleum *noun* a building which contains the grave of a famous person.

mauve *noun, adjective* pale purple.

maximise; also spelt **maximize** *verb* To maximise something is to make it as great or effective as possible.

maximum *adjective* 1 The maximum amount is the most that is possible. ▶ *noun* 2 The maximum is the most that is possible.

> **maximum** *adjective*
> 1 = top, utmost
> ▶ *noun* 2 = ceiling, height, most, upper limit, utmost

may *verb* 1 If something may happen, it is possible that it will happen. 2 If someone may do something, they are allowed to do it. 3 You can use 'may' when saying that although something is true, something else is also true: *This may be true, but it is only part of the story.* 4 (*formal*) You also use 'may' to express a wish that something will happen: *May you live to be a hundred.* ▶ *noun* 5 May is the fifth month of the year. It has 31 days.

maybe *adverb* You use 'maybe' when you are stating a possibility that you are not certain about.

m

maybe adverb
= conceivably, it could be,
perhaps, possibly

mayhem noun You can refer to a
confused and chaotic situation as
mayhem.

mayonnaise noun Mayonnaise is
a thick salad dressing made with
egg yolks and oil.

mayor noun a person who has
been elected to lead and represent
the people of a town.

maze noun a system of
complicated passages which it is
difficult to find your way
through.

MBE noun a British honour
granted by the King or Queen.
MBE is an abbreviation for
'Member of the Order of the
British Empire'.

MD an abbreviation for 'Doctor of
Medicine' or 'Managing Director'.

me pronoun A speaker or writer
uses 'me' to refer to himself or
herself.

meadow noun a field of grass.

meagre adjective very small and
poor.

meagre adjective
= inadequate, measly (informal),
paltry, scant, sparse

meal noun an occasion when
people eat, or the food they eat at
that time.

meal noun
= banquet, dinner, feast, kai
(New Zealand; informal)

mean means, meaning, meant
verb 1 If you ask what something
means, you want to know what it
refers to or what its message is.
2 If you mean what you say, you

are serious. 3 If something means
a lot to you, it is important to you.
4 If one thing means another, it
shows that the second thing is
true or will happen. 5 If you mean
to do something, you intend to do
it. 6 If something is meant to be
true, it is supposed to be true.
▶ adjective 7 Someone who is mean
is unwilling to spend much
money. 8 Someone who is mean
is unkind or cruel. ▶ noun
9 (in plural) A means of doing
something is a method or object
which makes it possible.
10 (in plural) Someone's means
are their money and income.
11 (MATHS) The mean of a set of
numbers is the result obtained by
adding all the numbers in the set
and dividing the total by the
number of members of the set.
> **meanly** adverb

mean verb
1 = denote, indicate, signify
5 = aim, intend, plan
▶ adjective 7 = miserly, snoep
(South African; informal), tight
(informal)

meander verb If a road or river
meanders, it has a lot of bends
in it.

meaning noun 1 The meaning
of a word is what it refers to or
expresses. 2 The meaning of what
someone says, or of a book or a
film, is the thoughts or ideas that
it is intended to express. 3 If
something has meaning, it seems
to be worthwhile and to have real
purpose. > **meaningful** adjective
> **meaningless** adjective

meaning noun
2 = drift, gist, message,
significance

means test noun a check of a person's money and income to see whether they need money or benefits from the government or other organisation.

meantime phrase In the meantime means in the period of time between two events.

meanwhile adverb Meanwhile means while something else is happening.

measles noun Measles is an infectious illness in which you have red spots on your skin.

measly adjective (informal) very small or inadequate.

measure verb 1 (MATHS) When you measure something, you find out how big it is. 2 (MATHS) If something measures a particular distance, its length or depth is that distance. ▶ noun 3 A measure of something is a certain amount of it. 4 (MATHS) a unit in which size, speed or depth is expressed. 5 Measures are actions carried out to achieve a particular result.

> **measure** verb
> 1 = gauge, survey
> ▶ noun 3 = amount, degree, portion, proportion
> 5 = expedient, manoeuvre, means, procedure, step

measured adjective careful and deliberate.

measurement noun 1 the result that you obtain when you measure something. 2 Measurement is the activity of measuring something. 3 Your measurements are the sizes of your chest, waist and hips that you use to buy the correct size of clothes.

meat noun Meat is the flesh of animals that is cooked and eaten.

Mecca noun (RE) Mecca is the holiest city of Islam, to which many Muslims make pilgrimages.

mechanic noun 1 a person who repairs and maintains engines and machines. 2 (in plural) The mechanics of something are the way in which it works or is done. 3 (in plural) Mechanics is also the scientific study of movement and the forces that affect objects.

mechanical adjective 1 A mechanical device has moving parts and is used to do a physical task. 2 A mechanical action is done automatically without thinking about it. > **mechanically** adverb

mechanism noun 1 (DGT) a part of a machine that does a particular task. 2 part of your behaviour that is automatic.

medal noun a small disc of metal given as an award for bravery or as a prize for sport.

medallion noun a round piece of metal worn as an ornament on a chain round the neck.

medallist noun a person who has won a medal in sport.

meddle verb To meddle is to interfere and try to change things without being asked.

media plural noun You can refer to the television, radio and newspapers as the media.

median adjective (MATHS) The median value of a set is the middle value when the set is arranged in order.

mediate verb If you mediate between two groups, you try to

m

settle a dispute between them.
> **mediation** noun > **mediator**
noun

medical adjective 1 relating to the prevention and treatment of illness and injuries. ▶ noun 2 a thorough examination of your body by a doctor.
> **medically** adverb

medication noun Medication is a substance that is used to treat illness.

medicinal adjective relating to the treatment of illness.

medicine noun 1 Medicine is the treatment of illness and injuries by doctors and nurses. 2 a substance that you drink or swallow to help cure an illness.

> **medicine** noun
> 2 = drug, medication, muti (South African; informal), remedy

medieval; also spelt **mediaeval** adjective (HISTORY) relating to the period between about 1100 AD and 1500 AD, especially in Europe.

mediocre adjective of rather poor quality. > **mediocrity** noun

meditate verb 1 If you meditate on something, you think about it very deeply. 2 If you meditate, you remain in a calm, silent state for a period of time, often as part of religious training. > **meditation** noun

Mediterranean noun 1 The Mediterranean is the large sea between southern Europe and northern Africa. ▶ adjective 2 relating to or typical of the Mediterranean or the European countries adjoining it.

medium mediums or media adjective 1 If something is of medium size or degree, it is neither large nor small. ▶ noun 2 a means that you use to communicate something. 3 a person who claims to be able to speak to the dead.

> **medium** adjective
> 1 = average, medium-sized, middling
> ▶ noun 2 = channel, vehicle

medley noun 1 a mixture of different things creating an interesting effect. 2 a number of different songs or tunes sung or played one after the other.

meek adjective A meek person is timid and does what other people say. > **meekly** adverb

> **meek** adjective
> = deferential, docile, mild, submissive, timid, unassuming

meet meets, meeting, met verb 1 If you meet someone, you happen to be in the same place as them and start talking to them. 2 If you meet a visitor, you go to be with them when they arrive. 3 When a group of people meet, they gather together for a purpose. 4 If something meets a need, it can fulfil it. 5 If something meets with a particular reaction, it gets that reaction from people.

> **meet** verb
> 1 = bump into (informal), come across, come upon, encounter, run across, run into
> 3 = assemble, congregate, convene, gather, get together
> 4 = answer, fulfil, satisfy

meeting noun 1 an event in which people discuss proposals and make decisions together. 2 When you meet someone, you can refer to this event as a meeting.

meeting noun
1 = audience, conference, congress, convention, gathering, get-together (informal), reunion
2 = assignation (formal), encounter, rendezvous, tryst (literary)

megabyte noun (ICT) a unit of computer memory size, equal to 1024 kilobytes.

melancholy adjective If you feel melancholy, you feel sad.

mellow adjective 1 Mellow light is soft and golden. 2 A mellow sound is smooth and pleasant to listen to. ▶ verb 3 If someone mellows, they become more pleasant or relaxed.

melodic adjective relating to melody.

melodious adjective pleasant to listen to.

melodrama noun a story or play in which people's emotions are exaggerated.

melodramatic adjective behaving in an exaggerated, emotional way.

melodramatic adjective
= histrionic, sensational, theatrical

melody melodies noun (MUSIC) a tune.

melon noun a large, juicy fruit with a green or yellow skin and many seeds inside.

melt verb 1 When something melts or when you melt it, it changes from a solid to a liquid because it has been heated. 2 If something melts, it disappears.

melt verb
1 = dissolve, thaw 2 = disappear, disperse, dissolve, evaporate, vanish

member noun 1 A member of a group is one of the people or things belonging to the group. 2 A member of an organisation is a person who has joined the organisation. ▶ adjective 3 A country belonging to an international organisation is called a member country or a member state.

membership noun 1 Membership of an organisation is the state of being a member of it. 2 The people who belong to an organisation are its membership.

membrane noun (SCIENCE) a very thin piece of skin or tissue which connects or covers plant or animal organs or cells.

meme noun something such as a video, picture or phrase that a lot of people send to each other on the internet.

memento mementos noun an object which you keep because it reminds you of a person or a special occasion.

memo memos noun a note from one person to another within the same organisation. Memo is short for 'memorandum'.

memoirs plural noun (ENGLISH) If someone writes their memoirs, they write a book about their life and experiences.

memorable adjective If something is memorable, it is likely to be remembered because it is special or unusual.

memorable adjective
= catchy, historic, notable, striking, unforgettable

memorandum memorandums or memoranda *noun* a memo.

memorial *noun* 1 a structure built to remind people of a famous person or event. ▸ *adjective* 2 A memorial event or prize is in honour of someone who has died, so that they will be remembered.

memory memories *noun* 1 Your memory is your ability to remember things. 2 something you remember about the past. 3 (ICT) the part in which information is stored in a computer.

> **memory** *noun*
> 1 = recall, remembrance (formal)

memory card *noun* a small device for storing information in a mobile phone or digital camera.

men the plural form of **man**.

menace *noun* 1 someone or something that is likely to cause serious harm. 2 Menace is the quality of being threatening. ▸ *verb* 3 If someone or something menaces you, they threaten to harm you.

menagerie *noun* a collection of different wild animals.

mend *verb* If you mend something that is broken, you repair it.

> **mend** *verb*
> = darn, fix, patch, renovate, repair, restore

menial *adjective* Menial work is boring and tiring and the people who do it have low status.

meningitis *noun* Meningitis is a serious infectious illness which affects your brain and spinal cord.

menopause *noun* The menopause is the time during which a woman gradually stops

menstruating. This usually happens when she is about fifty.

-ment *suffix* '-ment' forms nouns which refer to a state or a feeling: *contentment*.

mental *adjective* 1 relating to the process of thinking or intelligence. 2 relating to the health of the mind. ▸ **mentally** *adverb*

mentality mentalities *noun* an attitude or way of thinking.

mention *verb* 1 If you mention something, you talk about it briefly. ▸ *noun* 2 a brief comment about someone or something.

> **mention** *verb*
> 1 = allude to, bring up, broach, hint, intimate, refer to, touch on, touch upon
> ▸ *noun* 2 = allusion, reference

mentor *noun* Someone's mentor is a person who teaches them and gives them advice. ▸ **mentorship** *noun*

menu *noun* 1 a list of the foods you can eat in a restaurant. 2 (ICT) a list of different options shown on a computer screen which the user must choose from.

MEP *noun* a person who has been elected to represent people in the European Parliament. MEP is an abbreviation for 'Member of the European Parliament'.

mercenary mercenaries *noun* 1 a soldier who is paid to fight for a foreign country. ▸ *adjective* 2 Someone who is mercenary is mainly interested in getting money.

merchandise *noun* (formal) Merchandise is goods that are sold.

merchant noun a trader who imports and exports goods.

merciful adjective 1 showing kindness. 2 showing forgiveness.

> **merciful** adjective
> 1 = compassionate, humane, kind 2 = forgiving, lenient

merciless adjective showing no kindness or forgiveness.

> **merciless** adjective
> = callous, cruel, heartless, implacable, ruthless

mercury noun 1 (SCIENCE) Mercury is a silver-coloured metallic element that is liquid at room temperature. It is used in thermometers. Its atomic number is 80 and its symbol is Hg. 2 Mercury is also the planet in the solar system which is nearest to the sun.

mercy mercies noun If you show mercy, you show forgiveness and do not punish someone as severely as you could.

> **mercy** noun
> = forgiveness, leniency

mere merest adjective used to emphasise how unimportant or small something is: It's a mere seven-minute journey by boat.
> **merely** adverb

merge verb When two things merge, they combine together to make one thing.

meringue noun a type of crisp, sweet cake made with egg whites and sugar.

merino merinos noun a breed of sheep, common in Australia and New Zealand, with long, fine wool.

merit noun 1 If something has

merit, it is good or worthwhile. 2 The merits of something are its advantages or good qualities.
▶ verb 3 If something merits a particular treatment, it deserves that treatment.

> **merit** noun
> 1 = excellence, value, virtue, worth 2 = advantage, asset, strength, strong point, virtue
> ▶ verb 3 = be entitled to, be worthy of, deserve, earn, warrant

mermaid noun In stories, a mermaid is a woman with a fish's tail instead of legs, who lives in the sea.

merry merrier, merriest adjective happy and cheerful.

merry-go-round noun a large rotating platform with models of animals or vehicles on it, on which children ride at a fair.

mesh noun Mesh is threads of wire or plastic twisted together like a net.

mess noun 1 something untidy. 2 a situation which is full of problems and trouble. 3 a room or building in which members of the armed forces eat. ▷ **messy** adjective ▷ **mess about** or **mess around** verb If you mess about or mess around, you do things without any particular purpose. ▷ **mess up** verb If you mess something up, you spoil it or do it wrong.

> **mess** noun
> 1 = chaos, disarray, disorder 2 = fix (informal), jam (informal), muddle, turmoil

message noun 1 a piece of information or a request that you send someone or leave for them.

2 an idea that someone tries to communicate to people, for example in a play or a speech.
▶ verb **3** If you message someone, you send them a text message.

> **message** noun
> **1** = bulletin, communication, despatch or dispatch, memo, memorandum, note, word
> ▶ verb **3** = email or e-mail, IM, instant message, text

messaging noun Messaging or text messaging is the sending and receiving of short pieces of information between mobile phones.

messenger noun someone who takes a message to someone for someone else.

> **messenger** noun
> = courier, envoy, runner

Messiah proper noun **1** (RE) For Jews, the Messiah is the king of the Jews, who will be sent by God. **2** (RE) For Christians, the Messiah is Jesus Christ.

met the past tense and past participle of **meet**.

metabolism noun Your metabolism is the chemical processes in your body that use food for growth and energy.
> **metabolic** adjective

metal noun (SCIENCE) a chemical element such as iron, steel, copper or lead. Metals are good conductors of heat and electricity and form positive ions. > **metallic** adjective

metamorphosis
metamorphoses noun (formal) When a metamorphosis occurs, a person or thing changes into something completely different.

metaphor noun (ENGLISH) an imaginative way of describing something as another thing, and so suggesting that it has the typical qualities of that other thing. For example, if you wanted to say that someone is shy, you might say they are a mouse.
> **metaphorical** adjective
> **metaphorically** adverb

meteor noun a piece of rock or metal that burns very brightly when it enters the earth's atmosphere from space.

meteoric adjective A meteoric rise to power or success happens very quickly.

meteorite noun a piece of rock from space that has landed on earth.

meteorological
adjective (GEOGRAPHY) relating to or involving the weather or weather forecasting. > **meteorology** noun

meter noun a device that measures and records something.

methane noun Methane is a colourless gas with no smell that is found in coal gas and produced by decaying vegetable matter.

method noun a particular way of doing something.

> **method** noun
> = approach, mode, procedure, technique, way

methodical adjective Someone who is methodical does things carefully and in an organised way.

Methodist noun (RE) someone who belongs to the Methodist Church, a Protestant church whose members worship God in a way begun by John Wesley and his followers.

M

meticulous *adjective* A meticulous person does things very carefully and with great attention to detail.

metre *noun* 1 a unit of length equal to 100 centimetres. 2 (ENGLISH) In poetry, metre is the regular and rhythmic arrangement of words and syllables. ▶ **metrical** *adjective*

metric *adjective* relating to the system of measurement that uses metres, grams and litres.

metropolis *noun* a very large city.

metropolitan *adjective* relating or belonging to a large, busy city.

mettle *noun* If you are on your mettle, you are ready to do something as well as you can because you know you are being tested or challenged.

Mexican *adjective* 1 belonging or relating to Mexico. ▶ *noun* 2 someone who comes from Mexico.

mg an abbreviation for 'milligram' or 'milligrams'.

mice the plural of **mouse**.

microchip *noun* a very small piece of silicon inside a computer with electronic circuits on it, which can hold large quantities of information or perform mathematical or logical operations.

microphone *noun* a device that is used to make sounds louder or to record them.

microprocessor *noun* a microchip which can be programmed to do a large number of tasks or calculations.

microscope *noun* (SCIENCE) a piece of equipment which magnifies very small objects so that you can study them.

microscopic *adjective* very small indeed.

microwave *noun* A microwave or microwave oven is a type of oven which cooks food very quickly by radiation.

mid- *prefix* 'Mid-' is used to form words that refer to the middle part of a place or period of time: *mid-Atlantic*.

midday *noun* Midday is twelve o'clock in the middle of the day.

middle *noun* 1 The middle of something is the part furthest from the edges, ends or outside surface. ▶ *adjective* 2 The middle one in a series or a row is the one that has an equal number of people or things on each side of it.

> **middle** *noun*
> 1 = centre, halfway point, midst
> ▶ *adjective* 2 = central, halfway

middle age *noun* Middle age is the period of your life when you are between about 40 and 60 years old.

Middle Ages *plural noun* (HISTORY) In European history, the Middle Ages were the period between about 1100 AD and 1500 AD.

middle class *noun* The middle classes are the people in a society who are not working-class or upper-class, for example managers and lawyers.

Middle East *noun* The Middle East consists of Iran and the countries in Asia to the west and south-west of Iran.

middle-of-the-road *adjective* Middle-of-the-road opinions are moderate.

middle school *noun* In England and Wales, a middle school is for

m

children aged between about 8 and 12.

middling *adjective* of average quality or ability.

midge *noun* a small flying insect which can bite people.

midget *noun* **1** a very small thing. **2** (*offensive*) a very small person.

midnight *noun* Midnight is twelve o'clock at night.

midriff *noun* the middle of your body between your waist and your chest.

midst *noun* If you are in the midst of a crowd or an event, you are in the middle of it.

midsummer *adjective* relating to the period in the middle of summer.

midway *adverb* in the middle of a distance or period of time.

midweek *adjective* happening in the middle of the week.

midwife midwives *noun* a nurse who is trained to help women at the birth of a baby. > **midwifery** *noun*

might *verb* **1** If you say something might happen, you mean that it is possible that it will happen. **2** If you say that someone might do something, you are suggesting that they do it. **3** Might is also the past tense of **may**. ▶ *noun* **4** (*literary*) Might is strength or power.

mighty mightier, mightiest *adjective* (*literary*) **1** very powerful or strong. **2** very large and impressive.

migraine *noun* a severe headache that makes you feel very ill.

migrant *noun* a person who moves from one place to another, especially to find work.

migrate *verb* **1** (GEOGRAPHY) If people migrate, they move from one place to another, especially to find work. **2** (SCIENCE) When birds or animals migrate, they move at a particular season to a different place, usually to breed or to find new feeding grounds. > **migration** *noun* > **migratory** *adjective*

mike *noun* (*informal*) a microphone.

mild *adjective* **1** Something that is mild is not strong and does not have any powerful or damaging effects. **2** Someone who is mild is gentle and kind. **3** Mild weather is warmer than usual. **4** Mild emotions or attitudes are not very great or extreme.

> **mild** *adjective*
> **1** = insipid, weak **2** = gentle, meek, placid **3** = balmy, temperate

mildew *noun* Mildew is a soft white fungus that grows on things when they are warm and damp.

mile *noun* a unit of distance equal to 1760 yards or about 1.6 kilometres.

mileage *noun* **1** Your mileage is the distance that you have travelled, measured in miles. **2** The amount of mileage that you get out of something is how useful it is to you.

militant *adjective* **1** A militant person is very active in trying to bring about extreme political or social change. ▶ *noun* **2** a person who tries to bring about extreme political or social change.

military *adjective* **1** related to or involving the armed forces of a country. ▶ *noun* **2** The military are the armed forces of a country. > **militarily** *adverb*

militia *noun* an organisation that operates like an army but whose members are not professional soldiers.

milk *noun* **1** Milk is the white liquid produced by female cows, goats and some other animals to feed their young. People drink milk and use it to make butter, cheese and yogurt. **2** Milk is also the white liquid that a baby drinks from its mother's breasts. ▶ *verb* **3** When someone milks a cow or a goat, they get milk from it by pulling its udders.

milky milkier, milkiest *adjective* **1** pale creamy white. **2** containing a lot of milk.

Milky Way *noun* The Milky Way is a strip of stars clustered closely together, appearing as a pale band in the sky.

mill *noun* **1** a building where grain is crushed to make flour. **2** a factory for making materials such as steel, wool or cotton. **3** a small device for grinding coffee or spices into powder.

millennium millennia or millenniums *noun* (*formal*) a period of 1000 years.

miller *noun* the person who operates a flour mill.

milligram *noun* a unit of weight equal to one thousandth of a gram.

millimetre *noun* a unit of length equal to one tenth of a centimetre or one thousandth of a metre.

million the number 1,000,000. > **millionth** *adjective*

millionaire *noun* a very rich person who has money or property worth millions of pounds or dollars.

millstone *phrase* If something is a millstone round your neck, it is an unpleasant problem or responsibility you cannot escape from.

mime *noun* **1** Mime is the use of movements and gestures to express something or to tell a story without using speech. ▶ *verb* **2** If you mime something, you describe or express it using mime.

mimic mimics, mimicking, mimicked *verb* **1** If you mimic someone's actions or voice, you imitate them in an amusing way. ▶ *noun* **2** a person who can imitate other people. > **mimicry** *noun*

mince *noun* **1** Mince is meat which has been chopped into very small pieces in a special machine. ▶ *verb* **2** If you mince meat, you chop it into very small pieces. **3** To mince about is to walk with small quick steps in an affected, effeminate way.

mind *noun* **1** Your mind is your ability to think, together with all the thoughts you have and your memory. ▶ *phrase* **2** If you **change your mind**, you change a decision that you have made or an opinion that you have. ▶ *verb* **3** If you do not mind something, you are not annoyed by it or bothered about it. **4** If you say that you wouldn't mind something, you mean that you would quite like it. **5** If you mind a child or mind something for someone, you look after it for a while.

> **mind** *noun*
> **1** = brain, head, imagination, intellect, psyche
> ▶ *verb* **3** = be bothered, care, object **5** = keep an eye on, look after, take care of, watch

m

mindful adjective (formal) If you are mindful of something, you think about it carefully before taking action.

mindless adjective 1 Mindless actions are regarded as stupid and destructive. 2 A mindless job or activity is simple and repetitive.

mine pronoun 1 'Mine' refers to something belonging or relating to the person who is speaking or writing: *a friend of mine.* ▸ noun 2 a series of holes or tunnels in the ground from which diamonds, coal or other minerals are dug out. 3 a bomb hidden in the ground or underwater, which explodes when people or things touch it. ▸ verb 4 To mine diamonds, coal or other minerals is to obtain these substances from underneath the ground. > **miner** noun

minefield noun an area of land or water where mines have been hidden.

mineral noun (D-G-T) (SCIENCE) a substance such as tin, salt or coal that is formed naturally in rocks and in the earth.

mineral water noun Mineral water is water which comes from a natural spring.

mingle verb If things mingle, they become mixed together.

miniature adjective 1 copying something on a much smaller scale. ▸ noun 2 a very small detailed painting, often of a person.

minibus noun a van with seats in the back which is used as a small bus.

minimal adjective very small in quality, quantity or degree.

minimise; also spelt **minimize** verb If you minimise something, you reduce it to the smallest amount possible.

minimum adjective 1 The minimum amount is the smallest amount that is possible. ▸ noun 2 The minimum is the smallest amount that is possible.

> **minimum** adjective
> 1 = least possible, minimal

minister noun 1 A minister is a person who is in charge of a particular government department. 2 A minister in a Protestant church is a member of the clergy.

ministerial adjective relating to a government minister or ministry.

ministry ministries noun 1 a government department that deals with a particular area of work. 2 Members of the clergy can be referred to as the ministry.

mink noun Mink is an expensive fur used to make coats or hats.

minnow noun a very small freshwater fish.

minor adjective 1 not as important or serious as other things. 2 (MUSIC) A minor key is one of the keys in which most European music is written. In a minor key the third note is three semitones higher than the first. ▸ noun 3 (formal) a young person under the age of 18.

> **minor** adjective
> 1 = lesser, petty, secondary, slight, trifling, trivial

minority minorities noun 1 The minority of people or things in a group is a number of them forming less than half of the whole. **2** A minority is a group of people of a particular race or religion living in a place where most people are of a different race or religion.

mint noun **1** Mint is a herb used for flavouring in cooking. **2** a peppermint-flavoured sweet. **3** The mint is the place where the official coins of a country are made. ▸ verb **4** When coins or medals are minted, they are made. ▸ adjective **5** If something is in mint condition, it is in very good condition, like new.

minus 1 You use 'minus' to show that one number is being subtracted from another. ▸ adjective **2** 'Minus' is used when talking about temperatures below 0°C or 0°F.

minuscule adjective very small indeed.

minute[1] noun **1** a unit of time equal to sixty seconds. **2** The minutes of a meeting are the written records of what was said and decided. ▸ verb **3** To minute a meeting is to write the official notes of it.

> **minute** noun
> 1 = flash, instant, moment, second, trice

minute[2] adjective extremely small.

> **minute** adjective
> = microscopic, negligible, slender, small, tiny

minutiae plural noun (formal) Minutiae are small, unimportant details.

miracle noun **1** (RE) a wonderful and surprising event, believed to have been caused by God. **2** any very surprising and fortunate

event. > **miraculous** adjective
> **miraculously** adverb

> **miracle** noun
> 2 = marvel, wonder

mirage noun an image which you can see in the distance in very hot weather, but which does not actually exist.

mire noun (literary) Mire is swampy ground or mud.

mirror noun **1** a piece of glass which reflects light and in which you can see your reflection. ▸ verb **2** To mirror something is to have similar features to it.

mirth noun (literary) Mirth is great amusement and laughter.

misbehave verb If a child misbehaves, he or she is naughty or behaves badly. > **misbehaviour** noun

miscarriage noun **1** If a woman has a miscarriage, her baby dies and she gives birth to it before it is properly formed. **2** A miscarriage of justice is a wrong decision made by a court, which causes an innocent person to be punished.

miscellaneous adjective A miscellaneous group is made up of people or things that are different from each other.

mischief noun Mischief is eagerness to have fun by teasing people or playing tricks.
> **mischievous** adjective

misconception noun a wrong idea about something.

misconduct noun Misconduct is bad or unacceptable behaviour by a professional person.

misdemeanour noun (formal) an act that is shocking or unacceptable.

m

miser noun a person who enjoys saving money but hates spending it. ▸ **miserly** adjective

miserable adjective 1 If you are miserable, you are very unhappy. 2 If a place or a situation is miserable, it makes you feel downhearted.

> **miserable** adjective
> 1 = dejected, depressed, down, downcast, low, melancholy (literary), mournful, sad, unhappy, wretched 2 = gloomy, pathetic, sorry, wretched

misery miseries noun Misery is great unhappiness.

> **misery** noun
> = despair, grief, melancholy (literary), sadness, sorrow, unhappiness, woe (formal)

misfire verb If a plan misfires, it goes wrong.

misfit noun a person who is not accepted by other people because of being rather strange or eccentric.

misfortune noun an unpleasant occurrence that is regarded as bad luck.

> **misfortune** noun
> = adversity, bad luck

misgiving noun If you have misgivings, you are worried or unhappy about something.

misguided adjective A misguided opinion or action is wrong because it is based on a misunderstanding or bad information.

misinterpret verb To misinterpret something is to understand it wrongly.

misjudge verb If you misjudge

someone or something, you form an incorrect idea or opinion about them.

mislead misleads, misleading, misled verb To mislead someone is to make them believe something which is not true.

misplaced adjective A misplaced feeling is inappropriate or directed at the wrong thing or person.

misrepresent verb To misrepresent someone is to give an inaccurate or misleading account of what they have said or done.

> **misrepresent** verb
> = distort, falsify, twist

miss verb 1 If you miss something, you do not notice it. 2 If you miss someone or something, you feel sad that they are no longer with you. 3 If you miss a chance or opportunity, you fail to take advantage of it. 4 If you miss a bus, plane or train, you arrive too late to catch it. 5 If you miss something, you fail to hit it when you aim at it. ▸ noun 6 an act of missing something that you were aiming at. 7 'Miss' is used before the name of a woman or girl who is not married as a form of address.

> **miss** verb
> 1 = fail to notice, mistake, overlook 2 = long for, pine for, yearn for

missile noun a weapon that moves long distances through the air and explodes when it reaches its target; also used of any object thrown as a weapon.

mission noun 1 an important task that you have to do. 2 a group of people who have been sent to a foreign country to carry out an official task. **3** a journey made by a military aeroplane or space rocket to carry out a task. **4** If you have a mission, there is something that you believe it is your duty to try to achieve. **5** the workplace of a group of Christians who are working for the Church.

missionary missionaries noun RE a Christian who has been sent to a foreign country to work for the Church.

missive noun (old-fashioned) a letter.

mist noun **1** Mist consists of a large number of tiny drops of water in the air, which make it hard to see clearly. ▶ verb **2** If your eyes mist, you cannot see very far because there are tears in your eyes. **3** If glass mists over or mists up, it becomes covered with condensation so that you cannot see through it.

mistake mistakes, mistaking, mistook, mistaken noun **1** an action or opinion that is wrong or is not what you intended. ▶ verb **2** If you mistake someone or something for another person or thing, you wrongly think that they are the other person or thing.

> **mistake** noun
> **1** = blunder, error, gaffe, oversight, slip
> ▶ verb **2** = confuse with, misinterpret as, mix up with, take for

mistaken adjective **1** If you are mistaken about something, you are wrong about it. **2** If you have a mistaken belief or opinion,

you believe something which is not true.

mistletoe noun Mistletoe is a plant which grows on trees and has white berries on it. It is used as a Christmas decoration.

mistook the past tense of **mistake**.

mistreat verb To mistreat a person or animal is to treat them badly and make them suffer.

> **mistreat** verb
> = abuse, ill-treat

mistress noun **1** A school mistress is a female teacher. **2** A servant's mistress is the woman who is the servant's employer.

mistrust verb **1** If you mistrust someone, you do not feel that you can trust them. ▶ noun **2** Mistrust is a feeling that you cannot trust someone.

misty mistier, mistiest adjective full of or covered with mist.

misunderstand misunderstands, misunderstanding, misunderstood verb If you misunderstand something, you do not properly understand what it means.

misunderstanding noun If two people have a misunderstanding, they have a slight quarrel or disagreement.

misuse noun **1** The misuse of something is the incorrect or dishonest use of it. ▶ verb **2** To misuse something is to use it incorrectly or dishonestly.

mite noun a very tiny creature that lives in the fur of animals.

mitigating adjective (formal) Mitigating circumstances make a crime easier to understand, and perhaps justify it.

mix *verb* If you mix things, you combine them or shake or stir them together. ▷ **mix up** *verb* If you mix up two things or people, you confuse them.

> **mix** *verb*
> = amalgamate, blend, combine, merge, mingle
> ▷ **mix up** = confuse, muddle

mixed *adjective* 1 consisting of several things of the same general kind. 2 involving people from different religions or ethnic groups. 3 Mixed education or accommodation is for both males and females.

mixed up *adjective* 1 If you are mixed up, you are confused. 2 If you are mixed up in a crime or a scandal, you are involved in it.

mixer *noun* a machine used for mixing things together.

mixture *noun* several different things mixed or shaken together.

> **mixture** *noun*
> = alloy, amalgamation, blend, combination, compound, fusion, medley

mix-up *noun* a mistake in something that was planned.

> **mix-up** *noun*
> = mistake, misunderstanding, muddle

ml an abbreviation for 'millilitre' or 'millilitres'.

mm an abbreviation for 'millimetre' or 'millimetres'.

moan *verb* 1 If you moan, you make a low, miserable sound because you are in pain or suffering. 2 (*informal*) If you moan about something, you complain about it. ▷ *noun* 3 a low cry of pain or misery.

> **moan** *verb*
> 1 = groan, grunt 2 = complain, groan, grumble, whine, whinge (*informal*)
> ▷ *noun* 3 = groan, grunt

moat *noun* a wide, water-filled ditch around a building such as a castle.

mob mobs, mobbing, mobbed *noun* 1 a large, disorganised crowd of people. ▷ *verb* 2 If a lot of people mob someone, they crowd around the person in a disorderly way.

mobile *adjective* 1 able to move or be moved freely and easily. 2 (PE) If you are mobile, you are able to travel or move about from one place to another. ▷ *noun* 3 a decoration consisting of several small objects which hang from threads and move around when a breeze blows. 4 a mobile phone. ▷ **mobility** *noun*

mobile phone *noun* a small portable telephone.

mock *verb* 1 If you mock someone, you say something scornful or imitate their foolish behaviour. ▷ *adjective* 2 not genuine. 3 A mock examination is one that you do as a practice before the real examination.

> **mock** *verb*
> 1 = deride (*formal*), laugh at, make fun of, poke fun at, ridicule, scoff at
> ▷ *adjective* 2 = artificial, bogus, counterfeit, dummy, fake, false, feigned, imitation, phoney or phony (*informal*), pretended, sham

mockery *noun* Mockery is the expression of scorn or ridicule of someone.

mockery *noun*
= derision, jeering, ridicule

mode *noun* **1** A mode of life or behaviour is a particular way of living or behaving. **2** (MATHS) The most frequently occurring in a set of values.

model models, modelling, modelled *noun* **1** a copy of something that shows what it looks like or how it works. **2** Something that is described as, for example, a model of clarity or a model of perfection, is extremely clear or absolutely perfect. **3** a type or version of a machine. **4** a person who poses for a painter or a photographer. **5** a person who wears the clothes that are being displayed at a fashion show or in a magazine. ▶ *adjective* **6** Someone who is described as, for example, a model student is an excellent student. ▶ *verb* **7** If you model yourself on someone, you copy their behaviour because you admire them. **8** To model clothes is to display them by wearing them. **9** To model shapes or figures is to make them out of clay or wood.

model *noun*
1 = dummy, replica, representation **2** = epitome, example, ideal, paragon
▶ *verb* **9** = carve, fashion, form, mould, sculpt, shape

modem *noun* (ICT) a piece of equipment that links a computer to the telephone system so that data can be transferred from one machine to another via the telephone line.

moderate *adjective* **1** Moderate views are not extreme. They

usually favour gradual changes rather than major ones. **2** A moderate amount of something is neither large nor small. ▶ *noun* **3** a person whose political views are not extreme. ▶ *verb* **4** If you moderate something or if it moderates, it becomes less extreme or violent.

moderate *adjective*
2 = average, fair, medium, middling, reasonable
▶ *verb* **4** = abate, curb, ease, relax, soften, temper, tone down

moderation *noun* Moderation is control of your behaviour that stops you acting in an extreme way.

modern *adjective* **1** relating to the present time. **2** new and involving the latest ideas and equipment.

modern *adjective*
1 = contemporary, current, present, present-day, recent
2 = latest, new, up-to-date, up-to-the-minute

modernise; also spelt **modernize** *verb* To modernise something is to introduce new methods or equipment to it.

modest *adjective* **1** quite small in size or amount. **2** Someone who is modest does not boast about their abilities or possessions. **3** shy and easily embarrassed. > **modestly** *adverb* > **modesty** *noun*

modest *adjective*
1 = limited, middling, moderate, small **2** = humble, unassuming

modification *noun* a small change made to improve something.

modify modifies, modifying, modified *verb* If you modify something, you change it slightly in order to improve it.

module *noun* 1 one of the parts which when put together form a whole unit or object. 2 (ICT) a part of a machine, system or program that does a particular task. 3 a part of a spacecraft which can do certain things away from the main body.

mohair *noun* Mohair is very soft, fluffy wool obtained from angora goats.

moist *adjective* slightly wet.

moisture *noun* Moisture is tiny drops of water in the air or on the ground.

mole *noun* 1 a dark, slightly raised spot on your skin. 2 a small animal with black fur. Moles live in tunnels underground. 3 (*informal*) a member of an organisation who is working as a spy for a rival organisation.

molecule *noun* (SCIENCE) the smallest amount of a substance that can exist. > **molecular** *adjective*

molest *verb* If someone molests you, they annoy or pester you.

mollify mollifies, mollifying, mollified *verb* To mollify someone is to do something to make them less upset or angry.

molten *adjective* Molten rock or metal has been heated to a very high temperature and has become a thick liquid.

moment *noun* 1 a very short period of time. 2 The moment at which something happens is the point in time at which it happens. ▸ *phrase* 3 If something

is happening **at the moment**, it is happening now.

> **moment** *noun*
> 1 = instant, minute, second, split second 2 = instant, point, time

momentary *adjective* Something that is momentary lasts for only a few seconds. > **momentarily** *adverb*

momentous *adjective* (*formal*) very important, often because of its future effect.

momentum *noun* 1 Momentum is the ability that something has to keep developing. 2 Momentum is also the ability that an object has to continue moving as a result of the speed it already has.

monarch *noun* (CITIZENSHIP) a queen, king or other royal person who reigns over a country.

monarchy monarchies *noun* a system in which a queen or king reigns in a country.

monastery monasteries *noun* a building in which monks live. > **monastic** *adjective*

Monday *noun* Monday is the day between Sunday and Tuesday.

money *noun* Money is the coins or banknotes that you use to buy something.

> **money** *noun*
> = capital, cash, dosh (*British, Australian and New Zealand; slang*), dough (*informal*), funds

mongrel *noun* a dog with parents of different breeds.

monitor *verb* 1 If you monitor something, you regularly check its condition and progress. ▸ *noun* 2 a machine used to check or record things. 3 (ICT) the visual display unit of a computer. **4** a school pupil chosen to do special duties by the teacher.

monk noun a member of a male religious community.

monkey noun an animal which has a long tail and climbs trees. Monkeys live in hot countries.

monogamy noun (formal) Monogamy is the custom of being married to only one person at a time. > **monogamous** adjective

monologue noun (ENGLISH) a long speech by one person during a play or a conversation.

monopoly monopolies noun control of most of an industry by one or a few large firms.

monotonous adjective having a regular pattern which is very dull and boring. > **monotony** noun

monsoon noun (GEOGRAPHY) the season of very heavy rain in South-east Asia.

monster noun **1** a large, imaginary creature that looks very frightening. **2** a cruel or frightening person. ▶ adjective **3** extremely large.

monstrosity monstrosities noun something that is large and extremely ugly.

monstrous adjective extremely shocking or unfair. > **monstrously** adverb

montage noun a picture or film consisting of a combination of several different items arranged to produce an unusual effect.

month noun one of the twelve periods that a year is divided into.

monthly adjective **1** happening or appearing once a month. ▶ adverb **2** once a month.

monument noun a large stone

structure built to remind people of a famous person or event.

monumental adjective **1** A monumental building or sculpture is very large and important. **2** very large or extreme.

mood noun the way you are feeling at a particular time.

> **mood** noun
> = frame of mind, humour, spirits, state of mind, temper

moody moodier, moodiest adjective **1** Someone who is moody is irritable or unhappy. **2** Someone who is moody often changes their mood for no apparent reason.

> **moody** adjective
> **1** = irritable, morose, sulky, sullen **2** = temperamental, volatile

moon noun The moon is an object moving round the earth which you see as a shining circle or crescent in the sky at night. Some other planets have moons.

moonlight moonlights, moonlighting, moonlighted noun **1** Moonlight is the light that comes from the moon at night. ▶ verb **2** (informal) If someone is moonlighting, they have a second job that they have not informed the tax office about. > **moonlit** adjective

moor noun **1** a high area of open land. ▶ verb **2** If a boat is moored, it is attached to the land with a rope.

mooring noun a place where a boat can be tied.

moose noun a large North American deer with flat antlers.

m

moot verb (formal) When something is mooted, it is suggested for discussion.

mop mops, mopping, mopped noun 1 a tool for washing floors, consisting of a sponge or string head attached to a long handle. 2 a large amount of loose or untidy hair. ▶ verb 3 To mop a floor is to clean it with a mop. 4 To mop a surface is to wipe it with a dry cloth to remove liquid.

moped noun a type of small motorcycle.

moral noun 1 (PSHE) (in plural) Morals are values based on beliefs about the correct and acceptable way to behave. ▶ adjective 2 concerned with whether behaviour is right or acceptable. > **morality** noun > **morally** adverb

morale noun Morale is the amount of confidence and optimism that you have.

morbid adjective having a great interest in unpleasant things, especially death.

more adjective 1 More means a greater number or extent than something else: He's got more chips than me. 2 used to refer to an additional thing or amount of something: He found some more clues. ▶ pronoun 3 a greater number or extent. ▶ adverb 4 to a greater degree or extent. 5 You can use 'more' in front of adjectives and adverbs to form comparatives: You look more beautiful than ever.

> **more** adjective
> 2 = added, additional, extra, further

moreover adverb used to introduce a piece of information that supports or expands the previous statement.

morgue noun a building where dead bodies are kept before being buried or cremated.

morning noun the part of the day between midnight and noon.

Moroccan adjective 1 belonging or relating to Morocco. ▶ noun 2 someone who comes from Morocco.

moron noun (informal) a very stupid person. > **moronic** adjective

morose adjective miserable and bad-tempered.

morphine noun Morphine is a drug which is used to relieve pain.

Morse or **Morse code** noun Morse or Morse code is a code used for sending messages in which each letter is represented by a series of dots and dashes. It is named after its American inventor, Samuel Morse.

morsel noun a small piece of food.

mortal adjective 1 unable to live forever. 2 A mortal wound is one that causes death. ▶ noun 3 an ordinary person.

mortality noun 1 Mortality is the fact that all people must die. 2 Mortality also refers to the number of people who die at any particular time.

mortar noun 1 a short cannon which fires missiles high into the air for a short distance. 2 Mortar is a mixture of sand, water and cement used to hold bricks firmly together.

mortgage noun 1 a loan which you get from a bank or a building society in order to buy a house. ▶ verb 2 If you mortgage your house, you use it as a guarantee to a company in order to borrow money from them. They can take the house from you if you do not pay back the money you have borrowed.

mortuary mortuaries *noun* a special room in a hospital where dead bodies are kept before being buried or cremated.

mosaic *noun* a design made of small coloured stones or pieces of coloured glass set into concrete or plaster.

mosque *noun* RE a building where Muslims go to worship.

mosquito mosquitoes or mosquitos *noun* Mosquitoes are small insects which bite people in order to suck their blood.

moss *noun* Moss is a soft, low-growing, green plant which grows on damp soil or stone.

most *adjective, pronoun* 1 Most of a group of things or people means nearly all of them. 2 The most means a larger amount than anyone or anything else: *She has the most talent.* ▶ *adverb* 3 You can use 'most' in front of adjectives or adverbs to form superlatives: *the most beautiful buildings in the world.*

mostly *adverb* 'Mostly' is used to show that a statement is generally true: *Her friends are mostly classmates.*

MOT *noun* In Britain, the MOT test is an annual test for road vehicles to check that they are safe to drive. MOT is an abbreviation for 'Ministry of Transport'.

motel *noun* a hotel providing overnight accommodation for people in the middle of a car journey.

moth *noun* an insect like a butterfly which usually flies at night.

mother *noun* 1 A person's mother is their female parent. ▶ *verb* 2 To mother someone is to look after them and bring them up.

motherhood *noun* Motherhood is the state of being a mother.

mother-in-law mothers-in-law *noun* Someone's mother-in-law is the mother of their husband or wife.

motif *noun* a design which is used as a decoration.

motion *noun* 1 Motion is the process of continually moving or changing position. 2 an action or gesture. 3 a proposal which people discuss and vote on at a meeting. ▶ *verb* 4 If you motion to someone, you make a movement with your hand in order to show them what they should do.

motionless *adjective* not moving at all.

motivate *verb* 1 If you are motivated by something, it makes you behave in a particular way. 2 If you motivate someone, you make them feel determined to do something. > **motivation** *noun*

> **motivate** *verb*
> 1 = drive, inspire, lead, move, prompt, provoke

motive *noun* a reason or purpose for doing something.

motley *adjective* A motley collection is made up of people or things of very different types.

motor *noun* 1 a part of a vehicle or a machine that uses electricity or fuel to produce movement so that the machine can work. ▶ *adjective* 2 concerned with or relating to vehicles with a petrol or diesel engine.

motorcycle noun a two-wheeled vehicle with an engine which is ridden like a bicycle.
> **motorcyclist** noun

motoring adjective relating to cars and driving.

motorist noun a person who drives a car.

motorway noun a wide road built for fast travel over long distances.

mottled adjective covered with patches of different colours.

motto mottoes or mottos noun a short sentence or phrase that is a rule for good or sensible behaviour.

mould verb 1 To mould someone or something is to influence them and change them so they develop in a particular way. 2 (DGT) To mould a substance into a particular shape. ▶ noun 3 (DGT) a container used to make something into a particular shape. 4 Mould is a soft grey or green substance that can form on old food or damp walls. > **mouldy** adjective

mound noun 1 a small man-made hill. 2 a large, untidy pile.

mount verb 1 To mount a campaign or event is to organise it and carry it out. 2 If something is mounting, it is increasing. 3 (formal) To mount something is to go to the top of it. 4 If you mount a horse, you climb on its back. 5 If you mount an object in a particular place, you fix it there to display it. ▶ noun 6 'Mount' is also used as part of the name of a mountain.

mountain noun 1 a very high piece of land with steep sides. 2 a large amount of something.

mountaineer noun a person who climbs mountains.

mountainous adjective A mountainous area has a lot of mountains.

mourn verb 1 If you mourn for someone who has died, you are very sad and think about them a lot. 2 If you mourn something, you are sad because you no longer have it.

mourner noun a person who attends a funeral.

mournful adjective very sad.

mourning noun If someone is in mourning, they wear special black clothes or behave in a quiet and restrained way because a member of their family has died.

mouse mice noun 1 a small rodent with a long tail. 2 (ICT) a small device moved by hand to control the position of the cursor on a computer screen.

mousse noun Mousse is a light, fluffy food made from whipped eggs and cream.

moustache noun A man's moustache is hair growing on his upper lip.

mouth noun 1 your lips, or the space behind them where your tongue and teeth are. 2 The mouth of a cave or a hole is the entrance to it. 3 (GEOGRAPHY) The mouth of a river is the place where it flows into the sea. ▶ verb 4 If you mouth something, you form words with your lips without making any sound.
> **mouthful** noun

mouthpiece noun 1 the part you speak into on a telephone. 2 the part of a musical instrument you put to your mouth. 3 The mouthpiece of an organisation is the person who publicly states its opinions and policies.

movable *adjective* Something that is movable can be moved from one place to another.

move *verb* 1 To move means to go to a different place or position. To move something means to change its place or position. 2 If you move, or move house, you go to live in a different house. 3 If something moves you, it causes you to feel a deep emotion. ▶ *noun* 4 a change from one place or position to another. 5 an act of moving house.

> **move** *verb*
> 1 = dart, dash, go, hurry
> 2 = migrate, move house, relocate 3 = affect, touch

movement *noun* 1 Movement involves changing position or going from one place to another. 2 *(in plural, formal)* Your movements are everything you do during a period of time. 3 a group of people who share the same beliefs or aims. 4 one of the major sections of a piece of classical music.

> **movement** *noun*
> 1 = flow, motion 3 = campaign, faction, group, organisation

movie *noun (informal)* a film.

moving *adjective* Something that is moving makes you feel deep sadness or emotion. > **movingly** *adverb*

> **moving** *adjective*
> = affecting, emotional, poignant, stirring, touching

mow mows, mowing, mowed, mown *verb* To mow grass is to cut it with a lawnmower.

mower *noun* a machine for cutting grass.

MP *noun* (CITIZENSHIP) a person who has been elected to represent people in a country's parliament. MP is an abbreviation for 'Member of Parliament'.

mpg an abbreviation for 'miles per gallon'.

mph an abbreviation for 'miles per hour'.

Mr *noun* 'Mr' is used before a man's name when you are speaking or referring to him.

Mrs *noun* 'Mrs' is used before the name of a married woman when you are speaking or referring to her.

Ms *noun* 'Ms' is used before a woman's name when you are speaking or referring to her. Ms does not specify whether a woman is married or not.

MSP *noun* a person who has been elected to represent people in the Scottish Parliament. MSP is an abbreviation for 'Member of the Scottish Parliament'.

much *adverb* 1 You use 'much' to emphasise that something is true to a great extent: *I feel much better now.* 2 If something does not happen much, it does not happen very often. ▶ *adjective, pronoun* 3 You use 'much' to ask questions or give information about the size or amount of something: *How much money do you need?*

muck *noun* 1 *(informal)* Muck is dirt or some other unpleasant substance. 2 Muck is also manure. > **mucky** *adjective* > **muck about** *verb (informal)* If you muck about, you behave stupidly and waste time.

mucus *noun* Mucus is a liquid produced in parts of your body, for example in your nose.

mud *noun* Mud is wet, sticky earth.

muddle *noun* 1 A muddle is a state of disorder or untidiness. ▶ *verb* 2 If you muddle things, you mix them up.

> **muddle** *noun*
> 1 = chaos, confusion, disarray, disorder, disorganisation, jumble, mess, tangle
> ▶ *verb* 2 = confuse, jumble, mix up

muddy muddier, muddiest *adjective* 1 covered in mud. 2 A muddy colour is dull and not clear.

muesli *noun* Muesli is a mixture of chopped nuts, cereal flakes and dried fruit that you can eat for breakfast with milk.

muffin *noun* 1 a small, flat, sweet bread roll, which you eat hot. 2 a small, domed cake, often containing fruit pieces or chocolate chips.

muffled *adjective* A muffled sound is quiet or difficult to hear.

mug mugs, mugging, mugged *noun* 1 a large, deep cup. 2 (*informal*) someone who is stupid and easily deceived. ▶ *verb* 3 (*informal*) If someone mugs you, they attack you in order to steal your money.

muggy muggier, muggiest *adjective* Muggy weather is unpleasantly warm and damp.

mule *noun* the offspring of a female horse and a male donkey.

mull *verb* If you mull something over, you think about it for a long time before making a decision.

mullet *noun* a common edible fish.

mulloway *noun* a large edible fish found in Australian waters.

multicultural *adjective* consisting of or relating to people of many different nationalities and cultures.

multimedia *noun* 1 (ICT) in computing, you use 'multimedia' to refer to products which use sound, pictures, film and ordinary text to convey information. 2 In the classroom, all the things like TV, computers and books which are used as teaching aids are called multimedia.

multinational *noun* a very large company with branches in many countries.

multiple *adjective* 1 having or involving many different functions or things. ▶ *noun* 2 The multiples of a number are other numbers that it will divide into exactly. For example, 6, 9 and 12 are multiples of 3.

multiple sclerosis *noun* Multiple sclerosis is a serious disease which attacks the nervous system, affecting your ability to move.

multiplication *noun* 1 (MATHS) Multiplication is the process of multiplying one number by another. 2 The multiplication of things is a large increase in their number.

multiplicity *noun* If there is a multiplicity of things, there is a large number or variety of them.

multiply multiplies, multiplying, multiplied *verb* 1 When something multiplies, it increases greatly in number. 2 (MATHS) When you multiply one number by another, you calculate the total you would get if you added the first number to itself a particular number of times. For example, two multiplied by three is equal to two plus two plus two, which equals six.

multiply *verb*
1 = increase, proliferate, spread

multitude *noun* (*formal*) a very large number of people or things.

mum (*informal*) *noun* 1 Your mum is your mother. ▶ *phrase* 2 If you **keep mum** about something, you keep it secret.

mumble *verb* If you mumble, you speak very quietly and indistinctly.

mumble *verb*
= murmur, mutter

mummy mummies *noun*
1 (*informal*) Your mummy is your mother. 2 a dead body which was preserved long ago by being rubbed with special oils and wrapped in cloth.

mumps *noun* Mumps is a disease that causes painful swelling in the neck glands.

munch *verb* If you munch something, you chew it steadily and thoroughly.

mundane *adjective* very ordinary and not interesting or unusual.

municipal *adjective* belonging to a city or town which has its own local government.

munitions *plural noun* Munitions are bombs, guns and other military supplies.

mural *noun* a picture painted on a wall.

murder *noun* 1 Murder is the deliberate killing of a person. ▶ *verb* 2 To murder someone is to kill them deliberately. > **murderer** *noun*

murder *noun*
1 = assassination, homicide, killing, manslaughter, slaughter, slaying (*literary*)
▶ *verb* 2 = assassinate, butcher, kill, slaughter, slay (*literary*), take the life of

murderous *adjective* likely to murder someone.

murky murkier, murkiest *adjective* dark or dirty and unpleasant.

murmur *verb* 1 If you murmur, you say something very softly. ▶ *noun* 2 something that someone says which can hardly be heard.

muscle *noun* 1 (SCIENCE) Your muscles are pieces of flesh which you can expand or contract in order to move parts of your body. An **agonistic muscle** is a muscle which is relaxed when another muscle is contracted; an **antagonistic muscle** is a muscle which is contracted when another muscle is relaxed, returning the limb to its original position; an **antagonistic pair of muscles** means two muscles which work together, for example one opening a joint and the other closing it. ▶ *verb* 2 (*informal*) If you muscle in on something, you force your way into a situation in which you are not welcome.

muscular *adjective* 1 involving or affecting your muscles. 2 Someone who is muscular has strong, firm muscles.

muse *verb* (*literary*) To muse is to think about something for a long time.

museum noun a building where many interesting or valuable objects are kept and displayed.

mush noun A mush is a thick, soft paste.

mushroom noun 1 a fungus with a short stem and a round top. Some types of mushroom are edible. ▶ verb 2 If something mushrooms, it appears and grows very quickly.

mushy mushier, mushiest adjective 1 Mushy fruits or vegetables are too soft. 2 (informal) Mushy stories are too sentimental.

music noun 1 Music is a pattern of sounds performed by people singing or playing instruments. 2 Music is also the written symbols that represent musical sounds.

musical adjective 1 relating to playing or studying music. ▶ noun 2 a play or film that uses songs and dance to tell the story.
> **musically** adverb

musician noun (MUSIC) a person who plays a musical instrument as their job or hobby.

musk noun Musk is a substance with a strong, sweet smell. It is used to make perfume. > **musky** adjective

musket noun an old-fashioned gun with a long barrel.

Muslim noun (RE) 1 a person who believes in Islam and lives according to its rules. ▶ adjective 2 relating to Islam.

muslin noun Muslin is a very thin cotton material.

mussel noun Mussels are a kind of shellfish with black shells.

must verb 1 If something must happen, it is very important or necessary that it happens. 2 If you tell someone they must do something, you are suggesting that they do it. ▶ noun 3 something that is absolutely necessary.

mustard noun Mustard is a spicy-tasting yellow or brown paste made from seeds.

muster verb If you muster something such as energy or support, you gather it together.

musty mustier, mustiest adjective smelling stale and damp.

mutate verb (SCIENCE) If something mutates, its structure or appearance alters in some way.
> **mutant** noun, adjective

mute (formal) adjective 1 not giving out sound or speech. ▶ verb 2 To mute a sound means to make it quieter.

muted adjective 1 Muted colours or sounds are soft and gentle. 2 A muted reaction is not very strong.

mutilate verb 1 If someone is mutilated, their body is badly injured. 2 If you mutilate something, you deliberately damage or spoil it. > **mutilation** noun

mutiny mutinies noun A mutiny is a rebellion against someone in authority.

mutter verb To mutter is to speak in a very low and perhaps cross voice.

mutton noun Mutton is the meat of an adult sheep.

mutual adjective used to describe something that two or more people do to each other or share.

mutually adverb Mutually describes a situation in which two or more people feel the same way about each other.

muzzle *noun* **1** the nose and mouth of an animal. **2** a cover or a strap for a dog's nose and mouth to prevent it from biting. **3** the open end of a gun through which the bullets come out. ▶ *verb* **4** To muzzle a dog is to put a muzzle on it.

my *adjective* 'My' refers to something belonging or relating to the person speaking or writing: *I held my breath.*

myriad *noun* (*literary*) a very large number of people or things.

myself *pronoun* **1** 'Myself' is used when the person speaking or writing does an action and is affected by it: *I congratulated myself.* **2** 'Myself' is also used to emphasise 'I': *I find it a bit odd myself.*

mysterious *adjective* **1** strange and not well understood. **2** secretive about something.

> **mysterious** *adjective*
> **1** = arcane (*formal*), baffling, cryptic, enigmatic, mystifying
> **2** = furtive, secretive

mystery **mysteries** *noun* something that is not understood or known about.

> **mystery** *noun*
> = conundrum, enigma, puzzle, riddle

mystic *noun* **1** a religious person who spends long hours meditating. ▶ *adjective* **2** Mystic means the same as mystical.
> **mysticism** *noun*

mystical *adjective* involving spiritual powers and influences.

mystify **mystifies**, **mystifying**, **mystified** *verb* If something mystifies you, you find it impossible to understand.

mystique *noun* Mystique is an atmosphere of mystery and importance associated with a particular person or thing.

myth *noun* **1** an untrue belief or explanation. **2** (ENGLISH) a story which was made up long ago to explain natural events and religious beliefs.

mythical *adjective* imaginary, untrue or existing only in myths.

mythology *noun* Mythology refers to stories that have been made up in the past to explain natural events or justify religious beliefs. > **mythological** *adjective*

m

Nn

nag nags, nagging, nagged verb
1 If you nag someone, you keep complaining to them about something. 2 If something nags at you, it keeps worrying you.

nail noun 1 a small piece of metal with a sharp point at one end, which you hammer into objects to hold them together. 2 Your nails are the thin hard areas covering the ends of your fingers and toes. ▶ verb 3 If you nail something somewhere, you fit it there using a nail. 4 (informal) If you nail someone who has done something wrong, you catch them and prove that they are guilty.

naive; also spelt **naïve** adjective foolishly believing that things are easier or less complicated than they really are. > **naively** adverb > **naivety** noun

naked adjective 1 not wearing any clothes or not covered by anything. 2 shown openly. > **nakedness** noun

name noun 1 a word that you use to identify a person, place or thing. 2 Someone's name is also their reputation. ▶ verb 3 If you name someone or something, you give them a name or you say their name. 4 If you name a price or a date, you say what you want it to be.

name noun
1 = designation, epithet, nickname, term, title
2 = character, reputation
▶ verb 3 = baptise, call, christen, dub, style, term

nameless adjective You describe someone or something as nameless when you do not know their name, or when a name has not yet been given to them.

namely adverb that is; used to introduce more detailed information about what you have just said: *The state stripped most of their rights, namely the right to own land.*

namesake noun Your namesake is someone with the same name as you.

nanny nannies noun a person whose job is looking after young children.

nap naps, napping, napped noun 1 a short sleep. ▶ verb 2 When you nap, you have a short sleep.

napkin noun a small piece of cloth or paper used to wipe your hands and mouth after eating.

nappy nappies noun a piece of towelling or paper worn round a baby's bottom.

narcotic noun a drug which makes you sleepy and unable to feel pain.

narrate verb If you narrate a story, you tell it. > **narration** noun

narrative noun (ENGLISH) a story or an account of events.

narrator noun 1 a person who is reading or telling a story out loud. 2 (ENGLISH) a character in a novel who tells the story.

narrow adjective 1 having a small distance from one side to the other. **2** concerned only with a few aspects of something and ignoring the important points. **3** A narrow escape or victory is one that you only just achieve. ▶ verb **4** To narrow means to become less wide. > **narrowly** adverb > **narrowness** noun

> **narrow** adjective
> **1** = fine, slender, slim, thin

narrow-minded adjective unwilling to consider new ideas or opinions.

> **narrow-minded** adjective
> = biased, bigoted, insular, opinionated, prejudiced

nasal adjective **1** relating to the nose. **2** Nasal sounds are made by breathing out through your nose as you speak.

nasty nastier, nastiest adjective very unpleasant. > **nastily** adverb > **nastiness** noun

> **nasty** adjective
> = disagreeable, disgusting, foul, horrible, repellent, unpleasant, vile

nation noun (GEOGRAPHY) a large group of people sharing the same history and language and usually inhabiting a particular country.

national (GEOGRAPHY) adjective **1** relating to the whole of a country. **2** typical of a particular country. ▶ noun **3** A national of a country is a citizen of that country. > **nationally** adverb

national anthem noun A country's national anthem is its official song.

nationalise; also spelt **nationalize** verb To nationalise an industry means to bring it under the control and ownership of the state. > **nationalisation** noun

nationalism noun **1** Nationalism is a desire for the independence of a country; also a political movement aiming to achieve such independence. **2** Nationalism is also love of your own country. > **nationalist** noun > **nationalistic** adjective

nationality nationalities noun Nationality is the fact of belonging to a particular country.

National Party noun In Australia and New Zealand, the National Party is a major political party.

national service noun National service is a compulsory period of service in the armed forces.

nationwide adjective, adverb happening all over a country.

native adjective **1** Your native country is the country where you were born. **2** Your native language is the language that you first learned to speak. **3** Animals or plants that are native to a place live or grow there naturally and have not been brought there by people. ▶ noun **4** A native of a place is someone who was born there.

Nativity noun In Christianity, the Nativity is the birth of Christ or the festival celebrating this.

natural adjective **1** normal and to be expected. **2** not trying to pretend or hide anything. **3** (DGT) existing or happening in nature. **4** A natural ability is one you were born with. **5** Your natural mother or father is your birth mother or father and not someone who has adopted you. ▶ noun **6** someone who is born with a particular ability. **7** In music, a natural is a note that is not a sharp or a flat.

It is represented by the symbol (♮).
> **naturally** adverb

> **natural** adjective
> 1 = common, everyday, normal, ordinary, typical, usual
> 2 = candid, frank, genuine, real, unaffected 4 = inborn, inherent, innate, instinctive, intuitive, native

nature noun 1 Nature is animals, plants and all the other things in the world not made by people. 2 The nature of a person or thing is their basic character.

> **nature** noun
> 2 = character, make-up, personality

naughty naughtier, naughtiest adjective 1 behaving badly. 2 rude or indecent. > **naughtily** adverb > **naughtiness** noun

> **naughty** adjective
> 1 = bad, disobedient, impish, mischievous, wayward

nausea noun Nausea is a feeling in your stomach that you are going to be sick. > **nauseous** adjective

nautical adjective relating to ships or navigation.

naval adjective relating to or having a navy.

navel noun the small hollow on the front of your body just below your waist.

navigate verb 1 When someone navigates, they work out the direction in which a ship, plane or car should go, using maps and sometimes instruments. 2 To navigate a stretch of water means to travel safely across it. > **navigation** noun > **navigator** noun

navy navies noun 1 the part of a country's armed forces that fights at sea. ▶ adjective 2 dark blue.

Nazi noun (HISTORY) The Nazis were members of the National Socialist German Workers' Party, which was led by Adolf Hitler.

NB You write NB to draw attention to what you are going to write next. NB is an abbreviation for the Latin 'nota bene', which means 'note well'.

near preposition 1 not far from. ▶ adjective 2 not far away in distance. 3 not far away in time. 4 You can also use 'near' to mean almost: a night of near disaster. ▶ verb 5 When you are nearing something, you are approaching it and will soon reach it. > **nearness** noun

> **near** preposition
> 1 = adjacent to, alongside, close to, next to, not far from
> ▶ adjective 2 = adjacent, adjoining, close, nearby
> 3 = approaching, forthcoming, imminent, looming, near at hand, nigh, upcoming

nearby adjective, adverb only a short distance away.

nearly adverb not completely but almost.

> **nearly** adverb
> = almost, as good as, just about, practically, virtually

neat adjective 1 tidy and smart. 2 A neat alcoholic drink does not have anything added to it. > **neatly** adverb > **neatness** noun

> **neat** adjective
> 1 = orderly, smart, spruce, tidy, trim

necessarily adverb Something that is not necessarily the case is not always or inevitably the case.

necessary adjective 1 Something that is necessary is needed or must be done. 2 (formal) Necessary also means certain or inevitable.

> **necessary** adjective
> 1 = essential, imperative, indispensable, required, vital
> 2 = certain, inevitable, inexorable, unavoidable

necessity necessities noun 1 Necessity is the need to do something. 2 Necessities are things needed in order to live.

neck noun 1 the part of your body which joins your head to the rest of your body. 2 the long narrow part at the top of a bottle.

necklace noun a piece of jewellery worn around the neck.

nectar noun Nectar is a sweet liquid produced by flowers that is attractive to insects.

need verb 1 If you need something, you believe that you must have it or do it. ▶ noun 2 Your needs are the things that you need to have. 3 a strong feeling that you must have or do something.

> **need** verb
> 1 = demand, require, want

needle noun 1 a small thin piece of metal with a pointed end and a hole at the other, which is used for sewing. 2 Needles are also long thin pieces of steel or plastic, used for knitting. 3 the part of a syringe which a doctor or nurse sticks into your body. 4 the thin piece of metal or plastic on a dial which moves to show a

measurement. 5 The needles of a pine tree are its leaves.
▶ verb 6 (informal) If someone needles you, they annoy or provoke you.

needless adjective unnecessary.
> **needlessly** adverb

needy needier, neediest adjective very poor.

negative adjective 1 A negative answer means 'no'. 2 Someone who is negative sees only problems and disadvantages. 3 If a medical or scientific test is negative, it shows that something has not happened or is not present. 4 (MATHS) A negative number is less than zero. ▶ noun 5 the image on film that is first produced when you take a photograph. > **negatively** adverb

neglect verb 1 If you neglect something, you do not look after it properly. 2 (formal) If you neglect to do something, you fail to do it.
▶ noun 3 Neglect is failure to look after something or someone properly. > **neglectful** adjective

> **neglect** verb
> 1 = ignore, overlook, turn your back on 2 = fail, forget, omit
> ▶ noun 3 = disregard, indifference, unconcern

negligent adjective not taking enough care. > **negligently** adverb
> **negligence** noun

negligible adjective very small and unimportant.

negotiable adjective able to be changed or agreed by discussion.

negotiate verb 1 When people negotiate, they have formal discussions in order to reach an agreement about something. 2 If you negotiate an obstacle, you manage to get over it or round it. > **negotiation** noun > **negotiator** noun

Negro Negroes noun (old-fashioned, offensive) a person with black skin who comes from Africa or whose ancestors come from Africa.

neighbour noun 1 Your neighbour is someone who lives next door to you or near you. 2 Your neighbour is also someone standing or sitting next to you.

neighbourhood noun a district where people live.

neighbouring adjective situated nearby.

neither adjective, pronoun used to indicate that a negative statement refers to one or more things or people: It's neither a play nor a musical.

nephew noun Someone's nephew is the son of their sister or brother.

Neptune noun Neptune is the planet in the solar system which is eighth from the sun.

nerve noun 1 a long thin fibre that sends messages between your brain and other parts of your body. 2 If you talk about someone's nerves, you are referring to how able they are to remain calm in a difficult situation. 3 Nerve is courage. 4 (informal) Nerve is boldness or rudeness. ▶ phrase 5 (informal) If someone **gets on your nerves**, they irritate you.

nerve-racking adjective making you feel very worried and tense.

nervous adjective 1 worried and frightened. 2 affecting your nerves. > **nervously** adverb > **nervousness** noun

nervous adjective
1 = anxious, apprehensive, edgy, jittery (informal), jumpy, on edge, tense, toey (Australian and New Zealand; slang), worried

nervous breakdown noun an illness in which someone suffers from severe depression or anxiety and needs psychiatric treatment.

nervous system noun (SCIENCE) Your nervous system is the nerves in your body together with your brain and spinal cord.

nest noun 1 a place that a bird makes to lay its eggs in; also a place that some insects and other animals make to rear their young in. ▶ verb 2 When birds nest, they build a nest and lay eggs in it.

nestle verb If you nestle somewhere, you settle there comfortably, often pressing up against someone else.

nestling noun a young bird that has not yet learned to fly and so has not left the nest.

net noun 1 a piece of material made of threads woven together with small spaces in between. 2 The net is the same as the **internet**. ▶ adjective 3 A net amount is final, after everything that should be subtracted from it has been subtracted. 4 The net weight of something is its weight without its wrapping.

netball noun Netball is a game played by two teams of seven players in which each team tries to score goals by throwing a ball through a net at the top of a pole.

netting noun Netting is material made of threads or metal wires woven together with small spaces in between.

nettle *noun* a wild plant covered with little hairs that sting.

network *noun* **1** a large number of lines or roads which cross each other at many points. **2** A network of people or organisations is a large number of them that work together as a system. **3** A television network is a group of broadcasting stations that all transmit the same programmes at the same time. **4** (ICT) a group of computers connected to each other.

neuron; also spelt **neurone** *noun* a cell that is part of the nervous system and conducts messages to and from the brain.

neurosis neuroses *noun* a mental condition that causes people to have strong fears and worries.

neurotic *adjective* having strong and unreasonable fears and worries.

neuter *verb* **1** When an animal is neutered, its reproductive organs are removed. ▶ *adjective* **2** In some languages, a neuter noun or pronoun is one which is not masculine or feminine.

neutral *adjective* **1** People who are neutral do not support either side in a disagreement or war. **2** (DGT) The neutral wire in an electric plug is the one that is not earth or live. **3** (ART) A neutral colour is not definite or striking, for example pale grey. **4** (SCIENCE) In chemistry, a neutral substance is neither acid nor alkaline. ▶ *noun* **5** a person or country that does not support either side in a disagreement or war. **6** (DGT) Neutral is the position between the gears of a vehicle in which the gears are not connected to the engine. > **neutrality** *noun*

neutral *adjective*
1 = disinterested, dispassionate, impartial, nonaligned

neutralise neutralises, neutralising, neutralised; also spelt **neutralize** *verb* **1** To neutralise something means to prevent it from working or taking effect, especially by doing or applying something that has the opposite effect. **2** (SCIENCE) If you neutralise a substance, you make it neither acid nor alkaline.

neutron *noun* (SCIENCE) an atomic particle that has no electrical charge.

never *adverb* at no time in the past, present or future.

never *adverb*
= at no time, not ever

nevertheless *adverb* in spite of what has just been said.

new *adjective* **1** recently made, created or discovered. **2** not used or owned before. **3** different or unfamiliar. > **newness** *noun*

new *adjective*
1 = advanced, current, fresh, ground-breaking, latest, modern, recent, ultra-modern, up-to-date, up-to-the-minute

newborn *adjective* born recently.

newcomer *noun* someone who has recently arrived in a place.

newly *adverb* recently.

new moon *noun* The moon is a new moon when it is a thin crescent shape at the start of its four-week cycle.

news *noun* News is information about things that have happened.

news noun
= bulletin, disclosure, dispatch, information, intelligence, latest (informal), tidings (formal), word

newsagent noun a person or shop that sells newspapers and magazines.

newspaper noun a publication, on large sheets of paper, that is produced regularly and contains news and articles.

New Testament noun (RE) The New Testament is the second part of the Bible, which deals with the life of Christ and with the early Church.

New Year noun New Year is the time when people celebrate the start of a year.

New Zealander noun someone who comes from New Zealand.

next adjective 1 coming immediately after something else. 2 in a position nearest to something. ▶ adverb 3 coming immediately after something else. ▶ phrase 4 If one thing is **next** to another, it is at the side of it.

next adjective
1 = ensuing, following, subsequent, succeeding
2 = adjacent, adjoining, closest, nearest, neighbouring
▶ adverb 3 = afterwards, subsequently

next door adjective, adverb in the house next to yours.

NHS In Britain, NHS is an abbreviation for 'National Health Service'.

nib noun the pointed end of a pen.

nibble verb 1 When you nibble something, you take small bites

of it. ▶ noun 2 a small bite of something.

nice adjective pleasant or attractive. ▶ **nicely** adverb ▶ **niceness** noun

nice adjective
= attractive, beautiful, charming, delightful, fantastic, fine, gorgeous, lovely

niche noun 1 a hollow area in a wall. 2 If you say that you have found your niche, you mean that you have found a job or way of life that is exactly right for you.

nick verb 1 If you nick something, you make a small cut in its surface. 2 (informal) To nick something also means to steal it. ▶ noun 3 a small cut in the surface of something.

nickel noun (SCIENCE) Nickel is a silver-coloured metallic element that is used in alloys. Its atomic number is 28 and its symbol is Ni.

nickname noun 1 an informal name given to someone. ▶ verb 2 If you nickname someone, you give them a nickname.

nicotine noun (SCIENCE) Nicotine is an addictive substance found in tobacco. It is named after Jacques Nicot, who first brought tobacco to France.

niece noun Someone's niece is the daughter of their sister or brother.

nifty niftier, niftiest adjective neat and pleasing or cleverly done.

Nigerian adjective 1 belonging or relating to Nigeria. ▶ noun 2 someone from Nigeria.

niggle verb 1 If something niggles you, it worries you slightly. ▶ noun 2 a small worry that you keep thinking about.

night *noun* Night is the time between sunset and sunrise when it is dark.

nightclub *noun* a place where people go late in the evening to drink and dance.

nightfall *noun* Nightfall is the time of day when it starts to get dark.

nightie *noun* (*informal*) a nightdress.

nightly *adjective, adverb* happening every night.

nightmare *noun* a very frightening dream; also used of any very unpleasant or frightening situation.
> **nightmarish** *adjective*

nil *noun* Nil means zero or nothing. It is used especially in sports scores.

nimble *adjective* 1 able to move quickly and easily. 2 able to think quickly and cleverly. > **nimbly** *adverb*

nine the number 9. > **ninth** *adjective*

nineteen the number 19.
> **nineteenth** *adjective*

ninety nineties the number 90.
> **ninetieth** *adjective*

nip nips, nipping, nipped *verb* 1 (*informal*) If you nip somewhere, you go there quickly. 2 To nip someone or something means to pinch or squeeze them slightly. ▶ *noun* 3 a light pinch.

nirvana *noun* (RE) Nirvana is the ultimate state of spiritual enlightenment which can be achieved in the Buddhist religion.

nitrogen *noun* (SCIENCE) Nitrogen is a chemical element usually found as a gas. It forms about 78 per cent of the earth's atmosphere. Nitrogen's atomic number is 7 and its symbol is N.

no *interjection* 1 used to say that something is not true or to refuse something. ▶ *adjective* 2 none at all or not at all. ▶ *adverb* 3 used with a comparative to mean 'not': *no later than July 24th*.

> **no** *interjection*
> 1 = absolutely not, certainly not, definitely not, not at all, of course not

no. a written abbreviation for **number**.

nobility *noun* 1 Nobility is the quality of being noble. 2 The nobility of a society are all the people who have titles and high social rank.

noble *adjective* 1 honest and brave, and deserving admiration. 2 very impressive. ▶ *noun* 3 a member of the nobility. > **nobly** *adverb*

> **noble** *adjective*
> 1 = generous, honourable, magnanimous, upright, virtuous, worthy
> ▶ *noun* 3 = aristocrat, lord, nobleman, peer

nobleman noblemen *noun* a man who is a member of the nobility.

noblewoman noblewomen *noun* a woman who is a member of the nobility.

nobody nobodies *pronoun* 1 not a single person. ▶ *noun* 2 Someone who is a nobody is not at all important.

nocturnal *adjective* 1 happening at night. 2 active at night.

nod nods, nodding, nodded *verb* 1 When you nod, you move your head up and down, usually to show agreement. ▶ *noun* 2 a movement of your head up and down. > **nod off** *verb* If you nod off, you fall asleep.

noise *noun* a sound, especially one that is loud or unpleasant.

> **noise** *noun*
> = commotion, din, hubbub, pandemonium, racket, row, uproar

noisy noisier, noisiest *adjective* making a lot of noise or full of noise. > **noisily** *adverb* > **noisiness** *noun*

> **noisy** *adjective*
> = deafening, loud, piercing, strident, tumultuous, vociferous

nomad *noun* a person who belongs to a tribe which travels from place to place rather than living in just one place. > **nomadic** *adjective*

nominal *adjective* 1 Something that is nominal is supposed to have a particular identity or status, but in reality does not have it. 2 A nominal amount of money is very small compared to the value of something. > **nominally** *adverb*

nominate *verb* If you nominate someone for a job or position, you formally suggest that they have it. > **nomination** *noun*

> **nominate** *verb*
> = name, propose, recommend, select, submit, suggest

non- *prefix* not: non-smoking.

nonchalant *adjective* seeming calm and not worried. > **nonchalance** *noun* > **nonchalantly** *adverb*

nondescript *adjective* Someone or something nondescript has no special or interesting qualities or details.

none *pronoun* not a single thing or person, or not even a small amount of something.

nonfiction *noun* (LIBRARY) Nonfiction is writing that gives facts and information rather than telling a story.

nonmetal *noun* (SCIENCE) a chemical element such as carbon, oxygen or sulphur. Nonmetals are poor conductors of heat and electricity and form negative ions.

nonplussed *adjective* confused and unsure about how to react.

nonsense *noun* Nonsense is foolish and meaningless words or behaviour. > **nonsensical** *adjective*

> **nonsense** *noun*
> = drivel, garbage (*informal*), inanity, rot, rubbish, waffle (*British; informal*)

nonstop *adjective, adverb* continuing without any pauses or breaks.

noodle *noun* Noodles are a kind of pasta shaped into long, thin pieces.

nook *noun* (*literary*) a small sheltered place.

noon *noun* Noon is midday.

no-one; also spelt **no one** *pronoun* not a single person.

noose *noun* a loop at the end of a piece of rope, with a knot that tightens when the rope is pulled.

nor *conjunction* used after 'neither' or after a negative statement, to add something else that the negative statement applies to: *They had neither the time nor the money.*

norm *noun* If something is the norm, it is the usual and expected thing.

normal *adjective* usual and ordinary. > **normality** *noun*

> **normal** *adjective*
> = average, conventional, habitual, ordinary, regular, routine, standard, typical, usual

normally *adverb* 1 usually. 2 in a way that is normal.

north *noun* 1 The north is the direction to your left when you are looking towards the place where the sun rises. 2 The north of a place or country is the part which is towards the north when you are in the centre. ▶ *adverb*, *adjective* 3 North means towards the north. ▶ *adjective* 4 A north wind blows from the north.

North America *noun* North America is the third largest continent, consisting of Canada, the United States and Mexico. > **North American** *adjective*

north-east *noun*, *adverb*, *adjective* North-east is halfway between north and east.

north-eastern *adjective* in or from the north-east.

northerly *adjective* 1 Northerly means to or towards the north. 2 A northerly wind blows from the north.

northern *adjective* in or from the north.

North Pole *noun* (GEOGRAPHY) The North Pole is the most northerly place on the surface of the earth.

northward or **northwards** *adverb* 1 Northward or northwards means towards the north. ▶ *adjective* 2 The northward part of something is the north part.

north-west *noun*, *adverb*, *adjective* North-west is halfway between north and west.

north-western *adjective* in or from the north-west.

Norwegian *adjective* 1 belonging or relating to Norway. ▶ *noun* 2 someone who comes from Norway. 3 Norwegian is the main language spoken in Norway.

nose *noun* 1 the part of your face above your mouth which you use for smelling and breathing. 2 the front part of a car or plane.

nostalgia *noun* Nostalgia is a feeling of affection for the past, and sadness that things have changed. > **nostalgic** *adjective*

nostril *noun* Your nostrils are the two openings in your nose which you breathe through.

nosy nosier, nosiest; also spelt **nosey** *adjective* trying to find out about things that do not concern you.

> **nosy** *adjective*
> = curious, eavesdropping, inquisitive, prying

not *adverb* used to make a sentence negative, to refuse something, or to deny something.

notable *adjective* important or interesting. > **notably** *adverb*

notch *noun* a small V-shaped cut in a surface.

note *noun* 1 a short letter. 2 a written piece of information that helps you to remember something. 3 In music, a note is a musical sound of a particular pitch, or a written symbol that represents it. 4 a banknote. 5 an atmosphere, feeling or quality: *There was a note of regret in his voice.* ▶ *verb* 6 If you note a fact, you become aware of it or you

n

mention it. ▶ phrase 7 If you take note of something, you pay attention to it. ▷ note down verb If you note something down, you write it down so that you will remember it.

> **note** noun
> 1 = communication (formal), letter, memo, memorandum, message, reminder 2 = account, jotting, record, register 5 = hint, tone, touch, trace ▶ verb 6 = mention, notice, observe, perceive, register, remark, see

notebook noun a small book for writing notes in.

noted adjective well-known and admired.

nothing pronoun not anything.

notice verb 1 If you notice something, you become aware of it. ▶ noun 2 Notice is attention or awareness. 3 a written announcement. 4 Notice is also advance warning about something. ▶ phrase 5 If you hand in your notice, you tell your employer that you intend to leave your job after a fixed period of time.

> **notice** verb
> 1 = detect, discern, note, observe, perceive, see, spot ▶ noun 3 = advertisement, bill, poster, sign 4 = advance warning, intimation, notification, warning

noticeable adjective obvious and easy to see. ▷ **noticeably** adverb

> **noticeable** adjective
> = conspicuous, evident, obvious, perceptible, unmistakable

noticeboard noun a board for notices.

notification noun 1 a formal announcement. 2 an indication to the user of a computer or smartphone that they have received a message, alert or update.

notify notifies, notifying, notified verb To notify someone of something means to officially inform them of it.

> **notify** verb
> = advise (formal), inform, tell, warn

notion noun an idea or belief.

notorious adjective well-known for something bad. ▷ **notoriously** adverb ▷ **notoriety** noun

> **notorious** adjective
> = disreputable, infamous, scandalous

notwithstanding preposition (formal) in spite of.

nought the number 0.

noun noun (ENGLISH) (MFL) a word which refers to a person, thing or idea. Examples of nouns are 'president', 'table', 'sun' and 'beauty'.

nourish verb To nourish people or animals means to provide them with food.

nourishing adjective Food that is nourishing makes you strong and healthy.

nourishment noun Nourishment is food that your body needs in order to remain healthy.

novel noun 1 (LIBRARY) a book that tells an invented story. ▶ adjective 2 new and interesting.

novelist noun a person who writes novels.

novelty novelties noun 1 Novelty is the quality of being new and interesting. 2 something new and interesting. 3 a small, unusual object sold as a gift or souvenir.

November noun November is the eleventh month of the year. It has 30 days.

novice noun 1 someone who is not yet experienced at something. 2 someone who is preparing to become a monk or nun.

now adverb 1 at the present time or moment. ▸ conjunction 2 as a result or consequence of a particular fact: *Things have got better now there is a new board.* ▸ phrase 3 Just now means very recently. 4 If something happens now and then, it happens sometimes but not regularly.

> **now** adverb
> 1 = at once, currently, immediately, nowadays, right now, straight away, without delay

nowadays adverb at the present time, in contrast with in the past.

nowhere adverb not anywhere.

noxious adjective harmful or poisonous.

nozzle noun a spout fitted onto the end of a pipe or hose to control the flow of a liquid.

nuance noun a small difference in sound, colour or meaning.

nuclear adjective 1 (SCIENCE) relating to the energy produced when the nuclei of atoms are split. 2 relating to weapons that explode using the energy released by atoms. 3 (SCIENCE) relating to the structure and behaviour of the nuclei of atoms.

nuclear reactor noun A nuclear reactor is a device which is used to obtain nuclear energy.

nucleus nuclei noun 1 (SCIENCE) The nucleus of an atom is the central part of it. It is positively charged and is made up of protons and neutrons. 2 (SCIENCE) The nucleus of a cell is the part that contains the chromosomes and controls the growth and reproduction of the cell. 3 The nucleus of something is the basic central part of it to which other things are added.

nude adjective 1 naked. ▸ noun 2 a picture or statue of a naked person. > **nudity** noun

nudge verb 1 If you nudge someone, you push them gently, usually with your elbow. ▸ noun 2 a gentle push.

nudist noun a person who believes in wearing no clothes.

nugget noun a small rough lump of something, especially gold.

nuisance noun someone or something that is annoying or inconvenient.

> **nuisance** noun
> = annoyance, bother, hassle (informal), inconvenience, irritation, pain (informal), pest

numb adjective 1 unable to feel anything. ▸ verb 2 If something numbs you, it makes you unable to feel anything.

> **numb** adjective
> 1 = dead, frozen, insensitive, paralysed
> ▸ verb 2 = dull, freeze, paralyse, stun

number noun 1 a word or a symbol used for counting or calculating.

2 Someone's number is the series of numbers that you use to telephone them. **3** A number of things is a quantity of them. **4** a song or piece of music. ▶ *verb* **5** If things number a particular amount, there are that many of them. **6** If you number something, you give it a number. **7** To be numbered among a particular group means to belong to it.

> **number** *noun*
> **1** = digit, figure, numeral
> **3** = collection, crowd, horde, multitude

numerical *adjective* expressed in numbers or relating to numbers.

numerous *adjective* existing or happening in large numbers.

> **numerous** *adjective*
> = lots of, many, several

nun *noun* a woman who has taken religious vows and lives in a convent.

nurse *noun* **1** a person whose job is to look after people who are ill. ▶ *verb* **2** If you nurse someone, you look after them when they are ill. **3** If you nurse a feeling, you feel it strongly for a long time.

nursery *nurseries noun* **1** a place where young children are looked after while their parents are working. **2** a room in which young children sleep and play. **3** a place where plants are grown and sold.

nursery school *noun* a school for children from three to five years old.

nursing home *noun* a privately run hospital, especially for elderly people.

nurture *verb (formal)* If you nurture a young child or a plant, you look after it carefully.

nut *noun* **1** a fruit with a hard shell and an edible centre that grows on certain trees. **2** a piece of metal with a hole in the middle which a bolt screws into.

nutmeg *noun* Nutmeg is a spice used for flavouring in cooking.

nutrient *noun* (SCIENCE) Nutrients are substances that help plants or animals to grow.

nutrition *noun* (DGT) Nutrition is the food that you eat, considered from the point of view of how it helps you to grow and remain healthy. > **nutritional** *adjective* > **nutritionist** *noun*

nutritious *adjective* containing substances that help you to grow and remain healthy.

nutty *nuttier, nuttiest adjective* **1** *(informal)* mad or very foolish. **2** tasting of nuts.

nylon *noun* **1** Nylon is a type of strong artificial material. **2** Nylons are stockings or tights.

Oo

oak *noun* a large tree which produces acorns. It has a hard wood which is often used to make furniture.

OAP *noun* In Britain, an OAP is a person who receives a pension. OAP is an abbreviation for 'old age pensioner'.

oar *noun* a wooden pole with a wide, flat end, used for rowing a boat.

oasis oases *noun* (GEOGRAPHY) a small area in a desert where water and plants are found.

oat *noun* Oats are a type of grain.

oath *noun* a formal promise, especially a promise to tell the truth in a court of law.

> **oath** *noun*
> = pledge, promise, vow

oatmeal *noun* Oatmeal is a rough flour made from oats.

OBE *noun* a British honour awarded by the King or Queen. OBE is an abbreviation for 'Officer of the Order of the British Empire'.

obedient *adjective* If you are obedient, you do what you are told to do. > **obediently** *adverb* > **obedience** *noun*

> **obedient** *adjective*
> = law-abiding, submissive, subservient

obese *adjective* extremely fat. > **obesity** *noun*

obey *verb* If you obey a person or an order, you do what you are told to do.

> **obey** *verb*
> = abide by, adhere to (*formal*), comply with, follow, observe

obituary obituaries *noun* a piece of writing about the life and achievements of someone who has just died.

object *noun* **1** anything solid that you can touch or see, and that is not alive. **2** an aim or purpose. **3** The object of your feelings or actions is the person that they are directed towards. **4** (MFL) In grammar, the object of a verb or preposition is the word or phrase which follows it and describes the person or thing affected. ▶ *verb* **5** If you object to something, you dislike it or disapprove of it.

> **object** *noun*
> **1** = article, thing **2** = aim, goal, idea, intention, objective, purpose
> ▶ *verb* **5** = oppose, protest

objection *noun* If you have an objection to something, you dislike it or disapprove of it.

> **objection** *noun*
> = opposition, protest

objectionable *adjective* unpleasant and offensive.

objective *noun* **1** an aim. ▶ *adjective* **2** If you are objective, you are not influenced by personal feelings or prejudices. > **objectively** *adverb* > **objectivity** *noun*

obligation *noun* something that you must do because it is your duty.

o

obligatory *adjective* required by a rule or law.

oblige *verb* 1 If you are obliged to do something, you have to do it. 2 If you oblige someone, you help them. > **obliging** *adjective*

oblique *adjective* 1 An oblique remark is not direct, and is therefore difficult to understand. 2 An oblique line slopes at an angle.

obliterate *verb* To obliterate something is to destroy it completely. > **obliteration** *noun*

oblivion *noun* Oblivion is unconsciousness or complete lack of awareness of your surroundings. > **oblivious** *adjective* > **obliviously** *adverb*

oblong *noun* 1 a four-sided shape with two parallel short sides, two parallel long sides, and four right angles. ▶ *adjective* 2 shaped like an oblong.

obnoxious *adjective* extremely unpleasant.

oboe *noun* a woodwind musical instrument with a double reed. > **oboist** *noun*

obscene *adjective* indecent and likely to upset people. > **obscenely** *adverb* > **obscenity** *noun*

obscure *adjective* 1 Something that is obscure is known by only a few people. 2 Something obscure is difficult to see or to understand. ▶ *verb* 3 To obscure something is to make it difficult to see or understand. > **obscurity** *noun*

> **obscure** *adjective*
> 1 = little-known, unknown
> 2 = arcane (*formal*), cryptic, opaque
> ▶ *verb* 3 = cloak, cloud, conceal, hide, mask, screen, shroud

observance *noun* The observance of a law or custom is the practice of obeying or following it.

observant *adjective* Someone who is observant notices things that are not easy to see.

> **observant** *adjective*
> = attentive, perceptive, vigilant, watchful

observation *noun* 1 Observation is the act of watching something carefully. 2 something that you have seen or noticed. 3 a remark. 4 Observation is the ability to notice things that are not easy to see.

observatory observatories *noun* a room or building containing telescopes and other equipment for studying the sun, moon and stars.

observe *verb* 1 To observe something is to watch it carefully. 2 To observe something is to notice it. 3 If you observe that something is the case, you make a comment about it. 4 To observe a law or custom is to obey or follow it. > **observer** *noun* > **observable** *adjective*

> **observe** *verb*
> 1 = monitor, scrutinise, study, survey, view, watch
> 2 = discover, note, notice, see, spot, witness 3 = comment, mention, remark, say, state

obsession *noun* If someone has an obsession about something, they cannot stop thinking about that thing. > **obsessional** *adjective* > **obsessed** *adjective* > **obsessive** *adjective*

> **obsession** *noun*
> = complex, fixation, mania, preoccupation, thing (*informal*)

obsolete *adjective* out of date and no longer used.

obstacle *noun* something which is in your way and makes it difficult to do something.

> **obstacle** *noun*
> = barrier, difficulty, hindrance, hurdle, impediment, obstruction

obstetrician *noun* An obstetrician is a doctor who specialises in the care of women during pregnancy and childbirth.

obstetrics *noun* Obstetrics is the branch of medicine concerned with pregnancy and childbirth.

obstinate *adjective* Someone who is obstinate is stubborn and unwilling to change their mind. > **obstinately** *adverb* > **obstinacy** *noun*

> **obstinate** *adjective*
> = dogged, headstrong, inflexible, intractable, stubborn, wilful

obstruct *verb* If something obstructs a road or path, it blocks it. > **obstruction** *noun* > **obstructive** *adjective*

> **obstruct** *verb*
> = bar, block, choke, clog

obtain *verb* If you obtain something, you get it. > **obtainable** *adjective*

> **obtain** *verb*
> = acquire, get, get hold of, get your hands on (*informal*), procure (*formal*), secure (*formal*)

obtuse *adjective* 1 Someone who is obtuse is stupid or slow to understand things. 2 (MATHS) An obtuse angle is between 90° and 180°.

obvious *adjective* easy to see or understand. > **obviously** *adverb*

> **obvious** *adjective*
> = apparent, blatant, clear, evident, overt, palpable, plain, self-evident

occasion *noun* 1 a time when something happens. 2 an important event. 3 An occasion for doing something is an opportunity for doing it.

> **occasion** *noun*
> 2 = affair, event 3 = chance, opportunity, time

occasional *adjective* happening sometimes but not often. > **occasionally** *adverb*

> **occasional** *adjective*
> = intermittent, odd, periodic, sporadic

occult *noun* The occult is the knowledge and study of supernatural and magical forces or powers.

occupancy *noun* The occupancy of a building is the act of living or working in it.

occupant *noun* The occupants of a building are the people who live or work in it.

occupation *noun* 1 a job or profession. 2 a hobby or something you do for pleasure. 3 The occupation of a country is the act of invading it and taking control of it. > **occupational** *adjective*

occupy *occupies, occupying, occupied verb* 1 The people who occupy a building are the people who live or work there. 2 When people occupy a place, they move into it and take control of it. 3 To occupy a position in a system

or plan is to have that position.
4 If something occupies you,
you spend your time doing it.
> **occupier** noun

occur occurs, occurring, occurred
verb **1** If something occurs, it
happens or exists. **2** If something
occurs to you, you suddenly think
of it.

> **occur** verb
> **1** = appear, arise, be present,
> exist, happen, take place
> **2** = cross your mind, dawn on,
> strike

occurrence noun **1** an event.
2 The occurrence of something
is the fact that it happens or
exists.

ocean noun **1** the sea. **2** The five
oceans are the five very large
areas of sea on the Earth's
surface. > **oceanic** adjective

o'clock adverb You use 'o'clock'
after the number of the hour to
say what the time is.

octagon noun (MATHS) a shape
with eight straight sides.
> **octagonal** adjective

octave noun **1** (MUSIC) the
difference in pitch between the
first note and the eighth note of a
musical scale. **2** (ENGLISH) eight
lines of poetry together.

October noun October is the tenth
month of the year. It has 31 days.

octopus octopuses noun a sea
creature with eight long tentacles
which it uses to catch food.

odd adjective **1** Something odd
is strange or unusual. **2** Odd
things do not match each other.
3 Odd numbers are numbers
that cannot be divided exactly
by two. ▶ adverb **4** You use 'odd'
after a number to say that it is

approximate. > **oddly** adverb
> **oddness** noun

> **odd** adjective
> **1** = bizarre, curious, funny,
> peculiar, queer (old-fashioned),
> singular (formal), strange, weird

oddity oddities noun something
very strange.

odds plural noun The odds of
something happening are how
likely it is to happen.

ode noun (ENGLISH) a poem written
in praise of someone or
something.

odious adjective extremely
unpleasant.

odour noun (formal) a strong smell.
> **odorous** adjective

odyssey noun An odyssey is a long
and eventful journey. The name
comes from Odysseus, the Greek
hero who wandered from
adventure to adventure for ten
years.

oesophagus oesophaguses noun
the tube that carries food from
your throat to your stomach.

oestrogen another spelling of
estrogen.

of preposition **1** consisting of or
containing: a collection of short
stories. **2** used when naming
something or describing a
characteristic of something: the
city of Canberra. **3** belonging to or
connected with: a friend of Rachel.

off preposition, adverb **1** indicating
movement away from or out of a
place: They had just stepped off the
plane. **2** indicating separation or
distance from a place: some islands
off the coast of Australia. **3** not
working. ▶ adverb, adjective
4 not switched on. ▶ adjective
5 cancelled or postponed.

6 Food that is off has gone sour or bad. ▶ *preposition* **7** not liking or not using something: *He went right off chocolate.*

offal *noun* Offal is liver, kidneys and internal organs of animals, which can be eaten.

offence *noun* **1** a crime. ▶ *phrase* **2** If something **gives offence**, it upsets people. If you **take offence**, you are upset by someone or something.

offend *verb* **1** If you offend someone, you upset them. **2** (*formal*) To offend or to offend against a law is to commit a crime. ▷ **offender** *noun*

> **offend** *verb*
> **1** = affront, insult, outrage

offensive *adjective* **1** Something offensive is rude and upsetting. **2** Offensive actions or weapons are used in attacking someone. ▶ *noun* **3** an attack. ▷ **offensively** *adverb*

> **offensive** *adjective*
> **1** = abusive, insulting, objectionable

offer *verb* **1** If you offer something to someone, you ask them if they would like it. ▶ *noun* **2** something that someone says they will give you or do for you if you want them to. **3** a specially low price for a product in a shop.

> **offer** *verb*
> **1** = hold out, tender
> ▶ *noun* **2** = proposition, tender

offering *noun* something that is offered or given to someone.

offhand *adjective* **1** If someone is offhand, they are unfriendly and slightly rude. ▶ *adverb* **2** If you know something offhand, you

know it without having to think very hard.

office *noun* **1** a room where people work at desks. **2** a government department. **3** a place where people can go for information, tickets or other services. **4** Someone who holds office has an important job or position in government or in an organisation.

officer *noun* a person with a position of authority in the armed forces, the police or a government organisation.

official *adjective* **1** approved by the government or by someone in authority. **2** done or used by someone in authority as part of their job. ▶ *noun* **3** a person who holds a position of authority in an organisation. ▷ **officially** *adverb*

> **official** *adjective*
> **1** = authorised, certified, formal, licensed
> ▶ *noun* **3** = executive, officer, representative

officialdom *noun* You can refer to officials in government or other organisations as officialdom, especially when you find them difficult to deal with.

officiate *verb* To officiate at a ceremony is to be in charge and perform the official part of the ceremony.

offing *phrase* If something is in the offing, it is likely to happen soon.

off-licence *noun* a shop which sells alcoholic drinks.

offline *adjective* **1** If a computer is offline, it is switched off or not connected to the internet. ▶ *adverb* **2** If you do something offline, you do it while not connected to the internet.

offset offsets, offsetting, offset
verb If one thing is offset by
another thing, its effect is
reduced or cancelled out by that
thing.

offshoot *noun* something that
has developed from another
thing.

offshore *adjective, adverb* in or
from the part of the sea near the
shore.

offside *adjective* If a soccer, rugby
or hockey player is offside, they
have broken the rules by moving
too far forward.

offspring *noun* A person's or
animal's offspring are their
children.

often *adverb* happening many
times or a lot of the time.

> **often** *adverb*
> = frequently, repeatedly

ogre *noun* a cruel, frightening
giant in a fairy story.

oil *noun* 1 Oil is a thick, sticky
liquid used as a fuel and for
lubrication. 2 Oil is also a thick,
greasy liquid made from plants or
animals. ▶ *verb* 3 If you oil
something, you put oil in it or on
it.

oil painting *noun* An oil painting
is a painting that has been
painted with oil paints.

oily oilier, oiliest *adjective*
Something that is oily is covered
with or contains oil.

ointment *noun* a smooth, thick
substance that you put on sore
skin to heal it.

okay; also spelt **OK** *adjective*
(*informal*) Okay means all right.

> **okay** *adjective*
> = acceptable, all right

old *adjective* 1 having lived or
existed for a long time. 2 'Old' is
used to give the age of someone or
something: *This photo is five years
old*. 3 'Old' also means former:
my old art teacher.

> **old** *adjective*
> 1 = aged, elderly, senior,
> venerable 3 = former, one-time,
> previous

olden *phrase* In the olden days
means long ago.

Old English *noun* Old English was
the English language from the
fifth century AD until about 1100.
Old English is also known as
Anglo-Saxon.

old-fashioned *adjective*
1 Something which is
old-fashioned is no longer
fashionable. 2 Someone who is
old-fashioned believes in the
values and standards of the past.

> **old-fashioned** *adjective*
> 1 = antiquated, archaic, dated,
> obsolete, outdated, outmoded,
> out of date, passé

Old Testament *noun* (RE) The Old
Testament is the first part of the
Christian Bible. It is also the holy
book of the Jewish religion and
contains writings which relate to
the history of the Jews.

olive *noun* 1 a small green or black
fruit containing a stone. Olives
are usually pickled and eaten as a
snack or crushed to produce oil.
▶ *adjective, noun* 2 dark
yellowish-green.

-ology *suffix* '-ology' is used to
form words that refer to the study
of something: *geology*.

Olympic Games *plural noun*
(*trademark*) The Olympic Games

are a set of sporting contests held in a different city every four years. It originated in Ancient Greece where a contest was regularly held in Olympia to honour the god Zeus.

ombudsman *noun* The ombudsman is a person who investigates complaints against the government or a public organisation.

omelette *noun* a dish made by beating eggs together and cooking them in a flat pan.

omen *noun* something that is thought to be a sign of what will happen in the future.

> **omen** *noun*
> = sign, warning

ominous *adjective* suggesting that something unpleasant is going to happen. > **ominously** *adverb*

> **ominous** *adjective*
> = sinister, threatening

omission *noun* something that has not been included or done.

omit omits, omitting, omitted *verb* 1 If you omit something, you do not include it. 2 (*formal*) If you omit to do something, you do not do it.

> **omit** *verb*
> 1 = exclude, leave out, miss out, skip

omnibus omnibuses *noun* 1 a book containing a collection of stories or articles by the same author or about the same subject. ▶ *adjective* 2 An omnibus edition of a radio or television show contains two or more programmes that were originally broadcast separately.

omnipotent *adjective* having very great or unlimited power. > **omnipotence** *noun*

on *preposition* 1 above and supported by, touching, or attached to something: *The woman was sitting on the sofa.* 2 If you are on a bus, plane or train, you are inside it. 3 If something happens on a particular day, that is when it happens. 4 If something is done on an instrument or machine, it is done using that instrument or machine. 5 A book or talk on a particular subject is about that subject. ▶ *adverb* 6 If you have a piece of clothing on, you are wearing it. ▶ *adjective* 7 A machine or switch that is on is working. 8 If an event is on, it is happening or taking place.

once *adverb* 1 If something happens once, it happens one time only. 2 If something was once true, it was true in the past, but is no longer true. ▶ *conjunction* 3 If something happens once another thing has happened, it happens immediately afterwards. ▶ *phrase* 4 If you do something at once, you do it immediately. If several things happen at once, they all happen at the same time.

one 1 the number 1. ▶ *adjective* 2 If you refer to the one person or thing of a particular kind, you mean the only person or thing of that kind: *My one aim is to look after the horses well.* ▶ *pronoun* 3 One refers to a particular thing or person: *Alf Brown's business was a good one.* 4 One also means people in general: *One likes to have the opportunity to chat.*

one-off *noun* something that happens or is made only once.

onerous *adjective* (*formal*) difficult or unpleasant.

oneself pronoun 'Oneself' is used when you are talking about people in general: *One could hardly hear oneself talk*.

one-sided adjective 1 If an activity or relationship is one-sided, one of the people has a lot more success or involvement than the other. 2 A one-sided argument or report considers the facts or a situation from only one point of view.

one-way adjective 1 One-way streets are streets along which vehicles can drive in only one direction. 2 A one-way ticket is one that you can use to travel to a place, but not to travel back again.

ongoing adjective continuing to happen.

onion noun a small, round vegetable with a brown skin like paper and a very strong taste.

online adjective 1 Online activity is carried out using the internet. 2 If a computer is online, it is switched on or connected to the internet. ▶ adverb 3 If you do something online, you do it while connected to the internet.

onlooker noun someone who is watching an event.

only adverb 1 You use 'only' to indicate the one thing or person involved. 2 You use 'only' to emphasise that something is unimportant or small. 3 You can use 'only' to introduce something which happens immediately after something else. ▶ adjective 4 If you talk about the only thing or person, you mean that there are no others. 5 If you are an only child, you have no brothers or sisters. ▶ conjunction 6 'Only' also means but or except. ▶ phrase

7 Only too means extremely.

only adverb
1 = just, merely, purely, simply, solely
▶ adjective 4 = one, sole

onomatopoeia noun (ENGLISH) the use of words which sound like the thing that they represent. 'Hiss' and 'buzz' are examples of onomatopoeia. > **onomatopoeic** adjective

onset noun The onset of something unpleasant is the beginning of it.

onslaught noun a violent attack.

onto; also spelt **on to** preposition If you put something onto an object, you put it on.

onus noun (formal) If the onus is on you to do something, it is your duty or responsibility to do it.

onwards or **onward** adverb 1 continuing to happen from a particular time. 2 travelling forwards.

ooze verb When a thick liquid oozes, it flows slowly.

opal noun a pale or whitish semiprecious stone used for making jewellery.

opaque adjective If something is opaque, you cannot see through it.

open verb 1 When you open something, or when it opens, you move it so that it is no longer closed. 2 When a shop or office opens, people are able to go in. 3 To open something also means to start it. ▶ adjective 4 Something that is open is not closed or fastened. 5 If you have an open mind, you are willing to consider new ideas or suggestions. 6 Someone who is open is honest

and frank. **7** When a shop or office is open, people are able to go in. **8** An open area of sea or land is a large, empty area. **9** If something is open to you, it is possible for you to do it. **10** If a situation is still open, it is still being considered. ▶ *phrase* **11** In **the open** means outside. **12** In the **open** also means not secret.
> **openly** *adverb*

> **open** *verb*
> **1** = uncover, undo, unlock
> ▶ *adjective* **4** = ajar, uncovered, undone, unlocked **6** = candid, frank, honest

opening *adjective* **1** Opening means coming first. ▶ *noun* **2** The opening of a book or film is the first part of it. **3** a hole or gap. **4** an opportunity.

> **opening** *adjective*
> **1** = first, inaugural (*formal*), initial, introductory
> ▶ *noun* **2** = beginning, commencement (*formal*), start **3** = chink, cleft, crack, gap, hole, slot, space, vent

open-minded *adjective* willing to consider new ideas and suggestions.

open-plan *adjective* An open-plan office or building has very few dividing walls inside.

opera *noun* a play in which the words are sung rather than spoken. > **operatic** *adjective*

operate *verb* **1** To operate is to work. **2** When you operate a machine, you make it work. **3** When surgeons operate, they cut open a patient's body to remove or repair a damaged part.

operation *noun* **1** a complex planned event. **2** a form of

medical treatment in which a surgeon cuts open a patient's body to remove or repair a damaged part. **3** (MATHS) any process in which a number or quantity is operated on according to a set of rules, for example addition, subtraction, multiplication and division. ▶ *phrase* **4** If something is in **operation**, it is working or being used.

operational *adjective* working or able to be used.

operative *adjective* Something that is operative is working or having an effect.

operator *noun* **1** someone who operates a machine. **2** someone who runs a business. **3** someone who connects telephone calls in places such as an office or hotel.

opinion *noun* a belief or view.

> **opinion** *noun*
> = assessment, belief, estimation, judgment, point of view, view, viewpoint

opinionated *adjective* Someone who is opinionated has strong views and refuses to accept that they might be wrong.

opium *noun* Opium is a drug made from the seeds of a poppy. It is used in medicine to relieve pain.

opponent *noun* someone who is against you in an argument or a contest.

opportune *adjective* (*formal*) happening at a convenient time.

opportunism *noun* Opportunism is taking advantage of any opportunity to gain money or power for yourself.
> **opportunist** *noun*

o

opportunity opportunities *noun*
a chance to do something.

oppose *verb* If you oppose
something, you disagree with it
and try to prevent it.

> **oppose** *verb*
> = fight against, resist, speak
> out against

opposed *adjective* 1 If you are
opposed to something, you
disagree with it. 2 Opposed also
means opposite or very different.
▶ *phrase* 3 If you refer to one thing
as opposed to another, you are
emphasising that it is the first
thing rather than the second
which concerns you.

opposite *preposition, adverb*
1 If one thing is opposite another,
it is facing it. ▶ *adjective* 2 The
opposite part of something is
the part farthest away from you.
3 If things are opposite, they are
completely different. ▶ *noun*
4 If two things are completely
different, they are opposites.

> **opposite** *adjective*
> 3 = conflicting, contrary,
> contrasting, opposed,
> reverse
> ▶ *noun* 4 = antithesis (*formal*),
> contrary, converse, reverse

opposition *noun* 1 If there is
opposition to something, people
disagree with it and try to prevent
it. 2 The political parties who are
not in power are referred to as the
opposition. 3 In a game or sports
event, the opposition is the
person or team that you are
competing against.

> **opposition** *noun*
> 1 = disapproval, hostility,
> resistance

oppressed *adjective* People who
are oppressed are treated cruelly
or unfairly. > **oppress** *verb*
> **oppressor** *noun*

> **oppressed** *adjective*
> = downtrodden, persecuted

oppression *noun* cruel and unfair
treatment of people.

> **oppression** *noun*
> = persecution, tyranny

oppressive *adjective* 1 If the
weather is oppressive, it is hot
and humid. 2 An oppressive
situation makes you feel
dispirited or concerned.
3 An oppressive system treats
people cruelly or unfairly.
> **oppressively** *adverb*

opt *verb* If you opt for something,
you choose it. If you opt out of
something, you choose not to be
involved in it.

optical *adjective* 1 (SCIENCE)
concerned with vision, light or
images. 2 relating to the
appearance of things.

optician *noun* someone who tests
people's eyes, and makes and sells
glasses and contact lenses.

optimism *noun* Optimism is a
feeling of hopefulness about the
future. > **optimist** *noun*

optimistic *adjective* hopeful
about the future. > **optimistically**
adverb

> **optimistic** *adjective*
> = buoyant, confident, hopeful,
> positive, sanguine

optimum *adjective* the best that is
possible.

option *noun* a choice between
two or more things.
> **optional** *adjective*

opulent *adjective* grand and expensive-looking. ▷ **opulence** *noun*

opus opuses or opera *noun*
1 (MUSIC) An opus is a musical composition. 'Opus' is often used with a number, indicating its position in a series of published works by the same composer.
2 (ART) An opus is also a great artistic work, such as a piece of writing or a painting.

or *conjunction* 1 used to link two different things: *I didn't know whether to laugh or cry.* 2 used to introduce a warning: *Do what I say or else I will fire.*

-or *suffix* '-or' is used to form nouns from verbs: *actor*.

oracle *noun* 1 In ancient Greece, an oracle was a place where a priest or priestess made predictions about the future.
2 a prophecy made by a priest or other person with great authority or wisdom.

oral *adjective* 1 spoken rather than written. 2 Oral describes things that are used in your mouth or done with your mouth. ▷ *noun*
3 an examination that is spoken rather than written. ▷ **orally** *adverb*

> **oral** *adjective*
> 1 = spoken, verbal

orange *noun* 1 a round citrus fruit that is juicy and sweet and has a thick reddish-yellow skin.
▶ *adjective, noun* 2 reddish-yellow.

orang-utan; also spelt **orang-utang** *noun* An orang-utan is a large ape with reddish-brown hair. Orang-utans come from the forests of Borneo and Sumatra.

orator *noun* someone who is good at making speeches.

oratory *noun* Oratory is the art and skill of making formal public speeches.

orbit *noun* 1 (SCIENCE) the curved path followed by an object going round a planet or the sun. ▶ *verb*
2 If something orbits a planet or the sun, it goes round and round it.

orchard *noun* a piece of land where fruit trees are grown.

orchestra *noun* (MUSIC) a large group of musicians who play musical instruments together.
▷ **orchestral** *adjective*

orchestrate *verb* 1 To orchestrate something is to organise it very carefully in order to produce a particular result. 2 To orchestrate a piece of music is to rewrite it so that it can be played by an orchestra. ▷ **orchestration** *noun*

orchid *noun* Orchids are plants with beautiful and unusual flowers.

ordain *verb* When someone is ordained, they are made a member of the clergy.

ordeal *noun* a difficult and extremely unpleasant experience.

> **ordeal** *noun*
> = hardship, nightmare, torture, trial, tribulation (*formal*)

order *noun* 1 a command given by someone in authority. 2 If things are arranged or done in a particular order, they are arranged or done in that sequence. 3 Order is a situation in which everything is in the correct place or done at the correct time. 4 something that you ask to be brought to you or sent to you.

5 An order is a division of living organisms that is smaller than a class and larger than a family.
▶ *verb* **6** To order someone to do something is to tell them firmly to do it. **7** When you order something, you ask for it to be brought or sent to you. ▶ *phrase* **8** If you do something in order to achieve a particular thing, you do it because you want to achieve that thing.

> **order** *noun*
> **1** = command, decree, dictate, directive, instruction
> **3** = harmony, regularity, symmetry
> ▶ *verb* **6** = command, decree, direct, instruct, ordain

orderly *adjective* Something that is orderly is organised or arranged well.

> **orderly** *adjective*
> = neat, regular, tidy

ordinarily *adverb* If something ordinarily happens, it usually happens.
ordinary *adjective* Ordinary means not special or different in any way.

> **ordinary** *adjective*
> = conventional, normal, regular, routine, standard, usual

ordination *noun* When someone's ordination takes place, they are made a member of the clergy.
ordnance *noun* Weapons and other military supplies are referred to as ordnance.
ore *noun* (GEOGRAPHY) Ore is rock or earth from which metal can be obtained.

oregano *noun* Oregano is a herb used for flavouring in cooking.
organ *noun* **1** (SCIENCE) Your organs are parts of your body that have a particular function, for example your heart or lungs. **2** a large musical instrument with pipes of different lengths through which air is forced. It has various keyboards which are played like a piano.
organic *adjective* **1** Something that is organic is produced by or found in plants or animals. **2** Organic food is produced without the use of artificial fertilisers or pesticides. > **organically** *adverb*
organisation; also spelt **organization** *noun* **1** any group or business. **2** The organisation of something is the act of planning and arranging it.
> **organisational** *adjective*

> **organisation** *noun*
> **1** = association, body, company, confederation, group, institution, outfit (*informal*)
> **2** = organising, planning, structuring

organise; also spelt **organize** *verb* **1** If you organise an event, you plan and arrange it. **2** If you organise things, you arrange them in a sensible order.
> **organised** *adjective* > **organiser** *noun*

> **organise** *verb*
> **1** = arrange, establish, jack up (*New Zealand*; *informal*), plan, set up

organism *noun* (SCIENCE) any living animal, plant, fungus or bacterium.
organist *noun* someone who plays the organ.

Orient noun (literary) The Orient is eastern and south-eastern Asia.

oriental adjective relating to eastern or south-eastern Asia.

orientated adjective If someone is interested in a particular thing, you can say that they are orientated towards it.

orientation noun You can refer to an organisation's activities and aims as its orientation.

oriented adjective Oriented means the same as orientated.

orienteering noun Orienteering is a sport in which people run from one place to another in the countryside, using a map and compass to guide them.

origin noun 1 You can refer to the beginning or cause of something as its origin or origins. 2 You can refer to someone's family background as their origin or origins.

> **origin** noun
> 1 = derivation, root, source
> 2 = ancestry, descent, extraction, lineage, stock

original adjective 1 Original describes things that existed at the beginning, rather than being added later, or things that were the first of their kind to exist. 2 Original means imaginative and clever. ▶ noun 3 A work of art or a document that is the one that was first produced, and not a copy. > **originally** adverb > **originality** noun

> **original** adjective
> 1 = first, initial 2 = fresh, new, novel

originate verb When something originates, or you originate it,

it begins to happen or exist.
> **originator** noun

ornament noun a small, attractive object that you display in your home or that you wear in order to look attractive.

> **ornament** noun
> = adornment, bauble, decoration, knick-knack (informal), trinket

ornamental adjective designed to be attractive rather than useful.

ornate adjective Something that is ornate has a lot of decoration on it.

orphan noun 1 a child whose parents are dead. ▶ verb 2 If a child is orphaned, its parents have died.

orphanage noun a place where orphans are looked after.

orthodox adjective 1 Orthodox beliefs or methods are the ones that most people have or use and that are considered standard. 2 People who are orthodox believe in the older, more traditional ideas of their religion or political party. 3 (RE) The Orthodox Church is the part of the Christian Church which separated from the western European Church in the 11th century and is the main church in Greece and Russia. > **orthodoxy** noun

osmosis noun (SCIENCE) Osmosis is the process by which a liquid moves through a semipermeable membrane from a weaker solution to a more concentrated one.

osprey noun a large bird of prey which catches fish with its feet.

ostensibly adverb If something is done ostensibly for a reason, that seems to be the reason for it.

ostentatious *adjective*
1 Something that is ostentatious is intended to impress people, for example by looking expensive.
2 People who are ostentatious try to impress other people with their wealth or importance.
> **ostentatiously** *adverb*
> **ostentation** *noun*

> **ostentatious** *adjective*
> 1 = extravagant, flamboyant, flashy, grandiose, pretentious, showy

ostrich *noun* The ostrich is the largest bird in the world. Ostriches cannot fly.

other *adjective, pronoun* 1 Other people or things are different people or things: *All the other children had gone home.* ▶ *phrase*
2 **The other day** or **the other week** means recently.

otherwise *adverb* 1 You use 'otherwise' to say a different situation would exist if a particular fact or occurrence was not the case: *You had to learn to swim pretty quickly, otherwise you sank.*
2 'Otherwise' means apart from the thing mentioned: *She had written to her daughter, but otherwise refused to take sides.* 3 'Otherwise' also means in a different way: *The majority voted otherwise.*

otter *noun* a small, furry animal with a long tail. Otters swim well and eat fish.

ought *verb* If you say that someone ought to do something, you mean that they should do it.

ounce *noun* a unit of weight equal to one sixteenth of a pound or about 28.35 grams.

our *adjective* 'Our' refers to something belonging or relating to the speaker or writer and one or more other people: *We recently sold our house.*

ours *pronoun* 'Ours' refers to something belonging or relating to the speaker or writer and one or more other people: *a friend of ours from Korea.*

ourselves *pronoun* 1 'Ourselves' is used when the same speaker or writer and one or more other people do an action and are affected by it: *We haven't damaged ourselves too badly.* 2 'Ourselves' is used to emphasise 'we': *We ourselves were delighted at the news.*

oust *verb* If you oust someone, you force them out of a job or a place.

out *adverb* 1 towards the outside of a place. 2 not at home. 3 in the open air. 4 no longer shining or burning. ▶ *adjective* 5 on strike. 6 unacceptable or unfashionable. 7 incorrect.

out-and-out *adjective* entire or complete.

outback *noun* In Australia, the outback is the remote parts where very few people live.

outbreak *noun* If there is an outbreak of something unpleasant, such as war, it suddenly occurs.

> **outbreak** *noun*
> = eruption, explosion

outburst *noun* a sudden, strong expression of an emotion, especially anger.

outcast *noun* someone who is rejected by other people.

outcome *noun* a result.

outcrop *noun* a large piece of rock that sticks out of the ground.

outcry **outcries** *noun* If there is an

outcry about something, a lot of people are angry about it.

outdated *adjective* no longer in fashion.

outdo outdoes, outdoing, outdid, outdone *verb* If you outdo someone, you do a particular thing better than they do.

> **outdo** *verb*
> = go one better than, outshine, surpass, top

outdoor *adjective* happening or used outside.

outdoors *adverb* outside.

outer *adjective* The outer parts of something are the parts furthest from the centre.

outer space *noun* Outer space is everything beyond the earth's atmosphere.

outfit *noun* 1 a set of clothes. 2 (*informal*) an organisation.

outgoing *adjective* 1 Outgoing describes someone who is leaving a job or place. 2 Someone who is outgoing is friendly and not shy.

outgrow outgrows, outgrowing, outgrew, outgrown *verb* 1 If you outgrow a piece of clothing, you grow too big for it. 2 If you outgrow a way of behaving, you stop it because you have grown older and more mature.

outhouse *noun* a small building in the grounds of a house to which it belongs.

outing *noun* a trip made for pleasure.

outlandish *adjective* very unusual or odd.

outlaw *verb* 1 If something is outlawed, it is made illegal. ▶ *noun* 2 In the past, an outlaw was a criminal.

outlay *noun* an amount of money spent on something.

outlet *noun* 1 An outlet for your feelings or ideas is a way of expressing them. 2 a hole or pipe through which water or air can flow away. 3 a shop which sells goods made by a particular manufacturer.

outline *verb* 1 If you outline a plan or idea, you explain it in a general way. 2 You say that something is outlined when you can see its shape because there is a light behind it. ▶ *noun* 3 a general explanation or description of something. 4 The outline of something is its shape.

> **outline** *verb*
> 1 = sketch, summarise
> ▶ *noun* 3 = rundown (*informal*), summary, synopsis
> 4 = contours, figure, form, shape, silhouette

outlive *verb* To outlive someone is to live longer than they do.

outlook *noun* 1 Your outlook is your general attitude towards life. 2 The outlook of a situation is the way it is likely to develop.

> **outlook** *noun*
> 1 = attitude, perspective, view
> 2 = future, prospects

outlying *adjective* Outlying places are far from cities.

outmoded *adjective* old-fashioned and no longer useful.

outnumber *verb* If there are more of one group than of another, the first group outnumbers the second.

out of *preposition* 1 If you do something out of a particular feeling, you are motivated by that feeling. **2** 'Out of' also means from. **3** If you are out of something, you no longer have any of it. **4** If you are out of the rain, sun or wind, you are sheltered from it. **5** You also use 'out of' to indicate proportion. For example, one out of five means one in every five.

out of date *adjective*
old-fashioned and no longer useful.

> **out of date** *adjective*
> = antiquated, archaic, obsolete, old-fashioned, outdated, outmoded

outpatient *noun* Outpatients are people who receive treatment in hospital without staying overnight.

outpost *noun* a small collection of buildings a long way from a main centre.

output *noun* **1** Output is the amount of something produced by a person or organisation. **2** (ICT) The output of a computer is the information that it produces.

outrage *verb* **1** If something outrages you, it angers and shocks you. ▶ *noun* **2** Outrage is a feeling of anger and shock. **3** something very shocking or violent. > **outrageous** *adjective* > **outrageously** *adverb*

outright *adjective* **1** absolute. ▶ *adverb* **2** in an open and direct way. **3** completely and totally.

outset *noun* The outset of something is the beginning of it.

outshine outshines, outshining, outshone *verb* If you outshine someone, you perform better than they do.

outside *noun* **1** The outside of something is the part which surrounds or encloses the rest of it. ▶ *preposition* **2** on or to the exterior of. **3** Outside also means not included in something: *outside office hours.* ▶ *adjective* **4** Outside means not inside. ▶ *adverb* **5** out of doors.

> **outside** *noun*
> **1** = exterior, facade, face, surface
> ▶ *adjective* **4** = exterior, external, outdoor, outer, outward, surface

outsider *noun* **1** someone who does not belong to a particular group. **2** a competitor considered unlikely to win in a race.

outsize or **outsized** *adjective* much larger than usual.

outskirts *plural noun* The outskirts of a city or town are the parts around the edge of it.

> **outskirts** *plural noun*
> = edge, perimeter, periphery

outspoken *adjective* Outspoken people give their opinions openly, even if they shock other people.

outstanding *adjective* **1** extremely good. **2** Money that is outstanding is still owed.

> **outstanding** *adjective*
> **1** = brilliant, excellent, exceptional, first-class, first-rate, great, superb **2** = due, overdue, owing, payable, unpaid

outstretched *adjective* If your arms are outstretched, they are stretched out as far as possible.

outstrip outstrips, outstripping, outstripped *verb* If one thing outstrips another thing, it becomes bigger or more successful or moves faster than the other thing.

outward *adjective, adverb*
1 Outward means away from a place or towards the outside.
▶ *adjective* 2 The outward features of someone are the ones they appear to have, rather than the ones they actually have.
> **outwardly** *adverb*

outwards *adverb* away from a place or towards the outside.

outweigh *verb* If you say that the advantages of something outweigh its disadvantages, you mean that the advantages are more important than the disadvantages.

outwit outwits, outwitting, outwitted *verb* If you outwit someone, you use your intelligence to defeat them.

oval *noun* 1 a round shape, similar to a circle but wider in one direction than the other.
▶ *adjective* 2 shaped like an oval.

ovary ovaries *noun* (SCIENCE) A woman's ovaries are the two organs in her body that produce eggs.

ovation *noun* a long burst of applause.

oven *noun* the part of a cooker that you use for baking or roasting food.

over *preposition* 1 Over something means directly above it or covering it. 2 A view over an area is a view across that area. 3 If something is over a road or river, it is on the opposite side of the road or river. 4 Something that is over a particular amount is more than that amount. 5 'Over' indicates a topic of discussion: *A customer was arguing over the bill.*

6 If something happens over a period of time, it happens during that period. ▶ *adverb, preposition*
7 If you lean over, you bend your body in a particular direction.
▶ *adverb* 8 'Over' is used to indicate a position: *over by the window.*
9 If something rolls or turns over, it is moved so that its other side is facing upwards. ▶ *adjective*
10 Something that is over is completely finished. ▶ *phrase*
11 All over a place means everywhere in that place. ▶ *noun*
12 In cricket, an over is a set of six balls bowled by a bowler from the same end of the pitch.

> **over** *preposition*
> 4 = above, exceeding, in excess of, more than
> ▶ *adjective* 10 = at an end, complete, done, finished, gone, past, up

overall *adjective* 1 Overall means taking into account all the parts or aspects of something. ▶ *adverb*
2 taking into account all the parts of something. ▶ *noun* 3 (*in plural*) Overalls are a piece of clothing that looks like trousers and a jacket combined. You wear overalls to protect your other clothes when you are working.
4 An overall is a piece of clothing like a coat that you wear to protect your other clothes when you are working.

overawed *adjective* If you are overawed by something, you are very impressed by it and a little afraid of it.

overbearing *adjective* trying to dominate other people.

overboard *adverb* If you fall overboard, you fall over the side of a ship into the water.

o

overcame the past tense of **overcome**.

overcast *adjective* If it is overcast, the sky is covered by cloud.

overcoat *noun* a thick, warm coat.

overcome overcomes, overcoming, overcame, overcome *verb* 1 If you overcome a problem or a feeling, you manage to deal with it or control it. ▶ *adjective* 2 If you are overcome by a feeling, you feel it very strongly.

> **overcome** *verb*
> 1 = conquer, get the better of, master, surmount, triumph over, vanquish (*literary*)

overcrowded *adjective* If a place is overcrowded, there are too many things or people in it.

overdo overdoes, overdoing, overdid, overdone *verb* If you overdo something, you do it too much or in an exaggerated way.

overdose *noun* a larger dose of a drug than is safe.

overdraft *noun* an agreement with a bank that allows someone to spend more money than they have in their account.

overdrawn *adjective* If someone is overdrawn, they have taken more money from their bank account than the account has in it.

overdue *adjective* If someone or something is overdue, they are late.

overestimate *verb* If you overestimate something, you think that it is bigger, more important or better than it really is.

overflow overflows, overflowing, overflowed, overflown *verb* If a liquid overflows, it spills over the edges of its container. If a river

overflows, it flows over its banks.

overgrown *adjective* A place that is overgrown is covered with weeds because it has not been looked after.

overhang overhangs, overhanging, overhung *verb* If one thing overhangs another, it sticks out sideways above it.

overhaul *verb* 1 If you overhaul something, you examine it thoroughly and repair any faults. ▶ *noun* 2 If you give something an overhaul, you examine it and repair or improve it.

overhead *adjective, adverb* Overhead means above you.

overhear overhears, overhearing, overheard *verb* If you overhear someone's conversation, you hear what they are saying to someone else.

overhung the past tense and past participle of **overhang**.

overjoyed *adjective* extremely pleased.

overland *adjective, adverb* travelling across land rather than going by sea or air.

overlap overlaps, overlapping, overlapped *verb* If one thing overlaps another, one part of it covers part of the other thing.

overload *verb* If you overload someone or something, you give them too much to do or to carry.

overlook *verb* 1 If a building or window overlooks a place, it has a view over that place. 2 If you overlook something, you ignore it or do not notice it.

> **overlook** *verb*
> 2 = disregard, forget, ignore, miss, neglect, turn a blind eye to

overnight adverb 1 during the night. 2 suddenly. ▶ adjective 3 during the night. 4 sudden. 5 for use when you go away for one or two nights.

overpower verb 1 If you overpower someone, you seize them despite their struggles, because you are stronger than them. 2 If a feeling overpowers you, it affects you very strongly. > **overpowering** adjective

overran the past tense of **overrun**.

overrate verb If you overrate something, you think that it is better or more important than it really is. > **overrated** adjective

overreact verb If you overreact, you react in an extreme way.

overriding adjective more important than anything else.

overrule verb To overrule a person or their decisions is to decide that their decisions are incorrect.

> **overrule** verb
> = overturn, reverse

overrun overruns, overrunning, overran, overrun verb 1 If an army overruns a country, it occupies it very quickly. 2 If animals or plants overrun a place, they spread quickly over it. 3 If an event overruns, it continues for longer than it was meant to.

oversaw the past tense of **oversee**.

overseas adverb 1 abroad. ▶ adjective 2 abroad. 3 from abroad.

oversee oversees, overseeing, oversaw, overseen verb To oversee a job is to make sure it is done properly. > **overseer** noun

> **oversee** verb
> = be in charge of, coordinate, direct, manage, preside, supervise

overshadow verb If something is overshadowed, it is made unimportant by something else that is better or more important.

oversight noun something which you forget to do or fail to notice.

overstate verb If you overstate something, you exaggerate its importance.

overstep oversteps, overstepping, overstepped phrase If you **overstep the mark**, you behave in an unacceptable way.

overt adjective open and obvious. > **overtly** adverb

overtake overtakes, overtaking, overtook, overtaken verb If you overtake someone, you pass them because you are moving faster than them.

overthrow overthrows, overthrowing, overthrew, overthrown verb If a government is overthrown, it is removed from power by force.

> **overthrow** verb
> = bring down, depose, oust, topple

overtime noun 1 Overtime is time that someone works in addition to their normal working hours. ▶ adverb 2 If someone works overtime, they do work in addition to their normal working hours.

overtones plural noun If something has overtones of an emotion or attitude, it suggests it without showing it openly.

overtook the past tense of **overtake**.

overture noun 1 a piece of music that is the introduction to an opera or play. 2 If you make overtures to someone, you approach them because you want to start a friendly or business relationship with them.

overturn verb 1 To overturn something is to turn it upside down or onto its side. 2 If someone overturns a legal decision, they change it by using their higher authority.

> **overturn** verb
> 1 = capsize, knock down, knock over, tip over, topple, upset
> 2 = overrule, reverse

overview noun a general understanding or description of a situation.

overweight adjective too fat, and therefore unhealthy.

> **overweight** adjective
> = fat, hefty, obese, stout

overwhelm verb 1 If you are overwhelmed by something, it affects you very strongly. 2 If one group of people overwhelms another, they gain complete control or victory over them.
> **overwhelming** adjective
> **overwhelmingly** adverb

overwork verb If you overwork, you work too hard.

overwrought adjective extremely upset.

owe verb 1 If you owe someone money, they have lent it to you and you have not yet paid it back. 2 If you owe a quality or skill to someone, they are responsible for giving it to you. 3 If you say that

you owe someone gratitude or loyalty, you mean that they deserve it from you.

owl noun Owls are birds of prey that hunt at night. They have large eyes and short, hooked beaks.

own adjective 1 If something is your own, it belongs to you or is associated with you. ▶ verb 2 If you own something, it belongs to you. ▶ phrase 3 On your own means alone.

> **own** adjective
> 1 = personal, private
> ▶ verb 2 = have, keep, possess
> ▶ phrase 3 on your own = alone, by yourself, independently, unaided

owner noun The owner of something is the person it belongs to.

> **owner** noun
> = possessor, proprietor

ownership noun If you have ownership of something, you own it.

ox oxen noun Oxen are cattle which are used for carrying or pulling things.

oxide noun a compound of oxygen and another chemical element.

oxygen noun (SCIENCE) Oxygen is a chemical element in the form of a colourless gas. It makes up about 21 per cent of the earth's atmosphere. With an extremely small number of exceptions, living things need oxygen to live, and things cannot burn without it. Oxygen's atomic number is 8 and its symbol is O.

oxymoron oxymora or **oxymorons** noun (ENGLISH) two words that contradict each other placed beside each other, for example 'deafening silence'.

oyster *noun* Oysters are large, flat shellfish. Some oysters can be eaten, and others produce pearls.

oz an abbreviation for 'ounce' or 'ounces'.

ozone *noun* Ozone is a form of oxygen that is poisonous and has a strong smell. There is a layer of ozone high above the earth's surface.

ozone layer *noun* The ozone layer is that part of the earth's atmosphere that protects living things from the harmful radiation of the sun.

Pp

p 1 an abbreviation for 'pence'. **2** a written abbreviation for 'page'. The plural is pp.

pa *noun* In New Zealand, a pa is a Māori village or settlement.

pace *noun* **1** The pace of something is the speed at which it moves or happens. **2** a step; also used as a measurement of distance. ▶ *verb* **3** If you pace up and down, you continually walk around because you are anxious or impatient.

pacemaker *noun* a small electronic device put into someone's heart to control their heartbeat.

Pacific *noun* The Pacific is the ocean separating North and South America from Asia and Australia.

pacifist *noun* someone who is opposed to all violence and war. > **pacifism** *noun*

pacify pacifies, pacifying, pacified *verb* If you pacify someone who is angry, you calm them.

> **pacify** *verb*
> = appease, calm, mollify, placate, soothe

pack *verb* **1** If you pack, you put things neatly into a suitcase, bag or box. **2** If people pack into a place, it becomes crowded with them. ▶ *noun* **3** a bag or rucksack carried on your back. **4** a packet or collection of something. **5** A pack of playing cards is a complete set. **6** A pack of dogs or wolves is a group of them. ▷ **pack in** verb (informal) If you pack something in, you stop doing it. ▷ **pack up** verb If you pack up your belongings, you put them in a bag because you are leaving.

package noun **1** a small parcel. **2** a set of proposals or offers presented as a whole. ▷ **packaged** adjective

packaging noun ⑅DGT⑆ Packaging is the container or wrapping in which an item is sold or sent.

packed adjective very full.

packet noun a thin cardboard box or paper container in which something is sold.

pact noun a formal agreement or treaty.

pad pads, padding, padded noun **1** a thick, soft piece of material. **2** a number of pieces of paper fixed together at one end. **3** The pads of an animal such as a cat or dog are the soft, fleshy parts on the bottom of its paws. **4** a flat surface from which helicopters take off or rockets are launched. ▷ verb **5** If you pad something, you put a pad inside it or over it to protect it or change its shape. **6** If you pad around, you walk softly. ▷ **padding** noun

paddle noun **1** a short pole with a broad blade at one or both ends, used to move a small boat or a canoe. ▷ verb **2** If someone paddles a boat, they move it using a paddle. **3** If you paddle, you walk in shallow water.

paddock noun a small field where horses are kept.

paddy paddies noun A paddy or paddy field is an area in which rice is grown.

padlock noun **1** a lock made up of a metal case with a U-shaped bar attached to it, which can be put through a metal loop and then closed. It is unlocked by turning a key in the lock on the case. ▶ verb **2** If you padlock something, you lock it with a padlock.

paediatrician; also spelt **pediatrician** noun a doctor who specialises in treating children.

paediatrics; also spelt **pediatrics** noun Paediatrics is the area of medicine which deals with children's diseases. ▷ **paediatric** adjective

pagan adjective **1** involving beliefs and worship outside the main religions of the world. ▶ noun **2** someone who believes in a pagan religion. ▷ **paganism** noun

page noun **1** one side of one of the pieces of paper in a book or magazine; also the piece of paper itself. **2** In medieval times, a page was a young boy servant who was learning to be a knight. ▶ verb **3** To page someone is to send a signal or message to a small electronic device which they are carrying.

pageant noun a grand, colourful show or parade.

paid the past tense and past participle of **pay**.

pail noun a bucket.

pain noun **1** Pain is an unpleasant feeling of physical hurt. **2** Pain is also an unpleasant feeling of deep unhappiness. ▶ verb **3** If something pains you, it makes you very unhappy. ▷ **painless** adjective ▷ **painlessly** adverb

pain *noun*
1 = ache, discomfort, irritation, soreness, trouble, twinge
2 = agony, anguish, distress, grief, misery

painful *adjective* 1 causing emotional pain. 2 causing physical pain. ▸ **painfully** *adverb*

painful *adjective*
1 = distressing, grievous, saddening, unpleasant
2 = aching, excruciating, sore, tender

painkiller *noun* a drug that reduces or stops pain.

painstaking *adjective* very careful and thorough.

paint *noun* 1 (ART) Paint is a coloured liquid used to decorate buildings, or to make a picture. ▸ *verb* 2 (ART) If you paint something or paint a picture of it, you make a picture of it using paint. 3 (DGT) When you paint something such as a wall, you cover it with paint. ▸ **painter** *noun* ▸ **painting** *noun*

pair *noun* 1 two things of the same type or that do the same thing. 2 You use 'pair' when referring to certain objects which have two main matching parts: *a pair of scissors*. ▸ *verb* 3 When people pair off, they become grouped in pairs. 4 If you pair up with someone, you agree to do something together.

Pakistani *adjective* 1 belonging or relating to Pakistan. ▸ *noun* 2 someone who comes from Pakistan.

pal *noun* (*informal*) a friend.

palace *noun* a large, grand house, especially the official home of a king or queen.

palatable *adjective* Palatable food tastes pleasant.

palate *noun* 1 the top of the inside of your mouth. 2 Someone's palate is their ability to judge good food and drink.

pale *adjective* rather white and without much colour or brightness.

pale *adjective*
= ashen, colourless, faded, sallow, wan, white

Palestinian *adjective* 1 belonging or relating to the region of Palestine, between the River Jordan and the Mediterranean. ▸ *noun* 2 an Arab who comes from Palestine.

palette *noun* a flat piece of wood on which an artist mixes colours.

pall *verb* 1 If something palls, it becomes less interesting or less enjoyable. ▸ *noun* 2 a thick cloud of smoke. 3 a cloth covering a coffin.

palm *noun* 1 A palm or palm tree is a tropical tree with no branches and a crown of long leaves. 2 the flat surface of your hand which your fingers bend towards.

palpable *adjective* obvious and easily sensed. ▸ **palpably** *adverb*

paltry *adjective* A paltry sum of money is a very small amount.

pamper *verb* If you pamper someone, you give them too much kindness and comfort.

pamphlet *noun* (ENGLISH) a very thin book in paper covers giving information about something.

pan *noun*, pans, panning, panned 1 a round metal container with a long handle, used for cooking things in on top of a cooker.

▶ verb 2 When a film camera pans, it moves in a wide sweep.
3 (informal) To pan something is to criticise it strongly.

panacea noun something that is supposed to cure everything.

panache noun Something that is done with panache is done confidently and stylishly.

pancake noun a thin, flat piece of fried batter which can be served with savoury or sweet fillings.

pancreas noun (SCIENCE) The pancreas is an organ in the body situated behind the stomach. It produces insulin and enzymes that help with digestion.

panda noun A panda or giant panda is a large animal rather like a bear that lives in China. It has black fur with large patches of white.

pandemonium noun Pandemonium is a state of noisy confusion.

pander verb If you pander to someone, you do everything they want.

pane noun a sheet of glass in a window or door.

panel noun 1 a small group of people who are chosen to do something. 2 a flat piece of wood that is part of a larger object. 3 A control panel is a surface containing switches and instruments to operate a machine. > **panelled** adjective

panelling noun Panelling is rectangular pieces of wood covering an inside wall.

pang noun a sudden strong feeling of sadness or pain.

panic panics, panicking, panicked noun 1 Panic is a sudden

overwhelming feeling of fear or anxiety. ▶ verb 2 If you panic, you become so afraid or anxious that you cannot act sensibly.

> **panic** noun
> 1 = alarm, dismay, fear, fright, hysteria, terror
> ▶ verb 2 = become hysterical, go to pieces, lose your nerve

panorama noun an extensive view over a wide area of land.
> **panoramic** adjective

pant verb If you pant, you breathe quickly and loudly through your mouth.

panther noun a large wild animal belonging to the cat family, especially the black leopard.

pantomime noun a musical play, usually based on a fairy story and performed at Christmas.

pantry pantries noun a small room where food is kept.

pants plural noun 1 Pants are a piece of underwear with holes for your legs and elastic around the waist or hips. 2 In American English, pants are trousers.

papaya noun a fruit with sweet yellow or reddish-orange flesh and small black seeds.

paper noun 1 Paper is a material made from wood pulp and used for writing on or wrapping things. 2 a newspaper. 3 (in plural) Papers are official documents, for example a passport for identification. 4 part of a written examination. ▶ verb 5 If you paper a wall, you put wallpaper on it.

paperback noun a book with a thin cardboard cover.

paperwork noun Paperwork is the part of a job that involves dealing with letters and records.

paprika *noun* Paprika is a red powder made from a kind of pepper.

par *phrase* 1 Something that is **on a par** with something else is similar in quality or amount.
2 Something that is **below par** or **under par** is below its normal standard. ▶ *noun* 3 In golf, par is the number of strokes which it is thought a good player should take for a hole or all the holes on a particular golf course.

parable *noun* (RE) a short story which makes a moral or religious point.

parachute *noun* a circular piece of fabric attached by lines to a person or package so that they can fall safely to the ground from an aircraft.

parade *noun* 1 a line of people or vehicles standing or moving together as a display. ▶ *verb*
2 When people parade, they walk together in a group as a display.

parade *noun*
1 = cavalcade, march, pageant, procession, tattoo

Paradise *noun* According to some religions, Paradise is a wonderful place where good people go when they die.

paradox *noun* something that contains two ideas that seem to contradict each other.
> **paradoxical** *adjective*

paraffin *noun* Paraffin is a strong-smelling liquid which is used as a fuel.

paragraph *noun* (ENGLISH) a section of a piece of writing. Paragraphs begin on a new line.

parallel *noun* 1 Something that is

a parallel to something else has similar qualities or features to it.
▶ *adjective* 2 (MATHS) If two lines are parallel, they are the same distance apart along the whole of their length.

parallelogram *noun* (MATHS) a four-sided shape in which each side is parallel to the opposite side.

paralyse *verb* If something paralyses you, it causes loss of feeling and movement in your body.

paralysis *noun* Paralysis is loss of the power to move.

paramedic *noun* a person who does some types of medical work, for example for the ambulance service.

parameter *noun* a limit which affects the way something is done.

paramilitary *adjective* A paramilitary organisation has a military structure but is not the official army of a country.

paramount *adjective* more important than anything else.

paranoia *noun* a mental condition in which someone believes that other people are trying to harm them.

paranoid *adjective* Someone who is paranoid believes wrongly that other people are trying to harm them.

parapet *noun* a low wall along the edge of a bridge or roof.

paraphernalia *noun* Someone's paraphernalia is all their belongings or equipment.

paraphrase *noun* 1 A paraphrase of a piece of writing or speech is the same thing said in a different

P

way. ▶ *verb* 2 If you paraphrase what someone has said, you express it in a different way.

parasite *noun* a small animal or plant that lives on or inside a larger animal or plant.
> **parasitic** *adjective*

paratroops or **paratroopers** *plural noun* Paratroops are soldiers trained to be dropped by parachute.

parcel parcels, parcelling, parcelled *noun* 1 something wrapped up in paper. ▶ *verb* 2 If you parcel something up, you make it into a parcel.

parched *adjective* 1 If the ground is parched, it is very dry and in need of water. 2 (*informal*) If you are parched, you are very thirsty.

parchment *noun* Parchment is thick yellowish paper of very good quality.

pardon *interjection* 1 You say **pardon** or **I beg your pardon** to express surprise or apology, or when you have not heard what someone has said. ▶ *verb* 2 If you pardon someone, you forgive them for doing something wrong.

pare *verb* When you pare fruit or vegetables, you cut off the skin.

parent *noun* Your parents are the people who caused you to be born and who usually look after you while you grow up. > **parental** *adjective*

parent *noun*
= father, mother, old (*Australian and New Zealand; informal*), patriarch

parentage *noun* A person's parentage is their parents and ancestors.

parish *noun* an area with its own church, and often its own elected council.

parishioner *noun* Parishioners are the people who live in a parish and attend its church.

parity *noun* (*formal*) If there is parity between things, they are equal.

park *noun* 1 a public area with grass and trees. 2 a private area of grass and trees around a large country house. ▶ *verb* 3 When someone parks a vehicle, they drive it into a position where it can be left. > **parked** *adjective* > **parking** *noun*

parliament *noun* (CITIZENSHIP) the group of elected representatives who make the laws of a country.
> **parliamentary** *adjective*

parlour *noun* (*old-fashioned*) a sitting room.

parochial *adjective* concerned only with local matters.

parody parodies, parodying, parodied *noun* 1 an amusing imitation of the style of an author or of a familiar situation. ▶ *verb* 2 If you parody something, you make a parody of it.

parody *noun*
1 = imitation, satire, spoof (*informal*), takeoff (*informal*)

parole *noun* When prisoners are given parole, they are released early on condition that they behave well.

parrot *noun* a brightly coloured tropical bird with a curved beak.

parry parries, parrying, parried *verb* 1 If you parry a question, you cleverly avoid answering it. 2 If you parry a blow, you push aside your attacker's arm to defend yourself.

parsley noun Parsley is a herb with curly or flat leaves used for flavouring in cooking.

parsnip noun a long, pointed, cream-coloured root vegetable.

part noun **1** one of the pieces or aspects of something. **2** one of the roles in a play or film, played by an actor or actress. **3** Someone's part in something is their involvement in it. ▶ phrase **4** If you **take part in** an activity, you do it together with other people. ▶ verb **5** If things that are next to each other part, they move away from each other. **6** If two people part, they leave each other.

> **part** noun
> **1** = bit, fraction, fragment, piece, portion, section
> **3** = capacity, duty, function, involvement, role
> ▶ phrase **4 take part in** = be instrumental in, be involved in, have a hand in, join in, participate in, play a part in

partake partakes, partaking, partook, partaken verb (formal) If you partake of food, you eat it.

partial adjective **1** not complete or whole. **2** liking something very much. **3** supporting one side in a dispute, rather than being fair and without bias. > **partially** adverb

participate verb (CITIZENSHIP) If you participate in an activity, you take part in it. > **participant** noun > **participation** noun

> **participate** verb
> = be involved in, engage in, enter into, join in, take part

particle noun **1** (SCIENCE) a basic unit of matter, such as an atom, molecule or electron. **2** a very small piece of something.

particular adjective **1** relating or belonging to only one thing or person: *That particular place is dangerous.* **2** especially great or intense: *Pay particular attention to the oral part of the exam.* **3** Someone who is particular has high standards and is not easily satisfied. > **particularly** adverb

> **particular** adjective
> **1** = distinct, exact, express, peculiar, precise, specific
> **2** = exceptional, marked, notable, singular, special, uncommon **3** = choosy (informal), exacting, fastidious, fussy, meticulous

parting noun an occasion when one person leaves another.

partisan adjective **1** favouring or supporting one person or group. ▶ noun **2** a member of an unofficial armed force fighting to free their country from enemy occupation.

partition noun **1** a screen separating one part of a room or vehicle from another. **2** Partition is the division of a country into independent areas. ▶ verb **3** To partition something is to divide it into separate parts.

partly adverb to some extent but not completely.

> **partly** adverb
> = in part (formal), in some measure (formal), partially, to some degree, to some extent

partner noun **1** Someone's partner is the person they are married to or are living with. **2** Your partner

p

is the person you are doing something with, for example in a dance or a game. **3** Business partners are joint owners of their business. ▶ *verb* **4** If you partner someone, you are their partner for a game or social occasion.
> **partnership** *noun*

> **partner** *noun*
> **1** = husband, mate, spouse, wife
> **2** = companion, date, plus-one (*informal*), team-mate

partridge *noun* a brown game bird with a round body and a short tail.

part-time *adjective* involving work for only a part of the working day or week.

party parties *noun* **1** a social event held for people to enjoy themselves. **2** (CITIZENSHIP) an organisation whose members share the same political beliefs and campaign for election to government. **3** a group who are doing something together. **4** (*formal*) one of the people involved in a legal agreement or dispute.

> **party** *noun*
> **1** = celebration, function, gathering, get-together (*informal*), hooley or hoolie (*New Zealand, Scottish and Irish*), reception **2** = alliance, clique, coalition, faction, grouping **3** = band, crew, gang, squad, team, unit

pass *verb* **1** To pass something is to move past it. **2** To pass in a particular direction is to move in that direction. **3** If you pass something to someone, you hand it to them or transfer it to them. **4** If you pass a period of time

doing something, you spend it that way. **5** When a period of time passes, it happens and finishes. **6** If you pass a test, you are considered to be of an acceptable standard. **7** When a new law or proposal is passed, it is formally approved. **8** When a judge passes sentence on someone, the judge states what the punishment will be. **9** If you pass the ball in a ball game, you throw, kick or hit it to another player in your team. ▶ *noun* **10** the transfer of the ball in a ball game to another player in the same team. **11** an official document that allows you to go somewhere. **12** a narrow route between mountains. > **pass away** or **pass on** *verb* Someone who has passed away has died. > **pass out** *verb* If someone passes out, they faint. > **pass up** *verb* (*informal*) If you pass up an opportunity, you do not take advantage of it.

> **pass** *verb*
> **1** = exceed, go beyond, outdo, outstrip, overtake, surpass
> **6** = get through, graduate, qualify, succeed
> ▶ *noun* **11** = identification, passport, ticket

passable *adjective* of an acceptable standard.

passage *noun* **1** a space that connects two places. **2** a long, narrow corridor. **3** a section of a book or piece of music.

> **passage** *noun*
> **1** = channel, course, path, road, route, way **2** = aisle, corridor, hall, lobby **3** = excerpt, extract, quotation, section

passenger *noun* a person travelling in a vehicle, aircraft or ship.

passer-by passers-by noun
someone who is walking past
someone or something.

passing adjective lasting only for
a short time.

passion noun 1 Passion is a very
strong feeling of attraction.
2 Passion is also any strong
emotion.

> **passion** noun
> 2 = emotion, excitement, fire,
> intensity, warmth, zeal

passionate adjective involving
very strong feelings about
something. > **passionately**
adverb

> **passionate** adjective
> = ardent, emotional, heartfelt,
> impassioned, intense, strong

passive adjective 1 remaining
calm and showing no feeling
when provoked. ▶ noun 2 (ENGLISH)
In grammar, the passive or
passive voice is the form of the
verb in which the person or thing
to which an action is being done
is the grammatical subject of the
sentence, and is given more
emphasis as a result. For
example, the passive of The
committee rejected your application is
Your application was rejected by the
committee. > **passively** adverb
> **passivity** noun

> **passive** adjective
> 1 = docile, receptive, resigned,
> submissive

Passover noun (RE) The Passover
is an eight-day Jewish festival
held in spring.

passport noun an official
identification document which
you need to show when you
travel abroad.

password noun 1 a secret word
known to only a few people. It
allows people on the same side to
recognise a friend. 2 (ICT) a word
or series of numbers and letters
that you need to know to get into
a computer, mobile phone,
security system, etc.

past noun 1 The past is the period
of time before the present.
▶ adjective 2 Past things are things
that happened or existed before
the present. 3 (ENGLISH) (MFL) The
past tense of a verb is the form
used to express something that
happened in the past. ▶ preposition,
adverb 4 You use 'past' when you
are telling the time: It was ten past
eleven. 5 If you go past something,
you move towards it and continue
until you are on the other side:
They drove rapidly past their cottage.
▶ preposition 6 Something that is
past a place is situated on the
other side of it.

> **past** noun
> 1 the past = antiquity, days gone
> by, former times, long ago
> ▶ adjective 2 = ancient, bygone,
> former, olden, previous
> ▶ preposition 6 = beyond, by, over

pasta noun Pasta is a dried
mixture of flour, eggs and water,
formed into different shapes.

paste noun 1 Paste is a soft, rather
sticky mixture that can be easily
spread. ▶ verb 2 If you paste
something onto a surface, you
stick it with glue.

pastel adjective 1 Pastel colours are
pale and soft. ▶ noun 2 (ART)
Pastels are small sticks of
coloured crayon, used for drawing
pictures.

pastime noun a hobby or something
you do just for pleasure.

p

pastime noun
= activity, diversion, hobby, recreation

pastor noun a member of the clergy in charge of a congregation.

pastoral adjective 1 characteristic of peaceful country life and landscape. 2 relating to the duties of the clergy in caring for the needs of their parishioners, or of a school in caring for the needs of its students.

pastry pastries noun 1 Pastry is a mixture of flour, fat and water, rolled flat and used for making pies. 2 a small cake.

past tense noun (ENGLISH) (MFL) In grammar, the past tense is the tense of a verb that you use mainly to refer to things that happened or existed before the time of writing or speaking.

pasture noun Pasture is an area of grass on which farm animals graze.

pasty pastier, pastiest; pasties adjective 1 Someone who is pasty looks pale and unhealthy. ▶ noun 2 a small pie containing meat and vegetables.

pat pats, patting, patted verb 1 If you pat something, you tap it lightly with your hand held flat. ▶ noun 2 a small lump of butter.

patch noun 1 a piece of material used to cover a hole in something. 2 an area of a surface that is different in appearance from the rest. ▶ verb 3 If you patch something, you mend it by fixing a patch over the hole. ▶ **patch up** verb If you patch something up, you mend it hurriedly or temporarily.

patchwork adjective 1 A patchwork quilt is made from many small pieces of material sewn together. ▶ noun 2 Something that is a patchwork is made up of many parts.

patchy patchier, patchiest adjective Something that is patchy is unevenly spread or incomplete in parts.

patent noun 1 an official right given to an inventor to be the only person or company allowed to make or sell a new product. ▶ verb 2 If you patent something, you obtain a patent for it. ▶ adjective 3 obvious. > **patently** adverb

paternal adjective relating to a father.

paternity noun Paternity is the state or fact of being a father.

path noun 1 a strip of ground for people to walk on. 2 Your path is the area ahead of you and the direction in which you are moving.

path noun
1 = footpath, pathway, towpath, track, trail, way 2 = course, direction, passage, route, way

pathetic adjective 1 If something is pathetic, it makes you feel pity. 2 Pathetic also means very poor or unsuccessful. > **pathetically** adverb

pathetic adjective
1 = heartbreaking, sad
2 = feeble, lamentable, pitiful, poor, sorry

pathological adjective extreme and uncontrollable.
> **pathologically** adverb

pathology noun Pathology is the study of diseases and the way they develop. > **pathologist** noun

pathos noun Pathos is a quality in literature or art that causes great sadness or pity.

pathway noun a path.

patience noun Patience is the ability to stay calm in a difficult or irritating situation.

> **patience** noun
> = calmness, composure, cool (slang), restraint, tolerance

patient adjective 1 If you are patient, you stay calm in a difficult or irritating situation. ▶ noun 2 a person receiving medical treatment from a doctor or in a hospital. > **patiently** adverb

> **patient** adjective
> 1 = calm, composed, long-suffering, philosophical, serene
> ▶ noun 2 = case, sick person

patio patios noun a paved area close to a house.

patriarch noun a man who is the head of a family in a society in which power passes from father to son. > **patriarchy** noun > **patriarchal** adjective

patrician adjective (formal) belonging to a family of high rank.

patriot noun someone who loves their country and feels very loyal towards it. > **patriotic** adjective > **patriotism** noun

patrol patrols, patrolling, patrolled verb 1 When soldiers, police or guards patrol an area, they walk or drive around to make sure there is no trouble. ▶ noun 2 a group of people patrolling an area.

patron noun 1 a person who supports or gives money to artists, writers or musicians. 2 The patrons of a hotel, pub or shop are the people who use it. > **patronage** noun

patronise; also spelt **patronize** verb 1 If someone patronises you, they treat you kindly, but in a way that suggests that you are less intelligent than them or inferior to them. 2 If you patronise a hotel, pub or shop, you are a customer there. > **patronising** adjective

patron saint noun The patron saint of a group of people or place is a saint who is believed to look after them.

patter verb 1 If something patters on a surface, it makes quick, light tapping sounds. ▶ noun 2 a series of light tapping sounds.

pattern noun 1 a decorative design of repeated shapes. 2 The pattern of something is the way it is usually done or happens. 3 a diagram or shape used as a guide for making something, for example clothes. > **patterned** adjective

> **pattern** noun
> 1 = design, motif 3 = design, diagram, plan, stencil, template

pauper noun (old-fashioned) a very poor person.

pause verb 1 If you pause, you stop what you are doing for a short time. ▶ noun 2 a short period when you stop what you are doing.

> **pause** verb
> 1 = break, delay, halt, rest, take a break, wait
> ▶ noun 2 = break, halt, interruption, interval, rest, stoppage

P

pave *verb* When an area of ground is paved, it is covered with flat blocks of stone or concrete.

pavement *noun* a path with a hard surface at the side of a road.

pavilion *noun* a building at a sports ground where players can wash and change.

paw *noun* 1 The paws of an animal such as a cat or bear are its feet with claws and soft pads. ▶ *verb* 2 If an animal paws something, it hits it or scrapes at it with its paws.

pawn *verb* 1 If you pawn something, you leave it with a pawnbroker in exchange for money. ▶ *noun* 2 the smallest and least valuable playing piece in chess.

pay pays, paying, paid *verb* 1 When you pay money to someone, you give it to them because you are buying something or owe it to them. 2 If it pays to do something, it is to your advantage to do it. 3 If you pay for something that you have done, you suffer as a result. 4 If you pay attention to something, you give it your attention. 5 If you pay a visit to someone, you visit them. ▶ *noun* 6 Someone's pay is their salary or wages.

> **pay** *verb*
> 1 = compensate, honour, settle
> 2 = be advantageous, be worthwhile
> ▶ *noun* 6 = earnings, fee, income, payment, salary, wages

payable *adjective* An amount of money that is payable has to be paid or can be paid.

payment *noun* 1 Payment is the act of paying money. 2 a sum of money paid.

> **payment** *noun*
> 2 = advance, deposit, instalment, premium, remittance

payroll *noun* Someone who is on an organisation's payroll is employed and paid by them.

PC *noun* 1 In Britain, PC is an abbreviation for 'police constable'. 2 a personal computer. ▶ *adjective* 3 short for **politically correct**.

PE an abbreviation for 'physical education'.

pea *noun* Peas are small, round, green seeds that grow in pods and are eaten as a vegetable.

peace *noun* 1 Peace is a state of calm and quiet when there is no disturbance of any kind. 2 When a country is at peace, it is not at war. > **peaceable** *adjective*

> **peace** *noun*
> 1 = calm, quiet, silence, stillness, tranquillity
> 2 = armistice, cessation of hostilities, truce

peaceful *adjective* quiet and calm. > **peacefully** *adverb*

> **peaceful** *adjective*
> = calm, placid, quiet, serene, still, tranquil

peach *noun* 1 a soft, round fruit with yellow flesh and a yellow and red skin. ▶ *adjective* 2 pale orange with a hint of pink.

peacock *noun* a large bird with green and blue feathers. The male has a long tail which it can spread out in a fan.

peak *noun* 1 The peak of an activity or process is the point at which it is strongest or most successful.

2 the pointed top of a mountain.
▶ verb **3** When something peaks, it reaches its highest value or its greatest level of success. > **peaked** adjective

> **peak** noun
> **1** = climax, culmination, high point, zenith **2** = brow, crest, pinnacle, summit, top
> ▶ verb **3** = be at its height, climax, come to a head, culminate, reach its highest point

peanut noun Peanuts are small oval nuts that grow under the ground.

pear noun a fruit which is narrow at the top and wide and rounded at the bottom.

pearl noun a hard, round, creamy-white object used to make jewellery. Pearls grow inside the shell of an oyster.

peasant noun in some countries, a person who works on the land.

peat noun Peat is dark-brown decaying plant material found in cool, wet regions. Dried peat can be used as fuel.

pebble noun a smooth, round stone.

peck verb **1** If a bird pecks something, it bites at it quickly with its beak. **2** If you peck someone on the cheek, you give them a quick kiss. ▶ noun **3** a quick bite by a bird. **4** a quick kiss on the cheek.

peculiar adjective **1** strange and perhaps unpleasant. **2** relating or belonging only to a particular person or thing: a gesture peculiar to her. > **peculiarly** adverb > **peculiarity** noun

peculiar adjective
1 = bizarre, curious, funny, odd, queer (old-fashioned), strange, weird **2** = distinctive, distinguishing, individual, personal, special, unique

pedal noun pedals, pedalling, pedalled
noun **1** a control lever on a machine or vehicle that you press with your foot. ▶ verb **2** When you pedal a bicycle, you push the pedals round with your feet to move along.

pedantic adjective If a person is pedantic, they are too concerned with unimportant details and traditional rules.

peddle verb Someone who peddles something sells it.

pedestal noun a base on which a statue stands.

pedestrian noun **1** someone who is walking. ▶ adjective **2** Pedestrian means ordinary and rather dull.

pedestrian crossing noun a specially marked place where you can cross the road safely.

pediatrician another spelling of **paediatrician**.

pediatrics another spelling of **paediatrics**.

pedigree adjective **1** A pedigree animal is descended from a single breed and its ancestors are known and recorded. ▶ noun **2** Someone's pedigree is their background or ancestry.

peek verb **1** If you peek at something, you have a quick look at it. ▶ noun **2** a quick look at something.

> **peek** verb
> **1** = glance, peep, snatch a glimpse, sneak a look
> ▶ noun **2** = glance, glimpse, look, peep

P

peel noun 1 The peel of a fruit is the skin when it has been removed. ▶ verb 2 When you peel fruit or vegetables, you remove the skin. 3 If a surface is peeling, it is coming off in thin layers. > **peelings** plural noun

peep verb 1 If you peep at something, you have a quick look at it. 2 If something peeps out from behind something else, a small part of it becomes visible. ▶ noun 3 a quick look at something.

peer verb 1 If you peer at something, you look at it very hard. ▶ noun 2 a member of the nobility. 3 Your peers are the people who are of the same age and social status as yourself.

peerage noun 1 The peers in a country are called the peerage. 2 A peerage is also the rank of being a peer.

peer group noun Your peer group is the people who are of the same age and social status as yourself.

peerless adjective so magnificent that nothing can equal it.

peg pegs, pegging, pegged noun 1 a plastic or wooden clip used for hanging wet clothes on a line. 2 a hook on a wall where you can hang things. ▶ verb 3 If you peg clothes on a line, you fix them there with pegs. 4 If a price is pegged at a certain level, it is fixed at that level.

pejorative adjective A pejorative word expresses criticism.

pelican noun a large water bird with a pouch beneath its beak in which it stores fish.

pellet noun a small ball of paper, lead or other material.

pelt verb 1 If you pelt someone with things, you throw the things with force at them. 2 (informal) If you pelt along, you run very fast. ▶ noun 3 the skin and fur of an animal.

pelvis noun the wide, curved group of bones at hip level at the base of your spine. > **pelvic** adjective

pen pens, penning, penned noun 1 a long, thin instrument used for writing with ink. 2 a small fenced area in which farm animals are kept for a short time. ▶ verb 3 (literary) If someone pens a letter or article, they write it. 4 If you are penned in or penned up, you have to remain in an uncomfortably small area.

penal adjective relating to the punishment of criminals.

penalise; also spelt **penalize** verb If you are penalised, you are made to suffer some disadvantage as a punishment for something.

penalty penalties noun 1 a punishment or disadvantage that someone is made to suffer. 2 In soccer, a penalty is a free kick at goal that is given to the attacking team if the defending team have committed a foul near their goal.

penance noun If you do penance, you do something unpleasant to show that you are sorry for something wrong that you have done.

pence a plural form of **penny**.

penchant noun (formal) If you have a penchant for something, you have a particular liking for it.

pencil noun a long, thin stick of wood with graphite in the centre, used for drawing or writing.

pendant noun a piece of jewellery attached to a chain and worn round the neck.

pending (formal) adjective
1 Something that is pending is waiting to be dealt with or will happen soon. ▸ preposition
2 Something that is done pending a future event is done until the event happens: *The army should stay in the west pending a future war.*

pendulum noun a rod with a weight at one end in a clock which swings regularly from side to side to control the clock.

penetrate verb To penetrate an area that is difficult to get into is to succeed in getting into it.
> **penetration** noun

penetrating adjective 1 loud and high-pitched. 2 having or showing deep understanding.

penguin noun A penguin is a black and white bird with webbed feet and small wings like flippers. Penguins are found mainly in the Antarctic.

penicillin noun Penicillin is a powerful antibiotic obtained from fungus and used to treat infections.

peninsula noun (GEOGRAPHY) an area of land almost surrounded by water.

penis noun (SCIENCE) A man's penis is the part of his body used for urination and reproduction.

pennant noun a triangular flag, especially one used by ships as a signal.

penniless adjective Someone who is penniless has no money.

penny pennies or pence noun a unit of currency in Britain and some other countries. In Britain a penny is worth one-hundredth of a pound.

pension noun a regular sum of money paid to an old or retired person.

pensioner noun an old or retired person who gets a pension paid by the state.

pensive adjective deep in thought.

pentagon noun (MATHS) a shape with five straight sides; a regular pentagon is a shape with five straight sides of the same length.
> **pentagonal** adjective

pentathlon noun a sports contest in which athletes compete in five different events.

penthouse noun a luxurious flat at the top of a building.

pent-up adjective Pent-up emotions have been held back for a long time without release.

> **pent-up** adjective
> = inhibited, repressed, suppressed

penultimate adjective The penultimate thing in a series is the one before the last.

people peoples, peopling, peopled
plural noun 1 People are men, women and children. ▸ noun 2 all the men, women and children of a particular country or race. ▸ verb
3 If an area is peopled by a particular group, that group of people live there.

> **people** plural noun
> 1 = human beings, humanity, humans, mankind
> ▸ noun 2 = citizens, inhabitants, population, public

pepper noun 1 a hot-tasting powdered spice used for flavouring in cooking. 2 a hollow green, orange, red or yellow fruit eaten as a vegetable, with sweet-flavoured flesh.

peppermint *noun* Peppermint is a plant with a strong taste. It is used for making sweets and in medicine.

per *preposition* 'Per' is used to mean 'each' when expressing rates and ratios: *The class meets two evenings per week.*

perceive *verb* If you perceive something that is not obvious, you see it or realise it.

per cent *phrase* You use **per cent** to talk about amounts as a proportion of a hundred. An amount that is 10 per cent (10%) of a larger amount is equal to 10 hundredths of the larger amount.

percentage *noun* (MATHS) A fraction expressed as a number of hundredths.

perceptible *adjective* Something that is perceptible can be seen.

perception *noun* 1 Perception is the recognition of things using the senses, especially the sense of sight. 2 Someone who has perception realises or notices things that are not obvious. 3 Your perception of something or someone is your understanding of them.

perceptive *adjective* Someone who is perceptive realises or notices things that are not obvious. > **perceptively** *adverb*

> **perceptive** *adjective*
> = acute, astute, aware, penetrating, sharp

perch *verb* 1 If you perch on something, you sit on the edge of it. 2 When a bird perches on something, it stands on it. ▶ *noun*

3 a short rod for a bird to stand on. 4 an edible freshwater fish.

percussion *adjective, noun* (MUSIC) Percussion instruments or percussion are musical instruments that you hit to produce sounds. > **percussionist** *noun*

perennial *adjective* continually occurring or never ending.

perfect *adjective* 1 of the highest standard and without fault. 2 complete or absolute: *They have a perfect right to say so.* 3 (ENGLISH) (MFL) In grammar, the perfect tenses of a verb are used to talk about things that happened before a particular time. The **present perfect** is formed in English with the present tense of 'have' and the past participle of the main verb, as in 'She has spoken'. The **past perfect** is formed with 'had' and the past participle of the main verb, as in 'She had spoken'. ▶ *verb* 4 If you perfect something, you make it as good as it can possibly be. > **perfectly** *adverb* > **perfection** *noun*

> **perfect** *adjective*
> 1 = expert, faultless, flawless, masterly, polished, skilled
> 2 = absolute, complete, consummate, sheer, unmitigated, utter
> ▶ *verb* 4 = hone, improve, polish, refine

perfectionist *noun* someone who always tries to do everything perfectly.

perforated *adjective* Something that is perforated has had small holes made in it. > **perforation** *noun*

perform verb 1 To perform a task or action is to do it. 2 (DRAMA) To perform is to act, dance or play music in front of an audience. > **performer** noun

> **perform** verb
> 1 = carry out, complete, do, execute, fulfil 2 = act, do, play, present, put on, stage

performance noun 1 (DRAMA) an entertainment provided for an audience. 2 The performance of a task or action is the doing of it.

perfume noun 1 Perfume is a pleasant-smelling liquid for putting on the body. 2 The perfume of something is its pleasant smell. > **perfumed** adjective

perfunctory adjective done quickly without interest or care.

perhaps adverb You use 'perhaps' when you are not sure whether something is true or possible.

> **perhaps** adverb
> = conceivably, it could be, maybe, possibly

peril noun (formal) Peril is great danger. > **perilous** adjective > **perilously** adverb

perimeter noun (MATHS) The perimeter of a closed figure or shape is the length of its boundary.

period noun 1 a particular length of time. 2 one of the parts the day is divided into at school. 3 A woman's period is the monthly bleeding from her womb. > **periodic** adjective > **periodically** adverb

> **period** noun
> 1 = interval, spell, stretch, term, time, while

periodical noun a magazine.

peripheral adjective 1 of little importance in comparison with other things. 2 on or relating to the edge of an area.

periphery peripheries noun The periphery of an area is its outside edge.

perish verb 1 (formal) If someone or something perishes, they are killed or destroyed. 2 If fruit or fabric perishes, it rots. > **perishable** adjective

perjury noun (Law) If someone commits perjury, they tell a lie in court while under oath. > **perjure** verb

perk noun 1 an extra, such as a company car, offered by an employer in addition to a salary. Perk is an abbreviation for 'perquisite'. ▶ verb 2 (informal) When someone perks up, they become more cheerful. > **perky** adjective

perm noun 1 If you have a perm, your hair is curled and treated with chemicals to keep the curls for several months. ▶ verb 2 To perm someone's hair means to put a perm in it.

permanent adjective lasting for ever, or present all the time. > **permanently** adverb > **permanence** noun

> **permanent** adjective
> = abiding, constant, enduring, eternal, lasting, perpetual

permeate verb To permeate something is to spread through it and affect every part of it.

permissible adjective allowed by the rules.

permission noun If you have permission to do something, you are allowed to do it.

P

permission noun
= approval, assent *(formal)*,
authorisation, consent,
go-ahead, licence

permissive *adjective* A permissive
society allows things which some
people disapprove of.
> **permissiveness** *noun*

permit permits, permitting,
permitted *verb* 1 To permit
something is to allow it or make
it possible. ▶ *noun* 2 an official
document which says that you
are allowed to do something.

permit *verb*
1 = allow, authorise, enable,
give the green light to, grant,
sanction
▶ *noun* 2 = authorisation,
licence, pass, passport,
permission, warrant

pernicious *adjective (formal)* very
harmful.

peroxide *noun* Peroxide is a
chemical used for bleaching hair
or as an antiseptic.

perpendicular *adjective* (MATHS)
upright, or at right angles to
a horizontal line.

perpetrate *verb (formal)* To
perpetrate a crime is to commit it.
> **perpetrator** *noun*

perpetual *adjective* never ending.
> **perpetually** *adverb* > **perpetuity**
noun

perpetuate *verb* To perpetuate a
situation or belief is to cause it to
continue.

perplexed *adjective* If you are
perplexed, you are puzzled and do
not know what to do.

persecute *verb* To persecute
someone is to treat them cruelly
and unfairly over a long period

of time. > **persecution** *noun*
> **persecutor** *noun*

persecute *verb*
= hound, ill-treat, oppress, pick
on, torment, torture

persevere *verb* If you persevere,
you keep trying to do something
and do not give up.
> **perseverance** *noun*

Persian *adjective, noun* an old word
for Iranian, used especially when
referring to the older forms of the
language.

persist *verb* 1 If something
undesirable persists, it continues
to exist. 2 If you persist in doing
something, you continue in spite
of opposition or difficulty.
> **persistence** *noun* > **persistent**
adjective

person noun or persons *noun*
1 a man, woman or child. 2 (MFL)
In grammar, the first person is
the speaker (I), the second person
is the person being spoken to
(you), and the third person is
anyone else being referred to
(he, she, they).

person *noun*
1 = human, human being,
individual, living soul, soul

personal *adjective* 1 Personal
means belonging or relating to a
particular person rather than to
people in general. 2 Personal
matters relate to your feelings,
relationships and health which
you may not wish to discuss with
other people. > **personally** *adverb*

personal *adjective*
1 = individual, own, particular,
peculiar, private, special

personality personalities *noun*
1 Your personality is your

character and nature. **2** a famous person in entertainment or sport.

personality noun
1 = character, identity, individuality, make-up, nature, psyche **2** = big name, celebrity, famous name, household name, star

personification noun **1** (ENGLISH) Personification is a form of imagery in which something inanimate is described as if it has human qualities, for example 'The trees sighed and whispered as the impatient breeze stirred their branches'. **2** Someone who is the personification of some quality is a living example of that quality.

personify personifies, personifying, personified verb
1 Someone who personifies a particular quality seems to be a living example of it. **2** If you personify a thing or concept, you write or speak of it as if it had human abilities or qualities, for example 'The sun is trying to come out'.

personnel noun The personnel of an organisation are the people who work for it.

perspective noun **1** A particular perspective is one way of thinking about something. **2** (ART) Perspective is a method artists use to make some people and things seem further away than others.

perspiration noun Perspiration is the moisture that appears on your skin when you are hot or frightened.

persuade verb If someone persuades you to do something or persuades you that something is true, they make you do it or believe it by giving you very good reasons. > **persuasion** noun > **persuasive** adjective

persuade verb
= bring round (informal), coax, induce, sway, talk into, win over

pertaining adjective (formal) If information or questions are pertaining to a place or thing, they are about that place or thing.

pertinent adjective especially relevant to the subject being discussed.

perturbed adjective Someone who is perturbed is worried.

Peruvian adjective **1** belonging or relating to Peru. ▶ noun **2** someone who comes from Peru.

pervade verb Something that pervades a place is present and noticeable throughout it. > **pervasive** adjective

perverse adjective Someone who is perverse deliberately does things that are unreasonable or harmful. > **perversely** adverb > **perversity** noun

pervert verb (formal) To pervert something is to interfere with it so that it is no longer what it should be.

perverted adjective **1** Someone who is perverted has disgusting or unacceptable behaviour or ideas. **2** Something that is perverted is completely wrong.

peso pesos noun the main unit of currency in several South American countries.

pessimism noun Pessimism is the tendency to believe that bad things will happen. > **pessimist** noun

pessimistic *adjective* believing
that bad things will happen.
> **pessimistically** *adverb*

> **pessimistic** *adjective*
> = despondent, gloomy, glum,
> hopeless

pest *noun* 1 an insect or small
animal which damages plants or
food supplies. 2 (*informal*)
someone who keeps bothering or
annoying you.

> **pest** *noun*
> 1 = bane, blight, scourge
> 2 = bane, bore, nuisance, pain
> (*informal*), pain in the neck
> (*informal*)

pester *verb* If you pester someone,
you keep bothering them or
asking them to do something.

> **pester** *verb*
> = annoy, badger, bother, bug
> (*informal*), drive someone up the
> wall (*slang*), get on someone's
> nerves (*informal*)

pesticide *noun* (SCIENCE)
Pesticides are chemicals sprayed
onto plants to kill insects and
grubs.

pet pets, petting, petted *noun*
1 a tame animal kept at home.
▶ *adjective* 2 Someone's pet theory
or pet project is something that
they particularly support or feel
strongly about. ▶ *verb* 3 If you pet
a person or animal, you stroke
them affectionately.

petal *noun* The petals of a flower
are the coloured outer parts.

petite *adjective* A woman who is
petite is small and slim.

petition *noun* 1 a document
demanding official action which
is signed by a lot of people. 2 a
formal request to a court for legal

action to be taken. ▶ *verb* 3 If you
petition someone in authority,
you make a formal request to
them.

petrified *adjective* If you are
petrified, you are very frightened.

petrol *noun* (SCIENCE) Petrol is a
liquid obtained from petroleum
and used as a fuel for motor
vehicles.

petroleum *noun* Petroleum is
thick, dark oil found under the
earth or under the sea bed.

petty pettier, pettiest *adjective*
1 Petty things are small and
unimportant. 2 Petty behaviour
consists of doing small things
which are selfish and unkind.

> **petty** *adjective*
> 1 = insignificant, measly
> (*informal*), trifling, trivial,
> unimportant 2 = cheap, mean,
> small-minded

petulant *adjective* showing
unreasonable and childish
impatience or anger. > **petulantly**
adverb > **petulance** *noun*

pew *noun* a long wooden seat with
a back, which people sit on in
church.

pewter *noun* Pewter is a
silvery-grey metal made from a
mixture of tin and lead.

pH *noun* (SCIENCE) The pH of a
solution or of the soil is a
measurement of how acid or
alkaline it is. Acid solutions have
a pH of less than 7 and alkaline
solutions have a pH greater than
7. pH is an abbreviation for
'potential of hydrogen'.

phantom *noun* 1 a ghost.
▶ *adjective* 2 imagined or unreal.

pharaoh *noun* The pharaohs were
kings of ancient Egypt.

pharmaceutical *adjective* connected with the industrial production of medicines.

pharmacist *noun* a person who is qualified to prepare and sell medicines.

pharmacy pharmacies *noun* a shop where medicines are sold.

phase *noun* **1** a particular stage in the development of something. ▶ *verb* **2** To phase something is to cause it to happen gradually in stages.

PhD *noun* a degree awarded to someone who has done advanced research in a subject. PhD is an abbreviation for 'Doctor of Philosophy'.

pheasant *noun* a large, long-tailed game bird.

phenomenal *adjective* extraordinarily great or good. > **phenomenally** *adverb*

phenomenon phenomena *noun* something that happens or exists, especially something remarkable or something being considered in a scientific way.

philanthropist *noun* someone who freely gives help or money to people in need. ▶ **philanthropic** *adjective* > **philanthropy** *noun*

philistine *noun* If you call someone a philistine, you mean that they do not like art, literature or music.

philosophical or **philosophic** *adjective* Someone who is philosophical does not get upset when disappointing things happen.

philosophy philosophies *noun* **1** Philosophy is the study or creation of ideas about existence, knowledge or beliefs. **2** a set of

beliefs that a person has. > **philosopher** *noun*

phobia *noun* a great fear or hatred of something. > **phobic** *adjective*

-phobia *suffix* '-phobia' means 'fear of': *claustrophobia*.

phoenix *noun* an imaginary bird which, according to myth, burns itself to ashes every five hundred years and rises from the fire again.

phone *noun* **1** a piece of electronic equipment which allows you to speak to someone in another place by keying in or dialling their number. ▶ *verb* **2** If you phone someone, you key in or dial their number and speak to them using a phone.

-phone *suffix* '-phone' means 'giving off sound': *telephone*.

phoney phonier, phoniest; phoneys; also spelt **phony** (*informal*) *adjective* **1** false and intended to deceive. ▶ *noun* **2** Someone who is a phoney pretends to have qualities they do not possess.

photo photos *noun* (*informal*) a photograph.

photocopier *noun* a machine which makes instant copies of documents by photographing them.

photocopy photocopies, photocopying, photocopied (LIBRARY) *noun* **1** a copy of a document produced by a photocopier. ▶ *verb* **2** If you photocopy a document, you make a copy of it using a photocopier.

photogenic *adjective* Someone who is photogenic always looks nice in photographs.

P

photograph noun 1 a picture
made using a camera. ▶ verb
2 When you photograph
someone, you take a picture of
them by using a camera.
> **photographer** noun
> **photography** noun

photographic adjective
connected with photography.

photosynthesis noun (SCIENCE)
Photosynthesis is the process by
which the action of sunlight on
the chlorophyll in plants
produces the substances that
keep the plants alive.

phrase noun 1 a group of words
considered as a unit. ▶ verb
2 If you phrase something in a
particular way, you choose those
words to express it.

physical adjective 1 concerning
the body rather than the mind.
2 relating to things that can be
touched or seen, especially with
regard to their size or shape.
> **physically** adverb

physical education noun
Physical education consists of
lessons in which gymnastics or
sports are taught.

physician noun a doctor.

physics noun Physics is the
scientific study of matter, energy,
gravity, electricity, heat and
sound. > **physicist** noun

physiology noun Physiology is
the scientific study of the way the
bodies of living things work.

physiotherapy noun
Physiotherapy is medical
treatment which involves
exercise and massage.
> **physiotherapist** noun

physique noun A person's physique
is the shape and size of their body.

pi noun (MATHS) Pi is a number,
approximately 3.142 and
symbolised by the Greek letter π.
Pi is the ratio of the
circumference of a circle to its
diameter.

piano pianos (MUSIC) noun 1 a
large musical instrument with a
row of black and white keys.
When the keys are pressed, little
hammers hit wires to produce the
different notes. 2 In music, piano
is an instruction to play or sing
something quietly. > **pianist** noun

pick verb 1 To pick something is to
choose it. 2 If you pick a flower or
fruit, or pick something from a
place, you remove it with your
fingers. 3 If someone picks a lock,
they open it with a piece of wire
instead of a key. ▶ noun 4 The pick
of a group of people or things are
the best ones in it. 5 a pickaxe.
> **pick on** verb If you pick on
someone, you criticise them
unfairly or treat them unkindly.
> **pick out** verb If you pick out
someone or something, you
recognise them when they are
difficult to see, or you choose
them from among other things.
> **pick up** verb If you pick someone
or something up, you collect
them from the place where they
are waiting.

> **pick** verb
> 1 = choose, decide upon,
> hand-pick, opt for, select, settle
> on 2 = gather, harvest, pluck
> ▶ noun 4 = elite, flower, pride
> ▶ **pick on** = bait, tease,
> torment

picket verb 1 When a group of
people picket a place of work, they
stand outside to persuade other
workers to join a strike. ▶ noun

2 someone who is picketing a place.

pickle noun **1** Pickle or pickles consists of vegetables or fruit preserved in vinegar or salt water. ▶ verb **2** To pickle food is to preserve it in vinegar or salt water.

picnic picnics, picnicking, picnicked noun **1** a meal eaten out of doors. ▶ verb **2** People who are picnicking are having a picnic.

pictorial adjective relating to or using pictures.

picture noun **1** a drawing, painting or photograph of someone or something. **2** If you have a picture of something in your mind, you have an idea or impression of it. ▶ verb **3** If someone is pictured in a newspaper or magazine, a photograph of them is printed in it. **4** If you picture something, you think of it and imagine it clearly.

> **picture** noun
> **1** = drawing, illustration, painting, photograph, portrait, selfie (informal), sketch
> ▶ verb **4** = conceive of, imagine, see, visualise

picturesque adjective A place that is picturesque is very attractive and unspoiled.

pie noun a dish of meat, vegetables or fruit covered with pastry.

piece noun **1** a portion or part of something. **2** something that has been written or created, such as a work of art or a musical composition. **3** a coin: a 50 pence piece. ▶ verb **4** If you piece together a number of things, you gradually put them together to make something complete.

piece noun
1 = bit, chunk, fragment, part, portion, slice **2** = article, composition, creation, study, work
▶ verb **4** = assemble, join, mend, patch together, repair, restore

piecemeal adverb, adjective done gradually and at irregular intervals.

pier noun a large structure which sticks out into the sea at a seaside town, and which people can walk along.

pierce verb If a sharp object pierces something, it goes through it, making a hole.

> **pierce** verb
> = bore, drill, lance, penetrate, puncture

piercing adjective **1** A piercing sound is high-pitched and unpleasant. **2** Someone with piercing eyes seems to look at you very intensely.

piety noun Piety is strong and devout religious belief or behaviour.

pig noun a farm animal kept for its meat. It has pinkish skin, short legs, and a snout.

> **pig** noun
> = hog, piggy (informal), porker, swine

pigeon noun a largish bird with grey feathers, often seen in towns.

pigeonhole noun one of the sections in a frame on a wall where letters can be left.

piggyback noun If you give someone a piggyback, you carry them on your back, supporting them under their knees.

pigment noun a substance that gives something a particular colour. ▸ **pigmentation** noun

pike noun 1 a large freshwater fish of northern countries with strong teeth. 2 a medieval weapon consisting of a pointed metal blade attached to a long pole.

pile noun 1 a quantity of things lying one on top of another. 2 the soft surface of a carpet consisting of many threads standing on end. 3 (in plural) Piles are painful swellings that appear in the veins inside or just outside a person's anus. ▸ verb 4 If you pile things somewhere, you put them one on top of the other.

> **pile** noun
> 1 = heap, hoard, mound, mountain, stack 2 = down, fur, nap
> ▸ verb 4 = heap, hoard, stack

pile-up noun (informal) a road accident involving several vehicles.

pilgrim noun (RE) a person who travels to a holy place for religious reasons. ▸ **pilgrimage** noun

pill noun 1 a small, hard tablet of medicine that you swallow. 2 The pill is a type of drug that women can take regularly to prevent pregnancy.

pillage verb If a group of people pillage a place, they steal from it using violence.

pillar noun 1 a tall, narrow, solid structure, usually supporting part of a building. 2 Someone who is described as a pillar of a particular group is an active and important member of it.

pillory pillories, pillorying, pilloried verb If someone is pilloried, they are criticised severely by a lot of people.

pillow noun a rectangular cushion which you rest your head on when you are in bed.

pilot noun 1 a person who is trained to fly an aircraft. 2 a person who goes on board ships to guide them through local waters to a port. ▸ verb 3 To pilot something is to control its movement or to guide it. 4 To pilot a scheme or product is to test it to see if it would be successful.

pin pins, pinning, pinned noun 1 a thin, pointed piece of metal used to fasten together things such as pieces of fabric or paper. ▸ verb 2 If you pin something somewhere, you fasten it there with a pin or a drawing pin. 3 If someone pins you in a particular position, they hold you there so that you cannot move. 4 If you try to pin something down, you try to get or give a clear and exact description of it or statement about it.

PIN noun a security number used by the holder of a cash card or credit card. PIN is an abbreviation for 'personal identification number'.

pinch verb 1 If you pinch something, you squeeze it between your thumb and first finger. 2 (informal) If someone pinches something, they steal it. ▸ noun 3 A pinch of something is the amount that you can hold between your thumb and first finger.

pinched adjective If someone's face is pinched, it looks thin and pale.

pine *noun* 1 A pine or pine tree is an evergreen tree with very thin leaves. ▶ *verb* 2 If you pine for something, you are sad because you cannot have it.

pineapple *noun* a large, oval fruit with sweet, yellow flesh and a thick, lumpy brown skin.

ping-pong *noun* the same as **table tennis**.

pink *adjective* pale reddish-white.

pinnacle *noun* 1 a tall pointed piece of stone or rock. 2 The pinnacle of something is its best or highest point.

pinpoint *verb* If you pinpoint something, you explain or discover exactly what or where it is.

pinstripe *adjective* Pinstripe cloth has very narrow vertical stripes.

pint *noun* a unit of liquid volume equal to one eighth of a gallon or about 0.568 litres.

pioneer *noun* 1 Someone who is a pioneer in a particular activity is one of the first people to develop it. ▶ *verb* 2 Someone who pioneers a new process or invention is the first person to develop it.

pious *adjective* very religious and moral.

pip *noun* Pips are the hard seeds in a fruit.

pipe *noun* 1 a long, hollow tube through which liquid or gas can flow. 2 an object used for smoking tobacco. It consists of a small hollow bowl attached to a tube. ▶ *verb* 3 To pipe a liquid or gas somewhere is to transfer it through a pipe.

pipeline *noun* a large underground pipe that carries oil or gas over a long distance.

piper *noun* a person who plays the bagpipes.

piping *noun* Piping consists of pipes and tubes.

pirate *noun* Pirates were sailors who attacked and robbed other ships.

Pisces *noun* Pisces is the twelfth sign of the zodiac, represented by two fish. People born between February 19th and March 20th are born under this sign.

pistol *noun* a small gun held in the hand.

piston *noun* a cylinder or disc that slides up and down inside a tube. Pistons make parts of engines move.

pit *noun* 1 a large hole in the ground. 2 a small hollow in the surface of something. 3 a coal mine.

> **pit** *noun*
> 1 = chasm, hole, pothole

pitch *noun* 1 (PE) an area of ground marked out for playing a game such as football. 2 (MUSIC) The pitch of a sound is how high or low it is. 3 a black substance used in road tar and also for making boats and roofs waterproof. ▶ *verb* 4 If you pitch something somewhere, you throw it with a lot of force. 5 If you pitch something at a particular level of difficulty, you set it at that level. 6 When you pitch a tent, you fix it in an upright position.

pitcher *noun* a large jug.

pitfall *noun* The pitfalls of a situation are its difficulties or dangers.

pith *noun* the white substance between the outer skin and the flesh of an orange or lemon.

pitiful adjective Someone or something that is pitiful is in such a sad or weak situation that you feel pity for them.

pittance noun a very small amount of money.

pitted adjective covered in small hollows.

pity pities, pitying, pitied verb 1 If you pity someone, you feel very sorry for them. ▶ noun 2 Pity is a feeling of being sorry for someone. 3 If you say that it is a pity about something, you are expressing your disappointment about it.

> **pity** verb
> 1 = feel for, feel sorry for, sympathise with
> ▶ noun 2 = charity, compassion, kindness, mercy, sympathy, understanding 3 = crime (informal), crying shame

pivot verb 1 If something pivots, it balances or turns on a central point. ▶ noun 2 the central point on which something balances or turns.

pivotal adjective A pivotal role, point or figure is very important to the success of something.

pixel noun (ICT) the smallest area on a computer screen which can be given a separate colour by the computer.

pixie noun an imaginary little creature in fairy stories.

pizza noun a flat piece of dough covered with cheese, tomato and other savoury food.

placard noun a large notice carried on a demonstration or displayed in a public place.

placate verb If you placate someone, you stop them feeling

angry by doing something to please them.

place noun 1 any point, building or area. 2 the position where something belongs: *She set the holder in its place on the table.* 3 If you have a place in a group or at a college, you are a member or are accepted as a student. 4 a particular point or stage in a sequence of things: *second place in the race.* ▶ phrase 5 **take place** means to happen. ▶ verb 6 If you place something somewhere, you put it there. 7 If you place an order, you order something.

> **place** noun
> 1 = area, location, point, position, site, spot
> ▶ phrase 5 **take place** = come about, go on, happen, occur
> ▶ verb 6 = deposit, locate, plant, position, put, situate

placebo placebos noun a substance given to a patient in place of a drug and from which, though it has no active ingredients, the patient may imagine they get some benefit.

placenta placentas noun (SCIENCE) The placenta is the mass of veins and tissues in the womb of a pregnant woman or animal. It gives the foetus food and oxygen.

placid adjective calm and not easily excited or upset. > **placidly** adverb

plagiarism noun Plagiarism is copying someone else's work or ideas and pretending that it is your own. > **plagiarist** noun > **plagiarise** verb

plague plagues, plaguing, plagued noun 1 Plague is a very infectious disease that kills large numbers of people. 2 A plague of unpleasant things is a large number of them occurring at the same time. ▶ verb 3 If problems plague you, they keep causing you trouble.

plaice noun an edible European flat fish.

plaid noun Plaid is woven material with a tartan design.

plain adjective 1 very simple in style with no pattern or decoration. 2 obvious and easy to recognise or understand. 3 A person who is plain is not at all beautiful or attractive. ▶ adverb 4 You can use 'plain' before a noun or adjective to emphasise it. ▶ noun 5 a large, flat area of land with very few trees. > **plainly** adverb

plain adjective
1 = austere, bare, spartan, stark
2 = clear, comprehensible, distinct, evident, obvious, unmistakable

plaintiff noun a person who has brought a court case against another person.

plan plans, planning, planned noun 1 a method of achieving something that has been worked out beforehand. 2 a detailed diagram or drawing of something that is to be made. ▶ verb 3 If you plan something, you decide in detail what it is to be and how to do it. 4 If you are planning to do something, you intend to do it.

plan noun
1 = method, proposal, scheme, strategy, system 2 = blueprint, diagram, layout, scale drawing
▶ verb 3 = arrange, design, devise, draft, formulate

plane noun 1 a vehicle with wings and engines that enable it to fly. 2 a flat surface. 3 You can refer to the standard at which something is done as a particular plane. 4 a tool with a flat bottom with a sharp blade in it. You move it over a piece of wood to remove thin pieces from the surface. ▶ verb 5 If you plane a piece of wood, you smooth its surface with a plane.

planet noun a round object in space which moves around the sun or a star and is lit by light from it. > **planetary** adjective

plank noun a long rectangular piece of wood.

plankton noun Plankton is a layer of tiny plants and animals that live just below the surface of a sea or lake.

plant noun 1 a living thing that grows in the earth and has stems, leaves and roots. 2 a factory or power station. ▶ verb 3 When you plant a seed or plant, you put it into the ground. 4 If you plant something somewhere, you put it there firmly or secretly.

plantation noun 1 a large area of land where crops such as tea, cotton or sugar are grown. 2 a large number of trees planted together.

plaque noun 1 a flat piece of metal which is fixed to a wall and has an inscription in memory of a famous person or event. 2 Plaque is a substance which forms around your teeth and consists of bacteria, saliva and food.

plasma noun Plasma is the clear fluid part of blood.

plaster noun 1 Plaster is a paste made of sand, lime and water, which is used to form a smooth surface for inside walls and ceilings. **2** a strip of sticky material with a small pad, used for covering cuts on your body. ▶ *verb* **3** To plaster a wall is to cover it with a layer of plaster. ▶ *phrase* **4** If your arm or leg is **in plaster**, it has a plaster cast on it to protect a broken bone. ▶ **plasterer** *noun*

plastered *adjective* **1** If something is plastered to a surface, it is stuck there. **2** If something is plastered with things, they are all over its surface.

plastic *noun* **1** Plastic is a substance made by a chemical process that can be moulded when soft to make a wide range of objects. ▶ *adjective* **2** made of plastic.

plastic surgery *noun* Plastic surgery is surgery to replace or repair damaged skin or to improve a person's appearance by changing the shape of their features.

plate *noun* **1** a flat dish used to hold food. **2** a flat piece of metal or other hard material used for various purposes in machinery or building. **3** (GEOGRAPHY) a large part of the earth's surface.

plateau plateaus or plateaux *noun* (GEOGRAPHY) a large area of high and fairly flat land.

platform *noun* **1** a raised structure on which someone or something can stand. **2** the raised area in a railway station where passengers get on and off trains.

platinum *noun* Platinum is a valuable silver-coloured metal. Its atomic number is 78 and its symbol is Pt.

platitude *noun* a statement made as if it were significant but which

has become meaningless or boring because it has been used so many times before.

platonic *adjective* A platonic relationship is simply one of friendship and does not involve romantic attraction.

platoon *noun* a small group of soldiers, commanded by a lieutenant.

platter *noun* a large serving plate.

platypus *noun* A platypus or duck-billed platypus is an Australian mammal which lives in rivers. It has brown fur, webbed feet, and a bill like a duck.

plaudits *plural noun* (formal) Plaudits are expressions of admiration.

plausible *adjective* An explanation that is plausible seems likely to be true. > **plausibility** *noun*

play *verb* **1** When children play, they take part in games or use toys. **2** When you play a sport or match, you take part in. **3** If an actor plays a character in a play or film, he or she performs that role. **4** If you play a musical instrument, you produce music from it. **5** If you play recorded music, you operate a machine in order to produce that music. ▶ *noun* **6** a piece of drama performed in the theatre or on television. > **player** *noun*

play *verb*
1 = amuse yourself, entertain yourself, frolic, have fun
2 = compete, participate, take on, take part, vie with
▶ *noun* **6** = comedy, drama, pantomime, show, tragedy

playboy *noun* a rich man who spends his time enjoying himself.

playful *adjective* **1** friendly and light-hearted. **2** lively. > **playfully** *adverb*

playground *noun* a special area for children to play in.

playgroup *noun* an informal kind of school for very young children where they learn by playing.

playing field *noun* an area of grass where people play sports.

playwright *noun* (ENGLISH) (DRAMA) a person who writes plays.

plaza *noun* an open square in a city.

plea *noun* **1** an emotional request. **2** In a court of law, someone's plea is their statement that they are guilty or not guilty.

plead *verb* **1** If you plead with someone, you ask them in an intense emotional way to do something. **2** When a person pleads guilty or not guilty, they state in court that they are guilty or not guilty of a crime.

> **plead** *verb*
> **1** = appeal, ask, beg, beseech (*literary*), implore

pleasant *adjective* **1** enjoyable or attractive. **2** friendly or charming. > **pleasantly** *adverb*

> **pleasant** *adjective*
> **1** = agreeable, delightful, enjoyable, lekker (*South African; slang*), lovely, nice, pleasurable
> **2** = affable, amiable, charming, friendly, likable *or* likeable, nice

please *adverb* **1** You say please when you are asking someone politely to do something.
> *verb* **2** If something pleases you, it makes you feel happy and satisfied.

> **please** *verb*
> **2** = amuse, charm, delight, entertain

pleased *adjective* happy or satisfied.

> **pleased** *adjective*
> = contented, delighted, glad, happy, satisfied

pleasing *adjective* attractive, satisfying or enjoyable.

pleasure *noun* **1** Pleasure is a feeling of happiness, satisfaction or enjoyment. **2** an activity that you enjoy. > **pleasurable** *adjective*

> **pleasure** *noun*
> **1** = amusement, enjoyment, happiness, joy, satisfaction

pleat *noun* a permanent fold in fabric made by folding one part over another.

plebiscite *noun* (*formal*) a vote on a matter of national importance in which all the voters in a country can take part.

pledge *noun* **1** a solemn promise.
> *verb* **2** If you pledge something, you promise that you will do it or give it.

plentiful *adjective* existing in large numbers or amounts and readily available. > **plentifully** *adverb*

> **plentiful** *adjective*
> = abundant, ample, bountiful, copious, infinite

plenty *noun* If there is plenty of something, there is a lot of it.

> **plenty** *noun*
> = enough, great deal, heaps (*informal*), lots (*informal*), plethora

plethora *noun* A plethora of something is an amount that is greater than you need.

P

pliable *adjective* **1** If something is pliable, you can bend it without breaking it. **2** Someone who is pliable can be easily influenced or controlled.

pliers *plural noun* Pliers are a small tool with metal jaws for holding small objects and bending wire.

plight *noun* Someone's plight is the very difficult or dangerous situation that they are in.

plinth *noun* a block of stone on which a statue or pillar stands.

plod plods, plodding, plodded *verb* If you plod somewhere, you walk there slowly and heavily.

plonk *verb* (informal) If you plonk something down, you put it down heavily and carelessly.

plot plots, plotting, plotted *noun* **1** a secret plan made by a group of people. **2** (ENGLISH) The plot of a novel or play is the story. **3** a small piece of land. ▶ *verb* **4** If people plot to do something, they plan it secretly. **5** If someone plots the course of a plane or ship on a map, or plots a graph, they mark the points in the correct places.

> **plot** *noun*
> **1** = conspiracy, intrigue, plan, scheme **2** = narrative, scenario, story, story line
> ▶ *verb* **4** = conspire, hatch, plan, scheme

plough *noun* **1** a large farming tool that is pulled across a field to turn the soil over before planting seeds. ▶ *verb* **2** When someone ploughs land, they use a plough to turn over the soil.

ploy *noun* a clever plan or way of behaving in order to get something that you want.

pluck *verb* **1** To pluck a fruit or flower is to remove it with a sharp pull. **2** To pluck a chicken or other dead bird means to pull its feathers out before cooking it. **3** When you pluck a stringed instrument, you pull the strings and let them go. ▶ *noun* **4** Pluck is courage. ▶ **plucky** *adjective*

plug plugs, plugging, plugged *noun* **1** a plastic object with metal prongs that can be pushed into a socket to connect an appliance to the electricity supply. **2** a disc of rubber or metal with which you block up the hole in a sink or bath. ▶ *verb* **3** If you plug a hole, you block it with something.

> **plug** *noun*
> **2** = bung, cork, stopper
> ▶ *verb* **3** = block, fill, seal

plum *noun* a small fruit with a smooth red or yellow skin and a large stone in the middle.

plumage *noun* A bird's plumage is its feathers.

plumber *noun* a person who connects and repairs water pipes.

plumbing *noun* The plumbing in a building is the system of water pipes, sinks and toilets.

plume *noun* a large, brightly coloured feather.

plummet plummets, plummeting, plummeted *verb* If something plummets, it falls very quickly.

plump *adjective* rather fat.

> **plump** *adjective*
> = beefy (informal), burly, chubby, fat, stout, tubby

plunder *verb* If someone plunders a place, they steal things from it.

plunge verb 1 If something plunges, it falls suddenly. 2 If you plunge an object into something, you push it in quickly. 3 If you plunge into an activity or state, you suddenly become involved in it or affected by it. ▶ noun 4 a sudden fall.

plural noun (ENGLISH) (MFL) the form of a word that is used to refer to two or more people or things, for example the plural of 'chair' is 'chairs', and the plural of 'mouse' is 'mice'.

pluralism noun Pluralism is the belief that it is possible for different social and religious groups to live together peacefully while keeping their own beliefs and traditions. > **pluralist** adjective, noun

plus 1 You use 'plus' to show that one number is being added to another. 2 You can use 'plus' when you mention an additional item: He wrote a history of Scotland plus a history of British literature. ▶ adjective 3 slightly more than the number mentioned: a career of 25 years plus.

plush adjective (informal) very expensive and smart.

Pluto noun Pluto is a dwarf planet in the solar system.

ply plies, plying, plied verb 1 If you ply someone with things or questions, you keep giving them things or asking them questions. 2 To ply a trade is to do a particular job as your work. ▶ noun 3 Ply is the thickness of wool or thread, measured by the number of strands it is made from.

plywood noun Plywood is wooden board made from several thin sheets of wood glued together under pressure.

p.m. used to specify times between 12 noon and 12 midnight, eg He went to bed at 9 p.m. It is an abbreviation for the Latin phrase 'post meridiem', which means 'after noon'.

pneumatic adjective (DGT) operated by or filled with compressed air.

pneumonia noun Pneumonia is a serious disease which affects a person's lungs and makes breathing difficult.

poach verb 1 If someone poaches animals from someone else's land, they illegally catch the animals for food. 2 When you poach food, you cook it gently in hot liquid. > **poacher** noun

pocket noun 1 a small pouch that forms part of a piece of clothing. 2 A pocket of something is a small area of it.

pocket money noun Pocket money is an amount of money given regularly to children by their parents.

pod noun a long, narrow seed container that grows on plants such as peas or beans.

podium noun a small platform, often one on which someone stands to make a speech.

poem noun a piece of writing in which the words are arranged in short rhythmic lines, often with a rhyme.

poet noun a person who writes poems.

poetic adjective 1 very beautiful and expressive. 2 relating to poetry. > **poetically** adverb

poetry noun Poetry is poems, considered as a form of literature.

P

poignant *adjective* Something that is poignant has a strong emotional effect on you, often making you feel sad.
> **poignancy** *noun*

point *noun* 1 an opinion or fact expressed by someone. 2 a quality: *Tact was never her strong point.* 3 the purpose or meaning something has. 4 a position or time. 5 a single mark in a competition. 6 the thin, sharp end of something such as a needle or knife. 7 The points of a compass are the 32 directions indicated on it. 8 The decimal point in a number is the dot separating the whole number from the fraction. 9 On a railway track, the points are the levers and rails which enable a train to move from one track to another.
▶ *verb* 10 If you point at something, you stick out your finger to show where it is. 11 If something points in a particular direction, it faces that way.

point *noun*
2 = attribute, characteristic, feature, quality, side, trait
3 = aim, goal, intention, object, purpose 6 = nib, prong, tip

point-blank *adjective*
1 Something that is shot at point-blank range is shot with a gun held very close to it. ▶ *adverb*
2 If you say something point-blank, you say it directly without explanation or apology.

pointed *adjective* 1 A pointed object has a thin, sharp end. 2 Pointed comments express criticism. > **pointedly** *adverb*

pointer *noun* a piece of information which helps you to understand something.

pointless *adjective* Something that is pointless has no purpose.
> **pointlessly** *adverb*

point of view points of view *noun* Your point of view is your opinion about something or your attitude towards it.

poise *noun* Someone who has poise is calm and dignified.

poised *adjective* If you are poised to do something, you are ready to do it at any moment.

poison *noun* 1 Poison is a substance that can kill people or animals if they swallow it or absorb it. ▶ *verb* 2 To poison someone is to try to kill them with poison.

poison *noun*
1 = toxin, venom

poisonous *adjective* containing something that causes death or illness.

poisonous *adjective*
= noxious, toxic, venomous

poke *verb* 1 If you poke someone or something, you push at them quickly with your finger or a sharp object. 2 Something that pokes out of another thing appears from underneath or behind it. ▶ *noun* 3 a sharp jab or prod.

poke *verb*
1 = dig, elbow, jab, nudge, prod, stab
▶ *noun* 3 = dig, jab, nudge, prod

poker *noun* 1 Poker is a card game in which the players make bets on the cards dealt to them. 2 a long metal rod used for moving coals or logs in a fire.

polar *adjective* relating to the area around the North and South Poles.

polar bear noun a large white bear which lives in the area around the North Pole.

pole noun 1 a long rounded piece of wood or metal. 2 The earth's poles are the two opposite ends of its axis.

Pole noun someone who comes from Poland.

pole vault noun The pole vault is an athletics event in which contestants jump over a high bar using a long flexible pole to lift themselves into the air.

police plural noun 1 (CITIZENSHIP) The police are the people who are officially responsible for making sure that people obey the law.
▶ verb 2 To police an area is to keep law and order by means of the police or an armed force.

policeman policemen noun a man who is a member of a police force.

policewoman policewomen noun a woman who is a member of a police force.

policy policies noun 1 a set of plans, especially in politics or business. 2 An insurance policy is a document which shows an agreement made with an insurance company.

polio noun Polio is an infectious disease that is caused by a virus and often results in paralysis. Polio is short for 'poliomyelitis'.

polish verb 1 If you polish something, you put polish on it or rub it with a cloth to make it shine. 2 If you polish a skill or technique you have, you work on it in order to improve it. ▶ noun 3 Polish is a substance that you put on an object to clean it and make it shine. 4 Something that has polish is elegant and of good quality. > **polished** adjective

> **polish** verb
> 1 = buff, shine, wax 2 = brush up, improve, perfect, refine
> ▶ noun 4 = class (informal), elegance, finesse, grace, refinement, style

Polish adjective 1 belonging or relating to Poland. ▶ noun 2 Polish is the main language spoken in Poland.

polite adjective 1 Someone who is polite has good manners and behaves considerately towards other people. 2 Polite society is cultivated and refined. > **politely** adverb

> **polite** adjective
> 1 = civil, courteous, respectful, well-behaved, well-mannered 2 = cultured, genteel, refined, sophisticated, urbane

politeness noun the quality of having good manners and behaving considerately.

> **politeness** noun
> = civility, courtesy, decency, etiquette

political adjective 1 (GEOGRAPHY) relating to the state, government or public administration. 2 relating to or interested in politics. > **politically** adverb

politically correct adjective careful not to offend or designed not to offend minority or disadvantaged groups.

politician noun a person involved in the government of a country.

politics noun (HISTORY) Politics is the activity and planning concerned with achieving power and control in a country or organisation.

P

polka noun a fast dance in which couples dance together in circles around the room.

poll noun 1 a survey in which people are asked their opinions about something. 2 (in plural) A political election can be referred to as the polls. ▶ verb 3 If you are polled on something, you are asked your opinion about it as part of a survey.

pollen noun (SCIENCE) Pollen is a fine yellow powder produced by flowers in order to fertilise other flowers of the same species.

pollutant noun a substance that causes pollution.

pollute verb To pollute water or air is to make it dirty and dangerous to use or live in. > **polluted** adjective

> **pollute** verb
> = contaminate, infect, poison, taint

pollution noun (GEOGRAPHY) Pollution of the environment happens when dirty, dangerous or unwanted substances get into the air, water or soil.

polo noun Polo is a game played between two teams of players on horseback. The players use wooden hammers with long handles to hit a ball.

polyester noun (DGT) A synthetic fibre, used especially to make clothes.

polygamy noun Polygamy is being more than one marriage at the same time. > **polygamous** adjective

polystyrene noun Polystyrene is a very light plastic, used especially as insulating material or to make containers.

polythene noun (SCIENCE) Polythene is a type of plastic that is used to make thin sheets or bags.

polyunsaturated adjective Polyunsaturated oils and margarines are made mainly from vegetable fats and are considered to be healthier than most other oils. > **polyunsaturate** noun

pomegranate noun a round fruit with a thick reddish skin. It contains a lot of small seeds.

pomp noun Pomp is the use of ceremony, fine clothes and decorations on special occasions.

pompous adjective behaving in a way that is too serious and self-important. > **pomposity** noun

> **pompous** adjective
> = arrogant, grandiose, ostentatious, pretentious, puffed up

pond noun a small, usually man-made area of water.

ponder verb If you ponder, you think about something deeply.

> **ponder** verb
> = brood, consider, contemplate, mull over, reflect, think

ponderous adjective dull, slow and serious. > **ponderously** adverb

pong noun (informal) an unpleasant smell.

pontiff noun (formal) The pontiff is the Pope.

pony ponies noun a small horse.

ponytail noun a hairstyle in which long hair is tied at the back of the head and hangs down like a tail.

poodle noun a type of dog with curly hair.

pool noun 1 a small area of still water. 2 Pool is a game in which players try to hit coloured balls into pockets around the table using long sticks called cues. 3 A pool of people, money or things is a group or collection used or shared by several people. 4 (in plural) The pools are a competition in which people try to guess the results of football matches. ▶ verb 5 If people pool their resources, they gather together the things they have so that they can be shared or used by all of them.

poor adjective 1 Poor people have very little money and few possessions. 2 Poor places are inhabited by people with little money and show signs of neglect. 3 You use 'poor' to show sympathy: *Poor you!* 4 'Poor' also means of a low quality or standard.

> **poor** adjective
> 1 = broke (informal), destitute, hard up (informal), impoverished, penniless, poverty-stricken 4 = feeble, inferior, mediocre, second-rate, shoddy, unsatisfactory

poorly adjective 1 feeling unwell or ill. ▶ adverb 2 badly.

pop pops, popping, popped noun 1 Pop is modern music played and enjoyed especially by young people. 2 (informal) You can refer to fizzy, nonalcoholic drinks as pop. 3 a short, sharp sound. ▶ verb 4 If something pops, it makes a sudden sharp sound. 5 (informal) If you pop something somewhere, you put it there quickly. 6 (informal) If you pop somewhere, you go there quickly.

popcorn noun Popcorn is a snack consisting of grains of maize heated until they puff up and burst.

Pope noun (RE) The Pope is the head of the Roman Catholic Church.

poppy poppies noun a plant with a large, red flower on a hairy stem.

populace noun (formal) The populace of a country is its people.

popular adjective 1 liked or approved of by a lot of people. 2 involving or intended for ordinary people. > **popularly** adverb > **popularity** noun > **popularise** verb

> **popular** adjective
> 1 = fashionable, favourite, in demand, in favour, sought-after, well-liked
> 2 = common, conventional, general, universal

populate verb The people or animals that populate an area live there.

population noun The population of a place is the people who live there, or the number of people living there.

porcelain noun Porcelain is a delicate, hard material used to make crockery and ornaments.

porch noun a covered area at the entrance to a building.

pore noun 1 The pores in your skin or on the surface of a plant are very small holes which allow moisture to pass through. ▶ verb 2 If you pore over a piece of writing or a diagram, you study it carefully.

pork noun Pork is meat from a pig which has not been salted or smoked.

P

porridge noun Porridge is a thick, sticky food made from oats cooked in water or milk.

port noun 1 a town or area which has a harbour or docks. 2 Port is a kind of strong, sweet red wine. ▶ adjective 3 The port side of a ship is the left side when you are facing the front.

portable adjective designed to be easily carried.

porter noun 1 a person whose job is to be in charge of the entrance of a building, greeting and directing visitors. 2 A porter in a railway station or hospital is a person whose job is to carry or move things.

portfolio portfolios noun 1 a thin, flat case for carrying papers. 2 A portfolio is also a group of selected duties, investments or items of artwork.

portion noun a part or amount of something.

> **portion** noun
> = bit, chunk, helping, part, piece, segment, serving

portrait noun (ART) a picture or photograph of someone.

portray verb When an actor, artist or writer portrays someone or something, they represent or describe them. > **portrayal** noun

Portuguese adjective 1 belonging or relating to Portugal. ▶ noun 2 someone who comes from Portugal. 3 Portuguese is the main language spoken in Portugal and Brazil.

pose verb 1 If something poses a problem, it is the cause of the problem. 2 If you pose a question, you ask it. 3 If you pose as

someone else, you pretend to be that person in order to deceive people. ▶ noun 4 a way of standing, sitting or lying.

> **pose** verb
> 2 = ask, put, submit
> 3 = impersonate, masquerade as, pass yourself off as, pretend to be

posh adjective (informal) 1 smart, fashionable and expensive. 2 upper-class.

> **posh** adjective
> 1 = classy (informal), elegant, exclusive, fashionable, smart, stylish, up-market
> 2 = aristocratic, genteel, upper-class

position noun 1 (DRAMA) The position of someone or something is the place where they are or ought to be. 2 When someone or something is in a particular position, they are sitting or lying in that way. 3 a job or post in an organisation. 4 The position that you are in at a particular time is the situation that you are in. ▶ verb 5 To position something somewhere is to put it there.

> **position** noun
> 1 = location, place, point, whereabouts
> ▶ verb 5 = arrange, lay out, locate, place, put

positive adjective 1 completely sure about something. 2 confident and hopeful. 3 showing approval or encouragement: I anticipate a positive response. 4 (MATHS) A positive number is greater than zero. > **positively** adverb

positive *adjective*
1 = certain, confident, convinced, sure
3 = constructive, helpful

possess *verb* 1 If you possess a particular quality, you have it. 2 If you possess something, you own it. 3 If a feeling or belief possesses you, it strongly influences you. > **possessor** *noun*

possess *verb*
1 = be blessed with, be born with, enjoy, have 2 = acquire, control, hold, occupy, seize, take over

possession *noun* 1 If something is in your possession or if you are in possession of it, you have it. 2 Your possessions are the things that you own or that you have with you.

possession *noun*
1 = control, custody, ownership, tenure 2 = assets, belongings, effects, estate, property, things

possessive *adjective* 1 A person who is possessive about someone or something wants to keep them to themselves. ▶ *noun* 2 In grammar, the possessive is the form of a noun or pronoun used to show possession: *my car*; *That's hers.*

possibility possibilities *noun* something that might be true or might happen.

possibility *noun*
= chance, hope, likelihood, odds, prospect, risk

possible *adjective* 1 likely to happen or able to be done. 2 likely or capable of being true or correct. > **possibly** *adverb*

possible *adjective*
1 = attainable, feasible, practicable, viable, workable 2 = conceivable, imaginable, likely, potential

possum *noun* In Australian and New Zealand English, a possum is a phalanger, a marsupial with thick fur and a long tail.

post *noun* 1 The post is the system by which letters and parcels are collected and delivered. 2 a job or official position in an organisation. 3 a strong, upright pole fixed into the ground. 4 a message or article published on a website. ▶ *verb* 5 If you post a letter, you send it to someone by putting it into a postbox. 6 If you are posted somewhere, you are sent by your employers to work there. 7 If you post a message or article, you publish it on a website. > **postal** *adjective*

post- *prefix* after a particular time or event: *his postwar career.*

postage *noun* Postage is the money that you pay to send letters and parcels by post.

postcard *noun* a card, often with a picture on one side, which you write on and send without an envelope.

postcode *noun* a short sequence of letters and numbers at the end of an address which helps the post office to sort the mail.

poster *noun* a large notice or picture that is stuck on a wall as an advertisement or for decoration.

posterior *noun* (humorous) A person's posterior is their bottom.

posterity *noun* (formal) You can refer to the future and the people who will be alive then as posterity.

posthumous *adjective* happening or awarded after a person's death. > **posthumously** *adverb*

postman postmen *noun* someone who collects and delivers letters and parcels sent by post.

postmortem *noun* a medical examination of a dead body to find out how the person died.

post office *noun* 1 The Post Office is the national organisation responsible for postal services. 2 a building where you can buy stamps and post letters.

postpone *verb* If you postpone an event, you arrange for it to take place at a later time than was originally planned. > **postponement** *noun*

> **postpone** *verb*
> = adjourn, defer, delay, put back, put off, shelve

posture *noun* Your posture is the position or manner in which you hold your body.

pot *noun* a deep round container; also used to refer to its contents.

potato potatoes *noun* a white vegetable that has a brown or red skin and grows underground.

potent *adjective* effective or powerful. > **potency** *noun*

potential *adjective* 1 capable of becoming the thing mentioned: *potential customers*. ▶ *noun* 2 Your potential is your ability to achieve success in the future. > **potentially** *adverb*

> **potential** *adjective*
> 1 = likely, possible, probable
> ▶ *noun* 2 = ability, aptitude, capability, capacity, power, wherewithal

pothole *noun* 1 a hole in the surface of a road caused by bad weather or traffic. 2 an underground cavern.

potion *noun* a drink containing medicine, poison or supposed magical powers.

potted *adjective* Potted meat or fish is cooked and put into a small sealed container to preserve it.

potter *noun* 1 a person who makes pottery. ▶ *verb* 2 If you potter about, you pass the time doing pleasant, unimportant things.

pottery *noun* 1 Pottery is pots, dishes and other items made from clay and fired in a kiln. 2 Pottery is also the craft of making pottery.

potty potties; pottier, pottiest *noun* 1 a bowl which a small child can sit on and use instead of a toilet. ▶ *adjective* 2 (*informal*) crazy or foolish.

pouch *noun* 1 a small, soft container with a fold-over top. 2 Animals like kangaroos have a pouch, which is a pocket of skin in which they carry their young.

poultry *noun* Chickens, turkeys and other birds kept for their meat or eggs are referred to as poultry.

pounce *verb* If an animal or person pounces on something, they leap and grab it.

pound *noun* 1 The pound is the main unit of currency in Britain and in some other countries. 2 a unit of weight equal to 16 ounces or about 0.454 kilograms. ▶ *verb* 3 If you pound something, you hit it repeatedly with your fist. 4 If you pound a substance, you crush it into a powder or paste. 5 If your heart is pounding, it is beating very strongly and quickly. **6** If you pound somewhere, you run there with heavy noisy steps.

pour verb **1** If you pour a liquid out of a container, you make it flow out by tipping the container. **2** If something pours somewhere, it flows there quickly and in large quantities. **3** When it is raining heavily, you can say that it is pouring.

> **pour** verb
> **2** = course, flow, gush, run, spout, stream

pout verb If you pout, you stick out your lips or bottom lip.

poverty noun (GEOGRAPHY) the state of being very poor.

> **poverty** noun
> = destitution, hardship, insolvency, want

powder noun **1** Powder consists of many tiny particles of a solid substance. ▶ verb **2** If you powder a surface, you cover it with powder. > **powdery** adjective

power noun **1** Someone who has power has a lot of control over people and activities. **2** Someone who has the power to do something has the ability to do it. **3** Power is also the authority to do something. **4** The power of something is the physical strength that it has to move things. **5** Power is energy obtained, for example, by burning fuel or using the wind or waves. **6** (MATHS) In maths, a power is the product of a number multiplied by itself a certain number of times. For example, the third power of 10 is 1000. **7** (SCIENCE) In physics, power is the energy transferred from one thing to

another in one second. It is measured in watts. ▶ verb **8** Something that powers a machine provides the energy for it to work.

> **power** noun
> **1** = ascendancy (formal), control, dominion (formal), sovereignty, supremacy **3** = authorisation, authority, licence, privilege, right **4** = brawn, might, strength, vigour

powerful adjective **1** able to control people and events. **2** having great physical strength. **3** having a strong effect. > **powerfully** adverb

> **powerful** adjective
> **1** = commanding, dominant, influential **2** = mighty, strapping, strong, sturdy, vigorous **3** = compelling, convincing, effective, forceful, persuasive, telling

powerless adjective unable to control or influence events.

> **powerless** adjective
> = helpless, impotent, incapable

power station noun a place where electricity is generated.

practicable adjective If a task or plan is practicable, it can be carried out successfully.

practical adjective **1** The practical aspects of something are those that involve experience and real situations rather than ideas or theories. **2** sensible and likely to be effective. **3** Someone who is practical is able to deal effectively and sensibly with problems. ▶ noun **4** an examination in which you make or perform something rather than simply write. > **practicality** noun

practical adjective
1 = applied, pragmatic
2 = functional, sensible
3 = accomplished, experienced,
proficient, seasoned, skilled,
veteran

practically adverb 1 almost but
not completely or exactly: *The
house was practically a wreck.* 2 in a
practical way.

practice noun 1 You can refer to
something that people do
regularly as a practice. 2 Practice
is regular training or exercise.
3 A doctor's or lawyer's practice
is his or her business.

practice noun
1 = custom, habit, method,
routine, way 2 = drill, exercise,
preparation, rehearsal,
training

practise verb 1 If you practise
something, you do it regularly in
order to improve. 2 People who
practise a religion, custom or
craft regularly take part in the
activities associated with it.
3 Someone who practises
medicine or law works as a
doctor or lawyer.

practise verb
1 = polish, rehearse, train 2 = do,
follow, observe

practised adjective Someone who
is practised at doing something is
very skilful at it.

pragmatic adjective A pragmatic
way of considering or doing
something is a practical rather
than theoretical way.
> **pragmatically** adverb
> **pragmatism** noun

prairie noun a large area of flat,
grassy land in North America.

praise verb 1 If you praise someone
or something, you express strong
approval of their qualities or
achievements. ▶ noun 2 Praise
is what is said or written in
approval of someone's qualities or
achievements.

praise verb
1 = admire, applaud, approve,
congratulate, pay tribute to
▶ noun 2 = accolade, approval,
commendation,
congratulation, tribute

pram noun a baby's cot on wheels.

prance verb Someone who is
prancing around is walking with
exaggerated movements.

prank noun a childish trick.

prawn noun a small, pink, edible
shellfish with a long tail.

pray verb (RE) When someone
prays, they speak to God to give
thanks or to ask for help.

prayer noun 1 (RE) Prayer is the
activity of praying. 2 (RE) the
words said when someone prays.

pre- prefix 'Pre-' means before a
particular time or event: *pre-war.*

preach verb When someone
preaches, they give a short talk on
a religious or moral subject as
part of a church service.
> **preacher** noun

precarious adjective 1 If your
situation is precarious, you may
fail in what you are doing at any
time. 2 Something that is
precarious is likely to fall because
it is not well balanced or secured.
> **precariously** adverb

precaution noun an action that is
intended to prevent something
from happening.
> **precautionary** adjective

P

precaution *noun*
= insurance, preventative measure, protection, provision, safeguard

precede *verb* 1 Something that precedes another thing happens or occurs before it. 2 If you precede someone somewhere, you go in front of them. > **preceding** *adjective*

precedence *noun* If something takes precedence over other things, it is the most important thing and should be dealt with first.

precedent *noun* An action or decision that is regarded as a precedent is used as a guide in taking similar action or decisions later.

precinct *noun* 1 A shopping precinct is a pedestrian shopping area. 2 (*in plural, formal*) The precincts of a place are its buildings and land.

precious *adjective* Something that is precious is valuable or very important and should be looked after or used carefully.

precious *adjective*
= expensive, invaluable, priceless, prized, valuable

precipice *noun* a very steep rock face.

precipitate *verb* (*formal*) If something precipitates an event or situation, it causes it to happen suddenly.

precipitation *noun* (GEOGRAPHY) Precipitation is any kind of moisture that falls from the sky; used especially when stating the amount that falls during a particular period.

precise *adjective* exact and accurate

in every detail. > **precisely** *adverb* > **precision** *noun*

precise *adjective*
= accurate, actual, correct, exact, particular, specific, very

preclude *verb* (*formal*) If something precludes an event or situation, it prevents it from happening.

precocious *adjective* Precocious children behave in a way that seems too advanced for their age.

preconceived *adjective* Preconceived ideas about something have been formed without any real experience or information. > **preconception** *noun*

precondition *noun* If something is a precondition for another thing, it must happen before the second thing can take place.

precursor *noun* A precursor of something that exists now is a similar thing that existed at an earlier time.

predator *noun* (SCIENCE) an animal that kills and eats other animals. > **predatory** *adjective*

predecessor *noun* Someone's predecessor is a person who used to do their job before.

predetermined *adjective* decided in advance or controlled by previous events rather than left to chance.

predicament *noun* a difficult situation.

predicament *noun*
= fix (*informal*), hot water (*informal*), jam (*informal*), scrape (*informal*), tight spot (*informal*)

predict *verb* If someone predicts an event, they say that it will happen in the future.

predict *verb*
= forecast, foresee, foretell, prophesy

prediction *noun* something that is forecast.

> **prediction** *noun*
> = forecast, prophecy

predominant *adjective* more important or more noticeable than anything else in a particular set of people or things.
> **predominantly** *adverb*

predominate *verb* If one type of person or thing predominates, it is the most common, frequent or noticeable. > **predominance** *noun*

pre-eminent *adjective* recognised as being the most important in a particular group. > **pre-eminence** *noun*

pre-empt *verb* (*formal*) If you pre-empt something, you prevent it by doing something else which makes it pointless or impossible.

preen *verb* When a bird preens its feathers, it cleans them using its beak.

preface *noun* an introduction at the beginning of a book explaining what the book is about or why it was written.

prefect *noun* a pupil who has special duties at a school.

prefer prefers, preferring, preferred *verb* If you prefer one thing to another, you like it better than the other thing.
> **preferable** *adjective* > **preferably** *adverb*

> **prefer** *verb*
> = be partial to, favour, go for, incline towards, like better

preference *noun* 1 If you have a preference for something, you

like it more than other things.
2 When making a choice, if you give preference to one type of person or thing, you try to choose that type.

preferential *adjective* A person who gets preferential treatment is treated better than others.

prefix *noun* (ENGLISH) a letter or group of letters added to the beginning of a word to make a new word, for example 'semi-', 'pre-' and 'un-'.

pregnant *adjective* A woman who is pregnant has a baby developing in her womb. > **pregnancy** *noun*

prehistoric *adjective* (HISTORY) existing at a time in the past before anything was written down.

prejudice *noun* 1 Prejudice is an unreasonable and unfair dislike or preference formed without carefully examining the facts.
2 Prejudice is also an intolerance towards certain people or groups.
> **prejudiced** *adjective* > **prejudicial** *adjective*

> **prejudice** *noun*
> 1 = bias, partiality, preconception 2 = bigotry, chauvinism, discrimination, racism, sexism

preliminary *adjective* Preliminary activities take place before something starts, in preparation for it.

prelude *noun* Something that is an introduction to a more important event can be described as a prelude to that event.

premature *adjective* happening too early, or earlier than expected.
> **prematurely** *adverb*

premeditated *adjective* planned in advance.

premier noun 1 The leader of a government is sometimes referred to as the premier. 2 In Australia, a premier is the leader of a State government. ▶ adjective 3 considered to be the best or most important.

premiere noun the first public performance of a new play or film.

premise noun 1 (in plural) The premises of an organisation are all the buildings it occupies on one site. 2 a statement which you suppose is true and use as the basis for an idea or argument.

premium noun 1 A sum of money paid regularly to an insurance company for an insurance policy. 2 an extra sum of money that has to be paid.

premonition noun a feeling that something unpleasant is going to happen.

> **premonition** noun
> = foreboding, funny feeling (informal), omen, sign

preoccupation noun If you have a preoccupation with something, it is very important to you and you keep thinking about it.

preoccupied adjective Someone who is preoccupied is deep in thought or totally involved with something.

> **preoccupied** adjective
> = absorbed, engrossed, immersed, oblivious, wrapped up

preparatory adjective Preparatory activities are done before doing something else in order to prepare for it.

prepare verb If you prepare something, you make it ready for a particular purpose or event. ▶ **preparation** noun

prepared adjective If you are prepared to do something, you are willing to do it.

preposterous adjective extremely unreasonable and ridiculous.

prerequisite noun (formal) Something that is a prerequisite for another thing must happen or exist before the other thing is possible.

prerogative noun (formal) Something that is the prerogative of a person is their special privilege or right.

prescribe verb When a doctor prescribes something, he or she states what treatment a patient should have.

prescription noun a piece of paper on which the doctor has written the name of a medicine needed by a patient.

presence noun 1 Someone's presence in a place is the fact of their being there. 2 If you are in someone's presence, you are in the same place as they are. 3 Someone who has presence has an impressive appearance or manner.

present adjective 1 If someone is present somewhere, they are there. 2 A present situation is one that exists now rather than in the past or the future. 3 (ENGLISH) (MFL) The present tense of a verb is the form used to express something that is happening in the present. ▶ noun 4 The present is the period of time that is taking place now. 5 something that you give to

someone for them to keep. ▶ *verb*
6 If you present someone with
something, you give it to them.
7 Something that presents a
difficulty or a challenge causes it
or provides it. **8** The person who
presents a radio or television
show introduces each part or each
guest. > **presenter** *noun*

present *adjective*
1 = at hand, here, in attendance,
there, to hand
▶ *noun* **5** = bonsela (*South African*),
donation, gift, offering
▶ *verb* **6** = award, bestow,
donate, give, grant, hand out

presentable *adjective* neat or
attractive and suitable for people
to see.

presentation *noun* **1** the act of
presenting or a way of presenting
something. **2** The presentation of
a piece of work is the way it looks
or the impression it gives. **3** To
give a presentation is to give a
talk or demonstration to an
audience of something you have
been studying or working on.

present-day *adjective* existing or
happening now.

presently *adverb* **1** If something
will happen presently, it will
happen soon. **2** Something that is
presently happening is
happening now.

present tense
noun (ENGLISH) (MFL) In grammar,
the present tense is the tense of a
verb that you use mainly to talk
about things that happen or exist
at the time of writing or
speaking.

preservative *noun* a substance
or chemical that stops things
decaying.

preserve *verb* **1** If you preserve
something, you take action so
that it remains as it is. **2** If you
preserve food, you treat it to
prevent it from decaying. ▶ *noun*
3 Preserves are foods such as jam
or chutney that have been made
with a lot of sugar or vinegar.
> **preservation** *noun*

preside *verb* A person who
presides over a formal event is in
charge of it.

president *noun* **1** In a country
which has no king or queen, the
president is the elected leader.
2 The president of an organisation
is the person who has the highest
position. > **presidency** *noun*
> **presidential** *adjective*

press *verb* **1** If you press
something, you push it or hold it
firmly against something else.
2 If you press clothes, you iron
them. **3** If you press for
something, you try hard to
persuade someone to agree to it.
4 If you press charges, you make
an accusation against someone
which has to be decided in a court
of law. ▶ *noun* **5** Newspapers and
the journalists who work for
them are called the press.

press *verb*
1 = compress, crush, mash,
push, squeeze **3** = beg, implore,
petition, plead, pressurise, urge

press conference *noun* When
someone gives a press conference,
they have a meeting to answer
questions put by reporters.

pressing *adjective* Something that
is pressing needs to be dealt with
immediately.

pressure *noun* **1** (SCIENCE)
Pressure is the force that is

produced by pushing on something. 2 (PSHE) If you are under pressure, you have too much to do and not enough time, or someone is trying hard to persuade you to do something.
▶ verb 3 If you pressure someone, you try hard to persuade them to do something.

pressurise; also spelt **pressurize** verb If you pressurise someone, you try hard to persuade them to do something.

prestige noun If you have prestige, people admire you because of your position.
> **prestigious** adjective

presumably adverb If you say that something is presumably the case, you mean you assume that it is.

presume verb If you presume something, you think that it is the case although you have no proof. > **presumption** noun

presumptuous adjective Someone who behaves in a presumptuous way does things that they have no right to do.

pretence noun a way of behaving that is false and intended to deceive people.

pretend verb If you pretend that something is the case, you try to make people believe that it is, although in fact it is not.

> **pretend** verb
= counterfeit, fake, falsify, feign, pass yourself off as

pretender noun A pretender to a throne or title is someone who claims it but whose claim is being questioned.

pretension noun Someone with pretensions claims that they are

more important than they really are.

pretentious adjective Someone or something that is pretentious is trying to seem important when in fact they are not.

> **pretentious** adjective
= affected, conceited, ostentatious, pompous, snobbish

pretext noun a false reason given to hide the real reason for doing something.

pretty prettier, prettiest adjective
1 attractive in a delicate way.
▶ adverb 2 (informal) quite or rather.
> **prettily** adverb > **prettiness** noun

> **pretty** adjective
1 = attractive, beautiful, cute, lovely
▶ adverb 2 = fairly, kind of (informal), quite, rather

prevail verb 1 If a custom or belief prevails in a particular place, it is normal or most common there.
2 If someone or something prevails, they succeed in their aims. > **prevailing** adjective

prevalent adjective very common or widespread. > **prevalence** noun

prevent verb If you prevent something, you stop it from happening or being done.
> **preventable** adjective
> **prevention** noun

> **prevent** verb
= avert, foil, hinder, impede, stop, thwart

preventive or **preventative** adjective intended to help prevent things such as disease or crime.

preview noun 1 an opportunity to see something, such as a film or exhibition, before it is shown to the public. **2** (ICT) a part of a computer program which allows you to look at what you have keyed or added to a document or spreadsheet as it will appear when it is printed.

previous adjective happening or existing before something else in time or position. ▸ **previously** adverb

> **previous** adjective
> = earlier, former, one-time, past, preceding, prior

prey noun **1** The creatures that an animal hunts and eats are called its prey. ▸ verb **2** An animal that preys on a particular kind of animal lives by hunting and eating it.

price noun **1** The price of something is the amount of money you have to pay to buy it. ▸ verb **2** To price something at a particular amount is to fix its price at that amount.

> **price** noun
> **1** = amount, charge, cost, fee, figure, value
> ▸ verb **2** = cost, estimate, put a price on, value

priceless adjective Something that is priceless is so valuable that it is difficult to work out how much it is worth.

pricey pricier, priciest adjective (informal) expensive.

prick verb **1** If you prick something, you stick a sharp pointed object into it. ▸ noun **2** a small, sharp pain caused when something pricks you.

pride noun **1** Pride is a feeling of satisfaction you have when you have done something well. **2** Pride is also a feeling of

being better than other people. **3** A pride of lions is a group of them. ▸ verb **4** If you pride yourself on a quality or skill, you are proud of it.

priest noun **1** (RE) a member of the clergy in some Christian Churches. **2** (RE) In many non-Christian religions, a priest is a man who has special duties in the place where people worship. ▸ **priestly** adjective

priestess noun a female priest in a non-Christian religion.

priesthood noun The priesthood is the position of being a priest.

prim primmer, primmest adjective Someone who is prim always behaves very correctly and is easily shocked by anything rude.

> **prim** adjective
> = proper, prudish, puritanical, strait-laced

primary adjective 'Primary' is used to describe something that is extremely important for someone or something: *the primary aim of his research*.

primary school noun a school for children aged up to 11.

primate noun **1** an archbishop. **2** a member of the group of animals which includes humans, monkeys and apes.

prime adjective **1** main or most important. **2** of the best quality. ▸ noun **3** Someone's prime is the stage when they are at their strongest, most active or most successful. ▸ verb **4** If you prime someone, you give them information about something in advance to prepare them.

prime *adjective*
1 = chief, leading, main, principal 2 = best, choice, first-rate, select, superior

prime minister *noun* The prime minister is the leader of the government.

prime number *noun* (MATHS)
A prime number is a whole number greater than 1 that cannot be divided exactly by any whole number except itself and 1. The numbers 2, 3, 7 and 11 are prime numbers.

primeval; also spelt **primaeval** *adjective* belonging to a very early period in the history of the world.

primitive *adjective* 1 connected with a society that lives very simply without industries or a writing system. 2 very simple, basic or old-fashioned.

primitive *adjective*
2 = crude, rough, rude, rudimentary, simple

primrose *noun* a small plant that has pale yellow flowers in spring.

prince *noun* a male member of a royal family, especially the son of a king or queen. > **princely** *adjective*

princess *noun* a female member of a royal family, usually the daughter of a king or queen, or the wife of a prince.

principal *adjective* 1 main or most important. ▶ *noun* 2 the person in charge of a school or college. > **principally** *adverb*

principal *adjective*
1 = chief, first, foremost, main, major, primary, prime

principality principalities *noun* a country ruled by a prince.

principle *noun* 1 a belief you have about the way you should behave. 2 a general rule or scientific law which explains how something happens or works.

principle *noun*
1 = conscience, integrity, morals, scruples, sense of duty 2 = axiom, canon, doctrine, fundamental, law

print *verb* 1 To print a newspaper or book is to reproduce it in large quantities using a mechanical or electronic copying process. 2 If you print when you are writing, you do not join the letters together. ▶ *noun* 3 The letters and numbers on the pages of a book or newspaper are referred to as the print. 4 a photograph, or a printed copy of a painting. 5 Footprints and fingerprints can be referred to as prints.

printer *noun* 1 a machine that can be connected to a computer to reproduce copies of documents or pictures on paper. 2 a person or company that prints newspapers or books.

printing *noun* the process of producing printed material such as books and newspapers.

prior *adjective* 1 planned or done at an earlier time. ▶ *phrase* 2 Something that happens **prior to** a particular time or event happens before it.

prioritise; also spelt **prioritize** *verb* To prioritise things is to decide which is the most important and deal with it first.

priority priorities *noun* something that needs to be dealt with first.

p

prise verb If you prise something open or away from a surface, you force it open or away.

prism noun 1 an object made of clear glass with many flat sides. It separates light passing through it into the colours of the rainbow. 2 (MATHS) A prism is any polyhedron with two identical parallel ends and sides which are parallelograms.

prison noun a building where criminals are kept in captivity.

> **prison** noun
> = dungeon, jail, nick (British, Australian and New Zealand; slang), penal institution

prisoner noun someone who is kept in prison or held in captivity against their will.

> **prisoner** noun
> = captive, convict, hostage

pristine adjective (formal) very clean or new and in perfect condition.

private adjective 1 for the use of one person rather than people in general. 2 taking place between a small number of people and kept secret from others. 3 owned or run by individuals or companies rather than by the state. ▶ noun 4 a soldier of the lowest rank. > **privacy** noun > **privately** adverb

> **private** adjective
> 1 = exclusive, individual, personal, special
> 2 = clandestine (formal), confidential, secret

private school noun a school that does not receive money from the government, and which parents pay for their children to attend.

privatise; also spelt **privatize** verb If the government privatises a state-owned industry or organisation, it allows it to be bought and owned by a private individual or group.

privilege noun a special right or advantage given to a person or group. > **privileged** adjective

privy adjective (formal) If you are privy to something secret, you have been told about it.

prize noun 1 a reward given to the winner of a competition or game. ▶ adjective 2 of the highest quality or standard. ▶ verb 3 Something that is prized is wanted and admired for its value or quality.

> **prize** noun
> 1 = accolade, award, honour, trophy
> ▶ adjective 2 = award-winning, first-rate, outstanding, top
> ▶ verb 3 = cherish, esteem, treasure, value

pro pros noun 1 (informal) a professional. ▶ phrase 2 The **pros and cons** of a situation are its advantages and disadvantages.

pro- prefix 'Pro-' means supporting or in favour of: pro-democracy protests.

probability probabilities noun 1 The probability of something happening is how likely it is to happen. 2 If something is a probability, it is likely to happen.

> **probability** noun
> 1 = chances, likelihood, odds, prospect

probable adjective Something that is probable is likely to be true or correct, or likely to happen.

probable *adjective*
= apparent, feasible, likely, on the cards, plausible

probably *adverb* Something that is probably the case is likely but not certain.

probably *adverb*
= doubtless, in all probability, likely, presumably

probation *noun* Probation is a period of time during which a person convicted of a crime is supervised by a probation officer instead of being sent to prison. > **probationary** *adjective*

probe *verb* 1 If you probe, you ask a lot of questions to discover the facts about something. ▶ *noun* 2 a long thin instrument used by doctors and dentists when examining a patient.

problem *noun* 1 an unsatisfactory situation that causes difficulties. 2 a puzzle or question that you solve using logical thought or mathematics. > **problematic** *adjective*

problem *noun*
1 = difficulty, predicament, quandary, trouble
2 = conundrum, puzzle, riddle

procedure *noun* a way of doing something, especially the correct or usual way. > **procedural** *adjective*

procedure *noun*
= method, policy, practice, process, strategy, system

proceed *verb* 1 If you proceed to do something, you start doing it, or continue doing it. 2 *(formal)* If you proceed in a particular direction, you move in that direction.

proceed *verb*
1 = begin, carry on, continue, get under way, go on, start
2 = advance, continue, go on, make your way, progress, travel

proceedings *plural noun* 1 You can refer to an organised and related series of events as the proceedings. 2 Legal proceedings are legal action taken against someone.

process *noun* 1 a series of actions intended to achieve a particular result or change. ▶ *phrase* 2 If you are **in the process** of doing something, you have started doing it but have not yet finished. ▶ *verb* 3 When food is processed, it is prepared in factories before it is sold. 4 When information is processed, it is put through a system or into a computer to organise it.

process *noun*
1 = course of action, means, method, procedure, system
▶ *verb* 3 = deal with, dispose of, handle, take care of

procession *noun* a group of people or vehicles moving in a line, often as part of a ceremony.

processor *noun* (ICT) In computing, a processor is the central chip in a computer which controls its operations.

proclaim *verb* If someone proclaims something, they announce it or make it known. > **proclamation** *noun*

procure *verb* *(formal)* If you procure something, you obtain it.

prod prods, prodding, prodded *verb* If you prod something, you give it a push with your finger or with something pointed.

prodigy prodigies noun someone who shows an extraordinary natural ability at an early age.

produce verb 1 To produce something is to make it or cause it. 2 If you produce something from somewhere, you bring it out so it can be seen. ▶ noun 3 Produce is food that is grown to be sold.

> **produce** verb
> 1 = construct, create, invent, make, manufacture
> 2 = advance, bring forward, bring to light, put forward

producer noun The producer of a record, film or show is the person in charge of making it or putting it on.

product noun 1 something that is made to be sold. 2 (MATHS) The product of two or more numbers or quantities is the result of multiplying them together. 3 (SCIENCE) a substance formed in a chemical reaction.

> **product** noun
> 1 = commodity, goods, merchandise, produce

production noun 1 (DGT) Production is the process of manufacturing or growing something in large quantities. 2 Production is also the amount of goods manufactured or food grown by a country or company. 3 A production of a play, opera or other show is a series of performances of it.

productive adjective 1 To be productive means to produce a large number of things. 2 If something such as a meeting is productive, good or useful things happen as a result of it.

productive adjective
1 = fertile, fruitful, prolific
2 = constructive, useful, valuable, worthwhile

productivity noun Productivity is the rate at which things are produced or dealt with.

profane adjective (formal) showing disrespect for a religion or religious things.

profess verb 1 (formal) If you profess to do or have something, you claim to do or have it. 2 If you profess a feeling or opinion, you express it.

profession noun a type of job that requires advanced education or training.

> **profession** noun
> = business, career, occupation

professional adjective
1 Professional means relating to the work of someone who is qualified in a particular profession. 2 Professional also describes activities when they are done to earn money rather than as a hobby. 3 A professional piece of work is of a very high standard. ▶ noun 4 a person who has been trained in a profession. 5 someone who plays a sport to earn money rather than as a hobby.

professor noun the senior teacher in a department of a British university. > **professorial** adjective

proficient adjective If you are proficient at something, you can do it well. > **proficiency** noun

> **proficient** adjective
> = able, accomplished, adept, capable, competent, efficient, skilful, skilled

profile noun 1 Your profile is the outline of your face seen from the side. 2 A profile of someone is a short description of their life and character.

profit noun 1 When someone sells something, the profit is the amount they gain by selling it for more than it cost them to buy or make. ▸ verb 2 If you profit from something, you gain or benefit from it. > **profitable** adjective

> **profit** noun
> 1 = earnings, proceeds, revenue, surplus, takings
> ▸ verb 2 = capitalise on, exploit, make the most of, take advantage of

profound adjective 1 great in degree or intensity. 2 showing great and deep intellectual understanding. > **profoundly** adverb > **profundity** noun

program programs, programming, programmed
(ICT) noun 1 a set of instructions that a computer follows to perform a particular task. ▸ verb 2 When someone programs a computer, they write a program and put it into the computer.
> **programmer** noun

programme noun 1 a planned series of events. 2 a particular piece presented as a unit on television or radio, such as a play, show or discussion. 3 a booklet giving information about a play, concert or show that you are attending.

> **programme** noun
> 1 = agenda, schedule, timetable
> 2 = broadcast, show

progress noun 1 Progress is the process of gradually improving or

getting near to achieving something. 2 The progress of something is the way in which it develops or continues. ▸ phrase 3 Something that is in progress is happening. ▸ verb 4 If you progress, you become more advanced or skilful. 5 To progress is to continue. > **progression** noun

> **progress** noun
> 1 = advance, breakthrough, headway, improvement
> ▸ verb 4 = advance, blossom, develop, improve

progressive adjective 1 having modern ideas about how things should be done. 2 happening gradually.

prohibit verb If someone prohibits something, they forbid it or make it illegal. > **prohibition** noun

> **prohibit** verb
> = ban, forbid, outlaw, prevent

prohibitive adjective If the cost of something is prohibitive, it is so high that people cannot afford it.

project noun 1 a carefully planned attempt to achieve something or to study something over a period of time. ▸ verb 2 Something that is projected is planned or expected to happen in the future. 3 To project an image onto a screen is to make it appear there using equipment such as a projector. 4 Something that projects sticks out beyond a surface or edge. > **projection** noun

projector noun a piece of equipment which produces a large image on a screen by shining light through a photographic slide or film strip.

proletariat noun (formal) Working-class people are sometimes

referred to as the proletariat.
> **proletarian** *adjective*

proliferate *verb* If things
proliferate, they quickly increase
in number. > **proliferation** *noun*

prolific *adjective* producing a lot of
something.

prologue *noun* a speech or section
that introduces a play or book.

prolong *verb* If you prolong
something, you make it last
longer. > **prolonged** *adjective*

prom *noun* (*informal*) a concert at
which some of the audience
stand.

promenade *noun* a road or path
next to the sea at a seaside resort.

prominent *adjective* 1 Prominent
people are well-known and
important. 2 Something that is
prominent is very noticeable.
> **prominence** *noun* > **prominently**
adverb

> **prominent** *adjective*
> 1 = eminent, famous,
> important, notable, noted,
> renowned, well-known
> 2 = conspicuous, eye-catching,
> jutting, noticeable, obvious,
> pronounced, striking

promise *verb* 1 If you promise to
do something, you say that you
will definitely do it. 2 Something
that promises to have a particular
quality shows signs that it will
have that quality. ▶ *noun* 3 a
statement made by someone that
they will definitely do
something. 4 Someone or
something that shows promise
seems likely to be very successful.
> **promising** *adjective*

> **promise** *verb*
> 1 = assure, give your word,
> guarantee, pledge, vow

2 = hint at, indicate, show signs of
▶ *noun* 3 = assurance, guarantee,
pledge, undertaking, vow

promontory promontories *noun*
an area of high land sticking out
into the sea.

promote *verb* 1 If someone
promotes something, they try to
make it happen. 2 If someone
promotes a product such as a film
or a book, they try to make it
popular by advertising. 3 If
someone is promoted, they are
given a more important job at
work. > **promoter** *noun*
> **promotion** *noun*

> **promote** *verb*
> 1 = back, support 2 = advertise,
> plug (*informal*), publicise
> 3 = elevate, upgrade

prompt *verb* 1 If something
prompts someone to do
something, it makes them decide
to do it. 2 If you prompt someone
when they stop speaking, you tell
them what to say next or
encourage them to continue.
▶ *adverb* 3 exactly at the time
mentioned: *Wednesday morning at
10.40 prompt.* ▶ *adjective* 4 A prompt
action is done without any delay.
> **promptly** *adverb*

> **prompt** *verb*
> 1 = cause, induce, inspire,
> motivate, spur 2 = coax, remind
> ▶ *adverb* 3 = exactly, on the dot,
> precisely, sharp
> ▶ *adjective* 4 = immediate,
> instant, instantaneous, quick,
> rapid, swift

prone *adjective* 1 If you are prone to
something, you have a tendency
to be affected by it or to do it. 2 If
you are prone, you are lying flat
and face downwards.

prone *adjective*
1 = disposed, given, inclined, liable, susceptible 2 = face down, prostrate

pronoun *noun* (ENGLISH) (MFL)
In grammar, a pronoun is a word that is used to replace a noun. 'He', 'she' and 'them' are all pronouns.

pronounce *verb* (ENGLISH) (MFL)
When you pronounce a word, you say it.

pronounced *adjective* very noticeable.

pronunciation *noun* the way a word is usually said.

proof *noun* If you have proof of something, you have evidence which shows that it is true or exists.

proof *noun*
= confirmation, evidence, testimony, verification

prop props, propping, propped
verb 1 If you prop an object somewhere, you support it or rest it against something. ▶ *noun*
2 A stick or other object used to support something. 3 The props in a play are all the objects and furniture used by the actors.

propaganda *noun* (HISTORY)
Propaganda is exaggerated or false information that is published or broadcast in order to influence people.

propagate *verb* 1 If people propagate an idea, they spread it to try to influence many other people. 2 If you propagate plants, you grow more of them from an original one. > **propagation** *noun*

propel propels, propelling, propelled *verb* To propel something is to cause it to move in a particular direction.

propeller *noun* a device on a boat or aircraft with rotating blades which make the boat or aircraft move.

propensity propensities *noun* (*formal*) a tendency to behave in a particular way.

proper *adjective* 1 real and satisfactory: *a proper job*. 2 correct or suitable: *Put things in their proper place*. 3 accepted or conventional: *a proper wedding*. > **properly** *adverb*

proper *adjective*
2 = appropriate, apt, correct, fitting, right, suitable
3 = accepted, conventional, orthodox

property properties *noun* 1 A person's property is the things that belong to them. 2 a building and the land belonging to it. 3 a characteristic or quality.

property *noun*
1 = assets, belongings, effects, estate, possessions
3 = attribute, characteristic, feature, hallmark, quality, trait

prophecy prophecies *noun* a statement about what someone believes will happen in the future.

prophet *noun* (RE) a person who predicts what will happen in the future.

prophetic *adjective* correctly predicting what will happen.

proportion *noun* 1 A proportion of an amount or group is a part of it. 2 The proportion of one amount to another is its size in comparison with the other amount. 3 (*in plural*) You can refer to the size of something as its proportions.

P

proportion noun
1 = percentage, quota, segment, share

proportional or **proportionate**
adjective If one thing is
proportional to another, it
remains the same size in
comparison with the other.
> **proportionally** or
proportionately adverb

proportional representation
noun Proportional representation
is a system of voting in elections
in which the number of
representatives of each party is in
proportion to the number of
people who voted for it.

proposal noun a plan that has
been suggested.

propose verb 1 If you propose a
plan or idea, you suggest it. 2 If
you propose to do something, you
intend to do it. 3 When someone
proposes a toast to a particular
person, they ask people to drink a
toast to that person. 4 If someone
proposes to another person, they
ask that person to marry them.

proposition noun 1 a statement
expressing a theory or opinion.
2 an offer or suggestion.

proprietor noun The proprietor of
a business is the owner.

propriety noun (formal) Propriety
is what is socially or morally
acceptable.

propulsion noun Propulsion is
the power that moves something.

prose noun Prose is ordinary
written language in contrast to
poetry.

prosecute verb If someone is
prosecuted, they are charged with
a crime and have to stand trial.
> **prosecutor** noun

prosecution noun The lawyers
who try to prove that a person on
trial is guilty are called the
prosecution.

prospect noun 1 If there is a
prospect of something
happening, there is a possibility
that it will happen. 2 Someone's
prospects are their chances of
being successful in the future.
▶ verb 3 If someone prospects for
gold or oil, they look for it.
> **prospector** noun

prospect noun
1 = expectation, hope, outlook,
promise

prospective adjective
'Prospective' is used to say that
someone wants to be or is likely to
be something. For example, the
prospective owner of something
is the person who wants to
own it.

prospectus noun a booklet giving
details about a college or a
company.

prosper verb When people or
businesses prosper, they are
successful and make a lot of
money. > **prosperous** adjective
> **prosperity** noun

prostrate adjective lying face
downwards on the ground.

protagonist noun (formal) 1 a
main character in a play or story.
2 Someone who is a protagonist of
an idea or movement is a leading
supporter of it.

protect verb To protect someone
or something is to prevent them
from being harmed or damaged.
> **protective** adjective > **protector**
noun

protection noun 1 the act of
preventing harm or damage.

2 something that keeps a person or thing safe.

> **protection** noun
> **2** = barrier, buffer, cover, safeguard, shelter

protein noun (SCIENCE) Protein is a complex compound consisting of amino acid chains, found in many foods and essential for all living things.

protest verb **1** If you protest about something, you say or demonstrate publicly that you disagree with it. ▶ noun **2** a demonstration or statement showing that you disagree with something. > **protester** noun

> **protest** verb
> **1** = complain, disagree, disapprove, object, oppose
> ▶ noun **2** = complaint, objection, outcry

Protestant noun, adjective (RE) (a member) of one of the Christian Churches which separated from the Catholic Church in the 16th century.

protestation noun a strong declaration that something is true or not true.

protocol noun Protocol is the system of rules about the correct way to behave in formal situations.

proton noun (SCIENCE) a particle which forms part of the nucleus of an atom and has a positive electrical charge.

prototype noun (DGT) a first model of something that is made so that the design can be tested and improved.

protracted adjective lasting longer than usual.

protrude verb (formal) If something is protruding from a surface or edge, it is sticking out. > **protrusion** noun

proud adjective **1** feeling pleasure and satisfaction at something you own or have achieved. **2** having great dignity and self-respect. > **proudly** adverb

> **proud** adjective
> **1** = gratified, honoured, pleased

prove proves, proving, proved or proven verb **1** To prove that something is true is to provide evidence that it is definitely true. **2** If something proves to be the case, it becomes clear that it is so.

> **prove** verb
> **1** = ascertain, confirm, demonstrate, establish, verify

proverb noun a short sentence which gives advice or makes a comment about life. > **proverbial** adjective

provide verb **1** If you provide something for someone, you give it to them or make it available for them. **2** If you provide for someone, you give them the things they need.

> **provide** verb
> **1** = contribute, equip, furnish, outfit, supply

providence noun Providence is God or a force which is believed to arrange the things that happen to us.

province noun **1** one of the areas into which some large countries are divided, each province having its own administration. **2** (in plural) You can refer to the parts of a country which are not near the capital as the provinces.

p

provincial adjective 1 connected with the parts of a country outside the capital. 2 narrow-minded and lacking sophistication.

provision noun 1 The provision of something is the act of making it available to people. 2 (in plural) Provisions are supplies of food.

provisional adjective A provisional arrangement has not yet been made definite and so might be changed.

proviso provisos noun a condition in an agreement.

provocation noun an act done deliberately to annoy someone.

provocative adjective intended to annoy people or make them react.

provoke verb 1 If you provoke someone, you deliberately try to make them angry. 2 If something provokes an unpleasant reaction, it causes it.

> **provoke** verb
> 1 = anger, annoy, enrage, goad, insult, irritate, tease 2 = cause, evoke, produce, prompt, rouse, set off, spark off

prowess noun Prowess is outstanding ability.

prowl verb If a person or animal prowls around, they move around quietly and secretly, as if hunting.

proximity noun (formal) Proximity is nearness to someone or something.

proxy phrase If you do something by proxy, someone else does it on your behalf.

prudent adjective behaving in a sensible and cautious way. > **prudence** noun
> **prudently** adverb

prune noun 1 a dried plum. ▶ verb 2 When someone prunes a tree or shrub, they cut back some of the branches.

pry pries, prying, pried verb If someone is prying, they are trying to find out about something secret or private.

> **pry** verb
> = interfere, intrude, poke your nose in (informal), poke your nose into (informal), snoop (informal)

PS PS is written before an additional message at the end of a letter. PS is an abbreviation for 'postscript'.

pseudonym noun a name an author uses rather than their real name.

psyche noun your mind and your deepest feelings.

psychiatry noun Psychiatry is the branch of medicine concerned with mental health. > **psychiatrist** noun > **psychiatric** adjective

psychic adjective having unusual mental powers such as the ability to read people's minds or predict the future.

psychoanalysis noun Psychoanalysis is the examination and treatment of someone who has mental health problems by encouraging them to talk about their feelings and past events in order to discover the cause of the illness.
> **psychoanalyst** noun
> **psychoanalyse** verb

psychology noun Psychology is the scientific study of the mind and of the reasons for people's behaviour. > **psychological** adjective > **psychologist** noun

psychopath noun a person with a psychiatric disorder who can commit antisocial or violent acts without feeling guilt. > **psychopathic** adjective

psychosis psychoses noun a severe mental condition that causes people to interpret reality in a different way from the people around them. > **psychotic** adjective

PTO PTO is an abbreviation for 'please turn over'. It is written at the bottom of a page to indicate that the writing continues on the other side.

pub noun a building where people go to buy and drink alcoholic or soft drinks.

puberty noun Puberty is the stage when a person's body changes from that of a child into that of an adult.

pubic adjective relating to the area around and above a person's genitals.

public noun 1 You can refer to people in general as the public. ▶ adjective 2 relating to people in general. 3 provided for everyone to use, or open to anyone. > **publicly** adverb

> **public** noun
> 1 = masses, nation, people, populace, society
> ▶ adjective 2 = civic, general, popular, universal
> 3 = communal, community, open to the public, universal

publican noun a person who owns or manages a pub.

publication noun 1 The publication of a book is the act of printing it and making it available. 2 a book or magazine.

3 a piece of content made available on the World Wide Web.

publicise; also spelt **publicize** verb When someone publicises a fact or event, they advertise it and make it widely known.

> **publicise** verb
> = advertise, plug (informal), promote

publicity noun Publicity is information or advertisements about an item or event.

> **publicity** noun
> = advertising, plug (informal), promotion

public school noun In Britain, a public school is a school that is privately run and that charges fees for the pupils to attend.

public servant noun In Australia and New Zealand, a public servant is someone who works in the public service.

public service noun In Australia and New Zealand, the public service is the government departments responsible for the administration of the country.

publish verb 1 (LIBRARY) When a company publishes a book, newspaper or magazine, they print copies of it and distribute it. 2 If you publish something on the World Wide Web, you make it available there. > **publishing** noun

> **publish** verb
> 1 = bring out, post, print, put out

publisher noun (LIBRARY) The publisher of a book, newspaper or magazine is the person or company that prints copies of it and distributes it.

P

pudding noun 1 a sweet cake mixture cooked with fruit or other flavouring and served hot. 2 You can refer to the sweet course of a meal as the pudding.

puddle noun a small shallow pool of liquid.

puerile adjective Puerile behaviour is silly and childish.

puff verb 1 To puff on a cigarette or pipe is to smoke it. 2 If you are puffing, you are breathing loudly and quickly with your mouth open. 3 If something puffs out or puffs up, it swells and becomes larger and rounder. ▶ noun 4 a small amount of air or smoke that is released.

pug noun a small, short-haired dog with a flat nose.

pull verb 1 When you pull something, you hold it and move it towards you. 2 When something is pulled by a vehicle or animal, it is attached to it and moves along behind it. 3 When you pull a curtain or blind, you move it so that it covers or uncovers the window. 4 If you pull a muscle, you injure it by stretching it too far or too quickly. 5 When a vehicle pulls away, pulls out or pulls in, it moves in that direction. ▶ noun 6 The pull of something is its attraction or influence. > **pull down** verb When a building is pulled down, it is deliberately destroyed. > **pull out** verb If you pull out of something, you leave it or decide not to continue with it. > **pull through** verb When someone pulls through, they recover from a serious illness.

pull verb
1 = drag, draw, haul, tow, tug, yank

▶ noun 6 = attraction, lure, magnetism

pulley noun (D&T) a device for lifting heavy weights. The weight is attached to a rope which passes over a wheel or series of wheels.

pullover noun a woollen piece of clothing that covers the top part of your body.

pulmonary adjective relating to the lungs or to the veins and arteries carrying blood between the lungs and the heart.

pulp noun If something is turned into a pulp, it is crushed until it is soft and moist.

pulpit noun the small raised platform in a church where a member of the clergy stands to preach.

pulse noun 1 Your pulse is the regular beating of blood through your body, the rate of which you can feel at your wrists and elsewhere. 2 The seeds of beans, peas and lentils are called pulses when they are used for food. ▶ verb 3 If something is pulsing, it is moving or vibrating with rhythmic, regular movements.

pummel pummels, pummelling, pummelled verb If you pummel something, you beat it with your fists.

pump noun 1 a machine that is used to force a liquid or gas to move in a particular direction. 2 Pumps are light shoes with flat soles which people wear for sport or leisure. ▶ verb 3 To pump a liquid or gas somewhere is to force it to flow in that direction, using a pump. 4 If you pump money into something, you put a lot of money into it.

pumpkin noun a very large, round, orange fruit eaten as a vegetable.

pun noun a clever and amusing use of words so that what you say has two different meanings, such as *my dog's a champion boxer.*

punch verb 1 If you punch someone, you hit them hard with your fist. ▶ noun 2 a hard blow with the fist. 3 a tool used for making holes. 4 Punch is a drink made from a mixture of wine, spirits and fruit.

punctual adjective arriving at the correct time. > **punctually** adverb > **punctuality** noun

> **punctual** adjective
> = in good time, on time, prompt

punctuate verb 1 Something that is punctuated by a particular thing is interrupted by it at intervals. 2 (ENGLISH) When you punctuate a piece of writing, you put punctuation into it.

punctuation noun (ENGLISH) The marks in writing such as full stops, question marks and commas are called punctuation or punctuation marks.

puncture noun 1 If a tyre has a puncture, a small hole has been made in it and it has become flat. ▶ verb 2 To puncture something is to make a small hole in it.

pungent adjective having a strong, often unpleasant, smell or taste. > **pungency** noun

punish verb To punish someone who has done something wrong is to make them suffer because of it.

> **punish** verb
> = discipline, penalise, rap someone's knuckles, sentence, throw the book at

punishment noun something unpleasant done to someone because they have done something wrong.

> **punishment** noun
> = penalty, retribution

punitive adjective harsh and intended to punish people.

Punjabi adjective 1 belonging or relating to the Punjab, a state in north-western India. ▶ noun 2 someone who comes from the Punjab. 3 Punjabi is a language spoken in the Punjab.

punk noun Punk or punk rock is an aggressive style of rock music.

punt noun a long, flat-bottomed boat. You move it along by pushing a pole against the river bottom.

puny punier, puniest adjective very small and weak.

> **puny** adjective
> = feeble, frail, sickly, skinny, weak

pup noun a young dog. Some other young animals such as seals are also called pups.

pupil noun 1 The pupils at a school are the children who go there. 2 Your pupils are the small, round, black areas in the centre of your eyes.

> **pupil** noun
> 1 = scholar (South African), schoolboy, schoolchild, schoolgirl, student

puppet noun a doll or toy animal that is moved by pulling strings or by putting your hand inside its body.

puppy puppies noun a young dog.

purchase verb 1 When you purchase something, you buy it. ▶ noun 2 something you have bought. ▷ **purchaser** noun

pure adjective 1 Something that is pure is not mixed with anything else. 2 Pure also means clean and free from harmful substances. 3 People who are pure have not done anything considered to be sinful. 4 Pure also means complete and total. ▷ **purity** noun

> **pure** adjective
> 2 = clean, germ-free, pasteurised, spotless, sterilised
> 4 = absolute, complete, outright, sheer, unmitigated, utter

purely adverb involving only one feature and not including anything else.

purge verb To purge something is to remove undesirable things from it.

purify purifies, purifying, purified verb To purify something is to remove all dirty or harmful substances from it. ▷ **purification** noun

purist noun someone who believes that something should be done in a particular, correct way.

puritan noun someone who believes in strict moral principles and avoids physical pleasures. ▷ **puritanical** adjective

purple noun, adjective reddish-blue.

purport verb (formal) Something that purports to be or have a particular thing claims to be or have it.

purpose noun 1 The purpose of something is the reason for it. 2 If you have a particular purpose, this is what you want to achieve.

▶ phrase 3 If you do something on purpose, you do it deliberately. ▷ **purposely** adverb ▷ **purposeful** adjective

> **purpose** noun
> 1 = aim, function, intention, object, point, reason
> ▶ phrase 3 on purpose = by design, deliberately, intentionally, knowingly, purposely

purr verb When a cat purrs, it makes a low vibrating sound because it is contented.

purse noun 1 a small leather or fabric container for carrying money. ▶ verb 2 If you purse your lips, you move them into a tight, rounded shape.

pursue pursues, pursuing, pursued verb 1 If you pursue an activity or plan, you do it or make efforts to achieve it. 2 If you pursue someone, you follow them to try to catch them. ▷ **pursuer** noun ▷ **pursuit** noun

purveyor noun (formal) A purveyor of goods or services is a person who sells them or provides them.

push verb 1 When you push something, you press it using force in order to move it. 2 If you push someone into doing something, you force or persuade them to do it. 3 (informal) Someone who pushes drugs sells them illegally. ▷ **push off** verb (informal) If you tell someone to push off, you are telling them rudely to go away.

> **push** verb
> 1 = press, ram, shove, thrust
> 2 = encourage, persuade, press, urge

pushchair noun a small folding chair on wheels in which a baby or toddler can be wheeled around.

pushover noun (informal)
1 something that is easy.
2 someone who is easily persuaded or defeated.

pushy pushier, pushiest adjective (informal) behaving in a forceful and determined way.

> **pushy** adjective
> = aggressive, ambitious, assertive, bossy (formal), forceful, obtrusive

pussy pussies noun (informal) a cat.

put puts, putting, put 1 When you put something somewhere, you move it into that place or position. 2 If you put an idea or remark in a particular way, you express it that way. 3 To put someone or something in a particular state or situation means to cause them to be in it. 4 You can use 'put' to express an estimate of the size or importance of something. > **put down** verb 1 To put someone down is to criticise them and make them appear foolish. 2 If an animal is put down, it is killed because it is very ill or dangerous. > **put off** verb 1 If you put something off, you delay doing it. 2 To put someone off is to discourage them. > **put out** verb 1 If you put a fire out or put the light out, you make it stop burning or shining. 2 If you are put out, you are annoyed or upset. > **put up** verb If you put up resistance to something, you argue or fight against it. > **put up with** verb If you put up with something, you tolerate it even though you disagree with it or dislike it.

put verb
1 = deposit, lay, place, position, rest 2 = phrase, word
▸ **put down** 1 = belittle, criticise, find fault with, humiliate ▸ **put off** 1 = defer, delay, postpone, put back, put on ice, reschedule
▸ **put up with** = abide, bear, stand, stand for, stomach, tolerate

putt noun In golf, a putt is a gentle stroke made when the ball is near the hole.

putting noun Putting is a game played on a small grass course with no obstacles. You hit a ball gently with a club so that it rolls towards one of a series of holes around the course.

putty noun Putty is a paste used to fix panes of glass into frames.

puzzle verb 1 If something puzzles you, it confuses you and you do not understand it. ▸ noun 2 A puzzle is a game or question that requires a lot of thought to complete or solve. > **puzzled** adjective > **puzzlement** noun

> **puzzle** verb
> 1 = baffle, bewilder, confuse, mystify, stump
> ▸ noun 2 = brain-teaser (informal), poser, problem, riddle

PVC noun PVC is a plastic used for making clothing, pipes and many other things. PVC is an abbreviation for 'polyvinyl chloride'.

pygmy pygmies; also spelt **pigmy** noun a very small person, especially one who belongs to a racial group in which all the people are small.

pyjamas *plural noun* Pyjamas are loose trousers and a jacket or top that you wear in bed.

pylon *noun* a very tall metal structure which carries overhead electricity cables.

pyramid *noun* 1 a three-dimensional shape with a flat base and flat triangular sides sloping upwards to a point.
2 (HISTORY) The Pyramids are ancient stone structures built over the tombs of Egyptian kings and queens.

python *noun* a large snake that kills animals by squeezing them with its body.

Qq

quack *verb* When a duck quacks, it makes a loud, harsh sound.

quadriceps *noun* (PE) a large muscle in four parts at the front of your thigh.

quadruple *verb* When an amount or number quadruples, it becomes four times as large as it was.

quagmire *noun* a soft, wet area of land which you sink into if you walk on it.

quail *noun* 1 a type of small game bird with a round body and short tail. ▶ *verb* 2 If you quail, you feel or look afraid.

quaint *adjective* attractively old-fashioned or unusual.
> **quaintly** *adverb*

quake *verb* If you quake, you shake and tremble because you are very frightened.

Quaker *noun* (RE) a member of a Christian group, the Society of Friends.

qualification *noun* 1 Your qualifications are your skills and achievements, especially as officially recognised at the end of a course of training or study.
2 something you add to a statement to make it less strong.

qualification *noun*
1 = ability, accomplishment, achievement, capability, quality, skill 2 = condition,

exception, modification, reservation

qualify qualifies, qualifying, qualified verb 1 (PE) When you qualify, you pass the examinations or tests that you need to pass to do a particular job or to take part in a sporting event. 2 If you qualify a statement, you add a detail or explanation to make it less strong. 3 If you qualify for something, you become entitled to have it.
> **qualified** adjective

> **qualify** verb
> 1 = become licensed, gain qualifications, get certified, graduate

quality qualities noun 1 The quality of something is how good it is. 2 a characteristic.

> **quality** noun
> 1 = calibre, distinction, grade, merit, value, worth 2 = aspect, characteristic, feature, mark, property, trait

qualm noun If you have qualms about what you are doing, you worry that it might not be right.

quandary quandaries noun If you are in a quandary, you cannot decide what to do.

quango quangos noun a body responsible for a particular area of public administration, which is financed by the government but is outside direct government control. Quango is short for 'quasi-autonomous non-governmental organisation'.

quantity quantities noun 1 an amount you can measure or count. 2 Quantity is the amount of something that there is.

quantity noun
1 = amount, number, part, sum
2 = extent, measure, size, volume

quarantine noun If an animal is in quarantine, it is kept away from other animals for a time because it might have an infectious disease.

quarrel quarrels, quarrelling, quarrelled noun 1 an angry argument. ▶ verb 2 If people quarrel, they have an angry argument.

> **quarrel** noun
> 1 = argument, disagreement, dispute, feud, fight, row, squabble
> ▶ verb 2 = argue, bicker, clash, fall out (informal), fight, row, squabble

quarry quarries, quarrying, quarried noun 1 a place where stone is removed from the ground by digging or blasting. 2 A person's or animal's quarry is the animal that they are hunting. ▶ verb 3 To quarry stone means to remove it from a quarry by digging or blasting.

quarter noun 1 one of four equal parts. 2 an American coin worth 25 cents. 3 You can refer to a particular area in a city as a quarter. 4 (in plural) A soldier's or a servant's quarters are the rooms that they live in.

quarterly quarterlies adjective 1 Quarterly means happening regularly every three months. ▶ noun 2 a magazine or journal published every three months.

quartet noun a group of four musicians who sing or play together; also a piece of music

q

written for four instruments or singers.

quartz noun Quartz is a kind of hard, shiny crystal used in making very accurate watches and clocks.

quash verb To quash a decision or judgment means to reject it officially.

quay noun a place where boats are tied up and loaded or unloaded.

queasy queasier, queasiest adjective feeling slightly sick.
> **queasiness** noun

> **queasy** adjective
> = ill, nauseous, queer (old-fashioned), sick, unwell

queen noun 1 a female monarch or a woman married to a king. 2 a female bee or ant which can lay eggs. 3 In chess, the queen is the most powerful piece and can move in any direction. 4 In a pack of cards, a queen is a card with a picture of a queen on it.

queer adjective Queer means very strange.

quell verb 1 To quell a rebellion or riot means to put an end to it by using force. 2 If you quell a feeling such as fear or grief, you stop yourself from feeling it.

quench verb If you quench your thirst, you have a drink so that you are no longer thirsty.

query queries, querying, queried noun 1 a question. ▶ verb 2 If you query something, you ask about it because you think it might not be right.

> **query** noun
> 1 = inquiry, question
> ▶ verb 2 = challenge, dispute, object to, question

quest noun a long search for something.

question noun 1 a sentence which asks for information. 2 If there is some question about something, there is doubt about it. 3 a problem that needs to be discussed. ▶ verb 4 If you question someone, you ask them questions. 5 If you question something, you express doubts about it. ▶ phrase 6 If something is out of the question, it is impossible.

> **question** noun
> 3 = issue, motion, point, subject, topic
> ▶ verb 4 = examine, interrogate, probe, quiz 5 = challenge, dispute, distrust, doubt, query, suspect

questionable adjective possibly not true or not honest.

question mark noun the punctuation mark (?) which is used at the end of a question.

questionnaire noun a list of questions which asks for information.

queue queues, queuing or queueing, queued noun 1 a line of people or vehicles waiting for something. ▶ verb 2 When people queue, they stand in a line waiting for something.

quibble verb 1 If you quibble, you argue about something unimportant. ▶ noun 2 a minor objection.

quiche noun a tart with a savoury filling.

quick adjective 1 moving with great speed. 2 lasting only a short time. 3 happening without any delay. 4 intelligent and able to understand things easily.

quick *adjective*
1 = brisk, fast, hasty, rapid, speedy, swift 2 = brief, cursory, hasty, hurried, perfunctory 3 = hasty, prompt, sudden

quickly *adverb* with great speed.

quickly *adverb*
= fast, hastily, hurriedly, rapidly, speedily, swiftly

quicksand *noun* an area of deep wet sand that you sink into if you walk on it.

quid quid *noun* (*informal*) In British English, a pound in money.

quiet *adjective* 1 Someone or something that is quiet makes very little noise or no noise at all. 2 Quiet also means peaceful. 3 A quiet event happens with very little fuss or publicity. ▶ *noun* 4 Quiet is silence. > **quietly** *adverb* > **quietness** *noun*

quiet *adjective*
1 = hushed, inaudible, low, silent, soft 2 = calm, mild, peaceful, restful, serene, tranquil
▶ *noun* 4 = calmness, peace, serenity, silence, stillness, tranquillity

quieten *verb* To quieten someone means to make them become quiet.

quill *noun* 1 A pen made from a feather. 2 A bird's quills are the large feathers on its wings and tail. 3 A porcupine's quills are its spines.

quilt *noun* A quilt for a bed is a cover, especially a cover that is padded.

quince *noun* a sour-tasting fruit used for making jam and marmalade.

quintessential *adjective* (*formal*) A person or thing that is quintessential seems to represent the basic nature of something in a pure, concentrated form.

quintet *noun* a group of five musicians who sing or play together; also a piece of music written for five instruments or singers.

quip quips, quipping, quipped *noun* 1 an amusing or clever remark. ▶ *verb* 2 To quip means to make an amusing or clever remark.

quirk *noun* 1 an odd habit or characteristic. 2 an unexpected event or development. > **quirky** *adjective*

quit quits, quitting, quit *verb* If you quit something, you leave it or stop doing it.

quit *verb*
= discontinue, give up, leave, resign, retire, stop

quite *adverb* 1 fairly but not very. 2 completely. ▶ *phrase* 3 You use quite a to emphasise that something is large or impressive.

quite *adverb*
1 = fairly, moderately, rather, reasonably, somewhat 2 = absolutely, completely, entirely, fully, perfectly, totally

quiver *verb* 1 If something quivers, it trembles. ▶ *noun* 2 a trembling movement.

quiz quizzes, quizzing, quizzed *noun* 1 a game in which the competitors are asked questions to test their knowledge. ▶ *verb* 2 If you quiz someone, you question them closely about something.

quizzical *adjective* amused and questioning.

q

quota *noun* a number or quantity of something which is officially allowed.

quotation *noun* an extract from a book or speech which is quoted.

quote *verb* **1** If you quote something that someone has written or said, you repeat their exact words. **2** If you quote a fact, you state it because it supports what you are saying. ▶ *noun* **3** an extract from a book or speech. **4** an estimate of how much a piece of work will cost.

> **quote** *verb*
> **1** = cite, extract, recite, repeat

quotient *noun* (MATHS) A quotient is the number that you get when you divide one number into another.

Qur'an another spelling of **Koran**.

Rr

RAAF In Australia, RAAF is an abbreviation for 'Royal Australian Air Force'.

rabbi *noun* a Jewish religious leader.

rabbit *noun* a small mammal with long ears.

rabble *noun* a noisy, disorderly crowd.

rabid *adjective* A rabid dog or other animal has rabies.

rabies *noun* an infectious disease which causes people and animals, especially dogs, to go mad and die.

raccoon; also spelt **racoon** *noun* a small North American mammal with a long striped tail.

race *noun* **1** a competition to see who is fastest, for example in running or driving. **2** one of the major groups that human beings can be divided into according to their physical features. ▶ *verb* **3** If you race someone, you compete with them in a race. **4** If you race something or if it races, it goes at its greatest rate. **5** If you race somewhere, you go there as quickly as possible. **> racing** *noun*

> **race** *noun*
> **2** = ethnic group, nation, people
> ▶ *verb* **5** = dash, fly, hurry, run, speed, tear

racecourse noun a grass track, sometimes with jumps, along which horses race.

racehorse noun a horse trained to run in races.

racial adjective relating to the different races that people belong to. > **racially** adverb

racism or **racialism** noun Racism or racialism is the treatment of some people as inferior because of their race or skin colour. > **racist** noun, adjective

rack noun 1 a piece of equipment for holding things or hanging things on. ▸ verb 2 If you are racked by something, you suffer because of it. ▸ phrase 3 (informal) If you **rack your brains**, you try hard to think of or remember something.

racket noun 1 If someone is making a racket, they are making a lot of noise. 2 an illegal way of making money. 3 Racket is another spelling of **racquet**.

> **racket** noun
> 1 = clamour, commotion, din, hubbub, noise, row, rumpus
> 2 = enterprise, fraud, scheme

racquet; also spelt **racket** noun a bat with strings across it used in tennis and similar games.

radar noun Radar is equipment used to track ships or aircraft that are out of sight by using radio signals that are reflected back from the object and shown on a screen.

radiant adjective 1 Someone who is radiant is so happy that it shows in their face. 2 glowing brightly. > **radiance** noun

radiate verb 1 If things radiate from a place, they form a pattern like lines spreading out from the centre of a circle. 2 If you radiate a quality or emotion, it shows clearly in your face and behaviour.

radiation noun (SCIENCE) the stream of particles given out by a radioactive substance.

radiator noun 1 a hollow metal device for heating a room, usually connected to a central heating system. 2 the part of a car that is filled with water to cool the engine.

radical noun 1 Radicals are people who think there should be great changes in society, and try to make them happen. ▸ adjective 2 very significant, important or basic. > **radically** adverb > **radicalism** noun

radio radios, radioing, radioed noun 1 Radio is a system of sending sound over a distance by transmitting electrical signals. 2 Radio is also the broadcasting of programmes to the public by radio. 3 a piece of equipment for listening to radio programmes. ▸ verb 4 To radio someone means to send them a message by radio.

radioactive adjective giving off powerful and harmful rays. > **radioactivity** noun

radiotherapy noun the treatment of diseases such as cancer using radiation. > **radiotherapist** noun

radish noun a small salad vegetable with a red skin and white flesh and a hot taste.

radius radii or radiuses noun (MATHS) The radius of a circle is the length of a straight line drawn from its centre to its circumference.

RAF In Britain, RAF is an abbreviation for 'Royal Air Force'.

raffle *noun* a competition in which people buy numbered tickets and win a prize if they have the ticket that is chosen.

raft *noun* a floating platform made from long pieces of wood tied together.

rafter *noun* Rafters are the sloping pieces of wood that support a roof.

rag *noun* 1 a piece of old cloth used to clean or wipe things. 2 If someone is dressed in rags, they are wearing old torn clothes.

rage *noun* 1 Rage is great anger. ▶ *verb* 2 To rage about something means to speak angrily about it. 3 If something such as a storm or battle is raging, it is continuing with great force or violence.

> **rage** *noun*
> 1 = anger, frenzy, fury, wrath
> ▶ *verb* 2 = be furious, fume, lose your temper, rave, storm 3 = be at its height, rampage, storm, surge

ragged *adjective* Ragged clothes are old and torn.

raid *verb* 1 To raid a place means to enter it by force to attack or steal something. ▶ *noun* 2 the raiding of a building or a place.

> **raid** *verb*
> 1 = assault, attack, break into, invade, plunder
> ▶ *noun* 2 = attack, break-in, foray

rail *noun* 1 a fixed horizontal bar used as a support or for hanging things on. 2 Rails are the steel bars which trains run along. 3 Rail is the railway considered as a means of transport.

railing *noun* Railings are a fence made from metal bars.

railway *noun* a route along which trains travel on steel rails.

rain *noun* 1 water falling from the clouds in small drops. ▶ *verb* 2 When it is raining, rain is falling. > **rainy** *adjective*

> **rain** *noun*
> 1 = deluge, downpour, drizzle, rainfall, showers
> ▶ *verb* 2 = drizzle, pour, teem

rainbow *noun* an arch of different colours that sometimes appears in the sky when it is raining.

raincoat *noun* a waterproof coat.

rainfall *noun* the amount of rain that falls in a place during a particular period.

rainforest *noun* (GEOGRAPHY) a dense forest of tall trees where there is a lot of rain.

rainwater *noun* rain that has been stored.

raise *verb* 1 If you raise something, you make it higher. 2 If you raise your voice, you speak more loudly. 3 To raise money for a cause means to get people to donate money towards it. 4 To raise a child means to look after it until it is grown up. 5 If you raise a subject, you mention it.

> **raise** *verb*
> 1 = elevate, heave, hoist, lift
> 4 = bring up, nurture, rear
> 5 = advance, bring up, broach, introduce, moot, suggest

raisin *noun* Raisins are dried grapes.

rake *noun* a garden tool with a row of metal teeth and a long handle. > **rake up** *verb* If you rake up something embarrassing from the past, you remind someone about it.

rally rallies, rallying, rallied noun
1 a large public meeting held to show support for something.
2 a competition in which vehicles are raced over public roads.
3 In tennis or squash, a rally is a continuous series of shots exchanged by the players.
▶ verb 4 When people rally to something, they gather together to continue a struggle or to support something.

ram rams, ramming, rammed verb
1 If one vehicle rams another, it crashes into it. 2 To ram something somewhere means to push it there firmly. ▶ noun
3 an adult male sheep.

RAM noun (ICT) a storage space which can be filled with data but which loses its contents when the machine is switched off. RAM stands for 'random access memory'.

Ramadan noun (RE) the ninth month of the Muslim year, during which Muslims eat and drink nothing during daylight.

ramble noun 1 a long walk in the countryside. ▶ verb 2 To ramble means to go for a ramble. 3 To ramble also means to talk in a confused way. ▶ **rambler** noun

> **ramble** noun
> 1 = excursion, hike, stroll, walk
> ▶ verb 2 = amble, stray, stroll, walk, wander 3 = babble, chatter

ramification noun The ramifications of a decision or plan are all its consequences and effects.

ramp noun a sloping surface connecting two different levels.

rampage verb 1 To rampage means to rush about wildly causing damage. ▶ phrase 2 To go **on the rampage** means to rush about in a wild or violent way.

> **rampage** verb
> 1 = go berserk, rage, run amok, run riot
> ▶ phrase 2 **on the rampage** = amok, berserk, wild

rampant adjective If something such as crime or disease is rampant, it is growing or spreading uncontrollably.

ramshackle adjective A ramshackle building is in very poor condition.

ran the past tense of **run**.

ranch noun a large farm where cattle or horses are reared, especially in the USA.

rancid adjective Rancid food has gone bad.

rancour noun (formal) Rancour is bitter hatred. ▶ **rancorous** adjective

rand noun The rand is the main unit of currency in South Africa.

random adjective 1 A random choice or arrangement is not based on any definite plan.
▶ phrase 2 If you do something **at random**, you do it without any definite plan. ▶ **randomly** adverb

> **random** adjective
> 1 = aimless, arbitrary, haphazard, indiscriminate, spot
> ▶ phrase 2 **at random** = aimlessly, arbitrarily, haphazardly, indiscriminate, randomly

rang the past tense of **ring**.

range noun 1 The range of something is the maximum distance over which it can reach things or detect things. 2 a number of different things of the same kind. 3 a set of values on a scale. 4 A range of mountains is a line of them. 5 A rifle range or firing range is a place where people practise shooting at targets. ▶ verb 6 When a set of things ranges between two points, they vary within these points on a scale.

> **range** noun
> 1 = bounds, extent, field, limits, province, scope 2 = assortment, class, gamut, selection, series, variety
> ▶ verb 6 = extend, go, run, stretch, vary

ranger noun someone whose job is to look after a forest or park.

rank noun 1 Someone's rank is their official level in a job or profession. 2 The ranks are the ordinary members of the armed forces, rather than the officers. 3 The ranks of a group are its members. 4 a row of people or things. ▶ verb 5 To rank as something means to have that status or position on a scale. ▶ adjective 6 complete and absolute. 7 having a strong, unpleasant smell.

> **rank** noun
> 1 = class, echelon, grade, level, standing, station, status
> 4 = column, file, line, row
> ▶ adjective 6 = absolute, complete, downright, sheer, unmitigated, utter

ransack verb To ransack a place means to disturb severely and leave it in a mess, in order to search for or steal something.

ransom noun money that is demanded to free someone who has been kidnapped.

rant verb To rant means to talk loudly in an excited or angry way.

rap raps, rapping, rapped verb 1 If you rap something, you hit it with a series of quick blows. ▶ noun 2 a quick knock or blow on something. 3 Rap is a style of poetry spoken to music with a strong rhythmic beat.

rapid adjective happening or moving very quickly. > **rapidly** adverb > **rapidity** noun

rapport noun (formal) If there is a rapport between two people, they find it easy to understand each other's feelings and attitudes.

rapt adjective If you are rapt, you are so interested in something that you are not aware of other things.

rapture noun Rapture is a feeling of extreme delight. > **rapturous** adjective > **rapturously** adverb

rare adjective 1 Something that is rare is not common or does not happen often. 2 Rare meat has been lightly cooked. > **rarely** adverb

> **rare** adjective
> 1 = exceptional, few, scarce, sparse, sporadic, uncommon, unusual

raring adjective If you are raring to do something, you are very eager to do it.

rarity rarities noun 1 something that is interesting or valuable because it is unusual. 2 The rarity of something is the fact that it is not common.

R

rash *adjective* 1 If you are rash, you do something hasty and foolish. ▶ *noun* 2 an area of red spots that appear on your skin when you are ill or have an allergy. 3 A rash of events is a lot of them happening in a short time. > **rashly** *adverb*

> **rash** *adjective*
> 1 = foolhardy, hasty, impetuous, impulsive, reckless
> ▶ *noun* 2 = eruption, outbreak
> 3 = epidemic, flood, plague, spate, wave

rasp *verb* 1 To rasp means to make a harsh unpleasant sound. ▶ *noun* 2 a coarse file with rows of raised teeth, used for smoothing wood or metal.

raspberry raspberries *noun* a small, red soft fruit that grows on a bush.

rat *noun* a long-tailed animal which looks like a large mouse.

rate *noun* 1 The rate of something is the speed or frequency with which it happens. 2 The rate of interest is its level. 3 the cost or charge for something. 4 In some countries, rates are a local tax paid by people who own buildings. ▶ *phrase* 5 If you say at **this rate** something will happen, you mean it will happen if things continue in the same way. 6 You say **at any rate** when you want to add to or amend what you have just said. ▶ *verb* 7 The way you rate someone or something is your opinion of them.

> **rate** *noun*
> 1 = frequency, pace, speed, tempo, velocity 3 = charge, cost, fee, price, tariff
> ▶ *verb* 7 = appraise, class, consider, count, rank, regard

rather *adverb* 1 Rather means to a certain extent: *We got along rather well.* ▶ *phrase* 2 If you **would rather** do a particular thing, you would prefer to do it. 3 If you do one thing **rather than** another, you choose to do the first thing instead of the second.

> **rather** *adverb*
> 1 = fairly, pretty (*informal*), quite, relatively, slightly, somewhat

ratify ratifies, ratifying, ratified *verb (formal)* To ratify a written agreement means to approve it formally, usually by signing it. > **ratification** *noun*

rating *noun* 1 a score based on the quality or status of something. 2 The ratings are statistics showing how popular each television programme is.

ratio ratios *noun* 1 a relationship which shows how many times one thing is bigger than another. 2 (MATHS) a relationship between two numbers, which shows how many times one number goes into another: *The ratio of 1 to 6 is shown as 1:6.*

ration *noun* 1 Your ration of something is the amount you are allowed to have. 2 Rations are the food given each day to a soldier or member of an expedition. ▶ *verb* 3 When something is rationed, you are only allowed a limited amount of it, because there is a shortage.

rational *adjective* When people are rational, their judgments are based on reason rather than emotion. > **rationally** *adverb* > **rationality** *noun*

> **rational** *adjective*
> = enlightened, logical, reasonable, sensible

r

rationale noun The rationale for a course of action or for a belief is the set of reasons on which it is based.

rattle verb 1 When something rattles, it makes short, regular knocking sounds. 2 If something rattles you, it upsets you. ▶ noun 3 the noise something makes when it rattles. 4 a baby's toy which makes a noise when it is shaken.

raucous adjective A raucous voice is loud and rough.

ravage (formal) verb 1 To ravage something means to seriously harm or damage it. ▶ noun 2 The ravages of something are its damaging effects.

rave verb 1 If someone raves, they talk in an angry, uncontrolled way. 2 (informal) If you rave about something, you talk about it very enthusiastically. ▶ adjective 3 (informal) If something gets a rave review, it is praised enthusiastically. ▶ noun 4 (informal) a large party with electronic dance music.

> **rave** verb
> 1 = babble, rage, rant 2 = be wild about (informal), enthuse, gush

raven noun 1 a large black bird with a deep, harsh call. ▶ adjective 2 Raven hair is black and shiny.

ravenous adjective very hungry.

ravine noun a deep, narrow valley with steep sides.

raving adjective 1 If someone is raving, they are speaking in a strange, wild way. ▶ noun 2 Someone's ravings are strange things they write or say.

ravioli noun Ravioli consists of small squares of pasta filled with meat or other ingredients and served with a sauce.

ravishing adjective Someone or something that is ravishing is very beautiful.

raw adjective 1 Raw food has not been cooked. 2 A raw substance is in its natural state. 3 If part of your body is raw, the skin has come off or been rubbed away. 4 Someone who is raw is too young or too new in a job or situation to know how to behave.

raw material noun Raw materials are the natural substances used to make something.

ray noun 1 a beam of light or radiation. 2 A ray of hope is a small amount that makes an unpleasant situation seem slightly better. 3 a large sea fish with eyes on the top of its body, and a long tail.

raze verb To raze a building, town or forest means to completely destroy it.

razor noun a tool that people use for shaving.

re- prefix 1 'Re-' is used to form nouns and verbs that refer to the repetition of an action or process: reread. 2 'Re-' is also used to form verbs that refer to going back to a previous condition: renew.

reach verb 1 When you reach a place, you arrive there. 2 When you reach for something, you stretch out your arm to it. 3 If something reaches a place or point, it extends as far as that place or point. 4 If something or someone reaches a stage or level, they get to it. 5 To reach an agreement or decision means

R

to succeed in achieving it.
▶ *phrase* 6 If a place is **within reach**, you can get there. 7 If something is **out of reach**, you cannot get it to it by stretching out your arm.

> **reach** *verb*
> 1 = arrive at, get as far as, get to, make 3 = extend to, go as far as 4 = arrive at, attain, climb to, fall to, rise to

react *verb* When you react to something, you behave in a particular way because of it.

reaction *noun* 1 Your reaction to something is what you feel, say or do because of it. 2 Your reactions are your ability to move quickly in response to something that happens. 3 If there is a reaction against something, it becomes unpopular.

> **reaction** *noun*
> 1 = acknowledgment, answer, feedback, response
> 3 = backlash, counterbalance

reactionary reactionaries *adjective* 1 Someone who is reactionary tries to prevent political or social change. ▶ *noun* 2 Reactionaries are reactionary people.

reactor *noun* a device which is used to produce nuclear energy.

read reads, reading, read *verb* 1 When you read, you look at something written and follow it or say it aloud. 2 If you can read someone's moods or mind, you can judge what they are feeling or thinking. 3 When you read a meter or gauge, you look at it and record the figure on it. 4 If you read a subject at university, you study it.

> **read** *verb*
> 1 = glance at, look at, pore over, scan, study 2 = comprehend, decipher, interpret

reader *noun* 1 The readers of a newspaper or magazine are the people who read it regularly. 2 At a university, a reader is a senior lecturer just below the rank of professor.

readership *noun* The readership of a newspaper or magazine consists of the people who read it regularly.

readily *adverb* 1 willingly and eagerly. 2 easily done or quickly obtainable.

reading *noun* 1 Reading is the activity of reading books. 2 The reading on a meter or gauge is the figure or measurement it shows.

readjust *verb* 1 If you readjust, you adapt to a new situation. 2 If you readjust something, you alter it to a different position.

ready *adjective* 1 having reached the required stage, or prepared for action or use. 2 willing or eager to do something. 3 easily produced or obtained. > **readiness** *noun*

> **ready** *adjective*
> 1 = organised, prepared, primed, ripe, set 2 = agreeable, eager, happy, keen, willing 3 = accessible, available, convenient, handy

ready-made *adjective* already made and therefore able to be used immediately.

reaffirm *verb* To reaffirm something means to state it again.

real *adjective* 1 actually existing and not imagined or invented.

2 genuine and not imitation.
3 true or actual and not mistaken.

> **real** adjective
> 1 = actual, authentic, concrete, factual, genuine, legitimate, tangible, true 2 = authentic, bona fide, dinkum (*Australian and New Zealand*; *informal*), genuine, honest, rightful, sincere, true, unaffected

real estate noun Real estate is property in the form of land and buildings rather than personal possessions.

realise; also spelt **realize** verb 1 If you realise something, you become aware of it. 2 (*formal*) If your hopes or fears are realised, what you hoped for or feared actually happens. > **realisation** noun

> **realise** verb
> 1 = appreciate, comprehend, grasp, recognise, understand

realism noun Realism is the recognition of the true nature of a situation. > **realist** noun

realistic adjective 1 recognising and accepting the true nature of a situation. 2 representing things in a way that is true to real life. > **realistically** adverb

> **realistic** adjective
> 1 = down-to-earth, level-headed, matter-of-fact, practical, sensible, sober 2 = authentic, faithful, lifelike, true

reality noun 1 Reality is the real nature of things, rather than the way someone imagines it. 2 If something has become reality, it actually exists or is actually happening.

reality noun
1 = authenticity, fact, realism, truth

really adverb 1 used to add emphasis to what is being said: *I'm not really surprised.* 2 used to indicate that you are talking about the true facts about something: *What was really going on?*

> **really** adverb
> 1 = absolutely, certainly, extremely, remarkably, terribly, truly, very 2 = actually, in fact, in reality, truly

realm noun (*formal*) 1 You can refer to any area of thought or activity as a realm. 2 a country with a king or queen.

reap verb 1 To reap a crop such as corn means to cut and gather it. 2 When people reap benefits or rewards, they get them as a result of hard work or careful planning. > **reaper** noun

reappear verb When people or things reappear, you can see them again, because they have come back. > **reappearance** noun

rear noun 1 The rear of something is the part at the back. ▶ verb 2 To rear children or young animals means to bring them up until they are able to look after themselves. 3 When a horse rears, it raises the front part of its body, so that its front legs are in the air.

rearrange verb To rearrange something means to organise or arrange it in a different way.

reason noun 1 The reason for something explains the fact or situation which explains why it happens or which causes it to happen. 2 If you have reason to believe or feel something, there are definite reasons why you believe it or feel it. **3** Reason is the ability to think and make judgments. ▶ verb **4** If you reason that something is true, you decide it is true after considering all the facts. **5** If you reason with someone, you persuade them to accept sensible arguments.

reason noun
1 = cause, grounds, incentive, motive, purpose **3** = intellect, judgment, rationality, reasoning, sense
▶ verb **5** = bring round (informal), persuade, win over

reasonable adjective **1** Reasonable behaviour is fair and sensible. **2** If an explanation is reasonable, there are good reasons for thinking it is correct. **3** A reasonable amount is a fairly large amount. **4** A reasonable price is fair and not too high.
> **reasonably** adverb

reasonable adjective
1 = fair, moderate, rational, sane, sensible, sober, steady, wise **2** = justifiable, legitimate, logical, sensible, sound, understandable **4** = cheap, competitive, fair, inexpensive, low, modest

reasoning noun Reasoning is the process by which you reach a conclusion after considering all the facts.

reassess verb If you reassess something, you consider whether it still has the same value or importance. > **reassessment** noun

reassure verb If you reassure someone, you say or do things that make them less worried.
> **reassurance** noun

reassure verb
= bolster, cheer up, comfort, encourage

rebate noun money paid back to someone who has paid too much tax or rent.

rebel rebels, rebelling, rebelled noun **1** (HISTORY) Rebels are people who are fighting their own country's army to change the political system. **2** Someone who is a rebel rejects society's values and behaves differently from other people. ▶ verb **3** To rebel means to fight against authority or reject accepted values.

rebel verb
3 = defy, mutiny, resist, revolt

rebellion noun (HISTORY) A rebellion is organised and often violent opposition to authority.

rebellion noun
= insurrection, mutiny, revolt, revolution, uprising

rebellious adjective unwilling to obey and likely to rebel against authority.

rebound verb When something rebounds, it bounces or springs back after hitting a solid surface.

rebuff verb **1** If you rebuff someone, you reject what they offer. ▶ noun **2** a rejection of an offer.

rebuild rebuilds, rebuilding, rebuilt verb When a town or building is rebuilt, it is built again after being damaged or destroyed.

rebuke verb To rebuke someone means to speak severely to them about something they have done.

recall verb 1 To recall something means to remember it. 2 If you are recalled to a place, you are ordered to return there. 3 If a company recalls products, it asks people to return them because they are faulty.

recap recaps, recapping, recapped verb 1 To recap means to repeat and summarise the main points of an explanation or discussion. ▶ noun 2 a summary of the main points of an explanation or discussion.

recapture verb 1 When you recapture a pleasant feeling, you experience it again. 2 When soldiers recapture a place, they capture it from the people who took it from them. 3 When animals or prisoners are recaptured, they are caught after they have escaped.

recede verb 1 When something recedes, it moves away into the distance. 2 If a man's hair is receding, he is starting to go bald at the front.

receipt noun 1 a piece of paper confirming that money or goods have been received. 2 In a shop or theatre, the money received is often called the receipts. 3 (formal) The receipt of something is the receiving of it.

receive verb 1 When you receive something, someone gives it to you, or you get it after it has been sent to you. 2 To receive something also means to have it happen to you: *injuries she received in a car crash.* 3 When you receive visitors or guests, you welcome them. 4 If something is received in a particular way, that is how people react to it.

receive verb
1 = accept, be given, get, pick up, take 2 = encounter, suffer, sustain, undergo 3 = entertain, greet, meet, take in, welcome

receiver noun the part of a telephone you hold near to your ear and mouth.

recent adjective Something recent happened a short time ago.
> **recently** adverb

recent adjective
= current, fresh, new, present-day, up-to-date

reception noun 1 In a hotel or office, reception is the place near the entrance where appointments or enquiries are dealt with. 2 a formal party. 3 The reception someone or something gets is the way people react to them. 4 If your radio or television gets good reception, the sound or picture is clear.

receptionist noun The receptionist in a hotel or office deals with people when they arrive, answers the telephone, and arranges appointments.

receptive adjective Someone who is receptive to ideas or suggestions is willing to consider them.

recess noun 1 a period when no work is done by a committee or parliament. 2 a place where part of a wall has been built further back than the rest.

recession noun a period when a country's economy is less successful and more people become unemployed.

recession noun
= decline, depression, downturn, slump

recharge *verb* To recharge a battery means to charge it with electricity again after it has been used.

recipe *noun* 1 (DGT) a list of ingredients and instructions for cooking something. 2 If something is a recipe for disaster or for success, it is likely to result in disaster or success.

recipient *noun* The recipient of something is the person receiving it.

reciprocal *adjective* A reciprocal agreement involves two people, groups or countries helping each other in a similar way.

reciprocate *verb* If you reciprocate someone's feelings or behaviour, you feel or behave in the same way towards them.

recital *noun* a performance of music or poetry, usually by one person.

recite *verb* If you recite a poem or something you have learnt, you say it aloud. > **recitation** *noun*

reckless *adjective* showing a complete lack of care about danger or damage. > **recklessly** *adverb* > **recklessness** *noun*

reckon *verb* 1 (*informal*) If you reckon that something is true, you think it is true. 2 To reckon an amount means to calculate it. 3 If you had not reckoned with something, you had not expected it and therefore were unprepared when it happened.

> **reckon** *verb*
> 1 = assume, believe, consider, judge, suppose, think
> 2 = calculate, count, estimate, figure out, work out

reclaim *verb* 1 When you reclaim something, you collect it after leaving it somewhere or losing it. 2 To reclaim land means to make it suitable for use, for example by draining it. > **reclamation** *noun*

recline *verb* To recline means to lie or lean back at an angle.

recluse *noun* Someone who is a recluse lives alone and avoids other people. > **reclusive** *adjective*

recognise; also spelt **recognize** *verb* 1 If you recognise someone or something, you realise that you know who or what they are. 2 To recognise something also means to accept and acknowledge it. > **recognition** *noun* > **recognisable** *adjective* > **recognisably** *adverb*

> **recognise** *verb*
> 1 = identify, know, place, spot
> 2 = acknowledge, appreciate, honour, salute

recoil *verb* To recoil from something means to draw back in shock or horror.

recommend *verb* If you recommend something to someone, you praise it and suggest they try it. > **recommendation** *noun*

reconcile *verb* 1 To reconcile two things that seem to oppose one another means to make them work or exist together successfully. 2 When people are reconciled, they become friendly again after a quarrel. 3 If you reconcile yourself to an unpleasant situation, you accept it. > **reconciliation** *noun*

reconnaissance *noun* Reconnaissance is the gathering of military information by soldiers, planes or satellites.

r

reconsider *verb* To reconsider something means to think about it again to decide whether to change it. ▶ **reconsideration** *noun*

reconstruct *verb* 1 To reconstruct something that has been damaged means to build it again. 2 To reconstruct a past event means to get a complete description of it from small pieces of information.
▶ **reconstruction** *noun*

> **reconstruct** *verb*
> 1 = rebuild, recreate, regenerate, renovate, restore 2 = build up, deduce, piece together

record *noun* 1 If you keep a record of something, you keep a written account or store information in a computer. 2 a round, flat piece of plastic on which music has been recorded. 3 an achievement which is the best of its type. 4 Your record is what is known about your achievements or past activities. ▶ *verb* 5 If you record information, you write it down or put it into a computer. 6 To record sound means to preserve it on tape or disc, or digitally. ▶ *adjective* 7 higher, lower, better or worse than ever before.

> **record** *noun*
> 1 = account, archive, file, journal, minute, register
> 4 = background, career, curriculum vitae, track record (*informal*)
> ▶ *verb* 5 = blog, document, enter, log, note, register, write down

recorder *noun* a small woodwind instrument.

recording *noun* A recording of something is a tape, disc etc of it.

recount *verb* 1 If you recount a story, you tell it. ▶ *noun* 2 a second count of votes in an election when the result is very close.

recoup *verb* If you recoup money that you have spent or lost, you get it back.

recourse *noun* (*formal*) If you have recourse to something, you use it to help you.

recover *verb* 1 To recover from an illness or unhappy experience means to get well again or get over it. 2 If you recover a lost object or your ability to do something, you get it back.

> **recover** *verb*
> 1 = convalesce, get better, get well, improve, recuperate, revive 2 = get back, recapture, recoup, regain, retrieve

recovery *noun* 1 the act of getting better again. 2 the act of getting something back.

> **recovery** *noun*
> 1 = healing, improvement, recuperation, revival
> 2 = recapture, reclamation, restoration, retrieval

recreate *verb* To recreate something means to succeed in making it happen or exist again.

recreation *noun* Recreation is all the things that you do for enjoyment in your spare time.
> **recreational** *adjective*

recrimination *noun* Recriminations are accusations made by people about each other.

recruit *verb* 1 To recruit people means to get them to join a group or help with something. ▶ *noun* 2 someone who has joined the

army or some other organisation.
> **recruitment** noun

recruit verb
1 = draft, enlist, enrol, muster
▶ noun 2 = beginner, convert,
novice, trainee

rectangle noun (MATHS) a four-
sided shape with four right
angles. > **rectangular** adjective

rectify rectifies, rectifying,
rectified verb (formal) If you rectify
something that is wrong, you put
it right.

rector noun a Church of England
priest in charge of a parish.

rectory rectories noun a house
where a rector lives.

rectum noun (technical) the bottom
end of the tube down which
waste food passes out of your
body. > **rectal** adjective

recuperate verb When you
recuperate, you gradually recover
after being ill or injured.
> **recuperation** noun

recur recurs, recurring, recurred
verb If something recurs, it
happens or occurs again.
> **recurrence** noun > **recurrent**
adjective

recurring adjective 1 happening or
occurring many times. 2 (MATHS)
A recurring digit is one that is
repeated over and over again after
the decimal point.

recycle verb (GEOGRAPHY) To
recycle used products means to
process them so that they can be
used again.

red redder, reddest noun, adjective
1 Red is the colour of blood or of a
ripe tomato. ▶ adjective 2 Red hair
is between red and brown in
colour.

redeem verb 1 If a feature redeems

an unpleasant thing or situation,
it makes it seem less bad. 2 If
you redeem yourself, you do
something that gives people a
good opinion of you again. 3 If
you redeem something, you get it
back by paying for it. 4 (RE) In
Christianity, Jesus Christ is said
to have redeemed the human race
by paying the price of his life to
save them from sin and death.

redemption noun Redemption is
the state of being redeemed.

red-handed phrase To catch
someone red-handed means to
catch them doing something
wrong.

red-hot adjective Red-hot metal
has been heated to such a high
temperature that it has turned
red.

redress (formal) verb 1 To redress a
wrong means to put it right.
▶ noun 2 If you get redress for
harm done to you, you are
compensated for it.

red tape noun Red tape is official
rules and procedures that seem
unnecessary and cause delay. In
the 18th century, red tape was
used to bind official government
documents.

reduce verb 1 To reduce
something means to make it
smaller in size or amount.
2 You can use 'reduce' to say
that someone or something is
changed to a weaker or inferior
state.

reduce verb
1 = curtail, cut, cut down,
decrease, diminish, lessen,
lower, shorten 2 = degrade,
demote, downgrade, drive,
force

reduction *noun* When there is a reduction in something, it is made smaller.

redundancy redundancies *noun* 1 Redundancy is the state of being redundant. 2 The number of redundancies is the number of people made redundant.

redundant *adjective* 1 When people are made redundant, they lose their jobs because there is no more work for them or no money to pay them. 2 When something becomes redundant, it is no longer needed.

reed *noun* 1 Reeds are hollow stemmed plants that grow in shallow water or wet ground. 2 a thin piece of cane or metal inside some wind instruments which vibrates when air is blown over it.

reef *noun* (GEOGRAPHY) a long line of rocks or coral close to the surface of the sea.

reek *verb* 1 To reek of something means to smell strongly and unpleasantly of it. ▶ *noun* 2 If there is a reek of something, there is a strong unpleasant smell of it.

reel *noun* 1 a cylindrical object around which you wrap something; often part of a device which you turn as a control. 2 a fast Scottish dance. ▶ *verb* 3 When someone reels, they move unsteadily as if they are going to fall. 4 If your mind is reeling, you are confused because you have too much to think about. ▶ **reel off** *verb* If you reel off information, you repeat it from memory quickly and easily.

re-elect *verb* When someone is re-elected, they win an election again and are able to stay in power.

refer refers, referring, referred *verb* 1 If you refer to something, you mention it. 2 If you refer to a book or record, you look at it to find something out. 3 When a problem or issue is referred to someone, they are formally asked to deal with it.

> **refer** *verb*
> 1 = allude, bring up, cite, mention 2 = consult, look up

referee *noun* 1 the official who controls a football game or a boxing or wrestling match. 2 someone who gives a reference to a person who is applying for a job.

reference *noun* 1 A reference to something or someone is a mention of them. 2 Reference is the act of referring to something or someone for information or advice. 3 a number or name that tells you where to find information or identifies a document. 4 If someone gives you a reference when you apply for a job, they write a letter about your abilities.

referendum referendums or referenda *noun* a vote in which all the people in a country are officially asked whether they agree with a particular proposal.

refine *verb* To refine a raw material such as oil or sugar means to process it to remove impurities.

refined *adjective* 1 very polite and well-mannered. 2 processed to remove impurities.

> **refined** *adjective*
> 1 = civilised, genteel, gentlemanly, ladylike, polite 2 = distilled, filtered, processed, pure, purified

refinement noun 1 Refinements are minor improvements. 2 Refinement is politeness and good manners.

refinery refineries noun a factory where substances such as oil or sugar are refined.

reflect verb 1 If something reflects an attitude or situation, it shows what it is like. 2 (SCIENCE) If something reflects light or heat, the light or heat bounces off it. 3 When something is reflected in a mirror or water, you can see its image in it. 4 (MATHS) If something reflects, its direction is reversed. 5 When you reflect, you think about something. > **reflective** adjective > **reflectively** adverb

reflection noun 1 If something is a reflection of something else, it shows what it is like. 2 an image in a mirror or water. 3 (SCIENCE) Reflection is the process by which light and heat are bounced off a surface. 4 (MATHS) In maths, reflection is also the turning over of something on itself. 5 Reflection is also thought.

reflex noun 1 A reflex or reflex action is a sudden uncontrollable movement that you make as a result of pressure or a blow. 2 If you have good reflexes, you respond very quickly when something unexpected happens. ▶ adjective 3 (MATHS) A reflex angle is between 180° and 360°.

reform noun 1 Reforms are major changes to laws or institutions. ▶ verb 2 When laws or institutions are reformed, major changes are made to them. 3 When people reform, they stop committing crimes or doing other unacceptable things. > **reformer** noun

> **reform** noun
> 1 = amendment, correction, improvement, rehabilitation
> ▶ verb 2 = amend, better, correct, rectify, rehabilitate

Reformation noun (HISTORY) The Reformation was a religious and political movement in Europe in the 16th century that began as an attempt to reform the Roman Catholic Church, but ended in the establishment of the Protestant Churches.

refrain verb 1 (formal) If you refrain from doing something, you do not do it. ▶ noun 2 (MUSIC) The refrain of a song is a short, simple part, repeated after each verse.

refresh verb 1 If something refreshes you when you are hot or tired, it makes you feel cooler or more energetic. ▶ phrase 2 To refresh someone's memory means to remind them of something they had forgotten.

> **refresh** verb
> 1 = brace, enliven, rejuvenate, revive, stimulate

refreshing adjective You say that something is refreshing when it is pleasantly different from what you are used to.

refreshment noun Refreshments are drinks and small amounts of food provided at an event.

refrigerator noun an electrically cooled container in which you store food to keep it fresh.

refuel refuels, refuelling, refuelled verb When an aircraft or vehicle is refuelled, it is filled with more fuel.

r

refuge noun 1 a place where you go for safety. 2 If you take refuge, you go somewhere for safety or behave in a way that will protect you.

> **refuge** noun
> 1 = asylum, harbour, haven, sanctuary, shelter

refugee noun Refugees are people who have been forced to leave their country and live elsewhere.

refund noun 1 money returned to you because you have paid too much for something or because you have returned goods. ▶ verb 2 To refund someone's money means to return it to them after they have paid for something with it.

refurbish verb (formal) To refurbish a building means to decorate it and repair damage.
> **refurbishment** noun

refusal noun A refusal is when someone says firmly that they will not do, allow or accept something.

refuse¹ verb 1 If you refuse to do something, you say or decide firmly that you will not do it. 2 If someone refuses something, they do not allow it or do not accept it.

> **refuse** verb
> 1 = abstain (formal), decline, withhold 2 = decline, reject, spurn, turn down

refuse² noun Refuse is rubbish or waste.

> **refuse** noun
> = garbage (informal), junk (informal), litter, rubbish, trash, waste

refute verb (formal) To refute a theory or argument means to prove that it is wrong.

regain verb To regain something means to get it back.

regal adjective very grand and suitable for a king or queen.
> **regally** adverb

regard verb 1 To regard someone or something in a particular way means to think of them in that way or have that opinion of them. 2 (literary) To regard someone in a particular way also means to look at them in that way. ▶ noun 3 If you have a high regard for someone, you have a very good opinion of them. ▶ phrase 4 Regarding, as regards, with regard to and in regard to are all used to indicate what you are talking or writing about. 5 'Regards' is used in various expressions to express friendly feelings.

> **regard** verb
> 1 = consider, judge, look on, see, think of, view 2 = contemplate, eye, gaze, look, scrutinise, watch

regardless preposition, adverb done or happening in spite of something else: He led from the front, regardless of the danger.

regatta noun a race meeting for sailing or rowing boats.

regenerate verb (formal) To regenerate something means to develop and improve it after it has been declining.
> **regeneration** noun

regent noun someone who rules in place of a king or queen who is ill or too young to rule.

reggae noun Reggae is a type of music, originally from Jamaica, with a strong beat.

regime noun a system of government, and the people who are ruling a country.

regiment noun a large group of soldiers commanded by a colonel. > **regimental** adjective

regimented adjective very strictly controlled. > **regimentation** noun

region noun 1 (GEOGRAPHY) a large area of land. 2 You can refer to any area or part as a region.
▶ phrase 3 **In the region of** means approximately. > **regional** adjective > **regionally** adverb

> **region** noun
> 1 = area, district, land, locality, quarter, sector, territory, tract, zone

register noun 1 an official list or record of things. 2 (technical) a style of speaking or writing used in particular circumstances or social occasions. ▶ verb 3 When something is registered, it is recorded on an official list. 4 If an instrument registers a measurement, it shows it. 5 If your face registers a feeling, it expresses it. > **registration** noun

registrar noun 1 a person who keeps official records of births, marriages and deaths. 2 At a college or university, the registrar is a senior administrative official. 3 a senior hospital doctor.

registration number noun the sequence of letters and numbers on the front and back of a motor vehicle that identify it.

registry registries noun a place where official records are kept.

regret regrets, regretting, regretted verb 1 If you regret something, you are sorry that it happened. ▶ noun 2 If you have regrets, you are sad or sorry about something. > **regretful** adjective > **regretfully** adverb

> **regret** verb
> 1 = be sorry, grieve, lament, mourn, repent
> ▶ noun 2 = grief, pang of conscience, penitence, remorse, repentance, sorrow

regrettable adjective unfortunate and undesirable. > **regrettably** adverb

regular adjective 1 even and equally spaced: soft music with a regular beat. 2 (MATHS) A regular shape has equal angles and equal sides. 3 Regular events or activities happen often and according to a pattern, for example each day or each week. 4 If you are a regular customer or visitor somewhere, you go there often. 5 usual or normal: It's way past his regular bedtime. 6 having a well balanced appearance. ▶ noun 7 People who go to a place often are known as its regulars. > **regularly** adverb > **regularity** noun

> **regular** adjective
> 1 = consistent, constant, even, periodic, rhythmic, steady, uniform 5 = customary, everyday, habitual, normal, ordinary, routine, typical, usual

regulate verb To regulate something means to control the way it operates. > **regulator** noun

regulation noun 1 Regulations are official rules. 2 Regulation is the control of something.

rehabilitate verb To rehabilitate someone who has been ill or in prison means to help them lead a normal life. > **rehabilitation** noun

rehearsal noun (DRAMA) a practice of a performance in preparation for the actual event.

rehearse verb (DRAMA) To rehearse a performance means to practise it in preparation for the actual event.

reign verb 1 When a king or queen reigns, he or she rules a country. 2 You can say that something reigns when it is a noticeable feature of a situation or period of time. ▶ noun 3 (HISTORY) The reign of a king or queen is the period during which he or she reigns.

rein noun 1 Reins are the thin leather straps which you hold when you are riding a horse. ▶ phrase 2 To **keep a tight rein on** someone or something means to control them firmly.

reincarnation noun (RE) People who believe in reincarnation believe that when you die, you are born again as another creature.

reindeer reindeer noun Reindeer are deer with large antlers that live in northern regions.

reinforce verb 1 To reinforce something means to strengthen it. 2 If something reinforces an idea or claim, it provides evidence to support it.

reinforcement noun 1 Reinforcements are additional soldiers sent to join an army in battle. 2 Reinforcement is the reinforcing of something.

reinstate verb 1 To reinstate someone means to give them back a position they have lost. 2 To reinstate something means to bring it back. > **reinstatement** noun

reiterate verb (formal) If you reiterate something, you say it again. > **reiteration** noun

reject verb 1 If you reject a proposal or request, you do not accept it or agree to it. 2 If you reject a belief, political system or way of life, you decide that it is not for you. ▶ noun 3 a product that cannot be used, because there is something wrong with it. > **rejection** noun

> **reject** verb
> 1 = decline, deny, rebuff, refuse, renounce (formal), say no to, spurn, turn down, unfollow, unfriend

rejoice verb To rejoice means to be very pleased about something.

> **rejoice** verb
> = be overjoyed, celebrate, delight, glory

rejoin verb If you rejoin someone, you go back to them soon after leaving them.

rejuvenate verb To rejuvenate someone means to make them feel young again. > **rejuvenation** noun

relapse noun If a sick person has a relapse, their health suddenly gets worse after improving.

relate verb 1 If something relates to something else, it is connected or concerned with it. 2 If you can relate to someone, you can understand their thoughts and feelings. 3 To relate a story means to tell it.

relation noun 1 If there is a relation between two things, they are similar or connected in some way. 2 Your relations are the members of your family. 3 Relations between people are their feelings and behaviour towards each other.

relation noun
1 = bearing, bond, connection, correlation, link, relationship
2 = kin, kinsman, kinswoman, relative

relationship noun 1 The relationship between two people or groups is the way they feel and behave towards each other.
2 (PSHE) a close friendship, especially one involving romantic feelings. 3 The relationship between two things is the way in which they are connected.

relationship noun
1 = affinity, association, bond, connection, rapport
3 = connection, correlation, link, parallel

relative adjective 1 compared to other things or people of the same kind: *The fighting resumed after a period of relative calm.* 2 You use 'relative' when comparing the size or quality of two things: *the relative strengths of the British and German forces.* ▶ noun 3 Your relatives are the members of your family.

relax verb 1 If you relax, you become calm and your muscles lose their tension. 2 If you relax your hold, you hold something less tightly. 3 To relax something also means to make it less strict or controlled. > **relaxation** noun

relax verb
1 = laze, rest, take it easy, unwind

relay noun 1 (PE) A relay race or relay is a race between teams, with each team member running one part of the race. ▶ verb 2 To relay a television or radio signal means to send it on. 3 If you relay

information, you tell it to someone else.

release verb 1 To release someone or something means to set them free or remove restraints from them. 2 To release something also means to issue it or make it available. ▶ noun 3 When the release of someone or something takes place, they are set free. 4 A press release or publicity release is an official written statement given to reporters. 5 A new release is a new film or record that has just become available.

release verb
1 = deliver, discharge, extricate, free, let go, liberate, set free
2 = issue, launch, publish, put out
▶ noun 3 = discharge, emancipation, freedom, liberation, liberty

relegate verb To relegate something or someone means to give them a less important position or status. > **relegation** noun

relent verb If someone relents, they agree to something they had previously not allowed.

relentless adjective never stopping and never becoming less intense. > **relentlessly** adverb

relentless adjective
= incessant, nonstop, persistent, sustained, unrelenting, unremitting

relevant adjective If something is relevant, it is connected with and is appropriate to what is being discussed. > **relevance** noun

relevant adjective
= applicable, apposite, appropriate, apt, pertinent

reliable *adjective* 1 Reliable people and things can be trusted to do what you want. 2 If information is reliable, you can assume that it is correct. > **reliably** *adverb* > **reliability** *noun*

> **reliable** *adjective*
> 1 = dependable, faithful, safe, sound, staunch, sure, true, trustworthy

reliant *adjective* If you are reliant on someone or something, you depend on them.

relic *noun* 1 Relics are objects or customs that have survived from an earlier time. 2 an object regarded as holy because it is thought to be connected with a saint.

relief *noun* 1 If you feel relief, you are glad and thankful because a bad situation is over or has been avoided. 2 Relief is also money, food or clothing provided for people in need.

relieve *verb* 1 If something relieves an unpleasant feeling, it makes it less unpleasant. 2 (*formal*) If you relieve someone, you do their job or duty for a period. 3 If someone is relieved of their duties, they are dismissed from their job. 4 If you relieve yourself, you urinate.

religion *noun* 1 (RE) Religion is the belief in a god or gods and all the activities connected with such beliefs. 2 (RE) a system of religious belief.

religious *adjective* 1 connected with religion. 2 (RE) Someone who is religious has a strong belief in a god or gods.

> **religious** *adjective*
> 1 = devotional, divine, doctrinal, holy, sacred, scriptural, spiritual, theological 2 = devout, God-fearing, godly, pious, righteous

religiously *adverb* If you do something religiously, you do it regularly as a duty.

relinquish *verb* (*formal*) If you relinquish something, you give it up.

relish *verb* 1 If you relish something, you enjoy it. ▶ *noun* 2 Relish is enjoyment. 3 Relish is also a savoury sauce or pickle.

relive *verb* If you relive a past experience, you remember it and imagine it happening again.

relocate *verb* If people or businesses are relocated, they are moved to a different place. > **relocation** *noun*

reluctant *adjective* If you are reluctant to do something, you are unwilling to do it. > **reluctance** *noun*

> **reluctant** *adjective*
> = averse, disinclined, hesitant, loath, slow, unwilling

reluctantly *adverb* If you do something reluctantly, you do it although you do not want to.

rely relies, relying, relied *verb* 1 If you rely on someone or something, you need them and depend on them. 2 If you can rely on someone to do something, you can trust them to do it.

remain *verb* 1 If you remain in a particular place, you stay there. 2 If you remain in a particular state, you stay the same and do not change. 3 Something that remains still exists or is left over.

remain verb
1 = be left, linger, stay behind, wait 2 = continue, endure, go on, last, stay, survive

remainder noun 1 The remainder of something is the part that is left. 2 the amount left over when one number cannot be exactly divided by another.

remainder noun
1 = balance, last, others, remains, remnants, rest

remand verb 1 If a judge remands someone who is accused of a crime, the trial is postponed and the person is ordered to come back at a later date. ▶ phrase 2 If someone is on remand, they are in prison waiting for their trial to begin.

remark verb 1 If you remark on something, you mention it or comment on it. ▶ noun 2 something you say, often in a casual way.

remark verb
1 = comment, mention, observe, say, state
▶ noun 2 = comment, observation, statement, utterance, word

remarkable adjective impressive and unexpected. > **remarkably** adverb

remarry remarries, remarrying, remarried verb If someone remarries, they get married again.

remedial adjective 1 Remedial activities are to help someone improve their health after they have been ill. 2 Remedial exercises are designed to improve someone's ability in something.

remedy remedies, remedying, remedied noun 1 a way of dealing with a problem. ▶ verb 2 If you remedy something that is wrong, you correct it.

remember verb 1 If you can remember someone or something from the past, you can bring them into your mind or think about them. 2 If you remember to do something, you do it when you intended to.

remember verb
1 = call to mind, recall, recognise, retain

remembrance noun If you do something in remembrance of a dead person, you are showing that they are remembered with respect and affection.

remind verb 1 If someone reminds you of a fact, they say something to make you think about it. 2 If someone reminds you of another person, they look similar and make you think of them.

remind verb
1 = bring back to, jog someone's memory, make someone remember, put in mind, refresh someone's memory

reminder noun 1 If one thing is a reminder of another, the first thing makes you think of the second. 2 a note sent to tell someone they have forgotten to do something.

reminiscent adjective Something that is reminiscent of something else reminds you of it.

remission noun When prisoners get remission for good behaviour, their sentences are reduced.

r

remit noun The remit of a person or committee is the subject or task they are responsible for.

remnant noun a small part of something left after the rest has been used or destroyed.

remorse noun (formal) Remorse is a strong feeling of guilt.
> **remorseful** adjective

remote adjective 1 Remote areas are far away from places where most people live. 2 far away in time. 3 If you say a person is remote, you mean they do not want to be friendly. 4 If there is only a remote possibility of something happening, it is unlikely to happen.
> **remoteness** noun

> **remote** adjective
> 1 = distant, far-off, inaccessible, isolated, lonely, outlying
> 2 = distant, far-off 3 = aloof, cold, detached, distant, reserved, withdrawn 4 = poor, slender, slight, slim, small

remote control noun Remote control is a system of controlling a machine or vehicle from a distance using radio or electronic signals.

remotely adverb used to emphasise a negative statement: He isn't remotely keen.

removal noun 1 The removal of something is the act of taking it away. 2 A removal company transports furniture from one building to another.

remove verb 1 If you remove something from a place, you take it off or away. 2 If you are removed from a position of authority, you are not allowed to continue your job. 3 If you remove an

undesirable feeling or attitude, you get rid of it. > **removable** adjective

> **remove** verb
> 1 = delete, detach, eject, eliminate, erase, extract, get rid of, take away, take off, take out, withdraw

Renaissance noun (HISTORY) The Renaissance was a period from the 14th to 16th centuries in Europe when there was a great revival in the arts and learning.

renal adjective concerning the kidneys.

rename verb If you rename something, you give it a new name.

render verb You can use 'render' to say that something is changed into a different state.

rendezvous noun 1 a meeting. 2 a place where you have arranged to meet someone.

rendition noun (formal) a performance of a play, poem or piece of music.

renew verb 1 To renew an activity or relationship means to begin it again. 2 To renew a licence or contract means to extend the period of time for which it is valid. > **renewal** noun

> **renew** verb
> 1 = begin again, recommence, re-establish, reopen, resume

renewable adjective 1 able to be renewed. ▶ noun 2 (GEOGRAPHY) a renewable form of energy, such as wind power or solar power.

renounce verb (formal) If you renounce something, you reject it or give it up. > **renunciation** noun

R

renounce *verb*
= disown, give up, reject, relinquish

renovate *verb* If you renovate an old building or machine, you repair it and restore it to good condition. > **renovation** *noun*

renovate *verb*
= do up, modernise, recondition, refurbish, repair, restore, revamp

renowned *adjective* well-known for something good. > **renown** *noun*

rent *verb* 1 If you rent something, you pay the owner a regular sum of money in return for being able to use it. ▶ *noun* 2 Rent is the amount of money you pay regularly to rent land or accommodation.

rental *adjective* 1 concerned with the renting out of goods and services. ▶ *noun* 2 the amount of money you pay when you rent something.

reorganise; also spelt **reorganize** *verb* To reorganise something means to organise it in a new way in order to make it more efficient or acceptable. > **reorganisation** *noun*

rep (*informal*) *noun* 1 A rep is a travelling salesperson. Rep is an abbreviation for **representative**. ▶ *phrase* 2 When actors work in **rep**, they are working with a repertory company.

repair *noun* 1 something you do to mend something that is damaged or broken. ▶ *verb* 2 If you repair something, you mend it.

repair *noun*
1 = darn, mend, patch, restoration
▶ *verb* 2 = fix, mend, patch, patch up, renovate, restore

repay repays, repaying, repaid *verb* 1 To repay money means to give it back to the person who lent it. 2 If you repay a favour, you do something to help the person who helped you. > **repayment** *noun*

repay *verb*
1 = pay back, refund, settle up

repeal *verb* If the government repeals a law, it cancels it so that it is no longer valid.

repeat *verb* 1 If you repeat something, you say, write or do it again. 2 If you repeat what someone has said, you tell someone else about it. ▶ *noun* 3 something which is done or happens again. > **repeated** *adjective* > **repeatedly** *adverb*

repeat *verb*
1 = echo, reiterate, say again

repel repels, repelling, repelled *verb* 1 If something repels you, you find it horrible and disgusting. 2 When soldiers repel an attacking force, they successfully defend themselves against it. 3 (SCIENCE) When a magnetic pole repels an opposite pole, it forces the opposite pole away.

repel *verb*
1 = disgust, offend, revolt, sicken 2 = drive off, repulse, resist

repellent *adjective* 1 (*formal*) horrible and disgusting.
▶ *noun* 2 Repellents are chemicals used to keep insects or other creatures away.

r

repent *verb* (formal) If you repent, you are sorry for something bad you have done. ▸ **repentance** *noun* ▸ **repentant** *adjective*

repercussion *noun* The repercussions of an event are the effects it has at a later time.

repertoire *noun* A performer's repertoire is all the pieces of music or dramatic parts he or she has learned and can perform.

repertory repertories *noun*
1 Repertory is the practice of performing a small number of plays in a theatre for a short time, using the same actors in each play. 2 In Australian, New Zealand and South African English, repertory is the same as **repertoire**.

repetition *noun* 1 If there is a repetition of something, it happens again. 2 (ENGLISH) Repetition is when a word, phrase or sound is repeated, for example to emphasise a point or to make sure it is understood, or for poetic effect.

repetitive *adjective* A repetitive activity involves a lot of repetition and is boring.

replace *verb* 1 When one thing replaces another, the first thing takes the place of the second. 2 If you replace something that is damaged or lost, you get a new one. 3 If you replace something, you put it back where it was before.

> **replace** *verb*
> 1 = succeed, supersede, supplant, take over from, take the place of

replacement *noun* 1 The replacement for someone or

something is the person or thing that takes their place. 2 The replacement of a person or thing happens when they are replaced by another person or thing.

> **replacement** *noun*
> 1 = proxy, stand-in, substitute, successor, surrogate

replay *verb* 1 If a match is replayed, the teams play it again. 2 If you replay a recording, you play it again. ▸ *noun* 3 a match that is played for a second time.

replenish *verb* (formal) If you replenish something, you make it full or complete again.

replica *noun* an accurate copy of something. ▸ **replicate** *verb*

reply replies, replying, replied *verb* 1 If you reply to something, you say or write an answer. ▸ *noun* 2 what you say or write when you answer someone.

> **reply** *verb*
> 1 = answer, counter, respond, retort, return
> ▸ *noun* 2 = answer, response, retort

report *verb* 1 If you report that something has happened, you tell someone about it or give an official account of it. 2 To report someone to an authority means to make an official complaint about them. 3 If you report to a person or place, you go there and say you have arrived. ▸ *noun* 4 an account of an event or situation.

> **report** *verb*
> 1 = cover, describe, inform of, notify, state
> ▸ *noun* 4 = account, description, statement

reporter *noun* someone who writes news articles or broadcasts news reports.

repossess *verb* If a shop or company repossesses goods that have not been paid for, they take them back.

represent *verb* 1 If you represent someone, you act on their behalf. 2 If a sign or symbol represents something, it stands for it. 3 To represent something in a particular way means to describe it in that way.

> **represent** *verb*
> 2 = mean, stand for, symbolise
> 3 = depict, describe, picture, portray, show

representation *noun*
1 Representation is the state of being represented by someone. 2 You can describe a picture or statue of someone as a representation of them.

representative *noun* 1 a person chosen to act on behalf of another person or a group. ▶ *adjective* 2 A representative selection is typical of the group it belongs to.

> **representative** *noun*
> 1 = agent, delegate, deputy, proxy, spokesman, spokeswoman
> ▶ *adjective* 2 = characteristic, illustrative, typical

repress *verb* 1 If you repress a feeling, you succeed in not showing or feeling it. 2 To repress people means to restrict their freedom and control them by force. > **repression** *noun*

repressive *adjective* Repressive governments use force and unjust laws to restrict and control people.

reprieve *verb* 1 If someone who has been sentenced to death is reprieved, their sentence is changed and they are not killed. ▶ *noun* 2 a delay before something unpleasant happens.

reprimand *verb* 1 If you reprimand someone, you officially tell them that they should not have done something. ▶ *noun* 2 something said or written by a person in authority when they are reprimanding someone.

reprisal *noun* Reprisals are violent actions taken by one group of people against another group that has harmed them.

reproach (*formal*) *noun* 1 If you express reproach, you show that you feel sad and angry about what someone has done. ▶ *verb* 2 If you reproach someone, you tell them, rather sadly, that they have done something wrong.
> **reproachful** *adjective*
> **reproachfully** *adverb*

reproduce *verb* 1 To reproduce something means to make a copy of it. 2 (SCIENCE) When living things reproduce, they produce more of their own kind.

reproduction *noun* 1 a modern copy of a painting or piece of furniture. 2 (SCIENCE) Reproduction is the process by which a living thing produces more of its kind.

reproductive *adjective* relating to the reproduction of living things.

reptile *noun* a cold-blooded animal, such as a snake or a lizard, which has scaly skin and lays eggs. > **reptilian** *adjective*

republic *noun* a country which has a president rather than a king

r

or queen. ▶ **republican** noun, adjective ▶ **republicanism** noun

repulsive adjective horrible and disgusting.

reputable adjective known to be good and reliable.

reputation noun The reputation of something or someone is the opinion that people have of them.

reputation noun
= character, name, renown, repute, standing, stature

reputed adjective If something is reputed to be true, some people say that it is true. ▶ **reputedly** adverb

request verb 1 If you request something, you ask for it politely or formally. ▶ noun 2 If you make a request for something, you request it.

request verb
1 = ask, beg, seek
▶ noun 2 = appeal, application, call, plea

require verb 1 If you require something, you need it. 2 If you are required to do something, you have to do it because someone says you must.

require verb
1 = be in need of, demand, depend on, need, want (informal)
2 = compel, demand, direct, instruct, oblige, order

requirement noun something that you must have or must do.

requirement noun
= demand, essential, necessity, need, specification

requisite (formal) adjective
1 necessary for a particular purpose. ▶ noun 2 something that

is necessary for a particular purpose.

rescue rescues, rescuing, rescued verb 1 If you rescue someone, you save them from a dangerous or unpleasant situation. ▶ noun 2 Rescue is help which saves someone from a dangerous or unpleasant situation. ▶ **rescuer** noun

research noun 1 Research is work that involves studying something and trying to find out facts about it. ▶ verb 2 If you research something, you try to discover facts about it. ▶ **researcher** noun

research noun
1 = analysis, examination, exploration, investigation, study
▶ verb 2 = analyse, examine, explore, google, investigate, study

resemblance noun If there is a resemblance between two things, they are similar to each other.

resemblance noun
= analogy, correspondence, likeness, parallel, similarity

resemble verb To resemble something means to be similar to it.

resemble verb
= bear a resemblance to, be like, be similar to, look like, parallel, take after

resent verb If you resent something, you feel bitter and angry about it.

resent verb
= be angry about, be offended by, dislike, object to, take offence at

R

resentful adjective bitter and angry. > **resentfully** adverb

> **resentful** adjective
> = aggrieved, angry, bitter, embittered, huffy, indignant, offended

resentment noun a feeling of anger or bitterness.

> **resentment** noun
> = anger, animosity, bitterness, grudge, huff, indignation, rancour (formal)

reservation noun 1 If you have reservations about something, you are not sure that it is right. 2 If you make a reservation, you book a place in advance. 3 an area of land set aside for a particular purpose or people.

reserve verb 1 If something is reserved for a particular person or purpose, it is kept specially for them. ▶ noun 2 a supply of something for future use. 3 In sport, a reserve is someone who is available to play in case one of the team is unable to play. 4 A nature reserve is an area of land where animals, birds or plants are officially protected. 5 If someone shows reserve, they keep their feelings hidden. > **reserved** adjective

> **reserve** verb
> 1 = hoard, hold, keep, put by, save, set aside, stockpile, store ▶ noun 2 = cache, fund, hoard, stock, stockpile, store, supply

reservoir noun a lake used for storing water before it is supplied to people.

reshuffle noun a reorganisation of people or things.

reside verb (formal) 1 If someone resides somewhere, they live there or are staying there. 2 If a quality resides in something, the quality is in that thing.

residence (formal) noun 1 A residence is a house. ▶ phrase 2 If you **take up residence** somewhere, you go and live there.

resident noun 1 A resident of a house or area is someone who lives there. ▶ adjective 2 If someone is resident in a house or area, they live there.

residential adjective 1 A residential area contains mainly houses rather than offices or factories. 2 providing accommodation.

residue noun a small amount of something that remains after most of it has gone: an increase in toxic residues found in drinking water. > **residual** adjective

resign verb 1 If you resign from a job, you formally announce that you are leaving it. 2 If you resign yourself to an unpleasant situation, you realise that you have to accept it. > **resigned** adjective

> **resign** verb
> 1 = abdicate, hand in your notice, leave, quit, step down (informal) 2 **resign oneself** = accept, bow, reconcile yourself

resignation noun 1 Someone's resignation is a formal statement of their intention to leave a job. 2 Resignation is the reluctant acceptance of an unpleasant situation or fact.

resilient adjective (PSHE) able to recover quickly from unpleasant or damaging events. > **resilience** noun

resin noun 1 Resin is a sticky substance produced by some trees. 2 Resin is also a substance produced chemically and used to make plastics.

resist verb 1 If you resist something, you refuse to accept it and try to prevent it. 2 If you resist someone, you fight back against them.

> **resist** verb
> 1 = defy, fight, oppose, refuse, struggle against

resistance noun 1 Resistance to something such as change is a refusal to accept it. 2 Resistance to an attack consists of fighting back. 3 Your body's resistance to germs or disease is its power to not be harmed by them.
4 (SCIENCE) Resistance is also the power of a substance to resist the flow of an electrical current through it.

resistant adjective 1 opposed to something and wanting to prevent it. 2 If something is resistant to a particular thing, it is not harmed or affected by it.

resolute adjective (formal) Someone who is resolute is determined not to change their mind.
> **resolutely** adverb

resolution noun 1 Resolution is determination. 2 If you make a resolution, you promise yourself to do something. 3 a formal decision taken at a meeting.
4 (ENGLISH) The resolution of a problem is the solving of it.

resolve verb 1 If you resolve to do something, you firmly decide to do it. 2 If you resolve a problem, you find a solution to it.
▶ noun 3 Resolve is absolute determination.

resolve verb
1 = decide, determine, intend, make up your mind 2 = clear up, find a solution to, overcome, solve, sort out, work out
▶ noun 3 = determination, resolution, tenacity

resonance noun 1 Resonance is sound produced by an object vibrating as a result of another sound nearby. 2 Resonance is also a deep, clear and echoing quality of sound.

resonate verb If something resonates, it vibrates and produces a deep, strong sound.

resort verb 1 If you resort to a course of action, you do it because you have no alternative. ▶ noun 2 a place where people spend their holidays. ▶ phrase 3 If you do something as a last resort, you do it because you can find no other way of solving a problem.

resounding adjective 1 loud and echoing. 2 A resounding success is a great success.

resource noun The resources of a country, organisation or person are the materials, money or skills they have.

resourceful adjective A resourceful person is good at finding ways of dealing with problems. > **resourcefulness** noun

respect verb 1 If you respect someone, you have a good opinion of their character or ideas. 2 If you respect someone's rights or wishes, you do not do things that they would not like, or would consider wrong. ▶ noun 3 If you have respect for someone, you have a good opinion of them. ▶ phrase 4 You can say in this respect to refer to a particular feature.

R

respect verb
1 = admire, have a good opinion of, have a high opinion of, honour, look up to, think highly of, venerate (formal)
▶ noun 3 = admiration, esteem, regard, reverence

respectable adjective 1 considered to be acceptable and morally correct. 2 adequate or reasonable.
> **respectability** noun
> **respectably** adverb

> **respectable** adjective
> 1 = decent, good, honourable, proper, reputable, upright, worthy 2 = appreciable, considerable, decent, fair, reasonable

respectful adjective showing respect for someone.
> **respectfully** adverb

respective adjective belonging or relating individually to the people or things just mentioned: They went into their respective rooms to pack.

respectively adverb in the same order as the items just mentioned: Amanda and Emily finished first and second respectively.

respiration noun (SCIENCE) Your respiration is your breathing.

respiratory adjective (SCIENCE) relating to breathing.

respite noun (formal) a short rest from something unpleasant.

respond verb When you respond to something, you react to it by doing or saying something.

respondent noun 1 a person who answers a questionnaire or a request for information. 2 In a court case, the respondent is the defendant.

response noun Your response to an event is your reaction or reply to it.

responsibility responsibilities noun 1 (PSHE) (CITIZENSHIP) If you have responsibility for something, it is your duty to deal with it or look after it. 2 If you accept responsibility for something that has happened, you agree that you caused it or were to blame.

> **responsibility** noun
> 1 = duty, obligation, onus
> 2 = blame, fault, guilt, liability

responsible adjective 1 If you are responsible for something, it is your job to deal with it. 2 If you are responsible for something bad that has happened, you are to blame for it. 3 If you are responsible to someone, that person is your boss and tells you what you have to do. 4 A responsible person behaves properly and sensibly without needing to be supervised. 5 A responsible job involves making careful judgments about important matters.
> **responsibly** adverb

> **responsible** adjective
> 1 = in charge, in control
> 2 = at fault, guilty, to blame
> 4 = dependable, level-headed, reliable, sensible, sound, trustworthy

responsive adjective 1 quick to show interest and pleasure. 2 taking notice of events and reacting in an appropriate way.

rest noun 1 The rest of something is all the remaining parts of it. 2 If you have a rest, you sit or lie quietly and relax. ▶ verb 3 If you rest, you relax and do not do anything active for a while.

rest noun
1 = balance, others, remainder, surplus 2 = break, holiday, leisure, relaxation, respite
▶ verb 3 = have a break, idle, laze, put your feet up, relax, sit down, take it easy

restaurant noun a place where you can buy and eat a meal.

restaurateur noun someone who owns or manages a restaurant.

restful adjective Something that is restful helps you feel calm and relaxed.

restless adjective finding it hard to remain still or relaxed because of boredom or impatience.
> **restlessly** adverb > **restlessness** noun

restless adjective
= edgy, fidgety, fretful, jumpy, on edge, unsettled

restore verb 1 To restore something means to cause it to exist again or to return to its previous state. 2 To restore an old building or work of art means to clean and repair it. > **restoration** noun

restore verb
1 = re-establish, reinstate, reintroduce, return 2 = fix up, mend, rebuild, reconstruct, refurbish, renovate, repair

restrain verb To restrain someone or something means to hold them back or prevent them from doing what they want to.

restrain verb
= contain, control, curb, hamper, hinder, hold back, inhibit

restrained adjective behaving in a controlled way.

restraint noun 1 Restraints are rules or conditions that limit something. 2 Restraint is calm, controlled behaviour.

restrict verb 1 If you restrict something, you prevent it becoming too large or varied. 2 To restrict people or animals means to limit their movement or actions. > **restrictive** adjective

restrict verb
2 = confine, contain, hamper, handicap, impede, inhibit, limit, restrain

restriction noun a rule or situation that limits what you can do.

restriction noun
= constraint, control, curb, limitation, regulation, restraint, stipulation

result noun 1 The result of an action or situation is the situation that is caused by it. 2 The result is also the final marks, figures or situation at the end of an exam, calculation or contest. ▶ verb 3 If something results in a particular event, it causes that event to happen. 4 If something results from a particular event, it is caused by that event. > **resultant** adjective

result noun
1 = consequence, effect, outcome, product, upshot
▶ verb 3 = bring about, cause, lead to 4 = arise, derive, develop, ensue, follow, happen, stem

resume verb If you resume an activity or position, you return to it after a break. > **resumption** noun

resurgence noun If there is a resurgence of an attitude or activity, it reappears and grows stronger. > **resurgent** adjective

resurrect verb If you resurrect something, you make it exist again after it has disappeared or ended. > **resurrection** noun

resuscitate verb If you resuscitate someone, you make them conscious again after an accident. > **resuscitation** noun

retail noun The retail price is the price at which something is sold in the shops. > **retailer** noun

retain verb To retain something means to keep it. > **retention** noun

retaliate verb If you retaliate, you do something to harm or upset someone because they have already acted in a similar way against you. > **retaliation** noun

> **retaliate** verb
> = get back (informal), get even (informal), get your own back (informal), hit back (informal), pay back, take revenge

rethink rethinks, rethinking, rethought verb If you rethink something, you think about how it should be changed.

reticent adjective Someone who is reticent is unwilling to tell people about things. > **reticence** noun

retina noun (SCIENCE) the light-sensitive part at the back of your eyeball, which receives an image and sends it to your brain.

retinue noun a group of helpers or friends travelling with an important person.

retire verb 1 When older people retire, they give up work. 2 (formal) If you retire, you leave

to go into another room, or to bed. > **retired** adjective > **retirement** noun

retort verb 1 To retort means to reply angrily. ▶ noun 2 a short, angry reply.

retract verb 1 If you retract something you have said, you say that you did not mean it. 2 When something is retracted, it moves inwards or backwards. > **retraction** noun

retreat verb 1 To retreat means to move backwards away from something or someone. 2 If you retreat from something difficult or unpleasant, you avoid doing it. ▶ noun 3 If an army moves away from the enemy, this is referred to as a retreat. 4 a quiet place where you can go to rest or do things in private.

> **retreat** verb
> 1 = back away, back off, draw back, pull back, withdraw
> ▶ noun 3 = departure, evacuation, flight, withdrawal
> 4 = haven, refuge, sanctuary

retribution noun (formal) Retribution is punishment.

retrieve verb If you retrieve something, you get it back. > **retrieval** noun

retriever noun a large dog often used by hunters to bring back birds and animals which have been shot.

retrospect phrase When you consider something in retrospect, you think about it afterwards and often have a different opinion from the one you had at the time.

retrospective adjective 1 concerning things that happened in the past. 2 taking effect from a date in the past. > **retrospectively** adverb

return verb 1 When you return to a place, you go back after you have been away. 2 If you return something to someone, you give it back to them. 3 When you return a ball during a game, you hit it back to your opponent. 4 When a judge or jury returns a verdict, they announce it. ▶ noun 5 Your return is your arrival back at a place. 6 The return on an investment is the profit or interest you get from it. 7 a ticket for the journey to a place and back again. ▶ phrase 8 If you do something **in return** for a favour, you do it to repay the favour.

> **return** verb
> 1 = come back, go back, reappear, turn back 2 = give back, pay back, refund, repay

reunion noun a party or meeting for people who have not seen each other for a long time.

reunite verb If people are reunited, they meet again after they have been separated for some time.

rev revs, revving, revved (informal) verb 1 When you rev the engine of a vehicle, you press the accelerator to increase the engine speed. ▶ noun 2 The speed of an engine is measured in revolutions per minute, referred to as revs.

revamp verb To revamp something means to improve or repair it.

reveal verb 1 To reveal something means to tell people about it. 2 If you reveal something that has been hidden, you uncover it.
▶ noun 3 an occasion when

something that has been kept secret is shown or explained.

> **reveal** verb
> 1 = announce, disclose, divulge, get off your chest (informal), let on 2 = bring to light, lay bare, uncover, unearth, unveil

revel revels, revelling, revelled verb If you revel in a situation, you enjoy it very much. > **revelry** noun

revelation noun 1 a surprising or interesting fact made known to people. 2 If an experience is a revelation, it makes you realise or learn something.

revenge noun 1 Revenge involves hurting someone who has hurt you. ▶ verb 2 If you revenge yourself on someone who has hurt you, you hurt them in return.

> **revenge** noun
> 1 = reprisal, retaliation, retribution, vengeance
> ▶ verb 2 = avenge, get even (informal), get your own back (informal), hit back (informal), pay back, retaliate

revenue noun Revenue is money that a government, company or organisation receives.

revered adjective If someone is revered, he or she is respected and admired.

reverence noun Reverence is a feeling of great respect.

Reverend adjective Reverend is a title used before the name of a member of the clergy.

reversal noun If there is a reversal of a process or policy, it is changed to the opposite process or policy.

reverse verb 1 When someone reverses a process, they change it to the opposite process. **2** If you reverse the order of things, you arrange them in the opposite order. **3** When you reverse a car, you drive it backwards. ▶ *noun* **4** The reverse is the opposite of what has just been said or done. ▶ *adjective* **5** Reverse means opposite to what is usual or to what has just been described.

> **reverse** *verb*
> **1** = change, invalidate, overrule, overturn, retract
> ▶ *noun* **4** = contrary, converse, opposite

reversible *adjective* Reversible clothing can be worn with either side on the outside.

revert *verb (formal)* To revert to a former state or type of behaviour means to go back to it.

review *noun* **1** an article or an item on television or radio, giving an opinion of a new book, play or film. **2** When there is a review of a situation or system, it is examined to decide whether changes are needed. ▶ *verb* **3** To review a book, play or film means to write an account expressing an opinion of it. **4** To review something means to examine it to decide whether changes are needed. > **reviewer** *noun*

> **review** *noun*
> **1** = commentary, criticism, notice **2** = analysis, examination, report, study, survey

revise *verb* **1** If you revise something, you alter or correct it. **2** When you revise for an examination, you go over your work to learn things thoroughly. > **revision** *noun*

revise *verb*
1 = amend, correct, edit, refresh, revamp, update

revive *verb* **1** When a feeling or practice is revived, it becomes active or popular again. **2** If someone who has fainted revives, they become conscious again. > **revival** *noun*

> **revive** *verb*
> **1** = rally, resuscitate

revolt *noun* **1** (HISTORY) a violent attempt by a group of people to change their country's political system. ▶ *verb* **2** (HISTORY) When people revolt, they fight against the authority that governs them. **3** If something revolts you, it is so horrible that you feel disgust.

revolting *adjective* horrible and disgusting.

revolution *noun* **1** (HISTORY) a violent attempt by a large group of people to change the political system of their country. **2** an important change in an area of human activity. **3** one complete turn in a circle.

revolutionary revolutionaries *adjective* **1** involving great changes. ▶ *noun* **2** a person who takes part in a revolution.

revolve *verb* **1** If something revolves round something else, it centres on that as the most important thing. **2** When something revolves, it turns in a circle around a central point.

revolver *noun* a small gun held in the hand.

revulsion *noun* Revulsion is a strong feeling of disgust or disapproval.

reward (PSHE) *noun* **1** something you are given because you have done something good. ▶ *verb* 2 If you reward someone, you give them a reward.

reward *noun*
1 = bonus, bounty, payment, prize

rewarding *adjective* Something that is rewarding gives you a lot of satisfaction.

rewind rewinds, rewinding, rewound *verb* If you rewind a tape on a tape recorder or video, you make the tape go backwards.

rhetoric *noun* Rhetoric is speech or writing that is intended to impress people.

rhetorical *adjective* 1 A rhetorical question is one which is asked in order to make a statement rather than to get an answer.
2 Rhetorical language is intended to be grand and impressive.

rhino rhinos (*informal*) a rhinoceros.

rhinoceros *noun* a large African or Asian animal with one or two horns on its nose.

rhododendron *noun* an evergreen bush with large coloured flowers.

rhubarb *noun* Rhubarb is a plant with long red stems which can be cooked with sugar and eaten.

rhyme (ENGLISH) *verb* 1 If two words rhyme, they have a similar sound. ▶ *noun* 2 a word that rhymes with another. 3 a short poem with rhyming lines.

rhythm *noun* 1 (MUSIC) Rhythm is a regular movement or beat. 2 a regular pattern of changes, for example, in the seasons.
> **rhythmic** *adjective*
> **rhythmically** *adverb*

rhythm *noun*
1 = beat, pulse, tempo, time

rib *noun* Your ribs are the curved bones that go from your backbone to your chest.

ribbon *noun* a long, narrow piece of cloth used for decoration.

rice *noun* Rice is a tall grass that produces edible grains. Rice is grown in warm countries on wet ground.

rich *adjective* 1 Someone who is rich has a lot of money and possessions. 2 Something that is rich in something contains a large amount of it. 3 Rich food contains a large amount of fat, oil or sugar. 4 Rich colours, smells and sounds are strong and pleasant. > **richness** *noun*

rich *adjective*
1 = affluent, loaded (*slang*), opulent, prosperous, wealthy, well off 2 = abundant, fertile, plentiful

richly *adverb* 1 If someone is richly rewarded, they are rewarded well with something valuable. 2 If you feel strongly that someone deserves something, you can say it is richly deserved.

rickety *adjective* likely to collapse or break.

rickshaw *noun* a hand-pulled cart used in Asia for carrying passengers.

ricochet ricochets, ricocheting or ricochetting, ricocheted or ricochetted *verb* When a bullet ricochets, it hits a surface and bounces away from it.

rid rids, ridding, rid *phrase* 1 When you **get rid of** something you do not want, you remove or destroy it. ▶ *verb* 2 (*formal*) To rid a place of something unpleasant means to succeed in removing it.

rid phrase
1 **get rid of** = dispose of, dump, eject, jettison, remove, weed out

ridden the past participle of **ride**.
riddle noun 1 a puzzle which seems to be nonsense, but which has an entertaining solution. 2 Something that is a riddle puzzles and confuses you.
ride rides, riding, rode, ridden verb 1 When you ride a horse or a bike, you sit on it and control it as it moves along. 2 When you ride in a car, you travel in it. ▶ noun 3 a journey on a horse or bike or in a vehicle.
rider noun 1 a person riding on a horse or bicycle. 2 an additional statement which changes or puts a condition on what has already been said.
ridge noun 1 a long, narrow piece of high land. 2 a raised line on a flat surface.
ridicule verb 1 To ridicule someone means to make fun of them in an unkind way. ▶ noun 2 Ridicule is unkind laughter and mockery.
ridiculous adjective very foolish. > **ridiculously** adverb

ridiculous adjective
= absurd, laughable, ludicrous, preposterous

rife adjective (formal) very common.
rifle noun 1 a gun with a long barrel. ▶ verb 2 When someone rifles something, they make a quick search through it to steal things.
rift noun 1 a serious quarrel between friends that damages

their friendship. 2 a split in something solid, especially in the ground.
rig rigs, rigging, rigged verb 1 If someone rigs an election or contest, they dishonestly arrange for a particular person to succeed. ▶ noun 2 a large structure used for extracting oil or gas from the ground or sea bed. > **rig up** verb If you rig up a device or structure, you make it quickly and fix it in place.
right adjective, adverb 1 correct and in accordance with the facts. 2 'Right' means on or towards the right side of something. ▶ adjective 3 The right choice or decision is the best or most suitable one. 4 The right side of something is the side intended to be seen and to face outwards. ▶ noun 5 'Right' is used to refer to principles of morally correct behaviour. 6 PSHE CITIZENSHIP If you have a right to do something, you are morally or legally entitled to do it. 7 The right is one of the two sides of something. For example, when you look at the word 'to', the 'o' is to the right of the 't'. 8 The Right refers to people who support the political ideas of capitalism and conservatism rather than socialism. ▶ adverb 9 'Right' is used to emphasise a precise place: I'm right here. 10 'Right' means immediately: I had to decide right then. ▶ verb 11 If you right something, you correct it or put it back in an upright position. > **rightly** adverb

right adjective, adverb
1 = accurate, correct, exact, factual, genuine, precise, strict, true, valid

r

▶ *adjective* 3 = acceptable,
appropriate, desirable, done,
fit, fitting, okay or OK (*informal*),
proper, seemly (*old-fashioned*),
suitable

▶ *noun* 5 = equity, fairness,
honour, integrity, justice,
legality, morality, virtue

right angle *noun* (MATHS) an
angle of 90°.

righteous *adjective* Righteous
people behave in a way that is
morally good and religious.

rightful *adjective* Someone's
rightful possession is one which
they have a moral or legal right
to. > **rightfully** *adverb*

right-handed *adjective, adverb*
Someone who is right-handed
does things such as writing and
painting with their right hand.

right-wing *adjective* believing
more strongly in capitalism or
conservatism, or less strongly in
socialism, than other members of
the same party or group.
> **right-winger** *noun*

right-wing *adjective*
= conservative, Tory (*British*)

rigid *adjective* 1 Rigid laws or
systems cannot be changed and
are considered severe. 2 A rigid
object is stiff and does not bend
easily. > **rigidly** *adverb* > **rigidity**
noun

rigid *adjective*
1 = fixed, inflexible, set, strict,
stringent 2 = firm, hard, solid,
stiff

rigorous *adjective* very careful and
thorough. > **rigorously** *adverb*

rigour *noun* (*formal*) The rigours of
a situation are the things which
make it hard or unpleasant.

rim *noun* the outside or top edge of
an object such as a wheel or a cup.
> **rimmed** *adjective*

rind *noun* Rind is the thick outer
skin of fruit, cheese or bacon.

ring rings, ringing, ringed, rang,
rung *verb* 1 If you ring someone,
you phone them. 2 When a bell
rings, it makes a clear, loud
sound. 3 To ring something
means to draw a circle around it.
4 If something is ringed with
something else, it has that thing
all the way around it. ▶ *noun* 5 the
sound made by a bell. 6 a small
circle of metal worn on your
finger. 7 an object or group of
things in the shape of a circle.
8 At a boxing match or circus, the
ring is the place where the fight
or performance takes place. 9 an
organised group of people who
are involved in an illegal activity.

ring *verb*
2 = chime, clang, peal, resonate,
toll
▶ *noun* 7 = band, circle, hoop,
loop, round 9 = band, cell,
clique, syndicate

ringer *noun* 1 a person or thing
that is almost identical to
another. 2 In Australian English,
a ringer is someone who works on
a sheep farm. 3 In Australian and
New Zealand English, a ringer is
also the fastest shearer in a
woolshed.

ringleader *noun* the leader of a
group of people who get involved
in mischief or crime.

rink *noun* a large indoor area for
ice-skating or roller-skating.

rinse *verb* 1 When you rinse
something, you wash it in clean
water. ▶ *noun* 2 a liquid you can

put on your hair to give it a different colour.

riot noun 1 When there is a riot, a crowd of people behave noisily and violently. ▶ verb 2 To riot means to behave noisily and violently. ▶ phrase 3 To **run riot** means to behave in a wild and uncontrolled way.

> **riot** noun
> 1 = anarchy, disorder, disturbance, mob violence, strife
> ▶ verb 2 = go on the rampage, rampage, run riot, take to the streets

rip rips, ripping, ripped verb 1 When you rip something, you tear it violently. 2 If you rip something away, you remove it quickly and violently. ▶ noun 3 a long split in cloth or paper.
> **rip off** verb (informal) If someone rips you off, they cheat you by charging you too much money.

RIP an abbreviation often written on gravestones, meaning 'rest in peace'.

ripe adjective 1 When fruit or grain is ripe, it is fully developed and ready to be eaten. 2 If a situation is ripe for something to happen, it is ready for it. > **ripeness** noun

ripen verb When crops ripen, they become ripe.

ripper noun (informal) In Australian and New Zealand English, a ripper is an excellent person or thing.

ripple noun 1 Ripples are little waves on the surface of calm water. 2 If there is a ripple of laughter or applause, people laugh or applaud for a short time. ▶ verb 3 When the surface of water ripples, little waves appear on it.

rise rises, rising, rose, risen verb 1 If something rises, it moves upwards. 2 (formal) When you rise, you stand up. 3 To rise also means to get out of bed. 4 When the sun rises, it first appears. 5 The place where a river rises is where it begins. 6 If land rises, it slopes upwards. 7 If a sound or wind rises, it becomes higher or stronger. 8 If an amount rises, it increases. 9 If you rise to a challenge or a remark, you respond to it rather than ignoring it. 10 When people rise up, they start fighting against people in authority. ▶ noun 11 an increase. 12 Someone's rise is the process by which they become more powerful or successful.

> **rise** verb
> 1 = ascend, climb, go up, move up 8 = go up, grow, increase, intensify, mount
> ▶ noun 11 = improvement, increase, upsurge

riser noun An early riser is someone who likes to get up early in the morning.

risk noun 1 (PSHE) a chance that something unpleasant or dangerous might happen.
▶ verb 2 If you risk something unpleasant, you do something knowing that the unpleasant thing might happen as a result: If he doesn't play, he risks losing his place in the team. 3 If you risk someone's life, you put them in a dangerous situation in which they might be killed. > **risky** adjective

> **risk** noun
> 1 = danger, gamble, peril, pitfall
> ▶ verb 2 = chance, dare, gamble, jeopardise, put in jeopardy

rite noun a religious ceremony.

ritual noun **1** a series of actions carried out according to the custom of a particular society or group. ▶ adjective **2** Ritual activities happen as part of a tradition or ritual. ▸ **ritualistic** adjective

rival rivals, rivalling, rivalled noun **1** Your rival is the person you are competing with. ▶ verb **2** If something rivals something else, it is of the same high standard or quality.

> **rival** noun
> **1** = adversary, antagonist, challenger, opponent
> ▶ verb **2** = be a match for, equal, match

rivalry rivalries noun Rivalry is active competition between people.

river noun a natural feature consisting of water flowing for a long distance between two banks.

rivet noun a short, round pin with a flat head which is used to fasten sheets of metal together.

riveting adjective If you find something riveting, you find it fascinating and it holds your attention.

road noun a long piece of hard ground specially surfaced so that people and vehicles can travel along it easily.

> **road** noun
> = motorway, route, street, track

road rage noun Road rage is aggressive behaviour by a driver as a reaction to the behaviour of another driver.

road train noun in Australia, a road train is a line of linked

trailers pulled by a truck, used for transporting cattle or sheep.

roadworks plural noun Roadworks are repairs being done on a road.

roam verb If you roam around, you wander around without any particular purpose.

roar verb **1** If something roars, it makes a very loud noise. **2** To roar with laughter or anger means to laugh or shout very noisily. **3** When a lion roars, it makes a loud, angry sound. ▶ noun **4** a very loud noise.

roast verb **1** When you roast meat or other food, you cook it using dry heat in an oven or over a fire. ▶ adjective **2** Roast meat has been roasted. ▶ noun **3** a piece of meat that has been roasted.

rob robs, robbing, robbed verb **1** If someone robs you, they steal your possessions. **2** If you rob someone of something they need or deserve, you deprive them of it.

> **rob** verb
> **1** = burgle, con (informal), defraud, loot, steal from, swindle

robber noun Robbers are people who steal money or property using force or threats.

robbery robberies noun Robbery is the act of stealing money or property using force or threats.

robe noun a long, loose piece of clothing which covers the body.

robin noun a small bird with a red breast.

robot noun **1** a machine which is programmed to move and perform tasks automatically. **2** in South African English, a robot is a set of traffic lights.

robust *adjective* very strong and healthy. ▸ **robustly** *adverb*

rock *noun* 1 Rock is the hard mineral substance that forms the surface of the earth. 2 a large piece of rock. 3 Rock or rock music is music with simple tunes and a very strong beat. 4 Rock is also a sweet shaped into long, hard sticks, sold in holiday resorts. ▸ *verb* 5 When something rocks or when you rock it, it moves regularly backwards and forwards or from side to side. 6 If something rocks people, it shocks and upsets them. ▸ *phrase* 7 If someone's marriage or relationship is **on the rocks**, it is unsuccessful and about to end.

rock and roll *noun* Rock and roll is a style of music with a strong beat that was especially popular in the 1950s.

rocket *noun* 1 a space vehicle, usually shaped like a long pointed tube. 2 an explosive missile. 3 a firework that explodes when it is high in the air. ▸ *verb* 4 If prices rocket, they increase very quickly.

rocking chair *noun* a chair on two curved pieces of wood that rocks backwards and forwards when you sit in it.

rocky rockier, rockiest *adjective* covered with rocks.

rod *noun* a long, thin pole or bar, usually made of wood or metal.

rode the past tense of **ride**.

rodent *noun* a small mammal with sharp front teeth which it uses for gnawing.

rodeo rodeos *noun* a public entertainment in which cowboys show different skills.

roe *noun* Roe is the eggs of a fish.

rogue *noun* 1 You can refer to a man who behaves dishonestly as a rogue. ▸ *adjective* 2 a vicious animal that lives apart from its herd or pack.

role; also spelt **rôle** *noun* 1 Someone's role is their position and function in a situation or society. 2 (DRAMA) An actor's role is the character that he or she plays.

roll *verb* 1 When something rolls or when you roll it, it moves along a surface, turning over and over. 2 When vehicles roll along, they move. 3 If you roll your eyes, you make them turn up or go from side to side. 4 If you roll something flexible into a cylinder or ball, you wrap it several times around itself. ▸ *noun* 5 A roll of paper or cloth is a long piece of it that has been rolled into a tube. 6 a small, rounded, individually baked piece of bread. 7 an official list of people's names. 8 A roll on a drum is a long, rumbling sound made on it. ▸ **roll up** *verb* 1 If you roll up something flexible, you wrap it several times around itself. 2 If you roll up your sleeves or trousers, you fold them over from the bottom to make them shorter. 3 (*informal*) If you roll up, you arrive.

roller *noun* 1 a cylinder that turns round in a machine or piece of equipment. 2 Rollers are tubes which you can wind your hair around to make it curly.

roller-coaster *noun* a pleasure ride at a fair, consisting of a small railway that goes up and down very steep slopes.

rolling pin noun a cylinder used for rolling pastry dough to make it flat.

ROM noun (ICT) ROM is a storage device that holds data permanently and cannot be altered by the programmer. ROM stands for 'read only memory'.

Roman Catholic (RE) adjective 1 relating or belonging to the branch of the Christian Church that accepts the Pope in Rome as its leader. ▸ noun 2 someone who belongs to the Roman Catholic Church. > **Roman Catholicism** noun

romance noun 1 a relationship between two people who are in love with each other. 2 Romance is the pleasure and excitement of doing something new and unusual. 3 (LIBRARY) A novel about a love affair.

Romanian; also spelt **Rumanian** adjective 1 belonging or relating to Romania. ▸ noun 2 someone who comes from Romania. 3 Romanian is the main language spoken in Romania.

romantic adjective 1 A romantic person has ideas that are not realistic, for example about love or about ways of changing society. 2 connected with love. 3 Something that is romantic is beautiful in a way that strongly affects your feelings.
> **romantically** adverb
> **romanticism** noun

romantic adjective
2 = amorous, loving, tender

roo roos noun (informal) In Australian English, a roo is a kangaroo.

roof noun 1 The roof of a building or car is the covering on top of it. 2 The roof of your mouth or of a cave is the highest part.

roofing noun Roofing is material used for covering roofs.

rooftop noun the outside part of the roof of a building.

room noun 1 a separate section in a building, divided from other rooms by walls. 2 If there is room somewhere, there is enough space for things to be fitted in or for people to do what they want to do.

room noun
1 = chamber, office 2 = capacity, elbow room, space

roost noun 1 a place where birds rest or build their nests. ▸ verb 2 When birds roost, they settle somewhere for the night.

root noun 1 The roots of a plant are the parts that grow under the ground. 2 The root of a hair is the part beneath the skin. 3 You can refer to the place or culture that you grew up in as your roots. 4 The root of something is its original cause or basis. ▸ verb 5 To root through things means to search through them, pushing them aside. > **root out** verb If you root something or someone out, you find them and force them out.

rooted adjective developed from or strongly influenced by something.

rope noun 1 a thick, strong length of twisted cord. ▸ verb 2 If you rope one thing to another, you tie them together with rope.

rosary rosaries noun a string of beads that Roman Catholics use for counting prayers.

rose 1 Rose is the past tense of **rise**. ▶ noun 2 a large garden flower which has a pleasant smell and grows on a bush with thorns. ▶ noun, adjective 3 reddish-pink.

rosemary noun Rosemary is a herb with fragrant spiky leaves, used for flavouring in cooking.

rosette noun a large badge of coloured ribbons gathered into a circle, which is worn as a prize in a competition or to support a political party.

roster noun a list of people who take it in turn to do a particular job.

rostrum rostrums or rostra noun a raised platform on which someone stands to speak to an audience or conduct an orchestra.

rosy rosier, rosiest adjective 1 reddish-pink. 2 If a situation seems rosy, it is likely to be good or successful. 3 If a person looks rosy, they have pink cheeks and look healthy.

rot rots, rotting, rotted verb 1 When food or wood rots, it decays and can no longer be used. 2 When something rots another substance, it causes it to decay. ▶ noun 3 Rot is the condition that affects things when they rot.

> **rot** verb
> 1 = decay, decompose, fester, spoil
> ▶ noun 3 = decay, deterioration, mould

rota noun a list of people who take turns to do a particular job.

rotate verb (MATHS) When something rotates, it turns with a circular movement.
> **rotation** noun

rotor noun 1 The rotor is the part of a machine that turns. 2 The rotors or rotor blades of a helicopter are the four long, flat pieces of metal on top of it which rotate and lift it off the ground.

rotten adjective 1 decayed and no longer of use. 2 (informal) of very poor quality. 3 (informal) very unfair, unkind or unpleasant.

> **rotten** adjective
> 1 = bad, decayed, decomposed, mouldy, sour 2 = inferior, lousy (slang), poor, unsatisfactory

rouble noun the main unit of currency in Russia.

rough adjective 1 uneven and not smooth. 2 not using enough care or gentleness. 3 difficult or unpleasant. 4 approximately correct: At a rough guess it is five times more profitable. 5 If the sea is rough, there are large waves because of bad weather. 6 A rough town or area has a lot of crime or violence. ▶ noun, adjective 7 A rough or a rough sketch is a drawing or description that shows the main features but does not show the details. > **roughly** adverb > **roughness** noun

> **rough** adjective
> 1 = bumpy, craggy, rocky, rugged, uneven 3 = difficult, hard, tough, unpleasant 4 = approximate, estimated, sketchy, vague

roulette noun Roulette is a gambling game in which a ball is dropped onto a revolving wheel with numbered holes in it.

round adjective 1 Something round is shaped like a ball or a circle. 2 complete or whole: round numbers. ▶ preposition, adverb 3 If something is round something else, it surrounds it. **4** The distance round something is the length of its circumference or boundary. **5** You can refer to an area near a place as the area round it. ▶ *preposition* **6** If something moves round you, it keeps moving in a circle with you in the centre. **7** When someone goes to the other side of something, they have gone round it. ▶ *adverb* **8** If you go round a place, you go to different parts of it to look at it. ▶ *adverb* **9** If you turn or look round, you turn so you are facing in a different direction. **10** When someone comes round, they visit you. ▶ *noun* **11** one of a series of events. **12** If you buy a round of drinks, you buy a drink for each member of the group you are with. > **round up** *verb* If you round up people or animals, you gather them together.

> **round** *adjective*
> **1** = circular, cylindrical, rounded, spherical
> ▶ *noun* **11** = lap, period, session, stage

roundabout *noun* **1** a meeting point of several roads with a circle in the centre which vehicles have to travel around. **2** a circular platform which rotates and which children can ride on in a playground. **3** the same as a merry-go-round.

rounded *adjective* curved in shape, without any points or sharp edges.

rounders *noun* a game played by two teams, in which a player scores points by hitting a ball and running around four sides of a square pitch.

round-the-clock *adjective* happening continuously.

rouse *verb* **1** If someone rouses you, they wake you up. **2** If you rouse yourself to do something, you make yourself get up and do it. **3** If something rouses you, it makes you feel very emotional and excited.

rout *verb* To rout your opponents means to defeat them completely and easily.

route *noun* a way from one place to another.

> **route** *noun*
> = channel, course, itinerary, path, road, way

router *noun* a piece of equipment which allows computers to access the internet.

routine *adjective* **1** Routine activities are done regularly. ▶ *noun* **2** the usual way or order in which you do things. **3** a boring repetition of tasks. > **routinely** *adverb*

> **routine** *adjective*
> **1** = everyday, normal, ordinary, regular, standard, typical, usual
> ▶ *noun* **2** = order, pattern, practice, procedure, programme, schedule, system

roving *adjective* wandering or roaming.

row[1] *noun* **1** A row of people or things is several of them arranged in a line. ▶ *verb* **2** When you row a boat, you use oars to make it move through the water.

> **row** *noun*
> **1** = bank, column, line, queue, rank

row[2] *noun* **1** a serious argument.

R

2 If someone is making a row, they are making too much noise.
▶ verb **3** If people are rowing, they are quarrelling noisily.

> **row** noun
> **1** = altercation, argument, quarrel, squabble

rowdy rowdier, rowdiest adjective rough and noisy.

> **rowdy** adjective
> = boisterous, noisy, unruly, wild

royal adjective **1** belonging to or involving a queen, a king or a member of their family. **2** 'Royal' is used in the names of organisations appointed or supported by a member of a royal family. ▶ noun **3** (informal) Members of the royal family are sometimes referred to as the royals.

> **royal** adjective
> **1** = imperial, regal, sovereign

royalist noun someone who supports their country's royal family.

royalty royalties noun **1** The members of a royal family are sometimes referred to as royalty. **2** Royalties are payments made to authors and musicians from the sales of their books or records.

rub rubs, rubbing, rubbed verb If you rub something, you move your hand or a cloth backwards and forwards over it. > **rub out** verb To rub out something written means to remove it by rubbing it with a rubber or a cloth.

rubber noun **1** Rubber is a strong elastic substance used for making tyres, boots and other products. **2** a small piece of rubber used to rub out pencil mistakes.

rubbish noun **1** Rubbish is unwanted or waste material. **2** (informal) You can refer to nonsense or something of very poor quality as rubbish.

> **rubbish** noun
> **1** = garbage, litter, refuse (formal), trash, waste **2** = drivel, garbage (informal), gibberish, nonsense

rubble noun Bits of old brick and stone are referred to as rubble.

ruby rubies noun a type of red jewel.

rucksack noun a bag with shoulder straps for carrying things on your back.

rudder noun a piece of wood or metal at the back of a boat or plane which is moved to make the boat or plane turn.

rude adjective **1** not polite. **2** embarrassing or offensive. **3** unexpected and unpleasant. > **rudely** adverb > **rudeness** noun

> **rude** adjective
> **1** = disrespectful, impertinent, impudent, insolent **3** = abrupt, unpleasant, violent

rudimentary adjective (formal) very basic or not basic.

ruff noun **1** a stiff circular collar with many pleats in it, worn especially in the 16th century. **2** a thick band of fur or feathers around the neck of a bird or animal.

ruffle verb **1** If you ruffle someone's hair, you move your hand quickly backwards and forwards over their head. **2** If something ruffles you, it makes you annoyed or upset. ▶ noun **3** Ruffles are small folds made in a piece of material for decoration.

r

rug noun 1 a small, thick carpet. 2 a blanket which you can use to cover your knees or for sitting on outdoors.

rugby noun Rugby is a game played by two teams, who try to kick and throw an oval ball to their opponents' end of the pitch. Rugby League is played with 13 players in each side; Rugby Union is played with 15 players in each side.

rugged adjective 1 rocky and wild. 2 having strong features.

ruin verb 1 If you ruin something, you destroy or spoil it completely. 2 If someone is ruined, they have lost all their money. ▶ noun 3 Ruin is the state of being destroyed or completely spoilt. 4 A ruin or the ruins of something refers to the parts that are left after it has been severely damaged.

> **ruin** verb
> 1 = break, damage, destroy, devastate, impair, mar, mess up, spoil, undo, wreck
> ▶ noun 3 = decay, destruction, devastation, disrepair, downfall, fall 4 = remains, shell, wreck

rule noun 1 Rules are statements which tell you what you are allowed to do. ▶ verb 2 To rule a country or group of people means to have power over it and be in charge of its affairs. 3 (formal) When someone in authority rules on a particular matter, they give an official decision about it. ▶ phrase 4 As a rule means usually or generally. > **rule out** verb 1 If you rule out an idea or course of action, you reject it. 2 If one thing rules out another, it prevents it from happening or being possible.

> **rule** noun
> 1 = decree, guideline, law, order, regulation
> ▶ verb 2 = administer, be in power, govern, lead, reign
> ▶ phrase 4 as a rule = generally, mainly, normally, on the whole, usually

ruler noun 1 a person who rules a country. 2 a long, flat piece of wood or plastic with straight edges marked in centimetres or inches, used for measuring or drawing straight lines.

> **ruler** noun
> 1 = commander, governor, head of state, leader, monarch, sovereign

rum noun Rum is a strong alcoholic drink made from sugar cane juice.

rumble verb 1 If something rumbles, it makes a continuous low noise. ▶ noun 2 a continuous low noise.

rummage verb If you rummage somewhere, you search for something, moving things about carelessly.

rumour noun 1 a story that people are talking about, which may or may not be true. ▶ verb 2 If something is rumoured, people are suggesting that it has happened.

> **rumour** noun
> 1 = gossip, hearsay, whisper, word

rump noun 1 An animal's rump is its rear end. 2 Rump or rump steak is meat cut from the rear end of a cow.

run runs, running, ran, run 1 When you run, you move quickly, leaving the ground during each stride. **2** If you say that a road or river runs in a particular direction, you are describing its course. **3** If you run your hand or an object over something, you move it over it. **4** If someone runs in an election, they stand as a candidate. **5** If you run a business or an activity, you are in charge of it. **6** If you run an experiment, a computer program, or a tape, you start it and let it continue. **7** To run a car means to have it and use it. **8** If you run someone somewhere in a car, you drive them there. **9** If you run water, you turn a tap to make it flow. **10** If your nose is running, it is producing a lot of mucus. **11** If the dye in something runs, the colour comes out when it is washed. **12** If a feeling runs through your body, it affects you quickly and strongly. **13** If an amount is running at a particular level, it is at that level. **14** If someone or something is running late, they have taken more time than was planned. **15** If an event or contract runs for a particular time, it lasts for that time. ▶ noun **16** If you go for a run, you run for pleasure or exercise. **17** a journey somewhere. **18** If a play or show has a run of a particular length of time, it is on for that time. **19** A run of success or failure is a series of successes or failures. **20** In cricket or baseball, a player scores one run by running between marked places on the pitch after hitting the ball. ▷ **run away** verb If you run away from a place, you leave it suddenly and secretly. ▷ **run down** verb **1** To run someone down means to criticise them strongly. **2** To run

down an organisation means to reduce its size and activity. ▷ **run out** verb If you run out of something, you have no more left. ▷ **run over** verb If someone is run over, they are hit by a moving vehicle.

run verb
1 = bolt, gallop, jog, sprint
5 = administer, be in charge of, control, direct, look after, manage

runaway noun a person who has escaped from a place or left it secretly and hurriedly.

rundown adjective **1** tired and not well. **2** neglected and in poor condition. ▶ noun **3** (informal) If you give someone the rundown on a situation, you tell them the basic, important facts about it.

rung **1** Rung is the past participle of **ring**. ▶ noun **2** The rungs on a ladder are the bars that form the steps.

runner noun **1** a person who runs, especially as a sport. **2** a person who takes messages or runs errands. **3** A runner on a plant such as a strawberry is a long shoot from which a new plant develops. **4** The runners on drawers and ice-skates are the thin strips on which they move.

runner-up runners-up noun a person or team that comes second in a race or competition.

running adjective **1** continuing without stopping over a period of time. **2** Running water is flowing rather than standing still.

runny runnier, runniest adjective **1** more liquid than usual. **2** If someone's nose or eyes are runny, liquid is coming out of them.

runway noun a long strip of ground used by aeroplanes for taking off or landing.

rupee noun the main unit of currency in India, Pakistan and some other countries.

rupture noun 1 a severe injury in which part of your body tears or bursts open. ▶ verb 2 To rupture part of your body means to cause it to tear or burst.

rural adjective (GEOGRAPHY) relating to or involving the countryside.

ruse noun (formal) an action which is intended to trick someone.

rush verb 1 To rush means to move fast or do something quickly. 2 If you rush someone into doing something, you make them do it without allowing them enough time to think. ▶ noun 3 A rush is a situation in which people go somewhere or do something very quickly. 4 If there is a rush for something, there is a sudden increase in demand for it. 5 Rushes are plants with long, thin stems that grow near water.

> **rush** verb
> 1 = dash, fly, gush, hasten, hurry, race, run, scurry, shoot
> 2 = hurry, hustle, press, pressurise, push
> ▶ noun 3 = bustle, dash, hurry, race, scramble, stampede

rush hour noun The rush hour is one of the busy parts of the day when most people are travelling to or from work.

Russian adjective 1 belonging or relating to Russia. ▶ noun 2 someone who comes from Russia. 3 Russian is the main language spoken in Russia.

rust noun 1 Rust is a reddish-brown substance that forms on iron or steel which has been in contact with water and which is decaying gradually. ▶ noun, adjective 2 reddish-brown. ▶ verb 3 When a metal object rusts, it becomes covered in rust.

rustic adjective simple in a way considered to be typical of the countryside.

rustle verb When something rustles, it makes soft sounds as it moves. > **rustling** adjective, noun

rusty rustier, rustiest adjective 1 affected by rust. 2 If someone's knowledge is rusty, it is not as good as it used to be because they have not used it for a long time.

rut noun 1 a deep, narrow groove in the ground made by the wheels of a vehicle. ▶ phrase 2 If someone is in a rut, they have become fixed in their way of doing things.

ruthless adjective very harsh or cruel. > **ruthlessness** noun > **ruthlessly** adverb

rye noun a type of grass that produces light brown grain.

Ss

Sabbath noun (RE) The Sabbath is the day of the week when members of some religious groups, especially Jews and Christians, do not work.

sabotage noun 1 the deliberate damaging of things such as machinery and railway lines. ▶ verb 2 If something is sabotaged, it is deliberately damaged. > **saboteur** noun

sabre noun 1 a heavy curved sword. 2 a light sword used in fencing.

sachet noun a small closed packet, containing a small amount of something such as sugar or shampoo.

sack noun 1 a large bag made of rough material used for carrying or storing goods. ▶ verb 2 (informal) If someone is sacked, they are dismissed from their job by their employer. ▶ phrase 3 (informal) If someone gets **the sack**, they are dismissed from their job by their employer.

> **sack** verb
> 2 = discharge, dismiss, fire (informal)
> ▶ phrase 3 **the sack** = discharge, dismissal, termination of employment (formal)

sacrament noun (RE) an important Christian ceremony such as communion, baptism or marriage.

sacred adjective holy, or connected with religion or religious ceremonies.

sacrifice verb 1 If you sacrifice something valuable or important, you give it up. 2 To sacrifice an animal means to kill it as an offering to a god. ▶ noun 3 the killing of an animal as an offering to a god or gods. 4 the action of giving something up. > **sacrificial** adjective

> **sacrifice** verb
> 1 = forego, forfeit, give up, surrender
> ▶ noun 4 = renunciation, self-denial

sacrilege noun Sacrilege is behaviour that shows great disrespect for something holy. > **sacrilegious** adjective

sad sadder, saddest adjective 1 If you are sad, you feel unhappy. 2 Something sad makes you feel unhappy. > **sadly** adverb

> **sad** adjective
> 1 = blue, dejected, depressed, dismal, down, downcast, gloomy, glum, grief-stricken, low, melancholy (literary), mournful, unhappy, wistful
> 2 = depressing, dismal, gloomy, harrowing, heart-rending, melancholy, mournful, moving, pathetic, poignant, tragic, upsetting

sadden verb If something saddens you, it makes you feel sad.

saddle noun 1 a leather seat that you sit on when you are riding a horse. 2 The saddle on a bicycle is the seat. ▶ verb 3 If you saddle a horse, you put a saddle on it.

sadism noun Sadism is the obtaining of pleasure from making people suffer pain or humiliation. > **sadist** noun > **sadistic** adjective > **sadistically** adverb

sadness noun the feeling of being unhappy.

sadness noun
= dejection, depression, despondency, melancholy (literary), unhappiness

safari safaris noun an expedition for hunting or observing wild animals, especially in Africa.

safe adjective 1 (PSHE) Something that is safe does not cause harm or danger. 2 If you are safe, you are not in any danger. 3 If it is safe to say something, you can say it with little risk of being wrong. ▶ noun 4 a strong metal box with special locks, in which you can keep valuable things. > **safely** adverb

safe adjective
1 = harmless, innocuous 2 = all right, in safe hands, okay or OK (informal), out of danger, out of harm's way, protected, safe and sound, secure

safeguard verb 1 To safeguard something means to protect it. ▶ noun 2 something designed to protect people or things.

safeguard verb
1 = defend, guard, look after, preserve, protect, save, shield ▶ noun 2 = barrier, cover, defence, protection

safekeeping noun If something is given to you for safekeeping, it is given to you to look after.

safety noun the state of being safe from harm or danger.

safety noun
= immunity, protection, security

sag sags, sagging, sagged verb When something sags, it hangs down loosely or sinks downwards in the middle. > **sagging** adjective

saga noun a very long story, usually with many different adventures.

sage noun 1 (literary) a very wise person. 2 Sage is also a herb used for flavouring in cooking.

Sagittarius noun Sagittarius is the ninth sign of the zodiac, represented by a creature who is half horse, half man, holding a bow and arrow. People born between November 22nd and December 21st are born under this sign.

said the past tense and past participle of **say**.

sail noun 1 Sails are large pieces of material attached to a ship's mast. The wind blows against the sail and moves the ship. ▶ verb 2 When a ship sails, it moves across water. 3 If you sail somewhere, you go there by ship.

sailor noun a member of a ship's crew.

saint noun a person who after death is formally recognised by a Christian Church as deserving special honour because of having lived a very holy life.

saintly adjective behaving in a very good or holy way.

sake phrase 1 If you do something for someone's sake, you do it to help or please them. 2 You use for the sake of to say why you are doing something: a one-off expedition for interest's sake.

salad noun a mixture of raw vegetables.

salami noun Salami is a kind of spicy sausage.

salary salaries noun a regular monthly payment to an employee. > **salaried** adjective

sale noun 1 The sale of goods is the selling of them. 2 an occasion when a shop sells things at reduced prices. 3 (in plural) The sales of a product are the numbers that are sold.

saleable adjective easy to sell or suitable for being sold.

salesman salesmen noun a man who sells products for a company.

saleswoman saleswomen noun a woman who sells products for a company.

salient adjective (formal) The salient points or facts are the important ones.

saliva noun Saliva is the watery liquid in your mouth that helps you chew and digest food.

salmon salmons or salmon noun a large edible silver-coloured fish with pink flesh.

salmonella noun Salmonella is a kind of bacteria which can cause severe food poisoning.

salon noun a place where hairdressers work.

saloon noun 1 a car with a fixed roof and a separate boot. 2 in the Wild West of America, a place where alcoholic drinks were sold and drunk.

salt noun 1 Salt is a white substance found naturally in sea water. It is used to flavour and preserve food. 2 (SCIENCE) a chemical compound formed from an acid base.

salty saltier, saltiest adjective containing salt or tasting of salt.

> **salty** adjective
> = brak (South African), briny, salted

salute noun 1 a formal sign of respect. Soldiers give a salute by raising their right hand to their forehead. ▶ verb 2 If you salute someone, you give them a salute.

salvage verb 1 If you salvage things, you save them, for example from a wrecked ship or a destroyed building. ▶ noun 2 You refer to things saved from a wrecked ship or destroyed building as salvage.

salvation noun 1 When someone's salvation takes place, they are saved from harm or evil. 2 To be someone's salvation means to save them from harm or evil.

salvo salvos or salvoes noun the firing of several guns or missiles at the same time.

same adjective (usually preceded by the) 1 If two things are the same, they are like one another. 2 Same means just one thing and not two different ones: They were born in the same town.

> **same** adjective
> 1 = alike, equal, equivalent, identical, indistinguishable

Samoan adjective 1 belonging or relating to Samoa. ▶ noun 2 someone who comes from Samoa.

sample noun 1 A sample of something is a small amount of it that you can try or test. ▶ verb 2 If you sample something, you try it.

samurai noun A samurai was a member of an ancient Japanese warrior class.

sanctimonious adjective pretending to be very religious and virtuous.

sanction verb 1 To sanction something means to officially approve of it or allow it. ▶ noun 2 Sanction is official approval of something. 3 a severe punishment or penalty intended to make people obey the law. 4 Sanctions are sometimes taken by countries against a country that has broken international law.

> **sanction** verb
> 1 = allow, approve, authorise, back, endorse, permit, support
> ▶ noun 2 = approval, authorisation, backing, blessing, permission, support
> 4 = ban, boycott, embargo, penalties

sanctity noun If you talk about the sanctity of something, you are saying that it should be respected because it is very important.

sanctuary sanctuaries noun 1 a place where you are safe from harm or danger. 2 a place where wildlife is protected.

sand noun 1 Sand consists of tiny pieces of stone. Beaches are made of sand. ▶ verb 2 If you sand something, you rub sandpaper over it to make it smooth.

sandal noun Sandals are light open shoes with straps, worn in warm weather.

sandpaper noun (DGT) Sandpaper is strong paper with a coating of sand on it, used for rubbing surfaces to make them smooth.

sandstone noun Sandstone is a type of rock formed from sand, often used for building.

sandwich noun 1 two slices of bread with a filling between them. ▶ verb 2 If one thing is sandwiched between two others, it is in a narrow space between them.

sandy sandier, sandiest adjective 1 A sandy area is covered with sand. 2 Sandy hair is light orange-brown.

sane adjective 1 If someone is sane, they have a normal and healthy mind. 2 A sane action is sensible and reasonable.

> **sane** adjective
> 1 = lucid, normal, rational
> 2 = judicious (formal), level-headed, rational, reasonable, sensible, sound

sang the past tense of **sing**.

sanguine adjective (formal) cheerful and confident.

sanitary adjective Sanitary means concerned with keeping things clean and hygienic.

sanitation noun Sanitation is the process of keeping places clean and hygienic, especially by providing a sewage system and clean water supply.

sanity noun Your sanity is your ability to think and act normally and reasonably.

sank the past tense of **sink**.

sap saps, sapping, sapped verb 1 If something saps your strength or confidence, it gradually weakens and destroys it. ▶ noun 2 Sap is the watery liquid in plants.

sapphire noun a blue precious stone.

sarcastic *adjective* saying or doing the opposite of what you really mean in order to mock or insult someone. > **sarcasm** *noun* > **sarcastically** *adverb*

> **sarcastic** *adjective*
> = caustic, ironic, sardonic, satirical

sardine *noun* a small edible sea fish.

sardonic *adjective* mocking or scornful. > **sardonically** *adverb*

sari saris *noun* a piece of clothing worn especially by Indian women, consisting of a long piece of material folded around the body.

sash *noun* a long piece of cloth worn round the waist or over one shoulder.

sat the past tense and past participle of **sit**.

Satan *noun* Satan is the Devil.

satanic *adjective* caused by or influenced by Satan.

satchel *noun* a leather or cloth bag with a long strap.

satellite *noun* 1 a spacecraft sent into orbit round the earth to collect information or as part of a communications system. 2 a natural object in space that moves round a planet or star.

satin *noun* Satin is a kind of smooth, shiny fabric.

satire *noun* Satire is the use of mocking or ironical humour, especially in literature, to show how foolish or wicked some people are. > **satirical** *adjective*

satisfaction *noun* Satisfaction is the feeling of pleasure you get when you do something you wanted or needed to do.

satisfactory *adjective* acceptable or adequate. > **satisfactorily** *adverb*

> **satisfactory** *adjective*
> = acceptable, adequate, all right, good enough, passable, sufficient

satisfied *adjective* happy because you have got what you want.

> **satisfied** *adjective*
> = content, contented, happy, pleased

satisfy satisfies, satisfying, satisfied *verb* 1 To satisfy someone means to give them enough of something to make them pleased or contented. 2 To satisfy someone that something is the case means to convince them of it. 3 To satisfy the requirements for something means to fulfil them.

> **satisfy** *verb*
> 1 = gratify, indulge, please
> 2 = convince, persuade, put someone's mind at rest, reassure 3 = fulfil, meet

satisfying *adjective* Something that is satisfying gives you a feeling of pleasure and fulfilment.

saturated *adjective* 1 very wet. 2 If a place is saturated with things, it is completely full of them. > **saturation** *noun*

Saturday *noun* the day between Friday and Sunday.

Saturn *noun* Saturn is the planet in the solar system which is sixth from the sun.

sauce *noun* a liquid eaten with food to give it more flavour.

saucepan *noun* a deep metal cooking pot with a handle and a lid.

s

saucer *noun* a small curved plate for a cup.

saucy saucier, sauciest *adjective* cheeky in an amusing way.

Saudi *adjective* 1 belonging or relating to Saudi Arabia. ▶ *noun* 2 someone who comes from Saudi Arabia.

sauna *noun* If you have a sauna, you go into a very hot room in order to sweat, then have a cold bath or shower.

saunter *verb* To saunter somewhere means to walk there slowly and casually.

sausage *noun* a mixture of minced meat and herbs formed into a tubular shape and served cooked.

savage *adjective* 1 cruel and violent. ▶ *noun* 2 If you call someone a savage, you mean that they are violent and uncivilised. ▶ *verb* 3 If an animal savages you, it attacks you and bites you.
> **savagely** *adverb*

> **savage** *adjective*
> 1 = barbaric, barbarous, brutal, cruel, ferocious, inhuman, vicious, violent
> ▶ *noun* 2 = barbarian, beast, brute, lout, monster
> ▶ *verb* 3 = attack, bite, maul

savagery *noun* Savagery is cruel and violent behaviour.

save *verb* 1 If you save someone, you rescue them. 2 If you save someone or something, you keep them safe. 3 If you save something, you keep it so that you can use it later. 4 To save time, money or effort means to prevent it from being wasted. ▶ *preposition* 5 (*formal*) Save means except.

save *verb*
1 = come to someone's rescue, deliver, redeem, rescue, salvage
2 = keep safe, preserve, protect, safeguard 3 = hoard, keep, put by, reserve, set aside

saving *noun* 1 a reduction in the amount of time or money used. 2 (*in plural*) Your savings are the money you have saved.

saviour *noun* 1 If someone saves you from danger, you can refer to them as your saviour. ▶ *proper noun* 2 (RE) In Christianity, the Saviour is Jesus Christ.

savour *verb* If you savour something, you take your time with it and enjoy it fully.

savoury *adjective* 1 Savoury is salty or spicy. 2 Something that is not very savoury is not very pleasant or respectable.

saw saws, sawing, sawed, sawn 1 Saw is the past tense of **see**. ▶ *verb* 2 If you saw something, you cut it with a saw. ▶ *noun* 3 a tool, with a blade with sharp teeth along one edge, for cutting wood.

sawdust *noun* Sawdust is the fine powder produced when you saw wood.

saxophone *noun* a curved metal wind instrument often played in jazz bands.

say says, saying, said *verb* 1 When you say something, you speak words. 2 'Say' is used to give an example: *a maximum fee of, say, a million*. ▶ *noun* 3 If you have a say in something, you can give your opinion and influence decisions.

say *verb*
1 = announce, declare, mention, remark, state, utter
▶ *noun* 3 = voice, vote

saying noun a well-known sentence or phrase that tells you something about human life.

> **saying** noun
> = adage, axiom, maxim, proverb

scab noun a hard, dry covering that forms over a wound.
> **scabby** adjective

scaffolding noun Scaffolding is a framework of poles and boards that is used by workers to stand on while they are working on the outside structure of a building.

scald verb 1 If you scald yourself, you burn yourself with very hot liquid or steam. ▶ noun 2 a burn caused by scalding.

scale noun 1 The scale of something is its size or extent. 2 a set of levels or numbers used for measuring things. 3 (GEOGRAPHY) The scale of a map, plan or model is the relationship between the size of something in the map, plan or model and its size in the real world. 4 (MUSIC) An upward or downward sequence of musical notes. 5 The scales of a fish or reptile are the small pieces of hard skin covering its body. 6 (in plural) Scales are a piece of equipment used for weighing things. ▶ verb 7 If you scale something high, you climb it.

scallop noun Scallops are edible shellfish with two flat fan-shaped shells.

scalp noun 1 Your scalp is the skin under the hair on your head. 2 the piece of skin and hair removed when someone is scalped. ▶ verb 3 To scalp someone means to remove the skin and hair from their head in one piece.

scalpel noun a knife with a thin, sharp blade, used by surgeons.

scaly scalier, scaliest adjective covered with scales.

scam noun (informal) an illegal trick, usually done to get money from a person.

scamper verb To scamper means to move quickly and lightly.

scan scans, scanning, scanned verb 1 If you scan something, you look at all of it carefully. 2 If you scan a piece of writing, you read it very quickly to find the important or interesting parts. 3 If a machine scans something, it examines it by means of a beam of light or X-rays. 4 (ENGLISH) If the words of a poem scan, they fit into a regular, rhythmical pattern. 5 (ENGLISH) If you scan a line of poetry you count the number of beats or metrical feet it has. ▶ noun 6 an examination or search by a scanner.

scandal noun a situation or event that people think is shocking and immoral. > **scandalous** adjective

Scandinavia noun Scandinavia is the name given to a group of countries in Northern Europe, including Norway, Sweden, Denmark and sometimes Finland and Iceland. > **Scandinavian** noun, adjective

scanner noun 1 a machine which is used to examine, identify or record things by means of a beam of light or X-rays. 2 (ICT) a machine which converts text or images into a form that can be stored on a computer.

scant adjective You use 'scant' to show that there is not as much of something as there should be.

scapegoat noun If someone is made a scapegoat, they are blamed for something, although it may not be their fault.

scar scars, scarring, scarred noun 1 a mark left on your skin after a wound has healed. 2 a permanent effect on someone's mind that results from a very unpleasant experience. ▶ verb 3 If an injury scars you, it leaves a permanent mark on your skin. 4 If an unpleasant experience scars you, it has a permanent effect on you.

scarce adjective If something is scarce, there is not very much of it. > **scarcity** noun

> **scarce** adjective
> = few, rare, uncommon, unusual

scarcely adverb Scarcely means hardly.

scare verb 1 If something scares you, it frightens you. ▶ noun 2 If something gives you a scare, it scares you. 3 If there is a scare about something, a lot of people are worried about it. > **scared** adjective

> **scare** verb
> 1 = alarm, frighten, give someone a fright, intimidate, startle, terrify, terrorise, unnerve
> ▶ noun 2 = fright, shock, start
> 3 = alert, hysteria, panic

scarecrow noun an object shaped like a person, put in a field to scare birds away.

scarf scarfs or scarves noun a piece of cloth worn round your neck or head to keep you warm.

scarlet noun, adjective bright red.

scary scarier, scariest adjective (informal) frightening.

> **scary** adjective
> = alarming, chilling, creepy (informal), eerie, frightening, hair-raising, spooky, terrifying, unnerving

scathing adjective harsh and scornful.

scatter verb 1 To scatter things means to throw or drop them all over an area. 2 If people scatter, they suddenly move away in different directions.

> **scatter** verb
> 1 = shower, sow, sprinkle, throw about

scattering noun A scattering of things is a small number of them spread over a large area.

scavenge verb If you scavenge for things, you search for them among waste and rubbish. > **scavenger** noun

scenario scenarios noun 1 (DRAMA) The scenario of a film or play is a summary of its plot. 2 the way a situation could possibly develop in the future.

scene noun 1 (ENGLISH) (DRAMA) part of a play or film in which a series of events happen in one place. 2 Pictures and views are sometimes called scenes. 3 The scene of an event is the place where it happened. 4 an area of activity: *the music scene.*

> **scene** noun
> 2 = landscape, panorama, view
> 3 = location, place, setting, site, spot 4 = arena, business, environment, world

scenery noun 1 In the countryside, you can refer to

everything you see as the scenery. **2** In a theatre, the scenery is the painted cloth on the stage which represents the place where the action is happening.

> **scenery** *noun*
> **1** = landscape, panorama, surroundings, terrain, view

scenic *adjective* A scenic place or route has nice views.

scent *noun* **1** a smell, especially a pleasant one. **2** Scent is perfume. ▶ *verb* **3** When an animal scents something, it becomes aware of it by smelling it.

sceptic *noun* someone who has doubts about things that other people believe. > **scepticism** *noun*

sceptical *adjective* If you are sceptical about something, you have doubts about it.
> **sceptically** *adverb*

schedule *noun* **1** a plan that gives a list of events or tasks, together with the times at which each thing should be done. ▶ *verb* **2** If something is scheduled to happen, it has been planned and arranged.

scheme *noun* **1** a plan or arrangement. ▶ *verb* **2** When people scheme, they make secret plans.

schism *noun* a split or division within a group or organisation.

schizophrenia *noun* Schizophrenia is a serious mental condition which prevents someone relating their thoughts and feelings to what is happening around them. > **schizophrenic** *adjective*

scholar *noun* **1** a person who studies an academic subject and knows a lot about it. **2** In South

African English, a scholar is a school pupil.

scholarly *adjective* having or showing a lot of knowledge.

scholarship *noun* **1** If you get a scholarship to a school or university, your studies are paid for by the school or university or by some other organisation. **2** Scholarship is academic study and knowledge.

school *noun* **1** a place where children are educated. **2** University departments and colleges are sometimes called schools. **3** You can refer to a large group of dolphins or fish as a school. ▶ *verb* **4** When someone is schooled in something, they are taught it.

schoolchild schoolchildren *noun* Schoolchildren are children who go to school. > **schoolboy** *noun* > **schoolgirl** *noun*

schooling *noun* Your schooling is the education you get at school.

schooner *noun* a sailing ship.

science *noun* **1** Science is the study of the nature and behaviour of natural things and the knowledge obtained about them. **2** a branch of science, for example physics or biology.

science fiction *noun* Stories about events happening in the future or in other parts of the universe are called science fiction.

scientific *adjective* **1** relating to science or to a particular science. **2** done in a systematic way, using experiments or tests.
> **scientifically** *adverb*

scientist *noun* an expert in one of the sciences who does work connected with it.

s

scintillating adjective lively and witty.

scissors plural noun Scissors are a cutting tool with two sharp blades.

scoff verb 1 If you scoff, you speak in a scornful, mocking way about something. 2 (informal) If you scoff food, you eat it quickly and greedily.

scold verb If you scold someone, you tell them off.

> **scold** verb
> = chide, lecture, rebuke, reprimand, tell off (informal), tick off (informal)

scone noun Scones are small cakes made from flour and fat and usually eaten with butter.

scoop verb 1 If you scoop something up, you pick it up using a spoon or the palm of your hand. ▶ noun 2 an object like a large spoon which is used for picking up food such as ice cream.

scooter noun 1 a small, light motorcycle. 2 a simple cycle which a child rides by standing on it and pushing the ground with one foot.

scope noun 1 If there is scope for doing something, the opportunity to do it exists. 2 The scope of something is the whole subject area which it deals with or includes.

-scope suffix '-scope' is used to form nouns meaning an instrument used for observing or detecting: microscope.

scorching adjective extremely hot.

score verb 1 If you score in a game, you get a goal, run or point. 2 To score in a game also means to record the score obtained by the

players. 3 If you score a success or victory, you achieve it. 4 To score a surface means to cut a line into it. ▶ noun 5 The score in a game is the number of goals, runs or points obtained by the two teams. 6 Scores of things means very many of them. 7 (old-fashioned) A score is twenty. 8 (MUSIC) The score of a piece of music is the written version of it. > **scorer** noun

scorn noun 1 Scorn is great contempt. ▶ verb 2 If you scorn someone, you treat them with great contempt. 3 (formal) If you scorn something, you refuse to accept it.

> **scorn** noun
> 1 = contempt, derision, disdain, mockery
> ▶ verb 2 = despise, disdain, look down on, slight

scornful adjective showing contempt. > **scornfully** adverb

> **scornful** adjective
> = contemptuous, disdainful, scathing, sneering, supercilious, withering

Scorpio noun Scorpio is the eighth sign of the zodiac, represented by a scorpion. People born between October 23rd and November 21st are born under this sign.

scorpion noun an animal that looks like a small lobster, with a long tail with a poisonous sting on the end.

Scot noun 1 a person who comes from Scotland. ▶ adjective 2 Scots means the same as **Scottish**.

scotch noun Scotch is whisky made in Scotland.

Scotsman Scotsmen noun a man who comes from Scotland.

Scotswoman Scotswomen *noun*
a woman who comes from
Scotland.

Scottish *adjective* belonging or
relating to Scotland.

scoundrel *noun (old-fashioned)*
a man who cheats and deceives
people.

scour *verb* 1 If you scour a place,
you look all over it in order to find
something. 2 If you scour
something such as a pan, you
clean it by rubbing it with
something rough.

scourge *noun* something that
causes a lot of suffering.

scout *noun* 1 a boy who is a
member of the Scout Association,
an organisation for boys which
aims to develop character and
responsibility. 2 someone who is
sent to an area to find out the
position of an enemy army.
▶ *verb* 3 If you scout around for
something, you look around
for it.

scowl *verb* 1 If you scowl, you
frown because you are angry.
▶ *noun* 2 an angry expression.

scrabble *verb* If you scrabble at
something, you scrape at it with
your hands or feet.

scramble *verb* 1 If you scramble
over something, you climb over it
using your hands to help you.
▶ *noun* 2 a motorcycle race over
rough ground.

scrap scraps, scrapping, scrapped
noun 1 A scrap of something is a
very small piece of it. 2 (*in plural*)
Scraps are pieces of leftover food.
▶ *adjective, noun* 3 Scrap metal or
scrap is metal from old
machinery or cars that can be
re-used. ▶ *verb* 4 If you scrap
something, you get rid of it.

scrapbook *noun* a book in which
you stick things such as pictures
or newspaper articles.

scrape *verb* 1 If you scrape a
surface, you rub a rough or sharp
object against it. 2 If something
scrapes, it makes a harsh noise by
rubbing against something.

> **scrape** *verb*
> 1 = graze, scour, scratch, scuff,
> skin 2 = grate, grind, rasp,
> scratch

scratch *verb* 1 To scratch
something means to make a
small cut on it accidentally. 2 If
you scratch, you rub your skin
with your nails because it is
itching. ▶ *noun* 3 a small cut.

scrawl *verb* 1 If you scrawl
something, you write it in a
careless and untidy way. ▶ *noun*
2 You can refer to careless and
untidy writing as a scrawl.

scrawny scrawnier, scrawniest
adjective thin and bony.

scream *verb* 1 If you scream,
you shout or cry in a loud,
high-pitched voice. ▶ *noun*
2 a loud, high-pitched cry.

> **scream** *verb*
> 1 = cry, howl, screech, shout,
> shriek, squeal, yell
> ▶ *noun* 2 = cry, howl, screech,
> shriek, squeal, yell

screech *verb* 1 To screech
means to make an unpleasant
high-pitched noise. ▶ *noun* 2 an
unpleasant high-pitched noise.

screen *noun* 1 a flat vertical
surface on which a picture is
shown. 2 a vertical panel used to
separate different parts of a room
or to protect something. ▶ *verb*
3 To screen a film or television

s

programme means to show it.
4 If you screen someone, you put something in front of them to protect them.

screenplay noun The screenplay of a film is the script.

screenshot noun A screenshot is an image copied from a computer screen at a particular moment.

screw noun **1** a small, sharp piece of metal used for fixing things together or for fixing something to a wall. ▶ verb **2** If you screw things together, you fix them together using screws. **3** If you screw something onto something else, you fix it there by twisting it round and round. > **screw up** verb If you screw something up, you twist it or squeeze it so that it no longer has its proper shape.

screwdriver noun a tool for turning screws.

scribble verb **1** If you scribble something, you write it quickly and roughly. **2** To scribble also means to make meaningless marks. ▶ noun **3** You can refer to something written or drawn quickly and roughly as a scribble.

script noun (DRAMA) the written version of a play or film.

scripture noun (RE) Scripture refers to sacred writings, especially the Bible. > **scriptural** adjective

scroll noun a long roll of paper or parchment with writing on it.

scrub scrubs, scrubbing, scrubbed verb **1** If you scrub something, you clean it with a stiff brush and water. ▶ noun **2** If you give something a scrub, you scrub it. **3** (GEOGRAPHY) Scrub consists of low trees and bushes.

scruff noun The scruff of your neck is the back of your neck or collar.

scruffy scruffier, scruffiest adjective dirty and untidy.

> **scruffy** adjective
> = ragged, seedy, shabby, tatty, unkempt

scrum noun When rugby players form a scrum, they form a group and push against each other with their heads down in an attempt to get the ball.

scrupulous adjective **1** always doing what is honest or morally right. **2** paying very careful attention to detail.
> **scrupulously** adverb

scrutinise; also spelt **scrutinize** verb If you scrutinise something, you examine it very carefully.

> **scrutinise** verb
> = examine, inspect, pore over, scan, search, study

scrutiny noun If something is under scrutiny, it is being observed very carefully.

scuba diving noun Scuba diving is the sport of swimming underwater while breathing from tanks of compressed air on your back.

scuff verb **1** If you scuff your feet, you drag them along the ground when you are walking. **2** If you scuff your shoes, you mark them by scraping or rubbing them.

scuffle noun **1** a short, rough fight. ▶ verb **2** When people scuffle, they fight roughly.

sculpt verb When something is sculpted, it is carved or shaped in stone, wood or clay.

sculptor noun someone who makes sculptures.

sculpture noun 1 a work of art produced by carving or shaping stone or clay. 2 Sculpture is the art of making sculptures.

scum noun Scum is a layer of a dirty substance on the surface of a liquid.

scurrilous adjective abusive and damaging to someone's good name.

scurry scurries, scurrying, scurried verb To scurry means to run quickly with short steps.

scuttle verb 1 To scuttle means to run quickly. 2 To scuttle a ship means to sink it deliberately by making holes in the bottom. ▶ noun 3 a container for coal.

scythe noun a tool with a long handle and a curved blade used for cutting grass or grain.

sea noun 1 The sea is the salty water that covers much of the earth's surface. 2 A sea of people or things is a very large number of them.

seagull noun Seagulls are common white, grey and black birds that live near the sea.

seal noun 1 an official mark on a document which shows that it is genuine. 2 a piece of wax fixed over the opening of a container. 3 a large mammal with flippers that lives partly on land and partly in the sea. ▶ verb 4 If you seal an envelope, you stick down the flap. 5 If you seal an opening, you cover it securely so that air, gas or liquid can't get through.

sea lion noun a type of large seal.

seam noun 1 a line of stitches joining two pieces of cloth. 2 A seam of coal is a long, narrow layer of it beneath the ground.

seaman seamen noun a sailor.

search verb 1 If you search for something, you look for it in several places. 2 If a person is searched their body and clothing are examined to see if they are hiding anything. ▶ noun 3 an attempt to find something.

> **search** verb
> 1 = comb, forage, fossick (Australian and New Zealand), google, hunt, look, scour, seek, sift
> ▶ noun 3 = hunt, quest

search engine noun a service on the internet which enables users to search for items of interest.

searing adjective A searing pain is very sharp.

seashore noun The seashore is the land along the edge of the sea.

seasick adjective feeling sick because of the movement of a boat. > **seasickness** noun

seaside noun The seaside is an area next to the sea.

season noun 1 The seasons are the periods into which a year is divided and which have their own typical weather conditions. The seasons are spring, summer, autumn and winter. 2 a period of the year when something usually happens: *the football season*. ▶ verb 3 If you season food, you add salt, pepper or spices to it.

seasonal adjective happening during one season or one time of the year.

seasoning noun Seasoning is flavouring such as salt and pepper.

season ticket noun a train or bus ticket that you can use as many times as you like within a certain period.

S

seat *noun* 1 something you can sit on. 2 The seat of a piece of clothing is the part that covers your bottom. 3 If someone wins a seat in parliament, they are elected. ▶ *verb* 4 If you seat yourself somewhere, you sit down. 5 If a place seats a particular number of people, it has enough seats for that number.

seat belt *noun* a strap that you fasten across your body for safety when travelling in a car or an aircraft.

seating *noun* The seating in a place is the number or arrangement of seats there.

seaweed *noun* Plants that grow in the sea are called seaweed.

secateurs *plural noun* Secateurs are small shears for pruning garden plants.

secluded *adjective* quiet and hidden from view. > **seclusion** *noun*

second *adjective* 1 The second item in a series is the one counted as number two. ▶ *noun* 2 one of the sixty parts that a minute is divided into. 3 Seconds are goods that are sold cheaply because they are slightly faulty. ▶ *verb* 4 If you second a proposal, you formally agree with it so that it can be discussed or voted on. 5 If you are seconded somewhere, you are sent there temporarily to work. > **secondly** *adverb*

secondary *adjective* 1 Something that is secondary is less important than something else. 2 Secondary education is education for pupils between the ages of eleven and eighteen.

secondary school *noun* a school for pupils between the ages of eleven and eighteen.

second-class *adjective* 1 Second-class things are regarded as less important than other things of the same kind. 2 Second-class services are cheaper and therefore slower or less comfortable than first-class ones.

second-hand *adjective, adverb* 1 Something that is second-hand has already been owned by someone else. 2 If you hear a story second-hand, you hear it indirectly, rather than from the people involved.

second-rate *adjective* of poor quality.

secret *adjective* 1 Something that is secret is told to only a small number of people and hidden from everyone else. ▶ *noun* 2 a fact told to only a small number of people and hidden from everyone else. > **secretly** *adverb* > **secrecy** *noun*

secret *adjective*
1 = closet (*informal*), confidential, covert, furtive, hidden, undercover, underground

secret agent *noun* a spy.

secretary secretaries *noun* 1 a person employed by an organisation to keep records, write letters, and do office work. 2 Ministers in charge of some government departments are also called secretaries. > **secretarial** *adjective*

secrete *verb* 1 When part of a plant or animal secretes a liquid, it produces it. 2 (*formal*) If you secrete something somewhere, you hide it. > **secretion** *noun*

secretive adjective Secretive people tend to hide their feelings and intentions.

> **secretive** adjective
> = cagey (informal), reserved, reticent

secret service noun A country's secret service is the government department in charge of espionage.

sect noun a religious or political group which has broken away from a larger group.

sectarian adjective strongly supporting a particular sect.

section noun A section of something is one of the parts it is divided into.

> **section** noun
> = division, instalment, part, piece, portion, segment

sector noun 1 A sector of something, especially a country's economy, is one part of it.
2 (MATHS) A sector of a circle is one of the two parts formed when you draw two straight lines from the centre to the circumference.

secular adjective having no connection with religion.

secure verb 1 (formal) If you secure something, you manage to get it. 2 If you secure a place, you make it safe from harm or attack. 3 To secure something also means to fasten it firmly. ▶ adjective 4 If a place is secure, it is tightly locked or well protected. 5 If an object is secure, it is firmly fixed in place. 6 If you feel secure, you feel safe and confident. > **securely** adverb

> **secure** verb
> 1 = acquire, gain, get, obtain, procure (formal) 2 = fortify, make

impregnable, make safe, strengthen 3 = attach, bind, fasten, fix, lock, moor, tie up
> ▶ adjective 4 = fortified, impregnable, protected, safe, shielded 5 = fastened, firm, fixed, locked, solid, stable, tight 6 = confident, protected, reassured, relaxed, safe

security noun 1 Security means all the precautions taken to protect a place. 2 A feeling of security is a feeling of being safe.

sedate adjective 1 quiet and dignified. ▶ verb 2 To sedate someone means to give them a drug to calm them down or make them sleep. > **sedately** adverb

sedative noun 1 a drug that calms you down or makes you sleep.
▶ adjective 2 having a calming or soothing effect. > **sedation** noun

sedentary adjective A sedentary occupation is one in which you spend most of your time sitting down.

sediment noun 1 Sediment is solid material that settles at the bottom of a liquid. 2 (GEOGRAPHY) Sediment is also small particles of rock that have been worn down and deposited together by water, ice and wind.

sedimentary
adjective (GEOGRAPHY) Sedimentary rocks are formed from fragments of shells or rocks that have become compressed. Sandstone and limestone are sedimentary rocks.

seduce verb If you are seduced into doing something, you are persuaded to do it because it seems very attractive.

seductive adjective Something seductive is very attractive and tempting. > **seductively** adverb

s

see sees, seeing, saw, seen verb
1 If you see something, you are looking at it or you notice it.
2 If you see someone, you visit them or meet them. 3 If you see someone to a place, you accompany them there. 4 To see something also means to realise or understand it. 5 If you say you will see what is happening, you mean you will find out. 6 If you say you will see if you can do something, you mean you will try to do it. 7 If you see that something is done, you make sure that it is done. 8 If you see to something, you deal with it.
9 'See' is used to say that an event takes place during a particular period of time: *The next couple of years saw two momentous developments.* ▶ phrase 10 (informal) Seeing that or seeing as means because: *I took John for lunch, seeing as it was his birthday.* ▶ noun
11 A bishop's see is his diocese.

> **see** verb
> 1 = behold, discern, glimpse, look, notice, observe, perceive, sight, spot 4 = appreciate, comprehend, follow, get, grasp, realise, understand
> 5 = ascertain, determine, discover, find out

seed noun 1 (SCIENCE) The seeds of a plant are the small, hard parts from which new plants can grow.
2 The seeds of a feeling or process are its beginning or origins.
seedling noun a young plant grown from a seed.
seedy seedier, seediest adjective untidy and shabby.
seek seeks, seeking, sought verb (formal) 1 To seek something means to try to find it, obtain it

or achieve it. 2 If you seek to do something, you try to do it.

> **seek** verb
> 1 = be after, hunt, look for, search for 2 = aim, aspire to, attempt, endeavour, strive, try

seem verb If something seems to be the case, it appears to be the case or you think it is the case.

> **seem** verb
> = appear, give the impression, look, look like

seep verb If a liquid or gas seeps through something, it flows through very slowly.
seething adjective If you are seething about something, you are very angry but it does not show.
segment noun 1 A segment of something is one part of it. 2 The segments of an orange or grapefruit are the sections which you can divide it into. 3 (MATHS) A segment of a circle is one of the two parts formed when you draw a straight line across it.
segregate verb To segregate two groups of people means to keep them apart from each other.
> **segregated** adjective
> **segregation** noun
seize verb 1 If you seize something, you grab it firmly. 2 To seize a place or to seize control of it means to take control of it quickly and suddenly. > **seize up** verb
1 If a part of your body seizes up, it becomes stiff and painful. 2 If an engine seizes up, it becomes jammed and stops working.

> **seize** verb
> 1 = grab, grasp, snatch
> 2 = annex, appropriate, confiscate, hijack, impound

S

seizure noun 1 a sudden violent attack of an illness, especially a heart attack or a fit. 2 If there is a seizure of power, a group of people suddenly take control using force.

seldom adverb not very often.

select verb 1 If you select something, you choose it.
▶ adjective 2 of good quality.
> **selector** noun

> **select** verb
> 1 = choose, decide on, opt for, pick, settle on, single out, take
> ▶ adjective 2 = choice, exclusive, first-class, first-rate, hand-picked, prime, special, superior

selection noun 1 Selection is the choosing of people or things. 2 A selection of people or things is a set of them chosen from a larger group. 3 The selection of goods in a shop is the range of goods available.

selective adjective choosing things carefully. > **selectively** adverb

self selves noun Your self is your basic personality or nature.

self- prefix 1 done to yourself or by yourself: self-help. 2 doing something automatically: a self-loading rifle.

self-assured adjective behaving in a way that shows confidence in yourself.

self-centred adjective thinking only about yourself and not about other people.

self-confessed adjective admitting to having bad habits or unpopular opinions.

self-confident adjective confident of your own abilities or worth.
> **self-confidence** noun

self-conscious adjective nervous and easily embarrassed, and worried about what other people think of you. > **self-consciously** adverb

self-control noun (PSHE) Self-control is the ability to restrain yourself and not show your feelings.

self-defence noun Self-defence is the use of special physical techniques to protect yourself when someone attacks you.

self-employed adjective working for yourself and organising your own finances, rather than working for an employer.

self-esteem noun (PSHE) Your self-esteem is your good opinion of yourself.

self-evident adjective Self-evident facts are completely obvious and need no proof or explanation.

selfie noun (informal) a photograph taken by pointing a camera at yourself.

self-indulgent adjective allowing yourself to do or have things you enjoy, especially as a treat.

self-interest noun If you do something out of self-interest, you do it for your own benefit rather than to help other people.

selfish adjective caring only about yourself, and not about other people. > **selfishly** adverb
> **selfishness** noun

> **selfish** adjective
> = egoistic or egoistical, egotistic or egotistical, greedy, self-centred

selfless adjective putting other people's interests before your own.

self-raising *adjective* Self-raising flour contains baking powder to make cakes and bread rise when they are baked.

self-respect *noun* Self-respect is a belief in your own worth and opinions.

self-righteous *adjective* convinced that you are better or more virtuous than other people. > **self-righteousness** *noun*

self-service *adjective* A self-service shop or restaurant is one where you serve yourself.

self-sufficient *adjective*
1 producing or making everything you need, and so not needing to buy things. 2 able to live in a way in which you do not need other people.

sell sells, selling, sold *verb* 1 If you sell something, you let someone have it in return for money.
2 If a shop sells something, it has it available for people to buy.
3 If something sells, people buy it. > **seller** *noun* > **sell out** *verb* If a shop has sold out of something, it has sold it all.

sell *verb*
1 = deal in, hawk, peddle, trade in 2 = deal in, stock, trade in

semblance *noun* If there is a semblance of something, it seems to exist, although it might not really exist.

semi- *prefix* 'Semi-' means half or partly: *semiskilled workers*.

semicircle *noun* a half of a circle, or something with this shape. > **semicircular** *adjective*

semifinal *noun* The semifinals are the two matches in a competition played to decide who plays in the final. > **semifinalist** *noun*

seminar *noun* a meeting of a small number of university students or teachers to discuss a particular topic.

Senate *noun* The Senate is the smaller, more important of the two councils in the government of some countries, for example Australia, Canada and the USA.

senator *noun* a member of a Senate.

send sends, sending, sent *verb* 1 If you send something to someone, you arrange for it to be delivered to them. 2 To send a radio signal or message means to transmit it. 3 If you send someone somewhere, you tell them to go there or arrange for them to go. 4 If you send for someone, you send a message asking them to come and see you. 5 If you send off for something, you write and ask for it to be sent to you. 6 To send people or things in a particular direction means to make them move in that direction. > **send up** *verb* If you send someone or something up, you imitate them and make fun of them.

send *verb*
1 = dispatch, forward, remit 2 = broadcast, stream, transmit

senile *adjective* If elderly people become senile, they become confused and cannot look after themselves. > **senility** *noun*

senior *adjective* 1 The senior people in an organisation or profession have the highest and most important jobs. ▶ *noun* 2 Someone who is your senior is older than you. > **seniority** *noun*

senior *adjective*
1 = best, better, high-ranking, superior

senior citizen *noun* an elderly person, especially one receiving a retirement pension.

sensation *noun* 1 a feeling, especially a physical feeling. 2 If something is a sensation, it causes great excitement and interest.

sensational *adjective* 1 causing great excitement and interest. 2 (*informal*) extremely good.
> **sensationally** *adverb*

sense *noun* 1 Your senses are the physical abilities of sight, hearing, smell, touch and taste. 2 a feeling. 3 A sense of a word is one of its meanings. 4 Sense is the ability to think and behave sensibly. ▶ *verb* 5 If you sense something, you become aware of it. ▶ *phrase* 6 If something **makes sense**, you can understand it or it seems sensible.

sense *noun*
2 = consciousness, feeling, impression 4 = brains (*informal*), common sense, intelligence, judgment, reason, wisdom
▶ *verb* 5 = be aware of, feel, get the impression, have a hunch, realise

senseless *adjective* 1 A senseless action has no meaning or purpose. 2 If someone is senseless, they are unconscious.

sensibility *noun* Your sensibility is your ability to experience deep feelings.

sensible *adjective* showing good sense and judgment.
> **sensibly** *adverb*

sensible *adjective*
= down-to-earth, judicious (*formal*), practical, prudent, rational, sound, wise

sensitive *adjective* 1 If you are sensitive to other people's feelings, you understand them. 2 If you are sensitive about something, you are worried or easily upset about it. 3 A sensitive subject or issue needs to be dealt with carefully because it can make people angry or upset. 4 Something that is sensitive to a particular thing is easily affected or harmed by it. > **sensitively** *adverb*

sensitive *adjective*
2 = easily offended, easily upset, thin-skinned, touchy

sensitivity *noun* 1 the quality of being sensitive. 2 the ability of a plant or animal to respond to external stimuli such as light, sound, movement or temperature.

sensor *noun* an instrument which reacts to physical conditions such as light or heat.

sensual *adjective* giving pleasure to your physical senses rather than to your mind. > **sensuality** *noun*

sensuous *adjective* giving pleasure through the senses.
> **sensuously** *adverb*

sentence *noun* 1 a group of words which make a statement, question or command. When written down a sentence begins with a capital letter and ends with a full stop. 2 In a law court, a sentence is a punishment given to someone who has been found guilty. ▶ *verb* 3 When a guilty

S

person is sentenced, they are told officially what their punishment will be.

sentiment *noun* 1 a feeling, attitude or opinion. 2 Sentiment consists of feelings such as tenderness or sadness.

sentimental *adjective* 1 feeling or expressing tenderness or sadness to an exaggerated extent. 2 relating to a person's emotions. 3 (ENGLISH) Sentimental literature is intended to provoke an emotional response to the story, rather than relying on the reader's own natural response. > **sentimentality** *noun*

> **sentimental** *adjective*
> 1 = maudlin, mushy (*informal*), nostalgic, sloppy (*informal*), slushy (*informal*)

sentinel *noun* (*old-fashioned*) a sentry.

sentry *noun* a soldier who keeps watch and guards a camp or building.

separate *adjective* 1 If something is separate from something else, the two things are not connected. ▶ *verb* 2 To separate people or things means to cause them to be apart from each other. 3 If people or things separate, they move away from each other. 4 If a married couple separate, they decide to live apart. > **separately** *adverb* > **separation** *noun*

> **separate** *adjective*
> 1 = detached, disconnected, discrete, divorced, isolated, unconnected
> ▶ *verb* 2 = detach, disconnect, divide 4 = break up, divorce, part, split up

sepia *adjective*, *noun* deep brown,

like the colour of old photographs.

September *noun* September is the ninth month of the year. It has 30 days.

septic *adjective* If a wound becomes septic, it becomes infected with poison.

sequel *noun* 1 A sequel to a book or film is another book or film which continues the story. 2 The sequel to an event is a result or consequence of it.

sequence *noun* 1 A sequence of events is a number of them coming one after the other. 2 The sequence in which things are arranged is the order in which they are arranged.

> **sequence** *noun*
> 1 = chain, course, cycle, progression, series, string, succession 2 = arrangement, order, pattern, progression, structure

sequin *noun* Sequins are small, shiny, coloured discs sewn on clothes to decorate them.

Serbian *adjective* 1 belonging or relating to Serbia. ▶ *noun* 2 someone who comes from Serbia.

serenade *verb* 1 If you serenade someone you love, you sing or play music to them outside their window. ▶ *noun* 2 a song sung outside a person's window by someone who loves them.

serene *adjective* peaceful and calm. > **serenely** *adverb* > **serenity** *noun*

sergeant *noun* 1 a noncommissioned officer of middle rank in the army or air force. 2 a police officer just above a constable in rank.

serial noun a story which is broadcast or published in a number of parts over a period of time.

series series noun 1 A series of things is a number of them coming one after the other. 2 A radio or television series is a set of programmes with the same title.

> **series** noun
> 1 = chain, run, sequence, string, succession

serious adjective 1 A serious problem or situation is very bad and worrying. 2 Serious matters are important and should be thought about carefully. 3 If you are serious about something, you are sincere about it. 4 People who are serious are thoughtful and quiet, and do not laugh much.
> **seriousness** noun

> **serious** adjective
> 1 = acute, alarming, bad, critical, dangerous, extreme, grave (formal), grievous, grim, intense, precarious, severe, worrying 2 = crucial, deep, difficult, far-reaching, grave (formal), important, momentous, pressing, profound, significant, urgent, weighty 3 = earnest, genuine, heartfelt, honest, in earnest, resolute, resolved, sincere 4 = earnest, grave, humourless, pensive, sober, solemn, staid, stern

seriously adverb 1 You say 'seriously' to emphasise that you mean what you say: *Seriously, though, something must be done.* ▶ phrase 2 If you **take something seriously**, you regard it as important.

sermon noun a talk on a religious or moral subject given as part of a church service.

serpent noun (literary) a snake.

servant noun someone who is employed to work in another person's house.

serve verb 1 If you serve a country, an organisation or a person, you do useful work for them. 2 To serve as something means to act or be used as that thing. 3 If something serves people in a particular place, it provides them with something they need. 4 If you serve food or drink to people, you give it to them. 5 To serve customers in a shop means to help them and provide them with what they want. 6 To serve a prison sentence or an apprenticeship means to spend time doing it. 7 When you serve in tennis or badminton, you throw the ball or shuttlecock into the air and hit it over the net to start playing. ▶ noun 8 the act of serving in tennis or badminton.

server noun (ICT) a computer or computer program which supplies information or resources to a number of computers on a network.

service noun 1 a system organised to provide something for the public: *the bus service.* 2 Some government organisations are called services: *the diplomatic service.* 3 The services are the army, the navy and the air force. 4 If you give your services to a person or organisation, you work for them or help them in some way. 5 In a shop or restaurant, service is the process of being served. 6 a religious ceremony. 7 When it is

your service in a game of tennis or badminton, it is your turn to serve. **8** (*in plural*) Motorway services consist of a petrol station, restaurant, shop and toilets.
▶ *verb* **9** When a machine or vehicle is serviced, it is examined and adjusted so that it will continue working efficiently.

serviceman servicemen *noun* a man in the army, navy or air force.

service station *noun* a garage that sells petrol, oil, spare parts and snacks.

servicewoman servicewomen *noun* a woman in the army, navy or air force.

serving *noun* **1** a helping of food.
▶ *adjective* **2** A serving spoon or dish is used for serving food.

session *noun* **1** a meeting of an official group. **2** The period during which an activity takes place can also be called a session.

set sets, setting, set *noun* **1** Several things make a set when they belong together or form a group. **2** (MATHS) In maths, a set is a collection of numbers or other things which are treated as a group. **3** A television set is a television. **4** The set for a play or film is the scenery or furniture on the stage or in the studio. **5** In tennis, a set is a group of six or more games. There are usually several sets in a match. ▶ *verb* **6** If something is set somewhere, that is where it is. **7** When the sun sets, it goes below the horizon. **8** When you set the table, you prepare it for a meal by putting plates and cutlery on it. **9** When you set a clock or a control, you adjust it to a particular point or position. **10** If you set someone a

piece of work or a target, you give it to them to do or to achieve. **11** When something such as jelly or cement sets, it becomes firm or hard. ▶ *adjective* **12** Something that is set is fixed and not varying. **13** If you are set to do something, you are ready or likely to do it. **14** If you are set on doing something, you are determined to do it. **15** If a play or story is set at a particular time or in a particular place, the events in it take place at that time or in that place. > **set about** *verb* If you set about doing something, you start doing it. > **set back** *verb* If something sets back a project or scheme, it delays it. > **set off** *verb* **1** When you set off, you start a journey. **2** To set something off means to cause it to start. > **set out** *verb* **1** When you set out, you start a journey. **2** If you set out to do something, you start trying to do it. > **set up** *verb* If you set something up, you make all the necessary preparations for it.

---

set *noun*
1 = batch, kit, outfit, series
▶ *verb* **6** = deposit, lay, locate, place, position, put, rest, stick
▶ *adjective* **12** = arranged, established, firm, fixed, predetermined, scheduled
14 = bent on, determined, intent on
▶ **set up** = arrange, establish, install, institute, organise

---

setback *noun* (PSHE) something that stops you from making progress.

settee *noun* a long comfortable seat for two or three people to sit on.

setter noun a long-haired breed of dog originally used in hunting.

setting noun 1 The setting of something is its surroundings or circumstances. 2 The settings on a machine are the different positions to which the controls can be adjusted.

settle verb 1 To settle an argument means to put an end to it. 2 If something is settled, it has all been decided and arranged. 3 If you settle on something or settle for it, you choose it. 4 When you settle a bill, you pay it. 5 If you settle in a place, you make it your permanent home. 6 If you settle yourself somewhere, you sit down and make yourself comfortable. 7 If something settles, it sinks slowly down and comes to rest. > **settle down** verb 1 When someone settles down, they start living a quiet life in one place, especially when they get married. 2 To settle down means to become quiet or calm.

> **settle** verb
> 1 = clear up, decide, dispose of, put an end to, reconcile, resolve, straighten out
> 2 = agree, arrange, decide on, determine, fix 5 = make your home, move to, people, populate

settlement noun 1 an official agreement between people who have been involved in a conflict. 2 (GEOGRAPHY) a place where people have settled and built homes.

settler noun someone who settles in a new country.

seven the number 7.

seventeen the number 17. > **seventeenth** adjective

seventh adjective 1 The seventh item in a series is the one counted as number seven. ▶ noun 2 one of seven equal parts.

seventy seventies the number 70. > **seventieth** adjective

sever verb 1 To sever something means to cut it off or cut right through it. 2 If you sever a connection with someone or something, you end it completely.

several adjective Several people or things means a small number of them.

> **several** adjective
> = assorted, some, sundry, various

severe adjective 1 extremely bad or unpleasant. 2 stern and harsh. > **severely** adverb > **severity** noun

> **severe** adjective
> 1 = acute, critical, deep, dire, extreme, grave (formal), intense, serious, terrible
> 2 = disapproving, grim, hard, harsh, stern, strict

sew sews, sewing, sewed, sewn verb (DGT) When you sew something together, you join them using a needle and thread. > **sewing** noun

sewage noun Sewage is dirty water and waste which is carried away in sewers.

sewer noun an underground channel that carries sewage to a place where it is treated to make it harmless.

sewerage noun Sewerage is the system by which sewage is carried away and treated.

sex noun 1 The sexes are the two groups, male and female, into which people and animals are divided. **2** The sex of a person or animal is their characteristic of being either male or female. **3** Sex is the physical activity by which people and animals produce young.

sexism noun Sexism is discrimination against the members of one sex, usually women. > **sexist** adjective, noun

sextet noun **1** (MUSIC) a group of six musicians who sing or play together; also a piece of music written for six instruments or singers. **2** (ENGLISH) six lines of poetry together, especially linked by a pattern of rhyme.

sexual adjective **1** connected with the act of sex or with people's desire for sex. **2** relating to the difference between males and females. **3** relating to the biological process by which people and animals produce young. > **sexually** adverb

sexuality noun **1** A person's sexuality is their ability to experience sexual feelings. **2** You can refer to a person's sexuality when you are talking about whether they are sexually attracted to people of the same sex or a different sex.

shabby shabbier, shabbiest adjective **1** old and worn in appearance. **2** dressed in old, worn-out clothes. **3** behaving in a mean or unfair way. > **shabbily** adverb

> **shabby** adjective
> **1** = dilapidated, ragged, scruffy, seedy, tatty, threadbare, worn
> **3** = contemptible, despicable, dirty, mean, rotten (informal)

shack noun a small hut.

shackle noun **1** In the past, shackles were two metal rings joined by a chain fastened around a prisoner's wrists or ankles. ▶ verb **2** To shackle someone means to put shackles on them. **3** (literary) If you are shackled by something, it restricts or hampers you.

shade noun **1** Shade is an area of darkness and coolness which the sun does not reach. **2** a lampshade. **3** The shades of a colour are its different forms. For example, olive green is a shade of green. ▶ verb **4** If a place is shaded by trees or buildings, they prevent the sun from shining on it. **5** If you shade your eyes, you put your hand in front of them to protect them from a bright light.

shadow noun **1** the dark shape made when an object prevents light from reaching a surface. **2** Shadow is darkness caused by light not reaching a place. ▶ verb **3** To shadow someone means to follow them and watch them closely.

shadow cabinet noun The shadow cabinet consists of the leaders of the main opposition party, each of whom is concerned with a particular policy.

shadowy adjective **1** A shadowy place is dark and full of shadows. **2** A shadowy figure or shape is difficult to see because it is dark or misty.

shady shadier, shadiest adjective A shady place is sheltered from sunlight by trees or buildings.

shaft noun **1** a vertical passage, for example one for a lift or one in a mine. **2** A shaft of light is a beam of light. **3** (DGT) A shaft in a machine is a rod which revolves and transfers movement in the machine.

shaggy shaggier, shaggiest *adjective* Shaggy hair or fur is long and untidy.

shake shakes, shaking, shook, shaken *verb* 1 To shake something means to move it quickly from side to side or up and down. 2 If something shakes, it moves from side to side or up and down with small, quick movements. 3 If your voice shakes, it trembles because you are nervous or angry. 4 If something shakes you, it shocks and upsets you. 5 When you shake your head, you move it from side to side in order to say 'no'. ▶ *noun* 6 If you give something a shake, you shake it. ▶ *phrase* 7 When you **shake hands** with someone, you grasp their hand as a way of greeting them.

> **shake** *verb*
> 1 = agitate, brandish, flourish, wave 2 = jolt, quake, quiver, shiver, shudder, tremble, vibrate 4 = distress, disturb, rattle (*informal*), shock, unnerve, upset

shaky shakier, shakiest *adjective* rather weak and unsteady.
> **shakily** *adverb*

> **shaky** *adjective*
> = rickety, tottering, trembling, unstable, unsteady, wobbly

shall *verb* 1 If I say I shall do something, I mean that I intend to do it. 2 If I say something shall happen, I am emphasising that it will definitely happen, or I am ordering it to happen. 3 'Shall' is also used in questions when you are asking what to do, or making

a suggestion: Shall we sit down?

shallow *adjective* 1 Shallow means not deep. 2 Shallow also means not involving serious thought or sincere feelings.

sham *noun* 1 Something that is a sham is not real or genuine. ▶ *adjective* 2 not real or genuine.

shambles *noun* (*informal*) If an event is a shambles, it is confused and badly organised.

shame *noun* 1 Shame is the feeling of guilt or embarrassment you get when you know you have done something wrong or foolish. 2 Shame is also something that makes people lose respect for you. 3 If you say something is a shame, you mean you are sorry about it. ▶ *interjection* 4 (*informal*) In South African English, you say 'Shame!' to show sympathy. ▶ *verb* 5 If something shames you, it makes you feel ashamed. 6 If you shame someone into doing something, you force them to do it by making them feel ashamed not to.

> **shame** *noun*
> 1 = embarrassment, humiliation, ignominy
> 2 = discredit, disgrace, dishonour, scandal
> ▶ *verb* 5 = disgrace, embarrass, humiliate

shameful *adjective* If someone's behaviour is shameful, they ought to be ashamed of it.
> **shamefully** *adverb*

shameless *adjective* behaving in an indecent or unacceptable way, but showing no shame.
> **shamelessly** *adverb*

> **shameless** *adjective*
> = barefaced, brazen, flagrant, unabashed, unashamed

s

shampoo noun 1 Shampoo is a soapy liquid used for washing your hair. ▶ verb 2 When you shampoo your hair, you wash it with shampoo.

shanty shanties noun 1 A small, rough hut. 2 A sea shanty is a song sailors used to sing.

shape noun 1 The shape of something is the form or pattern of its outline, for example whether it is round or square. 2 (MATHS) something with a definite form, for example a circle or triangle. 3 The shape of something such as an organisation is its structure and size. ▶ verb 4 If you shape an object, you form it into a particular shape. 5 To shape something means to cause it to develop in a particular way.

> **shape** noun
> 1 = contours, figure, form, lines, outline
> ▶ verb 4 = fashion, form, make, model, mould

shapeless adjective not having a definite shape.

shapely adjective having an attractive figure.

shard noun a small fragment of pottery, glass or metal.

share verb 1 If two people share something, they both use it, do it or have it. 2 If you share an idea or a piece of news with someone, you tell it to them. ▶ noun 3 A share of something is a portion of it. 4 The shares of a company are the equal parts into which its ownership is divided. People can buy shares as an investment. > **share out** verb If you share something out, you

give it out equally among a group of people.

> **share** verb
> 1 = divide, split
> ▶ noun 3 = allotment, portion, quota, ration

shareholder noun a person who owns shares in a company.

shark noun 1 Sharks are large, powerful fish with sharp teeth. 2 (informal) a person who cheats people out of money.

sharp adjective 1 A sharp object has a fine edge or point that is good for cutting or piercing things. 2 A sharp outline or distinction is easy to see. 3 A sharp person is quick to notice or understand things. 4 A sharp change is sudden and significant. 5 If you say something in a sharp way, you say it firmly and rather angrily. 6 A sharp sound is short, sudden and quite loud. 7 A sharp pain is a sudden pain. 8 A sharp taste is slightly sour. 9 A musical instrument or note that is sharp is slightly too high in pitch. ▶ adverb 10 If something happens at a certain time sharp, it happens at that time precisely. ▶ noun 11 In music, a sharp is a note or key a semitone higher than that described by the same letter. It is represented by the symbol (♯). > **sharply** adverb > **sharpness** noun

> **sharp** adjective
> 1 = jagged, keen, pointed, razor-sharp 3 = alert, astute, bright, observant, perceptive, quick, quick-witted 4 = abrupt, marked, sudden

sharpen verb 1 To sharpen an object means to make its edge or point sharper. **2** If your senses or abilities sharpen, you become quicker at noticing or understanding things. **3** If you voice sharpens, you begin to speak more angrily or harshly. **4** If something sharpens the disagreements between people, it makes them greater.

shatter verb **1** If something shatters, it breaks into a lot of small pieces. **2** If something shatters your hopes or beliefs, it destroys them completely. **3** If you are shattered by an event or piece of news, you are shocked and upset by it.

shattered adjective (informal) completely exhausted.

shave verb **1** When a person shaves, they remove hair from a part of their body with a razor. **2** If you shave off part of a piece of wood, you cut thin pieces from it. ▶ noun **3** When a man has a shave, he shaves.

shaven adjective If part of someone's body is shaven, it has been shaved.

shawl noun a large piece of woollen cloth worn round a person's head or shoulders or used to wrap a baby in.

she pronoun 'She' is used to refer to a woman or girl whose identity is clear. 'She' is also used to refer to a country, a ship or a car.

sheaf sheaves noun **1** A sheaf of papers is a bundle of them. **2** A sheaf of corn is a bundle of ripe corn tied together.

shear shears, shearing, shorn verb To shear a sheep means to cut off its wool.

shearer noun someone whose job is to shear sheep.

sheath noun a covering for the blade of a knife.

shed sheds, shedding, shed noun **1** a small building used for storing things. ▶ verb **2** When an animal sheds hair or skin, some of its hair or skin drops off. When a tree sheds its leaves, its leaves fall off. **3** (formal) To shed something also means to get rid of it. **4** If a lorry sheds its load, the load falls off the lorry onto the road. **5** If you shed tears, you cry.

sheen noun a gentle brightness on the surface of something.

sheep sheep noun A sheep is a farm animal with a thick woolly coat. Sheep are kept for meat and wool.

sheepdog noun a breed of dog often used for controlling sheep.

sheepish adjective If you look sheepish, you look embarrassed because you feel shy or foolish. > **sheepishly** adverb

sheepskin noun Sheepskin is the skin and wool of a sheep, used for making rugs and coats.

sheer adjective **1** Sheer means complete and total. **2** A sheer cliff or drop is vertical. **3** Sheer fabrics are very light and delicate.

> **sheer** adjective
> **1** = absolute, complete, pure, total, unqualified, utter
> **2** = perpendicular, steep, vertical **3** = delicate, fine, lightweight, thin

sheet noun **1** a large rectangular piece of cloth used to cover a bed. **2** A sheet of paper is a rectangular piece of it. **3** A sheet of glass or metal is a large, flat piece of it.

sheik; also spelt **sheikh** noun an Arab chief or ruler.

S

shelf shelves *noun* a flat piece of wood, metal or glass fixed to a wall and used for putting things on.

shell *noun* 1 The shell of an egg or nut is its hard covering. 2 The shell of a tortoise, snail or crab is the hard protective covering on its back. 3 The shell of a building or other structure is its frame. 4 a container filled with explosives that can be fired from a gun. ▶ *verb* 5 If you shell peas or nuts, you remove their natural covering. 6 To shell a place means to fire large explosive shells at it.

shellfish shellfish or shellfishes *noun* a small sea creature with a shell.

shelter *noun* 1 a small building made to protect people from bad weather or danger. 2 If a place provides shelter, it provides protection from bad weather or danger. ▶ *verb* 3 If you shelter in a place, you stay there and are safe. 4 If you shelter someone, you provide them with a place to stay when they are in danger.

---

shelter *noun*
1 = hostel, refuge, sanctuary
2 = asylum, cover, harbour, haven, protection, refuge, safety, sanctuary
▶ *verb* 3 = hide, huddle, take cover 4 = harbour, hide, protect, shield

---

sheltered *adjective* 1 A sheltered place is protected from wind and rain. 2 If you lead a sheltered life, you do not experience unpleasant or upsetting things. 3 Sheltered accommodation is accommodation designed for elderly or disabled people.

shelve *verb* If you shelve a plan, you decide to postpone it for a while.

shepherd *noun* 1 a person who looks after sheep. ▶ *verb* 2 If you shepherd someone somewhere, you accompany them there.

sheriff *noun* 1 In America, a sheriff is a person elected to enforce the law in a county. 2 In Australia, a sheriff is an administrative officer of the Supreme Court who carries out writs and judgments.

sherry sherries *noun* Sherry is a kind of strong wine.

shield *noun* 1 a large piece of a strong material like metal or plastic which soldiers or police officers carry to protect themselves. 2 If something is a shield against something, it gives protection from it. ▶ *verb* 3 To shield someone means to protect them from something.

shift *verb* 1 If you shift something, you move it. If something shifts, it moves. 2 If an opinion or situation shifts, it changes slightly. ▶ *noun* 3 A shift in an opinion or situation is a slight change. 4 a set period during which people work.

shilling *noun* a former British, Australian and New Zealand coin worth one-twentieth of a pound.

shimmer *verb* 1 If something shimmers, it shines with a faint, flickering light. ▶ *noun* 2 a faint, flickering light.

shin shins, shinning, shinned *noun* 1 Your shin is the front part of your leg between your knee and your ankle. ▶ *verb* 2 If you shin up a tree or pole, you climb it quickly by gripping it with your hands and legs.

shine shines, shining, shone *verb*
1 When something shines, it gives out or reflects a bright light.
2 If you shine a torch or lamp somewhere, you point it there.

> **shine** *verb*
> 1 = beam, gleam, glow, radiate, shimmer, sparkle

shingle *noun* 1 (GEOGRAPHY) Shingle consists of small pebbles on the seashore. 2 Shingles are small wooden roof tiles.
3 Shingles is a disease that causes a painful red rash, especially around the waist.

shining *adjective* 1 Shining things are very bright, usually because they are reflecting light. 2 A shining example of something is a very good or typical example of that thing.

> **shining** *adjective*
> 1 = bright, brilliant, gleaming, luminous, radiant, shimmering, sparkling

shiny shinier, shiniest *adjective* Shiny things are bright and look as if they have been polished.

ship ships, shipping, shipped *noun*
1 a large boat which carries passengers or cargo. ▶ *verb* 2 If people or things are shipped somewhere, they are transported there.

-ship *suffix* '-ship' is used to form nouns that refer to a condition or position: *fellowship*.

shipment *noun* 1 a quantity of goods that are transported somewhere. 2 The shipment of goods is the transporting of them.

shipping *noun* 1 Shipping is the transport of cargo on ships.
2 You can also refer to ships generally as shipping.

shipwreck *noun* When there is a shipwreck, a ship is destroyed in an accident at sea.

shipyard *noun* a place where ships are built and repaired.

shire *noun* 1 In Britain, 'shire' is an old word for a county.
2 In Australia, a shire is a rural district with its own local council.

shirk *verb* To shirk a task means to avoid doing it.

shirt *noun* a piece of clothing worn on the upper part of the body, with a collar, sleeves, and buttons down the front.

shiver *verb* 1 When you shiver, you tremble slightly because you are cold or scared. ▶ *noun* 2 a slight trembling caused by cold or fear.

shoal *noun* A shoal of fish is a large group of them swimming together.

shock *noun* 1 If you have a shock, you have a sudden upsetting experience. 2 Shock is a person's emotional and physical condition when something very unpleasant or upsetting has happened to them. 3 In medicine, shock is a serious physical condition in which the blood cannot circulate properly because of an injury. 4 a slight movement in something when it is hit by something else. 5 A shock of hair is a thick mass of it. ▶ *verb* 6 If something shocks you, it upsets you because it is unpleasant and unexpected.
7 You can say that something shocks you when it offends you because it is rude or immoral.
> **shocked** *adjective*

s

shock noun
1 = blow, bombshell, distress, trauma
▶ verb 6 = numb, paralyse, shake, stagger, stun, traumatise 7 = appal, disgust, offend, outrage

shocking adjective 1 (informal) very bad. 2 disgusting or horrifying.

shod the past tense and past participle of **shoe**.

shoddy shoddier, shoddiest adjective badly made or done.

shoe shoes, shoeing, shod noun
1 Shoes are strong coverings for your feet. They cover most of your foot, but not your ankle. ▶ verb
2 To shoe a horse means to fix horseshoes onto its hooves.

shoestring noun (informal) If you do something on a shoestring, you do it using very little money.

shone the past tense and past participle of **shine**.

shook the past tense of **shake**.

shoot shoots, shooting, shot verb
1 To shoot a person or animal means to kill or injure them by firing a gun at them. 2 To shoot an arrow means to fire it from a bow. 3 If something shoots in a particular direction, it moves there quickly and suddenly.
4 When a film is shot, it is filmed.
5 In games such as football or hockey, to shoot means to kick or hit the ball towards the goal.
▶ noun 6 an occasion when people hunt animals or birds with guns.
7 a plant that is beginning to grow, or a new part growing from a plant.

shooting noun an incident in which someone is shot.

shop shops, shopping, shopped noun 1 a place where goods are sold. 2 a place where a particular type of work is done: a bicycle repair shop. ▶ verb 3 When you shop, you go to the shops to buy things.
> **shopper** noun

shop noun
1 = boutique, market, store, supermarket

shopkeeper noun someone who owns or manages a small shop.

shoplifting noun Shoplifting is stealing goods from shops.
> **shoplifter** noun

shopping noun Your shopping is the goods you have bought from the shops.

shore noun 1 The shore of a sea, lake or wide river is the land along the edge of it. ▶ verb 2 If you shore something up, you reinforce it or strengthen it.

shoreline noun the edge of a sea, lake or wide river.

shorn 1 Shorn is the past participle of **shear**. ▶ adjective
2 Grass or hair that is shorn is cut very short.

short adjective 1 not lasting very long. 2 small in length, distance or height. 3 not using many words. 4 If you are short with someone, you speak to them crossly. 5 If you have a short temper, you get angry very quickly. 6 If you are short of something, you do not have enough of it. 7 If a name is short for another name, it is a short version of it. ▶ noun 8 (in plural) Shorts are trousers with short legs. ▶ adverb 9 If you stop short of a place, you do not quite reach it.
▶ phrase 10 Short of is used to say

that a level or amount has not quite been reached.

short *adjective*
1 = brief, fleeting, momentary, short-lived **2** = diminutive, little, small, tiny **3** = brief, concise, succinct, terse

shortage *noun* If there is a shortage of something, there is not enough of it.

shortage *noun*
= dearth, deficiency, lack, scarcity, shortfall, want

shortcoming *noun* Shortcomings are faults or weaknesses.

shortcut *noun* **1** a quicker way of getting somewhere than the usual route. **2** a quicker way of doing something.

shorten *verb* If you shorten something or if it shortens, it becomes shorter.

shorten *verb*
= abbreviate, cut, trim

shortfall *noun* If there is a shortfall in something, there is less than you need.

shorthand *noun* Shorthand is a way of writing in which signs represent words or syllables. It is used to write down quickly what someone is saying.

short-list *noun* **1** a list of people selected from a larger group, from which one person is finally selected for a job or prize. ▶ *verb* **2** If someone is short-listed for a job or prize, they are put on a short-list.

shortly *adverb* **1** Shortly means soon. **2** If you speak to someone shortly, you speak to them in a cross and impatient way.

short-sighted *adjective* **1** If you are short-sighted, you cannot see things clearly when they are far away. **2** A short-sighted decision does not take account of the way things may develop in the future.

short-term *adjective* happening or having an effect within a short time or for a short time.

shot **1** Shot is the past tense and past participle of **shoot**. ▶ *noun* **2** the act of firing a gun. **3** Someone who is a good shot can shoot accurately. **4** In football, golf and tennis, a shot is the act of kicking or hitting the ball. **5** a photograph or short film sequence. **6** (*informal*) If you have a shot at something, you try to do it.

shotgun *noun* a gun that fires a lot of small pellets all at once.

shot put *noun* In athletics, the shot put is an event in which the contestants throw a heavy metal ball called a shot as far as possible. ▶ **shot putter** *noun*

should *verb* **1** You use 'should' to say that something ought to happen: *Ward should have done better.* **2** You also use 'should' to say that you expect something to happen: *He should have heard by now.* **3** 'Should' is used in conditional sentences: *If you should see Kerr, tell him I have his umbrella.* **4** 'Should' is sometimes used in 'that' clauses: *It is inevitable that you should go.*

shoulder *noun* **1** Your shoulders are the parts of your body between your neck and the tops of your arms. ▶ *verb* **2** If you shoulder something heavy, you put it across one of your shoulders to carry it. **3** If you shoulder the responsibility or blame for something, you accept it.

s

shout noun **1** a loud call or cry.
▶ verb **2** If you shout something, you say it very loudly.
> **shout down** verb If you shout someone down, you prevent them from being heard by shouting at them.

shout noun
1 = bellow, cry, roar, scream, yell
▶ verb **2** = bawl, bellow, call, cry, roar, scream, yell

shove verb **1** If you shove someone or something, you push them roughly. ▶ noun **2** a rough push.
> **shove off** verb (informal) If you tell someone to shove off, you are telling them angrily and rudely to go away.

shovel shovels, shovelling, shovelled noun **1** a tool like a spade, used for moving earth or snow. ▶ verb **2** If you shovel earth or snow, you move it with a shovel.

show shows, showing, showed, shown verb **1** To show that something exists or is true means to prove it. **2** If a picture shows something, it represents it. **3** If you show someone something, you let them see it. **4** If you show someone to a room or seat, you lead them there. **5** If you show someone how to do something, you demonstrate it to them.
6 If something shows, it is visible.
7 If something shows a quality or characteristic, you can see that it has it. **8** If you show your feelings, you let people see them.
9 If you show affection or mercy, you behave in an affectionate or merciful way. **10** To show a film or television programme means to let the public see it. ▶ noun **11** a form of light entertainment at the theatre or on television. **12** an exhibition. **13** A show of a feeling or attitude is behaviour in which you show it. ▶ phrase **14** If something is on show, it is being exhibited for the public to see.
> **show off** verb (informal) If someone is showing off, they are trying to impress people.
> **show up** verb **1** (informal) If you show up, you arrive at a place. **2** If something shows up, it can be seen clearly.

show verb
1 = demonstrate, prove
5 = demonstrate, instruct, teach
7 = demonstrate, display, indicate, manifest (formal), reveal
▶ noun **12** = display, exhibition, presentation **13** = air, display, pose, pretence, semblance

show business noun Show business is entertainment in the theatre, films and television.

showdown noun (informal) a major argument or conflict intended to end a dispute.

shower noun **1** a device which sprays you with water so that you can wash yourself. **2** If you have a shower, you wash yourself by standing under a shower. **3** a short period of rain. **4** You can refer to a lot of things falling at once as a shower. ▶ verb **5** If you shower, you have a shower.
6 If you are showered with a lot of things, they fall on you.

showing noun A showing of a film or television programme is a presentation of it so that the public can see it.

showjumping noun Showjumping is a horse-riding competition in which the horses jump over a series of high fences.

show-off noun (informal) someone who tries to impress people with their knowledge or skills.

showroom noun a shop where goods such as cars or electrical appliances are displayed.

showy showier, showiest adjective large or bright and intended to impress people.

shrank the past tense of **shrink**.

shrapnel noun Shrapnel consists of small pieces of metal scattered from an exploding shell.

shred shreds, shredding, shredded verb 1 If you shred something, you cut or tear it into very small pieces. ▶ noun 2 A shred of paper or material is a small, narrow piece of it. 3 If there is not a shred of something, there is absolutely none of it.

shrewd adjective Someone who is shrewd is intelligent and makes good judgments. > **shrewdly** adverb > **shrewdness** noun

> **shrewd** adjective
> = astute, canny, crafty, perceptive, sharp, smart

shriek noun 1 a high-pitched scream. ▶ verb 2 If you shriek, you make a high-pitched scream.

shrill adjective A shrill sound is unpleasantly high-pitched and piercing. > **shrilly** adverb

> **shrill** adjective
> = penetrating, piercing, sharp

shrimp noun a small edible shellfish with a long tail and many legs.

shrine noun (RE) a place of worship associated with a sacred person or object.

shrink shrinks, shrinking, shrank, shrunk verb 1 If something shrinks, it becomes smaller. 2 If you shrink from something, you move away from it because you are afraid of it. > **shrinkage** noun

> **shrink** verb
> 1 = contract, diminish, dwindle, get smaller, narrow

shrivel shrivels, shrivelling, shrivelled verb When something shrivels, it becomes dry and withered.

shroud noun 1 a cloth in which a dead body is wrapped before it is buried. ▶ verb 2 If something is shrouded in darkness or fog, it is hidden by it.

shrub noun a low, bushy plant.

shrug shrugs, shrugging, shrugged verb 1 If you shrug your shoulders, you raise them slightly as a sign of indifference of if you don't know something. ▶ noun 2 If you give a shrug of your shoulders, you shrug them.

shrunk the past participle of **shrink**.

shrunken adjective (formal) Someone or something that is shrunken has become smaller than it used to be.

shudder verb 1 If you shudder, you tremble with fear or horror. 2 If a machine or vehicle shudders, it shakes violently. ▶ noun 3 a shiver of fear or horror.

shuffle verb 1 If you shuffle, you walk without lifting your feet properly off the ground. 2 If you shuffle about, you move about and fidget because you feel uncomfortable or embarrassed. 3 If you shuffle a pack of cards, you mix them up before you begin

s

a game. ▶ noun 4 the way someone walks when they shuffle.

shun shuns, shunning, shunned verb If you shun someone or something, you deliberately avoid them.

shunt verb (informal) If you shunt people or things to a place, you move them there.

shut shuts, shutting, shut verb 1 If you shut something, you close it. 2 When a shop or pub shuts, it is closed and you can no longer go into it. ▶ adjective 3 If something is shut, it is closed. > **shut down** verb When a factory or business is shut down, it is closed permanently. > **shut up** verb (informal) If you shut up, you stop talking.

> **shut**
> 1 = close, fasten, slam
> ▶ adjective 3 = closed, fastened, sealed

shutter noun Shutters are hinged wooden or metal covers fitted on the outside or inside of a window.

shuttle adjective 1 A shuttle service is an air, bus or train service which makes frequent journeys between two places. ▶ noun 2 a plane used in a shuttle service.

shy shyer, shyest; shies, shying, shied adjective 1 A shy person is nervous and uncomfortable in the company of other people. ▶ verb 2 When a horse shies, it moves away suddenly because something has frightened it. 3 If you shy away from doing something, you avoid doing it because you are afraid or nervous. > **shyly** adverb > **shyness** noun

> **shy** adjective
> 1 = bashful, reserved, retiring, self-conscious, timid

sibling noun (formal) Your siblings are your brothers and sisters.

sick adjective 1 If you are sick, you are ill. 2 If you feel sick, you feel as if you are going to vomit. If you are sick, you vomit. 3 (informal) If you are sick of doing something, you feel you have been doing it too long. 4 (informal) A sick joke or story deals with death or suffering in an unpleasantly frivolous way. ▶ phrase 5 If something makes you sick, it makes you angry. > **sickness** noun

> **sick** adjective
> 1 = ailing, laid up (informal), poorly (British; informal), under the weather (informal), unwell 2 = ill, nauseous, queasy 3 sick of = bored, fed up, tired, weary

sicken verb If something sickens you, it makes you feel disgusted. > **sickening** adjective

sickle noun a tool with a short handle and a curved blade used for cutting grass or grain.

sickly sicklier, sickliest adjective 1 A sickly person or animal is weak and unhealthy. 2 Sickly also means very unpleasant to smell or taste.

side noun 1 Side refers to a position to the left or right of something. 2 The sides of a boundary or barrier are the two areas it separates. 3 Your sides are the parts of your body from your armpits down to your hips. 4 The sides of something are its outside surfaces, especially the surfaces which are not its front or back. 5 The sides of a hill or valley are the parts that slope. **6** The two sides in a war, argument or relationship are the two people or groups involved. **7** A particular side of something is one aspect of it. ▶ *adjective* **8** situated on a side of a building or vehicle. **9** A side road is a small road leading off a larger one. **10** A side issue is an issue that is less important than the main one. ▶ *verb* **11** If you side with someone in an argument, you support them.

> **side** noun
> 1 = edge, verge 6 = camp, faction, party, team
> ▶ *verb* 11 = agree with, stand up for, support, take the part of

sideboard *noun* **1** a long, low cupboard for plates and glasses. **2** (*in plural*) A man's sideboards are his sideburns.

sideburns *plural noun* A man's sideburns are areas of hair growing on his cheeks in front of his ears.

side effect *noun* The side effects of a drug are the effects it has in addition to its main effects.

sidekick *noun* (*informal*) Someone's sidekick is their close friend who spends a lot of time with them.

sideline *noun* an extra job in addition to your main job.

sideshow *noun* Sideshows are stalls at a fairground.

sidestep sidesteps, sidestepping, sidestepped *verb* If you sidestep a difficult problem or question, you avoid dealing with it.

sidewalk *noun* In American English, a sidewalk is a pavement.

sideways *adverb* **1** from or towards the side of something or someone.

▶ *adjective* **2** to or from one side.

siding *noun* a short railway track beside the main tracks, where engines and carriages are left when not in use.

siege *noun* (HISTORY) a military operation in which an army surrounds a place and prevents food or help from reaching the people inside.

sieve *noun* **1** a kitchen tool of mesh, used for sifting or straining things. ▶ *verb* **2** If you sieve a powder or liquid, you pass it through a sieve.

sift *verb* **1** If you sift a powdery substance, you pass it through a sieve to remove lumps. **2** If you sift through something such as evidence, you examine it all thoroughly.

sigh *verb* **1** When you sigh, you let out a deep breath. ▶ *noun* **2** the breath you let out when you sigh.

sight *noun* **1** Sight is the ability to see. **2** something you see. **3** (*in plural*) Sights are interesting places which tourists visit.
▶ *verb* **4** If you sight someone or something, you see them briefly or suddenly. ▶ *phrase* **5** If something is **in sight**, you can see it. If it is **out of sight**, you cannot see it.

> **sight** noun
> 1 = eyesight, visibility, vision
> 2 = display, scene, spectacle
> ▶ *verb* 4 = see, spot

sighted *adjective* Someone who is sighted can see.

sighting *noun* A sighting of something rare or unexpected is an occasion when it is seen.

sightseeing *noun* Sightseeing is visiting the interesting places

that tourists usually visit.
> **sightseer** noun

sign noun **1** a mark or symbol that always has a particular meaning, for example in mathematics or music. **2** a gesture with a particular meaning. **3** A sign can also consist of words, a picture or a symbol giving information or a warning. **4** A sign is an event or happening that some people believe God has sent as a warning or instruction to an individual or to people in general. **5** If there are signs of something, there is evidence that it exists or is happening. ▶ verb **6** If you sign a document, you write your name on it. **7** If you sign, you communicate by using sign language. > **sign on** verb **1** If you sign on for a job or course, you officially agree to do it by signing a contract. **2** When people sign on, they officially state that they are unemployed and claim benefit from the state. > **sign up** verb If you sign up for a job or course, you officially agree to do it.

sign noun
1 = character, emblem, logo, mark, symbol **3** = board, notice, placard **5** = clue, evidence, hint, indication, symptom, token, trace

signal signals, signalling, signalled noun **1** a gesture, sound, action or device intended to give a message to someone. **2** A railway signal is a piece of equipment beside the track which tells train drivers whether to stop or not. ▶ verb **3** If you signal to someone, you make a gesture or sound to give them a message.

signal noun
1 = beacon, cue, gesture, sign
▶ verb **3** = beckon, gesticulate, gesture, motion, nod, sign, wave

signature noun If you write your signature, you write your name the way you usually write it.

significant adjective large or important. > **significance** noun > **significantly** adverb

significant adjective
= considerable, important, impressive, marked, notable, pronounced, striking

signify signifies, signifying, signified verb A gesture that signifies something has a particular meaning.

sign language noun Sign language is a way of communicating using your hands, used especially by deaf people.

signpost noun a road sign with information on it such as the name of a town and how far away it is.

Sikh noun (RE) a person who believes in Sikhism, an Indian religion which separated from Hinduism in the 16th century and which teaches that there is only one God. > **Sikhism** noun

silence noun **1** Silence is quietness. **2** Someone's silence about something is their failure or refusal to talk about it. ▶ verb **3** To silence someone or something means to stop them talking or making a noise.

silence noun
1 = calm, hush, lull, peace, quiet, stillness **2** = dumbness, muteness, reticence, speechlessness

S

▶ *verb* 3 = deaden, gag, muffle, quiet, quieten, stifle, still, suppress

silent *adjective* 1 If you are silent, you are not saying anything. 2 If you are silent about something, you do not tell people about it. 3 When something is silent, it makes no noise. 4 A silent film has only pictures and no sound. > **silently** *adverb*

silent *adjective*
1 = dumb, mute, speechless, taciturn, wordless
3 = hushed, quiet, soundless, still

silhouette *noun* the outline of a dark shape against a light background. > **silhouetted** *adjective*

silicon *noun* (SCIENCE) Silicon is an element found in sand, clay and stone. It is used to make glass and also to make parts of computers. Its atomic number is 14 and its symbol is Si.

silk *noun* Silk is a fine, soft cloth made from a substance produced by silkworms.

silken *adjective* (*literary*) smooth and soft.

silky silkier, silkiest *adjective* smooth and soft.

sill *noun* a ledge at the bottom of a window.

silly sillier, silliest *adjective* foolish or childish.

silly *adjective*
= absurd, daft (*British; informal*), foolish, idiotic, inane, ridiculous, stupid

silt *noun* (GEOGRAPHY) Silt is fine sand or soil which is carried along by a river.

silver *noun* 1 (SCIENCE) Silver is a valuable greyish-white metallic element used for making jewellery and ornaments. Its atomic number is 47 and its symbol is Ag. 2 Silver is also coins made from silver or from silver-coloured metal. 3 In a house, the silver is all the things made from silver, especially the cutlery.
▶ *adjective, noun* 4 greyish-white.

silver medal *noun* a medal made from silver awarded to the competitor who comes second in a competition.

similar *adjective* 1 If one thing is similar to another, or if two things are similar, they are like each other. 2 In maths, two triangles are similar if the angles in one correspond exactly to the angles in the other. > **similarly** *adverb*

similar *adjective*
1 = alike, analogous, comparable, like, uniform

similarity *noun* If there is a similarity between things, they are alike in some way.

similarity *noun*
= analogy, likeness, resemblance, sameness

simmer *verb* When food simmers, it cooks gently at just below boiling point.

simple *adjective* 1 Something that is simple is uncomplicated and easy to understand or do. 2 Simple also means plain and not elaborate in style. 3 A simple way of life is uncomplicated. 4 You use 'simple' to emphasise that what you are talking about is the only important thing: *simple stubbornness*. 5 In grammar, a simple sentence consists of one

s

main clause and no subordinate clause. > **simplicity** noun

simple adjective
1 = easy, elementary, straightforward, uncomplicated, understandable 2 = basic, classic, clean, plain, severe

simplify simplifies, simplifying, simplified verb To simplify something means to make it easier to do or understand. > **simplification** noun

simplify verb
= make simpler, streamline

simplistic adjective too simple or naive.

simply adverb 1 Simply means merely: It was simply a question of making the decision. 2 You use 'simply' to emphasise what you are saying: It is simply not true. 3 If you say or write something simply, you do it in a way that makes it easy to understand.

simulate verb To simulate something means to imitate it.

simulation noun 1 Simulation is the process of simulating something or the result of simulating it. 2 (technical) A simulation is an attempt to solve a problem by representing it mathematically, often on a computer.

simulator noun A simulator is a device designed to reproduce actual conditions, for example in order to train pilots or astronauts.

simultaneous adjective Things that are simultaneous happen at the same time. > **simultaneously** adverb

sin sins, sinning, sinned noun 1 (RE) Sin is wicked and immoral behaviour. ▶ verb 2 To sin means to do something wicked and immoral.

sin noun
1 = crime, evil, offence, wickedness, wrong
▶ verb 2 = do wrong

since preposition, conjunction, adverb 1 Since means from a particular time until now: I've been waiting patiently since half past three. ▶ adverb 2 Since also means at some time after a particular time in the past: The band split up and he has since gone solo. ▶ conjunction 3 Since also means because: I'm forever on a diet, since I put on weight easily.

sincere adjective If you are sincere, you say things that you really mean. > **sincerity** noun

sincere adjective
= genuine, heartfelt, real, wholehearted

sincerely adverb 1 If you say or feel something sincerely, you mean it or feel it genuinely. ▶ phrase 2 You write Yours sincerely before your signature at the end of a letter in which you have named the person you are writing to in the greeting at the beginning of the letter. For example, if you began your letter 'Dear Mr Brown' you would use 'Yours sincerely'.

sinful adjective (RE) wicked and immoral.

sing sings, singing, sang, sung verb 1 When you sing, you make musical sounds with your voice, usually producing words that fit a tune. 2 When birds or insects sing, they make pleasant sounds. > **singer** noun

single adjective 1 Single means only one and not more. 2 People who are single are not married. 3 A single bed or bedroom is for one person. 4 A single ticket is a one-way ticket. ▶ noun 5 a recording of one or two short pieces of music on a small record, CD or download. 6 Singles is a game of tennis, badminton or squash between just two players. > **single out** verb If you single someone out from a group, you give them special treatment.

> **single** adjective
> 1 = lone, one, only, sole, solitary
> 2 = unattached, unmarried
> 3 = individual, separate

single-handed adverb If you do something single-handed, you do it on your own, without any help.

single-minded adjective A single-minded person has only one aim and is determined to achieve it.

singly adverb If people do something singly, they do it on their own or one by one.

singular noun 1 (MFL) In grammar, the singular is the form of a word that refers to just one person or thing. ▶ adjective 2 (formal) unusual and remarkable. > **singularity** noun > **singularly** adverb

> **singular** adjective
> 2 = exceptional, extraordinary, rare, remarkable, uncommon, unique, unusual

sinister adjective seeming harmful or evil.

> **sinister** adjective
> = evil, forbidding, menacing, ominous, threatening

sink sinks, sinking, sank, sunk noun 1 a basin with taps supplying water, usually in a kitchen or bathroom. ▶ verb 2 If something sinks, it moves downwards, especially through water. 3 To sink a ship means to cause it to sink by attacking it. 4 If an amount or value sinks, it decreases. 5 If you sink into an unpleasant state, you gradually pass into it. 6 To sink something sharp into an object means to make it go deeply into it. > **sink in** verb When a fact sinks in, you fully understand it or realise it.

sinner noun someone who has committed a sin.

sinus noun Your sinuses are the air passages in the bones of your skull, just behind your nose.

sip sips, sipping, sipped verb 1 If you sip a drink, you drink it by taking a small amount at a time. ▶ noun 2 a small amount of drink that you take into your mouth.

siphon; also spelt **syphon** verb If you siphon off a liquid, you draw it out of a container through a tube and transfer it to another place.

sir noun 1 Sir is a polite, formal way of addressing a man. 2 Sir is also the title used in front of the name of a knight or baronet.

siren noun a warning device, for example on a police car, which makes a loud wailing noise.

sirloin noun Sirloin is a prime cut of beef from the lower part of a cow's back.

sister noun 1 Your sister is a girl or woman who has the same parents as you. 2 a member of a female religious order. 3 In a hospital, a sister is a senior nurse who supervises a ward.

S

sisterhood noun Sisterhood is a strong feeling of companionship between women.

sister-in-law sisters-in-law noun Someone's sister-in-law is the sister of their husband or wife, or their sibling's wife.

sit sits, sitting, sat verb 1 If you are sitting, your weight is supported by your buttocks rather than your feet. 2 When you sit or sit down somewhere, you lower your body until you are sitting. 3 If you sit an examination, you take it. 4 (formal) When a parliament, law court or other official body sits, it meets and officially carries out its work.

sitcom noun (informal) a television comedy series which shows characters in amusing situations that are similar to everyday life.

site noun 1 a piece of ground where a particular thing happens or is situated. 2 A site is the same as a website. ▶ verb 3 If something is sited in a place, it is built or positioned there.

sitting noun 1 one of the times when a meal is served. 2 one of the occasions when a parliament or law court meets and carries out its work.

sitting room noun a room in a house where people sit and relax.

situated adjective If something is situated somewhere, that is where it is.

situation noun 1 what is happening in a particular place at a particular time. 2 The situation of a building or town is its surroundings.

> **situation** noun
> 1 = case, circumstances, plight, scenario, state of affairs

six the number 6.

sixteen the number 16.
> **sixteenth** adjective

sixth adjective 1 The sixth item in a series is the one counted as number six. ▶ noun 2 one of six equal parts.

sixth sense noun You say that someone has a sixth sense when they know something instinctively, without having any evidence of it.

sixty sixties the number 60.
> **sixtieth** adjective

sizable; also spelt **sizeable** adjective fairly large.

size noun 1 The size of something is how big or small it is. 2 The size of something is also the fact that it is very large. 3 one of the standard graded measurements of clothes and shoes. > **size up** verb If you size up people or situations, you look at them carefully and make a judgment about them.

> **size** noun
> 1 = dimensions, extent, proportions 2 = bulk, immensity

sizzle verb If something sizzles, it makes a hissing sound like the sound of frying food.

skate noun 1 Skates are ice skates or roller skates. 2 a flat edible sea fish. ▶ verb 3 If you skate, you move about on ice wearing ice skates. 4 If you skate round a difficult subject, you avoid discussing it.

skateboard noun a narrow board on wheels, which you stand on and ride for fun.

skeleton noun Your skeleton is the framework of bones in your body.

sketch noun 1 (ART) a quick, rough

drawing. **2** A sketch of a situation or incident is a brief description of it. **3** a short, humorous piece of acting, usually forming part of a comedy show. ▶ verb **4** If you sketch something, you draw it quickly and roughly.

sketchy sketchier, sketchiest *adjective* giving only a rough description or account.

skew or **skewed** *adjective* in a slanting position, rather than straight or upright.

skewer *noun* **1** a long metal pin used to hold pieces of food together during cooking. ▶ verb **2** If you skewer something, you push a skewer through it.

ski skis, skiing, skied *noun* **1** Skis are long pieces of wood, metal or plastic that you fasten to special boots so you can move easily on snow. ▶ verb **2** When you ski, you move on snow wearing skis, especially as a sport.

skid skids, skidding, skidded *verb* If a vehicle skids, it slides in an uncontrolled way, for example because the road is wet or icy.

skilful *adjective* If you are skilful at something, you can do it very well. **> skilfully** *adverb*

> **skilful** *adjective*
> = able, accomplished, adept, competent, expert, masterly, proficient, skilled

skill *noun* **1** Skill is the knowledge and ability that enables you to do something well. **2** a type of work or technique which requires special training and knowledge.

> **skill** *noun*
> **1** = ability, competence, dexterity, expertise, facility, knack, proficiency

skilled *adjective* **1** A skilled person has the knowledge and ability to do something well. **2** Skilled work is work which can only be done by people who have had special training.

> **skilled** *adjective*
> **1** = able, accomplished, competent, experienced, expert, masterly, professional, proficient, skilful, trained

skim skims, skimming, skimmed *verb* **1** If you skim something from the surface of a liquid, you remove it. **2** If something skims a surface, it moves along just above it. **3** If you skim a piece of writing, you read through it quickly and without taking in the details.

skimmed milk *noun* Skimmed milk has had the cream removed.

skin skins, skinning, skinned *noun* **1** Your skin is the natural covering of your body. An animal skin is the skin and fur of a dead animal. **2** The skin of a fruit or vegetable is its outer covering. **3** a solid layer which forms on the surface of a liquid. ▶ verb **4** If you skin a dead animal, you remove its skin. **5** If you skin a part of your body, you accidentally graze it.

skinny skinnier, skinniest *adjective* extremely thin.

> **skinny** *adjective*
> = bony, emaciated, lean, scrawny, thin, underfed, undernourished

skip skips, skipping, skipped *verb* **1** If you skip along, you move along jumping from one foot to the other. **2** (*informal*) If you skip something, you miss it out or avoid doing it. ▶ noun **3** Skips are the movements you make when you skip. **4** a large metal container for holding rubbish and rubble.

skipper noun (*informal*) The skipper of a ship or boat is its captain.

skirmish noun a short, rough fight.

skirt noun **1** A skirt is a piece of clothing which fastens at the waist and hangs down over the legs. ▶ verb **2** Something that skirts an area is situated around the edge of it. **3** If you skirt something, you go around the edge of it.

skull noun Your skull is the bony part of your head which surrounds your brain.

skunk noun a small black and white mammal from North America which gives off an unpleasant smell when it is frightened.

sky skies noun The sky is the space around the earth which you can see when you look upwards.

skylight noun a window in a roof or ceiling.

skyline noun The skyline is the line where the sky meets buildings and the ground.

Skype noun (*trademark*) **1** a computer program for making phone calls and video calls on the internet. ▶ verb **2** If you Skype someone, you use a computer program to speak to them on the internet.

skyscraper noun a very tall building.

slab noun a thick, flat piece of something.

slack adjective **1** Something that is slack is loose and not firmly stretched or positioned. **2** A slack period is one in which there is not much work to do. ▶ noun **3** The slack in a rope is the part that hangs loose. **4** (*in plural, old-fashioned*) Slacks are casual trousers. > **slackness** noun

slacken verb **1** If something slackens, it becomes slower or less intense. **2** To slacken also means to become looser.

slag slags, slagging, slagged noun **1** Slag is the waste material left when ore has been melted down to remove the metal. ▶ verb **2** (*informal*) To slag someone off means to criticise them in an unpleasant way, usually behind their back.

slain the past participle of **slay**.

slalom noun a skiing competition in which the competitors have to twist and turn quickly to avoid obstacles.

slam slams, slamming, slammed verb **1** If you slam a door or if it slams, it shuts noisily and with great force. **2** If you slam something down, you put it down violently.

slander noun **1** Slander is something untrue and malicious said about someone. ▶ verb **2** To slander someone means to say untrue and malicious things about them. > **slanderous** adjective

slander noun
1 = libel, scandal, slur, smear
▶ verb **2** = libel, malign, smear

slang noun Slang consists of very informal words and expressions.

slant verb **1** If something slants, it slopes. **2** If news or information is slanted, it is presented in a biased way. ▶ noun **3** a slope. **4** A slant on a subject is one way of looking at it, especially a biased one.

slap slaps, slapping, slapped verb
1 If you slap someone, you hit them with the palm of your hand. 2 If you slap something onto a surface, you put it there quickly and noisily. ▶ noun
3 If you give someone a slap, you slap them.

slash verb 1 If you slash something, you make a long, deep cut in it. 2 (informal) To slash money means to reduce it greatly. ▶ noun 3 A diagonal line that separates letters, words or numbers, for example in the number 340/21/K.

slate noun 1 Slate is a dark grey rock that splits easily into thin layers. 2 Slates are small, flat pieces of slate used for covering roofs. ▶ verb 3 (informal) If critics slate a play, film or book, they criticise it severely.

slaughter verb 1 To slaughter a large number of people means to kill them unjustly or cruelly. 2 To slaughter farm animals means to kill them for meat. ▶ noun 3 Slaughter is the killing of many people.

slave noun 1 someone who is forced to work for another person. ▶ verb 2 If you slave for someone, you work very hard for them.
> **slavery** noun

slay slays, slaying, slew, slain verb (literary) To slay someone means to kill them.

sleazy sleazier, sleaziest adjective A sleazy place looks dirty, run-down and not respectable.

sled or **sledge** noun a vehicle on runners used for travelling over snow.

sledgehammer noun a large, heavy hammer.

sleek adjective 1 Sleek hair is smooth and shiny. 2 Someone who is sleek looks rich and dresses elegantly.

sleep sleeps, sleeping, slept noun
1 Sleep is the natural state of rest in which your eyes are closed and you are unconscious. 2 If you have a sleep, you sleep for a while. ▶ verb 3 When you sleep, you rest in a state of sleep. ▶ phrase 4 If a sick or injured animal **is put to sleep**, it is painlessly killed.

> **sleep** noun
> 1 = doze, hibernation, kip (British; slang), nap, slumber, snooze (informal)
> ▶ verb 3 = doze, hibernate, kip (British; slang), slumber, snooze (informal), take a nap

sleeper noun 1 You use 'sleeper' to say how deeply someone sleeps: I'm a very heavy sleeper. 2 a bed on a train, or a train which has beds on it. 3 Railway sleepers are the large beams that support the rails of a railway track.

sleeping bag noun a large, warm bag for sleeping in, especially when you are camping.

sleepover noun a gathering or party at which friends spend the night at another friend's house.

sleepy sleepier, sleepiest adjective
1 tired and ready to go to sleep. 2 A sleepy town or village is very quiet.
> **sleepily** adverb > **sleepiness** noun

> **sleepy** adjective
> 1 = drowsy, lethargic, sluggish
> 2 = dull, quiet

sleet noun Sleet is a mixture of rain and snow.

sleeve noun The sleeves of a piece of clothing are the parts that cover your arms. > **sleeveless** adjective

sleigh noun a sledge.

slender adjective 1 attractively thin and graceful. 2 small in amount or degree.

> **slender** adjective
> 1 = lean, slight, slim 2 = faint, remote, slight, slim, small

slept the past tense and past participle of **sleep**.

sleuth noun (old-fashioned) a detective.

slew verb 1 Slew is the past tense of **slay**. 2 If a vehicle slews, it slides or skids.

slice noun 1 A slice of cake, bread or other food is a piece of it cut from a larger piece. 2 a kitchen tool with a broad, flat blade. 3 In sport, a slice is a stroke in which the player makes the ball go to one side, rather than straight ahead. ▶ verb 4 If you slice food, you cut it into thin pieces. 5 To slice through something means to cut or move through it quickly, like a knife.

slick adjective 1 A slick action is done quickly and smoothly. 2 A slick person speaks easily and persuasively but is not sincere. ▶ noun 3 An oil slick is a layer of oil floating on the surface of the sea or a lake.

slide slides, sliding, slid verb 1 When something slides, it moves smoothly over or against something else. ▶ noun 2 a small piece of photographic film which can be projected onto a screen so that you can see the picture. 3 a small piece of glass on which you

put something that you want to examine through a microscope. 4 In a playground, a slide is a structure with a steep, slippery slope for children to slide down.

slight adjective 1 Slight means small in amount or degree. 2 A slight person has a slim body. ▶ verb 3 If you slight someone, you insult them by behaving rudely towards them. ▶ noun 4 A slight is an example of rude or insulting behaviour. > **slightly** adverb

> **slight** adjective
> 1 = insignificant, minor, negligible, small, trivial

slim slimmer, slimmest; slims, slimming, slimmed adjective 1 A slim person is attractively thin. 2 A slim object is thinner than usual. 3 If there is only a slim chance that something will happen, it is unlikely to happen. ▶ verb 4 If you are slimming, you are trying to lose weight. > **slimmer** noun

slime noun Slime is an unpleasant, thick, slippery substance.

slimy slimier, slimiest adjective 1 covered in slime. 2 Slimy people are friendly and pleasant in an insincere way.

sling slings, slinging, slung verb 1 (informal) If you sling something somewhere, you throw it there. 2 If you sling a rope between two points, you attach it so that it hangs loosely between them. ▶ noun 3 a piece of cloth tied round a person's neck to support a broken or injured arm. 4 a device made of ropes or cloth used for carrying things.

slip slips, slipping, slipped verb 1 If you slip, you accidentally slide and lose your balance. **2** If something slips, it slides out of place accidentally. **3** If you slip somewhere, you go there quickly and quietly. **4** If you slip something somewhere, you put it there quickly and quietly. **5** If something slips to a lower level or standard, it falls to that level or standard. ▶ *noun* **6** a small mistake. **7** A slip of paper is a small piece of paper. **8** a piece of clothing worn under a dress or skirt. ▷ **slip up** *verb* (*informal*) If you slip up, you make a mistake.

> **slip** *verb*
> **3** = creep, sneak, steal
> ▶ *noun* **6** = blunder, error, mistake

slipper *noun* Slippers are loose, soft shoes that you wear indoors.

slippery *adjective* **1** smooth, wet or greasy, and difficult to hold or walk on. **2** (*informal*) You describe a person as slippery when they cannot be trusted.

slipstream *noun* The slipstream of a car or plane is the flow of air directly behind it.

slit slits, slitting, slit *verb* **1** If you slit something, you make a long, narrow cut in it. ▶ *noun* **2** a long, narrow cut or opening.

slither *verb* To slither somewhere means to move there by sliding along the ground in an uneven way.

sliver *noun* a small, thin piece of something.

slob *noun* (*informal*) a lazy, untidy person.

slog slogs, slogging, slogged *verb* (*informal*) **1** If you slog at something, you work hard and steadily at it. **2** If you slog

somewhere, you move along with difficulty.

slogan *noun* a short, easily remembered phrase used in advertising or by a political party.

> **slogan** *noun*
> = jingle, motto

slop slops, slopping, slopped *verb* **1** If a liquid slops, it spills over the edge of a container in a messy way. ▶ *noun* **2** (*in plural*) Slops can refer to dirty water or liquid waste as slops.

slope *noun* **1** a flat surface that is at an angle, so that one end is higher than the other. **2** The slope of something is the angle at which it slopes. ▶ *verb* **3** If a surface slopes, it is at an angle. **4** If something slopes, it leans to one side rather than being upright.

> **slope** *noun*
> **1** = gradient, incline, ramp
> ▶ *verb* **3** = fall, rise, slant

sloppy sloppier, sloppiest *adjective* (*informal*) **1** very messy or careless. **2** foolishly sentimental. ▷ **sloppily** *adverb* ▷ **sloppiness** *noun*

slot slots, slotting, slotted *noun* **1** a narrow opening in a machine or container, for example for putting coins in. ▶ *verb* **2** When you slot something into something else, you put it into a space where it fits.

sloth *noun* **1** (*formal*) Sloth is laziness. **2** a South and Central American animal that moves very slowly and hangs upside down from the branches of trees.

slouch *verb* If you slouch, you stand or sit with your shoulders and head drooping forwards.

Slovak *adjective* 1 belonging or relating to Slovakia. ▶ *noun* 2 someone who comes from Slovakia. 3 Slovak is the language spoken in Slovakia.

Slovene *adjective* 1 belonging or relating to Slovenia. ▶ *noun* 2 someone who comes from Slovenia. 3 Slovene is the language spoken in Slovenia.

slow *adjective* 1 moving, happening or doing something with very little speed. 2 Someone who is slow is not very clever. 3 If a clock or watch is slow, it shows a time earlier than the correct one. ▶ *verb* 4 If something slows, slows down or slows up, it moves or happens more slowly.
> **slowness** *noun*

> **slow** *adjective*
> 1 = gradual, leisurely, lingering, ponderous, sluggish, unhurried
> ▶ *verb* 4 = check, decelerate

slowly *adverb* not quickly or hurriedly.

> **slowly** *adverb*
> = by degrees, gradually, unhurriedly

slow motion *noun* Slow motion is movement which is much slower than normal, especially in a film.

sludge *noun* Sludge is thick mud or sewage.

slug *noun* 1 a small, slow-moving creature with a slimy body, like a snail without a shell. 2 (*informal*) A slug of a strong alcoholic drink is a mouthful of it.

sluggish *adjective* moving slowly and without energy.
> **sluggishly** *adverb*

slum *noun* a poor, run-down area of a city.

slumber (*literary*) *noun* 1 Slumber is sleep. ▶ *verb* 2 When you slumber, you sleep.

slump *verb* 1 If an amount or a value slumps, it falls suddenly by a large amount. 2 If you slump somewhere, you fall or sit down heavily. ▶ *noun* 3 a sudden, severe drop in an amount or value. 4 a time when there is economic decline and high unemployment.

slung the past tense and past participle of **sling**.

slur slurs, slurring, slurred *noun* 1 an insulting remark. ▶ *verb* 2 When people slur their speech, they do not say their words clearly, often because they are drunk or ill.

slush *noun* 1 Slush is wet melting snow. 2 (*informal*) You can refer to sentimental love stories as slush.
> **slushy** *adjective*

sly slyer or slier, slyest or sliest *adjective* 1 A sly expression or remark shows that you know something other people do not know. 2 A sly person is cunning and good at deceiving people.
> **slyly** *adverb*

> **sly** *adjective*
> 2 = crafty, cunning, devious, scheming, underhand, wily

smack *verb* 1 If you smack someone, you hit them with your open hand. 2 If something smacks of something else, it reminds you of it. ▶ *noun* 3 If you give someone a smack, you smack them. 4 a loud, sharp noise.

small *adjective* 1 Small means not large in size, number or amount. 2 Small means not important or significant. ▶ noun **3** The small of your back is the narrow part where your back curves slightly inwards. > **smallness** noun

small adjective
1 = little, miniature, minute, minuscule, tiny
2 = inconsequential, insignificant, little, minor, negligible, petty, slight, trifling, trivial, unimportant

smallpox noun Smallpox is a serious contagious disease that causes a fever and a rash.

small talk noun Small talk is conversation about unimportant things.

smart adjective **1** A smart person is clean and neatly dressed. **2** Smart means clever. **3** A smart movement is quick and sharp. **4** A smart machine or system is one that uses computer technology.
▶ verb **5** If a wound smarts, it stings. **6** If you are smarting from criticism or unkindness, you are feeling upset by it. > **smartly** adverb > **smartness** noun

smart adjective
1 = chic, elegant, neat, spruce, stylish 2 = astute, bright, canny, clever, ingenious, intelligent, shrewd

smarten verb If you smarten something up, you make it look neater and tidier.

smartphone noun a mobile phone allowing access to the internet.

smash verb **1** If you smash something, you break it into a lot of pieces by hitting it or dropping it. **2** To smash through something such as a wall means to go through it by breaking it.

3 To smash against something means to hit it with great force.
▶ noun **4** (informal) If a play or film is a smash or a smash hit, it is very successful. **5** a car crash. **6** In tennis, a smash is a stroke in which the player hits the ball downwards very hard.

smashing adjective (informal) If you describe something as smashing, you mean you like it very much.

smattering noun A smattering of knowledge or information is a very small amount of it.

smear noun **1** a dirty, greasy mark on a surface. **2** an untrue and malicious rumour. ▶ verb **3** If something smears a surface, it makes dirty, greasy marks on it. **4** If you smear a surface with a thick substance, you spread a layer of the substance over the surface.

smell smells, smelling, smelled or smelt noun **1** The smell of something is a quality it has which you perceive through your nose. **2** Your sense of smell is your ability to smell things. ▶ verb **3** If something smells, it has a quality you can perceive through your nose, especially an unpleasant quality. **4** If you smell something, you become aware of it through your nose. **5** If you can smell something such as danger or trouble, you feel it is present or likely to happen.

smell noun
1 = aroma, fragrance, odour, perfume, pong (British and Australian; informal), reek, scent, stench, stink
▶ verb 4 = scent, sniff

smelly smellier, smelliest adjective having a strong, unpleasant smell.

smelly *adjective*
= foul, reeking, stinking

smelt *verb* To smelt a metal ore means to heat it until it melts, so that the metal can be extracted.

smile *verb* 1 When you smile, the corners of your mouth move outwards and slightly upwards because you are pleased or amused. ▶ *noun* 2 the expression you have when you smile.

smile *verb*
1 = beam, grin, smirk
▶ *noun* 2 = beam, grin, smirk

smirk *verb* 1 When you smirk, you smile in a sneering or sarcastic way. ▶ *noun* 2 a sneering or sarcastic smile.

smith *noun* someone who makes things out of iron, gold or another metal.

smitten *adjective* If you are smitten with someone or something, you are very impressed with or enthusiastic about them.

smock *noun* a loose garment like a long blouse.

smog *noun* Smog is a mixture of smoke and fog which occurs in some industrial cities.

smoke *noun* 1 Smoke is a mixture of gas and small particles sent into the air when something burns. ▶ *verb* 2 If something is smoking, smoke is coming from it. 3 When someone smokes a cigarette or pipe, they suck smoke from it into their mouth and blow it out again. 4 To smoke fish or meat means to hang it over burning wood so that the smoke preserves it and gives it a pleasant flavour. > **smoker** *noun* > **smoking** *noun*, *adjective*

smoky smokier, smokiest *adjective* A smoky place is full of smoke.

smooth *adjective* 1 A smooth surface has no roughness and no holes in it. 2 A smooth liquid or mixture has no lumps in it. 3 A smooth movement or process happens evenly and steadily. 4 Smooth also means successful and without problems. ▶ *verb* 5 If you smooth something, you move your hands over it to make it smooth and flat. > **smoothly** *adverb* > **smoothness** *noun*

smooth *adjective*
1 = glassy, glossy, polished, silky, sleek

smoothie *noun* a thick type of drink made in an electric blender from, or example, milk, fruit and crushed ice, or from vegetables.

smother *verb* 1 If you smother a fire, you cover it with something to put it out. 2 To smother a person means to cover their face with something so that they cannot breathe. 3 To smother someone also means to give them too much love and protection. 4 If you smother an emotion, you control it so that people do not notice it.

smoulder *verb* 1 When something smoulders, it burns slowly, producing smoke but no flames. 2 If a feeling is smouldering inside you, you feel it very strongly but do not show it.

smudge *noun* 1 a dirty or blurred mark or a smear on something. ▶ *verb* 2 If you smudge something, you make it dirty or messy by touching it or marking it.

smug smugger, smuggest *adjective* Someone who is smug is very pleased with how good or clever they are. > **smugly** *adverb* > **smugness** *noun*

> **smug** *adjective*
> = complacent, conceited,
> self-satisfied, superior

smuggle *verb* To smuggle things or people into or out of a place means to take them there illegally or secretly.

smuggler *noun* someone who smuggles goods illegally into a country.

snack *noun* a light, quick meal.

snag snags, snagging, snagged *noun* **1** a small problem or disadvantage. **2** (*informal*) In Australian and New Zealand English, a snag is a sausage. > *verb* **3** If you snag your clothing, you damage it by catching it on something sharp.

> **snag** *noun*
> **1** = catch (*informal*), difficulty,
> disadvantage, drawback,
> problem

snail *noun* a small, slow-moving creature with a long, slimy body and a shell on its back.

snake *noun* **1** a long, thin, scaly reptile with no legs. > *verb* **2** Something that snakes moves in long winding curves.

snap snaps, snapping, snapped *verb* **1** If something snaps or if you snap it, it breaks with a sharp cracking noise. **2** If you snap something into a particular position, you move it there quickly with a sharp sound. **3** If an animal snaps at you, it shuts its jaws together quickly as if to bite you. **4** If someone snaps at you, they speak in a sharp, unfriendly way. **5** If you snap

someone, you take a quick photograph of them. > *noun* **6** the sound of something snapping. **7** (*informal*) a photograph taken quickly and casually. > *adjective* **8** A snap decision or action is taken suddenly without careful thought.

snapper *noun* a fish with edible pink flesh, found in waters around Australia, New Zealand and the US.

snapshot *noun* a photograph taken quickly and casually.

snare *noun* **1** a trap for catching birds or small animals. > *verb* **2** To snare an animal or bird means to catch it using a snare.

snarl *verb* **1** When an animal snarls, it bares its teeth and makes a fierce growling noise. **2** If you snarl, you say something in a fierce, angry way. > *noun* **3** the noise an animal makes when it snarls.

snatch *verb* **1** If you snatch something, you reach out for it quickly and take it. **2** If you snatch an amount of time or an opportunity, you quickly make use of it. > *noun* **3** If you make a snatch at something, you reach out for it quickly to try to take it. **4** A snatch of conversation or song is a very small piece of it.

sneak *verb* **1** If you sneak somewhere, you go there quickly trying not to be seen or heard. **2** If you sneak something somewhere, you take it there secretly. > *noun* **3** (*informal*) someone who tells people in authority that someone else has done something wrong.

> **sneak** *verb*
> **1** = lurk, sidle, slip, steal **2** = slip,
> smuggle, spirit

sneaker noun Sneakers are casual shoes with rubber soles.

sneaking adjective If you have a sneaking feeling about something or someone, you have this feeling rather reluctantly.

sneaky sneakier, sneakiest adjective (informal) Someone who is sneaky does things secretly rather than openly.

> **sneaky** adjective
> = crafty, deceitful, devious, dishonest, mean, slippery, sly, untrustworthy

sneer verb 1 If you sneer at someone or something, you show by your expression and your comments that you think they are stupid or inferior. ▶ noun 2 the expression on someone's face when they sneer.

sneeze verb 1 When you sneeze, you suddenly take in breath and blow it down your nose noisily, because something has irritated the inside of your nose. ▶ noun 2 an act of sneezing.

snide adjective A snide comment or remark criticises someone in a nasty but indirect way.

sniff verb 1 When you sniff, you breathe in air through your nose hard enough to make a sound. 2 If you sniff something, you smell it by sniffing. ▶ noun 3 the noise you make when you sniff. 4 A sniff of something is a smell of it.

snigger verb 1 If you snigger, you laugh in a quiet, disrespectful way. ▶ noun 2 a quiet, disrespectful laugh.

snip snips, snipping, snipped verb 1 If you snip something, you cut it with scissors or shears in a single quick action. ▶ noun 2 a small cut made by scissors or shears.

snippet noun A snippet of something such as information or news is a small piece of it.

snob noun 1 someone who admires upper-class people and looks down on lower-class people. 2 someone who believes that they are better than other people. > **snobbery** noun > **snobbish** adjective

snooker noun Snooker is a game played on a large table covered with smooth green cloth. Players score points by hitting different coloured balls into side pockets using a long stick called a cue.

snoop verb (informal) Someone who is snooping is secretly looking round a place to find out things.

snooze (informal) verb 1 If you snooze, you sleep lightly for a short time, especially during the day. ▶ noun 2 a short, light sleep.

snore verb 1 When a sleeping person snores, they make a loud noise each time they breathe. ▶ noun 2 the noise someone makes when they snore.

snorkel noun a tube you can breathe through when you are swimming just under the surface of the sea. > **snorkelling** noun

snort verb 1 When people or animals snort, they force breath out through their nose in a noisy way. ▶ noun 2 the noise you make when you snort.

snout noun An animal's snout is its nose.

snow noun 1 Snow consists of flakes of ice crystals which fall from the sky in cold weather. ▶ verb 2 When it snows, snow falls from the sky.

S

snowball noun 1 a ball of snow for throwing. ▶ verb 2 When something such as a project snowballs, it grows rapidly.

snowman snowmen noun a large mound of snow moulded into the shape of a person.

snub snubs, snubbing, snubbed verb 1 To snub someone means to behave rudely towards them, especially by making an insulting remark or ignoring them. ▶ noun 2 an insulting remark or a piece of rude behaviour. ▶ adjective 3 A snub nose is short and turned-up.

snuff noun Snuff is powdered tobacco which people take by sniffing it up their noses.

snug snugger, snuggest adjective A snug place is warm and comfortable. If you are snug, you are warm and comfortable.
> **snugly** adverb

snuggle verb If you snuggle somewhere, you cuddle up more closely to something or someone.

so adverb 1 'So' is used to refer to what has just been mentioned: *Had he locked the car? If so, where were the keys?* 2 'So' is used to mean also: *Jarvis laughed, and so did Jarvis.* 3 'So' can be used to mean 'therefore': *It's a bit expensive, so I don't think I will get one.* 4 'So' is used when you are talking about the degree or extent of something: *Why are you so cruel?* 5 'So' is used before words like 'much' and 'many' to say that there is a definite limit to something: *There are only so many questions that can be asked about the record.*
▶ phrase 6 So that and so as are used to introduce the reason for doing something: *to die so that you might live.*

soak verb 1 To soak something or leave it to soak means to put it in a liquid and leave it there. 2 When a liquid soaks something, it makes it very wet. 3 When something soaks up a liquid, the liquid is drawn up into it.

> **soak** verb
> 2 = bathe, permeate, steep, wet

soaked adjective extremely wet.

soaking adjective If something is soaking, it is very wet.

soap noun Soap is a substance made of natural oils and fats and used for washing yourself.
> **soapy** adjective

soap opera noun a popular television drama serial about people's daily lives.

soar verb 1 If an amount soars, it quickly increases by a great deal. 2 If something soars into the air, it quickly goes up into the air.
> **soaring** adjective

sob sobs, sobbing, sobbed verb 1 When someone sobs, they cry in a noisy way, breathing in short breaths. ▶ noun 2 the noise made when you cry.

sober adjective 1 If someone is sober, they are not drunk. 2 Sober also means serious and thoughtful. 3 Sober colours are plain and rather dull. > **soberly** adverb > **sober up** verb To sober up means to become sober after being drunk.

so-called adjective You use 'so-called' to say that the name by which something is called is incorrect or misleading.

soccer noun Soccer is a game played by two teams of eleven players who try to kick or head a ball into the opposing team's net.

s

sociable adjective Sociable people are friendly and enjoy talking to other people. > **sociability** noun

> **sociable** adjective
> = friendly, gregarious, outgoing

social adjective 1 to do with society or life within a society. 2 to do with leisure activities that involve meeting other people. > **socially** adverb

socialise; also spelt **socialize** verb When people socialise, they meet other people socially, for example at parties.

socialism noun Socialism is the political belief that the state should own industries on behalf of the people and that everyone should be equal. > **socialist** adjective, noun

social media plural noun (ICT) websites and applications used by large groups of people to share information and to develop social and professional contacts.

social networking site noun (ICT) a website where users can connect with other people to chat and share photographs and videos.

social security noun Social security is a system by which the government pays money regularly to people who have no other income or only a very small income.

social work noun Social work involves giving help and advice to people with serious financial or family problems. > **social worker** noun

society **societies** noun
1 (CITIZENSHIP) Society is the people in a particular country or region. 2 an organisation for people who have the same interest or aim. 3 Society is also rich, upper-class, fashionable people.

> **society** noun
> 1 = civilisation, culture
> 2 = association, circle, club, fellowship, group, guild, institute, league, organisation, union

sociology noun Sociology is the study of human societies and the relationships between groups in these societies. > **sociological** adjective > **sociologist** noun

sock noun Socks are pieces of clothing covering your foot and ankle.

socket noun 1 a place on a wall or on a piece of electrical equipment into which you can put a plug or bulb. 2 Any hollow part or opening into which another part fits can be called a socket.

sod noun (literary) The sod is the surface of the ground, together with the grass and roots growing in it.

soda noun 1 Soda is the same as **soda water**. 2 Soda is also sodium in the form of crystals or a powder, and is used for baking or cleaning.

soda water noun Soda water is fizzy water used for mixing with alcoholic drinks or fruit juice.

sodden adjective soaking wet.

sodium noun (SCIENCE) Sodium is a silvery-white chemical element which combines with other chemicals. Salt is a sodium compound. Sodium's atomic number is 11 and its symbol is Na.

sofa noun a long comfortable seat with a back and arms for two or three people.

soft *adjective* **1** Something soft is not hard, stiff or firm. **2** Soft also means very gentle. **3** A soft sound or voice is quiet and not harsh. **4** A soft colour or light is not bright. > **softly** *adverb*

> **soft** *adjective*
> **1** = flexible, pliable, squashy, supple, yielding **3** = gentle, low, mellow, muted, quiet, subdued

soft drink *noun* any cold, nonalcoholic drink.

soften *verb* **1** If something is softened or softens, it becomes less hard, stiff or firm. **2** If you soften, you become more sympathetic and less critical.

software *noun* (ICT) Computer programs are known as software.

soggy soggier, soggiest *adjective* unpleasantly wet or full of water.

soil *noun* **1** Soil is the top layer on the surface of the earth in which plants grow. ▶ *verb* **2** If you soil something, you make it dirty. > **soiled** *adjective*

> **soil** *noun*
> **1** = clay, dirt, earth, ground ▶ *verb* **2** = dirty, foul, pollute, smear, spatter, stain

solace *noun* (literary) Solace is something that makes you feel less sad.

solar *adjective* **1** (SCIENCE) relating or belonging to the sun. **2** using the sun's light and heat as a source of energy.

solar system *noun* The solar system is the sun and all the planets, comets and asteroids that orbit round it.

sold the past tense and past participle of **sell**.

soldier *noun* a person in an army.

sole soles, soling, soled *adjective* **1** The sole thing or person of a particular type is the only one of that type. ▶ *noun* **2** The sole of your foot or shoe is the underneath part. **3** a flat seawater fish which you can eat. ▶ *verb* **4** When a shoe is soled, a sole is fitted to it.

solely *adverb* If something involves solely one thing, it involves that thing and nothing else.

solemn *adjective* Solemn means serious rather than cheerful or humorous. > **solemnly** *adverb* > **solemnity** *noun*

> **solemn** *adjective*
> = earnest, grave (formal), serious, sober, staid

solicitor *noun* a lawyer who gives legal advice and prepares legal documents and cases.

solid *adjective* **1** A solid substance or object is hard or firm, and not in the form of a liquid or gas. **2** You say that something is solid when it is not hollow. **3** You say that a structure is solid when it is strong and not likely to fall down. **4** You use 'solid' to say that something happens for a period of time without interruption. ▶ *noun* **5** a solid substance or object. > **solidly** *adverb*

> **solid** *adjective*
> **1** = firm, hard **3** = stable, strong, sturdy, substantial

solidarity *noun* If a group of people show solidarity, they show unity and support for each other.

soliloquy soliloquies *noun* (ENGLISH) a speech in a play made by a character who is alone on the stage.

S

solitary *adjective* 1 A solitary activity is one that you do on your own. 2 A solitary person or animal spends a lot of time alone. 3 If there is a solitary person or object somewhere, there is only one.

solitary confinement *noun* A prisoner in solitary confinement is being kept alone in a prison cell.

solitude *noun* Solitude is the state of being alone.

> **solitude** *noun*
> = isolation, loneliness, privacy, seclusion

solo **solos** *noun* 1 a piece of music played or sung by one person alone. ▶ *adjective* 2 A solo performance or activity is done by one person alone. ▶ *adverb* 3 Solo means alone.

soloist *noun* a person who performs a solo.

solstice *noun* one of the two times in the year when the sun is at its furthest point south or north of the equator.

soluble *adjective* (SCIENCE) A soluble substance is able to dissolve in liquid.

solution *noun* 1 a way of dealing with a problem or difficult situation. 2 The solution to a riddle or a puzzle is the answer. 3 (SCIENCE) a liquid in which a solid substance has been dissolved.

solve *verb* If you solve a problem or a question, you find a solution or answer to it.

> **solve** *verb*
> = clear up, crack, decipher, get to the bottom of, resolve, work out

solvent *adjective* 1 If a person or company is solvent, they have enough money to pay all their debts. ▶ *noun* 2 (SCIENCE) a liquid that can dissolve other substances. > **solvency** *noun*

Somali **Somalis** *adjective* 1 belonging or relating to Somalia. ▶ *noun* 2 The Somalis are a group of people who live in Somalia. 3 Somali is the language spoken by Somalis.

sombre *adjective* 1 Sombre colours are dark and dull. 2 A sombre person is serious, sad or gloomy.

some 1 You use 'some' to refer to a quantity or number when you are not stating the quantity or number exactly: *There's some money on the table.* 2 You use 'some' to emphasise that a quantity or number is fairly large: *She had been there for some days.* ▶ *adverb* 3 You use 'some' in front of a number to show that it is not exact: *a fishing village some seven miles north.*

somebody *pronoun* You use 'somebody' to refer to a person without saying exactly who you mean.

some day *adverb* Some day means at a date in the future that is unknown or that has not yet been decided.

somehow *adverb* 1 You use 'somehow' to say that you do not know how something was done or will be done: *You'll find a way of doing it somehow.* 2 You use 'somehow' to say that you do not know the reason for something: *Somehow it didn't feel quite right.*

someone *pronoun* You use 'someone' to refer to a person without saying exactly who you mean.

somersault noun a forwards or backwards roll in which the head is placed on the ground and the body is brought over it.

something pronoun You use 'something' to refer to anything that is not a person without saying exactly what you mean.

sometime adverb 1 at a time in the future or the past that is unknown or that has not yet been fixed: *He has to find out sometime.*
▶ adjective 2 (formal) 'Sometime' is used to say that a person had a particular job or role in the past: *a sometime actor, dancer and singer.*

sometimes adverb occasionally, rather than always or never.

> **sometimes** adverb
> = at times, every now and then, every so often, from time to time, now and again, now and then, occasionally, once in a while

somewhat adverb to some extent or degree.

somewhere adverb 1 'Somewhere' is used to refer to a place without stating exactly where it is.
2 'Somewhere' is used when giving an approximate amount, number or time: *somewhere between the winter of 2009 and the summer of 2011.*

son noun Someone's son is their male child.

sonar noun Sonar is equipment on a ship which calculates the depth of the sea or the position of an underwater object using sound waves.

sonata noun (MUSIC) a piece of classical music, usually in three or more movements, for piano or for another instrument with or without piano.

song noun a piece of music with words that are sung to the music.

songbird noun a bird that produces musical sounds like singing.

son-in-law sons-in-law noun Someone's son-in-law is the husband of their grown-up child.

sonnet noun (ENGLISH) a poem with 14 lines, in which lines rhyme according to fixed patterns.

soon adverb If something is going to happen soon, it will happen in a very short time.

> **soon** adverb
> = any minute now, before long, in a minute, in the near future, presently, shortly

soot noun Soot is black powder which rises in the smoke from a fire. > **sooty** adjective

soothe verb 1 If you soothe someone who is angry or upset, you make them calmer.
2 Something that soothes pain makes the pain less severe.
> **soothing** adjective

sophisticated adjective
1 Sophisticated people have refined or cultured tastes or habits. 2 A sophisticated machine or device is made using advanced and complicated methods. > **sophistication** noun

> **sophisticated** adjective
> 1 = cosmopolitan, cultivated, cultured, refined, urbane
> 2 = advanced, complex, complicated, elaborate, intricate, refined

soppy soppier, soppiest adjective (informal) silly or foolishly sentimental.

s

soprano sopranos noun (MUSIC) a woman, girl or boy with a singing voice in the highest range of musical notes.

sorcerer noun a person who performs magic by using the power of evil spirits.

sorcery noun Sorcery is magic that uses the power of evil spirits.

sordid adjective 1 dishonest or immoral. 2 dirty, unpleasant or miserable.

sore adjective 1 If part of your body is sore, it causes you pain and discomfort. ▶ noun 2 a painful place where your skin has become infected. > **soreness** noun

> **sore** adjective
> 1 = inflamed, painful, raw, sensitive, smarting, tender

sorghum noun a type of tropical grass that is grown for hay, grain and syrup.

sorrow noun 1 Sorrow is deep sadness or regret. 2 Sorrows are things that cause sorrow.

> **sorrow** noun
> 1 = grief, heartache, melancholy (literary), misery, mourning, pain, regret, sadness, unhappiness, woe (formal)
> 2 = hardship, heartache, misfortune, trouble, woe (formal), worry

sorry sorrier, sorriest adjective 1 If you are sorry about something, you feel sadness or regret about it. 2 feeling sympathy for someone. 3 'Sorry' is used to describe people and things that are in a bad physical or mental state.

> **sorry** adjective
> 1 = apologetic, penitent, regretful, remorseful, repentant 2 = moved, sympathetic 3 = deplorable, miserable, pathetic, pitiful, poor, sad, wretched

sort noun 1 The different sorts of something are the different types of it. ▶ verb 2 To sort things means to arrange them into different groups or sorts. > **sort out** verb If you sort out a problem or misunderstanding, you deal with it and find a solution to it.

> **sort** noun
> 1 = brand, category, class, group, kind, make, species, style, type, variety
> ▶ verb 2 = arrange, categorise, classify, divide, grade, group, separate

SOS noun An SOS is a signal that you are in danger and need help.

so-so adjective (informal) neither good nor bad.

soufflé; also spelt **souffle** noun a light, fluffy food made from beaten egg whites and other ingredients that is baked in the oven.

sought the past tense and past participle of **seek**.

soul noun 1 (RE) A person's soul is the spiritual part of them that is supposed to continue after their body is dead. 2 People also use 'soul' to refer to a person's mind, character, thoughts and feelings. 3 'Soul' can be used to mean person. 4 Soul is a type of pop music.

sound noun 1 SCIENCE Sound is everything that can be heard. It is caused by vibrations travelling through air or water to your ear.

S

2 A particular sound is something that you hear. **3** The sound of someone or something is the impression you have of them through what other people have told you: *I like the sound of your father's grandfather*. ▶ *verb* **4** If something sounds or if you sound it, it makes a noise. **5** To sound something deep, such as a well or the sea, means to measure how deep it is using a weighted line or sonar. ▶ *adjective* **6** in good condition. **7** reliable and sensible. > **soundly** *adverb*

> **sound** *noun*
> 1 = din, hubbub, noise, racket, tone
> ▶ *verb* 4 = blow, chime, clang, peal, ring, set off, toll
> ▶ *adjective* 6 = all right, fine, fit, healthy, in good condition, intact, robust 7 = down-to-earth, good, reasonable, reliable, sensible, solid, valid

soundtrack *noun* The soundtrack of a film is the part you hear, especially the music.

soup *noun* Soup is liquid food made by cooking meat, fish or vegetables in water.

sour *adjective* **1** If something is sour, it has a sharp, acid taste. **2** Sour milk has an unpleasant taste because it is no longer fresh. **3** A sour person is bad-tempered and unfriendly. ▶ *verb* **4** If a friendship, situation or attitude sours or if something sours it, it becomes less friendly, enjoyable or hopeful.

> **sour** *adjective*
> 1 = acid, bitter, pungent, sharp, tart 2 = curdled, off, rancid
> 3 = disagreeable, embittered, jaundiced, tart

source *noun* **1** The source of something is the person, place or thing that it comes from. **2** A source is a person or book that provides information for a news story or for research.
3 (GEOGRAPHY) The source of a river or stream is the place where it begins.

> **source** *noun*
> 1 = beginning, cause, derivation, origin, originator

sour grapes *plural noun* You describe someone's behaviour as sour grapes when they say something is worthless but secretly want it and cannot have it.

south *noun* **1** The south is the direction to your right when you are looking towards the place where the sun rises. **2** The south of a place or country is the part which is towards the south when you are in the centre. ▶ *adverb, adjective* **3** South means towards the south. ▶ *adjective* **4** A south wind blows from the south.

South America *noun* South America is the fourth largest continent. It has the Pacific Ocean on its west side, the Atlantic on the east, and the Antarctic to the south. South America is joined to Central America by the Isthmus of Panama. > **South American** *adjective*

south-east *noun, adverb, adjective* South-east is halfway between south and east.

south-eastern *adjective* in or from the south-east.

southerly *adjective* **1** Southerly means to or towards the south.

s

2 A southern wind blows from the south.

southern *adjective* in or from the south.

Southern Cross *noun* The Southern Cross is a small group of stars which can be seen from the southern part of the earth, and which is represented on the national flags of Australia and New Zealand.

South Pole *noun* (GEOGRAPHY) The South Pole is the most southerly place on the surface of the earth.

southward or **southwards** *adverb* 1 Southward or southwards means towards the south.
▶ *adjective* 2 The southward part of something is the south part.

south-west *noun, adverb, adjective* South-west is halfway between south and west.

south-western *adjective* in or from the south-west.

souvenir *noun* something you keep to remind you of a holiday, place or event.

> **souvenir** *noun*
> = keepsake, memento, relic, reminder

sovereign *noun* 1 a king, queen or royal ruler of a country. 2 In the past, a sovereign was a British gold coin worth one pound.
▶ *adjective* 3 A sovereign state or country is independent and not under the authority of any other country.

sovereignty *noun* Sovereignty is the political power that a country has to govern itself.

Soviet (HISTORY) *adjective* 1 belonging or relating to the Soviet Union, a former country consisting of Russia and

neighbouring states. ▶ *noun* 2 The people and the government of the Soviet Union were sometimes referred to as the Soviets.

sow[1] sows, sowing, sowed, sown *verb* 1 To sow seeds or sow an area of land with seeds means to plant them in the ground. 2 To sow undesirable feelings or attitudes means to cause them.

sow[2] sows *noun* an adult female pig.

soya *noun* Soya flour, margarine, oil and milk are made from soya beans.

spa *noun* a place where water containing minerals bubbles out of the ground, at which people drink or bathe in the water to improve their health.

space *noun* 1 Space is the area that is empty or available in a place, building or container. 2 Space is the area beyond the earth's atmosphere surrounding the stars and planets. 3 a gap between two things. 4 Space can also refer to a period of time: *two incidents in the space of a week.* ▶ *verb* 5 If you space a series of things, you arrange them with gaps between them.

> **space** *noun*
> 1 = accommodation, capacity, room 3 = blank, distance, gap, interval 4 = interval, period, span, time, while

spacecraft *noun* a rocket or other vehicle that can travel in space.

spaceship *noun* a spacecraft that carries people through space.

spacious *adjective* having or providing a lot of space.

> **spacious** *adjective*
> = ample, broad, expansive, extensive, huge, large, vast

s

spade noun 1 a tool with a flat metal blade and a long handle used for digging. 2 Spades is one of the four suits in a pack of playing cards. It is marked by a black symbol like a heart-shaped leaf with a stem.

spaghetti noun Spaghetti consists of long, thin pieces of pasta.

spam noun unwanted emails, usually containing advertising.

span spans, spanning, spanned noun 1 the period of time during which something exists or functions. 2 The span of something is the total length of it from one end to the other. ▶ verb 3 If something spans a particular length of time, it lasts throughout that time. 4 A bridge that spans something stretches right across it.

Spaniard noun someone who comes from Spain.

spaniel noun a dog with long drooping ears and a silky coat.

Spanish adjective 1 belonging or relating to Spain. ▶ noun 2 Spanish is the main language spoken in Spain, and is also spoken by many people in Central and South America.

spanner noun a tool with a specially shaped end that fits round a nut to turn it.

spar spars, sparring, sparred verb 1 When boxers spar, they hit each other with light punches for practice. 2 To spar with someone also means to argue with them, but not in an unpleasant or serious way. ▶ noun 3 a strong pole that a sail is attached to on a yacht or ship.

spare adjective 1 extra to what is needed. ▶ noun 2 a thing that is extra to what is needed. ▶ verb 3 If you spare something for a particular purpose, you make it available. 4 If someone is spared an unpleasant experience, they are prevented from suffering it.

> **spare** adjective
> 1 = extra, free, superfluous, surplus
> ▶ verb 3 = afford, give, let someone have 4 = let off (informal), pardon, relieve of, save from

sparing adjective If you are sparing with something, you use it in very small quantities. > **sparingly** adverb

spark noun 1 a tiny, bright piece of burning material thrown up by a fire. 2 a small flash of light caused by electricity. 3 A spark of feeling is a small amount of it. ▶ verb 4 If something sparks, it throws out sparks. 5 If one thing sparks another thing off, it causes the second thing to start happening.

sparkle verb 1 If something sparkles, it shines with a lot of small, bright points of light. ▶ noun 2 Sparkles are small, bright points of light. > **sparkling** adjective

> **sparkle** verb
> 1 = gleam, glisten, glitter, shimmer, twinkle

sparrow noun a common small bird with brown and grey feathers.

sparse adjective small in number or amount and spread out over an area. > **sparsely** adverb

spartan adjective A spartan way of life is very simple with no luxuries.

S

spasm noun 1 a sudden tightening of the muscles. 2 a sudden, short burst of something.

spat the past tense and past participle of **spit**.

spate noun A spate of things is a large number of them that happen or appear in a rush.

spatial adjective to do with size, area or position.

spawn noun 1 Spawn is a jelly-like substance containing the eggs of fish or amphibians. ▸ verb 2 When fish or amphibians spawn, they lay their eggs. 3 If something spawns something else, it causes it.

speak speaks, speaking, spoke, spoken verb 1 When you speak, you use your voice to say words. 2 If you speak a foreign language, you know it and can use it. ▸ **speak out** verb 2 To speak out about something means to publicly state an opinion about it.

speaker noun 1 a person who is speaking, especially someone making a speech. 2 A speaker on a device that reproduces sound is a loudspeaker.

spear noun 1 a weapon consisting of a long pole with a sharp point. ▸ verb 2 To spear something means to push or throw a spear or other pointed object into it.

spearhead verb If someone spearheads a campaign, they lead it.

special adjective 1 Something special is more important or better than other things of its kind. 2 Special describes someone who is officially appointed, or something that is needed for a particular purpose: *Karen actually had to get special permission to go there.*

3 Special also describes something that belongs or relates to only one particular person, group or place.

> **special** adjective
> 1 = exceptional, important, significant, unique
> 3 = characteristic, distinctive, individual, particular, peculiar, specific

specialise; also spelt **specialize** verb If you specialise in something, you make it your speciality. ▸ **specialisation** noun

specialised; also spelt **specialized** adjective developed for a particular purpose or trained in a particular area of knowledge.

specialist noun 1 someone who has a particular skill or who knows a lot about a particular subject. ▸ adjective 2 having a skill or knowing a lot about a particular subject. ▸ **specialism** noun

speciality specialities noun A person's speciality is something they are especially good at or know a lot about.

specially adverb If something has been done specially for a particular person or purpose, it has been done only for that person or purpose.

species species noun (SCIENCE) a division of plants or animals whose members have the same characteristics and are able to breed with each other.

specific adjective 1 particular. 2 precise and exact. ▸ **specifically** adverb

specification noun (DGT) a detailed description of what is needed for something, such as the necessary features in the design of something.

specify specifies, specifying, specified verb To specify something means to state or describe it precisely.

> **specify** verb
> = be specific about, indicate, name, spell out, state, stipulate

specimen noun A specimen of something is an example or small amount of it which gives an idea of what the whole is like.

speck noun a very small stain or amount of something.

speckled adjective Something that is speckled is covered in very small marks or spots.

spectacle noun 1 a strange or interesting sight or scene. 2 a grand and impressive event or performance.

spectacular adjective 1 Something spectacular is very impressive or dramatic. ▶ noun 2 a grand and impressive show or performance.

spectator noun a person who is watching something.

> **spectator** noun
> = bystander, eyewitness, observer, onlooker, witness

spectre noun 1 a frightening idea or image. 2 a ghost.

spectrum spectra or spectrums noun 1 (ART) The spectrum is the range of different colours produced when light passes through a prism or a drop of water. A rainbow shows the colours in a spectrum. 2 A spectrum of opinions or emotions is a range of them.

speculate verb If you speculate

about something, you think about it and form opinions about it. ▶ **speculation** noun

speculative adjective A speculative piece of information is based on guesses and opinions rather than known facts.

speech noun 1 Speech is the ability to speak or the act of speaking. 2 a formal talk given to an audience. 3 In a play, a speech is a group of lines spoken by one of the characters.

> **speech** noun
> 2 = address, discourse, lecture, talk

speechless adjective Someone who is speechless is unable to speak for a short time because something has shocked them.

speed speeds, speeding, sped or speeded noun 1 The speed of something is the rate at which it moves or happens. 2 Speed is very fast movement or travel. ▶ verb 3 If you speed somewhere, you move or travel there quickly. 4 Someone who is speeding is driving a vehicle faster than the legal speed limit.

> **speed** noun
> 1 = haste, hurry, momentum, pace, rapidity, swiftness, velocity
> ▶ verb 3 = career, flash, gallop, race, rush, tear

speedboat noun a small, fast motorboat.

speed limit noun The speed limit is the maximum speed at which vehicles are legally allowed to drive on a particular road.

speedway noun Speedway is the sport of racing lightweight motorcycles on special tracks.

speedy speedier, speediest
adjective done very quickly.
> **speedily** *adverb*

spell spells, spelling, spelt or
spelled *verb* 1 When you spell a
word, you name or write its
letters in order. 2 When letters
spell a word, they form that word
when put together in a particular
order. 3 If something spells a
particular result, it suggests that
this will be the result. ▶ *noun*
4 A spell of something is a short
period of it. 5 a word or sequence
of words used to perform magic.
> **spell out** *verb* If you spell
something out, you explain
it in detail.

spellbound *adjective* so fascinated
by something that you cannot
think about anything else.

spelling *noun* The spelling of a
word is the correct order of letters
in it.

spend spends, spending, spent
verb 1 When you spend money, you
buy things with it. 2 To spend
time or energy means to use it.

spent *adjective* 1 Spent describes
things which have been used and
therefore cannot be used again.
2 If you are spent, you are
exhausted and have no energy
left.

sperm *noun* a cell produced in the
reproductive organ of a male
animal which can enter a female
animal's egg and fertilise it.

spew *verb* 1 When things spew
from something or when it spews
them out, they come out of it in
large quantities. 2 (*informal*) To
spew means to vomit.

sphere *noun* 1 a perfectly round
object, such as a ball. 2 An area of
activity or interest can be referred

to as a sphere of activity or
interest. ▶ **spherical** *adjective*

spice *noun* 1 Spice is powder or
seeds from a plant added to food
to give it flavour. 2 Spice is
something which makes life
more exciting. ▶ *verb* 3 To spice
food means to add spice to it.
4 If you spice something up, you
make it more exciting or lively.

spicy spicier, spiciest *adjective*
strongly flavoured with spices.

spider *noun* a small insect-like
creature with eight legs that
spins webs to catch insects for
food.

spike *noun* 1 a long pointed piece
of metal. 2 The spikes on a sports
shoe are the pointed pieces of
metal attached to the sole.
3 Some other long pointed objects
are called spikes.

spiky spikier, spikiest *adjective*
Something spiky has sharp
points.

spill spills, spilling, spilled or
spilt *verb* 1 If you spill something or if it
spills, it accidentally falls or runs
out of a container. 2 If people or
things spill out of a place, they
come out of it in large numbers.

spillage *noun* the spilling of
something, or something that
has been spilt.

spin spins, spinning, spun *verb* 1 If
something spins, it turns quickly
around a central point. 2 When
spiders spin a web, they give out a
sticky substance and make it into
a web. 3 When people spin, they
make thread by twisting together
pieces of fibre using a machine.
4 If your head is spinning, you
feel dizzy or confused. ▶ *noun* 5 a
rapid turn around a central point.
> **spin out** *verb* If you spin

something out, you make it last longer than it otherwise would.

spin *verb*
1 = pirouette, revolve, rotate, turn, whirl

spinach *noun* Spinach is a vegetable with large green leaves.

spinal *adjective* to do with the spine.

spine *noun* 1 Your spine is your backbone. 2 Spines are long, sharp points on an animal's body or on a plant.

spin-off *noun* something useful that unexpectedly results from an activity.

spinster *noun* (*old-fashioned*) a woman who has never married.

spiny spinier, spiniest *adjective* covered with spines.

spiral spirals, spiralling, spiralled *noun* 1 a continuous curve which winds round and round, with each curve above or outside the previous one. ▶ *adjective* 2 in the shape of a spiral. ▶ *verb* 3 If something spirals, it moves up or down in a spiral curve. 4 If an amount or level spirals, it rises or falls quickly at an increasing rate.

spire *noun* The spire of a church is the tall cone-shaped structure on top.

spirit *noun* 1 Your spirit is the part of you that is not physical and that is connected with your deepest thoughts and feelings. 2 RE The spirit of a dead person is a nonphysical part that is believed to remain alive after death. 3 a supernatural being, such as a ghost. 4 Spirit is liveliness, energy and self-confidence. 5 Spirit can refer to an attitude: *his old fighting spirit*. 6 (*in plural*) Spirits can describe how happy or unhappy someone is: *in good spirits*. 7 Spirits are strong alcoholic drinks such as whisky and gin. ▶ *verb* 8 If you spirit someone or something into or out of a place, you get them in or out quickly and secretly.

spirit *noun*
1 = life force, soul 3 = apparition, ghost, phantom, spectre, sprite 4 = animation, energy, enthusiasm, fire, force, vigour, zest

spirited *adjective* showing energy and courage.

spiritual *adjective* 1 to do with people's thoughts and beliefs, rather than their bodies and physical surroundings. 2 RE to do with people's religious beliefs. ▶ *noun* 3 a religious song originally sung by enslaved Black people in America. > **spiritually** *adverb* > **spirituality** *noun*

spit spits, spitting, spat *noun* 1 Spit is saliva. 2 a long thin stick made of metal or wood which is pushed through a piece of meat so that it can be hung over a fire and cooked. 3 GEOGRAPHY a long, flat, narrow piece of land sticking out into the sea. ▶ *verb* 4 If you spit, you force saliva or some other substance out of your mouth. 5 (*informal*) When it is spitting, it is raining very lightly.

spite *phrase* 1 If you do something in spite of something else, you do the first thing even though the second thing is unpleasant or difficult. ▶ *verb* 2 If you do something to spite someone, you do it deliberately to hurt or annoy them. ▶ *noun* 3 If you do something out of spite, you do it to hurt or annoy someone.

s

spite *phrase*
1 **in spite of** = despite, even though, notwithstanding, regardless of, though,
▶ *noun* 3 = ill will, malevolence, malice, spitefulness, venom

spiteful *adjective* A spiteful person does or says nasty things to people deliberately to hurt them.

spiteful *adjective*
= catty (*informal*), cruel, malevolent, malicious, nasty, snide, venomous, vindictive

splash *verb* 1 If you splash around in water, your movements disturb the water in a noisy way. 2 If liquid splashes something, it scatters over it in a lot of small drops. ▶ *noun* 3 A splash is the sound made when something hits or falls into water. 4 A splash of liquid is a small quantity of it that has been spilt on something. > **splash out** *verb* To splash out on something means to spend a lot of money on it.

splatter *verb* When something is splattered with a substance, the substance is splashed all over it.

spleen *noun* Your spleen is an organ near your stomach which controls the quality of your blood.

splendid *adjective* 1 very good indeed. 2 beautiful and impressive. > **splendidly** *adverb*

splendid *adjective*
1 = cracking (*British, Australian and New Zealand; informal*), excellent, fantastic (*informal*), fine, glorious, great (*informal*), marvellous, wonderful
2 = gorgeous, grand, imposing, impressive, magnificent, superb

splendour *noun* 1 If something has splendour, it is beautiful and impressive. 2 (*in plural*) The splendours of something are its beautiful and impressive features.

splint *noun* a long piece of wood or metal fastened to a broken limb to hold it in place.

splinter *noun* 1 a thin, sharp piece of wood or glass which has broken off a larger piece. ▶ *verb* 2 If something splinters, it breaks into thin, sharp pieces.

split splits, splitting, split *verb* 1 If something splits or if you split it, it divides into two or more parts. 2 If something such as wood or fabric splits, a long crack or tear appears in it. 3 If people split something, they share it between them. ▶ *noun* 4 A split in a piece of wood or fabric is a crack or tear. 5 A split between two things is a division or difference between them. > **split up** *verb* If two people split up, they end their relationship or marriage.

split *verb*
1 = diverge, fork, part, separate
2 = burst, come apart, crack, rip
▶ *noun* 4 = crack, fissure, rip, tear 5 = breach, breakup, divergence, division, rift, schism

split second *noun* an extremely short period of time.

splitting *adjective* A splitting headache is a very painful headache.

splutter *verb* 1 If someone splutters, they speak in a confused way because they are embarrassed. 2 If something splutters, it makes a series of short, sharp sounds.

s

spoil spoils, spoiling, spoiled or spoilt *verb* **1** If you spoil something, you prevent it from being successful or satisfactory. **2** To spoil children means to give them everything they want, with harmful effects on their character. **3** To spoil someone also means to give them something nice as a treat.

> **spoil** *verb*
> **1** = damage, destroy, harm, impair, mar, mess up, ruin, wreck **2** = cosset, indulge, pamper

spoke **1** Spoke is the past tense of **speak**. ▶ *noun* **2** The spokes of a wheel are the bars which connect the hub to the rim.

spoken the past participle of **speak**.

spokesperson *noun* someone who speaks on behalf of another person or a group. > **spokesman** *noun* > **spokeswoman** *noun*

sponge *noun* **1** a sea creature with a body made up of many cells. **2** part of the very light skeleton of a sponge, used for bathing and cleaning. **3** A sponge or sponge cake is a very light cake. ▶ *verb* **4** If you sponge something, you clean it by wiping it with a wet sponge.

sponsor *verb* **1** To sponsor something, such as an event or someone's training, means to support it financially. **2** If you sponsor someone who is doing something for charity, you agree to give them a sum of money for the charity if they manage to do it. **3** If you sponsor a proposal or suggestion, you officially put it forward and support it. ▶ *noun* **4** a person or organisation sponsoring something or someone. > **sponsorship** *noun*

spontaneous *adjective* **1** Spontaneous acts are not planned or arranged in advance. **2** A spontaneous event happens because of processes within something rather than being caused by things outside it. > **spontaneously** *adverb* > **spontaneity** *noun*

spoof *noun* something such as an article or television programme that seems to be about a serious matter but is actually a joke.

spooky spookier, spookiest *adjective* eerie and frightening.

> **spooky** *adjective*
> = creepy (*informal*), eerie, frightening, ghostly, haunted, scary (*informal*), supernatural, uncanny

spool *noun* a cylindrical object onto which thread, tape or film can be wound.

spoon *noun* an object shaped like a small shallow bowl with a long handle, used for eating, stirring and serving food.

spoonful spoonfuls or spoonsful *noun* the amount held by a spoon.

sporadic *adjective* happening at irregular intervals. > **sporadically** *adverb*

spore *noun* (SCIENCE) Spores are cells produced by bacteria and nonflowering plants such as fungi which develop into new bacteria or plants.

sport *noun* **1** Sports are games and other enjoyable activities which need physical effort and skill. **2** (*informal*) You say that someone is a sport when they accept defeat or teasing cheerfully. ▶ *verb* **3** If you sport something noticeable or unusual, you wear it.

s

sporting adjective 1 relating to sport. 2 behaving in a fair and decent way.

sports car noun A low, fast car, usually with room for only two people.

sportsman sportsmen noun a man who takes part in sports and is good at them.

sportsmanship noun Sportsmanship is the behaviour and attitudes of a good sportsman or sportswoman, for example fairness, generosity and cheerfulness when losing.

sportsperson sportspeople noun a person who takes part in sports and is good at them.

sportswoman sportswomen noun a woman who takes part in sports and is good at them.

sporty sportier, sportiest adjective 1 A sporty car is fast and flashy. 2 A sporty person is good at sports.

spot spots, spotting, spotted noun 1 Spots are small, round, coloured areas on a surface. 2 Spots on a person's skin are small lumps, usually caused by an infection or allergy. 3 A spot of something is a small amount of it. 4 A place can be called a spot. ▶ verb 5 If you spot something, you notice it. ▶ phrase 6 If you do something on the spot, you do it immediately.

> **spot** noun
> 1 = blemish, blot, blotch, mark, smudge, speck 4 = location, place, point, position, scene, site
> ▶ verb 5 = catch sight of, detect, discern, observe, see, sight

spotless adjective perfectly clean.
> **spotlessly** adverb

spotlight spotlights, spotlighting, spotlit or spotlighted noun 1 (DRAMA) a powerful light which can be directed to light up a small area. ▶ verb 2 If something spotlights a situation or problem, it draws the public's attention to it.

spot-on adjective (informal) exactly correct or accurate.

spotted adjective Something spotted has a pattern of spots on it.

spotty spottier, spottiest adjective Someone who is spotty has spots or pimples on their skin, especially on their face.

spouse noun Someone's spouse is the person they are married to.

spout verb 1 When liquid or flame spouts out of something, it shoots out in a long stream. 2 When someone spouts what they have learned, they say it in a boring way. ▶ noun 3 a tube with a lip-like end for pouring liquid.

sprain verb 1 If you sprain a joint, you accidentally damage it by twisting it violently. ▶ noun 2 the injury caused by spraining a joint.

sprang the past tense of **spring**.

sprawl verb 1 If you sprawl somewhere, you sit or lie there with your legs and arms spread out. 2 A place that sprawls is spread out over a large area.
> **sprawling** adjective

spray noun 1 Spray consists of many drops of liquid splashed or forced into the air. 2 Spray is also a liquid kept under pressure in a can or other container. 3 A spray of flowers or leaves consists of several of them on one stem. ▶ verb 4 To spray a liquid over something means to cover it with drops of the liquid.

spread spreads, spreading, spread
verb 1 If you spread something out, you open it out or arrange it so that it can be seen or used easily. 2 If you spread a substance on a surface, you put a thin layer on the surface. 3 If something spreads, it gradually reaches or affects more people. 4 If something spreads over a period of time, it happens regularly or continuously over that time. 5 If something such as work is spread, it is distributed evenly. ▶ *noun* 6 The spread of something is the extent to which it gradually reaches or affects more people. 7 A spread of ideas, interests or other things is a wide variety of them. 8 soft food put on bread: *cheese spread*.

> **spread** *verb*
> 1 = extend, fan out, open, sprawl, unfold, unfurl, unroll
> 2 = apply, coat, cover, overlay, plaster, smear, smother
> 3 = circulate, grow, expand, increase, proliferate, travel
> ▶ *noun* 6 = diffusion, expansion, extent, growth, increase, progression, proliferation, upsurge

spreadsheet *noun* (ICT) a computer program that is used for entering and arranging figures, used mainly for financial planning.

spree *noun* a period of time spent doing something enjoyable.

sprig *noun* 1 a small twig with leaves on it. 2 In Australian and New Zealand English, sprigs are studs on the sole of a football boot.

sprightly sprightlier, sprightliest
adjective lively and active.

spring springs, springing, sprang, sprung *noun* 1 Spring is the season between winter and summer. 2 a coil of wire which returns to its natural shape after being pressed or pulled. 3 a place where water comes up through the ground. 4 an act of springing. ▶ *verb* 5 To spring means to jump upwards or forwards. 6 If something springs in a particular direction, it moves suddenly and quickly. 7 If one thing springs from another, it is the result of it.

springboard *noun* 1 a flexible board on which a diver or gymnast jumps to gain height. 2 If something is a springboard for an activity or enterprise, it makes it possible for it to begin.

springbok *noun* 1 a small South African antelope which moves in leaps. 2 A Springbok is a person who has represented South Africa in a sports team.

spring onion *noun* a small onion with long green shoots, often eaten raw in salads.

sprinkle *verb* If you sprinkle a liquid or powder over something, you scatter it over it.

sprinkling *noun* A sprinkling of something is a small quantity of it.

sprint *noun* 1 a short, fast race. ▶ *verb* 2 To sprint means to run fast over a short distance.

sprinter *noun* an athlete who runs fast over short distances.

sprout *verb* 1 When something sprouts, it grows. 2 If things sprout up, they appear rapidly. ▶ *noun* 3 A sprout is the same as a **Brussels sprout**.

spruce noun 1 an evergreen tree with needle-like leaves. ▶ adjective 2 Someone who is spruce is very neat and smart. ▶ verb 3 To spruce something up means to make it neat and smart.

sprung the past participle of **spring**.

spun the past tense and past participle of **spin**.

spur spurs, spurring, spurred verb 1 If something spurs you to do something or spurs you on, it encourages you to do it. ▶ noun 2 Something that acts as a spur encourages a person to do something. 3 Spurs are sharp metal points attached to the heels of a rider's boots and used to urge a horse on. ▶ phrase 4 If you do something **on the spur of the moment**, you do it suddenly, without planning it.

spurious adjective not genuine or real.

spurn verb If you spurn something, you refuse to accept it.

spurt verb 1 When a liquid or flame spurts out of something, it comes out quickly in a thick, powerful stream. ▶ noun 2 A spurt of liquid or flame is a thick powerful stream of it. 3 A spurt of activity or effort is a sudden, brief period of it.

spy spies, spying, spied noun 1 a person sent to find out secret information about a country or organisation. ▶ verb 2 Someone who spies tries to find out secret information about another country or organisation. 3 If you spy on someone, you watch them secretly. 4 If you spy something, you notice it.

squabble verb 1 When people squabble, they quarrel about something trivial. ▶ noun 2 a quarrel.

> **squabble** verb
> 1 = argue, bicker, fall out (informal), feud, fight, quarrel, row, wrangle
> ▶ noun 2 = altercation, argument, barney (British, Australian and New Zealand; informal), disagreement, dispute, fight, quarrel, row, tiff

squad noun a small group chosen to do a particular activity.

squadron noun a section of one of the armed forces, especially the air force.

squalid adjective 1 dirty, untidy and in bad condition. 2 Squalid activities are unpleasant and often dishonest.

squall noun a brief, violent storm.

squalor noun Squalor consists of bad or dirty conditions or surroundings.

squander verb To squander money or resources means to waste them.

square noun 1 (MATHS) a shape with four equal sides and four right angles. 2 In a town or city, a square is a flat, open place, bordered by buildings or streets. 3 (MATHS) The square of a number is the number multiplied by itself. For example, the square of 3, written 3^2, is 3×3. ▶ adjective 4 shaped like a square. 5 'Square' is used before units of length when talking about the area of something: 24 square metres. 6 'Square' is used after units of length when you are giving the length of each side of something square: *a towel measuring a foot square.* ▶ verb 7 (MATHS) If you square a number, you multiply it by itself.

squarely adverb 1 Squarely means directly rather than indirectly or at an angle. 2 If you approach a subject squarely, you consider it fully, without trying to avoid unpleasant aspects of it.

squash verb 1 If you squash something, you press it, so that it becomes flat or loses its shape. ▶ noun 2 If there is a squash in a place, there are a lot of people squashed in it. 3 Squash is a game in which two players hit a small rubber ball against the walls of a court using rackets. 4 Squash is a drink made from fruit juice, sugar and water.

squat squats, squatting, squatted; squatter, squattest verb 1 If you squat down, you crouch, balancing on your feet with your legs bent. 2 A person who squats in an unused building lives there as a squatter. ▶ noun 3 a building used by squatters. ▶ adjective 4 short and thick.

squatter noun 1 a person who lives in an unused building without permission and without paying rent. 2 In Australian English, a squatter is someone who owns a large amount of land for sheep or cattle farming. 3 In Australia and New Zealand in the past, a squatter was someone who rented land from the King or Queen.

squawk verb 1 When a bird squawks, it makes a loud, harsh noise. ▶ noun 2 a loud, harsh noise made by a bird.

squeak verb 1 If something squeaks, it makes a short, high-pitched sound. ▶ noun 2 a short, high-pitched sound. > **squeaky** adjective

squeal verb 1 When things or people squeal, they make long, high-pitched sounds. ▶ noun 2 a long, high-pitched sound.

squeamish adjective easily upset by unpleasant sights or situations.

squeeze verb 1 When you squeeze something, you press it firmly from two sides. 2 If you squeeze something into a small amount of time or space, you manage to fit it in. ▶ noun 3 If you give something a squeeze, you squeeze it. 4 If getting into something is a squeeze, it is just possible to fit into it.

squid noun a sea creature with a long soft body and many tentacles.

squint verb 1 If you squint at something, you look at it with your eyes screwed up. ▶ noun 2 If someone has a squint, their eyes look in different directions from each other.

squire noun (HISTORY) In a village, the squire was a gentleman who owned a large house with a lot of land.

squirm verb If you squirm, you wriggle and twist your body about, usually because you are nervous or embarrassed.

squirrel noun a small furry mammal with a long bushy tail.

squirt verb 1 If a liquid squirts, it comes out of a narrow opening in a thin, fast stream. ▶ noun 2 a thin, fast stream of liquid.

s

Sri Lankan adjective 1 belonging or relating to Sri Lanka. ▶ noun 2 someone who comes from Sri Lanka.

stab stabs, stabbing, stabbed verb 1 To stab someone means to wound them by pushing a knife into their body. 2 To stab at something means to push at it sharply with your finger or with something long and narrow. ▶ phrase 3 (informal) If you **have a stab** at something, you try to do it. ▶ noun 4 You can refer to a sudden unpleasant feeling as a stab of something.

stable adjective 1 not likely to change or come to an end suddenly. 2 firmly fixed or balanced and not likely to move, wobble or fall. ▶ noun 3 a building in which horses are kept. > **stability** noun > **stabilise** verb

staccato adjective consisting of a series of short, sharp, separate sounds.

stack noun 1 A stack of things is a pile of them, one on top of the other. ▶ verb 2 If you stack things, you arrange them one on top of the other in a pile.

stadium noun a sports ground with rows of seats around it.

staff noun 1 The staff of an organisation are the people who work for it. ▶ verb 2 To staff an organisation means to find and employ people to work in it. 3 If an organisation is staffed by particular people, they are the people who work for it.

staff noun
1 = employees, personnel, team, workers, workforce

stag noun an adult male deer.

stage noun 1 a part of a process that lasts for a period of time. 2 (DRAMA) In a theatre, the stage is a raised platform where the actors or entertainers perform. 3 (DRAMA) You can refer to the profession of acting as the stage. ▶ verb 4 If someone stages a play or event, they organise it and present it or take part in it.

stage noun
1 = lap, period, phase, point, step
▶ verb 4 = arrange, engineer, mount, orchestrate, organise

stagger verb 1 If you stagger, you walk unsteadily, for example because you are ill. 2 If something staggers you, it amazes you. 3 If events are staggered, they are arranged so that they do not all happen at the same time. > **staggering** adjective > **staggered** adjective

stagnant adjective Stagnant water is not flowing and is unhealthy and dirty.

staid adjective serious and dull.

stain noun 1 a mark on something that is difficult to remove. ▶ verb 2 If a substance stains something, the thing becomes marked or coloured by it.

stain noun
1 = blot, mark, spot
▶ verb 2 = dirty, mark, soil, spot

stained glass noun Stained glass is coloured pieces of glass held together with strips of lead.

stainless steel noun Stainless steel is a metal made from steel and chromium which does not rust.

stair *noun* Stairs are a set of steps inside a building going from one floor to another.

staircase *noun* a set of stairs.

stairway *noun* a set of stairs.

stake *phrase* 1 If something is **at stake**, it might be lost or damaged if something else is not successful. ▶ *verb* 2 If you say you would stake your money, life or reputation on the success or truth of something, you mean you would risk it. ▶ *noun* 3 If you have a stake in something such as a business, you own part of it and its success is important to you. 4 a pointed wooden post that can be hammered into the ground and used as a support. 5 (*in plural*) The stakes involved in something are the things that can be lost or gained.

stale *adjective* 1 Stale food or air is no longer fresh. 2 If you feel stale, you have no new ideas and are bored.

> **stale** *adjective*
> 1 = flat, old, sour, stagnant

stalemate *noun* 1 Stalemate is a situation in which neither side in an argument or contest can win. 2 In chess, stalemate is a situation in which a player cannot make any move permitted by the rules, so that the game ends and no-one wins.

stalk *noun* 1 The stalk of a flower or leaf is its stem. ▶ *verb* 2 To stalk a person or animal means to follow them quietly in order to catch, kill or observe them. 3 If someone stalks into a room, they walk in a stiff, proud or angry way.

stall *noun* 1 a large table containing goods for sale or information. 2 (*in plural*) In a theatre, the stalls are the seats at the lowest level, in front of the stage. ▶ *verb* 3 When a vehicle stalls, the engine suddenly stops. 4 If you stall when someone asks you to do something, you try to avoid doing it until a later time.

stallion *noun* an adult male horse that can be used for breeding.

stamina *noun* Stamina is the physical or mental energy needed to do something for a very long time.

stammer *verb* 1 When someone stammers, they speak with difficulty, repeating words and sounds and hesitating awkwardly. ▶ *noun* 2 Someone who has a stammer tends to stammer when they speak.

stamp *noun* 1 a small piece of gummed paper which you stick on a letter or parcel before posting it. 2 a small block with a pattern cut into it, which you press onto an inky pad and make a mark with it on paper; also the mark made by the stamp. 3 If something bears the stamp of a particular quality or person, it shows clear signs of that quality or of the person's style or characteristics. ▶ *verb* 4 If you stamp a piece of paper, you make a mark on it using a stamp. 5 If you stamp, you lift your foot and put it down hard on the ground. > **stamp out** *verb* To stamp something out means to put an end to it.

stampede *verb* 1 When a group of animals stampede, they run in a wild, uncontrolled way. ▶ *noun* 2 a group of animals stampeding.

s

stance noun Your stance on a particular matter is your attitude and way of dealing with it.

stand stands, standing, stood verb 1 If you are standing, you are upright, your legs are straight, and your weight is supported by your feet. When you stand up, you get into a standing position. 2 If something stands somewhere, that is where it is. 3 If you stand something somewhere, you put it there in an upright position. 4 If a decision or offer stands, it is still valid. 5 You can use 'stand' when describing the state or condition of something: *Youth unemployment stands at 35 per cent.* 6 If a letter stands for a particular word, it is an abbreviation for that word. 7 If you say you will not stand for something, you mean you will not tolerate it. 8 If something can stand a situation or test, it is good enough or strong enough not to be damaged by it. 9 If you cannot stand something, you cannot bear it. 10 If you stand in an election, you are one of the candidates. ▶ phrase 11 When someone **stands trial**, they are tried in a court of law. ▶ noun 12 a stall or very small shop outdoors or in a large public building. 13 a large structure at a sports ground, where the spectators sit. 14 a piece of furniture designed to hold something: *an umbrella stand.* ▶ **stand by** verb 1 If you stand by to provide help or take action, you are ready to do it if necessary. 2 If you stand by while something happens, you do nothing to stop it. ▶ **stand down** verb If someone stands down, they resign from their job or position. ▶ **stand in** verb If you stand in for someone,

you take their place while they are ill or away. ▶ **stand out** verb If something stands out, it can be easily noticed or is more important than other similar things. ▶ **stand up** verb 1 If something stands up to rough treatment, it is not damaged or harmed. 2 If you stand up to someone who is criticising or attacking you, you defend yourself.

standard noun 1 a level of quality or achievement that is considered acceptable. 2 (in plural) Standards are moral principles of behaviour. ▶ adjective 3 usual, normal and correct.

> **standard** noun
> 1 = calibre, criterion, guideline, level, norm, quality, requirement 2 = ethics, ideals, morals, principles, rules, scruples, values
> ▶ adjective 3 = accepted, correct, customary, normal, orthodox, regular, usual

standardise; also spelt **standardize** verb To standardise things means to change them so that they all have a similar set of features.

stand-by noun 1 something available for use when you need it. ▶ adjective 2 A stand-by ticket is a cheap ticket that you buy just before a theatre performance or a flight if there are any seats left.

stand-in noun someone who takes a person's place while the person is ill or away.

standing noun 1 A person's standing is their status and reputation. 2 'Standing' is used to say how long something has existed: *a friend of 20 years' standing.*

standpoint noun If you consider something from a particular standpoint, you consider it from that point of view.

standstill noun If something comes to a standstill, it stops completely.

stank the past tense of **stink**.

stanza noun (ENGLISH) A verse of a poem.

staple noun 1 Staples are small pieces of wire that hold sheets of paper firmly together. You insert them with a stapler. ▶ verb 2 If you staple sheets of paper, you fasten them together with staples. ▶ adjective 3 A staple food forms a regular and basic part of someone's everyday diet.

star stars, starring, starred noun 1 a large ball of burning gas in space that appears as a point of light in the sky at night. 2 a shape with four or more points sticking out in a regular pattern. 3 Famous actors, sports players and musicians are referred to as stars. ▶ verb 4 If an actor or actress stars in a film or if the film stars that person, he or she has one of the most important parts in it.

star noun
3 = celebrity, idol, luminary (literary)

starboard adjective The starboard side of a ship is the right-hand side when you are facing the front.

starch noun 1 Starch is a substance used for stiffening fabric such as cotton and linen. 2 (SCIENCE) Starch is a carbohydrate found in foods such as bread and potatoes. ▶ verb 3 To starch fabric means to stiffen it with starch.

stare verb 1 If you stare at something, you look at it for a long time. ▶ noun 2 a long fixed look at something.

stare verb
1 = gaze, look

starfish starfishes or starfish noun a flat, star-shaped sea creature with five limbs.

stark adjective 1 harsh, unpleasant and plain. ▶ phrase 2 If someone is stark naked, they have no clothes on at all.

start verb 1 If something starts, it begins to take place or comes into existence. 2 If you start to do something, you begin to do it. 3 If you start something, you cause it to begin or to come into existence. 4 If you start a machine or car, you operate the controls to make it work. 5 If you start, your body suddenly jerks because of surprise or fear. ▶ noun 6 The start of something is the point or time at which it begins. 7 If you do something with a start, you do it with a sudden jerky movement because of surprise or fear.

start verb
1 = arise, begin, come into being, come into existence, commence (formal), get under way, originate 2 = begin, commence (formal), embark upon, proceed, set about 3 = begin, create, establish, found, get going, inaugurate (formal), initiate, instigate, institute, introduce, launch, open, pioneer, set in motion, set up, trigger
▶ noun 6 = beginning, birth, commencement (formal), dawn, foundation, inauguration

s

(formal), inception (formal), initiation (formal), onset, opening, outset

starter noun a small quantity of food served as the first part of a meal.

startle verb If something sudden and unexpected startles you, it surprises you and makes you slightly frightened. > **startled** adjective > **startling** adjective

starve verb 1 If people are starving, they are suffering from a serious lack of food and are likely to die. 2 To starve a person or animal means to prevent them from having any food. 3 (informal) If you say you are starving, you mean you are very hungry. 4 If someone or something is starved of something they need, they are suffering because they are not getting enough of it. > **starvation** noun

stash verb (informal) If you stash something away in a secret place, you store it there to keep it safe.

state noun 1 The state of something is its condition, what it is like, or its circumstances. 2 Countries are sometimes referred to as states. 3 Some countries are divided into regions called states which make some of their own laws. 4 You can refer to the government or administration of a country as the state. ▶ phrase 5 If you are in a state, you are nervous or upset and unable to control your emotions. ▶ adjective 6 A state ceremony involves the ruler or leader of a country. ▶ verb 7 If you state something, you say it or write it, especially in a formal way.

state noun
1 = circumstances, condition, plight, position, predicament, shape, situation 2 = country, kingdom, land, nation, republic
▶ verb 7 = affirm, articulate, assert, declare, express, say, specify

stately home noun In Britain, a stately home is a very large old house which belongs to an upper-class family.

statement noun 1 something you say or write when you give facts or information in a formal way. 2 a document provided by a bank showing all the money paid into and out of an account during a period of time.

statement noun
1 = account, announcement, bulletin, declaration, explanation, proclamation, report, testimony

state school noun a school maintained and financed by the government in which education is free.

statesman statesmen noun an important and experienced politician.

static adjective 1 never moving or changing. ▶ noun 2 (SCIENCE) Static or static electricity is an electrical charge caused by friction. It builds up in metal objects.

station noun 1 a building and platforms where trains stop for passengers. 2 A bus or coach station is a place where some buses start their journeys. 3 A radio station is the frequency on which a particular company broadcasts. **4** In Australian and New Zealand English, a station is a large sheep or cattle farm. **5** (old-fashioned) A person's station is their position or rank in society. ▶ verb **6** Someone who is stationed somewhere is sent there to work or do a particular job.

stationary adjective not moving.

stationery noun Stationery is paper, pens and other writing equipment.

statistic noun **1** Statistics are facts obtained by analysing numerical information. **2** Statistics is the branch of mathematics that deals with the analysis of numerical information. > **statistical** adjective > **statistically** adverb

statistician noun a person who studies or works with statistics.

statue noun a sculpture of a person or animal.

stature noun **1** Someone's stature is their height and size. **2** Someone's stature is also their importance and reputation.

status noun **1** A person's status is their position and importance in society. **2** Status is also the official classification given to someone or something.

> **status** noun
> **1** = position, prestige, rank, standing

status quo noun The status quo is the situation that exists at a particular time.

statute noun a law. > **statutory** adjective

staunch adjective **1** A staunch supporter is a strong and loyal supporter. ▶ verb **2** If you staunch blood, you stop it from flowing out of a wound.

stave noun **1** (MUSIC) A stave is the five lines that music is written on. ▶ verb **2** If you stave something off, you try to delay or prevent it.

stay verb **1** If you stay in a place, you do not move away from it. **2** If you stay at a hotel or a friend's house, you spend some time there as a guest or visitor. **3** If you stay in a particular state, you continue to be in it. **4** In Scottish and South African English, to stay in a place can also mean to live there. ▶ noun **5** a short time spent somewhere.

> **stay** verb
> **1** = hang around (informal), linger, loiter, remain, tarry, wait

stead phrase (formal) Something that will stand someone in good stead will be useful to them in the future.

steadfast adjective refusing to change or give up. > **steadfastly** adverb

> **steadfast** adjective
> = constant, faithful, firm, immovable, resolute, staunch, steady, unshakable

steady steadier, steadiest; steadies, steadying, steadied adjective **1** continuing or developing gradually without major interruptions or changes. **2** firm and not shaking or wobbling. **3** A steady look or voice is calm and controlled. **4** Someone who is steady is sensible and reliable. ▶ verb **5** When you steady something, you hold on to prevent it from shaking or wobbling. **6** When you steady yourself, you control and calm yourself. > **steadily** adverb

s

steady *adjective*
1 = consistent, constant, continuous, even, nonstop, regular, uninterrupted
2 = firm, secure, stable
▶ *verb* 5 = brace, secure, stabilise, support

steak *noun* 1 Steak is good-quality beef without much fat. 2 A fish steak is a large piece of fish.

steal steals, stealing, stole, stolen *verb* 1 To steal something means to take it without permission and without intending to return it. 2 To steal somewhere means to move there quietly and secretively.

steal *verb*
1 = appropriate, nick (*British, Australian and New Zealand; slang*), pilfer, pinch (*informal*), swipe (*slang*), take 2 = creep, slip, sneak, tiptoe

stealth *noun* If you do something with stealth, you do it quietly and secretively. ▶ **stealthy** *adjective* ▶ **stealthily** *adverb*

steam *noun* 1 Steam is the hot vapour formed when water boils. ▶ *adjective* 2 Steam engines are operated using steam as a means of power. ▶ *verb* 3 If something steams, it gives off steam. 4 To steam food means to cook it in steam. ▶ **steamy** *adjective*

steamer *noun* 1 a ship powered by steam. 2 a container with small holes in the bottom in which you steam food.

steel *noun* 1 Steel is a very strong metal containing mainly iron with a small amount of carbon. ▶ *verb* 2 To steel yourself means to prepare to deal with something unpleasant.

steep *adjective* 1 A steep slope rises sharply and is difficult to go up. 2 larger than is reasonable. ▶ *verb* 3 To steep something in a liquid means to soak it thoroughly. ▶ **steeply** *adverb*

steep *adjective*
1 = sheer, vertical 2 = excessive, extortionate, high, unreasonable
▶ *verb* 3 = immerse, marinate, soak

steeple *noun* a tall pointed structure on top of a church tower.

steeplechase *noun* a long horse race in which the horses jump over obstacles such as hedges and water jumps.

steer *verb* 1 To steer a vehicle or boat means to control it so that it goes in the right direction. 2 To steer someone towards a particular course of action means to influence and direct their behaviour or thoughts.

stem stems, stemming, stemmed *noun* 1 The stem of a plant is the long, thin central part above the ground that carries the leaves and flowers. 2 The stem of a glass is the long, narrow part connecting the bowl to the base. ▶ *verb* 3 If a problem stems from a particular situation, that situation is the original starting point or cause of the problem. 4 If you stem the flow of something, you restrict it or stop it from spreading.

stench *noun* a very strong, unpleasant smell.

stencil stencils, stencilling, stencilled *noun* 1 a thin sheet with a cut-out pattern through which ink or paint passes to form the

pattern on the surface below.
▶ *verb* **2** To stencil a design on a surface means to create it using a stencil.

step steps, stepping, stepped *noun*
1 If you take a step, you lift your foot and put it down somewhere else. **2** one of a series of actions that you take in order to achieve something. **3** a raised flat surface, usually one of a series that you can walk up or down. ▶ *verb* **4** If you step in a particular direction, you move your foot in that direction. **5** If someone steps down or steps aside from an important position, they resign. > **step in** *verb* If you step in, you become involved in a difficult situation in order to help to resolve it. > **step up** *verb* If you step up the rate of something, you increase it.

stepping stone *noun* **1** Stepping stones are a line of large stones that you walk on to cross a shallow river. **2** a job or event that is regarded as a stage in your progress, especially in your career.

stereo *adjective* A stereo recording or music system is one in which the sound is directed through two speakers.

stereotype (PSHE) *noun* **1** a fixed image or set of characteristics that people consider to represent a particular type of person or thing. ▶ *verb* **2** If you stereotype someone, you assume they are a particular type of person and will behave in a particular way.

sterile *adjective* **1** Sterile means completely clean and free from germs. **2** A sterile person or animal is unable to produce offspring. > **sterility** *noun*

sterile *adjective*
1 = antiseptic, germ-free, sterilised **2** = barren, unproductive

sterilise; also spelt **sterilize** *verb*
1 To sterilise something means to make it completely clean and free from germs, usually by boiling it or treating it with an antiseptic. **2** If a person or animal is sterilised, they have an operation that makes it impossible for them to produce offspring.

sterling *noun* **1** Sterling is the money system of the United Kingdom. ▶ *adjective* **2** excellent in quality.

stern *adjective* **1** very serious and strict. ▶ *noun* **2** The stern of a boat is the back part.

steroid *noun* Steroids are chemicals that occur naturally in your body. Sometimes sportsmen and sportswomen illegally take them as drugs to improve their performance.

stethoscope *noun* a device used by doctors to listen to a patient's heart and breathing, consisting of earpieces connected to a hollow tube and a small disc.

stew *noun* **1** a dish of small pieces of savoury food cooked together slowly in a liquid. ▶ *verb* **2** To stew meat, vegetables or fruit means to cook them slowly in a liquid.

steward *noun* **1** a man who works on a ship or plane looking after passengers and serving meals. **2** a person who helps to direct the public at a race, march or other event.

stewardess *noun* a woman who works on a ship or plane looking after passengers and serving meals.

s

stick sticks, sticking, stuck *noun*
1 a long, thin piece of wood.
2 A stick of something is a long, thin piece of it. ▶ *verb* 3 If you stick a long or pointed object into something, you push it in.
4 If you stick one thing to another, you attach it with glue or sticky tape. 5 If one thing sticks to another, it becomes attached and is difficult to remove. 6 If a movable part of something sticks, it becomes fixed and will no longer move or work properly.
7 (*informal*) If you stick something somewhere, you put it there.
8 If you stick by someone, you continue to help and support them. 9 If you stick to something, you keep to it and do not change to something else. 10 When people stick together, they stay together and support each other.
> **stick out** *verb* 1 If something sticks out, it projects from something else. 2 To stick out also means to be very noticeable. > **stick up** *verb* 1 If something sticks up, it points upwards from a surface.
2 (*informal*) If you stick up for a person or principle, you support or defend them.

> **stick** *noun*
1 = bat, cane, mace, pole, rod, truncheon, twig, wand
> ▶ *verb* 3 = dig, insert, jab, poke, push, put, ram, shove, stuff, thrust 4 = attach, bond, fix, fuse, glue, paste 5 = adhere (*formal*), bond, cling, fuse 6 = catch, jam, lodge, snag

sticker *noun* a small piece of paper or plastic with writing or a picture on it, that you stick onto a surface.

sticky stickier, stickiest *adjective*
1 A sticky object is covered with a substance that can stick to other things. 2 Sticky paper or tape has glue on one side so that you can stick it to a surface. 3 (*informal*) A sticky situation is difficult or embarrassing to deal with.
4 Sticky weather is unpleasantly hot and humid.

> **sticky** *adjective*
1 = adhesive, tacky

stiff *adjective* 1 (DGT) Something that is stiff is firm and not easily bent. 2 If you feel stiff, your muscles or joints ache when you move. 3 Stiff behaviour is formal and not friendly or relaxed. 4 Stiff also means difficult or severe: *stiff competition for places.* 5 A stiff breeze is blowing strongly. ▶ *adverb*
6 (*informal*) If you are bored stiff or scared stiff, you are very bored or very scared. > **stiffly** *adverb*
> **stiffness** *noun*

> **stiff** *adjective*
1 = firm, hard, rigid, solid, taut
3 = cold, forced, formal, stilted, unnatural, wooden 4 = arduous, difficult, exacting, formidable, hard, rigorous, tough

stiffen *verb* 1 If you stiffen, you suddenly stop moving and your muscles become tense. 2 If your joints or muscles stiffen, they become sore and difficult to bend or move. 3 If fabric or material is stiffened, it is made firmer so that it does not bend easily.

stifle *verb* 1 If the atmosphere stifles you, you feel you cannot breathe properly. 2 To stifle something means to stop it from happening or continuing.
> **stifling** *adjective*

stigma noun If something has a stigma attached to it, people consider it unacceptable or a disgrace.

stiletto stilettos noun Stilettos are women's shoes with very high, narrow heels.

still adverb 1 If a situation still exists, it has continued to exist and it exists now. 2 If something could still happen, it might happen although it has not happened yet. 3 'Still' emphasises that something is the case in spite of other things: *Whatever you think of him, he's still your father.* ▸ adverb, adjective 4 Still means staying in the same position without moving. ▸ adjective 5 A still place is quiet and peaceful with no signs of activity. ▸ noun 6 a photograph taken from a film or video. > **stillness** noun

> **still** adverb, adjective
> 4 = calm, inert, motionless,
> stationary, tranquil

stillborn adjective A stillborn baby is dead when it is born.

stilt noun 1 Stilts are long upright poles on which a building is built, for example on wet land. 2 Stilts are also two long pieces of wood or metal on which people balance and walk.

stilted adjective formal, unnatural and rather awkward.

stimulant noun A drug or other substance that makes your body work faster, increasing your heart rate and making it difficult to sleep.

stimulate verb 1 To stimulate something means to encourage it to begin or develop. 2 If something stimulates you, it gives you new

ideas and enthusiasm.
> **stimulating** adjective
> **stimulation** noun

stimulus stimuli noun something that causes a process or event to begin or develop.

sting stings, stinging, stung verb 1 If a creature or plant stings you, it pricks your skin and injects a substance which causes pain. 2 If a part of your body stings, you feel a sharp tingling pain there. 3 If someone's remarks sting you, they make you feel upset and hurt. ▸ noun 4 A creature's sting is the part it stings you with.

stink stinks, stinking, stank, stunk verb 1 Something that stinks smells very unpleasant. ▸ noun 2 a very unpleasant smell.

stint noun a period of time spent doing a particular job.

stipulate verb (formal) If you stipulate that something must be done, you state clearly that it must be done. > **stipulation** noun

stir stirs, stirring, stirred verb 1 When you stir a liquid, you move it around using a spoon or a stick. 2 To stir means to move slightly. 3 If something stirs you, it makes you feel strong emotions. ▸ noun 4 If an event causes a stir, it causes general excitement or shock.

stirring adjective causing excitement, emotion and enthusiasm.

stitch verb 1 When you stitch pieces of material together, you use a needle and thread to sew them together. 2 To stitch a wound means to use a special needle and thread to hold the edges of skin together. ▸ noun 3 one of the pieces of thread that can be seen where material has been sewn. **4** one of the pieces of thread that can be seen where a wound has been stitched. **5** If you have a stitch, you feel a sharp pain at the side of your abdomen, usually because you have been running or laughing.

stock noun **1** Stocks are shares bought as an investment in a company; also the amount of money raised by the company through the issue of shares. **2** A shop's stock is the total amount of goods it has for sale. **3** If you have a stock of things, you have a supply ready for use. **4** The stock an animal or person comes from is the type of animal or person they are descended from. **5** Stock is farm animals. **6** Stock is a liquid made from boiling meat, bones or vegetables together in water. Stock is used as a base for soups, stews and sauces. ▶ verb **7** A shop that stocks particular goods keeps a supply of them to sell. **8** If you stock a shelf or cupboard, you fill it with food or other things. ▶ adjective **9** A stock expression or way of doing something is one that is commonly used. > **stock up** verb If you stock up on something, you buy a supply of it.

> **stock** noun
> **1** = bonds, investments, shares
> **2** = goods, merchandise (*formal*)
> **3** = reserve, reservoir, stockpile, store, supply **4** = ancestry, descent, extraction, lineage, origin, parentage
> ▶ verb **7** = deal in, sell, supply, trade in
> ▶ adjective **9** = hackneyed, overused, routine, standard, stereotyped, typical, usual

stockbroker noun A stockbroker is a person whose job is to buy and sell shares for people who want to invest money.

stock exchange noun a place where there is trading in stocks and shares.

stocking noun Stockings are long pieces of thin clothing that cover the leg.

stockman stockmen noun a man who looks after sheep or cattle on a farm.

stock market noun The stock market is the organisation and activity involved in buying and selling stocks and shares.

stockpile verb **1** If someone stockpiles something, they store large quantities of it for future use. ▶ noun **2** a large store of something.

> **stockpile** verb
> **1** = accumulate, amass, collect, gather, hoard, save, stash (*informal*), store up
> ▶ noun **2** = arsenal, cache, hoard, reserve, stash (*informal*), stock, store

stocky stockier, stockiest adjective A stocky person is rather short, but broad and solid-looking.

> **stocky** adjective
> = chunky, solid, sturdy

stoke verb To stoke a fire means to keep it burning by moving or adding fuel.

stole the past tense of **steal**.

stolen the past participle of **steal**.

stomach noun **1** Your stomach is the organ inside your body where food is digested. **2** You can refer to the front part of your body above your waist as your stomach.

▶ *verb* **3** If you cannot stomach something, you strongly dislike it and cannot accept it.

stomach *noun*
2 = belly, paunch, puku (*New Zealand*), tummy (*informal*)

stone *noun* **1** Stone is the hard solid substance found in the ground and used for building. **2** A small piece of rock. **3** The stone in a fruit such as a plum or cherry is the large seed in the centre. **4** a unit of weight equal to 14 pounds or about 6.35 kilograms. **5** You can refer to a jewel as a stone. ▶ *verb* **6** To stone something or someone means to throw stones at them.

stony stonier, stoniest *adjective* **1** Stony ground is rough and contains a lot of stones or rocks. **2** If someone's expression is stony, it shows no friendliness or sympathy.

stood the past tense and past participle of **stand**.

stool *noun* a seat with legs but no back or arms.

stoop *verb* **1** If you stoop, you stand or walk with your shoulders bent forwards. **2** If you would not stoop to something, you would not disgrace yourself by doing it.

stop stops, stopping, stopped *verb* **1** If you stop doing something, you no longer do it. **2** If an activity or process stops, it comes to an end or no longer happens. **3** If a machine stops, it no longer functions or it is switched off. **4** To stop something means to prevent it. **5** If people or things that are moving stop, they no longer move. **6** If you stop somewhere, you stay there for a short while. ▶ *phrase* **7** To put a

stop to something means to prevent it from happening or continuing. ▶ *noun* **8** a place where a bus, train or other vehicle stops during a journey. **9** If something that is moving comes to a stop, it no longer moves.

stop *verb*
1 = cease, cut out (*informal*), desist, discontinue, end, quit **2** = cease, come to an end, conclude, end, finish, halt **4** = arrest, check, prevent

stoppage *noun* If there is a stoppage, people stop work because of a disagreement with their employer.

stopper *noun* a piece of glass or cork that fits into the neck of a jar or bottle.

stopwatch *noun* a watch that can be started and stopped by pressing buttons, which is used to time events.

storage *noun* **1** The storage of something is the keeping of it somewhere until it is needed. **2** ⓘCT Storage is the process of storing information in a computer.

store *noun* **1** a shop. **2** A store of something is a supply kept for future use. **3** a place where things are kept while they are not used. ▶ *verb* **4** When you store something somewhere, you keep it there until it is needed. ▶ *phrase* **5** Something that is in store for you is going to happen to you in the future.

store *noun*
2 = cache, fund, hoard, reserve, reservoir, stock, stockpile, supply **3** = depot, storeroom, warehouse

s

▶ verb 4 = hoard, keep, save, stash (informal), stockpile

storeroom noun a room where things are kept until they are needed.

storey storeys noun A storey of a building is one of its floors or levels.

storm noun 1 When there is a storm, there is heavy rain, a strong wind, and often thunder and lightning. 2 If something causes a storm, it causes an angry or excited reaction. ▶ verb 3 If someone storms out, they leave quickly, noisily and angrily. 4 To storm means to say something in a loud, angry voice. 5 If people storm a place, they attack it. > **stormy** adjective

story stories noun 1 (ENGLISH) a description of imaginary people and events written or told to entertain people. 2 The story of something or someone is an account of the important events that have happened to them.

> **story** noun
> 1 = account, anecdote, legend, narrative, tale, yarn

stout adjective 1 rather fat. 2 thick, strong and sturdy. 3 determined, firm and strong. > **stoutly** adverb

stove noun a piece of equipment for heating a room or for cooking.

stow verb 1 If you stow something somewhere or stow it away, you store it until it is needed. 2 If someone stows away in a ship or plane, they hide in it to go somewhere secretly without paying.

straddle verb 1 If you straddle something, you stand or sit with one leg on either side of it.

2 If something straddles a place, it crosses it, linking different parts together.

straight adjective, adverb
1 continuing in the same direction without curving or bending. 2 upright or level rather than sloping or bent. ▶ adverb 3 immediately and directly: We will go straight to the hotel. ▶ adjective 4 neat and tidy. 5 honest, frank and direct. 6 A straight choice involves only two options.

> **straight** adjective, adverb
> 2 = erect, even, horizontal, level, perpendicular, upright, vertical
> ▶ adjective 5 = blunt, candid, forthright, frank, honest, outright, plain, point-blank

straightaway adverb If you do something straightaway, you do it immediately.

straighten verb 1 To straighten something means to remove any bends or curves from it. 2 To straighten something also means to make it neat and tidy. 3 To straighten out a confused situation means to organise and deal with it.

straightforward adjective 1 easy and involving no problems. 2 honest, open and frank.

> **straightforward** adjective
> 1 = basic, easy, elementary, lo-fi, routine, simple, uncomplicated
> 2 = candid, direct, forthright, frank, honest, open, plain, straight

strain noun 1 Strain is worry and nervous tension. 2 If a strain is put on something, it is affected by a strong force which may damage it. 3 You can refer to an aspect of someone's character, remarks or

S

work as a strain. **4** You can refer
to distant sounds of music as
strains of music. **5** A particular
strain of plant is a variety of it.
▶ *verb* **6** To strain something
means to force it or use it more
than is reasonable or normal. **7** If
you strain a muscle, you injure it
by moving awkwardly. **8** To strain
food means to pour away the
liquid from it.

> **strain** noun
> 1 = anxiety, pressure, stress,
> tension
> ▶ *verb* 6 = overwork, tax

strained *adjective* **1** worried and
anxious. **2** If a relationship is
strained, people feel unfriendly
and do not trust each other.

strait *noun* **1** You can refer to a
narrow strip of sea as a strait or
the straits. **2** (*in plural*) If someone
is in a bad situation, you can say
they are in difficult straits.

straitjacket *noun* a special jacket
used to tie the arms of a violent
person tightly around their body.

strand *noun* **1** A strand of thread
or hair is a single long piece of it.
2 You can refer to a part of a
situation or idea as a strand of it.

stranded *adjective* If someone or
something is stranded somewhere,
they are stuck and cannot leave.

strange *adjective* **1** unusual or
unexpected. **2** not known, seen or
experienced before. > **strangely**
adverb > **strangeness** *noun*

> **strange** adjective
> 1 = abnormal, bizarre, curious,
> extraordinary, funny, odd,
> peculiar, queer (*old-fashioned*),
> uncommon, weird 2 = alien,
> exotic, foreign, new, novel,
> unfamiliar

stranger *noun* **1** someone you
have never met before. **2** If you are
a stranger to a place or situation,
you have not been there or
experienced it before.

strangle *verb* To strangle someone
means to kill them by squeezing
their throat. > **strangulation** *noun*

strangled *adjective* A strangled
sound is unclear and muffled.

stranglehold *noun* To have a
stranglehold on something means
to have control over it and
prevent it from developing.

strap straps, strapping, strapped
noun **1** a narrow piece of leather or
cloth, used to fasten or hold
things together. ▶ *verb* **2** To strap
something means to fasten it
with a strap.

strapping *adjective* tall, strong
and healthy-looking.

strata the plural of **stratum**.

strategic *adjective* planned or
intended to achieve something or
to gain an advantage.
> **strategically** *adverb*

strategy strategies *noun* **1** (PSHE)
a plan for achieving something.
2 Strategy is the skill of planning
the best way to achieve
something, especially in war.
> **strategist** *noun*

stratum strata *noun* (SCIENCE)
The strata in the earth's surface
are the different layers of rock.

straw *noun* **1** Straw is the dry,
yellowish stalks from cereal
crops. **2** a hollow tube of paper or
plastic which you use to suck a
drink into your mouth. ▶ *phrase*
3 If something is **the last straw**,
it is the latest in a series of bad
events and makes you feel you
cannot stand any more.

strawberry strawberries noun a small red fruit with tiny seeds in its skin.

stray verb 1 When people or animals stray, they wander away from where they should be. 2 If your thoughts stray, you stop concentrating. ▶ adjective 3 A stray dog or cat is one that has wandered away from home. 4 Stray things are separated from the main group of things of their kind. ▶ noun 5 a stray dog or cat.

streak noun 1 a long mark or stain. 2 If someone has a particular streak, they have that quality in their character. 3 A lucky or unlucky streak is a series of successes or failures. ▶ verb 4 If something is streaked with a colour, it has lines of the colour in it. 5 To streak somewhere means to move there very quickly. > **streaky** adjective

stream noun 1 a small river. 2 You can refer to a steady flow of something as a stream. 3 In a school, a stream is a group of children of the same age and ability. ▶ verb 4 To stream somewhere means to move in a continuous flow in large quantities. 5 To stream video or audio material is to send it over the internet so that the receiving system can play it almost simultaneously.

streamline verb 1 To streamline a vehicle, aircraft or boat means to improve its shape so that it moves more quickly and efficiently. 2 To streamline an organisation means to make it more efficient by removing parts of it.

street noun a road in a town or village, usually with buildings along it.

strength noun 1 Your strength is your physical energy and the power of your muscles. 2 Strength can refer to the degree of someone's confidence or courage. 3 You can refer to power or influence as strength. 4 Someone's strengths are their good qualities and abilities. 5 The strength of an object is the degree to which it can stand rough treatment. 6 The strength of a substance is the amount of other substances that it contains. 7 The strength of a feeling or opinion is the degree to which it is felt or supported. 8 The strength of a relationship is its degree of closeness or success.

strength noun
1 = brawn, might, muscle, stamina 7 = force, intensity, potency, power, vehemence, vigour

strengthen verb 1 To strengthen something means to give it more power, influence or support and make it more likely to succeed. 2 To strengthen an object means to improve it or add to its structure so that it can withstand rough treatment.

strengthen verb
1 = consolidate, encourage, harden, stiffen, toughen 2 = bolster, brace, fortify, reinforce, support

strenuous adjective involving a lot of effort or energy. > **strenuously** adverb

stress noun 1 Stress is worry and nervous tension. 2 Stresses are strong physical forces applied to an object. 3 (ENGLISH) Stress is emphasis put on a word or part of a word when it is pronounced, making it slightly louder. ▶ verb **4** If you stress a point, you emphasise it and draw attention to its importance. > **stressful** adjective

stress noun
1 = anxiety, hassle (informal), pressure, strain, tension, worry
▶ verb **4** = accentuate, emphasise, repeat, underline

stretch verb **1** Something that stretches over an area extends that far. **2** When you stretch, you hold out part of your body as far as you can. **3** To stretch something soft or elastic means to pull it to make it longer or bigger. ▶ noun **4** A stretch of land or water is an area of it. **5** A stretch of time is a period of time.

stretch verb
1 = continue, cover, extend, go on, hang, last, reach, spread
2 = extend, reach, straighten
▶ noun **4** = area, expanse, extent, sweep, tract **5** = period, run, space, spell, stint, term, time

stretcher noun a long piece of material with a pole along each side, used to carry an injured person.

strewn adjective If things are strewn about, they are scattered about untidily.

stricken adjective severely affected by something unpleasant.

strict adjective **1** Someone who is strict controls other people very firmly. **2** A strict rule must always be obeyed absolutely. **3** The strict meaning of something is its precise and accurate meaning. **4** You can use 'strict' to describe someone who never breaks the

rules or principles of a particular belief.

strict adjective
1 = authoritarian, firm, rigid, rigorous, stern, stringent
3 = accurate, exact, meticulous, particular, precise, true

strictly adverb Strictly means only for a particular purpose: I was in it strictly for the money.

stride strides, striding, strode, stridden verb **1** To stride along means to walk quickly with long steps. ▶ noun **2** a long step; also the length of a step.

strident adjective loud, harsh and unpleasant.

strife noun (formal) Strife is trouble, conflict and disagreement.

strike strikes, striking, struck noun **1** If there is a strike, people stop working as a protest. **2** A hunger strike is a refusal to eat anything as a protest. A rent strike is a refusal to pay rent. **3** a military attack. ▶ verb **4** To strike someone or something means to hit them. **5** If an illness, disaster or enemy strikes, it suddenly affects or attacks someone. **6** If a thought strikes you, it comes into your mind. **7** If you are struck by something, you are impressed by it. **8** When a clock strikes, it makes a sound to indicate the time. **9** To strike a deal with someone means to come to an agreement with them. **10** If someone strikes oil or gold, they discover it in the ground. **11** If you strike a match, you rub it against something to make it burst into flame. > **strike off** verb If a professional person is struck off for bad behaviour, their name is removed from an official register

s

and they are not allowed to practise their profession. > **strike out** verb If someone strikes out, they go off to do something different on their own. > **strike up** verb To strike up a conversation or friendship means to begin it.

striker noun 1 Strikers are people who are refusing to work as a protest. 2 In soccer, a player whose function is to attack and score goals.

striking adjective very noticeable because of being unusual or very attractive. > **strikingly** adverb

string strings, stringing, strung noun 1 String is thin cord made of twisted threads. 2 You can refer to a row or series of similar things as a string of them. 3 The strings of a musical instrument are tightly stretched lengths of wire or nylon which vibrate to produce the notes. 4 (in plural) The section of an orchestra consisting of stringed instruments is called the strings. > **string along** verb (informal) To string someone along means to deceive them by letting them believe you have the same desires, hopes or plans as them. > **string out** verb 1 If things are strung out, they are spread out in a long line. 2 To string something out means to make it last longer than necessary.

stringent adjective Stringent laws or conditions are very severe or are strictly controlled.

strip strips, stripping, stripped noun 1 A strip of something is a long, narrow piece of it. 2 A comic strip is a series of drawings which tell a story. 3 A sports team's strip is the clothes worn by the team

when playing a match. ▶ verb 4 If you strip, you take off all your clothes. 5 To strip something means to remove whatever is covering its surface. 6 To strip someone of their property or rights means to take their property or rights away from them officially.

stripe noun Stripes are long, thin lines, usually of different colours. > **striped** adjective

strive strives, striving, strove, striven verb If you strive to do something, you make a great effort to achieve it.

---

strive verb
= attempt, do your best, do your utmost, endeavour (formal), make an effort, seek, try

---

strode the past tense of **stride**.

stroke verb 1 If you stroke something, you move your hand smoothly and gently over it. ▶ noun 2 If someone has a stroke, they suddenly lose consciousness as a result of a blockage or rupture in a blood vessel in the brain. A stroke can result in damage to speech and paralysis. 3 The strokes of a brush or pen are the movements that you make with it. 4 The strokes of a clock are the sounds that indicate the hour. 5 A swimming stroke is a particular style of swimming. ▶ phrase 6 If you have **a stroke of luck**, then you are lucky and something good happens to you.

stroll verb 1 To stroll along means to walk slowly in a relaxed way. ▶ noun 2 a slow, pleasurable walk.

stroller noun In Australian and American English, a stroller is a pushchair.

strong *adjective* 1 Someone who is strong has powerful muscles. 2 You also say that someone is strong when they are confident and have courage. 3 Strong objects are able to withstand rough treatment. 4 Strong also means great in degree or intensity. 5 A strong argument or theory is supported by a lot of evidence. 6 If a group or organisation is strong, it has a lot of members or influence. 7 You can use 'strong' to say how many people there are in a group: *The audience was about two dozen strong.* 8 Your strong points are the things you are good at. 9 A strong economy or currency is stable and successful. 10 A strong liquid or drug contains a lot of a particular substance. ▶ *adverb* 11 If someone or something is still going strong, they are still healthy or working well after a long time. > **strongly** *adverb*

> **strong** *adjective*
> 1 = athletic, brawny, burly, muscular, powerful, strapping, well-built 3 = durable, hard-wearing, heavy-duty, reinforced, sturdy, substantial, tough, well-built 4 = acute, ardent, deep, fervent, fierce, intense, keen, passionate, profound, vehement, violent, zealous

stronghold *noun* 1 a place that is held and defended by an army. 2 A stronghold of an attitude or belief is a place in which the attitude or belief is strongly held.

strove the past tense of **strive**.

struck the past tense and past participle of **strike**.

structure *noun* 1 (DGT) The structure of something is the way it is made, built or organised. 2 something that has been built or constructed. ▶ *verb* 3 (DGT) To structure something means to arrange it into an organised pattern or system. > **structural** *adjective* > **structurally** *adverb*

> **structure** *noun*
> 1 = arrangement, construction, design, make-up, organisation 2 = building, construction, edifice

struggle *verb* 1 If you struggle to do something, you try hard to do it in difficult circumstances. 2 When people struggle, they twist and move violently during a fight. ▶ *noun* 3 Something that is a struggle is difficult to achieve and takes a lot of effort. 4 a fight.

> **struggle** *verb*
> 1 = strain, strive, toil, work
> ▶ *noun* 3 = effort, labour, toil, work

strum strums, strumming, strummed *verb* To strum a guitar means to play it by moving your fingers backwards and forwards across all the strings.

strung the past tense and past participle of **string**.

strut struts, strutting, strutted *verb* 1 To strut means to walk in a stiff, proud way with your chest out and your head high. ▶ *noun* 2 a piece of wood or metal which strengthens or supports part of a building or structure.

Stuart (HISTORY) *noun* Stuart was the family name of the monarchs who ruled Scotland from 1371 to 1714 and England from 1603 to 1714.

stub stubs, stubbing, stubbed
noun 1 The stub of a pencil or cigarette is the short piece that remains when the rest has been used. 2 The stub of a ticket is the small part that you keep. ▶ *verb* 3 If you stub your toe, you hurt it by accidentally kicking something. ▶ **stub out** *verb* To stub out a cigarette means to put it out by pressing the end against something.

stubble *noun* 1 The short stalks remaining in the ground after a crop is harvested are called stubble. 2 If a man has stubble on his face, he has very short hair growing there because he has not shaved recently.

stubborn *adjective* 1 Someone who is stubborn is determined not to change their opinion or course of action. 2 A stubborn stain is difficult to remove.
> **stubbornly** *adverb*
> **stubbornness** *noun*

> **stubborn** *adjective*
> 1 = dogged, inflexible, obstinate, tenacious, wilful

stuck 1 Stuck is the past tense and past participle of **stick**. ▶ *adjective* 2 If something is stuck in a particular position, it is fixed or jammed and cannot be moved. 3 If you are stuck, you are unable to continue what you were doing because it is too difficult. 4 If you are stuck somewhere, you are unable to get away.

stud *noun* 1 a small piece of metal fixed into something. 2 A male horse or other animal that is kept for stud is kept for breeding purposes.

studded *adjective* decorated with small pieces of metal or precious stones.

student *noun* a person studying at university or college.

studied *adjective* A studied action or response has been carefully planned and is not natural.

studio studios *noun* 1 a room where a photographer or painter works. 2 a room containing special equipment where records, films or radio or television programmes are made.

studious *adjective* spending a lot of time studying.

studiously *adverb* carefully and deliberately.

study studies, studying, studied
verb 1 If you study a particular subject, you spend time learning about it. 2 If you study something, you look at it carefully. ▶ *noun* 3 Study is the activity of studying a subject. 4 Studies are subjects which are studied. 5 a piece of research on a particular subject. 6 a room used for writing and studying.

> **study** *verb*
> 1 = learn, read up, swot (*British, Australian and New Zealand; informal*) 2 = contemplate, examine, pore over
> ▶ *noun* 3 = lessons, research, school work, swotting (*British, Australian and New Zealand; informal*)

stuff *noun* 1 You can refer to a substance or group of things as stuff. ▶ *verb* 2 (*informal*) If you stuff something somewhere, you push it there quickly and roughly. 3 If you stuff something with a substance or objects, you fill it with the substance or objects.

stuff *noun*
1 = apparatus, belongings, equipment, gear, kit, material, substance, tackle, things
▶ *verb* 2 = cram, force, jam, push, ram, shove, squeeze, thrust 3 = cram, fill, load, pack

stuffing *noun* Stuffing is a mixture of small pieces of food put inside poultry or a vegetable before it is cooked.

stuffy stuffier, stuffiest *adjective*
1 very formal and old-fashioned.
2 If it is stuffy in a room, there is not enough fresh air.

stuffy *adjective*
1 = dull, formal, old-fashioned, staid, strait-laced 2 = close, heavy, muggy, oppressive, stale, stifling

stumble *verb* 1 If you stumble while you are walking or running, you trip and almost fall. 2 If you stumble when speaking, you make mistakes when pronouncing the words. 3 If you stumble across something or stumble on it, you find it unexpectedly.

stump *noun* 1 a small part of something that is left when the rest has been removed. 2 In cricket, the stumps are the three upright wooden sticks that support the bails, forming the wicket. ▶ *verb* 3 (*informal*) If a question or problem stumps you, you cannot think of an answer or solution.

stun stuns, stunning, stunned *verb*
1 If you are stunned by something, you are very shocked by it. 2 To stun a person or animal means to knock them unconscious with a blow to the head.

stung the past tense and past participle of **sting**.

stunk the past participle of **stink**.

stunning *adjective* very beautiful or impressive.

stunt *noun* 1 an unusual or dangerous and exciting action that someone does to get publicity or as part of a film. ▶ *verb* 2 To stunt the growth or development of something means to prevent it from developing as it should.

stupendous *adjective* very large or impressive. > **stupendously** *adverb*

stupid *adjective* showing lack of good judgment or intelligence and not at all sensible. > **stupidly** *adverb*

stupid *adjective*
= absurd, daft (*British; informal*), dim, foolish, idiotic, inane, obtuse (*formal*), thick

stupidity *noun* a lack of intelligence or good judgment.

stupidity *noun*
= absurdity, folly, foolishness, inanity, silliness

sturdy sturdier, sturdiest *adjective* strong and firm and unlikely to be damaged or injured.

sturdy *adjective*
= durable, hardy, robust, solid, substantial, stout, strong, well-built

sturgeon *noun* a large edible fish, the eggs of which are also eaten and are known as caviar.

stutter *noun* 1 Someone who has a stutter finds it difficult to speak smoothly and often repeats sounds through being unable to complete a word. ▸ *verb* 2 When someone stutters, they hesitate or repeat sounds when speaking.

style *noun* 1 The style of something is the general way in which it is done or presented, often showing the attitudes of the people involved. 2 A person or place that has style is smart, elegant and fashionable. 3 The style of something is its design. ▸ *verb* 4 To style a piece of clothing or a person's hair means to design and create its shape.

> **style** *noun*
> 1 = approach, manner, method, mode, technique, way 2 = chic, elegance, flair, sophistication, taste

stylised; also spelt **stylized** *adjective* using a particular artistic or literary form as a basis rather than being natural or spontaneous.

stylish *adjective* smart, elegant and fashionable. > **stylishly** *adverb*

suave *adjective* charming, polite and confident.

subconscious *noun* 1 Your subconscious is the part of your mind that can influence you without your being aware of it. ▸ *adjective* 2 happening or existing in someone's subconscious and therefore not directly realised or understood by them. > **subconsciously** *adverb*

subcontinent *noun* a large mass of land, often consisting of several countries, and forming part of a continent.

subdue subdues, subduing, subdued *verb* 1 To subdue a person or group of people is to bring

them under control by using force. 2 To subdue a colour, light or emotion means to make it less bright or strong.

> **subdue** *verb*
> 1 = crush, defeat, overcome, overpower, quell, vanquish (*literary*)

subdued *adjective* 1 rather quiet and sad. 2 not very noticeable or bright.

subject *noun* 1 The subject of writing or a conversation is the thing or person being discussed. 2 (MFL) In grammar, the subject is the word or words representing the person or thing doing the action expressed by the verb. For example, in the sentence 'My cat keeps catching birds', 'my cat' is the subject. 3 an area of study. 4 The subjects of a king or queen are the people who are ruled by them. ▸ *verb* 5 To subject someone to something means to make them experience it. ▸ *adjective* 6 Someone or something that is subject to something is affected by it.

> **subject** *noun*
> 1 = issue, matter, object, point, question, theme, topic
> ▸ *verb* 5 = expose, put through

subjective *adjective* influenced by personal feelings and opinion rather than based on fact or rational thought.

sublime *adjective* Something that is sublime is wonderful and affects people emotionally.

submarine *noun* a ship that can travel beneath the surface of the sea.

submerge *verb* 1 To submerge means to go beneath the surface of a liquid. **2** If you submerge yourself in an activity, you become totally involved in it.

submission noun **1** Submission is a state in which someone accepts the control of another person. **2** The submission of a proposal or application is the act of sending it for consideration.

submissive adjective behaving in a quiet, obedient way.

submit submits, submitting, submitted verb **1** If you submit to something, you accept it because you are not powerful enough to resist it. **2** If you submit an application or proposal, you send it to someone for consideration.

> **submit** verb
> **1** = agree, bow, capitulate, comply, give in, surrender, yield
> (formal) **2** = hand in, present, propose, put forward, send in, table, tender

subordinate noun **1** A person's subordinate is someone who is in a less important position than them. ▶ adjective **2** If one thing is subordinate to another, it is less important. ▶ verb **3** To subordinate one thing to another means to treat it as being less important.

subscribe verb **1** If you subscribe to a particular belief or opinion, you support it or agree with it. **2** If you subscribe to a magazine, you pay to receive regular copies. > **subscriber** noun

subscription noun a sum of money that you pay regularly to belong to an organisation or to receive regular copies of a magazine.

subsequent adjective happening or coming into existence at a later time than something else: *the December uprising and the subsequent political violence.* > **subsequently** adverb

subservient adjective Someone who is subservient does whatever other people want them to do.

subside verb **1** To subside means to become less intense or quieter. **2** If water or the ground subsides, it sinks to a lower level.

subsidence noun If a place is suffering from subsidence, parts of the ground have sunk to a lower level.

subsidiary subsidiaries noun **1** a company which is part of a larger company. ▶ adjective **2** treated as being of less importance and additional to another thing.

subsidise; also spelt **subsidize** verb To subsidise something means to provide part of the cost of it. > **subsidised** adjective

subsidy subsidies noun a sum of money paid to help support a company or provide a public service.

substance noun **1** Anything which is a solid, a powder, a liquid or a paste can be referred to as a substance. **2** If a speech or piece of writing has substance, it is meaningful or important.

> **substance** noun
> **1** = element, fabric, material, stuff

substantial adjective **1** very large in degree or amount. **2** large and strongly built.

substantially adverb Something that is substantially true is generally or mostly true.

S

substitute verb 1 To substitute one thing for another means to use it instead of the other thing or to put it in the other thing's place. 2 (MATHS) To replace one mathematical element with another. ▶ noun 3 If one thing is a substitute for another, it is used instead of it or put in its place.
> **substitution** noun

> **substitute** verb
> 1 = exchange, interchange, replace, swap, switch
> ▶ noun 3 = deputy, proxy, replacement, representative, surrogate

subterfuge noun Subterfuge is the use of deceitful or dishonest methods.

subtitle noun A film with subtitles has a printed translation of the dialogue at the bottom of the screen.

subtle adjective 1 very fine, delicate or small in degree. 2 using indirect methods to achieve something. > **subtly** adverb > **subtlety** noun

subtract verb If you subtract, you remove one number from another.

> **subtract** verb
> = deduct, take away, take from

suburb noun an area of a town or city that is away from its centre.

suburban adjective 1 relating to a suburb or suburbs. 2 dull and conventional.

suburbia noun You can refer to the suburbs of a city as suburbia.

subversive adjective intended to destroy or weaken a political system. > **subversion** noun

subvert verb (formal) To subvert something means to cause it to weaken or fail.

subway noun 1 a footpath that goes underneath a road. 2 an underground railway.

succeed verb 1 To succeed means to achieve the result you intend. 2 To succeed someone means to be the next person to have their job. 3 If one thing succeeds another, it comes after it in time.
> **succeeding** adjective

> **succeed** verb
> 1 = be successful, do well, flourish, make it (informal), prosper, thrive, triumph, work
> 2 = replace, take over from

success noun 1 Success is the achievement of something you have been trying to do. 2 Someone who is a success has achieved an important position or made a lot of money.

> **success** noun
> 1 = celebrity, eminence, fame, prosperity, triumph, victory, wealth 2 = celebrity, hit, sensation, star, triumph, winner

successful adjective having achieved what you intended to do. > **successfully** adverb

> **successful** adjective
> = flourishing, lucrative, profitable, rewarding, thriving, top

succession noun 1 A succession of things is a number of things occurring one after the other. 2 When someone becomes the next person to have an important position, you can refer to this event as their succession to this position. ▶ *phrase* **3** If something happens a number of weeks, months or years **in succession**, it happens that number of times without a break.

successive *adjective* occurring one after the other without a break.

successor *noun* Someone's successor is the person who takes their job when they leave.

succinct *adjective* expressing something clearly and in very few words. > **succinctly** *adverb*

succulent *adjective* Succulent food is juicy and delicious.

succumb *verb* If you succumb to something, you are unable to resist it any longer.

such *adjective, pronoun* **1** You use 'such' to refer to the person or thing you have just mentioned, or to someone or something similar: *Naples or Palermo or some such place.* ▶ *phrase* **2** You can use **such as** to introduce an example of something: *herbal teas such as camomile.* **3** You can use **such and such** when you want to refer to something that is not specific: *A good trick is to ask whether they have seen such and such a film.* ▶ *adjective* **4** 'Such' can be used for emphasising: *I have such a terrible sense of guilt.*

suck *verb* **1** If you suck something, you hold it in your mouth and pull at it with your cheeks and tongue, usually to get liquid out of it. **2** To suck something in a particular direction means to draw it there with a powerful force. > **suck up** *verb* (*informal*) To suck up to someone means to do things to please them in order to obtain praise or approval.

sucker *noun* **1** (*informal*) If you call

someone a sucker, you mean that they are easily fooled or cheated. **2** Suckers are pads on the bodies of some animals and insects which they use to cling to a surface. **3** A sucker is also a cup-shaped piece of plastic or rubber on an object that sticks to a surface when pressed flat.

suction *noun* **1** Suction is the force involved when a substance is drawn or sucked from one place to another. **2** Suction is the process by which two surfaces stick together when the air between them is removed.

Sudanese *adjective* **1** belonging or relating to the Sudan. ▶ *noun* **2** someone who comes from the Sudan.

sudden *adjective* happening quickly and unexpectedly. > **suddenly** *adverb* > **suddenness** *noun*

> **sudden** *adjective*
> = abrupt, hasty, quick, swift, unexpected

sue sues, suing, sued *verb* To sue someone means to start a legal case against them, usually to claim money from them.

suede *noun* Suede is a thin, soft leather with a rough surface.

suffer *verb* **1** If someone is suffering pain, or suffering as a result of an unpleasant situation, they are badly affected by it. **2** If something suffers as a result of neglect or a difficult situation, its condition or quality becomes worse. > **sufferer** *noun* > **suffering** *noun*

> **suffer** *verb*
> **1** = bear, endure, experience, go through, sustain, undergo

s

suffice verb (formal) If something suffices, it is enough or adequate for a purpose.

sufficient adjective If a supply or quantity is sufficient for a purpose, there is enough of it available. > **sufficiently** adverb

sufficient adjective
= adequate, ample, enough

suffix noun (ENGLISH) a group of letters which is added to the end of a word to form a new word, for example '-ology' or '-itis'.

suffocate verb To suffocate means to die as a result of having too little air or oxygen to breathe. > **suffocation** noun

suffrage noun Suffrage is the right to vote in political elections.

suffused adjective (literary) If something is suffused with light or colour, light or colour has gradually spread over it.

sugar noun Sugar is a sweet substance used to sweeten food or drinks. Sugar is obtained from sugar cane or sugar beet.

sugar cane noun a tropical plant with thick stems from which sugar is obtained.

suggest verb 1 If you suggest a plan or idea to someone, you mention it as a possibility for them to consider. 2 If something suggests a particular thought or impression, it makes you think in that way or gives you that impression.

suggest verb
1 = advise, advocate, propose, recommend 2 = hint, imply, indicate, insinuate, intimate

suggestion noun 1 a plan or idea that is mentioned as a possibility for someone to consider. 2 A suggestion of something is a very slight indication or faint sign of it.

suggestion noun
1 = plan, proposal, proposition, recommendation 2 = hint, indication, insinuation, intimation, trace

suggestive adjective Something that is suggestive of a particular thing gives a slight hint or sign of it. > **suggestively** adverb

suicidal adjective 1 People who are suicidal want to kill themselves. 2 Suicidal behaviour is so dangerous that it is likely to result in death. > **suicidally** adverb

suicide noun People who die by suicide deliberately kill themselves.

suicide bomber noun a terrorist who carries out a bomb attack, knowing that he or she will be killed in the explosion. > **suicide bombing** noun

suit noun 1 a matching jacket and trousers or skirt. 2 In a court of law, a suit is a legal action taken by one person against another. 3 one of four different types of card in a pack of playing cards. The four suits are hearts, clubs, diamonds and spades. ▶ verb 4 If a situation or course of action suits you, it is appropriate or acceptable for your purpose. 5 If a piece of clothing or a colour suits you, you look good when you are wearing it. 6 If you do something to suit yourself, you do it because you want to and without considering other people.

suit verb
4 = be acceptable to, do, please, satisfy

suitable *adjective* right or acceptable for a particular purpose or occasion. ▷ **suitability** *noun* ▷ **suitably** *adverb*

> **suitable** *adjective*
> = acceptable, appropriate, apt, fit, fitting, proper, right, satisfactory

suitcase *noun* a case in which you carry your clothes when you are travelling.

suite *noun* 1 In a hotel, a suite is a set of rooms. 2 a set of matching furniture or bathroom fittings.

suited *adjective* right or appropriate for a particular purpose or person.

suitor *noun* (*old-fashioned*) A person's suitor is someone who wants to marry them.

sulk *verb* Someone who is sulking is showing their annoyance by being silent and moody.

sulky sulkier, sulkiest *adjective* showing annoyance by being silent and moody.

> **sulky** *adjective*
> = huffy, moody, petulant, resentful, sullen

sullen *adjective* behaving in a bad-tempered and disagreeably silent way. ▷ **sullenly** *adverb*

sulphur *noun* (SCIENCE) Sulphur is a pale yellow nonmetallic element which burns with a very unpleasant smell. Its atomic number is 16 and its symbol is S.

sultan *noun* In some Muslim countries, the ruler of the country is called the sultan.

sum sums, summing, summed *noun* 1 an amount of money. 2 In arithmetic, a sum is a calculation. 3 The sum of something is the total amount of it. ▷ **sum up** *verb* If you sum something up, you briefly describe its main points.

> ▶ **sum up** = recapitulate, summarise

summarise; also spelt **summarize** *verb* (EXAM TERM) To summarise something means to give a short account of its main points.

summary summaries *noun* 1 A summary of something is a short account of its main points. ▶ *adjective* 2 A summary action is done without delay or careful thought. ▷ **summarily** *adverb*

> **summary** *noun*
> 1 = outline, review, rundown, summing-up, synopsis

summer *noun* Summer is the season between spring and autumn.

summit *noun* 1 The summit of a mountain is its top. 2 a meeting between leaders of different countries to discuss particular issues.

summon *verb* 1 If someone summons you, they order you to go to them. 2 If you summon up strength or energy, you make a great effort to be strong or energetic.

summons summonses *noun* 1 an official order to appear in court. 2 an order to go to someone.

sumptuous *adjective* Something that is sumptuous is magnificent and obviously very expensive.

sum total *noun* The sum total of a number of things is all of them added or considered together.

sun suns, sunning, sunned *noun* 1 The sun is the star providing heat and light for the planets revolving around it in our solar system. **2** You refer to heat and light from the sun as sun. ▶ *verb* **3** If you sun yourself, you sit in the sunshine.

sunbathe *verb* If you sunbathe, you sit in the sunshine to get a suntan.

sunburn *noun* Sunburn is sore red skin on someone's body due to too much exposure to the rays of the sun. > **sunburnt** *adjective*

Sunday *noun* Sunday is the day between Saturday and Monday.

Sunday school *noun* Sunday school is a special class held on Sundays to teach children about Christianity.

sundry *adjective* **1** 'Sundry' is used to refer to several things or people of various sorts. ▶ *phrase* **2** All and sundry means everyone.

sunflower *noun* a tall plant with very large yellow flowers.

sung the past participle of **sing**.

sunglasses *plural noun* Sunglasses are spectacles with dark lenses that you wear to protect your eyes from the sun.

sunk the past participle of **sink**.

sunken *adjective* **1** having sunk to the bottom of the sea, a river, or a lake. **2** A sunken object or area has been constructed below the level of the surrounding area. **3** curving inwards.

sunlight *noun* Sunlight is the bright light produced when the sun is shining. > **sunlit** *adjective*

sunny sunnier, sunniest *adjective* When it is sunny, the sun is shining.

sunrise *noun* Sunrise is the time in the morning when the sun

first appears, and the colours produced in the sky at that time.

sunset *noun* Sunset is the time in the evening when the sun disappears below the horizon, and the colours produced in the sky at that time.

sunshine *noun* Sunshine is the bright light produced when the sun is shining.

suntan *noun* If you have a suntan, the sun has turned your skin brown. > **suntanned** *adjective*

super *adjective* very nice or very good.

superb *adjective* very good indeed. > **superbly** *adverb*

superb *adjective*
= breathtaking, excellent, exquisite, magnificent, marvellous, outstanding, splendid, superior, unrivalled, wonderful

superficial *adjective* **1** involving only the most obvious or most general aspects of something: *a superficial knowledge of music.* **2** not having a deep, serious or genuine interest in anything. **3** Superficial wounds are not very deep or severe. > **superficially** *adverb*

superfluous *adjective* (*formal*) unnecessary or no longer needed.

superhuman *adjective* having much greater power or ability than is normally expected of humans.

superintendent *noun* **1** a police officer above the rank of inspector. **2** a person whose job is to be responsible for a particular thing.

superior *adjective* **1** better or of higher quality than other similar things. **2** in a position of higher

authority than another person.
3 showing too much pride and
self-importance. ▶ *noun* **4** Your
superiors are people who are in a
higher position than you in
society or an organisation.
> **superiority** *noun*

> **superior** *adjective*
> **1** = better, choice, de luxe,
> exceptional, first-rate,
> surpassing, unrivalled
> **3** = condescending, disdainful,
> haughty, lofty, patronising,
> snobbish, stuck-up (*informal*),
> supercilious
> ▶ *noun* **4** = boss, manager,
> senior, supervisor

superlative *noun* **1** (ENGLISH) In
grammar, the superlative is the
form of an adjective which
indicates that the person or thing
described has more of a particular
quality than anyone or anything
else. For example, 'quickest', 'best'
and 'easiest' are all superlatives.
▶ *adjective* **2** (*formal*) very good
indeed.

supermarket *noun* a shop selling
food and household goods
arranged so that you can help
yourself and pay for everything at
a till by the exit.

supernatural *adjective*
1 Something that is supernatural,
for example ghosts or witchcraft,
cannot be explained by normal
scientific laws. ▶ *noun* **2** You can
refer to supernatural things as
the supernatural.

superpower *noun* a very powerful
and influential country such as
the USA.

supersede *verb* If something
supersedes another thing,
it replaces it because it is
more modern.

supersonic *adjective* A supersonic
aircraft can travel faster than the
speed of sound.

superstar *noun* You can refer to a
very famous entertainer or sports
player as a superstar.

superstition *noun* Superstition is a
belief in things like magic and
powers that bring good or bad
luck. > **superstitious** *adjective*

supervise *verb* To supervise
someone means to check and
direct what they are doing to
make sure that they do it
correctly. > **supervision** *noun*
> **supervisor** *noun*

> **supervise** *verb*
> = be in charge of, direct, have
> charge of, keep an eye on,
> manage, oversee, run

supper *noun* Supper is a meal
eaten in the evening or a snack
eaten before you go to bed.

supplant *verb* (*formal*) To supplant
someone or something means to
take their place.

supple *adjective* able to bend and
move easily.

supplement *verb* **1** To supplement
something means to add
something to it to improve it.
▶ *noun* **2** something that is added
to something else to improve it.
3 a separate part of a newspaper or
magazine, often dealing with a
particular subject.

> **supplement** *verb*
> **1** = add to, augment,
> complement, reinforce, top up
> ▶ *noun* **2** = addition, appendix,
> complement, extra

supplementary *adjective*
added to something else to
improve it.

supplier *noun* a firm which provides particular goods.

supply supplies, supplying, supplied *verb* 1 To supply someone with something means to provide it or send it to them. ▶ *noun* 2 A supply of something is an amount available for use. 3 (*in plural*) Supplies are food and equipment for a particular purpose.

> **supply** *verb*
> 1 = equip, furnish, give, provide
> ▶ *noun* 2 = cache, fund, hoard, reserve, stock, stockpile, store
> 3 = equipment, provisions, rations, stores

support *verb* 1 If you support someone, you agree with their aims and want them to succeed. 2 If you support someone who is in difficulties, you are kind, encouraging and helpful to them. 3 If something supports an object, it is underneath it and holding it up. 4 To support someone or something means to prevent them from falling by holding them. 5 To support someone financially means to provide them with money. ▶ *noun* 6 an object that is holding something up. 7 (PSHE) Moral support is encouragement given to someone to help them do something difficult. 8 Financial support is money that is provided for someone or something.
> **supportable** *adjective*

> **support** *verb*
> 1 = back, champion, defend, promote, second, side with, uphold 2 = encourage, help 3 = bolster, brace, hold up, prop up, reinforce
> ▶ *noun* 6 = brace, foundation, pillar, post, prop

supporter *noun* a person who agrees with or helps someone.

> **supporter** *noun*
> = adherent (*formal*), advocate, ally, champion, fan, follower, sponsor

supportive *adjective* A supportive person is encouraging and helpful to someone who is in difficulties.

suppose *verb* 1 If you suppose that something is the case, you think that it is likely. ▶ *phrase* 2 You can say I suppose when you are not entirely certain or enthusiastic about something: *Yes, I suppose he could come.* ▶ *conjunction* 3 You can use 'suppose' or 'supposing' when you are considering or suggesting a possible situation or action: *Supposing he were to break down under interrogation?*

> **suppose** *verb*
> 1 = assume, believe, expect, guess, imagine, presume, think

supposed *adjective* 1 'Supposed' is used to express doubt about something that is generally believed: *the supposed culprit.* 2 If something is supposed to be done or to happen, it is planned, expected or required to be done or to happen. 3 Something that is supposed to be the case is generally believed or thought to be so. ▷ **supposedly** *adverb*

> **supposed** *adjective*
> 2 = expected, meant, obliged, required 3 = alleged, assumed, believed, meant, presumed, reputed, rumoured

supposition *noun* something that is believed or assumed to be true.

suppress *verb* 1 If an army or government suppresses an activity, it prevents people from doing it. 2 If someone suppresses a piece of information, they prevent it from becoming generally known. 3 If you suppress your feelings, you stop yourself expressing them.
> **suppression** *noun*

> **suppress** *verb*
> 1 = crush, quash, quell, stamp out, stop 3 = conceal, contain, curb, repress, restrain, smother, stifle

supremacy *noun* If a group of people has supremacy over others, it is more powerful than the others.

supreme *adjective* 1 'Supreme' is used as part of a title to indicate the highest level of an organisation or system. 2 'Supreme' is used to emphasise the greatness of something.
> **supremely** *adverb*

> **supreme** *adjective*
> 2 = chief, foremost, greatest, highest, leading, paramount, pre-eminent, principal, top, ultimate

surcharge *noun* an additional charge.

sure *adjective* 1 If you are sure about something, you have no doubts about it. 2 If you are sure of yourself, you are very confident. 3 If something is sure to happen, it will definitely happen. 4 Sure means reliable or accurate. ▶ *phrase* 5 If you **make sure** about something, you check it or take action to see that it is done. ▶ *interjection* 6 Sure is an informal way of saying 'yes'.

> **sure** *adjective*
> 1 = certain, clear, convinced, definite, positive, satisfied
> 4 = definite, dependable, foolproof, infallible, reliable, trustworthy, undeniable

surely *adverb* 'Surely' is used to emphasise the belief that something is the case: *Surely these people here knew that?*

surf *verb* 1 When you surf, you take part in the sport of surfing. 2 When you surf the internet, you go from website to website reading the information. ▶ *noun* 3 Surf is the white foam that forms on the top of waves when they break near the shore.

surface *noun* 1 The surface of something is the top or outside area of it. 2 The surface of a situation is what can be seen easily rather than what is hidden or not immediately obvious. ▶ *verb* 3 If someone surfaces, they come up from under water to the surface.

surfboard *noun* a long narrow lightweight board used for surfing.

surf club *noun* In Australia, a surf club is an organisation of lifesavers in charge of safety on a particular beach, and which often provides leisure facilities.

surfeit *noun* If there is a surfeit of something, there is too much of it.

surfing *noun* Surfing is a sport which involves riding towards the shore on the top of a large wave while standing on a surfboard.

surge *noun* 1 a sudden great increase in the amount of

s

something. ▶ *verb* **2** If something surges, it moves suddenly and powerfully.

surgeon *noun* a doctor who performs operations.

surgery **surgeries** *noun* **1** Surgery is medical treatment involving cutting open part of the patient's body to treat the damaged part. **2** The room or building where a doctor or dentist works is called a surgery. **3** A period of time during which a doctor is available to see patients is called surgery.

surgical *adjective* used in or involving a medical operation. > **surgically** *adverb*

surly **surlier, surliest** *adjective* rude and bad-tempered. > **surliness** *noun*

surmise *verb* (*formal*) To surmise something means to guess it.

surname *noun* Your surname is your last name, which you share with other members of your family.

surpass *verb* (*formal*) To surpass someone or something means to be better than them.

surplus *noun* If there is a surplus of something there is more of it than is needed.

surprise *noun* **1** an unexpected event. **2** Surprise is the feeling caused when something unexpected happens. ▶ *verb* **3** If something surprises you, it gives you a feeling of surprise. **4** If you surprise someone, you do something they were not expecting. > **surprising** *adjective*

surprise *noun*
1 = bombshell, revelation, shock, start **2** = amazement, astonishment, incredulity, wonder

▶ *verb* **3** = amaze, astonish, astound, jolt, stagger, stun, take aback

surreal *adjective* very strange and dreamlike.

surrender *verb* **1** To surrender means to stop fighting and agree that the other side has won. **2** If you surrender to a temptation or feeling, you let it take control of you. **3** To surrender something means to give it up to someone else. ▶ *noun* **4** Surrender is a situation in which one side in a fight agrees that the other side has won and gives in.

surrender *verb*
1 = capitulate, give in, submit, succumb (*formal*), yield (*formal*) **3** = cede, give up, relinquish, renounce, yield (*formal*)
▶ *noun* **4** = capitulation, submission

surreptitious *adjective* A surreptitious action is done secretly or so that no-one will notice. > **surreptitiously** *adverb*

surrogate *adjective* **1** acting as a substitute for someone or something. ▶ *noun* **2** a person or thing that acts as a substitute.

surround *verb* **1** To surround someone or something means to be situated all around them. ▶ *noun* **2** The surround of something is its outside edge or border.

surround *verb*
1 = encircle, enclose, encompass, envelop, hem in

surrounding *adjective* The surrounding area of a particular place is the area around it.

surveillance *noun* Surveillance is the close watching of a person's activities by the police or army.

survey *verb* 1 To survey something means to look carefully at the whole of it. 2 To survey a building or piece of land means to examine it carefully in order to make a report or plan of its structure and features. ▶ *noun* 3 A survey of something is a detailed examination of it, often in the form of a report.

surveyor *noun* a person whose job is to survey buildings or land.

survival *noun* Survival is being able to continue living or existing in spite of great danger or difficulties.

survive *verb* To survive means to continue to live or exist in spite of great danger or difficulties. > **survivor** *noun*

> **survive** *verb*
> = endure, last, live, outlive, pull through

susceptible *adjective* If you are susceptible to something, you are likely to be influenced or affected by it. > **susceptibility** *noun*

suspect *verb* 1 If you suspect something, you think that it is likely or is probably true. 2 If you suspect something, you have doubts about its reliability or genuineness. 3 If you suspect someone of doing something wrong, you think that they have done it. ▶ *noun* 4 someone who is thought to be guilty of a crime. ▶ *adjective* 5 If something is suspect, it cannot be trusted or relied upon.

> **suspect** *verb*
> 1 = believe, feel, guess, suppose
> 2 = distrust, doubt, mistrust
> ▶ *adjective* 5 = dodgy (*British, Australian and New Zealand; informal*), doubtful, dubious, fishy (*informal*), questionable

suspend *verb* 1 If something is suspended, it is hanging from somewhere. 2 To suspend an activity or event means to delay it or stop it for a while. 3 If someone is suspended from their job, they are told not to do it for a period of time, usually as a punishment.

suspense *noun* Suspense is a state of excitement or anxiety caused by having to wait for something.

suspension *noun* 1 The suspension of something is the delaying or stopping of it. 2 A person's suspension is their removal from a job for a period of time, usually as a punishment. 3 The suspension of a vehicle consists of springs and shock absorbers which provide a smooth ride. 4 a liquid mixture in which very small bits of a solid material are contained and are not dissolved.

suspicion *noun* 1 Suspicion is the feeling of not trusting someone or the feeling that something is wrong. 2 a feeling that something is likely to happen or is probably true.

> **suspicion** *noun*
> 1 = distrust, doubt, misgiving, mistrust, scepticism 2 = hunch, idea, impression

suspicious *adjective* 1 If you are suspicious of someone, you do not trust them. 2 'Suspicious' is used to describe things that make you think that there is something wrong with a situation: *suspicious circumstances*. > **suspiciously** adverb

> **suspicious** adjective
> 1 = apprehensive, distrustful, doubtful, sceptical, wary
> 2 = dodgy (*British, Australian and New Zealand; informal*), doubtful, dubious, fishy (*informal*), funny, questionable, shady (*informal*), suspect

sustain verb 1 To sustain something means to continue it for a period of time. 2 If something sustains you, it gives you energy and strength. 3 (*formal*) To sustain an injury or loss means to suffer it.

sustainable adjective 1 capable of being sustained. 2 If economic development or energy resources are sustainable they are capable of being maintained at a steady level without exhausting natural resources or causing ecological damage.

sustenance noun (*formal*) Sustenance is food and drink.

swab swabs, swabbing, swabbed noun 1 a small piece of cotton wool used for cleaning a wound. ▶ verb 2 To swab something means to clean it using a large mop and a lot of water. 3 To swab a wound means to clean it or take specimens from it using a swab.

swag (*informal*) 1 goods or valuables, especially ones which have been gained dishonestly. 2 in Australian and New Zealand English, a swag is the bundle of possessions belonging to a tramp. 3 In Australian and New Zealand English, swags of something is lots of it.

swagger verb 1 To swagger means to walk in a proud, exaggerated way. ▶ noun 2 an exaggerated walk.

swallow verb 1 If you swallow something, you make it go down your throat and into your stomach. 2 When you swallow, you move your throat muscles as if you were swallowing something, especially when you are nervous. ▶ noun 3 a bird with pointed wings and a long forked tail.

swam the past tense of **swim**.

swamp noun 1 an area of permanently wet land. ▶ verb 2 If something is swamped, it is covered or filled with water. 3 If you are swamped by things, you have more than you are able to deal with. > **swampy** adjective

swan noun a large, usually white, bird with a long neck that lives on rivers or lakes.

swap swaps, swapping, swapped verb To swap one thing for another means to replace the first thing with the second, often by making an exchange with another person.

> **swap** verb
> = barter, exchange, interchange, switch, trade

swarm noun 1 A swarm of insects is a large group of them flying together. ▶ verb 2 When bees or other insects swarm, they fly together in a large group. 3 If people swarm somewhere, a lot of people go there quickly and at the same time. 4 If a place is swarming with people, there are a lot of people there.

swashbuckling adjective 'Swashbuckling' is used to

describe people who have the exciting behaviour or appearance of pirates.

swastika noun a symbol in the shape of a cross with each arm bent over at right angles. It was the official symbol of the Nazis in Germany, but in India it is a good luck sign.

swat swats, swatting, swatted verb To swat an insect means to hit it sharply in order to kill it.

swathe noun 1 a long strip of cloth that is wrapped around something. 2 A swathe of land is a long strip of it.

swathed adjective If someone is swathed in something, they are wrapped in it.

sway verb 1 To sway means to lean or swing slowly from side to side. 2 If something sways you, it influences your judgment. ▸ noun 3 (literary) Sway is the power to influence people.

swear swears, swearing, swore, sworn verb 1 To swear means to say words that are considered to be very rude or blasphemous. 2 If you swear to something, you state solemnly that you will do it or that it is true. 3 If you swear by something, you firmly believe that it is a reliable cure or solution. ▸ **swear in** verb When someone is sworn in to a new position, they solemnly promise to fulfil the duties and are officially appointed.

sweat noun 1 Sweat is the salty liquid produced by your body when you are hot or afraid. ▸ verb 2 When you sweat, sweat comes through the pores in your skin in order to lower the temperature of your body.

sweater noun a knitted piece of clothing covering your upper body and arms.

sweatshirt noun a piece of clothing made of thick cotton, covering your upper body and arms.

sweaty sweatier, sweatiest adjective covered or soaked with sweat.

Swede noun someone who comes from Sweden.

Swedish adjective 1 belonging or relating to Sweden. ▸ noun 2 Swedish is the main language spoken in Sweden.

sweep sweeps, sweeping, swept verb 1 If you sweep the floor, you use a brush to gather up dust or rubbish from it. 2 To sweep things off a surface means to push them all off with a quick, smooth movement. 3 If something sweeps from one place to another, it moves there very quickly. 4 If an attitude or new fashion sweeps a place, it spreads rapidly through it. ▸ noun 5 If you do something with a sweep of your arm, you do it with a wide curving movement of your arm.

sweeping adjective 1 A sweeping curve or movement is long and wide. 2 A sweeping statement is based on a general assumption rather than on careful thought. 3 affecting a lot of people to a great extent: *sweeping changes*.

sweet adjective 1 containing a lot of sugar. 2 pleasant and satisfying. 3 A sweet smell is soft and fragrant. 4 A sweet sound is gentle and tuneful. 5 attractive and pleasant. ▸ noun 6 Things such as toffees, chocolates and mints are sweets. 7 a dessert.

> **sweetly** adverb > **sweetness** noun

sweet adjective
1 = cloying, sugary, sweetened
3 = aromatic, fragrant, perfumed, sweet-smelling
4 = harmonious, mellow, melodious, musical, tuneful
▶ noun 6 = candy (American), confectionery, lolly (Australian and New Zealand), sweetie

sweet corn noun Sweet corn is a long stalk covered with juicy yellow seeds that can be eaten as a vegetable.

sweeten verb To sweeten food means to add sugar or another sweet substance to it.

sweetener noun A very sweet, artificial substance that can be used instead of sugar.

sweetheart noun 1 You can call someone who you are very fond of 'sweetheart'. 2 (old-fashioned) A young person's sweetheart is their boyfriend or girlfriend.

sweet tooth noun If you have a sweet tooth, you like sweet food very much.

swell swells, swelling, swelled, swollen verb 1 If something swells, it becomes larger and rounder. 2 If an amount swells, it increases in number. ▶ noun 3 The regular up and down movement of the waves at sea can be called a swell.

swelling noun 1 an enlarged area on your body as a result of injury or illness. 2 The swelling of something is an increase in its size.

sweltering adjective If the weather is sweltering, it is very hot.

swept the past tense and past participle of **sweep**.

swerve verb To swerve means to suddenly change direction to avoid colliding with something.

swerve verb
= swing, turn, veer

swift adjective 1 happening or moving very quickly. ▶ noun 2 a bird with narrow crescent-shaped wings. > **swiftly** adverb > **swiftness** noun

swift adjective
1 = brisk, express, fast, hurried, prompt, quick, rapid, speedy

swig swigs, swigging, swigged (informal) verb 1 To swig a drink means to drink it in large mouthfuls, usually from a bottle. ▶ noun 2 If you have a swig of a drink, you take a large mouthful of it.

swill verb 1 To swill something means to pour water over it to clean it. ▶ noun 2 Swill is a liquid mixture containing waste food that is fed to pigs.

swim swims, swimming, swam, swum verb 1 To swim means to move through water using various movements with parts of the body. 2 If things are swimming, it seems as if everything you see is moving and you feel dizzy. ▶ noun 3 If you go for a swim, you go into water to swim for pleasure. > **swimmer** noun

swimming noun Swimming is the activity of moving through water using your arms and legs.

swimming pool noun a large hole that has been tiled and filled with water for swimming.

swimsuit noun a piece of clothing worn for swimming.

swindle verb 1 To swindle someone means to deceive them to obtain money or property. ▶ noun 2 a trick in which someone is cheated out of money or property. > **swindler** noun

swine noun 1 (old-fashioned) A swine is another name for a pig. 2 (informal) If you call someone a swine, you mean they are nasty and spiteful.

swing swings, swinging, swung verb 1 If something swings, it moves repeatedly from side to side from a fixed point. 2 If someone or something swings in a particular direction, they turn quickly or move in a sweeping curve in that direction. ▶ noun 3 a seat hanging from a frame or a branch, which you sit on and move backwards and forwards. 4 A swing in opinion is a significant change in people's opinion.

swipe verb 1 To swipe at something means to try to hit it making a curving movement with the arm. 2 (informal) To swipe something means to steal it. 3 To swipe a credit card means to pass it through a machine that electronically reads the information stored in the card. ▶ noun 4 To take a swipe at something means to swipe at it.

swirl verb To swirl means to move quickly in circles.

swish verb 1 To swish means to move quickly through the air making a soft sound. ▶ noun 2 the sound made when something swishes.

Swiss Swiss adjective 1 belonging or relating to Switzerland. ▶ noun 2 someone who comes from Switzerland.

switch noun 1 a small control for an electrical device or machine. 2 a change. ▶ verb 3 To switch to a different task or topic means to change to it. 4 If you switch things, you exchange one for the other. > **switch off** verb To switch off a light or machine means to stop it working by pressing a switch. > **switch on** verb To switch on a light or machine means to start it working by pressing a switch.

switchboard noun The switchboard of an organisation is the part where all telephone calls are received.

swivel swivels, swivelling, swivelled verb 1 To swivel means to turn round on a central point. ▶ adjective 2 A swivel chair or lamp is made so that you can move the main part of it while the base remains in a fixed position.

swollen past participle of **swell**.

swoon verb (literary) To swoon means to faint as a result of strong emotion.

swoop verb To swoop means to move downwards through the air in a fast curving movement.

swop another spelling of **swap**.

sword noun a weapon consisting of a very long blade with a short handle.

swordfish swordfishes or swordfish noun a large sea fish with an upper jaw which sticks out like a sword.

swore the past tense of **swear**.

sworn the past participle of **swear**.

swum the past participle of **swim**.

swung the past tense and past participle of **swing**.

sycamore noun a tree that has large leaves with five points.

syllable noun (ENGLISH) a part of a word that contains a single vowel sound and is pronounced as a unit. For example, 'book' has one syllable and 'reading' has two.

syllabus syllabuses or syllabi noun The subjects that are studied for a particular course or examination are called the syllabus.

symbol noun a shape, design or idea that is used to represent something.

> **symbol** noun
> = emblem, emoticon, figure, logo, mark, representation, sign, token

symbolic adjective Something that is symbolic has a special meaning that is considered to represent something else.

symbolise; also spelt **symbolize** verb If a shape, design or idea symbolises something, it is regarded as being a symbol of it. > **symbolism** noun

symmetrical adjective (MATHS) If something is symmetrical, it could be split into two halves, one being the exact reflection of the other. > **symmetrically** adverb

symmetry noun (MATHS) Something that has symmetry is symmetrical.

sympathetic adjective 1 A sympathetic person shows kindness and understanding to other people. 2 If you are sympathetic to a proposal or an idea, you approve of it.

sympathise; also spelt **sympathize** verb To sympathise with someone who is in difficulties means to show them understanding and care.

sympathiser; also spelt **sympathizer** noun People who support a particular cause can be referred to as sympathisers.

sympathy sympathies noun 1 Sympathy is kindness and understanding towards someone who is in difficulties. 2 If you have sympathy with someone's ideas or actions, you agree with them. ▶ phrase 3 If you do something in sympathy with someone, you do it to show your support for them.

> **sympathy** noun
> 1 = compassion, empathy, pity, understanding

symphony symphonies noun a piece of music for an orchestra, usually in four movements.

symptom noun 1 something wrong with your body that is a sign of an illness. 2 Something that is considered to be a sign of a bad situation can be referred to as a symptom of it. > **symptomatic** adjective

synagogue noun (RE) a building where Jewish people meet for worship and religious instruction.

synchronise; also spelt **synchronize** verb 1 To synchronise two actions means to do them at the same time and speed. 2 To synchronise watches means to set them to show exactly the same time as each other. > **synchronisation** noun

syndicate *noun* an association of business people formed to carry out a particular project.

syndrome *noun* **1** a medical condition characterised by a particular set of symptoms. **2** You can refer to a typical set of characteristics as a syndrome.

synod *noun* a council of church leaders which meets regularly to discuss religious and moral issues.

synonym *noun* (ENGLISH) If two words have the same or a very similar meaning, they are synonyms.

synonymous *adjective* **1** Two words that are synonymous have the same or very similar meanings. **2** If two things are closely associated, you can say that one is synonymous with the other.

synopsis synopses *noun* a summary of a book, play or film.

syntax *noun* (ENGLISH) The syntax of a language is its grammatical rules and the way its words are arranged.

synthesis syntheses *noun* A synthesis of different ideas or styles is a blended combination of them. ▶ **synthesise** *verb*

synthetic *adjective* made from artificial substances rather than natural ones.

Syrian *adjective* **1** belonging or relating to Syria. ▶ *noun* **2** someone who comes from Syria.

syringe *noun* a hollow tube with a part which is pushed down inside and a fine hollow needle at one end, used for injecting or extracting liquids.

syrup *noun* a thick sweet liquid made by boiling sugar with water. ▶ **syrupy** *adjective*

system *noun* **1** (LIBRARY) an organised way of doing or arranging something according to a fixed plan or set of rules. **2** People sometimes refer to the government and administration of the country as the system. **3** You can also refer to a set of equipment as a system. **4** In biology, a system of a particular kind is the set of organs that perform that function.

> **system** *noun*
> **1** = arrangement, method, procedure, routine, structure, technique

systematic *adjective* following a fixed plan and done in an efficient way. ▶ **systematically** *adverb*

s

tab | 704

Tt

tab *noun* a small extra piece that is attached to something, for example on a curtain so it can be hung on a pole.

tabby tabbies *noun* a cat whose fur has grey, brown or black stripes.

table *noun* 1 a piece of furniture with a flat horizontal top supported by one or more legs. 2 a set of facts or figures arranged in rows or columns. ▶ *verb* 3 If you table something such as a proposal, you say formally that you want it to be discussed.

tablecloth *noun* a cloth used to cover a table and keep it clean.

tablespoon *noun* a large spoon used for serving food; also the amount that a tablespoon contains.

tablet *noun* 1 any small, round pill made of powdered medicine. 2 a slab of stone with words cut into it. 3 (ICT) a small mobile personal computer with a screen that is manipulated by swiping or tapping with the hand.

table tennis *noun* Table tennis is a game for two or four people in which you use bats to hit a small hollow ball over a low net across a table.

tabloid *noun* (ENGLISH) a newspaper with small pages, short news stories, and lots of photographs.

taboo taboos *noun* 1 a social custom that some words, subjects or actions must be avoided because they are considered embarrassing or offensive. 2 a religious custom that forbids people to do something. ▶ *adjective* 3 forbidden or disapproved of.

tacit *adjective* understood or implied without actually being said or written. > **tacitly** *adverb*

taciturn *adjective* Someone who is taciturn does not talk very much and so seems unfriendly.

tack *noun* 1 a short nail with a broad, flat head. 2 If you change tack, you start to use a different method for dealing with something. ▶ *verb* 3 If you tack something to a surface, you nail it there with tacks. 4 If you tack a piece of fabric, you sew it with long loose stitches.

tackle *verb* 1 If you tackle a difficult task, you start dealing with it in a determined way. 2 If you tackle someone in a game such as soccer, you try to get the ball away from them. 3 If you tackle someone about something, you talk to them about it in order to get something changed or dealt with. ▶ *noun* 4 A tackle in sport is an attempt to get the ball away from your opponent. 5 Tackle is the equipment used for fishing.

tacky tackier, tackiest *adjective* 1 slightly sticky to touch. 2 (*informal*) badly made and in poor taste.

tact *noun* Tact is the ability to see when a situation is difficult or delicate and to handle it without upsetting people. > **tactless** *adjective* > **tactlessly** *adverb*

T

tact noun
= delicacy, diplomacy, discretion, sensitivity

tactful adjective behaving with or showing tact. > **tactfully** adverb

tactful adjective
= diplomatic, discreet, sensitive

tactic noun 1 Tactics are the methods you use to achieve what you want, especially to win a game. 2 Tactics are also the ways in which troops and equipment are used in order to win a battle.

tactical adjective relating to or using tactics. > **tactically** adverb

tactile adjective involving the sense of touch.

taffeta noun Taffeta is a stiff, shiny fabric.

tag tags, tagging, tagged noun 1 a small label made of cloth, paper or plastic. ▶ verb 2 If you tag something, you attach a tag to it.

tail noun 1 The tail of an animal, bird or fish is the part extending beyond the end of its body. 2 Tail can be used to mean the end part of something: *the tail of the plane*. ▶ verb 3 (informal) If you tail someone, you follow them in order to find out where they go and what they do. ▶ adjective, adverb 4 The 'tails' side of a coin is the side which does not have a person's head. > **tail off** verb If something tails off, it becomes gradually less.

tailback noun a long queue of traffic stretching back from whatever is blocking the road.

tailor noun 1 a person who makes, alters and repairs clothes, especially for men. ▶ verb 2 If something is tailored for a

particular purpose, it is specially designed for it.

tailor-made adjective suitable for a particular person or purpose, or specifically designed for them.

taint verb 1 To taint something is to spoil it by adding something undesirable to it. ▶ noun 2 an undesirable quality in something which spoils it.

take takes, taking, took, taken verb 1 'Take' is used to show what action or activity is being done: *Amy took a bath.* 2 If something takes a certain amount of time, or a particular quality or ability, it requires it. 3 If you take something, you put your hand round it and hold it or carry it. 4 If you take someone somewhere, you drive them there by car or lead them there. 5 If you take something that is offered to you, you accept it. 6 If you take the responsibility or blame for something, you accept responsibility or blame for it. 7 If you take something that does not belong to you, you steal it. 8 If you take pills or medicine, you swallow them. 9 If you can take something painful, you can bear it. 10 If you take someone's advice, you do what they say you should do. 11 If you take a person's temperature or pulse, you measure it. 12 If you take a car or train, or a road or route, you use it to go from one place to another. ▶ phrase 13 If you **take care of** someone or something, you look after them. 14 If you **take care of** a problem or situation, you deal with it and get it sorted. > **take after** verb If you take after someone in your family, you look or behave like them. > **take down**

verb If you take down what someone is saying, you write it down.
> **take in** *verb* 1 If someone is taken in, they are deceived. 2 If you take something in, you understand it.
> **take off** *verb* When an aeroplane takes off, it leaves the ground and begins to fly. > **takeoff** *noun*
> **take over** *verb* To take something over means to start controlling it. > **takeover** *noun*
> **take to** *verb* If you take to someone or something, you like them immediately.

take *verb*
2 = demand, require 3 = bear (*formal*), bring, carry, convey (*formal*), ferry, fetch, transport 4 = bring, conduct (*formal*), escort, guide, lead, usher
▶ *phrase* 13 = care for, look after, mind, nurse, protect, tend, watch 14 = attend to, cope with, deal with, handle, manage, see to
▶ **take in** 1 = con (*informal*), deceive, dupe, fool, mislead, trick 2 = absorb, appreciate, assimilate, comprehend, digest, get, grasp, understand

takeaway *noun* 1 a shop or restaurant that sells hot cooked food to be eaten elsewhere. 2 a hot cooked meal bought from a takeaway.

takings *plural noun* Takings are the money that a shop or cinema gets from selling its goods or tickets.

tale *noun* a story.

talent *noun* Talent is the natural ability to do something well.
> **talented** *adjective*

talent *noun*
= ability, aptitude, capacity, flair, genius, gift, knack

talisman *noun* an object which you believe has magic powers to protect you or bring luck.

talk *verb* 1 When you talk, you say things to someone. 2 If you talk on or about something, you make a speech about it.
▶ *noun* 3 Talk is discussion or gossip. 4 an informal speech about something. > **talk down** *verb* If you talk down to someone, you talk to them in a way that shows that you think you are more important or clever than them.

talk *noun*
3 = chat, chatter, conversation 4 = address, discourse, lecture, sermon, speech

talkative *adjective* talking a lot.

talkative *adjective*
= chatty, communicative, long-winded

tall *adjective* 1 of more than average or normal height. 2 having a particular height: *a wall ten metres tall.* ▶ *phrase* 3 If you describe something as a tall story, you mean that it is difficult to believe because it is so unlikely.

tall *adjective*
1 = high, lanky, lofty, soaring, towering

tally tallies, tallying, tallied *noun* 1 an informal record of amounts which you keep adding to as you go along. ▶ *verb* 2 If numbers or statements tally, they are exactly the same or they give the same results or conclusions.

tambourine *noun* a percussion instrument made of a skin stretched tightly over a circular frame, with small round pieces of metal around the edge that jingle when the tambourine is beaten or shaken.

tame *adjective* 1 A tame animal or bird is not afraid of people and is not violent towards them. 2 Something that is tame is uninteresting and lacks excitement or risk. ▸ *verb* 3 If you tame people or things, you bring them under control. 4 To tame a wild animal or bird is to train it to be obedient and live with humans.

tamper *verb* If you tamper with something, you interfere or meddle with it.

tan tans, tanning, tanned *noun* 1 If you have a tan, your skin is darker than usual because you have been in the sun. ▸ *verb* 2 To tan an animal's hide is to turn it into leather by treating it with chemicals. ▸ *adjective* 3 Something that is tan is of a light yellowish-brown colour.

tandem *noun* A bicycle designed for two riders sitting one behind the other.

tang *noun* A strong, sharp smell or flavour. > **tangy** *adjective*

tangerine *noun* 1 A type of small sweet orange with a loose rind. ▸ *noun, adjective* 2 reddish-orange.

tangible *adjective* Clear or definite enough to be easily seen or felt.

tangle *noun* 1 A mass of things such as hairs or fibres knotted or coiled together and difficult to separate. ▸ *verb* 2 If you are tangled in wires or ropes, you are caught or trapped in them so that it is difficult to get free.

tangle *noun*
1 = jumble, knot, mass, mat, muddle, web
▸ *verb* 2 = catch, jumble, knot, twist

tango tangos *noun* A tango is a Latin American dance using long gliding steps and dramatic pauses; also a piece of music composed for this dance.

tank *noun* 1 A large container for storing liquid or gas. 2 An armoured military vehicle which moves on tracks and is equipped with guns or rockets.

tanker *noun* A ship or lorry designed to carry large quantities of gas or liquid.

tannin *noun* A brown or yellow substance found in plants and used in making leather.

tantalising; also spelt **tantalizing** *adjective* Something that is tantalising makes you feel hopeful and excited, although you know that you probably will not be able to have what you want.

tantamount *adjective* If you say that something is tantamount to something else, you mean that it is almost the same as it.

tantrum *noun* A noisy and sometimes violent outburst of temper, especially by a child.

Tanzanian *adjective* 1 Belonging or relating to Tanzania. ▸ *noun* 2 Someone who comes from Tanzania.

tap taps, tapping, tapped *noun* 1 A device that you turn to control the flow of liquid or gas from a pipe or container. 2 The action of hitting something lightly; also the sound that this action makes.

▶ *verb* **3** If you tap something or tap on it, you hit it lightly. **4** If a telephone is tapped, a device is fitted to it so that someone can listen secretly to the calls.

tape *noun* **1** Tape is plastic ribbon covered with a magnetic substance and used to record sounds, pictures and computer data. **2** A tape is a recording of sounds, pictures or computer data. **3** Tape is a long, thin strip of fabric that is used for binding or fastening. **4** Tape is also a strip of sticky plastic which you use for sticking things together. ▶ *verb* **5** If you tape sounds or television pictures, you record them. **6** If you tape one thing to another, you attach them using sticky tape.

tape measure *noun* a strip of plastic or metal that is marked off in inches or centimetres and used for measuring things.

taper *verb* **1** Something that tapers becomes thinner towards one end. ▶ *noun* **2** a thin candle.

tape recorder *noun* a machine used for recording sounds onto magnetic tape, and for playing these sounds back.

tapestry tapestries *noun* a piece of heavy cloth with designs woven into it.

tar *noun* Tar is a thick, black, sticky substance which is used in making roads.

target *noun* **1** something which you aim at when firing weapons. **2** The target of an action or remark is the person or thing at which it is directed. **3** Your target is the result that you are trying to achieve.

tariff *noun* **1** a tax that a government collects on imported goods. **2** any list of prices or charges.

tarmac *noun* Tarmac is a material used for making road surfaces. It consists of crushed stones mixed with tar.

tarnish *verb* **1** If metal tarnishes, it becomes stained and loses its shine. **2** If something tarnishes your reputation, it spoils it and causes people to lose their respect for you.

tarpaulin *noun* a sheet of heavy waterproof material used as a protective covering.

tarragon *noun* Tarragon is a herb with narrow green leaves used in cooking.

tart *noun* **1** a pastry case with a sweet filling. ▶ *adjective* **2** Something that is tart is sour or sharp to taste. **3** A tart remark is unpleasant and cruel.

tartan *noun* Tartan is a woollen fabric from Scotland with checks of various colours and sizes, depending on which clan it belongs to.

task *noun* any piece of work which has to be done.

> **task** *noun*
> = assignment, chore, duty, job, mission, undertaking

Tasmanian devil *noun* a black-and-white marsupial of Tasmania, which eats flesh.

taste *noun* **1** Your sense of taste is your ability to recognise the flavour of things in your mouth. **2** The taste of something is its flavour. **3** If you have a taste of food or drink, you have a small amount of it to see what it is like.

4 If you have a taste for something, you enjoy it. **5** If you have a taste of something, you experience it. **6** A person's taste is their choice in the things they like to buy or have around them. ▸ *verb* **7** When you can taste something in your mouth, you are aware of its flavour. **8** If you taste food or drink, you have a small amount of it to see what it is like. **9** If food or drink tastes of something, it has that flavour.

> **taste** noun
> **2** = flavour, tang **3** = bite, mouthful, sip **4** = appetite, fondness, liking, penchant (formal)

tasteful adjective attractive and elegant. ▸ **tastefully** adverb

tasteless adjective **1** vulgar and unattractive. **2** A tasteless remark or joke is offensive. **3** Tasteless food has very little flavour.

> **tasteless** adjective
> **1** = flashy, garish, gaudy, tacky (informal), tawdry, vulgar **3** = bland, insipid

tasty tastier, tastiest adjective having a pleasant flavour.

> **tasty** adjective
> = appetising, delicious, lekker (South African; slang), luscious, palatable

tatters phrase Clothes that are in tatters are badly torn. ▸ **tattered** adjective

tattoo tattoos, tattooing, tattooed verb **1** If someone tattoos you or tattoos a design on you, they draw it on your skin by pricking little holes and filling them with coloured dye. ▸ noun **2** a picture or design tattooed on

someone's body. **3** a public military display of exercises and music.

tatty tattier, tattiest adjective worn out or untidy and rather dirty.

taught the past tense and past participle of **teach**.

taunt verb **1** To taunt someone is to speak to them about their weaknesses or failures in order to make them angry or upset. ▸ noun **2** an offensive remark intended to make a person angry or upset.

Taurus noun Taurus is the second sign of the zodiac, represented by a bull. People born between April 20th and May 20th are born under this sign.

taut adjective stretched very tight.

tavern noun (old-fashioned) a pub.

tawdry tawdrier, tawdriest adjective cheap, gaudy and of poor quality.

tawny noun, adjective brownish-yellow.

tax noun **1** Tax is an amount of money that the people in a country have to pay to the government so that it can provide public services such as health care and education. ▸ verb **2** If a sum of money is taxed, a certain amount of it has to be paid to the government. **3** If goods are taxed, a certain amount of their price has to be paid to the government. **4** If a person or company is taxed, they have to pay a certain amount of their income to the government. **5** If something taxes you, it makes heavy demands on you. ▸ **taxation** noun

tax noun
1 = duty, excise, levy (formal), tariff
▶ verb 5 = drain, exhaust, sap, strain, stretch

taxi taxis, taxiing, taxied noun 1 a car with a driver which you hire to take you to where you want to go. ▶ verb 2 When an aeroplane taxis, it moves slowly along the runway before taking off or after landing.

tea noun 1 Tea is the dried leaves of an evergreen shrub found in Asia. 2 Tea is a drink made by brewing the leaves of the tea plant in hot water; also a cup of this. 3 Tea is also any drink made with hot water and leaves or flowers. 4 Tea is a meal taken in the late afternoon or early evening.

teach teaches, teaching, taught verb 1 If you teach someone something, you give them instructions about it or know how to do it. 2 If you teach a subject, you help students learn about a subject at school, college or university.
> **teaching** noun

teach verb
1 = coach, drill, educate, instruct, school, train, tutor

teacher noun a person who teaches other people, especially children.

teacher noun
= coach, don, guru, instructor, lecturer, master, mistress, professor, tutor

teak noun Teak is a hard wood which comes from a large Asian tree.

team noun 1 a group of people who work together or play together against another group in a sport or game. ▶ verb 2 If you team up with someone, you join them and work together with them.

team noun
1 = band, crew, gang, group, side, squad, troupe
▶ verb 2 = collaborate, cooperate, join forces, link up, pair up, unite, work together

teamwork noun Teamwork is the ability of a group of people to work well together.

teapot noun a round pot with a handle, a lid and a spout, used for brewing and pouring tea.

tear[1] noun Tears are the drops of salty liquid that come out of your eyes when you cry.

tear[2] tears, tearing, tore, torn noun 1 a hole that has been made in something. ▶ verb 2 If you tear something, it is damaged by being pulled so that a hole appears in it. 3 If you tear somewhere, you rush there.

tear noun
1 = hole, ladder, rip, rupture, scratch, split
▶ verb 2 = ladder, rip, rupture, scratch, shred, split 3 = charge, dart, dash, fly, race, shoot, speed, zoom

tearaway noun someone who is wild and uncontrollable.

tearful adjective about to cry or crying gently. > **tearfully** adverb

tease verb 1 If you tease someone, you deliberately make fun of them or embarrass them because it amuses you. ▶ noun 2 someone who enjoys teasing people.

tease verb
1 = make fun of, mock, needle (informal), taunt

teaspoon noun a small spoon used for stirring drinks; also the amount that a teaspoon holds.

tea tree noun a tree found in Australia and New Zealand with leaves that yield an oil used as an antiseptic.

tech noun (informal) a technical college.

technical adjective 1 involving machines, processes and materials used in industry, transport and communications. 2 skilled in practical and mechanical things rather than theories and ideas. 3 involving a specialised field of activity: I never understood the technical jargon.

technicality technicalities noun The technicalities of a process or activity are the detailed methods used to do it.

technically adverb If something is technically true or correct, it is true or correct when you consider only the facts, rules or laws, but may not be important or relevant in a particular situation.

technician noun someone whose job involves skilled practical work with scientific equipment.

technique noun 1 a particular method of doing something. 2 Technique is skill and ability in an activity which is developed through training and practice.

technology technologies noun (D&T) Technology is the study of the application of science and scientific knowledge for practical purposes in industry, farming, medicine or business.

> **technological** adjective
> **technologically** adverb

teddy teddies noun A teddy or teddy bear is a stuffed toy that looks like a friendly bear.

tedious adjective boring and lasting for a long time.

tedium noun the quality of being boring and lasting for a long time.

tee tees, teeing, teed noun the small wooden or plastic peg on which a golf ball is placed before the golfer first hits it. > **tee off** verb To tee off is to hit the golf ball from the tee, or to start a round of golf.

teem verb 1 If a place is teeming with people or things, there are a lot of them moving about. 2 If it teems, it rains very heavily.

teenage adjective 1 aged between thirteen and nineteen. 2 typical of people aged between thirteen and nineteen. > **teenager** noun

teens plural noun Your teens are the period of your life when you are between thirteen and nineteen years old.

teeter verb To teeter is to shake or sway slightly in an unsteady way and seem about to fall over.

teeth the plural of **tooth**.

teetotal adjective Someone who is teetotal never drinks alcohol. > **teetotaller** noun

telecommunications noun Telecommunications is the science and activity of sending signals and messages over long distances using electronic equipment.

telegram noun a message sent by telegraph.

telegraph noun The telegraph is a

system of sending messages over long distances using electrical or radio signals.

telephone *noun* **1** a piece of electrical equipment for talking directly to someone who is in a different place. ▶ *verb* **2** If you telephone someone, you speak to them using a telephone.

telescope *noun* a long instrument shaped like a tube which has lenses which make distant objects appear larger and nearer.

televise *verb* If an event is televised, it is filmed and shown on television.

television *noun* a piece of electronic equipment which receives pictures and sounds by electrical signals over a distance.

tell tells, telling, told *verb* **1** If you tell someone something, you let them know about it. **2** If you tell someone to do something, you order or advise them to do it. **3** If you can tell something, you are able to judge correctly what is happening or what the situation is: *I could tell he was scared.* **4** If an unpleasant or tiring experience begins to tell, it begins to have a serious effect.

> **tell** *verb*
> **1** = inform, notify
> **2** = command, direct (*formal*), instruct, order **3** = discern, see

teller *noun* a person who receives or gives out money in a bank.

telling *adjective* Something that is telling has an important effect, often because it shows the true nature of a situation.

telltale *adjective* A telltale sign reveals information: *the sad telltale signs of a recent accident.*

telly tellies *noun* (*informal*) a television.

temerity *noun* If someone has the temerity to do something, they do it even though it upsets or annoys other people.

temp *noun* (*informal*) an employee who works for short periods of time in different places.

temper *noun* **1** Your temper is the frame of mind or mood you are in. **2** a sudden outburst of anger. ▶ *phrase* **3** If you **lose your temper**, you become very angry. ▶ *verb* **4** To temper something is to make it more acceptable or suitable.

temperament *noun* Your temperament is your nature or personality, shown in the way you react towards people and situations.

temperamental *adjective* Someone who is temperamental has moods that change often and suddenly.

temperate *adjective* (GEOGRAPHY) A temperate place has weather that is neither extremely hot nor extremely cold.

temperature *noun* **1** (SCIENCE) The temperature of something is how hot or cold it is. **2** Your temperature is the temperature of your body. ▶ *phrase* **3** If you **have a temperature**, the temperature of your body is higher than it should be, because you are ill.

tempest *noun* (*literary*) a violent storm.

tempestuous *adjective* violent or strongly emotional.

template *noun* a shape or pattern cut out in wood, metal, plastic or card which you draw or cut around to reproduce that shape or pattern.

temple *noun* 1 (RE) A building used for the worship of a god in various religions. 2 Your temples are the flat parts on each side of your forehead.

tempo tempos *or* tempi *noun* 1 The tempo of something is the speed at which it happens. 2 (MUSIC) The tempo of a piece of music is its speed.

temporary *adjective* lasting for only a short time. > **temporarily** *adverb*

> **temporary** *adjective*
> = ephemeral (*formal*), fleeting, interim, momentary, passing, provisional, transient (*formal*), transitory

tempt *verb* 1 If you tempt someone, you try to persuade them to do something by offering them something they want. 2 If you are tempted to do something, you want to do it but you think it might be wrong or harmful.

> **tempt** *verb*
> 1 = entice, lure, seduce

temptation *noun* 1 Temptation is the state you are in when you want to do or have something, even though you know it might be wrong or harmful. 2 something that you want to do or have, even though you know it might be wrong or harmful.

ten the number 10. > **tenth** *adjective*

tenacious *adjective* determined and not giving up easily. > **tenaciously** *adverb* **tenacity** *noun*

tenant *noun* someone who pays rent for the place they live in, or for land or buildings that they use. > **tenancy** *noun*

tend *verb* 1 If something tends to happen, it happens usually or often. 2 If you tend someone or something, you look after them.

> **tend** *verb*
> 1 = be apt, be inclined, be liable, be prone, have a tendency
> 2 = care for, look after, nurse, take care of

tendency tendencies *noun* a trend or type of behaviour that happens very often.

> **tendency** *noun*
> = inclination, leaning, propensity

tender *adjective* 1 Someone who is tender has gentle and caring feelings. 2 If someone is at a tender age, they are young and do not know very much about life. 3 Tender meat is easy to cut or chew. 4 If a part of your body is tender, it is painful and sore. ▸ *verb* 5 If someone tenders an apology or their resignation, they offer it. ▸ *noun* 6 a formal offer to supply goods or to do a job for a particular price.

> **tender** *adjective*
> 1 = affectionate, caring, compassionate, gentle, kind, loving, sensitive, warm
> 4 = aching, bruised, inflamed, painful, raw, sensitive, sore
> ▸ *verb* 5 = hand in, offer
> ▸ *noun* 6 = bid, estimate, package, submission

tendon *noun* (SCIENCE) a strong cord of tissue which joins a muscle to a bone.

tenement *noun* a large house or building divided into many flats.

tenet *noun* The tenets of a theory or belief are the main ideas it is based upon.

t

tenner noun (informal) a ten-pound or ten-dollar note.

tennis noun Tennis is a game played by two or four players on a rectangular court in which a ball is hit by players over a central net.

tenor noun 1 a man who sings in a fairly high voice. 2 The tenor of something is the general meaning or mood that it expresses. ▶ adjective 3 A tenor recorder, saxophone or other musical instrument has a range of notes of a fairly low pitch.

tense adjective 1 If you are tense, you are nervous and cannot relax. 2 A tense situation or period of time is one that makes people nervous and worried. 3 If your body is tense, your muscles are tight. ▶ verb 4 If you tense, or if your muscles tense, your muscles become tight and stiff. ▶ noun 5 The tense of a verb is the form which shows whether you are talking about the past, present or future.

> **tense** adjective
> 1 = anxious, edgy, jittery (informal), jumpy, nervous, uptight (informal) 2 = anxious, nerve-racking, stressful 3 = rigid, strained, taut, tight

tension noun 1 Tension is the feeling of nervousness or worry that you have when something dangerous or important is happening. 2 (DGT) The tension in a rope or wire is how tightly it is stretched.

tent noun a shelter made of canvas or nylon held up by poles and pinned down with pegs and ropes.

tentacle noun The tentacles of an animal such as an octopus are the long, thin parts that it uses to feel and hold things.

tentative adjective acting or speaking cautiously because of being uncertain or afraid.
> **tentatively** adverb

tenterhooks plural noun If you are on tenterhooks, you are nervous and excited about something that is going to happen.

tenuous adjective If an idea or connection is tenuous, it is so slight and weak that it may not really exist or may easily cease to exist.

tenure noun 1 Tenure is the legal right to live in a place or to use land or buildings for a period of time. 2 Tenure is the period of time during which someone holds an important job.

tepid adjective Tepid liquid is only slightly warm.

term noun 1 a fixed period of time. 2 one of the periods of time that each year is divided into at a school or college. 3 a name or word used for a particular thing. 4 (in plural) The terms of an agreement are the conditions that have been accepted by the people involved in it. 5 If you express something in particular terms, you express it using a particular type of language or in a way that clearly shows your attitude. ▶ phrase 6 If you come to terms with something difficult or unpleasant, you learn to accept it. ▶ verb 7 To term something is to give it a name or to describe it.

> **term** noun
> 1 = period, session, spell, stretch, time 3 = designation,

expression, name, word
4 = conditions, provisions,
proviso, stipulations

terminal adjective **1** A terminal
illness or disease cannot be cured
and causes death gradually.
▶ noun **2** a place where vehicles,
passengers or goods begin or end
a journey. **3** A computer terminal
is a keyboard and a visual display
unit that is used to put
information into or get
information out of a computer.
4 one of the parts of an electrical
device through which electricity
enters or leaves. > **terminally**
adverb

terminate verb When you
terminate something or when it
terminates, it stops or ends.
> **termination** noun

terminology terminologies noun
The terminology of a subject is
the set of special words and
expressions used in it.

terminus noun a place where a
bus or train route ends.

termite noun Termites are small
white insects that feed on wood.

terrace noun **1** a row of houses
joined together. **2** a flat area of
stone next to a building where
people can sit.

terracotta noun a type of brown
pottery with no glaze.

terrain noun The terrain of an area
is the type of land there.

terrestrial adjective involving the
earth or land.

terrible adjective **1** serious and
unpleasant. **2** (informal) very bad
or of poor quality.

> **terrible** adjective
> **1** = appalling, awful, desperate,
> dreadful, frightful

(old-fashioned), horrendous,
horrible, horrid (old-fashioned),
rotten (informal) **2** = abysmal,
appalling, awful, dire,
dreadful, horrible, rotten
(informal)

terribly adverb very or very much.

terrier noun a small, short-bodied
dog.

terrific adjective **1** (informal) very
pleasing or impressive. **2** great in
amount, degree or intensity.
> **terrifically** adverb

terrify terrifies, terrifying,
terrified verb If something
terrifies you, it makes you feel
extremely frightened.

territorial adjective involving or
relating to the ownership of a
particular area of land or water.

territory territories noun **1** The
territory of a country is the land
that it controls. **2** An animal's
territory is an area which it
regards as its own and defends
when other animals try to enter it.

> **territory** noun
> **1** = area, country, district,
> domain, dominion, land,
> province, state

terror noun **1** Terror is great fear or
panic. **2** something that makes
you feel very frightened.

terrorise; also spelt **terrorize**
verb If someone terrorises you,
they frighten you by threatening
you or being violent to you.

terrorism noun Terrorism is the
use of violence for political
reasons. > **terrorist** noun, adjective

terse adjective A terse statement is
short and rather unfriendly.

tertiary adjective **1** third in order
or importance. **2** Tertiary education

t

is education at university or college level.

test *verb* **1** When you test something, you try it to find out what it is, what condition it is in, or how well it works. **2** If you test someone, you ask them questions to find out how much they know. ▶ *noun* **3** a deliberate action or experiment to find out whether something works or how well it works. **4** a set of questions or tasks given to someone to find out what they know or can do.

> **test** *verb*
> **1** = assess, check, try, try out
> ▶ *noun* **3** = assessment, check, trial

testament *noun* **1** (*Law*) a will. **2** a copy of either the Old or the New Testament of the Bible.

test case *noun* a legal case that becomes an example for deciding other similar cases.

testicle *noun* (SCIENCE) A man's testicles are the two sex glands beneath the penis that produce sperm.

testify testifies, testifying, testified *verb* **1** When someone testifies, they make a formal statement, especially in a court of law. **2** To testify to something is to show that it is likely to be true.

testimonial *noun* a statement saying how good someone or something is.

testimony testimonies *noun* A person's testimony is a formal statement they make, especially in a court of law.

test match *noun* one of a series of international cricket or rugby matches.

testosterone *noun* Testosterone is a hormone that produces male characteristics.

test tube *noun* a small cylindrical glass container that is used in chemical experiments.

tetanus *noun* Tetanus is a painful infectious disease caused by germs getting into wounds.

tether *verb* **1** If you tether an animal, you tie it to a post. ▶ *phrase* **2** If you are **at the end of your tether**, you are extremely tired and have no more patience or energy left to deal with your problems.

Teutonic *adjective* (*formal*) involving or related to German people.

text *noun* **1** The text of a book is the main written part of it, rather than the pictures or index. **2** Text is any written material. **3** a book or other piece of writing used for study or an exam at school or college. **4** Text is short for 'text message'. ▶ *verb* **5** If you text someone, you send them a text message. > **textual** *adjective*

textbook *noun* a book about a particular subject for students to use.

textile *noun* (DGT) a woven cloth or fabric.

text message *noun* a written message sent using a mobile phone.

texture *noun* The texture of something is the way it feels when you touch it.

> **texture** *noun*
> = consistency, feel

Thai Thais *adjective* **1** belonging or relating to Thailand. ▶ *noun* **2** someone who comes from

Thailand. **3** Thai is the main language spoken in Thailand.

than *preposition, conjunction* **1** You use 'than' to link two parts of a comparison: *She was older than me.* **2** You use 'than' to link two parts of a contrast: *Players would rather play than train.*

thank *verb* When you thank someone, you show that you are grateful for something, usually by saying 'thank you'.

thankful *adjective* happy and relieved about something.
> **thankfully** *adverb*

thankless *adjective* A thankless job or task involves doing a lot of hard work that other people do not notice or are not grateful for.

thanks *plural noun* **1** When you express your thanks to someone, you tell or show them how grateful you are for something.
▶ *interjection* **2** You say 'thanks' to show that you are grateful for something.

thanksgiving *noun*
1 Thanksgiving is an act of thanking God, especially in prayer or in a religious ceremony. **2** In the United States, Thanksgiving is a public holiday in the autumn.

thank you *interjection* You say 'thank you' to show that you are grateful to someone for something.

that *adjective, pronoun* **1** 'That' or 'those' is used to refer to things or people already mentioned or known about: *That man was waving.* ▶ *conjunction* **2** 'That' is used to introduce a clause: *I said that I was coming home.* **3** 'That' is also used to introduce a relative clause: *I followed Alex to a door that led inside.*

thatch *noun* **1** Thatch is straw and reeds used to make roofs. ▶ *verb* **2** To thatch a roof is to cover it with thatch.

thaw *verb* **1** When snow or ice thaws, it melts. **2** When you thaw frozen food, or when it thaws, it returns to its normal state in a warmer atmosphere. **3** When people who are unfriendly thaw, they begin to be more friendly and relaxed. ▶ *noun* **4** A period of warmer weather in winter when snow or ice melts.

the The definite article 'the' is used when you are talking about something that is known about, that has just been mentioned, or that you are going to give details about.

theatre *noun* **1** (DRAMA) a building where plays and other entertainments are performed on a stage. **2** Theatre is work such as writing, producing and acting in plays. **3** An operating theatre is a room in a hospital designed and equipped for surgical operations.

theatrical *adjective* **1** (DRAMA) involving the theatre or performed in a theatre. **2** Theatrical behaviour is exaggerated, unnatural and done for effect. ▶ **theatrically** *adverb*

thee *pronoun* (*old-fashioned*) Thee means you.

theft *noun* Theft is the crime of stealing.

> **theft** *noun*
> = robbery, stealing, thieving

their *adjective* 'Their' refers to something belonging or relating to people or things, other than yourself or the person you are talking to, which have already been mentioned: *It was their fault.*

theirs pronoun 'Theirs' refers to something belonging or relating to people or things, other than yourself or the person you are talking to, which have already been mentioned: *Amy had been Helen's friend, not theirs.*

them pronoun 'Them' refers to things or people, other than yourself or the people you are talking to, which have already been mentioned: *He picked up the pillows and threw them to the floor.*

theme noun 1 (ENGLISH) a main idea or topic in a piece of writing, painting, film or music. 2 a tune, especially one played at the beginning and end of a television or radio programme.

themselves pronoun
1 'Themselves' is used when people, other than yourself or the person you are talking to, do an action and are affected by it: *They think they've made a fool of themselves.* 2 'Themselves' is used to emphasise 'they': *He was as excited as they themselves were.*

then adverb at a particular time in the past or future: *I'd left home by then.*

theologian noun someone who studies religion and the nature of God.

theology noun (RE) Theology is the study of religion and God.
> **theological** adjective

theoretical adjective 1 based on or to do with ideas of a subject rather than the practical aspects. 2 not proved to exist or be true.
> **theoretically** adverb

theory theories noun 1 an idea or set of ideas that is meant to explain something. 2 Theory is the set of rules and ideas that a

particular subject or skill is based upon. ▶ *phrase* 3 You use **in theory** to say that although something is supposed to happen, it may not in fact happen.

> **theory** noun
> 1 = conjecture (*formal*), hypothesis (*formal*), supposition, surmise (*formal*)

therapeutic adjective 1 If something is therapeutic, it helps you to feel happier and more relaxed. 2 In medicine, therapeutic treatment is designed to treat a disease or to improve a person's health.

therapy noun Therapy is the treatment of mental or physical health problems, often without the use of drugs or operations.
> **therapist** noun

there adverb 1 in, at or to that place, point or case: *He's sitting over there.* ▶ *pronoun* 2 'There' is used to say that something exists or does not exist, or to draw attention to something: *There are flowers on the table.*

therefore adverb as a result.

> **therefore** adverb
> = as a result, consequently, for that reason, hence (*formal*), so, thus

thermal adjective 1 to do with or caused by heat. 2 Thermal clothes are specially designed to keep you warm in cold weather.

thermometer noun (SCIENCE) an instrument for measuring the temperature of a room or a person's body.

thermostat noun a device used to control temperature, for example on a central heating system.

thesaurus thesauruses
noun (LIBRARY) A reference book in which words with similar meanings are grouped together.

these the plural of **this**.

thesis theses noun A long piece of writing, based on research, that is done as part of a university degree.

they pronoun 1 'They' refers to people or things, other than you or the people you are talking to, that have already been mentioned: *They married two years later.* 2 'They' is sometimes used instead of 'he' or 'she' where the gender of the person is unknown or unspecified. Some people consider this to be incorrect: *Someone could have a nasty accident if they tripped over that.*

thick adjective 1 Something thick has a large distance between its two opposite surfaces. 2 If something is a particular amount thick, it measures that amount between its two sides. 3 Thick means growing or grouped closely together and in large quantities. 4 Thick liquids contain little water and do not flow easily. 5 (informal) A thick person is stupid or slow to understand things.

> **thick** adjective
> 1 = fat, wide 3 = bristling, dense, lush, luxuriant 4 = clotted, concentrated, condensed

thicken verb If something thickens, it becomes thicker.

> **thicken** verb
> = clot, condense, congeal, set

thicket noun A small group of trees growing closely together.

thief thieves noun A person who steals.

> **thief** noun
> = burglar, crook (informal), mugger (informal), pickpocket, robber, shoplifter

thieving noun Thieving is the act of stealing.

thigh noun Your thighs are the top parts of your legs, between your knees and your hips.

thin thinner, thinnest; thins, thinning, thinned adjective 1 Something that is thin is much narrower than it is long. 2 A thin person or animal has very little fat on their body. 3 Thin liquids contain a lot of water. ▶ verb 4 If you thin something such as paint or soup, you add water or other liquid to it.

> **thin** adjective
> 1 = fine, narrow, slim 3 = dilute or diluted, runny, watery, weak

thing noun 1 An object, rather than a plant, an animal or a human being. 2 (in plural) Your things are your clothes or possessions.

> **thing** noun
> 1 = article, object
> 2 = belongings, effects, gear (informal), possessions, stuff

think thinks, thinking, thought verb 1 When you think about ideas or problems, you use your mind to consider them. 2 If you think something, you have the opinion that it is true or the case. 3 If you think of something, you remember it or it comes into your mind. 4 If you think a lot of someone or something, you admire them or think they are good.

t

think verb
1 = consider, contemplate, deliberate, meditate, mull over, muse (literary), ponder, reflect
2 = believe, consider, deem (formal), hold, imagine, judge, reckon (informal)

third adjective 1 The third item in a series is the one counted as number three. ▶ noun 2 one of three equal parts.

Third World noun The poorer countries of Africa, Asia and South America are sometimes referred to as the Third World.

thirst noun 1 If you have a thirst, you feel a need to drink something. 2 A thirst for something is a very strong desire for it. > **thirsty** adjective > **thirstily** adverb

thirteen the number 13.
> **thirteenth** adjective

thirty thirties the number 30.
> **thirtieth** adjective

this adjective, pronoun 1 'This' is used to refer to something or someone that is nearby or has just been mentioned: This is Robert. 2 'This' is used to refer to the present time or place: this week.

thistle noun a wild plant with prickly-edged leaves and purple flowers.

thong noun a long narrow strip of leather.

thorn noun one of many sharp points growing on some plants and trees.

thorny thornier, thorniest adjective 1 covered with thorns. 2 A thorny subject or question is difficult to discuss or answer.

thorough adjective 1 done very carefully and completely.

2 A thorough person is very careful in what they do and makes sure nothing has been missed out. > **thoroughly** adverb

thorough adjective
1 = complete, comprehensive, exhaustive, full, intensive, meticulous, painstaking, scrupulous

thoroughbred noun an animal that has parents that are of the same high quality breed.

thoroughfare noun a main road in a town.

those the plural of **that**.

thou pronoun (old-fashioned) Thou means you.

though conjunction 1 despite the fact that: Meg felt cold, even though the sun was out. 2 if: It looks as though you were right.

thought 1 Thought is the past tense and past participle of **think**. ▶ noun 2 an idea that you have in your mind. 3 Thought is the activity of thinking.

thought noun
2 = idea, notion, opinion, view
3 = consideration, contemplation, deliberation, meditation, reflection, thinking

thoughtful adjective 1 When someone is thoughtful, they are quiet and serious because they are thinking about something. 2 A thoughtful person remembers what other people want or need, and tries to be kind to them. > **thoughtfully** adverb

thoughtful adjective
1 = contemplative, pensive, reflective 2 = attentive, caring, considerate, kind

T

thoughtless *adjective* A thoughtless person forgets or ignores what other people want, need or feel. > **thoughtlessly** *adverb*

> **thoughtless** *adjective*
> = insensitive, tactless

thousand the number 1000. > **thousandth** *adjective*

thrash *verb* 1 To thrash someone is to beat them by hitting them with something. 2 To thrash someone in a contest or fight is to defeat them completely. 3 To thrash out a problem or an idea is to discuss it in detail until a solution is reached.

thread *noun* 1 a long, fine piece of cotton, silk, nylon or wool. 2 The thread on something such as a screw at the top of a container is the raised spiral line of metal or plastic round it. 3 The thread of an argument or story is an idea or theme that connects the different parts of it. 4 On the internet, a thread is a series of messages from different people about a particular subject. ▸ *verb* 5 When you thread something, you pass thread, tape or cord through it. 6 If you thread your way through people or things, you carefully make your way through them.

threadbare *adjective* Threadbare cloth or clothing is old and thin.

threat *noun* 1 a statement that someone will harm you, especially if you do not do what they want. 2 anything or anyone that seems likely to harm you. 3 If there is a threat of something unpleasant happening, it is very possible that it will happen.

threat *noun*
1 = menace, threatening remark
2 = hazard, menace, risk

threaten *verb* 1 If you threaten to harm someone or threaten to do something that will upset them, you say that you will do it. 2 If someone or something threatens a person or thing, they are likely to harm them.

> **threaten** *verb*
> 1 = make threats to, menace
> 2 = endanger, jeopardise, put at risk, put in jeopardy

three the number 3.

three-dimensional *adjective* (MATHS) A three-dimensional object or shape is not flat, but has height or depth as well as length and width.

threesome *noun* a group of three.

threshold *noun* 1 the doorway or the floor at the entrance to a building or room. 2 The threshold of something is the lowest amount, level or limit at which something happens or changes.

threw the past tense of **throw**.

thrice *adverb* (old-fashioned) If you do something thrice, you do it three times.

thrift *noun* Thrift is the practice of saving money and not wasting things.

thrifty thriftier, thriftiest *adjective* A thrifty person saves money and does not waste things.

> **thrifty** *adjective*
> = careful, economical, frugal, prudent

thrill *noun* 1 a sudden feeling of great excitement, pleasure or fear; also any event or experience that gives you such a feeling.

▶ **verb 2** If something thrills you, or you thrill to it, it gives you a feeling of great pleasure and excitement. > **thrilled** adjective > **thrilling** adjective

> **thrill** noun
> **1** = high (informal), kick (informal)
> ▶ verb **2** = excite, give a kick (informal)

thriller noun a book, film or play that tells an exciting story about dangerous or mysterious events.

thrive thrives, thriving, thrived or throve verb When people or things thrive, they are healthy, happy or successful. > **thriving** adjective

> **thrive** verb
> = do well, flourish, prosper

throat noun **1** the back of your mouth and the top part of the passages inside your neck. **2** the front part of your neck.

throb throbs, throbbing, throbbed verb **1** If a part of your body throbs, you feel a series of strong beats or dull pains. **2** If something throbs, it vibrates and makes a loud, rhythmic noise.

throes plural noun Throes are a series of violent pangs or movements.

thrombosis thromboses noun a blood clot which blocks the flow of blood in the body. Thromboses are dangerous and often fatal.

throne noun **1** a ceremonial chair used by a king or queen on important official occasions. **2** The throne is a way of referring to the position of being king or queen.

throng noun **1** a large crowd of people. ▶ verb **2** If people throng somewhere or throng a place, they go there in great numbers.

throttle verb To throttle someone is to kill or injure them by squeezing their throat.

through preposition **1** moving all the way from one side of something to the other: a path through the woods. **2** because of: He had been exhausted through lack of sleep. **3** during: He has to work through the summer. **4** If you go through an experience, it happens to you. ▶ adjective **5** If you are through with something, you have finished doing it or using it.

throughout preposition **1** during: I stayed awake throughout the night. ▶ adverb **2** happening or existing through the whole of a place: The house was painted brown throughout.

throw throws, throwing, threw, thrown verb **1** When you throw something you are holding, you move your hand quickly and let it go, so that it moves through the air. **2** If you throw yourself somewhere, you move there suddenly and with force. **3** To throw someone into an unpleasant situation is to put them there. **4** If something throws light or shadow on something else, it makes that thing have light or shadow on it. **5** If you throw yourself into an activity, you become actively and enthusiastically involved in it. **6** If you throw a fit or tantrum, you suddenly begin behaving in an uncontrolled way.

> **throw** verb
> **1** = cast, chuck (informal), fling, hurl, lob, pitch, sling, toss

throwback noun something which has the characteristics of something that existed a long time ago.

thrush *noun* a small brown songbird.

thrust thrusts, thrusting, thrust *verb* 1 If you thrust something somewhere, you push or move it there quickly with a lot of force. 2 If you thrust your way somewhere, you move along, pushing between people or things. ▶ *noun* 3 a sudden forceful movement. 4 The main thrust of an activity or idea is the most important part of it.

thud thuds, thudding, thudded *noun* 1 a dull sound, usually made by a solid, heavy object hitting something soft. ▶ *verb* 2 If something thuds somewhere, it makes a dull sound, usually by hitting something else.

thug *noun* a very rough and violent person.

> **thug** *noun*
> = bandit, hooligan, tough, tsotsi (South African)

thumb *noun* 1 the short, thick finger on the side of your hand. ▶ *verb* 2 If someone thumbs a lift, they stand at the side of the road and stick out their thumb until a driver stops and gives them a lift.

thump *verb* 1 If you thump someone or something, you hit them hard with your fist. 2 If something thumps somewhere, it makes a fairly loud, dull sound, usually when it hits something else. 3 When your heart thumps, it beats strongly and quickly. ▶ *noun* 4 a hard hit. 5 a fairly loud, dull sound.

thunder *noun* 1 Thunder is a loud cracking or rumbling noise caused by expanding air which is suddenly heated by lightning.

2 Thunder is any loud rumbling noise. ▶ *verb* 3 When it thunders, a loud cracking or rumbling noise occurs in the sky after a flash of lightning. 4 If something thunders, it makes a loud continuous noise.

thunderbolt *noun* a flash of lightning, accompanied by thunder.

thunderous *adjective* A thunderous noise is very loud.

Thursday *noun* Thursday is the day between Wednesday and Friday.

thus *adverb* (formal) 1 in this way: *I sat thus for nearly half an hour.* 2 therefore: *She is more experienced than him, thus better paid.*

thwart *verb* To thwart someone or their plans is to prevent them from doing or getting what they want.

thy *adjective* (old-fashioned) Thy means your.

thyme *noun* Thyme is a bushy herb with very small leaves.

tiara *noun* a semicircular crown of jewels worn by a woman on formal occasions.

Tibetan *adjective* 1 belonging or relating to Tibet. ▶ *noun* 2 someone who comes from Tibet.

tic *noun* a twitching of a group of muscles, especially the muscles in the face.

tick *noun* 1 a written mark to show that something is correct or has been dealt with. 2 The tick of a clock is the series of short sounds it makes when it is working. 3 a tiny, blood-sucking, insect-like creature that usually lives on the bodies of people or animals. ▶ *verb* 4 To tick something written on a piece of paper is to put a tick next to it. **5** When a clock ticks, it makes a regular series of short sounds as it works. > **ticking** noun > **tick off** verb (informal) If you tick someone off, you speak angrily to them because they have done something wrong.

ticket noun a piece of paper or card which shows that you have paid for a journey or have paid to enter a place of entertainment.

tickle verb **1** When you tickle someone, you move your fingers lightly over their body in order to make them laugh. **2** If something tickles you, it amuses you or gives you pleasure.

tidal adjective to do with or produced by tides.

tidal wave noun (GEOGRAPHY) a very large wave, often caused by an earthquake, that comes over land and destroys things.

tide noun **1** The tide is the regular change in the level of the sea on the shore, caused by the gravitational pull of the sun and the moon. **2** The tide of opinion or fashion is what the majority of people think or do at a particular time. **3** A tide of something is a large amount of it. > **tide over** verb If something will tide someone over, it will help them through a difficult period of time.

tidings plural noun (formal) Tidings are news.

tidy tidier, tidiest; tidies, tidying, tidied adjective **1** Something that is tidy is neat and arranged in an orderly way. **2** Someone who is tidy always keeps their things neat and arranged in an orderly way. **3** (informal) A tidy amount of money is a fairly large amount

of it. ▶ verb **4** To tidy a place is to make it neat by putting things in their proper place.

tidy adjective
1 = neat, orderly
▶ verb **4** = spruce up, straighten

tie ties, tying, tied verb **1** If you tie one thing to another or tie it in a particular position, you fasten it using cord of some kind. **2** If you tie a knot or a bow in a piece of cord or cloth, you fasten the ends together to make a knot or bow. **3** Something or someone that is tied to something else is closely linked with it. **4** If you tie with someone in a competition or game, you have the same number of points. ▶ noun **5** a long, narrow piece of cloth worn around the neck under a shirt collar and tied in a knot at the front. **6** a connection or feeling that links you with a person, place or organisation.

tie verb
1 = bind, fasten, knot, lash, rope, secure, tether, truss **4** = be level, draw
▶ noun **6** = affiliation, affinity, bond, connection, relationship

tied up adjective If you are tied up, you are busy.

tier noun one of a number of rows or layers of something.

tiff noun (informal) a small unimportant quarrel.

tiger noun a large meat-eating animal of the cat family. It comes from Asia and has an orange coloured coat with black stripes.

tight adjective **1** fitting closely. **2** firmly fastened and difficult to move. **3** stretched or pulled so as not to be slack. **4** A tight plan or arrangement allows only the minimum time or money needed to do something. ▶ adverb **5** held firmly and securely. > **tightly** adverb > **tightness** noun

tight adjective
1 = constricted, cramped, snug
2 = firm, secure **3** = rigid, taut, tense

tighten verb **1** If you tighten your hold on something, you hold it more firmly. **2** If you tighten a rope or chain, or if it tightens, it is stretched or pulled until it is straight. **3** If someone tightens a rule or system, they make it stricter or more efficient.

tightrope noun a tightly stretched rope on which an acrobat balances and performs tricks.

tights plural noun Tights are a piece of clothing made of thin stretchy material that fit closely round a person's hips, legs and feet.

tile noun **1** a small flat square piece of something, for example slate or carpet, that is used to cover surfaces. ▶ verb **2** To tile a surface is to fix tiles to it. > **tiled** adjective

till preposition, conjunction **1** Till means the same as until. ▶ noun **2** a drawer or box in a shop where money is kept, usually in a cash register. ▶ verb **3** To till the ground is to plough it for raising crops.

tiller noun the handle fixed to the top of the rudder for steering a boat.

tilt verb **1** If you tilt an object or it tilts, it changes position so that one end or side is higher than the other. ▶ noun **2** a position in which one end or side of something is higher than the other.

tilt verb
1 = incline, lean, slant, slope, tip
▶ noun **2** = angle, gradient, incline, slant, slope

timber noun **1** Timber is wood that has been cut and prepared ready for building and making furniture. **2** The timbers of a ship or house are the large pieces of wood that have been used to build it.

timbre noun (MUSIC) The timbre of a musical instrument, voice or sound is the particular quality or characteristic it has.

time noun **1** Time is what is measured in hours, days and years. **2** 'Time' is used to mean a particular period or point: I enjoyed my time in Durban. **3** If you say it is time for something or it is time to do it, you mean that it ought to happen or be done now. **4** 'Times' is used after numbers to indicate how often something happens: I saw my father four times a year. **5** 'Times' is used in arithmetic to link numbers that are multiplied together: Two times three is six. ▶ verb **6** If you time something for a particular time, you plan that it should happen then. **7** If you time an activity or action, you measure how long it lasts.

time noun
2 = interval, period, spell, stretch, while
▶ verb **6** = schedule, set

timeless adjective Something timeless is so good or beautiful that it cannot be affected by the passing of time or by changes in fashion.

timely adjective happening at just the right time.

timer *noun* a device that measures time, especially one that is part of a machine.

timescale *noun* The timescale of an event is the length of time during which it happens.

timetable *noun* 1 a plan of the times when particular activities or jobs should be done. 2 a list of the times when particular trains, boats, buses or aeroplanes arrive and depart.

timid *adjective* shy and having no courage or self-confidence. > **timidity** *noun* > **timidly** *adverb*

> **timid** *adjective*
> = bashful, cowardly, diffident, nervous, shy

timing *noun* 1 Someone's timing is their skill in judging the right moment at which to do something. 2 The timing of an event is when it actually happens.

tin *noun* 1 (SCIENCE) Tin is a soft, silvery-white metallic element used in alloys. Its atomic number is 50, and its symbol is Sn. 2 A tin is a metal container which is filled with food and then sealed in order to preserve the food. 3 A tin is a small metal container which may have a lid.

tinge *noun* a small amount of something. > **tinged** *adjective*

tingle *verb* 1 When a part of your body tingles, you feel a slight prickling feeling in it. ▶ *noun* 2 a slight prickling feeling. > **tingling** *noun, adjective*

tinker *noun* 1 a person who travels from place to place mending metal pots and pans or doing other small repair jobs. ▶ *verb* 2 If you tinker with something, you make a lot of small changes to it in order to repair or improve it.

tinned *adjective* Tinned food has been preserved by being sealed in a tin.

tinsel *noun* Tinsel is long threads with strips of shiny paper attached, used as a decoration at Christmas.

tint *noun* 1 a small amount of a particular colour. ▶ *verb* 2 If a person tints their hair, they change its colour by adding a weak dye to it. > **tinted** *adjective*

tiny tinier, tiniest *adjective* extremely small.

> **tiny** *adjective*
> = diminutive, microscopic, miniature, minute, negligible, wee (Scottish)

tip tips, tipping, tipped *noun* 1 the end of something long and thin. 2 a place where rubbish is dumped. 3 If you give someone such as a waiter a tip, you give them some money to thank them for their services. 4 a useful piece of advice or information. ▶ *verb* 5 If you tip an object, you move it so that it is no longer horizontal or upright. 6 If you tip something somewhere, you pour it there quickly or carelessly. > **tipped** *adjective*

tipple *noun* A person's tipple is the alcoholic drink that they normally drink.

tipsy tipsier, tipsiest *adjective* slightly drunk.

tiptoe tiptoes, tiptoeing, tiptoed *verb* If you tiptoe somewhere, you walk there very quietly on your toes.

tirade *noun* a long, angry speech in which you criticise someone or something.

tire verb 1 If something tires you, it makes you use a lot of energy so that you want to rest or sleep. 2 If you tire of something, you become bored with it.

> **tire** verb
> 1 = drain, exhaust, fatigue

tired adjective having little energy.
> **tiredness** noun

> **tired** adjective
> = drained, drowsy, exhausted, fatigued, sleepy, tuckered out (*American, Australian and New Zealand; informal*), weary, worn out

tireless adjective Someone who is tireless has a lot of energy and never seems to need a rest.

tiresome adjective A person or thing that is tiresome makes you feel irritated or bored.

tiring adjective Something that is tiring makes you tired.

tissue noun 1 (SCIENCE) The tissue in plants and animals consists of cells that are similar in appearance and function. 2 Tissue is thin paper that is used for wrapping breakable objects. 3 a small piece of soft paper that you use as a handkerchief.

titanic adjective very big or important.

title noun 1 the name of a book, film or piece of music. 2 a word that describes someone's rank or job. 3 the position of champion in a sports competition.

titled adjective Someone who is titled has a high social rank and has a title such as 'Princess', 'Lord', 'Lady' or 'Sir'.

TNT noun TNT is a type of powerful explosive. It is an abbreviation for 'trinitrotoluene'.

to preposition 1 'To' is used to indicate the place that someone or something is moving towards or pointing at: *They are going to China.* 2 'To' is used to indicate the limit of something: *Goods to the value of 500 pounds.* 3 'To' is used in ratios and rates when saying how many units of one type there are for each unit of another: *I only get about 30 kilometres to the gallon from it.* ▶ adverb 4 If you push or shut a door to, you close it but do not shut it completely.

toad noun an amphibian that looks like a frog but has a drier skin and lives less in the water.

toast noun 1 Toast is slices of bread made brown and crisp by cooking at a high temperature. 2 To drink a toast to someone is to drink an alcoholic drink in honour of them. ▶ verb 3 If you toast bread, you cook it at a high temperature so that it becomes brown and crisp. 4 If you toast yourself, you sit in front of a fire so that you feel pleasantly warm. 5 To toast someone is to drink an alcoholic drink in honour of them.

toaster noun a piece of electrical equipment used for toasting bread.

tobacco noun Tobacco is the dried leaves of the tobacco plant which people smoke in pipes, cigarettes and cigars.

today adverb, noun 1 Today means the day on which you are speaking or writing. 2 Today also means the present period of history.

toddler noun a small child who has just learned to walk.

to-do to-dos *noun* A to-do is a situation in which people are very agitated or confused.

toe *noun* 1 Your toes are the five movable parts at the end of your foot. 2 The toe of a shoe or sock is the part that covers the end of your foot.

toff *noun* (*informal, old-fashioned*) a rich person or one from an aristocratic family.

toffee *noun* Toffee is a sticky, chewy sweet made by boiling sugar and butter together with water.

together *adverb* 1 If people do something together, they do it with each other. 2 If two things happen together, they happen at the same time. 3 If things are joined or fixed together, they are joined or fixed to each other. 4 If things or people are together, they are very near to each other.

> **together** *adverb*
> 1 = collectively, en masse, in unison, jointly, shoulder to shoulder, side by side 2 = as one, at once, concurrently (*formal*), simultaneously, with one accord

togetherness *noun* Togetherness is a feeling of closeness and friendship.

toil *verb* 1 When people toil, they work hard doing unpleasant, difficult or tiring tasks or jobs. ▶ *noun* 2 Toil is unpleasant, difficult or tiring work.

toilet *noun* 1 a large bowl, connected by a pipe to the drains, which you use when you want to get rid of urine or faeces. 2 a small room containing a toilet.

toiletries *plural noun* Toiletries are the things you use when cleaning and taking care of your body, such as soap and talc.

token *noun* 1 a piece of paper or card that is worth a particular amount of money and can be exchanged for goods. 2 a flat round piece of metal or plastic that can sometimes be used instead of money. 3 If you give something to someone as a token of your feelings for them, you give it to them as a way of showing those feelings. ▶ *adjective* 4 If something is described as token, it shows that it is not being treated as important.

told Told is the past tense and past participle of **tell**.

tolerable *adjective* 1 able to be put up with. 2 fairly satisfactory or reasonable.

> **tolerable** *adjective*
> 1 = acceptable, bearable
> 2 = acceptable, adequate, okay or OK (*informal*), passable, reasonable, so-so (*informal*)

tolerance *noun* 1 A person's tolerance is their ability to accept or put up with something which may not be enjoyable or pleasant for them. 2 Tolerance is the quality of allowing other people to have their own attitudes or beliefs, or to behave in a particular way, even if you do not agree or approve.

tolerant *adjective* accepting of different views and behaviour.

> **tolerant** *adjective*
> = broad-minded, liberal, open-minded, understanding

tolerate *verb* 1 If you tolerate things that you do not approve of or agree with, you allow them. **2** If you can tolerate something, you accept it, even though it is unsatisfactory or unpleasant. > **toleration** noun

> **tolerate** verb
> **1** = accept, put up with **2** = bear, endure, stand

toll noun **1** The death toll in an accident is the number of people who have died in it. **2** a sum of money that you have to pay in order to use a particular bridge or road. ▶ verb **3** When someone tolls a bell, it is rung slowly, often as a sign that someone has died.

tom noun a male cat.

tomato tomatoes noun a small round red fruit, used as a vegetable and often eaten raw in salads.

tomb noun a large grave for one or more corpses.

> **tomb** noun
> = grave, mausoleum, sarcophagus, sepulchre (literary), vault

tomboy noun a girl who likes playing rough or noisy games.

tome noun (formal) a very large heavy book.

tomorrow adverb, noun **1** Tomorrow means the day after today. **2** You can refer to the future, especially the near future, as tomorrow.

ton noun **1** a unit of weight equal to 2240 pounds or about 1016 kilograms. **2** (in plural, informal) If you have tons of something, you have a lot of it.

tonal adjective involving the quality or pitch of a sound or of music.

tone noun **1** Someone's tone is a quality in their voice which shows what they are thinking or feeling. **2** (MUSIC) The tone of a musical instrument or a singer's voice is the kind of sound it has. **3** (ENGLISH) The tone of a piece of writing is its style and the ideas or opinions expressed in it. **4** (ART) a lighter, darker or brighter shade of the same colour. > **tone down** verb If you tone down something, you make it less forceful or severe.

tongs plural noun Tongs consist of two long narrow pieces of metal joined together at one end. You press the pieces together to pick an object up.

tongue noun **1** Your tongue is the soft part in your mouth that you can move and use for tasting, licking and speaking. **2** a language. **3** Tongue is the cooked tongue of an ox. **4** The tongue of a shoe or boot is the piece of leather underneath the laces.

tonic noun **1** Tonic or tonic water is a colourless, fizzy drink that has a slightly bitter flavour and is often mixed with alcoholic drinks. **2** a medicine that makes you feel stronger, healthier and less tired. **3** anything that makes you feel stronger or more cheerful.

tonight adverb, noun Tonight is the evening or night that will come at the end of today.

tonne noun a unit of weight equal to 1000 kilograms.

tonsillitis noun Tonsillitis is a painful swelling of your tonsils caused by an infection.

too adverb **1** also or as well: You were there too. **2** more than a desirable, necessary or acceptable amount: We had spent too long in the sun.

too adverb
1 = as well, besides, in addition, into the bargain, likewise, moreover 2 = excessively, over-, overly, unduly, unreasonably

took the past tense of **take**.

tool noun 1 any hand-held instrument or piece of equipment that you use to help you do a particular kind of work. 2 an object, skill or idea that is needed or used for a particular purpose.

tool noun
1 = implement, instrument, utensil

tooth teeth noun 1 Your teeth are the hard, enamel-covered objects in your mouth that you use for biting and chewing food. 2 The teeth of a comb, saw or zip are the parts that stick out in a row on its edge.

toothbrush noun a small brush that you use for cleaning your teeth.

toothpaste noun Toothpaste is a substance which you use to clean your teeth.

top tops, topping, topped noun 1 The top of something is its highest point, part or surface. 2 The top of a bottle, jar or tube is its cap or lid. 3 a piece of clothing worn on the upper half of your body. 4 a toy with a pointed end on which it spins. ▶ adjective 5 The top thing of a series of things is the highest one. ▶ verb 6 If someone tops a poll or popularity chart, they do better than anyone else in it. 7 If something tops a particular amount, it is greater than that amount. ▷ **top up** verb To top something up is to add

something to it in order to keep it at an acceptable or usable level.

top hat noun a tall hat with a narrow brim that men wear on special occasions.

topic noun a particular subject that you write about or discuss.

topical adjective involving or related to events that are happening at the time you are speaking or writing.

topping noun food that is put on top of other food in order to decorate it or add to its flavour.

topple verb If something topples, it becomes unsteady and falls over.

top-secret adjective meant to be kept completely secret.

topsy-turvy adjective in a confused state.

Torah noun (RE) The Torah is Jewish law and teaching.

torch noun 1 a small electric light carried in the hand and powered by batteries. 2 a long stick with burning material wrapped around one end.

tore the past tense of **tear²**.

torment noun 1 Torment is extreme pain or unhappiness. 2 something that causes extreme pain and unhappiness. ▶ verb 3 If something torments you, it causes you extreme unhappiness.

torn 1 Torn is the past participle of **tear²**. ▶ adjective 2 If you are torn between two or more things, you cannot decide which one to choose and this makes you unhappy.

tornado tornadoes or tornados noun a violent storm with strong circular winds around a funnel-shaped cloud.

T

torpedo torpedoes, torpedoing, torpedoed noun 1 a tube-shaped bomb that travels underwater and explodes when it hits a target. ▶ verb 2 If a ship is torpedoed, it is hit, and usually sunk, by a torpedo.

torrent noun 1 When a lot of water is falling very rapidly, it can be said to be falling in torrents. 2 A torrent of speech is a lot of it directed continuously to someone.

torrential adjective Torrential rain pours down very rapidly and in great quantities.

torrid adjective 1 Torrid weather is very hot and dry. 2 If something is described as torrid, it involves very strong emotions.

torso torsos noun the main part of your body, excluding your head, arms and legs.

tortoise noun a slow-moving reptile with a large hard shell over its body into which it can pull its head and legs for protection.

tortuous adjective 1 A tortuous road is full of bends and twists. 2 A tortuous piece of writing is long and complicated.

torture noun 1 Torture is great pain that is deliberately caused to someone to punish them or get information from them. ▶ verb 2 If someone tortures another person, they deliberately cause that person great pain to punish them or get information. 3 To torture someone is also to cause them to suffer mentally.
> **torturer** noun

Tory Tories noun In Britain, a Tory is a member or supporter of the Conservative Party.

toss verb 1 If you toss something somewhere, you throw it there lightly and carelessly. 2 If you toss a coin, you decide something by throwing a coin into the air and guessing which side will face upwards when it lands. 3 If you toss your head, you move it suddenly backwards, especially when you are angry or annoyed or want your own way. 4 To toss is to move repeatedly from side to side.

tot tots, totting, totted noun 1 a very young child. 2 a small amount of strong alcohol such as whisky. ▶ verb 3 To tot up numbers is to add them together.

total totals, totalling, totalled noun 1 the number you get when you add several numbers together. ▶ adjective 2 Total means complete. ▶ verb 3 When you total a set of numbers or objects, you add them all together. 4 If several numbers total a certain figure, that is the figure you get when all the numbers are added together.
> **totally** adverb

total noun
1 = aggregate, sum, whole
▶ adjective 2 = absolute, complete, out-and-out, outright, unconditional, undivided, unmitigated, unqualified, utter
▶ verb 4 = add up to, amount to, come to

totalitarian adjective A totalitarian political system is one in which one political party controls everything and does not allow any other parties to exist.
> **totalitarianism** noun

tote (informal) noun 1 The tote is a system of betting money on horses at a racetrack, in which all

the money is divided among the people who have bet on the winning horses. Tote is an abbreviation for 'totalisator'.
▶ verb 2 To tote a gun means to carry it.

totter verb When someone totters, they walk in an unsteady way.

touch verb 1 If you touch something, you put your fingers or hand on it. 2 When two things touch, their surfaces come into contact. 3 If you are touched by something, you are emotionally affected by it. ▶ noun 4 Your sense of touch is your ability to tell what something is like by touching it. 5 A detail which is added to improve something. 6 a small amount of something.
▶ phrase 7 If you are in touch with someone, you are in contact with them.

> **touch** verb
> 1 = feel, finger, handle
> 2 = brush, graze, meet 3 = affect, move, stir

touchdown noun Touchdown is the landing of an aircraft.

touching adjective causing feelings of sadness and sympathy.

> **touching** adjective
> = affecting (literary), moving, poignant

touchscreen noun a computer screen that allows the user to give commands by touching parts of the screen instead of using a keyboard or mouse.

touchy touchier, touchiest adjective 1 If someone is touchy, they are easily upset or irritated. 2 A touchy subject is one that

needs to be dealt with carefully, because it might upset or offend people.

> **touchy** adjective
> 1 = easily offended, sensitive, toey (Australian and New Zealand; slang)

tough adjective 1 A tough person is strong and independent and able to put up with hardship. 2 A tough substance is difficult to break. 3 A tough task, problem or way of life is difficult or full of hardship. 4 Tough policies or actions are strict and firm.
> **toughly** adverb > **toughness** noun > **toughen** verb

> **tough** adjective
> 1 = hardened, hardy, resilient, robust, rugged, strong
> 2 = durable, hard-wearing, leathery, resilient, robust, rugged, solid, strong, sturdy
> 3 = arduous, difficult, exacting, hard

tour noun 1 a long journey during which you visit several places. 2 a short trip round a place such as a city or famous building.
▶ verb 3 If you tour a place, you go on a journey or a trip round it.

tourism noun Tourism is the business of providing services for people on holiday, for example hotels and sightseeing trips.

tourist (GEOGRAPHY) noun a person who visits places for pleasure or interest.

tournament noun (PE) a sports competition in which players who win a match play further matches, until just one person or team is left.

tousled adjective Tousled hair is untidy.

tout verb 1 If someone touts something, they try to sell it. 2 If someone touts for business or custom, they try to obtain it in a very direct way. ▶ noun 3 someone who sells tickets outside a sports ground or theatre, charging more than the original price.

tow verb 1 If a vehicle tows another vehicle, it pulls it along behind it. ▶ noun 2 To give a vehicle a tow is to tow it. ▶ phrase 3 If you have someone **in tow**, they are with you because you are looking after them.

towards preposition 1 in the direction of: He turned towards the door. 2 about or involving: My feelings towards Susan have changed. 3 as a contribution for: a huge donation towards the new opera house. 4 near to: We sat towards the back.

towel noun a piece of thick, soft cloth that you use to dry yourself.

towelling noun Towelling is thick, soft cloth that is used for making towels.

tower noun 1 a tall, narrow building, sometimes attached to a larger building such as a castle or church. ▶ verb 2 Someone or something that towers over other people or things is much taller than them. > **towering** adjective

town noun 1 a place with many streets and buildings where people live and work. 2 Town is the central shopping and business part of a town rather than the suburbs.

toxic adjective poisonous.

toxin noun (SCIENCE) a poison, especially one produced by bacteria and very harmful to living creatures.

toy noun 1 any object made to play with. ▶ verb 2 If you toy with an idea, you consider it without being very serious about it. 3 If you toy with an object, you fiddle with it.

trace verb 1 If you trace something, you find it after looking for it. 2 (EXAM TERM) To trace the development of something is to find out or describe how it developed. 3 If you trace a drawing or a map, you copy it by covering it with a piece of transparent paper and drawing over the lines underneath. ▶ noun 4 a sign which shows you that someone or something has been in a place. 5 a very small amount of something. > **tracing** noun

> **trace** verb
> 1 = locate, track down
> ▶ noun 4 = evidence, hint, indication, record, sign, suggestion, whiff 5 = dash, drop, remnant, suspicion, tinge, touch, vestige

track noun 1 a narrow road or path. 2 a strip of ground with rails on it that a train travels along. 3 a piece of ground, shaped like a ring, which horses, cars or athletes race around. 4 (in plural) Tracks are marks left on the ground by a person or animal. ▶ adjective 5 In an athletics competition, the track events are the races on a running track. ▶ verb 6 If you track animals or people, you find them by following their footprints or other signs that they have left behind. > **track down** verb If you track down someone or something, you find them by searching for them.

t

track record noun The track record of a person or a company is their past achievements or failures.

tracksuit noun a loose, warm suit of trousers and a top, worn for outdoor sports.

tract noun 1 A tract of land or forest is a large area of it.
2 a pamphlet which expresses a strong opinion on a religious, moral or political subject.
3 a system of organs and tubes in an animal's or person's body that has a particular function.

traction noun Traction is a form of medical treatment given to an injured limb which involves pulling it gently for long periods of time using a system of weights and pulleys.

tractor noun a vehicle with large rear wheels that is used on a farm for pulling machinery and other heavy loads.

trade noun 1 Trade is the activity of buying, selling or exchanging goods or services between people, firms or countries. 2 Someone's trade is the kind of work they do, especially when it requires special training in practical skills. ▶ verb 3 When people, firms or countries trade, they buy, sell or exchange goods or services. 4 If you trade things, you exchange them.

> **trade** noun
> 1 = business, commerce
> 2 = business, line, line of work, occupation, profession
> ▶ verb 3 = deal, do business, traffic

trademark noun a name or symbol that a manufacturer always uses on its products. Trademarks are usually protected by law so that no-one else can use them.

trader noun a person whose job is to buy and sell goods.

> **trader** noun
> = broker, dealer, merchant

tradesman tradesmen noun a person, for example a shopkeeper, whose job is to sell goods.

trade union noun an organisation of workers that tries to improve the pay and conditions in a particular industry.

tradition noun a custom or belief that has existed for a long time without changing.

> **tradition** noun
> = convention, custom

traditional adjective 1 Traditional customs or beliefs have existed for a long time without changing.
2 A traditional organisation or institution is one in which older methods are used rather than modern ones. > **traditionally** adverb

> **traditional** adjective
> 1 = conventional, established

traditionalist noun someone who supports the established customs and beliefs of their society, and does not want to change them.

traffic traffics, trafficking, trafficked noun 1 Traffic is the movement of vehicles or people along a route at a particular time.
2 Traffic in something such as drugs is an illegal trade in them.
▶ verb 3 Someone who traffics in drugs or other goods buys and sells them illegally.

traffic light *noun* Traffic lights are the set of red, amber and green lights at a road junction which control the flow of traffic.

tragedy tragedies *noun* **1** an event or situation that is disastrous or very sad. **2** a serious story or play, that usually ends with the death of the main character.

tragic *adjective* **1** Something tragic is very sad because it involves death, suffering or disaster. **2** Tragic films, plays and books are sad and serious. > **tragically** *adverb*

> **tragic** *adjective*
> **1** = distressing, heartbreaking, heart-rending

trail *noun* **1** a rough path across open country or through forests. **2** a series of marks or other signs left by someone or something as they move along. ▶ *verb* **3** If you trail something or it trails, it drags along behind you as you move, or it hangs down loosely. **4** If someone trails along, they move slowly, without any energy or enthusiasm. **5** If a voice trails away or trails off, it gradually becomes more hesitant until it stops completely.

trailer *noun* a small vehicle which can be loaded with things and pulled behind a car.

train *noun* **1** a number of carriages or trucks which are pulled by a railway engine. **2** A train of thought is a connected series of thoughts. **3** A train of vehicles or people is a line or group following behind something or someone. ▶ *verb* **4** If you train someone, you teach them how to do something. **5** If you train, you learn how to do a particular job. **6** If you train for a sports match or a race, you prepare for it by doing exercises. > **training** *noun*

> **train** *verb*
> **4** = coach, drill, educate, instruct, school, teach, tutor

trainee *noun* someone who is being taught how to do a job.

trainers *plural noun* Trainers are shoes with thick rubber soles, originally designed for running.

trait *noun* a particular characteristic or tendency. In literature, a trait is an aspect of a character in a story, for example, kind, greedy, funny or stupid.

traitor *noun* (HISTORY) someone who betrays their country or the group which they belong to.

trajectory trajectories *noun* The trajectory of an object moving through the air is the curving path that it follows.

tram *noun* a vehicle which runs on rails along the street and is powered by electricity from an overhead wire.

tramp *noun* **1** a person who has no home, no job, and very little money. **2** a long country walk. ▶ *verb* **3** If you tramp from one place to another, you walk with slow, heavy footsteps.

trample *verb* **1** If you trample on something, you tread heavily on it so that it is damaged. **2** If you trample on someone or on their rights or feelings, you behave in a way that shows you don't care about them.

trampoline *noun* a piece of gymnastic equipment consisting of a large piece of strong cloth held taut by springs in a frame, on which a person jumps for exercise or fun.

t

trance *noun* a mental state in which someone seems to be asleep but is conscious enough to be aware of their surroundings and to respond to questions and commands.

tranquil *adjective* calm and peaceful. ▸ **tranquillity** *noun*

transaction *noun* a business deal which involves buying and selling something.

transcend *verb* If one thing transcends another, it goes beyond it or is superior to it.

transcript *noun* a written copy of something that is spoken.

transfer transfers, transferring, transferred *verb* 1 If you transfer something from one place to another, you move it. 2 If you transfer to a different place or job, or are transferred to it, you move to a different place or job within the same organisation. ▸ *noun* 3 the movement of something from one place to another. 4 a piece of paper with a design on one side which can be ironed or pressed onto cloth, paper or china. ▸ **transferable** *adjective*

transfixed *adjective* If a person is transfixed by something, they are so impressed or frightened by it that they cannot move.

transform *verb* 1 If something is transformed, it is changed completely. 2 (MATHS) To transform a shape is to change how it looks, for example by translation, reflection, rotation or enlargement. ▸ **transformation** *noun*

> **transform** *verb*
> 1 = alter, change, convert, reform, revolutionise

transfusion *noun* A transfusion or blood transfusion is a process in which blood from a healthy person is injected into the body of another person who is badly injured or ill.

transgender *adjective* Someone who is transgender has a gender identity which does not fully correspond to the sex assigned to them at birth.

transient *adjective* Something transient does not stay or exist for very long. ▸ **transience** *noun*

transistor *noun* 1 a small electrical device in something such as a television or radio which is used to control electric currents. 2 A transistor or a transistor radio is a small portable radio.

transit *noun* Transit is the carrying of goods or people by vehicle from one place to another.

transition *noun* (PSHE) a change from one form, state or stage of life to another.

transitional *adjective* A transitional period or stage is one during which something changes from one form or state to another.

transitory *adjective* lasting for only a short time.

translate *verb* 1 To translate something that someone has said or written is to say it or write it in a different language. 2 (MATHS) To translate a shape is to move it up or down, or from side to side, but not change it in any other way. ▸ **translation** *noun* ▸ **translator** *noun*

translucent *adjective* If something is translucent, light passes through it so that it seems to glow.

transmission noun 1 The transmission of something involves passing or sending it to a different place or person. 2 The transmission of television or radio programmes is the broadcasting of them. 3 a broadcast.

transmit transmits, transmitting, transmitted verb 1 When a message or an electronic signal is transmitted, it is sent by radio waves. 2 To transmit something to a different place or person is to pass it or send it to the place or person. > **transmitter** noun

transparency transparencies noun 1 a small piece of photographic film which can be projected onto a screen. 2 Transparency is the quality that an object or substance has if you can see through it.

transparent adjective If an object or substance is transparent, you can see through it.
> **transparently** adverb

> **transparent** adjective
> = clear, crystalline (literary), sheer, translucent

transpire verb 1 (formal) When it transpires that something is the case, people discover that it is the case. 2 When something transpires, it happens.

transplant noun 1 a process of removing something from one place and putting it in another. ▶ verb 2 When something is transplanted, it is moved to a different place.

transport noun 1 Vehicles that you travel in are referred to as transport. 2 Transport is the moving of goods or people from one place to another. ▶ verb

3 When goods or people are transported from one place to another, they are moved there.

> **transport** noun
> 2 = removal, shipment, transportation
> ▶ verb 3 = carry, convey (formal), ship, transfer

transportation noun Transportation is the transporting of people and things from one place to another.

trap traps, trapping, trapped noun 1 a piece of equipment or a hole that is carefully positioned in order to catch animals or birds. 2 a trick that is intended to catch or deceive someone. ▶ verb 3 Someone who traps animals catches them using traps. 4 If you trap someone, you trick them so that they do or say something which they did not want to. 5 If you are trapped somewhere, you cannot move or escape because something is blocking your way or holding you down. 6 If you are trapped, you are in an unpleasant situation that you cannot easily change. > **trapper** noun

> **trap** noun
> 1 = net, snare
> ▶ verb 3 = catch, corner, snare
> 4 = dupe, trick

trapeze noun a bar of wood or metal hanging from two ropes on which acrobats and gymnasts swing and perform skilful movements.

trappings plural noun The trappings of a particular rank, position or state are the clothes or equipment that go with it.

trash noun 1 Trash is rubbish. 2 (informal) If you say that something

t

such as a book, painting or film is trash, you mean that it is not very good.

trash noun
1 = garbage, refuse, rubbish, waste **2** = garbage (informal), rubbish

trauma noun a very upsetting experience which causes great stress.

traumatic adjective A traumatic experience is very upsetting.

travel travels, travelling, travelled verb **1** To travel is to go from one place to another. **2** When something reaches one place from another, you say that it travels there. ▶ noun **3** Travel is the act of travelling. **4** (in plural) Someone's travels are the journeys that they make to places a long way from their home. ▷ **traveller** noun ▷ **travelling** adjective

travel verb
1 = go, journey (formal), make your way, take a trip

traverse verb (formal) If you traverse an area of land or water, you go across it or over it.

travesty travesties noun a very bad or ridiculous representation or imitation of something.

trawl verb When fishermen trawl, they drag a wide net behind a boat in order to catch fish.

trawler noun a fishing boat that is used for trawling.

tray noun a flat object with raised edges which is used for carrying food or drinks.

treacherous adjective **1** A treacherous person is likely to betray you and cannot be trusted.

2 The ground or the sea can be described as treacherous when it is dangerous or unreliable. ▷ **treacherously** adverb

treacherous adjective
1 = disloyal, faithless, unfaithful, untrustworthy **2** = dangerous, hazardous, perilous (literary)

treachery noun Treachery is behaviour in which someone betrays their country or a person who trusts them.

treacle noun Treacle is a thick, sweet syrup used to make cakes and toffee.

tread treads, treading, trod, trodden verb **1** If you tread on something, you walk on it or step on it. **2** If you tread something into the ground or into a carpet, you crush it in by stepping on it. ▶ noun **3** A person's tread is the sound they make with their feet as they walk. **4** The tread of a tyre or shoe is the pattern of ridges on it that stops it slipping.

treadmill noun **1** an exercise machine with a continuous moving belt for walking or running on. **2** Any task or job that you must keep doing even though it is unpleasant or tiring can be referred to as a treadmill.

treason noun Treason is the crime of betraying your country, for example by helping its enemies.

treasure noun **1** Treasure is a collection of gold, silver, jewels or other precious objects, especially one that has been hidden. **2** Treasures are valuable works of art. ▶ verb **3** If you treasure something, you are very pleased that you have it and regard it as very precious. ▸ **treasured** *adjective*

> **treasure** *verb*
> 3 = cherish, hold dear, prize, value

treasurer *noun* a person who is in charge of the finance and accounts of an organisation.

Treasury *noun* The Treasury is the government department that deals with the country's finances.

treat *verb* 1 If you treat someone in a particular way, you behave that way towards them. 2 If you treat something in a particular way, you deal with it that way or see it that way. 3 When a doctor treats a patient or an illness, he or she gives them medical care and attention. 4 If something such as wood or cloth is treated, a special substance is put on it in order to protect it or give it special properties. 5 If you treat someone, you buy or arrange something special for them which they will enjoy. ▸ *noun* 6 If you give someone a treat, you buy or arrange something special for them which they will enjoy. > **treatment** *noun*

> **treat** *verb*
> 1 = act towards, behave towards, deal with 3 = care for, nurse

treatise *noun* a long formal piece of writing about a particular subject.

treaty **treaties** *noun* a written agreement between countries in which they agree to do something or to help each other.

treble *verb* 1 If something trebles or is trebled, it becomes three times greater in number or

amount. ▸ *adjective* 2 Treble means three times as large or three times as strong as previously.

tree *noun* a large plant with a hard woody trunk, branches and leaves.

trek **treks, trekking, trekked** *verb* 1 If you trek somewhere, you go on a long and difficult journey. ▸ *noun* 2 a long and difficult journey, especially one made by walking.

trellis *noun* a frame made of horizontal and vertical strips of wood or metal and used to support plants.

tremble *verb* 1 If you tremble, you shake slightly, usually because you are frightened or cold. 2 If something trembles, it shakes slightly. 3 If your voice trembles, it sounds unsteady, usually because you are frightened or upset. > **trembling** *adjective*

tremendous *adjective* 1 large or impressive. 2 (*informal*) very good or pleasing. > **tremendously** *adverb*

tremor *noun* 1 a shaking movement of your body which you cannot control. 2 an unsteady quality in your voice, for example when you are upset. 3 a small earthquake.

trench *noun* a long narrow channel dug into the ground.

trenchant *adjective* Trenchant writings or comments are bold and firmly expressed.

trend *noun* 1 a change towards doing or being something different. ▸ *verb* 2 If a topic is trending on a social media site, it is being discussed by a large number of users.

trendy trendier, trendiest adjective (informal) Trendy things or people are fashionable.

> **trendy** adjective
> = fashionable, in (slang), in fashion, in vogue, latest, stylish

trepidation noun (formal) Trepidation is fear or anxiety.

trespass verb If you trespass on someone's land or property, you go onto it without their permission. > **trespasser** noun

tresses plural noun (old-fashioned) A woman's tresses are her long flowing hair.

trestle noun a wooden or metal structure that is used as one of the supports for a table.

trevally trevallies noun an Australian and New Zealand fish that is caught for both food and sport.

triad noun 1 (formal) a group of three similar things. 2 (MUSIC) In music, a triad is a chord of three notes consisting of the tonic and the third and fifth above it.

trial noun 1 the legal process in which a judge and jury decide whether a person is guilty of a particular crime after listening to all the evidence about it. 2 an experiment in which something is tested.

triangle noun 1 (MATHS) a shape with three straight sides. 2 a percussion instrument consisting of a thin steel bar bent in the shape of a triangle. > **triangular** adjective

triathlon noun a sports contest in which athletes compete in three different events.

tribe noun a group of people of the same race, who have the same customs, religion, language or land, especially when they are thought to be primitive. > **tribal** adjective

tribulation noun (formal) Tribulation is trouble or suffering.

tribunal noun a special court or committee appointed to deal with particular problems.

tributary tributaries noun (GEOGRAPHY) a stream or river that flows into a larger river.

tribute noun 1 A tribute is something said or done to show admiration and respect for someone. 2 If one thing is a tribute to another, it is the result of the other thing and shows how good it is.

> **tribute** noun
> 1 = accolade (formal), compliment, honour, praise, testimony

trick noun 1 an action done to deceive someone. 2 Tricks are clever or skilful actions done in order to entertain people. ▶ verb 3 If someone tricks you, they deceive you.

> **trick** noun
> 1 = con (informal), deception, hoax, ploy, ruse
> ▶ verb 3 = con (informal), deceive, dupe, fool, take in (informal)

trickery noun Trickery is deception.

trickle verb 1 When a liquid trickles somewhere, it flows slowly in a thin stream. 2 When people or things trickle somewhere, they move there slowly in small numbers or quantities. ▶ noun **3** a thin stream of liquid. **4** A trickle of people or things is a small number or quantity of them.

tricky trickier, trickiest adjective difficult to do or deal with.

> **tricky** adjective
> = complex, complicated, delicate, difficult, hard, problematic, puzzling, sensitive

tricycle noun a vehicle similar to a bicycle but with two wheels at the back and one at the front.

trifle noun **1** A trifle means a little. **2** Trifles are things that are not very important or valuable. **3** a cold pudding made of layers of sponge cake, fruit, jelly and custard. ▶ verb **4** If you trifle with someone or something, you treat them in a disrespectful way.

trifling adjective small and unimportant.

trigger noun **1** the small lever on a gun which is pulled in order to fire it. ▶ verb **2** If something triggers an event or triggers it off, it causes it to happen.

trillion noun **1** A trillion is a million million. This is shown as one followed by twelve zeros. **2** (informal) Trillions of things means an extremely large number of them.

trilogy trilogies noun a series of three books or plays that have the same characters or are on the same subject.

trim trimmer, trimmest; trims, trimming, trimmed adjective **1** neat, tidy and attractive. ▶ verb **2** To trim something is to clip small amounts off it. **3** If you trim

off parts of something, you cut them off because they are not needed. ▶ noun **4** If something is given a trim, it is cut a little. **5** a decoration on something, especially along its edges.
> **trimmed** adjective

trimming noun Trimmings are extra parts added to something for decoration or as a luxury.

trinity noun **1** (RE) In the Christian religion, the Trinity is the joining of God the Father, God the Son, and God the Holy Spirit. **2** (literary) A trinity is a group of three things or people.

trinket noun a cheap ornament or piece of jewellery.

trio trios noun **1** a group of three musicians who sing or play together; also a piece of music written for three instruments or singers. **2** any group of three things or people together.

trip trips, tripping, tripped noun **1** a journey made to a place. ▶ verb **2** If you trip, you catch your foot on something and fall over. **3** If you trip someone or trip them up, you make them fall over by making them catch their foot on something.

> **trip** noun
> **1** = excursion, jaunt, journey, outing, voyage
> ▶ verb **2** = fall over, lose your footing, stumble

tripe noun Tripe is the stomach lining of a pig, cow or ox, which is cooked and eaten.

triple adjective **1** consisting of three things or three parts. ▶ verb **2** If you triple something or if it triples, it becomes three times greater in number or size.

t

triplet noun Triplets are three children born at the same time to the same mother.

tripod noun a stand with three legs used to support something like a camera or telescope.

trite adjective dull and not original.

triumph noun 1 a great success or achievement. 2 Triumph is a feeling of great satisfaction when you win or achieve something. ▶ verb 3 If you triumph, you win a victory or succeed in overcoming something.

> **triumph** noun
> 1 = success, victory
> ▶ verb 3 = come out on top (informal), prevail, succeed, win

triumphal adjective done or made to celebrate a victory or great success.

triumphant adjective Someone who is triumphant feels very happy because they have won a victory or have achieved something.

trivia plural noun Trivia are unimportant things.

trivial adjective Something trivial is unimportant.

> **trivial** adjective
> = insignificant, minor, negligible, paltry, petty, slight, trifling, unimportant

trod the past tense of **tread**.

trodden the past participle of **tread**.

troll noun 1 an imaginary creature in Scandinavian mythology that lives in caves or mountains and is believed to turn to stone at daylight. 2 (slang) a person who makes offensive or provocative posts on a website. ▶ verb 3 (slang) If you troll, you deliberately make offensive or provocative posts on a website.

trolley noun 1 a small table on wheels. 2 a small cart on wheels used for carrying heavy objects.

trombone noun a brass wind instrument with a U-shaped slide which you move to produce different notes.

troop noun 1 Troops are soldiers. 2 A troop of people or animals is a group of them. ▶ verb 3 If people troop somewhere, they go there in a group.

trooper noun a low-ranking soldier in the cavalry.

trophy trophies noun 1 a cup or shield given as a prize to the winner of a competition. 2 something you keep to remember a success or victory.

tropical adjective belonging to or typical of the tropics.

tropics plural noun (GEOGRAPHY) The tropics are the hottest parts of the world, between two lines of latitude, the Tropic of Cancer, $23\frac{1}{2}°$ north of the equator, and the Tropic of Capricorn, $23\frac{1}{2}°$ south of the equator.

trot trots, trotting, trotted verb 1 When a horse trots, it moves at a speed between a walk and a canter, lifting its feet quite high off the ground. 2 If you trot, you run or jog using small quick steps. ▶ noun 3 When a horse breaks into a trot, it starts trotting.

trotter noun A pig's trotters are its feet.

trouble noun 1 Troubles are difficulties or problems. 2 If there is trouble, people are quarrelling or fighting. ▶ phrase 3 If you are in trouble, you are in a situation where you may be punished because you have done something wrong. ▶ verb 4 If something troubles you, it makes you feel worried or anxious. 5 If you trouble someone for something, you disturb them in order to ask them for it. > **troubling** adjective > **troubled** adjective

> **trouble** noun
> 1 = bother, difficulty, hassle (informal), problem
> ▶ verb 4 = agitate, bother, disturb, worry 5 = bother, disturb, impose upon, inconvenience, put out

troublesome adjective causing problems or difficulties.

trough noun a long, narrow container from which animals drink or feed.

trounce verb If you trounce someone, you defeat them completely.

troupe noun a group of actors, singers or dancers who work together and often travel around together.

trousers plural noun Trousers are a piece of clothing covering the body from the waist down, enclosing each leg separately.

trout trout noun a type of freshwater fish.

trowel noun 1 a small garden tool with a curved, pointed blade used for planting or weeding. 2 a small tool with a flat blade used for spreading cement or plaster.

truant noun 1 a child who stays away from school without permission. ▶ phrase 2 If children **play truant**, they stay away from school without permission. > **truancy** noun

truce noun an agreement between two people or groups to stop fighting for a short time.

truck noun 1 a large motor vehicle used for carrying heavy loads. 2 an open vehicle used for carrying goods on a railway.

truculent adjective bad-tempered and aggressive. > **truculence** noun

trudge verb 1 If you trudge, you walk with slow, heavy steps. ▶ noun 2 a slow tiring walk.

true truer, truest adjective 1 A true story or statement is based on facts and is not made up. 2 'True' is used to describe things or people that are genuine. 3 True feelings are sincere and genuine. ▶ phrase 4 If something comes true, it actually happens. > **truly** adverb

> **true** adjective
> 1 = accurate, correct, factual
> 2 = authentic, bona fide, genuine, real

truffle noun 1 a soft, round sweet made from chocolate. 2 a round mushroom-like fungus which grows underground and is considered very good to eat.

trump noun In a game of cards, trumps is the suit with the highest value.

trumpet noun 1 a brass wind instrument with a narrow tube ending in a bell-like shape. ▶ verb 2 When an elephant trumpets, it makes a sound like a very loud trumpet.

truncated adjective Something that is truncated is made shorter.

trundle verb If you trundle something or it trundles somewhere, it moves or rolls along slowly.

t

trunk noun 1 the main stem of a tree from which the branches and roots grow. 2 the main part of your body, excluding your head, neck, arms and legs. 3 the long flexible nose of an elephant. 4 a large, strong case or box with a hinged lid used for storing things. 5 (in plural) A man's trunks are his bathing pants or shorts.

truss verb To truss someone or truss them up is to tie them up so that they cannot move.

trust verb 1 If you trust someone, you believe that they are honest and will not harm you. 2 If you trust someone to do something, you believe they will do it successfully or properly. 3 If you trust someone with something, you give it to them or trust it to them. 4 If you do not trust something, you feel that it is not safe or reliable. ▶ noun 5 Trust is the responsibility you are given to deal with or look after important or secret things. 6 A financial arrangement in which an organisation looks after and invests money for someone. > **trusting** adjective

> **trust** verb
> 2 = count on, depend on, have confidence in, have faith in, place your trust in, rely upon

trustee noun someone who is allowed by law to control money or property they are keeping or investing for another person.

trustworthy adjective A trustworthy person is reliable and responsible and can be trusted.

trusty trustier, trustiest adjective Trusty things and animals are considered to be reliable because

they have always worked well in the past.

> **trusty** adjective
> = dependable, faithful, firm, reliable, solid, staunch, true, trustworthy

truth noun 1 The truth is the facts about something, rather than things that are imagined or made up. 2 an idea or principle that is generally accepted to be true.

> **truth** noun
> 1 = fact, reality

truthful adjective A truthful person is honest and tells the truth. > **truthfully** adverb

try tries, trying, tried verb 1 To try to do something is to make an effort to do it. 2 If you try something, you use it or do it to test how useful or enjoyable it is. 3 When a person is tried, they appear in court and a judge and jury decide if they are guilty after hearing the evidence. ▶ noun 4 an attempt to do something. 5 a test of something. 6 In rugby, a try is scored when someone carries the ball over the goal line of the opposing team and touches the ground with it.

> **try** verb
> 1 = attempt, endeavour (formal), make an attempt, make an effort, seek, strive 2 = check out, sample, test, try out
> ▶ noun 4 = attempt, effort, endeavour (formal), go (informal), shot (informal)

trying adjective A trying person or thing is difficult to deal with and makes you feel impatient or annoyed.

T

tryst noun an appointment or meeting, especially between lovers in a quiet, secret place.

tsar; also spelt **czar** noun a Russian emperor or king between 1547 and 1917.

T-shirt; also spelt **tee shirt** noun a simple short-sleeved cotton shirt with no collar.

tsunami tsunamis noun (GEOGRAPHY) a large, often destructive sea wave, caused by an earthquake or volcanic eruption under the sea.

tub noun a wide circular container.

tuba noun a large brass musical instrument that can produce very low notes.

tubby tubbier, tubbiest adjective rather fat.

> **tubby** adjective
> = chubby, fat, overweight, plump, podgy, portly, stout

tube noun 1 a round, hollow pipe. 2 a soft metal or plastic cylindrical container with a screw cap at one end. > **tubing** noun

tuberculosis noun Tuberculosis is a serious infectious disease affecting the lungs.

tubular adjective in the shape of a tube.

TUC In Britain, the TUC is an association of trade unions. TUC is an abbreviation for 'Trades Union Congress'.

tuck verb 1 If you tuck something somewhere, you put it there so that it is safe or comfortable. 2 If you tuck a piece of fabric into or under something, you push the loose ends inside or under it to make it tidy.

tucker (informal) noun 1 In Australian and New Zealand English, tucker is food. ▶ verb 2 In American, New Zealand and American English, if you are tuckered out you are tired out.

Tudor (HISTORY) noun Tudor was the family name of the English monarchs who reigned from 1485 to 1603.

Tuesday noun Tuesday is the day between Monday and Wednesday.

tug tugs, tugging, tugged verb 1 To tug something is to give it a quick, hard pull. ▶ noun 2 a quick, hard pull. 3 a small, powerful boat which tows large ships.

> **tug** verb
> 1 = drag, draw, haul, heave, jerk, pluck, pull, wrench, yank
> ▶ noun 2 = heave, jerk, pull, wrench, yank

tug of war noun A tug of war is a sport in which two teams test their strength by pulling against each other on opposite ends of a rope.

tuition noun Tuition is the teaching of a subject, especially to one person or to a small group.

tulip noun a brightly coloured spring flower.

tumble verb 1 To tumble is to fall with a rolling or bouncing movement. ▶ noun 2 a fall.

tumbler noun a drinking glass with straight sides.

tummy tummies noun (informal) Your tummy is your stomach.

tumour noun a mass of diseased or abnormal cells that has grown in a person's or animal's body.

tumultuous adjective A tumultuous event or welcome is very noisy because people are happy or excited.

t

tuna tuna noun Tuna are large fish that live in warm seas and are caught for food.

tundra noun (GEOGRAPHY) The tundra is a vast treeless Arctic region.

tune noun 1 a series of musical notes arranged in a particular way. ▶ verb 2 To tune a musical instrument is to adjust it so that it produces the right notes. 3 To tune an engine or machine is to adjust it so that it works well. 4 If you tune to a particular radio or television station you turn or press the controls to select the station you want to listen to or watch. ▶ phrase 5 If your voice or an instrument is in tune, it produces the right notes.

tune noun
1 = melody, strains

tuneful adjective having a pleasant and easily remembered tune.

tuner noun A piano tuner is a person whose job it is to tune pianos.

tunic noun a garment covering the top part of the body and reaching to the hips, thighs or knees.

Tunisian adjective 1 belonging or relating to Tunisia. ▶ noun 2 someone who comes from Tunisia.

tunnel tunnels, tunnelling, tunnelled noun 1 a long underground passage. ▶ verb 2 To tunnel is to make a tunnel.

turban noun a head-covering worn by a Hindu, Muslim or Sikh man, consisting of a long piece of cloth wound round his head.

turbine noun a machine or engine in which power is produced when a stream of air, gas, water or steam pushes the blades of a wheel and makes it turn round.

turbulent adjective 1 A turbulent period of history is one where there is much uncertainty, and possibly violent change. 2 Turbulent air or water currents make sudden changes of direction. > **turbulence** noun

turf turves; turfs, turfing, turfed noun Turf is short, thick, even grass and the layer of soil beneath it. > **turf out** verb (informal) To turf someone out is to force them to leave a place.

turgid adjective (literary) A turgid play, film or piece of writing is difficult to understand and rather boring.

Turk noun someone who comes from Turkey.

turkey turkeys noun a large bird kept for food; also the meat of this bird.

Turkish adjective 1 belonging or relating to Turkey. ▶ noun 2 Turkish is the main language spoken in Turkey.

turmoil noun Turmoil is a state of confusion, disorder or great anxiety.

turn verb 1 When you turn, you move so that you are facing or going in a different direction. 2 When you turn something or when it turns, it moves or rotates so that it faces in a different direction or is in a different position. 3 If you turn your attention or thoughts to someone or something, you start thinking about them or discussing them. 4 When something turns or is turned into something else, it becomes something different. ▶ noun 5 an act of turning

T

something so that it faces in a different direction or is in a different position. **6** a change in the way something is happening or being done. **7** If it is your turn to do something, you have the right, chance or duty to do it. ▶ *phrase* **8 In turn** is used to refer to people, things or actions that are in sequence one after the other. ▷ **turn down** *verb* If you turn down someone's request or offer, you refuse or reject it. ▷ **turn up** *verb* **1** If someone or something turns up, they arrive or appear somewhere. **2** If something turns up, it is found or discovered.

turn *verb*
2 = rotate, spin, swivel, twirl, twist 4 = change, convert, mutate, transform
▶ *noun* 7 = chance, go, opportunity

turning *noun* a road which leads away from the side of another road.

turning point *noun* the moment when decisions are taken and events start to move in a different direction.

turnip *noun* a round root vegetable with a white or yellow skin.

turnout *noun* The turnout at an event is the number of people who go to it.

turnover *noun* **1** The turnover of people in a particular organisation or group is the rate at which people leave it and are replaced by others. **2** The turnover of a company is the value of the goods or services sold during a particular period.

turnstile *noun* a revolving mechanical barrier at the entrance to places like football grounds or zoos.

turquoise *noun, adjective* **1** light bluish-green. ▶ *noun* **2** Turquoise is a bluish-green stone used in jewellery.

turret *noun* a small narrow tower on top of a larger tower or other buildings.

turtle *noun* a large reptile with a thick shell covering its body and flippers for swimming. It lays its eggs on land but lives the rest of its life in the sea.

tussle *noun* an energetic fight or argument between two people, especially about something they both want.

tutor *noun* **1** a teacher at a college or university. **2** a private teacher. ▶ *verb* **3** If someone tutors a person or subject, they teach that person or subject.

tutorial *noun* a teaching session involving a tutor and a small group of students.

tutu *noun* a short, stiff skirt worn by female ballet dancers.

TV *noun* **1** TV is television. **2** a television set.

twang *noun* **1** a sound like the one made by pulling and then releasing a tight wire. **2** A twang is a nasal quality in a person's voice. ▶ *verb* **3** If a tight wire or string twangs or you twang it, it makes a sound as it is pulled and then released.

tweak *verb* **1** If you tweak something, you twist it or pull it. ▶ *noun* **2** a short twist or pull of something.

twee *adjective* sweet and pretty but in bad taste or sentimental.

tweed *noun* Tweed is a thick woollen cloth.

tweet verb 1 When a small bird tweets, it makes a short, high-pitched sound. 2 If you tweet, you send a message on the social networking site Twitter. ▶ noun 3 a short high-pitched sound made by a small bird. 4 a message sent on the social networking site Twitter.

tweezers plural noun Tweezers are a small tool with two arms which can be closed together and are used for pulling out hairs or picking up small objects.

twelve the number 12. > **twelfth** adjective

twenty twenties the number 20. > **twentieth** adjective

twice adverb Twice means two times.

twig noun a very small thin branch growing from a main branch of a tree or bush.

twilight noun 1 Twilight is the time after sunset when it is just getting dark. 2 The twilight of something is the final stages of it.

twin noun 1 If two people are twins, they have the same mother and were born on the same day. 2 'Twin' is used to describe two similar things that are close together or happen together.

twine noun 1 Twine is strong smooth string. ▶ verb 2 If you twine one thing round another, you twist or wind it round.

twinge noun 1 a sudden, unpleasant feeling. 2 a sudden sharp pain.

twinkle verb 1 If something twinkles, it sparkles or seems to sparkle with an unsteady light.
▶ noun 2 a sparkle or brightness that something has.

twirl verb If something twirls, or if you twirl it, it spins or twists round and round.

twist verb 1 When you twist something, you turn one end of it in one direction while holding the other end or turning it in the opposite direction. 2 When something twists or is twisted, it moves or bends into a strange shape. 3 If you twist a part of your body, you injure it by turning it too sharply or in an unusual direction. 4 If you twist something that someone has said, you change the meaning slightly.
▶ noun 5 a twisting action or motion. 6 an unexpected development or event in a story or film, especially at the end.

> **twist** verb
> 1 = bend, curl, twine, weave, wring 2 = distort, mangle, screw up 3 = sprain, wrench

twisted adjective 1 Something twisted has been bent or moved into a strange shape. 2 If someone's mind or behaviour is twisted, it is unpleasantly abnormal.

twit noun (informal) a silly person.

twitch verb 1 If you twitch, you make little jerky movements which you cannot control. 2 If you twitch something, you give it a little jerk in order to move it. ▶ noun 3 a little jerky movement.

twitter verb When birds twitter, they make short high-pitched sounds.

two the number 2.

two-faced adjective A two-faced person is not honest in the way

they behave towards other
people.

two-faced *adjective*
= deceitful, dishonest, disloyal,
false, hypocritical, insincere,
treacherous

twofold *adjective* Something
twofold has two equally
important parts or reasons.

twosome *noun* two people or
things that are usually seen
together.

two-time *verb (informal)* If you
two-time your boyfriend or
girlfriend, you deceive them, by
having a romantic relationship
with someone else without
telling them.

two-up *noun* In Australia and
New Zealand, two-up is a popular
gambling game in which two
coins are tossed and bets are
placed on whether they land
heads or tails.

tycoon *noun* a person who is
successful in business and has
become rich and powerful.

type *noun* 1 A type of something is
a class of it that has common
features and belongs to a larger
group of related things. 2 A
particular type of person has a
particular appearance or quality.
▶ *verb* 3 If you type something, you
use a typewriter or computer
keyboard to write it.

type *noun*
1 = brand, breed, class, group,
kind, make, sort, species, style,
variety

typewriter *noun* a machine with
a keyboard with individual keys
which are pressed to produce
letters and numbers on a page.

typhoid *noun* Typhoid, or typhoid
fever, is an infectious disease
caused by dirty water or food. It
produces fever and can kill.

typhoon *noun* (GEOGRAPHY) a very
violent tropical storm.

typical *adjective* showing the most
usual characteristics or
behaviour. ▶ **typically** *adverb*

typical *adjective*
= average, characteristic,
normal, regular,
representative, standard, stock,
usual

typify typifies, typifying, typified
verb If something typifies a
situation or thing, it is
characteristic of it or a typical
example of it.

typing *noun* Typing is the work or
activity of producing something
on a typewriter or computer
keyboard.

typist *noun* a person whose job is
typing.

tyranny tyrannies *noun* 1 A
tyranny is cruel and unjust rule of
people by a person or group. 2 You
can refer to something which is
not human but is harsh as
tyranny. ▶ **tyrannical** *adjective*

tyrant *noun* a person who treats
the people he or she has authority
over cruelly and unjustly.

tyre *noun* a thick ring of rubber
fitted round each wheel of a
vehicle and filled with air.

t

Uu

ubiquitous *adjective* Something that is ubiquitous seems to be everywhere at the same time.

UFO *noun* a strange object seen in the sky, which some people believe to be a spaceship from another planet. UFO is an abbreviation for 'unidentified flying object'.

Ugandan *adjective* 1 belonging or relating to Uganda. ▶ *noun* 2 someone who comes from Uganda.

ugly uglier, ugliest *adjective* very unattractive in appearance.

> **ugly** *adjective*
> = plain, unattractive, unsightly

UK an abbreviation for **United Kingdom**.

ulcer *noun* a sore area on the skin or inside the body, which takes a long time to heal. > **ulcerous** *adjective*

ulterior *adjective* If you have an ulterior motive for doing something, you have a hidden reason for it.

ultimate *adjective* 1 final or eventual. 2 most important or powerful. ▶ *noun* 3 You can refer to the best or most advanced example of something as the ultimate. > **ultimately** *adverb*

> **ultimate** *adjective*
> 1 = eventual, final, last

2 = greatest, paramount, supreme, utmost
▶ *noun* 3 = epitome, extreme, height, peak

ultimatum *noun* a warning stating that unless someone meets your conditions, you will take action against them.

ultrasound *noun* (SCIENCE) Ultrasound is sound which cannot be heard by the human ear because its frequency is too high.

ultraviolet *adjective* (SCIENCE) Ultraviolet light is not visible to the human eye. It is a form of radiation that causes your skin to darken after being exposed to the sun.

umbilical cord *noun* (SCIENCE) the tube of blood vessels which connects an unborn baby to its mother and through which the baby receives nutrients and oxygen.

umbrella *noun* a device that you use to protect yourself from the rain. It consists of a folding frame covered in cloth attached to a long stick.

umpire *noun* 1 The umpire in cricket or tennis is the person who makes sure that the game is played according to the rules and who makes a decision if there is a dispute. ▶ *verb* 2 If you umpire a game, you are the umpire.

umpteen *adjective* (*informal*) very many. > **umpteenth** *adjective*

unable *adjective* If you are unable to do something, you cannot do it.

unacceptable *adjective* If you find something unacceptable, you disapprove of it because you think it is of a very low standard.

unaccompanied *adjective* alone.

unaccustomed *adjective* If you are unaccustomed to something, you are not used to it.

unaffected *adjective* 1 not changed in any way by a particular thing. 2 behaving in a natural and genuine way.

unaided *adverb, adjective* without help.

unambiguous *adjective* An unambiguous statement has only one meaning.

unanimous *adjective* When people are unanimous, they all agree about something.
> **unanimously** *adverb*
> **unanimity** *noun*

unannounced *adjective* happening unexpectedly and without warning.

unarmed *adjective* not carrying any weapons.

unassuming *adjective* modest and quiet.

unattached *adjective* An unattached person is not married and is not having a steady relationship with someone.

unattended *adjective* not being watched or looked after.

unauthorised; also spelt **unauthorized** *adjective* done without official permission.

unavoidable *adjective* unable to be prevented or avoided.

unaware *adjective* If you are unaware of something, you do not know about it.

> **unaware** *adjective*
> = ignorant, oblivious,
> unconscious, unsuspecting

unawares *adverb* If something catches you unawares, it happens when you are not expecting it.

unbalanced *adjective* 1 with more weight or emphasis on one side than the other. 2 slightly mad. 3 made up of parts that do not work well together. 4 An unbalanced account of something is an unfair one because it emphasises some things and ignores others.

unbearable *adjective* Something unbearable is so unpleasant or upsetting that you feel you cannot stand it. > **unbearably** *adverb*

> **unbearable** *adjective*
> = intolerable, oppressive,
> unacceptable

unbeatable *adjective* Something that is unbeatable is the best thing of its kind.

unbelievable *adjective*
1 extremely great or surprising. 2 so unlikely that you cannot believe it. > **unbelievably** *adverb*

> **unbelievable** *adjective*
> 1 = colossal, incredible,
> stupendous 2 = implausible,
> improbable, inconceivable,
> incredible, preposterous,
> unconvincing

unborn *adjective* not yet born.

unbroken *adjective* continuous or complete.

uncanny *adjective* strange and difficult to explain.

uncertain *adjective* 1 not knowing what to do. 2 doubtful or not known. > **uncertainty** *noun*

> **uncertain** *adjective*
> 1 = doubtful, dubious, unclear,
> undecided 2 = ambiguous,
> doubtful, indefinite,
> indeterminate

u

unchallenged adjective accepted without any questions being asked.

uncharacteristic adjective not typical or usual.

uncle noun Your uncle is the brother of your mother or father, or the husband of one of your parents' siblings.

unclear adjective confusing and not obvious.

> **unclear** adjective
> = ambiguous, confused, vague

uncomfortable adjective 1 If you are uncomfortable, you are not physically relaxed and feel slight pain or discomfort. 2 Uncomfortable also means slightly worried or embarrassed. > **uncomfortably** adverb

> **uncomfortable** adjective
> 1 = awkward, cramped, disagreeable, ill-fitting, painful 2 = awkward, embarrassed, ill at ease, self-conscious, uneasy

uncommon adjective not happening often or not seen often. > **uncommonly** adverb

> **uncommon** adjective
> = exceptional, extraordinary, few, infrequent, out of the ordinary, rare, scarce, sparse, unusual

uncompromising adjective determined not to change an opinion or aim in any way. > **uncompromisingly** adverb

unconcerned adjective not interested in something or not worried about it.

unconditional adjective with no conditions or limitations. > **unconditionally** adverb

unconscious adjective 1 Someone who is unconscious is asleep or in a state similar to sleep as a result of a shock, accident or injury. 2 If you are unconscious of something, you are not aware of it. > **unconsciously** adverb > **unconsciousness** noun

> **unconscious** adjective
> 1 = asleep, senseless, stunned 2 = oblivious, unaware, unknowing, unsuspecting

uncontrollable adjective If someone or something is uncontrollable, they or it cannot be controlled or stopped. > **uncontrollably** adverb

unconventional adjective not behaving in the same way as most other people.

uncouth adjective bad-mannered and unpleasant.

uncover verb 1 If you uncover a secret, you find it out. 2 To uncover something is to remove the cover or lid from it.

> **uncover** verb
> 1 = bring to light, expose, reveal, show up, unearth 2 = expose, lay bare, open, reveal, unearth, unveil, unwrap

undaunted adjective If you are undaunted by something disappointing, you are not discouraged by it.

undecided adjective If you are undecided, you have not yet made a decision about something.

undemanding adjective not difficult to do or deal with.

undeniable adjective certainly true. > **undeniably** adverb

under preposition 1 below or beneath. 2 You can use 'under' to say that a person or thing is affected by a particular situation or condition: *The country was under threat.* **3** If someone studies or works under a particular person, that person is their teacher or their boss. **4** less than: *under five kilometres.* ▶ *phrase* **5 Under way** means already started.

under *preposition*
1 = below, beneath, underneath

underarm *adjective* **1** under your arm. ▶ *adverb* **2** If you throw a ball underarm, you throw it without raising your arm over your shoulder.

undercarriage *noun* the part of an aircraft, including the wheels, that supports the aircraft when it is on the ground.

underclass *noun* The underclass is the people in society who are the most poor and whose situation is unlikely to improve.

undercover *adjective* involving secret work to obtain information.

undercurrent *noun* a weak, partly hidden feeling that may become stronger later.

undercut undercuts, undercutting, undercut *verb* **1** To undercut someone's prices is to sell a product more cheaply than they do. **2** If something undercuts your attempts to achieve something, it prevents them from being effective.

underdeveloped *adjective* An underdeveloped country does not have modern industries, and usually has a low standard of living.

underdog *noun* The underdog in a competition is the person who seems likely to lose.

underestimate *verb* If you underestimate something or someone, you do not realise how large, great or capable they are.

underfoot *adjective, adverb* under your feet.

undergo undergoes, undergoing, underwent, undergone *verb* If you undergo something unpleasant, it happens to you.

undergo *verb*
= be subjected to, endure, experience, go through, suffer

underground *adjective, adverb* **1** below the surface of the ground. **2** secret, unofficial and usually illegal. ▶ *noun* **3** The underground is a railway system in which trains travel in tunnels below ground.

undergrowth *noun* Small bushes and plants growing under trees are called the undergrowth.

underhand *adjective* secret and dishonest.

underlie underlies, underlying, underlay, underlain *verb* The thing that underlies a situation is the cause or basis of it. > **underlying** *adjective*

underline *verb* **1** If something underlines a feeling or a problem, it emphasises it. **2** If you underline a word or sentence, you draw a line under it.

undermine *verb* To undermine an idea, feeling or system is to make it less strong or secure.

undermine *verb*
= impair, sap, subvert, weaken

underneath *preposition* **1** below or beneath. ▶ *adjective* **2** The underneath part of something is the part that touches or faces the ground.

u

underpants *plural noun*
Underpants are a piece of clothing worn by men and boys under their trousers.

underpass *noun* a road or footpath that goes under a road or railway.

underpin underpins, underpinning, underpinned *verb*
If something underpins something else, it helps it to continue by supporting and strengthening it.

underprivileged *adjective*
Underprivileged people have less money and fewer opportunities than other people.

underrate *verb* If you underrate someone, you do not realise how clever or valuable they are.

understand understands, understanding, understood *verb*
1 If you understand what someone says, you know what they mean. 2 If you understand a situation, you know what is happening and why. 3 If you say that you understand that something is the case, you mean that you have heard that it is the case.

> **understand** *verb*
> 1 = catch on (*informal*), comprehend, follow, get, grasp, see, take in 2 = appreciate, comprehend, fathom, grasp, realise 3 = believe, gather, hear, learn

understandable *adjective* If something is understandable, people can easily understand it.
> **understandably** *adverb*

understanding *noun* 1 If you have an understanding of something, you have some

knowledge about it. 2 an informal agreement between people. ▶ *adjective* 3 kind and sympathetic.

> **understanding** *noun*
> 1 = appreciation, comprehension, grasp, knowledge, perception
> 2 = accord (*formal*), agreement, pact
> ▶ *adjective* 3 = compassionate, considerate, sensitive, sympathetic

understatement *noun* a statement that does not say fully how true something is.

understood the past tense and past participle of **understand**.

understudy understudies *noun* someone who has learnt a part in a play so that they can act it if the main actor or actress is ill.

undertake undertakes, undertaking, undertook, undertaken *verb* When you undertake a task or job, you agree to do it.

undertaker *noun* someone whose job is to prepare bodies for burial and arrange funerals.

undertaking *noun* a task which you have agreed to do.

> **undertaking** *noun*
> = affair, business, endeavour, enterprise, job, operation, project, task, venture

undertone *noun* 1 If you say something in an undertone, you say it very quietly. 2 If something has undertones of a particular kind, it indirectly suggests ideas of this kind.

undertook the past tense of **undertake**.

undervalue undervalues, undervaluing, undervalued *verb* If you undervalue something, you think it is less important than it really is.

underwater *adverb, adjective*
1 beneath the surface of the sea, a river or a lake. ▸ *adjective*
2 designed to work in water.

underwear *noun* Your underwear is the clothing that you wear under your other clothes, next to your skin.

underwent the past tense of **undergo**.

undesirable *adjective* unwelcome and likely to cause harm.

undid the past tense of **undo**.

undisputed *adjective* definite and without any doubt.

undivided *adjective* If you give something your undivided attention, you concentrate on it totally.

undo undoes, undoing, undid, undone *verb* 1 If you undo something that is tied up, you untie it. 2 If you undo something that has been done, you reverse the effect of it.

undoing *noun* If something is someone's undoing, it is the cause of their failure.

undoubted *adjective* You use 'undoubted' to emphasise something: *The event was an undoubted success.* ▸ **undoubtedly** *adverb*

undress *verb* When you undress, you take off your clothes.

undue *adjective* greater than is reasonable. ▸ **unduly** *adverb*

undulating *adjective* (formal) moving gently up and down.

undying *adjective* lasting forever.

unearth *verb* If you unearth something that is hidden, you discover it.

unearthly *adjective* strange and unnatural.

uneasy *adjective* If you are uneasy, you feel worried that something may be wrong. ▸ **unease** *noun* ▸ **uneasily** *adverb* ▸ **uneasiness** *noun*

> **uneasy** *adjective*
> = agitated, anxious, nervous, perturbed, worried

unemployed *adjective* without a job.

> **unemployed** *adjective*
> = idle, jobless, redundant

unemployment *noun* Unemployment is the state of being without a job.

unending *adjective* Something unending has continued for a long time and seems as if it will never stop.

unenviable *adjective* An unenviable situation is one that you would not like to be in.

unequal *adjective* 1 An unequal society does not offer the same opportunities and privileges to all people. 2 Unequal things are different in size, strength or ability.

uneven *adjective* 1 An uneven surface is not level or smooth. 2 not the same or consistent. ▸ **unevenly** *adverb*

> **uneven** *adjective*
> 1 = bumpy, not level, not smooth, rough 2 = fluctuating, inconsistent, irregular, patchy, variable

u

uneventful adjective An uneventful period of time is one when nothing interesting happens.

unexpected adjective Something unexpected is surprising because it was not thought likely to happen. > **unexpectedly** adverb

> **unexpected** adjective
> = astonishing, chance, surprising, unforeseen

unfailing adjective continuous and not weakening as time passes.

unfair adjective not right or just. > **unfairly** adverb

> **unfair** adjective
> = unjust, wrong, wrongful

unfaithful adjective If someone is unfaithful, they are not loyal.

unfamiliar adjective If something is unfamiliar to you, or if you are unfamiliar with it, you have not seen or heard it before.

> **unfamiliar** adjective
> = alien, exotic, foreign, new, novel, strange, unknown

unfashionable adjective Something that is unfashionable is not popular or is no longer used by many people.

unfavourable adjective not encouraging or promising, or not providing any advantage.

unfit adjective 1 If you are unfit, your body is not in good condition because you have not been taking enough exercise. 2 Something that is unfit for a particular purpose is not suitable for that purpose.

unfold verb 1 When a situation unfolds, it develops and becomes known. 2 If you unfold

something that has been folded, you open it out so that it is flat.

unforeseen adjective happening unexpectedly.

unforgettable adjective Something unforgettable is so good or so bad that you are unlikely to forget it. > **unforgettably** adverb

unforgivable adjective Something unforgivable is so bad or cruel that it can never be forgiven or justified. > **unforgivably** adverb

unfortunate adjective 1 Someone who is unfortunate is unlucky. 2 If you describe an event as unfortunate, you mean that it is a pity that it happened. > **unfortunately** adverb

unfounded adjective Something that is unfounded has no evidence to support it.

unfriendly adjective 1 A person who is unfriendly is not pleasant to you. 2 A place that is unfriendly makes you feel uncomfortable or is not welcoming.

> **unfriendly** adjective
> 1 = aloof, antagonistic, cold, disagreeable, hostile, unkind

ungainly adjective moving in an awkward or clumsy way.

ungrateful adjective not grateful or thankful.

> **ungrateful** adjective
> = unappreciative, unthankful

unhappy adjective unhappier, unhappiest adjective 1 sad and downhearted. 2 not pleased or satisfied. 3 If you describe a situation as an unhappy one, you are sorry that it exists. > **unhappily** adverb > **unhappiness** noun

unhappy *adjective*
1 = depressed, despondent, down, miserable, sad

unhealthy *adjective* 1 likely to cause illness. 2 An unhealthy person is often ill.

unhealthy *adjective*
1 = bad for you, harmful, insanitary, noxious, unwholesome 2 = ailing, crook (*Australian and New Zealand*; *informal*), ill, not well, poorly (*British*; *informal*), sick, unwell

unhurried *adjective* Unhurried is used to describe actions or movements that are slow and relaxed.

unicorn *noun* an imaginary animal that looks like a white horse with a straight horn growing from its forehead.

unidentified *adjective* You say that someone or something is unidentified when nobody knows who or what they are.

uniform *noun* 1 a special set of clothes worn by people at work or school. ▶ *adjective* 2 Something that is uniform does not vary but is even and regular throughout.
> **uniformity** *noun*

unify unifies, unifying, unified *verb*
If you unify a number of things, you bring them together.
> **unification** *noun*

unilateral *adjective* A unilateral decision or action is one taken by only one of several groups involved in a particular situation.
> **unilaterally** *adverb*

unimaginable *adjective* impossible to imagine or understand properly.

unimportant *adjective* having very little significance or importance.

unimportant *adjective*
= insignificant, minor, paltry, slight, trivial

uninhabited *adjective* An uninhabited place is a place where nobody lives.

uninhibited *adjective* If you are uninhibited, you behave freely and naturally and show your true feelings.

unintelligible *adjective* (*formal*) impossible to understand.

uninterested *adjective* If you are uninterested in something, you are not interested in it.

uninterested *adjective*
= apathetic, bored, impassive, indifferent, nonchalant, passive, unconcerned

uninterrupted *adjective* continuing without breaks or interruptions.

union *noun* 1 an organisation of people or groups with mutual interests, especially workers aiming to improve their pay and conditions. 2 When the union of two things takes place, they are joined together to become one thing.

union *noun*
1 = association, coalition, confederation, federation, league 2 = amalgamation, blend, combination, fusion, mixture

unique *adjective* 1 being the only one of its kind. 2 If something is unique to one person or thing, it concerns or belongs to that person or thing only. > **uniquely** *adverb* > **uniqueness** *noun*

unisex *adjective* designed to be used by both men and women.

u

unison *noun* If a group of people do something in unison, they all do it together at the same time.

unit *noun* 1 If you consider something as a unit, you consider it as a single complete thing. 2 a group of people who work together at a particular job. 3 a machine or piece of equipment which has a particular function. 4 A unit of measurement is a fixed standard that is used for measuring things.

unite *verb* If a number of people unite, they join together and act as a group.

> **unite** *verb*
> = collaborate, combine, join, join forces, link up, merge, pull together, work together

United Kingdom *noun* The United Kingdom consists of Great Britain and Northern Ireland.

United Nations *noun* The United Nations is an international organisation which tries to encourage peace, cooperation and friendship between countries.

unity *noun* Where there is unity, people are in agreement and act together for a particular purpose.

universal *adjective* concerning or relating to everyone in the world or every part of the universe.
> **universally** *adverb*

> **universal** *adjective*
> = common, general, unlimited, widespread, worldwide

universe *noun* The universe is the whole of space, including all the stars and planets.

university universities *noun* a place where students study for degrees.

unjust *adjective* not fair or reasonable. > **unjustly** *adverb*

unjustified *adjective* If a belief or action is unjustified, there is no good reason for it.

unkempt *adjective* untidy and not looked after properly.

unkind *adjective* unpleasant and rather cruel. > **unkindly** *adverb*
> **unkindness** *noun*

> **unkind** *adjective*
> = cruel, malicious, mean, nasty, spiteful, thoughtless

unknown *adjective* 1 If someone or something is unknown, people do not know about them or have not heard of them. ▶ *noun* 2 You can refer to the things that people in general do not know about as the unknown.

> **unknown** *adjective*
> 1 = humble, obscure, unfamiliar, unsung

unlawful *adjective* not legal.

unleaded *adjective* Unleaded petrol has a reduced amount of lead in it in order to reduce the pollution from cars.

unleash *verb* When a powerful or violent force is unleashed, it is released.

unless *conjunction* You use 'unless' to introduce the only circumstances in which something will not take place or is not true: *Unless it was raining, they played in the little garden.*

unlike *preposition* 1 You can use 'unlike' to show how two people, things or situations are different from each other: *Unlike me, she enjoys ballet.* ▶ *adjective* 2 If one thing is unlike another, the two things are different.

U

unlike *adjective*
2 = different from, dissimilar to, distinct from, divergent from (*formal*), far from

unlikely *adjective* 1 If something is unlikely, it is probably not true or probably will not happen. 2 strange and unexpected.

unlikely *adjective*
1 = implausible, incredible, unbelievable, unconvincing

unlimited *adjective* If a supply of something is unlimited, you can have as much as you want or need.

unload *verb* If you unload things from a container or vehicle, you remove them.

unlock *verb* If you unlock a door or container, you open it by turning a key in the lock.

unlucky *adjective* Someone who is unlucky has bad luck. > **unluckily** *adverb*

unlucky *adjective*
= cursed, hapless, luckless, unfortunate, wretched

unmarked *adjective* 1 with no marks of damage or injury. 2 with no signs or marks of identification.

unmistakable; also spelt **unmistakeable** *adjective* Something unmistakable is so obvious that it cannot be mistaken for something else. > **unmistakably** *adverb*

unmitigated *adjective* (*formal*) You use unmitigated to describe a situation or quality that is completely bad: *an unmitigated disaster*.

unmoved *adjective* not emotionally affected.

unnatural *adjective* 1 strange and rather frightening because it is not usual. 2 artificial and not typical. > **unnaturally** *adverb*

unnecessary *adjective* If something is unnecessary, there is no need for it to happen or be done. > **unnecessarily** *adverb*

unnecessary *adjective*
= needless, pointless, uncalled-for

unnerve *verb* If something unnerves you, it frightens or startles you. > **unnerving** *adjective*

unobtrusive *adjective* Something that is unobtrusive does not draw attention to itself.

unoccupied *adjective* not occupied. For example, if a house is unoccupied, there is nobody living in it.

unofficial *adjective* without the approval or permission of a person in authority. > **unofficially** *adverb*

unorthodox *adjective* unusual and not generally accepted.

unpack *verb* When you unpack, you take everything out of a suitcase or bag.

unpaid *adjective* 1 If you do unpaid work, you do not receive any money for doing it. 2 An unpaid bill has not yet been paid.

unpalatable *adjective*
1 Unpalatable food is unpleasant to eat. 2 An unpalatable idea is so unpleasant that it is difficult to accept.

unparalleled *adjective* greater than anything else of its kind.

unpleasant *adjective* 1 Something unpleasant causes you to have bad feelings, for example by making you uncomfortable or

u

upset. **2** An unpleasant person is unfriendly or rude.
> **unpleasantly** adverb
> **unpleasantness** noun

unpleasant adjective
1 = bad, disagreeable, distasteful, nasty, repulsive, unpalatable **2** = disagreeable, horrid (old-fashioned), objectionable, obnoxious, rude, unfriendly

unpopular adjective disliked by most people.

unpopular adjective
= detested, disliked, shunned, undesirable

unprecedented adjective (formal) Something that is unprecedented has never happened before or is the best of its kind so far.

unpredictable adjective If someone or something is unpredictable, you never know how they will behave or react.

unpredictable adjective
= chance, doubtful, hit and miss (informal), unforeseeable

unprepared adjective If you are unprepared for something, you are not ready for it and are therefore surprised or at a disadvantage when it happens.

unproductive adjective not producing anything useful.

unqualified adjective **1** having no qualifications or not having the right qualifications for a particular job. **2** total: an unqualified success.

unquestionable adjective so obviously true or real that nobody can doubt it.
> **unquestionably** adverb

unravel unravels, unravelling, unravelled verb **1** If you unravel something such as a twisted and knotted piece of string, you unwind it so that it is straight. **2** If you unravel a mystery, you work out the answer to it.

unreal adjective so strange that you find it difficult to believe.

unrealistic adjective **1** An unrealistic person does not face the truth about something or deal with it in a practical way. **2** Something unrealistic is not true to life.

unreasonable adjective unfair and difficult to deal with or justify. > **unreasonably** adverb

unrelated adjective Things that are unrelated have no connection with each other.

unrelenting adjective continuing in a determined way.

unreliable adjective If people, machines or methods are unreliable, you cannot rely on them.

unremitting adjective never stopping.

unrest noun If there is unrest, people are angry and dissatisfied.

unrivalled adjective better than anything else of its kind.

unruly adjective difficult to control or organise.

unsatisfactory adjective not good enough.

unsatisfactory adjective
= disappointing, inadequate, mediocre, poor, unacceptable

unscathed adjective not injured or harmed as a result of a dangerous experience.

U

unscrupulous *adjective* willing to behave dishonestly in order to get what you want.

unseemly *adjective* Unseemly behaviour is not suitable for a particular situation and shows a lack of control and good manners.

unseen *adjective* You use 'unseen' to describe things that you cannot see or have not seen.

unsettle *verb* If something unsettles you, it makes you restless or worried.

unshakable; also spelt **unshakeable** *adjective* An unshakable belief is so strong that it cannot be destroyed.

unsightly *adjective* very ugly.

unskilled *adjective* Unskilled work does not require any special training or ability.

unsolicited *adjective* given or happening without being asked for.

unsound *adjective* 1 If a conclusion or method is unsound, it is based on ideas that are likely to be wrong. 2 An unsound building is likely to collapse.

unspeakable *adjective* very unpleasant.

unspecified *adjective* You say that something is unspecified when you are not told exactly what it is.

unspoilt or **unspoiled** *adjective* If you describe a place as unspoilt or unspoiled, you mean it has not been changed and it is still in its natural or original state.

unspoken *adjective* An unspoken wish or feeling is one that is not mentioned to other people.

unstable *adjective* 1 likely to change suddenly and create difficulty or danger. 2 not firm or

fixed properly and likely to wobble or fall.

unsteady *adjective* 1 having difficulty in controlling the movement of your legs or hands. 2 not held or fixed securely and likely to fall over. > **unsteadily** *adverb*

> **unsteady** *adjective*
> 2 = precarious, rickety, shaky, tottering, unsafe, unstable, wobbly

unstuck *adjective* separated from the thing that it was stuck to.

unsuccessful *adjective* If you are unsuccessful, you do not succeed in what you are trying to do. > **unsuccessfully** *adverb*

unsuitable *adjective* not right or appropriate for a particular purpose. > **unsuitably** *adverb*

> **unsuitable** *adjective*
> = improper, inappropriate, unacceptable, unfit

unsuited *adjective* not appropriate for a particular task or situation.

unsure *adjective* uncertain or doubtful.

unsuspecting *adjective* having no idea of what is happening or going to happen.

untangle *verb* If you untangle something that is twisted together, you undo the twists.

untenable *adjective* (*formal*) A theory, argument or position that is untenable cannot be successfully defended.

unthinkable *adjective* so shocking or awful that you cannot imagine it to be true.

untidy **untidier**, **untidiest** *adjective* not neat or well arranged. > **untidily** *adverb*

u

untidy adjective
= bedraggled, chaotic, cluttered, jumbled, messy, unkempt

until preposition, conjunction 1 If something happens until a particular time, it happens before that time and stops at that time. 2 If something does not happen until a particular time, it does not happen before that time and only starts happening at that time.

untimely adjective happening too soon or sooner than expected.

unto preposition (old-fashioned) Unto means the same as to.

untold adjective You use untold to emphasise how great or extreme something is: *The island possessed untold wealth.*

untouched adjective 1 not changed, moved or damaged. 2 If a meal is untouched, none of it has been eaten.

untoward adjective unexpected and causing difficulties.

untrue adjective not true.

untrue adjective
= erroneous (formal), false, fictitious, inaccurate, incorrect, misleading, mistaken

unused adjective 1 not yet used. 2 If you are unused to something, you have not often done or experienced it.

unusual adjective Something that is unusual does not occur very often. > **unusually** adverb

unusual adjective
= curious, exceptional, extraordinary, rare, uncommon, unconventional

unveil verb When someone unveils a new statue or plaque,

they draw back a curtain that is covering it.

unwanted adjective Unwanted things are not desired or wanted, either by a particular person or by people in general.

unwarranted adjective (formal) not justified or not deserved.

unwelcome adjective not wanted.

unwell adjective If you are unwell, you are ill.

unwell adjective
= ailing, crook (Australian and New Zealand; informal), ill, poorly (British; informal), queasy, sick

unwieldy adjective difficult to move or carry because of being large or an awkward shape.

unwilling adjective If you are unwilling to do something, you do not want to do it. > **unwillingly** adverb

unwilling adjective
= averse, grudging, loath, reluctant

unwind unwinds, unwinding, unwound verb 1 When you unwind after working hard, you relax. 2 If you unwind something that is wrapped round something else, you undo it.

unwise adjective foolish or not sensible.

unwise adjective
= daft (British; informal), foolish, idiotic, irresponsible, rash, senseless, silly, stupid

unwitting adjective Unwitting describes someone who becomes involved in something without realising what is really happening. > **unwittingly** adverb

U

unworthy adjective (formal)
Someone who is unworthy of
something does not deserve it.

unwound the past tense and past
participle of **unwind**.

unwrap unwraps, unwrapping,
unwrapped verb When you
unwrap something, you take off
the paper or covering around it.

unwritten adjective An unwritten
law is one which is generally
understood and accepted without
being officially laid down.

up adverb, preposition 1 towards or
in a higher place. 2 towards or in
the north. ▶ preposition 3 If you go
up a road or river, you go along it.
4 You use 'up to' to say how large
something can be or what level
it has reached: traffic jams up to
15 kilometres long. 5 (informal) If
someone is up to something,
they are secretly doing something
they should not be doing. 6 If it is
up to someone to do something,
it is their responsibility. ▶ adjective
7 If you are up, you are not in bed.
8 If a period of time is up, it has
come to an end. ▶ adverb 9 If an
amount of something goes up, it
increases.

up-and-coming adjective
Up-and-coming people are likely
to be successful.

upbringing noun Your
upbringing is the way that your
parents have taught you to
behave.

update verb If you update
something, you make it more
modern or add new information
to it.

upgrade verb If a person or their
job is upgraded, they are given
more responsibility or status and
usually more money.

upheaval noun a big change
which causes a lot of trouble.

upheld the past tense and past
participle of **uphold**.

uphill adverb 1 If you go uphill, you
go up a slope. ▶ adjective 2 An
uphill task requires a lot of effort
and determination.

uphold upholds, upholding,
upheld verb If someone upholds a
law or a decision, they support
and maintain it.

upholstery noun Upholstery is
the soft covering on chairs and
sofas that makes them
comfortable.

upkeep noun The upkeep of
something is the continual
process and cost of keeping it in
good condition.

> **upkeep** noun
> = keep, maintenance, overheads,
> preservation, running

upland adjective 1 An upland area
is an area of high land. ▶ noun
2 (in plural) Uplands are areas of
high land.

uplifting adjective Something that
is uplifting makes you feel happy.

upload (ICT) verb 1 If you upload
data, you transfer it from the
memory of a computer to a larger
computer system. ▶ noun 2 a piece
of data transferred in this way.

upon preposition (formal) 'Upon'
means on.

upper adjective 1 referring to
something that is above
something else, or the higher
part of something. ▶ noun 2 the
top part of a shoe.

upper class noun The upper
classes are people who belong to a
very wealthy or aristocratic group
in a society.

u

uppermost adjective, adverb 1 on top or in the highest position.
▶ adjective 2 most important.

upright adjective, adverb 1 standing or sitting up straight, rather than bending or lying down.
2 behaving in a very respectable and moral way.

uprising noun If there is an uprising, a large group of people begin fighting against the existing government to bring about political changes.

uproar noun If there is uproar or an uproar, there is a lot of shouting and noise, often because people are angry.

uproot verb 1 If someone is uprooted, they have to leave the place where they have lived for a long time. 2 If a tree is uprooted, it is pulled out of the ground.

upset upsets, upsetting, upset adjective 1 worried or unhappy.
▶ verb 2 If something upsets you, it makes you feel worried or unhappy. 3 If you upset something, you turn it over or spill it accidentally. ▶ noun 4 A stomach upset is a slight stomach illness caused by an infection or by something you have eaten.

> **upset** adjective
> 1 = agitated, distressed, frantic, hurt, troubled, unhappy
> ▶ verb 2 = agitate, bother, distress, disturb, grieve, ruffle
> 3 = capsize, knock over, overturn, spill

upshot noun The upshot of a series of events is the final result.

upside down adjective, adverb the wrong way up.

upstage verb If someone upstages you, they draw people's attention away from you by being more attractive or interesting.

upstairs adverb 1 If you go upstairs in a building, you go up to a higher floor. ▶ adjective, adverb 2 on a higher floor or on the top floor. ▶ noun 3 The upstairs of a building is its upper floor or floors.

upstart noun someone who has risen too quickly to an important position and is too arrogant.

upstream adverb towards the source of a river.

upsurge noun An upsurge of something is a sudden large increase in it.

uptake noun You can say that someone is quick on the uptake if they understand things quickly.

uptight adjective (informal) tense or annoyed.

up-to-date adjective 1 being the newest thing of its kind. 2 having the latest information.

up-to-the-minute adjective Up-to-the-minute information is the latest available information.

upturn noun an improvement in a situation.

upturned adjective 1 pointing upwards. 2 upside down.

upwards adverb 1 If you move or look upwards, you move or look towards the sky or towards a higher level. 2 If an amount or rate moves upwards, it increases.
> **upward** adjective

uranium noun (SCIENCE) Uranium is a radioactive metallic element used in the production of nuclear power and weapons. Its atomic number is 92 and its symbol is U.

Uranus noun Uranus is the planet in the solar system which is seventh from the sun.

urban adjective (GEOGRAPHY) relating to a town or city.

urbane adjective well-mannered, and comfortable in social situations.

Urdu noun Urdu is the official language of Pakistan. It is also spoken by many people in India.

urge noun 1 If you have an urge to do something, you have a strong wish to do it. ▶ verb 2 If you urge someone to do something, you try hard to persuade them to do it.

> **urge** noun
> 1 = compulsion, desire, drive, impulse, longing, wish
> ▶ verb 2 = beg, beseech (literary), implore, plead, press

urgent adjective needing to be dealt with as soon as possible. > **urgently** adverb > **urgency** noun

> **urgent** adjective
> = compelling, immediate, imperative, pressing

urinal noun a bowl or trough fixed to the wall in a public toilet for men to urinate in.

urinate verb When you urinate, you go to the toilet and get rid of urine from your body.

urine noun the waste liquid that you get rid of from your body when you go to the toilet.

URL noun (ICT) A URL is a technical name for an internet address. URL is an abbreviation for 'uniform resource locator'.

urn noun a decorated container, especially one that is used to hold the ashes of a person who has been cremated.

us pronoun A speaker or writer uses us to refer to himself or herself

and one or more other people: Why don't you tell us?

US or **USA** an abbreviation for 'United States (of America)'.

usage noun 1 the degree to which something is used, or the way in which it is used. 2 the way in which words are actually used.

USB noun (ICT) a socket on a computer or other electronic device where you can connect another piece of equipment, such as a keyboard, camera or flash drive. USB is an abbreviation for 'universal serial bus'.

use verb 1 If you use something, you do something with it in order to do a job or achieve something. 2 If you use someone, you take advantage of them by making them do things for you. ▶ noun 3 The use of something is the act of using it. 4 If you have the use of something, you have the ability or permission to use it. 5 If you find a use for something, you find a purpose for it. > **usable**; also spelt **useable** adjective > **user** noun

> **use** verb
> 1 = apply, employ, operate, utilise
> ▶ noun 3 = application, employment, operation, usage
> 5 = end, object, point, purpose

used verb 1 Something that used to be done or used to be true was done or was true in the past. ▶ phrase 2 If you are **used to** something, you are familiar with it and have often experienced it. ▶ adjective 3 A used object has had a previous owner.

useful adjective If something is useful, you can use it in order to do something or to help you in

some way. ▷ **usefully** adverb
▷ **usefulness** noun

> **useful** adjective
> = beneficial, effective, helpful,
> practical, valuable, worthwhile

useless adjective 1 If something is
useless, you cannot use it because
it is not suitable or helpful. 2 If a
course of action is useless, it will
not achieve what is wanted.

> **useless** adjective
> 1 = futile, impractical,
> unproductive, unsuitable,
> worthless

username noun a name that
someone uses when logging into
a computer or website.

usher verb 1 If you usher someone
somewhere, you show them
where to go by going with them.
▶ noun 2 a person who shows
people where to sit at a wedding
or a concert.

USSR (HISTORY) an abbreviation
for 'Union of Soviet Socialist
Republics', a country which was
made up of a lot of smaller
countries including Russia, but
which is now broken up.

usual adjective 1 happening,
done or used most often.
▶ phrase 2 If you do something
as usual, you do it in the way that
you normally do it, or you do
something that you do regularly.
▷ **usually** adverb

> **usual** adjective
> 1 = accustomed, common,
> customary, habitual, normal,
> regular, standard

usurp verb (formal) If someone
usurps another person's job or
title they take it when they have
no right to do so.

ute noun (informal) In Australian
and New Zealand English, a ute is
a utility truck.

utensil noun Utensils are tools.

uterus noun (SCIENCE) A woman's
uterus is her womb.

utilise; also spelt **utilize** verb
(formal) To utilise something is to
use it. ▷ **utilisation** noun

utility utilities noun 1 The utility
of something is its usefulness.
2 a service, such as water or gas,
that is provided for everyone.

utmost adjective used to
emphasise a particular quality:
I have the utmost respect for Richard.

utter verb 1 When you utter
sounds or words, you make or say
them. ▶ adjective 2 Utter means
complete or total. ▷ **utterly** adverb

> **utter** adjective
> 2 = absolute, complete,
> consummate, out-and-out,
> outright, perfect, pure, sheer,
> thorough, total

utterance noun something that
is said.

u

Vv

vacant *adjective* 1 If something is vacant, it is not occupied or being used. 2 If a job or position is vacant, no-one holds it at present. 3 A vacant look suggests that someone does not understand something or is not very intelligent. > **vacancy** *noun* > **vacantly** *adverb*

vacate *verb* (formal) If you vacate a room or job, you leave it and it becomes available for someone else.

vacation *noun* 1 the period between academic terms at a university or college. 2 a holiday.

vaccinate *verb* To vaccinate someone means to give them a vaccine, usually by injection, to protect them against a disease. > **vaccination** *noun*

vaccine *noun* a substance made from the germs that cause a disease, given to people to make them immune to that disease.

vacuum *noun* 1 (SCIENCE) a space containing no air, gases or other matter. ▶ *verb* 2 If you vacuum something, you clean it using a vacuum cleaner.

vacuum cleaner *noun* an electric machine which cleans by sucking up dirt.

vagina *noun* (SCIENCE) A woman's vagina is the passage that connects her outer sex organs to her womb.

vague *adjective* 1 If something is vague, it is not expressed or explained clearly, or you cannot see or remember it clearly. 2 Someone looks or sounds vague if they are not concentrating or thinking clearly. > **vaguely** *adverb* > **vagueness** *noun*

> **vague** *adjective*
> 1 = hazy, indefinite, indistinct, loose, uncertain, unclear

vain *adjective* 1 A vain action or attempt is one which is not successful. 2 A vain person is very proud of their looks, intelligence or other qualities. ▶ *phrase* 3 If you do something **in vain**, you do not succeed in achieving what you intend. > **vainly** *adverb*

> **vain** *adjective*
> 1 = abortive, fruitless, futile, unproductive, useless
> 2 = conceited, egotistical, ostentatious, proud, stuck-up (informal)
> ▶ *phrase* 3 **in vain** = fruitless, to no avail, unsuccessful, wasted

valentine *noun* 1 Your valentine is someone you love and send a card to on Saint Valentine's Day, February 14th. 2 A valentine or a valentine card is the card you send to the person you love on Saint Valentine's Day.

valet *noun* a male servant who is employed to look after another man, particularly caring for his clothes.

valiant *adjective* very brave. > **valiantly** *adverb*

valid *adjective* 1 Something that is valid is based on sound reasoning. 2 A valid ticket or document is one which is officially accepted. > **validity** *noun*

V

validate verb If something validates a statement or claim, it proves that it is true or correct.

valley noun (GEOGRAPHY) a long stretch of land between hills, often with a river flowing through it.

valour noun Valour is great bravery.

valuable adjective 1 having great importance or usefulness. 2 worth a lot of money.

> **valuable** adjective
> 1 = beneficial, helpful, important, prized, useful, worthwhile 2 = costly, expensive, precious

valuation noun a judgment about how much money something is worth or how good it is.

value values, valuing, valued noun 1 The value of something is its importance or usefulness. 2 The value of something you own is the amount of money that it is worth. 3 The values of a group or a person are the moral principles and beliefs that they think are important. ▶ verb 4 If you value something, you think it is important and you appreciate it. 5 When experts value something, they decide how much money it is worth. > **valued** adjective
> **valuer** noun

> **value** noun
> 1 = advantage, benefit, effectiveness, importance, merit, use, usefulness, virtue, worth 2 = cost, market price, price, selling price, worth
> ▶ verb 4 = appreciate, cherish, have a high opinion of, prize, rate highly, respect, treasure
> 5 = appraise, assess, cost, estimate, evaluate, price

valve noun 1 a part attached to a pipe or tube which controls the flow of gas or liquid. 2 a small flap in your heart or in a vein which controls the flow and direction of blood.

vampire noun In horror stories, vampires are corpses that come out of their graves at night and suck the blood of living people.

van noun a covered vehicle larger than a car but smaller than a lorry, used for carrying goods.

vandal noun someone who deliberately damages or destroys things, particularly public property. > **vandalise** verb
> **vandalism** noun

vanguard noun If someone is in the vanguard of something, they are in the most advanced part of it.

vanilla noun Vanilla is a flavouring for food such as ice cream, which comes from the pods of a tropical plant.

vanish verb 1 If something vanishes, it disappears. 2 If something vanishes, it ceases to exist.

> **vanish** verb
> 1 = become invisible, be lost to view, disappear, fade, recede
> 2 = become extinct, cease, cease to exist, die out, dissolve, evaporate, fade away, go away, melt away, pass

vanity noun Vanity is a feeling of excessive pride about your looks or abilities.

vanquish verb (literary) To vanquish someone means to defeat them completely.

> **vanquish** verb
> = beat, conquer, crush, defeat, overcome, rout, trounce

vapour *noun* (SCIENCE) Vapour is a mass of tiny drops of water or other liquids in the air which looks like mist.

variable *adjective* 1 Something that is variable is likely to change at any time. ▶ *noun* 2 In any situation, a variable is something in it that can change. 3 (MATHS) a symbol such as x which can represent any value or any one of a set of values.
> **variability** *noun*

variance *noun* If one thing is at variance with another, the two seem to contradict each other.

variant *noun* 1 A variant of something has a different form from the usual one, for example *gaol* is a variant of *jail*. ▶ *adjective* 2 alternative or different.

variation *noun* 1 a change from the normal or usual pattern. 2 a change in level, amount or quantity.

> **variation** *noun*
> 1 = alteration, change, departure, deviation, difference, diversion

varicose veins *plural noun* Varicose veins are swollen painful veins in the legs.

varied *adjective* of different types, quantities or sizes.

variety *noun* **varieties** *noun* 1 If something has variety, it consists of things which are not all the same. 2 A variety of things is a number of different kinds of them. 3 A variety of something is a particular type of it. 4 Variety is a form of entertainment consisting of short unrelated acts, such as singing, dancing and comedy.

> **variety** *noun*
> 2 = array, assortment, collection, medley, mixture, range 3 = category, class, kind, sort, strain, type

various *adjective* Various means of several different types.
> **variously** *adverb*

> **various** *adjective*
> = assorted, different, disparate, diverse, miscellaneous, sundry

varnish *noun* 1 a liquid which when painted onto a surface gives it a hard, clear, shiny finish. ▶ *verb* 2 If you varnish something, you paint it with varnish.

vary **varies**, **varying**, **varied** *verb* 1 If things vary, they change. 2 If you vary something, you introduce changes in it.
> **varied** *adjective*

> **vary** *verb*
> 1 = alter, alternate, change, fluctuate 2 = alternate, diversify, modify

vascular *adjective* relating to tubes or ducts that carry fluids within animals or plants.

vase *noun* a glass or china jar for flowers.

vasectomy **vasectomies** *noun* an operation to sterilise a man by cutting the tube in his body that carries the sperm.

Vaseline *noun* (trademark) Vaseline is a soft, clear jelly made from petroleum and used as an ointment or as grease.

vast *adjective* extremely large.
> **vastly** *adverb* > **vastness** *noun*

> **vast** *adjective*
> = colossal, enormous, giant, gigantic, great, huge, immense, massive

v

vat *noun* a large container for liquids.

VAT *noun* In Britain, VAT is a tax which is added to the costs of making or providing goods and services. VAT is an abbreviation for 'value-added tax'.

vault *noun* 1 a strong secure room, often underneath a building, where valuables are stored, or underneath a church where people are buried. 2 an arched roof, often found in churches. ▸ *verb* 3 If you vault over something, you jump over it using your hands or a pole to help.

veal *noun* Veal is the meat from a calf.

Veda *noun* an ancient sacred text of the Hindu religion; also these texts as a collection. ▸ **Vedic** *adjective*

veer *verb* If something which is moving veers in a particular direction, it suddenly changes course.

vegan *noun* someone who does not eat any food made from animal products, such as meat, eggs, cheese or milk.

vegetable *noun* 1 Vegetables are edible roots or leaves such as carrots or cabbage. ▸ *adjective* 2 Vegetable is used to refer to any plants in contrast to animals or minerals.

vegetarian *noun* a person who does not eat meat, poultry or fish. ▸ **vegetarianism** *noun*

vegetation *noun* (GEOGRAPHY) Vegetation is the plants in a particular area.

vehement *adjective* Someone who is vehement has strong feelings or opinions and expresses them forcefully. ▸ **vehemence** *noun* ▸ **vehemently** *adverb*

vehicle *noun* 1 a machine, often with an engine, used for transporting people or goods. 2 something used to achieve a particular purpose or as a means of expression. ▸ **vehicular** *adjective*

veil *noun* a piece of thin, soft cloth that women sometimes wear over their heads. ▸ **veiled** *adjective*

vein *noun* 1 Your veins are the tubes in your body through which your blood flows to your heart. 2 Veins are the thin lines on leaves or on insects' wings. 3 A vein of a metal or a mineral is a layer of it in rock. 4 Something that is in a particular vein is in that style or mood.

veld *noun* The veld is flat high grassland in Southern Africa.

velocity *noun* (technical) Velocity is the speed at which something is moving in a particular direction.

velvet *noun* Velvet is a very soft material which has a thick layer of fine short threads on one side. ▸ **velvety** *adjective*

vendetta *noun* a long-lasting bitter quarrel in which people try to harm each other.

vendor *noun* a person who sells something.

veneer *noun* 1 You can refer to a superficial quality that someone has as a veneer of that quality. 2 Veneer is a thin layer of wood or plastic used to cover a surface.

venerable *adjective* 1 A venerable person is someone you treat with respect because they are old and wise. 2 Something that is venerable is impressive because it is old or important historically.

V

vengeance noun 1 Vengeance is the act of harming someone because they have harmed you. ▶ phrase 2 If something happens **with a vengeance**, it happens to a much greater extent than was expected.

venison noun Venison is the meat from a deer.

venom noun 1 The venom of a snake, scorpion or spider is its poison. 2 Venom is a feeling of great bitterness or spitefulness towards someone. > **venomous** adjective

vent noun 1 a hole in something through which gases and smoke can escape and fresh air can enter. ▶ verb 2 If you vent strong feelings, you express them. ▶ phrase 3 If you **give vent** to strong feelings, you express them.

ventilate verb To ventilate a room means to allow fresh air into it. > **ventilated** adjective

ventilation noun 1 Ventilation is the process of breathing air in and out of the lungs. 2 A ventilation system supplies fresh air into a building.

ventilator noun a machine that helps people breathe when they cannot breathe naturally, for example if they are very ill.

ventriloquist noun an entertainer who can speak without moving their lips so that the words seem to come from a dummy. > **ventriloquism** noun

venture noun 1 something new which involves the risk of failure or of losing money. ▶ verb 2 If you venture something such as an opinion, you say it cautiously or hesitantly because you are afraid it might be foolish or wrong.

3 If you venture somewhere that might be dangerous, you go there.

venue noun The venue for an event is the place where it will happen.

Venus noun Venus is the planet in the solar system which is second from the sun.

veranda; also spelt **verandah** noun a platform with a roof that is attached to an outside wall of a house at ground level.

verb noun (ENGLISH) (MFL) In grammar, a verb is a word that expresses actions and states, for example 'be', 'become', 'take' and 'run'.

verbal adjective 1 (ENGLISH) You use 'verbal' to describe things connected with words and their use. 2 'Verbal' describes things which are spoken rather than written. > **verbally** adverb

verdict noun 1 In a law court, a verdict is the decision which states whether a prisoner is guilty or not guilty. 2 If you give a verdict on something, you give your opinion after thinking about it.

> **verdict** noun
> 2 = conclusion, decision, finding, judgment, opinion

verge noun 1 The verge of a road is the narrow strip of grassy ground at the side. ▶ phrase 2 If you are **on the verge** of something, you are going to do it soon or it is likely to happen soon. ▶ verb 3 Something that verges on something else is almost the same as it.

verify verifies, verifying, verified verb If you verify something, you check that it is true. > **verifiable** adjective > **verification** noun

veritable *adjective* You use veritable to emphasise something: *a veritable jungle of shops.*

vermin *plural noun* Vermin are small animals or insects, such as rats and cockroaches, which carry disease and damage crops.

vernacular *noun* The vernacular of a particular country or district is the language widely spoken there.

versatile *adjective* 1 If someone is versatile, they have many different skills. 2 If a tool or material is versatile, it can be used for many different purposes.
> **versatility** *noun*

verse *noun* 1 Verse is another word for poetry. 2 one part of a poem or song, or a chapter of the Bible.

versed *adjective* If you are versed in something, you know a lot about it.

version *noun* 1 A version of something is a form of it in which some details are different from earlier or later forms. 2 Someone's version of an event is their personal description of what happened.

versus *preposition* Versus is used to indicate that two people or teams are competing against each other.

vertebra vertebrae *noun* (SCIENCE) Vertebrae are the small bones which form a person's or animal's backbone.

vertebrate *noun* (SCIENCE) Vertebrates are any creatures which have a backbone.

vertical *adjective* (MATHS) Something that is vertical points straight up and forms a ninety-degree angle with the surface on which it stands.
> **vertically** *adverb*

vertigo *noun* Vertigo is a feeling of dizziness caused by looking down from a high place.

verve *noun* Verve is lively and forceful enthusiasm.

very *adverb* 1 to a great degree. ▶ *adjective* 2 'Very' is used before words to emphasise them: *the very end of the book.* ▶ *phrase* 3 You use 'not very' to mean that something is the case only to a small degree.

> **very** *adverb*
> 1 = deeply, extremely, greatly, highly, really, terribly

vessel *noun* 1 a ship or large boat. 2 (*literary*) any bowl or container in which a liquid can be kept. 3 a thin tube along which liquids such as blood or sap move in animals and plants.

vest *noun* a piece of underwear worn for warmth on the top half of the body.

vestige *noun* (*formal*) A vestige is a tiny part of something that is left over when the rest has been used up.

vet vets, vetting, vetted *noun* 1 a doctor for animals. ▶ *verb* 2 If you vet someone or something, you check them carefully to see if they are acceptable.

veteran *noun* 1 someone who has served in the armed forces, particularly during a war. 2 someone who has been involved in a particular activity for a long time.

veterinary *adjective* Veterinary is used to describe the work of a vet and the medical treatment of animals.

veterinary surgeon *noun* the same as a **vet**.

veto vetoes, vetoing, vetoed *verb*
1 If someone in authority vetoes something, they say no to it.
▶ *noun* 2 Veto is the right that someone in authority has to say no to something.

> **veto** *verb*
> 1 = ban, forbid, prohibit
> ▶ *noun* 2 = ban, prohibition

vexed *adjective* If you are vexed, you are annoyed, worried or puzzled.

VHF *noun* VHF is a range of high radio frequencies. VHF is an abbreviation for 'very high frequency'.

via *preposition* 1 If you go to one place via another, you travel through that place to get to your destination. 2 Via also means done or achieved by making use of a particular thing or person.

viable *adjective* Something that is viable is capable of doing what it is intended to do without extra help or financial support.
> **viability** *noun*

viaduct *noun* a long, high bridge that carries a road or railway across a valley.

vibrant *adjective* Something or someone that is vibrant is full of life, energy and enthusiasm.
> **vibrantly** *adverb* > **vibrancy** *noun*

vibrate *verb* (SCIENCE) If something vibrates, it moves a tiny amount backwards and forwards very quickly. > **vibration** *noun*

vicar *noun* a priest in the Church of England.

vicarage *noun* a house where a vicar lives.

vice *noun* 1 a serious moral fault in someone's character, such as greed, or a weakness, such as smoking. 2 a tool with a pair of jaws that hold an object tightly while it is being worked on.

vice versa *adverb* 'Vice versa' is used to indicate that the reverse of what you have said is also true.

vicinity *noun* If something is in the vicinity of a place, it is in the surrounding or nearby area.

vicious *adjective* cruel and violent.
> **viciously** *adverb* > **viciousness** *noun*

victim *noun* someone who has been harmed or injured by someone or something.

victor *noun* The victor in a fight or contest is the person who wins.

Victorian *adjective* 1 (HISTORY) Victorian describes things that happened or were made during the reign of Queen Victoria (1837–1901). 2 Victorian also describes people or things connected with the state of Victoria in Australia.

victory victories *noun* a success in a battle or competition.
> **victorious** *adjective*

> **victory** *noun*
> = laurels, success, superiority, triumph, win

video videos, videoing, videoed *noun* 1 Video is the recording and showing of films and events. 2 a sound and picture recording which can be played back. 3 a short film recorded by a pop singer or group to accompany a song. ▶ *verb* 4 If you video something, you record it for later viewing.

vie vies, vying, vied *verb* (formal) If you vie with someone, you compete to do something sooner than or better than they do.

v

Vietnamese *adjective* 1 belonging or relating to Vietnam. ▶ *noun* 2 someone who comes from Vietnam. 3 Vietnamese is the main language spoken in Vietnam.

view *noun* 1 Your views are your personal opinions. 2 everything you can see from a particular place. ▶ *verb* 3 If you view something in a particular way, you think of it in that way. ▶ *phrase* 4 You use **in view of** to specify the main fact or event influencing your actions or opinions: *He wore a lighter suit in view of the heat.* 5 If something is **on view**, it is being shown or exhibited to the public.

> **view** *noun*
> 1 = attitude, belief, conviction, feeling, opinion, point of view
> 2 = aspect, landscape, panorama, perspective, scene, spectacle
> ▶ *verb* 3 = consider, deem (*formal*), judge, regard

viewer *noun* Viewers are the people who watch television.

viewpoint *noun* 1 Your viewpoint is your attitude towards something. 2 a place from which you get a good view of an area or event.

> **viewpoint** *noun*
> 1 = attitude, belief, conviction, feeling, opinion, point of view

vigil *noun* a period of time, especially at night, when you stay quietly in one place, for example because you are making a political protest or praying.

vigilant *adjective* careful and alert to danger or trouble. > **vigilance** *noun* > **vigilantly** *adverb*

vigilante *noun* Vigilantes are unofficially organised groups of people who try to protect their community and catch and punish criminals.

vigorous *adjective* energetic or enthusiastic. > **vigorously** *adverb* > **vigour** *noun*

Viking *noun* (HISTORY) The Vikings were seamen from Scandinavia who raided parts of north-western Europe from the 8th to the 11th centuries.

vile *adjective* unpleasant or disgusting.

villa *noun* a house, especially a pleasant holiday home in a country with a warm climate.

village *noun* a collection of houses and other buildings in the countryside. > **villager** *noun*

villain *noun* 1 someone who harms others or breaks the law. 2 the main evil character in a story. > **villainous** *adjective* > **villainy** *noun*

vindicate *verb* (*formal*) If someone is vindicated, their views or ideas are proved to be right. > **vindication** *noun*

vindictive *adjective* Someone who is vindictive is deliberately hurtful to someone, often as an act of revenge. > **vindictiveness** *noun*

vine *noun* a trailing or climbing plant which winds itself around and over a support, especially one which produces grapes.

vinegar *noun* Vinegar is a sharp-tasting liquid made from sour wine, beer or cider, which is used for salad dressing. > **vinegary** *adjective*

vineyard *noun* an area of land where grapes are grown.

vintage *adjective* 1 A vintage wine is a good quality wine which has been stored for a number of years to improve its quality. 2 Vintage describes something which is the best or most typical of its kind. 3 A vintage car is one made between 1918 and 1930.

vinyl *noun* Vinyl is a strong plastic used to make things such as furniture and floor coverings.

viola *noun* a musical instrument like a violin, but larger and with a lower pitch.

violate *verb* 1 If you violate an agreement, law or promise, you break it. 2 If you violate someone's peace or privacy, you disturb it. 3 If you violate a place, especially a holy place, you treat it with disrespect or violence. > **violation** *noun*

violence *noun* 1 Violence is behaviour that is intended to hurt or kill people. 2 If you do or say something with violence, you use a lot of energy in doing or saying it, often because you are angry.

violence *noun*
1 = bloodshed, brutality, cruelty, force, savagery, terrorism
2 = fervour, force, harshness, intensity, severity, vehemence

violent *adjective* 1 If someone is violent, they try to hurt or kill people. 2 A violent event happens unexpectedly and with great force. 3 Something that is violent is said, felt or done with great force. > **violently** *adverb*

violent *adjective*
1 = bloodthirsty, brutal, cruel, murderous, savage, vicious

2 = powerful, raging, rough, strong, turbulent, wild
3 = acute, furious, intense, powerful, severe, strong

violet *noun* 1 a plant with dark purple flowers. ▶ *noun, adjective* 2 bluish purple.

violin *noun* a musical instrument with four strings that is held under the chin and played with a bow. > **violinist** *noun*

VIP *noun* VIPs are famous or important people. VIP is an abbreviation for 'very important person'.

viral *adjective* 1 relating to or caused by a virus. ▶ *adverb* 2 If a story or a video goes viral, it spreads quickly and widely among users of the internet.

virgin *adjective* Something that is virgin is fresh and unused.

Virgo *noun* Virgo is the sixth sign of the zodiac, represented by a girl. People born between August 23rd and September 22nd are born under this sign.

virile *adjective* A virile man has all the qualities that a man is traditionally expected to have, such as strength. > **virility** *noun*

virtual *adjective* 1 Virtual means that something has all the characteristics of a particular thing, but it is not formally recognised as being that thing. 2 (ICT) Virtual objects and activities are generated by a computer to simulate real objects and activities. > **virtually** *adverb*

virtual reality *noun* (ICT) Virtual reality is a situation or setting that has been created by a computer and that looks real to the person using it.

v

virtue noun 1 Virtue is thinking and doing what is morally right and avoiding what is wrong. 2 a good quality in someone's character. 3 A virtue of something is an advantage. ▶ phrase 4 (formal) By virtue of means because of.

> **virtue** noun
> 1 = goodness, integrity, morality
> 3 = advantage, asset, attribute, merit, plus (informal), strength
> ▶ phrase 4 by virtue of = as a result of, because of, by dint of, on account of, thanks to

virtuoso virtuosos or virtuosi noun someone who is exceptionally good at something, particularly playing a musical instrument.

virtuous adjective behaving with or showing moral virtue.
> **virtuously** adverb

virus noun 1 (SCIENCE) a kind of germ that can cause disease. 2 (ICT) a program that alters or damages the information stored in a computer system.

visa noun an official stamp, usually put in your passport, that allows you to visit a particular country.

visibility noun You use visibility to say how far or how clearly you can see in particular weather conditions.

visible adjective 1 able to be seen. 2 noticeable or evident: There was little visible excitement. > **visibly** adverb

> **visible** adjective
> 1 = clear, conspicuous, distinguishable, in sight, observable, perceptible
> 2 = apparent, evident, manifest (formal), noticeable, obvious, plain

vision noun 1 Vision is the ability to see clearly. 2 a mental picture, in which you imagine how things might be different. 3 Vision is also imaginative insight. 4 an unusual experience that some people claim to have, in which they see things that other people cannot see. > **visionary** noun, adjective

> **vision** noun
> 2 = conception, daydream, dream, fantasy, ideal, image
> 3 = foresight, imagination, insight, intuition 4 = apparition, hallucination, illusion, mirage, phantom, spectre

visit verb 1 If you visit someone, you go to see them and spend time with them. 2 If you visit a place, you go to see it. ▶ noun 3 a trip to see a person or place.
> **visitor** noun

> **visit** verb
> 1 = call on, go to see, look up
> ▶ noun 3 = call, stay, stop

visor noun a transparent movable shield attached to a helmet, which can be pulled down to protect the eyes or face.

visual adjective relating to sight.

visualise; also spelt **visualize** verb If you visualise something, you form a mental picture of it.

vital adjective 1 necessary or very important. 2 energetic, exciting and full of life. > **vitally** adverb

> **vital** adjective
> 1 = central, critical, crucial, essential, important, indispensable, necessary, pivotal 2 = active, dynamic, energetic, lively, spirited, sprightly, vivacious

V

vitality noun People who have vitality are energetic and lively.

vitamin noun (SCIENCE) Vitamins are organic compounds which you need in order to remain healthy. They occur naturally in food.

vivacious adjective A vivacious person is attractively lively and high-spirited. > **vivacity** noun

vivid adjective very bright in colour or clear in detail. > **vividly** adverb > **vividness** noun

vixen noun a female fox.

vocabulary vocabularies noun 1 (ENGLISH) Someone's vocabulary is the total number of words they know in a particular language. 2 (ENGLISH) The vocabulary of a language is all the words in it.

vocal adjective 1 You say that someone is vocal if they express their opinions strongly and openly. 2 (MUSIC) Vocal means involving the use of the human voice, especially in singing. > **vocalist** noun > **vocally** adverb

vocation noun 1 a strong wish to do a particular job, especially one which involves serving other people. 2 a profession or career.

vocational adjective 'Vocational' is used to describe the skills needed for a particular job or profession.

vociferous adjective (formal) Someone who is vociferous speaks a lot, or loudly, because they want to make a point strongly. > **vociferously** adverb

vodka noun a strong clear alcoholic drink which originally came from Russia.

vogue phrase If something is the **vogue** or in **vogue**, it is

fashionable and popular.

voice noun 1 Your voice is the sounds produced by your vocal cords, or the ability to make such sounds. ▸ verb 2 If you voice an opinion or an emotion, you say what you think or feel.

void noun 1 a situation which seems empty because it has no interest or excitement. 2 a large empty hole or space.

volatile adjective liable to change often and unexpectedly.

volcanic adjective A volcanic region has many volcanoes or was created by volcanoes.

volcano volcanoes noun (GEOGRAPHY) a hill with an opening through which lava, gas and ash burst out from inside the earth onto the surface.

volition noun (formal) If you do something of your own volition, you do it because you have decided for yourself, without being persuaded by others.

volley noun 1 A volley of shots or gunfire is a lot of shots fired at the same time. 2 In tennis, a volley is a stroke in which the player hits the ball before it bounces.

volleyball noun Volleyball is a game in which two teams hit a large ball back and forth over a high net with their hands. The ball is not allowed to bounce on the ground.

volt noun (SCIENCE) A volt is a unit of electrical force. One volt produces one amp of electricity when the resistance is one ohm.

voltage noun The voltage of an electric current is its force measured in volts.

volume noun 1 (MATHS) The volume of something is the amount of space it contains or occupies. 2 The volume of something is also the amount of it that there is. 3 The volume of a radio, TV or MP3 player is the strength of the sound that it produces. 4 a book, or one of a series of books.

voluminous adjective very large or full in size or quantity.

voluntary adjective 1 Voluntary actions are ones that you do because you choose to do them and not because you have been forced to do them. 2 Voluntary work is done by people who are not paid for what they do.
> **voluntarily** adverb

volunteer noun 1 (CITIZENSHIP) someone who does work for which they are not paid.
2 someone who chooses to join the armed forces, especially during wartime. ▸ verb
3 (CITIZENSHIP) If you volunteer to do something, you offer to do it rather than being forced into it.
4 If you volunteer information, you give it without being asked.

voluptuous adjective having a figure which is considered to be full and attractive.
> **voluptuously** adverb
> **voluptuousness** noun

vomit verb 1 If you vomit, food and drink comes back up from your stomach and out through your mouth. ▸ noun 2 Vomit is partly digested food and drink that has come back up from someone's stomach and out through your mouth.

vomit verb
1 = be sick, bring up, regurgitate

voodoo noun Voodoo is a form of magic practised in the Caribbean, especially in Haiti.

vote noun 1 (CITIZENSHIP) Someone's vote is their choice in an election, or at a meeting where decisions are taken. 2 When a group of people have a vote, they make a decision by allowing each person in the group to say what they would prefer. 3 In an election, the vote is the total number of people who have made their choice. 4 If people have the vote, they have the legal right to vote in an election. ▸ verb
5 (CITIZENSHIP) When people vote, they indicate their choice or opinion, usually by writing on a piece of paper or by raising their hand. 6 If you vote that a particular thing should happen, you are suggesting it should happen. > **voter** noun

vote noun
2 = ballot, plebiscite (formal), polls, referendum
▸ verb 5 = cast a vote, go to the polls, opt, return 6 = propose, recommend, suggest

vouch verb 1 If you say that you can vouch for something, you mean that you have evidence from your own experience that it is true or correct. 2 If you say that you can vouch for someone, you mean that you are sure that you can guarantee their good behaviour or support.

voucher noun a piece of paper that can be used instead of money to pay for something.

vow verb 1 If you vow to do something, you make a solemn promise to do it. ▸ noun
2 a solemn promise.

vowel noun (ENGLISH) a sound made without your tongue touching the roof of your mouth or your teeth, or one of the letters a, e, i, o, u, which represent such sounds.

voyage noun a long journey on a ship or in a spacecraft. > **voyager** noun

vulgar adjective 1 socially unacceptable or offensive. 2 showing a lack of taste or quality. > **vulgarity** noun > **vulgarly** adverb

> **vulgar** adjective
> 1 = coarse, rude, uncouth
> 2 = common, flashy, gaudy, tacky (informal), tasteless, tawdry

vulnerable adjective weak and without protection. > **vulnerably** adverb > **vulnerability** noun

> **vulnerable** adjective
> = exposed, sensitive, susceptible, weak

vulture noun a large bird which lives in hot countries and eats the flesh of dead animals.

vying the present participle of **vie**.

Ww

wacky wackier, wackiest adjective (informal) odd or crazy.

wad noun 1 A wad of papers or banknotes is a thick bundle of them. 2 A wad of something is a lump of it.

wade verb 1 If you wade through water or mud, you walk slowly through it. 2 If you wade through a book or document, you spend a lot of time and effort reading it because you find it dull or difficult.

wafer noun 1 a thin, crisp, sweet biscuit often eaten with ice cream. 2 a thin disc of special bread used in the Christian service of Holy Communion.

waffle verb 1 When someone waffles, they talk or write a lot without being clear or without saying anything of importance. ▶ noun 2 Waffle is vague and lengthy speech or writing. 3 a thick, crisp pancake with squares marked on it, often eaten with syrup poured over it.

waft verb If a sound or scent wafts or is wafted through the air, it moves gently through it.

wag wags, wagging, wagged verb 1 When a dog wags its tail, it shakes it repeatedly from side to side. 2 If you wag your finger, you move it repeatedly up and down.

w

wage noun 1 A wage or wages is the regular payment made to someone each week for the work they do, especially for manual or unskilled work. ▶ verb 2 If a person or country wages a campaign or war, they start it and carry it on over a period of time.

wager noun a bet.

wagon; also spelt **waggon** noun 1 a strong four-wheeled vehicle for carrying heavy loads, usually pulled by a horse or tractor. 2 Wagons are also the containers for freight pulled by a railway engine.

waif noun a young, thin person who looks hungry and homeless.

wail verb 1 To wail is to cry loudly with sorrow or pain. ▶ noun 2 a long, unhappy cry.

waist noun the middle part of your body where it narrows slightly above your hips.

waistcoat noun a sleeveless piece of clothing, often worn under a suit or jacket, which buttons up the front.

wait verb 1 If you wait, you spend time, usually doing little or nothing, before something happens. 2 If something can wait, it is not urgent and can be dealt with later. 3 If you wait on people in a restaurant, it is your job to serve them food. ▶ noun 4 a period of time before something happens. ▶ phrase 5 If you **can't wait** to do something, you are very excited and eager to do it.

wait verb
1 = linger, pause, remain, stand by, stay
▶ noun 4 = delay, interval, pause

waiter noun a person who works in a restaurant, serving people with food and drink.

waiting list noun a list of people who have asked for something which cannot be given to them immediately, for example medical treatment.

waitress noun a woman who works in a restaurant, serving people with food and drink.

waive verb If someone waives something such as a rule or a right, they decide not to insist on it being applied.

wake wakes, waking, woke, woken verb 1 When you wake or when something wakes you, you become conscious again after being asleep. ▶ noun 2 The wake of a boat or other object moving in water is the track of waves it leaves behind it. 3 a gathering of people who have got together to mourn someone's death. ▶ phrase 4 If one thing follows in the wake of another, it follows it as a result of it, or in imitation of it.
> **wake up** verb 1 When you wake up or something wakes you up, you become conscious again after being asleep. 2 If you wake up to a dangerous situation, you become aware of it.

wake verb
1 = awake, come to, rouse, stir, waken

walk verb 1 When you walk, you move along by putting one foot in front of the other on the ground. 2 If you walk away with or walk off with something such as a prize, you win it or achieve it easily. ▶ noun 3 a journey made by walking. 4 Your walk is the way you walk. > **walk out** verb 1 If you walk out on someone, you leave them suddenly. **2** If workers walk out, they go on strike.

walk *verb*
1 = amble, hike, march, ramble, step, stride, stroll, wander
▶ *noun* **3** = hike, march, ramble, stroll, trek **4** = carriage, gait, pace, stride

walkabout *noun* **1** an informal walk amongst crowds in a public place by royalty or by some other well-known person. **2** a period when an Aboriginal Australian wanders in the bush to return to a traditional way of life.

walker *noun* a person who walks, especially for pleasure or to keep fit.

walking stick *noun* a wooden stick which people can lean on while walking.

walkover *noun* (*informal*) a very easy victory in a competition or contest.

walkway *noun* a passage between two buildings for people to walk along.

wall *noun* **1** one of the vertical sides of a building or a room. **2** a long, narrow vertical structure made of stone or brick that surrounds or divides an area of land. **3** a lining or membrane enclosing a bodily cavity or structure.

wallaby wallabies *noun* an Australian animal like a small kangaroo.

wallet *noun* a small, flat case made of leather or plastic, used for keeping paper money and sometimes credit cards.

wallop *verb* (*informal*) If you wallop someone, you hit them very hard.

wallow *verb* **1** If you wallow in an unpleasant feeling or situation, you allow it to continue longer than is reasonable or necessary because you are getting a kind of enjoyment from it. **2** When an animal wallows in mud or water, it lies or rolls about in it slowly for pleasure.

wallpaper *noun* Wallpaper is thick coloured or patterned paper for pasting onto the walls of rooms in order to decorate them.

walnut *noun* **1** an edible nut with a wrinkled shape and a hard, round, light-brown shell. **2** Walnut is wood from the walnut tree which is often used for making expensive furniture.

walrus walruses *noun* an animal which lives in the sea and which looks like a large seal with a tough skin, coarse whiskers, and two tusks.

waltz *noun* **1** a dance which has a rhythm of three beats to the bar. ▶ *verb* **2** If you waltz with someone, you dance a waltz with them. **3** (*informal*) If you waltz somewhere, you walk there in a relaxed and confident way.

wan *adjective* pale and tired-looking.

wand *noun* a long, thin rod that magicians wave when they are performing tricks and magic.

wander *verb* **1** If you wander in a place, you walk around in a casual way. **2** If your mind wanders or your thoughts wander, you lose concentration and start thinking about other things. ▷ **wanderer** *noun*

wander *verb*
1 = cruise, drift, ramble, range, roam, stroll

w

wane *verb* If a condition, attitude or emotion wanes, it becomes gradually weaker.

want *verb* 1 If you want something, you feel a desire to have it. 2 If something is wanted, it is needed or needs to be done. 3 If someone is wanted, the police are searching for them. ▶ *noun* 4 (*formal*) A want of something is a lack of it.

> **want** *verb*
> 1 = covet, crave, desire, wish
> 2 = be deficient in, demand, lack, need, require
> ▶ *noun* 4 = absence, deficiency, lack, scarcity, shortage

wanting *adjective* If you find something wanting or if it proves wanting, it is not as good in some way as you think it should be.

wanton *adjective* A wanton action deliberately causes unnecessary harm or waste.

war *wars, warring, warred* *noun* 1 a period of fighting between countries or states when weapons are used and many people may be killed. 2 a competition between groups of people, or a campaign against something. ▶ *verb* 3 When two countries war with each other, they are fighting a war against each other. ▶ **warring** *adjective*

> **war** *noun*
> 1 = combat, conflict, fighting, hostilities, strife, warfare
> ▶ *verb* 3 = battle, clash, fight

waratah *noun* an Australian shrub with dark green leaves and large clusters of crimson flowers.

ward *noun* 1 a room in a hospital which has beds for several people who need similar treatment. 2 an area or district which forms a separate part of a political constituency or local council. 3 A ward or a ward of court is a child who is officially put in the care of an adult or a court of law, because their parents are dead or because they need protection. > **ward off** *verb* If you ward off a danger or an illness, you do something to prevent it from affecting or harming you.

-ward or **-wards** *suffix* '-ward' and '-wards' form adverbs or adjectives that show the way something is moving or facing: *homeward*.

warden *noun* 1 a person in charge of a building or institution such as a youth hostel or prison. 2 an official who makes sure that certain laws or rules are obeyed in a particular place or activity.

warder *noun* a person who is in charge of prisoners in a jail.

wardrobe *noun* 1 a tall cupboard in which you can hang your clothes. 2 Someone's wardrobe is their collection of clothes.

ware *noun* 1 Ware is manufactured goods of a particular kind: *kitchenware*. 2 Someone's wares are the things they sell, usually in the street or in a market.

warehouse *noun* a large building where raw materials or manufactured goods are stored.

warfare *noun* Warfare is the activity of fighting a war.

warhead *noun* the front end of a bomb or missile, where the explosives are carried.

warm *adjective* 1 Something that is warm has some heat, but not enough to be hot. 2 Warm clothes

or blankets are made of a material which protects you from the cold. **3** Warm colours or sounds are pleasant and make you feel comfortable and relaxed. **4** A warm person is friendly and affectionate. ▶ *verb* **5** If you warm something, you heat it up gently so that it stops being cold.
> **warmly** *adverb* ▶ **warm up** *verb* If you warm up for an event or an activity, you practise or exercise gently to prepare for it.

> **warm** *adjective*
> **1** = balmy, heated, lukewarm, pleasant, tepid **4** = affectionate, amiable, cordial, friendly, genial, loving
> ▶ *verb* **5** = heat, heat up, melt, thaw, warm up

warm-blooded *adjective* An animal that is warm-blooded has a relatively high body temperature which remains constant and does not change with the surrounding temperature.

warmth *noun* **1** Warmth is a moderate amount of heat. **2** Someone who has warmth is friendly and affectionate.

warn *verb* **1** If you warn someone about a possible problem or danger, you tell them about it in advance so that they are aware of it. **2** If you warn someone not to do something, you advise them not to do it, in order to avoid possible danger or punishment.
> **warn off** *verb* If you warn someone off, you tell them to go away or to stop doing something.

> **warn** *verb*
> **1** = alert, caution, forewarn, notify

warning *noun* something said or written to tell people of a possible problem or danger.

> **warning** *noun*
> = alarm, alert, caution, notice, premonition

warp *verb* **1** If something warps or is warped, it becomes bent, often because of the effect of heat or water. **2** If something warps someone's mind or character, it makes them abnormal or corrupt. ▶ *noun* **2** an official document which gives permission to the police to do something.

warrant *verb* **1** (*formal*) If something warrants a particular action, it makes the action seem necessary. ▶ *noun* **2** an official document which gives permission to the police to do something.

warranty warranties *noun* a guarantee.

warren *noun* a group of holes under the ground connected by tunnels, which rabbits live in.

warrior *noun* a fighting man or soldier, especially in former times.

warship *noun* a ship built with guns and used for fighting in wars.

wart *noun* a small, hard piece of skin which can grow on someone's face or hands.

wartime *noun* Wartime is a period of time during which a country is at war.

wary warier, wariest *adjective* cautious and on one's guard.
> **warily** *adverb* ▶ **wariness** *noun*

> **wary** *adjective*
> = cautious, distrustful, guarded, suspicious, vigilant

was a past tense of **be**.

wash *verb* **1** If you wash something, you clean it with water and soap. **2** If you wash, you clean yourself using soap and water. **3** If something is washed somewhere, it is carried there gently by water. ▶ *noun* **4** The wash is all the clothes and bedding that are washed together at one time. **5** The wash in water is the disturbance and waves produced at the back of a moving boat. ▶ *phrase* **6** If you **wash your hands** of something or someone, you refuse to have anything more to do with it or them. > **wash up** *verb* **1** If you wash up, you wash the dishes, pans and cutlery used in preparing and eating a meal. **2** If something is washed up on land, it is carried by a river or sea and left there.

> **wash** *verb*
> **1** = bathe, cleanse, launder, rinse, scrub, shampoo **3** = carry off, erode, sweep away

washable *adjective* able to be washed without being damaged.

washer *noun* **1** a thin, flat ring of metal or plastic which is placed over a bolt before the nut is screwed on, so that it is fixed more tightly. **2** In Australian English, a washer is a small piece of towelling for washing yourself.

washing *noun* Washing consists of clothes and bedding which need to be washed or are in the process of being washed and dried.

washing machine *noun* a machine for washing clothes in.

washing-up *noun* If you do the washing-up, you wash the dishes, pans and cutlery which have been used in the cooking and eating of a meal.

wasp *noun* an insect with yellow and black stripes across its body, which can sting like a bee.

wastage *noun* Wastage is loss and misuse of something.

waste *verb* **1** If you waste time, money or energy, you use too much of it on something that is not important or necessary. **2** If you waste an opportunity, you do not take advantage of it when it is available. ▶ *noun* **3** If an activity is a waste of time, money or energy, it is not important or necessary. **4** Waste is the use of more money or some other resource than is necessary. **5** Waste is also material that is no longer wanted, or material left over from a useful process. ▶ *adjective* **6** unwanted in its present form. **7** Waste land is land which is not used or looked after by anyone. > **waste away** *verb* If someone is wasting away, they are becoming very thin and weak because they are ill or not eating properly.

> **waste** *verb*
> **1** = fritter away, squander, throw away
> ▶ *noun* **4** = extravagance, misuse, squandering
> ▶ *adjective* **6** = leftover, superfluous, unused

wasteful *adjective* extravagant or causing waste by using something in a careless and inefficient way.

> **wasteful** *adjective*
> = extravagant, uneconomical

wasteland *noun* A wasteland is land which is of no use because it is infertile or has been misused.

wasting *adjective* A wasting disease is one that gradually reduces the strength and health of the body.

watch noun **1** a small clock usually worn on a strap on the wrist. **2** a period of time during which a guard is kept over something. ▶ verb **3** If you watch something, you look at it for some time and pay close attention to what is happening. **4** If you watch someone or something, you take care of them. **5** If you watch a situation, you pay attention to it or are aware of it. > **watch out** verb **1** If you watch out for something, you keep alert to see if it is near you. **2** If you tell someone to watch out, you are warning them to be very careful.

watchdog noun **1** a dog used to guard property. **2** a person or group whose job is to make sure that companies do not act illegally or irresponsibly.

watchful adjective careful to notice everything that is happening.

watchman watchmen noun a person whose job is to guard property.

water noun **1** Water is a clear, colourless, tasteless and odourless liquid that is necessary for all plant and animal life. **2** You use 'water' or 'waters' to refer to a large area of water, such

as a lake or sea. ▶ verb **3** If you water a plant or an animal, you give it water to drink. **4** If your eyes water, you have tears in them because they are hurting. **5** If your mouth waters, it produces extra saliva, usually because you think of or can smell something appetising.
> **water down** verb If you water something down, you make it weaker.

watercolour noun **1** Watercolours are paints for painting pictures, which are diluted with water or put on the paper using a wet brush. **2** a picture that has been painted using watercolours.

watercress noun Watercress is a small plant which grows in streams and pools. Its leaves taste hot and are eaten in salads.

waterfall noun (GEOGRAPHY) A waterfall is water from a river or stream as it flows over the edge of a steep cliff in hills or mountains and falls to the ground below.

waterfront noun a street or piece of land next to an area of water such as a river or harbour.

waterlogged adjective Land that is waterlogged is so wet that the soil cannot contain any more water, so that some water remains on the surface of the ground.

watermelon noun a large, round fruit which has a hard green skin and red juicy flesh.

waterproof adjective **1** not letting water pass through. ▶ noun **2** a coat which keeps water out.

watershed noun an event or period which marks a turning point or the beginning of a new way of life.

w

water-skiing noun Water-skiing is the sport of skimming over the water on skis while being pulled by a boat.

water table noun (GEOGRAPHY) The water table is the level below the surface of the ground at which water can be found.

watertight adjective 1 Something that is watertight does not allow water to pass through. 2 An agreement or an argument that is watertight has been so carefully put together that nobody should be able to find a fault in it.

waterway noun a canal, river or narrow channel of sea which ships or boats can sail along.

watery adjective 1 pale or weak. 2 Watery food or drink contains a lot of water or is thin like water.

watt noun (SCIENCE) a unit of power equal to one joule per second. It is named after James Watt (1736–1819), the inventor of the modern steam engine.

wattle noun an Australian acacia tree with spikes of brightly coloured flowers.

wave verb 1 If you wave your hand, you move it from side to side, usually to say hello or goodbye. 2 If you wave someone somewhere or wave them on, you make a movement with your hand to tell them which way to go. 3 If you wave something, you hold it up and move it from side to side.
▶ noun 4 a ridge of water on the surface of the sea caused by wind or by tides. 5 A wave is the form in which some types of energy such as heat, light or sound travel through a substance. 6 A wave

of sympathy, alarm or panic is a steady increase in it which spreads through you or through a group of people. 7 an increase in a type of activity or behaviour.

> **wave** verb
> 3 = brandish, flap, flourish, flutter, shake
> ▶ noun 4 = breaker, ripple, swell
> 7 = flood, movement, rush, surge, trend, upsurge

wavelength noun 1 (SCIENCE) the distance between the same point on two adjacent waves of energy. 2 the size of radio wave which a particular radio station uses to broadcast its programmes.

waver verb 1 If you waver or if your confidence or beliefs waver, you are no longer as firm, confident or sure in your beliefs. 2 If something wavers, it moves slightly.

wavy wavier, waviest adjective having waves or regular curves.

wax noun 1 Wax is a solid, slightly shiny substance made of fat or oil and used to make candles and polish. 2 Wax is also the sticky yellow substance in your ears.
▶ verb 3 If you wax a surface, you treat it or cover it with a thin layer of wax, especially to polish it. 4 (formal) If you wax eloquent, you talk in an eloquent way.

way noun 1 A way of doing something is the manner of doing it. 2 The ways of a person or group are their customs or their normal behaviour. 3 The way you feel about something is your attitude to it or your opinion about it. 4 If you have a way with people or things, you are very skilful at dealing with them. 5 The way to a particular place is the route that you take to get there. **6** If you go or look a particular way, you go or look in that direction. **7** If you divide something a number of ways, you divide it into that number of parts. **8** Way is used with words such as 'little' or 'long' to say how far off in distance or time something is: *They lived a long way away.* ▶ phrase **9** If something or someone is **in the way**, they prevent you from moving freely or seeing clearly. **10** You say **by the way** when adding something to what you are saying. **11** If you **go out of your way** to do something, you make a special effort to do it.

way *noun*
1 = approach, manner, means, method, procedure, technique
2 = conduct, custom, manner, practice, style **5** = channel, course, lane, path, road, route

wayside *phrase* If someone or something **falls by the wayside**, they fail in what they are trying to do, or become forgotten and ignored.

wayward *adjective* difficult to control and likely to change suddenly.

WC *noun* a toilet. WC is an abbreviation for 'water closet'.

we *pronoun* A speaker or writer uses 'we' to refer to himself or herself and one or more other people: *We are going to see Eddie.*

weak *adjective* **1** not having much strength. **2** If something is weak, it is likely to break or fail. **3** If you describe someone as weak, you mean they are easily influenced by other people. > **weakly** *adverb*

weak *adjective*
1 = delicate, faint, feeble, frail, puny, sickly, wasted
2 = deficient, faulty, inadequate
3 = powerless, spineless

weaken *verb* **1** If someone weakens something, or it weakens, it becomes less strong or certain. **2** If someone weakens, they become less certain about something.

weaken *verb*
1 = diminish, fail, flag, lessen, reduce, sap, undermine, wane

weakness *noun* **1** Weakness is lack of moral or physical strength. **2** If you have a weakness for something, you have a great liking for it.

weakness *noun*
1 = defect, flaw, fragility, frailty, imperfection, vulnerability
2 = fondness, liking, passion, penchant (*formal*)

wealth *noun* **1** (GEOGRAPHY) Wealth is the large amount of money or property which someone owns. **2** A wealth of something is a lot of it.

wealth *noun*
1 = affluence, fortune, means, money, prosperity, riches, substance **2** = abundance, bounty, plenty, store

wealthy wealthier, wealthiest *adjective* having a large amount of money, property or other valuable things.

wealthy *adjective*
= affluent, comfortable, opulent, prosperous, rich, well-to-do

w

wean *verb* To wean a baby or animal is to start feeding it food other than its mother's milk.

weapon *noun* 1 an object used to kill or hurt people in a fight or war. 2 anything which can be used to get the better of an opponent. > **weaponry** *noun*

wear wears, wearing, wore, worn *verb* 1 When you wear something such as clothes, make-up or jewellery, you have them on your body or face. 2 If you wear a particular expression, it shows on your face. 3 If something wears, it becomes thinner or worse in condition. ▶ *noun* 4 You can refer to clothes that are suitable for a particular time or occasion as a kind of wear: *beach wear*. 5 Wear is the amount or type of use that something has and which causes damage or change to it.
> **wear down** *verb* If you wear people down, you weaken them by repeatedly doing something or asking them to do something.
> **wear off** *verb* If a feeling such as pain wears off, it gradually disappears. > **wear on** *verb* If time wears on, it seems to pass very slowly or boringly. > **wear out** *verb* 1 When something wears out or when you wear it out, it is used so much that it becomes thin, weak and no longer usable.
2 (*informal*) If you wear someone out, you make them feel extremely tired.

wear *verb*
1 = be clothed in, be dressed in, don, have on, put on, sport (*informal*) 3 = corrode, erode, fray, rub, wash away
▶ *noun* 5 = corrosion, deterioration, erosion, use

▶ **wear out** 2 = exhaust, tire, weary

wear and tear *noun* Wear and tear is the damage caused to something by normal use.

wearing *adjective* Someone or something that is wearing makes you feel extremely tired.

weary wearier, weariest; wearies, wearying, wearied *adjective* 1 very tired. ▶ *verb* 2 If you weary of something, you become tired of it. > **wearily** *adverb* > **weariness** *noun*

weary *adjective*
1 = drained, exhausted, fatigued, tired, tuckered out (*American, Australian and New Zealand; informal*), worn out

weasel *noun* a small wild mammal with a long, thin body and short legs.

weather *noun* 1 The weather is the condition of the atmosphere at any particular time and the amount of rain, wind or sunshine occurring. ▶ *verb* 2 If something such as rock or wood weathers, it changes colour or shape as a result of being exposed to the wind, rain or sun. 3 If you weather a problem or difficulty, you come through it safely.
▶ *phrase* 4 If you are **under the weather**, you feel slightly ill.

weave weaves, weaving, wove, woven *verb* 1 To weave cloth is to make it by crossing threads over and under each other, especially by using a machine called a loom. 2 If you weave your way somewhere, you go there by moving from side to side through and round the obstacles.

weaver *noun* a person who weaves cloth.

web *noun* 1 a fine net of threads that a spider makes from a sticky substance which it produces in its body. 2 something that has a complicated structure or pattern. 3 The Web is the same as the **World Wide Web**.

webcam *noun* a video camera that takes pictures which can be viewed on a website.

website *noun* a publication on the World Wide Web which contains information about a particular subject.

wed weds, wedding, wedded or **wed** *verb (old-fashioned)* If you wed someone or if you wed, you get married.

wedding *noun* a marriage ceremony.

wedge *verb* 1 If you wedge something, you force it to remain somewhere by holding it there tightly, or by fixing something next to it to prevent it from moving. ▶ *noun* 2 a piece of something such as wood, metal or rubber with one pointed edge and one thick edge which is used to wedge something. 3 a piece of something that has a thick triangular shape.

wedlock *noun (old-fashioned)* Wedlock is the state of being married.

Wednesday *noun* Wednesday is the day between Tuesday and Thursday.

wee *adjective* In Scotland, a term for small.

weed *noun* 1 a wild plant that prevents cultivated plants from growing properly. ▶ *verb* 2 If you weed a place, you remove the weeds from it. > **weed out** *verb* If you weed out unwanted things, you get rid of them.

week *noun* 1 a period of seven days, especially one beginning on a Sunday and ending on a Saturday. 2 The week can refer to the part of a week that does not include Saturday and Sunday: *They are working during the week.*

weekday *noun* any day except Saturday and Sunday.

weekend *noun* Saturday and Sunday.

weekly weeklies *adjective* 1 happening or appearing once a week. ▶ *adverb* 2 once a week. ▶ *noun* 3 A weekly is a newspaper or magazine that is published once a week.

weep weeps, weeping, wept *verb* 1 If someone weeps, they cry. 2 If something such as a wound weeps, it oozes blood or other liquid.

weigh *verb* 1 If something weighs a particular amount, that is how heavy it is. 2 If you weigh something, you measure how heavy it is using scales. 3 If you weigh facts or words, you think about them carefully before coming to a decision or before speaking. 4 If a problem weighs on you or weighs upon you, it makes you very worried. > **weigh down** *verb* 1 If a load weighs you down, it stops you moving easily. 2 If you are weighed down by a difficulty, it is making you very worried. > **weigh up** *verb* If you weigh up a person or a situation, you make an assessment of them.

weight *noun* 1 The weight of something is its heaviness. 2 a metal object which has a certain known heaviness. Weights are used with sets of scales in order to weigh things. **3** any heavy object. **4** The weight of something is its large amount or importance which makes it hard to fight against or contradict. ▶ *verb* **5** If you weight something or weight it down, you make it heavier, often so that it cannot move. ▶ *phrase* **6** If you **pull your weight**, you work just as hard as other people involved in the same activity.

weighted *adjective* A system that is weighted in favour of a particular person or group is organised in such a way that this person or group will have an advantage.

weightless *adjective* (SCIENCE) Something that is weightless has no weight or very little weight, for example because it is in space and not affected by the Earth's gravity. > **weightlessness** *noun*

weightlifting *noun* Weightlifting is the sport of lifting heavy weights in competition or for exercise. > **weightlifter** *noun*

weighty **weightier, weightiest** *adjective* serious or important.

weir *noun* a low dam which is built across a river to raise the water level, control the flow of water, or change its direction.

weird *adjective* strange or odd. > **weirdly** *adverb*

> **weird** *adjective*
> = bizarre, curious,
> extraordinary, funny, odd,
> peculiar, queer (*old-fashioned*),
> singular (*formal*), strange

weirdo **weirdos** *noun* (*informal*) If you call someone a weirdo, you mean they behave in a strange way.

welcome *verb* **1** If you welcome a visitor, you greet them in a friendly way when they arrive. **2** 'Welcome' can be said as a greeting to a visitor who has just arrived. **3** If you welcome something, you approve of it and support it. ▶ *noun* **4** a greeting to a visitor. ▶ *adjective* **5** If someone is welcome at a place, they will be warmly received there. **6** If something is welcome, it brings pleasure or is accepted gratefully. **7** If you tell someone they are welcome to something or welcome to do something, you mean they are willing for them to have or to do it. > **welcoming** *adjective*

weld *verb* To weld two pieces of metal together is to join them by heating their edges and fixing them together so that when they cool they harden into one piece. > **welder** *noun*

welfare *noun* **1** The welfare of a person or group is their general state of health and comfort. **2** Welfare services are provided to help with people's living conditions and financial problems.

welfare state *noun* The welfare state is a system in which the government uses money from taxes to provide health care and education services, and to give benefits to people who are old, unemployed or sick.

well **better, best; wells, welling, welled** *adverb* **1** If something goes well, it happens in a satisfactory way. **2** in a good, skilful or pleasing way: *He draws well.* **3** thoroughly and completely: *well established.* **4** kindly: *We treat our* *employees well.* **5** If something may well or could well happen, it is likely to happen. **6** You use 'well' to emphasise an adjective, adverb or phrase: *He was well aware of that.* ▶ *adjective* **7** If you are well, you are healthy. ▶ *phrase* **8 As well** means also. **9 As well as** means in addition to. **10** If you say you **may as well** or **might as well** do something, you mean you will do it, not because you are keen to, but because there is nothing better to do. ▶ *noun* **11** a hole drilled in the ground from which water, oil or gas is obtained. ▶ *verb* **12** If tears well or well up, they appear in someone's eyes.

> **well** *adverb*
> **1** = satisfactorily, smoothly, splendidly, successfully
> **2** = ably, adequately, admirably, competently, effectively, efficiently, expertly, professionally, skilfully
> **3** = amply, closely, completely, fully, highly, meticulously, rigorously, thoroughly
> **4** = compassionately, considerately, favourably, humanely, kindly, with consideration
> ▶ *adjective* **7** = blooming, fit, healthy, in good condition, in good health, robust, sound, strong

well-balanced *adjective* sensible and without serious emotional problems.

wellbeing *noun* (PSHE) Someone's wellbeing is their health and happiness.

well-earned *adjective* thoroughly deserved.

well-heeled *adjective* (*informal*) wealthy.

well-informed *adjective* having a great deal of knowledge about a subject or subjects.

well-meaning *adjective* A well-meaning person tries to be helpful but is often unsuccessful.

well-off *adjective* (*informal*) quite wealthy.

well-to-do *adjective* quite wealthy.

well-worn *adjective* **1** A well-worn expression or saying has been used too often and has become boring. **2** A well-worn object or piece of clothing has been used and worn so much that it looks old and shabby.

Welsh *adjective* **1** belonging or relating to Wales. ▶ *noun* **2** Welsh is a language spoken in parts of Wales.

Welshman Welshmen *noun* a man who comes from Wales.

Welshwoman Welshwomen *noun* a woman who comes from Wales.

welter *noun* (*formal*) A welter of things is a large number of them that happen or appear together in a state of confusion.

wend, wends, wending, wended *verb* (*literary*) If you wend your way in a particular direction, you walk slowly in that direction.

went the past tense of **go**.

wept the past tense and past participle of **weep**.

were a past tense of **be**.

werewolf werewolves *noun* In horror stories, a werewolf is a person who changes into a wolf.

west *noun* **1** The west is the direction in which you look to see the sun set. **2** The west of a place or country is the part which is towards the west when you are in

w

the centre. **3** The West refers to the countries of North America and western and southern Europe. ▶ *adverb, adjective* **4** West means towards the west.
▶ *adjective* **5** A west wind blows from the west.

westerly *adjective* **1** Westerly means to or towards the west. **2** A westerly wind blows from the west.

western *adjective* **1** in or from the west. **2** coming from or associated with the countries of North America and western and southern Europe. ▶ *noun* **3** a book or film about life in the west of America in the 19th century.

westward or **westwards** *adverb* **1** Westward or westwards means towards the west. ▶ *adjective* **2** The westward part of something is the west part.

wet wetter, wettest; wets, wetting, wet or wetted *adjective* **1** If something is wet, it is covered in water or another liquid. **2** If the weather is wet, it is raining. **3** If something such as paint, ink or cement is wet, it is not yet dry or solid. ▶ *noun* **4** In Australia, the wet is the rainy season. ▶ *verb* **5** To wet something is to put water or some other liquid over it. **6** If people wet themselves or wet their beds, they urinate in their clothes or bed because they cannot control their bladder.
> **wetness** *noun*

wet *adjective*
1 = damp, drenched, moist, saturated, soaked, sodden, waterlogged **2** = humid, misty, rainy, showery
▶ *verb* **5** = dampen, irrigate, moisten, soak, spray, water

whack *verb* If you whack someone or something, you hit them hard.

whale *noun* a very large sea mammal which breathes through a hole on the top of its head.

whaling *noun* Whaling is the work of hunting and killing whales for oil or food.

wharf wharves *noun* a platform beside a river or the sea, where ships load or unload.

what *pronoun* **1** 'What' is used in questions: *What time is it?* **2** 'What' is used in indirect questions and statements: *I don't know what you mean.* **3** 'What' can be used at the beginning of a clause to refer to something with a particular quality: *It is impossible to decide what is real and what is invented.* ▶ *adjective* **4** You say 'what' to emphasise an opinion or reaction: *What nonsense!* ▶ *phrase* **5** You say **what about** at the beginning of a question when you are making a suggestion or offer: *What about a drink?*

whatever *pronoun* **1** You use 'whatever' to refer to anything or everything of a particular type: *He said he would do whatever he could.* **2** You use 'whatever' when you do not know the precise nature of something: *Whatever it is, I don't like it.* ▶ *conjunction* **3** You use 'whatever' to mean no matter what: *Whatever happens, you have to behave decently.* ▶ *adverb* **4** You use 'whatever' to emphasise a negative statement or a question: *You have no proof whatever.*

whatsoever *adverb* You use 'whatsoever' to emphasise a negative statement: *I have no memory of it whatsoever.*

wheat noun Wheat is a cereal plant grown for its grain, which is used to make flour.

wheel noun 1 (DGT) a circular object which turns on a rod attached to its centre. Wheels are fixed underneath vehicles so that they can move along. 2 (DGT) The wheel of a car is its steering wheel. ▶ verb 3 If you wheel something such as a bicycle, you push it. 4 If someone or something wheels, they move round in the shape of a circle.

wheelbarrow noun a small cart with a single wheel at the front, used for carrying things in the garden.

wheelchair noun a chair with wheels in which sick or injured people, or people with certain disabilities, can move around.

wheeze verb If someone wheezes, they breathe with difficulty, making a whistling sound, usually because they have a chest complaint such as asthma. > **wheezy** adjective

when adverb 1 You use 'when' to ask what time something happened or will happen: When are you leaving? ▶ conjunction 2 You use 'when' to refer to a time in the past: I met him when I was sixteen. 3 You use 'when' to introduce the reason for an opinion, comment or question: How did you pass the exam when you hadn't studied for it? 4 'When' is used to mean although: He drives when he could walk.

whence adverb, conjunction (old-fashioned) 'Whence' means from where.

whenever conjunction 'Whenever' means at any time, or every time that something happens: I still go on courses whenever I can.

where adverb 1 You use 'where' to ask which place something is in, is coming from, or is going to: Where is Philip? ▶ conjunction, pronoun, adverb 2 You use 'where' when asking about or referring to something: I hardly know where to begin. ▶ conjunction 3 You use 'where' to refer to the place in which something is situated or happening: I don't know where we are. 4 'Where' can introduce a clause that contrasts with the other part of the sentence: Some people took music lessons, where others learned dance.

whereabouts noun 1 The whereabouts of a person or thing is the place where they are. ▶ adverb 2 You use 'whereabouts' when you are asking more precisely where something is: Whereabouts in Canada are you from?

whereas conjunction 'Whereas' introduces a comment that contrasts with the other part of the sentence: Her eyes were blue, whereas mine were brown.

whereby pronoun (formal) 'Whereby' means by which: a new system whereby you pay the bill quarterly.

whereupon conjunction (formal) 'Whereupon' means at which point: His enemies rejected his message, whereupon he tried again.

wherever conjunction 1 'Wherever' means in every place or situation: Alex heard the same thing wherever he went. 2 You use 'wherever' to show that you do not know where a place or person is: the nearest police station, wherever that is.

wherewithal noun If you have the wherewithal to do something,

whet | 794

you have enough money to do it.

whet whets, whetting, whetted *phrase* To **whet someone's appetite** for something means to increase their desire for it.

whether *conjunction* You use 'whether' when you are talking about two or more alternatives: *I don't know whether that's true or false.*

which *adjective, pronoun* **1** You use 'which' to ask about alternatives or to refer to a choice between alternatives: *Which room are you in?* ▶ *pronoun* **2** 'Which' at the beginning of a clause identifies the thing you are talking about or gives more information about it: *certain wrongs which exist in our society.*

whichever *adjective, pronoun* You use 'whichever' when you are talking about different alternatives or possibilities: *Make your pizzas round or square, whichever you prefer.*

whiff *noun* **1** a slight smell of something. **2** a slight sign or trace of something.

while *conjunction* **1** If something happens while something else is happening, the two things happen at the same time. **2** While also means but: *The first issue is free, while the second costs £5.* ▶ *noun* **3** a period of time: *a little while earlier.* ▶ *phrase* **4** If an action or activity is **worth your while**, it will be helpful or useful to you if you do it. > **while away** *verb* If you while away the time in a particular way, you pass the time that way because you have nothing else to do.

whilst *conjunction* Whilst means the same as while.

whim *noun* a sudden desire or fancy.

whim *noun* = craze, fad (*informal*), fancy, impulse, urge

whimper *verb* **1** When children or animals whimper, they make soft, low, unhappy sounds. **2** If you whimper something, you say it in an unhappy or frightened way, as if you are about to cry.

whimsical *adjective* unusual and slightly playful.

whine *verb* **1** To whine is to make a long, high-pitched noise, especially one which sounds sad or unpleasant. **2** If someone whines about something, they complain about it in an annoying way. ▶ *noun* **3** A whine is the noise made by something or someone whining.

whinge whinges, whingeing, whinged If someone whinges about something, they complain about it in an annoying way.

whip whips, whipping, whipped *noun* **1** a thin piece of leather or rope attached to a handle, which is used for hitting people or animals. ▶ *verb* **2** If you whip a person or animal, you hit them with a whip. **3** When the wind whips something, it strikes it. **4** If you whip something out or off, you take it out or off very quickly. **5** If you whip cream, you beat it until it is thick and frothy or stiff. > **whip up** *verb* If you whip up a strong emotion, you make people feel it.

whirl *verb* **1** When something whirls, or when you whirl it around, it turns round very fast. ▶ *noun* **2** You can refer to a lot of intense activity as a whirl of activity.

whirlpool noun a small circular area in a river or the sea where the water is moving quickly round and round so that objects floating near it are pulled into its centre.

whirlwind noun 1 a tall column of air which spins round and round very fast. ▶ adjective 2 more rapid than usual.

whisk verb 1 If you whisk someone or something somewhere, you take them there quickly. 2 If you whisk eggs or cream, you stir air into them quickly. ▶ noun 3 a kitchen tool used for quickly stirring air into eggs or cream.

whisker noun The whiskers of an animal such as a cat or mouse are the long, stiff hairs near its mouth.

whisky whiskies noun Whisky is a strong alcoholic drink made from grain such as barley.

whisper verb 1 When you whisper, you talk to someone very quietly, using your breath and not your throat. ▶ noun 2 If you talk in a whisper, you whisper.

whistle verb 1 When you whistle a tune or whistle, you produce a clear musical sound by forcing your breath out between your lips. 2 If something whistles, it makes a loud, high sound. ▶ noun 3 A whistle is the sound something or someone makes when they whistle. 4 a small metal tube that you blow into to produce a whistling sound.

white noun, adjective 1 White is the lightest possible colour. 2 Someone who is white has a pale skin and is of European origin. ▶ adjective 3 If someone goes white, their face becomes very pale because they are afraid, shocked or ill. 4 White coffee contains milk or cream. ▶ noun 5 The white of an egg is the transparent liquid which turns white when it is cooked. > **whiteness** noun

whiteboard noun a white board on which people can write or draw using special coloured pens.

white-collar adjective White-collar workers work in offices rather than doing manual work.

whitewash noun 1 Whitewash is a mixture of lime and water used for painting walls white. 2 an attempt to hide unpleasant facts.

whiting noun a sea fish related to the cod.

whittle verb If you whittle a piece of wood, you shape it by shaving or cutting small pieces off it. > **whittle away** or **whittle down** verb To whittle away at something or to whittle it down means to make it smaller or less effective.

whizz; also spelt **whiz** (informal) verb 1 If you whizz somewhere, you move there quickly. ▶ noun 2 If you are a whizz at something, you are very good at it.

who pronoun 1 You use 'who' when you are asking about someone's identity: Who gave you that black eye? 2 'Who' at the beginning of a clause refers to the person or people you are talking about: a shipyard worker who wants to be a postman.

whoever pronoun 1 'Whoever' means the person who: Whoever bought it for you has to make the claim. 2 'Whoever' also means no matter who: I pity him, whoever he is. 3 'Whoever' is used in questions to give emphasis to 'who': *Whoever thought of such a thing?*

whole *adjective* **1** indicating all of something: *Have the whole cake.* ▶ *noun* **2** the full amount of something. ▶ *adverb* **3** in one piece. ▶ *phrase* **4** You say **on the whole** to mean that something is generally true: *On the whole, we should be glad they are gone.* > **wholeness** *noun*

> **whole** *adjective*
> **1** = complete, entire, full, total, uncut, undivided
> ▶ *noun* **2** = aggregate, all, everything, lot, sum total, total

wholehearted *adjective* enthusiastic and totally sincere. > **wholeheartedly** *adverb*

wholemeal *adjective* Wholemeal flour is made from the complete grain of the wheat plant, including the husk.

wholesale *adjective, adverb* **1** Wholesale refers to the activity of buying goods cheaply in large quantities and selling them again, especially to shopkeepers. ▶ *adjective* **2** Wholesale also means done to an excessive extent. > **wholesaler** *noun*

wholesome *adjective* **1** Something that is wholesome is good and likely to improve your life, behaviour or health. **2** If you describe a person as wholesome, you mean that their appearance suggests health and wellbeing.

wholly *adverb* completely.

whom *pronoun* 'Whom' is the object form of 'who': *the girl whom Albert would marry.*

whoop *verb* **1** If you whoop, you shout loudly in a happy or excited way. ▶ *noun* **2** a loud cry of happiness or excitement.

whooping cough *noun* Whooping cough is an acute infectious disease which makes people cough violently and produce a loud sound when they breathe.

whose *pronoun* **1** You use 'whose' to ask who something belongs to: *Whose pen is this?* **2** You use 'whose' at the beginning of a clause which gives information about something relating or belonging to the thing or person you have just mentioned: *a wealthy aristocrat whose mansion is for sale.*

why *adverb, pronoun* You use 'why' when you are asking about the reason for something, or talking about it: *Why did you do it?*

wick *noun* the cord in the middle of a candle, which you set alight.

wicked *adjective* **1** very bad. **2** mischievous in an amusing or attractive way. > **wickedly** *adverb* > **wickedness** *noun*

> **wicked** *adjective*
> **1** = atrocious, bad, depraved, evil, sinful, vicious **2** = impish, mischievous, naughty

wicker *adjective* A wicker basket or chair is made from twigs, canes or reeds that have been woven together.

wicket *noun* **1** In cricket, the wicket is one of the two sets of stumps and bails at which the bowler aims the ball. **2** The grass between the wickets on a cricket pitch is also called the wicket.

wide *adjective* **1** measuring a large distance from one side to the other. **2** If there is a wide variety, range or selection of something, there are many different kinds of it. ▶ *adverb* **3** If you open or spread something wide, you open it to its fullest extent. > **widely** *adverb*

wide *adjective*
1 = ample, baggy, broad, expansive, full, immense, large, roomy, spacious, sweeping, vast, voluminous 2 = ample, broad, catholic, comprehensive, encyclopedic, exhaustive, extensive, far-ranging, immense, inclusive, large, vast, wide-ranging
▶ *adverb* 3 = completely, fully, right out

widen *verb* 1 If something widens or if you widen it, it becomes bigger from one side to the other. 2 You can say that something widens when it becomes greater in size or scope.

wide-ranging *adjective* extending over a variety of different things or over a large area.

widespread *adjective* existing or happening over a large area or to a great extent.

widespread *adjective*
= broad, common, extensive, pervasive, prevalent, rife

widow *noun* a woman whose spouse has died.

widowed *adjective* If someone is widowed, their husband or wife has died.

widower *noun* a man whose spouse has died.

width *noun* The width of something is the distance from one side or edge to the other.

wield *verb* 1 If you wield a weapon or tool, you carry it and use it. 2 If someone wields power, they have it and are able to use it.

wife wives *noun* A person's wife is the woman they are married to.

Wi-Fi *noun* (ICT) a system of accessing the internet from machines such as laptop computers that are not physically connected to a network.

wig *noun* a false head of hair worn to cover someone's own hair or to hide their baldness.

wiggle *verb* 1 If you wiggle something, you move it up and down or from side to side with small jerky movements. ▶ *noun* 2 a small jerky movement.

wild *adjective* 1 Wild animals, birds and plants live and grow in natural surroundings and are not looked after by people. 2 Wild land is natural and has not been cultivated. 3 Wild weather or sea is stormy and rough. 4 Wild behaviour is excited and uncontrolled. 5 A wild idea or scheme is original and crazy. ▶ *noun* 6 The wild is a free and natural state of living. 7 The wilds are remote areas where few people live, far away from towns. > **wildly** *adverb*

wild *adjective*
1 = fierce, free, natural, uncultivated, undomesticated, untamed, warrigal (*Australian*; *literary*) 3 = howling, raging, rough, stormy, violent 4 = boisterous, rowdy, turbulent, uncontrolled, wayward

wilderness *noun* an area of natural land which is not cultivated.

wildfire *noun* If something spreads like wildfire, it spreads very quickly.

wildlife noun Wildlife means wild animals and plants.

Wild West noun The Wild West was the western part of the United States when it was first being settled by Europeans.

wiles plural noun Wiles are clever or crafty tricks used to persuade people to do something.

wilful adjective 1 Wilful actions or attitudes are deliberate and often intended to hurt someone. 2 Someone who is wilful is obstinate and determined to get their own way. > **wilfully** adverb

will[1] verb 1 You use 'will' to form the future tense: *Robin will be quite annoyed.* 2 You use 'will' to say that you intend to do something: *I will not deceive you.* 3 You use 'will' when asking or telling someone to do something: *Will you do me a favour?*

will[2] verb 1 If you will something to happen, you try to make it happen by mental effort. 2 If you will something to someone, you leave it to them when you die. ▶ noun 3 Will is the determination to do something. 4 If something is the will of a person or group, they want it to happen. 5 a legal document in which you say what you want to happen to your money and property when you die. ▶ phrase 6 If you can do something **at will**, you can do it whenever you want.

> **will** verb
> 2 = bequeath, leave, pass on
> ▶ noun 3 = determination, purpose, resolution, resolve, willpower 4 = choice, inclination, mind, volition, wish

willing adjective ready and eager to do something. > **willingly** adverb > **willingness** noun

> **willing** adjective
> = agreeable, eager, game (*informal*), happy, prepared, ready

willow noun A willow or willow tree is a tree with long, thin branches and narrow leaves that often grows near water.

wilt verb 1 If a plant wilts, it droops because it needs more water or is dying. 2 If someone wilts, they gradually lose strength or confidence.

wily wilier, wiliest adjective clever and cunning.

wimp noun (*informal*) someone who is feeble and timid.

win wins, winning, won verb 1 If you win a fight, game or argument, you defeat your opponent. 2 If you win something, you succeed in obtaining it. ▶ noun 3 a victory in a game or contest. > **win over** verb If you win someone over, you persuade them to support you.

> **win** verb
> 1 = be victorious, come first, prevail, succeed, triumph
> 2 = achieve, attain, gain, get, secure (*formal*)
> ▶ noun 3 = success, triumph, victory

wince verb When you wince, the muscles of your face tighten suddenly because of pain, fear or distress.

winch noun 1 a machine used to lift heavy objects. It consists of a cylinder around which a rope or chain is wound. ▶ verb 2 If you winch an object or person somewhere, you lift, lower or pull them using a winch.

wind¹ *noun* **1** a current of air moving across the earth's surface. **2** Your wind is the ability to breathe easily. **3** Wind is air swallowed with food or drink, or gas produced in your stomach, which causes discomfort. **4** (MUSIC) The wind section of an orchestra is the group of musicians who play wind instruments.

wind² *winds, winding, wound* *verb* **1** If a road or river winds in a particular direction, it twists and turns in that direction. **2** When you wind something round something else, you wrap it round it several times. **3** When you wind a clock or machine or wind it up, you turn a key or handle several times to make it work. > **wind up** *verb* **1** When you wind up something such as an activity or a business, you finish it or close it. **2** If you wind up in a particular place, you end up there.

windfall *noun* a sum of money that you receive unexpectedly.

windmill *noun* a machine for grinding grain or pumping water. It is driven by vanes or sails turned by the wind.

window *noun* a space in a wall or roof or in the side of a vehicle, usually with glass in it so that light can pass through and people can see in or out.

windowsill *noun* a ledge along the bottom of a window, either on the inside or outside of a building.

windpipe *noun* Your windpipe is the tube which carries air into your lungs when you breathe. The technical name for windpipe is **trachea**.

windscreen *noun* the glass at the front of a vehicle through which the driver looks.

windsurfing *noun* Windsurfing is the sport of moving along the surface of the sea or a lake standing on a board with a sail on it.

windswept *adjective* A windswept place is exposed to strong winds.

windy *windier, windiest adjective* If it is windy, there is a lot of wind.

wine *noun* Wine is the red or white alcoholic drink which is normally made from grapes.

wing *noun* **1** A bird's or insect's wings are the parts of its body that it uses for flying. **2** An aeroplane's wings are the long, flat parts on each side that support it while it is in the air. **3** A wing of a building is a part which sticks out from the main part or which has been added later. **4** A wing of an organisation, especially a political party, is a group within it with a particular role or particular beliefs. **5** (in *plural*) The wings in a theatre are the sides of the stage which are hidden from the audience. > **winged** *adjective*

wink *verb* **1** When you wink, you close one eye briefly, often as a signal that something is a joke or a secret. ▶ *noun* **2** The closing of your eye when you wink.

winner *noun* The winner of a prize, race or competition is the person or thing that wins it.

w

winner noun
= champion, conqueror, victor

winning adjective 1 The winning team or entry in a competition is the one that has won. 2 attractive and charming.

winter noun Winter is the season between autumn and spring.

wintry adjective Something wintry has features that are typical of winter.

wipe verb 1 If you wipe something, you rub its surface lightly to remove dirt or liquid. 2 If you wipe dirt or liquid off something, you remove it using a cloth or your hands. ▸ **wipe out** verb To wipe out people or places is to destroy them completely.

wire noun 1 Wire is metal in the form of a long, thin, flexible thread which can be used to make or fasten things or to conduct an electric current. ▸ verb 2 If you wire one thing to another, you fasten them together using wire. 3 (DGT) If you wire something or wire it up, you connect it so that electricity can pass through it. > **wired** adjective

wireless noun 1 (old-fashioned) a radio. ▸ adjective 2 communicating without connecting wires.

wiring noun The wiring in a building is the system of wires that supply electricity to the rooms.

wiry wirier, wiriest adjective 1 Wiry people are thin but with strong muscles. 2 Wiry things are stiff and rough to the touch.

wisdom noun 1 Wisdom is the ability to use experience and knowledge in order to make sensible decisions or judgments. 2 If you talk about the wisdom of an action or a decision, you are talking about how sensible it is.

wisdom noun
1 = discernment, insight, judgment, knowledge, reason

wise adjective Someone who is wise can use their experience and knowledge to make sensible decisions and judgments.

wise adjective
= informed, judicious (formal), perceptive, rational, sensible, shrewd

wisecrack noun a clever remark, intended to be amusing but often unkind.

wish noun 1 a longing or desire for something, often something difficult to achieve or obtain. 2 something desired or wanted. 3 (in plural) Good wishes are expressions of hope that someone will be happy or successful. ▸ verb 4 If you wish to do something, you want to do it. 5 If you wish something were the case, you would like it to be the case, but know it is not very likely.

wish noun
1 = desire, hankering, hunger, longing, urge, want
▸ verb 4 = desire, hunger, long, thirst, want, yearn

wishbone noun a V-shaped bone in the breast of most birds.

wishful thinking noun If someone's hope or wish is wishful thinking, it is unlikely to come true.

wistful adjective sadly thinking about something, especially something you want but cannot have. > **wistfully** adverb

W

wit noun 1 Wit is the ability to use words or ideas in an amusing and clever way. 2 Wit means sense. 3 (in plural) Your wits are the ability to act quickly in a difficult situation.

witch noun a woman claimed to have magic powers and to be able to use them for good or evil.

witchcraft noun Witchcraft is the skill or art of using magic powers, especially evil ones.

with preposition 1 If you are with someone, you are in their company. 2 'With' is used to show who your opponent is in a fight or competition: *next week's game with Brazil*. 3 'With' can mean using or having: *Apply the colour with a brush*. 4 'With' can mean concerning: *a problem with her telephone bill*.

withdraw withdraws, withdrawing, withdrew, withdrawn verb 1 If you withdraw something, you remove it or take it out. 2 If you withdraw to another place, you leave where you are and go there. 3 If you withdraw from an activity, you back out of it.

> **withdraw** verb
> 1 = draw out, extract, remove, take out 3 = back out, leave, pull out, retire, retreat

withdrawal noun 1 The withdrawal of something is the act of taking it away. 2 The withdrawal of a statement is the act of saying formally that you wish to change or deny it. 3 an amount of money you take from your bank or building society account.

withdrawn 1 Withdrawn is the past participle of **withdraw**.

▶ adjective 2 unusually shy or quiet.

withdrew the past tense of **withdraw**.

wither verb 1 When something withers or withers away, it becomes weaker until it no longer exists. 2 If a plant withers, it wilts or shrivels up and dies.

> **wither** verb
> 1 = decline, fade 2 = droop, shrivel, wilt

withering adjective A withering look or remark makes you feel ashamed, stupid or inferior.

withhold withholds, withholding, withheld verb (formal) If you withhold something that someone wants, you do not let them have it.

within preposition, adverb 1 Within means in or inside. ▶ preposition 2 Within can mean not going beyond certain limits: *Stay within the budget*. 3 Within can mean before a period of time has passed: *You must write back within fourteen days*.

without preposition 1 Without means not having, feeling or showing. 2 Without can mean not using. 3 Without can mean not in someone's company. 4 Without can indicate that something does not happen when something else happens.

withstand withstands, withstanding, withstood verb When something or someone withstands a force or action, they survive it or do not give in to it.

witness noun 1 someone who has seen an event such as an accident and can describe what happened. 2 someone who appears in a court of law to say what they know

w

about a crime or other event.
3 someone who writes their name on a document that someone else has signed, to confirm that it is really that person's signature.
▶ verb **4** (formal) If you witness an event, you see it.

> **witness** noun
> **1** = bystander, eyewitness, observer, onlooker, spectator
> ▶ verb **4** = be present at, observe, see, watch

witty wittier, wittiest adjective amusing in a clever way.
> **wittily** adverb

> **witty** adjective
> = amusing, brilliant, clever, funny, humorous, sparkling

wives the plural of **wife**.

wizard noun a man in a fairy story who has magic powers.

wizardry noun Wizardry is something that is very cleverly done.

wobble verb If something wobbles, it shakes or moves from side to side because it is loose or unsteady.

wobbly wobblier, wobbliest adjective unsteady.

woe (literary) noun **1** Woe is great unhappiness or sorrow. **2** (in plural) Someone's woes are their problems or misfortunes.

wok noun a large bowl-shaped metal pan used for Chinese-style cooking.

woke the past tense of **wake**.

woken the past participle of **wake**.

wolf wolves; wolfs, wolfing, wolfed noun **1** a wild animal related to the dog. Wolves hunt in packs and kill other animals for food. ▶ verb **2** (informal) If you wolf

food or wolf it down, you eat it up quickly and greedily.

woman women noun an adult female human being.

> **woman** noun
> = female, girl, lady, lass, sheila (Australian and New Zealand; informal), vrou (South African)

womanhood noun Womanhood is the state of being a woman rather than a girl.

womb noun A woman's womb is the part inside her body where her unborn baby grows.

wombat noun a short-legged furry Australian mammal which eats plants.

women the plural of **woman**.

won the past tense and past participle of **win**.

wonder verb **1** If you wonder about something, you think about it with curiosity or doubt.
2 If you wonder at something, you are surprised and amazed at it.
▶ noun **3** Wonder is a feeling of surprise and amazement.
4 something or someone that surprises and amazes people.

> **wonder** verb
> **1** = ask yourself, ponder, puzzle, speculate **2** = be amazed, be astonished, boggle, marvel
> ▶ noun **4** = marvel, miracle, phenomenon, spectacle

wonderful adjective **1** making you feel very happy and pleased. **2** very impressive. > **wonderfully** adverb

> **wonderful** adjective
> **1** = excellent, great (informal), marvellous, superb, tremendous **2** = amazing, astounding, incredible, magnificent, remarkable

W

wondrous adjective (literary) amazing and impressive.

wont adjective (old-fashioned) If someone is wont to do something, they do it often.

woo verb 1 If you woo people, you try to get them to help or support you. 2 (old-fashioned) If you woo someone you are attracted to, you try to get them to marry you.

wood noun 1 Wood is the substance which forms the trunks and branches of trees. 2 a large area of trees growing near each other.

wooded adjective covered in trees.

wooden adjective made of wood.

woodland noun Woodland is land that is mostly covered with trees.

woodwind adjective Woodwind instruments are musical instruments such as flutes, oboes, clarinets and bassoons, that are played by being blown into.

woodwork noun 1 Woodwork refers to the parts of a house, such as stairs, doors or window-frames, that are made of wood. 2 Woodwork is the craft or skill of making things out of wood.

woody woodier, woodiest adjective 1 Woody plants have hard tough stems. 2 A woody area has a lot of trees in it.

wool noun 1 Wool is the hair that grows on sheep and some other animals. 2 Wool is also yarn spun from the wool of animals which is used to knit, weave and make such things as clothes, blankets and carpets.

woollen adjective 1 made from wool. ▶ noun 2 Woollens are clothes made of wool.

woolly woollier, woolliest adjective 1 made of wool or looking like wool. 2 If you describe people or their thoughts as woolly, you mean that they seem confused and unclear.

word noun 1 a single unit of language in speech or writing which has a meaning. 2 a remark. 3 a brief conversation. 4 A word can also be a message. 5 Your word is a promise. 6 The word can be a command. 7 (in plural) The words of a play or song are the spoken or sung text. ▶ verb 8 When you word something, you choose your words in order to express your ideas accurately or acceptably.

> **word** noun
> 2 = comment, remark, statement, utterance 3 = chat, conversation, discussion, talk 4 = announcement, bulletin, communication, information, intelligence, message, news 5 = assurance, oath, pledge, promise, word of honour

word class noun a group of words that behave in the same way in terms of grammar, for example nouns, adjectives or verbs.

wording noun The wording of a piece of writing or a speech is the words used in it, especially when these words have been carefully chosen to have a certain effect.

word processor noun (ICT) a computer program or a computer which is used to produce printed documents.

wore the past tense of **wear**.

work verb 1 People who work have a job which they are paid to do.

w

2 When you work, you do the tasks that your job involves. **3** To work the land is to cultivate it. **4** If someone works a machine, they control or operate it. **5** If a machine works, it operates properly and effectively. **6** If something such as an idea or a system works, it is successful. **7** If something works its way into a particular position, it gradually moves there. ▸ noun **8** People who have work or who are in work have a job which they are paid to do. **9** Work is the tasks that have to be done. **10** something done or made. **11** (SCIENCE) In physics, work is transfer of energy. It is calculated by multiplying a force by the distance moved by the point to which the force has been applied. Work is measured in joules. **12** (in plural) A works is a place where something is made by an industrial process. **13** Works are large-scale building, digging or general construction activities. ▸ **work out** verb **1** If you work out a solution to a problem, you find the solution. **2** If a situation works out in a particular way, it happens in that way. ▸ **work up** verb **1** If you work up to something, you gradually progress towards it. **2** If you work yourself up or work someone else up, you make yourself or the other person very upset or angry about something. ▸ **worked up** adjective

> **work** verb
> **2** = labour, slave, slog away, toil
> ▸ noun **8** = craft, employment, job, livelihood, occupation, profession **9** = assignment, business, chore, duty, job, task, yakka (Australian and New Zealand; informal)

> ▸ **work out** **1** = calculate, figure out, resolve, solve **2** = develop, go, happen, turn out

workable adjective Something workable can operate successfully or can be used for a particular purpose.

workaholic noun a person who finds it difficult to stop working and do other things.

worker noun a person employed in a particular industry or business.

> **worker** noun
> = craftsman, employee, labourer, workman

workforce noun The workforce is all the people who work in a particular place.

working class noun The working class or working classes are the group of people in society who do not own much property and who do jobs which involve physical rather than intellectual skills.

workload noun the amount of work that a person or a machine has to do.

workman workmen noun a man whose job involves using physical rather than intellectual skills.

workmanship noun Workmanship is the skill with which something is made or a job is completed.

workmate noun Someone's workmate is the fellow worker with whom they do their job.

workout noun a session of physical exercise or training.

workshop noun **1** a room or building that contains tools or machinery used for making or repairing things. **2** a period of discussion or practical work in which a group of people learn about a particular subject.

world *noun* 1 The world is the earth, the planet we live on. 2 You can use 'world' to refer to people generally: *The eyes of the world are upon me.* 3 Someone's world is the life they lead and the things they experience. 4 A world is a division or section of the earth, its history, or its people, such as the Arab World or the Ancient World. 5 A particular world is a field of activity and the people involved in it.

worldly worldlier, worldliest *adjective* 1 relating to the ordinary activities of life rather than spiritual things. 2 experienced and knowledgeable about life.

world war *noun* a war that involves countries all over the world.

worldwide *adjective* throughout the world.

World Wide Web *noun* The World Wide Web is a system of linked documents accessed via the internet.

worm *noun* 1 a small thin animal without bones or legs, which lives in the soil or off other creatures. 2 an insect such as a beetle or moth at a very early stage in its life. 3 a computer program that makes many copies of itself within a network, usually harming the system. ▶ *verb* 4 If you worm an animal, you give it medicine in order to kill the worms that are living as parasites in its intestines. > **worm out** *verb* If you worm information out of someone, you gradually persuade them to give it to you.

worn 1 Worn is the past participle of **wear**. ▶ *adjective* 2 damaged or thin because of long use. 3 looking old or exhausted.

worn-out *adjective* 1 used until it is too thin or too damaged to be of further use. 2 extremely tired.

> **worn-out** *adjective*
> 1 = broken-down, tattered, threadbare, worn
> 2 = exhausted, fatigued, prostrate, tired, weary

worried *adjective* unhappy and anxious about a problem or about something unpleasant that might happen.

> **worried** *adjective*
> = anxious, bothered, concerned, nervous, troubled, uneasy

worry worries, worrying, worried *verb* 1 If you worry, you feel anxious and fearful about a problem or about something unpleasant that might happen. 2 If something worries you, it causes you to feel uneasy or fearful. 3 If you worry someone with a problem, you disturb or bother them by telling them about it. 4 If a dog worries sheep or other animals, it frightens or harms them by chasing them or biting them. ▶ *noun* 5 Worry is a feeling of unhappiness and unease caused by a problem or by thinking of something unpleasant that might happen. 6 a person or thing that causes you to feel anxious or uneasy. > **worrying** *adjective*

> **worry** *verb*
> 1 = be anxious, brood, feel uneasy, fret 3 = bother, hassle (*informal*), pester, plague, trouble

w

▶ noun 5 = anxiety, apprehension, concern, fear, misgiving, unease

worse adjective, adverb 1 Worse is the comparative form of **bad** and **badly**. 2 If someone who is ill gets worse, they become more ill than before.

worsen verb If a situation worsens, it becomes more difficult or unpleasant.

> **worsen** verb
> = decline, degenerate, deteriorate, go downhill (informal)

worse off adjective If you are worse off, you have less money or are in a more unpleasant situation than before.

worship worships, worshipping, worshipped verb 1 (RE) If you worship a god, you show your love and respect by praying or singing hymns. 2 If you worship someone or something, you love them or admire them very much. ▶ noun 3 Worship is the feeling or expression of respect, love or admiration you feel for something or someone.
> **worshipper** noun

> **worship** verb
> 1 = glorify, honour, praise, pray to, venerate (formal) 2 = adore, idolise, love
> ▶ noun 3 = admiration, adoration, adulation, devotion, homage, praise

worst adjective, adverb the superlative of **bad** and **badly**.

worth preposition 1 If something is worth a sum of money, it has that value. 2 If something is worth doing, it deserves to be done.

▶ noun 3 A particular amount of money's worth of something is the quantity of it that you can buy for that money. 4 Someone's worth is the value or usefulness they are considered to have.

worthless adjective having no real value or use.

> **worthless** adjective
> = meaningless, paltry, poor, trifling, trivial, useless, valueless

worthwhile adjective important enough to justify the time, money or effort spent on it.

worthy worthier, worthiest adjective If someone or something is worthy of something, they deserve it.

would verb 1 You use 'would' to say what someone thought was going to happen: We were sure it would be a success. 2 You use 'would' when you are referring to the result or effect of a possible situation: If readers can help I would be most grateful. 3 You use 'would' when referring to someone's willingness to do something: I wouldn't change places with him if you paid me. 4 You use 'would' in polite questions: Would you like some lunch?

would-be adjective wanting to be or claiming to be something.

wound¹ noun 1 an injury to part of your body, especially a cut in your skin and flesh. ▶ verb 2 If someone wounds you, they damage your body using a gun, knife or other weapon. 3 If you are wounded by what someone says or does, your feelings are hurt. > **wounded** adjective

wound² the past tense and past participle of **wind**².

wove the past tense of **weave**.

woven the past participle of **weave**.

wow interjection Wow is an expression of admiration or surprise.

wraith, wraiths noun (literary) A wraith is a ghost or apparition: *The child flitted about like a wraith.*

wrangle verb 1 If you wrangle with someone, you argue noisily or angrily, often about something unimportant. ▶ noun 2 an argument that is difficult to settle. > **wrangling** noun

wrap wraps, wrapping, wrapped verb 1 If you wrap something or wrap something up, you fold a piece of paper or cloth tightly around it to cover or enclose it. 2 If you wrap paper or cloth round something, you put or fold the paper round it. 3 If you wrap your arms, fingers or legs round something, you coil them round it. > **wrap up** verb If you wrap up, you put on warm clothes on.

wrapped up adjective (informal) If you are wrapped up in a person or thing, you give that person or thing all your attention.

wrapper noun a piece of paper, plastic or foil which covers and protects something that you buy.

wrapping noun Wrapping is the material used to cover and protect something.

wrath noun (literary) Wrath is great anger.

wreak verb To wreak havoc or damage is to cause it.

wreath noun an arrangement of flowers and leaves, often in the shape of a circle, which is put on a grave as a sign of remembrance for the dead person.

wreck verb 1 If someone wrecks something, they break it, destroy it, or spoil it completely. 2 If a ship is wrecked, it has been so badly damaged that it can no longer sail. ▶ noun 3 a vehicle which has been badly damaged in an accident. > **wrecked** adjective

wreckage noun Wreckage is what remains after something has been badly damaged or destroyed.

wrench verb 1 If you wrench something, you give it a sudden and violent twist or pull. 2 If you wrench a limb or a joint, you twist and injure it. ▶ noun 3 a metal tool with parts which can be adjusted to fit around nuts or bolts to loosen or tighten them. 4 a painful parting from someone or something.

wrest verb (formal) If you wrest something from someone else you take it from them violently or with effort.

wrestle verb 1 If you wrestle someone or wrestle with them, you fight by holding or throwing them, but not hitting them. 2 When you wrestle with a problem, you try to deal with it. > **wrestler** noun

wrestling noun Wrestling is a sport in which two people fight and try to win by throwing or holding their opponent on the ground.

wretched adjective 1 very unhappy or unfortunate. 2 (informal) You use wretched to describe something or someone you feel angry about or dislike.

wriggle verb 1 If someone wriggles, they twist and turn their body or a part of their body using quick movements. **2** If you wriggle somewhere, you move there by twisting and turning. > **wriggly** adjective

wring wrings, wringing, wrung verb **1** When you wring a wet cloth or wring it out, you squeeze the water out of it by twisting it. **2** If you wring your hands, you hold them together and twist and turn them, usually because you are worried or upset. **3** If someone wrings a bird's neck, they kill the bird by twisting and breaking its neck.

wrinkle noun **1** Wrinkles are lines in someone's skin, especially on the face, which form as they grow old. ▶ verb **2** If something wrinkles, folds or lines develop on it. **3** When you wrinkle your nose, forehead or eyes, you tighten the muscles in your face so that the skin folds into lines. > **wrinkled** adjective > **wrinkly** adjective

wrist noun the part of your body between your hand and your arm which bends when you move your hand.

writ noun a legal document that orders a person to do or not to do a particular thing.

write writes, writing, wrote, written verb **1** When you write something, you use a pen or pencil to form letters, words or numbers on a surface. **2** If you write something such as a poem, a book or a piece of music, you create it. **3** When you write to someone or write them a letter, you express your feelings in a letter. **4** When someone writes something such as a cheque, they put the necessary information on it and sign it. **5** When you write

data you transfer it to a computer's memory.
> **write down** verb If you write something down, you record it on a piece of paper. > **write up** verb If you write up something, you write a full account of it, often using notes that you have made.

writer noun **1** a person who writes books, stories or articles as a job. **2** The writer of something is the person who wrote it.

writhe verb If you writhe, you twist and turn your body, often because you are in pain.

writing noun **1** Writing is something that has been written or printed. **2** Your writing is the way you write with a pen or pencil. **3** Writing is also a piece of written work, especially the style of language used. **4** An author's writings are his or her written works.

written 1 Written is the past participle of **write**. ▶ adjective **2** taken down in writing.

wrong adjective **1** unsatisfactory or not working properly. **2** not correct: *the wrong answer; a wrong diagnosis.* **3** bad or immoral. ▶ noun **4** an unjust action or situation. ▶ verb **5** If someone wrongs you, they treat you in an unfair or unjust way. > **wrongly** adverb

---

wrong adjective
2 = false, faulty, incorrect, mistaken, unsound, untrue
3 = bad, crooked, evil, illegal, immoral, unfair, unjust
▶ noun **4** = abuse, crime, grievance, injustice, sin

---

wrongful adjective A wrongful act is regarded as illegal, unfair or immoral. > **wrongfully** adverb

wrote the past tense of **write**.

wrought iron *noun* Wrought iron is a pure type of iron that is formed into decorative shapes.

wrung the past tense and past participle of **wring**.

wry *adjective* A wry expression shows that you find a situation slightly amusing because you know more about it than other people. > **wryly** *adverb* > **wryness** *noun*

X or x **1** 'X' is used to represent the name of an unknown or secret person or place. **2** In algebra, 'x' is used as a symbol to represent a number whose value is not known. **3** People sometimes write 'X' on a map to mark a precise position. **4** 'X' is used to represent a kiss at the bottom of a letter, a vote on a ballot paper, or the signature of someone who cannot write.

xenophobia *noun* a fear or strong dislike of people from other countries. > **xenophobic** *adjective*

Xerox *noun* (*trademark*) **1** a machine that makes photographic copies of sheets of paper with writing or printing on them. **2** a copy made by a Xerox machine.

Xmas *noun* (*informal*) Xmas means the same as Christmas.

X-ray *noun* **1** a stream of radiation of very short wavelength that can pass through some solid materials. X-rays are used by doctors to examine the bones or organs inside a person's body. **2** a picture made by sending X-rays through someone's body in order to examine the inside of it. ▶ *verb* **3** If you are X-rayed, a picture is made of the inside of your body by passing X-rays through it.

x

xylophone *noun* a musical instrument made of a row of wooden bars of different lengths. It is played by hitting the bars with special hammers.

Yy

-y *suffix* -y forms nouns: *anarchy*.

yacht *noun* a boat with sails or an engine, used for racing or for pleasure trips.

yachting *noun* Yachting is the sport or activity of sailing a yacht.

yachtsman yachtsmen *noun* a man who sails a yacht.

yachtswoman yachtswomen *noun* a woman who sails a yacht.

yak *noun* a type of long-haired ox with long horns, found mainly in Tibet.

yakka or **yacker** *noun* (*informal*) In Australian and New Zealand English, yakka or yacker is work.

yank (*informal*) *verb* 1 If you yank something, you pull or jerk it suddenly with a lot of force. ▶ *noun* 2 A Yank is an American.

Yankee *noun* (*informal*) the same as a Yank.

yard *noun* 1 a unit of length equal to 36 inches or about 91.4 centimetres. 2 an enclosed area that is usually next to a building and is often used for a particular purpose.

yardstick *noun* someone or something you use as a standard against which to judge other people or things.

yarn *noun* 1 DGT Yarn is thread used for knitting or making cloth. 2 (*informal*) a story that someone tells, often with invented details to make it more interesting or exciting.

yawn verb 1 When you yawn, you open your mouth wide and take in more air than usual. You often yawn when you are tired or bored. 2 A gap or opening that yawns is large and wide. ▶ noun 3 an act of yawning.

yawning adjective A yawning gap or opening is very wide.

ye (old-fashioned) pronoun 1 Ye is used to mean 'you'. ▶ adjective 2 Ye is also used to mean 'the'.

yeah interjection (informal) Yeah means 'yes'.

year noun 1 a period of twelve months or 365 days (366 days in a leap year), which is the time taken for the earth to travel once around the sun. 2 a period of twelve consecutive months, not always January to December, on which administration or organisation is based.

yearling noun an animal between one and two years old.

yearn verb If you yearn for something, you want it very much indeed. ▷ **yearning** noun

yeast noun (SCIENCE) Yeast is a kind of fungus which is used to make bread rise, and to make liquids ferment in order to produce alcohol.

yell verb 1 If you yell, you shout loudly, usually because you are angry, excited or in pain. ▶ noun 2 a loud shout.

yellow noun, adjective 1 Yellow is the colour of buttercups, egg yolks and lemons. ▶ verb 2 When something yellows or is yellowed, it becomes yellow, often because it is old. ▶ adjective 3 (informal) If

you say someone is yellow, you mean they are cowardly. ▷ **yellowish** adjective

yellow fever noun Yellow fever is a serious infectious disease that is found in tropical countries. It causes fever and jaundice.

yelp verb 1 When people or animals yelp, they give a sudden, short cry. ▶ noun 2 a sudden, short cry.

yen noun 1 The yen is the main unit of currency in Japan. 2 (informal) If you have a yen to do something, you have a strong desire to do it.

yes interjection You use 'yes' to agree with someone, to say that something is true, or to accept something.

> **yes** interjection
> = aye (Scottish; informal), okay or OK (informal), sure (informal), ya (South African), yeah (informal), yup (informal)

yesterday noun, adverb 1 Yesterday is the day before today. 2 You also use 'yesterday' to refer to the past: Leave yesterday's sadness behind you.

yet adverb 1 If something has not happened yet, it has not happened up to the present time. 2 If something should not be done yet, it should not be done now, but later. 3 'Yet' can mean there is still a possibility that something can happen. 4 You can use 'yet' when you want to say how much longer a situation will continue. 5 'Yet' can be used for emphasis. ▶ conjunction 6 You can use 'yet' to introduce a fact which is rather surprising.

yew noun an evergreen tree with bright red berries.

Yiddish *noun* Yiddish is a language derived mainly from German, which many Jewish people of European origin speak.

yield *verb* 1 If you yield to someone or something, you stop resisting and give in to them. 2 If you yield something that you have control of or responsibility for, you surrender it. 3 If something yields, it breaks or gives way. 4 To yield something is to produce it.
▶ *noun* 5 A yield is an amount of food, money or profit produced from a given area of land or from an investment.

yob *noun* (informal) a noisy, badly behaved boy or young man.

yoga *noun* Yoga is a Hindu method of mental and physical exercise or discipline.

yogurt; also spelt **yoghurt** *noun* Yogurt is a slightly sour thick liquid made from milk that has had bacteria added to it.

yoke *noun* 1 a wooden bar attached to two collars which is laid across the necks of animals such as oxen to hold them together, and to which a plough or other tool may be attached. 2 (literary) If people are under a yoke of some kind, they are being oppressed.

yolk *noun* the yellow part in the middle of an egg.

Yom Kippur *noun* (RE) Yom Kippur is an annual Jewish religious holiday, which is a day of fasting and prayers. It is also called the Day of Atonement.

yonder *adverb, adjective* (old-fashioned) over there.

yore *phrase* (old-fashioned) Of yore means existing a long time ago.

you *pronoun* 1 'You' refers to the person or group of people that a person is speaking or writing to. 2 'You' also refers to people in general: *You can get a two-bedroom villa quite cheaply here.*

young *adjective* 1 A young person, animal or plant has not lived very long and is not yet mature.
▶ *plural noun* 2 The young are young people in general. 3 The young of an animal are its babies.

> **young** *adjective*
> 1 = adolescent, immature, infant, junior, juvenile, little, youthful
> ▶ *plural noun* 3 = babies, brood, family, litter, little ones, offspring

youngster *noun* a child or young person.

your *adjective* 1 'Your' means belonging or relating to the person or group of people that someone is speaking to: *I do like your name.* 2 'Your' is used to show that something belongs or relates to people in general: *Some of these chemicals can cause serious damage to your health.*

yours *pronoun* 'Yours' refers to something belonging or relating to the person or group of people that someone is speaking to: *His hair is longer than yours.*

yourself yourselves *pronoun* 1 'Yourself' is used when the person being spoken to does the action and is affected by it: *Why can't you do it yourself?* 2 'Yourself' is used to emphasise 'you': *Do you yourself want to go?*

youth *noun* 1 Someone's youth is the period of their life before they are a fully mature adult. 2 Youth is the quality or condition of being young and often inexperienced. **3** a boy or young man. **4** The youth are young people thought of as a group. > **youthful** *adjective*

yo-yo yo-yos *noun* a round wooden or plastic toy attached to a piece of string. You play by making the yo-yo rise and fall on the string.

Yule *noun* (*old-fashioned*) Yule means Christmas.

yuppie *noun* A yuppie is a young, middle-class person who earns a lot of money which he or she spends on himself or herself.

Zz

Zambian *adjective* **1** belonging or relating to Zambia. ▶ *noun* **2** someone who comes from Zambia.

zany zanier, zaniest *adjective* (*informal*) odd and ridiculous.

zap zaps, zapping, zapped *verb* (*informal*) **1** To zap someone is to kill them, usually by shooting. **2** To zap also is to move somewhere quickly.

zeal *noun* Zeal is very great enthusiasm. > **zealous** *adjective* > **zealously** *adverb*

zealot *noun* a person who acts with very great enthusiasm, especially in following a political or religious cause.

zebra *noun* a type of African wild horse with black and white stripes over its body.

Zen or **Zen Buddhism** *noun* (RE) Zen is a form of Buddhism that concentrates on learning through meditation and intuition.

zenith *noun* (*literary*) The zenith of something is the time when it is at its most successful or powerful.

zero zeros or zeroes, zeroing, zeroed **1** nothing or the number 0. **2** Zero is freezing point, 0° Centigrade. > **zero in** *verb* To zero in on a target is to aim at or to move towards it.

z

zero noun
1 = nil, nothing, nought

zest noun 1 Zest is a feeling of pleasure and enthusiasm. 2 Zest is a quality which adds extra flavour or interest to something. 3 The zest of an orange or lemon is the outside of the peel which is used to flavour food or drinks.

zigzag zigzags, zigzagging, zigzagged noun 1 A zigzag is a line which has a series of sharp, angular turns to the right and left in it, like a continuous series of 'W's. ▶ verb 2 To zigzag is to move forward by going at an angle first right and then left.

Zimbabwean adjective
1 belonging or relating to Zimbabwe. ▶ noun 2 someone who comes from Zimbabwe.

zinc noun (SCIENCE) Zinc is a bluish-white metallic element used in alloys and to coat other metals to stop them rusting. Its atomic number is 30 and its symbol is Zn.

zip zips, zipping, zipped noun 1 a long narrow fastener with two rows of teeth that are closed or opened by a small clip pulled between them. ▶ verb 2 When you zip something or zip it up, you fasten it using a zip.

zipper noun the same as a **zip**.

zodiac noun The zodiac is an imaginary strip in the sky which contains the planets and stars which astrologers think are important influences on people. It is divided into 12 sections, each with a special name and symbol.

zombie noun 1 (informal) If you refer to someone as a zombie, you mean that they seem to be unaware of what is going on around them and to act without thinking about them and to act without thinking about what they are doing. 2 In voodoo, a zombie is a dead person who has been brought back to life by witchcraft.

zone noun an area that has particular features or properties.

zoo zoos noun a place where live animals are kept so that people can look at them.

zoology noun Zoology is the scientific study of animals. > **zoological** adjective > **zoologist** noun

zoom verb 1 To zoom is to move very quickly. 2 If a camera zooms in on something, it gives a close-up picture of it.

zucchini plural noun Zucchini are small vegetable marrows with dark green skin. They are also called **courgettes**.

Zulu Zulus noun 1 The Zulus are a group of Black people who live in southern Africa. 2 Zulu is the language spoken by the Zulus.

z

Get It Right: Grammar, Punctuation, and Spelling

Grammar

Grammar is a set of rules about a language that tell you how we organise words to make sentences.

> ## ☆ How does grammar help us?
> - It helps us to work out how to use language in order to create the effect we want.
> - It helps us to work out why something 'doesn't sound right', and to put it right.
> - It helps us to learn other languages.

Word classes

Nouns

Nouns name a person, an animal, a thing, or a place.

   celebrity   *snake*   *laptop*   *park*

There are a few different types of noun.

Common nouns

Common nouns can be **concrete**, **abstract**, or **collective**:

- A **concrete noun** is a person, thing, or animal that you can actually touch.
   pen   *dog*   *house*   *teacher*

- An **abstract noun** is used for talking about an idea or a feeling.
   happiness   *beauty*   *imagination*

- A **collective noun** is used for talking about a group or collection of things or animals.
   pack   *bunch*   *flock*

Proper nouns

Proper nouns refer to a particular person, place, or thing. Remember that they always start with a capital letter.

Tom Holland   *Italy*   *Tower Bridge*

Possessive nouns

This form of the noun shows that a person or thing 'owns' something. You add **'s** to the noun to make the possessive form.

my mum's glasses   *Kirsty's football boots*
the dog's water bowl   *the mug's handle*

If the noun is a plural that already ends in **s**, you just add an apostrophe.

the soldiers' uniforms   *those boys' bikes*

☆ Don't do it!

Never use **'s** to make a plural.

Adjectives

Adjectives are words that tell people about a noun. We use adjectives to describe nouns in lots of different ways:

- how they feel or what they are like:
  a hungry caterpillar, a funny story, a strange coincidence
- what they look like:
  a huge cake, a stripy t-shirt, an idyllic beach
- what they sound, smell, taste, or feel like:
  a noisy party, smelly feet, a delicious pudding, slimy seaweed
- what colour they are: *a red purse, blonde hair, black trainers*
- where they come from:
  our German cousins, my American friends, a Scottish accent
- what something is made from:
  chocolate cake, a wooden box, a velvet scarf

3

☆ Astounding adjectives

You can make your writing come alive by using adjectives with your nouns.

*He gave us an **angelic** smile.*
*A **pungent** smell came from the kitchen.*

Comparative and superlative forms

To compare people or things using an adjective, we use the comparative and the superlative forms of the adjective:

*Holly is **tall**. She is **taller** than Rebecca.* (comparative form)
*Actually, Holly is **the tallest** girl in the class.* (superlative form)

☆ Forget the rules!

A few adjectives don't follow the rules.

Adjective	Comparative form	Superlative form
good	better	best
bad	worse	worst
far	further	furthest

Verbs

Verbs are words that we use to talk about an action or a state.

*Emily **plays** the guitar.   The cows **wandered** over to see us.*
*We always **listen** to the radio in the car.   I **feel** exhausted.*

Tense

The tense of a verb tells us *when* the action takes place, for example, if it has already happened or if it is happening now.

1. The present

The present tense has two forms:

4

- the **simple present**:
  *I **like** poodles.   You always **say** that!*
  *Max never **brushes** his hair.*
- the **progressive** (the '-ing' form):
  *We**'re trying** to concentrate.*
  *Look! I**'m wearing** my new jeans!*

2. The past
The past tense has two forms:
- the **simple past**:
  *Mary **had** a baby.   I **screamed** and **fainted**.*
  *Dad nearly **hit** the roof.*
- the **progressive**:
  *I **was doing** my homework when Bethany messaged me.*

3. The future
We can talk about the future in lots of different ways.
We can use:
- will: *I promise I **will** be there on time.*
- shall: *We **shall** see!*
- going to: *I**'m going to** get you!*
- the progressive form of the present tense:
  *They**'re leaving** on Sunday.*
- the simple present tense: *The train **leaves** at 4 p.m.*

Adverbs
Adverbs tell us something about a verb. Adverbs can tell us:
- how someone does something. This type of adverb often
  ends in **-ly**:
  *She woke up **suddenly**.   They walked home **slowly**.*
- where something happens:
  *We live **here**.   She went **upstairs**.*
- when something happens:
  *We're leaving **tomorrow**.   Call the police **now**!*

5

- the extent to which something is true:
  I **really** want to see that film.   He was **absolutely** furious.
- how often something happens: We **never** go there any more.
  I **often** wonder what happened to her.

> ### ☆ Amazing adverbs
>
> You can create vivid images in your writing by using adverbs with your verbs.
>
> 'I got an A in my test!' she declared **triumphantly**.
> For a while, I just stared **vacantly** out of the window.

Prepositions

We use prepositions before a noun or a pronoun. A preposition can tell us about:
- where a person or thing is: **on** the table   **under** the bed
- movement: The train came **into** the station.
  She ran **across** the road.
- time: It's twenty **to** six.   I've been here **since** midday.

Conjunctions

Conjunctions join two words or two parts of a sentence together.
- **Coordinating conjunctions** join two ideas that are equally important.
  I love fish **and** chips.   You can have a biscuit **or** a cake.
  It was dry **so** I walked home.   I like maths **but** I don't like physics.
- **Subordinating conjunctions** introduce a clause which is less important than the main part of the sentence.
  Mark read his book **while** he was waiting.
  Some dogs go a bit crazy **when** it's windy.

Pronouns

We use pronouns in place of nouns. We use them instead of repeating the name of a person, place, or thing.

- **Personal pronouns** are used instead of the subject or object of a sentence.
  She is good at maths.   *I don't like **him**.*
- **Possessive pronouns** are used to show that something belongs to a person or thing.
  *Hey, that's **mine**!*   *Excuse me, I think this is **yours**.*
- **Relative pronouns** are used to refer back to a noun that was mentioned earlier.
  *I have an aunt **who** lives in Australia.*
  *We took the road **that/which** leads to the sea.*

Determiners

We often use determiners in front of nouns.

- **Articles**: **a** and **an** are known as 'indefinite articles' and **the** is known as the 'definite article'.
- Other determiners tell you who owns something: ***my** bag*; how far something is from the speaker: ***this** book*, ***that** aeroplane*; how much of something there is: ***some** sugar*, ***a lot of** people*, ***one** melon*.

Sentences

Sentence types

- A **statement** tells you something. It ends with a full stop: *Berlin is the capital of Germany.*
- A **question** asks something. It ends with a question mark: *Have you seen my keys?*
- A **command** gives orders or instructions: *Come here, please.*
- An **exclamation** expresses strong feeling. It ends with an exclamation mark: *What a laugh! Hooray! Oh no!*

Sentence structure

- A **simple sentence** contains just one clause. *Patrick threw the ball.*
- A **compound sentence** contains two or more clauses joined by a conjunction. *Patrick threw the ball and Sara caught it.*
- A **complex sentence** has a main clause and one or more subordinate clauses. *Patrick threw the ball to Sara, who was standing on the other side of the pitch.*

> ### ☆ A change of pace
>
> Vary your sentence structures to change the pace in your writing.
>
> Compound and complex sentences can slow things down: *I should have gone to football training, but I just sat in front of the TV, watching anything that was on, before I decided it was time for bed.*
>
> Simple sentences can speed things up: *I got home. I wolfed down my dinner. I dashed out to football training.*

Parts of a sentence

- **Subject**: the person or thing that carries out the action:
  Louise fell asleep.
- **Verb**: all sentences have a verb:
  *Angus **fainted**.*
- **Object**: the person or thing that 'receives' the action of the verb. (Not all sentences have an object.):
  *Kim loves **chocolate**.*
- **Complement**: a word or phrase that tells you about the subject:
  *The boys felt **silly**.*   *Laura is an **architect**.*
- **Adverbial**: a word or phrase that tells you how the action is happening:
  ***Suddenly**, it started to rain.*   *The door closed **with a loud bang**.*

☆ A change of emphasis

By moving the parts of your sentence around, you can change what you emphasise and create different effects.

Placing the adverbial at the start of your sentence gives it emphasis:
***With a deafening crash**, the plates fell from the table.*

Moving the subject of your sentence to the end can create tension:
*Down the alley, onto the street and across the road, **Karl** ran for his life.*

Active and passive voice

In an **active voice** sentence, the subject of the sentence does the action:

<u>Nina</u> <u>fed</u> the rabbit.

    | |

subject   verb

In a **passive voice** sentence, the subject of the sentence has the action done to it:

<u>The rabbit</u> <u>was fed</u> by Nina.

    | |

subject   verb

Punctuation

☆ How does punctuation help us?

We use punctuation marks to make our writing easier to read and understand. Sometimes it is essential to add punctuation or the meaning of a sentence won't be clear:
Anika, thinks Oliver, is really annoying.
Anika thinks Oliver is really annoying.

Full stop (.)

We put a full stop:

- at the end of a sentence:
  I mustn't forget that appointment.
- at the end of a word or phrase that can stand on its own:
  Sorry.   Good morning.   Not much.

Question mark (?)

We put a question mark at the end of a question:
Did I leave my phone at your house?

Exclamation mark (!)

We put an exclamation mark at the end of a sentence:

- to show strong feeling like anger, surprise, or excitement:
  That's ridiculous!   I can't believe it!   We're getting a puppy!
- when we are telling someone to do something:
  Don't touch that!   Look over here!

Comma (,)

We use a comma:

- to separate items in a list:
  We need to pack shorts, swimming costumes, T-shirts, and trainers.

11

- to mark a short pause between parts of a sentence:
  After a while, the sun came out.
- when we are quoting someone:
  'I've never been here before,' said Emily.
  Ricky shouted, 'It's on fire!'
- to mark off parts of a sentence:
  My cousin, who lives in New York, is coming to stay next week.

Apostrophe (')

- **Possession**: apostrophes show possession of something:
  Callum's bag   Britain's castles   the car's windscreen
  James's hat   Mr Jones's golf clubs
  the children's notebooks   men's shoes   women's fashions

  In formal writing, when a name already ends in 's', people sometimes just add an apostrophe.

  This is a statue of Prince Charles' grandfather, King George VI.

- **Contraction**: apostrophes show that one or more letters have been removed from a word or sequence of words:
  can't (= cannot)   *I'll* (= I will/I shall)
  she'd (= she would/she had)

Inverted commas (' ' or " ")

We put inverted commas (or 'speech marks') before and after words to show exactly what someone is saying:

'You can all go home early,' said the teacher.
"Help me!" cried the man.

> ### ☆ Look!
>
> A punctuation mark such as a full stop, comma, or exclamation mark comes *inside* the inverted commas at the end of a piece of spoken text.

Brackets ( )

We use brackets to separate off extra information in a sentence. The sentence still makes sense without the information in the brackets.

Bring some snacks (like chocolate or popcorn) to the sleepover.
My grandmother (my mother's mother) was born in Dundee.

Dash (–)

A dash is a short line that is longer than a hyphen. It goes above the line, and has a space either side of it. You use a dash:

- to show a break in a sentence: *Don't leave your plate there – put it in the dishwasher.*
- to mark off separate information in the same way that brackets do:
  Peter and I – the others can't make it – are going skating on Friday.

> ### ☆ Look!
> When you use dashes to mark off extra information, you need to use a dash before *and* after the extra information.

Semicolon (;)

We use a semicolon:

- to separate items in a list, when the items are longer than one or two words:
  The flight was late; the hotel was dirty; the food was horrible; it rained every day; and I got an ear infection.
- to mark a break in a sentence, especially when you are showing a contrast between two things:
  Jack loves football; his brother hates it.

Colon (:)

We use a colon:

- to introduce a list: *The Jamaican flag contains three colours: black, green, and gold.*
- to introduce a reason for something: *You should take an umbrella: it's going to rain.*

Hyphen (-)

We use a hyphen to join two words together to make one:

- to avoid having two vowels next to each other:
  pro-independence   *re-elect*   *anti-ageing cream*
- to avoid confusion about how the word should be pronounced:
  no-nonsense   *mis-sell*   *non-negotiable*
- to avoid confusion with another word:
  re-creation (recreation) *re-cover* (recover) *re-count* (recount)
- to avoid confusion about what a phrase means:
  fish-eating seabirds (different from *fish eating seabirds*)
  20-odd books (different from *20 odd books*)

Ellipsis (...)

The ellipsis is made up of three dots. We use it to:

- show that some words are missing, for example, in a long quotation:
  'I have a dream that one day, even the state of Mississippi ... will be transformed into an oasis of freedom and justice.'
- represent a pause in someone's speech:
  Well ... I ... I'm not sure.
- create a dramatic ending to a story:
  Two red eyes appeared in the cave ...

Spelling

Commonly misspelt words

Here is a list of some commonly misspelt words with advice on how to avoid the difficult parts of these words.

accommodation	has double **c** and double **m**
achieve	put the **i** before **e**
across	has only one **c**
basically	ends in **ally**
believe	put the **i** before **e**
business	starts with **bus**
calendar	ends in **ar**
Caribbean	has one **r** and two **b**s
cemetery	ends in **ery**
committee	has a double **m**, a double **t**, and double **e**
completely	ends in **ely**
conscious	has **sc** in the middle
definitely	has **ite**, not **ate**, in the middle
dilemma	has one **l** and two **m**s
disappear	has one **s** and two **p**s
disappoint	has one **s** and two **p**s
embarrass	has double **r** and double **s**
environment	put an **n** before the **m**
finally	has double **l**
foreign	put the **e** before **i**
forty	has **o**, not **ou**, in the middle
friend	put the **i** before **e**
glamorous	ends in **orous**
government	put an **n** before the **m**
guard	has **ua** after **g**, not just **a**
happened	ends in **ened**
humorous	ends in **orous**

immediately	has double **m**
independent	ends in **ent**
knowledge	ends in **edge**
liaise	has an **i** in the middle
necessary	has one **c** and two **s**s
occasion	has two **c**s and one **s**
occurred, occurring	double **c**, double **r**
piece	**i** before **e**
possession	has two sets of double **s**
preferred, preferring	has one **f** and two **r**s
really	has double **l**
receive	put the **e** before **i**
referred, referring	has one **f** and two **r**s
separate	has **par**, not **per**, in the middle
successful	has double **c** and double **s**
tomorrow	has one **m** and two **r**s
tongue	ends in **gue**
until	has only one **l** at the end
weird	put the **e** before **i**
which	starts with **wh**

☆ Remember!

The ending **-ful** always has only one **l**.
beautiful hopeful faithful painful grateful